ANTARCTICA IN INTERNATIONAL LAW

Edited by

Ben Saul and Tim Stephens

•HART•

OXFORD • LONDON • NEW YORK • NEW DELHI • SYDNEY

HART PUBLISHING
Bloomsbury Publishing Plc
Kemp House, Chawley Park, Cumnor Hill, Oxford, OX2 9PH, UK
1385 Broadway, New York, NY 10018, USA

First published in Great Britain 2015

A catalogue record for this book is available from the British Library.

Library of Congress Cataloging-in-Publication Data

ISBN: 978-1-84946-731-5

Typeset by Criteria International

CONTENTS

List of Documents

PART 1:
International Instruments of the Antarctic Treaty System (ATS)

PART 2:

Secretariat of the Antarctic Treaty

PART 3:

Antarctic Treaty Consultative Meetings (ATCM) (1963–2013)

Other Selected ATCM Instruments

PART 6:
Council of Managers of National Antarctic Programs (COMNAP)

PART 7:
Other International Instruments Relevant to Antarctica

Treaties

PART 9:

Other United Nations Documents

PART 10:
Judicial Proceedings

PART 11:

National Submissions to the Commission on the Limits of the Continental Shelf (CLSC) concerning Antarctic Territorial Claims

ABBREVIATIONS

AAT	Australian Antarctic Territory
ASPA	Antarctic Specially Protected Area
ATCM	Antarctic Treaty Consultative Meeting
ATCP	Antarctic Treaty Consultative Party
ATME	Antarctic Treaty Meetings of Experts
ATS	Antarctic Treaty System
BAT	British Antarctic Territory
CCAMLR	Convention on the Conservation of Antarctic Marine Living Resources 1980
CCAS	Convention for the Conservation of Antarctic Seals 1972
CEE	Comprehensive Environmental Evaluation
CEMP	CCMALR Ecosystem Monitoring Program
CEP	Committee for Environmental Protection
CLCS	Commission on the Limits of the Continental Shelf
CO2	carbon dioxide
COMNAP	Council of Managers of National Antarctic Programs
CRAMRA	Convention on the Regulation of Antarctic Mineral Resources 1988
EEZ	exclusive economic zone
EIA	Environmental Impact Assessment
FAO	Food and Agriculture Organization
ICJ	International Court of Justice
ICRW	International Convention for the Regulation of Whaling 1946
IMO	International Maritime Organization
IPY	International Polar Year
IUU	illegal, unreported and unregulated fishing
MARPOL	International Convention on the Prevention of Pollution from Ships 1973
MPA	Marine Protected Area
nm	nautical mile
SAR Convention	International Convention on Maritime Search and Rescue 1979
SATCM	Special Antarctic Treaty Consultative Meetings
SCAR	Scientific Commission on Antarctic Research
SOLAS	Safety of Life at Sea (Convention) 1974
TAAF	Terres australes et antarctiques françaises
UNCLOS	United Nations Convention on the Law of the Sea 1982
UNGA	United Nations General Assembly
UNTS	United Nations Treaty Series
VMS	Vessel Monitoring Systems

ACKNOWLEDGEMENTS

We thank our research assistants at Sydney Law School for their considerable assistance in the preparation of this volume: Alexander Horne, Alice Gardoll, Harrison Grace, Ella Alexander, Kathleen Heath, Naomi Hart, Katherine Bones, Sarah Schwartz, Jackson Wherrett and Hannah Ryan. We also thank Sydney Law School and our colleagues at the Sydney Centre for International Law for their support for this project. For translations of Spanish documents into English, we thank Katherine Bones, Nicole Dicker, Patricia Gonzales and Josue Castro.

CHRONOLOGY OF LEGALLY SIGNIFICANT EVENTS[1]

1739

Pierre Bouvet de Lozier, leading a French expedition, sights what is now called Bouvet Island. Prior to the 18th century, exploration had primarily been carried out for commercial purposes. Increasingly it becomes an area of political rivalry, particularly between England and France. The increased number of expeditions is also due to growing public demand for travel logs. This follows growing interest in the sciences with the establishment of the Royal Society and Academie des Sciences in the late 17th century.

1772

A French expedition during January and February takes possession of the Crozet and Kerguelen Islands in the name of the King of France.

1773

On 17 January, an expedition led by English Captain James Cook is the first to cross the Antarctic Circle (66° 33′ 39″ south of the equator) but does not sight mainland Antarctica.

1775

On 17 January, Captain James Cook claims possession of the 'Isle of Georgia', now South Georgia. On 31 January he discovers 'Sandwich Land', now the South Sandwich Islands.

1819

On 19 February, Englishman William Smith claims to sight the mainland. In October, acting in his private capacity, he discovers and takes possession of 'New South Britain', the South Shetland Islands, for Britain.

[1] In addition to the primary sources mentioned here, this chronology draws upon and acknowledges these key sources: David Day, *Antarctica: A Biography* (Random House, North Sydney, 2012); John Stewart, *Antarctica: An Encyclopedia* (McFarland, Jefferson, 1990); Robert Headland, *Chronological List of Antarctic Expeditions and Related Historical Events* (Cambridge University Press, Cambridge, 1989); and W.M. Bush, *Antarctica and International Law: A Collection of Inter-State and National Documents* (Oceana, London, 1982). This chronology was prepared by Alexander Horne, Ella Alexander, Kathleen Heath, Ben Saul and Tim Stephens.

1820

Edward Bransfield, a British naval lieutenant, with Smith as his pilot, sails to the South Shetlands to chart and claim them for Britain, claiming King George Island and the Clarence Islands on 22 January and 4 February respectively. He also sees 'high mountains covered with snow' which are the peaks of Trinity Land, on the mainland.

In November, American sealer Nathaniel B. Palmer sights the Antarctic mainland.

A Russian expedition led by Fabian Gottlieb von Bellingshausen may be the first to sight mainland Antarctica on 27 January.

1821

In January, von Bellingshausen discovers Peter I Island and Alexander I Island, the first discovery of land below the Antarctic Circle. This expedition is the basis of Russian claims in the Antarctic.

On 7 February, American Captain John Davis makes what is generally thought to be the first landing on the Antarctic continent itself, apparently remarking that he thinks 'this southern land to be a continent'.

1829

British Acts of Possession are performed by Captain Foster of the *Chanticleer* on Hoseason Island.

1840

On 21 January, Dumont d'Urville takes possession of Adélie Land for France. An expedition led by American Charles Wilkes discovers Wilkes Land and declares it to be a part of the Antarctic continent, having identified the land as such.

1841

The expedition led by Sir James Clark Ross becomes the first to enter the Ross Sea, breaking through the pack ice on 9 January. On 11 January, Ross sights the Admiralty Islands; the furthest south land has ever been seen. On this voyage, Ross lands a party on Possession Island, discovers Victoria Land and McMurdo Sound, claims Franklin Island for the British Crown and discovers Ross Island.

1878
Britain begins to regulate sealing in its colonies following a declining population of seals in the region. Sealing, which began following Cook's expedition, reached its peak in 1800 with the killing of 57,000 fur seals. By 1822, seal species were nearly extinct. The regulations (including the British Seals Fisheries Protection Act of 1878 and the Falkland Islands Seal Fishery Ordinance of 1881) purport to prohibit seal hunting for specified periods in the British Colony and its dependencies, though were reportedly ineffective.

1892
A Buenos Aires company requests from the Argentine government fishing rights off Graham Land and the South Shetland, South Orkney and South Sandwich Islands. The company argues that the islands' geographic position makes them the rightful property of Argentina. The company asserts that 'no act of sovereignty had been performed there' and that Argentina should therefore take possession. Neither the British nor the Argentine government seek to annex the islands at this time.

1895
Norwegian Henrik Johan Bull leads a whaling expedition and on 24 January lands at Cape Adare with Carsten Borchgrevnik and Leonard Kristensen; the first confirmed landing on the continent. They raise the Norwegian flag; which is the first time a flag is raised over the continent itself.

In July, London hosts the Sixth International Geographical Congress with the hope of increasing Antarctic exploration for scientific purposes.

1898
In January, Norwegian Roald Amundsen leads the first sledding expedition in Antarctica.

American explorer Frederick Cook writes, after an expedition to Antarctica, that the islands 'belong to nobody; at least, there are no valid claims filed, except for those which accrue from the right of discovery.'

1899
Norwegian explorer Carsten Borchgrevink, leading a 'British' expedition, erects the first man-made structures on the Antarctic continent – two Norwegian pine huts. On 2 March, he hoists a British flag and tells the assembled officers and men that he is 'hoisting the first flag on the great Antarctic Continent'. News of this venture attracts less than the hoped for attention in Britain, due to the outbreak of the Boer War in the same year.

1902
On 30 January, Scott discovers Edward VII Peninsula. This discovery is the first significant discovery in Antarctica of the twentieth century.

On 4 February, Scott goes up in a balloon to 790 feet; the first aerial view of the Antarctic.

1903
Scottish explorer William Speirs Bruce establishes a land station on Laurie Island.

The *Antarctic*, a Swedish expedition's vessel, is crushed by the ice and sinks. Its crew are rescued and taken to Buenos Aires.

1904
Argentina takes over the shore station on Laurie Island as a permanent meteorological station. As part of the establishment of their permanent presence in the South Orkney Islands, Argentina creates a post office in the stone house on the island and designates one of its nationals as postmaster. Argentina will argue that this constitutes an effective exercise of authority on the island and, through it, the South Orkney Islands.

In December, Norwegian Carl Larsen leads an Argentinian company to South Georgia to establish a whaling station. 183 whales are killed and processed in the first summer.

1905
France begins an extended exchange of notes with Great Britain concerning their claims to the Crozet and Kerguelen Islands and Adélie Land.

1906
In February, Britain sends a frigate to Antarctica to assert its sovereignty over South Georgia Island. The Governor of the Falkland Islands had granted a mining and pastoral lease over South Georgia to a Falkland Islands company. When the holders of the lease arrived, they found a small Argentine settlement servicing

Larsen's Buenos Aires-based company. Larsen does not contest British sovereignty and is granted a lease over five hundred acres.

In May, Britain informs Norway, in response to a Norwegian enquiry, that the South Shetlands, South Georgia, South Orkneys and 'Graham Land' are owned by Britain, and that whales could only be caught in those waters with the permission of the governor of the Falkland Islands. Britain's claims are based on acts of possession performed by Captain Foster of the *Chanticleer* in 1829 and Sir John Ross in 1843.

A Chilean Governor gives a Norwegian-Chilean company authority to establish a whaling station on Deception Island in the South Shetland Islands, which Chile considers to be its territory.

On 10 June, Argentina produces a letter to Chile protesting a Chilean decree authorising the occupation of certain Antarctic territories

A Memorial of 18 September is issued by the Chilean Ministry of Foreign Affairs reporting that discussions with Argentina on interests in the Antarctic Territories have progressed cordially.

In December, Argentina refers to the South Orkney Islands as 'Southern Argentine lands' in a decree authorising the payment of salaries to meteorological observers.

1907

Britain and Argentina begin an extended exchange of notes and letters regarding their respective claims to the South Orkney Islands.

1908

On 10 March, Mount Erebus is climbed for the first time by Douglas Mawson, T. W. Edgeworth David and Alistair Mackay.

On 21 July, the British King issues Letters Patent, claiming ownership of the Sandwich Islands, the South Orkneys, the South Shetlands, South Georgia and Graham's Land. These territories, covering 17 per cent of the continent, are named 'the Falkland Islands Dependencies' and placed under the administration of the Falkland Islands Governor.

Following this, Britain establishes an administrative post in South Georgia next to the largely Norwegian settlement, Grytviken. While not provoking an official protest, this action leads to a violent press campaign in Argentina.

On 17 October, Professor T. W. Edgeworth David takes possession of Victoria Land for the British Empire.

1909

British explorer Ernest Shackleton reaches the 'Furthest South', approximately 100 miles from the South Pole. He claims the South Polar Plateau for Britain and names the area King Edward VII Plateau.

1910

'Charcot Land', on the western side of the Antarctic Peninsula, is discovered and charted by Jean-Baptiste Charcot. It is later discovered to be an island rather than part of the continent.

On 24 October, the first court case in Antarctica is heard by the Falkland Islands Dependencies Magistrate on South Georgia.

1911

British diplomats in Argentina suggest trading the South Orkneys for a parcel of land in Buenos Aires on which to build a new British legation. Although an agreement is drawn up, the new Argentinian government in 1914 objects to paying for something they consider to already be under their sovereignty.

Commander Prestrud of Norway claims King Edward VII Land from the summit 'Scott's Nunatakker' and records this claim in his account of 8 December.

On 14 December, Amundsen's party raises the Norwegian flag at the South Pole (or as close to it as can be reckoned using his instruments), becoming the first to achieve the feat. He records his claiming of the South Polar Plateau for Norway, giving it the name 'King Haakon VII's Plateau' in his account of the same date.

1912

Over February and March Scott and his companions perish on their return from the South Pole.

Paul Sarasin, chairman of a Provisional Commission for the Protection of Nature and a father of the Antarctic conservation movement, convinces the Society of German Scientists and Physicians to call on the German government to support the creation of nature reserves for whales and seals through international agreements.

A Japanese expedition claims an area they designate as 'Yamato Setsugen' for Japan, despite its being a floating ice shelf and having been traversed by a number of other explorers.

In 1911 Britain had asked France whether it claimed the part of the continent known as Wilkes Land, which extends between 52°E and 160°E. This is the coastline along which d'Urville had sailed at the same time as Wilkes, but while Wilkes had not formally claimed the territory for the US, d'Urville had stepped onto an offshore islet and raised the French flag. In April 1912, the French government responds that 'these lands were taken possession of in the name of France in 1840 and that [France] has no intention of renouncing its rights over them'.

1917

Great Britain issues Letters patent of 28 March providing for the further definition and administration of the Falkland Islands Dependencies, in which it clarifies its territorial claim.

1919

At the Paris Peace Conference, Germany is forced to relinquish any claims it might have over those parts of Antarctica discovered by German explorers.

1921

The UK issues The Seal Fishery (Consolidation) Ordinance 1921, providing for the regulation and licencing of sealing within its territories.

1922

In June, Carl Larsen's Norwegian whaling company requests British permission to hunt whales in the Ross Sea, inducing Britain to act concerning its sovereignty over the area.

1923

The UK cedes the 'Ross-Dependency', an area representing approximately 14 per cent of the continent, to New Zealand with an Order in Council of 30 July. This area was part of Victoria Land, which had been claimed by the English Captain James Clark Ross in 1841. The reason for the issuing of an Order in Council rather than Letters Patent was that the latter were generally used when annexing new territory. The former allowed Britain to purport to have long enjoyed an inchoate title, to be cemented by the performance of acts of ownership.

On 14 November, New Zealand passes regulations applying New Zealand Law to the Ross Dependency.

1924

A Ministerial Declaration of 26 March places the French Antarctic territories within specialized naval zones.

On 27 March, France responds to the earlier British pronouncement by issuing a decree concerning its Antarctic territory entitled a Decree Reserving Certain Rights in French Antarctic Territories to French Citizens.

The US Secretary of State writes a letter of 13 May to A. W. Prescott of the Republican Publicity Association concerning the claims of other countries to Antarctica and the American attitude to them.

On 6 August France notifies the UK of its Decree regulating the economic exploitation of the Crozet Islands and Adélie Land.

On 21 November, France decrees that its Antarctic territories will be administered as part of its Madagascar colony.

1925

Norway introduces Law No. 11 of 17 July on Svalbard (later made applicable to Antarctic by Law No. 3 of 27 February 1930) providing for the regulations applicable to its territory.

A new type of whaling ship is introduced into the Antarctic, with a sloping ramp at its rear. These ships can winch blue whales straight onto the flensing deck, meaning the carcass can be processed aboard the ship. This technological development not only reduces fuel costs and avoids the problem of putrefaction, but also means that the ships can remain beyond the three mile territorial limit at which licence fees and duties must be paid.

1926

At the British Imperial Conference, the Dominion Prime Ministers devise a program of action for acquiring territory in the Antarctic.

1927

A delegate of the Argentine post office represents to the International Postal Bureau at Berne, Switzerland, that South Georgia falls within Argentina's territorial jurisdiction.

Following the Imperial Conference, Norway questions Britain's right to include the Ross Ice Barrier within its territory. This is because it rests on water and is mostly more than the three mile distance from the actual coastline which, at the time, was the territorial limit.

In August, however, British officials suggest in Oslo that the Ross Ice Shelf, being a permanent ice barrier, should be regarded as coastline, even though it rests on water. The motive for this assertion is that the delineation of the coastline determines whether Britain controls the Ross Sea and the Norwegian whalers seeking to operate within it.

In December, Harald Horntvedt lands on and claims Bouvet Island for Norway. A hut is erected, which is a traditional Norwegian method of asserting ownership over new lands.

1928

In January, Britain grants a licence to hunt for seals and whales in the waters of Bouvet and Thompson Islands. Its authority to do so is, it claims, based on the British sealer George Norris' having landed on Bouvet Island and naming it 'Liverpool Island'. Norway immediately announce they have already claimed Bouvet Island and reject the British claim, arguing that even if Liverpool Island and Bouvet Island were one and the same, the British had failed to effectively maintain their sovereignty. This dispute results in an extended exchange of notes regarding the nations' respective claims and their basis.

In November, the British recognise Norway's claim to Bouvet Island, whilst reminding them of all the areas Britain claims by right of discovery. The Norwegians agree not to occupy any of these areas.

On 20 December, Australian aviator Hubert Wilkins pilots the first flight in the Antarctic.

1929

In February, Norwegian Nils Larsen, Captain of the *Norvegia*, 'occupies' Peter I Island for Norway by erecting a small hut and raising their flag.

A Royal Commission dated 21 August 1929 is granted in favour of Sir Hubert Wilkins to claim territory between the western boundary of the Falkland Islands Dependencies and the Ross Dependency. His first recorded claim is of 29 December.

On 28 November, American aviator Richard Byrd flies over the South Pole and drops an American flag. Byrd claims Marie Byrd Land, a region outside the Ross Dependency, for the US and this claim is recorded and confirmed on 21 December.

Norway passes the Norwegian Whaling Act and the Bureau of International Whaling Statistics is established by the Norwegian Government.

1930

The Australian explorer Sir Douglas Mawson lands on Proclamation Island on 13 January asserting, in the name of the King, 'the full sovereignty of the territory of Enderby Land, Kemp Land, MacRobertson Land' and all the islands between 73°E and 47°E.

Mawson reads a Proclamation from the air over the Antarctic continent near Proclamation Island on 25 January.

Norway issues its Law No. 3 of 27 February concerning the administration as dependencies of Bouvet Island, Peter Island and Queen Maud Land providing for the application of Norwegian law within these territories. This is accompanied by the Royal Decree of 19 September providing for the administration of Bouvet Island.

A Resolution is introduced on 30 June into the US Senate which would direct the President to claim areas in Antarctica discovered or explored by American citizens.

The first edition of the British Admiralty's *Antarctic Pilot* is published.

The Bureau of International Whaling Statistics publishes the first issue of *International Whaling Statistics*.

1931

Sir Douglas Mawson, as part of the BANZARE expedition, reads Proclamations claiming territory in the name of Great Britain at Cape Denison, King George V Land on 5 January; at Scullin Monolith, Mac. Robertson Land on 13 February; and at Cape Bruce, Mac. Robertson Land on 18 February. The ceremony at Cape

Denison is filmed for English and Australian audiences.

In February, a Norwegian plane flies over an as yet un-claimed section of Antarctica, dropping a flag and documents and claiming the area for Norway. Permission having been granted by King Haakon VII, it is named after the monarch's granddaughter; Princess Ragnhild.

Norway issues its Royal proclamation of 1 May placing Peter I Island under Norwegian sovereignty. This is accompanied by its Royal decree of the same day providing for the exercise of police authority on Peter I Island.

Britain, in a note of 6 August, recognises Norway's sovereignty over Peter I Island.

Under the auspices of the League of Nations, the Convention for the Regulation of Whaling is signed by 22 nations. However, some of the major whaling nations, including Germany and Japan, do not sign the Convention.

The Second International Polar Year begins. No IPY stations, however, are operated in the Antarctic.

1933

The UK makes the largest territorial claim; over almost half of the Antarctic continent. This portion of territory is ceded to Australia by way of a British Order in council on 7 February and the passing of the Australian Antarctic Territory Acceptance Act of 13 June. This creates the 'Australian Antarctic Territory'. This leads to an exchange of notes between the UK and France regarding the limits of Adélie Land.

Norway issues its Law No. 1 of 24 March amending Law No. 3 of 27 February 1930 concerning Bouvet Island by including Peter I Island.

1934

In January in response to the US's establishing an official post office at 'Little America', situated within the Ross Dependency, the British Ambassador in Washington informs the US State Department that this infringes 'British sovereignty and New Zealand administrative rights in the Dependency.' The US Secretary of State, Cordell Hull, acknowledges the note, whilst reserving 'all rights which the US or its citizens may have with respect to this matter.'

In October, the British Ambassador in Washington unofficially requests an explanation regarding what could be construed as the USA's assertion of sovereignty in sending an official postmaster to Little America. The US Secretary of State responds that 'mere discovery' of a place, such as the Ross Dependency, was insufficient to substantiate a claim of ownership and that what is required is that discovery be accompanied by 'occupancy and use'.

A British note of 23 October to the Norwegian Government expresses the Empire's governments' view that an Antarctic conference would not be desirable and containing an assurance concerning British intentions as regards the region lying between the Australian Antarctic Territory and Coats Land.

1935

American aviator Lincoln Ellsworth requests permission from the Governor of the Falkland Islands to use a harbour as a base. After having realised the possible implications of accepting this permission, the American State Department informs the British Foreign Office that this acceptance of authority 'cannot in any way be implied to have any bearing on the question as to what country or countries may validly claim ownership of or title to the various territories embraced within the term 'dependencies''. Britain declines to reply. Ellsworth makes a number of claims, by dropping flags, extending Marie Byrd Land to a part now known as Ellsworth Land.

1936

A US Act of 16 June authorising the presentation by the President to Lincoln Ellsworth of his second Congressional Gold Medal confirms his having claimed land on behalf of the US.

The UK's Whale Fishery (Consolidation) Ordinance 1936 updates the laws relating to whaling in the Falkland Islands and its Dependencies.

On 24 August 1936 the Australian Antarctic Territory is formally promulgated.

1937

On 29 January, four Norwegian women become the first women to set foot on the Antarctic continent.

In June, the enormous expansion of the Pelagic whaling industry leads to the International Whaling Conference, held in London. The International Agreement for the Regulation of Whaling is signed. This agreement regulates date limits for the Antarctic whaling season and the minimum size limit for various species. It also prohibits whaling in certain areas.

Argentina makes a reservation of rights as they stand concerning the Falkland Islands Dependencies.

1938

A French Decree of 1 April defines the limits of Adélie land.

Another International Whaling Conference is held in June in London. A whale sanctuary is established south of 40°S, between 70°W and 160°W. This is maintained until 1955.

The UK, Australia, New Zealand and France exchange Notes on 25 October regarding aerial navigation in the Antarctic.

A British letter of 11 November to Norway renews an assurance concerning British intentions in Antarctica and seeks recognition of the boundaries of the Australian Antarctic Territory.

1939

Norway issues a Royal Proclamation of 14 January defining the area of Norwegian sovereignty in Antarctica as extending between the boundary of Coats Land in the west and the limits of the Australian Antarctic Dependency in the east. The US, Germany, the USSR and Chile communicate their reservations to Norway. Following a suggestion regarding clarification of the border of the territory by the UK, Norway agrees to it in a Note of 3 October.

Between February and May, France and the US exchange letters regarding the basis of France's claim to Adélie land.

A German Report of 11 April records the discoveries and claims made by the German Antarctic Expedition of 1938–1939. No official claim is formulated on the basis of the Report.

The US issues instructions of 11 December to diplomatic officers of the US in the American Republics proposing a common Inter-American policy with reference to the Antarctic.

Nazi Germany claims territory claimed by the Norwegians on the basis of discovery, arguing that it was discovered and fully investigated by Germany.

1940

In January, a German naval operation in the Indian Ocean captures a Norwegian whaling fleet near Antarctic waters. After one of these ships, the *Pinguin*, which is being used by the Germans, is sunk by HMS *Cornwall* off the Persian Gulf in May 1941, Southern Ocean pelagic whaling ceases for the duration of the war.

Argentina's Decree No. 61852-M.97 of 30 April establishes its National Antarctic Commission.

Chile's Decree No. 1723 of 2 November entrusts to the Ministry of Foreign Affairs and Trade responsibility for Antarctic matters.

Chile's Decree No. 1747 of 6 November declares the limits of the Chilean Antarctic Territory it claims for itself, at longitudes 53°W and 90°W. It is accompanied by notes informing Argentina, the US and the UK of its claim.

Japan issues a note of 13 November reserving the Japanese position with regard to the Chilean decree. Chile responds with a refusal to accept that reservation.

Following a Chilean note of 3 December to Argentina giving further details of the bases of Chilean claims and inviting Argentine authorities to take part in discussions in Santiago, a series of Notes are exchanged between the two countries regarding their Antarctic claims from 1940–1943.

Following the raising of an American flag at their East Base, the British Ambassador in Washington informs the State Department that he hopes this has 'no political significance'. The State Department does not reply.

The government of Argentina suggests to the UK that an international Antarctic conference be held to discuss the various international claims.

1941

On 25 February, the UK informs Chile that its claim includes part of the Falkland Islands Dependencies and that the UK does not recognise the November 6 Decree as conferring any title with respect to those territories on the Government of Chile.

A conference of Chilean and Argentine legal advisors leads to an agreement concerning the territory disputed between them.

On 14 November, Argentina decrees the establishment of a permanent post office on Laurie Island.

1942

The Chilean government issues Decree No. 548 of 27 March establishing the composition and functions of the Chilean Antarctic Commission, which is to handle all questions relating to Chilean Antarctic interests.

The government of Argentina sends a transport ship, the *Primero de Mayo*, to Deception Island, where its crew perform acts of possession.

In June, the British Foreign Secretary, Anthony Eden, notifies the Argentine government that Britain will not recognise any mail originating from the Argentine post office on Laurie Island.

1943

The US Navy's Hydrographic Office issues the *Sailing Directions for Antarctica 1943*.

Argentina notifies the UK of its taking formal possession of the areas visited on the voyage of the *Primero de Mayo* the year before.

In January, Britain sends a ship to Deception Island to counter Argentina's claim and removes the Argentine marks of sovereignty left there. The ship then sails on to the South Orkneys to raise the British flag over Signy Island.

In March, an Argentine expedition visits Stonington Island and removes materials left by the US. The expedition also visits Deception Island and removes British emblems and repaints the Argentinian flag.

1944

In February, an International Whaling Conference is held in London, proposing new principles and regulations to limit the total annual catch at a sustainable level.

A British Appointment dated 1 May appoints a person to hold the post of Magistrate and other offices in Graham Land and the South Orkney Islands and the South Shetland Islands.

The UK issues its Fisheries Ordinance 1944 with regard to regulating fishing in the Falkland Islands.

Britain establishes post offices at their bases in the Falkland Dependencies and issues new stamps for the Dependencies. Protests are received from Argentina and Chile.

1945

The Charter of the UN is signed on 26 June.

1946

During the summer of 1945–6, Britain establishes two more bases in the Falkland Islands Dependencies, bringing its total to five.

In November, the US announces a naval expedition, 'Operation Highjump', to Antarctica with its purpose to 'train members of the Navy and to test ships, aircraft and other military equipment under frigid conditions'.

In December, the International Convention for the Regulation of Whaling is concluded and opened for signature. The agreement aims to protect all whale species from overhunting and establish a system of international regulation that ensures proper conservation and development of whale stocks. The Convention establishes the International Whaling Commission (IWC), an intergovernmental body charged with the conservation of whales and the management of whaling. The 1946 Convention follows multiple unsuccessful attempts at preventing exploitation, ranging from the issuing of licenses by the British Government from 1906, the signing of a Convention for the Regulation of Whaling in 1931 and certain domestic pieces of legislation, for example the UK's Whale Fishery (Consolidation) Ordinance 1936.

Chile's Decree No. 6378 of 4 December authorises the issue of postage stamps bearing a map of the Chilean Antarctic Territory.

The US Acting Secretary of State sends a letter on 14 December to the Secretary of the Navy setting out the US policy of exploration and use of Antarctic areas with a view to making a claim.

In response to the actions of Britain and the US, Argentina's President, Juan Perón, issues a decree in September prohibiting the publication of maps of Argentina that 'do not show the Argentine Antarctic'. In October, the President issues a decree 'declaring Argentine sovereignty over the Antarctic submarine platform and the water covering it'.

Chile responds, announcing in December that it will send three naval ships to reinforce its claims and issuing a decree asserting its right to exploit any uranium found in its Antarctic territory.

1947

Chile's Resolution No. 29 of 6 January establishes a post office in the Chilean Antarctic Territory. It is accompanied by another Resolution on 20 December establishing one at O' Higgins Base.

Argentina issues a Statement of 15 January on the work of the National Antarctic Commission and the grounds for Argentine Antarctic Claims.

Chilean Decree No. 118 of 20 January appoints a Naval Governor of the Chilean Antarctic Territory.

On 21 January Chile's Minister for Foreign Affairs delivers a speech to the Senate concerning the grounds of Chile's claim to Antarctica.

Chile inaugurates its 'Soberania' base in the South Shetland Islands on 6 February, provoking a protest in the form of a British note of 17 December to Chile protesting at the establishment of base and outlining the grounds of a claim to the International Court of Justice (ICJ).

On 12 March, the Argentine Government extends its Antarctic claim to a sector between longitudes 25°W and 74°W.

On 23 June the Chilean government issues a Presidential Declaration that claims sovereignty over the continental shelf off Chilean territories and including territorial waters extending 200 nautical miles from the coast.

Chile and Argentina issue a Joint Declaration on 12 July concerning the South American Antarctic in which both countries assert their 'unquestionable rights' to the South American Antarctic and state their desire to conclude a treaty between them regarding the demarcation of their respective boundaries in the South American Antarctic. A similar Declaration is made on 4 March 1948.

On 2 September, the Inter-American Treaty of Reciprocal Assistance is signed in Rio de Janeiro. It provides that an armed attack on an American state will be considered an attack on all of them. While the region covered by the treaty extends from the North to the South Pole, Argentina, Chile and the US make reservations relating to the Antarctic sector between longitudes 24°W and 90°W.

In October, the CIA prepares a secret map of Antarctica which shows all the areas America intends to claim.

In November, and despite a protest from the British magistrate, the Argentinians erect a base on Deception Island, where Britain already has a base.

A Chilean commander performs the acts of possession on Greenwich Island on 6 December.

On 17 December, the UK invites the Argentine and Chilean governments to submit their dispute regarding sovereignty in the Antarctic to the ICJ. This proposal is rejected by both governments.

On 26 December, Britain transfers sovereignty over Heard Island and the McDonald Islands to the Australian government.

Argentina erects a lighthouse at the entrance to Port Lockroy on Doumer Island, where Britain's main base in the region is located.

In December, the Australian National Antarctic Research Expedition establishes a research station on Heard Island.

On 29 December, a South African naval expedition formally raises the country's flag on Marion Island and establishes a permanent meteorological station.

Chile issues two stamps celebrating its recent voyage in the Antarctic. They are printed with a map of the 'Chilean Antarctic' with its boundary set between 53°W and 90°W.

The Japanese Whales Research Institute is founded.

1948

On 4 January, a South African naval expedition formally raises the country's flag on Prince Edward Island. On the same day, the South African Government issues a Proclamation concerning Marion Island and Prince Edward Island, affirming that the rights in these islands would now be exercised by the Imperial government of South Africa rather than that of the UK.

On 25 January, Argentina establishes a new station on Deception Island.

A Chilean note of 31 January to the UK rejects their protest at the establishment of the Chilean station in the South Shetland Islands and declines to submit the matter to the ICJ. This is accompanied by a Chilean statement of February 1948 of reasons for their refusal to accept settlement by the ICJ.

On 18 February, a Chilean expedition establishes a new station on the Trinity Peninsula.

On 4 March, Argentina and Chile issue a further joint statement regarding their claims in the Antarctic, despite their having been unable to resolve their dispute regarding their respective borders in the South American Antarctic as envisaged by the joint declaration of the previous year.

In March, the UK suggests talks between Argentina, Chile, the US and the UK concerning the Falkland Island Dependencies. This proposal is rejected.

Also in March, the second Australian National Antarctic Research Expedition establishes a research station on Macquarie Island.

Argentina issues a memorandum of 21 April setting out the grounds for the Argentine claims to the Falkland Islands and Antarctic Territories.

In June, the US produces a number of draft agreements regarding the formulation of US policy in Antarctica, placing Antarctica under UN trusteeship and providing for a condominium over Antarctica.

A US Department of State paper in August outlines proposed US territorial claims in Antarctica.

On 10 November, the International Convention for the Regulation of Whaling enters into force.

France issues an Order on 24 November establishing a post office in Adélie land, open for ordinary and registered mail.

An Australian mission to Heard Island performs a claiming ceremony and designates a tent its post office.

The President of Chile visits the 'Chilean Antarctic' territories aboard an armed troopship and returns to Chile to inform the public that he has defended and consolidated 'Chilean sovereignty in the Antarctic'.

Britain, Chile and Argentina agree not to send warships below 60° S latitude during the coming summer, except for warship movements that have been 'customary for a number of years'.

The Falkland Islands Internal Air Service is inaugurated.

The UK issues the Falkland Islands Letters Patent 1948 which further provide for the government of the Falkland Islands.

1949

The agreement not to send warships below 60° S is confirmed in the Tripartite Naval Declarations of 18 January between Argentina, Chile and the UK.

A Resolution of 10 February concerning Antarctica is adopted by the All-Soviet Geographical Society of the USSR which notes that '[n]o solution of the problem of a regime for the Antarctic without the participation of the Soviet Union can have legal force, and the U.S.S.R. has every reason not to recognize any such solution.'

On 24 March, France produces its Official Study concerning territories claimed by France in Southern Regions and on 12 April this is followed by a Parliamentary Report concerning territories claimed by France in southern regions.

1950

On 18 January, France establishes a research station at Port Martin, Terre Adélie. A post office is opened with overprinted Madagascar stamps.

A Soviet Memorandum of 7–8 June on the Participation of the Soviet Union in any International Settlement Concerning Antarctica notes that the USSR 'cannot agree to such a question as that of the Antarctic regime being settled without its participation'. Both the Argentine and Chilean Notes in response seem to interpret the USSR's memorandum as making a claim in the Antarctic and both reject it on those grounds.

The US issues its Draft Declaration to establish a regime of international cooperation and a moratorium of claims in Antarctica.

On 19 December there is an exchange of Notes constituting an Agreement regarding the transfer of Heard Island and McDonald Islands from His Majesty's Government in the UK to His Majesty's Government in the Commonwealth of Australia.

1951

Argentina issues its Declaration of 1 February of Sovereignty for Deposit in the Argentine Antarctic Sector.

In April, the British again invite the Governments of Argentina and Chile to submit their dispute regarding sovereignty in the Antarctic to the ICJ. This proposal is rejected.

On 8 September, a treaty of peace with Japan is signed by 49 nations in San Francisco. Its terms include Japan's renunciation of all territorial rights or claims in the Antarctic.

Between 1951 and 1953 Chile and the UK continue to exchange notes regarding their respective bases in the Antarctic.

Norway issues its Seal Fishery Law No. 1 of 14 December for the regulation of Antarctic sealing.

The International Meteorological Organization is reorganized within the UN. It becomes the World Meteorological Organization.

1952

In February, the British vessel, the *John Biscoe*, arrives to resupply and man the British base at Hope Bay, on the tip of the Antarctic Peninsula. The Commander of the Argentinian base established there orders shots be fired over the heads of the British as they unload their supplies. The British retreat to their vessel. A British Frigate with Royal Marines is sent to the base. A British protest regarding the incident is met with an apology by the president of Argentina.

On 10 March, a Japanese transport vessel, the *Settsu-Maru*, sinks in the Southern Ocean with 3800 tonnes of whale oil aboard.

1953

In February, the British again invite the Governments of Argentina and Chile to submit their dispute regarding sovereignty in the Antarctic to the ICJ. This proposal is rejected.

On 14 April the first criminal law case heard in the region subsequently covered by the Antarctic Treaty takes place before the Magistrate on Deception Island. It concerns the protection of wildlife.

On 27 March the Australian Government passes the Heard Island and McDonald Islands Act which provides for the administration of this island group.

On 10 September the Australian Government issues a Proclamation claiming sovereign rights over the continental shelf of Australia and its Territories, including the Australian Antarctic Territory, Heard Island, the McDonald Islands and Macquarie Island.

Disagreement over the erection of structures on Deception Island by Argentina and Chile leads to Britain sending a frigate to the island. On board are the Falkland Islands Governor, two police officers and 15 Royal Marines, who dismantle the structures and deport two Argentinians.

1954

On 1 November, Australia passes the Australian Antarctic Territory Act providing for the administration of the Australian Antarctic Territory.

In December, the British again invite the Governments of Argentina and Chile to submit their dispute regarding sovereignty in the Antarctic to the ICJ. This proposal is rejected.

Campbell Island is declared a Flora and Fauna Reserve by the UK.

1955

On 17 February Australia appoints a coroner for the Australian Antarctic Territory.

The UK requests the ICJ to recognise the validity of its claims of sovereignty over the portions of its Antarctic territory also claimed by Argentina and Chile. The claim is based upon Letters Patent of 1908 and 1917 which designate the territory as dependencies of the Falkland Islands. However, neither Chile nor Argentina accepts the Court's jurisdiction. Argentina refuses to accept adjudication concerning sovereignty over the Antarctic territories without the disputed title to the Falkland Islands also being resolved.

In May, the British produce their application instituting proceedings against the Argentine Republic and Chile before the ICJ.

A Chilean note of 4 May to the UK gives its reasons for rejecting British proposals to submit the dispute to judicial settlement.

Chile's Law No. 11846 of 27 June places the Chilean Antarctic Territory under the administration of the Intendent of Magallanes.
A Chilean letter of 15 July to the ICJ declines to accept the jurisdiction of the Court in respect of the British application.
A press statement on 30 July by the Australian Minister of External Affairs welcomes the interest of other states with regard to activities within the Australian Antarctic Territory within the International Geophysical Year (IGY).
On 1 August Argentina sends a letter to the ICJ embodying a note declining to accept the jurisdiction of the court in respect of the British application.
France's Law No. 55-1502 of 6 August establishes the territory of French Southern and Antarctic Lands and endows it with financial and administrative autonomy.
In a Note to the ICJ on 31 August the British comment upon the refusal of Argentina and Chile to accept the jurisdiction of the Court.
America establishes a base on the coast of Queen Maud Land.
A French expedition introduces the first reindeer to Illes Kerguelen. Myxomytosis is also introduced in an attempt to reduce the rabbit population.
The Commonwealth Trans-Antarctic Expedition commences.
The US confirms that it recognizes no claims to territory advanced in the Antarctic.

1956

France's Decree No. 56-32 of 13 January establishes the financial system for the French Southern and Antarctic Lands.
Argentina's Decree-law No. 1311 of 26 January establishes the Argentine Antarctic Institute.
A Chilean note of 22 March to the UK protests at the establishment of British bases within the Chilean Antarctic Territory. It is met with a British note rejecting the protest.
Chile's Decree No. 298 of 17 July enacts a Statute for the Chilean Antarctic Territory.
France issues Decree No. 56-935 of 18 September concerning the administrative organization of the French Southern and Antarctic Lands.
A Soviet expedition establishes IGY station 'Mirnyy' on the mainland of Queen Mary Land.
A US expedition establishes IGY station 'Little America V' on the Ross Ice Shelf.
India requests that the question of Antarctica be included on the agenda for the 11th session of the General Assembly. Chile opposes this request and the two countries produce explanatory documents outlining their respective positions.
The Antarctica case, *United Kingdom v Argentina*, Removal from the list, Order, (1956) ICJ Rep 12; ICGJ 178 (ICJ 1956) is handed down.
The Antarctica case, *United Kingdom v Chile*, Removal from the list, Order, (1956) ICJ Rep 15; ICGJ 177 (ICJ 1956) is handed down.
The US establishes a base at the Geographical South Pole (later named the Amundsen-Scott Base).
On 22 December, the Chilean national airline flies the first Antarctic tourist flight; a non-stop flight from Chacabuco over the South Shetland Islands and Trinity Peninsula.

1957

Argentina's Decree-law No. 2191 of 28 February re-establishes the National Territory of Tierra del Fuego, Antarctica and Islands of the South Atlantic.
Norway's Law No. 1 of 21 June amends Law No. 3 of 27 February 1930 concerning Bouvet Island and Peter I island by including Queen Maud Land.
The IGY, from July 1957 to December 1958, leads to international scientific cooperation in the region under the auspices of the International Council of Scientific Unions. Twelve countries are actively involved, including Argentina, Australia, Belgium, Chile, France, Japan, New Zealand, Norway, South Africa, the Soviet Union, the UK and the US.
New Zealand opens a post office at the Ross Island Base and issues four Ross Dependency stamps.
On 15 October, the first commercial flight arrives in Antarctica. It is a Pan American Airways flight from Christchurch to McMurdo Sound.

On 16 December, the South Geomagnetic Pole is reached for the first time, by a USSR tractor traverse.

1958

In February, the Scientific Commission on Antarctic Research (SCAR) conducts its first meeting.

On 18 February, Chile issues a statement concerning proposals to establish an international regime for Antarctica.

Talks between Britain, Australia, New Zealand and the US culminate in the US issuing a note to the eleven other IGY nations in April inviting them to attend an Antarctic conference to conclude a treaty.

On 15 July, the Indian Delegate to the UN proposes that 'the question of Antarctica' should be debated. This proposal is withdrawn on 14 November.

On 23 December, New Zealand and the US issue a Joint Announcement concerning the maintenance of bases beyond the IGY. The next day, the two governments exchange Notes constituting an Agreement regarding the provision of facilities in New Zealand for US Antarctic expeditions. This Agreement is extended in 1960.

1959

It is the Year of International Geophysical Cooperation, continuing the work of the IGY.

A Chilean note of 9 March to Australia informs Australia of the extent of the Chilean Antarctic Territory. This occurs in connection with a map published in an official Australian publication showing it as British.

In October, the Antarctic Conference begins in Washington, DC.

In December, the Antarctic Treaty is concluded and opened for signature. The twelve original signatory States are Argentina, Australia, Belgium, Chile, France, Japan, New Zealand, Norway, South Africa, the Soviet Union, the UK and the US. The signatories agree to hold all territorial claims and disputes concerning the region south of latitude 60°S in abeyance, to exchange information freely, to guarantee freedom of access for scientific research and not to conduct military activities except in support of scientific research. In the discussions surrounding the Treaty, the participating governments comment upon and make reservations concerning a number of the provisions especially with regard to their effect on their and others' existing territorial claims.

Phillip G Law discovers the Mawson Peninsula.

1960

A Chilean note of 19 January to the UK reserves Chilean rights before the entry into force of the Antarctic Treaty in relation to British maps and documents indicating as British parts of the Chilean Antarctic Territory.

On 31 May, Britain ratifies the Antarctic Treaty.

On 25 May, the Government of the Falkland Islands enacts the 'Oil in Territorial Waters Ordinance' to prevent oil pollution in the sea.

Norway's Law No. 2 of 2 June amends Law No. 3 of 27 February 1930 by providing for the implementation of the Antarctic treaty.

On 21 October, New Zealand's Antarctica Act brings the Antarctic Treaty into force for the Ross Dependency and regulates the conduct of New Zealand citizens in the unclaimed portions.

On 2 November, the Australian Antarctic Treaty Act brings the Antarctic Treaty into force for the Australian Antarctic Territory.

1961

The first Antarctic Treaty Consultative Meeting (ATCM) is held in Canberra.

On 23 June, the Antarctic Treaty enters into force. Article IV 'freezes' the territorial claims of States to the continent, effectively preserving the legal situation at the time of the conclusion of the treaty.

On 10 November, the Government of New Zealand designates the Snares Islands 'Reserve for the Preservation of Fauna and Flora'.

On 12 December, the first Antarctic nuclear plant arrives by ship at McMurdo Station.

1962

The British Antarctic Territory is constituted as a new colony comprising that part of the Falkland Islands Dependencies that lies south of latitude 60°S by the Antarctic Treaty Order in Council of 26 February. The Royal Letters Patent of 2 April provide for South Georgia and the South Sandwich Islands to remain Dependencies of the Falkland Islands.

In March, the US Navy builds nuclear power station PM-3A at McMurdo base. There are hundreds of malfunctions and radiation leaks before it is shut down in 1972. The site is left with thousands of cubic metres of radioactive earth and contaminated soil and it is not declared uncontaminated until May 1988.

On 21 May, South Africa's 'Citizens in Antarctica Act' make its laws applicable to South African citizens in Antarctica.

On 14 June, Czechoslovakia accedes to the Antarctic Treaty.

From 18–28 July, the second Antarctic Treaty Consultative Meeting is held in Buenos Aires.

Chile's Decree 363 of 13 September creates the National Committee of the Scientific Committee for Antarctic Research (SCAR), and establishes its functions.

1964

Parties to the Antarctic Treaty conclude the Agreed Measures for the Conservation of Antarctic Fauna and Flora (Recommendation III-VIII), providing for the establishment of specially protected areas.

The UK issues its Penguin and Albatross Regulations 1964 regulating the collecting of the species' eggs.

Chile's Decree No. 103 of 28 February approves the organic regulations of the Chilean Antarctic Institute.

The Third Consultative Meeting of the Antarctic Treaty is held in Brussels from 2–13 June. It recommends the 'Agreed measures for the Conservation of Antarctic Fauna and Flora' to member governments.

On 13 November, the UN Organization 'Committee of Twenty-Four' adopts a recommendation that urges Argentina and the UK to hold discussions with a view to finding a peaceful solution to the Falkland Islands problem.

1965

At a Special Meeting of the International Whaling Commission, taking place from 3–6 June, it recommends, for the first time, a quota on the number of whales permitted to be caught.

A Norwegian Royal Decree of 4 June prohibits the catching of fur seals and sea elephants in Antarctic regions.

The International Hydrological Decade begins.

On 16 December, UN General Assembly Resolution 2065 (XX) invites Britain and Argentina to negotiate a peaceful solution regarding their conflict in the Falkland Islands.

1966

From 23 February to 3 March the First Session of the World Meteorological Organization is held in Melbourne.

The first commercially organized American tourist cruise, offered by Lindblad Travel, arrives in Antarctica.

In November, the first resolution on Antarctic tourism is passed by ATCM, encouraging states to withhold permission for tourist groups to visit Antarctic stations unless assurances are given of compliance with the provisions of the Treaty, Recommendations of ATCM and any conditions imposed by the station.

The Symposium on Antarctic Oceanography is held in Santiago from 13–16 September.

The fourth Consultative Meeting of the Antarctic Treaty is held from 3–18 November.

On 8 December Australia appoints Deputy Coroners and Justices of the Peace for the Australian Antarctic Territory.

On 17 December a private mountaineering expedition reaches the peak of Vinson Massif, the highest peak in Antarctica.

1967

Britain's Antarctic Treaty Act gives effect to the Measures for the Conservation of Antarctic Fauna and Flora agreed upon by parties to the Antarctic Treaty.

On 4 January the Argentine Government approves a law claiming sovereignty over seas adjacent to Argentine territory to 200 nautical miles from the coast. A decree is issued to regulate fishing by foreign vessels within this territory.

On 27 January the Treaty on Principles Governing the Activities of States in the Exploration and Use of Outer Space, including the Moon and other Celestial Bodies is signed. Many of its provisions are analogous to those of the earlier Antarctic Treaty.

The Ecuadorian 'Asamblea Constituyente' declares Ecuador's right over the Antarctic sector between 84°30' W and 96°30' W. This declaration, while published in the Official Register 78 of 6 March, is not supported by the Ecuadorian Government.

On 30 March, the Netherlands accedes to the Antarctic Treaty.

On 4 December there is a volcanic eruption on Deception Island causing the rapid evacuation of the Chilean, British and Argentine stations.

On 28 December, the first fossilized land animals are found in Antarctica.

1968

In the US Tax Court case of Martin v Commissioner of Inland Revenue (1968) 50 TC No. 9 the Court, after noting that the State Department does 'not consider Antarctica to be under the sovereignty of any government' decides that Antarctica is not a foreign country.

The International Symposium on Antarctic Glaciological Exploration is held at Dartmouth College from 3–6 September.

The fifth Consultative Meeting of the Antarctic Treaty is held in Paris from 18–29 November.

1969

The first expedition ship *MS Explorer* is built, and the modern expedition cruise industry is born.

The volcano on Deception Island erupts again, causing the Argentine, British and Chilean stations to be evacuated.

1970

The Scientific Committee on Antarctic Research holds its second Symposium on Antarctic Geology and Solid Earth Geophysics in Oslo from 6–15 August.

The Sixth Consultative Meeting of the Antarctic Treaty is held in Tokyo from 19–31 October.

Regular flights from Argentina to Antarctica begin.

New Zealand and the UK first raise the issue of control over future mining of mineral resources after they are approached by mineral companies.

Chile issues its Decree No. 566 of 12 August concerning the depiction of Chilean territory on maps distributed within the country.

Chile's Decree No. 735 of 23 October establishes the Chilean Antarctic Commission.

1971

Between June and December, France pronounces a collection of laws, orders and decrees in relation to French Southern and Antarctic lands extending the continental shelf, applying French penal law and procedure and limiting the rights of foreign fishing vessels.

In August, the Scientific Committee on Antarctic Research, in conjunction with the International Commission on Polar Meteorology, holds a Symposium on Energy Fluxes over Polar Surfaces in Moscow.

The International Antarctic Glaciological Programme begins. It is a collaborative effort lasting ten years between Australian, British, French, Soviet Union and US scientists to study the ice cap of Greater Antarctica.

On 15 September, Romania accedes to the Antarctic Treaty.

On 15 December, the US Government bans whaling (except subsistence whaling) within its territories.

Norway enacts Regulations on 17 December for the protection of Bouvet Island with adjacent territorial waters as a nature reserve. On the same day, a Norwegian Royal Proclamation declares Bouvetøya a Nature Reserve.

Macquarie Island is proclaimed a State Reserve by the Tasmanian state government in Australia.

1972

France's Order No. 5 of 13 January promulgates legislation concerning the delimitation of the French territorial sea.

France's Order No. 16 of 14 April promulgates in French Southern and Antarctic Lands laws No. 68-1181 of 30 December 1968 and decree No. 70-988 relating to exploitation of the continental shelf.

In June, the Convention for the Conservation of Antarctic Seals (CCAS) is opened for signature. The convention is a response to the near extinction of populations of Antarctic seals resulting from commercial exploitation, and limits or prohibits the catch of certain species of seals.

The 'Biological Investigations of Marine Antarctic Systems and Stocks' (BIOMASS) series of coordinated international studies begins, collecting data on birds, fish, krill, seals, squid and other marine life in the Southern Ocean.

1973

The International Convention on the Prevention of Pollution from Ships (MARPOL

Convention) is adopted at the International Maritime Organization (IMO). The convention is aimed at preventing and minimizing pollution from ships.

A discovery of natural gas pockets in the continental shelf off the western Antarctic coast leads to increased oil and gas speculation and receives wide press coverage. The oil crisis of October 1973 intensifies this scrutiny.

The UK Government bans the importation of whale products, except sperm whale oil, spermaceti wax, ambergris and those products which have already been incorporated into manufactured goods overseas.

The Scientific Committee on Antarctic Research establishes the International Glaciological Programme for the Antarctic Peninsula.

1974

On 19 November, the DDR accedes to the Antarctic Treaty.

On 14 December, the UN General Assembly in its Resolution 3160 (XXVIII) urges Argentina and the UK to accelerate the negotiations called for in Resolution 2065 (XX) of 1965 to resolve their dispute regarding the Falkland Islands.

1975

On 15 May, the US issues a Statement of Policy Objectives in Antarctica.

On 16 May, Brazil accedes to the Antarctic Treaty.

On 12 June, the US issues a Statement concerning claims to sovereignty and the exploitation of Antarctic mineral resources.

In June, the Eighth Antarctic Treaty Consultative Meeting is held in Norway with parties discussing the issue of the exploitation of mineral resources in Antarctica. The parties adopt Recommendation VIII-14 which calls for the preparation of a report on the environmental impact of mining and resolving to hold a special meeting on the subject in 1976.

Article 5 of Chilean Decree 1230 includes the Chilean Antarctic Territory in its XII Region.

1976

France's Order No. 07 of 19 January re-enacts regulations concerning marine fishing and the exploitation of the produce of the sea in the French Southern and Antarctic Lands.

On 4 February, an Argentine destroyer, the *Almirante Storni*, intercepts an unarmed British research vessel, the *RRS Shackleton*, and commands it to stop because it is in Argentine territorial waters. The captain refuses and continues on to Port Stanley, despite several warning shots being fired over the bow of the British vessel.

In May, the oil tanker *Urquiola* damages her hull on a shoal, and spills an estimated 100,000 tonnes of crude oil off the coast of Spain.

In June, the special meeting on mineral resources in Paris reveals divergent views on the subject among parties to the Antarctic Treaty.

Argentina establishes naval station *Corbeta Uruguay* in the South Sandwich Islands. The UK protests the establishment of the base through diplomatic channels but does not close it down until 1982, following the Falklands War.

France issues Law No. 76-655 of 16 July concerning the economic zone in the seas off the coasts of its territory.

1977

At the Ninth Antarctic Treaty Consultative Meeting, parties adopt 1977 Recommendation IX-1 which imposes a 'voluntary' moratorium on mineral activities in Antarctica pending the adoption of a regime to be agreed upon amongst the Consultative Parties.

Poland becomes a consultative party to the Antarctic Treaty, and can formally participate in ATCMs.

Airborne tourism begins in Antarctica using long range passenger aircraft flying from Australia and New Zealand.

In February, the oil tanker *Hawaiian Patriot* spills 95,000 tonnes of crude oil off the coast of Hawaii as a result of a hull crack sustained during a storm.

In July, the first Special Consultative Meeting of the Antarctic Treaty is held in London. Poland is admitted as a Consultative Party.

In August, the Third Symposium on Antarctic Geology and Geophysics is held in Wisconsin.

In September, the ninth Consultative Meeting of the Antarctic Treaty is held in London.

In December, a maritime accident involving sister ships *Venpet* and *Venoil* results in the spillage of almost 30,000 tonnes of crude oil off the coast of South Africa.

1978

Belgium, a non-claimant State, issues its Law of 12 January relating to the protection of fauna and flora in the Antarctic, which support the Agreed Measures for the Conservation of Antarctic Fauna and Flora, recommended by the Antarctic Treaty consultative parties.

France's Decree No. 78-144 of 3 February establishes an economic zone in the sea off the coasts of French Southern Lands.

On 11 March, the Convention for the Conservation of Antarctic Seals enters into force.

The MARPOL Protocol of 1978 is adopted by the IMO, as a response to a series of tanker accidents in 1976–77. The MARPOL Convention had not yet entered into force and so the Protocol is absorbed into the parent Convention. The instrument combining the Convention and Protocol enters into force on 2 October 1983.

Australia makes its Proclamation of Australian Fishing Zone 1978, which still provides the basis for Fisheries Management Act and exempts the Australian Antarctic Territory.

The US Antarctic Conservation Act of 1978 implements the Agreed Measures for the Conservation of Antarctic Flora and Fauna, as recommended by the Consultative Parties to the Antarctic Treaty.

Emilio Palma, the son of an Argentine Base Commander, becomes the first person to be born on the Antarctic continent. He is declared the 'first Argentine Antarctic citizen'.

1979

Chile's Decree with Force of Law 82 of 22 January approves the organic law of the 'Instituto Antartico Chileno' (INACH). This entity will plan, coordinate, direct, and control scientific and technological activities carried out by the State or authorized individuals in the Antarctic Territory or the rest of the Antarctic continent. The organization and powers of the agency are provided.

At the 31st annual meeting of the International Whaling Commission in London between 9–13 July, a ban is placed on the catching of all whales in the Southern Ocean, except Minke whales by factory ships. Australia proclaims the Australian Fishing Zone 200 nautical miles from its territory, though certain Antarctic areas are excluded.

The tenth Consultative Meeting of the Antarctic Treaty is held in Washington from 17 September to 5 October.

Chile's Decree-Law 2958 of 20 November approves, with reservation, the Convention for Conservation of Antarctic Seals, signed in London on 28 December 1972.

In November, an Air New Zealand tourist flight crashes on Mount Erebus, Ross Island, resulting in the loss of 257 lives. A resolution is passed in an ATCM to declare the site of the accident a 'tomb' to be left in peace.

1980

On 11 January, Uruguay accedes to the Antarctic Treaty.

In August, the Convention on the Conservation of Antarctic Marine Living Resources (CAMLR Convention) is opened for signature. The convention is a response to concerns that unregulated increases in krill catches in the Southern Ocean could have a detrimental impact on Antarctic marine ecosystems. It fosters the conservation of krill fishery resources in the Southern Ocean, and establishes the Commission for the Conservation of Antarctic Marine Living Resources.

Australia passes a number of laws aimed at protecting and conserving the Antarctic environment; applying the Antarctic Treaty Endangered Species Ordinance and the Migratory Birds Ordinance to the Australian Antarctic Territory.

The Scientific Committee on Antarctic Research holds its sixteenth meeting in Queenstown, New Zealand from 13–24 October.

1981

Germany (DDR) becomes a consultative party to the Antarctic Treaty, and can formally participate in ATCMs.

New Zealand and the Federal Republic of Germany exchange letters comprising an agreement between them on Antarctic Cooperation.

The Australian Antarctic Marine Living Resources Conservation Act 1981 applies the CAMLR Convention to the Antarctic Territory.

New Zealand's Antarctic Marine Living Resources Act 1981 implements the CAMLR Convention.

On 16 March, Papua New Guinea succeeds to the Antarctic Treaty after having become independent from Australia. Italy and Peru accede to the Treaty, on 18 March and 10 April respectively.

Chile's Decree 662 of 24 July promulgates the agreement of the conservation of the Antarctic marine live resources subscribed in Canberra, Australia on 11 September 1980.

The third Special Consultative Meeting of the Antarctic Treaty is held is Buenos Aires. The BRD is admitted to Consultative Status.

The eleventh Consultative Meeting of the Antarctic Treaty is held in Buenos Aires between 23 June and 7 July. Recommendation No. XI-1 is adopted by the Consultative Parties to the Antarctic Treaty which, in effect, begins the process of mineral negotiations which eventually lead to the Convention on the Regulation of Antarctic Mineral Resource Activities of 1988.

1982

The IWC adopts a moratorium on commercial whaling. However, whaling quotas are set for aboriginal subsistence whaling and member nations may issue 'Scientific Permits' to their citizens.

On 2 April, the long-term dispute between Argentina and the UK over the Falkland Islands and South Georgia and South Sandwich Islands escalates when Argentine forces invade Stanley and rapidly overcome the small garrison of British marines posted there. On 3 April the Argentine ships *Bahia Paraiso* and *Guerrico* attack the British Antarctic Survey scientific station at King Edward Point, South Georgia. On 3 April the UN Security Council passes Resolution 502, requiring Argentina to cease hostilities and withdraw its forces. This is refused. Britain acts under Article 51 of the UN Charter to restore the Government of the Falkland Islands and its Dependencies.

The Falklands War continues until Argentina surrenders on 14 June. South Georgia Island was occupied by the Argentine military from 3–25 April. On 20 June the Royal Navy shuts down Argentina's naval base Corbeta Uruguay on the South Sandwich Islands, which had operated since 1976.

On 7 April, the CAMLR Convention enters into force.

The Scientific Committee on Antarctic Research holds its seventeenth meeting in Leningrad between 28 June and 9 July.

On 10 December, the UN Convention on the Law of the Sea (UNCLOS) is signed in Montego Bay.

1983

On 12 September, the fifth Special Consultative Meeting of the Antarctic Treaty is held in Canberra. Brazil and India are admitted to Consultative Status. ATCMs become open to acceding non-consultative parties, although they are unable to vote at the meetings.

The 12th Consultative Meeting is held in Canberra from 13–27 September.

On 2 October, the combined MARPOL Convention and Protocol enters into force.

On 15 December, the UN General Assembly requests the Secretary-General to prepare a report on all aspects of Antarctica, including the Antarctic Treaty System. This resolution begins the practice of the Secretary-General submitting a report to the General Assembly on a periodic basis, which continues until 2006.

Australia enacts the Protection of Sea (Prevention of Pollution from Ships) Act 1983.

In the US, *Beattie et al v USA* (1984) 756 F. 2d. 91 is handed down. It concerns the 1979 Mt Erebus disaster in Antarctica. The court hears the case in its civil jurisdiction.

1985

On 1 January, a Chilean tourist flight crashes on King George Island, killing the ten people aboard.

On 20 March, the UK's Interim Administration Act of 1982 is repealed and the South Georgia and the South Sandwich Islands Order is made. The designation 'Falkland Islands Dependencies' is abolished and replaced by 'South Georgia and the South Sandwich Islands' and is defined as all territories between 20° W and 50° W from 50° S to 60° S. It therefore also includes the Shag rocks.

The Commission for the Conservation of Antarctic Marine Living Resources sets up the Ecosystem Monitoring Programme (CEMP) to monitor the effects of fishing and harvesting of species in the area.

On 7 October, the sixth Special Consultative Meeting of the Antarctic Treaty is held in Brussels. China and Uruguay are admitted to Consultative Status.

From 8–19 October, the thirteenth Consultative Meeting of the Antarctic treaty is held in Brussels.

Australia issues its Poisons and Narcotic Drugs Ordinance 1985 of the Australian Antarctic Territory and Poisons Ordinance 1985 of the Australian Antarctic Territory.

The Territory of the South Georgia and South Sandwich Islands is formed, having previously been administered as a Falkland Island Dependency.

The Travel Corporation of America begins a series of tourist flights from Chile to King George Island.

1986

In January, the UN General Assembly passes a resolution affirming that 'any exploitation of the resources of Antarctica should ensure the maintenance of international peace and security in Antarctica, the protection of its environment, the non-appropriation and conservation of its resources and the international management and equitable sharing of the benefits of such exploitation.'

Japan begins to issue 'Scientific Permits' to its citizens, allowing whaling to continue under the IWC moratorium.

From 16–27 June, the nineteenth meeting of the Scientific Committee on Antarctic Research is held in San Diego. China is admitted to membership.

On 28 November, South Korea accedes to the Antarctic Treaty.

In December, the UN General Assembly passes a resolution requesting that the Antarctic Treaty Consultative Parties impose a moratorium on the negotiations to establish a minerals regime in Antarctica, owing to concerns that not all members of the international community can participate in such negotiations.

1987

Antarctic Treaty Consultative Meetings become open to observers and experts from international organizations may attend on invitation.

Greece, North Korea, Austria and Ecuador accede to the Antarctic Treaty on 8 January, 21 January, 25 August and 15 September respectively.

Spain, Sweden, Peru, Italy, the Netherlands, Sweden and Uruguay become associate members of the Scientific Committee on Antarctic Research on 15 January, 24 March, 14 April, 19 May, 20 May, 16 June and 29 July respectively.

On 5 October, the seventh Special Consultative Meeting of the Antarctic Treaty is held in Rio de Janeiro. The DDR and Italy are admitted to Consultative Status.

From 6 to 16 October, the fourteenth Consultative Meeting of the Antarctic Treaty is held in Rio de Janeiro.

In November, the UN General Assembly again calls for a moratorium on the negotiation of a minerals regime in Antarctica.

The first commercial base is established in the Antarctic by Antarctic Airways (a Canadian company), in territory contested by Chile and Britain.

Greenpeace establishes a base on Ross Island.

New Zealand and Sweden exchange of letters comprising an Agreement between them on Antarctic Cooperation.

New Zealand's Conservation Act 1987 establishes a Department of Conservation which, inter alia, covers issues relating to Antarctica and New Zealand's sub-Antarctic islands.

1988

In the winter of this year there are fifty scientific stations open in the Antarctic region. There are twenty on the peri-Antarctic islands and 30 on Antarctica.

On 4 May, Canada accedes to the Antarctic Treaty.

On 2 June, the Convention on the Regulation of Antarctic Mineral Resource Activities (CRAMRA) is signed. The convention is intended to establish rules of liability for operators undertaking Antarctic mineral resource activities. However, it never enters into force.

Finland and Ecuador become associate members of the Scientific Committee on Antarctic Research on 1 July and 12 September respectively.

From 12–19 September the Scientific Committee on Antarctic Research holds its twentieth meeting in Hobart. Italy, Sweden and Uruguay are admitted as full members.

At the eighth Special Consultative Meeting of the Antarctic Treaty, held in Paris from 20–22 September, Spain and Sweden become consultative parties to the Antarctic Treaty, and can formally participate in ATCMs.

In December, the UN General Assembly expresses its 'deep regret' at the adoption of the CRAMRA, in light of the calls for a moratorium on the negotiation of such a regime.

In London, a meeting reviewing the operation of the CCAS concludes that the operation of the Convention has been satisfactory.

New Zealand and Italy exchange letters comprising an Agreement between them on Antarctic Cooperation.

1989

In January, the Argentinian vessel *Bahia Paraiso* runs aground in Antarctic waters spilling 830,000 litres of diesel fuel and lubricants.

Also in January, Greenpeace members visiting a French base bring to the attention of the world an international airstrip being built on the site of a penguin rookery in contravention of the agreed measures to protect wildlife. The project is eventually abandoned.

The *Exxon Valdez* oil spill occurs in Alaska.

Finland, Korea and Peru become consultative parties to the Antarctic Treaty, and can formally participate in ATCMs.

The Basel Convention on the Control of Transboundary Movements of Hazardous Wastes and their Disposal is signed on 22 March. It is a response to growing concerns regarding the export of waste, especially from developed to developing countries, typified in a number of scandals in the preceding years, such as the *Khian Sea* waste disposal incident and the Koko case.

The Australian and French governments, under intense pressure from environmental groups and following diplomatic discussions, announce that they will not sign the CRAMRA on the grounds that they disagree with mining activities tacitly approved in the CRAMRA.

In December, the UN General Assembly passes a resolution expressing regret at the continuing exclusion of the Secretary General from ATCMs. The resolution expresses that any regime relating to Antarctica should be 'negotiated with the full participation of all members of the international community, and recommends the establishment of Antarctica as a nature reserve or a world park'.

1990

Ecuador and The Netherlands become consultative parties to the Antarctic Treaty, and can formally participate in ATCMs.

Chile's Decree 641 of 25 June supersedes the Regulation of the 'Comite Nacional de Investigaciones Antarticas', contained in Supreme Decree 434 of 8 July 1974. The Committee shall represent the national scientific community before the Scientific Committee of Antarctica Research (SCAR), agency operating within the jurisdiction of the International Council of Scientific Unions (ICSU); the Committee shall also provide advice to the 'Instituto Antartico Chileno' in the programming of its scientific and technological activities.

Argentina's Decree 2316/90 of 5 November 1990 approves and establishes the National Policy on Antarctica.

In December, the UN General Assembly passes a resolution requesting the Secretary-General to undertake a study on the establishment of a UN sponsored scientific station in Antarctica.

1991

The Protocol on Environmental Protection to the Antarctic Treaty (the Environmental Protocol) is opened for signature. The protocol was negotiated after the failure of the CRAMRA. Its aim, as provided in Article 2, is to provide a framework for the 'comprehensive protection of the Antarctic environment and dependent and associated ecosystems'. The protocol designates Antarctica as a natural reserve devoted to peace and science, and places a moratorium on mining for mineral resources in Antarctica for 50 years.

The International Association of Antarctic Tour Operators (IAATO) is founded.

Australia's Fisheries Management Act 1991 defines the high seas to include waters 'inside the outer limits of the exclusive economic zone adjacent to the coast of the Australian Antarctic Territory' meaning the Australian Antarctic Territory is not part of the Australian Fishing Zone, following its 1978 Proclamation to that effect.

The UK's Antarctic Treaty (Specially Protected Areas) Order 1991 provides that Cape Shirreff, Livingston Island and the South Shetland Islands are no longer Specially Protected Areas for the purposes of the Antarctic Treaty. It is now protected as a Site of Special Scientific Interest under administrative arrangements made pursuant to Recommendation XV-7 of the Fifteenth Antarctic Treaty Consultative Meeting.

Chile's Decree 266 of 6 March creates the 'Consejo Asesor del Instituto Antartico Chileno' (INACH) to integrate the national scientific and logistic support community and to provide advice in the direction and coordination of the scientific, technological, environmental protection, and scientific publication activities performed by Chile in the Antarctic.

The UN Secretary-General issues Report A/46/590 on 25 October on the Question of Antarctica concerning the environment in Antarctica and its impact on the global system. On the same day, the Secretary-General issues Report A/46/583, which is a study on the establishment of a UN-sponsored station in Antarctica.

1992

On 5 May, the Basel Convention on the Control of Transboundary Movements of Hazardous Wastes and their Disposal enters into force.

In November, the ATCM expresses concern about the increase of tourism and non-governmental expeditions in Antarctica. While agreeing that emergency assistance is a humanitarian obligation, assistance to such activities is expensive, disruptive to research programs and sometimes hazardous. No agreement is reached as to where responsibility for non-governmental expeditions should lie.

The UN Secretary-General issues his Question of Antarctica Report A/47/624 on 11 November regarding the State of the Environment in Antarctica.

In December, the UN General Assembly passes a resolution welcoming the ban on prospecting and mining in Antarctica, but calling for it to be made permanent, and encouraging greater international cooperation on conservation measures.

Section 23AA is inserted into the Australian Crimes Act 1914 in December, modifying the application of that Act regarding criminal procedure to the Antarctic territories.

The UK's Extradition (British Antarctic Territory) (Commonwealth Countries, Colonies and Republic of Ireland) Order 1992 extends the application of the Extradition Act 1989 to the British Antarctic Territory.

France's Law No. 92-1318 of 18 December authorizes approval of the Protocol on Environmental Protection to the Antarctic Treaty.

1993

The UK proclaims a 200 mile maritime zone for South Georgia and the South Sandwich Islands.

Australia's Antarctic Treaty (Environment Protection) (Environmental Impact Assessment) Regulations 1993 provide for environmental impact assessments concerning proposed activities in Antarctica.

Australia's Criminal Procedure Ordinance 1993 (AAT) provides for the application of certain aspects of criminal procedure in the Australian Antarctic Territory.

France's Decree No. 93-740 of 29 March establishes a Committee for Polar Environment. This Decree is modified by Decree No. 2002-496 of 9 April 2002.

Chile's Decree 67 of 14 April promulgates the Treaty with Argentina on the environment and its additional protocols on the protection of the Antarctic environment and shared resources.

Argentina's Law 24216 of 11 June approves the Environmental Protocol to the Antarctic Treaty.

In the Australian case of Re Richards and Commission for the Safety, Rehabilitation and Compensation of Commonwealth Employees [1993] AATA 164 it was decided that an Australian carpenter injured while working in Antarctica should have his income assessed as if he were working at the same level (GS06) in Australia.

The US case of Environmental Defense Fund Inc v Massey (1993) 986 F.2d 528 is decided. It concerns waste disposal in Antarctica. Following an alleged violation of the National Environmental Policy Act 1969, the court considers the legal status of Antarctica and extra-territorial application of NEPA.

1994

Australia enacts the Maritime Legislation Amendment Act 1994, which claims for Australia an exclusive economic zone at its Antarctic territory. There is debate about whether this is compatible with Article IV of the Antarctic Treaty.

The IWC establishes the Southern Ocean Whale Sanctuary surrounding the continent of Antarctica. The establishment of the sanctuary is opposed by Japan.

In November, UNCLOS enters into force. Its precise relation to the Antarctic Treaty System remains unclear.

At the Antarctic Treaty Consultative Meeting in Kyoto, Recommendation XVIII-1 is adopted in response to growing concerns from the scientific research community active in Antarctica, containing directives for tourists and tour operators.

New Zealand's Antarctica (Environmental Protection) Act 1994 implements the Protocol on Environmental Protection to the Antarctic Treaty.

The Governments of New Zealand and France conclude an Agreement between them on Antarctic Cooperation.

An Australian Proclamation made on 26 July sets the outer limit of Australia's exclusive economic zone. It is made under the Seas and Submerged Lands Act 1973.

Australia passes the Antarctic Marine Living Resources Conservation Regulations 1994; Antarctic Treaty (Environment Protection) (Waste Management) Regulations 1994; and the Antarctic Marine Living Resources Conservation Regulations 1994 all concerning the protection and regulation of the Antarctic environment.

The UK passes the Antarctic Act 1994 concerning the application of the Antarctic Treaty, the Protocol on Environmental Protection to the Antarctic Treaty and the CAMLR Convention.

Argentina's Law 24388 of 22 November approves a bilateral treaty on cooperation in Antarctic matters with Italy, signed in Rome on 6 October 1992.

1995

In January, the UN General Assembly urges the Antarctic Treaty Parties to extend an invitation to the Executive Director of the UN Environment Programme (UNEP).

Decision No. 1 adopted by the XIXth ATCM in Seoul concerning the legal effect of Antarctic 'Recommendations' distinguishes between 'measures', designating 'a text which contains provisions intended to be legally binding' and 'resolutions', designating 'a hortatory text'.

The Government of the UK passes The Antarctic Act (Overseas Territories) Order 1995; The Antarctic Act (Guernsey) Order 1995; The Antarctic Act (Jersey) Order 1995; The Antarctic Act (Isle of Man) Order 1995; The Antarctic Regulations 1995; and The Antarctic (Amendments) Regulations 1995 concerning the application of its Antarctic legislation to its external territories.

Chile's Decree 396 of 3 April promulgates the Protocol to the Antarctic Treaty on Conservation of the Environment, adopted in Madrid, Spain, on 4 October 1991.

Norway enacts its Regulations relating to protection of the Environment in Antarctica.

1996

The New Zealand Antarctic Institute Act 1996 establishes the New Zealand Antarctic Institute.

Chile's Decree 681 of 17 May promulgates the agreement on Antarctic Cooperation between Chile and the Russian Federation, signed in Moscow on 14 February 1995.

Argentina's Law 24712 enacted on 25 September and promulgated on 18 October approves the Agreement of Antarctic Affairs, signed in Lima, Peru on 10 November 1994 between the Argentine Republic and the Republic of Peru.

1997

The UK issues the Antarctic (Guernsey) Regulations 1997; Antarctic (Jersey)

Regulations 1997; and the Antarctic (Isle of Man) Regulations 1997.

The UK passes The Merchant Shipping (Oil Pollution) (British Antarctic Territory) Order 1997 applying certain provisions of the Merchant Shipping Act 1995, relating to the prevention of and liability for oil pollution, to the British Antarctic Territory.

France issues Decree No. 97-610 of 31 May, publishing amendments to the Annex to the 1978 Protocol on the International Convention of 1973 for the Prevention of Pollution by Ships (designation of the Antarctic area as a special area and lists of liquid substances indicated in Annex II) (Resolution MEPC. 57 [33]), adopted in London on 30 October 1992.

1998

The Environmental Protocol enters into force, along with its six Annexes.

Bulgaria becomes a consultative party to the Antarctic Treaty, and can formally participate in ATCMs.

New Zealand issues the Marine Protection Rules Part 160 – Prevention of Pollution by Sewage from Ships in the Antarctic Treaty Area (Deemed Regulation) to discharge its obligation with regard to the Environmental Protocol.

The UK issues The Antarctic (Amendments) Regulations 1998 providing for the protection of certain Restricted Areas in Antarctica.

France issues Decree No. 98-861 of 18 September on the publication of the Protocol on Environmental Protection to the Antarctic Treaty, signed in Madrid on 4 October 1991.

France's Order of 10 December relative to the organization of the Central division of Ministry of Foreign Affairs gives the Sub-division on the Law of the Sea, Fisheries and Antarctica of the Legal division at the Ministry of Foreign Affairs jurisdiction over any issue relating to Antarctica.

1999

In July, there is a fuel oil spill of between 700 and 2,330 litres at Casey Base Station in the Australian Antarctic Territory.

Australia passes the Environment Protection and Biodiversity Conservation Act 1999, which includes Antarctica in its purview.

In the Australian case of *Re Spurr and Comcare* (1999) 28 AAR 424, which refers to *Re Richards and Commission for the Safety, Rehabilitation and Compensation of Commonwealth Employees* [1993] AATA 164, mentioned above, a plumber is awarded compensation at a rate reflecting his wage in Antarctica (which was different to that he would have earned for the same work in Tasmania, where he was usually employed), following an injury sustained while working there.

2000

The International Hydrographic Organization (IHO) delimited as the world's fifth ocean a vast body of water encircling Antarctica, and linking the Indian, Atlantic and Pacific Oceans, naming it the Southern Ocean.

Australia issues the Environment Protection and Biodiversity Conservation Regulations 2000.

The UK issues The Antarctic (Amendments) Regulations 2000 which add further Restricted Areas and an Historic Site to the 1995 Regulations.

Chile's Decree 429 of 28 March approves its National Antarctica Policy.

Argentina's Law 25260 of 15 June approves the Annex V of the Environmental Protocol to the Antarctic Treaty.

Argentina's Disposicion No. 87/2000 of 3 August regulates the content of Laws 24216 and 25260, which are procedures for environmental impact statements.

2001

The Agreement on the Conservation of Albatrosses and Petrels is concluded and opened for signature. The agreement seeks to conserve albatrosses and petrels by mitigating known threats to their populations. Parties agree to take measures to reduce bycatch of seabirds while fishing, protect breeding colonies and control and remove introduced species from breeding islands.

Australia's Weapons Ordinance 2001 (AAT) prohibits the possession of automatic and semi-automatic weapons in the Australian Antarctic Territory and the Territory of Heard Island and the McDonald Islands.

The UN passes General Assembly Resolution A/RES/55/33 on 12 January concerning a nuclear free southern hemisphere and adjacent areas, which mentions the Antarctic Treaty.

2002

The IMO's *Guidelines for Ships Operating in Arctic Ice-covered Waters* are adopted.

The UK issues The Antarctic (Amendments) Regulations 2002 which add further Restricted Areas, giving effect to measures and recommendations from Antarctic Treaty Consultative Meetings.

Argentina enacts Law 25617 on 17 July and promulgates it on 9 August. It concerns a Cooperation Agreement about Antarctica between the Government of the Argentine Republic and the Government of the Republic of Peru, signed in the city of Lima, Republic of Peru, on 1 March 2001.

2003

The ATCM recommends Measure 1 (2003), which provides for the establishment of a Secretariat of the Antarctic Treaty, and creates regulations governing the financial administration and employment relations of the Secretariat.

A Treaty between the Government of Australia and the Government of the French Republic is concluded on cooperation in the maritime areas adjacent to the French Southern and Antarctic Territories (TAAF), Heard Island and the McDonald Islands.

The UK issues The Antarctic (Amendments) Regulations 2003 which add further Restricted Areas to the 1995 Regulations.

Argentina's Resolution 91 of 2003 outlines the National Strategy for Biological Diversity. Objetivo 2.2 affirms its commitment regarding Antarctica.

France passes Constitutional Law No. 2003-276 of 23 March relative to the decentralized organization of the Republic. This law registers the French Southern and Antarctic Territories under Article 72-3 of the 1958 French Constitution.

France's Environmental Code is modified to include protection of the Antarctic environment by the inclusion of French Environmental Code Article L.711-1 to 713-9 R.712-3. These are included by Law No. 2003-347 dated 15 April relative to the protection of the Antarctic environment. This is completed by Decree No. 2005-403 of 28 April 2005 relative to the protection of the Antarctic environment and modifying the Environmental Code. On 23 May 2006 France issues an Order defining the list of activities regulated under Article R. 712-3 of the Environmental Code.

2004

The UN General Assembly passes Resolution A/RES/58/49 on 8 January. It concerns a nuclear free southern hemisphere and adjacent areas and mentions the Antarctic Treaty.

In February, the Agreement on the Conservation of Albatrosses and Petrels enters into force.

In September, the Antarctic Treaty Secretariat is founded in Buenos Aires, Argentina. The first Executive Secretary is Johannes Huber.

Bulgaria becomes a consultative party to the Antarctic Treaty, and can formally participate in ATCMs.

Australia makes a submission to the Commission on the Limits of the Continental Shelf which is responded to by India, Japan, The Netherlands and the US.

The UK issues The Antarctic (Amendments) Regulations 2004 which provide for further Restricted Areas.

Argentina's Law 25955 is enacted on 10 November and promulgated on 25 November. It modifies Article 1 of Law 23272 (La Pampa Province is integrated to the Patagonian Region) stipulating that for the purposes of national laws, decrees, regulations, resolutions and other legal provisions, the Province of La Pampa, together with the Provinces of Río Negro, Chubut, Neuquén, Santa Cruz, Tierra del Fuego, Antarctica and South Atlantic Islands, and the department of Patagones in the Province of Buenos Aires, are considered the Patagonian Region.

In December, the US sends a diplomatic note to the UN Secretary-General stating that it 'does not recognize any State's claim to territory in Antarctica'.

2005

France's Law No. 2005-495 of 19 May authorizes approval of the Agreement on the Conservation of Albatross and Petrels. On the same day, Law No. 2005-501 authorizes approval of Annex V to the Protocol on Environmental Protection to the Antarctic Treaty regarding Area Protection and Management.

In June, the ACTM adopts Annex VI to the Environmental Protocol. The annex makes liable an operator who 'fails to take prompt and effective response action to environmental emergencies arising from its activities.'

French Decree No. 2005-1075 of 23 August publishes Annex V to the Protocol on Environmental Protection to the Antarctic Treaty–Area Protection and Management, adopted in Bonn on 18 October 1991.

French Decree No. 2005-1510 of 1 December publishes the Agreement on the Conservation of Albatross and Petrels (two annexes altogether), signed in Canberra on 19 June 2001.

In the UK case of *R v Secretary of State for Foreign and Commonwealth Affairs; ex parte Quark Fishing* [2005] UKHL 57 the judicial review of denial of a licence to fish in South Georgia and South Sandwich Islands territory is guided by CAMLR Convention. An appeal from this decision to the European Court of Human Rights is rejected in *Quark Fishing Ltd v United Kingdom* [2006] ECHR 841 because the Court did not have jurisdiction to decide the matter.

2006

In a submission to the Commission on the Limits of the Continental Shelf, New Zealand affirms the legitimacy of Australia's claim to the exclusive economic zone at its Antarctic territory.

New Zealand police declare that they are unable to issue warrants for American witnesses during their investigation of the death of Australian researcher Dr Rodney Marks from methanol poisoning at US Amundsen-Scott South Pole Station in 2000.

The Edinburgh Antarctic Declaration on the International Polar Year 2007–2008 states the cooperative goals for the year.

The practice of reporting on the 'Question of Antarctica' to the UN General Assembly is discontinued, and is no longer included on the General Assembly's agenda.

The XXIX ACTM adopts Measure 4 (2006) on Specially Protected Species: Fur Seals.

In a Note accompanying a Submission to the Commission on the Limits of the Continental Shelf New Zealand reserves its right to make a claim relating to Antarctica. This is responded to by Japan and The Netherlands.

New Zealand issues its Antarctica (Environmental Protection) Regulations 2006.

Chile's Decree 229 issued by the Ministry of Foreign Relations on 1 June promulgates the Antarctica Cooperation Agreement between Chile and Bulgaria, signed in Santiago, on 3 January.

2007

The International Polar Year (IPY) begins.

France's Organic Law No. 2007-223 of 21 February establishes institutional and statutory provisions relevant to overseas territories. On the same day, Law No. 2007-224 also establishes institutional and statutory provisions relevant to overseas territories.

In November, the *MS Explorer* is holed by ice and sinks, spilling an unknown quantity of fuel. The *MS Explorer* was both the first ship to take a commercial expedition to Antarctica in 1969, and the first commercial ship to sink there.

In the same month, there is a fire on board a whale processing vessel, the *Nisshin Maru.*

The Governments of Australia and the French Republic conclude an Agreement on Cooperative Enforcement of Fisheries Law in the Maritime Areas Adjacent to the French Southern and Antarctic Territories, Heard Island and the McDonald Islands.

Australia makes the Antarctic Treaty (Environment Protection) Proclamation 2007 concerning Specially Protected Areas. It also makes the Antarctic Treaty (Environment Protection – Historic Sites and Monuments) Proclamation 2007 concerning the preservation of historic sites and monuments. It also issues the Antarctic Seals Conservation Repeal Regulations 2007, repealing the Antarctic Seals Conservation Regulations 1986, because they are substantially incorporated into the Antarctic Treaty (Environment Protection) Act 1980.

The UK issues The Antarctic (Amendments) Regulations 2008 amending certain requirements concerning Restricted Areas.

2008

In a Submission to the Commission on the Limits of the Continental Shelf, the UK affirms the legitimacy of Australia's claim to the exclusive economic zone at its Antarctic territory. It also reserves the right to make a claim relating to Antarctica. This is responded to by Japan and the Netherlands.

In December, the *MV Ushuaia* runs aground on the north-west Antarctic Peninsula.

In the Australian case of *Humane Society International Inc v Kyodo Senpaku Kaisha Ltd* [2008] FCA 3; (2008) 244 ALR 161 the Court finds that the defendant, a Japanese whaling company, killed whales in the Australian Whale Sanctuary, in contravention of the Environment Protection and Biodiversity Conservation Act 1999 (Cth). The Court orders that the defendant be restrained from doing so in the future.

In the New Zealand case of *Omunkete Fishing (Pty) Limited v the Minister of Fisheries and Anor* [2008] NZHC 968 a Namibian fishing boat seeks an injunction to prevent New Zealand acting on information obtained which could indicate that it had contravened CAMLR Convention. In *Omunkete Fishing (Pty) Limited v the Minister of Fisheries and Anor* [2008] NZHC 1011 there is judicial review of whether the conditions imposed, the search of the boat and the subsequent actions taken were lawful.

2009

In February, the *Ocean Nova* runs aground on the Western Antarctic Peninsula.

In the Antarctic Treaty Consultative Meeting XXXII in Washington, D.C. on 6 April and despite global concerns regarding energy security, the 28 Antarctic Treaty Consultative Parties reaffirm their commitment to the moratorium on mineral exploitation.

The ATCM adopts the Washington Declaration on the International Polar Year and Polar Science, encouraging continued cooperation and collaboration on scientific research.

In November, the Russian icebreaker *Kapitan Khlebnikoc* is stuck in ice for several days with 184 passengers, staff and crew on board.

From November to December, the Smithsonian Institute hosts an Antarctic Treaty Summit.

In December, the IMO Assembly adopts Guidelines for Ships Operating in Polar Waters. The guidelines supplement the MARPOL Convention and Protocol by taking into account the particular climatic conditions of Polar waters, and recommend standards of maritime safety and pollution prevention beyond existing provisions. The guidelines are intended to precede a mandatory code.

A French Note accompanying its Submission to the Commission on the Limits of the Continental Shelf reserves its right to make a claim relating to Antarctica. This is responded to by Japan and The Netherlands. Norway also makes a Submission, responded to by the US, Russia, India, Japan and The Netherlands. Argentina also makes a Submission, generating a response from the US, Russia, India, Japan, The Netherlands and the UK. Argentina responds to the UK, which generates a second response.

New Zealand issues the Fisheries (High Seas Fishing Notifications – Commission for the Conservation of Antarctic Marine Living Resources) Notice 2009 concerning the application of conservation and management measures adopted by the Commission for the Conservation of Antarctic Marine Living Resources.

New Zealand's Antarctica (Environmental Protection: Liability Annex) Amendment Bill implements its obligation under Annex VI to the Protocol on Environmental Protection to the Antarctic Treaty.

The UK issues The Antarctic (Amendments) Regulations 2009 providing for further Restricted Areas and implementing certain measures adopted at Consultative Meetings of the Antarctic Treaty.

2010

The IMO amends Annex I of the MARPOL Protocol of 1978 to include a new Chapter 9- Special Requirements for the Use or Carriage of Oils in the Antarctic Area, which prohibits the carriage and use of heavy fuel oil on vessels operating in the Antarctic area.

An amendment to Australia's Fisheries Management Act 1991 inserts Section 84B, which implements the Agreement on Cooperative Enforcement of Fisheries Laws between the Government of Australia and the Government of the French Republic in the Maritime Areas Adjacent to the French Southern and Antarctic Territories, Heard Island and the McDonald Islands that was done at Paris on 8 January 2007.

In October, a Declaration of a Specially Protected Species (*Ommatophoca rossii*) made under the Australian Antarctic Treaty (Environmental Protection) Act 1980 declares the Ross Seal to be a protected species under the Act.

A Chinese delegation, including the Chinese Minister for Land and Resources, visits Antarctica to survey China's growing Antarctic operations and explore untapped mineral resources.

2011

In February, Japan suspends its whale season due to harassment from conservation groups. In July, it announces that it will send its fleet back to Antarctica to continue the season.

The largest cruise ships are banned from Antarctic waters by the IMO.

On 31 October Malaysia, a long-term detractor from the Antarctic Treaty System, accedes to the Antarctic Treaty.

2012

Chile's Decree 126 of 30 January promulgates an agreement between Chile and Colombia on cooperation on Antarctic matters.

In the Australian case of *Commonwealth of Australia v Vero Insurance Limited* [2012] FCA 826, which concerned an insurance claim relating to the oil spill at Casey Base in Antarctica, the Court considers whether the land formed part of the Australian Government's real property for the purposes of domestic law. Having considered the application of the Australian Antarctic Territory Acceptance Act 1933 and the Antarctic Treaty, the Court holds that it does, because while the Treaty freezes the territorial claim for the purposes of international law, it has no such domestic application.

In January, Chile announces plans to expand its presence in Antarctica. Plans include the construction of new scientific research stations and military bases and the development of tourism in areas over which Chile asserts sovereignty.

In June, Australia hosts the 35th Antarctic Treaty Consultative Meeting. The Australian Federal Opposition and various interest groups agitate for world heritage listing for Antarctica.

In August, an Australian plane collects an American requiring emergency medical attention from McMurdo Station in Antarctica and flies him to New Zealand. This is heralded by the US National Science Foundation as 'an excellent example of the benefits of long-standing co-operation [among] Antarctic partners'.

In August, the Governments of New Zealand and the Republic of Korea conclude an Agreement on Antarctic Cooperation to facilitate cooperation on Antarctic policy, scientific research and logistical activities.

A Memorandum of Understanding on Cooperation in Antarctica is signed by Russia and the US on 8 September.

In October, an Australian Senate Estimates Committee hears that there is multinational research under way measuring the rapid expansion of Antarctic sea ice. Scientists report unprecedented changes in the ocean flows that affect global climate patterns.

In November, proposals at a CCAMLR Conference for the establishment of a network of new marine reserves in east Antarctica fail following 11 days of intense discussion. This is in spite of unanticipated agreement between the US and New Zealand for the establishment of a Marine Protected Area in the Ross Sea (which would be the world's largest protected marine zone). The failure is attributed to conflicting interests among CAMLR Convention parties including China's concern about access to ocean resources. Parties decide to call an extra meeting in June 2014 to discuss the issue further.

In December, the British Government names Queen Elizabeth Land in honour of the Queen's Diamond Jubilee despite overlapping claims from Argentina and Chile in this area. In response, Argentina presents a formal note in protest stating Argentina's 'firmest rejection of the recently announced pretension of the government of the United Kingdom of Great Britain and Northern Ireland of naming an area of the Argentine Antarctic Sector' in contravention of the spirit of the Antarctic Treaty.

Australia's Environment Minister Tony Burke becomes the first Australian minister to visit Antarctica.

2013

The UK's Antarctic Act 2013 provides, *inter alia*, for the application of Annex VI to the Protocol on Environmental Protection to the Antarctic Treaty.

In April, a Chinese ship fishing for krill catches fire off the coast of Antarctica. The ship had authorisation to fish in the area from the Commission for the Conservation of Antarctic Marine Living Resources.

In May, Russia and India disclose in an Antarctic Treaty meeting that more than 150 tonnes of diesel was spilt on to the Antarctic sea floor during a fuel transfer operation in early 2012 when an ice shelf that had held tanks full of fuel broke away.

INTRODUCTION

Ben Saul and Tim Stephens

The historian David Day has described Antarctica as 'a mirror on which centuries of human hopes, fears and desires have been projected.'[1] These projections have taken a myriad of legal forms, as states initially explored and claimed parts of the Antarctic continent and its adjacent waters, and from 1959 onwards put territorial ambitions to one side in favour of cooperative management under the *Antarctic Treaty*.[2] Fears that Antarctica would become a new front in the Cold War catalysed agreement on that treaty and the Antarctic Treaty System (ATS) built around it, and provided the foundations for surprisingly harmonious and effective governance of the frozen continent.

There are, however, new anxieties for the continent, and the Southern Ocean that surrounds it. Antarctica already feels the early effects of climate change and ocean acidification. Claimant states assert rights to the Antarctic continental shelf and competitive interest in Antarctic resources grows. Tourism is spreading, bringing environmental and safety risks. China and other new powers are significantly increasing their presence on the continent, and some question the old consensus of the 'Antarctic club'. Security concerns too are increasingly discussed, despite the dedication of Antarctica to peaceful purposes over the past 50 years.

As the primary legal materials in this book show, however, Antarctica's legal and regulatory arrangements have constantly and effectively adapted to meet new challenges, evolving into an increasingly sophisticated, inclusive, dynamic and responsive governance regime. To set the scene for the materials that follow, this introductory essay explains the background, context and development of the cooperative legal regimes governing the Antarctic continent, its adjacent waters, continental shelf and islands, and the unique environment and living and non-living resources found there.

Antarctic Geography and Ecology

Most of the Antarctic continent falls within Antarctic Circle (at 66°33'44"S, the northernmost latitude where the sun does not rise in winter and does not set in summer). Unlike the Arctic, which is surrounded by five nearby coastal states, most of the Antarctic continent is extremely remote, with the exception of the Antarctic Peninsula that stretches northwards towards Cape Horn, the southern tip of the South American continent.

The Antarctic continent covers an area of around 14 million km^2, and almost all of its surface is covered by the Antarctic ice sheet. At the littoral edge of the continent there are large ice shelves that extend seawards, in some cases by many hundreds of kilometres. The Ross ice shelf is the largest, with an area around the size of France. Antarctic ice sheets

[1] David Day, 'Ice Works: Three Portraits of Antarctica' *The Monthly*, March 2012, 56. See further David Day, *Antarctica: A Biography* (Vintage, Sydney, 2013).

[2] Antarctic Treaty, adopted 1 December 1959, 402 UNTS 71 (entered into force 23 June 1961).

(on the Antarctic continent), ice shelves (where glaciers flow onto adjacent seas) and sea ice (which forms at sea) are undergoing substantial changes as a result of human-induced climate change. In summary, while seasonal sea ice is increasing in area, the ice sheets and shelves are losing volume.

Ecologically, the Antarctic bioregion extends from the continent into the sea, taking in areas of adjacent seas in the Southern Ocean extending beyond the sea ice fringing the continent and well into the Southern Temperate Zone. Whereas the biomass on the Antarctic continent itself is limited (there is, for instance, virtually no plant life on Antarctica), the Antarctic coastline and Southern Ocean supports extensive marine and seabird life, such as marine mammals (whales and seals), lower order fauna species such as toothfish and krill, and birdlife including penguins and albatrosses.

A key biophysical boundary that distinguishes the Antarctic is the Antarctic Convergence (or 'Polar Front'), the oceanic boundary, variably occurring between 45°S and 60°S, where colder Antarctic waters meet warmer northern seas. There is evidence that as the world's oceans absorb heat, the Antarctic Convergence, or Antarctic Polar Front, is moving southwards, and the Southern Ocean is becoming less alkaline under the influence of ocean acidification (as the oceans absorb CO_2 from the atmosphere).[3] The effects upon Southern Ocean are likely to be severe unless greenhouse gas emissions are very significantly reduced.

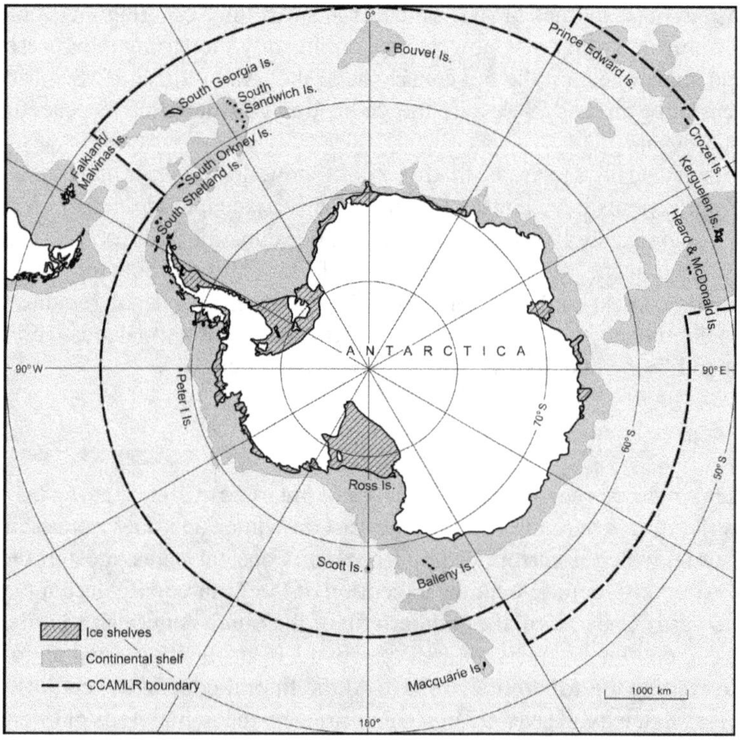

[3] John Turner et al, 'Antarctic Climate Change and the Environment: An Update' (2014) 50 *Polar Record 237*. See also, Tim Stephens, 'Warming Waters and Souring Seas: Climate Change and Ocean Acidification' in Donald R. Rothwell, Alex G. Oude Elferink, Karen N. Scott, Tim Stephens (eds), *The Oxford Handbook of the Law of the Sea* (OUP, Oxford, forthcoming, 2015).

Territorial Claims to Antarctica

The early legal history of Antarctica mirrors the history of other frontier areas subject to discovery, territorial claims and occupation. The expeditions of the British explorer Captain James Cook, who made a circumpolar voyage in the 1770s, provided the first persuasive evidence that a 'Great Southern Land' lay at high latitudes in the Southern Ocean. However, it was not until the 1820s that the continent was first sighted, at around the same time, by Russian and British discoverers and an American sealer. The early nineteenth century witnessed extensive activities by sealers and whalers, who pursued rich stocks of these species that Cook and others had reported on returning from their voyages. There was a frenzy of activity at the beginning of the twentieth century, leading to stunning new discoveries, but also disastrous tragedies. Both features of Antarctic exploration were on display in the race to the South Pole, won by a Norwegian team lead by Roald Amundsen. British explorer Robert Falcon Scott arrived at the geographic South Pole a month later, but perished with four others in his Terra Nova expedition during the return journey to the edge of the continent.

Further government sponsored voyages of discovery followed, and these soon turned to expeditions directed at claiming formal, legal possession of parts of Antarctica. From the early twentieth century until the 1950s, seven states made claims to Antarctica: Argentina, Australia, Chile, France, New Zealand, Norway and the United Kingdom. These resulted in most of the continent coming under one (or several) claims to territorial sovereignty, with the exception of Ellsworth Land and Marine Byrd Land, which to this day remain unclaimed (and indeed are the only land areas on Earth that have not been subject to sovereign claim). The United Kingdom maintains the earliest claim to Antarctica, which is closely linked to its claims to the sub-Antarctic South Georgia Island (over which Cook proclaimed sovereignty), and the Falkland Islands further north. The extent of the British claim, which embraces the Antarctic Peninsula, was set out in Letters Patent in 1908,[4] and in 1962 the claimed sector between 20°W and 80°W was named the British Antarctic Territory (BAT).[5] Claims by Argentina and Chile overlap with most of the BAT.

The titles to Antarctica claimed by Australia and New Zealand derive from various discoveries and proclamations of sovereignty made on behalf of Britain, and later independently of British claims. The Australian geologist and explorer, Douglas Mawson, who led the Australasian Antarctic Expedition between 1911 and 1914, and later the British, Australian and New Zealand Antarctic Expedition between 1929 and 1931, made claims to large areas of Antarctica. New Zealand's claimed sector, the Ross Dependency, was created by the British government and transferred to New Zealand administration in 1923.[6] Ten years later, the Australian Antarctic Territory (AAT) was recognised by the British government and placed under the administration of the Commonwealth of Australia.[7]

Australia's Antarctic claim remains the largest of the seven claimants, covering approximately 42 per cent of the continent. Within the AAT lies a slender sector claimed by France, Adelie Land. The eastern and western boundaries of Adelie Land were settled between Britain and France in 1938.[8] Norway's claims to Antarctic territory emerged at around the time that the extent of the French claim was clarified. Based upon Amundsen's

[4] 'Letters Patent Providing for the Government of the Falkland Islands Dependencies', 21 July 1908.
[5] British Antarctic Territory Order 1962 (UK).
[6] Order in Council under the British Settlements Act 1887 (UK).
[7] Australian Antarctic Territory Acceptance Act 1933 (Australia).
[8] Decree Defining the Limits of Adelie Land, 1 April 1938 (France).

discovery of the South Pole, Norway asserted priority of claim over those territories where the conditions of effective occupation could be fulfilled, and in 1939 issued a proclamation over a lengthy area of the Antarctic coast between the Australian and British Antarctic Territories, and inland areas explored by Amundsen. Chile's and Argentina's claims to Antarctica were proclaimed in the early 1940s, and overlap between each other, and also with areas of the British Antarctic Territory.

The Antarctic continent is fringed by a large number of coastal islands and a smaller number of offshore islands and groups. Except for islands adjacent to the unclaimed sector of Antarctica, all of these islands have been subject to territorial claims, sometimes by several states (such as the South Shetlands, which are claimed by Argentina, Chile and the United Kingdom). The sovereign claims over Sub Antarctic islands have not been subject to any general opposition (that is to say it is generally accepted that the islands may be claimed, even if there is dispute in relation to some of them among several overlapping claimants). The same cannot be said for the Antarctic continent itself.

The validity of the territorial claims to Antarctic territory is recognised only by the claimants themselves. The claimants insist that general principles of international law concerning the acquisition of territory, as set out in the *Island of Palmas Arbitration*[9] and the *Eastern Greenland Case*,[10] also apply in the Antarctic context. Discovery, followed by formal proclamation of title and an ongoing display of authority through effective occupation, is the *sine qua non* for sovereignty over *terrae nullius.* The obvious difficulty in meeting the effective occupation requirement in Antarctica is the great distance from the claimant states and the hostile environment, which make settlement beyond isolated research stations impractical. However, the claimants have contended that a lesser standard of effective occupation is accepted in the *Island of Palmas Arbitration* and *Eastern Greenland Case* in respect of remote areas, such that a reasonable level of state activity and administration, given the circumstances, will be sufficient to meet the requisite standard.[11]

The Antarctic Treaty System

The Antarctic Conference and the Antarctic Treaty

In 1948 the United States, which had not claimed territory in Antarctica, proposed placing Antarctica under United Nations trusteeship.[12] The proposal was rejected by some claimant states, which insisted on their sovereign rights, while other claimants (such as Britain) did not want the Soviet Union to gain a foothold in Antarctica under United Nations auspices. A revised United States proposal for a multi-power condominium over Antarctica also faced a mixed reception.[13]

By the middle of the twentieth century there was however a decisive shift in the international legal treatment of Antarctica, from being a domain of territorial claims to

[9] *Netherlands v United States* (1928) 2 RIAA 829.

[10] *Legal Status of Eastern Greenland (Norway v Denmark)* (1933) PCIJ Rep Ser A/B No. 53.

[11] Donald R. Rothwell, *The Polar Regions and the Development of International Law* (CUP, Cambridge, 1996), 59-61.

[12] United States Draft Agreement for Placing Antarctica under a United Nations Trusteeship, June 1948, in W.M. Bush, *Antarctica and International Law: A Collection of Inter-state and National Documents* (Oceana Publications, New York, 1988), vol. III, 461-464.

[13] United States Draft Agreement for Providing for a Condominium over Antarctica, July 1948, in Bush, ibid, 464-465.

one of international concern and management through the *Antarctic Treaty*. A number of factors explain this shift, including the increased prominence given to cooperative scientific investigation in Antarctica, as exemplified by the International Geophysical Year of 1957-58, as well as fears of superpower competition during the Cold War.

The international legal framework for the Antarctic is provided by the Antarctic Treaty System, the centrepiece of which is the *Antarctic Treaty*, which was agreed in 1959 in Washington DC. The Preamble to the *Antarctic Treaty* recognises that 'it is in the interest of all mankind that Antarctica shall continue forever to be used exclusively for peaceful purposes and shall not become the scene or object of international discord.' Concluded at the height of the Cold War between the United States and Soviet Union, the *Antarctic Treaty* addresses the key issues of concern to the international community in the management of Antarctica: the demilitarisation of Antarctica, the promotion of scientific research and, most critically of all, the freezing of claims to territorial sovereignty.

The original parties to the *Antarctic Treaty* were the twelve states participating in the Antarctic Conference: Argentina, Australia, Belgium, Chile, France, Japan, New Zealand, Norway, South Africa, the Soviet Union, the United Kingdom and the United States. These states had the most significant interests in Antarctica, including the two superpowers, and all seven states that had made territorial claims to Antarctica. Admittedly, original membership was still somewhat politicised; China's was explicitly excluded by a United States veto.[14] The *Antarctic Treaty* establishes a regime that is, however, also open to participation by all states, even those without particular Antarctic interests.

The *Antarctic Treaty* nevertheless bestows some privileges upon the most active Antarctic states by creating a two-tier membership structure: Antarctic Treaty Consultative Parties (ATCPs) and non-consultative parties. The ATCPs are the original members in addition to those states subsequently joining the treaty that have demonstrated an interest in the Antarctic by undertaking substantial research activity there.[15] There are now 28 ATCPs and these members are entitled to attend and participate in decision-making at annual Antarctic Treaty Consultative Meetings (ATCMs). This is in contrast to the 22 Non-Consultative parties that are permitted to attend ATCMs but not vote upon decisions. The latest state to join the *Antarctic Treaty* is Pakistan, which became a Non-Consultative party in March 2012, taking the total number of state parties to 50 – about one quarter of all states, with 80 per cent of the world's population.[16] There are also three ATCM Observers.[17]

The *Antarctic Treaty* was presented by the claimants and the ATCPs as an objective regime, that is one having legal effect upon all states, including non-parties. However this was contested by a number of states, notably Malaysia which was behind the placing, in 1983,[18] of the 'Question of Antarctica' on the agenda of each annual meeting of the First Committee of the United Nations General Assembly (UNGA). Malaysia argued that Antarctica should be regarded as the common heritage of humankind of similar status to the high seas.

Malaysia's position shifted in the early 2000s from being opposed to the ATS to being actively engaged with it. Following a Malaysian initiative, from 2005 the General Assembly

---

[14] Anne-Marie Brady, 'China's Rise in Antarctica?' (2010) 50 *Asian Survey* 759, 761.

[15] Antarctic Treaty, Art. 9(2).

[16] Karen Scott, 'Institutional Developments within the Antarctic Treaty System' (2003) 52 *International and Comparative Law Quarterly* 473, 476.

[17] The Scientific Committee on Antarctic Research (SCAR), Commission for the Conservation of Antarctic Marine Living Resources and Council of Managers of National Antarctic Programs (COMNAP).

[18] See UN General Assembly Resolution 38/77 (15 December 1983).

remained 'seized' of the 'Question of Antarctica' but no longer considers it annually on the Assembly's agenda or receives regular reports.[19] Malaysia has since become increasingly active in Antarctic science programs, and acceded to the *Antarctic Treaty* in 2011.

Core Elements of the Antarctic Treaty

The *Antarctic Treaty* has three main elements. First, the Treaty establishes that Antarctica is to be used exclusively for peaceful purposes, and prohibits the deployment of military forces in Antarctica unless used for scientific research or other peaceful purposes.[20] A right to inspect others' scientific bases has, however, been little used. Second, the Treaty seeks to facilitate and promote the freedom of scientific investigation, and requires states to co-operate to the greatest extent possible in their research endeavours.[21]

Third, and perhaps most significantly, the Treaty includes a very carefully drafted provision that freezes sovereign claims for the life of the treaty, and prohibits the enlargement of existing claims or the making of new claims.[22] Non-claimant states are therefore free to undertake scientific research and establish scientific stations in the purported 'territory' of claimant states, just as claimant states can establish bases in the 'territories' of other claimant states.

Another consequence of the suspension of sovereignty is that claimant states cannot exercise their usual civil, criminal and enforcement jurisdiction over the territories they claim. Instead, Article VIII of the *Antarctic Treaty* permits states to exercise nationality jurisdiction, that is, to regulate only the activities of their own citizens in Antarctica.[23] Later treaties recognise certain forms of jurisdiction for specific purposes, such as environmental protection or ensuring the safety of aerial or maritime navigation. But in general a state cannot exercise jurisdiction over non-nationals, potentially giving rise to gaps in law enforcement where another state party to the *Antarctic Treaty* does not enforce its laws against its nationals, or where nationals of non-party states are involved.

The *Antarctic Treaty* defines its area of operation to be south of 60°S,[24] which captures the landmass and also significant adjacent sea areas. This 'Antarctic Treaty area' (ATA) sets the boundary which applies in respect of all except one of the treaties that make up the ATS. The 1980 *Convention for the Conservation of Antarctic Marine Living Resources*[25] (CAMLR) adopts a more northerly boundary, which extends that treaty's operation up to a circumpolar line that roughly approximates the Antarctic Convergence, discussed above.[26]

The Antarctic Treaty System

A significant feature of the *Antarctic Treaty* was that it was intended to establish an evolving international legal regime that would grow over time to deal with Antarctic questions as

[19] Peter J. Beck, 'The United Nations and Antarctica, 2005: The End of the "Question of Antarctica"?' (2006) 42(3) *Polar Record* 217.

[20] Antarctic Treaty, Art. 1.

[21] Ibid, Arts. 2 and 3.

[22] Ibid, Art. 4.

[23] See generally Donald R. Rothwell, 'Law Enforcement in Antarctica' in Alan Hemmings, Donald R. Rothwell and Karen Scott (eds), *Antarctic Security in the Twenty-First Century* (Routledge, London, 2012), 135.

[24] Antarctic Treaty, Art. 6.

[25] Convention on the Conservation of Antarctic Marine Living Resources, adopted 20 May 1980, 1329 UNTS 47 (entered into force 7 April 1982).

[26] Ibid, Art. 1(4).

they arose. The *Antarctic Treaty* laid the legal foundations for what was to become the ATS, first clearly defined in the 1991 *Protocol on Environmental Protection to the Antarctic Treaty* (*Environmental Protocol*)[27] as 'the Antarctic Treaty, the measures in effect under the Treaty, its associated separate international instruments in force and the measures in effect under those instruments.'[28]

From 1959 onwards the Antarctic regime was developed first through the adoption of recommendations by ATCMs (which now number in the hundreds), including the 1964 Agreed Measures on the Conservation of Antarctic Fauna and Flora.[29] Later the ATS was augmented by new treaties, the first being the 1972 *Convention for the Conservation of Antarctic Seals* (CCAS),[30] later the CCAMLR, and most recently the Environmental Protocol. The CCAMLR *and the Environmental Protocol* regimes have themselves undergone significant evolution.

Agreement on the *Antarctic Treaty* crystallised in large part because of security concerns during the Cold War. There was another equally important turning point in the late 1980s which led to the adoption of the *Environmental Protocol.* The *Antarctic Treaty* did not deal with mineral resource issues, and it was not clear how mining in the Antarctic could occur. To resolve the uncertainty and in an effort to open up Antarctica to mining, the 1988 *Convention on the Regulation of Antarctic Mineral Resources*[31] (CRAMRA) was adopted. However, there was a quick turn-around in international attitudes towards Antarctic mining, with Australia and France reversing support for CRAMRA and pushing instead for a comprehensive treaty to protect the Antarctic environment. This led in a short time to the effective abandonment of CRAMRA, which never entered into force, and the adoption instead of the Environmental Protocol which provides in Article 7 that '[a]ny activity relating to mineral resources, other than scientific research, shall be prohibited.'

The ATS is somewhat unique among international regimes in not having strong central institutions for management and governance. The *Antarctic Treaty* establishes regular ATCMs to discuss Antarctic affairs, held biennially until 1991 (often with inter-sessional preparatory meetings) and annually thereafter (without preparatory meetings). There are also occasional Special Consultative Meetings and Meetings of Experts.

Over time the agenda of ATCMs has become fuller and more diverse, and its working methods and outputs more systematised. ATCMs exercise law-making, administrative, and non-binding standard setting powers.[32] In 1995 the ATCM adopted Decision 1 on Measures, Decisions and Resolutions, which sets out the legal status of ATCM texts. Only 'measures' are legally binding, once approved by all ATCPs. ATCM 'decisions' are operative only in respect of internal organisational matters. 'Resolutions' have only a recommendatory effect.

In recent practice, legally binding measures tend to be confined to the technical or scientific designation of specific protected areas and historic sites.[33] Where there is less consensus, as

[27] Protocol on Environmental Protection to the Antarctic Treaty, adopted 4 October 1991, 30 ILM 1455 (entered into force 14 January 1998) (Environmental Protocol).

[28] Environmental Protocol, Art. 1(e).

[29] Agreed Measures on the Conservation of Antarctic Fauna and Flora, 1964, ATCM III–VIII.

[30] Convention for the Conservation of Antarctic Seals, adopted 1 June 1972, 1080 UNTS 175 (entered into force 11 March 1978) (CCAS).

[31] Convention on the Regulation of Antarctic Mineral Resources, adopted 2 June 1988, 27 ILM 868 (never entered into force) (CRAMRA).

[32] Alan Hemmings, 'The Antarctic Treaty System' (2012) 10 *New Zealand Yearbook of International Law* 39, 42.

[33] Ibid, 40.

on more political or policy-oriented issues, non-binding resolutions are more common.[34] Even so, such 'soft' law can still shape behaviour on the ground amongst the relatively small social community of states and actors in Antarctica. Precisely because resolutions do not have immediate legal effects, they may be easier to agree upon and reflect nascent normative agreements. Even if they do not coalesce into 'harder' norms over time, they can still continue to influence community expectations of good Antarctic practice.

The *Environmental Protocol* also establishes an additional forum for the governance of Antarctic environmental matters: The Committee for Environmental Protection (CEP). The CEP is 'to provide advice and formulate recommendations to the Parties in connection with the implementation of this Protocol, including the operation of its Annexes'.[35] A significant number of ATCM texts relate to CEP matters. The CCAMLR Commission also possesses certain law-generating and standards setting powers. Its Conservation Measures are binding on all members and apply in the CCAMLR Convention area. Its resolutions are non-binding but complement or supplement its Measures, and parties are urged to implement them.

The ATS contrasts significantly with the more primitive governance arrangements in the Arctic polar region. In the Arctic, there is 'no firm legal structure, or regulatory functions assumed by a regional body, and only limited capacity to influence the development of Arctic policy'.[36] The difference is partly explained by geography. There is no Arctic landmass, undisputed sovereign territories fringe Arctic waters, and Arctic states exercise the usual legal rights and powers of sovereigns. The number of states directly involved in Arctic affairs is also fairly small – eight – lessening the pressures for a more participatory regime open to a wider group of interested states. The geopolitical and other factors driving a special Antarctic regime and stronger Antarctic cooperation are not the same in the Arctic, even if the Arctic presents its own unique coordination and governance challenges (such as the increase in shipping resulting from rapidly declining sea ice, overfishing, and overlapping maritime and continental shelf zones).

Sovereignty Issues

Article 4 of the *Antarctic Treaty* places to one side the sovereignty question for the life of the Treaty; existing claims are neither recognised nor rejected, while no new claims or the enlargement of existing claims are permitted. It is this delicate and ambiguous compromise that is central to the stability of the ATS, allowing parties to manage Antarctic affairs in a co-operative manner without having either to defend or protest territorial interests.[37] By precluding new claims, however, the ATS preserves a status quo that is more favourable to existing claimant states than would-be Antarctic powers.

Disputes over Antarctic sovereignty have been deferred but are not forgotten, nor resolved. Indeed, the very terms of Article 4 have been the subject of discussion and debate. For instance, Article 4 issues have arisen after some claimant states purported to establish maritime zones adjacent to their Antarctic territories.[38] Those who made these maritime

[34] Ibid, 42.

[35] Environmental Protocol, Art. 12.

[36] Tim Stephens, 'The Arctic and Antarctic Regimes and the Limits of Polar Comparativism' (2012) 54 *German Yearbook of International Law* 315, 316.

[37] Gillian D. Triggs, *International Law and Australian Sovereignty* (Legal Books, Sydney, 1986), 137.

[38] Patrizia Vigni, 'Antarctic Maritime Claims: "Frozen Sovereignty" and the Law of the Sea', in Alex G. Oude Elferink and Donald R. Rothwell (eds), *The Law of the Sea and Polar Maritime Delimitation and Jurisdiction* (Martinus Nijhoff, Leiden, 2001), 69.

claims sought to explain them on the basis that they are permitted under the law of the sea and the *Antarctic Treaty,* because the latter does not prevent states from simply declaring existing legal entitlements that flow from territorial claims. This argument has merit in relation to the territorial sea and the continental shelf, both of which are inherent maritime zones belonging automatically to coastal states.[39] A number of non-claimants, most notably the United States, have strongly protested these claims, but on the basis that the territorial claims upon which they are dependent are themselves not legally sound.[40]

Claimants made various maritime claims from the 1960s onwards, but matters have now come to a head with the territorial claimants submitting data on the extent of their Antarctic continental shelves to the Commission on the Limits of the Continental Shelf (CLCS), through the process established by the *United Nations Convention on the Law of the Sea* (UNCLOS). This process has, to date, been handled diplomatically and has not been elevated to a dispute before an international court or tribunal.

There have been only two cases in the International Court of Justice to touch upon Antarctic issues, and neither led to an engagement with sovereignty issues. In the first, the *Antarctica Case,* the United Kingdom asserted its sovereignty over the Falkland Island Dependencies, which included its Antarctic territorial claim, and contested the competing claims by Argentina and Chile. However, the Court did not have jurisdiction and the case was removed from the Court's docket in 1956.[41]

In the recent *Whaling in the Antarctic* case between Australia and Japan, Australia contended that Japanese scientific whaling was unlawful under the terms of the *International Convention for the Regulation of Whaling* (ICRW),[42] rather than basing the argument on any claim to jurisdiction over whales and living resources generally within waters adjacent to the AAT. Consistent with the way in which the case was argued by the parties, it is unnecessary for the Court to consider Antarctic sovereignty issues.

Antarctic Continental Shelf Submissions

Ordinarily, coastal states enjoy sovereign rights to explore and exploit living and non-living natural resources in their continental shelf under Article 77 of UNCLOS. Article 76(1) sets the limits of this zone to either 200 nautical miles (nm) from the coastal state's baselines, or to the outer edge of the continental margin if it extends beyond 200 nm. All seven Antarctic claimants are parties to the ATS and UNCLOS and assert that by virtue of being coastal states they are entitled to define their continental shelves where their margins extend from the landmass beyond 200 nm.

In this respect Article 76 affords coastal states two options for identifying the outer limits of their continental shelves. They may delineate lines by reference to the outermost fixed points at each of which the thickness of the sedimentary rocks is at least one per cent of

[39] United Nations Convention on the Law of the Sea, adopted 10 December 1982, 1833 UNTS 3 (entered into force 16 November 1994), Art. 77(3) (UNCLOS). Stuart B. Kaye, 'The Outer Continental Shelf in the Antarctic', in Alex G. Oude Elferink and Donald R. Rothwell (eds), *The Law of the Sea and Polar Maritime Delimitation and Jurisdiction* (Martinus Nijhoff, Leiden, 2001), 69, 125–137.

[40] However note that the United Kingdom sought to bring proceedings against two other claimants, Argentina and Chile, in relation to disputed Antarctic and sub-Antarctic territories: ICJ, *Antarctica (United Kingdom v Argentina; United Kingdom v Chile)*, Order of 16 March 1956, [1956] ICJ Rep 12; [1956] ICJ Rep 15.

[41] *Antarctica (United Kingdom v Argentina; United Kingdom v Chile)*, Order of 16 March 1956, [1956] ICJ Rep 12; [1956] ICJ Rep 15.

[42] *International Convention for the Regulation of Whaling*, opened for signature 2 December 1946, 161 UNTS 72 (entered into force 10 November 1948).

the shortest distance from the point to the foot of the continental slope.[43] Alternatively they may apply a combined geomorphological and geographical approach, specifying a line by reference to fixed points not more than 60 nm from the foot of the continental slope.[44] While states are entitled to adopt either approach in various sectors of their continental margins to give themselves the widest shelf, there are important ultimate limits. Article 76(5) of the UNCLOS provides that the lines adopted may not exceed 350 nm from the territorial sea baselines, or 100 nm from the 2500 metre isobath (which in some cases will exceed 350 nm). The UNCLOS does not leave it to coastal states alone to establish outer continental shelf limits. Instead they are required to submit information to the CLCS, an independent scientific and technical body, within 10 years of the entry into force of the UNCLOS for those states.[45] Once it has scrutinised the data received, the UNCLOS makes recommendations on the establishment of the outer limits of the continental shelf, and the limits so established by a state on the basis of such recommendations are final and binding.[46]

It soon became clear that the submission deadline would be unrealistic for many, particularly developing, states. Accordingly, in 2001 a meeting of state parties to the LOSC resolved that for those states for which the UNCLOS entered into force prior to 13 May 1999 the 10 year period would begin to run from that date.[47] As all Antarctic claimants had joined the UNCLOS before this time, they were required to meet the 2009 deadline and all did so except Chile. Because of technical and financial constraints Chile has submitted only 'Preliminary Information'. In so doing Chile relies on another decision of the states parties in 2008 that the deadline will be complied with by submitting initial information, to be followed at a later stage by a full submission.[48]

The claimants' submissions have taken somewhat different approaches in addressing the sensitive sovereignty question. The first claimant to make a submission was Australia, which included extensive data for the continental shelf of the AAT.[49] Conscious that few states recognise Australia's Antarctic claim, Australia requested the CLCS not to consider the Antarctica component of its submission for the time being. When handing down its recommendations, accepting most of Australia's outer continental shelf, the CLCS duly avoided addressing the Antarctic data.[50] Several ATCPs lodged an objection with the CLCS to Australia's submission of data with respect to Antarctica,[51] including the United States. The United States insisted that while it did not recognise any state's claim to Antarctica or its continental shelf areas, it did acknowledge 'with appreciation Australia's request to the Commission that it not take any action on that portion of its

[43] UNCLOS, Art. 76 (4)(a)(i).

[44] UNCLOS, Art. 76 (4)(a)(ii).

[45] Pursuant to LOSC, Article 76 and Annex II. See also Ted L. McDorman, 'The Role of the Commission on the Limits of the Continental Shelf: A Technical Body in a Political World' (2002) 17(3) *International Journal of Marine and Coastal Law* 301.

[46] UNCLOS, Art. 76 (8).

[47] UNCLOS, Annex II, Art. 4. In 2001 a meeting of states parties to the Convention resolved that for those states for which the UNCLOS entered into force prior to 13 May 1999, the 10 year period would begin to run from that date: UN Doc. SPLOS/72 (2001).

[48] UN Doc. SPLOS/183 (2008).

[49] Continental Shelf Submission of Australia: Executive Summary, 15 November 2004, available at http://www.un.org/depts/los/clcs_new/submissions_files/aus04/Documents/aus_doc_es_web_delivery.pdf (accessed on 22 November 2011).

[50] Summary of the recommendations of the Commission on the Limits of the Continental Shelf in regard to the submission made by Australia on 15 November 2004, adopted 9 April 2008, at http://www.un.org/Depts/los/clcs_new/submissions_files/aus04/aus_summary_of_recommendations.pdf (accessed on 22 November 2011).

[51] Germany, India, Japan, Netherlands, the Russian Federation and the United States.

submission relating to areas of the seabed and subsoil adjacent to Antarctica.'[52] Other states similarly commended Australia for taking an approach that was consistent with the spirit of the ATS.

In its 2006 submission New Zealand took a different approach from Australia, making no reference to continental shelf areas offshore of its Antarctic territory, the Ross Dependency. New Zealand identified the 'special legal and political status of Antarctica' and stated that it is open to states pursuant to the LOSC to make a partial submission, and that a submission relating to Antarctic shelf 'may be made later'.[53]

The United Kingdom followed the same approach in reserving its capacity to make an Antarctic submission at a later date. It has lodged several partial submissions alone and with other states, including its May 2009 partial submission in relation to the Falkland Islands, South Georgia and the South Sandwich Islands.[54] In that submission it did not include continental shelf data for the British Antarctic sector. Instead it relied on its statement in 2008, when submitting its partial submission in relation to Ascension Island, that it recognised 'the special legal and political status of Antarctica' and may in the future make a submission for the British Antarctic sector.

France addressed its Antarctic territory, Adélie Land, in its CLCS submission in a similar fashion to New Zealand and the United Kingdom. In France's partial submission in 2009, in relation to the subantarctic Kerguelen Island and the French Antilles, it advised that it did not include areas of the continental shelf that adjoin Antarctica, 'for which a submission may later be made'.[55]

In Norway's first partial submission to the CLCS in 2006, in relation to the northeast Atlantic and the Arctic, Norway preferred complete silence on Antarctic issues while expressly keeping open the possibility of future continental shelf submissions.[56] This was followed by Norway's May 2009 partial submission relating specifically to its Antarctic possessions, the sub-Antarctic island Bouvetøya (Bouvet) and its continental territory of Dronning Maud Land[57] (the latter claimed in part to thwart Nazi Germany's Antarctic aspirations[58]). Norway included data in relation to Dronning Maud Land but, like Australia, requested the CLCS not to take any action for the time being in relation to the continental shelf appurtenant to Antarctica. The submission of Norway that included data for Dronning Maud Land attracted a similar response from other ATCPs as Australia's submission had done.

By contrast to the other claimants, Argentina's 2009 submission took a very assertive approach.[59] Argentina made a full submission to the CLCS, including the Argentine Antarctic sector and the Islas Malvinas, Georgias del Sur and Sandwich del Sur. Unlike Australia and

[52] See further Christopher C. Joyner, 'United States Foreign Policy Interests in the Antarctic' (2011) 1 *The Polar Journal* 17.

[53] Note from the Permanent Mission of New Zealand to the Secretary-General of the United Nations Accompanying the Lodgement of New Zealand's Submission, 19 April 2006.

[54] United Kingdom Submission in respect of the Falkland Islands, and of South Georgia and the South Sandwich Islands: Executive Summary, 2009.

[55] The French Continental Shelf: Partial Submission to the Commission on the Limits of the Continental Shelf in Respect of the Areas of the French Antilles and Kerguelen, 5 February 2009.

[56] Continental Shelf Submission of Norway in Respect of Areas in the Arctic Ocean, the Barents Sea and the Norwegian Sea: Executive Summary, 2006.

[57] Continental Shelf Submission of Norway in respect of Bouvetøya and Dronning Maud Land: Executive Summary, 2006.

[58] Klaus Dodds and Alan Hemmings, 'Britain and the British Antarctic Territory in the Wider Geopolitics of the Antarctic and the Southern Ocean' (2013) 89 *International Affairs* 1429, 1442.

[59] Outer limit of the continental shelf: Argentine submission: executive summary, 2009, at http://www.un.org/Depts/los/clcs_new/submissions_files/arg25_09/arg2009e_summary_eng.pdf (accessed on 22 November 2011).

Norway, Argentina did not request the CLCS not to consider its Antarctic data. For this and other reasons (including because it covered the disputed Falkland/Malvinas, South Georgia and South Sandwich islands) the Argentinian submission excited objections from several states, including India, Russia and the United States. They stated their expectation that the CLCS would not take any action in relation to the Antarctic component of Argentina's submission. This protest means that there no prospect that the CLCS will consider the Antarctic component of Argentina's submission, as Article 5(a) of Annex I of the CLCS's rules of procedure preclude the CLCS from considering and qualifying a submission where a land or maritime dispute exists, unless prior consent is given by all parties to the dispute.[60]

The making of Antarctic maritime claims has not produced major difficulties, mainly because the claims have been made largely in the abstract. While maintaining their entitlement to sovereignty as coastal states, with all that entails for the claiming of maritime zones, the claimants have not sought to assert jurisdiction inconsistently with the *Antarctic Treaty*.[61] A second reason that there has not been an open challenge made to the *Antarctic Treaty*'s compromise on sovereignty is that Antarctic claimants have mostly (though not uniformly) shown exceptional deference to both the letter and spirit of the ATS, as seen in the careful way submissions have been made to the CLCS on Antarctic continental shelf areas. Moreover there has been restraint on the part of non-claimants, who have not taken every possible objection to the making of Antarctic maritime claims. This is seen in the tolerance towards the 'claims' to extended continental shelves from sub-Antarctic islands even though these extend in some cases within the ATA and therefore are at odds with the ATS.[62]

Antarctic Resource Management

Mining may not be carried out in Antarctica unless and until the prohibition under the *Environmental Protocol* is lifted. This prohibition on mining applies not only to the Antarctic continent, but throughout the ATA, and will remain in force until such time as the Protocol is amended to overturn it, which is possible at any time but not likely until the 2048 review conference at the earliest.[63] The mining ban applies to the maritime zones, including the continental shelves of the territorial claimants.

While mining is not permitted, there is extensive exploitation of a number of species of living organism in the Southern Ocean, and even active bio-prospecting programs for organisms found on and adjacent to the Antarctic continent. The Southern Ocean holds rich fishing grounds for some species, and there is a lengthy history of the exploitation of Antarctic marine living resources, including extensive whaling and sealing operations, and fishing for a range of species from krill to Antarctic toothfish.

Sealing is comprehensively regulated in the Antarctic under the CCAS, but as there is no longer any commercial sealing in the Antarctic, the CCAS has fallen into disuse. Commercial whaling has also been phased out in the Southern Ocean, as a result of the moratorium adopted in 1982 and the establishment of the Southern Ocean Sanctuary in

[60] Kaye, above note 39, 126.

[61] Tim Stephens and Ben Boer, 'Enforcement and Compliance in the Australian Antarctic Territory: Legal and Policy Dilemmas' in Lorne K. Kriwoken, Julia Jabour and Alan D. Hemmings (eds), *Looking South: Australia's Antarctic Agenda* (Federation Press, Sydney, 2007), 54, 58–59.

[62] Alan D. Hemmings and Tim Stephens, 'Reconciling Regional and Global Dispensations: The Implications of Sub-Antarctic Extended Continental Shelf Penetration of the Antarctic Treaty Area' (2009) *New Zealand Yearbook of International Law*, 273.

[63] See Environmental Protocol, Art. 24.

1994, both under the ICRW. The only whaling that continues is controversially conducted by Japan, which purports to rely on Article 8 of the ICRW, which allows parties to take whales for the purposes of scientific research.

As regards marine living resources other than mammals, the CCAMLR establishes an extensive regulatory framework that applies to all Antarctic marine living resources found south of the Antarctic Convergence, including finfish, molluscs and crustaceans.[64] It is generally judged to have been an effective regional fisheries management organisation, having adopted many conservation measures to protect heavily targeted species and associated and dependent organisms. However illegal, unreported and unregulated (IUU) fishing remains a challenge that has only partially been addressed.[65] Another challenge is harmonising the CCAMLR Convention regime with the international fisheries law that has expanded substantially since the CCAMLR Convention was concluded, as best exemplified by the *Fish Stocks Agreement*, which adopts a precautionary approach to the management of highly migratory and straddling fish stocks.[66]

One of the interesting dynamics in the operation of the regime for Antarctic marine living resources is that it applies in both areas over which sovereignty is not recognised or exercised, and areas adjacent to sub-Antarctic islands over which sovereignty is accepted. This has led national authorities to apply and enforce CCAMLR standards against vessels fishing unlawfully in the exclusive economic zones of sovereign territorial islands such as Heard and McDonald Islands (Australia) and Kerguelen (France). Antarctic states have also sought to develop innovative arrangements for cooperative enforcement to address the practical difficulties of enforcement in these remote areas.[67]

Environmental Protection

One of the great strengths of the ATS is its extensive and effective system for protecting the Antarctic environment. Environmental protection has been a focal point for Antarctic cooperation from the 1960s onwards. It was raised to particular prominence by the *Environmental Protocol*, under which states committed to 'comprehensive protection of the Antarctic environment and dependent and associated ecosystems' and also designated 'Antarctica as a natural reserve, devoted to peace and science.'[68]

The *Environmental Protocol* takes an ecosystem approach and applies throughout the ATA. It requires parties to cooperate in planning and conducting activities in the ATA,[69] undertake environmental impact assessments (EIA) for potentially harmful activities[70] according to detailed procedures set out in Annex I to the Protocol, and establishes the

[64] CCAMLR Convention, Art. 1(2).

[65] Rachel J. Baird, *Aspects of Illegal, Unreported and Unregulated Fishing in the Southern Ocean* (Springer, Netherlands, 2006).

[66] Agreement for the Implementation of the Provisions of the United Nations Convention on the Law of the Sea of 10 December 1982 Relating to the Conservation and Management of Straddling Fish Stocks and Highly Migratory Fish Stocks, adopted 4 August 1995, 2167 UNTS 3 (entered into force 11 December 2001). See Gregory Rose and Ben Milligan, 'Law for the Management of Antarctic Marine Living Resources: From Normative Conflicts towards Integrated Governance?' (2009) 20(1) *Yearbook of International Environmental Law* 41.

[67] Warwick Gullett and Clive Schofield, 'Pushing the Limits of the Law of the Sea Convention: Australian and French Cooperative Surveillance and Enforcement in the Southern Ocean' (2007) 22 *International Journal of Marine and Coastal Law* 545, 567.

[68] Environmental Protocol, Art 2.

[69] Environmental Protocol, Art. 6.

[70] Environmental Protocol, Art. 8.

CEP to provide advice in connection with the implementation of the Protocol.[71] Drawing from the model provided by the *Antarctic Treaty* itself, it also sets up a system of inspection to ensure compliance.[72]

One of the most important features of the *Environmental Protocol* is its Annexes, which form an integral part of the Protocol and have been significantly developed over time.[73] In addition to EIA (Annex I), these deal with the conservation of Antarctic Fauna and Flora (Annex II), waste disposal (Annex III), marine pollution (Annex IV), protected areas (Annex V) and liability arising from environmental emergencies (Annex VI). Although legitimate questions are raised about operational issues in the implementation of aspects of the *Environmental Protocol* (such as EIA[74]) and how it deals with specific activities (such as tourism[75]) and threats (such as invasive species[76]), overall it provides a highly effective, ecosystem-based system for Antarctic environmental management.

There nonetheless loom significant challenges for effective Antarctic environmental protection. Two examples are shipping and climate change/ocean acidification. In relation to shipping, the Southern Ocean has not been used for significant merchant traffic since the Clipper Route fell into disuse with the opening of the Panama Canal in 1914. However, the number and type of fishing, tourist and research vessels operating in the Antarctic has increased significantly in recent decades. This increased shipping activity poses risks for the Antarctic environment, as illustrated by several casualties involving fishing and cruise vessels, including the sinking of the *MS Explorer* in 2007, and the trapping of a Russian research vessel, the *Akademik Shokalskiy*, in sea ice in 2013-14.

Both the Arctic and the Antarctic have been the subject of attention from the International Maritime Organization (IMO) for several decades. In 2009 the IMO Assembly adopted revised guidelines that applied to both Arctic and Antarctic areas: the Guidelines for Ships Operating in Polar Waters.[77] While providing extensive provisions for protecting the Antarctic environment the efficacy of the guidelines is limited because they are only recommendatory. Turning the guidelines into a legally binding 'Polar Code' is currently being negotiated within the IMO. Issues that have been sticking points include the geographical coverage (whether in the Antarctic they will apply only to the ATA or to the Antarctic Convergence) and the type of vessels to be included (whether all vessels, including fishing vessels, or only larger vessels).

Undoubtedly the most significant environmental challenge facing the Antarctic is one driven by external rather than localised risks, namely climate change and ocean acidification.[78] The Fifth Assessment Report of the Intergovernmental Panel on Climate Change in 2013 included the following conclusions in relation to the Antarctic:[79]

---

[71] Environmental Protocol, Art. 12.

[72] Environmental Protocol, Art. 14. See further Tim Stephens and Ben Boer, above note 61.

[73] Environmental Protocol, Art. 9.

[74] See Alan D. Hemmings and Lorne K. Kriwoken, 'High Level Antarctic EIA under the Madrid Protocol: State Practice and the Effectiveness of the Comprehensive Environmental Evaluation Process' (2010) 10(3) *International Environmental Agreements: Politics, Law and Economics* 187.

[75] Murray P. Johnson and Lorne K. Kriwoken, 'Emerging Issues of Australian Antarctic Tourism: Legal and Policy Directions' in Kriwoken et al (eds), above note 61, 85.

[76] Sandra Potter, 'Protecting Antarctica from Non-Native Species: The Imperatives and the Impediments' (2009) 1 *The Yearbook of Polar Law* 383.

[77] IMO, *Guidelines for Ships Operating in Polar* Waters, IM Doc. A 26/Res.1024, 2 December 2009.

[78] Duncan French and Karen Scott, 'International Legal Implications of Climate Change for the Polar Regions: Too Much, Too Little, Too Late?' (2009) 10(2) *Melbourne Journal of International Law* 631.

[79] David G Vaughan et al, 'Chapter 4: Observations: Cryosphere', in *Working Group I Contribution to the IPCC Fifth Assessment Report* (2013), at http://www.climatechange2013.org/images/uploads/WGIAR5_WGI-12Doc2b_FinalDraft_Chapter04.pdf (accessed on 19 February 2014).

- It is very likely that the annual Antarctic sea ice extent increased at a rate of between 1.2 and 1.8 per cent per decade between 1979 and 2012. There was a greater increase in sea ice area, due to a decrease in the percentage of open water within the ice pack. There is high confidence that there are strong regional differences in this annual rate, with some regions increasing in extent/area and some decreasing;
- The Antarctic ice sheet has been losing ice during the last two decades. There is very high confidence that these losses are mainly from the northern Antarctic Peninsula and the Amundsen Sea sector of West Antarctica, and high confidence that they result from the acceleration of outlet glaciers;
- The average rate of ice loss from Antarctica likely increased from 30 to 147 gigatonnes per year between 1992 and 2011, causing global sea levels to rise; and
- In parts of Antarctica, floating ice shelves are undergoing substantial changes. There is medium confidence that ice shelves are thinning in the Amundsen Sea region of West Antarctica, and low confidence that this is due to high ocean heat flux. There is high confidence that ice shelves round the Antarctic Peninsula continue a long-term trend of retreat and partial collapse that began decades ago.

While climate change has been a major focus of Antarctic research, and has attracted considerable attention within the CEP and is a core part of its five-year work plan,[80] there have been limited policy initiatives and no concrete legal steps taken to deal with adaptation or other climate change issues.[81]

The Documents in this Collection

This book brings together the key legal materials that are the product of multilateral efforts expended since 1959 to regulate the Antarctic continent, its adjacent maritime areas, and resources. As a sophisticated and active regime, the ATS has given rise to voluminous documentation, and it would not be possible to reproduce all international documents relevant to Antarctica within this volume. The more modest purpose of this collection is to provide governments, researchers, and students with an accessible and up-to-date compendium of the treaties, decisions, resolutions, recommendations, conservation measures, guidelines and other documents that are of central relevance to contemporary Antarctic governance. In so doing, we wish to acknowledge the path-breaking work by others, most notably W M Bush, Donald R Rothwell, and Ruth Davis,[82] that has been of tremendous assistance to us as we selected the most appropriate documents for inclusion.

The collection is divided into ten parts. In Part 1, we set out the framework treaties of the ATS, namely the *Antarctic Treaty*, the CCAS, the CAMLR Convention, and the *Environmental Protocol*. Also included is CRAMRA; although this mining regime did not enter into force, it remains of relevance in an era in which there is increasing interest in the mineral resource potential of the Antarctic continent. The ATS treaties

[80] See Report of the Committee for Environmental Protection, CEPXIV, 2011, 38.

[81] French and Scott, above note 78, 649–650.

[82] W.M. Bush, *Antarctica and International Law: A Collection of Inter-state and National Documents* (Oceana Publications, New York), vols. I (1982), II (1982), III (1988) and IV (1991); Donald R. Rothwell and Ruth Davis (eds), *Antarctic Environmental Protection: A Collection of Australian and International Instruments* (Federation Press, Sydney, 1997).

are accompanied by selected documents from the *travaux préparatoires,* including drafting records.

Part 2 of the book collects the legal and administrative arrangements establishing and governing the Antarctic Treaty Secretariat. The Antarctic Treaty Secretariat was only established in 2004,[83] after a string of proposals over the years – some as early as 1959 – to create a central ATS institution.[84] The Secretariat provides a focal point for Antarctic cooperation and is based in Buenos Aires, Argentina. The tasks of the Secretariat are to support the annual meetings of the ATCMs and the CEP, to assist the exchange of information between parties, to collect and archive ATCM and CEP documentation, and to disseminate information about the ATS to the world at large.

In Parts 3 and 4 the book sets out the core documentary outputs of ATCMs and the CEP. Crucial to the functioning and adaptability of the ATS are the recommendations, measures, decisions and resolutions of the ATCM, including those adopted by the ATCM and designated as relating to the CEP. The book provides a complete chronological list of this mix of hard and soft law instruments that address a diversity of regulatory subjects.[85] Between 1961 and 2014, the ATCM adopted 543 instruments in total, of which 74 are no longer current.[86] the book reproduces the text of many of the most significant normative or standard-setting instruments.

For reasons of space, the book omits instruments which are no longer current. It also omits the many materials relating to specific specially protected areas, which concern particular local sites rather than having broader, Antarctic-wide, standard-setting relevance. Where multiple instruments over subsequent years address the same subject, the book typically includes only those instruments which most comprehensively address the area. These are often more recent instruments, signifying the increasing sophistication of regulation over time. Earlier documents on a given subject are sometimes included to illustrate the historical emergence of regulatory interest in a subject.

In a similar vein, Part 5 lists all instruments of the CCAMLR and reproduces most (53 of 85) of its Conservation Measures and resolutions, chiefly omitting those (35) narrowly targeted at a particular species.[87] Part 6 includes the Constitution of the Council of Managers of National Antarctic Programs Constitution (COMNAP), which dedicates COMNAP to serve its scientific role in supporting scientific research and cooperation under the ATS. It also includes a list and map of national scientific bases in Antarctica.

Other relevant 'hard' international treaty provisions, outside the ATS, are set out in Part 7, including those relating to whaling in the Southern Ocean, the safety of fishing vessels in ice areas, shipping pollution in Antarctic waters, the conservation of albatrosses and petrels, and regional fisheries conservation agreements applying to areas adjacent to the ATS and CCAMLR Convention areas.[88] Of course, many other international treaties of general application are relevant to state activities in Antarctica and its surrounds, but not reproduced here, from the UNCLOS, to international environmental and human rights treaties.

---

[83] See ATCM Measure 1 (2003) (the Secretariat became operative on 1 September 2004).

[84] See Scott, above note 16, 478-487.

[85] All ATCM documents are online at http://www.ats.aq/e/ats_meetings_atcm.htm. CEP documents are available at http://www.ats.aq/e/cep_handbook.htm.

[86] As a result of Decision 1 (2011), Annex.

[87] All CCAMLR documents are available at https://www.ccamlr.org/en/conservation-and-management/conservation-measures.

[88] See Dodds and Hemmings, above note 58, 1435-6.

Particularly relevant 'soft' law materials outside the ATS are also included in Part 7, such as IMO standards on fishing vessels in ice areas, passenger ships in remote areas, intact stability of shipping in ice areas, and shipping generally in polar waters. Standards continue to evolve in this area; the IMO is continuing work on a binding International Code of Safety for Ships in Polar Waters, building on its existing non-binding guidelines.

The episodic interest in Antarctica of the United Nations General Assembly is the focus of Parts 8 and 9. The book includes periodic resolutions on the 'Question of Antarctica' between 1983 and 2006, along with the reports of the United Nations Secretary General on various scientific, environmental, legal and political issues connected with Antarctica. These materials also provide a flavour of the controversies in the Assembly, including over discrete issues (such as the role of apartheid South Africa) and big picture debates (such as whether Antarctica should be declared the common heritage of humankind and subject to a universal regime, or left to by regulated by the smaller group of ATS parties).

For reasons of space, the book is unable to include all relevant legal materials on Antarctica.

Consistent with its focus on multilateral arrangements, the book omits the many national legal and policy instruments which purport to evidence sovereign claims to Antarctic territory. However, some of the documents that have been included do shed significant light on sovereign claims. Some of the claimants' recent continental shelf submissions, summaries of which are included in Part 11 of the book, provide information on the extent and the history of territorial and maritime claims. Moreover, Part 10 reproduces materials from International Court of Justice proceeding concerning the British-Argentine dispute over sovereignty in the Falkland Islands/Malvinas.

The book also excludes national laws on with Antarctica, much of which domestically implements ATS instruments. Part 10 of the book does, however, include some key national judicial decisions which discuss international law issues pertaining to Antarctica. Many of the legal materials not found in this book can be found in the comprehensive, three-volume collection of W.M. Bush in 1991.[89] While now dated, it contains an excellent selection of historical and national materials.

Conclusion

In a highly creative way the ATS defused the risks of sovereign competition which arose from the early era of exploration in Antarctica, and were later brought to a head in the early years of the Cold War. On the whole it has produced a peaceful, stable, effective and widely accepted regime for cooperation on a range of scientific, environmental, and related issues. Rising powers, such as China (which joined in 1983), have been brought into the system. The ATS has proven sufficiently flexible to accommodate new challenges and risks, even as the number of state parties has expanded, thus making consensus on many issues more difficult to achieve. Above all the ATS has, at least for now, seen off challenges to its normative and institutional authority in the United Nations General Assembly.

There is nonetheless ongoing speculation about the future of the Antarctic regime, including rising concerns about security risks.[90] The prospect of military confrontation

[89] W.M. Bush, *Antarctica and International Law: A Collection of Inter-state and National Documents* (Oceana Publications, New York, 1991).

[90] Australian Strategic Policy Institute, *Cold Calculations: Australia's Antarctic Challenges*, ASPI Strategic Insights, October 2013; Ellie Fogarty, *Antarctica: Assessing and Protecting Australia's National Interests*, Policy Brief, Lowy Institute for International Policy, August 2011.

in Antarctica is remote. How one views the security landscape, however, depends on how security is conceptualised, for instance, as 'human', 'environmental', 'resource', 'maritime', 'regime' or 'national' security and so on.[91]

Some are legitimately concerned about the use of militaries for non-peaceful purposes, such as the use of satellite installations for intelligence gathering, weapons targeting, or the militarisation of space. There is a debate about whether China's growing presence in Antarctica is a threat, or simply commensurate with its renewed place in the world. On one view China's interests and behaviour in Antarctica are little different from those of the hegemonic Western powers in Antarctica over many years.[92] There is also renewed debate about living and non-living resources in Antarctica. A 'cold rush' for oil, gas and minerals has not yet eventuated, despite the proliferation of extended continental shelf submissions by the Antarctic claimant states. But there are certainly risks of mineral exploitation disguised as scientific research, and growing interest in bio-prospecting for commercial purposes. Some environmental disagreements are sharp, such as over marine protected areas, illegal fishing and non-cooperation in its investigation, and dangerous skirmishes at sea between Japanese whalers and anti-whaling protesters. Above all climate change and ocean acidification pose perhaps the greatest challenge to Antarctic governance in the long term, not least because they are changing the productivity and range of valuable fisheries in the Southern Ocean.

So far there is no serious evidence that tensions arising from these issues threaten to unravel the half-century consensus on the Antarctic regime. To the contrary, the growing number of states participating in the ATS is testament to its vitality, and it has weathered efforts by some states in the General Assembly to replace the ATS it with a more universal arrangement that would truly vest the Antarctic continent in humanity as a whole. In the long term, the persisting uncertainty about the final status of sovereign territorial, maritime and continental shelf claims will present the greatest challenge to Antarctic stability. The ATS embodies an uneasy truce and cannot indefinitely defer disputes over sovereign title (and thus sovereign rights to exploit Antarctica's riches). The time will come when it may be necessary to reconsider sovereign claims and to desire an alternative legal architecture for securing Antarctica's future.[93] Until such a time comes (and even when it does) we hope this volume will be of assistance in understanding the origins and the practical operation of the Antarctic regime.

Sydney, September 2014

[91] For different approaches, see Donald R. Rothwell and Hitoshi Nasu, 'Antarctica and International Security Discourse: A Primer' (2008) 6 *New Zealand Yearbook of International Law* 3; and the chapters in Hemmings et al (eds), above note 23.

[92] Dodds and Hemmings, above note 58.

[93] Alan Hemmings, 'Beyond Claims: Towards a Non-Territorial Antarctic Security Prism for Australia and New Zealand' (2008) 6 *New Zealand Yearbook of International Law* 77.

PART 1
INTERNATIONAL INSTRUMENTS OF THE ANTARCTIC TREATY SYSTEM (ATS)

The Antarctic Treaty[1]

The Governments of Argentina, Australia, Belgium, Chile, the French Republic, Japan, New Zealand, Norway, the Union of South Africa, the Union of Soviet Socialist Republics, the United Kingdom of Great Britain and Northern Ireland, and the United States of America,

Recognizing that it is in the interest of all mankind that Antarctica shall continue for ever to be used exclusively for peaceful purposes and shall not become the scene or object of international discord;

Acknowledging the substantial contributions to scientific knowledge resulting from international cooperation in scientific investigation in Antarctica;

Convinced that the establishment of a firm foundation for the continuation and development of such cooperation on the basis of freedom of scientific investigation in Antarctica as applied during the International Geophysical Year accords with the interests of science and the progress of all mankind;

Convinced also that a treaty ensuring the use of Antarctica for peaceful purposes only and the continuance of international harmony in Antarctica will further the purposes and principles embodied in the Charter of the United Nations;

Have agreed as follows:

Article I

1. Antarctica shall be used for peaceful purposes only. There shall be prohibited, inter alia, any measures of a military nature, such as the establishment of military bases and fortifications, the carrying out of military manoeuvres, as well as the testing of any type of weapons.

2. The present Treaty shall not prevent the use of military personnel or equipment for scientific research or for any other peaceful purpose.

Article II

Freedom of scientific investigation in Antarctica and cooperation toward that end, as applied during the International Geophysical Year, shall continue, subject to the provisions of the present Treaty.

Article III

1. In order to promote international cooperation in scientific investigation in Antarctica, as provided for in Article II of the present Treaty, the Contracting Parties agree that, to the greatest extent feasible and practicable:

(a) information regarding plans for scientific programs in Antarctica shall be exchanged to permit maximum economy and efficiency of operations;

(b) scientific personnel shall be exchanged in Antarctica between expeditions and stations;

(c) scientific observations and results from Antarctica shall be exchanged and made freely available.

2. In implementing this Article, every encouragement shall be given to the establishment of cooperative working relations with those Specialized Agencies of the United Nations and other international organizations having a scientific or technical interest in Antarctica.

[1] Adopted 1 December 1959, entered into force 23 June 1961, 402 UNTS 71.

Article IV

1. Nothing contained in the present Treaty shall be interpreted as:

(a) a renunciation by any Contracting Party of previously asserted rights of or claims to territorial sovereignty in Antarctica;

(b) a renunciation or diminution by any Contracting Party of any basis of claim to territorial sovereignty in Antarctica which it may have whether as a result of its activities or those of its nationals in Antarctica, or otherwise;

(c) prejudicing the position of any Contracting Party as regards its recognition or non-recognition of any other State's right of or claim or basis of claim to territorial sovereignty in Antarctica.

2. No acts or activities taking place while the present Treaty is in force shall constitute a basis for asserting, supporting or denying a claim to territorial sovereignty in Antarctica or create any rights of sovereignty in Antarctica. No new claim, or enlargement of an existing claim, to territorial sovereignty in Antarctica shall be asserted while the present Treaty is in force.

Article V

1. Any nuclear explosions in Antarctica and the disposal there of radioactive waste material shall be prohibited.

2. In the event of the conclusion of international agreements concerning the use of nuclear energy, including nuclear explosions and the disposal of radioactive waste material, to which all of the Contracting Parties whose representatives are entitled to participate in the meetings provided for under Article IX are parties, the rules established under such agreements shall apply in Antarctica.

Article VI

The provisions of the present Treaty shall apply to the area south of 60° South Latitude, including all ice shelves, but nothing in the present Treaty shall prejudice or in any way affect the rights, or the exercise of the rights, of any State under international law with regard to the high seas within that area.

Article VII

1. In order to promote the objectives and ensure the observance of the provisions of the present Treaty, each Contracting Party whose representatives are entitled to participate in the meetings referred to in Article IX of the Treaty shall have the right to designate observers to carry out any inspection provided for by the present Article. Observers shall be nationals of the Contracting Parties which designate them. The names of observers shall be communicated to every other Contracting Party having the right to designate observers, and like notice shall be given of the termination of their appointment.

2. Each observer designated in accordance with the provisions of paragraph 1 of this Article shall have complete freedom of access at any time to any or all areas of Antarctica.

3. All areas of Antarctica, including all stations, installations and equipment within those areas, and all ships and aircraft at points of discharging or embarking cargoes or personnel in Antarctica, shall be open at all times to inspection by any observers designated in accordance with paragraph 1 of this Article.

4. Aerial observation may be carried out at any time over any or all areas of Antarctica by any of the Contracting Parties having the right to designate observers.

5. Each Contracting Party shall, at the time when the present Treaty enters into force for it, inform the other Contracting Parties, and thereafter shall give them notice in advance, of

(a) all expeditions to and within Antarctica, on the part of its ships or nationals, and all expeditions to Antarctica organized in or proceeding from its territory;

(b) all stations in Antarctica occupied by its nationals; and

(c) any military personnel or equipment intended to be introduced by it into Antarctica subject to the conditions prescribed in paragraph 2 of Article I of the present Treaty.

Article VIII

1. In order to facilitate the exercise of their functions under the present Treaty, and without prejudice to the respective positions of the Contracting Parties relating to jurisdiction over all other persons in Antarctica, observers designated under paragraph 1 of Article VII and scientific personnel exchanged under subparagraph 1(b) of Article III of the Treaty, and members of the staffs accompanying any such persons, shall be subject only to the jurisdiction of the Contracting Party of which they are nationals in respect of all acts or omissions occurring while they are in Antarctica for the purpose of exercising their functions.

2. Without prejudice to the provisions of paragraph 1 of this Article, and pending the adoption of measures in pursuance of subparagraph 1(e) of Article IX, the Contracting Parties concerned in any case of dispute with regard to the exercise of jurisdiction in Antarctica shall immediately consult together with a view to reaching a mutually acceptable solution.

Article IX

1. Representatives of the Contracting Parties named in the preamble to the present Treaty shall meet at the City of Canberra within two months after the date of entry into force of the Treaty, and thereafter at suitable intervals and places, for the purpose of exchanging information, consulting together on matters of common interest pertaining to Antarctica, and formulating and considering, and recommending to their Governments, measures in furtherance of the principles and objectives of the Treaty, including measures regarding:

(a) use of Antarctica for peaceful purposes only;
(b) facilitation of scientific research in Antarctica;
(c) facilitation of international scientific cooperation in Antarctica;
(d) facilitation of the exercise of the rights of inspection provided for in Article VII of the Treaty;
(e) questions relating to the exercise of jurisdiction in Antarctica;
(f) preservation and conservation of living resources in Antarctica.

2. Each Contracting Party which has become a party to the present Treaty by accession under Article XIII shall be entitled to appoint representatives to participate in the meetings referred to in paragraph 1 of the present Article, during such time as that Contracting Party demonstrates its interest in Antarctica by conducting substantial scientific research activity there, such as the establishment of a scientific station or the despatch of a scientific expedition.

3. Reports from the observers referred to in Article VII of the present Treaty shall be transmitted to the representatives of the Contracting Parties participating in the meetings referred to in paragraph 1 of the present Article.

4. The measures referred to in paragraph 1 of this Article shall become effective when approved by all the Contracting Parties whose representatives were entitled to participate in the meetings held to consider those measures.

5. Any or all of the rights established in the present Treaty may be exercised as from the date of entry into force of the Treaty whether or not any measures facilitating the exercise of such rights have been proposed, considered or approved as provided in this Article.

Article X

Each of the Contracting Parties undertakes to exert appropriate efforts, consistent with the Charter of the United Nations, to the end that no one engages in any activity in Antarctica contrary to the principles or purposes of the present Treaty.

Article XI

1. If any dispute arises between two or more of the Contracting Parties concerning the interpretation or application of the present Treaty, those Contracting Parties shall consult among themselves with a view to having the dispute resolved by negotiation, inquiry, mediation, conciliation, arbitration, judicial settlement or other peaceful means of their own choice.

2. Any dispute of this character not so resolved shall, with the consent, in each case, of all parties to the dispute, be referred to the International Court of Justice for settlement; but failure to reach agreement on reference to the International Court shall not absolve parties to the dispute from the responsibility of continuing to seek to resolve it by any of the various peaceful means referred to in paragraph 1 of this Article.

Article XII

1.

(a) The present Treaty may be modified or amended at any time by unanimous agreement of the Contracting Parties whose representatives are entitled to participate in the meetings provided for under Article IX. Any such modification or amendment shall enter into force when the depositary Government has received notice from all such Contracting Parties that they have ratified it.

(b) Such modification or amendment shall thereafter enter into force as to any other Contracting Party when notice of ratification by it has been received by the depositary Government. Any such Contracting Party from which no notice of ratification is received within a period of two years from the date of entry into force of the modification or amendment in accordance with the provisions of subparagraph 1(a) of this Article shall be deemed to have withdrawn from the present Treaty on the date of the expiration of such period.

2.

(a) If after the expiration of thirty years from the date of entry into force of the present Treaty, any of the Contracting Parties whose representatives are entitled to participate in the meetings provided for under Article IX so requests by a communication addressed to the depositary Government, a Conference of all the Contracting Parties shall be held as soon as practicable to review the operation of the Treaty.

(b) Any modification or amendment to the present Treaty which is approved at such a Conference by a majority of the Contracting Parties there represented, including a majority of those whose representatives are entitled to participate in the meetings provided for under Article IX, shall be communicated by the depositary Government to all the Contracting Parties immediately after the termination of the Conference and shall enter into force in accordance with the provisions of paragraph 1 of the present Article.

(c) If any such modification or amendment has not entered into force in accordance with the provisions of subparagraph 1(a) of this Article within a period of two years after the date of its communication to all the Contracting Parties, any Contracting Party may at any time after the expiration of that period give notice to the depositary Government of its withdrawal from the present Treaty; and such withdrawal shall take effect two years after the receipt of the notice by the depositary Government.

Article XIII

1. The present Treaty shall be subject to ratification by the signatory States. It shall be open for accession by any State which is a Member of the United Nations, or by any other State which may be invited to accede to the Treaty with the consent of all the Contracting Parties whose representatives are entitled to participate in the meetings provided for under Article IX of the Treaty.

2. Ratification of or accession to the present Treaty shall be effected by each State in accordance with its constitutional processes.

3. Instruments of ratification and instruments of accession shall be deposited with the Government of the United States of America, hereby designated as the depositary Government.

4. The depositary Government shall inform all signatory and acceding States of the date of each deposit of an instrument of ratification or accession, and the date of entry into force of the Treaty and of any modification or amendment thereto.

5. Upon the deposit of instruments of ratification by all the signatory States, the present Treaty shall enter into force for those States and for States which have deposited instruments of accession. Thereafter the Treaty shall enter into force for any acceding State upon the deposit of its instrument of accession.

6. The present Treaty shall be registered by the depositary Government pursuant to Article 102 of the Charter of the United Nations.

Article XIV

The present Treaty, done in the English, French, Russian and Spanish languages, each version being equally authentic, shall be deposited in the archives of the Government of the United States of America, which shall transmit duly certified copies thereof to the Governments of the signatory and acceding States.

SELECTED *TRAVAUX PREPARATOIRES* OF THE ANTARCTIC TREATY

Chilean Report of the Proceedings during 1958 of the Preparatory Working Group for the Conference on Antarctica[2]

The Government of the United States of America accepted the Chilean suggestion contained in the note of response, in the sense that a Preparatory Working Group of the Conference ought to be established. Thereupon it invited the other eleven participating countries to appoint a delegate before it.

Chile appointed for that purpose Mr Enrique Gajardo Villarroel, who remained in Washington from the 24th of June to the 20th of August of this year. On his return to the country, the Minister Councillor Mr Horacio Suarez H and the Councillor Mr Manuel Bianchi continued to act as alternate delegates.

In the Working Group, the representative of the United States of America, Ambassador Paul Daniels, materialized the ideas contained in the North American note of invitation in a draft that he submitted, in his personal capacity, as kind of guidelines for the deliberations.

The matters that ought to occupy the Working Group are the following: a) Agenda of the Conference; b) Its date; c) Headquarters; d) Regulations; e) Other technical details; and f) Preparation of a draft treaty.

The Working Group held continuous sessions for the rest of the year in order to focus on studying the matters abovementioned, however the session ended with no definitive resolutions on any of these points.

During the course of this exchange of ideas between the delegates of the countries invited to take part in the Conference, which always had an informal character, the Delegate of Chile, Mr Enrique Gajardo Villarroel as the alternate delegates, clearly and firmly set out the position of Chile. This was defined in the following terms:

1. Chile considers that its Antarctic sector forms an integral part of its national territory and, accordingly, its position is distinct from other countries that have colonial possessions or overseas territories there;

2. Chile does not accept for its Antarctic territory any form of internationalisation, nor an interference of the United Nations or whichever other international organisation that violates its rights of sovereignty in that territory or that interferes with its internal jurisdiction.

3. Chile has accepted the invitation of President Eisenhower, of the 2nd of May 1958, to take part in an Antarctic Conference and sign a treaty, within the framework of the principles

[2] Reproduced from W.M. Bush, *Antarctica and International Law: A Collection of Inter-state and National Documents*, vol. I (Oceana Publications, New York, 1991), 27–28 (translated from Spanish) by permission of Oxford University Press, USA.

contained in that invitation and with the attendance of the eleven countries mentioned therein;

4. The aim of Chile's participation is to establish whether there is enough level of agreement with the principles so as to ensure the success of the Conference;

5. Chile considers that the three principles contained in the invitation of President Eisenhower are inseparable: scientific collaboration, peaceful use and freezing of territorial claims.

6. Chile desires that scientific collaboration in Antarctica be open to all countries that wish to participate. However, it considers that the general principles for such collaboration should be established exclusively by the 12 Antarctic powers, without this being an obstacle to the practical modalities of such collaboration being agreed with third party countries.

7. The freezing of territorial claims, in other words, the establishment of a status quo on this matter, is a necessary complement to the peaceful use of Antarctica.

8. The presence of bases maintained or supplied by units of the armed forces of the Antarctic powers, is not contrary to the peaceful purposes pursued by this Treaty, provided that those activities do not assume the character of preparation for belligerent objectives, and remain in the logistical character as they have to date.

9. The Treaty must be as simple and general as possible, with the aim of proposed unanimous approval by the participants.

10. The administrative arrangements to be adopted for the proper functioning of compliance with the Treaty must not be of a nature that jeopardizes Chile's sovereignty and jurisdiction in its Antarctic sector.

11. The geographical definition of Antarctica must be left to scientific researchers and institutes. For the purposes of the Treaty, it will suffice to refer to its 'field of application'.

The Chilean proposal of creating an Antarctic Institute for Scientific Research was approved by a majority of Delegations. However, the representative of the United States of America expressed concern that this project would be opposed by existing scientific organisations, and scientists in general, who are opposed to the intervention by other states in scientific activities. It was considered, on the other hand, that this resistance would be neutralised if this Institute dedicated itself to private activity, or if it sought to gather together scientific institutions, as is the case with SCAR.

Chilean Report of the Proceedings during 1959 of the Preparatory Working Group for the Conference of Antarctica[3]

Meetings of the Working Group on Preparatory Work for the Antarctic Conference

The Working Group on Preparatory Work for the Antarctic Conference began its work – informally – in June of last year, and continued its meetings throughout 1959.

After more than one year of continuous work, the Working Group completed its work, and set the date for the start of the Conference as 15 October of this year, to be held in the city of Washington.

Its prolonged debates on the projects proposed by the North American delegate enabled the Working Group to more closely understand the thinking of the invited Governments with respect to the fundamental questioned raised therein.

During the sessions of the Working Group, the British representative presented a Draft Protocol, to be signed as an annex to the Antarctic Treaty, which aim to ensure the participation of third party states in scientific research in Antarctica, and in other purposes of the Treaty.

Our Government rejected the amendment made to the draft, insofar as it departed from Chile's idea to facilitate the conclusion of an international instrument to secure relations between the signatories, and third party states, exclusively in respect of scientific collaboration.

[3] Reproduced from W.M. Bush, *Antarctica and International Law: A Collection of Inter-state and National Documents,* vol. I (Oceana Publications, New York, 1991), 29–30 (translated from Spanish) by permission of Oxford University Press, USA.

Likewise, the North American delegate suggested to the Working Group a draft Modus Vivendi, intended to allow the administrative and consultative mechanism between Governments to commence without having to wait for all ratifications of the Treaty and its entry into force. This draft will be discussed in detail during the Conference itself.

At the end of its deliberations the Working Group tabled the following official documents for consideration at the Conference:

(a) Provisional agenda;
(b) Provisional rules; and
(c) Important issues to be considered in the draft Antarctic Treaty.

Statements by State Representatives at the Opening Plenary Session of the Conference on Antarctica, 15 October 1959[4]

Morning Meeting (11.00am–12.30pm)
Secretary of State Christian A. Herter, Presiding
Welcoming Statement by Secretary of State Herter

It is a pleasure and an honor for me, on behalf of the Government of the United States, to welcome to Washington the distinguished representatives and advisers who compose the delegations to the Conference on Antarctica.

We are meeting here for the purpose of reaching an agreement concerning a vast continent. Long a mystery, later the scene of heroic adventure and exploration, this continent is now an area of the world in which international scientific cooperation, for the benefit of mankind, has been successfully demonstrated to an outstanding degree by the brave men of the nations here represented who participated in the Antarctic programs of the International Geophysical Year.

My Government is dedicated to the principle that the continuation of this cooperation should be assured, and that Antarctica should be used for peaceful purposes only, should not become an object of political conflict, and should be open for the conduct of scientific investigations.

The exertions of the explorers and scientists of nations represented here have made possible this opportunity to formulate and give legal effect to certain high principles which, in consonance with the Charter of the United Nations, would ensure peace and cooperation in a vast area of the world. The Conference will undertake this task with confidence.

The United States, as host country, welcomes you. We wish you a pleasant stay here and look forward to a successful conference.

[Editorial Note: At this point Mr. Phleger was elected Permanent Chairman of the Conference and Henry E. Allen was appointed Secretary General. Mr. Herter relinquished the chair to Mr. Phleger.]

Statement by Mr. Phleger (United States)

Governor Herter has other pressing engagements and must now leave. Thank you, Secretary Herter, for your words of welcome and your good wishes for the success of our deliberations. Will Ambassador Daniels please take the seat of Representative of the United States of America.

First, may I express my appreciation of the high honor which you have conferred upon me in electing me Chairman of this International Conference on Antarctica. I realize, or course, that my selection is as a representative of the United States of America, and that the honor is one bestowed upon my country, the host country, an honor which is deeply appreciated.

This is indeed a unique and important conference convened as it is to deal with the vital subjects of the pursuit of peace and international cooperation in the field of scientific research. There is added challenge in that the subject of our deliberations is the vast continent of Antarctica. I

[4] Note: footnote numbering restarts on each page of the original.

know our efforts will draw inspiration from the example of the heroic explorers and scientists who dedicated their lives to the discovery of the secrets of this great continent.

At this time it would seem appropriate to read the invitation issued in connection with the convening of this conference. On May 3[2], 1958, Ambassadors of the United States delivered to each of the governments represented here, identical notes reading as follows:

Excellency: I have the honor to refer to the splendid example of international cooperation which can now be observed in many parts of the world because of the coordinated efforts of scientists of many countries in seeking a better understanding of geophysical phenomena during the current International Geophysical Year. These coordinated efforts of the scientists of many lands have as their objective a greatly increased knowledge of the planet on which we live and will no doubt contribute directly and indirectly to the welfare of the human race for generations to come.

Among the various portions of the globe where these cooperative scientific endeavors are being carried on with singular success and with a sincere consciousness of the high ideals of mankind to which they are dedicated is the vast and relatively remote continent of Antarctica. The scientific research being conducted in that continent by the cooperative efforts of distinguished scientists from many countries is producing information of practical as well as theoretical value for all mankind.

The International Geophysical Year comes to a close at the end of 1958. The need for coordinated scientific research in Antarctica, however, will continue for many more years into the future. Accordingly, it would appear desirable for those countries participating in the Antarctic program of the International Geophysical Year to reach agreement among themselves on a program to assure the continuation of the fruitful scientific cooperation referred to above. Such an arrangement could have the additional advantage of preventing unnecessary and undesirable political rivalries in that continent, the uneconomic expenditure of funds to defend individual national interests, and the recurrent possibility of international misunderstanding. It would appear that if harmonious agreement can be reached among the countries directly concerned in regard to friendly cooperation in Antarctica, there would be advantages not only to those countries but to all other countries as well.

The present situation in Antarctica is characterized by diverse legal, political, and administrative concepts which render friendly cooperation difficult in the absence of an understanding among the countries involved. Seven countries have asserted claims of sovereignty to portions of Antarctica, some of which overlap and give rise to occasional frictions. Other countries have a direct interest in that continent based on past discovery and exploration, geographical proximity, sea and air transportation routes, and other considerations.

The United States for many years has had, and at the present time continues to have, direct and substantial rights and interests in Antarctica. Throughout a period of many years, commencing in the early eighteen-hundreds, many areas of the Antarctic region have been discovered, sighted, explored and claimed on behalf of the United States by nationals of the United States and by expeditions carrying the flag of the United States. During this period, the Government of the United States and its nationals have engaged in well-known and extensive activities in Antarctica.

In view of the activities of the United States and its national referred to above, my Government reserves all of the rights of the United States with respect to the Antarctic region, including the right to assert a territorial claim or claims.

It is the opinion of my Government, however, that the interests of mankind would best be served, in consonance with the high ideals of the Charter of the United Nations, if the countries which have a direct interest in Antarctica were to join together in the conclusion of a treaty which would have the following peaceful purposes:

(a) Freedom of scientific investigation throughout Antarctica by citizens, organizations, and governments of all countries; and a continuation of the international scientific cooperation which is being carried out so successfully during the current International Geophysical Year.

(b) International agreement to ensure that Antarctica be used for peaceful purposes only.

(c) Any other peaceful purposes not inconsistent with the Charter of the United Nations.

The Government of the United States is prepared to discuss jointly with the Governments of the other countries having a direct interest in Antarctica the possibility of concluding an agreement, which would be in the form of a treaty, for the purpose of giving legal effect to these high principles. It is believed that such a treaty can be concluded without requiring any participating nation to renounce whatever basic rights it may have in Antarctica, or whatever claims of sovereignty it may have asserted. It could be specifically provided that such basic rights and such claims would remain unaffected while the treaty is in force, and that no new rights would be acquired and no new claims made by any country during the duration of the treaty. In other words, the legal status quo in Antarctica would be frozen for the duration of the treaty, permitting cooperation in scientific and administrative matters to be carried out in a constructive manner without being hampered or affected in any way by political considerations. Provision could likewise be made for such joint administrative arrangements as might be necessary and desirable to ensure the successful accomplishment of the agreed objectives. The proposed treaty would be deposited with the United Nations, and the cooperation of the specialized technical agencies of the United Nations would be sought. Such an arrangement would provide a firm and favourable foundation for a continuation of the productive activities which have thus far distinguished the International Geophysical Year; would provide an agreed basis for the maintenance of peaceful and orderly conditions in Antarctica during years to come; and would avoid the possibility of that continent becoming the scene of international discord.

In the hope that the countries having a direct interest in Antarctica will agree on the desirability of the aforesaid high objectives, and will work together in an effort to convert them into practical realities, the Government of the United States has the honor to invite the Government of ________ to participate in a Conference for this purpose to be convened at an early date at such place as may be mutually agreeable.

Accept, Excellency, the renewed assurances of my highest consideration.

This is the time and place agreed upon by the participating governments for the convening of the conference.

Statement by Mr. Louw (Union of South Africa)

Mr. Chairman, may I convey to you, on my own behalf, and also on behalf of the members of my delegation, our sincere congratulations on your unanimous election as Chairman of this Conference. Your eminence as a jurist; your wide experience in international affairs; your ability and your wisdom are well known. It is a matter of satisfaction to know that in seeking their common objective the delegates attending this Conference will have the benefit of your wise guidance.

I would also wish to thank the Honourable the Secretary of State, Mr. Herter, for the welcome which he has extended to us. I personally am glad to have the opportunity of being once more in this beautiful city, where I had the honour to be my country's first diplomatic representative from 1929–1933.

Mr. Chairman, my Government is deeply appreciative of the initiative which the United States Government has taken in calling this Conference, and in providing the necessary facilities for holding it in Washington.

The Government of the Union of South Africa has long felt the need for an international cooperative approach to the "question-mark" of Antarctica, in order that this continent may be divorced from the discord and national rivalries which so often have bedevilled cooperation among nations in other parts of the world. We therefore welcomed the proposal of the United

States Government, that a Conference be held which could draw up a multilateral Treaty, embodying two fundamental principles, viz., that Antarctica shall be used for peaceful purposes only, and secondly that there shall be freedom of, and international cooperation in, scientific investigation in Antarctica.

I am sure that I am voicing the sentiments of all present when I express appreciation of the excellent work that has been done by the representatives of the Governments concerned, during the preliminary discussions. These discussions have helped to clarify our thoughts as to the form of the proposed treaty and prepared the way for consideration of the various problems with which we are faced.

The twelve nations represented at this Conference all have a special interest in the Antarctica area. These nations comprise Great Powers and smaller Powers; countries in the Northern, as well as in the Southern Hemisphere. Their interests are based on a variety of considerations, such as discovery, exploration, scientific activity and geographical situation. It is gratifying, and also encouraging that they have been willing to get together in order to seek agreement and also coordination of their activities, and of their respective policies, and above all, that they have agreed that the basis of our approach to this matter should be adherence to the principles of peaceful use, and the freedom of scientific investigation, on an international cooperative basis. These two principles my delegation regards as fundamental to any multilateral agreement in regard to Antarctica. Indeed these principles are mutually dependent and complementary. The South African delegation attaches as much importance to the one, as to the other.

By virtue of South Africa's geographical situation at the Southern end of Africa, and thus the nearest part of that continent to Antarctica, it stands to reason that we in South Africa regard events and developments in the Antarctic continent – our Southern neighbour – as of particular importance and of direct and special concern to us.

The strategic importance of Antarctica has become increasingly evident during recent years. Today South Africa is only a few hours flying time away from the Antarctic Continent. The main, and in fact the only sure sea route between the West and the East is around the Cape of Good Hope. Thus, not only for South Africa, but also for all peace-loving nations, it is imperative that this sea route should remain open to the shipping of all nations.

Mr. Chairman, in the discussion which lie ahead, it will be the purpose of my delegation, in cooperation with other delegations, to seek mutually acceptable means of ensuring that the principle of the peaceful use of Antarctica is assured. "Peaceful use" means non-military use, and it should be our aim to ensure non-militarisation of the Antarctic area to the fullest extent possible, consistent with the objectives of the Treaty.

It is only on the basis of an international agreement that Antarctica will not be used for military purposes, and that it will not be the scene of political and international rivalries, that it will be possible to secure international cooperation in scientific investigation and research in that area.

It is a reassuring fact that since the discovery of Antarctica its slow but steady penetration by a number of countries has been characterized by very little friction or dispute. The emphasis has been more on cooperative effort than on political rivalry.

No doubt, that cooperation was made easier by the difficulties and hardships inseparable from the exploration of an unknown and barren area of the world. What is important, however, is that we *have* this basis upon which cooperative effort can be built. This basis for future cooperation was greatly strengthened by the joint activities of the recently concluded International Geophysical Year, in which the twelve countries here represented, participated.

It will readily be agreed that the tempo of scientific and geographic progress was given a tremendous impetus by the International Geophysical Year. There is little doubt that the international cooperation which characterized the International Geophysical Year, largely contributed towards solving some of the scientific problems which have exercised men's minds since time immemorial. Many problems still remain to be solved, and the solution of some may be found in Antarctica. It is our earnest hope that by the cooperative effort of the nations here represented, the success of this undertaking will be assured.

South Africa is eager to play its part in scientific investigation and research in Antarctica. Our scientists have, even in the distant past, shown a keen interest in the Continent, and although we may not have achieved spectacular results, I think I can claim that the records of international cooperation in the scientific investigation of Antarctica will show that the part played by South Africa has not been insignificant.

Because of its geographical position in relation to Antarctica, Cape Town was an important port of call for the early Antarctic explorers of the Nineteenth Century. In the early years of this century South African commercial enterprise turned its attention to the rich harvest which the Antarctic seas offered in whales and seals, and many South African vessels ventured into the dangerous waters of Antarctica and the contiguous islands.

Not only did the South African Government contribute to the funds of the Scott Expedition of 1910, but the South African public, whose imagination was stirred by the explorations then taking place, responded generously to an appeal for funds for the expedition. It was in fact at Cape Town that Captain Scott boarded the "Terra Nova" on his last voyage to Antarctica.

A deeper and more extensive scientific knowledge of Antarctica is of the greatest concern to South Africa, not only for the solution of the more important scientific problems of the Southern Hemisphere and in the furtherance of pure research, but also for the purpose of increasing our knowledge and understanding of the natural phenomena of South Africa in various fields – for example, geology, geomagneticism, meteorology, climatology and oceanography. There are geophysical problems which occur in the everyday life of our country, the solution of which, it is believed, will be substantially helped by the results of scientific investigations in Antarctica. It is there, for instance, that our climate is largely fashioned.

Immediately after the first World War the South African Association for the Advancement of Science, in cooperation with our Universities and other scientific institutions, organised a South African Expedition to that part of Antarctica which lies due south of South Africa. It was planned that the Expedition – consisting of about 65 men divided into five parties – would remain on the mainland for three years, in order to undertake geographical and biological research on the mainland, and also in the surrounding seas, particular attention being paid to meteorology and oceanography. Planning for the Expedition had reached an advanced stage, when unfortunately the impact of the first post-war depression prevented its being carried out.

South African interest in Antarctica did not however wane. In 1921 the South African Government nominated Professor Goddard of Stellenbosch University, who had been the prime mover behind the proposed Expedition, to serve on the Overseas Committee for the Shackleton-Rowett Expedition. The South African Government also became an early contributor to the funds of the Scott Polar Research Institute. In 1925, in his presidential address to the British Association for the Advancement of Science, General Smuts made a plea for a coordinated programme of meteorological observation through the establishment by the nations of the Southern Hemisphere of weather stations on Antarctica. Later, in the nineteen thirties, South African scientists participated in the programme of the International Polar Year.[5]

A South African geologist, Dr. A. L. du Toit, took a prominent part in the establishment of the principles of the Continental Drift. In particular, his comparison of the geologies of South America and South Africa led to the general acceptance of the theory of the former contiguity of these continents. According to the same theory, the lands which formerly lay east of South Africa now constitute the eastern side of the Weddell Sea in Antarctica. Rock formations that occur in South Africa occur also in Antarctica.

[5] This international effort was also called the Second Polar Year (1932–33) in commemoration of the Jubilee of the First International Polar Year (1882–83).

It was therefore not surprising that the Geological Society of South Africa should take the initiative in 1944 in the formation of a South African Antarctic Research Committee to consider the possibility of a South African Expedition to the Antarctic after the Second World War. The Committee worked actively for a number of years, but again the plans could not be realised.

The fact that imaginative and ambitious plans for independent South African Expeditions to Antarctica could not be realised, illustrates the difficulties facing small countries that wish to undertake a complicated and costly enterprise. Indeed, it was because of these difficulties that South Africa's manifestation of interest in Antarctic research has in the past taken the form of the contribution of men and money to the undertakings of other countries. Thus our participation in the Antarctic programme of the International Geophysical Year was confined to weather observations at Marion, Tristan da Cunha and Gough, and also to contributions to the Commonwealth Trans-Antarctic Expedition.[6] South African meteorologists also were seconded to the British base at Halley Bay; and our Weather Bureau has produced a voluminous and authoritative work entitled "The Meteorology of Antarctica" which has been well received in scientific circles.[7] Furthermore the World Meteorological Office has commissioned the compilation of three weather maps of the world, and the map for that part of the world which is south of the equatorial belt has been entrusted to South Africa's meteorologists.

Against this background it gives me great pleasure now to inform the Conference that the South African Government has recently decided to send a purely South African Scientific Expedition to the mainland of Antarctica. Barring unforeseen circumstances the Expedition will sail from Cape Town next month and will remain on the mainland during the Antarctic winter of 1960. It will be under the leadership of Mr. Hannes Le Grange who was a member of Sir Vivian Fuchs' Commonwealth Trans-Antarctic Expedition. There will be approximately ten men in the party leaving this year, but it is our hope that we shall, within the limits of our resources of manpower and funds, be able to increase this number in future years. In the preparation for this Expedition we have had the willing cooperation of the Norwegian government and we are negotiating with them for the use of their buildings in Queen Maud Land. A long-term programme of scientific work is being drawn up in consultation with our scientists, and we are confident that the Expedition will make an effective and valuable contribution to the scientific investigation of Antarctica. We are also continuing our activities in the contiguous islands, and hope also to undertake in due course another reconnaissance of Bouvet Island, with a view to investigating the prospects of establishing a weather station there. With this network of island weather stations, together with the station on Antarctica itself, we shall be in a position to make an even more valuable contribution than in the past to the meteorology of these parts.

The South African Government looks forward with confidence to continuing to play its part in the investigation of the scientific phenomena of Antarctica, and sincerely hopes that the fruitful cooperation of past years between the nations represented at this Conference will continue in the future under the shelter of the Treaty for the negotiation of which we are now meeting at Washington. Constructive and cooperative endeavour will, we believe, contribute substantially towards men's conquest of the unknown, and also towards ensuring that Antarctica is only used for peaceful purposes.

On behalf of the South African Government I wish to express the sincere hope that the proceedings of this Conference will successfully terminate in the conclusion of a Treaty which will enshrine the two fundamental principles to which all the Governments represented here subscribe – that Antarctica shall be used for peaceful purposes only and that there shall be freedom of scientific investigation throughout Antarctica.

[6] This expedition took place in the years 1955–58.

[7] *Meteorology of the Antarctic*, edited by M. P. van Rooy (Pretoria: Weather Bureau, Department of Transport, 1957).

The South African Government extends its best wishes to the Conference in the assurance that its deliberations will be conducted in a constructive spirit so that we may achieve the goal we have set ourselves.

Statement by Mr. McIntosh (New Zealand)

On behalf of the New Zealand delegation, I should like to express our appreciation of the welcome extended to use this morning by the Secretary of State.

If the arrangements and hospitality offered by the United States Government can be regarded as an augury, we can be assured of a successful conference.

In making this statement on behalf of my Prime Minister, Mr. Walter Nash, I have been asked to convey to other delegates his deep regret at not being able to be present for the opening of the Conference, and to state his views.

This regret is all the keener by reason of the fact that Mr. Nash has for many years taken, and continues to take, a day to day interest in proposals for joint international action in respect of Antarctica.

New Zealand has, in recent years, advocated international action to ensure the future use of Antarctica for the welfare of all nations.

As other delegates will no doubt be aware, Mr. Nash has made it clear that the New Zealand Government, for its part, would be prepared to consider the relinquishment of national rights and claims in Antarctica if such a step towards the establishment of a wider régime were generally agreed.

This does not mean that New Zealand is in any sense doubtful about the validity of its title to the Ross Dependency, or is unwilling to maintain its responsibilities for the administration of that area.

New Zealand's claim to the Ross Dependency is firmly grounded upon a substantial record of early British exploration in Antarctica, beginning with the great voyage of discovery of Captain Cook in the southern oceans. It was Cook who first used New Zealand's essential base and staging facilities; and for nearly two centuries since many other Antarctic explorers have met their staging needs in New Zealand. The area over which New Zealand claims jurisdiction was the scene of intensive exploratory work by Sir James Clark Ross between 1839 and 1843 and by the expeditions of Scott, Shackleton and other British parties at the beginning of the present century.

Since jurisdiction over the Dependency was formally transferred to New Zealand by the United Kingdom in 1923, legal title has been supported by administrative acts to regulate whaling and other activities in the territory, and in more recent years by further exploratory and scientific expeditions.

This is a brief record of the basis of the New Zealand claim, which we are confident will stand the closest scrutiny. In saying this I am of course aware that other countries with claims as well as those which have not made or recognized claims can advance substantial arguments about their national interests in Antarctica.

But, in this issue, it is not enough to adhere to past attitudes. This is why my Prime Minister has put forward the view that the establishment of a completely international régime for Antarctica would require countries to forego their national claims.

In Mr. Nash's view, it is only on this basis that a fully effective administration of the whole of Antarctica could be achieved – an administration which could coordinate all activities and ensure the permanent neutralization of the area. Such an international régime could prepare for the eventual use of the resources of Antarctica in a regulated and orderly manner.

New Zealand would, as Mr. Nash has also publicly stated, envisage the establishment of an organic relationship between such an Antarctic régime and the United Nations, in the belief that joint international action in Antarctica could provide a practical demonstration of the principles for which the United Nations stands.

The New Zealand Government recognizes, however, that at the present time it may not be possible to secure general agreement to an Antarctic settlement of this scope and nature.

Accordingly, while this broader concept remains the basis of the New Zealand approach to Antarctic problems, the New Zealand Government is prepared to join in more limited discussions, directed towards specific objectives on which a general measure of agreement is possible.

The convening of the present Conference suggests that there is in fact a widespread – and most welcome – willingness to discuss specific problems affecting international cooperation in Antarctica.

Although the whole world will benefit in due course from the comprehensive and fascinating exploration of our environment known as the International Geophysical Year, the twelve countries represented at this Conference have particular reason to acknowledge the value of the I.G.Y.

That experiment in global scientific cooperation has had, in respect of Antarctica, a two-fold result. It has provided a precedent for similar cooperation on an intergovernmental level. At the same time it has shown the need for such cooperation.

The New Zealand delegation at this Conference would wish to see a Treaty concluded which would meet four main objectives:

1. It should provide a basis for avoiding rivalries and quarrels over territorial claims and conflicting national interests in Antarctic
2. It should ensure that Antarctica remains permanently "sealed off" from the tensions of the Cold War and free from war or the threat of war.
3. It should assist continuing cooperation in scientific activities in Antarctica, and affirm the principle of the widest freedom of access to Antarctica for peaceful purposes.
4. It should be associated with the United Nations in an appropriate manner

As I have already mentioned, the New Zealand Government believes that the only final solution to territorial disputes and rivalries may eventually prove to be an agreement to relinquish national rights and claims in respect of Antarctica.

Since this is clearly not possible at the present time, the New Zealand delegation would for its part accept a simple arrangement to "freeze" the existing legal status quo as a way of ensuring that peaceful cooperation can continue unhampered by such disputes and rivalries.

There will surely also be general agreement on the need to keep Antarctica free from any form of militarization or warlike preparations.

It is accordingly our confident hope that this principle will be stated in treaty form, with provision also for methods of ensuring that the principle is scrupulously observed.

In particular, the New Zealand Government would wish to make quite clear its opposition to any nuclear testing or other testing of weapons in the Antarctic area.

We trust that it will also prove possible to agree on political arrangements to safeguard the excellent cooperative relationships already established in the scientific field.

New Zealand believes that such cooperation should be extended on the widest possible basis, with the sole qualification of an insistence that only activities directed towards peaceful purposes should be permitted.

In this manner, the New Zealand delegation considers that the nations at this Conference can demonstrate that there is nothing exclusive or restrictive about our motives in considering the future of Antarctica.

Treaty provisions of the kind I have suggested would be fully in accordance with the principles and purposes of the United Nations to which all the states participating in the Conference have subscribed.

The New Zealand Government considers that in any treaty which is drawn up there should be specific recognition of the relationship which it would wish to see established with the United

Nations. My delegation will have some detailed suggestions to offer to the Conference on this question.

We believe that these are objectives which all governments throughout the world would support; but the twelve countries participating in this Conference have a special role to play in achieving them.

They include all those states which have existing rights or claims in Antarctica, and all those other states at present active there.

This Conference should accordingly be able to give a lead to the world by agreeing to remove from Antarctica the conditions in which rivalries flourish and tensions develop. We must, moreover, keep in mind the responsibilities we owe to the rest of the world.

There will no doubt be differences of view. There will naturally be difficulties in reaching agreement on a Treaty which all can regard as satisfactory.

In seeking solutions of the problems confronting this Conference, we cannot do better than remind ourselves of the manner in which the tremendous physical hardships and difficulties of the Antarctic Continent have over the years been met and conquered by the great explorers of many nations.

Antarctica gives us a unique opportunity to take an initiative which could offer a hopeful prospect for similar cooperative relationships in other and more troubled areas of the world.

This vast and icy waste of 6,000,000 square miles, lying more in darkness than in light, has no permanent inhabitants. It can be explored and developed only with the resources of our advanced civilization. Its animosities, generated from outside, are potential rather than historic. It is only now being threatened by the tensions and rivalries that disturb the peace of the world elsewhere. As we see it the immediate task is to prevent such difficulties from developing and to let Antarctica remain in that peaceful state which, ironically, is the characteristic of areas unknown to man.

The leaders of the Great Powers have in recent weeks given encouraging indications of their desire for peace, and have declared their willingness to seek a general improvement in international relations.

It is my Prime Minister's earnest hope and that of the New Zealand Government and people that this Conference on Antarctica will provide a demonstration of what can be done – despite considerable difficulties and natural hesitations – when there is the need and the will to cooperate.

Statement by Mr. Asakai (Japan)

First of all I want to offer my congratulations to our Chairman Mr. Phleger, on his election to that post. I hope to see smooth sailing for this conference and a safe arrival in port with him as our pilot.

I would like to express my gratitude to the Honorable Secretary of State of the United States for the opening speech in which he welcomed us so warmly. Mr. Herter inspires us with a hopeful confidence in the noble and significant cause of this conference.

The need for international cooperation in Antarctica is of great significance. The Government of the United States has acted most happily for all countries concerned by inviting our attention to this need. I'm sure I speak for all of us when I say we are grateful to the United States Government for convening this conference here in Washington at this time.

I would also like to pay high tribute to the members of the preliminary conference. Thanks to their painstaking spadework our task is made smoother; the promise of ultimate success is brighter.

Now, Mr. Chairman, I would like to speak a few words about the policies and the fundamental thinking of my Government on the subject of this conference.

You all know, of course, how Japan secluded herself from the world for a long time. You know also that it was only in the middle of the last century that Japan opened her doors to foreign friendship and commerce. Only fifty years after this, the Japanese people began to show their interest in Antarctica.

From 1910 through 1912 a Japanese expedition under Captain Shirase explored the Ross Sea and areas adjacent to it as far south as the 80 degrees of latitude. Since 1934 our fleets have been actively engaged in whaling operations there, except for their suspension during the war years. More recently we have dispatched scientific expeditions to Antarctica every year since 1956 under the International Geophysical Year program.

I wish to point out here that, despite all this activity in the area, never in her history has Japan made territorial claim to any part of Antarctica. Logically Japan might have taken advantage of the achievements of the Shirase expedition to institute political claims, but it has never been our intention to do so, even without the provisions of Article 2 of the San Francisco Peace Treaty.[8]

Nevertheless, the Japanese people have consistently entertained a deep attachment to and a keen interest in Antarctica and they still do. The Showa Base on the coast of Prince Harald could not have been established successfully without the united and powerful support of the entire nation of Japan.

Our experience leads the people and the Government of Japan earnestly to hope that Antarctica will be used for peaceful purposes only without being subject to the conflicts and disturbances of world politics. The invitation to the conference to conclude a treaty on Antarctica, issued by the United States Government in May of last year,[9] was in complete harmony with the aspirations of the people and the Government of Japan. For this reason my Government accepted that invitation whole-heartedly, along with the other ten countries.

As the invitation of the American Government says, our twelve countries have pursued useful international cooperation for scientific purposes in Antarctica under the International Geophysical Year project. The treaty we have in mind has as its main purpose to provide a legal basis for the existing structure of international cooperation and to ensure for the future that Antarctica will always and only be used for peaceful and scientific purposes and that it will be kept open for those purposes.

International cooperation such as we have effected under the International Geophysical Year program has no parallel in any other region of the world or in any other field of activity. We should be proud of this. At this moment, Mr. Chairman, I can think of no other example of such a wholehearted international cooperation, anywhere else in this strife-torn world. It is like a beacon on the road to world peace. We, here, must do our best to raise that beacon so it may throw its peaceful light on more and more of the world's peoples.

With this in mind, I submit that the freedom to use Antarctica for peaceful purposes and scientific research, which it is the chief purpose of our Treaty to ensure, should not be monopolized by these twelve countries. To achieve our principal purpose most effectively it is essential that we keep the Treaty open for accession by all countries which have a bona fide interest in Antarctica and which are willing to subscribe to the conditions of our Treaty.

Another factor that calls for our attention is this: the drafting of our Treaty on Antarctica involves a number of entirely novel elements in the realm of the existing principles of international law. The freezing of territorial claims on Antarctica, the complex composition of Antarctica, the nonmilitarization of Antarctica and observation and inspection for that purpose, criminal and civil jurisdiction in Antarctica – these are among the questions difficult of regulation on the basis of the concepts of international law we now know.

Take for example the question of the zone of application of our Treaty. Research under the International Geophysical Year program shows that the Antarctic continent is composed of

[8] For the text of the Treaty of Peace with Japan, signed on Sept. 8, 1951, see *Treaties and Other International Acts Series* 2490 (3 UST, pt. 3, p. 3169); also printed in *American Foreign Policy, 1950–1955: Basic Documents* (Department of State publication 6446), vol. I, pp. 425–550.

[9] See *ante*, pp. 2–4.

small areas of exposed land, large expanses permanently covered with ice, and some areas seasonally frozen. Not only the limits of these several areas, but even the border lines of the whole Antarctic region cannot presently be established scientifically. Neither do we know if the soil bed under the permanent ice lies above sea level or below. How do we apply to these complex actualities our established ideas of international law relating to territorial waters, inland waters, the high seas?

Also, to establish America as a completely non-military area under proper observation and inspection poses a real challenge. It will be the first time in history such an attempt has been made on so large a scale and in an area so sparsely populated. Should we succeed here, we provide a hopeful precedent for the solution of one of the most important problems now facing the whole world.

With these points in mind, I submit that we have to make a totally flexible approach in grappling with the task of drafting our Treaty on Antarctica, and I want to assure you, Mr. Chairman, that the Japanese delegation participates in the deliberations throughout this conference with a very flexible and open-minded attitude.

The Government and the people of Japan earnestly and confidently hope that this conference will exhibit fully the spirit of peaceful cooperation already attained by our twelve countries relative to Antarctica. We hope this conference will conclude such a treaty as will in future be a model of international cooperation in other fields of activity.

Statement by Mr. Mora (Chile)

I should like first of all on behalf of the Chilean Delegation, to congratulate the distinguished Ambassador, Mr. Herman Phleger, on his appointment as Chairman of this Conference. For our part, we rejoice that the proposal we made in favour of Ambassador Phleger was unanimously accepted, for we are certain that with his experience and wisdom as a jurist and diplomat, he will be able to lead our discussions skilfully and surely along the pathway of success.

It is with the deepest interest that Chile joins in the important work of this Conference, and therefore my country offers its fullest cooperation in attaining the lofty objectives that inspired President Eisenhower to convoke it.

This interest in the Antarctic Continent on the part of Chile is certainly not something of today or yesterday. It goes back to the days, now far remote, when shortly after the Republic was established the country was able, to the extent of its capabilities, to broaden and strengthen its activities of all kinds in those regions.

This Conference has before it, therefore, a task that is undoubtedly of transcendental importance – that of clarifying as far as possible what has been termed the Antarctic problem, a complex problem, since it involves at the same time scientific, economic, strategic and political aspects.

From a geographical standpoint I wish to emphasize a well-known fact: my country is the closest one to the Antarctic Continent, for between the Antarctic Continent and its southernmost insular possessions in the Americas the distance is hardly more than 428 nautical miles, clear proof that the southern extreme of the American hemisphere and the Antarctic Continent of today were joined together in another age.

The government of Chile considers that the Chilean Antarctic sector, the limits of which were fixed by Supreme Decree No. 1747 of November 6, 1940, which I had the honor to sign during the Aguirre Cerda administration[10] in my capacity as Minister of Foreign Relations at the time, forms an integral part of the territory of the nation and constitutes a natural extension thereof toward the South Pole.

From a political standpoint, my government fully shares the view of the host government that the Antarctic problem must not be linked with other problems of today, but rather must be faced with realism and with respect for territorial sovereignties, because I take the liberty of saying

[10] Pedro Aguirre Cerda was President of the Republic of Chile, December 1938–November 1941.

that our Antarctic regions formed a part of the Chilean domain a long time before our country won its independence in 1810.

In this conversation, the reply which my government had the honor to give to the invitation to attend this Conference stated that the case of Chile presents distinctive characteristics because the Chilean Antarctic territory does not have the character of a colonial possession but is part of its metropolitan territory and form part of its southernmost province. It was added on the above-mentioned occasion that Chile saw two distinct basic objectives in the invitation: one, of a scientific type, and the other, of a political nature. With respect to the first [*second?*], it was stated in advance that Chile could not accept any formula that might imply the internationalization of its Antarctic territory because that would be contrary to the normal exercise of its sovereignty and would contravene clearly stated provisions of its Constitution.

Our Foreign Office also stated that it viewed with satisfaction the aim to continue the scientific cooperation set up on the occasion of the International Geophysical Year, but that it should be continued in conformity with the principles and procedures agreed upon at that time.

With regard to the second objective, Chile is not opposed to the possibility of studying an international commitment aimed at guaranteeing the peaceful use of the Antarctic Continent but rather much to the contrary, in accordance with its traditional peaceful policy, will gladly cooperate to that end. But it fears that an agreement of this nature may weaken the provisions of the Inter-American Treaty of Reciprocal Assistance signed at Rio de Janeiro in 1947[11] if the necessary precautions are not taken. As we know, part of the American Antarctic is included within the "Continental Security Zone" created by the said Treaty for which reason Chile considers that it would be advisable to state in the pertinent part that the provisions of the Antarctic Treaty in no way affect the principles contained in the aforementioned international instrument.

Lastly, my government suggested in its reply that it would be useful to supplement those objectives with an agreement on the conservation of the Antarctic maritime resources.

The government of Chile also thinks that the diplomatic instrument or instruments resulting from this meeting should, in their final wording, be as specific as possible and consider complications that might arise with respect to other international agreements into which we have entered. For example, it is well to reflect carefully on whether such an Antarctic agreement will enter the sphere of the so-called "Regional Agreements" referred to in Chapter VIII of the United Nations Charter, or whether it will better fall within another type of international pact. The question is important in our opinion, and it is therefore our obligation not to avoid giving a specific pronouncement in this connection.

We could make other observations regarding certain ideas that were exchanged in the preliminary stage of this meeting; we also could dwell more extensively, as some other Delegates have done, on detailed considerations concerning the bases of various kinds that lend special strength to our claims and rights concerning the portion of the Antarctic Territory that belongs to us; but my Delegation prefers to avail itself of the opportunity to express those observations and arguments in the course of the discussions to come, as a constructive contribution to the greater success of this Conference, which is starting today under such favourable auspices.

I do not wish to conclude without expressing our sincere gratitude for the cordial hospitality given our Delegation by the government of the United States, and our conviction that our deliberations and decisions must be inspired by the concept which the countries of our hemisphere expressed in one of their most significant periodical meetings: "Peace is the fulfilment of Justice sustained by the moral order and having the guarantee of Law."

---

[11] For text, see *Treaties and Other International Acts Series* 1838 (62 Stat., pt. 2, p. 1681); also printed in *Department of State Bulletin*, Sept. 21, 1947, pp. 565–567.

Statement by Mr. Koht (Norway)

First of all I want to thank the Secretary of State for his kind words of welcome.

Norway has during the years been actively engaged in the polar reasons, both for reasons of exploration and pure science, and not least have those parts of the world afforded us considerable economic support. It is sufficient to draw the attention to the Norwegian whaling fleet, which, since the beginning of this century, has been active in the waters of Antarctic and which was the main reason for Norwegian presence in the area.

There should be no need to remind anyone of the achievements of the distinguished explorer Roald Amundsen, who, together with four other Norwegians, was the first to set foot on the geographic South Pole on December 14th, 1911, planting the Norwegian flag there and naming the area Haakon the Seventh's plateau. Numerous other expeditions from Norway visited that area of Antarctica which was later to be named Queen Maud Land, during the thirties. The most prominent of these expeditions were under the sponsorship of Lars Christensen, one of the pioneers of international whaling.

These accomplishments, as well as those of expeditions from other nations, are the more remarkable when we consider the tremendous difficulties the pioneers of Antarctic exploration had to overcome. Some lost their lives in this world of ice and snow. I wish to pay tribute to those men of different nationalities who were the predecessors of today's scientists and explorers in these same regions.

Things have changed. The advanced technical civilization of the present day has made it possible to launch large-scale scientific operations in Antarctica, which little by little is yielding its secrets. Thus, time has clearly come for a new era to break in this vast continent, an era of international cooperation and mutual understanding in order to solve those problems which will naturally and inevitably arise where nations with different backgrounds and experiences are actively engaged in the same field. In Antarctica this aim should be the easier to reach as we all would have one common interest: that of securing the peaceful development of the continent.

I want to extend my Government's thanks and appreciation for the initiative taken by the President of the United States in inviting the nations which have a principal interest in the area to participate in a conference with a view to establish an international arrangement for the initiative taken by the President of the United States in inviting the nations which have a principal interest in an area to participate in a conference with a view to establish an international arrangement for Antarctica. In the invitation three main principles for the future arrangement are outlined, viz:

1. International cooperation and coordination of scientific research
2. Antarctica is to be used for purely peaceful purposes only, and
3. The legal status quo in Antarctica should be frozen for the duration of the arrangement reached, as far as rights and claims to territorial sovereignty are concerned. The Government of Norway in its reply to the United States' invitation expressed its willingness to participate in a conference as proposed and also its adherence to the basic principles which the United States has outlined.

I am happy to be able to say that Norway already has had the opportunity to practise international cooperation in the field of Antarctic scientific research. Starting in 1949 and terminating in 1952 a scientific team consisting of several nationalities[12] under Norwegian leadership built and manned "Maudheim", the name given to their headquarters in Queen Maud Land. The scientific knowledge gathered by their activities was considerable.

Norway Station, which is our IGY-station, and which is also situated in Queen Maud Land, is to be discontinued from the beginning of next year. Some time ago the Norwegian Government offered to lend this station to the Union of South Africa, and negotiations are taking place in this connection. It is hoped that it will prove possible to have the station

[12] Norwegian-British-Swedish Antarctic expedition, 1949–52.

manned by scientists from the Union of South Africa when our expedition is withdrawn. I can assure our South-African friends that Norway takes great pleasure in being able to assist the cause of science in this way.

To end let me express the hope that the conference which we now are about to begin will be successful and that we shall be able to reach those aims we have set in order to further a peaceful and orderly development in the future of Antarctica.

As far as Norway is concerned, we promise to do our utmost to succeed in what we are all now about to undertake.

Afternoon Meeting (3:00–4:30 p.m.)
Mr. Phleger, Presiding
Statement by Mr. Kuznetsov (Soviet Union)

Allow me, on behalf of the Soviet delegation, to express our greetings to the representatives of the countries assembled here at the Conference on Antarctica.

The present Conference has been convened to discuss important questions concerning Antarctica and to work out an international treaty which would contribute to the further development of fruitful cooperation among states in this part of the globe.

It is known that Antarctica is a vast area in the center of our planet, a continent with a territory surpassing that of Europe in size.

At present when we stand on the threshold of man's penetration into outer space we still have considerable gaps in our knowledge about the nature of our planet. Of vast area, Antarctica has not yet revealed all its secrets. This makes more difficult the solution of major geophysical problems on a world scale. The solution of these problems, however, would permit even wider use of the forces of nature for the benefit of mankind.

The economic potential of the Antarctic continent has not yet been sufficiently studied, but there is reason to believe that in the future, in conjunction with a more detailed exploration of Antarctica and the development of means of communication, this continent will be of still greater importance. The Antarctic waters are abundant in organic sea life and intensive fishing is carried on there, accounting for about 9/10 of the total world catch of whales.

Having in mind the geographic, economic, historic and other conditions, the Soviet Government has always proceeded from the premise that it is expedient to settle the question of the régime for Antarctica on an international basis with a view to attaining an agreement that would respond to the legitimate interests of all states. It is known that the Soviet Government has moved to invite to the Conference on Antarctica all the states which might wish to take part. The participation of the greatest possible number of states in the treaty under consideration would contribute to its effectiveness.

At this Conference those states are represented that are at present directly conducting scientific research in Antarctica. The convening of an International Conference on Antarctica is, undoubtedly, a positive factor, and it may play a substantial role in the further development of international cooperation in this area of the world.

The convening of this Conference indicates that its participants agree that a régime for Antarctica should be established on an international basis with due consideration to mutual interests and rights.

Our Conference is the first in history held on Antarctica, the exploration of which began many years ago. It should lay the foundation for an international régime of Antarctica.

In the view of the Soviet Government, the Conference in working out an international treaty must proceed on the basis of the main task now facing mankind. This task is to maintain and consolidate peace among all states, to develop and strengthen friendship among all nations.

Proceeding from the above, the Soviet Government considers that there should be established in Antarctica an international régime that would contribute to the strengthening of peace and would exclude the possibility of this area being turned into a source of frictions and tensions in the relations between states.

Therefore, it is important, first of all, to come to an agreement providing for the use of Antarctica for peaceful purposes only. This means that the carrying out in Antarctica of any measures of military nature, in particular the construction of military bases and installations, the conducting of military, naval and air exercises and the testing of any types of weapons, should be prohibited.

The conclusion of an international treaty will, undoubtedly, open up the prospects for a more effective exploration of that region.

Gentlemen, Russia has made a great contribution to the common cause of exploration of Antarctica. As is known, its navigators and scientists, Bellingshausen and Lazarev, were the first to discover the sixth continent at the beginning of the Nineteenth Century.[13]

The Soviet Union is taking an active part in the exploration of Antarctica by conducting extensive research there. The work that has been assigned to Soviet scientists concerns the exploration of those almost inaccessible areas of the Antarctic continent, namely, its hinterland, of which mankind knew nothing until recently.

Soviet explorers penetrated into those regions of the Antarctic continent that lie furthest from the coast, they reached the South geomagnetic pole and the pole of relative inaccessibility and stayed in these regions during winter periods. They discovered the pole of cold of our planet where an air temperature of 87.6° below zero centigrade was registered.

The Soviet scientists were working under unusually difficult conditions, which were to a certain extent similar to those expected in outer space where much exploration has already been done by Soviet scientists as well as by scientists of other countries.

The selfless work of Soviet explorers in Antarctica gives valuable scientific data, which becomes available to the scientists of all countries.

The Soviet scientists, naturally, realize that the results of their research work constitute only a part of what has recently been done by all of the scientists working in Antarctica.

We are glad to note that in Antarctica – this coldest region of our planet – exceptionally warm relations have developed between scientists from different countries. A wide exchange of the results of research work and observations, close contacts between expeditions, unselfish aid and mutual assistance in surmounting difficulties – these are characteristic features of scientific cooperation in Antarctica. It may be said without exaggeration that, as a result of this international scientific cooperation, mankind has learned more about Antarctica in the last three or four years than in all the 130 years since the day of its discovery.

To ensure still closer and wider international cooperation it is necessary to consolidate the existing principle of freedom of scientific exploration in Antarctica. This principle, which has gained general recognition in the carrying out of the International Geophysical Year, means that governments, organizations and citizens of all countries may conduct scientific research in Antarctica on the basis of equality.

As to the question of the territorial claims in Antarctica, the position of the Soviet Union was laid down in the Soviet Government's note of June 2, 1958, which stated in particular:

The Soviet Union reserves for itself all of the rights based on the discoveries and explorations of Russian seafarers and scientists, including the right to make appropriate territorial claims in Antarctica.

Realizing the complex and delicate character of the territorial problems in Antarctica, the Soviet Union supports the agreement on this question arrived at in the course of the preliminary negotiations which took place in connection with preparations for this Conference.

[13] This refers to the voyage of Adm. Thaddeus von Bellingshausen, accompanied by Lt. Mikhail Petrovich Lazarev, in the *Mirny* and *Vostok*, 1819–21.

Fellow Delegates, at present favourable conditions are emerging in the world for more active cooperation of all states in the interests of consolidating universal peace and security. The historic visit of the Chairman of the Council of Ministers of the U.S.S.R., N.S. Khrushchev, to the United States of America[14] and his talks with the U.S. President, Dwight D. Eisenhower, was an important contribution to the improvement of the international situation.

Our Conference is meeting at a time when the trend towards warmer relations between states is discernible, and, figuratively speaking, this fair wind that has appeared in the international atmosphere is favourable for our Conference and must assist in the happy sailing of our ship.

Mr. Chairman, Gentlemen, as is known, since June of last year preliminary negotiations between representatives of the states participating in this Conference have been held in Washington, during which a considerable amount of work has been done.

We note with satisfaction that these negotiations were conducted in a spirit of business-like cooperation and mutual understanding. The Soviet delegation expresses its hope that this constructive cooperation will continue also at the Conference that opened today.

Availing myself of this opportunity, I would like to express our appreciation of the efforts of the Government of the United States in convening this Conference and to thank Secretary of State Christian Herter for his warm words of welcome spoken here.

The Soviet delegation hopes that this Conference will successfully solve the tasks facing it, will work out an international treaty on Antarctica, which will be in harmony with the aims and spirit of the U.N. Charter, and will promote to the maximum extent the peaceful cooperation of states in this area.

For its part, the Soviet Government will make every effort to contribute to the success of the Conference.

Statement by Mr. Casey (Australia)

I first wish to express my thanks to Mr. Herter for his kind words of welcome and to say that the Australian Government greatly appreciates the American Government's invitation to hold this Conference in Washington.

I fully agree that this Conference for the settlement of Antarctic problems is one of the most promising developments in recent history, and if it is brought to a successful conclusion it will constitute an important and indeed unique step forward in international relations.

I must confess that when informal negotiations were first begun over a year ago for an Antarctic Treaty, the Australian Government was not optimistic that a satisfactory basis of agreement could be found among all the countries with interests in the Antarctic. These countries are very diverse in their national backgrounds and in the past have tended to follow different courses in the Antarctic. In fact, in some cases there have been direct conflicts of national interest. It seemed unlikely therefore that sufficient common ground could be found to provide the basis for an Antarctic Treaty. The Australian Government believed that unless such common ground could be found it would be unwise to call a Conference. This would have raised unfounded hopes and might well have sharpened rather than diminished existing conflicts of interest. From the outset of the informal negotiations we therefore urged strongly that all Governments should seek a basic measure of agreement before calling a formal conference.

The Australian Government has been glad to find that, contrary to its earlier expectations, an important and valuable area of common agreement has been established among the twelve governments represented at this Conference. Although the informal discussions which have preceded the Conference are not necessarily binding on Governments, they have nevertheless enabled our representatives to define and formulate substantial agreement in all the important fields. I would go so far as to say that if all the informal understandings arrived at in the

[14] Sept. 15–27, 1959.

Working Group are upheld by the delegations to this Conference, the successful conclusion of the Treaty is assured.

The Leaders of Delegations who have already spoken have presented in eloquent terms the broad principles on which it is hoped the Antarctic Treaty will be based. I need only say that the Australian Government is in full accord with these principles. We have for many years favoured the widest possible scientific cooperation in the area and the fullest exchange of scientific information. We have always made the information which we have acquired through our own activities in the Antarctic freely available to the rest of the world. We also emphatically endorse the principle that the whole of the Antarctic region should be reserved for peaceful uses only – and that no dispute of any kind shall be allowed to disturbed the pax Antarctica. I might say that the more completely this principle is applied the happier the Australian Government will be. We are confident that all parties will pledge themselves to the principle that there should be no militarization of the Antarctic and I also am encouraged to believe that agreement will be reached on arrangements for observation and inspection which will ensure that this principle is carried out.

I believe that another important aspect of ensuring peace in the Antarctic is the elimination of potential causes of international rivalry and conflict. In the past the principal cause of such differences has been the question of territorial claims. It is therefore the Australian Government's profound conviction that everything possible should be done to eliminate this source of conflict. We realise that it would be optimistic to expect that the question of territorial claims could be settled at the present time. We have therefore come to the conclusion that the best solution is to include provisions in the Treaty which would preserve the status quo. This means that countries such as Australia who have made great efforts over many years in their own territories in the Antarctic will not be obliged to relinquish any of their rights and claims. At the same time we recognise that countries who have not made claims are entitled to maintain that their own position should not be worsened under the Treaty. I have been most gratified at the fact that in the informal discussions that have already taken place, general acceptance has been indicated of those concepts. I might in fact say that such acceptance has always been considered by the Australian Government as an essential prerequisite of a satisfactory treaty. It was only when it became clear that there was fairly general agreement on this point that we believed that the calling of a Conference was justified.

One of the primary objectives of the Treaty must be to eliminate suspicions in the Antarctic. I do not wish to imply that at the present time there are any such suspicions; in fact, in recent years co-operation in the area has been marked by the most complete international goodwill. We want to keep it that way. As realists we must recognise that as the importance of the area grows and as national activities continue to develop, the possibilities of disagreement are likely to increase. Only by signing a treaty on the lines at present contemplated can we keep the Antarctic from becoming a breeding ground for suspicion – which is the great corroder.

The Antarctic's geographical relationship with the Antarctic continent means that it is of special importance to us. Australia's coastline of 2000 miles runs parallel to the Antarctic coastline only 2000 or 3000 miles to the south. The weather of Australia is greatly affected by Antarctic meteorological conditions. As a country largely concerned with agricultural and pastoral production Australia has an important economic interest in a close knowledge of Antarctic weather conditions.

Australia has a long history of exploration and scientific activity in the Antarctic and the Australian territory makes up almost one third of the continent. In the nineteenth century a number of Australians participated in exploration and whaling activity in the region. In 1909 two of the three members of Sir Ernest Shackleton's expedition who reached the South Magnetic Pole were Australians. These were Sir Douglas Mawson and Sir Edgeworth David whose names have since become famous in the annals of Antarctic exploration. Mawson led the

Australasian Antarctic expedition of 1911/1914 which discovered and explored King George V and Queen Mary Lands, explored Adélie Land and sledged to the South Magnetic Pole area. He also led the British, Australian, New Zealand Antarctic Research Expedition of 1929/31. This expedition discovered MacRobertson Land and the BANZARE Coast, and visited Kemp and Enderby Lands.

Sir Hubert Wilkins, an Australian who spent many years of his life in the United States, went on expeditions to the Antarctic several times and explored Graham Land from the air in 1928–30. During 1934–37 another Australian, John Rymill, led the British Graham Land Expedition which discovered and surveyed much of the coast of Graham Land and its off-lying islands.

Australian post-war Antarctic activities began in the summer of 1947–48, when the Australian National Antarctic Research Expedition under the leadership of Stuart Campbell made a reconnaissance of the coast-line King George V Land in the "Wyatt Earp". In December, 1947 a scientific research station was established on Heard Island, and another one on Macquarie Island in March 1948.

Since 1953 the Australian National Antarctic Research Expedition under the direction of Phillip Law, has carried out extensive exploration along the coast of the Australian Antarctic Territory. It is now true to say that practically the whole of the coastline of the Australian sector has been explored and photographed from the air.

In February 1954 our first permanent base on the Antarctic mainland, Mawson, was set up in MacRobertson Land. In January 1957, a second mainland base, Davis, was established in the Vestfold Hills area, and in January 1958, an automatic weather station was set up on Lewis Island, just to the west of the French territory of Adélie Land.

In February 1959 the Australians took over operation of the Wilkes Station which had been established by the United States on the Budd Coast.

Australia is most conscious of the importance of scientific research in the Antarctic. I have already mentioned the effect of Antarctic meteorology on Australia but we are also deeply interested in many other fields of scientific endeavour. I would like to mention, I hope with all proper modesty, that Australia may be regarded as one of the six or eight most advanced scientific nations in the world. We have made important contributions to scientific development in a number of fields and are already equipped to develop our research in several important directions. Research in the Antarctic will be an important complement to these efforts. This is particularly true in such fields as geophysics, geomagnetism, cosmic rays and the ionosphere. I would emphasize that scientific data of great importance to research workers studying the upper atmosphere can be gained from observations in the Antarctic. Such work has recently been greatly stimulated by the remarkable discoveries of Van Allen[15] and others of zones of intense radiation which exist in doughnut form near the earth. The holes in these doughnuts are above the geomagnetic polar regions – which may be of significance as scientific effort develops.

Another aspect of Antarctic research which may be of great ultimate importance to the rest of the world is the study of the nutritive wealth of the Antarctic seas. In view of the astronomical increase in the world demand for food that is likely to occur within the next fifty years it is quite conceivable that mankind will have to turn to the Antarctic zones as a source of protein food for both animals and human beings.

Work in a number of scientific disciplines is carried out at our four main bases – at Macquarie Island, Mawson, Davis and Wilkes, and in the field. The Australian base at Heard Island was closed down in March 1955, when our scientific research work there was completed. In addition, our automatic weather station on Lewis Island is of considerable interest and scientific usefulness.

[15] Dr James Alfred Van Allen, professor and head of Physics Department, State University of Iowa.

Australia has of course participated fully in the work of the Special Committee on Antarctic Research (SCAR)[16] and considerable scientific work on the Antarctic is carried out in Australia under the auspices of this organization. The permanent Secretary of the Working Group on Cartography is an Australian and the function of this group is to co-ordinate information about mapping of the Antarctic to prevent unnecessary duplication of effort. At the invitation of SCAR Australia has also set up the International Antarctic Weather Analysis Centre in Melbourne.

In view of our efforts in the Antarctic over several decades, I feel that I am justified in claiming that Australia has made an important contribution to the opening up of this difficult and inhospitable continent. We have not however engaged in these activities solely in our national interest. We have always sought to share with others the results of our efforts. We co-operated wholeheartedly in the International Geophysical Year and we fully support one of the main objectives of the proposed Antarctic Treaty, which is to facilitate the continuation and expansion of international scientific co-operation in the area. There is nothing exclusive about the proposed Treaty. The twelve countries gathered at this conference are the ones with direct interests and responsibilities in the area and it is right and proper that they should have the task of drawing up a treaty for the area. As far as Australia is concerned however we do not believe that membership of such a treaty need necessarily be limited to the present twelve. For example, any member of the United Nations who is prepared to undertake the considerable effort of maintaining operations in the Antarctic area should perhaps be able to join the Treaty. But even those countries who do not join it will stand to benefit greatly from it. Apart from the world-wide importance of the establishment of an area of permanent peace in the Antarctic, the whole world will benefit from the scientific co-operation among the signatories to the Treaty.

It would therefore like to say in conclusion, Mr. Chairman, that if this conference succeeds in drawing up a treaty for the Antarctic it will be of very great benefit not only to the signatories but to the whole of mankind.

Statement of Mr. Charpentier (France)

Mr. Chairman, it is a joy for me to be able to express publicly the cordial thanks of my Government for the reception accorded us in Washington and for the words of welcome you have addressed to us.

The step taken by the Government of the United States – and I should like to stress it at this time – appears to us extremely felicitous.

The Antarctic portion of the work of the International Geophysical Year was carried out in an atmosphere of understanding and harmony, untroubled by any rivalry. The pathway of scientific cooperation among many nations on which this experience has started us is full of promise. It would have been most regrettable if such an effort had not been followed up, and we congratulate ourselves on the agreement reached by the interested governments to strengthen the results obtained and to extend into the future an activity as fruitful as this has been.

The French Government, which has already furnished poof of its intentions in that regard, is ready to give its full assistance to the development of scientific cooperation among nations with respect to the Antarctic Continent. It sees in the emulation of the courageous explorers who, despite the harshness of the climate, are working together to increase the sum total of human knowledge, a shining example of what can be accomplished by good understanding among nations.

France has been in the forefront of the countries that are engaged in scientific cooperation in the Antarctic. It takes pride in this and intends to continue its work. It actively participated in the work of the Scientific Committee on Antarctic Research since that body was established and

[16] Special Committee on Antarctic Research, established by the International Council of Scientific Unions to meet the need for further international organization of scientific activity in Antarctica beyond the IGY.

its scientists are keeping in close touch with the foreign scientific missions that have undertaken the study of the southern continent. It is willing to increase its efforts in that field.

Military neutralization of the Antarctic regions, which the Conference proposes to bring about, also meets with the full approval of my country. The French expeditions in the Antarctic have never served to support any activity of a military nature, and the programs drawn up for the next few years in that region of the world are concerned only with the development of scientific research. We agree that controlled military neutralization of the Antarctic should be instituted in the form of a convention and should be the subject of solemn commitments on the part of all interested governments.

France attaches all the more importance to the work of the Conference, since for many years it has been represented on the southern seas and in the Antarctic. Its sovereignty over Adélie Land, discovered in 1840 by Dumont d'Urville who flew the tricolor there for the first time, explored by Charcot[17] at the beginning of this century, and crossed in recent years by the French polar expeditions, rests on solid foundations. The French Government is proud, in addition to having undisputable historical claims, to be able to rely on a permanent occupation which, if it affirms our rights, serves at the same time the higher interests of science.

Such are the reasons for which my country is anxious to express its satisfaction at taking part in the work which we are undertaking today; such are the reasons for which it expresses the hope of seeing this work succeed in the interest of cooperation among nations, and in the interest of science and of peace.

Statement by Mr. Scilingo (Argentina)

The Conference that is opening today upon the invitation of the Government of the United States of America and at which the countries that participated in the activities of the International Geophysical Year are represented, has been convened to deal with the question of the exclusively peaceful use of and scientific cooperation in Antarctica.

The area that the discussions will cover includes a sector forming the subject of an Argentine-Chilean declaration of recognition of mutual rights, which, as a natural extension of the Argentine Republic, has, for many decades, formed an integral part of its territory. Argentina installed in Antarctica the first permanent observatory in 1904.[18] Since then, not to mention activities prior to that year, it has been establishing bases, stations, refuges, lighthouses, buoys, post offices, and radio-telegraph stations. Argentine military men and Argentine men of science have performed many deeds of heroism in the Antarctic wilderness and some have given their lives in the unceasing process of their outstanding technical and scientific work. Under those circumstances, Mr. Chairman, it can be a surprise to no one that Antarctica has taken root and established an awareness in the soul of the Argentine nation.

The Argentine Republic, the first actual and continuous occupant of the area, which has been incorporated administratively for some time into the Tierra del Fuego Government District, which is only a few hundred nautical miles from the Antarctic, is attending this Conference with all these rights. They indicate the measure of its interest in the discussions that are beginning and of the importance that it attaches to this Conference. They also determine its line of action and its responsibility.

This Conference – and it is fitting that we set forth these ideas clearly – has not been convened to institute regimes or to create structures. It is not its mission to change or alter anything. Nothing that is done here or is the consequence of what is agreed upon here will give rise, affect or will disregard rights. The objective of this Conference is to reach an agreement, with the express concurrence of all the parties, upon the peaceful use and of scientific cooperation in the Antarctic area within the geographic boundary that may be agreed upon. With that clear understanding, Argentina will take part in the work with a sincere desire to cooperate.

[17] Dr. Jean B. Charcot led French Antarctic expeditions in 1903–05 and in 1908–10.

[18] On Laurie Island in the South Orkney group.

The nuclear world in which we live, in which science, ever working wonders, is constantly producing new forms and instruments of massive destruction, would make the consequences of an armed conflict far worse than the human mind could conceive. War, and the danger or threat of war, have been casting their dark shadows over a humanity that is far from desiring its own holocaust; a humanity that knows that those same media that are conspiring against its existence, if used for peaceful purposes, would create possibilities for development that could radically transform its living conditions.

Recent events and the mutual public recognition by two statement of their sincere reciprocal desire for peace are tending to create a new atmosphere in which a new spirit could take root. In this situation, if the Conference solemnly agrees on the exclusively peaceful use of the geographic area coming within its jurisdiction, it will have accomplished, by that fact alone, a historic task. This would be the first great step toward the realization of the hopes of the world.

If, at the same time, it establishes scientific cooperation as an end in itself, applicable to the area where it was begun and carried out under conditions that made it perfectly possible during the International Geophysical Year, which was mentioned in calling the Conference, it will, in the opinion of the Argentine Delegation, have fully accomplished its objectives.

Argentina will support those principles, whether they take the form of a declaration or treaty. Both principles flow from its tradition and its history. To mention but one or two precedents, I should like to recall that several years ago Argentina pledged itself, along with two other countries taking part in the Conference, not to send warships south of parallel 60 and that it has scrupulously kept that commitment and is still doing so. In its broad exploratory work in the Antarctic region it has always practiced both general and scientific cooperation. For over fifty years it has often had the privilege of giving its support to technical expeditions in difficult situations and has felt itself more than repaid by the expressions of public gratitude.

The Argentine Delegation will make its point of view known in the Committees. There it will express its concurrence or disagreement with such proposals as may be submitted and it will present some of its own.

Mr. Chairman, if we should work widely in a spirit of mutual understanding, we could, provided we rise about dissimilar interests and situations, reach a satisfactory agreement.

I sincerely hope that this will be accomplished and I pledge the loyal cooperation of the Delegation of which I have the honour to be Chairman.

Statement by Viscount Obert de Thieusies (Belgium)

The Belgian delegation is very happy to pay tribute to President Eisenhower's initiative in calling a conference of the interested powers with a view to preparing a provisional statute for the Antarctic. It considers this step a very concrete effort towards promoting international understanding and cooperation wherever possible.

The Antarctic has shown, in a field that is of course geographically limited but nevertheless vast, just how possible it is to cooperate in a very friendly spirit.

Belgium, whose Antarctic expedition of 1958 owes much to the spontaneous and generous aid of the Russians and Americans, is particularly aware of that fact.

Hence, it is a really enticing prospect – that of bringing together the powers that have knowledge of the Antarctic, the problems that arise there, and the difficulties that must be overcome there in order to establish and perpetuate, by a deliberative agreement, the spirit of understanding that has continually manifested itself with respect to the Antarctic. Those who have had to surmount the same obstacles are always ready to understand one another.

Belgium expresses the wish that the present negotiations will end in unanimous agreement, which would thus set an example that might be followed in other fields.

Belgium has the right to be invited to these sessions. It is proud of this. Its contribution to the scientific exploration of the Antarctic is not, as a matter of fact, entirely recent. The Adrien de

Gerlache expedition of 1898 was the first to spend the winter within the polar circle; next month the fourth Belgian expedition will set out for this still mysterious continent. This expresses all the interest it has shown and will continue to show in the Antarctic. The Belgian delegation, therefore, wishes to emphasize that it is specifically in the name of that interest that it hopes the planned agreement will be successfully concluded.

Statement of Sir Esler Denning (United Kingdom)

Mr. Chairman, one behalf of the United Kingdom Delegation, I should like to express our warm thanks to Mr. Herter, Secretary of State of the United States, for presiding over the preliminary proceedings of this Conference and for his kind words of welcome to the Delegates. I should also like to congratulate you, Sir, on your election to your responsible office, just as we congratulate ourselves on having made available to us the benefits of your wisdom and your experience. We are grateful too to the U.S. Government for the facilities and organisation they have so kindly placed at our disposal for the smooth and speedy transaction of the business which lies before us. As to the nature of that business other distinguished Delegates have already made reference to the spirit of cooperation and the considerable measure of agreement achieved by the Working Group, and I should like to pay tribute to the extent of their accomplishment.

The U.K. Delegation approaches the present Conference in no rigid or inflexible spirit. Her Majesty's Government in the United Kingdom have for many years been in favour of the conclusion of an agreement between countries actively interested in the Antarctic, if only because of the peculiar and indeed unique conditions which prevail there, and because of the special nature of the benefits which mankind may expect to derive from the area. For these reasons, as long ago as 1948, they indicated their readiness to accept proposals put forward by the United States Government for an international regime in the Antarctic.[19] Ten years later, they welcome equally the invitation of President Eisenhower, extended in May 1958, to participate in this present Conference.

We are wholly in agreement with the United States as to the high value to be attached to the close international cooperation achieved during the International Geophysical Year in the Antarctic, and we warmly welcome the prospect of ensuring the continuance of the scientific cooperation which has already added measurably to our knowledge of this remote area of the earth's surface.

The object of the Conference which meets here today for the first time is, as we see it, to consider and agree upon the terms of a Treaty, which will not only promote continuing international cooperation in the field of scientific research in the Antarctic, but will facilitate such cooperation by eliminating, as far as lies in the power of the countries represented here, the possibility of political dispute, or military menace, which might otherwise impede or retard international progress in the search for knowledge.

Of the 12 countries who have a special interest in the conclusion of a Treaty for the purposes indicated, the United Kingdom has a long record of Antarctic exploration. We were amongst the first in this field, and also amongst the first to establish permanent settlements for scientific investigation and the regulation of whaling activities. The Antarctic Circle was first crossed by Captain Cook in 1773. From 1900 onwards many points in the Antarctic were occupied at various times by British wintering parties. Continuous occupation of a number of research stations started in 1944. Our first formal territorial claims to parts of the continent were made as long ago as 1841. Throughout the period a large number of major expeditions of discovery and research have set out from the United Kingdom and a vast corpus of knowledge relating to certain parts of Antarctica has been amassed and made public; all these records are freely available at the Scott Polar Research Institute in England. Our surveys have been made by

[19] See *Department of State Bulletin*, Sept. 5, 1948, p. 301.

pioneer efforts over land and on the ice as well as from the air, often in circumstances of great difficulty and danger.

In keeping with the continuity of our interest, United Kingdom sovereignty over the area in which our activities had been, and were to be displayed, was consolidated in 1908 and 1917. The fact that this sovereignty has since been contested by rival claims gives substance to one of the matters which this Conference expects to discuss.

While we fully maintain the indisputable rights to sovereignty to which the U.K. is entitled we recognise the need to ensure that knowledge of the Antarctic and freedom of access to it should not be limited by political considerations. We are accordingly prepared to subscribe to a clause in the Treaty which will maintain the legal *status quo* throughout the area of the Antarctic. Indeed we consider such a clause to be an essential part of the Treaty if its main aims are to be secured.

There are other Powers represented at this Conference who have rights and claims in other areas of the Antarctic. The suggestion is that the Treaty should provide full protection for the present juridical position of all the Powers concerned, while they, for their part, will accept the obligations involved by adherence to the Treaty as a whole. In this way it is hoped to ensure that, for the duration of the Treaty, political disputes arising from territorial claims can be avoided.

We come next to the important principle that the Antarctic should be used for peaceful purposes only. In our view the Treaty must contain provisions for ensuring that this principle is observed in practice, for while we have, of course, no reason to doubt the good faith of the parties signatory to it, the principle of non-militarisation is still so new in international practice, that it would surely be wise to eliminate from the outset, the possibility that the actions of one or other of the parties, including the United Kingdom, can give rise to doubt or suspicion amongst other Powers as to whether the principle is being observed. We hope, therefore, that approval will be given to proposals for a system of observation and inspection sufficient, in the special conditions prevailing in the Antarctic, to ensure that the basic purpose of preserving the area from military activities is achieved. At the same time it seems important to bear in mind the relevance of certain practical considerations. Antarctic expeditions already work under very difficult conditions, and we must not add to the burdens of climate and geography, by imposing unacceptable conditions in the Treaty. We have particularly in mind the need to limit requirements as regards the attachment of observers to expeditions and bases, as well as the possible need of certain countries to provide logistic support for their scientific expeditions from military sources. It would be difficult to ban such support, though it must be made clear that military personnel and equipment can only be employed for peaceful purposes.

There are two further matters which are not only of close concern to this Conference, but which may well require clarification for the benefit of other countries who are not parties to our present deliberations. The first concerns any organisation which may set up under 12-Power Treaty which we are now about to negotiate, and the second, which is interlinked with it, relates to participation by other Powers and access to the Antarctic by other nations of the world.

As to the first, the participants of this Conference other than the United States are those who accepted the invitation of the United States Government, and they include on the one hand the group of Powers having territorial rights or claims in the general area of the Antarctic, and on the other, a number of Powers who, through their scientific expeditions and association with the Antarctic, can justifiably claim to participate in any arrangements which may be agreed upon to make a Treaty effective. The short answer to those who might ask why the drafting of a Treaty should be confined to 12 Powers would seem to be that a beginning must be made somewhere, and that the 12 are, by reason of their association in the Antarctic during the International Geophysical Year, well qualified to make that beginning. It was originally the view of the United Kingdom that some organisation vested with more effective and comprehensive powers than that which is now contemplated, would have been desirable, but in deference to the views of others we are prepared to subscribe to a less far-reaching scheme in the interests of general agreement. We feel, however, that the Treaty arrangements should be made as effective as possible, for if too many matters are left undecided they can give rise to subsequent disputes, which may prejudice the international harmony we are all anxious to promote. We therefore believe that the Treaty should include firm provisions for such matters as jurisdiction and the settlement of disputes between the parties. We should also regard the Treaty as unsatisfactory if it failed to set up some form of continuing organisation to promote its aims.

The other interlinked question is how to safeguard the interests of countries other than those represented at this Conference. We are concerned that no misunderstanding should arise as to the motives of the Twelve Powers; we should not wish our deliberations to raise doubts in the minds of other nations, and particularly of those who, although hitherto not actively interested in the Antarctic, may question the right of any single group of countries even to give the appearance of legislating on a matter of worldwide concern.

We believe, however, that a Treaty on the lines of that which is now proposed would provide a just and effective method of achieving the aim of preserving the Antarctic as a heritage from nature for the benefit of mankind in general, by freeing it as far as possible from the ambitions and disputes of nations and groups of nations. The Treaty is, in fact, to be almost entirely a self-denying ordinance on the part of the signatures, who will derive from it virtually no privileges but only obligations. In order to ensure the smooth working of the practical arrangements, which will give effect to the principles underlying the Treaty, it is desirable that these arrangements should be in the hands of those Powers having experience of physical conditions in the Antarctic. The Twelve Powers participating in this Conference have that experience, and it is surely reasonable that they should be charged, initially, with the responsibilities which will devolve upon them, as a consequence of the Treaty.

On the other hand, it is highly important in the interests of all nations – including those represented here – that any other country, which may wish to engage in activities in the Antarctic, should be able to associate itself with the terms of the Treaty and agree to abide by the principles which underlie it. Insofar as these principles are in conformity with the spirit of the United Nations, we may hope that no member of the United Nations would decline to accept them, but there are various ways in which acceptance might be indicated, and this is a matter which, it seems to us, will merit further consideration by the delegates to this Conference. There is, I am sure, no need for other nations to fear that we shall fail to take their position into account, in the course of our discussions.

In conclusion, it is the belief of Her Majesty's Government in the United Kingdom that, if the principles which I have tried to outline can be accepted, it should be possible to devise a Treaty which will take fully into account the various and contrasting features; which are part of the picture: the need to preserve the legal position of the signatories; the need to protect the rights of non-signatories; the need for effectively preserving the Antarctic for peaceful uses; and, finally, the need to avoid anything which might unduly limit the activities of genuinely scientific expeditions. If we can forge an instrument which will maintain the balance between these considerations, I believe that we shall have made a real contribution to the future not only of the Antarctic, but also of the whole world. For here we have an opportunity to demonstrate the effectiveness of international cooperation, and if we are able, as a result of this Treaty, to transform an ideal into a reality, in a region which is admittedly remote and empty of people, may it not be, that the practice and the example which it will establish, will guide us towards a settlement of some of the graver problems which afflict the rest of the world, and to which we have so far failed to find a solution.

Statement of Mr. Daniels (United States)

Earlier this day you heard the general statement given by the Secretary of State which summarised the thinking of this Government in regard to the conference which is now convening. It gave our philosophy and summarised our objectives. Subsequently our Chairman, Ambassador Phleger, read our note of invitation which was addressed to all your governments and which sets forth in more detail the thinking, the objectives, the policies of the United States Government. There is little that I need add to those statements at this time. I should be remiss in my duty, however, were I to let pass this occasion without expressing on behalf of the Delegation of the United States of America, our very sincere appreciation for the kind references which previous speakers have made to President Eisenhower, to the Secretary of State, and to our Chairman. I thank you all.

With reference to activities of countries in Antarctica over past years, it is not my intention to go into detail on that subject at this time. I have listened with interest and attention to the activities which many countries have pursued in Antarctica over past years. Were I to attempt to recount American activities over the past 140 years since the days of Captain Nathaniel Palmer of Connecticut, I would keep you here to an unseemly late hour and I shall refrain from doing so. I do wish, however, to make of record the fact that those activities have indeed been extensive and over a long period of time.

Having listened now to the eleven previous speakers it has become apparent that there does indeed exist wide areas of agreement among all of us in regard to the nature of the proposed treaty which we all hope will be concluded as a result of this conference. There is agreement – I think it has been expressed unanimously – with the proposition that Antarctica should be used for peaceful purposes only, and similarly there have been many good words in support of a continuation of the fruitful type of international scientific cooperation which has been going on there in recent years and which we hope can be continued indefinitely.

Other points have been mentioned and it has been quite apparent to me at least, and I hope to all of us, that indeed there is a very wide measure of agreement. That gives rise to a note of optimism and one on which I should like to conclude my brief statement today. That optimism is based not only on the substance of what previous speakers have said, but also on a recognition on our part of the very high calibre of statesmen which have been sent by eleven governments to participate in these debates. We are delighted to find with us distinguished gentlemen of such high calibre and I believe that that, combined with what I have just said, augurs well for the success of this Conference on Antarctica. It is our hope that not only will we conclude successfully a treaty along the general lines that have been outlined and which we will further refine, but also, having concluded that treaty, we hope that there will radiate forth from it and from Antarctica and into an otherwise troubled world, a little additional warmth of understanding, additional light and knowledge, and added hope for peace.

Conference on Antarctica Press Releases Nos. 1 to 5[20]

Press Release No. 1, October 16

The Conference, in its Second Plenary Session on October 16, adopted its Rules of Procedure and organized itself into two main committees, one of which [Committee II] will consider legal and political problems. The other committee [Committee I] will deal primarily with scientific matters.

Committee I held its first meeting during the afternoon.

[20] Reproduced from US Department of State, *The Conference on Antarctica: Washington October 15–December 1 1959* (US Government Printing Office, Washington DC, 1959), 40–42. There were two other Conference press releases: press release No. 6, which summarized the main points contained in the treaty, was cancelled, and instead the full text of the treaty was made available to the press; press release No. 7, dated Nov. 30, announced that, agreement having been reached on the preamble and articles of the treaty and on the final act, final accord on the treaty as a whole would be considered at a plenary session on Dec. 1, to be followed by a signing ceremony.

Press Release No. 2, October 20

Committee II of the Conference on Antarctica, which is concerned with legal and political subjects, held its second committee meeting the afternoon of October 20. This Committee, the same as Committee I, consists of delegates representing all 12 countries participating in the Conference.

Following the practice of rotating chairmen, the Right Honorable Richard Gardiner Casey, C.H., Minister for External Affairs and head of the Australian delegation, presided.

In this committee session general agreement was reached that Antarctica should be used for peaceful purposes only and that all measures of a military nature should be prohibited.

It is anticipated this topic will become Article I of the treaty being negotiated.

Press Release No. 3, October 23

The Conference on Antarctica in which 12 nations are participating and which completed its seventh full working day Friday, October 23, announced that a spirit of cooperation prevails and that satisfactory progress is being made. During this period, the Conference has reached complete agreement on two topics. Numerous points involved in other topics of discussion have been agreed or clarified.

On October 20 it was announced that general agreement was reached that Antarctica should be used for peaceful purposes only and that all measures of a military nature should be prohibited.

General agreement has also been reached on international cooperation in scientific investigation in Antarctica. This topic is concerned with the exchange of information about plans for scientific programs, the exchange of scientific personnel between expeditions and stations, and the exchange of scientific observations and results.

During the seven working days there have been six Committee I meetings and five Committee II meetings. Committee I deals with scientific matters and Committee II with legal and political subjects.

Press Release No. 4, November 5

The Conference on Antarctica, approaching the end of three weeks of deliberations, has entered a new phase.

Committees I and II, having completed discussion of the items on their respective agendas, have been combined into a Committee of the Whole which is now considering the different positions expressed during the Committee meetings.

During the course of the Conference the Heads of Delegation have held a number of informal meetings to expedite discussions of substantive topics of the Treaty which is being negotiated.

Up to now there have been eleven Committee I and nine Committee II sessions. Committee I has concerned itself with scientific and technical subjects and Committee II with legal and political matters.

The following are among the topics which have been the subject of discussion at the Conference:

Preamble.

Use of Antarctica for peaceful purposes.

Freedom of scientific investigation in Antarctica.

International cooperation in scientific investigation in Antarctica.

Questions of rights and claims in Antarctica.

Observation and inspection for purposes of ensuring peaceful use and observance of the treaty's provisions.

Relationship of treaty to countries which are not parties.

Zone of application of the treaty.

Settlement of disputes arising under the treaty.

Provision for consultation.

Questions relating to jurisdiction in Antarctica.

Preliminary agreement has been reached on many of these items, subject to acceptance of the provisions as a whole.

It is hoped that by early next week the discussions will have proceeded to a point where there will be general agreement in principle between delegations, subject to final drafting and reference to governments

Press Release No .5, November 25

The Heads of Delegation met this morning to consider agreement on the remaining questions at issue. It had been hoped that it would be possible to reach final agreement this morning so a treaty could be signed on Friday [27 November]. However, owing to the failure to receive instructions, final agreement has not been possible. A further meeting of Heads of Delegation will be held at 10:30 a.m. Friday, at which time it is hoped that all representatives will have received their instructions.

Chilean Report of the Organisation of the Conference on Antarctica from 15 October–1 December 1959[21]

In the plenary meeting the rules of the Conference were approved, which enshrined the highly important principle that, in order for the Treaty to be signed, the text would require unanimous approval.

Two committees were established, termed the First and Second Committees, each charged with studying and approving the different tasks of the Conference. It was resolved that the committees would be presided over by the delegation heads, rotating in alphabetical order.

These committees met on an alternating basis, one in the morning, the other in the afternoon. This enabled committee members to attend both committee meetings at their convenience.

Each committee was assigned issues for consideration, as follows:

First Committee

1. Freedom of scientific research in the Antarctic.
2. International cooperation on scientific research in the Antarctic.
5. Monitoring and inspection to ensure the peaceful use and observance of the terms of the terms of the Treaty.
3. Application of the Treaty to non-party states.
4. Area of application of the Treaty.

Second Committee

1. Questions of rights and claims in the Antarctic.
2. Use of the Antarctic for peaceful means.
3. Resolution of disputes that arise from the Treaty.
4. Jurisdiction over and transgressions committed in the Antarctic.
5. Final provisions.
6. Preamble.
7. Consultations until the entry into force of the Treaty.

The Committees took as a point of departure for their discussion of these themes: the working documents that the committee had produced, albeit without official commitment from any Government; the Working Group convened in Washington since June 1958; and the specifications issued by the different Delegations.

Subsequently, the First Committee was merged with the Second Committee on the basis that at times it was necessary to discuss and to take into account the Treaty in its totality or generally,

[21] Reproduced from W.M. Bush, *Antarctica and International Law: A Collection of Inter-state and National Documents*, vol. I (Oceana Publications, New York, 1991), 30–32 (translated from Spanish) by permission of Oxford University Press, USA.

without direct relevance to the themes assigned to each Committee. The two Committees met in joint sessions under the title of 'Plenary Committee'.

That which was agreed unanimously by the Plenary Committee had the status of text approved in-principle. It was then presented for final approval to the respective Governments in the Plenary Session of the Conference.

The Plenary Committee held seven meetings between 3 and 30 November.

Likewise, sessions were held between the Heads of Delegation. These 12-person meetings discussed the conclusions, or final arrangements, that had been arrived at on the key issues.

The Conference proceeded via the following organisation:

Plenary Sessions, assigned responsibility for solemn activities and for discussion and approval of final agreements.

Plenary Committee, for general discussion of Treaty provisions, whose in-principle approval would enable their discussion and final agreement in the Conference.

First and Second Committee, for separate consideration and approval of the issues assigned to them.

Meetings of Heads of Delegation, for resolving difficulties that arose in relation with key issues in the Treaty, specifying amendments of ideas that, once unanimously agreed to, were sent to the Plenary Committee for approval.

These organs were supported by the Editorial Sub-Committee and the Style Sub-Committee.

Throughout November the Plenary Committee and the Heads of Delegation meetings were convened, in which the articles of the Antarctic Treaty were debated in detail.

The final session of the Plenary Committee was held on 30 November. After a briefing on the work done by the Heads of Delegation was read, each of the 14 articles of the Treaty was discussed.

After approving each article, each delegation was allowed to speak, to make whatever declarations they deemed appropriate.

The final Plenary Session was held on 1 December, under the presidency of Ambassador Hermann Phleger, Head of the North American Delegation and President of the Conference.

On that occasion, the Final Act was approved, in the first vote and unanimously, and then signed by each Head of Delegation.

Marking the solemnity of the occasion, the President offered the opportunity to each Head of Delegation to speak, in alphabetical order. The speech of Ambassador don Marcial Mora Moranda, President of the Chilean Delegation, was transcribed is transcribed below. [...]

At the end of the speeches the session was closed in order to commence the ceremony marking the signing of the Antarctic Treaty.

Statements of the Contracting Parties Made on 30 November 1959 Concerning Particular Articles of the Antarctic Treaty[22]

Final Plenary Session, December 1
(10:00–11:43 a.m.)
Mr. Phleger, Presiding

[EDITORIAL NOTE: Before the representatives made their concluding statements, the Chairman requested each delegation to indicate its formal approval of the text of the Treaty. Each representative in turn then signified his approval. The Conference thus unanimously adopted the Antarctic Treaty and opened it for signature.]

[22] Reproduced from W.M. Bush, *Antarctica and International Law: A Collection of Inter-state and National Documents,* vol. I (Oceana Publications, New York, 1991), 38–43. By permission of Oxford University Press, USA. Note: footnote numbering restarts on each page of the original.

Statement by Mr. Scilingo (Argentina)[23]

On October 15, precisely one month and a half ago today, the sessions of the Antarctic Conference began, as a result of the initiative of one of the Parties in calling for such a conference on May 2, 1958.[24]

The list of topics was an arduous one and the objectives were, indeed, ambitious. Some of them called for decisions of principle and policy, which would come to bear upon some of the most serious contemporary problems. The Conference had before it a limited number of draft articles, which had been the object of discussions at sixty meetings of a working group made up of the representatives of the twelve participating countries. It had not yet been possible to reach common agreement on most of these.

During the inaugural session, the Heads of Delegations expressed a desire to reach agreement, thus overcoming obstacles arising from dissimilar positions and situations, with regard to a body of rules and formulae that might constitute a mutually satisfactory and unanimously acceptable Antarctic Treaty.

The document we are signing today, is the fruitful outcome of lengthy deliberations undertaken in an atmosphere of reciprocal good will, but it is, above all, the fruitful result of the foresight of the respective Governments, in response to something that, after all, was a challenge.

The Treaty establishes principles and precedents of historical significance. It neutralizes the Antarctic from the military standpoint, it forbids nuclear explosions and the disposal of radioactive waste throughout the whole area, it sets up a system of observation and control, and it provides for scientific research and cooperation together with the exchange of personnel and information, within a juridical framework that does not affect in any way the original positions of the Parties.

In one field, the nuclear one, the Treaty goes beyond the greatest expectations. The Argentine Delegation considers it as its duty to express its utmost satisfaction because of the significance of the decision and the spirit that inspired it.

Time will tell if the hopes that are based on the transcendental provisions of the Treaty are to be fully realized. Time will also tell whether the good examples they set forth, shall also achieve the desired results in broader fields of endeavor.

For the sake of Antarctica, to whose destiny and peaceful development it is indissolubly linked, and for the sake of the peace of the world, no other country wishes this to be so more ardently and tenaciously than the Argentine Republic.

Statement by Mr. Beale (Australia)[25]

Mr. Chairman, I should, first of all, like to congratulate you, Sir, upon the skilful, impartial, and courteous way in which you have presided over this Conference; also the Secretary General, Mr. Allen, and his Secretariat for their faithful and assiduous labours. May I also compliment all delegates here upon the contributions which they each have made to our deliberations, and on the tolerance, goodwill, and understanding which they have exhibited. This has been a fine Conference in which sincerity and the spirit of reasonableness have been abundantly manifest.

The Australian Government very gladly joins in this Treaty. Twelve nations, meeting in a spirit of genuine co-operation, have reached agreement upon four great principles. Firstly, that the vast Antarctic region shall be used only for peaceful purposes; there are to be no military measures in the Antarctica and, to ensure this, there is to be complete mutual inspection throughout the area.

Secondly, that there shall be freedom of scientific investigation and full co-operation among all the parties to this Treaty, to the end that mankind's knowledge of this part of the earth may go forward for the benefit of present and future generations.

[23] Conf. doc. 25, Annex A, December 1, 1959

[24] See *ante*, pp. 2–4.

[25] Conf. doc. 25, Annex B, December 1, 1959.

Thirdly, that the rights and claims to sovereignty of various parties shall not be renounced or prejudiced by the Treaty; nor shall the position be affected of those who may dispute such rights and claims.

Lastly we have reached agreement on the question of nuclear explosions in the Antarctic. The testing of nuclear weapons for military purposes is forbidden; and, pending general international agreements on the subject, non-military nuclear explosions also.

Mr. Chairman, let no man underestimate the importance of what has been done around this table. It is true that the Antarctic is a remote, lonely and inhospitable place with far more penguins on it than people; but it comprises a large part of this earth's surface; it is strategically important; and from its frozen wastes comes much of the weather of the nations of the Southern Hemisphere. Moreover, for all we know now, it may also be a great reservoir of raw materials capable some day of being exploited in the service of man. To have pledged the honour of all of the twelve nations present that this region shall remain free from international strife and rivalry and be the scene only of peaceful scientific and economic developments, is a major achievement. Such a document as this may well become a model for international agreements relating to other parts of this earth, and perhaps to the outer marches of space itself.

This is the belief which has carried us forward here, and we present this Treaty to the world confident that mankind will benefit greatly from it.

Statement by Viscount Obert de Thieusies (Belgium)[26]

Speaking in the name of the Belgian Delegation I would like to state the great satisfaction derived by us from our participation in the preparation of the Antarctic Treaty.

I have already had the opportunity on an earlier occasion to state the interest which always was and continues to be that of Belgium in the Antarctic Continent, and to say to what point my country is happy to be associated in an undertaking, the importance of which, we, like the other States represented here today, understand fully.

This Treaty will permit, or at least we hope so, to make that part of the world safe from any intrigue, whether military or otherwise. It will also make it possible for the various nations to carry on, in a spirit of sincere cooperation and mutual respect, the tasks of scientific research to which so many scientists from our various countries devoted their energies during the International Geophysical Year.

Belgium was happy to participate in this work, and will likewise be happy in the future to bring its share of effort to all the undertakings capable of contributing to the scientific and peaceful development of Antarctica. And if one day that Continent, which despite all efforts remains full of mystery, were to prove itself rich in unsuspected resources and capabilities, Belgium will consider it her duty to continue contributing in the undertakings of the other Nations interested in the development of Antarctica.

It is in such a spirit that we took part in the work of this Conference; it is in such a spirit that we will sign the Treaty which is the outcome of its deliberations, and it is in such a spirit that we will participate in the future in the meetings of the consultative committee the establishment of which is contemplated, and the duties of which are defined in Article IX of the Treaty.

Finally, I would like in my own name and in that of the other members of the Belgium Delegation to say how much we appreciated the friendly relations which we enjoyed with the members of the other delegations and of the Secretariat, and to express to our American hosts our deep gratitude for the hospitality extended to us.

Statement by Mr. Mora (Chile)[27]

With the signing of the Antarctic Treaty the bases have been laid down for a new system for the coexistence of nations separated geographically, with different political, social and economic

[26] Conf. doc. 25, Annex C, December 1, 1959.
[27] Conf. doc. 25, Annex D, December 1, 1959.

systems, of different strength, and even of varied racial origins; but with similar purposes and interests within a Continent of exceptional characteristics.

It has not been easy to reach this agreement, because not all of us meeting here had disciplined our spirits to the management of ideas such as that of freedom of scientific research, as that of a controlled peace, that of the prohibition of tests of weapons of war, and of nuclear explosions, that of the freezing of rights, in a formula that without impairing neither titles nor sovereignties, guards against all danger that a tranquil coexistence might be disturbed.

Someone said, during a debate, that we were drafting a document that could mean the beginning of a new era for the world. And, doubtless, it must be so if good will and reciprocal trust contribute to faithful compliance with the common principles that we have here codified.

Given such a noble example, we may see all the peoples of mankind at a time not too far off, enjoying as in the Antarctic, the results of a cooperation fruitful in accomplishment for the common good, of an enduring peace that lifts from the heart of man distrust and fear, and of the permanent enjoyment of loyal friendship that will permit the solution of all differences without discord.

Chile places its signature to this Antarctic Treaty with lofty intentions and with full confidence that all the obligations hereby undertaken of collaboration, of reciprocity, of peace, of mutual respect for the rights of each other, and of progress and general welfare, will be complied with in the degree necessary so that none of the noble inspirations we have pursued here so tenaciously, will be frustrated.

If it turns out this way, then we would have the satisfaction of seeing the Antarctic converted into a better region than the rest of the world, and into a precedent worthy of imitation

Statement by Mr. Charpentier (France)[28]

The care with which the French Government followed the work of the Conference on Antarctica reflects the interest that it attached to the success of our negotiations. The Treaty which we are about to sign will make it possible for scientists of all countries to carry on, in the harsh climate of the South Pole, the task undertaken during the International Geophysical Year and to probe into the mysteries which Nature defends so fiercely in the South Polar Continent.

As we look back, we can justly feel that it is an exceptional success to have been able to conquer so many obstacles which, to us, seemed as insurmountable as those with which the daring explorers of Antarctica had to cope. We had so many interests and such serious political problems to take into consideration; we had to be careful not to arouse the fears that anyone of us could come to feel, and to reconcile our decisions with the actual facts of the internal or the foreign policy of our own country. Each day that went by could bring about the failure of the Conference, but each day that passed brought to us a strengthened hope of success. And it is with the thought that we were all working for the peace and welfare of mankind that we persevered in the task before us, that we avoided clashes, that we succeeded in sparing the feelings of the parties involved and that we finally succeeded in concluding the Treaty in [*on*] Antarctica.

For nearly one hundred and twenty years France has been present in Adélie Land, over which it has sovereignty and the Government of the Republic, to the extent to which its indefeasible rights are respected, is determined to do its part in the peaceful task that will be undertaken in Antarctica by scientists and research workers, in accordance with the Treaty.

The fact that the Treaty prohibits any military installation and activity in the South Polar Continent and that it is in full consonance with the efforts of mankind to solve the problems relating to the maintenance of peace in the world, is most gratifying to my country. In order to ensure the observance of the non-militarization in Antarctica the French Government, bearing in mind the particular conditions prevailing in this area, has accepted that simplified forms of

[28] Conf. doc. 25, Annex E, December 1, 1959.

inspection be applied for the time being. These latter, in its opinion, must some day be replaced by a genuine international control within the framework of a world disarmament organization, which it is our hope will soon come into being.

The French delegation has particularly appreciated the spirit of mutual understanding, goodwill and, I shall even say friendship, in which our negotiations were held. Our success is a good omen on the eve of the important meeting on which rest the hopes of mankind.

May I be permitted in concluding to express the gratitude of the French Government for the Statesman who is at the origin of our success, since it is upon his invitation that this Conference was held. May I be allowed to extend my thanks to President Eisenhower and the Government of the United States for the excellent organization of our work and for the cordial welcome we received in Washington

Statement by Mr. Asakai (Japan) [29]

We are gratified to be here to affix our signatures to the Antarctic Treaty.

We have met for the past six weeks and have succeeded in establishing the principles of peaceful use of Antarctica and freedom of scientific research there. It is virtually unprecedented to provide for non-militarization with inspection in such a vast expanse as that of Antarctica. In view of the great strategic potential there, this would be a bold and welcome step towards the promotion of world peace.

Underlying these principles, Mr. Chairman, is the legal formula we have so carefully worked out whereby opposing positions of claimant and non-claimant countries are frozen in connection with territorial rights on Antarctica. It is on this firm legal foundation that all parties have been able to agree to such advanced and progressive measures as non-militarization, inspection to that end, the control of nuclear explosions and freedom of scientific research there.

Our as yet unexplored Antarctica has boundless potentialities. So has our new Treaty. Politically, legally and scientifically the importance of this Treaty is inestimable; its future is bright with promise. How bright that future actually becomes, however, depends upon our faithfulness and sincerity. No matter how flawless a treaty may be, the participating countries must implement and promote the purposes and principles of that treaty in practice, or it fails. You may be sure, Mr. Chairman, that the Government and people of Japan will abide by the provisions of our Treaty in good faith and with good grace.

Statement by Mr. White (New Zealand)[30]

We have completed our work and are agreed on the terms of the Antarctic Treaty.

The twelve nations represented here are clearly entitled to take pride in what they have accomplished. My Prime Minister, the Right Honourable Walter Nash, who led the New Zealand delegation during the earlier stages of the negotiations, has asked me to convey to the Conference his keen personal satisfaction at the successful conclusion of the Treaty.

The Treaty we are signing today will ensure that Antarctica will forever remain an area of peace, free from war and warlike preparations, shielded against political rivalries and devoted to pursuits which will be of benefit to all mankind.

We have just recently been reminded that the enlargement of our knowledge about Antarctica, even in today's conditions, has its own hardships and dangers. A few weeks ago, during the course of this Conference, a tractor carrying three New Zealanders fell down a hidden crevasse in Antarctica. One man was killed and two were badly injured. A United States party in the area lent valuable assistance in rescuing the injured. These men were on scientific expeditions and were risking their lives, as many other brave men have done before in Antarctica, in seeking to add to what is known about the southern continent.

[29] Conf. doc. 25, Annex F, December 1, 1959

[30] Conf. doc. 25, Annex G, December 1, 1959.

It has always been the New Zealand view that scientific activity in Antarctica should be carried out in future, as it has been in the past, in peaceful conditions, by cooperative means, and for the benefit of all. The present Treaty will assure these objectives. The New Zealand Government therefore believes its conclusion to be a step of the greatest significance.

New Zealand is geographically close to Antarctica. New Zealand has a lengthy record of Antarctic achievement. We have asserted our claim to sovereignty. We have conducted exploration and scientific research both in our own right and in cooperation with other countries, for example in the epic trans-Antarctic expedition of 1957, in the International Geophysical Year, and in programmes of mutual assistance to American expeditions at present operating in Antarctica.

However, we look towards future cooperation with other countries also. The Treaty provides for the accession of additional countries who may wish to subscribe to its objectives. It does not endeavor to set up a monopolistic regime for the original twelve signatory parties.

We believe that this Treaty conforms with the principles and purposes of the United Nations Charter. Provision has also been made to bring it into consonance with future international agreements concerning, for example, the uses of fissionable material. The testing of nuclear weapons is to be prohibited completely in Antarctica and the peaceful use of nuclear explosions for scientific or developmental purposes is to be deferred until a more far-reaching international agreement can be concluded ensuring the safety of such activity.

The negotiation of this Treaty has not been a simple task. We have had to overcome many difficulties of detail in drafting a precise text. We have worked intensively for many weeks, even after allowing for months of preparatory work extending back to early 1958. But we have never lost sight of our major objectives. Therefore today we can be justifiably proud of our achievement and can confidently commend the Antarctic Treaty for the approval of the rest of the world.

In doing so, we are encouraged to hope that the spirit which has animated the conclusion of this Treaty will prevail in other areas of international negotiation.

Statement by Mr. Koht (Norway)[31]

I would like to join with those who have spoken before me in expressing the satisfaction of my Government with the results achieved at this Conference.

We set out to guarantee that a vast continent should be used for peaceful purposes only and that there should be freedom of scientific investigation and international scientific co-operation in Antarctica. Like all members of expeditions into unchartered territory we have had to go through periods of adjustment, and my Government, in the same way as others represented here, has had to accept certain provisions that it would have preferred to be different. I think, however, it may safely be said that the Conference never lost sight of its goal, and that we did reach it. I shall therefore be most happy to recommend to my Government that the Treaty be ratified in accordance with the Norwegian Constitution.

The thrilling saga of Antarctica has inspired men everywhere with its emphasis on basic human values—courage, patience and willingness to work together towards a common goal. I hope that the chapter which we have added here, will not be found to be entirely void of these values, and that it may inspire men to undertake similar ventures to promote peace and international cooperation in other fields.

I cannot conclude these remarks without expressing my deep-felt gratitude to the Government of the United States for its hospitality, to you Mr. Chairman for your distinguished and always tactful conduct of our negotiations, and to the Secretary General and his able staff for courteous and efficient service.

[31] Conf. doc. 25, Annex H, December 1, 1959.

Statement by Mr. du Plessis (Union of South Africa)[32]

Mr. Chairman, nearly seven weeks have passed since we commenced our deliberations on the Treaty we are about to sign. These deliberations have been marked by frank exchanges of views and opinions and it is a tribute to the refreshing spirit of enquiry and of cooperation, and where necessary of compromise, displayed by my colleagues, the Heads of the various national delegations, that those negotiations have been carried to so successful a conclusion. We are all conscious of our debt to you Sir, for successfully guiding us through the intricacies of negotiation. Both as Conference Chairman and as Chairman of the meetings of Heads of Delegations your wisdom, your understanding and your example have been an encouragement to all of us who have laboured for what we believed to be necessary and equitable arrangements governing our relations in Antarctica. The Secretary-General and his staff have worked hard and diligently to keep the Conference arrangements on a smooth and even course. We extend sincere thanks also to them.

In so far as the Treaty itself is concerned I need not, I trust, emphasise the great importance which my country attaches to the principles of non-militarization and of international scientific cooperation for peaceful purposes which are enshrined in it. As a country whose nearest overseas neighbour is precisely the continent of Antarctica, the Union of South Africa and indeed all of Southern Africa, cannot but have a high sense of appreciation for what has been achieved at this Conference.

It is comforting to know that our national Antarctic expedition which sailed from Cape Town for the remote South a few days ago, will have commenced its odyssey at almost the precise moment that this Treaty ushers in what we all, I am sure, hope will be an enduring era of peaceful cooperation in Antarctica, from which not only the nations whose representatives are gathered around this table, but all mankind, must profit.

For the first time in history the opportunity has been created for one of the continents of this world, admittedly the most barren and desolate one, to be freed from the threat of destructive war. It is my hope that this beginning will not only be a contribution to the relaxation of tensions and to the breaking down of the cold war but that it might establish a pattern also in other spheres of international life through which universal understanding and cooperation might be ushered in. If the olive branch of peace has to be carried into the world from the barren wastes of Antarctica then, paradoxical as it may seem, it is as good a starting place as any for so momentous a mission.

Statement by Mr. Kuznetsov (Soviet Union)[33]

The Conference on Antarctica is ending its work today. The Conference proceeded in an atmosphere of business-like cooperation and mutual understanding which yielded fruitful results. An international treaty on Antarctica has been worked out.

The treaty stipulates that Antarctica may be used for peaceful purposes only, that no measures of a military nature, including the establishment or military bases and fortifications, the carrying out of military maneuvres and the testing of any type of weapons may be undertaken in this area.

Agreement has also been reached on the prohibition of any nuclear explosion in Antarctica and of the disposal of radioactive materials in this area.

These treaty provisions serve the main objective now facing mankind, namely, to preserve and strengthen peace among all nations. At the same time they open broad prospects for the development of cooperation between states in the exploration of Antarctica.

The principle of scientific investigation in Antarctica is an important provision of the treaty. This principle, universally recognized during the International Geophysical Year, means that

[32] Conf. doc. 25, Annex I, December 1, 1959.
[33] Conf. doc. 25, Annex J, December 1, 1959.

governments, organizations and citizens of all countries may carry out scientific investigations in Antarctica on an equal basis, which will undoubtedly promote a more effective exploration of this area.

Fruitful international scientific cooperation in Antarctica will be promoted by the confirmation and further development in the treaty of the established specific forms of cooperation between scientists of different countries, including reciprocal exchange of scientific personnel. Joint efforts of scientists from as many countries as possible, wide exchange of results of observations, and close contacts between expeditions in Antarctica will permit sooner the revelation of the secrets of the Antarctic Continent, which have so far been insufficiently explored.

The achievement of agreement on such a complicated and delicate problem as territorial claims in Antarctica was the result of efforts to cooperate on the part of all participants in the Conference. The treaty provides that the positions of signatory States shall not be impaired in this respect. Such a solution should contribute to the situation where the possibility of conflicts arising between states in Antarctica would be prevented.

The Conference has successfully resolved the question of the adoption of measures to enforce the treaty, which include the establishment of an inspection system, a consultative procedure for the solution of operational problems, etc.

There is every reason to believe that the treaty as worked out by the Conference will be an important contribution to the cause of further development of scientific cooperation in Antarctica and will promote confidence between states. The Conference on Antarctica is an additional evidence of the fact that states, if they are ready to cooperate, can successfully achieve through negotiations mutually acceptable solutions of international problems in the interest of universal peace and progress.

Both the Conference and the treaty on Antarctica reflect a definite improvement in international situations and constitute in themselves a positive contribution to the cause of further development of mutual understanding between states.

On behalf of the Soviet Delegation I congratulate all participants in the Conference on Antarctica upon its successful termination.

Allow me also to express to the gratitude to the Government of the United States of America for its hospitality and for providing the facilities necessary for the work of the Conference.

Statement by Sir Harold Caccia (United Kingdom)[34]

In his statement at the opening plenary Session of the Conference, Sir Esler Dening, speaking as leader of the United Kingdom Delegation, pointed out that Her Majesty's Government in the United Kingdom had for many years been in favour of the conclusion of an agreement between the countries actively interested in the Antarctic. He also expressed the hope that the Conference would be able to devise a Treaty which would take fully into account the interests of all the powers concerned, or likely to be concerned, with the area. I think that we can fairly say that that object has been achieved.

No Treaty of course ever gives complete satisfaction to all its signatories. We in the United Kingdom Delegation fully realise that others have made concessions in the interest of mutual agreement just as we have ourselves. It is because of the conciliatory spirit that has been displayed throughout the Conference that we are now about to sign the Antarctic Treaty.

The International Geophysical Year showed what could be achieved by international co-operation in scientific research in the Antarctic. It is our belief that the present Treaty will serve as a firm framework within which co-operation will continue in the scientific field and be extended to others.

We also attach great importance to the requirement that the Antarctic shall be used for peaceful purposes only and to the provisions designed to ensure that friendly international relations shall

[34] Conf. doc. 25, Annex K, December 1, 1959

not be disturbed by political disputes arising from the area. The Treaty is, of course, not merely a statement of principles; it also contains provisions, appropriate to the special conditions in the Antarctic, to ensure that its terms are observed in practice.

I need hardly remind you that the principles on which the Treaty is based are those set out in President Eisenhower's original invitation. I should like to take this opportunity to pay tribute to the United States Government for the part which they have played in making this Treaty a reality. I also wish, on behalf of the United Kingdom Delegation, to thank the United States Government for making available to the Conference the Secretariat who have served us so well.

The problems of this remote and unpeopled region might be thought to be of little relevance to the great issues that concern the world to-day. But they are problems to which the 12 nations represented here have attached importance and which have created real difficulties for some of them. It is our hope that the successful conclusion of this Treaty will be a good omen and will contribute to the establishment of a climate more favourable to the settlement of other international questions. In that case, the Treaty will have had an importance far transcending the Antarctic.

Statement of Mr. Daniels (United States) [35]

Today we have brought to successful conclusion our joint efforts to conclude the first treaty covering the vast expanse of Antarctica. All of us will long remember this historic occasion. Furthermore, the conclusion of this unusual and unprecedented treaty will be deeply engraved in the annals of history.

This is no treaty of selfish monopoly. This treaty is not of a monopolistic or colonialistic character. It is neither land-grabbing nor land-dividing. Rather, it is aimed at achieving rational and constructive solutions in Antarctica. This treaty is of a broad and generous character. The significance of its three major objectives is readily apparent:

1. We have agreed that Antarctica shall be used for peaceful purposes only. In the world today peace, like war, tends to become indivisible. Accordingly, in reaching this solemn agreement among ourselves, we have thereby contributed to the establishment of peace in the world at large. This is of advantage to peoples everywhere.

2. We have agreed that there shall be freedom of scientific cooperation in Antarctica and international cooperation to that end. The beneficial results of this international scientific cooperation will be enjoyed by all of the countries participating in it. Even more, since science has a tendency to surmount nationalistic barriers, the contributions we make to science in Antarctica, by making it freely available, will be of obvious benefit to all countries and contribute to the enlightenment of man.

3. A third major objective has been successfully achieved, namely, the prohibition on all nuclear explosions in Antarctica for the purpose of preventing radioactive fallout. This achievement, in which have all agreed today, is of obvious benefit to all regions in the world, and not solely to those of use which have signed this solemn agreement. The little speck of radioactive dust drifting in the upper air does not known when it comes to earth whether it will light on a section of the map colored black or white or brown or yellow or red. Certainly we do not wish it to fall on our lands; nor do we wish it to fall on anyone else's land.

In these three major ways we have concluded basic agreements which will be of benefit to ourselves, and of benefit to all mankind. It is in that spirit that the United States has been proud to associate itself with the other countries represented at this Conference in concluding these broad and far-reaching agreements on Antarctica.

[35] Conf. doc. 25, Annex L, December 1, 1959

Statements by State Representatives at the Final Plenary Session of the Conference on Antarctica, 1 December 1959[36]

Article One

[1] Chile:

"The Chilean Delegation interprets paragraph 2 of article I as meaning that Chile will be able to maintain and supply its Antarctic bases, both present and future, by means of its regular armed forces and that none of the provisions of the article referred to in any way impair the right of legitimate individual and collective self defence explicitly enshrined in the Charter of the United Nations."

Article Four

[2] Argentina:

"The Argentine Republic declares that in accordance with article IV(1)(a) of the Treaty, none of its stipulations should be interpreted or applied to affect its rights, based on juridical titles, acts of possession, geological contiguity and continuity in the area situated south of the sixtieth parallel over which it proclaims and maintains its sovereignty."

[3] Australia:

"The Government of Australia is pleased to indicate its agreement with this article, the provisions of which guarantee that nothing in the Treaty can be interpreted as a renunciation by Australia of any of its rights and claims to territorial sovereignty in Antarctica, and that no act or activity that may take place while the Treaty is in force, impairs those said rights and claims."

[4] U.S.S.R.:

"With respect to the declaration of the Argentine Republic on article IV, the position of the Delegation of the Union of Soviet Socialist Republics with reference to claims of territorial sovereignty is well known. In particular, it was explained in a note verbale dated 2 June 1958 from the Soviet Government to the Government of the United States of America. The Soviet Delegation would also like to point out that the Antarctic Treaty contains clear and specific provisions to the points mentioned in the declaration of the Argentine delegation."

"Furthermore, the Soviet Delegation believes that it is also necessary to point out that in accordance with the generally accepted rules of International Law, the unilateral interpretation of any Treaty does not bind the other contracting parties, nor exempt the party making that interpretation from the obligations undertaken in the said Treaty."

"The Delegation of the Soviet Union does not consider that any of the declarations referring to article IV can modify in any way at all the provisions of that article with respect to the rights and obligations of the High Contracting Parties."

[5] Great Britain:

"One of the principal objectives of the Treaty is, of course, to avoid disputes over territorial sovereignty. This conference would not be, therefore, a suitable forum for a dispute concerning this question and, what is more, until now has been free of such disputes. Consequently, in reply to what has been expressed by some previous speakers in regard to the sovereignty which their countries assert in the Antarctic region, I will only say that the Government of the United Kingdom, for its part, does not consider that the sovereignty which the United Kingdom has affirmed and exercised in the area for many years is open to discussion."

"In so far as article IV is concerned, I would like to associate myself with the words of my distinguished Australian colleague."

[6] France:

"On the occasion of signing the Antarctic Treaty, the French Republic wishes to reaffirm the sovereignty it exercises over Adelie Land; it recalls the historic and juridical grounds on which such rights are based as well as the laws which have sanctioned them."

[36] Reproduced from US Department of State, *The Conference on Antarctica: Washington October 15–December 1, 1959* (US Government Printing Office, Washington DC, 1959), 38–43.

[7] Chile:

"The Government of Chile on the occasion of the adoption of the present Treaty declares that it maintains its sovereignty over the Chilean Antarctic Territory virtue of its clear geographical, historical, juridical and other rights and that nothing in the present Treaty can be interpreted as an abandonment or impairment of its exercise in the region referred to."

"In this connection it will continue to implement the full range of peaceful activities which it has hitherto carried out and any other activities of the same character."

[8] Belgium:

"The Belgian Delegation wishes to emphasise that none of the declarations relating to article IV modify in any way the provisions of this article relating to the rights of the Contracting Parties."

[9] Japan:

"The Representative of Japan expressed the agreement of his Delegation with the remarks of the Belgian Representative."

[10] South Africa:

"The Representative of South Africa declared that his Delegation wished to express its agreement with the points of view expressed by the Representatives of Belgium and Japan."

[11] U.S.S.R.:

"The Soviet Delegation does not intend to enter into discussions on the substance of the declarations of the Delegation of Chile on articles I and IV, which, of course, should not be interpreted as agreement on the part of the Soviet Union with the interpretation of the provisions of the treaty expressed in such declarations.

"Even so, the Soviet Delegation considers it necessary to refer once more on this occasion to its declarations relating to what was expressed by the Delegation of Argentina on article IV, in which the Delegation of the Soviet Socialist Republics pointed out that in accordance with generally accepted rules of International Law any unilateral interpretation of an international Treaty does not bind the other contracting parties to the said Treaty, nor exempt the party which subscribes to that interpretation from the fulfilment of its obligations contracted under the said Treaty."

Article V

[12] U.S.A.:

"The Delegation of the United States accepts Article V because it is evident that it does not contain any prohibition on the peaceful use of nuclear material in Antarctica, with the exception of its use for explosions, which will be regulated by any other general international agreement on this matter to which the parties of the Treaty become parties."

[13] Australia and France:

The representatives of Australia and France indicated that their Delegations adhered to the declaration made by the Representative of the United States.

[14] U.S.S.R.:

"With respect to the declarations relating to article V, the Delegation of the Soviet Union considers it necessary to point out that no declaration concerning Article V can modify in any way the obligations which are contained in this Article."

Article VI

[15] Japan:

"I wish to take this opportunity to reiterate the understanding of the Japanese Delegation, as was already confirmed in the course of the deliberations on the zone of application of this Treaty, that the term 'ice shelves' is interpreted as including all zones more or less permanently covered by ice, including the air space above and the waters below such zones."

Article VII

[16] France:

"In giving its approval to the provisions of Article VII of the Antarctic Treaty, the French delegation wishes to point out that the French Government remains faithful to the international methods of disarmament control."

[17] U.S.A.:

"Paragraph 5 of article VII provides that the Contracting Parties will inform the other Parties in advance of the expeditions, bases, personnel, and military equipment in the Antarctic. The Delegation of the United States wishes to point out that normally plans for activities in the said region are made many months in advance. They can be changed due to unforeseen circumstances, such as budgetary limitations, the weather, and damages to ships and equipment.

"For this reason, the Delegation of the United States wishes to point out that information given in advance should not be considered as an obligation to carry out any particular plan, but that it can be modified or revised as notified to the Contracting Parties."

[18] Belgium:

"The Delegate of Belgium wished to declare that the Belgian Government, accepting without reservations the dispositions of the Treaty, maintains itself faithful to the forms of international disarmament control."

[19] Japan and Great Britain:

Their representatives declared that they joined with the declaration of the representatives of France and Belgium.

Article VIII

[20] Great Britain:

"The Delegation of the United Kingdom presented at the beginning of the Conference a proposal that would have provided for a more complete system of jurisdiction. As this proposal was not generally accepted, we presented a compromise solution with reference to the immunity of observers and exchanged scientists which formed the basis of the proposal that was agreed to. We considered that this was a method of dealing with those cases which in practice would be those which were more likely to cause difficulties. We still believe that the general problem of jurisdiction, if not resolved as soon as possible, could well cause international disputes of the kind that this Treaty has as its objective to avoid. Consequently, we hope that pursuant to paragraph (1) of article IX the designated representatives, in conformity with this article will consider and present recommendations to their Governments on this matter as soon as possible after they begin their meetings."

[21] South Africa:

"In expressing its acceptance of this article the Delegation of South Africa wishes to reaffirm its declaration respecting the position of the Government of South Africa which appears in the record of an earlier session, to the effect that the Government of South Africa is not able to foresee that it will be possible to renounce its jurisdiction over its nationals in any place in Antarctica."

[22] Norway:

"The Delegation of Norway believes that the attempt to resolve the problem jurisdiction in Antarctica is a matter of some complexity and, for that purpose it would be preferable for many reasons, that a smaller group of experts formulate norms at a future date.

"We believe, nevertheless, that any person in the Antarctic should be subject to the penal jurisdiction of the country of which he is a national and this principle should have been embodied in the treaty. We are therefore disappointed that the principle which was outlined in the proposal of the United Kingdom and in that of Japan as well, has not found the necessary support of all Delegations.

"We understand that it is difficult for some Delegations to accept a solution of this kind at this moment. The deliberations over jurisdiction, with the exception of those concerning the condition of the observers and exchanged scientific personnel, are left now within the charge of the consultative body. I would like it to be clearly understood that my Delegation assumes that nothing contained in the article on the condition of the observers etc. or in articles IV and IX, can prejudice in any way the agreement on jurisdiction which it is hoped will be established by the administrative body or the committee of experts nominated by it.

"The Delegation of Norway understands that the matter of exercise of jurisdiction will be considered by the consultative body on the entry into force of the Treaty and we hope that it will be possible to find a prompt and satisfactory solution."

[23] France:

"With respect to the declarations which have just been made in relation to article VIII, in particular those made by the Delegation of Norway and by the Delegation of South Africa, the French Delegation wishes to make clear that it does not renounce any of the privileges of its sovereignty in Adelie Land, especially in those which concern the general power of jurisdiction which it exercises over said territory."

[24] Chile and Argentina:

Declared that they wished to adhere to the declarations made by the representative of France.

[25] Japan:

"As was indicated in our proposal presented at the beginning of the Conference relating to the question of jurisdiction, the Delegation of Japan continues in its belief that all personnel in Antarctica should be subject only to the jurisdiction of the country of which they are nationals. Consequently, we are confident that this principle will be respected in the formulation of future regulations."

[26] Belgium:

Its representative declared his Delegation wished to associate itself with the declaration made by the representative of Japan.

[27] U.S.S.R :

"In relation to the declarations made today in relation to article VIII, the Soviet Delegation considers it necessary to indicate the position of the Soviet Union with respect to the subject of jurisdiction in Antarctica which was expressed during the sessions of the Committee. The Soviet Union has considered and continues to consider that Soviet citizens in the Antarctic are subject to the jurisdiction of the Soviet Union alone."

Article IX

[28] Great Britain:

"The Delegation of the United Kingdom understands that the requirement of paragraph 2 that reference to the International Court of Justice should be subject to the consent, in each case, of all the parties to the dispute, does not mean to say that the dispute could be referred to the Court only if such consent were given ad hoc. In other words, when a dispute is of such a nature that it falls within the acceptances of the compulsory jurisdiction of the Court previously put forward by the parties to the dispute, this paragraph cannot be interpreted in the sense that a further consent is required before a reference can be made."

[29] South Africa:

"On expressing its approval of this article, the Delegation of South Africa wishes to refer to a declaration it made in a previous session with respect to the acceptance by the South African Government of the compulsory jurisdiction of the International Court, subject to certain reservations."

[30] France:

Its Delegation associated itself with the declaration made by the representative of Great Britain.

Article XII

[31] Chile:

"The Delegation of Chile lends its support to the article of the Antarctic Treaty relative to revision on the understanding that if any Contracting Party withdraws from the Treaty, its provisions will not be applicable to that Party from the time of this withdrawal and that with respect to the provisions of article IV, the Parties will return to the previous status quo."

Article XIII

[32] Japan:

"The Delegation of Japan regrets that the class of members of the specialised agencies of the United Nations has been excluded from the right of free adherence to this Treaty especially in view of the fact that it has been possible for Japan, owing to its character as a member of some specialised agencies of the United Nations, to participate in various international activities even before being admitted to the United Nations. We therefore trust that the provisions which we have accepted reluctantly will not be repeated in future international agreements."

[33] U.S.A.:

"The United States is in agreement with the paragraph on adherence contained in article XIII which does not include the members of the specialised agencies of the United Nations for the reason that it is the only possible way of arriving at a treaty.

"This conference has adopted the rule of consensus. Since one of the participating States has adopted the position of not being in favour of permitting members of the Specialised Agencies of the United Nations to adhere, the United States either accepts this position thus ensuring a treaty, or refuses to accept it thus preventing it being finalised.

"The United States is of the opinion that this Treaty is of great significance, not only for the 12 participating States but for all humanity, and therefore, accepts a paragraph on adherence which does not contain a provision which permits the adherence on the part of the members of Specialised Agencies.

"In the light of these circumstances it is evident that the paragraph on adherence which forms part of the Treaty does not constitute a precedent for other Treaties or conferences."

[34] France:

"The Delegation of France wishes to associate itself with the declaration of the representative of Japan. In its opinion, the exclusion from the paragraph on accession to the Treaty, of those States which are members of the specialised agencies of the United Nations does not in any way establish a precedent.

[35] USSR:

"The Soviet Delegation has considered and continues to consider that the best solution to the problem of accession to the Treaty would be to *give* an opportunity to accede to the Treaty to every State that wishes to do so.

"Nevertheless, taking into account that some of the participants in the Conference have adopted a position that the signing of the Treaty will only be achieved by limiting the number of States which have the right to accede, the Soviet Delegation, with the aim of arriving at an agreement has consented to accept article XIII in its present form."

[36] Australia:

Its delegation associated itself with the declarations made by the representatives of Japan and the USA.

OTHER INTERNATIONAL INSTRUMENTS OF THE ATS

Convention for the Conservation of Antarctic Seals (CCAS) (1972)[37]

The Contracting Parties,

Recalling the Agreed Measures for the Conservation of Antarctic Fauna and Flora, adopted under the Antarctic Treaty signed at Washington on 1 December 1959;

[37] Adopted 1 June 1972, entered into force 11 March 1978, 1080 UNTS 175.

Recognizing the general concern about the vulnerability of Antarctic seals to commercial exploitation and the consequent need for effective conservation measures;

Recognizing that the stocks of Antarctic seals are an important living resource in the marine environment which requires an international agreement for its effective conservation;

Recognizing that this resource should not be depleted by over-exploitation, and hence that any harvesting should be regulated so as not to exceed the levels of the optimum sustainable yield;

Recognizing that in order to improve scientific knowledge and so place exploitation on a rational basis, every effort should be made both to encourage biological and other research on Antarctic seal populations and to gain information from such research and from the statistics of future sealing operations, so that further suitable regulations may be formulated;

Noting that the Scientific Committee on Antarctic Research of the International Council of Scientific Unions (SCAR) is willing to carry out the tasks requested of it in this Convention;

Desiring to promote and achieve the objectives of protection, scientific study and rational use of Antarctic seals, and to maintain a satisfactory balance within the ecological system,

Have agreed as follows:

Article 1 Scope

1. This Convention applies to the seas south of 60° South Latitude, in respect of which the Contracting Parties affirm the provisions of Article IV of the Antarctic Treaty.

2. This Convention may be applicable to any or all of the following species:

   Southern elephant seal *Mirounga leonina*,
   Leopard seal *Hydrurga leptonyx*,
   Weddell seal *Leptonychotes weddelli*,
   Crabeater seal *Lobodon carcinophagus*,
   Ross seal *Ommatophoca rossi*,
   Southern fur seals *Arctocephalus sp.*

3. The Annex to this Convention forms an integral part thereof.

Article 2 Implementation

1. The Contracting Parties agree that the species of seals enumerated in Article 1 shall not be killed or captured within the Convention area by their nationals or vessels under their respective flags except in accordance with the provisions of this Convention.

2. Each Contracting Party shall adopt for its nationals and for vessels under its flag such laws, regulations and other measures, including a permit system as appropriate, as may be necessary to implement this Convention.

Article 3 Annexed Measures

1. This Convention includes an Annex specifying measures which the Contracting Parties hereby adopt. Contracting Parties may from time to time in the future adopt other measures with respect to the conservation, scientific study and rational and humane use of seal resources, prescribing *inter alia*:

(a) permissible catch;
(b) protected and unprotected species;
(c) open and closed seasons;
(d) open and closed areas, including the designation of reserves;
(e) the designation of special areas where there shall be no disturbance of seals;
(f) limits relating to sex, size, or age for each species;
(g) restrictions relating to time of day and duration, limitations of effort and methods of sealing;
(h) types and specifications of gear and apparatus and appliances which may be used;
(i) catch returns and other statistical and biological records;
(j) procedures for facilitating the review and assessment of scientific information;
(k) other regulatory measures including an effective system of inspection.

2. The measures adopted under paragraph (1) of this Article shall be based upon the best scientific and technical evidence available.

3. The Annex may from time to time be amended in accordance with the procedures provided for in Article 9.

Article 4 Special Permits

1. Notwithstanding the provisions of this Convention, any Contracting Party may issue permits to kill or capture seals in limited quantities and in conformity with the objectives and principles of this Convention for the following purposes:

(a) to provide indispensable food for men or dogs;

(b) to provide for scientific research; or

(c) to provide specimens for museums, educational or cultural institutions.

2. Each Contracting Party shall, as soon as possible, inform the other Contracting Parties and SCAR of the purpose and content of all permits issued under paragraph (1) of this Article and subsequently of the numbers of seals killed or captured under these permits.

Article 5 Exchange of Information and Scientific Advice

1. Each Contracting Party shall provide to the other Contracting Parties and to SCAR the information specified in the Annex within the period indicated therein.

2. Each Contracting Party shall also provide to the other Contracting Parties and to SCAR before 31 October each year information on any steps it has taken in accordance with Article 2 of this Convention during the preceding period 1 July to 30 June.

3. Contracting Parties which have no information to report under the two preceding paragraphs shall indicate this formally before 31 October each year.

4. SCAR is invited:

(a) to assess information received pursuant to this Article; encourage exchange of scientific data and information among the Contracting Parties; recommend programmes for scientific research; recommend statistical and biological data to be collected by sealing expeditions within the Convention area; and suggest amendments to the Annex; and

(b) to report on the basis of the statistical, biological and other evidence available when the harvest of any species of seal in the Convention area is having a significantly harmful effect on the total stocks of such species or on the ecological system in any particular locality.

5. SCAR is invited to notify the Depositary which shall report to the Contracting Parties when SCAR estimates in any sealing season that the permissible catch limits for any species are likely to be exceeded and, in that case, to provide an estimate of the date upon which the permissible catch limits will be reached. Each Contracting Party shall then take appropriate measures to prevent its nationals and vessels under its flag from killing or capturing seals of that species after the estimated date until the Contracting Parties decide otherwise.

6. SCAR may if necessary seek the technical assistance of the Food and Agriculture Organization of the United Nations in making its assessments.

7. Notwithstanding the provisions of paragraph (1) of Article 1 the Contracting Parties shall, in accordance with their internal law, report to each other and to SCAR, for consideration, statistics relating to the Antarctic seals listed in paragraph (2) of Article 1 which have been killed or captured by their nationals and vessels under their respective flags in the area of floating sea ice north of 60° South Latitude.

Article 6 Consultations between Contracting Parties

1. At any time after commercial sealing has begun a Contracting Party may propose through the Depositary that a meeting of Contracting Parties be convened with a view to:

(a) establishing by a two-thirds majority of the Contracting Parties, including the concurring votes of all States signatory to this Convention present at the meeting, an effective system of control, including inspection, over the implementation of the provisions of this Convention;

(b) establishing a commission to perform such functions under this Convention as the Contracting Parties may deem necessary; or
(c) considering other proposals, including:
 (i) the provision of independent scientific advice;
 (ii) the establishment, by a two-thirds majority, of a scientific advisory committee which may be assigned some or all of the functions requested of SCAR under this Convention, if commercial sealing reaches significant proportions;
 (iii) the carrying out of scientific programmes with the participation of the Contracting Parties; and
 (iv) the provision of further regulatory measures, including moratoria.

2. If one-third of the Contracting Parties indicate agreement the Depositary shall convene such a meeting, as soon as possible.

3. A meeting shall be held at the request of any Contracting Party, if SCAR reports that the harvest of any species of Antarctic seal in the area to which this Convention applies is having a significantly harmful effect on the total stocks or the ecological system in any particular locality.

Article 7 Review of Operations

The Contracting Parties shall meet within five years after the entry into force of this Convention and at least every five years thereafter to review the operation of the Convention.

Article 8 Amendments to the Convention

1. This Convention may be amended at any time. The text of any amendment proposed by a Contracting Party shall be submitted to the Depositary, which shall transmit it to all the Contracting Parties.

2. If one-third of the Contracting Parties request a meeting to discuss the proposed amendment the Depositary shall call such a meeting.

3. An amendment shall enter into force when the Depositary has received instruments of ratification or acceptance thereof from all the Contracting Parties.

Article 9 Amendments to the Convention

1. Any Contracting Party may propose amendments to the Annex to this Convention. The text of any such proposed amendment shall be submitted to the Depositary which shall transmit it to all Contracting Parties.

2. Each such proposed amendment shall become effective for all Contracting Parties six months after the date appearing on the notification from the Depositary to the Contracting Parties, if within 120 days of the notification date, no objection has been received and two-thirds of the Contracting Parties have notified the Depositary in writing of their approval.

3. If an objection is received from any Contracting Party within 120 days of the notification date, the matter shall be considered by the Contracting Parties at their next meeting. If unanimity on the matter is not reached at the meeting, the Contracting Parties shall notify the Depositary within 120 days from the date of closure of the meeting of their approval or rejection of the original amendment or of any new amendment proposed by the meeting. If, by the end of this period, two-thirds of the Contracting Parties have approved such amendment, it shall become effective six months from the date of the closure of the meeting for those Contracting Parties which have by then notified their approval.

4. Any Contracting Party which has objected to a proposed amendment may at any time withdraw that objection, and the proposed amendment shall become effective with respect to such Party immediately if the amendment is already in effect, or at such time as it becomes effective under the terms of this Article.

5. The Depositary shall notify each Contracting Party immediately upon receipt of each approval or objection, of each withdrawal of objection, and of the entry into force of any amendment.

6. Any State which becomes a Party to this Convention after an amendment to the Annex has entered into force shall be bound by the Annex as so amended. Any State which becomes a Party

to this Convention during the period when a proposed amendment is pending may approve or object to such an amendment within the time limits applicable to other Contracting Parties.

Article 10 Signature

This Convention shall be open for signature at London from 1 June to 31 December 1972 by States participating in the Conference on the Conservation of Antarctic Seals held at London from 3 to 11 February 1972.

Article 11 Ratification

This Convention is subject to ratification or acceptance. Instruments of ratification or acceptance shall be deposited with the Government of the United Kingdom of Great Britain and Northern Ireland, hereby designated as the Depositary.

Article 12 Accession

This Convention shall be open for accession by any State which may be invited to accede to this Convention with the consent of all the Contracting Parties.

Article 13 Entry into Force

1. This Convention shall enter into force on the thirtieth day following the date of deposit of the seventh instrument of ratification or acceptance.

2. Thereafter this Convention shall enter into force for each ratifying, accepting or acceding State on the thirtieth day after deposit by such State of its instrument of ratification, acceptance or accession.

Article 14 Withdrawal

Any Contracting Party may withdraw from this Convention on 30 June of any year by giving notice on or before 1 January of the same year to the Depositary, which upon receipt of such a notice shall at once communicate it to the other Contracting Parties. Any other Contracting Party may, in like manner, within one month of the receipt of a copy of such a notice from the Depositary, give notice of withdrawal, so that the Convention shall cease to be in force on 30 June of the same year with respect to the Contracting Party giving such notice.

Article 15 Notifications by the Depositary

The Depositary shall notify all signatory and acceding States of the following:

(a) signatures of this Convention, the deposit of instruments of ratification, acceptance or accession and notices of withdrawal;

(b) the date of entry into force of this Convention and of any amendments to it or its Annex.

Article 16 Certified Copies and Registration

1. This Convention, done in the English, French, Russian and Spanish languages, each version being equally authentic, shall be deposited in the archives of the Government of the United Kingdom of Great Britain and Northern Ireland, which shall transmit duly certified copies thereof to all signatory and acceding States.

2. This Convention shall be registered by the Depositary pursuant to Article 102 of the Charter of the United Nations.

IN WITNESS WHEREOF, the undersigned, duly authorized, have signed this Convention.

DONE at London, this 1st day of June 1972

Annex[38]

1. Permissible Catch

The Contracting Parties shall in any one year, which shall run from 1 March to the last day in February inclusive, restrict the total number of seals of each species killed or captured to the numbers specified below. These numbers are subject to review in the light of scientific assessments:

(a) in the case of Crabeater seals *Lobodon carcinophagus*, 175,000;

(b) in the case of Leopard seals *Hydrurga leptonyx*, 12,000;

[38] Text as amended in the CCAS Review Meeting (London, 12–16 September 1988). The amendments became effective on 27 March 1990.

(c) in the case of Weddell seals *Leptonychotes weddelli*, 5,000.

2. Protected Species

(a) It is forbidden to kill or capture Ross seals *Ommatophoca rossi*, Southern elephant seals *Mirounga leonina*, or fur seals of the genus *Arctocephalus*.

(b) In order to protect the adult breeding stock during the period when it is most concentrated and vulnerable, it is forbidden to kill or capture any Weddell seal *Leptonychotes weddelli* between 1 September and 31 January inclusive.

3. Closed Season and Sealing Season

The period between 1 March and 31 August inclusive is a Closed Season, during which the killing or capturing of seals is forbidden. The period 1 September to the last day in February constitutes a Sealing Season.

4. Sealing Zones

Each of the sealing zones listed in this paragraph shall be closed in numerical sequence to all sealing operations for the seal species listed in paragraph 1 of this Annex for the period 1 September to the last day of February inclusive. Such closures shall begin with the same zone as is closed under paragraph 2 of Annex B to Annex 1 of the Report of the Fifth Antarctic Treaty Consultative Meeting at the moment the Convention enters into force. Upon the expiration of each closed period, the affected zone shall reopen:

Zone 1 – between 60° and 120° West Longitude

Zone 2 – between 0° and 60° West Longitude, together with that part of the Weddell Sea lying westward of 60° West Longitude

Zone 3 – between 0° and 70° East Longitude

Zone 4 – between 70° and 130° East Longitude

Zone 5 – between 130° East Longitude and 170° West Longitude

Zone 6 – between 120° and 170° West Longitude.

5. Seal Reserves

It is forbidden to kill or capture seals in the following reserves, which are seal breeding areas or the site of long-term scientific research:

(a) The area around the South Orkney Islands between 60°20' and 60°56' South Latitude and 44°05' and 46°25' West Longitude.

(b) The area of the southwestern Ross Sea south of 76° South Latitude and west of 170° East Longitude.

(c) The area of Edisto Inlet south and west of a line drawn between Cape Hallett at 72°19' South Latitude, 170°18' East Longitude, and Helm Point, at 72°11' South Latitude, 170°00' East Longitude.

6. Exchange of Information

(a) Contracting Parties shall provide before 30 June each year to other Contracting Parties and to SCAR a summary of statistical information on all seals killed or captured by their nationals and vessels under their respective flags in the Convention area, in respect of the preceding period 1 March to the last day in February. This information shall include by zones and months:

(i) The gross and nett tonnage, brake horse-power, number of crew, and number of days' operation of vessels under the flag of the Contracting Party;

(ii) The number of adult individuals and pups of each species taken.

When specially requested, this information shall be provided in respect of each ship, together with its daily position at noon each operating day and the catch on that day.

(b) When an industry has started, reports of the number of seals of each species killed or captured in each zone shall be made to SCAR in the form and at the intervals (not shorter than one week) requested by that body.

(c) Contracting Parties shall provide to SCAR biological information, in particular:

(i) Sex
(ii) Reproductive condition
(iii) Age
SCAR may request additional information or material with the approval of the Contracting Parties.

(d) Contracting Parties shall provide to other Contracting Parties and to SCAR at least 30 days in advance of departure from their home ports, information on proposed sealing expeditions.

7. Sealing Methods

(a) SCAR is invited to report on methods of sealing and to make recommendations with a view to ensuring that the killing or capturing of seals is quick, painless and efficient. Contracting Parties, as appropriate, shall adopt rules for their nationals and vessels under their respective flags engaged in the killing and capturing of seals, giving due consideration to the views of SCAR.

(b) In the light of the available scientific and technical data, Contracting Parties agree to take appropriate steps to ensure that their nationals and vessels under their respective flags refrain from killing or capturing seals in the water, except in limited quantities to provide for scientific research in conformity with the objectives and principles of this Convention. Such research shall include studies as to the effectiveness of methods of sealing from the viewpoint of the management and humane and rational utilization of the Antarctic seal resources for conservation purposes. The undertaking and the results of any such scientific research programme shall be communicated to SCAR and the Depositary which shall transmit them to the Contracting Parties.

8. Cooperation

The Contracting Parties to this Convention shall, as appropriate, cooperate and exchange information with the other Contracting Parties to the other international instruments within the Antarctic Treaty System and their respective institutions.

Report of the 1988 Meeting to Review the Operation of the CCAS, London 12–16 September 1998 including Special Permits for the Killing or Capturing of Seals [39]

Opening of the meeting

1. A meeting to review the operation of the Convention for the Conservation of Antarctic Seals, convened in accordance with Article 7 of the Convention, was held in London from 12 to 16 September 1988.

2. All the Contracting Parties to the Convention were represented: Argentina, Australia, Belgium, Chile, France, Federal Republic of Germany, Japan, Norway, Poland, South Africa, Union of Soviet Socialist Republics, United Kingdom of Great Britain and Northern Ireland and the United States of America.

3. Brazil, Canada, New Zealand, Peru and Sweden participated as observers by invitation of the Contracting Parties.

4. The Commission for the Conservation of Antarctic Marine Living Resources (CCAMLR) and the Scientific Committee on Antarctic Research (SCAR) were also present as observers. At the special invitation of the Contracting Parties the International Union for Nature and Natural Resources (IUCN) provided an expert to assist the Meeting in its consideration of the conservation aspects of the Convention's operation.

5. A list of participants is at Annex A [not reproduced].

6. The Meeting was opened by Mr Tim Eggar, MP, Parliamentary Under-Secretary of State for Foreign and Commonwealth Affairs. The text of this speech is at Annex B [not reproduced].

[39] Including at paragraph 17 Special Permits for the Killing or Capturing of Seals.

Election of Officers

7. Mr David Edwards (United Kingdom) was elected Chairman of the Meeting. Mr Michael Snell (United Kingdom) was appointed Secretary.

Opening addresses

8. Opening addresses made by Heads of Delegations are reproduced at Annex C [not reproduced].

Adoption of agenda

9. The Provisional Agenda was adopted. A copy of the agenda is at Annex D [not reproduced].

Adoption of Rules of Procedure

10. The Provisional Rules of Procedure were adopted. A copy of these Rules is at Annex E [reproduced].

Review of the operation of the Convention

11. In accordance with the requirement laid upon the Contracting Parties by the terms of Article 7 of the Convention to review the operation of the Convention at regular intervals since its entry into force (on 11 March 1978) the Meeting considered the number of seals that had been taken under special permit and the expedition that had taken place during this period.

12. The Meeting noted the conclusion of the SCAR Group of Specialists on Seals that the number of seals killed or captured under special permit had been low and could not be considered to have had any significant adverse effect on any seal populations. The numbers of seals killed and captured in the Antarctic over the 21 year period 1964–1985 had been tabulated by Dr R. M. Laws (CCAS/RM88/INF2 reproduced at Annex F [not reproduced]). Over the 21 year period, 10, 142 seals had been reported killed or captured under the system of special permits. This was an average of 483 seals per year. When the data were considered for two sub-periods, the following facts emerge. For the decade 1964/65 – 1973/74, 6949 seals were reported taken, an average of 695 per year: for the eleven year period 1974/75 – 1984/85, 3193 seals were reported taken, an average of 290 per year, less than half that for the previous decade. This reduction in the average take reflects the reduction in seals killed as food for dog teams as they were replaced by mechanical transport. The Meeting noted that the SCAR Group of Specialists had previously reported that it saw no cause for concern that these catches were having a significantly harmful effect on the total stocks of the species concerned, nor on the ecological system in any particular locality and that the Group had seen no reason to change that view given the sustained reduction in the second period.

13. The Meeting noted that the reporting of seals killed or captured under special permit had been incomplete and therefore reminded all Contracting Parties of their reporting obligations under Article 4(2) (see paragraph 17 below).

14. The Meeting noted that during the 1986/87 austral summer, two vessels had been active in the vicinity of the Balleny Islands and the Ninnis and Mertz Glaciers (approximately 145°E to 165°E and 66°S). A report of this expedition was made available to the Meeting. It was noted that a programme of scientific research had been carried out. The Meeting heard with interest that the results of this expedition had been such as to indicate that the initiation of commercial sealing within the next five to ten years was not at all likely. In this context delegations indicated that their countries were unlikely to engage in commercial sealing in the foreseeable future.

15. In concluding its consideration of this element of the operation of the Convention the Meeting generally felt that, on the basis of the information it had before it, there was no evidence to suggest that the Convention had not operated in a reasonably satisfactory manner. Some delegations, however, felt that it would be advisable to review and improve various elements of the Convention, more especially with respect to the Annex, to ensure the more effective operation of the Convention in the event of more sustained sealion activity than had occurred hitherto.

16. Papers submitted by the delegations were initially discussed in Plenary. On the proposal of the Chairman it was then agreed that two open-ended working groups should be established

to examine these matters further. A Working Group on the Annex was convened under Dr John Heap (United Kingdom) to consider sub-items 6(i), 6(ii), 6(iii) and the question of a review of protected species as proposed by Australia under sub-item 6(vi). The second group, the Chairman's Working Group, took subitems 6(iv) and 6(v). It also considered the remaining matters tabled for consideration under sub-item 6(vi) consisting of proposals by the United Kingdom to clarify the means by which suggestions made by SCAR under Article 5(4)(a) of the Convention for amendments to the Annex might be handled and for a consideration of the current accession procedures under Article 12 of the Convention.

Special Permits (Agenda item 6(i))

17. The Meeting discussed the operation of Article 4 of the Convention, including the proposals by Australia aimed at clarification of the objectives of this Article and at ensuring its effective implementation. The Meeting agreed:

A. When considering the issue of a special permit, each Contracting Party should:

(a) ensure that the number of seals permitted to be killed or captured is strictly limited to the minimum necessary to meet the purpose for which the permit is sought;

(b) for permits for scientific research, take all feasible steps to encourage co-operative planning and to minimise wasteful duplication; and, for all permits, take all feasible steps to maximise the scientific benefits derived. To these ends, permits should be issued as far in advance as possible of the commencement of activity under the permit.

B. Contracting Parties should provide to other Contracting Parties and SCAR the following information in respect of each permit:

(a) without delay after a permit is issued:

(i) the purpose of the permit, including the specific objectives of the research for which a scientific research permit is being issued;

(ii) the content of the permit including the locality, time period, number, species and relative age of seals permitted to be killed or captured;

(b) annually, by 30 June, a report describing activities undertaken under special permits in the previous year, including, as appropriate, the following information for each seal killed or captured:

(i) Specimen number
(ii) Species
(iii) Collection date
(iv) Collection location
(v) Sex
(vi) Relative age or size
(vii) Reproductive condition (immature, mature, pregnant, lactating)
(viii) Type of specimen material collected (eg teeth, reproductive organs, skeletal material, stomach contents, tissue samples, blood, urine, organs etc.)

Exchange of information (Agenda Item 6(ii))

18. The Meeting considered the existing provisions for the exchange of information on seals killed or captured (other than under special permit) as set down in Section 6 of the Annex to the Convention. The Meeting had before it a number of proposals as well as the results of an examination of this matter by the SCAR Group of Specialists on Seals at their 1988 meeting.

19. The Meeting recognized that exchanges of information were an important element of the Convention. It therefore felt that proposals for amendment should be considered with particular care. While there was a considerable measure of agreement as to changes that could be made with advantage, there was not enough time to give adequate consideration to other proposals based on papers which had been circulated only a short while before the Meeting or which had not been available until the Meeting opened. (In the case of the report of the SCAR Group of Specialists on Seals this had occurred because the Review Meeting, for unavoidable reasons,

had had to be scheduled a short time after the relevant SCAR meeting.) The matters on which there was concordance were as follows:

(a) The existing requirement for information to be provided by SCAR by 31 October each year meant that the Contracting Parties would not be able to have the benefit of SCAR's advice until after a further sealing season had begun. Since this had implications for the proper operation of the Convention, it was considered that the following dates could, with advantage, be changed to overcome this problem:
   - Section 1: for 1 July to 30 June read 1 March to the last day in February.
   - Section 6(a): for 31 October read 30 June and for 1 July to 30 June read 1 March to the last day in February;

(b) data on the number, sex, reproductive condition, and relative age (adult, juvenile, pup) of each species of seal taken could with advantage be reported by areas of one half degree latitude by one degree longitude (as determined by the noon position of the vessel each day) and by 10-day reporting periods;

(c) careful consideration should be given to providing for the collection of biological information from a statistically valid random sample of seals taken along the lines proposed in paragraph 3.2.2 of the Report of the SCAR Group of Specialists on Seals;

(d) if such provision were made it should be followed by a requirement for the results of the analyses of specimen material from the sample to be reported to SCAR within 12 months of the end of the sealing season, including the ages for each individual in the sample as estimated from teeth and the results of macroscopic analysis of ovaries (counts and size of corpora and large follicles);

(e) the advance notice of the departure of sealing expeditions from their home ports under Section 6(d) of the Annex could, with advantage, be increased from 30 to 60 days and that information might be provided on the location(s) of proposed seal harvesting and the name of vessel(s), gross and net tonnage, brake horsepower and number of crew;

(f) connection with paragraphs 6(a)(i) of the Annex, which requires Contracting Parties to provide certain information on vessels under their flags engaged in sealing, it was agreed that they would also provide the information required under paragraph 6(a)(i) in the case of vessels chartered by their nationals, wherever possible.

20. Other matters in this context upon which the meeting was not able to complete discussion were:

(a) the precise extent to which (if at all) the Annex to the Convention applied to the capture and killing of seals undertaken in accordance with a special permit issued under Article 4;

(b) the desirability of introducing requirements (cf paragraph 17 above) dealing with activity under special permits as a new section of the Annex to the Convention.

21. Representatives, pursuant to paragraph 19(a) above, agreed to recommend for approval by their respective Governments, that the Annex be changed in the following way:
   - Section 1: for 1 July to 30 June read 1 March to the last day in February.
   - Section 6(a) for 31 October read 30 June and for 1 July to 30 June read 1 March to the last day in February.

Sealing Zones and Catch Concentration (Agenda Item 6(iii))

22. The Meeting noted that since the conclusion of the Convention, further information had been gathered on the distribution of seals in relation to the pack ice. There have also been advances in understanding of the broad physical and biological processes operating in the Southern Ocean ecosystem, affording an ecological basis for distinguishing semi-discrete sub-systems or zones. The present information suggests that the boundaries of the sealing zones as specified in the Convention are not fully consistent with the current knowledge about the stock structure of the seal populations, and alternative boundaries might be preferable.

23. At the same time it was recognized that information was far from complete, and that new information might suggest further amendments to the boundaries. It was therefore premature to recommend changes to the boundaries as set out in Section 4 of the Annex to the Convention. In the meantime it is important that information on catches, particularly any large-scale catches taken, should be reported by small areas, so that they can be allocated to existing, or alternative, sealing zones or to sub-divisions within these zones.

24. In view of the current uncertainty the Meeting recommended that the scientists of the Contracting Parties and SCAR should keep the question of appropriate boundaries under review with the aim of re-defining zones in a manner more suitable for maintaining a satisfactory balance within the ecological system in a particular locality, as expressed in the preamble to the Convention and in Articles 5(4)(b) and 6(3).

25. As the Convention and the Convention for the Conservation of Antarctic Marine Living Resources share common ground in such an ecosystem approach, communication should be maintained between the Parties to these Conventions in reviewing zones.

26. The Meeting noted that the distribution of any future commercial sealing was unlikely to be evenly spread through the Antarctic. There was therefore a possibility that sealing could have a negative impact on local seal stocks of one or other species or on the local ecosystem, even when the catches for the Antarctic as a whole are well within the limits set in Section 1 of the Annex to the Convention. It further noted that, under Article 5(4)b, SCAR was invited 'to report when the harvest of any species of seal in the Convention Area [was] having significantly harmful effect on the total stocks of seal species or on the ecological system in any particular locality'. However, if the Convention is to operate in a predictive rather than a reactive manner, it would be essential to receive reports, not only when such effects had been clearly demonstrated to be occurring, but when there was a significant probability that they might be occurring, or could occur in the near future.

27. The Meeting therefore recognized the need for regular reviews of current information on the distribution and magnitude of localised stocks of each species of seal, and on current catches, and likely future catches. These reviews should inter alia examine the annual and cumulative catches of each species by moderately small areas, chosen to reflect available knowledge of the population structure of seal stocks, and other information relevant to seal population dynamics (eg the distribution of krill), likely future trends in these catches and the relation of these catches to available estimates of population abundance of seals of each species in these areas.

28. SCAR was invited to carry out studies and to report:

(a) on measures that could be taken to avoid the possible adverse effects of sealing being concentrated in one or a few areas, and;

(b) when it appeared to it that there was a significant risk of the occurrence of the harmful effects referred to in Article 5(4)(b). It was further invited to report on any additional information eg on seal biology, or on commercial activities, which might be provided, and which might facilitate these studies.

Commercial Sealing (Agenda Item 6(iv))

29. The Meeting discussed the question of when commercial sealing should be deemed to have begun for the purpose of Article 6 of the Convention, in the absence of notice by a Contracting Party that it or its nationals are commencing commercial sealing. The Meeting concluded that it was unnecessary to amend the Convention at this time to specify any particular criterion and that the matter was one for determination by Contracting Parties, in the light of all the circumstances, in accordance with the procedure set out in Article 6. It was recognized, however, that in reaching a determination that commercial sealing had begun, Contracting Parties would need to take into account, in particular, the following factors:

(a) that in any sealing season the number of seals of any species taken exceed what could reasonably be required for the purposes described in Article 4(1) of the Convention; and

(b) the number of seasons in which the taking of seals in such numbers has occurred.

Consistency and Co-operation with Other Components of the Antarctic Treaty System (Agenda Item 6(v))

30. Representatives reviewed developments in the Antarctic Treaty System since the Convention came into force in 1978. They considered it desirable and appropriate that there should be cooperation between the Contracting Parties to the separate instruments within the System. They agreed that such cooperation would best be expressed by the fullest possible exchange of information between the Contracting Parties to these instruments, relevant institutions of the Antarctic Treaty System, such as the Commission for the Conservation of Antarctic Marine Living Resources, and SCAR.

31. Accordingly, they agreed on the text of the following amendment to the Annex (new paragraph 8) which they recommended to the Governments of Contracting Parties for their approval.

'8: Cooperation. The Contracting Parties to this Convention shall, as appropriate, cooperate and exchange information with the Contracting Parties to the other international instruments within the Antarctic Treaty System and their respective institutions.'

Other Matters (Agenda Item 6(vi))

a. Procedures for dealing with amendments to the Annex to the Convention that may be suggested by SCAR

32. The Meeting discussed the procedure to be followed for dealing with any amendment of the Annex to the Convention which SCAR might suggest in pursuance of Article 5(4)(a) of the Convention. The Meeting concluded that any such suggested amendment should be treated in accordance with Article 9 of the Convention provided that it is submitted to the Depositary by a Contracting Party in accordance with paragraph (1) of that Article.

b. Accession Procedures

33. The Meeting discussed means to facilitate the procedure for considering the issue of invitations to States wishing to accede to the Convention in accordance with Article 12. The Meeting agreed that it would be appropriate, whenever the Depositary notifies Contracting Parties of the wish of a State to accede to the Convention, that the Depositary should issue an invitation to that State if it receives no objection from any Contracting Party within 120 days of the date of the notification.

c. Protected Species

34. The Meeting considered the proposal by Australia to extend the protection already given to the adult breeding stock of Weddell seals to include the pups, and also to afford similar protection to crabeater seals during the breeding season.

35. In the case of Weddell seals, it was agreed that locally concentrated stocks are highly vulnerable during the breeding season, warranting the extension of protection at that time to include the pups.

36. Representatives, noting that they agreed on the desirability of extending the protection afforded to Weddell seals to include pups during the breeding season, agreed to recommend to Governments the deletion in paragraph 2 of the Annex of the words 'one year old or older'.

37. With regard to the protection of crabeater seals during the breeding season, Representatives agreed to refer this to their scientists and to SCAR for further consideration and advice.

d. Avoidance of the Accidental Introduction of Infectious Diseases

38. During the Meeting much concern was expressed about evidence that the recent deaths of many thousands of harbour seals (Phoca vitulina) in the North Sea might have been caused by a viral disease and it was recognized that this had emphasised the vulnerability of Antarctic seal populations to infectious diseases originating outside Antarctica. While noting that there are measures already in place under Annexes C and D of the Agreed Measures for the Conservation of Antarctic Fauna and Flora aimed at reducing the risk of accidental introduction of such diseases, it was agreed to draw the attention of Antarctic Treaty Consultative Parties and the

Executive Secretary of CCAMLR, to the concern that all possible steps be taken to reduce the risk of accidental introduction into Antarctica of viruses potentially lethal to native mammals or birds. SCAR was invited to consider what pathways there might be for the accidental introduction of such virus infections into Antarctica and to advise as to what steps might be taken to render such introductions less likely.

39. Meanwhile Representatives urged that steps should be taken to:

(a) avoid as far as possible the introduction into the Antarctic of any potential virus carrier;

(b) minimise contact between dogs and seals in the Convention area;

(c) quarantine sick dogs and carry out post mortem examination of all dogs and those seals which are believed to have died from unusual causes;

(d) cremate or remove all dead domestic animals from the Antarctic in sealed containers.

Adoption of the final report

40. The Final Report was adopted by consensus. The Meeting requested the Depositary to transmit the Recommendations contained in paragraphs 21, 31 and 36 of this Report to all Contracting Parties in accordance with Article 9(2) of the Convention.

41. In view of the relevance of this Report to the interpretation and application of the Convention, the Meeting decided to request the Depositary to transmit a copy of this Report to all Contracting Parties, to observers invited to the Meeting, and to the Government of any State which indicates a wish to accede to the Convention.

Closing of the Meeting

42. The Meeting warmly expressed its gratitude to the SCAR Group of Specialists on Seals for the important work they had done since 1972 to improve understanding of the scientific basis for the Conservation of Antarctic Seals and, in particular, for the Report prepared by the Group, at its meeting in Hobart in August this year specifically for consideration at their review meeting. The Meeting also thanked Professor Don Siniff for his expert assistance to the Meeting. Following a closing address by the delegation of Australia, on behalf of all delegations, expressing warm thanks to the Government of the United Kingdom, to the Chairman, and to the Secretary and his staff, the Meeting was closed at 5.15 pm on 16 September.

Convention on the Conservation of Antarctic Marine Living Resources[40]

The Contracting Parties,

Recognising the importance of safeguarding the environment and protecting the integrity of the ecosystem of the seas surrounding Antarctica;

Noting the concentration of marine living resources found in Antarctic waters and the increased interest in the possibilities offered by the utilization of these resources as a source of protein;

Conscious of the urgency of ensuring the conservation of Antarctic marine living resources;

Considering that it is essential to increase knowledge of the Antarctic marine ecosystem and its components so as to be able to base decisions on harvesting on sound scientific information;

Believing that the conservation of Antarctic marine living resources calls for international co-operation with due regard for the provisions of the Antarctic Treaty and with the active involvement of all States engaged in research or harvesting activities in Antarctic waters;

Recognising the prime responsibilities of the Antarctic Treaty Consultative Parties for the protection and preservation of the Antarctic environment and, in particular, their responsibilities under Article IX, paragraph 1(f) of the Antarctic Treaty in respect of the preservation and conservation of living resources in Antarctica;

Recalling the action already taken by the Antarctic Treaty Consultative Parties including in particular the Agreed Measures for the Conservation of Antarctic Fauna and Flora, as well as the provisions of the Convention for the Conservation of Antarctic Seals;

[40] Adopted 20 May 1980, entered into force 7 April 1982, 1329 UNTS 47.

Bearing in mind the concern regarding the conservation of Antarctic marine living resources expressed by the Consultative Parties at the Ninth Consultative Meeting of the Antarctic Treaty and the importance of the provisions of Recommendation IX-2 which led to the establishment of the present Convention;

Believing that it is in the interest of all mankind to preserve the waters surrounding the Antarctic continent for peaceful purposes only and to prevent their becoming the scene or object of international discord;

Recognising, in the light of the foregoing, that it is desirable to establish suitable machinery for recommending, promoting, deciding upon and co-ordinating the measures and scientific studies needed to ensure the conservation of Antarctic marine living organisms;

Have agreed as follows:

Article I

1. This Convention applies to the Antarctic marine living resources of the area south of 60° South latitude and to the Antarctic marine living resources of the area between that latitude and the Antarctic Convergence which form part of the Antarctic marine ecosystem.

2. Antarctic marine living resources means the populations of fin fish, molluscs, crustaceans and all other species of living organisms, including birds, found south of the Antarctic Convergence.

3. The Antarctic marine ecosystem means the complex of relationships of Antarctic marine living resources with each other and with their physical environment.

4. The Antarctic Convergence shall be deemed to be a line joining the following points along parallels of latitude and meridians of longitude:

50°S, 0°; 50°S, 30°E; 45°S, 30°E; 45°S, 80°E; 55°S, 80°E; 55°S, 150°E; 60°S, 150°E; 60°S, 50°W; 50°S, 50°W; 50°S, 0°.

Article II

1. The objective of this Convention is the conservation of Antarctic marine living resources.

2. For the purposes of this Convention, the term "conservation" includes rational use.

3. Any harvesting and associated activities in the area to which this Convention applies shall be conducted in accordance with the provisions of this Convention and with the following principles of conservation:

(a) prevention of decrease in the size of any harvested population to levels below those which ensure its stable recruitment. For this purpose its size should not be allowed to fall below a level close to that which ensures the greatest net annual increment;

(b) maintenance of the ecological relationships between harvested, dependent and related populations of Antarctic marine living resources and the restoration of depleted populations to the levels defined in sub-paragraph (a) above; and

(c) prevention of changes or minimization of the risk of changes in the marine ecosystem which are not potentially reversible over two or three decades, taking into account the state of available knowledge of the direct and indirect impact of harvesting, the effect of the introduction of alien species, the effects of associated activities on the marine ecosystem and of the effects of environmental changes, with the aim of making possible the sustained conservation of Antarctic marine living resources.

Article III

The Contracting Parties, whether or not they are Parties to the Antarctic Treaty, agree that they will not engage in any activities in the Antarctic Treaty area contrary to the principles and purposes of that Treaty and that, in their relations with each other, they are bound by the obligations contained in Articles I and V of the Antarctic Treaty.

Article IV

1. With respect to the Antarctic Treaty area, all Contracting Parties, whether or not they are Parties to the Antarctic Treaty, are bound by Articles IV and VI of the Antarctic Treaty in their relations with each other.

2. Nothing in this Convention and no acts or activities taking place while the present Convention is in force shall:

(a) constitute a basis for asserting, supporting or denying a claim to territorial sovereignty in the Antarctic Treaty area or create any rights of sovereignty in the Antarctic Treaty area;

(b) be interpreted as a renunciation or diminution by any Contracting Party of, or as prejudicing, any right or claim or basis of claim to exercise coastal state jurisdiction under international law within the area to which this Convention applies;

(c) be interpreted as prejudicing the position of any Contracting Party as regards its recognition or non-recognition of any such right, claim or basis of claim;

(d) affect the provision of Article IV, paragraph 2, of the Antarctic Treaty that no new claim, or enlargement of an existing claim, to territorial sovereignty in Antarctica shall be asserted while the Antarctic Treaty is in force.

Article V

1. The Contracting Parties which are not Parties to the Antarctic Treaty acknowledge the special obligations and responsibilities of the Antarctic Treaty Consultative Parties for the protection and preservation of the environment of the Antarctic Treaty area.

2. The Contracting Parties which are not Parties to the Antarctic Treaty agree that, in their activities in the Antarctic Treaty area, they will observe as and when appropriate the Agreed Measures for the Conservation of Antarctic Fauna and Flora and such other measures as have been recommended by the Antarctic Treaty Consultative Parties in fulfilment of their responsibility for the protection of the Antarctic environment from all forms of harmful human interference.

3. For the purposes of this Convention, "Antarctic Treaty Consultative Parties" means the Contracting Parties to the Antarctic Treaty whose Representatives participate in meetings under Article IX of the Antarctic Treaty.

Article VI

Nothing in this Convention shall derogate from the rights and obligations of Contracting Parties under the International Convention for the Regulation of Whaling and the Convention for the Conservation of Antarctic Seals.

Article VII

1. The Contracting Parties hereby establish and agree to maintain the Commission for the Conservation of Antarctic Marine Living Resources (hereinafter referred to as "the Commission").

2. Membership in the Commission shall be as follows:

(a) each Contracting Party which participated in the meeting at which this Convention was adopted shall be a Member of the Commission;

(b) each State Party which has acceded to this Convention pursuant to Article XXIX shall be entitled to be a Member of the Commission during such time as that acceding party is engaged in research or harvesting activities in relation to the marine living resources to which this Convention applies;

(c) each regional economic integration organization which has acceded to this Convention pursuant to Article XXIX shall be entitled to be a Member of the Commission during such time as its States members are so entitled;

(d) a Contracting Party seeking to participate in the work of the Commission pursuant to sub-paragraphs (b) and (c) above shall notify the Depositary of the basis upon which it seeks to become a Member of the Commission and of its willingness to accept conservation measures in force. The Depositary shall communicate to each member of the Commission such notification and accompanying information. Within two months of receipt of such communication from the Depositary, any Member of the Commission may request that a special meeting of the Commission be held to consider the matter. Upon receipt of such request, the Depositary shall call such a meeting. If there is no request for a meeting, the Contracting Party submitting the notification shall be deemed to have satisfied the requirements for Commission Membership.

3. Each Member of the Commission shall be represented by one representative who may be accompanied by alternate representatives and advisers.

Article VIII

The Commission shall have legal personality and shall enjoy in the territory of each of the States Parties such legal capacity as may be necessary to perform its function and achieve the purposes of this Convention. The privileges and immunities to be enjoyed by the Commission and its staff in the territory of a State Party shall be determined by agreement between the Commission and the State Party concerned.

Article IX

1. The function of the Commission shall be to give effect to the objective and principles set out in Article II of this Convention. To this end, it shall:

(a) facilitate research into and comprehensive studies of Antarctic marine living resources and of the Antarctic marine ecosystem;

(b) compile data on the status of and changes in population of Antarctic marine living resources and on factors affecting the distribution, abundance and productivity of harvested species and dependent or related species or populations;

(c) ensure the acquisition of catch and effort statistics on harvested populations;

(d) analyse, disseminate and publish the information referred to in sub-paragraphs (b) and (c) above and the reports of the Scientific Committee;

(e) identify conservation needs and analyse the effectiveness of conservation measures;

(f) formulate, adopt and revise conservation measures on the basis of the best scientific evidence available, subject to the provisions of paragraph 5 of this Article;

(g) implement the system of observation and inspection established under Article XXIV of this Convention;

(h) carry out such other activities as are necessary to fulfil the objective of this Convention.

2. The conservation measures referred to in paragraph 1(f) above include the following:

(a) the designation of the quantity of any species which may be harvested in the area to which this Convention applies;

(b) the designation of regions and sub-regions based on the distribution of populations of Antarctic marine living resources;

(c) the designation of the quantity which may be harvested from the populations of regions and sub-regions;

(d) the designation of protected species;

(e) the designation of the size, age and, as appropriate, sex of species which may be harvested;

(f) the designation of open and closed seasons for harvesting;

(g) the designation of the opening and closing of areas, regions or sub-regions for purposes of scientific study or conservation, including special areas for protection and scientific study;

(h) regulation of the effort employed and methods of harvesting, including fishing gear, with a view, inter alia, to avoiding undue concentration of harvesting in any region or sub-region;

(i) the taking of such other conservation measures as the Commission considers necessary for the fulfilment of the objective of this Convention, including measures concerning the effects of harvesting and associated activities on components of the marine ecosystem other than the harvested populations.

3. The Commission shall publish and maintain a record of all conservation measures in force.

4. In exercising its functions under paragraph 1 above, the Commission shall take full account of the recommendations and advice of the Scientific Committee.

5. The Commission shall take full account of any relevant measures or regulations established or recommended by the Consultative Meetings pursuant to Article IX of the Antarctic Treaty or by existing fisheries commissions responsible for species which may enter the area to which this Convention applies, in order that there shall be no inconsistency between the rights and obligations of a Contracting Party under such regulations or measures and conservation measures which may be adopted by the Commission.

6. Conservation measures adopted by the Commission in accordance with this Convention shall be implemented by Members of the Commission in the following manner:

(a) the Commission shall notify conservation measures to all Members of the Commission;

(b) conservation measures shall become binding upon all Members of the Commission 180 days after such notification, except as provided in sub-paragraphs (c) and (d) below;

(c) if a Member of the Commission, within ninety days following the notification specified in sub-paragraph (a), notifies the Commission that it is unable to accept the conservation measure, in whole or in part, the measure shall not, to the extent stated, be binding upon that Member of the Commission;

(d) in the event that any Member of the Commission invokes the procedure set forth in sub-paragraph (c) above, the Commission shall meet at the request of any Member of the Commission to review the conservation measure. At the time of such meeting and within thirty days following the meeting, any Member of the Commission shall have the right to declare that it is no longer able to accept the conservation measure, in which case the Member shall no longer be bound by such measure.

Article X

1. The Commission shall draw the attention of any State which is not a Party to this Convention to any activity undertaken by its nationals or vessels which, in the opinion of the Commission, affects the implementation of the objective of this Convention.

2. The Commission shall draw the attention of all Contracting Parties to any activity which, in the opinion of the Commission, affects the implementation by a Contracting Party of the objective of this Convention or the compliance by that Contracting Party with its obligations under this Convention.

Article XI

The Commission shall seek to cooperate with Contracting Parties which may exercise jurisdiction in marine areas adjacent to the area to which this Convention applies in respect of the conservation of any stock or stocks of associated species which occur both within those areas and the area to which this Convention applies, with a view to harmonizing the conservation measures adopted in respect of such stocks.

Article XII

1. Decisions of the Commission on matters of substance shall be taken by consensus. The question of whether a matter is one of substance shall be treated as a matter of substance.

2. Decisions on matters other than those referred to in paragraph 1 above shall be taken by a simple majority of the Members of the Commission present and voting.

3. In Commission consideration of any item requiring a decision, it shall be made clear whether a regional economic integration organization will participate in the taking of the decision and, if so, whether any of its member States will also participate. The number of Contracting Parties so participating shall not exceed the number of member States of the regional economic integration organization which are Members of the Commission.

4. In the taking of decisions pursuant to this Article, a regional economic integration organization shall have only one vote.

Article XIII

1. The headquarters of the Commission shall be established at Hobart, Tasmania, Australia.

2. The Commission shall hold a regular annual meeting. Other meetings shall also be held

at the request of one-third of its members and as otherwise provided in this Convention. The first meeting of the Commission shall be held within three months of the entry into force of this Convention, provided that among the Contracting Parties there are at least two States conducting harvesting activities within the area to which this Convention applies. The first meeting shall, in any event, be held within one year of the entry into force of this Convention. The Depositary shall consult with the signatory States regarding the first Commission meeting, taking into account that a broad representation of such States is necessary for the effective operation of the Commission.

3. The Depositary shall convene the first meeting of the Commission at the headquarters of the Commission. Thereafter, meetings of the Commission shall be held at its headquarters, unless it decides otherwise.

4. The Commission shall elect from among its members a Chairman and Vice-Chairman, each of whom shall serve for a term of two years and shall be eligible for re-election for one additional term. The first Chairman shall, however, be elected for an initial term of three years. The Chairman and Vice-Chairman shall not be representatives of the same Contracting Party.

5. The Commission shall adopt and amend as necessary the rules of procedure for the conduct of its meetings, except with respect to the matters dealt with in Article XII of this Convention.

6. The Commission may establish such subsidiary bodies as are necessary for the performance of its functions.

Article XIV

1. The Contracting Parties hereby establish the Scientific Committee for the Conservation of Antarctic Marine Living Resources (hereinafter referred to as "the Scientific Committee") which shall be a consultative body to the Commission. The Scientific Committee shall normally meet at the headquarters of the Commission unless the Scientific Committee decides otherwise.

2. Each Member of the Commission shall be a member of the Scientific Committee and shall appoint a representative with suitable scientific qualifications who may be accompanied by other experts and advisers.

3. The Scientific Committee may seek the advice of other scientists and experts as may be required on an ad hoc basis.

Article XV

1. The Scientific Committee shall provide a forum for consultation and co-operation concerning the collection, study and exchange of information with respect to the marine living resources to which this Convention applies. It shall encourage and promote cooperation in the field of scientific research in order to extend knowledge of the marine living resources of the Antarctic marine ecosystem.

2. The Scientific Committee shall conduct such activities as the Commission may direct in pursuance of the objective of this Convention and shall:

(a) establish criteria and methods to be used for determinations concerning the conservation measures referred to in Article IX of this Convention;

(b) regularly assess the status and trends of the populations of Antarctic marine living resources;

(c) analyse data concerning the direct and indirect effects of harvesting on the populations of Antarctic marine living resources;

(d) assess the effects of proposed changes in the methods or levels of harvesting and proposed conservation measures;

(e) transmit assessments, analyses, reports and recommendations to the Commission as requested or on its own initiative regarding measures and research to implement the objective of this Convention;

(f) formulate proposals for the conduct of international and national programs of research into Antarctic marine living resources.

3. In carrying out its functions, the Scientific Committee shall have regard to the work of other relevant technical and scientific organizations and to the scientific activities conducted within the framework of the Antarctic Treaty.

Article XVI

1. The first meeting of the Scientific Committee shall be held within three months of the first meeting of the Commission. The Scientific Committee shall meet thereafter as often as may be necessary to fulfil its functions.

2. The Scientific Committee shall adopt and amend as necessary its rules of procedure. The rules and any amendments thereto shall be approved by the Commission. The rules shall include procedures for the presentation of minority reports.

3. The Scientific Committee may establish, with the approval of the Commission, such subsidiary bodies as are necessary for the performance of its functions.

Article XVII

1. The Commission shall appoint an Executive Secretary to serve the Commission and Scientific Committee according to such procedures and on such terms and conditions as the Commission may determine. His term of office shall be for four years and he shall be eligible for re-appointment.

2. The Commission shall authorize such staff establishment for the Secretariat as may be necessary and the Executive Secretary shall appoint, direct and supervise such staff according to such rules and procedures and on such terms and conditions as the Commission may determine.

3. The Executive Secretary and Secretariat shall perform the functions entrusted to them by the Commission.

Article XVIII

The official languages of the Commission and of the Scientific Committee shall be English, French, Russian and Spanish.

Article XIX

1. At each annual meeting, the Commission shall adopt by consensus its budget and the budget of the Scientific Committee.

2. A draft budget for the Commission and the Scientific Committee and any subsidiary bodies shall be prepared by the Executive Secretary and submitted to the Members of the Commission at least sixty days before the annual meeting of the Commission.

3. Each Member of the Commission shall contribute to the budget. Until the expiration of five years after the entry into force of this Convention, the contribution of each Member of the Commission shall be equal. Thereafter the contribution shall be determined in accordance with two criteria: the amount harvested and an equal sharing among all Members of the Commission. The Commission shall determine by consensus the proportion in which these two criteria shall apply.

4. The financial activities of the Commission and Scientific Committee shall be conducted in accordance with financial regulations adopted by the Commission and shall be subject to an annual audit by external auditors selected by the Commission.

5. Each Member of the Commission shall meet its own expenses arising from attendance at meetings of the Commission and of the Scientific Committee.

6. A Member of the Commission that fails to pay its contributions for two consecutive years shall not, during the period of its default, have the right to participate in the taking of decisions in the Commission.

Article XX

1. The Members of the Commission shall, to the greatest extent possible, provide annually to the Commission and to the Scientific Committee such statistical, biological and other data and information as the Commission and Scientific Committee may require in the exercise of their functions.

2. The Members of the Commission shall provide, in the manner and at such intervals as may be prescribed, information about their harvesting activities, including fishing areas and vessels, so as to enable reliable catch and effort statistics to be compiled.

3. The Members of the Commission shall provide to the Commission at such intervals as may be prescribed information on steps taken to implement the conservation measures adopted by the Commission.

4. The Members of the Commission agree that in any of their harvesting activities, advantage shall be taken of opportunities to collect data needed to assess the impact of harvesting.

Article XXI

1. Each Contracting Party shall take appropriate measures within its competence to ensure compliance with the provisions of this Convention and with conservation measures adopted by the Commission to which the Party is bound in accordance with Article IX of this Convention.

2. Each Contracting Party shall transmit to the Commission information on measures taken pursuant to paragraph 1 above, including the imposition of sanctions for any violation.

Article XXII

1. Each Contracting Party undertakes to exert appropriate efforts, consistent with the Charter of the United Nations, to the end that no one engages in any activity contrary to the objective of this Convention.

2. Each Contracting Party shall notify the Commission of any such activity which comes to its attention.

Article XXIII

1. The Commission and the Scientific Committee shall co-operate with the Antarctic Treaty Consultative Parties on matters falling within the competence of the latter.

2. The Commission and the Scientific Committee shall co-operate, as appropriate, with the Food and Agriculture Organisation of the United Nations and with other Specialised Agencies.

3. The Commission and the Scientific Committee shall seek to develop co-operative working relationships, as appropriate, with inter-governmental and non-governmental organizations which could contribute to their work, including the Scientific Committee on Antarctic Research, the Scientific Committee on Oceanic Research and the International Whaling Commission.

4. The Commission may enter into agreements with the organizations referred to in this Article and with other organizations as may be appropriate. The Commission and the Scientific Committee may invite such organizations to send observers to their meetings and to meetings of their subsidiary bodies.

Article XXIV

1. In order to promote the objective and ensure observance of the provisions of this Convention, the Contracting Parties agree that a system of observation and inspection shall be established.

2. The system of observation and inspection shall be elaborated by the Commission on the basis of the following principles:

(a) Contracting Parties shall cooperate with each other to ensure the effective implementation of the system of observation and inspection, taking account of the existing international practice. This system shall include, inter alia, procedures for boarding and inspection by observers and inspectors designated by the Members of the Commission and procedures for flag state prosecution and sanctions on the basis of evidence resulting from such boarding and inspections. A report of such prosecutions and sanctions imposed shall be included in the information referred to in Article XXI of this Convention;

(b) in order to verify compliance with measures adopted under this Convention, observation and inspection shall be carried out on board vessels engaged in scientific research or harvesting of marine living resources in the area to which this Convention applies, through observers and inspectors designated by the Members of the Commission and operating under terms and conditions to be established by the Commission;

(c) designated observers and inspectors shall remain subject to the jurisdiction of the Contracting Party of which they are nationals. They shall report to the Member of the Commission by which they have been designated which in turn shall report to the Commission.

3. Pending the establishment of the system of observation and inspection, the Members of the Commission shall seek to establish interim arrangements to designate observers and inspectors and such designated observers and inspectors shall be entitled to carry out inspections in accordance with the principles set out in paragraph 2 above.

Article XXV

1. If any dispute arises between two or more of the Contracting Parties concerning the interpretation or application of this Convention, those Contracting Parties shall consult among themselves with a view to having the dispute resolved by negotiation, inquiry, mediation, conciliation, arbitration, judicial settlement or other peaceful means of their own choice.

2. Any dispute of this character not so resolved shall, with the consent in each case of all Parties to the dispute, be referred for settlement to the International Court of Justice or to arbitration; but failure to reach agreement on reference to the International Court or to arbitration shall not absolve Parties to the dispute from the responsibility of continuing to seek to resolve it by any of the various peaceful means referred to in paragraph 1 above.

3. In cases where the dispute is referred to arbitration, the arbitral tribunal shall be constituted as provided in the Annex to this Convention.

Article XXVI

1. This Convention shall be open for signature at Canberra from 1 August to 31 December 1980 by the States participating in the Conference on the Conservation of Antarctic Marine Living Resources held at Canberra from 7 to 20 May 1980.

2. The States which so sign will be the original signatory States of the Convention.

Article XXVII

1. This Convention is subject to ratification, acceptance or approval by signatory States.

2. Instruments of ratification, acceptance or approval shall be deposited with the Government of Australia, hereby designated as the Depositary.

Article XXVIII

1. This Convention shall enter into force on the thirtieth day following the date of deposit of the eighth instrument of ratification, acceptance or approval by States referred to in paragraph 1 of Article XXVI of this Convention.

2. With respect to each State or regional economic integration organization which subsequent to the date of entry into force of this Convention deposits an instrument of ratification, acceptance, approval or accession, the Convention shall enter into force on the thirtieth day following such deposit.

Article XXIX

1. This Convention shall be open for accession by any State interested in research or harvesting activities in relation to the marine living resources to which this Convention applies.

2. This Convention shall be open for accession by regional economic integration organizations constituted by sovereign States which include among their members one or more States Members of the Commission and to which the States members of the organization have transferred, in whole or in part, competences with regard to the matters covered by this Convention. The accession of such regional economic integration organizations shall be the subject of consultations among Members of the Commission.

Article XXX

1. This Convention may be amended at any time.

2. If one-third of the Members of the Commission request a meeting to discuss a proposed amendment the Depositary shall call such a meeting.

3. An amendment shall enter into force when the Depositary has received instruments of ratification, acceptance or approval thereof from all the Members of the Commission.

4. Such amendment shall thereafter enter into force as to any other Contracting Party when notice of ratification, acceptance or approval by it has been received by the Depositary. Any such Contracting Party from which no such notice has been received within a period of one year from the date of entry into force of the amendment in accordance with paragraph 3 above shall be deemed to have withdrawn from this Convention.

Article XXXI

1. Any Contracting Party may withdraw from this Convention on 30 June of any year, by giving written notice no later than 1 January of the same year to the Depositary, which, upon receipt of such a notice, shall communicate it forthwith to the other Contracting Parties.

2. Any other Contracting Party may, within sixty days of the receipt of a copy of such a notice from the Depositary, give written notice of withdrawal to the Depositary in which case the Convention shall cease to be in force on 30 June of the same year with respect to the Contracting Party giving such notice.

3. Withdrawal from this Convention by any Member of the Commission shall not affect its financial obligations under this Convention.

Article XXXII

The Depositary shall notify all Contracting Parties of the following:

(a) signatures of this Convention and the deposit of instruments of ratification, acceptance, approval or accession;

(b) the date of entry into force of this Convention and of any amendment thereto.

Article XXXIII

1. This Convention, of which the English, French, Russian and Spanish texts are equally authentic, shall be deposited with the Government of Australia which shall transmit duly certified copies thereof to all signatory and acceding Parties.

2. This Convention shall be registered by the Depositary pursuant to Article 102 of the Charter of the United Nations.

Drawn up at Canberra this twentieth day of May 1980.

IN WITNESS WHEREOF the undersigned, being duly authorized, have signed this Convention.

Annex for an Arbitral Tribunal

The arbitral tribunal referred to in paragraph 3 of Article XXV shall be composed of three arbitrators who shall be appointed as follows:

The Party commencing proceedings shall communicate the name of an arbitrator to the other Party which, in turn, within a period of forty days following such notification, shall communicate the name of the second arbitrator. The Parties shall, within a period of sixty days following the appointment of the second arbitrator, appoint the third arbitrator, who shall not be a national of either Party and shall not be of the same nationality as either of the first two arbitrators. The third arbitrator shall preside over the tribunal.

If the second arbitrator has not been appointed within the prescribed period, or if the Parties have not reached agreement within the prescribed period on the appointment of the third arbitrator, that arbitrator shall be appointed, as the request of either Party, by the Secretary-General of the Permanent Court of Arbitration, from among persons of international standing not having the nationality of a State which is a Party to this Convention.

The arbitral tribunal shall decide where its headquarters will be located and shall adopt its own rules of procedure.

The award of the arbitral tribunal shall be made by a majority of its members, who may not abstain from voting.

Any Contracting Party which is not a Party to the dispute may intervene in the proceedings with the consent of the arbitral tribunal.

The award of the arbitral tribunal shall be final and binding on all Parties to the dispute and on any Party which intervenes in the proceedings and shall be complied with without delay. The arbitral tribunal shall interpret the award at the request of one of the Parties to the dispute or of any intervening Party.

Unless the arbitral tribunal determines otherwise because of the particular circumstances of the case, the expenses of the tribunal, including the remuneration of its members, shall be borne by the Parties to the dispute in equal shares.

Final Act of the Conference on the Conservation of Antarctic Marine Living Resources, 20 May 1980

I

The Governments of Argentina, Australia, Belgium, Chile, The French Republic, German Democratic Republic, Germany, Federal Republic of, Japan, New Zealand, Norway, Poland, The Republic of South Africa, The Union of Soviet Socialist Republics, The United Kingdom of Great Britain and Northern Ireland, and The United States of America;

having accepted the invitation extended to them by the Government of Australia to participate in a Conference on the Conservation of Antarctic Marine Living Resources, appointed their representatives, advisers and observers who are listed below:

[List of representatives omitted]

The Conference met at Canberra on 7 May 1980 under the Chairmanship of Mr J.E. Ryan, Representative of the delegation of Australia. The Secretary-General was Mr R.H. Wyndham.

A Drafting Committee established under the Rules of Procedure of the Conference was constituted as follows:

[List of representatives omitted]

The Final Session was held on 20 May 1980. As a result of its deliberations the Conference has established and drawn up for signature a "Convention of the Conservation of Antarctic Marine Living Resources" the text of which is annexed hereto.

The Conference also decided to include in the Final Act the text of the following statement made by the Chairman on 19 May 1980 regarding the application of the Convention on the Conservation of Antarctic Marine Living Resources to the waters adjacent to Kerguelen and Crozet over which France has jurisdiction and to waters adjacent to other islands within the area to which this Convention applies over which the existence of State sovereignty is recognized by all Contracting parties.

"1. Measures for the conservation of Antarctic marine living resources of the waters adjacent to Kerguelen and Crozet, over which France has jurisdiction, adopted by France prior to the entry into force of the Convention, would remain in force after the entry into force of the Convention until modified by France acting within the framework of the Commission or otherwise.

2. After the Convention has come into force, each time the Commission should undertake examination of the conservation needs of the marine living resources of the general area in which the waters adjacent to Kerguelen and Crozet are to be found, it would be open to France either to agree that the waters in question should be included in the area of application of any specific conservation measure under consideration or to indicate that they should be excluded. In the latter event, the Commission would not proceed to the adoption of the specific conservation measure in a form applicable to the waters in question unless France removed its objection to it. France could also adopt such national measures as it might deem appropriate for the waters in question.

3. Accordingly, when specific conservation measures are considered within the framework of the commission and with the participation of France, then:

(a) France would be bound by any conservation measures adopted by consensus with its participation for the duration of those measures. This would not prevent France from promulgating national measures that were more strict that the Commission's measures or which dealt with other matters;

(b) In the absence of consensus, France could promulgate any national measures it might deem appropriate.

4. Conservation measures, whether national measures or measures adopted by the Commission, in respect of the waters adjacent to Kerguelen and Crozet, would be enforced by France. The system of observation and inspection foreseen by the Convention would not be implemented in the waters adjacent to Kerguelen and Crozet except as agreed by France and in the manner so agreed.

5. The understandings, set forth in paragraphs 1–4 above, regarding the application of the Convention to waters adjacent to the Islands of Kerguelen and Crozet, also apply to waters adjacent to the islands within the area to which this Convention applies over which the existence of State sovereignty is recognized by all Contracting Parties."

No objection to the statement was made.

II

The Conference on the Conservation of Antarctic Marine Living Resources,

Noting that a definitive regime for the conservation of Antarctic marine living resources has been elaborated, and desiring to have that regime enter into force as quickly as possible;

Recognizing that harvesting of Antarctic marine living resources is presently taking place and underlining the importance of the objectives of the Convention on the Conservation of Antarctic Marine Living Resources;

Recognizing the need to identify, emphasize and co-operate in carrying out research activities that will facilitate the effective operation of the Convention;

Desiring further to facilitate the implementation of the Convention by emphasizing and co-ordinating the collecting of scientific and fisheries data needed for the Scientific Committee to be constituted under the terms of the Convention to begin effective work upon entry into force of the Convention;

Calls upon the Parties entitled to become Members of the Commission:

1. To take all possible steps to bring the Convention on the Conservation of Antarctic Marine Living Resources into force as soon as possible;

2. To show the greatest possible care and concern, bearing in mind the principles and objectives of Article II of the Convention, in any harvesting of Antarctic marine living resources in the period prior to entry into force of the Convention and examination of the status of stocks by the Scientific Committee to be established by the Convention on the Conservation of Antarctic Marine Living Resources;

3. To the greatest extent practicable and feasible to co-operate broadly and comprehensively in the continued development of the scientific and fisheries data necessary for the effective operation of the Convention on the Conservation of Antarctic Marine Living Resources, and to this end:

(a) to intensify research related to Antarctic marine living resources;

(b) to identify the specific scientific and fisheries data needed and how those data should be collected and recorded to facilitate the work of the Scientific Committee to be established by the Convention; and

(c) to compile scientific and fisheries data identified pursuant to sub-paragraph (b) above in order to distribute those data to the Contracting Parties upon entry into force of the Convention on the Conservation of Antarctic Marine Living Resources.

III

The Conference on the Convention for the Conservation of Antarctic Marine Living Resources,

Having agreed on a text of the Convention which would establish a Commission and Scientific Committee for the Conservation of Antarctic Marine Living Resources and an Executive Secretariat;

Recognising the need to examine working methods for the Executive Secretary and Secretariat so that they may begin their work as soon as possible after entry into force of the Convention;

Takes note of the intention of the Depositary to convene a meeting of representatives of Parties entitled to become Members of the Commission within one year after expiration of the period during which the Convention is open for signature for the purpose of considering steps which might be taken to facilitate the early operation of the Commission, Scientific Committee and Executive Secretariat when these bodies are established.

IV

The Conference on the Conservation of Antarctic Marine Living Resources resolves:

1. to express its gratitude to the Australian Government for its initiative in convening the present Conference and for its preparation;

2. to express to its Chairman, Mr J.E. Ryan, its deep appreciation for the admirable manner in which he has guided the Conference;

3. to express to the officers and staff of the Secretariat its appreciation for their untiring efforts in contributing to the attainment of the objectives of the Conference.

V

The Conference on the Conservation of Antarctic Marine Living Resources resolves:

That the Government of Australia be authorised to publish the Final Act of this Conference and the text of the Convention annexed hereto.

VI

The Conference on the Conservation of Antarctic Marine Living Resources resolves:

To express its deep appreciation to the Australian Government for its offer to provide a site for the Headquarters of the Commission to be established under the Convention.

Done at Canberra, this Twentieth Day of May 1980, in a single original copy to be deposited in the archives of the Government of Australia which will transmit a certified copy thereof to all the other Participants in the Conference.

In witness whereof, the following representatives have signed this Final Act.

Convention on the Regulation of Antarctic Mineral Resource Activities[41]

Preamble

The States Parties to this Convention, hereinafter referred to as the Parties,

Recalling the provisions of the Antarctic Treaty;

Convinced that the Antarctic Treaty system has proved effective in promoting international harmony in furtherance of the purposes and principles of the Charter of the United Nations, in ensuring the absence of any measures of a military nature and the protection of the Antarctic environment and in promoting freedom of scientific research in Antarctica;

Reaffirming that it is in the interest of all mankind that the Antarctic Treaty area shall continue forever to be used exclusively for peaceful purposes and shall not become the scene or object of international discord;

Noting the possibility that exploitable mineral resources may exist in Antarctica;

Bearing in mind the special legal and political status of Antarctica and the special responsibility of the Antarctic Treaty Consultative Parties to ensure that all activities in Antarctica are consistent with the purposes and principles of the Antarctic Treaty;

[41] Never entered into force.

Bearing in mind also that a regime for Antarctic mineral resources must be consistent with Article IV of the Antarctic Treaty and in accordance therewith be without prejudice and acceptable to those States which assert rights of or claims to territorial sovereignty in Antarctica, and those States which neither recognise nor assert such rights or claims, including those States which assert a basis of claim to territorial sovereignty in Antarctica;

Noting the unique ecological, scientific and wilderness value of Antarctica and the importance of Antarctica to the global environment;

Recognising that Antarctic mineral resource activities could adversely affect the Antarctic environment or dependent or associated ecosystems;

Believing that the protection of the Antarctic environment and dependent and associated ecosystems must be a basic consideration in decisions taken on possible Antarctic mineral resource activities;

Concerned to ensure that Antarctic mineral resource activities, should they occur, are compatible with scientific investigation in Antarctica and other legitimate uses of Antarctica;

Believing that a regime governing Antarctic mineral resource activities will further strengthen the Antarctic Treaty system;

Convinced that participation in Antarctic mineral resource activities should be open to all States which have an interest in such activities and subscribe to a regime governing them and that the special situation of developing country Parties to the regime should be taken into account.

Believing that the effective regulation of Antarctic mineral resource activities is in the interest of the international community as a whole;

Have agreed as follows:

Chapter I: General Provisions

Article 1 Definitions

For the purposes of this Convention:

1. 'Antarctic Treaty' means the Antarctic Treaty done at Washington on 1 December 1959.

2. 'Antarctic Treaty Consultative Parties' means the Contracting Parties to the Antarctic Treaty entitled to appoint representatives to participate in the meetings referred to in Article IX of that Treaty.

3. 'Antarctic Treaty area' means the area to which the provisions of the Antarctic Treaty apply in accordance with Article VI of that Treaty.

4. 'Convention for the Conservation of Antarctic Seals' means the Convention done at London on 1 June 1972.

5. 'Convention on the Conservation of Antarctic Marine Living Resources' means the Convention done at Canberra on 20 May 1980.

6. 'Mineral resources' means all non-living natural non-renewable resources, including fossil fuels, metallic and non-metallic minerals.

7. 'Antarctic mineral resource activities' means prospecting, exploration or development, but does not include scientific research activities within the meaning of Article III of the Antarctic Treaty.

8. 'Prospecting' means activities, including logistic support, aimed at identifying areas of mineral resource potential for possible exploration and development, including geological, geochemical and geophysical investigations and field observations, the use of remote sensing techniques and collection of surface, seafloor and sub-ice samples. Such activities do not include dredging and excavations, except for the purpose of obtaining small-scale samples, or drilling, except shallow drilling into rock and sediment to depths not exceeding 25 metres, or such other depth as the Commission may determine for particular circumstances.

9. 'Exploration' means activities, including logistic support, aimed at identifying and evaluating specific mineral resource occurrences or deposits, including exploratory drilling, dredging and other surface or subsurface excavations required to determine the nature and

size of mineral resource deposits and the feasibility of their development, but excluding pilot projects or commercial production.

10. 'Development' means activities, including logistic support, which take place following exploration and are aimed at or associated with exploitation of specific mineral resource deposits, including pilot projects, processing, storage and transport activities.

11. 'Operator' means:

(a) a Party; or
(b) an agency or instrumentality of a Party; or
(c) a juridical person established under the law of a Party; or
(d) a joint venture consisting exclusively of any combination of any of the foregoing,
(e) which is undertaking Antarctic mineral resource activities and for which there is a Sponsoring State.

12. 'Sponsoring State' means the Party with which an Operator has a substantial and genuine link, through being:

(a) in the case of a Party, that Party;
(b) in the case of an agency or instrumentality of a Party, that Party;
(c) in the case of a juridical person other than an agency or instrumentality of a Party, the Party:
  (i) under whose law that juridical person is established and to whose law it is subject, without prejudice to any other law which might be applicable, and
  (ii) in whose territory the management of that juridical person is located, and
  (iii) to whose effective control that juridical person is subject;
(d) in the case of a joint venture not constituting a juridical person:
  (i) where the managing member of the joint venture is a Party or an agency or instrumentality of a Party, that Party; or
  (ii) in any other case, where in relation to a Party the managing member of the joint venture satisfies the requirements of subparagraph (c) above, that Party.

13. 'Managing member of the joint venture' means that member which the participating members in the joint venture have by agreement designated as having responsibility for central management of the joint venture, including the functions of organising and supervising the activities to be undertaken, and controlling the financial resources involved.

14. 'Effective control' means the ability of the Sponsoring State to ensure the availability of substantial resources of the Operator for purposes connected with the implementation of this Convention, through the location of such resources in the territory of the Sponsoring State or otherwise.

15. 'Damage to the Antarctic environment or dependent or associated ecosystems' means any impact on the living or non-living components of that environment or those ecosystems, including harm to atmospheric, marine or terrestrial life, beyond that which is negligible or which has been assessed and judged to be acceptable pursuant to this Convention.

16. 'Commission' means the Antarctic Mineral Resources Commission established pursuant to Article 18.

17. 'Regulatory Committee' means an Antarctic Mineral Resources Regulatory Committee established pursuant to Article 29.

18. 'Advisory Committee' means the Scientific, Technical and Environmental Advisory Committee established pursuant to Article 23.

19. 'Special Meeting of Parties' means the Meeting referred to in Article 28.

20. 'Arbitral Tribunal' means an Arbitral Tribunal constituted as provided for in the Annex, which forms an integral part of this Convention.

Article 2 Objectives and General Principles

1. This Convention is an integral part of the Antarctic Treaty system, comprising the Antarctic Treaty, the measures in effect under that Treaty, and its associated separate legal instruments, the

prime purpose of which is to ensure that Antarctica shall continue forever to be used exclusively for peaceful purposes and shall not become the scene or object of international discord. The Parties provide through this Convention, the principles it establishes, the rules it prescribes, the institutions it creates and the decisions adopted pursuant to it, a means for:

(a) assessing the possible impact on the environment of Antarctic mineral resource activities;
(b) determining whether Antarctic mineral resource activities are acceptable;
(c) governing the conduct of such Antarctic mineral resource activities as may be found acceptable; and
(d) ensuring that any Antarctic mineral resource activities are undertaken in strict conformity with this Convention.

2. In implementing this Convention, the Parties shall ensure that Antarctic mineral resource activities, should they occur, take place in a manner consistent with all the components of the Antarctic Treaty system and the obligations flowing therefrom.

3. In relation to Antarctic mineral resource activities, should they occur, the Parties acknowledge the special responsibility of the Antarctic Treaty Consultative Parties for the protection of the environment and the need to:

(a) protect the Antarctic environment and dependent and associated ecosystems;
(b) respect Antarctica's significance for, and influence on, the global environment;
(c) respect other legitimate uses of Antarctica;
(d) respect Antarctica's scientific value and aesthetic and wilderness qualities;
(e) ensure the safety of operations in Antarctica;
(f) promote opportunities for fair and effective participation of all Parties; and
(g) take into account the interests of the international community as a whole.

Article 3 Prohibition of Antarctic Mineral Resource Activities Outside this Convention

No Antarctic mineral resource activities shall be conducted except in accordance with this Convention and measures in effect pursuant to it and, in the case of exploration or development, with a Management Scheme approved pursuant to Article 48 or 54.

Article 4 Principles Concerning Judgments on Antarctic Mineral Resource Activities

1. Decisions about Antarctic mineral resource activities shall be based upon information adequate to enable informed judgments to be made about their possible impacts and no such activities shall take place unless this information is available for decisions relevant to those activities.

2. No Antarctic mineral resource activity shall take place until it is judged, based upon assessment of its possible impacts on the Antarctic environment and on dependent and on associated ecosystems, that the activity in question would not cause:

(a) significant adverse effects on air and water quality;
(b) significant changes in atmospheric, terrestrial or marine environments;
(c) significant changes in the distribution, abundance or productivity of populations of species of fauna or flora;
(d) further jeopardy to endangered or threatened species or populations of such species; or
(e) degradation of, or substantial risk to, areas of special biological, scientific, historic, aesthetic or wilderness significance.

3. No Antarctic mineral resource activity shall take place until it is judged, based upon assessment of its possible impacts, that the activity in question would not cause significant adverse effects on global or regional climate or weather patterns.

4. No Antarctic mineral resource activity shall take place until it is judged that:

(a) technology and procedures are available to provide for safe operations and compliance with paragraphs 2 and 3 above;
(b) there exists the capacity to monitor key environmental parameters and ecosystem components so as to identify any adverse effects of such activity and to provide for the modification of operating procedures as may be necessary in the light of the results

of monitoring or increased knowledge of the Antarctic environment or dependent or associated ecosystems; and

(c) there exists the capacity to respond effectively to accidents, particularly those with potential environmental effects.

5. The judgments referred to in paragraphs 2, 3 and 4 above shall take into account the cumulative impacts of possible Antarctic mineral resource activities both by themselves and in combination with other such activities and other uses of Antarctica.

Article 5 Area of Application

1. This Convention shall, subject to paragraphs 2, 3 and 4 below, apply to the Antarctic Treaty area.

2. Without prejudice to the responsibilities of the Antarctic Treaty Consultative Parties under the Antarctic Treaty and measures pursuant to it, the Parties agree that this Convention shall regulate Antarctic mineral resource activities which take place on the continent of Antarctica and all Antarctic islands, including all ice shelves, south of 60° south latitude and in the seabed and subsoil of adjacent offshore areas up to the deep seabed.

3. For the purposes of this Convention 'deep seabed' means the seabed and subsoil beyond the geographic extent of the continental shelf as the term continental shelf is defined in accordance with international law.

4. Nothing in this Article shall be construed as limiting the application of other Articles of this Convention in so far as they relate to possible impacts outside the area referred to in paragraphs 1 and 2 above, including impacts on dependent or on associated ecosystems.

Article 6 Cooperation and International Participation

In the implementation of this Convention cooperation within its framework shall be promoted and encouragement given to international participation in Antarctic mineral resource activities by interested Parties which are Antarctic Treaty Consultative Parties and by other interested Parties, in particular, developing countries in either category. Such participation may be realised through the Parties themselves and their Operators.

Article 7 Compliance with this Convention

1. Each Party shall take appropriate measures within its competence to ensure compliance with this Convention and any measures in effect pursuant to it.

2. If a Party is prevented by the exercise of jurisdiction by another Party from ensuring compliance in accordance with paragraph 1 above, it shall not, to the extent that it is so prevented, bear responsibility for that failure to ensure compliance.

3. If any jurisdictional dispute related to compliance with this Convention or any measure in effect pursuant to it arises between two or more Parties, the Parties concerned shall immediately consult together with a view to reaching a mutually acceptable solution.

4. Each Party shall notify the Executive Secretary, for circulation to all other Parties, of the measures taken pursuant to paragraph 1 above.

5. Each Party shall exert appropriate efforts, consistent with the Charter of the United Nations, to the end that no one engages in any Antarctic mineral resource activities contrary to the objectives and principles of this Convention.

6. Each Party may, whenever it deems it necessary, draw the attention of the Commission to any activity which in its opinion affects the implementation of the objectives and principles of this Convention.

7. The Commission shall draw the attention of all Parties to any activity which, in the opinion of the Commission, affects the implementation of the objectives and principles of this Convention or the compliance by any Party with its obligations under this Convention and any measures in effect pursuant to it.

8. The Commission shall draw the attention of any State which is not a Party to this Convention to any activity undertaken by that State, its agencies or instrumentalities, natural or juridical

persons, ships, aircraft or other means of transportation which, in the opinion of the Commission, affects the implementation of the objectives and principles of this Convention. The Commission shall inform all Parties accordingly.

9. Nothing in this Article shall affect the operation of Article 127 of this Convention or Article VIII of the Antarctic Treaty.

Article 8 Response Action and Liability

1. An Operator undertaking any Antarctic mineral resource activity shall take necessary and timely response action, including prevention, containment, clean up and removal measures, if the activity results in or threatens to result in damage to the Antarctic environment or dependent or associated ecosystems. The Operator, through its Sponsoring State, shall notify the Executive Secretary, for circulation to the relevant institutions of this Convention and to all Parties, of action taken pursuant to this paragraph.

2. An Operator shall be strictly liable for:

(a) damage to the Antarctic environment or dependent or associated ecosystems arising from its Antarctic mineral resource activities, including payment in the event that there has been no restoration to the status quo ante;

(b) loss of or impairment to an established use, as referred to in Article 15, or loss of or impairment to an established use of dependent or associated ecosystems, arising directly out of damage described in subparagraph (a) above;

(c) loss of or damage to property of a third party or loss of life or personal injury of a third party arising directly out of damage described in subparagraph (a) above; and

(d) reimbursement of reasonable costs by whomsoever incurred relating to necessary response action, including prevention, containment, clean up and removal measures, and action taken to restore the status quo ante where Antarctic mineral resource activities undertaken by that Operator result in or threaten to result in damage to the Antarctic environment or dependent or associated ecosystems.

3.

(a) Damage of the kind referred to in paragraph 2 above which would not have occurred or continued if the Sponsoring State had carried out its obligations under this Convention with respect to its Operator shall, in accordance with international law, entail liability of that Sponsoring State. Such liability shall be limited to that portion of liability not satisfied by the Operator or otherwise.

(b) Nothing in subparagraph (a) above shall affect the application of the rules of international law applicable in the event that damage not referred to in that subparagraph would not have occurred or continued if the Sponsoring State had carried out its obligations under this Convention with respect to its Operator.

4. An Operator shall not be liable pursuant to paragraph 2 above if it proves that the damage has been caused directly by, and to the extent that it has been caused directly by:

(a) an event constituting in the circumstances of Antarctica a natural disaster of an exceptional character which could not reasonably have been foreseen; or

(b) armed conflict, should it occur notwithstanding the Antarctic Treaty, or an act of terrorism directed against the activities of the Operator, against which no reasonable precautionary measures could have been effective.

5. Liability of an Operator for any loss of life, personal injury or loss of or damage to property other than that governed by this Article shall be regulated by applicable law and procedures.

6. If an Operator proves that damage has been caused totally or in part by an intentional or grossly negligent act or omission of the party seeking redress, that Operator may be relieved totally or in part from its obligation to pay compensation in respect of the damage suffered by such party.

7.

(a) Further rules and procedures in respect of the provisions on liability set out in this Article shall be elaborated through a separate Protocol which shall be adopted by consensus by the members of the Commission and shall enter into force according to the procedure provided for in Article 62 for the entry into force of this Convention.

(b) Such rules and procedures shall be designed to enhance the protection of the Antarctic environment and dependent and associated ecosystems.

(c) Such rules and procedures:

(i) may contain provisions for appropriate limits on liability, where such limits can be justified;

(ii) without prejudice to Article 57, shall prescribe means and mechanisms such as a claims tribunal or other fora by which claims against Operators pursuant to this Article may be assessed and adjudicated;

(iii) shall ensure that a means is provided to assist with immediate response action, and to satisfy liability under paragraph 2 above in the event, *inter alia*, that an Operator liable is financially incapable of meeting its obligation in full, that it exceeds any relevant limits of liability, that there is a defence to liability or that the loss or damage is of undetermined origin. Unless it is determined during the elaboration of the Protocol that there are other effective means of meeting these objectives, the Protocol shall establish a Fund or Funds and make provision in respect of such Fund or Funds, *inter alia*, for the following:

- financing by Operators or on industry wide bases;
- ensuring the permanent liquidity and mandatory supplementation thereof in the event of insufficiency;
- reimbursement of costs of response action, by whomsoever incurred.

8. Nothing in paragraphs 4, 6 and 7 above or in the Protocol adopted pursuant to paragraph 7 shall affect in any way the provisions of paragraph 1 above.

9. No application for an exploration or development permit shall be made until the Protocol provided for in paragraph 7 above is in force for the Party lodging such application.

10. Each Party, pending the entry into force for it of the Protocol provided for in paragraph 7 above, shall ensure, consistently with Article 7 and in accordance with its legal system, that recourse is available in its national courts for adjudicating liability claims pursuant to paragraphs 2, 4 and 6 above against Operators which are engaged in prospecting. Such recourse shall include the adjudication of claims against any Operator it has sponsored. Each Party shall also ensure, in accordance with its legal system, that the Commission has the right to appear as a party in its national courts to pursue relevant liability claims under paragraph 2(a) above.

11. Nothing in this Article or in the Protocol provided for in paragraph 7 above shall be construed as to:

(a) preclude the application of existing rules on liability, and the development in accordance with international law of further such rules, which may have application to either States or Operators; or

(b) affect the right of an Operator incurring liability pursuant to this Article to seek redress from another party which caused or contributed to the damage in question.

12. When compensation has been paid other than under this Convention liability under this Convention shall be offset by the amount of such payment.

Article 9 Protection of Legal Positions under the Antarctic Treaty

Nothing in this Convention and no acts or activities taking place while this Convention is in force shall:

(a) constitute a basis for asserting, supporting or denying a claim to territorial sovereignty in the Antarctic Treaty area or create any rights of sovereignty in the Antarctic Treaty area;

(b) be interpreted as a renunciation or diminution by any Party of, or as prejudicing, any right or claim or basis of claim to territorial sovereignty in Antarctica or to exercise coastal state jurisdiction under international law;
(c) be interpreted as prejudicing the position of any Party as regards its recognition or non-recognition of any such right, claim or basis of claim; or
(d) affect the provision of Article IV(2) of the Antarctic Treaty that no new claim, or enlargement of an existing claim, to territorial sovereignty in Antarctica shall be asserted while the Antarctic Treaty is in force.

Article 10 Consistency with the other Components of the Antarctic Treaty System

1. Each Party shall ensure that Antarctic mineral resource activities take place in a manner consistent with the components of the Antarctic Treaty system, including the Antarctic Treaty, the Convention for the Conservation of Antarctic Seals and the Convention on the Conservation of Antarctic Marine Living Resources and the measures in effect pursuant to those instruments.

2. The Commission shall consult and cooperate with the Antarctic Treaty Consultative Parties, the Contracting Parties to the Convention for the Conservation of Antarctic Seals, and the Commission for the Conservation of Antarctic Marine Living Resources with a view to ensuring the achievement of the objectives and principles of this Convention and avoiding any interference with the achievement of the objectives and principles of the Antarctic Treaty, the Convention for the Conservation of Antarctic Seals or the Convention on the Conservation of Antarctic Marine Living Resources, or inconsistency between the measures in effect pursuant to those instruments and measures in effect pursuant to this Convention.

Article 11 Inspection under the Antarctic Treaty

All stations, installations and equipment, in the Antarctic Treaty area, relating to Antarctic mineral resource activities, as well as ships and aircraft supporting such activities at points of discharging or embarking cargoes or personnel at such stations and installations, shall be open at all times to inspection by observers designated under Article VII of the Antarctic Treaty for the purposes of that Treaty.

Article 12 Inspection under this Convention

1. In order to promote the objectives and principles and to ensure the observance of this Convention and measures in effect pursuant to it, all stations, installations and equipment relating to Antarctic mineral resource activities in the area in which these activities are regulated by this Convention, as well as ships and aircraft supporting such activities at points of discharging or embarking cargoes or personnel anywhere in that area shall be open at all times to inspection by:
(a) observers designated by any member of the Commission who shall be nationals of that member; and
(b) observers designated by the Commission or relevant Regulatory Committees.

2. Aerial inspection may be carried out at any time over the area in which Antarctic mineral resource activities are regulated by this Convention.

3. The Commission shall maintain an up-to-date list of observers designated pursuant to paragraph 1(a) and (b) above.

4. Reports from the observers shall be transmitted to the Commission and to any Regulatory Committee having competence in the area where the inspection has been carried out.

5. Observers shall avoid interference with the safe and normal operations of stations, installations and equipment visited and shall respect measures adopted by the Commission to protect confidentiality of data and information.

6. Inspections undertaken pursuant to paragraph 1(a) and (b) above shall be compatible and reinforce each other and shall not impose an undue burden on the operation of stations, installations and equipment visited.

7. In order to facilitate the exercise of their functions under this Convention, and without prejudice to the respective positions of the Parties relating to jurisdiction over all other persons

in the area in which Antarctic mineral resource activities are regulated by this Convention, observers designated under this Article shall be subject only to the jurisdiction of the Party of which they are nationals in respect of all acts or omissions occurring while they are in that area for the purpose of exercising their functions.

8. No exploration or development shall take place in an area identified pursuant to Article 41 until effective provision has been made for inspection in that area.

Article 13 Protected Areas

1. Antarctic mineral resource activities shall be prohibited in any area designated as a Specially Protected Area or a Site of Special Scientific Interest under Article IX(1) of the Antarctic Treaty. Such activities shall also be prohibited in any other area designated as a protected area in accordance with Article IX(1) of the Antarctic Treaty, except to the extent that the relevant measure provides otherwise. Pending any designation becoming effective in accordance with Article IX(4) of the Antarctic Treaty, no Antarctic mineral resource activities shall take place in any such area which would prejudice the purpose for which it was designated.

2. The Commission shall also prohibit or restrict Antarctic mineral resource activities in any area which, for historic, ecological, environmental, scientific or other reasons, it has designated as a protected area.

3. In exercising its powers under paragraph 2 above or under Article 41 the Commission shall consider whether to restrict or prohibit Antarctic mineral resource activities in any area, in addition to those referred to in paragraph 1 above, protected or set aside pursuant to provisions of other components of the Antarctic Treaty system, to ensure the purposes for which they are designated.

4. In relation to any area in which Antarctic mineral resource activities are prohibited or restricted in accordance with paragraph 1, 2 or 3 above, the Commission shall consider whether, for the purposes of Article 4(2)(e), it would be prudent, additionally, to prohibit or restrict Antarctic mineral resource activities in adjacent areas for the purpose of creating a buffer zone.

5. The Commission shall give effect to Article 10(2) in acting pursuant to paragraphs 2, 3 and 4 above.

6. The Commission shall, where appropriate, bring any decisions it takes pursuant to this Article to the attention of the Antarctic Treaty Consultative Parties, the Contracting Parties to the Convention for the Conservation of Antarctic Seals, the Commission for the Conservation of Antarctic Marine Living Resources and the Scientific Committee on Antarctic Research.

Article 14 Non-Discrimination

In the implementation of this Convention there shall be no discrimination against any Party or its Operators.

Article 15 Respect for Other Uses of Antarctica

1. Decisions about Antarctic mineral resource activities shall take into account the need to respect other established uses of Antarctica, including:

(a) the operation of stations and their associated installations, support facilities and equipment in Antarctica;
(b) scientific investigation in Antarctica and cooperation therein;
(c) the conservation, including rational use, of Antarctic marine living resources;
(d) tourism;
(e) the preservation of historic monuments; and
(f) navigation and aviation,

that are consistent with the Antarctic Treaty system.

2. Antarctic mineral resource activities shall be conducted so as to respect any uses of Antarctica as referred to in paragraph 1 above.

Article 16 Availability and Confidentiality of Data and Information

Data and information obtained from Antarctic mineral resource activities shall, to the greatest extent practicable and feasible, be made freely available, provided that:

(a) as regards data and information of commercial value deriving from prospecting, they may be retained by the Operator in accordance with Article 37;

(b) regards data and information deriving from exploration or development, the Commission shall adopt measures relating, as appropriate, to their release and to ensure the confidentiality of data and information of commercial value.

Article 17 Notifications and Provisional Exercise of Functions of the Executive Secretary

1. Where in this Convention there is a reference to the provision of information, a notification or a report to any institution provided for in this Convention and that institution has not been established, the information, notification or report shall be provided to the Executive Secretary who shall circulate it as required.

2. Where in this Convention a function is assigned to the Executive Secretary and no Executive Secretary has been appointed under Article 33, that function shall be performed by the Depositary.

Chapter II: Institutions

Article 18 Commission

1. There is hereby established the Antarctic Mineral Resources Commission.

2. Membership of the Commission shall be as follows:

(a) each Party which was an Antarctic Treaty Consultative Party on the date when this Convention was opened for signature; and

(b) each other Party during such time as it is actively engaged in substantial scientific, technical or environmental research in the area to which this Convention applies directly relevant to decisions about Antarctic mineral resource activities, particularly the assessments and judgments called for in Article 4; and

(c) each other Party sponsoring Antarctic mineral resource exploration or development during such time as the relevant Management Scheme is in force.

3. A Party seeking to participate in the work of the Commission pursuant to subparagraph (b) or (c) above shall notify the Depositary of the basis upon which it seeks to become a member of the Commission. In the case of a Party which is not an Antarctic Treaty Consultative Party, such notification shall include a declaration of intent to abide by recommendations pursuant to Article IX(1) of the Antarctic Treaty. The Depositary shall communicate to each member of the Commission such notification and accompanying information.

4. The Commission shall consider the notification at its next meeting. In the event that a Party referred to in paragraph 2(b) above submitting a notification pursuant to paragraph 3 above is an Antarctic Treaty Consultative Party, it shall be deemed to have satisfied the requirements for Commission membership unless more than one-third of the members of the Commission object at the meeting at which such notification is considered. Any other Party submitting a notification shall be deemed to have satisfied the requirements for Commission membership if no member of the Commission objects at the meeting at which such notification is considered.

5. Each member of the Commission shall be represented by one representative who may be accompanied by alternate representatives and advisers.

6. Observer status in the Commission shall be open to any Party and to any Contracting Party to the Antarctic Treaty which is not a Party to this Convention.

Article 19 Commission Meetings

1.

(a) The first meeting of the Commission, held for the purpose of taking organisational, financial and other decisions necessary for the effective functioning of this Convention and its institutions, shall be convened within six months of the entry into force of this Convention.

(b) After the Commission has held the meeting or meetings necessary to take the decisions referred to in subparagraph (a) above, the Commission shall not hold further meetings except in accordance with paragraph 2 or 3 below.

2. Meetings of the Commission shall be held within two months of:

(a) receipt of a notification pursuant to Article 39;

(b) a request by at least six members of the Commission; or

(c) a request by a member of a Regulatory Committee in accordance with Article 49(1).

3. The Commission may establish a regular schedule of meetings if it determines that it is necessary for the effective functioning of this Convention.

4. Unless the Commission decides otherwise, its meetings shall be convened by the Executive Secretary.

Article 20 Commission Procedure

1. The Commission shall elect from among its members a Chairman and two Vice-Chairmen, each of whom shall be a representative of a different Party.

2.

(a) Until such time as the Commission has established a regular schedule of meetings in accordance with Article 19(3), the Chairman and Vice-Chairmen shall be elected to serve for a period of two years, provided that if no meeting is held during that period they shall continue to serve until the conclusion of the first meeting held thereafter.

(b) When a regular schedule of meetings has been established, the Chairman and Vice-Chairmen shall be elected to serve for a period of two years.

3. The Commission shall adopt its rules of procedure. Such rules may include provisions concerning the number of terms of office which the Chairman and Vice-Chairmen may serve and for the rotation of such offices.

4. The Commission may establish such subsidiary bodies as are necessary for the performance of its functions.

5. The Commission may decide to establish a permanent headquarters which shall be in New Zealand.

6. The Commission shall have legal personality and shall enjoy in the territory of each Party such legal capacity as may be necessary to perform its functions and achieve the objectives of this Convention.

7. The privileges and immunities to be enjoyed by the Commission, the Secretariat and representatives attending meetings in the territory of a Party shall be determined by agreement between the Commission and the Party concerned.

Article 21 Functions of the Commission

1. The functions of the Commission shall be:

(a) to facilitate and promote the collection and exchange of scientific, technical and other information and research projects necessary to predict, detect and assess the possible environmental impact of Antarctic mineral resource activities, including the monitoring of key environmental parameters and ecosystem components;

(b) to designate areas in which Antarctic mineral resource activities shall be prohibited or restricted in accordance with Article 13, and to perform the related functions assigned to it in that Article;

(c) to adopt measures for the protection of the Antarctic environment and dependent and associated ecosystems and for the promotion of safe and effective exploration and development techniques and, as it may deem appropriate, to make available a handbook of such measures;

(d) to determine, in accordance with Article 41, whether or not to identify an area for possible exploration and development, and to perform the related functions assigned to it in Article 42;

(e) to adopt measures relating to prospecting applicable to all relevant Operators:
  (i) to determine for particular circumstances maximum drilling depths in accordance with Article 1(8);
  (ii) to restrict or prohibit prospecting consistently with Articles 13, 37 and 38;
(f) to ensure the effective application of Articles 12(4), 37(7) and (8), 38(2) and 39(2), which require the submission to the Commission of information, notifications and reports;
(g) to give advance public notice of matters upon which it is requesting the advice of the Advisory Committee;
(h) to adopt measures relating to the availability and confidentiality of data and information, including measures pursuant to Article 16;
(i) to elaborate the principle of non-discrimination set forth in Article 14;
(j) to adopt measures with respect to maximum block sizes;
(k) to perform the functions assigned to it in Article 29;
(l) to review action by Regulatory Committees in accordance with Article 49;
(m) to adopt measures in accordance with Articles 6 and 41(1)(d) related to the promotion of cooperation and to participation in Antarctic mineral resource activities;
(n) to adopt general measures pursuant to Article 51(6);
(o) to take decisions on budgetary matters and adopt financial regulations in accordance with Article 35;
(p) to adopt measures regarding fees payable in connection with notifications submitted pursuant to Articles 37 and 39 and applications lodged pursuant to Articles 44 and 53, the purpose of which fees shall be to cover the administrative costs of handling such notifications and applications;
(q) to adopt measures regarding levies payable by Operators engaged in exploration and development, the principal purpose of which levies shall be to cover the costs of the institutions of this Convention;
(r) to determine in accordance with Article 35(7) the disposition of revenues, if any, accruing to the Commission which are surplus to the requirements for financing the budget pursuant to Article 35;
(s) to perform the functions assigned to it in Article 7(7) and (8);
(t) to perform the functions relating to inspection assigned to it in Article 12;
(u) to consider monitoring reports received pursuant to Article 52;
(v) to perform the functions relating to dispute settlement assigned to it in Article 59;
(w) to perform the functions relating to consultation and cooperation assigned to it in Articles 10(2) and 34;
(x) to keep under review the conduct of Antarctic mineral resource activities with a view to safeguarding the protection of the Antarctic environment in the interest of all mankind; and
(y) to perform such other functions as are provided for elsewhere in this Convention.

2. In performing its functions the Commission shall seek and take full account of the views of the Advisory Committee provided in accordance with Article 26.

3. Each measure adopted by the Commission shall specify the date on which it comes into effect.

4. The Commission shall, subject to Article 16 and measures in effect pursuant to it and paragraph 1(h) above, ensure that a publicly available record of its meetings and decisions and of information, notifications and reports submitted to it is maintained.

Article 22 Decision Making in the Commission

1. The Commission shall take decisions on matters of substance by a three-quarters majority of the members present and voting. When a question arises as to whether a matter is one of substance or not, that matter shall be treated as one of substance unless otherwise decided by a three-quarters majority of the members present and voting.

2. Notwithstanding paragraph 1 above, consensus shall be required for the following:

(a) the adoption of the budget and decisions on budgetary and related matters pursuant to Article 21(1)(p), (q) and (r) and Article 35(1), (2), (3), (4) and (5);

(b) decisions taken pursuant to Article 21(1)(i);

(c) decisions taken pursuant to Article 41(2).

3. Decisions on matters of procedure shall be taken by a simple majority of the members present and voting.

4. Nothing in this Article shall be interpreted as preventing the Commission, in taking decisions on matters of substance, from endeavouring to reach a consensus.

5. For the purposes of this Article, consensus means the absence of a formal objection. If, with respect to any decision covered by paragraph 2(c) above, the Chairman of the Commission determines that there would be such an objection he shall consult the members of the Commission. If, as a result of these consultations, the Chairman determines that an objection would remain, he shall convene those members most directly interested for the purpose of seeking to reconcile the differences and producing a generally acceptable proposal.

Article 23 Advisory Committee

1. There is hereby established the Scientific, Technical and Environmental Advisory Committee.

2. Membership of the Advisory Committee shall be open to all Parties.

3. Each member of the Advisory Committee shall be represented by one representative with suitable scientific, technical or environmental competence who may be accompanied by alternate representatives and by experts and advisers.

4. Observer status in the Advisory Committee shall be open to any Contracting Party to the Antarctic Treaty or to the Convention on the Conservation of Antarctic Marine Living Resources which is not a Party to this Convention.

Article 24 Advisory Committee Meetings

1. Unless the Commission decides otherwise, the Advisory Committee shall be convened for its first meeting within six months of the first meeting of the Commission. It shall meet thereafter as necessary to fulfil its functions on the basis of a schedule established by the Commission.

2. Meetings of the Advisory Committee, in addition to those scheduled pursuant to paragraph 1 above, shall be convened at the request of at least six members of the Commission or pursuant to Article 40(1).

3. Unless the Commission decides otherwise, the meetings of the Advisory Committee shall be convened by the Executive Secretary.

Article 25 Advisory Committee Procedure

1. The Advisory Committee shall elect from among its members a Chairman and two Vice-Chairmen, each of whom shall be a representative of a different Party.

2.

(a) Until such time as the Commission has established a schedule of meetings in accordance with Article 24(1), the Chairman and Vice-Chairmen shall be elected to serve for a period of two years, provided that if no meeting is held during that period they shall continue to serve until the conclusion of the first meeting held thereafter.

(b) When a schedule of meetings has been established, the Chairman and Vice-Chairmen shall be elected to serve for a period of two years.

3. The Advisory Committee shall give advance public notice of its meetings and of matters to be considered at each meeting so as to permit the receipt and consideration of views on such matters from international organisations having an interest in them. For this purpose the Advisory Committee may, subject to review by the Commission, establish procedures for the transmission of relevant information to these organisations.

4. The Advisory Committee shall, by a two-thirds majority of the members present and voting, adopt its rules of procedure. Such rules may include provisions concerning the number of

terms of office which the Chairman and Vice-Chairmen may serve and for the rotation of such offices. The rules of procedure and any amendments thereto shall be subject to approval by the Commission.

5. The Advisory Committee may establish such subcommittees, subject to budgetary approval, as may be necessary for the performance of its functions.

Article 26 Functions of the Advisory Committee

1. The Advisory Committee shall advise the Commission and Regulatory Committees, as required by this Convention, or as requested by them, on the scientific, technical and environmental aspects of Antarctic mineral resource activities. It shall provide a forum for consultation and cooperation concerning the collection, exchange and evaluation of information related to the scientific, technical and environmental aspects of Antarctic mineral resource activities.

2. It shall provide advice to:

(a) the Commission relating to its functions under Articles 21(1)(a) to (f), (u) and (x) and 35(7)(a) (in matters relating to scientific research) as well as on the implementation of Article 4; and

(b) Regulatory Committees with respect to:

(i) the implementation of Article 4;

(ii) scientific, technical and environmental aspects of Articles 43(3) and (5), 45, 47, 51, 52 and 54;

(iii) data to be collected and reported in accordance with Articles 47 and 52; and

(iv) the scientific, technical and environmental implications of reports and reported data provided in accordance with Articles 47 and 52.

3. It shall provide advice to the Commission and to Regulatory Committees on:

(a) criteria in respect of the judgments required under Article 4(2) and (3) for the purposes of Article 4(1);

(b) types of data and information required to carry out its functions, and how they should be collected, reported and archived;

(c) scientific research which would contribute to the base of data and information required in subparagraph (b) above;

(d) effective procedures and systems for data and information analysis, evaluation, presentation and dissemination to facilitate the judgments referred to in Article 4; and

(e) possibilities for scientific, technical and environmental cooperation amongst interested Parties which are developing countries and other Parties.

4. The Advisory Committee, in providing advice on decisions to be taken in accordance with Articles 41, 43, 45 and 54 shall, in each case, undertake a comprehensive environmental and technical assessment of the proposed actions. Such assessments shall be based on all information, and any amplifications thereof, available to the Advisory Committee, including the information provided pursuant to Articles 39(2)(e), 44(2)(b)(iii) and 53(2)(b). The assessments of the Advisory Committee shall, in each case, address the nature and scope of the decisions to be taken and shall include consideration, as appropriate, of, *inter alia*:

(a) the adequacy of existing information to enable informed judgments to be made;

(b) the nature, extent, duration and intensity of likely direct environmental impacts resulting from the proposed activity;

(c) possible indirect impacts;

(d) means and alternatives by which such direct or indirect impacts might be reduced, including environmental consequences of the alternative of not proceeding;

(e) cumulative impacts of the proposed activity in the light of existing or planned activities;

(f) capacity to respond effectively to accidents with potential environmental effects;

(g) the environmental significance of unavoidable impacts; and

(h) the probabilities of accidents and their environmental consequences.

5. In preparing its advice the Advisory Committee may seek information and advice from other scientists and experts or scientific organisations as may be required on an ad hoc basis.

6. The Advisory Committee shall, with a view to promoting international participation in Antarctic mineral resource activities as provided for in Article 6, provide advice concerning the availability to interested developing country Parties and other Parties, of the information referred to in paragraph 3 above, of training programmes related to scientific, technical and environmental matters bearing on Antarctic mineral resource activities, and of opportunities for cooperation among Parties in these programmes.

Article 27 Reporting by the Advisory Committee

The Advisory Committee shall present a report on each of its meetings to the Commission and to any relevant Regulatory Committee. The report shall cover all matters considered at the meeting and shall reflect the conclusions reached and all the views expressed by members of the Advisory Committee. The report shall be circulated by the Executive Secretary to all Parties, and to observers attending the meeting, and shall thereupon be made publicly available.

Article 28 Special Meeting of Parties

1. A Special Meeting of Parties shall, as required, be convened in accordance with Article 40(2) and shall have the functions, in relation to the identification of an area for possible exploration and development, specified in Article 40(3).

2. Membership of a Special Meeting of Parties shall be open to all Parties, each of which shall be represented by one representative who may be accompanied by alternate representatives and advisers.

3. Observer status at a Special Meeting of Parties shall be open to any Contracting Party to the Antarctic Treaty which is not a Party to this Convention.

4. Each Special Meeting of Parties shall elect from among its members a Chairman and Vice-Chairmen, each of whom shall serve for the duration of that meeting. The Chairman and Vice-Chairman shall not be representatives of the same Party.

5. The Special Meeting of Parties shall, by a two-thirds majority of the members present and voting, adopt its rules of procedure. Until such time as this has been done the Special Meeting of Parties shall apply provisional rules of procedure drawn up by the Commission.

6. Unless the Commission decides otherwise, a Special Meeting of Parties shall be convened by the Executive Secretary and shall be held at the same venue as the meeting of the Commission convened to consider the identification of an area for possible exploration and development.

Article 29 Regulatory Committees

1. An Antarctic Mineral Resources Regulatory Committee shall be established for each area identified by the Commission pursuant to Article 41.

2. Subject to paragraph 6 below, each Regulatory Committee shall consist of 10 members. Membership shall be determined by the Commission in accordance with this Article and, taking into account Article 9, shall include:

(a) the member, if any, or if there are more than one, those members of the Commission identified by reference to Article 9(b) which assert rights or claims in the identified area;

(b) the two members of the Commission also identified by reference to Article 9(b) which assert a basis of claim in Antarctica;

(c) other members of the Commission determined in accordance with this Article so that the Regulatory Committee shall, subject to paragraph 6 below, consist, in total, of 10 members:

   (i) four members identified by reference to Article 9(b) which assert rights or claims, including the member or members, if any, referred to in subparagraph (a) above and

   (ii) six members which do not assert rights or claims as described in Article 9(b), including the two members referred to in subparagraph (b) above.

3. Upon the identification of an area in accordance with Article 41(2), the Chairman of the Commission shall, as soon as possible and in any event within 90 days, make a recommendation to the Commission concerning the membership of the Regulatory Committee. To this end the Chairman shall consult, as appropriate, with the Chairman of the Advisory Committee and all members of the Commission. Such recommendation shall comply with the requirements of paragraphs 2 and 4 of this Article and shall ensure:

(a) the inclusion of members of the Commission which, whether through prospecting, scientific research or otherwise, have contributed substantial scientific, technical or environmental information relevant to the identification of the area by the Commission pursuant to Article 41;

(b) adequate and equitable representation of developing country members of the Commission, having regard to the overall balance between developed and developing country members of the Commission, including at least three developing country members of the Commission;

(c) that account is taken of the value of a rotation of membership of Regulatory Committees as a further means of ensuring equitable representation of members of the Commission.

4.

(a) When there are one or more members of the Regulatory Committee referred to in paragraph 2(a) above, the Chairman of the Commission shall make the recommendation in respect of paragraph 2(c)(i) above upon the nomination, if any, of such member or members which shall take into account paragraph 3 above, in particular subparagraph (b) of that paragraph.

(b) In making the recommendation in respect of paragraph 2(c)(ii) above, the Chairman of the Commission shall give full weight to the views (which shall take into account paragraph 3 above) which may be presented on behalf of those members of the Commission which do not assert rights of or claims to territorial sovereignty in Antarctica and, with reference to the requirements of paragraph 3(b) above, to the views which may be presented on behalf of the developing countries among them.

5. The recommendation of the Chairman of the Commission shall be deemed to have been approved by the Commission if it does not decide otherwise at the same meeting as the recommendation is submitted. In taking any decision in accordance with this Article the Commission shall ensure that the requirements of paragraphs 2 and 3 above are complied with and that the nomination, if any, referred to in paragraph 4(a) above is given effect.

6.

(a) If a member of the Commission which has sponsored prospecting in the identified area and submitted the notification pursuant to Article 39 upon which the Commission based its identification of the area pursuant to Article 41, is not a member of the Regulatory Committee by virtue of paragraphs 2 and 3 above, that member of the Commission shall be a member of the Regulatory Committee until such time as an application for an exploration permit is lodged pursuant to Article 44.

(b) If a Party lodging an application for an exploration permit pursuant to Article 44 is not a member of the Regulatory Committee by virtue of paragraphs 2 and 3 above, that Party shall be a member of the Regulatory Committee for its consideration of that application. Should such application result in approval of a Management Scheme pursuant to Article 48, the Party in question shall remain a member of the Regulatory Committee during such time as that Management Scheme is in force with the right to take part in decisions on matters affecting that Management Scheme.

7. Nothing in this Article shall be interpreted as affecting Article IV of the Antarctic Treaty.

Article 30 Regulatory Committee Procedure

1. The first meeting of each Regulatory Committee shall be convened by the Executive Secretary in accordance with Article 43(1). Each Regulatory Committee shall meet thereafter when and where necessary to fulfil its functions.

2. Each member of a Regulatory Committee shall be represented by one representative who may be accompanied by alternate representatives and advisers.

3. Each Regulatory Committee shall elect from among its members a Chairman and Vice-Chairman. The Chairman and Vice-Chairman shall not be representatives of the same Party.

4. Any Party may attend meetings of a Regulatory Committee as an observer.

5. Each Regulatory Committee shall adopt its rules of procedure. Such rules may include provisions concerning the period and number of terms of office which the Chairman and Vice-Chairman may serve and for the rotation of such offices.

Article 31 Functions of Regulatory Committees

1. The functions of each Regulatory Committee shall be:

(a) to undertake the preparatory work provided for in Article 43;

(b) to consider applications for exploration and development permits in accordance with Articles 45, 46 and 54;

(c) to approve Management Schemes and issue exploration and development permits in accordance with Articles 47, 48 and 54;

(d) to monitor exploration and development activities in accordance with Article 52;

(e) to perform the functions assigned to it in Article 51;

(f) to perform the functions relating to inspection assigned to in Article 12;

(g) to perform the functions relating to dispute settlement assigned to it in Article 47(r); and

(h) to perform such other functions as are provided for elsewhere in this Convention.

2. In performing its functions each Regulatory Committee shall seek and take full account of the views of the Advisory Committee provided in accordance with Article 26.

3. Each Regulatory Committee shall, subject to Article 16 and measures in effect pursuant to it and Article 21(1)(h), ensure that a publicly available record of its decisions, and of Management Schemes in force, is maintained.

Article 32 Decision Making in Regulatory Committees

1. Decisions by a Regulatory Committee pursuant to Articles 48 and 54(5) shall be taken by a two-thirds majority of the members present and voting, which majority shall include a simple majority of those members present and voting referred to in Article 29(2)(c)(i) and also a simple majority of those members present and voting referred to in Article 29(2)(c)(ii).

2. Decisions by a Regulatory Committee pursuant to Article 43(3) and (5) shall be taken by a two-thirds majority of the members present and voting, which majority shall include at least half of those members present and voting referred to in Article 29(2)(c)(i) and also at least half of those members present and voting referred to in Article 29(2)(c)(ii).

3. Decisions on all other matters of substance shall be taken by a two-thirds majority of the members present and voting. When a question arises as to whether a matter is one of substance or not, that matter shall be treated as one of substance unless otherwise decided by a two-thirds majority of the members present and voting.

4. Decisions on matters of procedure shall be taken by a simple majority of the members present and voting.

5. Nothing in this Article shall be interpreted as preventing a Regulatory Committee, in taking decisions on matters of substance, from endeavouring to reach a consensus.

Article 33 Secretariat

1. The Commission may establish a Secretariat to serve the Commission, Regulatory Committees, the Advisory Committee, the Special Meeting of Parties and any subsidiary bodies established.

2. The Commission may appoint an Executive Secretary, who shall be the head of the Secretariat, according to such procedures and on such terms and conditions as the Commission may determine. The Executive Secretary shall serve for a four year term and may be reappointed.

3. The Commission may, with due regard to the need for efficiency and economy, authorise such staff establishment for the Secretariat as may be necessary. The Executive Secretary shall appoint, direct and supervise the staff according to such rules and procedures and on such terms and conditions as the Commission may determine.

4. The Secretariat shall perform the functions specified in this Convention and, subject to the approved budget, the tasks entrusted to it by the Commission, Regulatory Committees, the Advisory Committee and the Special Meeting of Parties.

Article 34 Cooperation with International Organisations

1. The Commission and, as appropriate, the Advisory Committee shall cooperate with the Antarctic Treaty Consultative Parties, the Contracting Parties to the Convention for the Conservation of Antarctic Seals, the Commission for the Conservation of Antarctic Marine Living Resources, and the Scientific Committee on Antarctic Research.

2. The Commission shall cooperate with the United Nations, its relevant Specialised Agencies, and, as appropriate, any international organisation which may have competence in respect of mineral resources in areas adjacent to those covered by this Convention.

3. The Commission shall also, as appropriate, cooperate with the International Union for the Conservation of Nature and Natural Resources, and with other relevant international organisations, including non-governmental organisations, having a scientific, technical or environmental interest in Antarctica.

4. The Commission may, as appropriate, accord observer status in the Commission and in the Advisory Committee to such relevant international organisations, including non-governmental organisations, as might assist in the work of the institution in question. Observer status at a Special Meeting of Parties shall be open to such organisations as have been accorded observer status in the Commission or the Advisory Committee.

5. The Commission may enter into agreements with the organisations referred to in this Article.

Article 35 Financial Provisions

1. The Commission shall adopt a budget, on an annual or other appropriate basis, for:

(a) its activities and the activities of Regulatory Committees, the Advisory Committee, the Special Meeting of Parties, any subsidiary bodies established and the Secretariat; and

(b) the progressive reimbursement of any contributions paid under paragraphs 5 and 6 below whenever revenues under paragraph 4 below exceed expenditure.

2. The first draft budget shall be submitted by the Depositary at least 90 days before the first meeting of the Commission. At that meeting the Commission shall adopt its first budget and decide upon arrangements for the preparation of subsequent budgets.

3. The Commission shall adopt financial regulations.

4. Subject to paragraph 5 below, the budget shall be financed, *inter alia*, by:

(a) fees prescribed pursuant to Articles 21(1)(p) and 43(2)(b);

(b) levies on Operators, subject to any measures adopted by the Commission in accordance with Article 21(1)(q), pursuant to Article 47(k)(i); and

(c) such other financial payments by Operators pursuant to Article 47(k)(ii) as may be required to be paid to the institutions of this Convention.

5. If the budget is not fully financed by revenues in accordance with paragraph 4 above, and subject to reimbursement in accordance with paragraph 1(b) above, the budget shall, to the extent of any shortfall and subject to paragraph 6 below, be financed by contributions from the members of the Commission. To this end, the Commission shall adopt as soon as possible a method of equitable sharing of contributions to the budget. The budget shall, in the meantime, to the extent of any shortfall, be financed by equal contributions from each member of the Commission.

6. In adopting the method of contributions referred to in paragraph 5 above the Commission shall consider the extent to which members of and observers at institutions of this Convention may be called upon to contribute to the costs of those institutions.

7. The Commission, in determining the disposition of revenues accruing to it, which are surplus to the requirements for financing the budget pursuant to this Article, shall:

(a) promote scientific research in Antarctica, particularly that related to the Antarctic environment and Antarctic resources, and a wide spread of participation in such research by all Parties, in particular developing country Parties;

(b) ensure that the interests of the members of Regulatory Committees having the most direct interest in the matter in relation to the areas in question are respected in any disposition of that surplus.

8. The finances of the Commission, Regulatory Committees, the Advisory Committee, the Special Meeting of Parties, any subsidiary bodies established and the Secretariat shall accord with the financial regulations adopted by the Commission and shall be subject to an annual audit by external auditors selected by the Commission.

9. Each member of the Commission, Regulatory Committees, the Advisory Committee, the Special Meeting of Parties and any subsidiary bodies established, as well as any observer at a meeting of any of the institutions of this Convention, shall meet its own expenses arising from attendance at meetings.

10. A member of the Commission that fails to pay its contribution for two consecutive years shall not, during the period of its continuing subsequent default, have the right to participate in the taking of decisions in any of the institutions of this Convention. If it continues to be in default for a further two consecutive years, the Commission shall decide what further action should be taken, which may include loss by that member of the right to participate in meetings of the institutions of this Convention. Such member shall resume the full enjoyment of its rights upon payment of the outstanding contributions.

11. Nothing in this Article shall be construed as prejudicing the position of any member of a Regulatory Committee on the outcome of consideration by the Regulatory Committee of terms and conditions in a Management Scheme pursuant to Article 47(k)(ii).

Article 36 Official and Working Languages

The official and working languages of the Commission, Regulatory Committees, the Advisory Committee, the Special Meeting of Parties and any meeting convened under Article 64 shall be English, French, Russian and Spanish.

Chapter III: Prospecting

Article 37 Prospecting

1. Prospecting shall not confer upon any Operator any right to Antarctic mineral resources.

2. Prospecting shall at all times be conducted in compliance with this Convention and with measures in effect pursuant to this Convention, but shall not require authorisation by the institutions of this Convention.

3.

(a) The Sponsoring State shall ensure that its Operators undertaking prospecting maintain the necessary financial and technical means to comply with Article 8(1), and, to the extent that any such Operator fails to take response action as required in Article 8(1), shall ensure that this is undertaken.

(b) The Sponsoring State shall also ensure that its Operators undertaking prospecting maintain financial capacity, commensurate with the nature and level of the activity undertaken and the risks involved, to comply with Article 8(2).

4. In cases where more than one Operator is engaged in prospecting in the same general area, the Sponsoring State or States shall ensure that those Operators conduct their activities with due regard to each others' rights.

5. Where an Operator wishes to conduct prospecting in an area identified under Article 41 in which another Operator has been authorised to undertake exploration or development, the Sponsoring State shall ensure that such prospecting is carried out subject to the rights of

any authorised Operator and any requirements to protect its rights specified by the relevant Regulatory Committee.

6. Each Operator shall ensure upon cessation of prospecting the removal of all installations and equipment and site rehabilitation. On the request of the Sponsoring State, the Commission may waive the obligation to remove installations and equipment.

7. The Sponsoring State shall notify the Commission at least nine months in advance of the commencement of planned prospecting. The notification shall be accompanied by such fees as may be established by the Commission in accordance with Article 21(1)(p) and shall:

(a) identify, by reference to coordinates of latitude and longitude or identifiable geographic features, the general area in which the prospecting is to take place;

(b) broadly identify the mineral resource or resources which are to be the subject of the prospecting;

(c) describe the prospecting, including the methods to be used, and the general programme of work to be undertaken and its expected duration;

(d) provide an assessment of the possible environmental and other impacts of the prospecting, taking into account possible cumulative impacts as referred to in Article 4(5).

(e) describe the measures, including monitoring programmes, to be adopted to avoid harmful environmental consequences or undue interference with other established uses of Antarctica, and outline the measures to be put into effect in the event of any accident and contingency plans for evacuation in an emergency;

(f) provide details on the Operator and certify that it:

(i) has a substantial and genuine link with the Sponsoring State as defined in Article 1(12); and

(ii) is financially and technically qualified to carry out the proposed prospecting in accordance with this Convention; and

(g) provide such further information as may be required by measures adopted by the Commission.

8. The Sponsoring State shall subsequently provide to the Commission:

(a) notification of any changes to the information referred to in paragraph 7 above;

(b) notification of the cessation of prospecting, including removal of any installations and equipment as well as site rehabilitation; and

(c) a general annual report on the prospecting undertaken by the Operator.

9. Notifications and reports submitted pursuant to this Article shall be circulated by the Executive Secretary without delay to all Parties and observers attending Commission meetings.

10. Paragraphs 7, 8 and 9 above shall not be interpreted as requiring the disclosure of data and information of commercial value.

11. The Sponsoring State shall ensure that basic data and information of commercial value generated by prospecting are maintained in archives and may at any time release part of or all such data and information, on conditions which it shall establish, for scientific or environmental purposes.

12. The Sponsoring State shall ensure that basic data and information, other than interpretative data, generated by prospecting are made readily available when such data and information are not, or are no longer, of commercial value and, in any event, no later than 10 years after the year the data and information were collected, unless it certifies to the Commission that the data and information continue to have commercial value. It shall review at regular intervals whether such data and information may be released and shall report the results of such reviews to the Commission.

13. The Commission may adopt measures consistent with this Article relating to the release of data and information of commercial value including requirements for certifications, the frequency of reviews and maximum time limits for extensions of the protection of such data and information.

Article 38 Consideration of Prospecting by the Commission

1. If a member of the Commission considers that a notification submitted in accordance with Article 37(7) or (8), or ongoing prospecting, causes concern as to consistency with this Convention or measures in effect pursuant thereto, that member may request the Sponsoring State to provide a clarification. If that member considers that an adequate response is not forthcoming from the Sponsoring State within a reasonable time, the member may request that the Commission be convened in accordance with Article 19(2)(b) to consider the question and take appropriate action.

2. If measures applicable to all relevant Operators are adopted by the Commission following a request made in accordance with paragraph 1 above, Sponsoring States that have submitted notifications in accordance with Article 37(7) or (8), and Sponsoring States whose Operators are conducting prospecting, shall ensure that the plans and activities of their Operators are modified to the extent necessary to conform with those measures within such time limit as the Commission may prescribe, and shall notify the Commission accordingly.

Chapter IV: Exploration

Article 39 Requests for Identification of an Area for Possible Exploration and Development

1. Any Party may submit to the Executive Secretary a notification requesting that the Commission identify an area for possible exploration and development of a particular mineral resource or resources.

2. Any such notification shall be accompanied by such fees as may be established by the Commission in accordance with Article 21(1)(p) and shall contain:

(a) a precise delineation, including coordinates, of the area proposed for identification;

(b) specification of the resource or resources for which the area would be identified and any relevant data and information, excluding data and information of commercial value, concerning that resource or those resources, including a geological description of the proposed area;

(c) a detailed description of the physical and environmental characteristics of the proposed area;

(d) a description of the likely scale of exploration and development for the resource or resources involved in the proposed area and of the methods which could be employed in such exploration and development;

(e) a detailed assessment of the environmental and other impacts of possible exploration and development for the resource or resources involved, taking into account Articles 15 and 26(4); and

(f) such other information as may be required pursuant to measures adopted by the Commission.

3. A notification under paragraph 1 above shall be referred promptly by the Executive Secretary to all Parties and shall be circulated to observers attending the meeting of the Commission to be convened pursuant to Article 19(2)(a).

Article 40 Action by the Advisory Committee and Special Meeting of Parties

1. The Advisory Committee shall meet as soon as possible after the meeting of the Commission convened pursuant to Article 19(2)(a) has commenced. The Advisory Committee shall provide advice to the Commission on the notification submitted pursuant to Article 39(1). The Commission may prescribe a time limit for the provision of such advice.

2. A Special Meeting of Parties shall meet as soon as possible after circulation of the report of the Advisory Committee and in any event not later than two months after that report has been circulated.

3. The Special Meeting of Parties shall consider whether identification of an area by the Commission in accordance with the request contained in the notification would be consistent with this Convention, and shall report thereon to the Commission as soon as possible and in any event not later than 21 days from the commencement of the meeting.

4. The report of the Special Meeting of Parties to the Commission shall reflect the conclusions reached and all the views expressed by Parties participating in the meeting.

Article 41 Action by the Commission

1. The Commission shall, as soon as possible after receipt of the report of the Special Meeting of Parties, consider whether or not it will identify an area as requested. Taking full account of the views and giving special weight to the conclusions of the Special Meeting of Parties, and taking full account of the views and the conclusions of the Advisory Committee, the Commission shall determine whether such identification would be consistent with this Convention. For this purpose:

(a) the Commission shall ensure that an area to be identified shall be such that, taking into account all factors relevant to such identification, including the physical, geological, environmental and other characteristics of such area, it forms a coherent unit for the purposes of resource management. The Commission shall thus consider whether an area to be identified should include all or part of that which was requested in the notification and, subject to the necessary assessments having been made, adjacent areas not covered by that notification;

(b) the Commission shall consider whether there are, within an area requested or to be identified, any areas in which exploration and development are or should be prohibited or restricted in accordance with Article 13;

(c) the Commission shall specify the mineral resource or resources for which the area would be identified;

(d) the Commission shall give effect to Article 6, by elaborating opportunities for joint ventures or different forms of participation, up to a defined level, including procedures for offering such participation, in possible exploration and development, within the area, by interested Parties which are Antarctic Treaty Consultative Parties and by other interested Parties, in particular, developing countries in either category;

(e) the Commission shall prescribe any additional associated conditions necessary to ensure that an area to be identified is consistent with other provisions of this Convention and may prescribe general guidelines relating to the operational requirements for exploration and development in an area to be identified including measures establishing maximum block sizes and advice concerning related support activities; and

(f) the Commission shall give effect to the requirement in Article 59 to establish additional procedures for the settlement of disputes.

2. After it has completed its consideration in accordance with paragraph 1 above, the Commission shall identify an area for possible exploration and development if there is a consensus of Commission members that such identification is consistent with this Convention.

Article 42 Revision in the Scope of an Identified Area

1. If, after an area has been identified in accordance with Article 41, a Party requests identification of an area, all or part of which is contained within the boundaries of the area already identified but in respect of a mineral resource or resources different from any resource in respect of which the area has already been identified, the request shall be dealt with in accordance with Articles 39, 40 and 41. Should the Commission identify an area in respect of such different mineral resource or resources, it shall have regard, in addition to the requirements of Article 41(1)(a), to the desirability of specifying the boundaries of the area in such a way that it can be assigned to the Regulatory Committee with competence for the area already identified.

2. In the light of increased knowledge bearing on the effective management of the area, and after seeking the views of the Advisory Committee and the relevant Regulatory Committee, the Commission may amend the boundaries of any area it has identified. In making any such amendment the Commission shall ensure that authorised exploration and development in the area are not adversely affected. Unless there are compelling reasons for doing so, the

Commission shall not amend the boundaries of an area it has identified in such a way as to involve a change in the composition of the relevant Regulatory Committee.

Article 43 Preparatory Work by Regulatory Committees

1. As soon as possible after the identification of an area pursuant to Article 41, the relevant Regulatory Committee established in accordance with Article 29 shall be convened.

2. The Regulatory Committee shall:

(a) subject to any measures adopted by the Commission pursuant to Article 21(1)(j) relating to maximum block sizes, divide its area of competence into blocks in respect of which applications for exploration and development may be submitted and make provision for a limit in appropriate circumstances on the number of blocks to be accorded to any Party;

(b) subject to any measures adopted by the Commission pursuant to Article 21(1)(p), establish fees to be paid with any application for an exploration or development permit lodged pursuant to Article 44 or 53;

(c) establish periods within which applications for exploration and development may be lodged, all applications received within each such period being considered as simultaneous;

(d) establish procedures for the handling of applications; and

(e) determine a method of resolving competing applications which are not resolved in accordance with Article 45(4)(a), which method shall, provided that all other requirements of this Convention are satisfied and consistently with measures adopted pursuant to Article 41(1)(d), include priority for the application with the broadest participation among interested Parties which are Antarctic Treaty Consultative Parties, in particular, developing countries in either category.

3. The Regulatory Committee shall adopt guidelines which are consistent with, and which taken together with, the provisions of this Convention and measures of general applicability adopted by the Commission, as well as associated conditions and general guidelines adopted by the Commission when identifying the area, shall, by addressing the relevant items in Article 47, identify the general requirements for exploration and development in its area of competence.

4. Upon adoption of guidelines under paragraph 3 above the Executive Secretary shall, without delay, inform all members of the Commission of the decisions taken by the Regulatory Committee pursuant to paragraphs 2 and 3 above and shall make them publicly available together with relevant measures, associated conditions and general guidelines adopted by the Commission.

5. The Regulatory Committee may from time to time revise guidelines adopted under paragraph 3 above, taking into account any views of the Commission.

6. In performing its functions under paragraphs 3 and 5 above, the Regulatory Committee shall seek and take full account of the views of the Advisory Committee provided in accordance with Article 26.

Article 44 Application for an Exploration Permit

1. Following completion of the work undertaken pursuant to Article 43, any Party, on behalf of an Operator for which it is the Sponsoring State, may lodge with the Regulatory Committee an application for an exploration permit within the periods established by the Regulatory Committee pursuant to Article 43(2)(c).

2. An application shall be accompanied by the fees established by the Regulatory Committee in accordance with Article 43(2)(b) and shall contain:

(a) a detailed description of the Operator, including its managerial structure, financial composition and resources and technical expertise, and, in the case of an Operator being a joint venture, the inclusion of a detailed description of the degree to which Parties are involved in the Operator through, inter alia, juridical persons with which Parties have substantial and genuine links, so that each component of the joint venture can be easily attributed to a Party or Parties for the purposes of identifying the level of Antarctic mineral resource activities thereof, which description of substantial and genuine links shall include a description of equity sharing;

(b) a detailed description of the proposed exploration activities and a description in as much detail as possible of proposed development activities, including:

  (i) an identification of the mineral resource or resources and the block to which the application applies;

  (ii) a detailed explanation of how the proposed activities conform with the general requirements referred to in Article 43(3);

  (iii) a detailed assessment of the environmental and other impacts of the proposed activities, taking into account Articles 15 and 26(4); and

  (iv) a description of the capacity to respond effectively to accidents, especially those with potential environmental effects;

(c) a certification by the Sponsoring State of the capacity of the Operator to comply with the general requirements referred to in Article 43(3).

(d) a certification by the Sponsoring State of the technical competence and financial capacity of the Operator and that the Operator has a substantial and genuine link with it as defined in Article 1(12);

(e) a description of the manner in which the application complies with any measures adopted by the Commission pursuant to Article 41(1)(d); and

(f) such further information as may be required by the Regulatory Committee or in measures adopted by the Commission.

Article 45 Examination of Applications

1. The Regulatory Committee shall meet as soon as possible after an application has been lodged pursuant to Article 44, for the purpose of elaborating a Management Scheme. In performing this function it shall:

(a) determine whether the application contains sufficient or adequate information pursuant to Article 44(2). To this end, it may at any time seek further information from the Sponsoring State consistent with Article 44(2);

(b) consider the exploration and development activities proposed in the application, and such elaborations, revisions or adaptations as necessary:

  (i) to ensure their consistency with this Convention as well as measures in effect pursuant thereto and the general requirements referred to in Article 43(3); and

  (ii) to prescribe the specific terms and conditions of a Management Scheme in accordance with Article 47.

2. At any time during the process of consideration described above, the Regulatory Committee may decline the application if it considers that the activities proposed therein cannot be elaborated, revised or adapted to ensure consistency with this Convention as well as measures in effect pursuant thereto and the general requirements referred to in Article 43(3).

3. In performing its functions under this Article, the Regulatory Committee shall seek and take full account of the views of the Advisory Committee. To that end the Regulatory Committee shall refer to the Advisory Committee all parts of the application which are necessary for it to provide advice pursuant to Article 26, together with any other relevant information.

4. If two or more applications meeting the requirements of Article 44(2) are lodged in respect of the same block:

(a) the competing applicants shall be invited by the Regulatory Committee to resolve the competition amongst themselves, by means of their own choice within a prescribed period;

(b) if the competition is not resolved pursuant to subparagraph (a) above it shall be resolved by the Regulatory Committee in accordance with the method determined by it pursuant to Article 43(2)(e).

Article 46 Management Scheme

In performing its functions under Article 45, including the preparation of a Management Scheme, and under Article 54, the Regulatory Committee shall have recourse to the Sponsoring State and the member or members, if any, referred to in Article 29(2)(a) and, as may be required, one or two additional members of the Regulatory Committee.

Article 47 Scope of the Management Scheme

The Management Scheme shall prescribe the specific terms and conditions for exploration and development of the mineral resource or resources concerned within the relevant block. Such terms and conditions shall be consistent with the general requirements referred to in Article 43(3), and shall cover, *inter alia*:

(a) duration of exploration and development permits;

(b) measures and procedures for the protection of the Antarctic environment and dependent and associated ecosystems, including methods, activities and undertakings by the Operator to minimise environmental risks and damage;

(c) provision for necessary and timely response action, including prevention, containment and clean up and removal measures, for restoration to the status quo ante, and for contingency plans, resources and equipment to enable such action to be taken;

(d) procedures for the implementation of different stages of exploration and development;

(e) performance requirements;

(f) technical and safety specifications, including standards and procedures to ensure safe operations;

(g) monitoring and inspection;

(h) liability;

(i) procedures for the development of mineral deposits which extend outside the area covered by a permit;

(j) resource conservation requirements;

(k) financial obligations of the Operator including:

(l) levies in accordance with measures adopted pursuant to Article 21(1)(q);

(m) payments in the nature of and similar to taxes, royalties or payments in kind;

(n) financial guarantees and insurance;

(o) assignment and relinquishment;

(p) suspension and modification of the Management Scheme, or cancellation of the Management Scheme, exploration or development permit, and the imposition of monetary penalties, in accordance with Article 51;

(q) procedures for agreed modifications;

(r) enforcement of the Management Scheme;

(s) applicable law to the extent necessary;

(t) effective additional procedures for the settlement of disputes;

(u) provisions to avoid and to resolve conflict with other legitimate uses of Antarctica;

(v) data and information collection, reporting and notification requirements;

(w) confidentiality; and

(x) removal of installations and equipment, as well as site rehabilitation.

Article 48 Approval of the Management Scheme

A Management Scheme prepared in accordance with Articles 45, 46 and 47 shall be subject to approval pursuant to Article 32. Such approval shall constitute authorisation for the issue without delay of an exploration permit by the Regulatory Committee. The exploration permit shall accord exclusive rights to the Operator to explore and, subject to Articles 53 and 54, to develop the mineral resource or resources which are the subject of the Management Scheme exclusively in accordance with the terms and conditions of the Management Scheme.

Article 49 Review

1. Any member of the Commission, or any member of a Regulatory Committee, may within one month of a decision by that Regulatory Committee to approve a Management Scheme or issue a development permit, request that the Commission be convened in accordance with Article 19(2)(b) or (c), as the case may be, to review the decision of the Regulatory Committee for consistency with the decision taken by the Commission to identify the area pursuant to Article 41 and any measures in effect relevant to that decision.

2. The Commission shall complete its consideration within three months of a request made pursuant to paragraph 1 above. In performing its functions the Commission shall not assume the functions of the Regulatory Committee, nor shall it substitute its discretion for that of the Regulatory Committee.

3. Should the Commission determine that a decision to approve a Management Scheme or issue a development permit is inconsistent with the decision taken by the Commission to identify the area pursuant to Article 41 and any measures in effect relevant to that decision, it may request that Regulatory Committee to reconsider its decision.

Article 50 Rights of Authorised Operators

1. No Management Scheme shall be suspended or modified and no Management Scheme, exploration or development permit shall be cancelled without the consent of the Sponsoring State except pursuant to Article 51, or Article 54 or the Management Scheme itself.

2. Each Operator authorised to conduct activities pursuant to a Management Scheme shall exercise its rights with due regard to the rights of other Operators undertaking exploration or development in the same identified area.

Article 51 Suspension, Modification or Cancellation of the Management Scheme and Monetary Penalties

1. If a Regulatory Committee determines that exploration or development authorised pursuant to a Management Scheme has resulted or is about to result in impacts on the Antarctic environment or dependent or associated ecosystems beyond those judged acceptable pursuant to this Convention, it shall suspend the relevant activities and as soon as possible modify the Management Scheme so as to avoid such impacts. If such impacts cannot be avoided by the modification of the Management Scheme, the Regulatory Committee shall suspend it, or cancel it and the exploration or development permit.

2. In performing its functions under paragraph 1 above a Regulatory Committee shall, unless emergency action is required, seek and taken into account the views of the Advisory Committee.

3. If a Regulatory Committee determines that an Operator has failed to comply with this Convention or with measures in effect pursuant to it or a Management Scheme applicable to that Operator, the Regulatory Committee may do all or any of the following:

(a) modify the Management Scheme;

(b) suspend the Management Scheme;

(c) cancel the Management Scheme and the exploration or development permit; and

(d) impose a monetary penalty.

4. Sanctions determined pursuant to paragraph 3(a) to (d) above shall be proportionate to the seriousness of the failure to comply.

5. A Regulatory Committee shall cancel a Management Scheme and the exploration or development permit if an Operator ceases to have a substantial and genuine link with the Sponsoring State as defined in Article 1(12).

6. The Commission shall adopt general measures, which may include mitigation, relating to action by Regulatory Committees pursuant to paragraphs 1 and 3 above and, as appropriate, to the consequences of such action. No application pursuant to Article 44 may be lodged until such measures have come into effect.

Article 52 Monitoring in relation to Management Schemes

1. Each Regulatory Committee shall monitor the compliance of Operators with Management Schemes within its area of competence.

2. Each Regulatory Committee, taking into account the advice of the Advisory Committee, shall monitor and assess the effects on the Antarctic environment and on dependent and on associated ecosystems of Antarctic mineral resource activities within its area of competence, particularly by reference to key environmental parameters and ecosystem components.

3. Each Regulatory Committee shall, as appropriate, inform the Commission and the Advisory Committee in a timely fashion of monitoring under this Article.

Chapter V: Development

Article 53 Application for a Development Permit

1. At any time during the period in which an approved Management Scheme and exploration permit are in force for an Operator, the Sponsoring State may, on behalf of that Operator, lodge with the Regulatory Committee an application for a development permit.

2. An application shall be accompanied by the fees established by the Regulatory Committee in accordance with Article 43(2)(b) and shall contain:

(a) an updated description of the planned development identifying any modifications proposed to the approved Management Scheme and any additional measures to be taken, consequent upon such modifications, to ensure consistency with this Convention, including any measures in effect pursuant thereto and the general requirements referred to in Article 43(3);

(b) a detailed assessment of the environmental and other impacts of the planned development, taking into account Articles 15 and 26(4);

(c) a recertification by the Sponsoring State of the technical competence and financial capacity of the Operator and that the Operator has a substantial and genuine link with it as defined in Article 1(12);

(d) a recertification by the Sponsoring State of the capacity of the Operator to comply with the general requirements referred to in Article 43(3);

(e) updated information in relation to all other matters specified in Article 44(2); and

(f) such further information as may be required by the Regulatory Committee or in measures adopted by the Commission.

Article 54 Examination of Applications and Issue of Development Permits

1. The Regulatory Committee shall meet as soon as possible after an application has been lodged pursuant to Article 53.

2. The Regulatory Committee shall determine whether the application contains sufficient or adequate information pursuant to Article 53(2). In performing this function it may at any time seek further information from the Sponsoring State consistent with Article 53(2).

3. The Regulatory Committee shall consider whether:

(a) the application reveals modifications to the planned development previously envisaged;

(b) the planned development would cause previously unforeseen impacts on the Antarctic environment or dependent or associated ecosystems, either as a result of any modifications referred to in subparagraph (a) above or in the light of increased knowledge.

4. The Regulatory Committee shall consider any modifications to the Management Scheme necessary in the light of paragraph 3 above to ensure that the development activities proposed would be undertaken consistently with this Convention as well as measures in effect pursuant thereto and the general requirements referred to in Article 43(3). However, the financial obligations specified in the approved Management Scheme may not be revised without the consent of the Sponsoring State, unless provided for in the Management Scheme itself.

5. If the Regulatory Committee in accordance with Article 32 approves modifications under paragraph 4 above, or if it does not consider that such modifications are necessary, the Regulatory Committee shall issue without delay a development permit.

6. In performing its functions under this Article, the Regulatory Committee shall seek and take full account of the views of the Advisory Committee. To that end the Regulatory Committee shall refer to the Advisory Committee all parts of the application which are necessary for it to provide advice pursuant to Article 26, together with any other relevant information.

Chapter VI: Disputes Settlement

Article 55 Disputes Between Two or More Parties

Articles 56, 57 and 58 apply to disputes between two or more Parties.

Article 56 Choice of Procedure

1. Each Party, when signing, ratifying, accepting, approving or acceding to this Convention, or at any time thereafter, may choose, by written declaration, one or both of the following means for the settlement of disputes concerning the interpretation or application of this Convention:

(a) the International Court of Justice;

(b) the Arbitral Tribunal.

2. A declaration made under paragraph 1 above shall not affect the operation of Article 57(1), (3), (4) and (5).

3. A Party that has not made a declaration under paragraph 1 above or in respect of which a declaration is no longer in force shall be deemed to have accepted the competence of the Arbitral Tribunal.

4. If the parties to a dispute have accepted the same means for the settlement of a dispute, the dispute may be submitted only to that procedure, unless the parties otherwise agree.

5. If the parties to a dispute have not accepted the same means for the settlement of a dispute, or if they have both accepted both means, the dispute may be submitted only to the Arbitral Tribunal, unless the parties otherwise agree.

6. A declaration made under paragraph 1 above shall remain in force until it expires in accordance with its terms or until 3 months after written notice of revocation has been deposited with the Depositary.

7. A new declaration, a notice of revocation or the expiry of a declaration shall not in any way affect proceedings pending before the International Court of Justice or the Arbitral Tribunal, unless the parties to the dispute otherwise agree.

8. Declarations and notices referred to in this Article shall be deposited with the Depositary who shall transmit copies thereof to all Parties.

Article 57 Procedure for Dispute Settlement

1. If a dispute arises concerning the interpretation or application of this Convention, the parties to the dispute shall, at the request of any one of them, consult among themselves as soon as possible with a view to having the dispute resolved by negotiation, enquiry, mediation, conciliation, arbitration, judicial settlement or other peaceful means of their choice.

2. If the parties to a dispute concerning the interpretation or application of this Convention have not agreed on a means for resolving it within 12 months of the request for consultation pursuant to paragraph 1 above, the dispute shall be referred, at the request of any party to the dispute, for settlement in accordance with the procedure determined by the operation of Article 56(4) and (5).

3. If a dispute concerning the interpretation or application of this Convention relates to a measure in effect pursuant to this Convention or a Management Scheme and the parties to such a dispute:

(a) have not agreed on a means for resolving the dispute within 6 months of the request for consultation pursuant to paragraph 1 above, the dispute shall be referred, at the request of any party to the dispute, for discussion in the institution which adopted the instrument in question;

(b) have not agreed on a means for resolving the dispute within 12 months of the request for consultation pursuant to paragraph 1 above, the dispute shall be referred for settlement, at the request of any party to the dispute, to the Arbitral Tribunal.

4. The Arbitral Tribunal shall not be competent to decide or otherwise rule upon any matter within the scope of Article 9. In addition, nothing in this Convention shall be interpreted as conferring competence or jurisdiction on the International Court of Justice or any other tribunal established for the purpose of settling disputes between Parties to decide or otherwise rule upon any matter within the scope of Article 9.

5. The Arbitral Tribunal shall not be competent with regard to the exercise by an institution of its discretionary powers in accordance with this Convention; in no case shall the Arbitral Tribunal substitute its discretion for that of an institution. In addition, nothing in this Convention shall be interpreted as conferring competence or jurisdiction on the International Court of Justice or any other tribunal established for the purpose of settling disputes between Parties with regard to the exercise by an institution of its discretionary powers or to substitute its discretion for that of an institution.

Article 58 Exclusion of Categories of Disputes

1. Any Party, when signing, ratifying, accepting, approving or acceding to this Convention, or at any time thereafter, may, by written declaration, exclude the operation of Article 57(2) or (3) without its consent with respect to a category or categories of disputes specified in the declaration. Such declaration may not cover disputes concerning the interpretation or application of:

(a) any provision of this Convention or of any measure in effect pursuant to it relating to the protection of the Antarctic environment or dependent or associated ecosystems;
(b) Article 7(1);
(c) Article 8;
(d) Article 12;
(e) Article 14;
(f) Article 15; or
(g) Article 37.

2. Nothing in paragraph 1 above or in any declaration made under it shall affect the operation of Article 57(1), (4) and (5).

3. A declaration made under paragraph 1 above shall remain in force until it expires in accordance with its terms or until 3 months after written notice of revocation has been deposited with the Depositary.

4. A new declaration, a notice of revocation or the expiry of a declaration shall not in any way affect proceedings pending before the International Court of Justice or the Arbitral Tribunal, unless the parties to the dispute otherwise agree.

5. Declarations and notices referred to in this Article shall be deposited with the Depositary who shall transmit copies thereof to all Parties.

6. A Party which, by declaration made under paragraph 1 above, has excluded a specific category or categories of disputes from the operation of Article 57(2) or (3) without its consent shall not be entitled to submit any dispute falling within that category or those categories for settlement pursuant to Article 57(2) or (3), as the case may be, without the consent of the other party or parties to the dispute.

Article 59 Additional Dispute Settlement Procedures

1. The Commission, in conjunction with its responsibilities pursuant to Article 41(1), shall establish additional procedures for third-party settlement, by the Arbitral Tribunal or through other similar procedures, of disputes which may arise if it is alleged that a violation of this Convention has occurred by virtue of:

(a) a decision to decline a Management Scheme;
(b) a decision to decline the issue of a development permit; or
(c) a decision to suspend, modify or cancel a Management Scheme or to impose monetary penalties.

2. Such procedures shall:

(a) permit, as appropriate, Parties and Operators under their sponsorship, but not both in respect of any particular dispute, to initiate proceedings against a Regulatory Committee;

(b) require disputes to which they relate to be referred in the first instance to the relevant Regulatory Committee for consideration;

(c) incorporate the rules in Article 57(4) and (5).

Chapter VII: Final Clauses

Article 60 Signature

This Convention shall be open for signature at Wellington from 25 November 1988 to 25 November 1989 by States which participated in the final session of the Fourth Special Antarctic Treaty Consultative Meeting.

Article 61 Ratification, Acceptance, Approval or Accession

1. This Convention is subject to ratification, acceptance or approval by Signatory States.

2. After 25 November 1989 this Convention shall be open for accession by any State which is a Contracting Party to the Antarctic Treaty.

3. Instruments of ratification, acceptance, approval or accession shall be deposited with the Government of New Zealand, hereby designated as the Depositary.

Article 62 Entry Into Force

1. This Convention shall enter into force on the thirtieth day following the date of deposit of instruments of ratification, acceptance, approval or accession by 16 Antarctic Treaty Consultative Parties which participated as such in the final session of the Fourth Special Antarctic Treaty Consultative Meeting, provided that number includes all the States necessary in order to establish all of the institutions of the Convention in respect of every area of Antarctica, including 5 developing countries and 11 developed countries.

2. For each State which, subsequent to the date of entry into force of this Convention, deposits an instrument of ratification, acceptance, approval or accession, the Convention shall enter into force on the thirtieth day following such deposit.

Article 63 Reservations, Declarations and Statements

1. Reservations to this Convention shall not be permitted. This does not preclude a State, when signing, ratifying, accepting, approving or acceding to this Convention, from making declarations or statements, however phrased or named, with a view, *inter alia*, to the harmonisation of its laws and regulations with this Convention, provided that such declarations or statements do not purport to exclude or to modify the legal effect of this Convention in its application to that State.

2. The provisions of this Article are without prejudice to the right to make written declarations in accordance with Article 58.

Article 64 Amendment

1. This Convention shall not be subject to amendment until after the expiry of 10 years from the date of its entry into force. Thereafter, any Party may, by written communication addressed to the Depositary, propose a specific amendment to this Convention and request the convening of a meeting to consider such proposed amendment.

2. The Depositary shall circulate such communication to all Parties. If within 12 months of the date of circulation of the communication at least one-third of the Parties reply favourably to the request, the Depositary shall convene the meeting.

3. The adoption of an amendment considered at such a meeting shall require the affirmative votes of two-thirds of the Parties present and voting, including the concurrent votes of the members of the Commission attending the meeting.

4. The adoption of any amendment relating to the Special Meeting of Parties or to the Advisory Committee shall require the affirmative votes of three-quarters of the Parties present and voting, including the concurrent votes of the members of the Commission attending the meeting.

5. An amendment shall enter into force for those Parties having deposited instruments of ratification, acceptance or approval thereof 30 days after the Depositary has received such instruments of ratification, acceptance or approval from all the members of the Commission.

6. Such amendment shall thereafter enter into force for any other Party 30 days after the Depositary has received its instrument of ratification, acceptance or approval thereof.

7. An amendment that has entered into force pursuant to this Article shall be without prejudice to the provisions of any Management Scheme approved before the date on which the amendment entered into force.

Article 65 Withdrawal

1. Any Party may withdraw from this Convention by giving to the Depositary notice in writing of its intention to withdraw. Withdrawal shall take effect two years after the date of receipt of such notice by the Depositary.

2. Any Party which ceases to be a Contracting Party to the Antarctic Treaty shall be deemed to have withdrawn from this Convention on the date that it ceases to be a Contracting Party to the Antarctic Treaty.

3. Where an amendment has entered into force pursuant to Article 64(5), any Party from which no instrument of ratification, acceptance or approval of the amendment has been received by the Depositary within a period of two years from the date of the entry into force of the amendment shall be deemed to have withdrawn from this Convention on the date of the expiration of a further two year period.

4. Subject to paragraphs 5 and 6 below, the rights and obligations of any Operator pursuant to this Convention shall cease at the time its Sponsoring State withdraws or is deemed to have withdrawn from this Convention.

5. Such Sponsoring State shall ensure that the obligations of its Operators have been discharged no later than the date on which its withdrawal takes effect.

6. Withdrawal from this Convention by any Party shall not affect its financial or other obligations under this Convention pending on the date withdrawal takes effect. Any dispute settlement procedure in which that Party is involved and which has been commenced prior to that date shall continue to its conclusion unless agreed otherwise by the parties to the dispute.

Article 66 Notifications by the Depositary

The Depositary shall notify all Contracting Parties to the Antarctic Treaty of the following:

(a) signatures of this Convention and the deposit of instruments of ratification, acceptance, approval or accession;

(b) the deposit of instruments of ratification, acceptance or approval of any amendment adopted pursuant to Article 64;

(c) the date of entry into force of this Convention and of any amendment thereto;

(d) the deposit of declarations and notices pursuant to Articles 56 and 58;

(e) notifications pursuant to Article 18; and

(f) the withdrawal of a Party pursuant to Article 65.

Article 67 Authentic Texts, Certified Copies and Registration with the United Nations

1. This Convention of which the Chinese, English, French, Russian and Spanish texts are equally authentic shall be deposited with the Government of New Zealand which shall transmit duly certified copies thereof to all Signatory and Acceding States.

2. The Depositary shall also transmit duly certified copies to all Signatory and Acceding States of the text of this Convention in any additional language of a Signatory or Acceding State which submits such text to the Depositary.

3. This Convention shall be registered by the Depositary pursuant to Article 102 of the Charter of the United Nations.

Done at Wellington this second day of June 1988.

In witness whereof, the undersigned, duly authorised, have signed this Convention.

Annex for an Arbitral Tribunal

Article 1

The Arbitral Tribunal shall be constituted and shall function in accordance with this Convention, including this Annex.

Article 2

1. Each Party shall be entitled to designate up to three Arbitrators, at least one of whom shall be designated within three months of the entry into force of this Convention for that Party. Each Arbitrator shall be experienced in Antarctic affairs, with knowledge of international law and enjoying the highest reputation for fairness, competence and integrity. The names of the persons so designated shall constitute the list of Arbitrators. Each Party shall at all times maintain the name of at least one Arbitrator on the list.

2. Subject to paragraph 3 below, an Arbitrator designated by a Party shall remain on the list for a period of five years and shall be eligible for redesignation by that Party for additional five year periods.

3. An Arbitrator may by notice given to the Party which designated that person withdraw his name from the list. If an Arbitrator dies or gives notice of withdrawal of his name from the list or if a Party for any reason withdraws from the list the name of an Arbitrator designated by it, the Party which designated the Arbitrator in question shall notify the Executive Secretary promptly. An Arbitrator whose name is withdrawn from the list shall continue to serve on any Arbitral Tribunal to which that Arbitrator has been appointed until the completion of proceedings before that Arbitral Tribunal.

4. The Executive Secretary shall ensure that an up-to-date list is maintained of the Arbitrators designated pursuant to this Article.

Article 3

1. The Arbitral Tribunal shall be composed of three Arbitrators who shall be appointed as follows:

(a) The party to the dispute commencing the proceedings shall appoint one Arbitrator, who may be its national, from the list referred to in Article 2 of this Annex. This appointment shall be included in the notification referred to in Article 4 of this Annex.

(b) Within 40 days of the receipt of that notification, the other party to the dispute shall appoint the second Arbitrator, who may be its national, from the list referred to in Article 2 of this Annex.

(c) Within 60 days of the appointment of the second Arbitrator, the parties to the dispute shall appoint by agreement the third Arbitrator from the list referred to in Article 2 of this Annex. The third Arbitrator shall not be either a national of, or a person designated by, a party to the dispute, or of the same nationality as either of the first two Arbitrators. The third Arbitrator shall be the Chairman of the Arbitral Tribunal.

(d) If the second Arbitrator has not been appointed within the prescribed period, or if the parties to the dispute have not reached agreement within the prescribed period on the appointment of the third Arbitrator, the Arbitrator or Arbitrators shall be appointed, at the request of any party to the dispute and within 30 days of the receipt of such request, by the President of the International Court of Justice from the list referred to in Article 2 of this Annex and subject to the conditions prescribed in subparagraphs (b) and (c) above. In performing the functions accorded him in this subparagraph, the President of the Court shall consult the parties to the dispute and the Chairman of the Commission.

(e) If the President of the International Court of Justice is unable to perform the functions accorded him in subparagraph (d) above or is a national of a party to the dispute, the functions shall be performed by the Vice-President of the Court, except that if the Vice-President is unable to perform the functions or is a national of a party to the dispute the functions shall be performed by the next most senior member of the Court who is available and is not a national of a party to the dispute.

2. Any vacancy shall be filled in the manner prescribed for the initial appointment.

3. In disputes involving more than two Parties, those Parties having the same interest shall appoint one Arbitrator by agreement within the period specified in paragraph 1(b) above.

Article 4

The party to the dispute commencing proceedings shall so notify the other party or parties to the dispute and the Executive Secretary in writing. Such notification shall include a statement of the claim and the grounds on which it is based. The notification shall be transmitted by the Executive Secretary to all Parties.

Article 5

1. Unless the parties to the dispute agree otherwise, arbitration shall take place at the headquarters of the Commission, where the records of the Arbitral Tribunal shall be kept. The Arbitral Tribunal shall adopt its own rules of procedure. Such rules shall ensure that each party to the dispute has a full opportunity to be heard and to present its case and shall also ensure that the proceedings are conducted expeditiously.

2. The Arbitral Tribunal may hear and decide counterclaims arising out of the dispute.

Article 6

1. The Arbitral Tribunal, where it considers that prima facie it has jurisdiction under this Convention, may:

(a) at the request of any party to a dispute, indicate such provisional measures as it considers necessary to preserve the respective rights of the parties to the dispute;

(b) prescribe any provisional measures which it considers appropriate under the circumstances to prevent serious harm to the Antarctic environment or dependent or associated ecosystems.

2. The parties to a dispute shall comply promptly with any provisional measures prescribed under paragraph 1(b) above pending an award under Article 9 of this Annex.

3. Notwithstanding Article 57(1), (2) and (3) of this Convention, a party to any dispute that may arise falling within the categories specified in Article 58(1)(a) to (g) of this Convention may at any time, by notification to the other party or parties to the dispute and to the Executive Secretary in accordance with Article 4 of this Annex, request that the Arbitral Tribunal be constituted as a matter of exceptional urgency to indicate or prescribe emergency provisional measures in accordance with this Article. In such case, the Arbitral Tribunal shall be constituted as soon as possible in accordance with Article 3 of this Annex, except that the time periods in Article 3(1)(b), (c) and (d) shall be reduced to 14 days in each case. The Arbitral Tribunal shall decide upon the request for emergency provisional measures within two months of the appointment of its Chairman.

4. Following a decision by the Arbitral Tribunal upon a request for emergency provisional measures in accordance with paragraph 3 above, settlement of the dispute shall proceed in accordance with Articles 56 and 57 of this Convention.

Article 7

Any Party which believes it has a legal interest, whether general or individual, which may be substantially affected by the award of an Arbitral Tribunal, may, unless the Arbitral Tribunal decides otherwise, intervene in the proceedings.

Article 8

The parties to the dispute shall facilitate the work of the Arbitral Tribunal and, in particular, in accordance with their law and using all means at their disposal, shall provide it with all relevant documents and information, and enable it, when necessary, to call witnesses or experts and receive their evidence.

Article 9

If one of the parties to the dispute does not appear before the Arbitral Tribunal or fails to defend its case, any other party to the dispute may request the Arbitral Tribunal to continue the proceedings and make its award.

Article 10

1. The Arbitral Tribunal shall decide, on the basis of this Convention and other rules of law not incompatible with it, such disputes as are submitted to it.

2. The Arbitral Tribunal may decide, *ex aequo et bono*, a dispute submitted to it, if the parties to the dispute so agree.

Article 11

1. Before making its award, the Arbitral Tribunal shall satisfy itself that it has competence in respect of the dispute and that the claim or counterclaim is well founded in fact and law.

2. The award shall be accompanied by a statement of reasons for the decision and shall be communicated to the Executive Secretary who shall transmit it to all Parties.

3. The award shall be final and binding on the parties to the dispute and on any Party which intervened in the proceedings and shall be complied with without delay. The Arbitral Tribunal shall interpret the award at the request of a party to the dispute or of any intervening Party.

4. The award shall have no binding force except in respect of that particular case.

5. Unless the Arbitral Tribunal decides otherwise, the expenses of the Arbitral Tribunal, including the remuneration of the Arbitrators, shall be borne by the parties to the dispute in equal shares.

Article 12

All decisions of the Arbitral Tribunal, including those referred to in Articles 5, 6 and 11 of this Annex, shall be made by a majority of the Arbitrators who may not abstain from voting.

Protocol on Environmental Protection to the Antarctic Treaty[42]

Preamble

The States Parties to this Protocol to the Antarctic Treaty, hereinafter referred to as the Parties,

Convinced of the need to enhance the protection of the Antarctic environment and dependent and associated ecosystems;

Convinced of the need to strengthen the Antarctic Treaty system so as to ensure that Antarctica shall continue forever to be used exclusively for peaceful purposes and shall not become the scene or object of international discord;

Bearing in mind the special legal and political status of Antarctica and the special responsibility of the Antarctic Treaty Consultative Parties to ensure that all activities in Antarctica are consistent with the purposes and principles of the Antarctic Treaty;

Recalling the designation of Antarctica as a Special Conservation Area and other measures adopted under the Antarctic Treaty system to protect the Antarctic environment and dependent and associated ecosystems;

Acknowledging further the unique opportunities Antarctica offers for scientific monitoring of and research on processes of global as well as regional importance;

Reaffirming the conservation principles of the Convention on the Conservation of Antarctic Marine Living Resources;

Convinced that the development of a comprehensive regime for the protection of the Antarctic environment and dependent and associated ecosystems is in the interest of mankind as a whole;

Desiring to supplement the Antarctic Treaty to this end;

Have agreed as follows:

Article 1 Definitions

For the purposes of this Protocol:

(a) "The Antarctic Treaty" means the Antarctic Treaty done at Washington on 1 December 1959;

(b) "Antarctic Treaty area" means the area to which the provisions of the Antarctic Treaty apply in accordance with Article VI of that Treaty;

[42] Adopted 4 October 1991, entered into force 14 January 1998, 30 ILM 1455 (1991).

(c) "Antarctic Treaty Consultative Meetings" means the meetings referred to in Article IX of the Antarctic Treaty;
(d) "Antarctic Treaty Consultative Parties" means the Contracting Parties to the Antarctic Treaty entitled to appoint representatives to participate in the meetings referred to in Article IX of that Treaty;
(e) "Antarctic Treaty system" means the Antarctic Treaty, the measures in effect under that Treaty, its associated separate international instruments in force and the measures in effect under those instruments;
(f) "Arbitral Tribunal" means the Arbitral Tribunal established in accordance with the Schedule to this Protocol, which forms an integral part thereof;
(g) "Committee" means the Committee for Environmental Protection established in accordance with Article 11.

Article 2 Objective and Designation

The Parties commit themselves to the comprehensive protection of the Antarctic environment and dependent and associated ecosystems and hereby designate Antarctica as a natural reserve, devoted to peace and science.

Article 3 Environmental Principles

1. The protection of the Antarctic environment and dependent and associated ecosystems and the intrinsic value of Antarctica, including its wilderness and aesthetic values and its value as an area for the conduct of scientific research, in particular research essential to understanding the global environment, shall be fundamental considerations in the planning and conduct of all activities in the Antarctic Treaty area.

2. To this end:

(a) activities in the Antarctic Treaty area shall be planned and conducted so as to limit adverse impacts on the Antarctic environment and dependent and associated ecosystems;
(b) activities in the Antarctic Treaty area shall be planned and conducted so as to avoid:
 (i) adverse effects on climate or weather patterns
 (ii) significant adverse effects on air or water quality;
 (iii) significant changes in the atmospheric, terrestrial (including aquatic), glacial or marine environments;
 (iv) detrimental changes in the distribution, abundance or productivity of species or populations of species of fauna and flora;
 (v) further jeopardy to endangered or threatened species or populations of such species; or
 (vi) degradation of, or substantial risk to, areas of biological, scientific, historic, aesthetic or wilderness significance;
(c) activities in the Antarctic Treaty area shall be planned and conducted on the basis of information sufficient to allow prior assessments of, and informed judgments about, their possible impacts on the Antarctic environment and dependent and associated ecosystems and on the value of Antarctica for the conduct of scientific research; such judgments shall take account of:
 (i) the scope of the activity, including its area, duration and intensity;
 (i) the cumulative impacts of the activity, both by itself and in combination with other activities in the Antarctic Treaty area;
 (ii) whether the activity will detrimentally affect any other activity in the Antarctic Treaty area;
 (iii) whether technology and procedures are available to provide for environmentally safe operations;
 (iv) whether there exists the capacity to monitor key environmental parameters and

ecosystem components so as to identify and provide early warning of any adverse effects of the activity and to provide for such modification of operating procedures as may be necessary in the light of the results of monitoring or increased knowledge of the Antarctic environment and dependent and associated ecosystems; and

(v) whether there exists the capacity to respond promptly and effectively to accidents, particularly those with potential environmental effects;

(d) regular and effective monitoring shall take place to allow assessment of the impacts of ongoing activities, including the verification of predicted impacts;

(e) regular and effective monitoring shall take place to facilitate early detection of the possible unforeseen effects of activities carried on both within and outside the Antarctic Treaty area on the Antarctic environment and dependent and associated ecosystems.

3. Activities shall be planned and conducted in the Antarctic Treaty area so as to accord priority to scientific research and to preserve the value of Antarctica as an area for the conduct of such research, including research essential to understanding the global environment.

4. Activities undertaken in the Antarctic Treaty area pursuant to scientific research programmes, tourism and all other governmental and non-governmental activities in the Antarctic Treaty area for which advance notice is required in accordance with Article VII (5) of the Antarctic Treaty, including associated logistic support activities, shall:

(a) take place in a manner consistent with the principles in this Article; and

(b) be modified, suspended or cancelled if they result in or threaten to result in impacts upon the Antarctic environment or dependent or associated ecosystems inconsistent with those principles.

Article 4 Relationship with the Other Components of the Antarctic Treaty System

1. This Protocol shall supplement the Antarctic Treaty and shall neither modify nor amend that Treaty.

2. Nothing in this Protocol shall derogate from the rights and obligations of the Parties to this Protocol under the other international instruments in force within the Antarctic Treaty system.

Article 5 Consistency with the Other Components of the Antarctic Treaty System

The Parties shall consult and co-operate with the Contracting Parties to the other international instruments in force within the Antarctic Treaty system and their respective institutions with a view to ensuring the achievement of the objectives and principles of this Protocol and avoiding any interference with the achievement of the objectives and principles of those instruments or any inconsistency between the implementation of those instruments and of this Protocol.

Article 6 Co-operation

1. The Parties shall co-operate in the planning and conduct of activities in the Antarctic Treaty area. To this end, each Party shall endeavour to:

(a) promote co-operative programmes of scientific, technical and educational value, concerning the protection of the Antarctic environment and dependent and associated ecosystems;

(b) provide appropriate assistance to other Parties in the preparation of environmental impact assessments;

(c) provide to other Parties upon request information relevant to any potential environmental risk and assistance to minimize the effects of accidents which may damage the Antarctic environment or dependent and associated ecosystems;

(d) consult with other Parties with regard to the choice of sites for prospective stations and other facilities so as to avoid the cumulative impacts caused by their excessive concentration in any location;

(e) where appropriate, undertake joint expeditions and share the use of stations and other facilities; and

(f) carry out such steps as may be agreed upon at Antarctic Treaty Consultative Meetings.

2. Each Party undertakes, to the extent possible, to share information that may be helpful to other Parties in planning and conducting their activities in the Antarctic Treaty area, with a view to the protection of the Antarctic environment and dependent and associated ecosystems.

3. The Parties shall co-operate with those Parties which may exercise jurisdiction in areas adjacent to the Antarctic Treaty area with a view to ensuring that activities in the Antarctic Treaty area do not have adverse environmental impacts on those areas.

Article 7 Prohibition of Mineral Resource Activities

Any activity relating to mineral resources, other than scientific research, shall be prohibited.

Article 8 Environmental Impact Assessment

1. Proposed activities referred to in paragraph 2 below shall be subject to the procedures set out in Annex I for prior assessment of the impacts of those activities on the Antarctic environment or on dependent or associated ecosystems according to whether those activities are identified as having:

(a) less than a minor or transitory impact;

(b) a minor or transitory impact; or

(c) more than a minor or transitory impact.

2. Each Party shall ensure that the assessment procedures set out in Annex I are applied in the planning processes leading to decisions about any activities undertaken in the Antarctic Treaty area pursuant to scientific research programmes, tourism and all other governmental and non-governmental activities in the Antarctic Treaty area for which advance notice is required under Article VII (5) of the Antarctic Treaty, including associated logistic support activities.

3. The assessment procedures set out in Annex I shall apply to any change in an activity whether the change arises from an increase or decrease in the intensity of an existing activity, from the addition of an activity, the decommissioning of a facility, or otherwise.

4. Where activities are planned jointly by more than one Party, the Parties involved shall nominate one of their number to coordinate the implementation of the environmental impact assessment procedures set out in Annex I.

Article 9 Annexes

1. The Annexes to this Protocol shall form an integral part thereof.

2. Annexes, additional to Annexes I-IV, may be adopted and become effective in accordance with Article IX of the Antarctic Treaty.

3. Amendments and modifications to Annexes may be adopted and become effective in accordance with Article IX of the Antarctic Treaty, provided that any Annex may itself make provision for amendments and modifications to become effective on an accelerated basis.

4. Annexes and any amendments and modifications thereto which have become effective in accordance with paragraphs 2 and 3 above shall, unless an Annex itself provides otherwise in respect of the entry into effect of any amendment or modification thereto, become effective for a Contracting Party to the Antarctic Treaty which is not an Antarctic Treaty Consultative Party, or which was not an Antarctic Treaty Consultative Party at the time of the adoption, when notice of approval of that Contracting Party has been received by the Depository.

5. Annexes shall, except to the extent that an Annex provides otherwise, be subject to the procedures for dispute settlement set out in Articles 18 to 20.

Article 10 Antarctic Treaty Consultative Meetings

1. Antarctic Treaty Consultative Meetings shall, drawing upon the best scientific and technical advice available:

(a) define, in accordance with the provisions of this Protocol, the general policy for the comprehensive protection of the Antarctic environment and dependent and associated ecosystems; and

(b) adopt measures under Article IX of the Antarctic Treaty for the implementation of this Protocol.

2. Antarctic Treaty Consultative Meetings shall review the work of the Committee and shall draw fully upon its advice and recommendations in carrying out the tasks referred to in paragraph 1 above, as well as upon the advice of the Scientific Committee on Antarctic Research.

Article 11 Committee for Environmental Protection

1. There is hereby established the Committee for Environmental Protection.

2. Each Party shall be entitled to be a member of the Committee and to appoint a representative who may be accompanied by experts and advisers.

3. Observer status in the Committee shall be open to any Contracting Party to the Antarctic Treaty which is not a Party to this Protocol.

4. The Committee shall invite the President of the Scientific Committee on Antarctic Research and the Chairman of the Scientific Committee for the Conservation of Antarctic Marine Living Resources to participate as observers at its sessions. The Committee may also, with the approval of the Antarctic Treaty Consultative Meeting, invite such other relevant scientific, environmental and technical organisations which can contribute to its work to participate as observers at its sessions.

5. The Committee shall present a report on each of its sessions to the Antarctic Treaty Consultative Meeting. The report shall cover all matters considered at the session and shall reflect the views expressed. The report shall be circulated to the Parties and to observers attending the session, and shall thereupon be made publicly available.

6. The Committee shall adopt its rules of procedure which shall be subject to approval by the Antarctic Treaty Consultative Meeting.

Article 12 Functions of the Committee

1. The functions of the Committee shall be to provide advice and formulate recommendations to the Parties in connection with the implementation of this Protocol, including the operation of its Annexes, for consideration at Antarctic Treaty Consultative Meetings, and to perform such other functions as may be referred to it by the Antarctic Treaty Consultative Meetings. In particular, it shall provide advice on:

(a) the effectiveness of measures taken pursuant to this Protocol;
(b) the need to update, strengthen or otherwise improve such measures;
(c) the need for additional measures, including the need for additional Annexes, where appropriate;
(d) the application and implementation of the environmental impact assessment procedures set out in Article 8 and Annex I;
(e) means of minimising or mitigating environmental impacts of activities in the Antarctic Treaty area;
(f) procedures for situations requiring urgent action, including response action in environmental emergencies;
(g) the operation and further elaboration of the Antarctic Protected Area system;
(h) inspection procedures, including formats for inspection reports and checklists for the conduct of inspections;
(i) the collection, archiving, exchange and evaluation of information related to environmental protection;
(j) the state of the Antarctic environment; and
(k) the need for scientific research, including environmental monitoring, related to the implementation of this Protocol.

2. In carrying out its functions, the Committee shall, as appropriate, consult with the Scientific Committee on Antarctic Research, the Scientific Committee for the Conservation of Antarctic Marine Living Resources and other relevant scientific, environmental and technical organizations.

Article 13 Compliance with this Protocol

1. Each Party shall take appropriate measures within its competence, including the adoption of laws and regulations, administrative actions and enforcement measures, to ensure compliance with this Protocol.

2. Each Party shall exert appropriate efforts, consistent with the Charter of the United Nations, to the end that no one engages in any activity contrary to this Protocol.

3. Each Party shall notify all other Parties of the measures it takes pursuant to paragraphs 1 and 2 above.

4. Each Party shall draw the attention of all other Parties to any activity which in its opinion affects the implementation of the objectives and principles of this Protocol.

5. The Antarctic Treaty Consultative Meetings shall draw the attention of any State which is not a Party to this Protocol to any activity undertaken by that State, its agencies, instrumentalities, natural or juridical persons, ships, aircraft or other means of transport which affects the implementation of the objectives and principles of this Protocol.

Article 14 Inspection

1. In order to promote the protection of the Antarctic environment and dependent and associated ecosystems, and to ensure compliance with this Protocol, the Antarctic Treaty Consultative Parties shall arrange, individually or collectively, for inspections by observers to be made in accordance with Article VII of the Antarctic Treaty.

2. Observers are:

(a) observers designated by any Antarctic Treaty Consultative Party who shall be nationals of that Party; and

(b) any observers designated at Antarctic Treaty Consultative Meetings to carry out inspections under procedures to be established by an Antarctic Treaty Consultative Meeting.

3. Parties shall co-operate fully with observers undertaking inspections, and shall ensure that during inspections, observers are given access to all parts of stations, installations, equipment, ships and aircraft open to inspection under Article VII (3) of the Antarctic Treaty, as well as to all records maintained thereon which are called for pursuant to this Protocol.

4. Reports of inspections shall be sent to the Parties whose stations, installations, equipment, ships or aircraft are covered by the reports. After those Parties have been given the opportunity to comment, the reports and any comments thereon shall be circulated to all the Parties and to the Committee, considered at the next Antarctic Treaty Consultative Meeting, and thereafter made publicly available.

Article 15 Emergency Response Action

1. In order to respond to environmental emergencies in the Antarctic Treaty area, each Party agrees to:

(a) provide for prompt and effective response action to such emergencies which might arise in the performance of scientific research programmes, tourism and all other governmental and non-governmental activities in the Antarctic Treaty area for which advance notice is required under Article VII (5) of the Antarctic Treaty, including associated logistic support activities; and

(b) establish contingency plans for response to incidents with potential adverse effects on the Antarctic environment or dependent and associated ecosystems.

2. To this end, the Parties shall:

(a) co-operate in the formulation and implementation of such contingency plans; and

(b) establish procedures for immediate notification of, and co-operative response to, environmental emergencies.

3. In the implementation of this Article, the Parties shall draw upon the advice of the appropriate international organisations.

Article 16 Liability

Consistent with the objectives of this Protocol for the comprehensive protection of the Antarctic environment and dependent and associated ecosystems, the Parties undertake to elaborate rules and procedures relating to liability for damage arising from activities taking place in the Antarctic Treaty area and covered by this Protocol. Those rules and procedures shall be included in one or more Annexes to be adopted in accordance with Article 9 (2).

Article 17 Report by Parties

1. Each Party shall report annually on the steps taken to implement this Protocol. Such reports shall include notifications made in accordance with Article 13 (3), contingency plans established in accordance with Article 15 and any other notifications and information called for pursuant to this Protocol for which there is no other provision concerning the circulation and exchange of information.

2. Reports made in accordance with paragraph 1 above shall be circulated to all Parties and to the Committee, considered at the next Antarctic Treaty Consultative Meeting, and made publicly available.

Article 18 Dispute Settlement

If a dispute arises concerning the interpretation or application of this Protocol, the parties to the dispute shall, at the request of any one of them, consult among themselves as soon as possible with a view to having the dispute resolved by negotiation, inquiry, mediation, conciliation, arbitration, judicial settlement or other peaceful means to which the parties to the dispute agree.

Article 19 Choice of Dispute Settlement Procedure

1. Each Party, when signing, ratifying, accepting, approving or acceding to this Protocol, or at any time thereafter, may choose, by written declaration, one or both of the following means for the settlement of disputes concerning the interpretation or application of Articles 7, 8 and 15 and, except to the extent that an Annex provides otherwise, the provisions of any Annex and, insofar as it relates to these Articles and provisions, Article 13:

(a) the International Court of Justice;

(b) the Arbitral Tribunal.

2. A declaration made under paragraph 1 above shall not affect the operation of Article 18 and Article 20 (2).

3. A Party which has not made a declaration under paragraph 1 above or in respect of which a declaration is no longer in force shall be deemed to have accepted the competence of the Arbitral Tribunal.

4. If the parties to a dispute have accepted the same means for the settlement of a dispute, the dispute may be submitted only to that procedure, unless the parties otherwise agree.

5. If the parties to a dispute have not accepted the same means for the settlement of a dispute, or if they have both accepted both means, the dispute may be submitted only to the Arbitral Tribunal, unless the parties otherwise agree.

6. A declaration made under paragraph 1 above shall remain in force until it expires in accordance with its terms or until three months after written notice of revocation has been deposited with the Depositary.

7. A new declaration, a notice of revocation or the expiry of a declaration shall not in any way affect proceedings pending before the International Court of Justice or the Arbitral Tribunal, unless the parties to the dispute otherwise agree.

8. Declarations and notices referred to in this Article shall be deposited with the Depositary who shall transmit copies thereof to all Parties.

Article 20 Dispute Settlement Procedure

1. If the parties to a dispute concerning the interpretation or application of Articles 7, 8 or 15 or, except to the extent that an Annex provides otherwise, the provisions of any Annex or, insofar as it relates to these Articles and provisions, Article 13, have not agreed on a means for

resolving it within 12 months of the request for consultation pursuant to Article 18, the dispute shall be referred, at the request of any party to the dispute, for settlement in accordance with the procedure determined by Article 19 (4) and (5).

2. The Arbitral Tribunal shall not be competent to decide or rule upon any matter within the scope of Article IV of the Antarctic Treaty. In addition, nothing in this Protocol shall be interpreted as conferring competence or jurisdiction on the International Court of Justice or any other tribunal established for the purpose of settling disputes between Parties to decide or otherwise rule upon any matter within the scope of Article IV of the Antarctic Treaty.

Article 21 Signature

This Protocol shall be open for signature at Madrid on the 4th of October 1991 and thereafter at Washington until the 3rd of October 1992 by any State which is a Contracting Party to the Antarctic Treaty.

Article 22 Ratification, Acceptance, Approval or Accession

1. This Protocol is subject to ratification, acceptance or approval by signatory States.

2. After the 3rd of October 1992 this Protocol shall be open for accession by any State which is a Contracting Party to the Antarctic Treaty.

3. Instruments of ratification, acceptance, approval or accession shall be deposited with the Government of the United States of America, hereby designated as the Depositary.

4. After the date on which this Protocol has entered into force, the Antarctic Treaty Consultative Parties shall not act upon a notification regarding the entitlement of a Contracting Party to the Antarctic Treaty to appoint representatives to participate in Antarctic Treaty Consultative Meetings in accordance with Article IX (2) of the Antarctic Treaty unless that Contracting Party has first ratified, accepted, approved or acceded to this Protocol.

Article 23 Entry into Force

1. This Protocol shall enter into force on the thirtieth day following the date of deposit of instruments of ratification, acceptance, approval or accession by all States which are Antarctic Treaty Consultative Parties at the date on which this Protocol is adopted.

2. For each Contracting Party to the Antarctic Treaty which, subsequent to the date of entry into force of this Protocol, deposits an instrument of ratification, acceptance, approval or accession, this Protocol shall enter into force on the thirtieth day following such deposit.

Article 24 Reservations

Reservations to this Protocol shall not be permitted.

Article 25 Modification or Amendment

1. Without prejudice to the provisions of Article 9, this Protocol may be modified or amended at any time in accordance with the procedures set forth in Article XII (1) (a) and (b) of the Antarctic Treaty.

2. If, after the expiration of 50 years from the date of entry into force of this Protocol, any of the Antarctic Treaty Consultative Parties so requests by a communication addressed to the Depositary, a conference shall be held as soon as practicable to review the operation of this Protocol.

3. A modification or amendment proposed at any Review Conference called pursuant to paragraph 2 above shall be adopted by a majority of the Parties, including 3/4 of the States which are Antarctic Treaty Consultative Parties at the time of adoption of this Protocol.

4. A modification or amendment adopted pursuant to paragraph 3 above shall enter into force upon ratification, acceptance, approval or accession by 3/4 of the Antarctic Treaty Consultative Parties, including ratification, acceptance, approval or accession by all States which are Antarctic Treaty Consultative Parties at the time of adoption of this Protocol.

5.

(a) With respect to Article 7, the prohibition on Antarctic mineral resource activities contained therein shall continue unless there is in force a binding legal regime on Antarctic mineral resource activities that includes an agreed means for determining whether, and, if so, under which conditions, any such activities would be acceptable. This regime shall fully safeguard the interests of all States referred to in Article IV of the Antarctic Treaty and apply the principles thereof. Therefore, if a modification or amendment to Article 7 is proposed at a Review Conference referred to in paragraph 2 above, it shall include such a binding legal regime.

(b) If any such modification or amendment has not entered into force within 3 years of the date of its adoption, any Party may at any time thereafter notify to the Depositary of its withdrawal from this Protocol, and such withdrawal shall take effect 2 years after receipt of the notification by the Depositary.

Article 26 Notifications by the Depositary

The Depositary shall notify all Contracting Parties to the Antarctic Treaty of the following:

(a) signatures of this Protocol and the deposit of instruments of ratification, acceptance, approval or accession;
(b) the date of entry into force of this Protocol and any additional Annex thereto;
(c) the date of entry into force of any amendment or modification to this Protocol;
(d) the deposit of declarations and notices pursuant to Article 19; and
(e) any notification received pursuant to Article 25 (5) (b).

Article 27 Authentic Texts and Registration with the United Nations

1. This Protocol, done in the English, French, Russian and Spanish languages, each version being equally authentic, shall be deposited in the archives of the Government of the United States of America, which shall transmit duly certified copies thereof to all Contracting Parties to the Antarctic Treaty.

2. This Protocol shall be registered by the Depositary pursuant to Article 102 of the Charter of the United Nations.

Schedule to the Protocol: Arbitration

Article 1

1. The Arbitral Tribunal shall be constituted and shall function in accordance with the Protocol, including this Schedule.

2. The Secretary referred to in this Schedule is the Secretary General of the Permanent Court of Arbitration.

Article 2

1. Each Party shall be entitled to designate up to three Arbitrators, at least one of whom shall be designated within three months of the entry into force of the Protocol for that Party. Each Arbitrator shall be experienced in Antarctic affairs, have thorough knowledge of international law and enjoy the highest reputation for fairness, competence and integrity. The names of the persons so designated shall constitute the list of Arbitrators. Each Party shall at all times maintain the name of at least one Arbitrator on the list.

2. Subject to paragraph 3 below, an Arbitrator designated by a Party shall remain on the list for a period of five years and shall be eligible for redesignation by that Party for additional five year periods.

3. A Party which designated an Arbitrator may withdraw the name of that Arbitrator from the list. If an Arbitrator dies or if a Party for any reason withdraws from the list the name of an Arbitrator designated by it, the Party which designated the Arbitrator in question shall notify the Secretary promptly. An Arbitrator whose name is withdrawn from the list shall continue to serve on any Arbitral Tribunal to which that Arbitrator has been appointed until the completion of proceedings before the Arbitral Tribunal.

4. The Secretary shall ensure that an up-to-date list is maintained of the Arbitrators designated pursuant to this Article.

Article 3

1. The Arbitral Tribunal shall be composed of three Arbitrators who shall be appointed as follows:

(a) The party to the dispute commencing the proceedings shall appoint one Arbitrator, who may be its national, from the list referred to in Article 2.

(b) Within 40 days of the receipt of that notification, the other party to the dispute shall appoint the second Arbitrator, who may be its national, from the list referred to in Article 2.

(c) Within 60 days of the appointment of the second Arbitrator, the parties to the dispute shall appoint by agreement the third Arbitrator from the list referred to in Article 2.
The third Arbitrator shall not be either a national of a party to the dispute, or a person designated for the list referred to in Article 2 by a party to the dispute, or of the same nationality as either of the first two Arbitrators. The third Arbitrator shall be the Chairperson of the Arbitral Tribunal.

(d) If the second Arbitrator has not been appointed within the prescribed period, or if the parties to the dispute have not reached agreement within the prescribed period on the appointment of the third Arbitrator, the Arbitrator or Arbitrators shall be appointed, at the request of any party to the dispute and within 30 days of the receipt of such request, by the President of the International Court of Justice from the list referred to in Article 2 and subject to the conditions prescribed in subparagraphs (b) and (c) above. In performing the functions accorded him or her in this subparagraph, the President of the Court shall consult the parties to the dispute.

(e) If the President of the International Court of Justice is unable to perform the functions accorded him or her in subparagraph (d) above or is a national of a party to the dispute, the functions shall be performed by the Vice-President of the Court, except that if the Vice-President is unable to perform the functions or is a national of a party to the dispute the functions shall be performed by the next most senior member of the Court who is available and is not a national of a party to the dispute.

2. Any vacancy shall be filled in the manner prescribed for the initial appointment.

3. In any dispute involving more than two Parties, those Parties having the same interest shall appoint one Arbitrator by agreement within the period specified in paragraph l (b) above.

Article 4

The party to the dispute commencing proceedings shall so notify the other party or parties to the dispute and the Secretary in writing. Such notification shall include a statement of the claim and the grounds on which it is based. The notification shall be transmitted by the Secretary to all Parties.

Article 5

1. Unless the parties to the dispute agree otherwise, arbitration shall take place at The Hague, where the records of the Arbitral Tribunal shall be kept. the Arbitral Tribunal shall adopt its own rules of procedure. Such rules shall ensure that each party to the dispute has a full opportunity to be heard and to present its case and shall also ensure that the proceedings are conducted expeditiously.

2. The Arbitral Tribunal may hear and decide counterclaims arising out of the dispute.

Article 6

1. The Arbitral Tribunal, where it considers that *prima facie* it has jurisdiction under the Protocol, may:

(a) at the request of any party to a dispute, indicate such provisional measures as it considers necessary to preserve the respective rights of the parties to the dispute;

(b) prescribe any provisional measures which it considers appropriate under the circumstances to prevent serious harm to the Antarctic environment or dependent or associated ecosystems.

2. The parties to the dispute shall comply promptly with any provisional measures prescribed under paragraph 1 (b) above pending an award under Article 10.

3. Notwithstanding the time period in Article 20 of the Protocol, a party to a dispute may at any time, by notification to the other party or parties to the dispute and to the Secretary in accordance with Article 4, request that the Arbitral Tribunal be constituted as a matter of exceptional urgency to indicate or prescribe emergency provisional measures in accordance with this Article. In such case, the Arbitral Tribunal shall be constituted as soon as possible in accordance with Article 3, except that the time periods in Article 3 (1) (b), (c) and (d) shall be reduced to 14 days in each case. The Arbitral Tribunal shall decide upon the request for emergency provisional measures within two months of the appointment of its Chairperson.

4. Following a decision by the Arbitral Tribunal upon a request for emergency provisional measures in accordance with paragraph 3 above, settlement of the dispute shall proceed in accordance with Articles 18, 19 and 20 of the Protocol.

Article 7

Any Party which believes it has a legal interest, whether general or individual, which may be substantially affected by the award of an Arbitral Tribunal, may, unless the Arbitral Tribunal decides otherwise, intervene in the proceedings.

Article 8

The parties to the dispute shall facilitate the work of the Arbitral Tribunal and, in particular, in accordance with their law and using all means at their disposal, shall provide it with all relevant documents and information, and enable it, when necessary, to call witnesses or experts and receive their evidence.

Article 9

If one of the parties to the dispute does not appear before the Arbitral Tribunal or fails to defend its case, any other party to the dispute may request the Arbitral Tribunal to continue the proceedings and make its award.

Article 10

1. The Arbitral Tribunal shall, on the basis of the provisions of the Protocol and other applicable rules and principles of international law that are not incompatible with such provisions, decide such disputes as are submitted to it.

2. The Arbitral Tribunal may decide, *ex aequo et bono*, a dispute submitted to it, if the parties to the dispute so agree.

Article 11

1. Before making its award, the Arbitral Tribunal shall satisfy itself that it has competence in respect of the dispute and that the claim or counterclaim is well founded in fact and law.

2. The award shall be accompanied by a statement of reasons for the decision and shall be communicated to the Secretary who shall transmit it to all Parties.

3. The award shall be final and binding on the parties to the dispute and on any Party which intervened in the proceedings and shall be complied with without delay. The Arbitral Tribunal shall interpret the award at the request of a party to the dispute or of any intervening Party.

4. The award shall have no binding force except in respect of that particular case.

5. Unless the Arbitral Tribunal decides otherwise, the expenses of the Arbitral Tribunal, including the remuneration of the Arbitrators, shall be borne by the parties to the dispute in equal shares.

Article 12

All decisions of the Arbitral Tribunal, including those referred to in Articles 5, 6 and 11, shall be made by a majority of the Arbitrators who may not abstain from voting.

Article 13

1. This Schedule may be amended or modified by a measure adopted in accordance with Article IX (1) of the Antarctic Treaty. Unless the measure specifies otherwise, the amendment

or modification shall be deemed to have been approved, and shall become effective, one year after the close of the Antarctic Treaty Consultative Meeting at which it was adopted, unless one or more of the Antarctic Treaty Consultative Parties notifies the Depositary, within that time period, that it wishes an extension of that period or that it is unable to approve the measure.

2. Any amendment or modification of this Schedule which becomes effective in accordance with paragraph 1 above shall thereafter become effective as to any other Party when notice of approval by it has been received by the Depositary.

Environment Protocol, Annex I: Environmental Impact Assessment

Article 1 Preliminary Stage

1. The environmental impacts of proposed activities referred to in Article 8 of the Protocol shall, before their commencement, be considered in accordance with appropriate national procedures.

2. If an activity is determined as having less than a minor or transitory impact, the activity may proceed forthwith.

Article 2 Initial Environmental Evaluation

1. Unless it has been determined that an activity will have less than a minor or transitory impact, or unless a Comprehensive Environmental Evaluation is being prepared in accordance with Article 3, an Initial Environmental Evaluation shall be prepared. It shall contain sufficient detail to assess whether a proposed activity may have more than a minor or transitory impact and shall include:

(a) a description of the proposed activity, including its purpose, location, duration and intensity; and

(b) consideration of alternatives to the proposed activity and any impacts that the activity may have, including consideration of cumulative impacts in the light of existing and known planned activities.

2. If an Initial Environmental Evaluation indicates that a proposed activity is likely to have no more than a minor or transitory impact, the activity may proceed, provided that appropriate procedures, which may include monitoring, are put in place to assess and verify the impact of the activity.

Article 3 Comprehensive Environmental Evaluation

1. If an Initial Environmental Evaluation indicates or if it is otherwise determined that a proposed activity is likely to have more than a minor or transitory impact, a Comprehensive Environmental Evaluation shall be prepared.

2. A Comprehensive Environmental Evaluation shall include:

(a) a description of the proposed activity including its purpose, location, duration and intensity, and possible alternatives to the activity, including the alternative of not proceeding, and the consequences of those alternatives;

(b) a description of the initial environmental reference state with which predicted changes are to be compared and a prediction of the future environmental reference state in the absence of the proposed activity;

(c) a description of the methods and data used to forecast the impacts of the proposed activity;

(d) estimation of the nature, extent, duration, and intensity of the likely direct impacts of the proposed activity;

(e) consideration of possible indirect or second order impacts of the proposed activity;

(f) consideration of cumulative impacts of the proposed activity in the light of existing activities and other known planned activities;

(g) identification of measures, including monitoring programmes, that could be taken to minimise or mitigate impacts of the proposed activity and to detect unforeseen impacts

and that could provide early warning of any adverse effects of the activity as well as to deal promptly and effectively with accidents;
(h) identification of unavoidable impacts of the proposed activity;
(i) consideration of the effects of the proposed activity on the conduct of scientific research and on other existing uses and values;
(j) an identification of gaps in knowledge and uncertainties encountered in compiling the information required under this paragraph;
(k) a non-technical summary of the information provided under this paragraph; and
(l) the name and address of the person or organization which prepared the Comprehensive Environmental Evaluation and the address to which comments thereon should be directed.

3. The draft Comprehensive Environmental Evaluation shall be made publicly available and shall be circulated to all Parties, which shall also make it publicly available, for comment. A period of 90 days shall be allowed for the receipt of comments.

4. The draft Comprehensive Environmental Evaluation shall be forwarded to the Committee at the same time as it is circulated to the Parties, and at least 120 days before the next Antarctic Treaty Consultative Meeting, for consideration as appropriate.

5. No final decision shall be taken to proceed with the proposed activity in the Antarctic Treaty area unless there has been an opportunity for consideration of the draft Comprehensive Environmental Evaluation by the Antarctic Treaty Consultative Meeting on the advice of the Committee, provided that no decision to proceed with a proposed activity shall be delayed through the operation of this paragraph for longer than 15 months from the date of circulation of the draft Comprehensive Environmental Evaluation.

6. A final Comprehensive Environmental Evaluation shall address and shall include or summarise comments received on the draft Comprehensive Environmental Evaluation. The final Comprehensive Environmental Evaluation, notice of any decisions relating thereto, and any evaluation of the significance of the predicted impacts in relation to the advantages of the proposed activity, shall be circulated to all Parties, which shall also make them publicly available, at least 60 days before the commencement of the proposed activity in the Antarctic Treaty area.

Article 4 Decisions to Be Based on Comprehensive Environmental Evaluations

Any decision on whether a proposed activity, to which Article 3 applies, should proceed, and, if so, whether in its original or in a modified form, shall be based on the Comprehensive Environmental Evaluation as well as other relevant considerations.

Article 5 Monitoring

1. Procedures shall be put in place, including appropriate monitoring of key environmental indicators, to assess and verify the impact of any activity that proceeds following the completion of a Comprehensive Environmental Evaluation.

2. The procedures referred to in paragraph 1 above and in Article 2 (2) shall be designed to provide a regular and verifiable record of the impacts of the activity in order, *inter alia*, to:
(a) enable assessments to be made of the extent to which such impacts are consistent with the Protocol; and
(b) provide information useful for minimising or mitigating impacts, and, where appropriate, information on the need for suspension, cancellation or modification of the activity.

Article 6 Circulation of Information

1. The following information shall be circulated to the Parties, forwarded to the Committee and made publicly available:
(a) a description of the procedures referred to in Article 1;
(b) an annual list of any Initial Environmental Evaluations prepared in accordance with Article 2 and any decisions taken in consequence thereof;
(c) significant information obtained, and any action taken in consequence thereof, from procedures put in place in accordance with Articles 2 (2) and 5; and
(d) information referred to in Article 3 (6).

2. Any Initial Environmental Evaluation prepared in accordance with Article 2 shall be made available on request.

Article 7 Cases of Emergency

1. This Annex shall not apply in cases of emergency relating to the safety of human life or of ships, aircraft or equipment and facilities of high value, or the protection of the environment, which require an activity to be undertaken without completion of the procedures set out in this Annex.

2. Notice of activities undertaken in cases of emergency, which would otherwise have required preparation of a Comprehensive Environmental Evaluation, shall be circulated immediately to all Parties and to the Committee and a full explanation of the activities carried out shall be provided within 90 days of those activities.

Article 8 Amendment or Modification

1. This Annex may be amended or modified by a measure adopted in accordance with Article IX (1) of the Antarctic Treaty. Unless the measure specifies otherwise, the amendment or modification shall be deemed to have been approved, and shall become effective, one year after the close of the Antarctic Treaty Consultative Meeting at which it was adopted, unless one or more of the Antarctic Treaty Consultative Parties notifies the Depositary, within that period, that it wishes an extension of that period or that it is unable to approve the measure.

2. Any amendment or modification of this Annex which becomes effective in accordance with paragraph 1 above shall thereafter become effective as to any other Party when notice of approval by it has been received by the Depositary.

Environment Protocol, Annex II: Conservation of Antarctic Fauna and Flora[43]

Article 1 – Definitions

For the purposes of this Annex:

(a) "native mammal" means any member of any species belonging to the Class Mammalia, indigenous to the Antarctic Treaty area or occurring there naturally through migrations;

(b) "native bird" means any member, at any stage of its life cycle (including eggs), of any species of the Class Aves indigenous to the Antarctic Treaty area or occurring there naturally through migrations;

(c) "native plant" means any member of any species of terrestrial or freshwater vegetation, including bryophytes, lichens, fungi and algae, at any stage of its life cycle (including seeds, and other propagules), indigenous to the Antarctic Treaty area;

(d) "native invertebrate" means any member of any species of terrestrial or freshwater invertebrate, at any stage of its life cycle, indigenous to the Antarctic Treaty area;

(e) "appropriate authority" means any person or agency authorised by a Party to issue permits under this Annex;

(f) "permit" means a formal permission in writing issued by an appropriate authority;

(g) "take" or "taking" means to kill, injure, capture, handle or molest a native mammal or bird, or to remove or damage such quantities of native plants or invertebrates that their local distribution or abundance would be significantly affected;

(h) "harmful interference" means:

  (i) flying or landing helicopters or other aircraft in a manner that disturbs concentrations of native birds or seals;

  (ii) using vehicles or vessels, including hovercraft and small boats, in a manner that disturbs concentrations of native birds or seals;

[43] Amended/revised version adopted by ATCM Measure 16 (2009).

(iii) using explosives or firearms in a manner that disturbs concentrations of native birds or seals;

(iv) wilfully disturbing breeding or moulting native birds or concentrations of native birds or seals by persons on foot;

(v) significantly damaging concentrations of native terrestrial plants by landing aircraft, driving vehicles, or walking on them, or by other means; and

(vi) any activity that results in the significant adverse modification of habitats of any species or population of native mammal, bird, plant or invertebrate.

(i) "International Convention for the Regulation of Whaling" means the Convention done at Washington on 2 December 1946.

(j) "Agreement on the Conservation of Albatrosses and Petrels" means the Agreement done at Canberra on 19 June 2001.

Article 2 – Cases of Emergency

1. This Annex shall not apply in cases of emergency relating to the safety of human life or of ships, aircraft, or equipment and facilities of high value, or the protection of the environment.

2. Notice of activities undertaken in cases of emergency that result in any taking or harmful interference shall be circulated immediately to all Parties and to the Committee.

Article 3 – Protection of Native Fauna and Flora

1. Taking or harmful interference shall be prohibited, except in accordance with a permit.

2. Such permits shall specify the authorised activity, including when, where and by whom it is to be conducted and shall be issued only in the following circumstances:

(a) to provide specimens for scientific study or scientific information;

(b) to provide specimens for museums, herbaria and botanical gardens, or other educational institutions or uses;

(c) to provide specimens for zoological gardens but, in respect of native mammals or birds, only if such specimens cannot be obtained from existing captive collections elsewhere, or if there is a compelling conservation requirement; and

(d) to provide for unavoidable consequences of scientific activities not otherwise authorised under sub-paragraphs (a), (b) or (c) above, or of the construction and operation of scientific support facilities.

3. The issue of such permits shall be limited so as to ensure that:

(a) no more native mammals, birds, plants or invertebrates are taken than are strictly necessary to meet the purposes set forth in paragraph 2 above;

(b) only small numbers of native mammals or birds are killed, and in no case more are killed from local populations than can, in combination with other permitted takings, normally be replaced by natural reproduction in the following season; and

(c) the diversity of species, as well as the habitats essential to their existence, and the balance of the ecological systems existing within the Antarctic Treaty area are maintained.

4. Any species of native mammals, birds, plants and invertebrates listed in Appendix A to this Annex shall be designated "Specially Protected Species", and shall be accorded special protection by the Parties.

5. Designation of a species as a Specially Protected Species shall be undertaken according to agreed procedures and criteria adopted by the ATCM.

6. The Committee shall review and provide advice on the criteria for proposing native mammals, birds, plants or invertebrates for designation as a Specially Protected Species.

7. Any Party, the Committee, the Scientific Committee on Antarctic Research or the Commission for the Conservation of Antarctic Marine Living Resources may propose a species for designation as a Specially Protected Species by submitting a proposal with justification to the ATCM.

8. A permit shall not be issued to a Specially Protected Species unless the taking:

(a) is for a compelling scientific purpose; and

(b) will not jeopardise the survival or recovery of that species or local population;

9. The use of lethal techniques on Specially Protected Species shall only be permitted where there is no suitable alternative technique.

10. Proposals for the designation of a species as a Specially Protected Species shall be forwarded to the Committee, the Scientific Committee on Antarctic Research and, for native mammals and birds, the Commission for the Conservation of Antarctic Marine Living Resources, and as appropriate, the Meeting of the Parties to the Agreement on the Conservation of Albatrosses and Petrels and other organisations. In formulating its advice to the ATCM on whether a species should be designated as a Specially Protected Species, the Committee shall take into account any comments provided by the Scientific Committee on Antarctic Research, and, for native mammals and birds, the Commission for the Conservation of Antarctic Marine Living Resources, and as appropriate, the Meeting of the Parties to the Agreement on the Conservation of Albatrosses and Petrels and other organisations.

11. All taking of native mammals and birds shall be done in the manner that involves the least degree of pain and suffering practicable.

Article 4 – Introduction of Non-native Species and Diseases

1. No species of living organisms not native to the Antarctic Treaty area shall be introduced onto land or ice shelves, or into water, in the Antarctic Treaty area except in accordance with a permit.

2. Dogs shall not be introduced onto land, ice shelves or sea ice.

3. Permits under paragraph 1 above shall:

(a) be issued to allow the importation only of cultivated plants and their reproductive propagules for controlled use, and species of living organisms for controlled experimental use; and

(b) specify the species numbers and, if appropriate, age and sex of the species to be introduced, along with a rationale, justifying the introduction and precautions to be taken to prevent escape or contact with fauna or flora.

4. Any species for which a permit has been issued in accordance with paragraphs 1 and 3 above shall, prior to expiration of the permit, be removed from the Antarctic Treaty area or be disposed of by incineration or equally effective means that eliminates risk to native fauna or flora. The permit shall specify this obligation.

5. Any species, including progeny, not native to the Antarctic Treaty area that is introduced into that area without a permit that has been issued in accordance with paragraph 1 and 3 above, shall be removed or disposed of whenever feasible, unless the removal or disposal would result in a greater adverse environmental impact. Such removal or disposal may include by incineration or by equally effective means, so as to be rendered sterile, unless it is determined that they pose no risk to native flora or fauna. In addition, all reasonable steps shall be taken to control the consequences of that introduction to avoid harm to native fauna or flora.

6. Nothing in this Article shall apply to the importation of food into the Antarctic Treaty area provided that no live animals are imported for this purpose and all plants and animal parts and products are kept under carefully controlled conditions and disposed of in accordance with Annex III to the Protocol.

7. Each Party shall require that precautions are taken to prevent the accidental introduction of micro-organisms (e.g., viruses, bacteria, yeasts, fungi) not present naturally in the Antarctic Treaty area.

8. No live poultry or other living birds shall be brought into the Antarctic Treaty area. All appropriate efforts shall be made to ensure that poultry or avian products imported into Antarctica are free from contamination by diseases (such as Newcastle's Disease, tuberculosis, and yeast infection) which might be harmful to native flora and fauna. Any poultry or avian products

not consumed shall be removed from the Antarctic Treaty area or disposed of by incineration or equivalent means that eliminates the risks of introduction of micro-organisms (e.g. viruses, bacteria, yeasts, fungi) to native flora and fauna.

9. The deliberate introduction of non-sterile soil into the Antarctic Treaty area is prohibited. Parties should, to the maximum extent practicable, ensure that non-sterile soil is not unintentionally imported into the Antarctic Treaty area.

Article 5 – Information

Each Party shall make publicly available information on prohibited activities and Specially Protected Species to all those persons present in or intending to enter the Antarctic Treaty area with a view to ensuring that such persons understand and observe the provisions of this Annex.

Article 6 – Exchange of Information

1. The Parties shall make arrangements for:

(a) collecting and annually exchanging records (including records of permits) and statistics concerning the numbers or quantities of each species of native mammal, bird, plant or invertebrate taken in the Antarctic Treaty area; and

(b) obtaining and exchanging information as to the status of native mammals, birds, plants, and invertebrates in the Antarctic Treaty area, and the extent to which any species or population needs protection.

2. As early as possible, after the end of each austral summer season, but in all cases before 1 October of each year, the Parties shall inform the other Parties as well as the Committee of any step taken pursuant to paragraph 1 above and of the number and nature of permits issued under this Annex in the preceding period of 1 April to 31 March.

Article 7 – Relationship with Other Agreements Outside the Antarctic Treaty System

Nothing in this Annex shall derogate from the rights and obligations of Parties under the International Convention for the Regulation of Whaling.

Article 8 – Review

The Parties shall keep under continuing review measures for the conservation of Antarctic fauna and flora, taking into account any recommendations from the Committee.

Article 9 – Amendment of Modification

1. This Annex may be amended or modified by a measure adopted in accordance with Article IX (1) of the Antarctic Treaty. Unless the measure specifies otherwise, the amendment or modification shall be deemed to have been approved, and shall become effective, one year after the close of the Antarctic Treaty Consultative Meeting at which it was adopted, unless one or more of the Antarctic Treaty Consultative Parties notifies the Depositary, within that time period, that it wishes an extension of that period or that it is unable to approve the measure.

2. Any amendment or modification of this Annex which becomes effective in accordance with paragraph 1 above shall thereafter become effective as to any other Party when notice of approval by it has been received by the Depositary.

Appendices to the Annex

Appendix A: Specially Protected Species

Ommatophoca rossii, Ross Seal.

Environment Protocol, Annex III: Waste Disposal and Waste Management

Article 1 General Obligations

1. This Annex shall apply to activities undertaken in the Antarctic Treaty area pursuant to scientific research programmes, tourism and all other governmental and non-governmental activities in the Antarctic Treaty area for which advance notice is required under Article VII (5) of the Antarctic Treaty, including associated logistic support activities.

2. The amount of wastes produced or disposed of in the Antarctic Treaty area shall be reduced as far as practicable so as to minimise impact on the Antarctic environment and to minimise

interference with the natural values of Antarctica, with scientific research and with other uses of Antarctica which are consistent with the Antarctic Treaty.

3. Waste storage, disposal and removal from the Antarctic Treaty area, as well as recycling and source reduction, shall be essential considerations in the planning and conduct of activities in the Antarctic Treaty area.

4. Wastes removed from the Antarctic Treaty area shall, to the maximum extent practicable, be returned to the country from which the activities generating the waste were organized or to any other country in which arrangements have been made for the disposal of such wastes in accordance with relevant international agreements.

5. Past and present waste disposal sites on land and abandoned work sites of Antarctic activities shall be cleaned up by the generator of such wastes and the user of such sites. This obligation shall not be interpreted as requiring:

(a) the removal of any structure designated as a historic site or monument; or

(b) the removal of any structure or waste material in circumstances where the removal by any practical option would result in greater adverse environmental impact than leaving the structure or waste material in its existing location.

Article 2 Waste Disposal by Removal from the Antarctic Treaty Area

1. The following wastes, if generated after entry into force of this Annex, shall be removed from the Antarctic Treaty area by the generator of such wastes:

(a) radio-active materials;

(b) electrical batteries;

(c) fuel, both liquid and solid;

(d) wastes containing harmful levels of heavy metals or acutely toxic or harmful persistent compounds;

(e) poly-vinyl chloride (PVC), polyurethane foam, polystyrene foam, rubber and lubricating oils, treated timbers and other products which contain additives that could produce harmful emissions if incinerated;

(f) all other plastic wastes, except low density polyethylene containers (such as bags for storing wastes), provided that such containers shall be incinerated in accordance with Article 3 (1);

(g) fuel drums; and

(h) other solid, non-combustible wastes;

provided that the obligation to remove drums and solid non-combustible wastes contained in subparagraphs (g) and (h) above shall not apply in circumstances where the removal of such wastes by any practical option would result in greater adverse environmental impact than leaving them in their existing locations.

2. Liquid wastes which are not covered by paragraph 1 above and sewage and domestic liquid wastes, shall, to the maximum extent practicable, be removed from the Antarctic Treaty area by the generator of such wastes.

3. The following wastes shall be removed from the Antarctic Treaty area by the generator of such wastes, unless incinerated, autoclaved or otherwise treated to be made sterile:

(a) residues of carcasses of imported animals;

(b) laboratory culture of micro-organisms and plant pathogens; and

(c) introduced avian products.

Article 3 Waste Disposal by Incineration

1. Subject to paragraph 2 below, combustible wastes, other than those referred to in Article 2 (1), which are not removed from the Antarctic Treaty area shall be burnt in incinerators which to the maximum extent practicable reduce harmful emissions. Any emission standards and equipment guidelines which may be recommended by, inter alia, the Committee and the Scientific Committee on Antarctic Research shall be taken into account. The solid residue of such incineration shall be removed from the Antarctic Treaty area.

2. All open burning of wastes shall be phased out as soon as practicable, but no later than the end of the 1998/1999 season. Pending the completion of such phase-out, when it is necessary to dispose of wastes by open burning, allowance shall be made for the wind direction and speed and the type of wastes to be burnt to limit particulate deposition and to avoid such deposition over areas of special biological, scientific, historic, aesthetic or wilderness significance including, in particular, areas accorded protection under the Antarctic Treaty.

Article 4 Other Waste Disposal on Land

1. Wastes not removed or disposed of in accordance with Articles 2 and 3 shall not be disposed of onto ice-free areas or into fresh water systems.

2. Sewage, domestic liquid wastes and other liquid wastes not removed from the Antarctic Treaty area in accordance with Article 2, shall, to the maximum extent practicable, not be disposed of onto sea ice, ice shelves or the grounded ice-sheet, provided that such wastes which are generated by stations located inland on ice shelves or on the grounded ice-sheet may be disposed of in deep ice pits where such disposal is the only practicable option. Such pits shall not be located on known ice-flow lines which terminate at ice-free areas or in areas of high ablation.

3. Wastes generated at field camps shall, to the maximum extent practicable, be removed by the generator of such wastes to supporting stations or ships for disposal in accordance with this Annex.

Article 5 Disposal of Waste in the Sea

1. Sewage and domestic liquid wastes may be discharged directly into the sea, taking into account the assimilative capacity of the receiving marine environment and provided that:

(a) such discharge is located, wherever practicable, where conditions exist for initial dilution and rapid dispersal; and

(b) large quantities of such wastes (generated in a station where the average weekly occupancy over the austral summer is approximately 30 individuals or more) shall be treated at least by maceration.

2. The by-product of sewage treatment by the Rotary Biological Contacter process or similar processes may be disposed of into the sea provided that such disposal does not adversely affect the local environment, and provided also that any such disposal at sea shall be in accordance with Annex IV to the Protocol.

Article 6 Storage of Waste

All wastes to be removed from the Antarctic Treaty area, or otherwise disposed of, shall be stored in such a way as to prevent their dispersal into the environment.

Article 7 Prohibited Products

No polychlorinated biphenyls (PCBs), non-sterile soil, polystyrene beads, chips or similar forms of packaging, or pesticides (other than those required for scientific, medical or hygiene purposes) shall be introduced onto land or ice shelves or into water in the Antarctic Treaty area.

Article 8 Waste Management Planning

1. Each Party which itself conducts activities in the Antarctic Treaty area shall, in respect of those activities, establish a waste disposal classification system as a basis for recording wastes and to facilitate studies aimed at evaluating the environmental impacts of scientific activity and associated logistic support. To that end, wastes produced shall be classified as:

(a) sewage and domestic liquid wastes (Group 1);

(b) other liquid wastes and chemicals, including fuels and lubricants (Group 2);

(c) solids to be combusted (Group 3);

(d) other solid wastes (Group 4); and

(e) radioactive material (Group 5).

2. In order to reduce further the impact of waste on the Antarctic environment, each such Party shall prepare and annually review and update its waste management plans (including waste

reduction, storage and disposal), specifying for each fixed site, for field camps generally, and for each ship (other than small boats that are part of the operations of fixed sites or of ships and taking into account existing management plans for ships):

(a) programmes for cleaning up existing waste disposal sites and abandoned work sites;

(b) current and planned waste management arrangements, including final disposal;

(c) current and planned arrangements for analysing the environmental effects of waste and waste management; and

(d) other efforts to minimise any environmental effects of wastes and waste management.

3. Each such Party shall, as far as is practicable, also prepare an inventory of locations of past activities (such as traverses, field depots, field bases, crashed aircraft) before the information is lost, so that such locations can be taken into account in planning future scientific programmes (such as snow chemistry, pollutants in lichens or ice core drilling).

Article 9 Circulation and Review of Waste Management Plans

1. The waste management plans prepared in accordance with Article 8, reports on their implementation, and the inventories referred to in Article 8 (3), shall be included in the annual exchanges of information in accordance with Articles III and VII of the Antarctic Treaty and related Recommendations under Article IX of the Antarctic Treaty.

2. Each Party shall send copies of its waste management plans, and reports on their implementation and review, to the Committee.

3. The Committee may review waste management plans and reports thereon and may offer comments, including suggestions for minimising impacts and modifications and improvement to the plans, for the consideration of the Parties.

4. The Parties may exchange information and provide advice on, inter alia, available low waste technologies, reconversion of existing installations, special requirements for effluents, and appropriate disposal and discharge methods.

Article 10 Management Practices

Each Party shall:

(a) designate a waste management official to develop and monitor waste management plans; in the field, this responsibility shall be delegated to an appropriate person at each site;

(b) ensure that members of its expeditions receive training designed to limit the impact of its operations on the Antarctic environment and to inform them of requirements of this Annex; and

(c) discourage the use of poly-vinyl chloride (PVC) products and ensure that its expeditions to the Antarctic Treaty are advised of any PVC products they may introduce into that area in order that these products may be removed subsequently in accordance with this Annex.

Article 11 Review

This Annex shall be subject to regular review in order to ensure that it is updated to reflect improvement in waste disposal technology and procedures and to ensure thereby maximum protection of the Antarctic environment.

Article 12 Cases of Emergency

1. This Annex shall not apply in cases of emergency relating to the safety of human life or of ships, aircraft or equipment and facilities of high value or the protection of the environment.

2. Notice of activities undertaken in cases of emergency shall be circulated immediately to all Parties and to the Committee.

Article 13 Amendment or Modification

1. This Annex may be amended or modified by a measure adopted in accordance with Article IX (1) of the Antarctic Treaty. Unless the measure specifies otherwise, the amendment or modification shall be deemed to have been approved, and shall become effective, one year after the close of the Antarctic Treaty Consultative Meeting at which it was adopted, unless one or more of the Antarctic Treaty Consultative Parties notifies the Depositary, within that time

period, that it wishes an extension of that period or that it is unable to approve the amendment.

2. Any amendment or modification of this Annex which becomes effective in accordance with paragraph 1 above shall thereafter become effective as to any other Party when notice of approval by it has been received by the Depositary.

Environment Protocol, Annex IV: Prevention of Marine Pollution

Article 1 Definitions

For the purposes of this Annex:

(a) "discharge" means any release howsoever caused from a ship and includes any escape, disposal, spilling, leaking, pumping, emitting or emptying;

(b) "garbage" means all kinds of victual, domestic and operational waste excluding fresh fish and parts thereof, generated during the normal operation of the ship, except those substances which are covered by Articles 3 and 4;

(c) "MARPOL 73/78" means the International Convention for the Prevention of Pollution from Ships, 1973, as amended by the Protocol of 1978 relating thereto and by any other amendment in force thereafter;

(d) "noxious liquid substance" means any noxious liquid substance as defined in Annex II of MARPOL 73/78;

(e) "oil" means petroleum in any form including crude oil, fuel oil, sludge, oil refuse and refined oil products (other than petrochemicals which are subject to the provisions of Article 4);

(f) "oily mixture" means a mixture with any oil content; and

(g) "ship" means a vessel of any type whatsoever operating in the marine environment and includes hydrofoil boats, air-cushion vehicles, submersibles, floating craft and fixed or floating platforms.

Article 2 Application

This Annex applies, with respect to each Party, to ships entitled to fly its flag and to any other ship engaged in or supporting its Antarctic operations, while operating in the Antarctic Treaty area.

Article 3 Discharge of Oil

1. Any discharge into the sea of oil or oily mixture shall be prohibited, except in cases permitted under Annex I of MARPOL 73/78. While operating in the Antarctic Treaty area, ships shall retain on board all sludge, dirty ballast, tank washing waters and other oily residues and mixtures which may not be discharged into the sea. Ships shall discharge these residues only outside the Antarctic Treaty area, at reception facilities or as otherwise permitted under Annex I of MARPOL 73/78.

2. This Article shall not apply to:

(a) the discharge into the sea of oil or oily mixture resulting from damage to a ship or its equipment:

 (i) provided that all reasonable precautions have been taken after the occurrence of the damage or discovery of the discharge for the purpose of preventing or minimising the discharge; and

 (ii) except if the owner or the Master acted either with intent to cause damage, or recklessly and with the knowledge that damage would probably result; or

(b) the discharge into the sea of substances containing oil which are being used for the purpose of combating specific pollution incidents in order to minimise the damage from pollution.

Article 4 Discharge of Noxious Liquid Substances

The discharge into the sea of any noxious liquid substance, and any other chemical or other substances, in quantities or concentrations that are harmful to the marine environment, shall be prohibited.

Article 5 Disposal of Garbage

1. The disposal into the sea of all plastics, including but not limited to synthetic ropes, synthetic fishing nets, and plastic garbage bags, shall be prohibited.

2. The disposal into the sea of all other garbage, including paper products, rags, glass, metal, bottles, crockery, incineration ash, dunnage, lining and packing materials, shall be prohibited.

3. The disposal into the sea of food wastes may be permitted when they have been passed through a comminuter or grinder, provided that such disposal shall, except in cases permitted under Annex V of MARPOL 73/78, be made as far as practicable from land and ice shelves but in any case not less than 12 nautical miles from the nearest land or ice shelf. Such comminuted or ground food wastes shall be capable of passing through a screen with openings no greater than 25 millimeters.

4. When a substance or material covered by this article is mixed with other such substance or material for discharge or disposal, having different disposal or discharge requirements, the most stringent disposal or discharge requirements shall apply.

5. The provisions of paragraphs 1 and 2 above shall not apply to:

(a) the escape of garbage resulting from damage to a ship or its equipment provided all reasonable precautions have been taken, before and after the occurrence of the damage, for the purpose of preventing or minimising the escape; or

(b) the accidental loss of synthetic fishing nets, provided all reasonable precautions have been taken to prevent such loss.

6. The Parties shall, where appropriate, require the use of garbage record books.

Article 6 Discharge of Sewage

1. Except where it would unduly impair Antarctic operations:

(a) each Party shall eliminate all discharge into the sea of untreated sewage ("sewage" being defined in Annex IV of MARPOL 73/78) within 12 nautical miles of land or ice shelves;

(b) beyond such distance, sewage stored in a holding tank shall not be discharged instantaneously but at a moderate rate and, where practicable, while the ship is en route at a speed of no less than 4 knots.

This paragraph does not apply to ships certified to carry not more than 10 persons.

2. The Parties shall, where appropriate, require the use of sewage record books.

Article 7 Cases of Emergency

1. Articles 3, 4, 5 and 6 of this Annex shall not apply in cases of emergency relating to the safety of a ship and those on board or saving life at sea.

2. Notice of activities undertaken in cases of emergency shall be circulated immediately to all Parties and to the Committee.

Article 8 Effect on Dependent and Associated Ecosystems

In implementing the provisions of this Annex, due consideration shall be given to the need to avoid detrimental effects on dependent and associated ecosystems, outside the Antarctic Treaty area.

Article 9 Ship Retention Capacity and Reception Facilities

1. Each Party shall undertake to ensure that all ships entitled to fly its flag and any other ship engaged in or supporting its Antarctic operations, before entering the Antarctic Treaty area, are fitted with a tank or tanks of sufficient capacity on board for the retention of all sludge, dirty ballast, tank washing water and other oily residues and mixtures, and have sufficient capacity on board for the retention of garbage, while operating in the Antarctic Treaty area and have concluded arrangements to discharge such oily residues and garbage at a reception facility after leaving that area. Ships shall also have sufficient capacity on board for the retention of noxious liquid substances.

2. Each Party at whose ports ships depart en route to or arrive from the Antarctic Treaty area undertakes to ensure that as soon as practicable adequate facilities are provided for the reception

of all sludge, dirty ballast, tank washing water, other oily residues and mixtures, and garbage from ships, without causing undue delay, and according to the needs of the ships using them.

3. Parties operating ships which depart to or arrive from the Antarctic Treaty area at ports of other Parties shall consult with those Parties with a view to ensuring that the establishment of port reception facilities does not place an inequitable burden on Parties adjacent to the Antarctic Treaty area.

Article 10 Design, Construction, Manning and Equipment of Ships

In the design, construction, manning and equipment of ships engaged in or supporting Antarctic operations, each Party shall take into account the objectives of this Annex.

Article 11 Sovereign Immunity

1. This Annex shall not apply to any warship, naval auxiliary or other ship owned or operated by a State and used, for the time being, only on government non-commercial service. However, each Party shall ensure by the adoption of appropriate measures not impairing the operations or operational capabilities of such ships owned or operated by it, that such ships act in a manner consistent, so far as is reasonable and practicable, with this Annex.

2. In applying paragraph 1 above, each Party shall take into account the importance of protecting the Antarctic environment.

3. Each Party shall inform the other Parties of how it implements this provision.

4. The dispute settlement procedure set out in Articles 18 to 20 of the Protocol shall not apply to this Article.

Article 12 Preventive Measures and Emergency Preparedness and Response

1. In order to respond more effectively to marine pollution emergencies or the threat thereof in the Antarctic Treaty area, the Parties, in accordance with Article 15 of the Protocol, shall develop contingency plans for marine pollution response in the Antarctic Treaty area, including contingency plans for ships (other than small boats that are part of the operations of fixed sites or of ships) operating in the Antarctic Treaty area, particularly ships carrying oil as cargo, and for oil spills, originating from coastal installations, which enter into the marine environment. To this end they shall:

(a) co-operate in the formulation and implementation of such plans; and

(b) draw on the advice of the Committee, the International Maritime Organization and other international organizations.

2. The Parties shall also establish procedures for cooperative response to pollution emergencies and shall take appropriate response actions in accordance with such procedures.

Article 13 Review

The Parties shall keep under continuous review the provisions of this Annex and other measures to prevent, reduce and respond to pollution of the Antarctic marine environment, including any amendments and new regulations adopted under MARPOL 73/78, with a view to achieving the objectives of this Annex.

Article 14 Relationship with MARPOL 73/78

With respect to those Parties which are also Parties to MARPOL 73/78, nothing in this Annex shall derogate from the specific rights and obligations thereunder.

Article 15 Amendment or Modification

1. This Annex may be amended or modified by a measure adopted in accordance with Article IX (1) of the Antarctic Treaty. Unless the measure specifies otherwise, the amendment or modification shall be deemed to have been approved, and shall become effective, one year after the close of the Antarctic Treaty Consultative Meeting at which it was adopted, unless one or more of the Antarctic Treaty Consultative Parties notifies the Depositary, within that time period, that it wishes an extension of that period or that it is unable to approve the measure.

2. Any amendment or modification of this Annex which becomes effective in accordance with paragraph 1 above shall thereafter become effective as to any other Party when notice of approval by it has been received by the Depositary.

Environment Protocol, Annex V: Area Protection and Management

Article 1 Definitions

For the purposes of this Annex:

(a) "appropriate authority" means any person or agency authorised by a Party to issue permits under this Annex;

(b) "permit" means a formal permission in writing issued by an appropriate authority;

(c) "Management Plan" means a plan to manage the activities and protect the special value or values in an Antarctic Specially Protected Area or an Antarctic Specially Managed Area.

Article 2 Objectives

For the purposes set out in this Annex, any area, including any marine area, may be designated as an Antarctic Specially Protected Area or an Antarctic Specially Managed Area. Activities in those Areas shall be prohibited, restricted or managed in accordance with Management Plans adopted under the provisions of this Annex.

Article 3 Antarctic Specially Protected Areas

1. Any area, including any marine area, may be designated as an Antarctic Specially Protected Area to protect outstanding environmental, scientific, historic, aesthetic or wilderness values, any combination of those values, or ongoing or planned scientific research.

2. Parties shall seek to identify, within a systematic environmental-geographical framework, and to include in the series of Antarctic Specially Protected Areas:

(a) areas kept inviolate from human interference so that future comparisons may be possible with localities that have been affected by human activities;

(b) representative examples of major terrestrial, including glacial and aquatic, ecosystems and marine ecosystems;

(c) areas with important or unusual assemblages of species, including major colonies of breeding native birds or mammals;

(d) the type locality or only known habitat of any species;

(e) areas of particular interest to ongoing or planned scientific research;

(f) examples of outstanding geological, glaciological or geomorphological features;

(g) areas of outstanding aesthetic and wilderness value;

(h) sites or monuments of recognised historic value; and

(i) such other areas as may be appropriate to protect the values set out in paragraph 1 above.

3. Specially Protected Areas and Sites of Special Scientific Interest designated as such by past Antarctic Treaty Consultative Meetings are hereby designated as Antarctic Specially Protected Areas and shall be renamed and renumbered accordingly.

4. Entry into an Antarctic Specially Protected Area shall be prohibited except in accordance with a permit issued under Article 7.

Article 4 Antarctic Specially Managed Areas

1. Any area, including any marine area, where activities are being conducted or may in the future be conducted, may be designated as an Antarctic Specially Managed Area to assist in the planning and co-ordination of activities, avoid possible conflicts, improve co-operation between Parties or minimise environmental impacts.

2. Antarctic Specially Managed Areas may include:

(a) areas where activities pose risks of mutual interference or cumulative environmental impacts; and

(b) sites or monuments of recognised historic value.

3. Entry into an Antarctic Specially Managed Area shall not require a permit.

4. Notwithstanding paragraph 3 above, an Antarctic Specially Managed Area may contain one or more Antarctic Specially Protected Areas, entry into which shall be prohibited except in accordance with a permit issued under Article 7.

Article 5 Management Plans

1. Any Party, the Committee, the Scientific Committee for Antarctic Research or the Commission for the Conservation of Antarctic Marine Living Resources may propose an area for designation as an Antarctic Specially Protected Area or an Antarctic Specially Managed Area by submitting a proposed Management Plan to the Antarctic Treaty Consultative Meeting.

2. The area proposed for designation shall be of sufficient size to protect the values for which the special protection or management is required.

3. Proposed Management Plans shall include, as appropriate:

(a) a description of the value or values for which special protection or management is required;

(b) a statement of the aims and objectives of the Management Plan for the protection or management of those values;

(c) management activities which are to be undertaken to protect the values for which special protection or management is required;

(d) a period of designation, if any;

(e) a description of the area, including:

- (i) the geographical co-ordinates, boundary markers and natural features that delineate the area;
- (ii) access to the area by land, sea or air including marine approaches and anchorages, pedestrian and vehicular routes within the area, and aircraft routes and landing areas;
- (iii) the location of structures, including scientific stations, research or refuge facilities, both within the area and near to it; and
- (iv) the location in or near the area of other Antarctic Specially Protected Areas or Antarctic Specially Managed Areas designated under this Annex, or other protected areas designated in accordance with measures adopted under other components of the Antarctic Treaty system;

(f) the identification of zones within the area, in which activities are to be prohibited, restricted or managed for the purpose of achieving the aims and objectives referred to in subparagraph (b) above;

(g) maps and photographs that show clearly the boundary of the area in relation to surrounding features and key features within the area;

(h) supporting documentation;

(i) in respect of an area proposed for designation as an Antarctic Specially Protected Area, a clear description of the conditions under which permits may be granted by the appropriate authority regarding:

- (i) access to and movement within or over the area;
- (ii) activities which are or may be conducted within the area, including restrictions on time and place;
- (iii) the installation, modification, or removal of structures;
- (iv) the location of field camps;
- (v) restrictions on materials and organisms which may be brought into the area;
- (vi) the taking of or harmful interference with native flora and fauna;
- (vii) the collection or removal of anything not brought into the area by the permit-holder;
- (viii) the disposal of waste;
- (ix) measures that may be necessary to ensure that the aims and objectives of the Management Plan can continue to be met; and
- (x) requirements for reports to be made to the appropriate authority regarding visits to the area;

(j) in respect of an area proposed for designation as an Antarctic Specially Managed Area, a code of conduct regarding:

(i) access to and movement within or over the area;
(ii) activities which are or may be conducted within the area, including restrictions on time and place;
(iii) the installation, modification, or removal of structures;
(iv) the location of field camps;
(v) the taking of or harmful interference with native flora and fauna;
(vi) the collection or removal of anything not brought into the area by the visitor;
(vii) the disposal of waste; and
(viii) any requirements for reports to be made to the appropriate authority regarding visits to the area; and

(k) provisions relating to the circumstances in which Parties should seek to exchange information in advance of activities which they propose to conduct.

Article 6 Designation Procedures

1. Proposed Management Plans shall be forwarded to the Committee, the Scientific Committee on Antarctic Research and, as appropriate, to the Commission for the Conservation of Antarctic Marine Living Resources. In formulating its advice to the Antarctic Treaty Consultative Meeting, the Committee shall take into account any comments provided by the Scientific Committee on Antarctic Research and, as appropriate, by the Commission for the Conservation of Antarctic Marine Living Resources. Thereafter Management Plans may be approved by the Antarctic Treaty Consultative Parties by a measure adopted at an Antarctic Treaty Consultative Meeting in accordance with Article IX(1) of the Antarctic Treaty. Unless the measure specifies otherwise, the Plan shall be deemed to have been approved 90 days after the close of the Antarctic Treaty Consultative Meeting at which it was adopted, unless one or more of the Consultative Parties notifies the Depositary, within that time period, that it wishes an extension of that period or is unable to approve the measure.

2. Having regard to the provisions of Articles 4 and 5 of the Protocol, no marine area shall be designated as an Antarctic Specially Protected Area or an Antarctic Specially Managed Area without the prior approval of the Commission for the Conservation of Antarctic Marine Living Resources.

3. Designation of an Antarctic Specially Protected Area or an Antarctic Specially Managed Area shall be for an indefinite period unless the Management Plan provides otherwise. A review of a Management Plan shall be initiated at least every five years. The Plan shall be updated as necessary.

4. Management Plans may be amended or revoked in accordance with paragraph 1 above.

5. Upon approval Management Plans shall be circulated promptly by the Depositary to all Parties. The Depositary shall maintain a record of all currently approved Management Plans.

Article 7 Permits

1. Each Party shall appoint an appropriate authority to issue permits to enter and engage in activities within an Antarctic Specially Protected Area in accordance with the requirements of the Management Plan relating to that Area. The permit shall be accompanied by the relevant sections of the Management Plan and shall specify the extent and location of the Area, the authorised activities and when, where and by whom the activities are authorised and any other conditions imposed by the Management Plan.

2. In the case of a Specially Protected Area designated as such by past Antarctic Treaty Consultative Meetings which does not have a Management Plan, the appropriate authority may issue a permit for a compelling scientific purpose which cannot be served elsewhere and which will not jeopardise the natural ecological system in that Area.

3. Each Party shall require a permit-holder to carry a copy of the permit while in the Antarctic Specially Protected Area concerned.

Article 8 Historic Sites and Monuments

1. Sites or monuments of recognised historic value which have been designated as Antarctic Specially Protected Areas or Antarctic Specially Managed Areas, or which are located within such Areas, shall be listed as Historic Sites and Monuments.

2. Any Party may propose a site or monument of recognised historic value which has not been designated as an Antarctic Specially Protected Area or an Antarctic Specially Managed Area, or which is not located within such an Area, for listing as a Historic Site or Monument. The proposal for listing may be approved by the Antarctic Treaty Consultative Parties by a measure adopted at an Antarctic Treaty Consultative Meeting in accordance with Article IX(1) of the Antarctic Treaty. Unless the measure specifies otherwise, the proposal shall be deemed to have been approved 90 days after the close of the Antarctic Treaty Consultative Meeting at which it was adopted, unless one or more of the Consultative Parties notifies the Depositary, within that time period, that it wishes an extension of that period or is unable to approve the measure.

3. Existing Historic Sites and Monuments which have been listed as such by previous Antarctic Treaty Consultative Meetings shall be included in the list of Historic Sites and Monuments under this Article.

4. Listed Historic Sites and Monuments shall not be damaged, removed or destroyed.

5. The list of Historic Sites and Monuments may be amended in accordance with paragraph 2 above. The Depositary shall maintain a list of current Historic Sites and Monuments.

Article 9 Information and Publicity

1. With a view to ensuring that all persons visiting or proposing to visit Antarctica understand and observe the provisions of this Annex, each Party shall make available information setting forth, in particular:

(a) the location of Antarctic Specially Protected Areas and Antarctic Specially Managed Areas;

(b) listing and maps of those Areas;

(c) the Management Plans, including listings of prohibitions relevant to each Area;

(d) the location of Historic Sites and Monuments and any relevant prohibition or restriction.

2. Each Party shall ensure that the location and, if possible, the limits, of Antarctic Specially Protected Areas, Antarctic Specially Managed Areas and Historic Sites and Monuments are shown on its topographic maps, hydrographic charts and in other relevant publications.

3. Parties shall co-operate to ensure that, where appropriate, the boundaries of Antarctic Specially Protected Areas, Antarctic Specially Managed Areas and Historic Sites and Monuments are suitably marked on the site.

Article 10 Exchange of Information

1. The Parties shall make arrangements for:

(a) collecting and exchanging records, including records of permits and reports of visits, including inspection visits, to Antarctic Specially Protected Areas and reports of inspection visits to Antarctic Specially Managed Areas;

(b) obtaining and exchanging information on any significant change or damage to any Antarctic Specially Managed Area, Antarctic Specially Protected Area or Historic Site or Monument; and

(c) establishing common forms in which records and information shall be submitted by Parties in accordance with paragraph 2 below.

2. Each Party shall inform the other Parties and the Committee before the end of November of each year of the number and nature of permits issued under this Annex in the preceding period of 1st July to 30th June.

3. Each Party conducting, funding or authorising research or other activities in Antarctic Specially Protected Areas or Antarctic Specially Managed Areas shall maintain a record of such activities and in the annual exchange of information in accordance with the Antarctic

Treaty shall provide summary descriptions of the activities conducted by persons subject to its jurisdiction in such areas in the preceding year.

4. Each Party shall inform the other Parties and the Committee before the end of November each year of measures it has taken to implement this Annex, including any site inspections and any steps it has taken to address instances of activities in contravention of the provisions of the approved Management Plan for an Antarctic Specially Protected Area or Antarctic Specially Managed Area.

Article 11 Cases of Emergency

1. The restrictions laid down and authorised by this Annex shall not apply in cases of emergency involving safety of human life or of ships, aircraft, or equipment and facilities of high value or the protection of the environment.

2. Notice of activities undertaken in cases of emergency shall be circulated immediately to all Parties and to the Committee.

Article 12 Amendment or Modification

1. This Annex may be amended or modified by a measure adopted in accordance with Article IX(1) of the Antarctic Treaty. Unless the measure specifies otherwise, the amendment or modification shall be deemed to have been approved, and shall become effective, one year after the close of the Antarctic Treaty Consultative Meeting at which it was adopted, unless one or more of the Antarctic Treaty Consultative Parties notifies the Depositary, within that time period, that it wishes an extension of that period or that it is unable to approve the measure.

2. Any amendment or modification of this Annex which becomes effective in accordance with paragraph 1 above shall thereafter become effective as to any other Party when notice of approval by it has been received by the Depositary.

Environment Protocol, Annex VI: Liability Arising From Environmental Emergencies

Preamble

The Parties,

Recognising the importance of preventing, minimising and containing the impact of environmental emergencies on the Antarctic environment and dependent and associated ecosystems;

Recalling Article 3 of the Protocol, in particular that activities shall be planned and conducted in the Antarctic Treaty area so as to accord priority to scientific research and to preserve the value of Antarctica as an area for the conduct of such research;

Recalling the obligation in Article 15 of the Protocol to provide for prompt and effective response action to environmental emergencies, and to establish contingency plans for response to incidents with potential adverse effects on the Antarctic environment or dependent and associated ecosystems;

Recalling Article 16 of the Protocol under which the Parties to the Protocol undertook consistent with the objectives of the Protocol for the comprehensive protection of the Antarctic environment and dependent and associated ecosystems to elaborate, in one or more Annexes to the Protocol, rules and procedures relating to liability for damage arising from activities taking place in the Antarctic Treaty area and covered by the Protocol;

Noting further Decision 3 (2001) of the XXIVth Antarctic Treaty Consultative Meeting regarding the elaboration of an Annex on the liability aspects of environmental emergencies, as a step in the establishment of a liability regime in accordance with Article 16 of the Protocol;

Having regard to Article IV of the Antarctic Treaty and Article 8 of the Protocol;

Have agreed as follows:

Article 1 Scope

This Annex shall apply to environmental emergencies in the Antarctic Treaty area which relate to scientific research programmes, tourism and all other governmental and non-governmental activities in the Antarctic Treaty area for which advance notice is required under Article VII(5) of the Antarctic Treaty, including associated logistic support activities. Measures and plans for preventing and responding to such emergencies are also included in this Annex. It shall apply to all tourist vessels that enter the Antarctic Treaty area. It shall also apply to environmental emergencies in the Antarctic Treaty area which relate to other vessels and activities as may be decided in accordance with Article 13.

Article 2 Definitions

For the purposes of this Annex:

(a) "Decision" means a Decision adopted pursuant to the Rules of Procedure of Antarctic Treaty Consultative Meetings and referred to in Decision 1 (1995) of the XIXth Antarctic Treaty Consultative Meeting;

(b) "Environmental emergency" means any accidental event that has occurred, having taken place after the entry into force of this Annex, and that results in, or imminently threatens to result in, any significant and harmful impact on the Antarctic environment;

(c) "Operator" means any natural or juridical person, whether governmental or non-governmental, which organises activities to be carried out in the Antarctic Treaty area. An operator does not include a natural person who is an employee, contractor, subcontractor, or agent of, or who is in the service of, a natural or juridical person, whether governmental or non-governmental, which organises activities to be carried out in the Antarctic Treaty area, and does not include a juridical person that is a contractor or subcontractor acting on behalf of a State operator;

(d) "Operator of the Party" means an operator that organises, in that Party's territory, activities to be carried out in the Antarctic Treaty area, and:

   (i) those activities are subject to authorisation by that Party for the Antarctic Treaty area; or

   (ii) in the case of a Party which does not formally authorise activities for the Antarctic Treaty area, those activities are subject to a comparable regulatory process by that Party.

   The terms "its operator", "Party of the operator", and "Party of that operator" shall be interpreted in accordance with this definition;

(e) "Reasonable", as applied to preventative measures and response action, means measures or actions which are appropriate, practicable, proportionate and based on the availability of objective criteria and information, including:

   (i) risks to the Antarctic environment, and the rate of its natural recovery;

   (ii) risks to human life and safety; and

   (iii) technological and economic feasibility;

(f) "Response action" means reasonable measures taken after an environmental emergency has occurred to avoid, minimise or contain the impact of that environmental emergency, which to that end may include clean-up in appropriate circumstances, and includes determining the extent of that emergency and its impact;

(g) "The Parties" means the States for which this Annex has become effective in accordance with Article 9 of the Protocol.

Article 3 Preventative Measures

1. Each Party shall require its operators to undertake reasonable preventative measures that are designed to reduce the risk of environmental emergencies and their potential adverse impact.

2. Preventative measures may include:

(a) specialised structures or equipment incorporated into the design and construction of facilities and means of transportation;
(b) specialised procedures incorporated into the operation or maintenance of facilities and means of transportation; and
(c) specialised training of personnel.

Article 4 Contingency Plans

1. Each Party shall require its operators to:
(a) establish contingency plans for responses to incidents with potential adverse impacts on the Antarctic environment or dependent and associated ecosystems; and
(b) co-operate in the formulation and implementation of such contingency plans.
2. Contingency plans shall include, when appropriate, the following components:
(a) procedures for conducting an assessment of the nature of the incident;
(b) notification procedures;
(c) identification and mobilisation of resources;
(d) response plans;
(e) training;
(f) record keeping; and
(g) demobilisation.
3. Each Party shall establish and implement procedures for immediate notification of, and co-operative responses to, environmental emergencies, and shall promote the use of notification procedures and co-operative response procedures by its operators that cause environmental emergencies.

Article 5 Response Action

1. Each Party shall require each of its operators to take prompt and effective response action to environmental emergencies arising from the activities of that operator.
2. In the event that an operator does not take prompt and effective response action, the Party of that operator and other Parties are encouraged to take such action, including through their agents and operators specifically authorised by them to take such action on their behalf.
3.
(a) Other Parties wishing to take response action to an environmental emergency pursuant to paragraph 2 above shall notify their intention to the Party of the operator and the Secretariat of the Antarctic Treaty beforehand with a view to the Party of the operator taking response action itself, except where a threat of significant and harmful impact to the Antarctic environment is imminent and it would be reasonable in all the circumstances to take immediate response action, in which case they shall notify the Party of the operator and the Secretariat of the Antarctic Treaty as soon as possible.
(b) Such other Parties shall not take response action to an environmental emergency pursuant to paragraph 2 above, unless a threat of significant and harmful impact to the Antarctic environment is imminent and it would be reasonable in all the circumstances to take immediate response action, or the Party of the operator has failed within a reasonable time to notify the Secretariat of the Antarctic Treaty that it will take the response action itself, or where that response action has not been taken within a reasonable time after such notification.
(c) In the case that the Party of the operator takes response action itself, but is willing to be assisted by another Party or Parties, the Party of the operator shall coordinate the response action.
4. However, where it is unclear which, if any, Party is the Party of the operator or it appears that there may be more than one such Party, any Party taking response action shall make best endeavours to consult as appropriate and shall, where practicable, notify the Secretariat of the Antarctic Treaty of the circumstances.

5. Parties taking response action shall consult and coordinate their action with all other Parties taking response action, carrying out activities in the vicinity of the environmental emergency, or otherwise impacted by the environmental emergency, and shall, where practicable, take into account all relevant expert guidance which has been provided by permanent observer delegations to the Antarctic Treaty Consultative Meeting, by other organisations, or by other relevant experts.

Article 6 Liability

1. An operator that fails to take prompt and effective response action to environmental emergencies arising from its activities shall be liable to pay the costs of response action taken by Parties pursuant to Article 5(2) to such Parties.

2.

(a) When a State operator should have taken prompt and effective response action but did not, and no response action was taken by any Party, the State operator shall be liable to pay the costs of the response action which should have been undertaken, into the fund referred to in Article 12.

(b) When a non-State operator should have taken prompt and effective response action but did not, and no response action was taken by any Party, the non-State operator shall be liable to pay an amount of money that reflects as much as possible the costs of the response action that should have been taken. Such money is to be paid directly to the fund referred to in Article 12, to the Party of that operator or to the Party that enforces the mechanism referred to in Article 7(3). A Party receiving such money shall make best efforts to make a contribution to the fund referred to in Article 12 which at least equals the money received from the operator.

3. Liability shall be strict.

4. When an environmental emergency arises from the activities of two or more operators, they shall be jointly and severally liable, except that an operator which establishes that only part of the environmental emergency results from its activities shall be liable in respect of that part only.

5. Notwithstanding that a Party is liable under this Article for its failure to provide for prompt and effective response action to environmental emergencies caused by its warships, naval auxiliaries, or other ships or aircraft owned or operated by it and used, for the time being, only on government non-commercial service, nothing in this Annex is intended to affect the sovereign immunity under international law of such warships, naval auxiliaries, or other ships or aircraft.

Article 7 Actions

1. Only a Party that has taken response action pursuant to Article 5(2) may bring an action against a non-State operator for liability pursuant to Article 6(1) and such action may be brought in the courts of not more than one Party where the operator is incorporated or has its principal place of business or his or her habitual place of residence. However, should the operator not be incorporated in a Party or have its principal place of business or his or her habitual place of residence in a Party, the action may be brought in the courts of the Party of the operator within the meaning of Article 2(d). Such actions for compensation shall be brought within three years of the commencement of the response action or within three years of the date on which the Party bringing the action knew or ought reasonably to have known the identity of the operator, whichever is later. In no event shall an action against a non-State operator be commenced later than 15 years after the commencement of the response action.

2. Each Party shall ensure that its courts possess the necessary jurisdiction to entertain actions under paragraph 1 above.

3. Each Party shall ensure that there is a mechanism in place under its domestic law for the enforcement of Article 6(2)(b) with respect to any of its non-State operators within the

meaning of Article 2(d), as well as where possible with respect to any non-State operator that is incorporated or has its principal place of business or his or her habitual place of residence in that Party. Each Party shall inform all other Parties of this mechanism in accordance with Article 13(3) of the Protocol. Where there are multiple Parties that are capable of enforcing Article 6(2)(b) against any given non-State operator under this paragraph, such Parties should consult amongst themselves as to which Party should take enforcement action. The mechanism referred to in this paragraph shall not be invoked later than 15 years after the date the Party seeking to invoke the mechanism became aware of the environmental emergency.

4. The liability of a Party as a State operator under Article 6(1) shall be resolved only in accordance with any enquiry procedure which may be established by the Parties, the provisions of Articles 18, 19 and 20 of the Protocol and, as applicable, the Schedule to the Protocol on Arbitration.

5.

(a) The liability of a Party as a State operator under Article 6(2)(a) shall be resolved only by the Antarctic Treaty Consultative Meeting and, should the question remain unresolved, only in accordance with any enquiry procedure which may be established by the Parties, the provisions of Articles 18, 19 and 20 of the Protocol and, as applicable, the Schedule to the Protocol on Arbitration.

(b) The costs of the response action which should have been undertaken and was not, to be paid by a State operator into the fund referred to in Article 12, shall be approved by means of a Decision. The Antarctic Treaty Consultative Meeting should seek the advice of the Committee on Environmental Protection as appropriate.

6. Under this Annex, the provisions of Articles 19(4), 19(5), and 20(1) of the Protocol, and, as applicable, the Schedule to the Protocol on Arbitration, are only applicable to liability of a Party as a State operator for compensation for response action that has been undertaken to an environmental emergency or for payment into the fund.

Article 8 Exemptions from Liability

1. An operator shall not be liable pursuant to Article 6 if it proves that the environmental emergency was caused by:

(a) an act or omission necessary to protect human life or safety;

(b) an event constituting in the circumstances of Antarctica a natural disaster of an exceptional character, which could not have been reasonably foreseen, either generally or in the particular case, provided all reasonable preventative measures have been taken that are designed to reduce the risk of environmental emergencies and their potential adverse impact;

(c) an act of terrorism; or

(d) an act of belligerency against the activities of the operator.

2. A Party, or its agents or operators specifically authorised by it to take such action on its behalf, shall not be liable for an environmental emergency resulting from response action taken by it pursuant to Article 5(2) to the extent that such response action was reasonable in all the circumstances.

Article 9 Limits of Liability

1. The maximum amount for which each operator may be liable under Article 6(1) or Article 6(2), in respect of each environmental emergency, shall be as follows:

(a) for an environmental emergency arising from an event involving a ship:

(i) one million SDR for a ship with a tonnage not exceeding 2,000 tons;

(ii) for a ship with a tonnage in excess thereof, the following amount in addition to that referred to in (i) above:

- for each ton from 2,001 to 30,000 tons, 400 SDR;
- for each ton from 30,001 to 70,000 tons, 300 SDR; and
- for each ton in excess of 70,000 tons, 200 SDR;

(b) for an environmental emergency arising from an event which does not involve a ship, three million SDR.

2.

(a) Notwithstanding paragraph 1(a) above, this Annex shall not affect:

(i) the liability or right to limit liability under any applicable international limitation of liability treaty; or

(ii) the application of a reservation made under any such treaty to exclude the application of the limits therein for certain claims;

provided that the applicable limits are at least as high as the following: for a ship with a tonnage not exceeding 2,000 tons, one million SDR; and for a ship with a tonnage in excess thereof, in addition, for a ship with a tonnage between 2,001 and 30,000 tons, 400 SDR for each ton; for a ship with a tonnage from 30,001 to 70,000 tons, 300 SDR for each ton; and for each ton in excess of 70,000 tons, 200 SDR for each ton.

(b) Nothing in subparagraph (a) above shall affect either the limits of liability set out in paragraph 1(a) above that apply to a Party as a State operator, or the rights and obligations of Parties that are not parties to any such treaty as mentioned above, or the application of Article 7(1) and Article 7(2).

3. Liability shall not be limited if it is proved that the environmental emergency resulted from an act or omission of the operator, committed with the intent to cause such emergency, or recklessly and with knowledge that such emergency would probably result.

4. The Antarctic Treaty Consultative Meeting shall review the limits in paragraphs 1(a) and 1(b) above every three years, or sooner at the request of any Party. Any amendments to these limits, which shall be determined after consultation amongst the Parties and on the basis of advice including scientific and technical advice, shall be made under the procedure set out in Article 13(2).

5. For the purpose of this Article:

(a) "ship" means a vessel of any type whatsoever operating in the marine environment and includes hydrofoil boats, air-cushion vehicles, submersibles, floating craft and fixed or floating platforms;

(b) "SDR" means the Special Drawing Rights as defined by the International Monetary Fund;

(c) a ship's tonnage shall be the gross tonnage calculated in accordance with the tonnage measurement rules contained in Annex I of the International Convention on Tonnage Measurement of Ships, 1969.

Article 10 State Liability

A Party shall not be liable for the failure of an operator, other than its State operators, to take response action to the extent that that Party took appropriate measures within its competence, including the adoption of laws and regulations, administrative actions and enforcement measures, to ensure compliance with this Annex.

Article 11 Insurance and Other Financial Security

1. Each Party shall require its operators to maintain adequate insurance or other financial security, such as the guarantee of a bank or similar financial institution, to cover liability under Article 6(1) up to the applicable limits set out in Article 9(1) and Article 9(2).

2. Each Party may require its operators to maintain adequate insurance or other financial security, such as the guarantee of a bank or similar financial institution, to cover liability under Article 6(2) up to the applicable limits set out in Article 9(1) and Article 9(2).

3. Notwithstanding paragraphs 1 and 2 above, a Party may maintain self-insurance in respect of its State operators, including those carrying out activities in the furtherance of scientific research.

Article 12 The Fund

1. The Secretariat of the Antarctic Treaty shall maintain and administer a fund, in accordance with Decisions including terms of reference to be adopted by the Parties, to provide, *inter alia*,

for the reimbursement of the reasonable and justified costs incurred by a Party or Parties in taking response action pursuant to Article 5(2).

2. Any Party or Parties may make a proposal to the Antarctic Treaty Consultative Meeting for reimbursement to be paid from the fund. Such a proposal may be approved by the Antarctic Treaty Consultative Meeting, in which case it shall be approved by way of a Decision. The Antarctic Treaty Consultative Meeting may seek the advice of the Committee of Environmental Protection on such a proposal, as appropriate.

3. Special circumstances and criteria, such as: the fact that the responsible operator was an operator of the Party seeking reimbursement; the identity of the responsible operator remaining unknown or not subject to the provisions of this Annex; the unforeseen failure of the relevant insurance company or financial institution; or an exemption in Article 8 applying, shall be duly taken into account by the Antarctic Treaty Consultative Meeting under paragraph 2 above.

4. Any State or person may make voluntary contributions to the fund.

Article 13 Amendment or Modification

1. This Annex may be amended or modified by a Measure adopted in accordance with Article IX(1) of the Antarctic Treaty.

2. In the case of a Measure pursuant to Article 9(4), and in any other case unless the Measure in question specifies otherwise, the amendment or modification shall be deemed to have been approved, and shall become effective, one year after the close of the Antarctic Treaty Consultative Meeting at which it was adopted, unless one or more Antarctic Treaty Consultative Parties notifies the Depositary, within that time period, that it wishes any extension of that period or that it is unable to approve the Measure.

3. Any amendment or modification of this Annex which becomes effective in accordance with paragraph 1 or 2 above shall thereafter become effective as to any other Party when notice of approval by it has been received by the Depositary.

List of State Parties to the ATS Treaties

Country	Entry into force	Consultative status	Environment Protocol	CCAS	CCAMLR
Argentina	23 Jun 1961	23 Jun 1961	14 Jan 1998	X	X
Australia	23 Jun 1961	23 Jun 1961	14 Jan 1998	X	X
Austria	25 Aug 1987				
Belarus	27 Dec 2006		15 Aug 2008		
Belgium	23 Jun 1961	23 Jun 1961	14 Jan 1998	X	X
Brazil	16 May 1975	27 Sep 1983	14 Jan 1998	X	X
Bulgaria	11 Sep 1978	05 Jun 1998	21 May 1998		X
Canada	04 May 1988		13 Dec 2003	X	X
Chile	23 Jun 1961	23 Jun 1961	14 Jan 1998	X	X
China	08 Jun 1983	07 Oct 1985	14 Jan 1998		X
Colombia	31 Jan 1989				
Cuba	16 Aug 1984				
Czech Republic	01 Sep 1993		24 Sep 2004		
Denmark	20 May 1965				
Ecuador	15 Sep 1987	19 Nov 1990	14 Jan 1998		
Estonia	17 May 2001				
Finland	15 May 1984	20 Oct 1989	14 Jan 1998		X
France	23 Jun 1961	23 Jun 1961	14 Jan 1998	X	X

Germany	19 Nov 1974	03 Mar 1981	14 Jan 1998	X	X
Greece	08 Jan 1987		14 Jan 1998		X
Guatemala	31 Jul 1991				
Hungary	27 Jan 1984				
India	19 Aug 1983	12 Sep 1983	14 Jan 1998		X
Italy	18 Mar 1981	05 Oct 1987	14 Jan 1998	X	X
Japan	23 Jun 1961	23 Jun 1961	14 Jan 1998	X	X
Korea (DPRK)	21 Jan 1987				
Korea (ROK)	28 Nov 1986	09 Oct 1989	14 Jan 1998		X
Monaco	30 May 2008		31 Jul 2009		
Netherlands	30 Mar 1967	19 Nov 1990	14 Jan 1998		X
New Zealand	23 Jun 1961	23 Jun 1961	14 Jan 1998		X
Norway	23 Jun 1961	23 Jun 1961	14 Jan 1998	X	X
Papua New Guinea	16 Sep 1975				
Peru	10 Apr 1981	09 Oct 1989	14 Jan 1998		X
Poland	23 Jun 1961	29 Jul 1977	14 Jan 1998	X	X
Portugal	29 Jan 2010				
Romania	15 Sep 1971		05 Mar 2003		
Russian Federation	23 Jun 1961	23 Jun 1961	14 Jan 1998	X	X
Slovak Republic	01 Jan 1993				
South Africa	23 Jun 1961	23 Jun 1961	14 Jan 1998	X	X
Spain	31 Mar 1982	21 Sep 1988	14 Jan 1998		X
Sweden	24 Apr 1984	21 Sep 1988	14 Jan 1998		X
Switzerland	15 Nov 1990				
Turkey	24 Jan 1996				
Ukraine	28 Oct 1992	05 Jun 2004	24 Jun 2001		X
United Kingdom	23 Jun 1961	23 Jun 1961	14 Jan 1998	X	X
United States	23 Jun 1961	23 Jun 1961	14 Jan 1998	X	X
Uruguay	11 Jan 1980	07 Oct 1985	14 Jan 1998		X
Venezuela	24 Mar 1999				

PART 2
SECRETARIAT OF THE ANTARCTIC TREATY

Measure 1 (2003) Secretariat of the Antarctic Treaty

The Representatives,

Recalling the Antarctic Treaty and the Protocol on Environmental Protection to the Antarctic Treaty (the Protocol);

Recognizing the need for a secretariat to assist the Antarctic Treaty Consultative Meeting (the ATCM) and the Committee for Environmental Protection (the CEP) in performing their functions;

Recalling Decision 1 (2001) of the XXIV ATCM on the establishment of the Secretariat of the Antarctic Treaty (the Secretariat) in Buenos Aires, Argentina;

Recommend to their Governments the following Measure for approval in accordance with paragraph 4 of Article IX of the Antarctic Treaty:

Article I Secretariat

The Secretariat shall constitute an organ of the ATCM. As such it shall be subordinated to the ATCM.

Article II Functions

1. The Secretariat shall perform those functions in support of the ATCM and the CEP which are entrusted to it by the ATCM.

2. Under the direction and supervision of the ATCM, the Secretariat shall, in particular:

(a) Provide, with assistance from the host government, secretariat support for meetings held under the Antarctic Treaty and the Protocol and other meetings in conjunction with the ATCM. Secretariat support shall include:

(i) Collation of information for ATCM/CEP meetings e.g. environmental impact assessments and management plans;

(ii) Preparatory work for and distribution of the meeting agendas and reports;

(iii) Translation of meeting documents;

(iv) Provision of interpretation services;

(v) Copying, organizing and distributing meeting documents; and

(vi) Assisting the ATCM, in drafting the meeting documents including the final report;

(b) Support inter-sessional work of the ATCM and the CEP by facilitating the exchange of information, organizing meeting facilities and providing other secretariat support as directed by the ATCM;

(c) Facilitate and coordinate communications and exchange of information amongst Parties on all exchanges required under the Antarctic Treaty and the Protocol;

(d) Under guidance from the ATCM, provide the necessary coordination and contact with other elements of the Antarctic Treaty system and other relevant international bodies and organizations as appropriate;

(e) Establish, maintain, develop and, as appropriate publish, databases relevant to the operation of the Antarctic Treaty and the Protocol;

(f) Circulate amongst the Parties any other relevant information and disseminate information on activities in Antarctica;

(g) Record, maintain and publish, as appropriate, the records of the ATCM and CEP and of other meetings convened under the Antarctic Treaty and the Protocol;

(h) Facilitate the availability of information about the Antarctic Treaty system;

(i) Prepare reports on its activities and present them to the ATCM;

(j) Assist the ATCM in reviewing the status of past Recommendations and Measures adopted under Article IX of the Antarctic Treaty;
(k) Under the guidance of the ATCM, take responsibility for maintaining and updating an Antarctic Treaty system "Handbook"; and
(l) Perform such other functions relevant to the purposes of the Antarctic Treaty and the Protocol as may be determined by the ATCM.

Article III Executive Secretary

1. The Secretariat shall be headed by an Executive Secretary who shall be appointed by the ATCM from among candidates who are nationals of Consultative Parties. The procedure for the selection of the Executive Secretary shall be determined by a Decision of the ATCM.

2. The Executive Secretary shall appoint staff members essential for the carrying out of the functions of the Secretariat and engage experts as appropriate. The Executive Secretary and other staff members shall serve in accordance with the procedures, terms and conditions set out in the Staff Regulations which shall be adopted by a Decision of the ATCM.

3. During the intersessional periods the Executive Secretary shall consult in a manner to be prescribed in the Rules of Procedure.

Article IV Budget

1. The Secretariat shall operate in a cost-effective manner.

2. The budget of the Secretariat shall be approved by the Representatives of all Consultative Parties present at the ATCM.

3. Each Consultative Party shall contribute to the budget of the Secretariat. One half of the budget shall be contributed equally by all Consultative Parties. The other half of the budget shall be contributed by the Consultative Parties based on the extent of their national Antarctic activities, taking into account their capacity to pay.

4. The method for calculating the scale of contributions is contained in Decision 1 (2003) and the Schedule attached to it. The ATCM may amend the proportion in which the abovementioned two criteria shall apply and the method for calculating the scale of contributions by means of a Decision.

5. Any Contracting Party may make a voluntary contribution at any time.

6. Financial Regulations shall be adopted by a Decision of the ATCM.

Article V Legal capacity and privileges and immunities

1. The legal capacity of the Secretariat as an organ of the ATCM as well as its privileges and immunities and those of the Executive Secretary and other staff members in the territory of the Argentine Republic shall be provided for in the Headquarters Agreement for the Secretariat of the Antarctic Treaty (the Headquarters Agreement) hereby adopted and annexed to this Measure, to be concluded between the ATCM and the Argentine Republic.

2. The ATCM hereby authorizes the person who holds the office of the Chair to sign the Headquarters Agreement on its behalf at the time this Measure becomes effective.

3. The Secretariat may exercise its legal capacity as provided for in Article 2 of the Headquarters Agreement only to the extent authorized by the ATCM. Within the budget approved by and in accordance with any other decision of the ATCM, the Secretariat is hereby authorized to contract, and to acquire and dispose of movable property in order to perform its functions as set out in Article 2 of this Measure.

4. The Secretariat may not acquire or dispose of immovable property or institute legal proceedings without the prior approval of the ATCM.

Decision 1 (2003): Apportioning Contributions to the Secretariat of the Antarctic Treaty

The Representatives,

Noting the references in Article 4 of Measure 1 (2003) to the contributions of Parties to the budget of the Secretariat of the Antarctic Treaty;

Noting further that one half of the budget will be financed through equal shares and one half through the Consultative Parties' contributions apportioned on a scale determined by the ATCM;

Decide:

1. That the scale of such apportioned contributions shall be determined in the manner described in the Schedule to this Decision;

2. That the Schedule may be adjusted by further Decisions of the ATCM;

3. That this Decision shall become operative on the date on which Measure 1 (2003) becomes effective.

Schedule: Method for Calculating the Scale of Contributions

1. A Consultative Party's contribution shall consist of an equal part and a variable part.

2. The equal part of a Consultative Party's contribution is the amount obtained by dividing one half of the budget by the number of Consultative Parties.

3. In order to determine the variable part of the Consultative Parties' contributions they will choose a category according to the procedures set out in paragraphs 6 and 7 hereunder. Each category will have a multiplier according to the following table:

Category	*Multiplier*
Category A	3,6
Category B	2,8
Category C	2,2
Category D	1,6
Category E	1

4. The variable part of the contribution shall be calculated according to the following method:

(a) The base rate is calculated as follows:

(i) identify the size of the half of the budget to be apportioned differentially between the Consultative Parties;

(ii) add together the multipliers of all Consultative Parties;

(iii) divide the figure from subparagraph (i) by the figure derived from subparagraph (ii).

(b) The variable part is the amount obtained by multiplying the base rate calculated in paragraph 4(a) by the multiplier listed in paragraph 3.

5. The total contribution of each Consultative Party shall be the sum of the equal part calculated according to paragraph 2 and the variable part calculated according to paragraph 4.

6. Each Consultative Party shall elect to be in one of the categories listed in paragraph 3 above by notification to the Depositary Government within two months of Measure 1 (2003) becoming effective.

7. A Consultative Party may choose to move to a higher category at any time by means of a notification to the Secretariat. This change will be taken into account in the calculation of the budget at the ATCM following the notification. Otherwise, determination of a category shall be valid for at least three years. After three years, a Consultative Party wishing to move to a lower category may do so by notification to the Secretariat at least six months before the ATCM

preceding the financial year in which the change is to take effect. Consultative Parties wishing to change their category are recommended to state the circumstances of the change.

Decision 3 (2003), Annex: Staff Regulations for the Secretariat of the Antarctic Treaty

Regulation 1 Preamble

1.1 These Staff Regulations establish the fundamental principles of employment, regulate the working relationships and establish the rights and duties of members of the staff of the Secretariat of the Antarctic Treaty (the Secretariat), and includes the Staff members who render their services in and receive remuneration from the Antarctic Secretariat.

Regulation 2 Duties, Obligations and Privileges

2.1 Staff members, upon accepting their appointments, shall pledge themselves to discharge their duties faithfully and to conduct themselves solely with the interests of the ATCM in mind. Their responsibilities as staff members are not national but are exclusively owed to the ATCM.

2.2 Staff members shall at all times conduct themselves in a manner in keeping with the Antarctic Treaty. They shall always bear in mind the loyalty, discretion and tact imposed on them by their responsibilities in the performance of their duties. They shall avoid all actions, statements or public activities which might be detrimental to the ATCM and its aims.

2.3 Staff members are not required to renounce either their national feelings or their political or religious convictions, but must ensure that such views or convictions do not adversely affect their official duties or the interests of the ATCM. Staff members shall uphold the highest standards of efficiency, competence, and integrity. The concept of integrity includes, but is not limited to, probity, impartiality, fairness, honesty, and truthfulness in all matters affecting their work and status.

2.4 In the performance of their duties, staff members may neither seek nor accept instructions from any government or authority other than the ATCM.

2.5 Staff members shall observe maximum discretion regarding official matters and shall abstain from making private use of information they possess by reason of their position. Authorisation for the release of information for official purposes shall lie with the ATCM or the Executive Secretary, as the case may require.

2.6 Staff members shall, in general, have no employment other than with the Secretariat. In special cases, staff members may accept other employment, provided that it does not interfere with their duties in the Secretariat, and that prior authorisation by the Executive Secretary has been obtained. The ATCM's prior authorisation shall be obtained in respect of the Executive Secretary.

2.7 No staff member may be associated in the management of a business, industry or other enterprise, or have a financial interest therein if, as a result of the official position held in the Secretariat, he/she may benefit from such association or interest. Ownership of non-controlling stock in a company shall not be considered to constitute a financial interest within the meaning of this Regulation.

2.8 Staff members shall enjoy the privileges and immunities granted to them under the Headquarters Agreement for the Secretariat of the Antarctic Treaty, pursuant to Article 5 of Measure 1 (2003) of the XXVI ATCM.

Regulation 3 Hours of Work

3.1 The normal working day shall be eight hours, Monday to Friday, for a total of forty hours per week.

3.2 The Executive Secretary shall establish the working hours, and may alter them for the benefit of the ATCM , as circumstances may require.

Regulation 4 Classification of Staff

4.1 Staff members shall be classified in either of the two following categories:

(a) Executive Category

Positions of high responsibility of an executive nature. These posts will be filled by appropriately qualified professionals, preferably with University qualifications or the equivalent. Staff members in this category will be recruited internationally but only among nationals of Consultative Parties.

(b) General Staff Category

All other staff, such as translators, interpreters, technical, administrative and auxiliary positions. Such staff members shall be recruited in Argentina from among nationals of Consultative Parties.

4.2 Persons employed under Regulation 11 shall not be classified as staff members.

Regulation 5 Salaries and Other Remuneration

5.1 The scale of salaries for staff members in the executive category is attached in Schedule A. The salaries of staff members in the executive category shall be paid in US currency.

5.2 The scale of salaries for staff members in the general category is attached in Schedule B. The salaries of staff members in the general category shall be paid in US currency.

5.3 For the purposes of these regulations the term 'dependent' means:

(a) any unsalaried child, who is born of, or adopted by, a staff member, his/her spouse, or their children, who is below the age of eighteen years and who is dependent on a staff member for main and continuing support;

(b) any child fulfilling the conditions laid down in paragraph (a) above, but who is between eighteen and twenty-five years of age and is receiving school or university education or vocational training;

(c) any handicapped child who is dependent on a staff member for main and continuing support;

(d) any other child who is given a home by and is dependent on a staff member for main and continuing support;

(e) any member of the family forming part of the household of the staff member, for whose main and continuing support a staff member is legally responsible.

5.4 The salaries of staff members in the executive category shall begin at Step 1 of the level at which they are appointed. They shall remain at that level for at least the first year of employment.

5.5 The promotion of the Executive Secretary and other staff members from one level to another requires the prior approval of the ATCM.

5.6 The Executive Secretary shall seek to make arrangements for any staff member in the executive category whose salary is subject to income tax in his/her home country, to be reimbursed for that tax. Such arrangements shall be made only on the basis that the direct costs of reimbursement are paid by the staff member's home country. Staff members in the general category will be responsible for the payment of income tax, if any on their salaries in their home country.

5.7 Staff members shall receive annual step increases, subject to satisfactory performance of their duties. Step increases shall cease once the staff member has reached the highest step in the level in which he/she is serving.

5.8 Only in very special cases, on the proposal of the Executive Secretary and with the approval of the ATCM, may a staff member in the executive category be appointed at a salary higher than Step 1 of the relevant level.

5.9 Staff members in the executive category are not entitled to overtime pay or compensatory leave.

5.10 Staff members in the general category required to work more than 40 hours during one week will be compensated:

(a) with compensatory leave equivalent to hours of overtime performed; or

(b) by remuneration per overtime hour, to be calculated at the rate of time and a half, or if the additional time is worked on a Sunday, or on holidays listed in Regulation 7.8, at the rate of double time.

5.11 The ATCM shall pay duly justified representation expenses incurred by the Executive Secretary in the performance of his/her duties within the limits prescribed annually in the budget.

Regulation 6 Recruitment and Appointment

6.1 In accordance with Article 3 of Measure 1 (2003), the ATCM shall appoint an Executive Secretary and shall establish the remuneration and such other entitlements as it deems appropriate. The Executive Secretary's term of office shall be for four years unless otherwise decided by the ATCM and the Executive Secretary shall be eligible for reappointment for one additional term. The total length of employment may not exceed eight years.

6.2 In accordance with Article 3 of Measure 1 (2003) the Executive Secretary shall appoint, direct, and supervise other staff members. The paramount consideration in the appointment, transfer or promotion of staff members shall be the need to secure the highest standards of efficiency, competence and integrity. Subject to this, due consideration should be given to recruiting Executive staff on as wide a basis as possible from among the nationals of Consultative Parties.

6.3 Upon selection, each staff member shall receive an offer of appointment stating:

(a) that the appointment is subject to these regulations and to changes which may be made to them from time to time;
(b) the nature of the appointment including a description of the duties of the position;
(c) the date on which the staff member is required to commence duty;
(d) the period of appointment, the notice required to terminate it and the period of probation;
(e) for executive staff the period of appointment, which shall not exceed four years, and which may be renewed in consultation with the ATCM;
(f) the category, level, commencing rate of salary and the scale of steps increases and the maximum salary attainable;
(g) the allowances attached to the appointment;
(h) any special terms and conditions which may be applicable.

6.4 Together with the offer of appointment, staff members shall be provided with a copy of these Regulations. Upon acceptance of the offer staff members shall state in writing that they are familiar with and accept the conditions set out in these Regulations.

Regulation 7 Leave

7.1 Staff members shall be entitled to 25 days annual leave during each working year of service, or for periods of less than a full calendar year at the rate of two work days for each completed month of service. Annual leave is cumulative, but at the end of each calendar year, not more than 15 workdays may be carried over to the following year.

7.2 The taking of leave shall not cause undue disruption to normal Secretariat operations. In accordance with this principle, leave dates shall be subject to the needs of the ATCM. Leave dates shall be approved by the Executive Secretary who shall, as far as possible, bear in mind the personal circumstances, needs and preferences of staff members.

7.3 Annual leave may be taken in one or more periods.

7.4 Any absence not approved within the terms of these Regulations shall be deducted from annual leave.

7.5 Staff members who, upon termination of their appointment, have accumulated annual leave which has not been taken shall receive the cash equivalent estimated on the basis of the last salary received to a limit of 30 days.

7.6 After 18 months of service the Secretariat shall, in accordance with Regulations 9.3 and 9.4, pay fares to the staff member's home country on annual leave for internationally recruited staff members and their dependents. Following this, home leave fares shall be granted at two-year intervals provided that:

(a) dependants who benefit from this grant have resided at Buenos Aires for at least 6 months prior to travel;
(b) it is expected that staff members will return to the Secretariat to continue rendering their services for a minimum additional period of 6 months.

7.7 The possibility of combining travel to home country on leave with official travel in Secretariat service may also be considered provided the functions of the Secretariat are not disadvantaged.

7.8 Staff shall be entitled to the holidays celebrated traditionally in Buenos Aires, i.e.:

Fixed Holidays

1 January	New Year's Day
	Holy Thursday
	Good Friday
	Easter Sunday
01 May	National Holiday
25 May	National Holiday
9 July	National Holiday
8 December	Immaculate Conception
25 December	Christmas Day

Moveable Holidays

02 April	National Holiday
20 June	National Holiday
17 August	National Holiday
12 October	National Holiday

7.9 If under special circumstances members of the staff are required to work on one of the aforementioned days, or if any one of the above holidays falls on a Saturday or Sunday, the holiday shall be observed on another day to be set by the Executive Secretary, who shall take into account the efficient functioning of the Secretariat.

Regulation 8 Social Security

8.1 It is a condition of employment that each staff member will contribute to a recognised retirement fund and have adequate medical, hospital, life and disability insurance cover to the satisfaction of the Executive Secretary. Such insurance cover shall include adequate provision for dependents. Staff members shall be responsible for the full payment of contributions to their retirement fund and insurance premiums.

8.2 Staff members shall not be granted sick leave for a period of more than three consecutive days and more than a total of seven working days in any calendar year without producing a medical certificate.

8.3 (a) Staff members shall be granted certified sick leave not exceeding 12 months in any four consecutive years. The first six months shall be on full salary and the second six months on half salary, except that no more than four months on full salary shall normally be granted in any period of 12 consecutive months.

(b) In the event of long term sickness, which prevents a staff member from continuing in their position with the Secretariat, the staff member and dependents shall be entitled to return travel and removal expenses to country of origin or former residence at the expense of the Secretariat.

8.4 After six months of employment in the Secretariat staff members shall be entitled to maternity leave. On the basis of medical advice that the confinement will probably take place within six weeks, staff members shall be entitled to be absent from duty until eight weeks after confinement. During this period staff members shall receive full pay and corresponding allowances.

8.5 In the event of death of a staff member following illness or surgery not resulting from an accident covered by the appropriate insurance, the right to salary, allowances and other corresponding benefits shall cease on the day on which death occurs, unless the deceased leaves dependents, in which case these shall be entitled to mortality allowances and return travel and removal expenses to their country of origin or former residence at the expense of the Secretariat.

8.6 Eligibility of the dependents of a deceased staff member for the payment of return travel and removal expenses shall lapse if the travel is not undertaken within six months of the date of the staff member's death.

8.7 The above mortality allowance for death shall be calculated in accordance with the following scale:

Years of Service	Months of Gross Salary Following Death
Less than 3 years	3 months
3 years and more, but less than 7 years	4 months
7 years and more, but less than 9 years	5 months
9 years and more	6 months

8.8 The Secretariat shall pay for customary and reasonable expenses for shipment of the staff member's body from the place of death to the place designated by the next of kin.

Regulation 9 Travel

9.1 Staff members may be required to undertake travel, including international travel, on behalf of the Secretariat. All official travel shall be authorised by the Executive Secretary in advance within the limits of the budget, and the itinerary and travelling conditions shall be those best suited for maximum effectiveness in the fulfilment of duties assigned.

9.2 With regard to official travel, a reasonable travel allowance shall be paid in advance for accommodation and daily living expenses.

9.3 Economy class shall be utilised, wherever feasible, for air travel. For journeys over nine hours in flying time, business class may be utilised.

9.4 First class may be utilised for land travel, but not for travel by sea or air.

9.5 Following completion of a journey for official purposes, staff members shall repay any travel allowances to which, in the event, they were not entitled. Where staff members have incurred expenses above and beyond those for which travel allowances have been paid, they shall be reimbursed, against receipts and vouchers, as long as such expenses were necessarily incurred in pursuit of their official duties.

9.6 On taking up an appointment in the Executive Category staff members shall be eligible for:

(a) payment of air fares (or equivalent) and travel allowance for themselves, their spouses and dependents to Buenos Aires;

(b) payment of removal costs, including the shipment of personal effects and household goods from place of residence to Buenos Aires, subject to a maximum volume of 30 cubic metres or one international standard shipping container;

(c) payment or reimbursement of sundry other reasonable expenses related to relocation, including insurance of goods in transit and excess baggage charges. Such payments shall be subject to prior approval by the Executive Secretary.

9.7 Staff members who, in the course of their duty, are required to use private motor vehicles for official travel purposes shall, with the prior authorisation of the Executive Secretary, be entitled to receive a reimbursement of the reasonable costs involved. The costs associated with normal daily travel to and from the place of work shall not be reimbursed.

Regulation 10 Separation from Service

10.1 Staff members may resign at any time upon giving three months notice or such lesser period as may be approved by the Executive Secretary (in the case of staff other than the Executive Secretary) or the ATCM (in the case of the Executive Secretary).

10.2 In the event of a staff member resigning without giving the required notice the Executive Secretary (in the case of staff members other than the Executive Secretary) or the ATCM (in the case of the Executive Secretary) reserves the right to decide whether repatriation expenses or any other allowance shall be paid.

10.3 Appointment of staff members may be terminated upon prior written notice at least three months in advance, by the Executive Secretary (and in the case of the Executive Secretary by the ATCM) when this is deemed to be for the benefit of the efficient functioning of the Secretariat due to restructuring of the Secretariat or if it is considered that the staff member does not give satisfactory service, fails to comply with the duties and obligations set out in these Regulations, or is incapacitated for service.

10.4 In the event of separation from service with the Secretariat, executive staff members shall be compensated at a rate of one month base pay for each year of service, beginning the second year, unless the cause of termination has been gross dereliction of duties imposed in Regulation 2.

10.5 In the event of involuntary termination of the appointment of a general staff member, he/she shall be paid the outstanding amount of his/her appointment except when the Executive Secretary considers that the staff member has not given satisfactory service, fails to comply with the duties and obligations set out in these Regulations, or is incapacitated for service.

10.6 On separation from service, an executive staff member shall be entitled to the following:

(a) payment of economy class air fares (or equivalent) to the staff member's country of origin or former residence, for the staff member and dependent members of his/her family; and
(b) payment of removal costs, including the shipment of personal effects and household goods from place of residence in Buenos Aires to the country of origin or former residence, subject to a maximum volume of 30 cubic metres or one international shipping container.

Regulation 11 Temporary Personnel Under Contract

11.1 The Executive Secretary may contract temporary personnel necessary to discharge special duties of a short term nature in the service of the Secretariat. Short term shall be defined as a contract lasting less than six months. Such personnel shall be classified as additional help and may be paid on an hourly basis.

11.2 Persons in this category may include additional translators, interpreters, typists, and other persons contracted for meetings, as well as those whom the Executive Secretary contracts for a specific task.

Regulation 12 Application and Amendment of Regulations

12.1 Any doubts arising from application of these Regulations shall be resolved by the Executive Secretary following consultation with the ATCM.

12.2 All matters not foreseen in these Regulations shall be brought to the attention of the ATCM by the Executive Secretary.

12.3 These Regulations including the schedules may be amended by a Decision of the ATCM.

[Note: Schedules A and B – Salary Scales – Omitted.]

Decision 4 (2003): Financial Regulations for the Secretariat of the Antarctic Treaty

Regulation 1 Applicability

1. These Regulations shall govern the financial administration of the Secretariat of the Antarctic Treaty (the Secretariat) established under Measure 1 (2003) of the XXVI ATCM (the Measure).

Regulation 2 Financial year

2. The financial year shall be for 12 months commencing 1 April and ending 31 March, both dates inclusive.

Regulation 3 The budget

3.1 A draft budget comprising estimates of receipts by the Secretariat and of expenditures by the Secretariat shall be prepared by the Executive Secretary for the ensuing financial year.

3.2 The draft budget shall include a statement of significant financial implications for subsequent financial years in respect of work programs presented by the ATCM in terms of administrative, recurrent and capital expenditure.

3.3 The draft budget shall be divided by functions into items and, where necessary or appropriate, into sub-items.

3.4 The draft budget shall be accompanied by details both of the appropriations made for the previous year and estimated expenditure against those appropriations, together with such supporting documents as may be required by Parties or deemed necessary or desirable by the Executive Secretary. The precise form in which the draft budget is to be presented shall be prescribed by the ATCM.

3.5 The Executive Secretary shall submit the draft budget to all Consultative Parties of the ATCM at least 60 days prior to the ATCM. At the same time, and in the same form as the draft budget, the Executive Secretary he shall prepare and submit to all Consultative Parties a forecast budget for the subsequent financial year.

3.6 The draft budget and the forecast budget shall be presented in United States currency.

3.7 At each annual meeting, the ATCM shall adopt the budget for the Secretariat. The budget shall be treated as a matter of substance and approved by a representative of all Consultative Parties present at the meeting. In determining the size of the budget the ATCM shall adhere to the principle of cost-effectiveness.

Regulation 4 Appropriations

4.1 The appropriations adopted by the ATCM shall constitute an authorisation for the Executive Secretary to incur obligations and make payments for the purposes for which the appropriations were adopted and up to the amounts so adopted.

4.2 All forward commitments shall be identified in annual budgets presented to the ATCM. Unless the ATCM decides otherwise, the Executive Secretary may incur obligations against future years before appropriations are adopted when such obligations are necessary for the continued effective functioning of the Secretariat, provided such obligations are restricted to administrative requirements of a continuing nature not exceeding the scale of such requirements as authorised in the budget of the current financial year. In other circumstances the Executive Secretary may incur obligations against future years only as authorised by the ATCM.

4.3 Appropriations shall be available for the financial year to which they relate. At the end of the financial year all appropriations shall lapse. Commitments remaining undischarged against previous appropriations at the end of a financial year shall be carried over and be included in the budget for the next financial year, unless the ATCM otherwise decides.

4.4 The Executive Secretary may make transfers within each of the main appropriation lines of the approved budget. The Executive Secretary may also make transfers between such appropriation lines up to 15 per cent of the appropriation lines. All such transfers must be reported by the Executive Secretary to the next annual meeting of the ATCM. The transfers authorised under these regulations shall not result in overall increase of the budget above that approved by the ATCM, nor will they result in increased expenditure in future years.

4.5 The ATCM shall prescribe the conditions under which unforeseen and extraordinary expenses may be incurred.

Regulation 5 Provision of funds

5.1 On approval of the budget for a financial year, the Executive Secretary shall send a copy thereof to all Consultative Parties notifying them of their contributions and the date they are due, and requesting them to remit their contributions due.

5.2 All contributions shall be made in United States currency.

5.3 Contribution from States that become Consultative Parties after the beginning of the financial period shall be made pro rata temporis for the balance of the financial period.

5.4 The Executive Secretary shall acknowledge pledges and contributions immediately upon receipt. The Executive Secretary shall report to each meeting of the ATCM on the receipt of contributions and the status of any arrears.

5.5 Contributions shall be due for payment on the first day of the financial year (i.e. the due date) and shall be paid not later than 90 days after that date. However, in the case referred to in Regulation 5.3, contributions by a new Consultative Party shall be made within 60 days following the date on which its accession becomes effective.

Regulation 6 Funds

6.1

(a) There shall be established a General Fund for the purpose of accounting for the income and expenditure of the Secretariat;

(b) Contributions paid by Consultative Parties pursuant to Article 4 of Measure 1 (2003) under and Miscellaneous Income as referred to in Regulation 7.1 shall be credited to the General Fund;

(c) An advance made by a Consultative Party shall be carried to the credit of the Party which has made the advance.

6.2

(a) There shall be established a Working Capital Fund in an amount of not more than one-sixth (1/6) of the budget of that financial year to ensure continuity of operations in the event of a temporary shortfall of cash and for other purposes to be determined by the ATCM from time to time. The Working Capital Fund shall initially be financed up to the specified level by a transfer from the General Fund, and thereafter from the fund determined appropriate by the Antarctic Treaty Consultative Meeting;

(b) Advances made from the Working Capital Fund to finance budgetary appropriations during a financial year shall be reimbursed as soon as possible, and to the extent that income is available for that purpose;

(c) Income derived from the investment of the Working Capital Fund shall be credited to Miscellaneous Income of the General Fund; and

(d) Trust and Special Funds may be established by the Secretariat at the direction of the ATCM for the purpose of receiving funds and making payments for purposes not covered by the General or Working Capital Fund of the Secretariat. The purposes and limits of each Trust and Special Fund shall be clearly defined by the ATCM. Unless otherwise provided by the ATCM, such Funds shall be administered in accordance with the present regulations.

6.3 The Secretariat shall notify the Consultative Parties of any cash surplus in the General Fund at the close of the financial year that is not required to meet undischarged commitments and of each Consultative Party's proportional share of that surplus. Those Parties that choose not to allow their portion of the surplus to be retained in the General Fund shall notify the Secretariat of that fact and shall have that portion credited against such Consultative Parties' contributions for the following year. Otherwise any cash surplus shall be retained in the General Fund.

6.4. Where contributions are received from new Consultative Parties after the commencement of the financial year and such contributions have not been taken into account in formulating the budget these shall be placed in the General Fund.

Regulation 7 Other income

7.1 All income other than contributions to the budget under Regulation 5, income derived from investment in the Working Capital Fund as provided in Regulation 6.2(c), and that referred to in Regulation 7.5 below, shall be classified as Miscellaneous Income and credited to the General Fund.

7.2 Profits and losses on exchange shall be credited and debited to Miscellaneous Income.

7.3 The use of Miscellaneous Income shall be subject to the same financial controls as activities financed from regular budget appropriations.

7.4 Voluntary contributions above and beyond Consultative Parties' budget contributions may be accepted by the Executive Secretary provided that the purposes for which the contributions are made are consistent with the policies, aims and activities of the ATCM. Voluntary contributions offered by non-Consultative Parties and non-Parties may be accepted, subject to agreement by the ATCM that the purposes of the contribution are consistent with the policies, aims and activities of the ATCM.

7.5 Voluntary contributions as referred to in Regulation 7.4 above shall be treated as Trust or Special Funds under Regulation 6.2(d).

Regulation 8 Custody of funds

8.1 The Executive Secretary shall designate a bank or banks in which the funds of the Secretariat shall be kept and shall report the identity of the bank or banks so designated to the ATCM.

8.2

(a) The Executive Secretary may make short-term investments of moneys not needed for the immediate requirements of the Secretariat. Such investments shall be restricted to securities and other investments issued by institutions or Government bodies with current ratings, provided by a rating body approved by the Secretariat's auditor and indicating a strong capacity to pay. The details of investment transactions and income derived shall be reported in the documents supporting the budget.

(b) With regard to moneys held in Trust or Special Funds for which use is not required for at least 12 months, longer-term investments may be authorised by the ATCM provided such action is consistent with the terms under which the moneys were lodged with the Secretariat. Such investments shall be restricted to securities and other investments issued by institutions or Government bodies with current ratings, provided by a rating body approved by the Secretariat's auditor and indicating a strong capacity to pay.

8.3 Income derived from investments shall be credited to the Fund from which the investment was made.

Regulation 9 Internal control

9.1 The Executive Secretary shall:

(a) establish detailed financial rules and procedures after consultation with the external auditor to ensure effective financial administration and the exercise of economy in the use of funds and effective custody of the physical assets of the Secretariat;

(b) cause all payments to be made on the basis of supporting vouchers and other documents which ensure that the goods or services have been received and that payment has not previously been made;

(c) designate officers who may receive moneys, incur obligations and make payments on behalf of the Secretariat; and

(d) maintain and be responsible for internal financial control to ensure:

- (i) the regularity of the receipt, custody and disposal of all funds and other financial resources of the Secretariat;
- (ii) the conformity of obligations and expenditures with the appropriations adopted by the ATCM; and
- (iii) the economic use of the resources of the Secretariat.

9.2 No obligations shall be incurred until allotments or other appropriate authorisations have been made in writing under the authority of the Executive Secretary.

9.3 The Executive Secretary may propose to the ATCM, after full investigation by him/her, the writing off of losses of assets, provided that the external auditor so recommends. Such losses shall be included in the annual accounts.

9.4 Tenders in writing for equipment, supplies and other requirements shall be invited by advertisement, or by direct requests for quotation from at least three persons or firms able to supply the equipment, supplies, or other requirements, if such exist, in connection with all purchases or contracts, the amounts of which exceed USD2,000. For amounts exceeding USD500, but less than USD2,000 competition shall be obtained either by the above means or by telephone or personal enquiry. The foregoing rules, shall, however, not apply in the following cases:

(a) where it has been ascertained that only a single supplier exists and that fact is so certified by the Executive Secretary;

(b) in case of emergency, or where, for any other reason, these rules would not be in the best financial interests of the Secretariat, and that fact is so certified by the Executive Secretary.

Regulation 10 The accounts

10.1 The Executive Secretary shall ensure that appropriate records and accounts are kept of the transactions and affairs of the Secretariat and shall ensure that all payments out of the Secretariat's moneys are correctly made and properly authorised. The Executive Secretary shall also ensure that adequate control is maintained over the assets of, or in the custody of, the Secretariat and over the incurring of liabilities by the Secretariat.

10.2 The Executive Secretary shall submit to the Consultative Parties, as soon as practicable but not later than 30 June immediately following the end of the financial year, annual financial statements showing, for the financial year to which they relate:

(a) the income and expenditure relating to all funds and accounts;

(b) the situation with regard to budget provisions, including:

(i) the original budget provisions;

(ii) the approved expenditure in excess of the original budget provisions;

(iii) any other income;

(iv) the amounts charged against these provisions and other income;

(c) the financial assets and liabilities of the Secretariat;

(d) details of the performance of the investments; and

(e) writing off of losses of assets proposed in accordance with Regulation 9.3.

10.3 The Executive Secretary shall also give such other information as may be appropriate to indicate the financial position of the Secretariat. These financial statements shall be prepared in a form approved by the ATCM after consultation with the external auditor.

10.4 The accounting transactions of the Secretariat shall be recorded in the currency in which they took place but the annual financial statements shall record all transactions in United States currency.

10.5 Appropriate separate accounts shall be kept for all Working Capital, Special and Trust Funds.

Regulation 11 External audit

11.1 The ATCM shall appoint an external auditor who shall be the Auditor-General or equivalent statutory authority from a Consultative Party of the ATCM and shall serve for a term of two years with the possibility of re-appointment. The ATCM will ensure the external auditor's independence of the Secretariat, and the Secretariat's staff. The ATCM shall fix the terms of office, appropriate funds to the external auditor and may consult him/her on the introduction or amendment of any financial regulations or detailed accounting methods as well as on all matters affecting auditing procedures and methodology.

11.2 The external auditor or a person or persons authorised by him/her shall be entitled at all reasonable times to full and free access to all accounts and records of the Secretariat relating directly or indirectly to the receipt or payment of moneys by the Secretariat or to the acquisition, receipt, custody or disposal of assets by the Secretariat. This applies also to allowances such as travel and representation expenses. The external auditor or a person or persons authorised by him/her may make copies of or take extracts from any such accounts or records.

11.3 If required by the ATCM to perform a full audit, the external auditor shall conduct his/her examination of the statements in conformity with generally accepted auditing standards and shall report to the ATCM on all relevant matters, including:

(a) whether, in his/her opinion, the statements are based on proper accounts and records;

(b) whether the statements are in agreement with the accounts and records;

(c) whether, in his/her opinion, the income, expenditure and investment of moneys and the acquisition and disposal of assets by the Secretariat during the year have been in accordance with these Regulations; and

(d) observations with respect to the efficiency and economy of the financial procedures and the conduct of business, the accounting system, internal financial controls and the administration and management of the Secretariat.

11.4 If required by the ATCM to perform a review audit, the external auditor shall review the statements and accounting controls in operation. The external auditor shall report to the ATCM whether anything has come to his/her attention which would cause him/her to doubt whether:

(a) the statements are based on proper accounts and records;

(b) the statements are in agreement with the accounts and records; or

(c) the income, expenditure and investment of moneys and the acquisition and disposal of assets by the Secretariat during the year have been in accordance with these Regulations.

11.5 The Executive Secretary shall provide the external auditor with the facilities he/she may require in the performance of the audit.

11.6 The Executive Secretary shall provide to the Parties of the ATCM a copy of the audit report and the audited financial statements within 30 days of their receipt.

11.7 The ATCM shall, if necessary, invite the external auditor to address the Meeting and to attend discussions on any item under scrutiny and consider recommendations arising out of his/her findings.

Regulation 12 Acceptance of annual financial statements

12.1 The ATCM shall, following consideration of the audited annual financial statements and audit report submitted to the Consultative Parties under Regulation 11 signify its acceptance of the audited annual financial statements or take such other action as it may consider appropriate.

Regulation 13 Insurance

13. The Secretariat shall take out suitable insurances with one or more reputable financial institution against normal risks to its assets.

Regulation 14 General provision

14.1 These Regulations may be amended by a Decision of the ATCM.

14.2 Where the ATCM is considering matters which may lead to a decision which has financial or administrative implications, it shall have before it an evaluation of those implications from the Executive Secretary.

Headquarters Agreement for the Secretariat of the Antarctic Treaty between the Antarctic Treaty Consultative Meeting and the Argentine Republic[1]

The Antarctic Treaty Consultative Meeting (ATCM) and the Argentine Republic,

Convinced of the need to strengthen the Antarctic Treaty system;

Bearing in mind the special legal and political status of Antarctica and the special responsibility of the Antarctic Treaty Consultative Parties to ensure that all activities in Antarctica are consistent with the purposes and principles of the Antarctic Treaty and its Protocol on Environmental Protection;

Having regard to Decision 1 (2001) of the XXIV ATCM and Measure 1 (2003) of the XXVI ATCM on the Secretariat of the Antarctic Treaty in Buenos Aires, Argentina;

Desiring to enable the Secretariat as an organ of the ATCM fully and efficiently to fulfill its purposes and functions; and

Desiring to define the legal capacity of the Secretariat as an organ of the ATCM as well as its privileges and immunities and those of the Executive Secretary and other staff members in the territory of the Argentine Republic;

[1] Adopted 10 May 2010.

Have agreed as follows:

Article 1 Definitions

For the purpose of this Agreement:

(a) "Antarctic Treaty" or "the Treaty" means the Antarctic Treaty done at Washington on 1 December 1959;

(b) "Appropriate Authorities" means the national, provincial or local authorities of the Argentine Republic in accordance with the laws of the Argentine Republic;

(c) "Archives" means all correspondence, documents, manuscripts, photographs, computer data storage, films, recordings and any other records, in paper, electronic or any other form, belonging to or held by the Secretariat;

(d) "Committee for Environmental Protection" or "CEP" means the Committee established under Article 11 of the Protocol;

(e) "Delegates" means Representatives, Alternate Representatives, Advisers and any other persons who represent the States Parties;

(f) "Executive Secretary" means the Executive Secretary appointed by the ATCM to head the Secretariat according to the instrument establishing the Secretariat;

(g) "Expert" means a person engaged to perform short term or temporary projects on behalf of the Secretariat or participate in the work of or perform a mission on behalf of the Secretariat without necessarily receiving remuneration from the Secretariat, but does not include staff members;

(h) "Government" means the Government of the Argentine Republic;

(i) "Headquarters" means the premises, including buildings or parts of buildings and any land ancillary thereto, irrespective of ownership, occupied by the Secretariat for the performance of its Official Activities;

(j) "Official Activities" means all activities undertaken pursuant to the Treaty and the Protocol including the Secretariat's administrative activities;

(k) "Protocol" means the Protocol on Environmental Protection to the Antarctic Treaty done at Madrid on 4 October 1991;

(l) "Secretariat" means the Secretariat of the Antarctic Treaty, established as a permanent organ of the ATCM;

(m) "Staff member" means the Executive Secretary and all other persons appointed for employment with the Secretariat and subject to its Staff Regulations, but does not include persons recruited locally and assigned to hourly rates of pay; and

(n) "States Parties" means the States Parties to the Antarctic Treaty.

Article 2 Legal Capacity

The Secretariat as an organ of the ATCM has legal personality and capacity to perform its functions in the territory of the Argentine Republic. It has, in particular, the capacity to contract, to acquire and dispose of movable and immovable property, and to institute and be a party to legal proceedings. The Secretariat may exercise its legal capacity only to the extent authorized by the ATCM.

Article 3 Headquarters

1. The Headquarters shall be inviolable and shall be under the full authority of the Secretariat.

2. The Government shall provide premises rent-free, in Buenos Aires, suitable as the Headquarters.

3. The Government shall take all appropriate steps to protect the Headquarters against any intrusion or damage and to prevent any impairment of its dignity.

4. The Government shall arrange for the Headquarters to be supplied by the appropriate authorities with available public services, such as electricity, water, sewerage, gas, mail, telephone, telegraph, drainage, garbage collection and fire protection, on terms no less favourable than those enjoyed by diplomatic missions in Argentine Republic.

5. Through the ATCM, the Secretariat shall make known to the Government the need for any changes to the location or extent of its permanent premises or archives and of any temporary occupation of premises for the performance of its Official Activities. Where any premises other than those provided under paragraph 2 above are used or occupied by the Secretariat for the performance of its Official Activities, such premises shall, with the concurrence of the Government, be accorded the status of official premises of the Secretariat. Where any permanent or temporary changes are made to the premises of the Secretariat in accordance with this paragraph, any additional premises occupied by the Secretariat shall not necessarily be provided by the Government rent-free.

6. Without prejudice to the terms of this Agreement, the Secretariat shall not permit the Headquarters to become a refuge from justice for persons avoiding arrest or service of legal process or against whom an order of extradition or deportation has been issued.

7. The Appropriate Authorities may enter the Headquarters to carry out their duties only with the consent of the Executive Secretary and under the conditions agreed by him/her. The Executive Secretary's consent shall be deemed to have been given in the case of fire or other exceptional emergencies which require immediate protective action.

Article 4 Immunities

1. Subject to what is provided for in the Treaty, the Protocol or this Agreement, the activities of the Secretariat in the Argentine Republic shall be governed by Argentine domestic law consistent with international law.

2. Within the scope of its Official Activities, the Secretariat as an organ of the ATCM and its property, premises and assets shall have immunity of jurisdiction in judicial and administrative proceedings except:

(a) to the extent that the ATCM expressly waives such immunity;

(b) in respect of any contract for the supply of goods or services and any loan or other transaction for the provision of finance and any guarantee or indemnity in respect of any such transaction or of any other financial obligation;

(c) in respect of a civil action by a third party for death, damage or personal injury arising from an accident caused by a motor vehicle belonging to, or operated on behalf of, the Secretariat to the extent that compensation is not recoverable from insurance;

(d) in respect of a motor vehicle offence involving a motor vehicle belonging to, or operated on behalf of, the Secretariat;

(e) in the event of a claim for salaries, wages or other emoluments owed by the Secretariat;

(f) in respect of a counter-claim directly connected with proceedings initiated by the Secretariat;

(g) in respect of claims made on real estate situated in the Argentine Republic; and

(h) in respect of actions based on the Secretariat's status as heir or beneficiary of property situated in the Argentine Republic.

3. The Secretariat's property, premises and assets shall have immunity from any form of restrictions or controls such as requisition, confiscation, expropriation or attachment. They shall also be immune from any form of administrative or judicial constraint provided that motor vehicles belonging to or operated on behalf of the Secretariat shall not be immune from administrative or judicial constraint when temporarily necessary in connection with the prevention of, and investigation into, accidents involving such motor vehicles.

4. Nothing in this Agreement shall impair, or shall be construed as a waiver of, immunity that States enjoy in the territory of other States.

Article 5 Objective and Waiver of Privileges and Immunities

1. Privileges and immunities provided for in this Agreement are granted to ensure the unimpeded functioning of the ATCM and the Secretariat and the complete independence of the persons to whom they are accorded. They are not granted for the personal benefit of the individuals themselves.

2. Except as provided in paragraph 3 below, the privileges and immunities provided in this Agreement may be waived by the ATCM. They should be waived in a particular case where the privilege and immunity in question would impede the course of justice and can be waived without prejudice to the purpose for which they are accorded.

3. In the case of Delegates, their privileges and immunities provided in this Agreement may be waived by the States Parties which they respectively represent.

Article 6 Archives

The Archives shall be inviolable.

Article 7 The Treaty Flag and Emblem

The Secretariat shall be entitled to display the Treaty flag and emblem on the premises and means of transport of the Secretariat and of the Executive Secretary.

Article 8 Exemption from Direct Taxes

Within the scope of its Official Activities, the Secretariat, its property, premises and assets, and its income (including contributions made to the Secretariat as the result of any agreement arrived at by the States Parties) shall be exempt from all direct taxes including income tax, capital gains tax and all State taxes. The Secretariat shall be exempt from municipal taxes with the exception of those which constitute payment for specific services rendered in accordance with paragraph 4 of Article 3 above.

Article 9 Exemption from Customs and Excise Duties and Value Added Tax

1. The property used by the Secretariat necessary for its Official Activities (including the ATCM publications, motor vehicles and items for official entertainment purposes) shall be exempt from all customs and excise duties.

2. The Secretariat shall be exempt from any value added tax or similar taxes for services and goods, including publications and other information material, motor vehicles and items for official entertainment purposes, if the services and goods so purchased by the Secretariat are necessary for its official use.

Article 10 Exemption from Restrictions and Prohibitions

Goods imported or exported for the Official Activities of the Secretariat shall be exempt from any prohibitions or restrictions applicable to such goods on grounds of national origin.

Article 11 Re-sale

Goods which have been acquired or imported by the Secretariat to which exemptions under Article 9 above apply and goods acquired or imported by the Executive Secretary or other staff members to which the exemptions under Article 16 or Article 17 below apply, shall not be given away, sold, lent, hired out or otherwise disposed of in the Argentine Republic, except under conditions agreed in advance with the Government.

Article 12 Currency and Exchange

The Secretariat shall be exempt from any currency or exchange restrictions, including those in respect of funds, currency and securities received, acquired, held or disposed of. The Secretariat may also operate without restrictions bank or other accounts for its official use in any currency, and have them transferred freely within the Argentine Republic or to any other country.

Article 13 Communications

1. With regard to its official communications and the transfer of all its documents, the Secretariat shall enjoy treatment not less favourable than that generally accorded by the Government to any other government, including the latter's diplomatic mission, in the matter of priorities, rates and taxes on mails and all forms of telecommunications.

2. The Secretariat may employ any appropriate means of communication, including encrypted messages. The Government shall not impose any restriction on the official communications of the Secretariat or on the circulation of its publications.

3. The Secretariat may install and use radio transmitters with the consent of the Government.

4. Official correspondence and other official communications of the Secretariat are not subject to censorship and shall enjoy all the guarantees established by Argentine domestic law.

Article 14 Publications

The importation and exportation of the Secretariat's publications and other information material imported or exported by the Secretariat within the scope of its Official Activities shall not be restricted in any way.

Article 15 Privileges and Immunities of Delegates

1. Delegates of the States Parties shall enjoy, during their stay in the Argentine Republic for exercising their official functions, the privileges and immunities of diplomatic agents as established in the Vienna Convention on Diplomatic Relations of 18 April 1961.

2. The provisions of paragraph 1 above shall be applicable irrespective of the relations existing between the governments which the persons referred to represent and the Government, and are without prejudice to any additional immunities to which such persons may be entitled in the Argentine Republic.

3. The privileges and immunities described in paragraph 1 above shall not be accorded to any delegate of the Government or to any national or permanent resident of the Argentine Republic.

4. The Government shall treat Delegates with all due respect and shall take all necessary measures to prevent encroachment on their person, freedom and dignity. Where it appears that an offence may have been committed against a Delegate, steps shall be taken in accordance with Argentine legal procedures to investigate the matter and to ensure that appropriate action is taken with respect to the prosecution of the alleged offender.

Article 16 Executive Secretary

In addition to the privileges, immunities, exemptions and facilities provided for in Article 17 below, the Executive Secretary, unless he or she is a national or a permanent resident of the Argentine Republic, shall enjoy the privileges, immunities, exemptions and facilities to which a diplomatic agent in the Argentine Republic is entitled, including privileges, immunities, exemptions and facilities in respect of the members of their family which form a part of the household, unless they are nationals or permanent residents of the Argentine Republic.

Article 17 Staff Members

1. Staff members of the Secretariat:

(a) shall have, even after the termination of their service with the Secretariat, immunity from suit and any other legal or administrative proceedings or judicial request in respect of acts and things done by them in the exercise of their official functions, including words written or spoken;

(b) immunities set out in the sub-paragraph above shall not, however, apply in the case of a motor vehicle offence committed by such a staff member or the Executive Secretary nor in the case of civil or administrative proceedings arising out of death, damage or personal injury caused by a motor vehicle belonging to or driven by him or her to the extent that compensation is not recoverable from insurance;

(c) shall be exempt from any obligations in respect of military service and all other kinds of mandatory service, unless they are nationals or permanent residents of the Argentine Republic;

(d) shall be exempt from the application of laws relating to the registration of aliens and immigration;

(e) unless they are nationals or permanent residents of the Argentine Republic, they shall be accorded the same exemption from currency and exchange restrictions as is accorded to an official of comparable rank from an international agency in the Argentine Republic;

(f) unless they are nationals or permanent residents of the Argentine Republic, they shall when taking up their post in the Argentine Republic for the first time, be exempt from customs duties and other such charges (except payments for services) in respect of import of furniture, motor vehicles and other personal effects in their ownership or possession or already ordered by them and intended for their personal use or for their establishment. Such goods shall be imported within six months of a staff member's first entry into the Argentine Republic but in exceptional circumstances an extension of this period shall be granted by the Government. Goods which have been acquired or imported by staff members and to which exemptions under this sub-paragraph apply shall not be given away, sold, lent, hired out, or otherwise disposed of except under conditions agreed in advance with the Government. Furniture and personal effects may be exported free of duties when leaving the Argentine Republic on the termination of the official functions of the staff member;

(g) shall be exempt from all taxes on income received from the Secretariat. This exemption shall not apply to staff members who are nationals or permanent residents of the Argentine Republic;

(h) shall have similar repatriation facilities as are accorded to representatives of international agencies in times of international crisis; and

(i) shall have personal inviolability with respect to any form of personal arrest or detention or seizure of their personal baggage unless they are nationals or permanent residents of the Argentine Republic.

2. Privileges and immunities applicable to a staff member in accordance with sub-paragraphs c), d), e), f), h) and i) of paragraph 1 above shall also apply to the members of his or her family forming a part of the household, unless they are nationals or permanent residents in the Argentine Republic.

Article 18 Experts

In the exercise of their functions experts shall enjoy the following privileges and immunities to the extent necessary for the carrying out of their functions, including while traveling in the Argentine Republic to that effect:

(a) immunity from suit and any other legal or administrative proceedings or judicial request in respect of acts and things done by them in the exercise of their official functions, including words written or spoken. This immunity shall not, however, apply in the case of a motor vehicle offence committed by such experts nor in the case of civil or administrative proceedings arising out of death, damage or personal injury caused by a motor vehicle belonging to or driven by him or her to the extent the compensation is not recoverable from insurance. Such immunity shall continue after the expert's function in relation to the Secretariat has ceased;

(b) inviolability for all their official papers and documents as well as other official materials, which are related to the performance of the functions of the Secretariat;

(c) unless they are nationals or permanent residents of the Argentine Republic, the same exemption from currency and exchange restrictions as is accorded to a representative of a foreign Government on a temporary mission in Argentina on behalf of that Government; and

(d) unless they are nationals or permanent residents of the Argentine Republic, immunity from personal arrest and detention and from attachment of personal luggage.

Article 19 Visas

1. All persons having official business with the Secretariat, namely Delegates and members of their families forming a part of the household, staff members of the Secretariat and any members of their families forming a part of the household, and the experts referred to in Article 18 above, shall have the right of entry into, stay in and exit from the Argentine Republic.

2. The Government shall take all measures necessary to facilitate the entry into the Argentine Republic, the sojourn on that territory and the exit therefrom of all persons mentioned in paragraph 1 above. Visas, where required, shall be granted without wait or delay, and without fee, on production of a certificate that the applicant is a person described in paragraph 1 above. In addition, the Government shall facilitate travel for such persons within the territory of the Argentine Republic.

Article 20 Cooperation

The Secretariat shall co-operate fully at all times with the appropriate Authorities in order to prevent any abuse of the privileges, immunities and facilities provided for in this Agreement. The Government reserves its sovereign right to take reasonable measures to preserve security. Nothing in this Agreement prevents the application of laws necessary for health and quarantine or, with respect to the Secretariat and its officials, laws relating to public order.

Article 21 Notification of appointments, identity cards

1. The ATCM shall notify the Government of the appointment of an Executive Secretary and the date when he or she is to take up or relinquish the post.
2. The Secretariat shall notify the Government when a staff member takes up or relinquishes his or her post or when an expert starts or finishes a project or mission.
3. The Secretariat shall twice a year send to the Government a list of all experts and staff members and the members of their families forming a part of the household in the Argentine Republic. In each case the Secretariat shall indicate whether such persons are nationals or permanent residents of the Argentine Republic.
4. The Government shall issue to all staff members and experts as soon as practicable after notification of their appointment, a card bearing the photograph of the holder and identifying him or her as a staff member or expert as the case may be. This card shall be accepted by the appropriate Authorities as evidence of identity and appointment. The members of their families forming a part of the household shall also be issued with an identity card. When the staff member or expert relinquishes his or her duties, the Secretariat shall return to the Government his or her identity card together with identity cards issued to members of his or her family forming a part of the household.

Article 22 Consultation

The Government and the Secretariat as an organ of the ATCM shall consult at the request of either of them concerning matters arising under this Agreement. If any such matter is not promptly resolved, the Secretariat shall refer it to the ATCM.

Article 23 Amendment

This Agreement may be amended by agreement between the Government and the ATCM.

Article 24 Settlement of disputes

Any dispute arising out of the interpretation or application of this Agreement shall be settled by consultation, negotiation or any other mutually acceptable method, which may include resort to binding arbitration.

Article 25 Entry into force and termination

1. This Agreement shall enter into force upon signature.
2. This Agreement may be terminated by written notification by either Party. Termination shall take effect two years after receipt of such notification unless otherwise agreed.

Done in Punta del Este, on the tenth day of May, 2010, in two originals, in the Spanish, English, French and Russian languages, both being equally authentic.

[*Signatories omitted.*]

PART 3
ANTARCTIC TREATY CONSULTATIVE MEETINGS (ATCM) (1963–2013)

List of All Measures, Decisions, Recommendations and Resolutions Adopted by the ATCM 1961–2014[1]*

ATCM I, Canberra, 10–24 July 1961

I Exchange of information on scientific programmes
II Exchange of scientific personnel
III Exchange of scientific data
IV SCAR
V International organizations
VI Exchange of information
*VII Exchange of information on logistic problems
VIII Conservation of fauna and flora
IX Historic sites
X Assistance in emergency
XI Telecommunications
XII Postal services
*XIII Exchange of information on nuclear equipment and techniques
XIV Administrative arrangements for Consultative Meetings
XV Second Consultative Meeting
XVI Preparations for Consultative Meetings

ATCM II, Buenos Aires, 18–28 July 1962

I Exchange of scientific data
*II Conservation of Antarctic fauna and flora
III Telecommunications
IV Exchange of information on operations
V Symposium/logistic problems
VI Exchange of information
VII Shipment of scientific materials
VIII International Year of the Quiet Sun (1964–65)
IX Consultative meeting recommendation
X Third Consultative Meeting

ATCM III, Brussels, 2–13 June 1964

I Information on facilities for the landing of aircraft
II Notification of unoccupied refuges
III Logistics
IV Next meeting
V Telecommunications
VI Questions concerning meeting of specialists
VII Acceptance of approved recommendations
*VIII Agreed Measures for the Conservation of Antarctic fauna and flora
IX Interim guidelines for the Conservation of Antarctic fauna and flora

* Denotes no longer in force (See Annex 1 to Decision 1 (1995))

[1] Between 1961–1994, instruments adopted by ATCM were described as Recommendations. By Decision 1 (1995) Parties agreed at the Consultative Meeting to a new nomenclature and numbering system for Recommendations.

*X SCAR interest in the Conservation of Antarctic fauna and flora
XI Pelagic sealing and the taking of fauna on pack ice

ATCM IV, Santiago, 3–18 November 1966

*1 Specially Protected Areas: Taylor Rookery
*2 Specially Protected Areas: Rookery Islands
*3 Specially Protected Areas: Ardery Island and Odbert Island
4 Specially Protected Areas: Sabrina Island, Balleny Islands
5 Specially Protected Areas: Beaufort Island, Ross Sea
6 Specially Protected Areas: Cape Crozier, Ross Island
7 Specially Protected Areas: Cape Hallett, Victoria Land
*8 Specially Protected Areas: Dion Islands
*9 Specially Protected Areas: Green Island
10 Specially Protected Areas: Byers Peninsula
11 Specially Protected Areas: Cape Shirreff
12 Specially Protected Areas: Fildes Peninsula
*13 Specially Protected Areas: Moe Island
14 Specially Protected Areas: Lynch Island
15 Specially Protected Areas: Southern Powell Island and adjacent islands
*16 Specially Protected Species: Fur Seals
*17 Specially Protected Species: Ross Seals
18 Cooperation in implementing Article VI of Agreed Measures for the Conservation of Fauna and Flora
*19 Implementation of Article XII(1)(d) of Agreed Measures
20 Interim guidelines for the Conservation of fauna and flora
21 Interim guidelines for the voluntary regulation of Antarctic pelagic sealing
22 SCAR interest in Antarctic pelagic sealing
23 Date of exchanges of information
24 Meetings of experts
25 Meeting on logistics
26 Telecommunications
27 Effects of Antarctic tourism
28 Next meeting

ATCM V, Paris, 18–29 November 1968

1 Commemorative stamp issue
*2 Measures for improving Antarctic telecommunications
3 Southern Ocean
4 Historic monuments
5 Specially Protected Areas: Fildes Peninsula
6 Modification of Agreed Measures
7 SCAR proposals for revision of Guidelines on Pelagic Sealing
8 Examination of Draft Convention for Regulation of Antarctic Pelagic Sealing
9 Sixth Consultative Meeting

ATCM VI, Tokyo, 19–31 October 1970

*1 Antarctic telecommunications
2 Exchange of information on telecommunications facilities
*3 Antarctic meteorology
*4 Man's impact on Antarctic environment
5 Use of radio-isotopes in the Antarctic
6 Coordination of Antarctic scientific investigations involving the use of radio-isotopes
7 Effects of tourists and non-government expeditions to the Antarctic Treaty area

*8 Permits for entry to Specially Protected Areas
*9 Data on the conservation of fauna and flora
10 Specially Protected Areas: Coppermine Peninsula, Robert Island
11 New islands
12 Scientific research rockets
13 Exchange of information on oceanographic research
14 Historic monuments
15 Seventh Consultative Meeting

ATCM VII, Wellington, 30 October–10 November 1972

*1 Man's impact on the environment
2 Review of Specially Protected Areas
3 Sites of Special Scientific Interest
4 Effects of tourists and non-governmental expeditions in the Antarctic Treaty Area
*5 Import of laboratory plants/animals
6 Antarctic resources: Effects of mineral exploration
7 Antarctic telecommunications
8 Cooperation in transport
*9 Historic monuments

ATCM VIII, Oslo, 9–20 June 1975

1 Specially Protected Areas: Litchfield Island
*2 Review of Specially Protected Areas
3 Sites of Special Scientific Interest
*4 Sites of Special Scientific Interest: interim guidelines
5 Permits for entry into Specially Protected Areas
6 Annual exchanges of information
7 Cooperation in transport
8 Activities of states that are not consultative parties
9 Effects of tourists and non-governmental expeditions in the Treaty Area
10 Antarctic marine living resources
*11 Man's impact on the environment
12 Disposal of nuclear wastes
*13 The Antarctic environment
14 Antarctic resources: effects of mineral exploitation

ATCM IX, London, 19 September–7 October 1977

1 Antarctic mineral resources
2 Antarctic marine living resources
3 Improvement of telecommunications in the Antarctic
4 Cooperation in transport
*5 Man's impact on the Antarctic environment
*6 Oil contamination of the Antarctic marine environment

ATCM X, Washington, 17 September–5 October 1979

1 Antarctic mineral resources
2 Antarctic marine living resources
3 Improvement of telecommunications in Antarctica and the collection and distribution of Antarctic meteorological data
*4 Man's impact on the Antarctic environment: collection of geological specimens
*5 Man's impact on the Antarctic environment: Sites of Special Scientific Interest: interim guidelines
*6 Man's impact on the Antarctic environment: Sites of Special Scientific Interest
*7 Oil contamination of the Antarctic marine environment

8 Effects of tourists and non-government expeditions in the Antarctic Treaty Area
9 Twentieth anniversary of the Antarctic Treaty

ATCM XI, Buenos Aires, 23 June–7 July 1981

1 Antarctic mineral resources
2 Antarctic marine living resources
3 Air disaster on Mount Erebus

ATCM XII, Canberra, 13–27 September 1983

*1 Collection and distribution of Antarctic meteorological data
2 Antarctic telecommunications
*3 Man's impact on the Antarctic environment
*4 Man's impact on the Antarctic environment: Code of conduct on waste disposal for Antarctic expeditions and station activities
*5 Sites of Special Scientific Interest: Extension of the expiry date of the designation of Sites 1–8
6 Operation of the Antarctic Treaty System
7 Historic sites and monuments
8 SCAR assistance to consultative parties

ATCM XIII, Brussels, 8–18 October 1985

1 Operation of the Antarctic Treaty System: information
2 Operation of the Antarctic Treaty System: overview
3 Exchange of information in accordance with the Antarctic Treaty: annual exchanges
*4 Man's impact on the Antarctic environment: code of conduct for Antarctic expeditions and station activities: waste disposal
5 Man's impact on the Antarctic environment: additional protective arrangements
6 Facilitation of scientific research: siting of stations
*7 Facilitation of scientific research: Sites of Special Scientific Interest: Interim guidelines: extension of designation
8 Facilitation of scientific research: Sites of Special Scientific Interest: Interim guidelines: additional Sites
*9 Facilitation of scientific research: Sites of Special Scientific Interest: Interim guidelines: SSSI No 1: Cape Royds, Ross Island: amendment to management plan
*10 Specially Protected Areas: North Coronation Island, South Orkney Islands
11 Specially Protected Areas: Lagotellerie Island, Marguerite Bay
*12 Specially Protected Areas: 'New College Valley', Caughley Beach, Cape Bird, Ross Island
13 Specially Protected Area No 7: Cape Hallett, Victoria Land: extension of boundaries
*14 Specially Protected Areas: interim guidelines
15 Matters relating to the appointment of observers at consultative meetings
16 Historic sites and monuments

ATCM XIV, Rio de Janeiro, 5–16 October 1987

1 Operation of Antarctic Treaty System; public availability of the documents of Consultative Meetings
*2 Man's impact on the Antarctic environment: environmental impact assessment
3 Man's impact on the Antarctic environment: safeguards for scientific drilling
*4 Facilitation of scientific research: Sites of Special Scientific Interest: Interim Guidelines: extension of designation
5 Facilitation of scientific research: Sites of Special Scientific Interest: Interim Guidelines: additional sites
6 Marine Sites of Special Scientific Interest
*7 Antarctic meteorology and telecommunications

8 Historic sites and monuments
9 Air safety in Antarctica
*10 Marine meteorological and sea ice information services for navigation in the Treaty Area of the Southern Ocean

ATCM XV, Paris, 9–20 October 1989

*1 Comprehensive Measures for the protection of the Antarctic environment and dependent and associated ecosystems
2 Comprehensive Measures for the protection of the Antarctic environment and dependent and associated ecosystems
*3 Human impact on the Antarctic environment: waste disposal
*4 Human impact on the Antarctic environment: prevention, control and response to marine pollution
5 Human impact on the Antarctic environment: environmental monitoring in Antarctica
*6 Antarctic Protected Area System: new Sites of Special Scientific Interest Nos. 29, 30, 31
*7 Antarctic Protected Area System: redesignation of Specially Protected Area No. 11, Cape Shirreff as Site of Special Scientific Interest No. 32
8 Antarctic Protected Area System: Agreed Measures for the Conservation of Antarctic Fauna and Flora: amendment to Article VIII (Management Plans for Specially Protected Areas)
9 Antarctic Protected Area System: Development of improved descriptions and management plans for Specially Protected Areas
10 Antarctic Protected Area System: Establishment of Specially Reserved Areas (SRAs)
11 Antarctic Protected Area System: Establishment of Multiple-use Planning Areas (MPAs)
12 Antarctic Protected Area System: new Historic Sites and Monuments
13 Antarctic Protected Area System: Historic Sites and Monuments (Amendment to description of HM 53)
14 Promotion of international scientific cooperation: a declaration
15 Promotion of international scientific cooperation
16 Facilitation of scientific research: comparability and accessibility of Antarctic scientific data
17 Facilitation of scientific research: siting of scientific stations
*18 Cooperation in meteorological and sea ice information services for maritime and air navigation in Antarctica
*19 Cooperation in hydrographic charting of Antarctic waters
20 Air safety in Antarctica
21 Uses of Antarctic ice
22 Antarctic Treaty thirtieth anniversary commemorative stamp

ATCM XVI, Bonn, 7–18 October 1991

1 Exchange of information
2 Antarctic Protected Area System, New Sites of Special Scientific Interest
3 Antarctic Protected Area System, New Marine Sites of Special Scientific Interest
*4 Antarctic Protected Area System, Specially Protected Areas No. 21
*5 Antarctic Protected Area System, Site of Special Scientific Interest No. 6: revised management plan
6 Antarctic Protected Area System, Specially Protected Areas: revised descriptions and management plans for Nos. 8, 9, 13, 14, 15, 16, 18, 19
7 Antarctic Protected Area System, Sites of Special Scientific Interest: Extension of Designation

*8 Antarctic Protected Area System, Specially Protected Area No. 22
9 Antarctic Protected Area System, Specially Protected Area No. 23
10 Antarctic Protected Area System, Review of the System: Annex V to the Protocol on Environmental Protection to the Antarctic Treaty: Area Protection and Management
11 Antarctic Protected Area System, New Historic Sites and Monuments
12 Accessibility of Antarctic Geophysical data
13 Tourism and non-governmental activities in the Antarctic Treaty Area

ATCM XVII, Venice, 11–20 November 1992

1 Environmental monitoring and data management
2 Revised descriptions and proposed management plans for Specially Protected Areas
3 Antarctic Protected Areas: New Historic Sites and Monuments
4 Global change research and international cooperation in Antarctica

ATCM XVIII, Kyoto, 11–22 April 1994

1 Tourism and non-Governmental Activities

ATCM XIX, Seoul, 8–19 May 1995

Measure 1 (1995) Revised Descriptions and Management Plans for Specially Protected Areas
*Measure 2 (1995) Revised Description and Management Plan for Sites of Special Scientific Interest
Measure 3 (1995) Antarctic Protected Area System: Specially Protected Areas
Measure 4 (1995) Antarctic Protected Area System: New Historic Sites and Monuments
Measure 5 (1995) Historic Sites and Monuments: Amendment – Short amendment to Resolution 9
Decision 1 (1995) Measures, Decisions and Resolutions
Decision 2 (1995) Rules of Procedure: Amendment
*Resolution 1 (1995) Strengthening Cooperation in Hydrographic Surveying and Charting of Antarctic Waters
Resolution 2 (1995) Nuclear Waste Disposal
Resolution 3 (1995) Reporting of Tourism and non-Governmental Activities
*Resolution 4 (1995) Fuel Storage and Handling
Resolution 5 (1995) Antarctic Inspection Checklists
*Resolution 6 (1995) Environmental Impact Assessment: Circulation of Information
*Resolution 7 (1995) Extension of the Expiry Dates for Sites of Special Scientific Interest
Resolution 8 (1995) New Historic Sites and Monuments: Suggested Guidelines for the Designation of Historic Sites
Resolution 9 (1995) Uniform Model for Management Plans

ATCM XX, Utrecht, 29 April–10 May 1996

Measure 1 (1996) Revised Description and Management Plan for Sites of Scientific Interest
Measure 2 (1996) Antarctic Protected Area System: New Historic Sites and Monuments
Resolution 1 (1996) Addition to Checklist A "Permanent Antarctic Stations and Associated Installations" attached to Resolution 5 (1995)
Resolution 2 (1996) Aesthetic Values of Antarctica
*Resolution 3 (1996) Extension of the Expiry Dates for Sites of Special Scientific Interest
Resolution 4 (1996) Effective Management and Conservation of Historic Sites and Monuments
*Resolution 5 (1996) Revised Renumbering of Antarctic Protected Areas

ATCM XXI, Christchurch, 19–30 May 1997

Measure 1 (1997) Antarctic Protected Areas System: Revised Description and Management Plan for Specially Protected Area, SPA 5 Beaufort Island

Measure 2 (1997)	Antarctic Protected Areas System: Management Plans for Specially Protected Areas, Number 25 Cape Evans Historic Site and its environs, Number 26 Lewis Bay Tomb
Measure 3 (1997)	Antarctic Protected Areas System: Revised Descriptions and Management Plans for Sites of Special Scientific Interest (SSSI)
Measure 4 (1997)	Antarctic Protected Areas System: Historic Sites and Monuments: Memorial Cross, Lewis Bay, Ross Island
Measure 5 (1997)	Antarctic Protected Areas System: Historic Sites and Monuments: Amendment Number 41: Stone Hut on Paulet Island
Decision 1 (1997)	Revised Rules of Procedure (1997)
Decision 2 (1997)	Consultative Status
Resolution 1 (1997)	Emergency Response Action and Contingency Planning
Resolution 2 (1997)	Comprehensive Environmental Evaluation (CEE): Methodology for Reviewing Activities for which a CEE has been Prepared
Resolution 3 (1997)	Standard Form for Advance Notification and Post-Visit Reporting on Tourism and Non-Governmental Activities in Antarctica
ATCM XXII, Tromsø, 25 May–5 June 1998	
Measure 1 (1998)	Antarctic Protected Areas System: Management Plan for Specially Protected Areas, Number 27: Cape Royds Historic Site and its environs, Number 28: Hut Point, Historic Site Number 29: Cape Adare Historic Site and its environs
Measure 2 (1998)	Antarctic Protected Areas System: Historic Sites and Monument, South-West Coast of Elephant Island, South Shetland Islands
Decision 1 (1998)	Recognition that the Republic of Bulgaria has fulfilled the requirements established in Article IX, paragraph 2
Decision 2 (1998)	Rules of Procedure for the Committee for Environmental Protection
*Decision 3 (1998)	Liability
Decision 4 (1998)	Marine Protected Areas
Resolution 1 (1998)	Annex V: Protected Areas
Resolution 2 (1998)	Guide to the Preparation of Management Plans for Antarctic Specially Protected Areas
Resolution 3 (1998)	International Code of Safety for Ships in Polar Waters
Resolution 4 (1998)	Antarctic Data Management
Resolution 5 (1998)	ATCM Home Page
*Resolution 6 (1998)	Emergency Response Action and Contingency Planning
ATCM XXIII, Lima, 24 May–4 June 1999	
Measure 1 (1999)	Antarctic Protected Areas System: Revised Management Plan for Site of Special Scientific Interest No. 23: Svarthamaren
Decision 1 (1999)	CEP Web Site
Decision 2 (1999)	Guidelines for Antarctic Shipping and Related Activities
*Resolution 1 (1999)	Guidelines for EIA in Antarctica
Resolution 2 (1999)	List of Specially Protected Species: Annex II to the Environmental Protocol
Resolution 3 (1999)	Support for CCAMLR
*Resolution 4 (1999)	Cooperation among Parties in Accordance with Article 6 of the Protocol on Environmental Protection to the Antarctic Treaty
Resolution 5 (1999)	Advice from COMNAP and SCAR
Resolution 6 (1999)	Adherence to the Environmental Protocol by Non-Consultative Parties
ATCM XXIV, St Petersburg, 9–20 July 2001	
Measure 1 (2001)	Antarctic Protected Areas System: Historic Sites and Monuments: "A

	Hut", Scott Base, Ross Sea Region
Measure 2 (2001)	Antarctic Protected Areas System: Historic Sites and Monuments: Ruins of the Base Pedro Aguirre Cerda, Pendulum Cove, Deception Island
Measure 3 (2001)	Antarctic Protected Areas System: Extension of Expiry Dates for Certain Sites of Special Scientific Interest
Decision 1 (2001)	[Site of Permanent Secretariat]
Decision 2 (2001)	Guidelines on Circulation and Handling of CEP Documents
*Decision 3 (2001)	Liability
Resolution 1 (2001)	[Table of Recommendations, Measures, Decisions and Resolutions]
Resolution 2 (2001)	Support for CCAMLR and its Measures to Combat Illegal, Unregulated and Unrestricted Fishing, Including a Catch Documentation Scheme for Dissostichus spp. (Toothfish)
Resolution 3 (2001)	Collection of meteorites in Antarctica
Resolution 4 (2001)	Historic Sites and Monuments
Resolution 5 (2001)	Guidelines for Handling of Pre-1958 Historic Remains whose Existence or Present Location is Not Known
Resolution 6 (2001)	Exchange of Information

ATCM XXV, Warsaw, 10–20 September 2002

Measure 1 (2002)	Antarctic Protected Area System: Management Plans for Antarctic Specially Protected Areas – Measures 1 relates to specific sites and so not included
Decision 1 (2002)	Naming and Numbering System for Antarctic Specially Protected Areas
Decision 2 (2002)	Emblem of the Antarctic Treaty
Decision 3 (2002)	The Status of ATCM Recommendation
Resolution 1 (2002)	Review of Conservation Status of Antarctic Species
Resolution 2 (2002)	Revision of Antarctic Specially Protected Area Management Plans
Resolution 3 (2002)	Support for CCAMLR and action to combat Illegal, Unreported and Unregulated Fishing for Dissostichus spp (toothfish)

ATCM XXVI, Madrid, 9–20 June 2003

Measure 1 (2003)	Secretariat of the Antarctic Treaty
Measure 2 (2003)	Antarctic Protected Area System: Management Plans for Antarctic Specially Protected Areas – not included, all in relation to particular areas
Measure 3 (2003)	Antarctic Protected Areas System: Revised List of Historic Sites and Monuments
Decision 1 (2003)	Apportioning Contributions to the Secretariat of the Antarctic Treaty
Decision 2 (2003)	Provisional Application of Measure 1
Decision 3 (2003)	Staff Regulations for the Secretariat of the Antarctic Treaty
Decision 4 (2003)	Financial Regulations for the Secretariat of the Antarctic Treaty
Decision 5 (2003)	Meeting of Experts on Tourism and Non-Governmental Activities
Resolution 1 (2003)	(untitled): on the inclusion of the Protocol on Environmental Protection to the Antarctic Treaty (1998) in advices to marines
Resolution 2 (2003)	Support of the ATCM for the International Polar Year 2007/8
*Resolution 3 (2003)	Co-operation in Hydrographic Survey and Charting of Antarctic Waters
Resolution 4 (2003)	Support for the Conservation of Albatrosses and Petrels

ATCM XXVII, Capetown, 24 May 2004–4 June 2004

Measure 1 (2004)	Antarctic Specially Managed Areas: Designations and Management Plans – not included, all in relation to particular areas
Measure 2 (2004)	Antarctic Specially Protected Areas: Designations and Management Plans – not included, all in relation to particular areas
Decision 1 (2004)	Revised Rules of Procedure

Decision 2 (2004)	Financial Considerations for the Secretariat of the Antarctic Treaty
Decision 3 (2004)	Appointment of the Executive Secretary
Decision 4 (2004)	Guidelines for Ships Operating in Arctic and Antarctic Ice-Covered Waters
Resolution 1 (2004)	Enhancing Prevention of Marine Pollution by Fishing Activities
Resolution 2 (2004)	Guidelines for the Operation of Aircraft Near Concentrations of Birds in Antarctica
*Resolution 3 (2004)	Tourism and Non-governmental Activities: Enhanced Co-operation Amongst Parties
Resolution 4 (2004)	Guidelines on Contingency Planning, Insurance and Other Matters for Tourist and Other Non-governmental Activities in the Antarctic Treaty Area
Resolution 5 (2004)	Establishment of an Intersessional Contact Group to Improve Exchange of Information
ATCM XXVIII, Stockholm, 6–17 June 2005	
Measure 1 (2005)	Annex VI to the Protocol on Environmental Protection to the Antarctic Treaty: Liability Arising From Environmental Emergencies
Measure 2 (2005)	Antarctic Specially Protected Areas: Designations and Management Plans – not included, all in relation to particular areas
Measure 3 (2005)	Antarctic Specially Managed Area and Antarctic Specially Protected Areas: Designation and Management Plans: Deception Island
Measure 4 (2005)	Antarctic Specially Protected Areas: Extension of Expiry Dates
Measure 5 (2005)	Antarctic Historic Sites and Monuments: Lillie Marleen Hut and Amundsen's Tent
Decision 1 (2005)	Annex VI on Liability Arising from Environmental Emergencies to the Protocol on Environmental Protection to the Antarctic Treaty
Decision 2 (2005)	Decision confirming the recognition of Ukraine as a Consultative Party
Decision 3 (2005)	Amendments to the Rules of Procedure
Decision 4 (2005)	Consultative Party Status
Decision 5 (2005)	Appointment of External Auditor
Decision 6 (2005)	Amendment to Financial Regulations for the Secretariat of the Antarctic Treaty
Decision 7 (2005)	Approval of the Work Programme and Budget of the Secretariat
Decision 8 (2005)	Use of Heavy Fuel Oil (HFO) in Antarctica
Decision 9 (2005)	Marine Protected Areas and other areas of interest to CCAMLR
Decision 10 (2005)	Establishment of an Electronic Information Exchange System
Resolution 1 (2005)	Environmental Impact Assessment: Circulation of Information
Resolution 2 (2005)	Practical Guidelines for Developing and Designing Environmental Monitoring Programs in Antarctica
Resolution 3 (2005)	Fuel Storage and Handling
Resolution 4 (2005)	Updating of Guidelines for Environmental Impact Assessment in Antarctica
Resolution 5 (2005)	Resolution on Site Guidelines for Visitors
Resolution 6 (2005)	Antarctic Post Visit Site Report Form
Resolution 7 (2005)	Biological Prospecting in Antarctica
ATCM XXIX, Edinburgh, 12–23 June 2006	
Measure 1 (2006)	Antarctic Specially Protected Areas: Designations and Management Plans – not included, all in relation to particular areas
Measure 2 (2006)	Antarctic Specially Managed Area: Designation and Management Plan: Admiralty Bay, King George Island

Measure 3 (2006)	Antarctic Historic Sites and Monuments: Rocher du Débarquement
Measure 4 (2006)	Specially Protected Species: Fur Seals
Decision 1 (2006)	Approval of Secretariat's Financial Reports for 2004/5 and 2005/6 and Programme and Budget for 2006/7
Decision 2 (2006)	Ballast Water Exchange in the Antarctic Treaty Area
Resolution 1 (2006)	CCAMLR in the Antarctic Treaty System
Resolution 2 (2006)	Resolution on Site Guidelines for Visitors
Resolution 3 (2006)	Ballast Water Exchange in the Antarctic Treaty Area
Resolution 4 (2006)	Conservation of Southern Giant Petrels
ATCM XXX, New Delhi, 30 April 2007–11 May 2007	
Measure 1 (2007)	Antarctic Specially Protected Areas: Revised Management Plans
Measure 2 (2007)	Antarctic Specially Managed Areas: Designations and Management Plans
Measure 3 (2007)	Antarctic Historic Sites and Monuments: Monument to the Antarctic Treaty
Decision 1 (2007)	Review of the Status of Measures Relating to Area Protection and Management
Decision 2 (2007)	Re-appointment of the Executive Secretary
Decision 3 (2007)	Appointment of an External Auditor
Decision 4 (2007)	Approval of the Secretariat's Programme and Budget for 2007/08
Resolution 1 (2007)	Resolution on Site Guidelines for Visitors
Resolution 2 (2007)	Conservation of Southern Giant Petrel *Macronectes giganteus*
Resolution 3 (2007)	Long-term Scientific Monitoring and Sustained Environmental Observation in Antarctica
Resolution 4 (2007)	Ship-based Tourism in the Antarctic Treaty Area
Resolution 5 (2007)	Tourism in the Antarctic Treaty Area
ATCM XXXI, Kyiv, 2–13 June 2008	
Measure 1 (2008)	Antarctic Specially Managed Area No 7: South-west Anvers Island and Palmer Basin
Measure 2 (2008)	Antarctic Specially Protected Area No 168: Mount Harding, Grove Mountains, East Antarctica
Measure 3 (2008)	Antarctic Specially Protected Area No 169: Amanda Bay, Ingrid Christensen Coast, Princess Elizabeth Land, East Antarctica
Measure 4 (2008)	Antarctic Specially Protected Area No 170: Marion Nunataks, Charcot Island, Antarctic Peninsula
Measure 5 (2008)	Antarctic Specially Protected Area No 118: (Summit of Mount Melbourne, Victoria Land): Revised Management Plan
Measure 6 (2008)	Antarctic Specially Protected Area No 123: (Barwick and Balham Valleys, Southern Victoria Land): Revised Management Plan
Measure 7 (2008)	Antarctic Specially Protected Area No 124: (Cape Crozier, Ross Island): Revised Management Plan
Measure 8 (2008)	Antarctic Specially Protected Area No 135: (North-East Bailey Peninsula, Budd Coast, Wilkes Land): Revised Management Plan
Measure 9 (2008)	Antarctic Specially Protected Area No 137: (North-west White Island, McMurdo Sound): Revised Management Plan
Measure 10 (2008)	Antarctic Specially Protected Area No 138: (Linnaeus Terrace, Asgard Range, Victoria Land): Revised Management Plan
Measure 11 (2008)	Antarctic Specially Protected Area No 154: (Botany Bay, Cape Geology, Victoria Land): Revised Management Plan
Measure 12 (2008)	Antarctic Specially Protected Area No 155: (Cape Evans, Ross Island): Revised Management Plan

Measure 13 (2008)	Antarctic Specially Protected Area No 160: (Frazier Islands, Windmill Islands, Wilkes Land, East Antarctica): Revised Management Plan
Measure 14 (2008)	Antarctic Specially Protected Area No 161: (Terra Nova Bay, Ross Sea): Revised Management Plan
Decision 1 (2008)	Amendment to the Rules of Procedure
Decision 2 (2008)	Approval of the Secretariat's Financial Report for 2006/07 and Programme and Budget for 2008/09
Decision 3 (2008)	Appointment of an External Auditor
Decision 4 (2008)	Procedure for Selection and Appointment of the Executive Secretary of the Secretariat of the Antarctic Treaty
Decision 5 (2008)	Electronic Information Exchange System
Resolution 1 (2008)	Guide to the Presentation of Working Papers Containing Proposals for Antarctic Specially Protected Areas, Antarctic Specially Managed Areas or Historic Sites and Monuments
Resolution 2 (2008)	Site Guidelines for Visitors
Resolution 3 (2008)	Environmental Domains Analysis for the Antarctic continent as a dynamic model for a systematic environmental geographic framework
Resolution 4 (2008)	Checklist to assist in the inspection of Antarctic Specially Protected Areas and Antarctic Specially Managed Areas
*Resolution 5 (2008)	Improving hydrographic surveying and charting to support safety of navigation and environmental protection in the Antarctic region
Resolution 6 (2008)	Enhancing the role of Maritime Rescue Coordination Centres with Search and Rescue Regions in the Antarctic Treaty Area

ATCM XXXII, Baltimore, 6–17 April 2009

Measure 1 (2009)	Antarctic Specially Managed Area No 3: (Cape Denison, Commonwealth Bay, George V Land, East Antarctica): revised Management Plan
Measure 2 (2009)	Antarctic Specially Managed Area No 7: (South-west Anvers Island and Palmer Basin): revised Management Plan
Measure 3 (2009)	Antarctic Specially Protected Area No 104: (Sabrina Island, Balleny Islands): Management Plan
Measure 4 (2009)	Antarctic Specially Protected Area No 113: (Litchfield Island, Arthur Harbour, Anvers Island, Palmer Archipelago): revised Management Plan
Measure 5 (2009)	Antarctic Specially Protected Area No 121: (Cape Royds, Ross Island): revised Management Plan
Measure 6 (2009)	Antarctic Specially Protected Area No 125: (Fildes Peninsula, King George Island, South Shetland Islands): revised Management Plan
Measure 7 (2009)	Antarctic Specially Protected Area No 136: (Clark Peninsula, Budd Coast, Wilkes Land): revised Management Plan
Measure 8 (2009)	Antarctic Specially Protected Area No 142: (Svarthamaren): revised Management Plan
Measure 9 (2009)	Antarctic Specially Protected Area No 150: (Ardley Island, Maxwell Bay, King George Island): revised Management Plan
Measure 10 (2009)	Antarctic Specially Protected Area No 152: (Western Bransfield Strait): revised Management Plan
Measure 11 (2009)	Antarctic Specially Protected Area No 153: (Eastern Dallmann Bay): revised Management Plan
Measure 12 (2009)	Antarctic Specially Protected Area No 162: (Mawson's Huts, Cape Denison, Commonwealth Bay, George V Land, East Antarctica): revised Management Plan

Measure 13 (2009)	Antarctic Specially Protected Area No 171: (Narybski Point, Barton Peninsula, King George Island): Management Plan
Measure 14 (2009)	Antarctic Historic Sites and Monuments: Base "W" and Hut at Damoy Point
Measure 15 (2009)	Landing of persons from passenger vessels in the Antarctic Treaty area
Measure 16 (2009)	Amendment of Annex II to the Protocol on Environmental Protection to the Antarctic Treaty: Conservation of Antarctic Fauna and Flora
Decision 1 (2009)	Meeting of Experts on Climate Change
Decision 2 (2009)	Renewal of the contract of the Secretariat's External Auditor
Decision 3 (2009)	Revised guidelines for the submission, translation and distribution of documents for the ATCM and the CEP
Decision 4 (2009)	Approval of Secretariat's Financial Report for 2007/08 and Programme and Budget for 2009/10
Decision 5 (2009)	Appointment of the Executive Secretary of the Antarctic Treaty Secretariat
Decision 6 (2009)	Revised Rules of Procedure for the Committee for Environmental Protection
Decision 7 (2009)	Meeting of Experts on the management of ship-borne tourism in the Antarctic Treaty area
Decision 8 (2009)	Letter to UNFCCC
Resolution 1 (2009)	Urging Parties to enhance environmental protection for the Antarctic ecosystem northward to the Antarctic Convergence
Resolution 2 (2009)	Role and place of COMNAP in the Antarctic Treaty system
Resolution 3 (2009)	Guidelines for the designation and protection of Historic Sites and Monuments
Resolution 4 (2009)	Site Guidelines for visitors
Resolution 5 (2009)	Protection of the southern giant petrel
Resolution 6 (2009)	Ensuring the legacy of the International Polar Year (IPY)
Resolution 7 (2009)	General principles of Antarctic tourism
Resolution 8 (2009)	Mandatory shipping code for vessels operating in Antarctic waters
Resolution 9 (2009)	Collection and use of Antarctic biological material

ATCM XXXIII, Punta del Este, 3–14 May 2010

Measure 1 (2010)	Antarctic Specially Protected Area No 101: (Taylor Rookery, MacRobertson Land): Revised Management Plan
Measure 2 (2010)	Antarctic Specially Protected Area No 102: (Rookery Islands, Holme Bay, MacRobertson Land): Revised Management Plan
Measure 3 (2010)	Antarctic Specially Protected Area No 103: (Ardery Island and Odbert Island, Budd Coast, Wilkes Land): Revised Management Plan
Measure 4 (2010)	Antarctic Specially Protected Area No 105: (Beaufort Island, McMurdo Sound, Ross Sea): Revised Management Plan
Measure 5 (2010)	Antarctic Specially Protected Area No 106: (Cape Hallett, Northern Victoria Land, Ross Sea): Revised Management Plan
Measure 6 (2010)	Antarctic Specially Protected Area No 119: (Davis Valley and Forlidas Pond, Dufek Massif, Pensacola Mountains): Revised Management Plan
Measure 7 (2010)	Antarctic Specially Protected Area No 139: (Biscoe Point, Anvers Island, Palmer Archipelago): Revised Management Plan
Measure 8 (2010)	Antarctic Specially Protected Area No 155: (Cape Evans, Ross Island): Revised Management Plan
Measure 9 (2010)	Antarctic Specially Protected Area No 157: (Backdoor Bay, Cape Royds, Ross Island): Revised Management Plan

Measure 10 (2010)	Antarctic Specially Protected Area No 158: (Hut Point, Ross Island): Revised Management Plan
Measure 11 (2010)	Antarctic Specially Protected Area No 159: (Cape Adare, Borchgrevink Coast): Revised Management Plan
Measure 12 (2010)	Antarctic Specially Protected Area No 163: (Dakshin Gangotri Glacier, Dronning Maud Land): Revised Management Plan
Measure 13 (2010)	Antarctic Specially Protected Area No 164: (Scullin and Murray Monoliths, MacRobertson Land): Revised Management Plan
Measure 14 (2010)	Antarctic Specially Managed Area No 7: (Southwest Anvers Island and Palmer Basin): Revised Management Plan
Measure 15 (2010)	Antarctic Historic Sites and Monuments: Plaque Commemorating the PM-3A Nuclear Power Plant at McMurdo Station
Decision 1 (2010)	Compilation of Key Documents of the Antarctic Treaty System
Decision 2 (2010)	Secretariat Reports, Programme and Budgets
Decision 3 (2010)	Revised Rules of Procedure for the Committee for Environmental Protection
Decision 4 (2010)	Liability arising from Environmental Emergencies
Decision 5 (2010)	Letters to UNFCCC, IPCC, WMO and IMO on the SCAR ACCE Report
Resolution 1 (2010)	Site Guidelines for visitors
*Resolution 2 (2010)	The contribution of the IPY to hydrographic knowledge of waters of the Antarctic Treaty area
Resolution 3 (2010)	Revised Antarctic inspection Checklist "A"
Resolution 4 (2010)	SCAR Antarctic Climate Change and the Environment Report
Resolution 5 (2010)	Co-ordination among Antarctic Treaty Parties on Antarctic proposals under consideration in the IMO
Resolution 6 (2010)	Improving the co-ordination of maritime search and rescue in the Antarctic Treaty area
Resolution 7 (2010)	Enhancement of port State control for passenger vessels bound for the Antarctic Treaty area

ATCM XXXIV, Buenos Aires, 20 June 2011–1 July 2011

Measure 1 (2011)	Antarctic Specially Protected Area No 116: (New College Valley, Caughley Beach, Cape Bird, Ross Island): Revised Management Plan
Measure 2 (2011)	Antarctic Specially Protected Area No 120: (Pointe-Géologie Archipelago, Terre Adélie): Revised Management Plan
Measure 3 (2011)	Antarctic Specially Protected Area No 122: (Arrival Heights, Hut Point Peninsula, Ross Island): Revised Management Plan
Measure 4 (2011)	Antarctic Specially Protected Area No 126: (Byers Peninsula, Livingston Island, South Shetland Islands): Revised Management Plan
Measure 5 (2011)	Antarctic Specially Protected Area No 127: (Haswell Island): Revised Management Plan
Measure 6 (2011)	Antarctic Specially Protected Area No 131: (Canada Glacier, Lake Fryxell, Taylor Valley, Victoria Land): Revised Management Plan
Measure 7 (2011)	Antarctic Specially Protected Area No 149: (Cape Shirreff and San Telmo Island, Livingston Island, South Shetland Islands): Revised Management Plan
Measure 8 (2011)	Antarctic Specially Protected Area No 165: (Edmonson Point, Wood Bay, Ross Sea): Revised Management Plan
Measure 9 (2011)	Antarctic Specially Protected Area No 167: (Hawker Island, Vestfold Hills, Ingrid Christensen Coast, Princess Elizabeth Land, East Antarctica): Revised Management Plan

Measure 10 (2011)	Antarctic Specially Managed Area No 2: (McMurdo Dry Valleys, Southern Victoria Land): Revised Management Plan
Measure 11 (2011)	Antarctic Historic Sites and Monuments: Monument to the Antarctic Treaty and Plaque
Measure 12 (2011)	Antarctic Historic Sites and Monuments: No 1 Building at Great Wall Station
Decision 1 (2011)	Measures designated as no longer current
Decision 2 (2011)	Revised Rules of Procedure for the Antarctic Treaty Consultative Meeting (2011); Revised Rules of Procedure for the Committee for Environmental Protection (2011); Guidelines for the Submission, Translation and Distribution of Documents for the ATCM and the CEP
Decision 3 (2011)	Secretariat Reports, Programme and Budgets
Resolution 1 (2011)	Strengthening Support for the Protocol on Environmental Protection to the Antarctic Treaty
Resolution 2 (2011)	Revised Guide to the Preparation of Management Plans for Antarctic Specially Protected Areas
Resolution 3 (2011)	General Guidelines for Visitors to the Antarctic
Resolution 4 (2011)	Site Guidelines for visitors
Resolution 5 (2011)	Revised Guide to the Presentation of Working Papers Containing Proposals for Antarctic Specially Protected Areas, Antarctic Specially Managed Areas or Historic Sites and Monuments
Resolution 6 (2011)	Non-native Species

ATCM XXXV, Hobart, 11–20 June 2012

Measure 1 (2012)	Antarctic Specially Protected Area No 109 (Moe Island, South Orkney Islands): Revised Management Plan
Measure 2 (2012)	Antarctic Specially Protected Area No 110 (Lynch Island, South Orkney Islands): Revised Management Plan
Measure 3 (2012)	Antarctic Specially Protected Area No 111 (Southern Powell Island and adjacent islands, South Orkney Islands): Revised Management Plan
Measure 4 (2012)	Antarctic Specially Protected Area No 112 (Coppermine Peninsula, Robert Island, South Shetland Islands): Revised Management Plan
Measure 5 (2012)	Antarctic Specially Protected Area No 115 (Lagotellerie Island, Marguerite Bay, Graham Land): Revised Management Plan
Measure 6 (2012)	Antarctic Specially Protected Area No 129 (Rothera Point, Adelaide Island): Revised Management Plan
Measure 7 (2012)	Antarctic Specially Protected Area No 133 (Harmony Point, Nelson Island, South Shetland Islands): Revised Management Plan
Measure 8 (2012)	Antarctic Specially Protected AREA No 140 (Parts of Deception Island): Revised Management Plan
Measure 9 (2012)	Antarctic Specially Protected Area No 172 (Lower Taylor Glacier and Blood Falls, Taylor Valley, McMurdo Dry Valleys, Victoria Land): Management Plan
Measure 10 (2012)	Antarctic Specially Managed Area No 4 (Deception Island): Revised Management Plan
Measure 11 (2012)	Antarctic Historic Sites and Monuments: No 4 Pole of Inaccessibility Station building, No 7 Ivan Khmara's Stone, No 8 Anatoly Shcheglov's Monument, No 9 Buromsky Island Cemetery, No 10 Soviet Oasis Station Observatory, No 11 Vostok Station Tractor, No 37 O'Higgins Historic Site
Decision 1 (2012)	Measures on Operational Matters designated as no longer current

Decision 2 (2012)	Secretariat Report, Programme and Budget
Decision 3 (2012)	The Development of a Multi-Year Strategic Work Plan for the Antarctic Treaty Consultative Meeting
Decision 4 (2012)	Electronic Information Exchange System
Resolution 1 (2012)	Strengthening Support for the Protocol on Environmental Protection to the Antarctic Treaty
Resolution 2 (2012)	Cooperation on questions related to the exercise of jurisdiction in the Antarctic Treaty area
Resolution 3 (2012)	Improving Cooperation in Antarctica
Resolution 4 (2012)	Site Guidelines for visitors
Resolution 5 (2012)	Barrientos Island (Aitcho Islands) visitor Site Guidelines
Resolution 6 (2012)	Antarctic Conservation Biogeographic Regions
Resolution 7 (2012)	Vessel Safety in the Antarctic Treaty Area
Resolution 8 (2012)	Improved Coordination of Maritime, Aeronautical and Land-Based Search and Rescue
Resolution 9 (2012)	The Assessment of Land-Based Expeditionary Activities
Resolution 10 (2012)	Yachting Guidelines
Resolution 11 (2012)	Checklist for visitors' in-field activities

ATCM XXXVI, Brussels, 20–29 May 2013

Measure 1 (2013)	Antarctic Specially Protected Area No 108 (Green Island, Berthelot Islands, Antarctic Peninsula): Revised Management Plan
Measure 2 (2013)	Antarctic Specially Protected Area No 117 (Avian Island, Marguerite Bay, Antarctic Peninsula): Revised Management Plan
Measure 3 (2013)	Antarctic Specially Protected Area No 123 (Barwick and Balham Valleys, Southern Victoria Land): Revised Management Plan
Measure 4 (2013)	Antarctic Specially Protected Area No 132 (Potter Peninsula, King George Island (Isla 25 de Mayo), South Shetland Islands): Revised Management Plan
Measure 5 (2013)	Antarctic Specially Protected Area No 134 (Cierva Point and offshore islands, Danco Coast, Antarctic Peninsula): Revised Management Plan
Measure 6 (2013)	Antarctic Specially Protected Area No 135 (North-east Bailey Peninsula, Budd Coast, Wilkes Land): Revised Management Plan
Measure 7 (2013)	Antarctic Specially Protected Area No 137 (Northwest White Island, McMurdo Sound): Revised Management Plan
Measure 8 (2013)	Antarctic Specially Protected Area No 138 (Linnaeus Terrace, Asgard Range, Victoria Land): Revised Management Plan
Measure 9 (2013)	Antarctic Specially Protected Area No 143 (Marine Plain, Mule Peninsula, Vestfold Hills, Princess Elizabeth Land): Revised Management Plan
Measure 10 (2013)	Antarctic Specially Protected Area No 147 (Ablation Valley and Ganymede Heights, Alexander Island): Revised Management Plan
Measure 11 (2013)	Antarctic Specially Protected Area No 151 (Lions Rump, King George Island (Isla 25 de Mayo), South Shetland Islands): Revised Management Plan
Measure 12 (2013)	Antarctic Specially Protected Area No 154 (Botany Bay, Cape Geology, Victoria Land): Revised Management Plan
Measure 13 (2013)	Antarctic Specially Protected Area No 156 (Lewis Bay, Mount Erebus, Ross Island): Revised Management Plan
Measure 14 (2013)	Antarctic Specially Protected Area No 160 (Frazier Islands, Windmill Islands, Wilkes Land, East Antarctica): Revised Management Plan

Measure 15 (2013)	Antarctic Specially Protected Area No 161 (Terra Nova Bay, Ross Sea): Revised Management Plan
Measure 16 (2013)	Antarctic Specially Protected Area No 170 (Marion Nunataks, Charcot Island, Antarctic Peninsula): Revised Management Plan
Measure 17 (2013)	Antarctic Specially Protected Area No 173 (Cape Washington and Silverfish Bay, Terra Nova Bay, Ross Sea): Management Plan
Measure 18 (2013)	Antarctic Historic Sites and Monuments: Location of the first permanently occupied German Antarctic research station "Georg Forster" at the Schirmacher Oasis, Dronning Maud Land
Measure 19 (2013)	Antarctic Historic Sites and Monuments: Professor Kudryashov's Drilling Complex Building, Vostok Station
Measure 20 (2013)	Antarctic Historic Sites and Monuments: Upper "Summit Camp", Mount Erebus
Measure 21 (2013)	Antarctic Historic Sites and Monuments: Lower "Camp E", Mount Erebus
Decision 1 (2013)	Recognition of the Czech Republic as a Consultative Party
Decision 2 (2013)	Re-appointment of the Executive Secretary
Decision 3 (2013)	Renewal of the Contract of the Secretariat's External Auditor
Decision 4 (2013)	Secretariat Report, Programme and Budget
Decision 5 (2013)	Multi-Year Strategic Work Plan for the Antarctic Treaty Consultative Meeting
Decision 6 (2013)	Information Exchange on Tourism and Non-Governmental Activities
Decision 7 (2013)	Additional availability of information on lists of Observers of the Consultative Parties through the Secretariat of the Antarctic Treaty
Resolution 1 (2013)	Air Safety in Antarctica
Resolution 2 (2013)	Antarctic Clean-Up Manual
Resolution 3 (2013)	Site Guidelines for visitors
Resolution 4 (2013)	Improved Collaboration on Search and Rescue (SAR) in Antarctica
Resolution 5 (2013)	International cooperation in cultural projects about Antarctica
Resolution 6 (2013)	Biological Prospecting in Antarctica
ATCM XXXVII, Brazil, 28 April–7 May 2014	
Measure 1 (2014)	Antarctic Specially Protected Area No 113 (Litchfield Island, Arthur Harbor, Anvers Island, Palmer Archipelago): Revised Management Plan
Measure 2 (2014)	Antarctic Specially Protected Area No 121 (Cape Royds, Ross Island): Revised Management Plan
Measure 3 (2014)	Antarctic Specially Protected Area No 124 (Cape Crozier, Ross Island): Revised Management Plan
Measure 4 (2014)	Antarctic Specially Protected Area No 128 (Western shore of Admiralty Bay, King George Island, South Shetland Islands): Revised Management Plan
Measure 5 (2014)	Antarctic Specially Protected Area No 136 (Clark Peninsula, Budd Coast, Wilkes Land, East Antarctica): Revised Management Plan
Measure 6 (2014)	Antarctic Specially Protected Area No 139 (Biscoe Point, Anvers Island, Palmer Archipelago): Revised Management Plan
Measure 7 (2014)	Antarctic Specially Protected Area No 141 (Yukidori Valley, Langhovde, Lützow-Holm Bay): Revised Management Plan
Measure 8 (2014)	Antarctic Specially Protected Area No 142 (Svarthamaren): Revised Management Plan

Measure 9 (2014)	Antarctic Specially Protected Area No 162 (Mawson's Huts, Cape Denison, Commonwealth Bay, George V Land, East Antarctica): Revised Management Plan
Measure 10 (2014)	Antarctic Specially Protected Area No 169 (Amanda Bay, Ingrid Christensen Coast, Princess Elizabeth Land, East Antarctica): Revised Management Plan
Measure 11 (2014)	Antarctic Specially Protected Area No 171 (Narębski Point, Barton Peninsula, King George Island): Revised Management Plan
Measure 12 (2014)	Antarctic Specially Protected Area No 174 (Stornes, Larsemann Hills, Princess Elizabeth Land): Management Plan
Measure 13 (2014)	Antarctic Specially Protected Area No 175 (High Altitude Geothermal sites of the Ross Sea region): Management Plan
Measure 14 (2014)	Antarctic Specially Managed Area No 1 (Admiralty Bay, King George Island): Revised Management Plan
Measure 15 (2014)	Antarctic Specially Managed Area No 6 (Larsemann Hills, East Antarctica): Revised Management Plan
Measure 16 (2014)	Antarctic Specially Protected Area No 114 (Northern Coronation Island, South Orkney Islands): Revoked Management Plan
Decision 1 (2014)	Measures on Operational Matters designated as no longer current
Decision 2 (2014)	Secretariat Report, Programme and Budget
Decision 3 (2014)	Multi-Year Strategic Work Plan for the Antarctic Treaty Consultative Meeting
Resolution 1 (2014)	Fuel Storage and Handling
Resolution 2 (2014)	Cooperation, Facilitation, and Exchange of Meteorological and Related Oceanographic and Cryospheric Environmental Information
Resolution 3 (2014)	Supporting the Polar Code
Resolution 4 (2014)	Site Guidelines for Visitors
Resolution 5 (2014)	Strengthening Cooperation in Hydrographic Surveying and Charting of Antarctic Waters
Resolution 6 (2014)	Toward a Risk-based Assessment of Tourism and Non-governmental Activities
Resolution 7 (2014)	Entering into force of Measure 4 (2004)

Thematic Index of All Measures, Decisions, Resolutions and Recommendations adopted by the ATCM (1961–2014)

Exchange of information, data, personnel	**Recommendations**: I-I (1961); I-II (1961); I-III (1961); I-VI (1961); I-VII (1961); I-XIII (1961); II-I (1962); II-IV (1962); II-VI (1962); IV-23 (1966); VI-2 (1970); VI-13 (1970); VIII-6 (1975); XIII-3 (1985); XVI-1 (1991); XVI-12 (1991) **Resolutions**: 4 (1998); 6 (2001); 5 (2004) **Decisions**: 10 (2005); 5 (2008); 4 (2012)
Scientific research (facilitation, cooperation)	**Recommendations**: I-IV (1961); I-V (1961); II-VII (1962); VI-3 (1970); VI-5 (1970); VI-6 (1970); VI-12 (1970); VII-5 (1972); XII-1 (1983); XIV-7 (1987); XV-15 (1989); XV-16 (1989); XVII-4 (1992) **Resolutions**: 3 (2001); 3 (2007); 3 (2008); 2 (2009); 2 (2014)
SCAR	**Recommendation** XII-8 (1983) **Resolutions**: 5 (1999); 4 (2010)

Conservation of fauna and flora	**Recommendations**: I-VIII (1961); II-II (1962); III-VIII (1964); III-IX (1964); III-X (1964); III-XI (1964); IV-18 (1966); IV-19 (1966); IV-20 (1966); IV-21 (1966); IV-22 (1966); V-7 (1968); V-8 (1968); VI-9 (1970); XV-8 (1989) **Resolutions**: 2 (1999); 2 (2001); 1 (2002); 3 (2002); 4 (2003); 2 (2004); 4 (2006); 2 (2007); 5 (2009); 6 (2011); 6 (2012) **Measure** 4 (2006)
Historic sites and monuments	**Recommendations**: I-IX (1961); V-4 (1968); VI-14 (1970); VII-9 (1972); XII-7 (1983); XIII-16 (1985); XIV-8 (1987); XV-12 (1989); XV-13 (1989); XVI-11 (1991); XVII-3 (1992) **Measures**: 4 (1995); 5 (1995); 5 (1997); 2 (1998); 1 (2001); 2 (2001); 2 (1996); 4 (1997); 3 (2003); 5 (2005); 3 (2006); 3 (2007); 14 (2009); 15 (2010); 11 (2011); 12 (2011); 11 (2012); 18 (2013); 19 (2013); 20 (2013); 21 (2013) **Resolutions**: 8 (1995); 4 (1996); 4 (2001); 5 (2001); 3 (2009)
Emergencies	**Recommendation** I-X (1961) **Resolutions**: 1 (1997); 6 (1998); 6 (2008); 6 (2010); 4 (2013); 8 (2012)
Telecommunications and postal services	**Recommendations:** I-XI (1961); I-XII (1961); II-III (1962); III-V (1964); IV-26 (1966); V-2 (1968); VI-1 (1970); VII-7 (1972); IX-3 (1977); X-3 (1979); XII-2 (1983)
Specially Protected Areas; the Antarctic Protected Area System (generally)	**Recommendations**: IV-1 (1966); IV-2 (1966); IV-3 (1966); IV-4 (1966); IV-5 (1966); IV-6 (1966); IV-7 (1966); IV-8 (1966); IV-9 (1966); IV-10 (1966); IV-11 (1966); IV-12 (1966); IV-13 (1966); IV-14 (1966); IV-15 (1966); IV-16 (1966); IV-17 (1966); V-5 (1968); VI-8 (1970); VI-10 (1970); VII-2 (1972); VIII-1 (1975); VIII-2 (1975); VIII-5 (1975); XIII-10 (1985); XIII-11 (1985); XIII-12 (1985); XIII-13 (1985); XIII-14 (1985); XV-7 (1989); XV-9 (1989); XV-10 (1989); XV-11 (1989); XVI-4 (1991); XVI-6 (1991); XVI-8 (1991); XVI-9 (1991); XVI-10 (1991); XVII-2 (1992) **Measures**: 1 (1995); 3 (1995); 1 (1997); 2 (1997); 1 (1998); 1 (2002); 2 (2003); 1 (2004); 2 (2004); 2 (2005); 3 (2005); 4 (2005); 1 (2006); 2 (2006); 1 (2007); 2 (2007); 1 (2008); 2 (2008); 3 (2008); 4 (2008); 5 (2008); 6 (2008); 7 (2008); 8 (2008); 9 (2008); 10 (2008); 11 (2008); 12 (2008); 13 (2008); 14 (2008); 1 (2009); 2 (2009); 3 (2009); 4 (2009); 5 (2009); 6 (2009); 7 (2009); 8 (2009); 9 (2009); 10 (2009); 11 (2009); 12 (2009); 13 (2009); 1 (2010); 2 (2010); 3 (2010); 4 (2010); 5 (2010); 6 (2010); 7 (2010); 8 (2010); 9 (2010); 10 (2010); 11(2010); 12 (2010); 13 (2010); 14 (2010); 1 (2011); 2 (2011); 3 (2011); 4 (2011); 5 (2011); 6 (2011); 7 (2011); 8 (2011); 9 (2011); 10 (2011); 1 (2012); 2 (2012); 3 (2012); 4 (2012); 5 (2012); 6 (2012); 7 (2012); 8 (2012); 9 (2012); 10 (2012); 1 (2013); 2 (2013); 3 (2013); 4 (2013); 5 (2013); 6 (2013); 7 (2013); 8 (2013); 9 (2013); 10 (2013); 11 (2013); 12 (2013); 13 (2013); 14 (2013); 15 (2013); 16 (2013); 17 (2013); 1 (2014); 2 (2014); 3 (2014); 4 (2014); 5 (2014); 6 (2014); 7 (2014); 8 (2014); 9 (2014); 10 (2014); 11 (2014); 12 (2014); 13 (2014); 14 (2014); 15 (2014); 16 (2014) **Resolutions**: 5 (1996); 1 (1998); 2 (1998); 2 (2002); 1 (2008); 4 (2008); 2 (2011) **Decisions**: 1 (2002); 1 (2007)

Sites of Special Scientific Interest	**Recommendations**: VII-3 (1972); VIII-3 (1975); VIII-4 (1975); X-5 (1979); X-6 (1979); XIII-6 (1985); XIII-7 (1985); XIII-8 (1985); XIII-9 (1985); XIV-4 (1987); XIV-5 (1987); XIV-6 (1987); XV-6 (1989); XV-14 (1989); XV-17 (1989); XVI-2 (1991); XVI-3 (1991); XVI-5 (1991); XVI-7 (1991) **Measures**: 2 (1995); 1 (1996); 1 (1999); 3 (2001); 3 (1997); **Resolutions**: 7 (1995); 3 (1996)
Tourism and non-government expeditions	**Recommendations**: IV-27 (1966); VI-7 (1970); VII-4 (1972); VIII-9 (1975); X-8 (1979); XII-5 (1983); XVI-13 (1991); XVIII-1 (1994) **Resolutions**: 3 (1995); 3 (1997); 3 (2004); 4 (2004); 4 (2007); 5 (2007); 7 (2009); 7 (2010); 3 (2011); 6 (2014); 7 (2014) **Decisions**: 5 (2003); 7 (2009); 6 (2013) **Measure** 15 (2009)
Site Visits	**Resolutions**: 5 (2005); 6 (2005); 2 (2006); 1 (2007); 2 (2008); 4 (2009); 1 (2010); 4 (2011); 5 (2011); 4 (2012); 5 (2012); 11 (2012); 3 (2013); 4 (2014)
Biological material/prospecting	**Resolutions**: 7 (2005); 9 (2009); 6 (2013)
Antarctic mineral resources/ effects of mineral exploration	**Recommendations**: VII-6 (1972); VIII-14 (1975); IX-1 (1977); X-1 (1979); XI-1 (1981)
The Antarctic environment (man's impact on; protection of)	**Recommendations**. VI-4 (1970); VII-1 (1972); VIII-11 (1975); VIII-13 (1975); IX-5 (1977); X-4 (1979); XII-3 (1983); XII-4 (1983); XIII-4 (1985); XIII-5 (1985); XIV-2 (1987); XIV-3 (1987); XV-1 (1989); XV-2 (1989); XV-3 (1989); XV-4 (1989) **Resolutions**: 2 (1996); 4 (1999); 1 (2009); 2 (2013)
Antarctic marine environment and resources	**Recommendations**: V-3 (1968); VIII-10 (1975); IX-2 (1977); IX-6 (1977); X-2 (1979); XI-2 (1981); X-7 (1979) **Decisions**: 4 (1998); 9 (2005) **Resolutions**: 3 (1999); 1 (2004); 1 (2006)
Fuel (use, storage and handling)	**Resolutions**: 4 (1995); 3 (2005); 1 (2014) **Decision** 8 (2005)
Protocol on Environmental Protection	**Recommendation** XV-5 (1989) **Resolutions**: 6 (1999); 1 (2003); 1 (2011); 1 (2012) **Measures**: 1 (2005); 16 (2009) **Decision** 1 (2005)
Environmental monitoring and data management; Environmental Impact Assessments	**Recommendation** XVII-1 (1992) **Resolutions**: 6 (1995); 2 (1997); 1 (1999); 1 (2005); 2 (2005); 4 (2005)
Disposal of nuclear wastes	**Recommendation** VIII-12 (1975) **Resolution** 2 (1995)
Aircraft; air safety in Antarctica	**Recommendations**: III-I (1964); XI-3 (1981); XIV-9 (1987); XV-20 (1989) **Resolution** 1 (2013)

Navigation; Hydrographic charting	**Recommendations**: XIV-10 (1987); XV-18 (1989); XV-19 (1989) **Resolutions**: 1 (1995); 3 (2003); 5 (2008); 2 (2010); 5 (2014)
Ships and boats operating in Arctic and Antarctic Waters	**Resolutions**: 3 (1998); 3 (2006); 8 (2009); 7 (2012); 10 (2012) **Decisions**: 2 (1999); 4 (2004); 2 (2006)
Antarctic Inspection Checklists	**Resolutions**: 5 (1995); 1 (1996); 3 (2010)
Measures, Recommendations, Decisions and Resolutions of ATCM and CEP	**Recommendations**: III-VII (1964); V-6 (1968) **Decisions**: 1 (1995); 3 (2002); 1 (2011); 1 (2012); 1 (2014) **Resolution** 1 (2001)
Rules of Procedure (amendments and revisions)	**Decisions**: 2 (1995); 1 (1997); 2 (1998); 1 (2004); 3 (2005); 1 (2008); 6 (2009); 3 (2010); 2 (2011)
Consultative Parties, observers, non-consultative parties	**Recommendation** VIII-8 (1975) **Decisions:** 2 (1997); 1 (1998); 2 (2005); 4 (2005); 1 (2013); 7 (2013)
Liability	**Decisions**: 3 (1998); 3 (2001); 4 (2010)
Secretariat	**Decisions**: 1 (2001); 1 (2003); 2 (2003); 3 (2003); 4 (2003); 3 (2004); 2 (2004); 6 (2005); 7 (2005); 1 (2006); 2 (2007); 4 (2007); 2 (2008); 4 (2008); 4 (2009); 5 (2009); 2 (2010); 3 (2011); 2 (2012); 2 (2013); 4 (2013); 2 (2014) **Measure** 1 (2003)
Circulation and Handling of CEP and ATCM Documents	**Decisions**: 2 (2001); 3 (2009); 1 (2010)
External Auditor	**Decisions**: 5 (2005); 3 (2007); 3 (2008); 2 (2009); 3 (2013)
Cooperation among Parties, International Organisations	**Recommendations**: VII-8 (1972); VIII-7 (1975); IX-4 (1977) **Resolutions**: 2 (2012); 3 (2012); 5 (2010); 5 (2013)
Consultative Meetings	**Recommendations**: I-XIV (1961); I-XV (1961); I-XVI (1961); II-IX (1962); II-X (1962); III-IV (1964); IV-24 (1966); IV-25 (1966); IV-28 (1966); V-9 (1968); VI-15 (1970); XIII-15 (1985) **Decisions**: 3 (2012); 5 (2013); 3 (2014)
Operation of the Antarctic Treaty System	**Recommendations**: XII-6 (1983); XIII-1 (1985); XIII-2 (1985); XIV-1 (1987)
Commemorative stamps/ anniversaries	**Recommendations**: II-VIII (1962); V-1 (1968); X-9 (1979); XV-22 (1989) **Decision** 2 (2002) **Resolutions**: 2 (2003); 6 (2009)
Miscellaneous	**Recommendations**: II-V (1962) and III-III (1964) (logistics); III-II (1964) (notification of unoccupied refuges); III-VI (1964) (meeting of specialists); XV-21 (1989) (Use of Antarctic ice); VI-11 (1989) (new islands) **Decisions**: 1 (1999) (ATCM and CEP websites); 1 (2009) (meeting of on climate change); Decision 8 (2009) (Letter to UNFCCC); Decision 5 (2010) (Correspondence) **Resolutions**: 9 (1995) (Uniform Model for Management Plans); 9 (2012) (The Assessment of Land-Based Expeditionary Activities)

Decision 1 (1995): Measures, Decisions, Resolutions and Recommendations

1. Measures
   (a) A text which contains provisions intended to be legally binding once it has been approved by all the Antarctic Treaty Consultative Parties will be expressed as a Measure recommended for approval in accordance with paragraph 4 of Article IX of the Antarctic Treaty, and referred to as a "Measure".
   (b) Measures will be numbered consecutively, followed by the year of adoption.
2. Decisions
   (a) A decision taken at an Antarctic Treaty Consultative Meeting on an internal organizational matter will be operative at adoption or at such other time as may be specified, and will be referred to as a "Decision".
   (b) Decisions will be numbered consecutively, followed by the year of adoption.
3. Resolutions
   (a) A hortatory text adopted at an Antarctic Treaty Consultative Meeting will be contained in a Resolution.
   (b) Resolutions will be numbered consecutively, followed by the year of adoption.
4. Final Reports of ATCMs
   (a) Part 11, Annex A of the Final Report of each Antarctic Treaty Consultative Meeting will contain the full text of Measures adopted at the Meeting.
   (b) Part 11, Annex B of the Final Report of each Antarctic Treaty Consultative Meeting will contain the full text of any Decisions adopted at that Meeting.
   (c) Part 11, Annex C of the Final Report of each Antarctic Treaty Consultative Meeting will contain the full text of any Resolutions adopted at that Meeting.
5. Nothing in this Decision affects in any way anything done by previous Antarctic Treaty Consultative Meetings.
6. This Decision will be operative at adoption.

Decision 2 (2011), Annex 1: ATCM Revised Rules of Procedure

1. Meetings held pursuant to Article IX of the Antarctic Treaty shall be known as Antarctic Treaty Consultative Meetings. Contracting Parties entitled to participate in those Meetings shall be referred to as "Consultative Parties"; other Contracting Parties which may have been invited to attend those Meetings shall be referred to as "non-Consultative Parties". The Executive Secretary of the Secretariat of the Antarctic Treaty shall be referred to as the "Executive Secretary".

2. The Representatives of the Commission for the Conservation of Antarctic Marine Living Resources, the Scientific Committee on Antarctic Research and the Council of Managers of National Antarctic Programs, invited to attend those Meetings in accordance with Rule 31, shall be referred to as "Observers".

Representation

3. Each Consultative Party shall be represented by a delegation composed of a Representative and such Alternate Representatives, Advisers and other persons as each State may deem necessary. Each non-Consultative Party which has been invited to attend a Consultative Meeting shall be represented by a delegation composed of a Representative and such other persons as it may deem necessary within such numerical limit as may from time to time be determined by the Host Government in consultation with the Consultative Parties. The Commission for the Conservation of Antarctic Marine Living Resources, the Scientific Committee on Antarctic Research and the Council of Managers of National Antarctic Programs shall be represented by their respective Chairman or President, or other persons appointed to this end. The names of

members of delegations and of the observers shall be communicated to the Host Government prior to the opening of the Meeting.

4. The order of precedence of the delegations shall be in accordance with the alphabet in the language of the Host Government, all delegations of non-Consultative Parties following after those of Consultative Parties, and all delegations of observers following after non-Consultative Parties.

Officers

5. A Representative of the Host Government shall be the Temporary Chairman of the Meeting and shall preside until the Meeting elects a Chairman.

6. At its inaugural session, a Chairman from one of the Consultative Parties shall be elected. The other Representatives of Consultative Parties shall serve as Vice-Chairmen of the Meeting in order of precedence. The Chairman normally shall preside at all plenary sessions. If he is absent from any session or part thereof, the Vice-Chairmen, rotating on the basis of the order of precedence as established by Rule 4, shall preside during each such session.

Secretariat

7. The Executive Secretary shall act as Secretary to the Meeting. He or she shall be responsible, with the assistance of the Host Government, for providing secretariat services for the meeting, as provided in Article 2 of Measure 1 (2003), as provisionally applied by Decision 2 (2003) until Measure 1 becomes effective.

Sessions

8. The opening plenary session shall be held in public, other sessions shall be held in private, unless the Meeting shall determine otherwise.

Committees and Working Groups

9. The Meeting, to facilitate its work, may establish such committees as it may deem necessary for the performance of its functions, defining their terms of reference.

10. The committees shall operate under the Rules of Procedure of the Meeting, except where they are inapplicable.

11. Working Groups may be established by the Meeting, or its committees to deal with various agenda items. The Chair(s) of the Working Group(s) will be appointed at the beginning of the Meeting or committee meeting. The Chair(s) will serve no more than four consecutive Meetings or committee meetings, unless otherwise decided. At the conclusion of each Meeting, the Meeting may decide as a preliminary matter which Working Group(s) are proposed for the subsequent Meeting.

Conduct of Business

12. A quorum shall be constituted by two-thirds of the Representatives of Consultative Parties participating in the Meeting.

13. The Chairman shall exercise the powers of his office in accordance with customary practice. He shall see to the observance of the Rules of Procedure and the maintenance of proper order. The Chairman, in the exercise of his functions, remains under the authority of the Meeting.

14. Subject to Rule 28, no Representative may address the Meeting without having previously obtained the permission of the Chairman and the Chairman shall call upon speakers in the order in which they signify their desire to speak. The Chairman may call a speaker to order if his remarks are not relevant to the subject under discussion.

15. During the discussion of any matter, a Representative of a Consultative Party may rise to a point of order and the point of order shall be decided immediately by the Chairman in accordance with the Rules of Procedure. A Representative of a Consultative Party may appeal against the ruling of the Chairman. The appeal shall be put to a vote immediately, and the Chairman's ruling shall stand unless over-ruled by a majority of the Representatives of Consultative Parties present and voting. A Representative of a Consultative party rising to a point of order shall not speak on the substance of the matter under discussion.

16. The Meeting may limit the time to be allotted to each speaker, and the number of times he may speak on any subject. When the debate is thus limited and a Representative has spoken his allotted time, the Chairman shall call him to order without delay.

17. During the discussion of any matter, a Representative of a Consultative Party may move the adjournment of the debate on the item under discussion. In addition to the proposer of the motion, Representatives of two Consultative Parties may speak in favour of, and two against, the motion, after which the motion shall be put to the vote immediately. The Chairman may limit the time to be allowed to speakers under this Rule.

18. A Representative of a Consultative Party may at any time move the closure of the debate in the item under discussion, whether or not any other Representative has signified his wish to speak. Permission to speak on the closure of the debate shall be accorded only to Representatives of two Consultative Parties opposing the closure, after which the motion shall be put to the vote immediately. If the Meeting is in favour of the closure, the Chairman shall declare the closure of the debate. The Chairman may limit the time to be allowed to speakers under this Rule. (This Rule shall not apply to debate in committees.)

19. During the discussion of any matter, a Representative of a Consultative Party may move the suspension or adjournment of the Meeting. Such motions shall not be debated, but shall be put to the vote immediately. The Chairman may limit the time to be allowed to the speaker moving the suspension or adjournment of the Meeting.

20. Subject to Rule 15, the following motions shall have precedence in the following order over all other proposals or motions before the Meeting:

(a) to suspend the Meeting;
(b) to adjourn the Meeting;
(c) to adjourn the debate on the item under discussion;
(d) for the closure of the debate on the item under discussion.

21. Decisions of the Meeting on all matters of procedure shall be taken by a majority of the Representatives of Consultative Parties participating in the Meeting, each of whom shall have one vote.

Languages

22. English, French, Russian and Spanish shall be the official languages of the Meeting.

23. Any Representative may speak in a language other than the official languages. However, in such cases he shall provide for interpretation into one of the official languages.

Measures, Decisions, and Resolutions and Final Report

24. Without prejudice to Rule 21, Measures, Decisions and Resolutions, as referred to in Decision 1 (1995), shall be adopted by the Representatives of all Consultative Parties present and will thereafter be subject to the provisions of Decision 1 (1995).

25. The final report shall also contain a brief account of the proceedings of the Meeting. It will be approved by a majority of the Representatives of Consultative Parties present and shall be transmitted by the Executive Secretary to Governments of all Consultative and non-Consultative Parties which have been invited to take part in the Meeting for their consideration.

26. Notwithstanding Rule 25, the Executive Secretary, immediately following the closure of the Consultative Meeting, shall notify all Consultative Parties of all Measures, Decisions and Resolutions taken and send them authenticated copies of the definitive texts in an appropriate language of the Meeting. In respect to a Measure adopted under the procedures of Article 6 or 8 of Annex V of the Protocol, the respective notification shall also include the time period for approval of that Measure.

Non-Consultative Parties

27. Representatives of non-Consultative Parties, if invited to attend a Consultative Meeting, may be present at:

(a) all plenary sessions of the Meeting; and

(b) all formal Committees or Working Groups, comprising all Consultative Parties, unless a Representative of a Consultative Party requests otherwise in any particular case.

28. The relevant Chairman may invite a Representative of a non-Consultative Party to address the Meeting, Committee or Working group which he is attending, unless a Representative of a Consultative Party requests otherwise. The Chairman shall at any time give priority to Representatives of Consultative Parties who signify their desire to speak and may, in inviting Representatives of non-Consultative Parties to address the Meeting, limit the time to be allotted to each speaker and the number of times he may speak on any subject.

29. Non-Consultative Parties are not entitled to participate in the taking of decisions.

30.

(a) Non-Consultative Parties may submit documents to the Secretariat for distribution to the Meeting as information documents. Such documents shall be relevant to matters under Committee consideration at the Meeting.

(b) Unless a Representative of a Consultative Party requests otherwise such documents shall be available only in the language or languages in which they were submitted.

Antarctic Treaty System Observers

31. The observers referred to in Rule 2 shall attend the Meetings for the specific purpose of reporting on:

(a) in the case of the Commission for the Conservation of Antarctic Marine Living Resources, developments in its area of competence.

(b) in the case of the Scientific Committee on Antarctic Research:

(i) the general proceedings of SCAR;

(ii) matters within the competence of SCAR under the Convention for the Conservation of Antarctic Seals;

(iii) such publications and reports as may have been published or prepared in accordance with Recommendations IX-19 and VI-9 respectively.

(c) in the case of the Council of Managers of National Antarctic Programs, the activities within its area of competence.

32. Observers may be present at:

(a) the plenary sessions of the Meeting at which the respective Report is considered;

(b) formal committees or working groups, comprising all Contracting Parties at which the respective Report is considered, unless a Representative of a Consultative Party requests otherwise in any particular case.

33. Following the presentation of the pertinent Report, the relevant Chairman may invite the observer to address the Meeting at which it is being considered once again, unless a Representative of a Consultative Party requests otherwise. The Chairman may allot a time limit for such interventions.

34. Observers are not entitled to participate in the taking of decisions.

35. Observers may submit their Report and/or documents relevant to matters contained therein to the Secretariat, for distribution to the Meeting as working papers.

Agenda for Consultative Meetings

36. At the end of each Consultative Meeting, the Host Government of that Meeting shall prepare a preliminary agenda for the next Consultative Meeting. If approved by the Meeting, the preliminary agenda for the next Meeting shall be annexed to the Final Report of the Meeting.

37. Any Contracting Party may propose supplementary items for the preliminary agenda by informing the Host Government for the forthcoming Consultative Meeting no later than 180 days before the beginning of the Meeting; each proposal shall be accompanied by an explanatory memorandum. The Host Government shall draw the attention of all Contracting Parties to this Rule no later than 210 days before the Meeting.

38. The Host Government shall prepare a provisional agenda for the Consultative Meeting. The provisional agenda shall contain:

(a) all items on the preliminary agenda decided in accordance with Rule 36; and

(b) all items the inclusion of which has been requested by a Contracting Party pursuant to Rule

37. Not later than 120 days before the Meeting, the Host Government shall transmit to all the Contracting Parties the provisional agenda, together with explanatory memoranda and any other papers related thereto.

Experts from International Organisations

39. At the end of each Consultative Meeting, the Meeting shall decide which international organisations having a scientific or technical interest in Antarctica shall be invited to designate an expert to attend the forthcoming Meeting in order to assist it in its substantive work.

40. Any Contracting Party may thereafter propose that an invitation be extended to other international organisations having a scientific or technical interest in Antarctica to assist the Meeting in its substantive work; each such proposal shall be submitted to the Host Government for that Meeting not later than 180 days before the beginning of the Meeting and shall be accompanied by a memorandum setting out the basis for the proposal.

41. The Host Government shall transmit these proposals to all Contracting Parties in accordance with the procedure in Rule 38. Any Consultative Party which wishes to object to a proposal shall do so not less than 90 days before the Meeting.

42. Unless such an objection has been received, the Host Government shall extend invitations to international organisations identified in accordance with Rules 39 and 40 and shall request each international organisation to communicate the name of the designated expert to the Host Government prior to the opening of the Meeting. All such experts may attend the Meeting during consideration of all items, except for those items relating to the operation of the Antarctic Treaty System which are identified by the previous Meeting or upon adoption of the agenda.

43. The relevant Chairman, with the agreement of all the Consultative Parties, may invite an expert to address the meeting he is attending. The Chairman shall at any time give priority to Representatives of Consultative Parties or non-Consultative Parties or Observers referred to in Rule 31 who signify their desire to speak, and may in inviting an expert to address the Meeting limit the time to be allotted to him and the number of times he may speak on any subject.

44. Experts are not entitled to participate in the taking of decisions.

45.

(a) Experts may, in respect of the relevant agenda item, submit documents to the Secretariat for distribution to the Meeting as information documents.

(b) Unless a Representative of a Consultative Party requests otherwise, such documents shall be available only in the language or languages in which they were submitted.

Intersessional Consultations

1. Intersessionally, the Executive Secretary shall, within his/her competence as established under Measure 1 (2003) and associated instruments that govern the operation of the Secretariat, consult the Consultative Parties, when legally required to do so under relevant instruments of the ATCM and when the exigencies of the circumstances require action to be taken before the opening of the next ATCM, using the following procedure:

(a) The Executive Secretary shall transmit the relevant information and any proposed action to all Consultative Parties through contact persons designated by them, indicating an appropriate date by which responses are requested;

(b) The Executive Secretary shall ensure that all Consultative Parties acknowledge the receipt of such transmission, and shall also ensure the list of contact persons is current;

(c) Each Consultative Party shall consider the matter and communicate their reply, if any, to the Executive Secretary through their respective contact person by the specified date;

(d) The Executive Secretary after informing the Consultative Parties of the result of the consultations, may proceed to take the proposed action if no Consultative Party has objected; and

(e) The Executive Secretary shall keep a record of the intersessional consultations, including their results and the actions taken by him/her and shall reflect these results and actions in his/her report to the ATCM for its review.

47. Intersessionally, when a request for information about the activities of the ATCM is received from an international organisation having a scientific or technical interest in Antarctica, the Executive Secretary shall coordinate a response, using the following procedure:

(a) The Executive Secretary shall transmit the request and a first draft response to all Consultative Parties through contact persons designated by them, proposing to answer the request, and including an appropriate date by which Consultative Parties should *either* (1) indicate that it would not be appropriate to answer, *or* (2) provide comments to the first draft response. The date shall give a reasonable amount of time to provide comments, taking into account any deadlines set by the initial requests for information. If a Consultative Party indicates that a response would not be appropriate, the Executive Secretary shall send only a formal response, acknowledging the request without going into the substance of the matter.

(b) If there is no objection to proceeding and if comments are provided before the date specified in the transmission referred to in paragraph (a) above, the Executive Secretary shall revise the response in light of the comments and transmit the revised response to all Consultative Parties, including an appropriate date by which reactions are requested;

(c) If any further comments are provided before the date specified in the transmission referred to in paragraph (b) above, the Executive Secretary shall repeat the procedure referred to in paragraph (b) above until no further comments are provided;

(d) If no comments are provided before the date specified in a transmission referred to in paragraph (a), (b) or (c) above, the Executive Secretary shall circulate a final version and shall request both an active digital "read"-confirmation and an active digital "accept"-confirmation from each Consultative Party, suggesting a date by which the "accept"-confirmation should be received. The Executive Secretary shall keep the Consultative Parties informed about the progress of received confirmations. After receipt of "accept"-confirmations from all Consultative Parties the Executive Secretary shall sign and send the response to the international organisation concerned, on behalf of all Consultative Parties, and shall provide a copy of the signed response to all Consultative Parties.

(e) Any Consultative Party may, at any stage of this process, ask for more time for consideration.

(f) Any Consultative Party may, at any stage of this process, indicate that it would not be appropriate to respond to the request. In this case the Executive Secretary shall send only a formal response, acknowledging the request without going into the substance of the matter.

Meeting Documents

48. Working Papers shall refer to papers submitted by Consultative Parties that require discussion and action at a Meeting and papers submitted by Observers referred to in Rule 2.

49. Secretariat Papers shall refer to papers prepared by the Secretariat pursuant to a mandate established at a Meeting, or which would, in the view of the Executive Secretary, help inform the Meeting or assist in its operation.

50. Information Papers shall refer to:

- Papers submitted by Consultative Parties or Observers that provide information in support of a Working Paper or that are relevant to discussions at a Meeting;
- Papers submitted by Non-Consultative Parties that are relevant to discussions at a Meeting; and
- Papers submitted by Experts that are relevant to discussions at a Meeting.

51. Background Papers shall refer to papers submitted by any participant that will not be introduced in a Meeting, but that are submitted for the purpose of formally providing information.

52. Procedures for the submission, translation and distribution of documents are annexed to these Rules of Procedure.

Amendments

53. These Rules of Procedure may be amended by a two-thirds majority of the Representatives of Consultative Parties participating in the Meeting. This Rule shall not apply to Rules 24, 27, 29, 34, 39–42, 44, and 46, amendments of which shall require the approval of the Representatives of all Consultative Parties present at the Meeting.

Decision 2 (2011), Annex 1: Procedures for the Submission, Translation and Distribution of Documents for the ATCM and the CEP

1. These procedures apply to the distribution and translation of official papers for the Antarctic Treaty Consultative Meeting (ATCM) and for the Committee on Environmental Protection (CEP) as defined in their respective Rules of Procedure. These papers consist of Working Papers, Secretariat Papers, Information Papers and Background Papers.

2. Documents to be translated are Working Papers, Secretariat Papers, reports submitted to the ATCM by ATCM Observers and invited Experts according to the provisions of Recommendation XIII-2, reports submitted to the ATCM in relation to Article III-2 of the Antarctic Treaty, and Information Papers that a Consultative Party requests be translated. Background Papers will not be translated.

3. Papers that are to be translated, with the exception of the reports of Intersessional Contact Groups (ICG) convened by the ATCM or CEP, Chair Reports from Antarctic Treaty Meetings of Experts, and the Secretariat's Report and Programme, should not exceed 1500 words. When calculating the length of a paper, proposed Measures, Decisions and Resolutions and their attachments are not included.

4. Papers that are to be translated should be received by the Secretariat no later than 45 days before the Consultative Meeting. If any such paper is submitted later than 45 days before the Consultative Meeting, it may only be considered if no Consultative Party objects.

5. The Secretariat should receive Information Papers for which no translation has been requested and Background Papers that participants wish to be listed in the Final Report no later than 30 days before the Meeting.

6. The Secretariat will indicate on each document submitted by a Contracting Party, an Observer, or an Expert the date it was submitted.

7. When a revised version of a Paper made after its initial submission is resubmitted to the Secretariat for translation, the revised text should indicate clearly the amendments that have been incorporated.

8. The Papers should be transmitted to the Secretariat by electronic means and will be uploaded to the ATCM Home Page established by the Secretariat. Working Papers received before the 45 day limit should be uploaded as soon as possible and in any case not later than 30 days before the Meeting. Papers will be uploaded initially to the password protected portion of the website, and moved to the non-password protected part once the Meeting has concluded.

9. Parties may agree to present any paper for which a translation has not been requested to the Secretariat during the Meeting for translation.

10. No paper submitted to the ATCM should be used as the basis for discussion at the ATCM or at the CEP unless it has been translated into the four official languages.

11. Within six months of the end of the Consultative Meeting the Secretariat will circulate through diplomatic channels and also post on the ATCM Home Page the Final Report of that Meeting in the four official languages.

OTHER SELECTED ATCM INSTRUMENTS

Recommendation I-I (1961): Exchange of Information on Scientific Programmes

The Representatives recommend to their Governments that they should facilitate the continuation of the exchange of information regarding plans for scientific programmes as now carried on through the Special Committee on Antarctic Research (SCAR) and through other member unions and committees of the International Council of Scientific Unions (ICSU) and by such other means as may ensure the availability of this information.

Recommendation I-II (1961): Exchange of Scientific Personnel

The Representatives recommend to their Governments that they should promote the continuation of the exchange, on a basis of bilateral arrangements, of scientific personnel amongst their expeditions, and should make available such of their facilities as may be helpful to this purpose.

Recommendation I-III (1961): Exchange of Scientific Data

The Representatives recommend to their Governments that they should promote the exchange and making available of observations and results from Antarctica through the recognized international data gathering centres and by such other means as may be appropriate to ensure the exchange and free availability of this information.

Recommendation I-IV (1961): Scientific Committee on Antarctic Research

The Representatives agree, without prejudice to the rights of Governments to make such arrangements as they may deem necessary to further the objectives of scientific co-operation set forth in the Treaty:

1. that the free exchange of information and views among scientists participating in SCAR, and the recommendations concerning scientific programmes and co-operation formulated by this body constitute a most valuable contribution to international scientific co-operation in Antarctica;

2. that since these activities of SCAR constitute the kind of activity contemplated in Article III of the Treaty, SCAR should be encouraged to continue this advisory work which has so effectively facilitated international co-operation in scientific investigation.

Recommendation I-V (1961): International Organizations

The Representatives recommend to their Governments that they should individually encourage the work of international organisations having a scientific or technical interest in Antarctica, including the specialised agencies of the United Nations, and should promote on a bilateral basis the establishment and development of co-operative working relations with these organisations.

In this connection, the Representatives take note of the letter to the Minister of State for External Affairs of Australia from the Secretary-General of the World Meteorological Organisation dated 28th June 1961, circulated at the Meeting. They welcome the offer made by the World Meteorological Organisation of co-operation in questions of meteorology and of the collection and relaying of meteorological data in the Antarctic, and recommend to their Governments that they should establish co-operation in these matters through their Representatives in that Organisation.

Recommendation I-VI (1961): Exchange of Information

The Representatives recommend to their Governments that information furnished in accordance with Article VII paragraph 5 should be exchanged between Governments through diplomatic channels as early in each year as possible, and in any case before the end of November each year, and should include—

1. the names, types, numbers, descriptions, and armaments of ships, aircraft and other vehicles, introduced, or to be introduced into Antarctica, and information on military equipment, if any, and its location in Antarctica;
2. dates of expeditions leaving for, and arriving in, Antarctica, duration of stay, itinerary to and from Antarctica and routes followed within Antarctica;
3. the names, location and date of opening of the Party's bases and subsidiary stations established or planned to be established in Antarctica, listed according to whether they arc for summer and/or winter operations;
4. the names of the officers in charge of each of these bases, subsidiary stations, ships and aircraft; the number and occupations and specialisation of personnel (including any designated by other governments), who are or will be stationed at each of these bases and subsidiary stations and on board these ships and aircraft, including the number of personnel who are members of the military services together with the rank of any officers and the names and professional affiliation of personnel engaged in scientific activities;
5. the number and types of armaments possessed by personnel;
6. the programme of work, including scientific investigation, being done and planned at each of these bases and subsidiary stations and on board those ships and aircraft; and also the area or areas of operation to be covered by such programme;
7. principal scientific equipment;
8. transportation facilities and communication equipment for use within Antarctica;
9. facilities for rendering assistance;
10. notice of any expeditions to Antarctica not organised by the Party but organised, in, or proceeding from, the Party's territory.

Recommendation I-IX (1961): Historic Sites

With due regard to Article IV of the Treaty, the Representatives recommend that —

1. Governments interested in any tombs, buildings or Objects of historic interest should consult together whenever appropriate on their resolution or preservation;
2. appropriate reports on the condition of such tombs, buildings or objects of historic interest as well as any restoration which might have been effected should be exchanged among Governments;
3. Governments adopt all adequate measures to protect such tombs, buildings or objects of historic interest, from damage and destruction.

Recommendation I-X (1961): Assistance in Emergency

The Representatives reaffirm the traditional Antarctic principle that expeditions render all assistance feasible in the event of an emergency request for help and recommend to their Governments that consideration should be given to arranging consultations among them, and to the matter being discussed at the appropriate time at any meeting of experts qualified to discuss it.

Recommendation I-XI (1961): Telecommunications

The Representatives recommend to their Governments:

1. that they convene as soon as practicable a meeting of specialists in Antarctic radio communications;
2. that this meeting of specialists should discuss the telecommunications facilities needed for scientific, technical and other purposes in the Treaty area, and their use;
3. that the meeting should take into consideration –
   (a) the requirements of governments;
   (b) the viewpoint of the United Nations Specialised Agencies and other International organisations having a scientific or technical interest in Antarctic communications;
   (c) the relevant recommendations of the communications working group of SCAR;
   (d) the experience of the various Antarctic expeditions;
4. that the meeting should examine and make recommendations regarding such matters as –
   (i) the routing required to meet demands of users most effectively;
   (ii) the modes of transmission;
   (iii) the power requirements for effective reception;
   (iv) the rationalisation of schedules and the evaluation of priorities for traffic in normal and post blackout conditions;
   (v) new developments in the field of communications relevant to Antarctic requirements;
   (vi) emergency radio procedures;
   (vii) such other matters of an engineering or traffic nature as may be appropriate;
5. that the Governments should consult regarding the date, place and definitive agenda of the meeting, and as to which specialised agencies and other international organisations referred to in paragraph 3 (b) should be informed of the meeting and be invited to send observers.

Recommendation I-XII (1961): Postal Services

The Representatives recommend to their Governments that they should:—

1. promote co-operation among expeditions in the Treaty area in the collection and distribution of mail for expedition members:
2. advise each other of opportunities for forwarding mail to and from stations in the Treaty area;
3. consult together with a view to reaching agreement on further practical measures for improving postal communications in the Treaty area.

Recommendation I-XIII (1961): Exchange of Information on Nuclear Equipment and Techniques

Taking into consideration the provisions established in Article V of the Antarctic Treaty, the Representatives recommend to their Governments that they exchange by all means deemed advisable information on the application of nuclear equipment and techniques in the Treaty area.

Recommendation III-VII (1964): Acceptance of Approved Recommendations

Since the Recommendations approved by the Contracting Parties entitled to participate in meetings held in accordance with Article IX of the Antarctic Treaty are so much a part of the overall structure of cooperation established by the Treaty, the Representatives recommend to their Governments that any new Contracting Party entitled to participate in such meetings should be urged to accept these recommendations and to inform other Contracting Parties of its intention to apply and be bound by them.

The Representatives recommend further that their Governments agree that existing Contracting parties and any new Contracting Parties other than those entitled to participate in meetings held in accordance with Article IX of the Treaty be invited to consider accepting these recommendations and to inform other Contracting Parties of their intention to apply and be bound by them.

Recommendation III-XI (1964): Pelagic Sealing and the Taking of Fauna on Pack Ice

The Representatives, at the time of adopting the Agreed Measures on the Conservation of Fauna and Flora,

1. *Considering* that appropriate voluntary regulation of pelagic sealing or the taking of fauna on pack ice is of great importance for the fulfilment of the purposes and principles of these Measures;

2. *Recommend* to their Governments that this matter be considered further by them on as broad a basis as practicable in preparing for the Fourth Consultative Meeting at Santiago, Chile, with a view to its inclusion on the Agenda for the Fourth Consultative Meeting;

3. *Recommend* to their Governments that when ships of their nationality engage in pelagic sealing or the taking of fauna on pack ice south of 60° South Latitude, each Government voluntarily regulate these activities to ensure the survival of any species being taken and to ensure that the nature ecological system is not seriously disturbed.

Recommendation IV-27 (1966): Effects of Antarctic Tourism

Recognizing that the effects of tourist activities may prejudice the conduct of scientific research, conservation of fauna and flora and the operation of Antarctic stations,

The Representatives recommend to their Governments that:

1. The Government of a country in which a tourist or other non-scientific expedition is being organized furnish notice of the expedition as soon as possible through diplomatic channels to any other Government whose station the expedition plans to visit;

2. A Government provide on request information as promptly as possible regarding the conditions upon which it would grant permission for tourist groups to visit Antarctic stations which it maintains; and

3. Such permission be withheld unless reasonable assurances are given of compliance with the provisions of the Treaty, the Recommendations then effective and the conditions applicable at stations to be visited.

Recommendation V-3 (1968): Southern Ocean

The Representatives,

Considering that the Southern Ocean is an integral part of the Antarctic environment and that the Consultative Governments have made substantial contributions towards knowledge of this ocean in the Treaty Area,

Noting that Resolution 5 of the Vth Session of the Intergovernmental Oceanographic Commission (IOC) established a Co-ordination Group for the Southern Ocean and that the terms of reference for this group include plans for the gradual development of a comprehensive study of the Southern Ocean;

Noting further the significant contribution which the Scientific Committee on Antarctic Research (SCAR) has made to these studies and that SCAR is invited to participate in the Co-ordination Group as an observer;

Welcome the proposed study of the Southern Ocean by the IOC with the participation of SCAR as well as other interested scientific organizations;

Recommend to their governments that they encourage SCAR through their National Committees to continue its interest in scientific matters related to the Southern Ocean and to make available scientific advice as appropriate to the IOC Coordination Group in order to aid in its development of plans for the comprehensive study of the Southern Ocean.

Recommendation V-4 (1968): Historic Monuments

The Representatives,

Recalling Recommendation I-9,

Recommend to their governments

1. that a list of historic monuments which should be preserved be drawn up;
2. that each government circulate a list of historic monuments through diplomatic channels to other Consultative Governments;
3. that this subject be considered further at the next Consultative Meeting;
4. that, in the meantime, they do what is feasible to ensure the survival as far as possible of any historic monument which has been included on any list circulated under paragraph 2.

Recommendation VI-5 (1970): Use of Radio-isotopes in the Antarctic

The Representatives,

Recognizing:

1. the need to minimise harmful disturbance to the Antarctic environment;
2. that the uncontrolled use of radio-isotopes in the course of scientific investigations may jeopardise the conduct of subsequent investigations;

Recommend to their Governments that through their National Antarctic Committees, they invite the Scientific Committee on Antarctic Research to consider the uses of radio-isotopes in Antarctic scientific investigations and to propose comprehensive principles for their control which can be considered under Article IX of the Antarctic Treaty.

Recommendation VI-6 (1970): Coordination of Antarctic Scientific Investigations Involving the Use of Radio-isotopes

The Representatives,

Recognising that experiments involving the use of radio-isotopes may jeopardize subsequent scientific investigations in the same locality;

Considering that:

1. prior notification of the use of radio-isotopes is necessary to allow time for consultations between Consultative Parties whose investigators may wish to carry out experiments in the same locality at a later date;
2. interim measures are required before agreement is reached on the controlled use of radio-isotopes in the Antarctic Treaty area;

Recommend to their Governments that, when experiments involving the use of radioisotopes in the Antarctic Treaty area are planned, they should provide appropriate information on such experiments to other Consultative Parties as early as possible, preferably six months in advance, but in any event annually.

Recommendation VI-7 (1970): Effects of Tourists and Non-government Expeditions to the Antarctic Treaty Area

The Representatives,

Noting the increase in recent years in the number of tourists and also in the number of visitors who are not sponsored by the Consultative Parties to the Antarctic Treaty area;

Considering that the activities of such visitors can have lasting and harmful effects on scientific programmes, on the Antarctic environment, particularly in Specially Protected Areas, and on historic monuments;

Desiring to ensure that such visitors are afforded the best view of stations in the Antarctic compatible with the research programmes being undertaken;

Recalling paragraph 5 of Article VII and Article X of the Antarctic Treaty and Recommendations I-VI and IV-27;

Recommend to their Governments that:

1. They should exert appropriate efforts to ensure that all tourists and other visitors do not engage in any activity in the Treaty area which is contrary to the principles and purposes or the Antarctic Treaty or Recommendations made under it;

2. They should inform, in so far as they are able, those responsible for expeditions to the Treaty area which are not organized by a Consultative Party but organized in, proceeding from, or calling at, their territory, of the following:

(a) that final arrangements to visit any station be made with that station between twenty four and seventy two hours in advance of the expected time of arrival;

(b) that all tourists and other visitors comply with any conditions or restrictions on their movements which the station commander may stipulate for their safety or to safeguard scientific programmes being undertaken at or near the station;

(c) that visitors must not enter Specially Protected Areas and must respect designated historic monuments;

3. Advance notice of all expeditions to the Treaty area not organized by a Consultative Party, but organized in, proceeding from or calling at that Party's territory, shall be given, in so far as is possible, to the other Consultative Parties. Such notice shall include the relevant information listed in Recommendation I-VI;

4. Until such time as this Recommendation becomes effective in accordance with Article IX of the Antarctic Treaty, it shall be considered, as far as feasible, as a guideline.

Recommendation VII-2 (1972): Review of Specially Protected Areas

The Representatives,

Recalling:

1. that the purpose of Specially Protected Areas is to preserve, in accordance with the Agreed Measures for the Conservation of Antarctic Fauna and Flora, the natural ecological systems of areas of outstanding scientific interest;

2. that Recommendation VI-8 has notably increased the protection afforded to Specially Protected Areas by prohibiting entry into them except in accordance with a permit;

Recognising that the existing Specially Protected Areas were designated under less strict provisions regarding entry;

Conscious of the need to review the existing Specially Protected Areas in the light of experience and the increased degree of protection they have been afforded;

Recalling Recommendation III-X which encouraged SCAR to continue its interest in and prepare reports from time to time on the conservation of Antarctic fauna and flora;

Noting the opinion of SCAR, expressed in the report produced at its Twelfth Meeting on the "Purposes and Designation of Special Areas", that the existing Specially Protected Areas are not fully representative of the major Antarctic land and freshwater ecological systems and that some of these ecological systems are over-represented in the series so far designated;

Recommend to their Governments that:

1. In due course they include in the series of Specially Protected Areas listed in Annex A of the Agreed Measures for the Conservation of Antarctic Fauna and Flora:
   (a) representative examples of the major Antarctic land and freshwater ecological systems;
   (b) areas with unique complexes of species;
   (c) areas which are the type locality or only known habitat of any plant or invertebrate species;
   (d) areas which contain specially interesting breeding colonies of birds or mammals;
   (e) areas which should be kept inviolate so that in the future they may be used for purposes of comparison with localities that have been disturbed by man;
2. They invite SCAR, through their National Committees, to review in the light of the criteria set out in paragraph 1 the existing Specially Protected Areas, and to make recommendations about:
   (a) the desirability of retaining each Area;
   (b) the desirability of redefining the limits of each Area retained;
   (c) creating such additional Areas as may be considered desirable;
3. The number of Specially Protected Areas should be kept to the minimum that will meet the criteria set out in paragraph 1;
4. The size of each Specially Protected Area should be the minimum required to serve the purpose for which the Area has been designated.

Recommendation VII-4 (1972): Effects of Tourists and Non-governmental Expeditions in the Antarctic Treaty Area

The Representatives,

Noting the increase in the Antarctic Treaty Area in the number of visitors who are not sponsored by Consultative Parties.

Considering that both Governments and such visitors would benefit from having available to them an agreed statement:

(a) of accepted practices in the Treaty Area including, *infer alia,* the need for self sufficiency and prior notification of intended arrival at a station, which such visitors would be expected to follow (to which could be appended the particular conditions imposed by each government for a visit to anyone of its stations); and
(b) of the relevant provisions of the Antarctic Treaty and of the Recommendations made under it;

Recalling Recommendations VI-7 and VI-II concerning the possible harmful effects of such visitors on scientific programmes and on the Antarctic environment;

Convinced of the need to avoid unnecessary interference with natural ecological systems which are not sufficiently understood and continue to be the subject of research;

Conscious that the Treaty Area contains many unique features of historical, scenic and general scientific interest;

Recommend to their Governments that:

1. They keep under review, in the light of existing Recommendations, the effects in the Treaty Area of tourists and other visitors who are not sponsored by Consultative Parties;
2. They consider drawing up at the Eighth Consultative Meeting a statement of those accepted practices and relevant provisions about which all visitors to the Treaty Area should be aware;

3. They consult each other well in advance about the possibility of designating at the Eighth Consultative Meeting an adequate number of areas of interest to which tourists could be encouraged to go, and about the criteria to be used to determine such areas;
4. They use their best efforts to ensure that the provisions of the Treaty and subsequent recommendations relating to the conservation of fauna and flora are applied in practice to all visitors who are not sponsored by Consultative Parties, as well as to tourists.

Recommendation VII-6 (1972): Antarctic Resources – Effects of Mineral Exploration

The Representatives,

Recalling the provisions and principles of the Antarctic Treaty;

Reaffirming that it is in the interest of all mankind that the Antarctic Treaty Area shall continue forever to be used exclusively for peaceful purposes and shall not become the scene or object of international discord;

Acknowledging that the Antarctic Treaty places a special responsibility upon the Contracting Parties to exert appropriate efforts, consistent with the Charter of the United Nations, to the end that no one engages in any activity in the Antarctic Treaty Area contrary to the principles or purposes of the Treaty;

Noting the technological developments in polar mineral exploration and the increasing interest in the possibility of there being exploitable minerals in the Antarctic Treaty Area;

Noting that there is a need for further study and deliberation amongst the Consultative Parties;

Recognising that mineral exploration is likely to raise problems of an environmental nature and that the Consultative Parties should assume responsibility for the protection of the environment and the wise use of resources;

Conscious of the special situation in the Antarctic arising from the particular regime of the Antarctic Treaty and the Recommendations adopted under it;

Recommend to their Governments that the subject "Antarctic Resources – Effects of Mineral Exploration" be carefully studied and included on the Agenda of the Eighth Consultative Meeting.

Recommendation VIII-3 (1975): Sites of Special Scientific Interest

The Representatives,

Recalling Article II of the Antarctic Treaty and Recommendation VII-3;

Conscious of the need to protect scientific investigations which might suffer from wilful or accidental interference;

Desiring to protect only sites where harmful interference is generally recognised to be likely;

Recognizing the need to protect such scientific investigations irrespective of their purpose;

Recognizing that a limited number of sites of exceptional scientific interest may require long-term protection from harmful interference;

Noting with appreciation the interim response of the Scientific Committee on Antarctic Research (SCAR) to paragraph 1 of Recommendation VII-3;

Recommend to their Governments that:

1. They invite SCAR, through their National Committees, to have regard to the following when considering proposals for Sites of Special Scientific Interest:
(a) Sites should only be proposed when:
 (i) Scientific investigations are being carried out or arc planned to begin before the following meeting of SCAR, and there is a demonstrable risk of interference which would jeopardise those scientific investigations; or

(ii) they are of exceptional scientific interest and therefore require long-term protection from harmful interference;

(b) Sites should be proposed for designation up to a specified date, which may be extended following a review by SCAR;

(c) Proposals for the designation of Sites should be accompanied by a management plan which should include, *inter alia,* and where applicable, the following details:

(i) a description of the Site, together with a map delimiting its boundaries and where applicable showing any existing or proposed demarcations on the Site;

(ii) a statement setting out the reasons in conformity with paragraphs 1(a) (i) and (ii) above for designation of the Site;

(iii) a summary of the scientific investigations being carried out or planned;

(iv) the proposed date at which the designation will expire unless extended;

(v) proposed points of access;

(vi) any proposed pedestrian and vehicular routes;

(vii) other kinds of scientific investigation which would not cause harmful interference with the investigations described at paragraph (c) (iii) above;

(viii) whether specific kinds of scientific sampling may take place and guidelines for such sampling;

(ix) any other restraints that may be needed

2. They invite SCAR, through their National Committees, to initiate review of those Sites whose designation is likely to terminate before the second following Antarctic Treaty Consultative Meeting;

3. They request their national offices responsible for the administration of Antarctic expeditions to maintain a record of activities within each Site of Special Scientific Interest in which their scientists are active;

4. Persons wishing to visit Sites of Special Scientific Interest should consult their national offices responsible for the administration of Antarctic expeditions;

5. Until such time as the Recommendations designating Sites of Special Scientific Interest become effective in accordance with Article IX of the Antarctic Treaty, they should, as far as possible, be considered as guidelines.

Recommendation VIII-6 (1975): Annual Exchanges of Information

The Representatives,

Recalling Articles III and VII of the Antarctic Treaty;

Noting that numerous recommendations of Consultative Meetings have established requirements for exchange of information between Governments;

Desiring to consolidate the requirements for periodic exchanges of information into a standard annual report;

Conscious that other Recommendations, including Recommendations I-I, I-III, I-VII, I-XIII, II-I, II-VIII, IV-27, VI-3, VI-7, and VII-7 provide for exchanges of information on an occasional basis or outside the annual reports exchanged between Governments;

Recommend to their Governments that:

1. They adopt the Annex to this Recommendation as the standard format for the annual exchanges of information between Governments:

2. They consider that the provisions set forth in the Annex satisfy the requirements for exchanges of information in Recommendations I-VI, II-IV, II-VI, III-I, III-II, IV-23, VI-2, VI-6, VI-12, and VI-13;

3. They exchange the report described in the Annex through diplomatic channels, not later than 30 November each year;

4. They report prior to 30 June in accordance with Recommendation II-VI on extensions, reductions or other modifications in the development of the activities previously reported;

5. Until such time as the Agreed Measures for the Conservation of Antarctic Fauna and Flora become effective, the information exchange requirements set forth in Recommendation IV-19 should be considered as an interim guideline and may be added to the Annex.

Annex: Standard Format for the Annual Exchanges of Information

1. Information in as complete a form as possible under the categories listed below is to be exchanged as early as possible but in no case later than 30 November each year.

2. Under Recommendation II-VI any extensions, reductions or other modifications of activities (in the categories marked below with an asterisk (*)) previously reported are to be furnished as soon as possible and in any case prior to 30 June following the season of activity.

3. If a category is not applicable to the activities of a particular country (for example, it has no airfields or does not intend to use research rockets) this fact should be stated.

I.* The names, types, numbers, descriptions, and armament of ships, aircraft, and other vehicles, introduced, or to be introduced, into the Antarctic Treaty Area, and information on military equipment, if any, and its location in the Area. (List only vehicles used for transport to and from Antarctica. Vehicles at individual stations are described under category VIII below.)

II.* Dates of expeditions leaving for, and arriving in, the Antarctic Treaty Area, duration of stay, itinerary to and from the Area and routes followed within the Area.

III.* The names, locations, and dates of opening of the Party's bases and subsidiary stations established or planned to be established in the Antarctic Treaty Area, listed according to whether they are for summer and/or winter operations.

IV.* The names of the officers in charge of each of these bases, subsidiary stations, ships and aircraft; the number, occupations and specialisations of personnel (including any designated by other Governments), who are or will be stationed at each of these bases and subsidiary stations and on board these ships and aircraft, including the number of personnel who are members of the military services, together with the rank of any officers and the names and professional affiliations of personnel engaged in scientific activities:

A.* Officers in charge of bases.

B.* Officers in charge of ships.

C.* Officers in charge of aircraft.

D.* Number, occupations and specialisations of personnel:

1.* Summer personnel (listed according to base or ship at which working);

2.* Winter personnel (listed according to base at which working).

E.* Number of personnel who are members of the military services together with rank of any officers.

F.* Names and professional affiliation of personnel engaged in scientific activities (listed according to base or ship at which working. It would be useful to list each person's scientific disciplines as well as his affiliation).

V.* The number and types of armaments possessed by personnel.

VI.* The programme of work, including scientific investigation, being done and planned at each of these bases and subsidiary stations and on board those ships and aircraft; and also the area or areas of operation to be covered by such programme (this may be included as an Annex).

VII.* Principal scientific equipment, which may be listed according to the base at which it is customarily used (this may be included as an Annex).

VIII. Transportation facilities and communication equipment for use within the Antarctic Treaty Area:

A.* Surface, marine, and air transport vehicles at each base.

B.* Description of communications facilities using the standard form in accordance with Recommendation VI-2.

C.* Description of airfields in accordance with Recommendation III-I, including particulars of location, operating conditions and limitations, radio aids to navigation, facilities for radio communications and instrument landing (this may be included as an Annex).

IX.* Facilities for rendering assistance (medical and transport services and shelter available in emergencies).

X.* Notice of any expeditions to Antarctica not organised by the Party but organised in, calling at, or proceeding from the Party's territory (including tourism in accordance with Recommendations IV-27 and VI-7).

XI.* Description of unoccupied refuges in accordance with Recommendation III-II, including name, position, description of location, dated established, date last examined and estimate of available accommodation, facilities, food, fuel, and supplies of other kinds (this may be included as an Annex).

XII. Annual return of the numbers of each species killed or captured in the Antarctic Treaty Area in accordance with Article XII of the Agreed Measures for the Conservation of Antarctic Fauna and Flora, using the format annexed to Recommendation IV-19 (this may be included as an Annex).

XIII. Notice of the intended use of radio-isotopes in scientific investigations in the Antarctic Treaty Area. (Note: under Recommendation VI-6 this information is to be provided by Consultative Parties as early as possible, preferably six months in advance, but in any case annually.)

XIV. Notice of intended use of scientific research rockets in the Antarctic Treaty Area in accordance with Recommendation VI-12 including *inter alia* geographical co-ordinates of the place of launching; the time and date of launching or, alternatively, the approximate period of time during which it is planned to carry out the launchings; the direction of launching; the planned maximum altitude; the planned impact area; the type and other specifications of the rockets to be launched, including possible residual hazards; the purpose and research programme of the rocket.

XV. Notice of ships which are carrying out substantial oceanographic research programmes in the Antarctic Treaty Area, in accordance with Recommendation VI-13 including information required under categories I, II, IV, VI, and VII above.

Recommendation VIII-7 (1975): Co-operation in Transport

The Representatives,

Recalling Recommendation VII-8;

Recognizing that access to Antarctica by long-range aircraft combined with intracontinental feeder routes by smaller aircraft would facilitate new levels of co-operation and flexibility in research;

Noting the interest taken by the Scientific Committee on Antarctic Research (SCAR) in the potential benefits to be derived from a co-operative air transport system;

Recommend to their Governments that:

1. They request their offices responsible for the administration of Antarctic expeditions to review their scientific programmes in order to identify the ways in which a co-operative air transport system might benefit them and to inform SCAR through their representatives on the SCAR Working Group on Logistics;

2. They request SCAR, through their National Antarctic Committees, to review the available transport resources and the potential requirements with respect to a co-operative air transport system and to bring their conclusions to the attention of the Consultative Parties.

Recommendation VIII-8 (1975): Activities of States that are not Consultative Parties

The Representatives,

Recalling the principles and purposes of the Antarctic Treaty;

Reaffirming that it is in the interest of all mankind that Antarctica shall continue forever to be used exclusively for peaceful purposes and shall not become the scene or object of international discord;

Recognising that the Antarctic Treaty places a special responsibility on the Contracting Parties to exert appropriate efforts, consistent with the Charter of the United Nations, to the end that no one engages in any activity in the Antarctic Treaty Area contrary to the principles or purposes of the Treaty;

Considering paragraphs 15 to 17 of the Final Report of the Seventh Antarctic Treaty Consultative Meeting regarding activities in the Treaty Area by States that are not Contracting Parties;

Considering further that it is desirable for acceding States to approve existing and future Recommendations, which form an integral part of the Treaty regime;

Recommend to their Governments that:

1. They reaffirm the principles set forth in paragraphs 15 to 17 of the Final Report of the Seventh Antarctic Treaty Consultative Meeting in respect of activities by States that are not Contracting Parties to the Antarctic Treaty;
2. They urge the States that have or will become Parties to the Antarctic Treaty to approve the Recommendations adopted at Consultative Meetings in pursuance of the Treaty and subsequently approved by all the Contracting Parties whose representatives were entitled to participate in the meetings held to consider those measures.

Recommendation VIII-10 (1975): Antarctic Marine Living Resources

The Representatives,

Recalling Article IX, paragraph 1(f), of the Antarctic Treaty;

Convinced that the Antarctic Treaty Area contains significant concentrations of marine living resources;

Recognizing the need to promote and achieve, within the framework of the Antarctic Treaty, the objectives of protection, scientific study and rational use of these marine living resources;

Aware of the inadequacy of the information concerning the stocks of these living resources and of the need to develop a good scientific foundation for appropriate conservation measures;

Recommend to their Governments that:

1. They initiate or expand, insofar as is practicable within their Antarctic scientific programmes, detailed studies of the biology, distribution, bio-mass and population dynamics and the ecology of Antarctic marine living resources;
2. They encourage further co-operation among the Consultative Parties in scientific studies of and programmes relating to Antarctic marine living resources;
3. They encourage studies which could lead to the development of effective measures for the conservation of Antarctic marine living resources in the Treaty Area;
4. They urge the Scientific Committee on Antarctic Research (SCAR), through their National Antarctic Committees, to continue its scientific work on these matters and to consider convening, as soon as practicable, a meeting to discuss current work and report on programmes for the study and conservation of Antarctic marine living resources;
5. They include the subject "Antarctic Marine Living Resources" on the agenda of the Ninth Consultative Meeting.

Recommendation VIII-12 (1975): Disposal of Nuclear Waste

The Representatives,

Recalling Article V of the Antarctic Treaty;

Noting the increasing production of nuclear materials and the growing concern about the disposal of nuclear waste;

Bearing in mind the undertaking of Contracting Parties in Article X of the Antarctic Treaty to exert appropriate efforts, consistent with the Charter of the United Nations, to the end that no one engages in any activity in Antarctica contrary to the principles or purposes of the Treaty;

Desiring to preserve the unique quality of the Antarctic environment;

Recommend to their Governments that they continue to exert appropriate efforts to the end that no one disposes of nuclear waste in the Antarctic Treaty Area.

Recommendation IX-1 (1977): Antarctic Mineral Resources

The Representatives,

Recalling the provisions of the Antarctic Treaty, which establishes a regime for international co-operation in Antarctica, with the objective of ensuring that Antarctica should continue forever to be used exclusively for peaceful purposes and should not become the scene or object of international discord;

Bearing in mind the provisions of Article IV of the Treaty;

Convinced that the framework established by the Antarctic Treaty has proved effective in promoting international harmony in furtherance of the purposes and principles of the United Nations Charter, in ensuring the protection of the Antarctic environment, and on promoting freedom of scientific research in Antarctica;

Noting with thanks the Report of the Scientific Committee on Antarctic Research (SCAR) Group of Specialists entitled Preliminary Assessment of the Environmental Impact of Mineral Exploration/Exploitation in Antarctica (EAMREA);

Recognising nevertheless that adequate scientific data concerning the harmful environmental effects of activities related to the exploration and exploitation of Antarctic mineral resources, should they occur, are not yet available;

Concerned that unregulated activities related to exploration and exploitation of mineral resources could adversely affect the unique environment of the Antarctic and other ecosystems dependent on the Antarctic environment;

Conscious that the Consultative Parties to the Antarctic Treaty in carrying out scientific research in the area have accumulated valuable experience and can substantially contribute to the protection of the environment and the rational use of Antarctic mineral resources, should exploration or exploitation thereof occur;

Aware of the special responsibilities of Consultative Parties to ensure that any activities in Antarctica, including commercial exploration and exploitation in the future, should they occur, should not become the cause of international discord, of danger to the unique Antarctic environment, of disruption to scientific investigation, or be otherwise contrary to the principles or purposes of the Antarctic Treaty;

Recommend to their Governments that;

1. They reaffirm the basic principles set forth in Recommendation VIII-14 of the Eighth Antarctic Treaty Consultative Meeting;

2. They take note with appreciation of the Report of the Group of Experts on Mineral Exploration and Exploitation annexed to the Report of the Ninth Consultative Meeting and make the best possible use of its conclusions and guidelines;

3. They continue to study the environmental implications of mineral resource activities in the Antarctic Treaty Area and hold at a time and place to be arranged through diplomatic channels a meeting of ecological, technological and other related experts, in accordance with Recommendation IV-24, with a view to developing scientific programmes aimed at:

(i) improving predictions of the impact of possible technologies for mineral exploration and exploitation in the Antarctic, as outlined in Section IIB of the Report of the Group of Experts, and in Section 5 of the SCAR / EAMREA Group Report;

(ii) developing measures for the prevention of damage to the environment or for its rehabilitation, in accordance with Section IIC of the Report of the Group of Experts;

4. They endorse the following principles elaborated at the Special Preparatory Meeting held in Paris from 28 June to 10 July 1976:

(i) the Consultative Parties will continue to play an active and responsible role in dealing with the question of the mineral resources of Antarctica;

(ii) the Antarctic Treaty must be maintained in its entirety;

(iii) protection of the unique Antarctic environment and of its dependent ecosystems should be a basic consideration;

(iv) the Consultative Parties, in dealing with the question of mineral resources in Antarctica, should not prejudice the interests of all mankind in Antarctica;

5. They note that the provisions of Article IV of the Antarctic Treaty shall not be affected by the regime. It should ensure that the principles embodied in Article IV of the Antarctic Treaty are safeguarded in application to the area covered by the Antarctic Treaty;

6. They study the content of a future regime based on the principles contained in paragraphs 4 and 5 and on such further principles, rules and arrangements as may be agreed, taking full account of all proposals submitted to the IXth Consultative Meeting;

7. The subject "Antarctic Resources – The Question of Mineral Exploration and Exploitation" be the subject of intensified consultation among them and they urge the host Government of the Tenth Consultative Meeting to convene a meeting to consider legal and political aspects of mineral resource issues; this meeting to report to the Tenth Consultative Meeting on the results of its work;

8. They urge their nationals and other States to refrain from all exploration and exploitation of Antarctic mineral resources while making progress towards the timely adoption of an agreed regime concerning Antarctic mineral resource activities. They will thus endeavour to ensure that, pending the timely adoption of agreed solutions pertaining to exploration and exploitation of mineral resources, no activity shall be conducted to explore or exploit such resources. They will keep these matters under continuing examination;

9. The subject "Antarctic Resources – The Question of Mineral Exploration and Exploitation" be placed on the Agenda of the Tenth Antarctic Treaty Consultative Meeting.

Recommendation X-8 (1979): Effect of Tourists and Non-government Expeditions in the Antarctic Treaty Area

The Representatives,

Recalling that Annex A to Recommendation VIII-9 was to be discussed at the Ninth Consultative Meeting and that a draft text of a Statement of Accepted Practices and the Relevant Provisions of the Antarctic Treaty was referred from the Ninth to the Tenth Consultative Meeting;

Recognizing that, in addition to the statement referred to in the previous paragraph which is primarily intended for the organizers of tourist expeditions, it would be helpful to the organizers of such expeditions to be able to provide to individual visitors a brief guide to good conduct in the Antarctic;

Noting that adventurous individuals organizing non-governmental expeditions to Antarctica may seek help or advice from offices administering Antarctic programs;

Recognizing, also, that in considering responses to requests for help from such expeditions, an important concern is the possibility that such expeditions may, in cases of emergency, involve the offices administering Antarctic programs in financial or material loss;

Recognizing that suitably qualified guides accompanying commercially organized Antarctic tours would both benefit the tourists and help to ensure that the conservation and environmental measures adopted by the Consultative Parties were observed;

Reaffirming the traditional principle in the Antarctic of rendering all assistance feasible in the event of an emergency request for help, but noting that commercial overflights of Antarctica are operating in a particularly hazardous environment, where aircraft operation systems normally available elsewhere in the world are at a minimum, and where emergencies could arise which are beyond the capacity of permanent Antarctic expeditions to respond adequately;

Recommend to their governments that:

I – Statement of accepted practices and the relevant provisions of the Antarctic Treaty

They insert the attached statement of Accepted Practices and the Relevant Provisions of the Antarctic Treaty into Annex A to Recommendation VIII-9 for the purposes set out in operative paragraph 1 of that Recommendation.

II – Non-Governmental Expeditions

If a non-governmental expedition approaches a Consultative Party for help or advice, that Consultative Party should inform the Contracting Party where the expedition to Antarctica is being organized and may request all relevant information about the expedition.

They urge non-governmental expeditions to carry adequate insurance cover against the risk of their incurring financial charges or material losses in the Antarctic Treaty Area.

III – Tour Guides

To the extent practicable, they encourage commercial tour operators to carry tour guides with experience of Antarctic conditions, who are aware of the considerations which underlie the Agreed Measures for the Conservation of Antarctic Fauna and Flora and for the protection of the Antarctic environment.

IV – Commercial Overflights in Antarctica

They notify commercial aircraft operators that the present level of tourist overflight activity:

(i) exceeds existing capabilities for air traffic control, communications and search and rescue in the Antarctic;

(ii) may interfere with normal operational flights in support of expeditions engaged in ongoing scientific programs in the Antarctic;

(iii) exceeds the capacity of their Antarctic operations to respond adequately to an unplanned emergency landing.

Statement of accepted principles and the relevant provisions of the Antarctic Treaty

Introduction

The following statement is intended for the guidance of all those who visit the Antarctic.

The Antarctic Treaty was negotiated in Washington in 1959 by the states which had established scientific stations in the Antarctic during the International Geophysical Year (1957–58) in order to perpetuate the close scientific cooperation which had marked that period. It provides, *inter alia*, that the Antarctic shall be used for peaceful purposes only and that any measures of a military nature shall be prohibited; that there shall be freedom of scientific investigation and that the results of such investigation shall be made freely available; that any nuclear explosions and the disposal of radioactive waste material in the Antarctic is prohibited; that notification of an expedition to the Antarctic shall be provided in advance; and that each of the Antarctic Treaty Contracting Parties shall exert appropriate efforts to the end that no one engages in any activity in the Antarctic contrary to the principles or purposes of the Antarctic Treaty.

Recommendations of Antarctic Treaty Consultative Meetings

The Treaty requires that meetings shall be held from time to time to consider and recommend measures in furtherance of its principles and objectives. Amongst these are measures of which all those who enter the Antarctic Treaty Area, both those sponsored by Governments and those not so sponsored, should be aware. The following notes indicate the nature of these measures and the reader is referred to the Recommendations of successive Consultative Meetings for the details.

Protection of the Antarctic Environment

The ecosystem of the Antarctic Treaty Area is particularly vulnerable to human interference and the Antarctic derives much of its importance from its uncontaminated and undisturbed condition and the effects it has on adjacent areas and the global environment. For these reasons the Consultative Parties recognise their special responsibility for the protection of the environment and the wise use of the Treaty Area.

Conservation of Wildlife

Animals in the Antarctic are in almost all cases tame and are therefore peculiarly vulnerable. Both animals and plants are living under extreme conditions and great care has to be taken to avoid upsetting the natural ecological system. They are protected by the following five mechanisms under the Agreed Measures for the Conservation of Antarctic Fauna and Flora:

(i) Protection of Native Fauna

The killing, wounding, capturing or molesting of any native mammal or native bird is prohibited except in an emergency or in accordance with a permit issued under the authority of a Participating Government. Any attempt to do any of these things is also prohibited under the same conditions.

(ii) Harmful Interference

Every effort shall be made to minimize harmful interference with the normal living conditions of any native mammal or bird.

(iii) Specially Protected Species

Two species of seal, Fur Seals and the Ross Seal have been designated as Specially Protected Species and permits may only be issued in relation to these species in accordance with certain restrictive criteria.

(iv) Specially Protected Areas

Certain areas of outstanding scientific interest have been designated as Specially Protected Areas in order to preserve their unique natural ecological system (see Annex I). No person may enter such an Area except in accordance with a permit issued under the authority of a Participating Government. Such permits may only be issued in accordance with certain restrictive criteria.

(v) Introduction of Non Indigenous Species, Parasites and Diseases

No species of animal or plant not indigenous to the Antarctic Treaty Area may be brought into the Area except in accordance with a permit issued under the authority of a Participating Government. Special precautions have to be taken to prevent the accidental introduction of parasites and diseases into the Treaty Area.

Pelagic Sealing

The Consultative Parties, having regard to the possibly damaging ecological consequences that might arise from the exploitation of Antarctic seals for commercial purposes, negotiated the Convention for the Conservation of Antarctic Seals. This Convention entered into force on 11 March 1978.

Waste Disposal

In addition to the measures for the conservation of Antarctic Fauna and Flora outlined above, the Consultative Parties have prepared a Code of Conduct for Antarctic Expeditions and Station Activities including, *inter alia*, recommended procedures for waste disposal (see Annex II).

Protection of Historic Monuments

Every effort should be made to prevent damage or destruction to any historic monuments. The Consultative Parties have listed a number of such monuments for special protection (see Annex III).

Facilitation of Scientific Research: Sites of Special Scientific Interest

There are many scientific investigations being carried out in the Antarctic which could suffer from accidental interference. For example, long term studies of the population dynamics of a penguin colony may require that visitors be kept to an absolute minimum. Intensive scientific work in one area may require that a nearby ecologically similar area be kept undisturbed and uncontaminated for reference purposes. Again, certain electromagnetically "quiet" areas, where sensitive instruments have been installed for recording minute signals associated with upper atmosphere studies, may require that visits to the site should be kept to a minimum.

For these and similar reasons the Consultative Parties have designated certain Sites of Special Scientific Interest in the Antarctic (see Annex IV). Each Site is subject to a management plan designed to protect the particular scientific investigations being undertaken. Persons wishing to visit Sites of Special Scientific Interest should, well in advance, consult the national office responsible for the administration of a permanent Antarctic scientific expedition or, if this is not possible, should consult the station commander of the scientific station nearest the site which it is intended to visit.

Tourism and Non-Governmental Expeditions to the Antarctic Treaty Area

An important feature of the Antarctic Treaty is that cooperation under it is facilitated by the prior exchange of information about planned activities. The Treaty commitment covers any expedition organised in or proceeding to the Antarctic from any state which is a Contracting Party to the Antarctic Treaty. A consolidated list of the information to be exchanged is attached at Annex V.

It is a traditional principle that expeditions render all assistance feasible in the event of an emergency. There is in the Antarctic a number of unoccupied huts and refuges which may be used by any expedition in an emergency, in which case the authorities who maintain the hut or refuge should be informed of what use has been made of it.

Special Measures Relating to Tourist and Non-Governmental Expeditions

The number of non-governmental expeditions to the Antarctic is steadily increasing and there is a tendency for these expeditions to concentrate on the more easily accessible parts of the Antarctic. Frequent visits to scientific stations or undue dependence on the facilities of such stations can prejudice their scientific work. It is therefore required that the organizers of a tourist or non-governmental expedition should furnish notice as soon as possible, through diplomatic channels, to any other Government whose station the expedition plans to visit. Any such Government may refuse to accept a visit to a station which it maintains or may lay down conditions upon which it would grant permission including *inter alia*, that:

(i) reasonable assurance be given of compliance with the provisions of the Antarctic Treaty, measures adopted under it and the conditions applicable at stations to be visited;

(ii) tour organizers should ensure that prior to the commencement of the tour or expedition, procedures and systems for adequate telecommunications have been confirmed with the offices administering the Antarctic stations to be visited;

(iii) final arrangements to visit any station be made with that station between twenty-four and seventy-two hours in advance of the expected time of arrival;

(iv) all tourists and other comply with any conditions or restrictions on their movements which the station commander may stipulate for their safety or to safeguard scientific programmes being undertaken at or near the station;

(v) visitors must not enter Specially Protected Areas and must respect designated historic monuments;

(vi) tour organizers should report to the Governments whose stations they have visited, after completion of the tour, the name and nationality of the ship, the name of the captain, the itinerary of each separate cruise, the number of tourists accompanying each cruise and the places and dates at which landings were made in the Antarctic Treaty Area, with the number of persons landed on each occasion.

List of Annexes

ANNEX I Specially Protected Areas. (Annex B to Recommendation Ill-B.)

ANNEX II Extract From the Code of Conduct for Antarctic Expeditions and Station Activities Relating to Waste Disposal. (Annex to Recommendation VIII-II.)

ANNEX III List of Historic Monuments. (Annex to Recommendation VII-9.)

ANNEX IV Sites of Special Scientific Interest. (Management Plans annexed to Recommendation VIII-4.)

ANNEX V Standard Format for the Annual Exchanges of Information. (Annex to Recommendation VIII-6.)

Guidance for visitors to the Antarctic

Antarctica and its surrounding islands are one of the few places in the world which are still relatively unchanged by man's activities. Scientists still know very little about the ecological situation in the Antarctic. At the present early stage in research on these matters, some restrictions and precautions may seem unnecessarily harsh, but preliminary studies indicate the need for great caution.

By following a few very simple requests, you can help preserve the unique environment of this region.

1. Avoid disturbing wildlife, in particular do not:
   - walk on vegetation;
   - touch or handle birds or seals;
   - startle or chase any bird from its nest;
   - wander indiscriminately through penguin or other bird colonies.

2. Litter of all types must be kept to a minimum. Retain all litter (film wrappers, tissue, food scraps, tins, lotion bottles, etc) in bag or pocket to be disposed of on board your ship. Avoid throwing tin cans and other trash off the ship near land.

3. Do not use sporting guns.

4. Do not introduce plants or animals into the Antarctic.

5. Do not collect eggs or fossils.

6. Do not enter any of the Specially Protected Areas and avoid Sites of Special Scientific Interest.

7. In the vicinity of scientific stations avoid interference with scientific work and do not enter unoccupied buildings or refuges except in an emergency.

8. Do not paint names or graffiti on rocks or buildings.

9. Take care of Antarctic historic monuments.

10. When ashore, keep together with your party.

Recommendation XI-3 (1981): Air Disaster on Mount Erebus

The Representatives,

Recalling with respect that in the years of exploration and research many have travelled to and worked in Antarctica and not returned,

Noting that on November 28, 1979, two hundred and fifty seven people of several nationalities lost their lives when the aircraft in which they were travelling crashed into the slopes of Mount Erebus, Ross Island, Antarctica;

Aware that in spite of the determined and courageous action of members of the New Zealand and United States Antarctic expeditions the bodies of some of those who died could not be recovered;

Aware, too, that no permanent memorial may be placed on the ice slopes at the site of the tragedy;

Express their deep sympathy with the relatives of those who died and with the Government and people of New Zealand, and

Recommend to their governments that the site on the northern slopes of Mount Erebus where the accident took place be declared a tomb and that they ensure that the area is left in peace.

Recommendation XII-6 (1983): Operation of the Antarctic Treaty System

The Representatives,

Noting that the Antarctic Treaty, based on principles of the United Nations Charter, in the interest of all mankind, establishes Antarctica as an area dedicated exclusively to peaceful purposes, to international harmony and to international scientific cooperation;

Noting further that the Antarctic Treaty, the numerous measures adopted in furtherance of the principles and objectives of the Treaty and other instruments and acts associated with it constitute a far-sighted and effective system of international co-operation, which promotes international peace and security, increase in scientific knowledge and understanding, and effective environmental protection;

Desiring to involve the Contracting Parties to the Antarctic Treaty which are not Consultative Parties more closely with the Antarctic Treaty System;

Conscious of the value of increasing public knowledge of the achievements and operation of the Antarctic Treaty System;

Recalling Article III, paragraph 2 of the Antarctic Treaty which encourages co-operative working relations with those Specialised Agencies of the United Nations and international organisations having a scientific and technical interest in Antarctica;

Recommend to their Governments that:

1. In addition to sending Consultative Parties certified copies of the Report as well as documents of Consultative Meetings as called for in Recommendation I-XIV, paragraph 1, the Government of the host country of each Consultative Meeting shall also send certified copies of the Report as well as documents of that meeting to all other Contracting Parties which were invited to that Meeting;

2. In furtherance of Article III, paragraph 2, of the Treaty, the Government of the host country shall:

(a) On behalf of the Consultative Parties send a certified copy of the Final Report and Recommendations of regular Consultative Meetings to the Secretary General of the United Nations, and

(b) As and when the Representatives of the Consultative Parties consider it appropriate, draw the attention of any Specialised Agency of the United Nations or other international organisation having a scientific or technical interest in Antarctica to any part of the Report of the Consultative Meeting, or any information document submitted to the Meeting and made available to the public, relevant to the scientific or technical interest which the agency or organisation has in Antarctica;

3. The 'Handbook of Measures in Furtherance of the Principles and Objectives of the Antarctic Treaty' be renamed the 'Handbook of the Antarctic Treaty' and:

(a) Be brought up to date by the host government as soon as possible after each Consultative Meeting.

(b) Contain an introduction outlining the background and history of the Antarctic Treaty as well as a preface to each section as appropriate giving a brief background to the measures set out in that section. The host government of the Twelfth Consultative Meeting will undertake the necessary consultations with a view to the early preparation of such introduction and prefaces, and

(c) Contain the final Report (excluding attachments and annexes) from each Consultative Meeting;

4.

(a) Starting with the Thirteenth regular Consultative Meeting, Delegations should indicate, when submitting an Information Document, if they intend that document to be publicly available;

(b) After the closure of the Meeting and provided no Consultative Party has objected, any Consultative Party or non-Consultative Party which has been invited to that Meeting may make such document publicly available on such terms as it may prescribe;

(c) As regards Conference Documents or Information Documents of the First to the Twelfth Consultative Meeting, and Conference Documents of the Thirteenth Consultative Meeting, and subsequent Meetings, as well as Information Documents that have not been identified in accordance with paragraph (a) above as intended to be publicly available, Consultative Parties will consider in what circumstances such Documents may be made publicly available, with a view to discussing the matter further at the Thirteenth Consultative Meeting;

5. Invite the depository Government to examine the question of information about the Antarctic Treaty System, including publicly available documents arising from Consultative Meetings, with a view to identifying and cataloguing publicly available information about the System and identifying the sources from which such information can be obtained; and

6. "The Operation of the Antarctic Treaty System" be included on the Agenda of the Thirteenth Consultative Meeting.

Recommendation XIII-1 (1985): Operation of the Antarctic Treaty System: Information

The Representatives.

Recalling Recommendation XII-6;

Recognizing the importance of accurate and adequate information regarding the Antarctic Treaty System,

Noting therefore the desirability of ensuring and facilitating the availability of information about the Antarctic Treaty System;

Recommend to their Governments that:

1. Efforts be continued to ensure that Final Reports of Consultative Meetings provide full and accurate records of these meetings, including:

(a) the general trends of discussion of the specific agenda items considered as well as specific steps or actions taken as a result of decisions or recommendations adopted at previous consultative meetings; and

(b) appropriate additional documentation of the meeting;

2. The Antarctic Treaty Handbook be regularly maintained as a current compilation of the recommendations and other actions agreed by Consultative Meetings;

3. To the greatest extent practicable and feasible and in accordance with national laws and regulations, the following be made available on request:

(a) Final Reports of Consultative Meetings,

(b) The Antarctic Treaty Handbook,

(c) Annual exchange of information they provide under the Antarctic Treaty;

4. Their national committees be encouraged to make available, on request and in accordance with national laws and regulations, annual activities reports which these committees submit to the Scientific Committee on Antarctic Research (SCAR);

5. On request and in accordance with national laws and regulations, up-to-date information be made available, to the greatest extent practicable and feasible, on:

(a) the location of depositories of data, samples and collections resulting from scientific research in Antarctica; and

(b) the nature and location of bibliographies or other information sources concerning reports and published works related to Antarctic matters, including those related to scientific research activities in Antarctica;

6. A national contact point, or contact points, be designated and charged with the functions referred to in paragraph 3 above and maintaining the information referred to in paragraph 5 above;

7. The names and addresses of the institutions or entities designated as national contact points, pursuant to paragraph 6 above, be published as an annex to the Final Report of each Consultative Meeting and the Antarctic Treaty Handbook and be otherwise publicly disseminated.

Recommendation XIII-2 (1985): Operation of the Antarctic Treaty System: Overview

The Representatives,

Recognizing the virtue of there being a regular overview of the Antarctic Treaty System, including the relationships among its components;

Believing that regular reports about the activities of these components at the Consultative Meetings would serve this objective;

Recommend to their Governments that:

1. An item "Operation of the Antarctic Treaty System: Reports" be included on the Agenda of each subsequent Consultative Meeting;

2. Under that item reports concerning developments in their respective areas of competence since the previous Consultative Meeting be received from the components of the System and that, to this end:

(a) they request the Chairman of any special Consultative Meeting, and any other meeting held pursuant to a recommendation of a Consultative Meeting, or a person designated by him, to present such a report;

(b) they invite the Commission for the Conservation of Antarctic Marine Living Resources to appoint its Chairman or other person to represent the Commission as an observer for the specific purpose of presenting such a report;

(c) through their National Committees, they invite the Scientific Committee on Antarctic Research (SCAR) to appoint its President or other person to represent the Committee as an observer for the specific purpose of reporting on:

(i) the general proceedings of SCAR;

(ii) matters within the competence of SCAR under the Convention for the Conservation of Antarctic Seals;

(iii) such publications and reports as may have been published or prepared in accordance with Recommendations IV-19 and VI-9 respectively;

(d) pending possible establishment of a Commission as provided for under the Convention for the Conservation of Antarctic Seals, they invite the Depositary Government of that Convention to report on the matters within the Depositary's competence under the Convention.

3. In preparing for each Consultative Meeting they consider, in relation to developments since the previous Consultative Meeting, whether, for the purpose of such overview, reports on any

such developments in, or bearing upon, the Antarctic Treaty System would be helpful and, through the host Government for that Consultative Meeting, act accordingly.

Recommendation XIII-6 (1985): Facilitation of Scientific Research: Siting of Stations

The Representatives,

Recalling Recommendations I-I, VI-4, VII-I, VII-8, VIII-II and XII-3;

Reaffirming that freedom of scientific investigation as set out in Article II of the Antarctic Treaty is one of the fundamental principles of the Treaty; and

Noting that nothing in this recommendation may be construed as prejudicing that provision of the Treaty;

Recognizing that, while there are scientific, environmental and logistic advantages to be gained from stations being in proximity to one another, there can also be disadvantages which can be avoided by appropriate consultation;

Recommend to their Governments that where stations have been established in the same vicinity the concerned national Antarctic operating agencies should consult together, by whatever means found appropriate, so as to safeguard existing scientific activities, avoid operational logistic difficulties and avoid undue adverse environmental effects arising from cumulative impacts.

Recommendation XIV-3 (1987): Human Impact on the Antarctic Environment: Safeguards for Scientific Drilling

The Representatives,

Recalling Article II of the Antarctic Treaty and Recommendations VIII-I3, IX-5, X-7, XII-3;

Recognizing the knowledge or the tectonic, geochemical and climatic evolution of the Antarctic region that can be obtained from Scientific Drilling;

Bearing in mind the potential risk to the Antarctic environment in cases where such drilling could result in hydrocarbons being released into the Antarctic environment;

Conscious of the need for adequate preparation and planning of such drilling to ensure the best possible scientific results and protection of the Antarctic environment;

Conscious also that planning such drilling will require preparation of a Comprehensive Environmental Evaluation as provided for in Recommendation XIV-2;

Recommend to their Governments that they adopt and use the following Guidelines to assist in evaluating and avoiding the potential risk for significant adverse environmental impacts resulting from such drilling:

Guidelines for Scientific Drilling in the Antarctic Treaty Area

(i) Before undertaking any scientific drilling that may have significant adverse environmental effects, adequately detailed geophysical surveys shall be performed of the sites in question to enable any potential hazard associated with any specific drill site within the area of interest to be evaluated along with any other information available about that particular site.

(ii) All feasible precautions shall be taken to locate such drill sites offstructure to reduce the possibility of encountering hydrocarbons.

(iii) Such planned drill sites and operational drilling plans, including the geophysical survey results and other information, shall be reviewed by a body of appropriate experts to identify potential hazards and to assess the potential risk to the environment resulting from the proposed drilling and how those risks can be minimized.

(iv) If any significant potential hazard is identified which cannot be avoided by modifying the planned drilling procedure or equipment, the location of the proposed drill site shall be abandoned and any recommendations of the reviewing body shall be considered in connection with the choice of an alternative site.

(v) Contingency plans shall be prepared to deal with any problems that may develop during the drilling process.

(vi) The drilling process shall be continuously monitored for potential hazards and necessary action shall be taken if problems occur.

(vii) Notification shall be provided to the responsible national agency by those conducting drilling operations of all hazards encountered, including the location of the site at which they were identified, and a description of the actions taken.

Recommendation XV-5 (1989): Human Impact on the Environment: Environmental Monitoring in Antarctica

The Representatives,

Recognizing that, because of its relatively pristine state, Antarctica provides an important natural laboratory to obtain baseline information on Antarctic environments and for detecting and monitoring some of the effects of human activities on the global environments and ecosystems upon which the welfare and survival of the human species depend;

Recognizing also that scientific research, related logistic support activities, tourism, natural resources exploration and development, and other human activities in Antarctica could have local, regional or global environmental effects, or compromise the scientific value of Antarctica;

Recalling the Scientific Committee on Antarctic Research (SCAR) response to Recommendation XII-3 and Recommendation XIV-2, which call upon the Antarctic Treaty Consultative Parties to establish programs for detecting and monitoring the effects of human activities on key components of Antarctic ecosystems;

Conscious that determining cause-effect relationships between certain human activities and observed changes in Antarctic environments will require knowledge of natural variation in Antarctic environments and accurate records of such things as the types and quantities of fuels used to supply heat and light to Antarctic stations and to operate aircraft and land vehicles in Antarctica;

Aware of the ecosystem monitoring program being developed to help meet the objectives of the Convention on the Conservation of Antarctic Marine Living Resources;

Desiring to identify and initiate cooperative, long-term monitoring programs necessary to verify the predicted effects and to detect and quantify the possible unforeseen effects of human activities on the Antarctic environment; and

Recognizing that the design and implementation of integrated, comprehensive, and cost-effective environmental monitoring programs in Antarctica serve both scientific and environmental protection purposes;

Recommend to their Governments that:

1. They encourage their national Antarctic programs, individually and collectively, to continue and, as appropriate, expand programs in Antarctica aimed at detecting and monitoring global environmental change, including its effects on the ozone layer over Antarctica, effects on Antarctic terrestrial, marine, and atmospheric environments and dependent and associated ecosystems as well as effects on Antarctic living resources.

2. They undertake, individually and collectively, to establish environmental monitoring programs to verify the predicted effects and to detect the possible unforeseen effects on Antarctic environments and living resources of activities in the Antarctic Treaty area, including:

(a) waste disposal

(b) contamination by oil or other hazardous or toxic substances;

(c) construction and operation of stations, field camps, and related ship, aircraft and other logistic support facilities;
(d) conduct of science programs;
(e) recreational activities; and
(f) those affecting the purposes of designated protected areas.

3. They take such steps as necessary to maintain accurate records of the activities of their national programs in Antarctica, including, among other things, maintaining accurate records of the types and quantities of fuels and other materials transported to and used to support their national programs in Antarctica, the types and quantities of materials subsequently removed from Antarctica, and the types and quantities of materials disposed of in Antarctica by various means, bearing in mind Recommendation XV-3.

4. They convene, in accordance with Recommendation IV-24, a meeting of experts to consider and provide advice on:
(a) The types of cooperative, long-term monitoring programs that would be useful for detecting, quantifying, monitoring, and determining the likely causes of observed changes in air quality, snow and water quality, and other key features of Antarctic environments and living resources;
(b) on the methods that should be used to collect, report, store, exchange, and analyze needed data; and
(c) on where and how frequently various environmental parameters should be measured.

To this end, they invite SCAR through their national committees, to consider and provide advice on the above matters.

5. They exchange information and establish cooperative working relations with those Specialized Agencies of the United Nations and other international organizations having a scientific or technical interest in Antarctica that are engaged in the planning and implementation of related scientific research and environmental monitoring programs.

Recommendation XV-14 (1989): Promotion of International Scientific Cooperation: A Declaration

The Representatives,

Recommend to their Governments that they approve the following declaration on scientific research in Antarctica:

The Governments participating in the XVth Consultative Meeting:

Deeply aware of the role that Antarctica and the Southern Ocean play in interactive physical, chemical and biological processes that regulate the total Earth System;

Recognizing that,
(a) the Antarctic region has a high negative radiation budget and so acts as one of the Earth's "refrigerators". Any changes in the budget will have global consequences on atmospheric and oceanic circulation;
(b) conditions beneath the ice shelves and the girdle of sea ice promote the formation of cold bottom water that drains northward;
(c) polar seas play an especially important role in the exchange of CO_2 between ocean and atmosphere since they may be large sinks for CO_2. These processes are controlled by the sea-ice formation, thermohaline convection and biological productivity;
(d) Antarctica provides unique conditions for investigating the impact of man-made pollutants on atmospheric ozone;
(e) a detailed record of past global climate and atmospheric chemistry extending over hundreds of millennia is preserved within the Antarctic ice sheet, and in the sediments of the Southern Ocean and the Antarctic continent;

(f) because climate change is predicted to be largest at high latitudes, detection of such change above the background of high natural variability is best sought in the polar regions;
(g) plant communities existing under polar conditions are sensitive to changes in temperature, and may be good indicators of climate change:
(h) the Antarctic ice sheet contains enough water to raise global sea level world-wide some 60 metres. Any green-house climate warning which makes even a small change to this volume of ice will have a significant impact on sea level;

Recognizing, with appreciation, that the contribution that Antarctic science can make to these scientific questions is the subject of intensive work within the scientific committee on Antarctic Research (SCAR) and that they have identified the following five major, interconnected, interdisciplinary research thrusts for the purpose of defining and encompassing research priorities:

(a) Detection of Changes of Global Importance Best Observed in Antarctica;
(b) Processes Linking Antarctic Ice and Biological Systems to the Global Ocean and Atmosphere;
(c) Antarctic Sources of Palaeoenvironmental Information;
(d) Ecology in the Changing Antarctic Environment;
(e) Monitoring Changes in Antarctica;

Recognising, moreover, that other scientific programmes which are not so directly relevant to issues of global change are of no less value to science;

Conscious of the need to ensure that all Antarctic activity is based on information adequate to ensure that informed judgements can be made about their environmental consequences;

Renew their commitment to the pursuit of scientific research in the Antarctic; and

Declare their intent:

1. Vigorously to pursue scientific research programmes in Antarctica in a manner which makes the most productive use of the resources available.

2. To ensure that their scientific endeavours contribute as much as possible to programmes of global significance being undertaken or being prepared by the International Council of Scientific Unions and by other international organisations.

3. To ensure that research results and observations are, in accordance with Article III of the Antarctic Treaty, made freely available and that the results of Antarctic programmes of global significance are brought to the attention of the international scientific community as rapidly as possible.

4. To ensure that activities in the Antarctic take full account of the global importance of the Antarctic as a scientific laboratory and as a place where aspects of global changes can most readily be monitored.

5. To ensure, in conformity with the declaration in Recommendation IX-5 on the Antarctic environment, that all Antarctic activity is based on information adequate to ensure that informed judgements can be made about their environmental consequences.

Recommendation XV-20 (1989): Air Safety in Antarctica

The Representatives,

Recalling Recommendations I-X and XIV-9;

Recognising the importance of ensuring safe air operations in the Antarctic, and:

(a) that there is a wide range of problems in air operations which are becoming more urgent with increasing activity;
(b) that the principal body of knowledge and experience of Antarctic air operations, and its current problems, lies with the operators of national Antarctic programmes;

Noting, with appreciation, the Report of the Meeting of Experts on Air Safety in Antarctica, held in Paris from 2 to 5 May 1989;

Recommend to their Governments that:

1. For the purpose of ensuring that measures for improved air safety apply to all flights in Antarctica, measures to improve air safety set out in paragraphs 2–10 below should be elaborated on the basis of ICAO criteria, taking due account of the specific features of Antarctica as well as of existing practices and services.

2. For the purpose of ensuring the safety of air operations in the Antarctic Treaty area, they exchange, preferably by 1 September and no later than 1 November each year, information about their planned air operations in accordance with the standardized format at Annex 1 to this Recommendation.

3. For the purpose of improving air safety in Antarctica, national Antarctic programmes operating aircraft in Antarctica and their aircrews should be provided with a continuously updated compendium ("Handbook") describing ground facilities, aircraft and aircraft operating procedures (including helicopters) and associated communications facilities operated by each national Antarctic programme (out of the use of which questions of liability will not arise) and, therefore, they should:

(a) prepare such a Handbook as a matter of urgency;

(b) facilitate the preparation of such a Handbook by their national Antarctic programme operators by collective action through the medium of the Council of Managers of National Antarctic Programmes (COMNAP) federated to SCAR;

(c) adopt a loose-leaf format in which information provided by each national operator is kept separate (unless facilities are jointly operated) so as to facilitate updating of information;

(d) request their national Antarctic operators to provide information for the purpose of compiling the Handbook in accordance with Annex 2 to this Recommendation.

4. For the purpose of ensuring mutual awareness of current air operations and exchanging information about them, they should designate:

(a) Primary Air Information stations (PAIS) which coordinate their own air information and information from their Secondary Air Information Stations (if any) for the purpose of notifying current air operations to other PAIS. These PAIS should have adequate communication facilities able to transmit "hard copy" information by means of an agreed HF data mode and/or INMARSAT; and

(b) Secondary Air Information Stations (SAIS) which comprise stations/bases (including field bases and ships) which provide air information to their parent coordinating PAIS.

5. For the purpose of avoiding air incidents in areas beyond the range of VHF radio coverage of primary and secondary stations, aircraft outside the areas covered by primary and secondary stations should use a specific radio frequency to apply the "TIBA" procedure laid down in Annex 11 to the Convention on International Civil Aviation.

6. So as to ensure compliance with Article VII, paragraph 5 to the Antarctic Treaty and also Recommendation X-8, Part IV, they should keep one another informed about nongovernmental flights and a reminder of the above provisions should be given to all pilots filing a flight plan for flights to Antarctica.

7. So as to provide for the improved collection from, and exchange within Antarctica of meteorological data and information of significance to the safety of Antarctic air operations, they should:

(a) encourage the World Meteorological organisation in their work towards this end; and

(b) take steps to improve meteorological services available in Antarctica, specifically to meet aviation requirements.

8. For the purpose of ensuring effective communications between primary Air Information stations (PAIS), they ensure that their PAIS have adequate facilities for communicating with other PAIS, and that, in this connection, they bear in mind the INHARSAT system.

9. For the purpose of locating aircraft in distress in Antarctica, and noting the possibilities offered by the COSPAS-SARSAT system for the location of Emergency-Locator-Beacons-Aircraft transmitting on 406 Mhz, they designate points of contact which are to be the addressees of emergency location messages relating to air operations in Antarctica generated by the COSPAS-SARSAT system.

10. For the purpose of enhancing the safety of operation of aircraft in the longer term, studies should be undertaken, at a suitable time, aimed at making use of a satellite communication and navigation system being developed within the framework of ICAO.

Recommendation XV-21 (1989): Uses of Antarctic Ice

The Representatives,

Considering that the ice existing in Antarctica represents the world's largest freshwater reserve;

Noting that, technological developments might one day make it possible to utilize icebergs detached from the continent for freshwater requirements, especially in coastal areas;

Recalling the principles enshrined in the Antarctic Treaty, which lay down a regime for international co-operation guaranteeing that Antarctica shall continue for ever to be used exclusively for peaceful purposes and shall not become the scene or object of international discord;

Convinced that the structure established under the Antarctic exploitation of Antarctic icebergs could also have an adverse effect on the unique Antarctic environment and its dependent and associated ecosystems;

Concerned that uncontrolled activities relating to the exploitation of Antarctic icebergs could also have an adverse effect on the unique Antarctic environment and its dependent and associated ecosystems;

Noting that sufficient scientific information is not yet available on the environment impacts, including global climate and weather, which might occur in the event of floating icebergs being used for that purpose;

Noting that the harvesting of ice in the coastal regions of Antarctica, especially if this were to require land-based installations, could give rise to a number of additional environmental or other issues;

Acknowledging that the Antarctic Treaty is the most appropriate framework for fostering international efforts to guarantee the protection of the environment and give impetus to the freedom of scientific research and co-operation in Antarctica;

Recognizing the desirability that commercial exploitation of Antarctic ice not occur, in any case, prior to examination by the contracting Parties to the Antarctic Treaty of the issues posed by such activity;

Recommend to their Governments that:

1. They exchange information on the feasibility of commercial exploitation of icebergs, relevant technologies and possible environmental impacts.

2. Through their national committees, they invite SCAR to provide advice, as appropriate, on the above-mentioned matters, and continue to co-ordinate research programmes in polar glaciology, biology, oceanography, and meteorology in relation to Antarctic ice.

3. They include an item on "Use of Antarctic Ice" on the agenda of the XVIth Consultative Meeting.

Recommendation XVIII-1 (1994): Tourism and Non-governmental Activities

The Representatives,

Reaffirming the exceptional character of the Antarctic environment given in particular the fragility of its fauna and flora and of the setting which the Antarctic offers for the conduct of scientific activities;

Acknowledging the increase in the development of tourist activities in the Antarctic;

Noting that those who visit the Antarctic and organise or conduct tourism and non-governmental activities in the Antarctic are currently subject to legally binding obligations pursuant to national legislation implementing the Antarctic Treaty and associated legal instruments;

Noting further that such visitors or organisers will be subject to additional legally binding obligations upon entry into force of the Protocol on Environmental Protection to the Antarctic Treaty;

Recognizing the need for visitors and organisers to have practical guidance on how best to plan and carry out any visits to the Antarctic;

Recalling the Final Act of the Eleventh Special Antarctic Treaty Consultative Meeting, at which the Protocol was adopted, in which the signatories of the Final Act decided that the Annexes of the Protocol should be applied in accordance with their legal systems and to the extent practicable;

Desiring to ensure that those who visit the Antarctic carry out their visits or tours strictly in accordance with existing obligations and in so far as is consistent with existing national law, in accordance with the Protocol, pending its entry into force;

Desiring further to facilitate the early entry into force of the Protocol and of the implementation of its provisions in relation to those who visit or organise tours to the Antarctic.

Recommend to their Governments that:

1. They circulate widely and as quickly as possible the Guidance for Visitors to the Antarctic, and the Guidance for Those Organising and Conducting Tourism and Non-governmental Activities in the Antarctic annexed to this Recommendation.

2. They urge those intending to visit or organise and conduct tourism and non-governmental activities in the Antarctic to act in accordance with the attached guidance consistent with the relevant provisions of their applicable national law.

Attachment: Guidance for Visitors

Activities in the Antarctic are governed by the Antarctic Treaty of 1959 and associated agreements, referred to collectively as the Antarctic Treaty system. The Treaty established Antarctica as a zone of peace and science.

In 1991, the Antarctic Treaty Consultative Parties adopted the Protocol on Environmental Protection to the Antarctic Treaty, which designates the Antarctic as a natural reserve. The Protocol sets out environmental principles, procedures and obligations for the comprehensive protection of the Antarctic environment, and its dependent and associated ecosystems. The Consultative Parties have agreed that, pending its entry into force, as far as possible and in accordance with their legal system, the provisions of the Protocol should be applied as appropriate.

The Environmental Protocol applies to tourism and non-governmental activities as well as governmental activities in the Antarctic Treaty Area. It is intended to ensure that these activities do not have adverse impacts on the Antarctic environment, or on its scientific and aesthetic values.

This **Guidance for Visitors to the Antarctic** is intended to ensure that all visitors are aware of, and are therefore able to comply with, the Treaty and the Protocol. Visitors are, of course, bound by national laws and regulations applicable to activities in the Antarctic.

A) Protect Antarctic Wildlife

Taking or harmful interference with Antarctic wildlife is prohibited except in accordance with a permit issued by a national authority.

1. Do not use aircraft, vessels, small boats, or other means of transport in ways that disturb wildlife, either at sea or on land.
2. Do not feed, touch, or handle birds or seals, or approach or photograph them in ways that cause them to alter their behavior. Special care is needed when animals are breeding or moulting.
3. Do not damage plants, for example by walking, driving, or landing on extensive moss beds or lichen-covered scree slopes.
4. Do not use guns or explosives. Keep noise to the minimum to avoid frightening wildlife.
5. Do not bring non-native plants or animals into the Antarctic (e.g. live poultry, pet dogs and cats, house plants).

B) Respect protected areas

A variety of areas in the Antarctic have been afforded special protection because of their particular ecological, scientific, historic or other values. Entry into certain areas may be prohibited except in accordance with a permit issued by an appropriate national authority. Activities in and near designated Historic Sites and Monuments and certain other areas may be subject to special restrictions.

1. Know the locations of areas that have been afforded special protection and any restrictions regarding entry and activities that can be carried out in and near them.
2. Observe applicable restrictions.
3. Do not damage, remove or destroy Historic Sites or Monuments, or any artefacts associated with them.

C) Respect scientific research

Do not interfere with scientific research, facilities or equipment.

1. Obtain permission before visiting Antarctic science and logistic support facilities; reconfirm arrangements 24–72 hours before arriving; and comply strictly with the rules regarding such visits.
2. Do not interfere with, or remove, scientific equipment or marker posts, and do not disturb experimental study sites, field camps, or supplies.

D) Be safe

Be prepared for severe and changeable weather. Ensure that your equipment and clothing meet Antarctic standards. Remember that the Antarctic environment is inhospitable, unpredictable and potentially dangerous.

1. Know your capabilities, the dangers posed by the Antarctic environment, and act accordingly. Plan activities with safety in mind at all times.
2. Keep a safe distance from all wildlife, both on land and at sea.
3. Take note of, and act on, the advice and instructions from your leaders; do not stray from your group.
4. Do not walk onto glaciers or large snow fields without proper equipment and experience; there is a real danger of falling into hidden crevasses.
5. Do not expect a rescue service; self-sufficiency is increased and risks reduced by sound planning, quality equipment, and trained personnel.
6. Do not enter emergency refuges (except in emergencies). If you use equipment or food from a refuge, inform the nearest research station or national authority once the emergency is over.
7. Respect any smoking restrictions, particularly around buildings, and take great care to safeguard against the danger of fire. This is a real hazard in the dry environment of Antarctica.

E) Keep Antarctica pristine

Antarctica remains relatively pristine, and has not yet been subjected to large scale human perturbations. It is the largest wilderness area on earth. Please keep it that way.

1. Do not dispose of litter or garbage on land. Open burning is prohibited.
2. Do not disturb or pollute lakes or streams. Any materials discarded at sea must be disposed of properly.
3. Do not paint or engrave names or graffiti on rocks or buildings.
4. Do not collect or take away biological or geological specimens or man-made artefacts as a souvenir, including rocks, bones, eggs, fossils, and parts or contents of buildings.
5. Do not deface or vandalise buildings, whether occupied, abandoned, or unoccupied, or emergency refuges.

Guidance for those Organising and Conducting Tourism and Non-governmental Activities in the Antarctic

Antarctica is the largest wilderness area on earth, unaffected by large scale human activities. Accordingly, this unique and pristine environment has been afforded special protection. Furthermore, it is physically remote, inhospitable, unpredictable and potentially dangerous. All activities in the Antarctic Treaty Area, therefore, should be planned and conducted with both environmental protection and safety in mind.

Activities in the Antarctic are subject to the Antarctic Treaty of 1959 and associated legal instruments, referred to collectively as the Antarctic Treaty system. These include the Convention for the Conservation of Antarctic Seals (CCAS' 1972), the Convention on the Conservation of Antarctic Marine Living Resources (CCAMLR' 1980) and the Recommendations and other measures adopted by the Antarctic Treaty Consultative Parties under the Antarctic Treaty.

In 1991, the Consultative Parties to the Antarctic Treaty adopted the Protocol on Environmental Protection to the Antarctic Treaty. This Protocol sets out environmental principles, procedures and obligations for the comprehensive protection of the Antarctic environment, and its dependent and associated ecosystems. The Consultative Parties have agreed that, pending its entry into force, as far as possible and in accordance with their legal systems, that the provisions of the Protocol should be applied as appropriate.

The Environmental Protocol designates Antarctica as a natural reserve devoted to peace and science, and applies to both governmental and non-governmental activities in the Antarctic Treaty Area. The Protocol seeks to ensure that human activities, including tourism, do not have adverse impacts on the Antarctic.

The Protocol states, as a matter of principle, that all activities are to be planned and conducted on the basis of information sufficient to evaluate their possible impact on the Antarctic environment and its associated ecosystems, and on the value of Antarctica for the conduct of scientific research. Organisers should be aware that the Environmental Protocol requires that "activities shall be modified, suspended or cancelled if they result in or threaten to result in impacts upon the Antarctic environment or dependent or associated ecosystems."

Those responsible for organising and conducting tourism and nongovernmental activities must comply fully with national laws and regulations which implement the Antarctic Treaty system, as well as other national laws and regulations implementing international agreements on environmental protection, pollution and safety that relate to the Antarctic Treaty Area. They should also abide by the requirements imposed on organisers and operators under the Protocol on Environmental Protection and its Annexes, in so far as they have not yet been implemented in national law.

Key Obligations on Organisers and Operators

1. Provide prior notification of, and reports on, their activities to the competent authorities of the appropriate Party or Parties.
2. Conduct an assessment of the potential environmental impacts of their planned activities.
3. Provide for effective response to environmental emergencies, especially with regard to marine pollution.
4. Ensure self-sufficiency and safe operations.

5. Respect scientific research and the Antarctic environment, including restrictions regarding protected areas, and the protection of flora and fauna.

6. Prevent the disposal and discharge of prohibited waste.

Procedures to be followed by organisers and operators

A) When planning to go to the Antarctic

Organisers and operators should:

1. Notify the competent national authorities of the appropriate Party or Parties of details of their planned activities with sufficient time to enable the Party(ies) to comply with their information exchange obligations under Article VII(5) of the Antarctic Treaty. The information to be provided is listed in Attachment A.

2. Conduct an environmental assessment in accordance with such procedures as may have been established in national law to give effect to Annex I of the Protocol, including, if appropriate, how potential impacts will be monitored.

3. Obtain timely permission from the national authorities responsible for any stations they propose to visit.

4. Provide information to assist in the preparation of: contingency response plans in accordance with Article 15 of the Protocol waste management plans in accordance with Annex III of the Protocol; and marine pollution contingency plans in accordance with Annex IV of the Protocol.

5. Ensure that expedition leaders and passengers are aware of the location and special regimes which apply to Specially Protected Areas and Sites of Special Scientific Interest (and on entry into force of the Protocol, Antarctic Specially Protected Areas and Antarctic Specially Managed Areas) and of Historic Sites and Monuments and, in particular, relevant management plans.

6. Obtain a permit, where required by national law, from the competent national authority of the appropriate Party or Parties, should they have a reason to enter such areas, or a monitoring site (CEMP Site) designated under CCAMLR.

7. Ensure that activities are fully self-sufficient and do not require assistance from Parties unless arrangements for it have been agreed in advance.

8. Ensure that they employ experienced and trained personnel, including a sufficient number of guides.

9. Arrange to use equipment, vehicles, vessels, and aircraft appropriate to Antarctic operations.

10. Be fully conversant with applicable communications, navigation, air traffic control and emergency procedures.

11. Obtain the best available maps and hydrographic charts, recognising that many areas are not fully or accurately surveyed.

12. Consider the question of insurance (subject to requirements of national law).

13. Design and conduct information and education programmes to ensure that all personnel and visitors are aware of relevant provisions of the Antarctic Treaty system.

14. Provide visitors with a copy of the Guidance for Visitors to the Antarctic.

B) When in the Antarctic Treaty Area

Organisers and operators should:

1. Comply with all requirements of the Antarctic Treaty system, and relevant national laws, and ensure that visitors are aware of requirements that are relevant to them.

2. Reconfirm arrangements to visit stations 24–72 hours before their arrival and ensure that visitors are aware of any conditions or restrictions established by the station.

3. Ensure that visitors are supervised by a sufficient number of guides who have adequate experience and training in Antarctic conditions and knowledge of the Antarctic Treaty system requirements.

4. Monitor environmental impacts of their activities, if appropriate, and advise the competent national authorities of the appropriate Party or Parties of any adverse or cumulative impacts resulting from an activity, but which were not foreseen by their environmental impact assessment.

5. Operate ships, yachts, small boats, aircraft, hovercraft, and all other means of transport safely and according to appropriate procedures, including those set out in the Antarctic Flight Information Manual (AFIM).

6. Dispose of waste materials in accordance with Annex III and IV of the Protocol. These annexes prohibit, among other things, the discharge of plastics, oil and noxious substances into the Antarctic Treaty Area; regulate the discharge of sewage and food waste; and require the removal of most wastes from the area.

7. Co-operate fully with observers designated by Consultative Parties to conduct inspections of stations, ships, aircraft and equipment under Article VII of the Antarctic Treaty, and those to be designated under Article 14 of the Environmental Protocol.

8. Co-operate in monitoring programmes undertaken in accordance with Article 3(2)(d) of the Protocol.

9. Maintain a careful and complete record of their activities conducted.

C) On completion of the activities

Within three months of the end of the activity, organisers and operators should report on the conduct of it to the appropriate national authority in accordance with national laws and procedures. Reports should include the name, details and state of registration of each vessel or aircraft used and the name of their captain or commander; actual itinerary; the number of visitors engaged in the activity; places, dates and purposes of landings and the number of visitors landed on each occasion; any meteorological observations made, including those made as part of the World Meteorological Organization (WMO) Voluntary Observing Ships Scheme; any significant changes in activities and their impacts from those predicted before the visit was conducted; and action taken in case of emergency.

D) Antarctic Treaty System Documents and Information

Most Antarctic Treaty Parties can provide, through their national contact points, copies of relevant provisions of the Antarctic Treaty system and information about national laws and procedures, including:

- The Antarctic Treaty (1959)
- Convention for the Conservation of Antarctic Seals (1972)
- Convention on the Conservation of Antarctic Marine Living Resources (1980)
- Protocol on Environmental Protection to the Antarctic Treaty (1991)
- Recommendations and other measures adopted under the Antarctic Treaty
- Final Reports of Consultative Meetings
- Handbook of the Antarctic Treaty System (1994)
- Handbook of the Antarctic Treaty System (in Spanish, 1991 edition)

Attachment A: Information to be provided in advance notice

Organisers should provide the following information to the appropriate national authorities in the format requested.

1. name, nationality, and contact details of the organiser;

2. where relevant, registered name and national registration and type of any vessel or aircraft to be used (including name of the captain or commander, call-sign, radio frequency, INMARSAT number);

3. intended itinerary including the date of departure and places to be visited in the Antarctic Treaty Area;

4. activities to be undertaken and purpose;

5. number and qualifications of crew and accompanying guides and expedition staff;

6. estimated number of visitors to be carried;

7. carrying capacity of vessel;

8. intended use of vessel;

9. intended use and type of aircraft;

10. number and type of other vessels, including small boats, to be used in the Antarctic Treaty Area;
11. information about insurance coverage;
12. details of equipment to be used, including for safety purposes, and arrangements for self-sufficiency;
13. and other matters required by national laws.

Resolution 2 (1995): Nuclear Waste Disposal

The Representatives,

Recalling the provisions of Article V of the Antarctic Treaty;

Recalling Recommendation VIII-12;

Aware that Article 4.6 of the Basel Convention on the Control of Transboundary Movements of Hazardous Wastes and their Disposal prohibits the export of hazardous wastes or other wastes for disposal within the area south of 60° South latitude, whether or not such wastes are subject to transboundary movement;

Aware also that, according to Article 1.3 of the Basel Convention, wastes which, as a result of being radioactive, are subject to other international control systems, applying specifically to radioactive materials, are excluded from the scope of this Convention;

Noting that in September 1994 the International Atomic Energy Agency's General Conference adopted a resolution inviting the Board of Governors and the Director General to commence preparations for a convention on the safety of radioactive waste management;

Urge their Governments to:

Coordinate their positions in any negotiations relating to the disposal of nuclear waste in which they participate, with the objective of the inclusion of provisions prohibiting the transfer of nuclear waste to, and the disposal of nuclear waste in, the Antarctic Treaty Area.

Resolution 3 (1995): Reporting of Tourism and Non-governmental Activities

The Representatives,

Considering that there would be an advantage in standardised reporting of information on tourism and non-governmental activities;

Noting that Attachment A to ATCM Recommendation XVTII-l outlines the requirements for advance notice of tourism and non-governmental activities but does not outline requirements for post-activity reports;

Acknowledging that there are obligations of national legislation such as environmental impact assessment and reporting that must be met by tourist and non-governmental operators.

Recommend that:

Tourist and non-governmental operators when reporting on visits to Antarctica should provide the following information to the relevant national authorities:

1. Name, details and state of registration of each vessel
2. Name of captain or commander of each vessel
3. Name and organisation of observer / Government representative (if present)
4. Actual itinerary
5. Number and nationalities of passengers, staff and crew
6. Places, dates and duration of ship landings, small boat cruises and/or flights, and the number of visitors landed
7. WMO meteorological report (yes/no)
8. Action taken in the event of an emergency
9. Comments (e.g., impacts observed, changes to planned itinerary)

Resolution 5 (1995): Antarctic Inspection Checklists

The Representatives,

Considering that inspection checklists are useful as guidelines for those planning and conducting inspections under Article VII of the Antarctic Treaty and in assessing implementation of the provisions of the Environmental Protocol pending its entry into force;

Noting that inspection checklists are not mandatory and are not to be used as a questionnaire;

Recommend that:

The Consultative Parties should encourage the use of the checklists attached:

Checklist A Permanent Antarctic Stations and Associated Installations

Checklist B Vessels within the Antarctic Treaty Area

Checklist C Abandoned Antarctic Stations and Associated Installations

Checklist D Waste Disposal Sites

Attachment: Antarctic Inspection Checklists

These checklists, which are not intended to be exhaustive, are designed to provide a guideline to observers conducting inspections in Antarctica in accordance with the provisions of Article VII of the Antarctic Treaty.

Not all items in the checklists are necessarily applicable to the activity being inspected or directly related to Article VII of the Antarctic Treaty or the requirements of the Protocol on Environmental Protection to the Antarctic Treaty. It is recognized that some of the items could be addressed through the Antarctic Treaty Exchange of Information. It is also recognized that the purpose of an inspection is to verify through observation. Therefore, any inspection report should clearly identify which information was observed and which was taken from documents.

It is recommended that observers seek out and examine all relevant documents prior to undertaking inspections, including the Antarctic Treaty Exchange of Information, the relevant national Annual Reports to SCAR and the COMNAP/SCALOP Advance Exchange of Information.

Checklist A: Permanent Antarctic Stations and Associated Installations

1. General Information

1.1 Name of station visited
1.2 Operating nation
1.3 Location
1.4 Date established
1.5 Primary aim of the station (scientific, logistic, etc.)
1.6 Plans for future use of the station
1.7 International logistic cooperation
1.8 Availability of the Antarctic Treaty Exchange of Information

2. Inspection Details

2.1 Date
2.2 Time of visit
2.3 Duration of visit
2.4 Last inspection (nation(s), date)

3. Personnel

3.1 Name of person in charge
3.2 Total number of personnel on station
3.3 Number of scientists on station
3.4 Number of over-wintering personnel
3.5 Maximum capacity of station
3.6 Responsible agencies or ministries
3.7 Training (survival, first-aid, environmental protection, etc.)

4. Scientific Research
4.1 Major scientific programmes supported by the station
4.2 Dedicated permanent scientific facilities on the station
4.3 Number and nationality of exchange scientists from other Antarctic programmes
4.4 Advance notice, use and control of radio-isotopes
5. Physical Description of Station
5.1 Area covered by station
5.2 Approximate number and type of buildings
5.3 Age and state of buildings
5.4 New or recent construction
5.5 Sketch or map of buildings
5.6 Major aerial systems
5.7 Landing or dock facilities
5.8 Roads
5.9 Airstrips
5.10 Helipads
5.11 Nearby facilities (refuges, field huts, etc)
6. Communications
6.1 Communication facilities
7. Transport
7.1 Number and type of ground vehicles
7.2 Number and type of small boats
7.3 Number and type of fixed and rotary wing aircraft
7.4 Number of aircraft movements per year
7.5 Cargo handling and earth moving equipment
7.6 Frequency and method of resupply
8. Station Facilities – Fuel Storage/Usage
8.1 Types, amount and use of fuel (diesel, petrol, aviation fuel, etc.)
8.2 Types and capacity of station storage containers
8.3 Monitoring of fuel pumping systems and storage tanks (method)
8.4 Background information on fuel pipe-work (material, above ground, gravity feed, valves, etc.)
8.5 Transfer of bulk fuel (include transfer method)
8.6 Methods of emptying fuel lines (gravity, compressed air, etc.)
8.7 Field fuel depots (quantity and type)
8.8 Responsibility for fuel management
8.9 Protection against leaks and spills
9. Station Facilities – Water System
9.1 Type of water supply and storage facility (RO, distillation, snow melt, chemical treatment, etc.)
9.2 Availability and quality of water supply
9.3 Consumption of water per person/day
10. Station Facilities – Power Generation
10.1 Number, type and capacity of generators
10.2 Annual fuel consumption for power generation (tones)
10.3 Alternative energy sources
10.4 Filtering and monitoring of emissions
11. Station Facilities – Medical
11.1 Medical facilities and personnel
11.2 Number of patient beds

12. Station Facilities – Hazardous Chemicals
12.1 Types and quantities of chemicals
12.2 Storage and monitoring arrangements
12.3 Protection against leaks and spills
13. Firearms/Explosives
13.1 Number, type and purpose of firearms and ammunition
13.2 Amount, type and use of explosives
13.3 Storage of explosives and method of disposal
14. Military Support Activities
14.1 Describe any military support to the station
14.2 Details of military equipment held at station
15. Antarctic Treaty Legislation
15.1 Understanding of the provisions of the Antarctic Treaty and related agreements
15.2 Availability of Antarctic Treaty documentation on station
16. Emergency Response Capability
16.1 General
a. Search and rescue capability
b. Incidents in the last year resulting m significant damage to station facilities or tbe environment
c. Method of reporting incidents
16.2 Medical
a. Mobile medical emergency response capability
b. Evacuation plan for medical emergencies
16.3 Fire
a. Fire emergency plan
b. Fire fighting equipment
c. Training of personnel for fire fighting
d. Fire fighting exercises (frequency)
16.4 Pollution (oil and chemical spills)
a. Risk assessment for spills
b. Spill response plan
c. Training of personnel to deal with spills
d. Spill response exercises (frequency)
e. Mobile spill response capability
17. Environmental Impact Assessment (EIA)
17.1 Awareness of station management personnel of the requirement to conduct an EIA for all new activities
17.2 EIAs prepared for activities currently being undertaken
17.3 Environmental monitoring of indicators of possible environmental impacts of the station or associated activities
18. Conservation of Flora and Fauna
18.1 Methods of making station personnel aware of the rules relating to the conservation of Antarctic flora and fauna
18.2 Details of any native mammals, birds or invertebrates that have been killed, injured, captured, handled, molested or disturbed during the past year; Methods used to kill, capture and or handle animals; Issue of permits and reasons for their issue
18.3 Harmful interference with animals and plants in the vicinity of the base; Issue of permits and reasons for their issue
18.4 Non-indigenous animals or plant species present; Issue of permits and reasons for their issue

18.5 Actions taken to avoid accidental introduction of non-indigenous species
18.6 Nearby, important wildlife or plant sites
18.7 Local guidelines controlling the use of aircraft and vehicles close to concentrations of wildlife

19. Waste Management

19.1 Waste management plan for the separation, reduction, collection, storage and disposal of wastes
19.2 Responsibility for waste management on the station
19.3 Production of an annual waste management report
19.4 Training of personnel in waste management and the need to minimize the impact of wastes on the environment
19.5 Publicly displayed notices concerning waste management
19.6 Current waste disposal methods:
- a. Radioactive materials
- b. Electrical batteries
- c. Fuel (both liquid and solid) and lubricants
- d. Wastes containing harmful levels of heavy metals or acutely toxic or harmful persistent compounds
- e. Poly-vinyl chloride (PVC), polyurethane foam, polystyrene foam, rubber
- f. Other plastics
- g. Treated wood
- h. Fuel drums
- i. Other solid, non-combustible wastes
- j. Organic wastes
  - Residues of carcasses of imported animals
  - Laboratory cultures of micro-organisms and plant pathogen
  - Introduced avian products
  - Other organic wastes (food waste, etc)
- k. Sewage and domestic liquid wastes
- l. Waste produced by field parties

19.7 Production of waste per person/day
19.8 Use of open burning; Disposal of ash; Alternatives planned for by 1998/99
19.9 Use of incineration; Disposal of ash; Control and monitoring of emissions
19.10 Treatment of sewage and domestic liquid wastes; Monitoring of effluent
19.11 Use of landfill or ice pit
19.12 Recycling of wastes
19.13 Measures taken to prevent wastes which are to be removed from the Treaty area being dispersed by wind or accessed by scavengers
19.14 Inventory of the locations of past activities (abandoned bases, old fuel depots, etc.)
19.15 Clean-up of past activities and future plans

20. Management of Protected Areas

20.1 Protected area(s) in the vicinity of, or containing, the station (type, name, site number)
20.2 Relevant management plans and maps of protected areas held on the station
20.3 Entry by station personnel to protected areas within the past year; Issue of permits and reasons for their issue
20.4 Problems with station personnel or visitors not observing the restrictions of protected areas
20.5 Marking of the protected area(s) in the vicinity of, or containing, the station
20.6 Monitoring or management of protected areas
20.7 Information as to whether the protected areas continue to serve the purpose for which they were designated

20.8 Additional steps that should be taken to protect the areas

21. Tourist and Non-Governmental Activities

21.1 Visits to the station by tourists or non-governmental expeditions during the past year
- Total number of people
- Numbers ashore at any one time
- Number of cruise ships
- Number of yachts
- Number of aircraft

21.2 Procedures developed to facilitate or control tourist and non-governmental activities

21.3 Advance permission required for visits to the station

21.4 Operational problems for the station caused by visitors (unannounced visits, etc)

21.5 Environmental impact of visitors at the station or nearby

Checklist B: Vessels within the Antarctic Treaty Area

Observers undertaking an inspection of a vessel in the Antarctic Treaty Area should bear in mind that:

(i) only a vessel flying the flag of a Treaty Party can be inspected;

(ii) an inspection can only be undertaken under the terms of Article VII (3) of the Antarctic Treaty which states that inspections can only be carried out at points of discharging or embarking cargoes or personnel in Antarctica, and;

(iii) Article VI of the Antarctic Treaty safeguards High Sea rights under international law within the Antarctic Treaty Area.

Inspections which are not in accord with (i) and (ii) above, including inspections of vessels chartered by Treaty Parties, can only be carried out with the explicit consent of the master of the vessel.

1. General Information

1.1 Name of ship visited

1.2 Radio call sign

1.3 State and/or Port of Registration

1.4 Owner, manager and/or charterer of vessel

1.5 Ship type (general cargo, scientific research, etc.)

1.6 Date launched, if known

1.7 Primary activity of vessel at time of inspection (scientific research, logistic support, tourism, etc.)

1.8 Planned itinerary

1.9 Expected length of annual operating period in the Antarctic

1.10 Area of operation in the Antarctic in past year

1.11 International logistic cooperation

1.12 Presence of mandatory documentation (e.g., IMO inspection reports),

2. Inspection Details

2.1 Date

2.2 Time of visit

2.3 Location of visit

2.4 Duration of visit

2.5 Last inspection (nation(s), date)

2.6 Persons conducting inspection

3. Personnel

3.1 Name of captain

3.2 Name of expedition leader or person in charge

3.3 Total number of personnel on board crew (e.g., captain, officers, crew and catering staff) staff (e.g., scientists, expedition or tour staff, helicopter pilots) passengers (e.g., members of the expedition that are not crew or staff)

3.4 Maximum accommodation capacity of vessel
3.5 Previous Antarctic experience of captain and deck officers
3.6 Previous Antarctic experience of other crew and staff
3.7 Training of crew, staff and passengers (safety, life-boat drills, emergency response, etc.)

4. Scientific Research

4.1 Principal scientific programmes undertaken by the vessel
4.2 Dedicated scientific facilities on the vessel
4.3 Number of research cruises planned during the season
4.4 Number and nationality of scientists
4.5 Advance notice, use and control of radio-isotopes

5. Physical Description of Vessel

5.1 Basic dimensions (gross tonnage, length, beam, draught, etc.)
5.2 Marine classification, including ice strengthening classification

6. Navigation Aids

6.1 Navigation aids and equipment (radar, sonar, depth sounding equipment, weather facsimile receiver, weather/ice satellite picture facilities, Global Positioning System (GPS) or similar)
6.2 Back-up or emergency equipment carried
6.3 Availability and currency of hydrographic chart
6.4 Availability and currency of Antarctic pilot reference material

7. Communications

7.1 Communication facilities
7.2 Presence of emergency beacons (EPIRBS, etc.)

8. Transport

8.1 Type and number of small craft (landing craft, inflatables, survey launches, etc.)
8.2 Total capacity of lifeboats and liferafts; whether lifeboats are motorised, open or enclosed, and covered by a relevant survey certificate
8.3 Type and number of helicopters
8.4 Number of helicopter movements per Antarctic season

9. Vessel Facilities – General Cargo

9.1 General cargo – types, amount
9.2 Presence and use of Cargo Record Book
9.3 Cargo handling equipment
9.4 Frequency and method of resupply to shore stations

10. Vessel Facilities – Fuel Bunkers and Cargo

10.1 Fuel bunkers – types, amount and use of fuel (marine gas oil, petrol, etc.)
10.2 Fuel cargo – types, amount (aviation fuel, etc.)
10.3 Types and capacity of fuel tanks, Use of double-bottomed tanks
10.4 Deck storage of fuel
10.5 Prevention and protection against leaks and spills
10.6 Monitoring of fuel pumping systems and storage tanks (method)
10.7 Transfer of bulk fuel (include transfer method)
10.8 Responsibility for fuel management
10.9 Processing of oily water (oily water separator, direct to storage tanks, etc.)
10.10 Capacity to retain on board all oily waste whilst in the Antarctic Treaty Area
10.11 Presence and use of Oil Record Book

11. Vessel Facilities – Engines and Power Generation

11.1 Number, type and capacity of engines and generators
11.2 Subsidiary propulsion (bow and/or stem thrusters, etc.)
11.3 Daily fuel consumption of engines and power generation (tones)

11.4 Filtering and monitoring of engine emissions (method)

12. Vessel Facilities – Medical

12.1 Medical facilities (e.g., numbers of patient beds)

12.2 Medical personnel

13. Vessel Facilities – Hazardous Substances

13.1 Responsibility for management of hazardous substances

13.2 Types and quantities of hazardous substances being transported or used on board ship

13.3 Storage and monitoring arrangements

13.4 Protection against leaks and spills

14. Firearms/Explosives

14.1 Number, type and purpose of firearms and ammunition

14.2 Amount, type and purpose of explosives

14.3 Storage of explosives and method of disposal

15. Military Support Activities

15.1 Describe any military support to the vessel (e.g., personnel)

15.2 Details of military equipment held on the vessel

16. Antarctic Treaty System Legislation

16.1 Availability of Antarctic Treaty System documentation on the vessel

16.2 Understanding and application of the provisions of the Antarctic Treaty and related agreements

17. Emergency Response Capability

17.1. General

a. Search and rescue capability

b. Incidents in the current Antarctic season resulting in damage to the vessel or impact on the Antarctic environment

c. Method of reporting incidents

17.2 Medical

a. Evacuation plan for medical emergencies

b. Ship's capacity to mobilise in support of medical emergencies elsewhere

17.3 Fire

a. Fire emergency plan

b. Fire fighting equipment

c. Training of personnel for fire fighting

d. Fire fighting exercises (frequency)

17.4 Pollution (oil and chemical spills)

a. Shipboard oil pollution contingency plan

b. Spill response materials and equipment available on board

c. Training of personnel to deal with spills

d. Spill response exercises (frequency)

e. Ship's capacity to mobilise in support of spill response elsewhere

18. Environmental Impact Assessment

18.1 Awareness of captain (and deck officers), and chief scientist and/or expedition leader of EIA

18.2 EIAs prepared for activities currently being undertaken (e.g., research cruise)

18.3 Environmental monitoring of activities undertaken by the vessel (e.g., monitoring of seismic surveys)

19. Conservation of Flora and Fauna

19.1 Methods of making crew, staff and passengers aware of prohibited activities and guidelines relating to the conservation of Antarctic flora and fauna

19.2 Vessel guidelines regarding the use of aircraft, small boats and ship's personnel close ton concentrations of wildlife

19.3 Details of any native mammals, birds or invertebrates that have been killed, injured, captured, handled or disturbed during the past year; Methods used to kill, capture and or handle animals; Issue of permits and reasons for their issue
19.4 Harmful interference with animals and plants due to vessel activities; Issue or permits and reasons for their issue
19.5 Whether non-indigenous animals or plants carried on board the vessel (dogs, birds, ornamental plants, etc.)
19.6 Actions taken to avoid accidental introduction of non-indigenous species (animals, plants, micro-organisms)

20. Waste Management

20.1 Waste management plan for the separation, reduction, collection, storage and disposal of wastes
20.2 Responsibility for waste management on the vessel
20.3 Availability of an up-to-date waste management report
20.4 Training of crew, staff and passengers in waste minimisation and management and the need to minimise the impact of shipboard wastes on the environment
20.5 Publicly displayed notices concerning waste management practices on board
20.6 Current waste disposal methods:
- a. Radioactive materials
- b. Electrical batteries
- c. Fuel (both liquid and solid) and lubricants
- d. Wastes containing harmful levels of heavy metals or acutely toxic or harmful persistent compounds
- e. Poly-vinyl chloride (PVC), polyurethane foam, polystyrene foam, rubber
- f. Other plastics
- g. Treated wood
- h. Fuel drums
- i. Other solid, non-combustible wastes
- j. Organic wastes
  - Residues of carcasses of imported animals
  - Laboratory cultures of micro-organisms and plant pathogens
  - Introduced avian products
  - Other organic wastes (food wastes, etc.)
- k. Sewage and domestic liquid wastes
- l. Waste produced by field parties

20.7 Adequate storage space on board to retain all wastes on board whilst in the Treaty Area
20.8 Equipment for waste management (compactors, shredders, comminuters, etc.)
20.9 Type of incineration; Disposal of ash; Control and monitoring of emissions
20.10 Type of sewage treatment; Disposal of sludge; Presence and currency of sewage record book
20.11 Recycling of wastes
20.12 Whether contractual arrangements have been made for the use of Port Reception facilities

21. Management of Protected Areas

21.1 Responsibility for ensuring compliance with management plans for protected areas
21.2 Current management plans and maps of relevant protected areas held on the vessel
21.3 Entry by crew, staff or passengers to protected areas during the current Antarctic season; Issue of permits and reasons for their issue
21.4 Problems with crew, staff or passengers not observing the restrictions of protected areas (e.g., lack of supervision)

21.5 Monitoring or management of protected areas

22. Tourist and Non-Governmental Activities

22.1 Advance notification provided as required under the Antarctic Treaty

22.2 Number of tourist or non-governmental expedition cruises already undertaken or planned by the vessel in the current Antarctic season

22.3 Location, date, number and nationality of research stations visited

22.4 Location, date and number of wildlife or other sites visited

22.5 Total number of tourists or expedition personnel carried

22.6 Number of tourists ashore at any one time

22.7 Normal ratio of staff to tourists during visits ashore

22.8 Procedures used to facilitate and control tourist and non-governmental activities, in implementation of Recommendation XVlII-1

22.9 Indications of environmental impact of crew, staff and passengers during visits ashore

22.10 Affiliation of tour organiser, ship owner or operator to any tourism association (e.g., International Association of Antarctic Tour Operators)

Checklist C: Abandoned Antarctic Stations and Associated Installations

This checklist is designed for abandoned Antarctic stations and associated installations which are considered to be stations which have been given up altogether and are now unused. The checklist does not cover stations which are operated each summer or infrequently used over a number of years.

1. General Information

1.1 Name of station visited

1.2 Location

1.3 Nation responsible, if known

1.4 Date established, if known

1.5 Date abandoned, if known

1.6 Reason for abandonment, if known

1.7 Plans for future use of the station, if known

1.8 Plans to clean up the station, if known

2. Inspection Details

2.1 Date

2.2 Time of visit

2.3 Duration of visit

2.4 Last inspection (nation(s), date),

2.5 Persons conducting inspection if known

3. Physical Description of Station

3.1 Area covered by station

3.2 Number and type of buildings

3.3 Sketch or map of buildings

3.4 Age and state of buildings (structural damage, state of roofing, state of fittings and fixtures, condition of internal walls and floors, internal accumulation of snow, ice, etc.)

3.5 Hazards to visitors (dangerous buildings, materials or wastes)

3.6 Notable historic buildings, facilities or artifacts

3.7 Evidence of measures to conserve notable historic buildings, facilities or artifacts

3.8 Signs of theft or vandalism, including graffiti

3.9 Use of information signs (interpretation, unsafe buildings, toxic waste, etc.)

3.10 Major aerial/antennae systems (structural damage, etc.)

3.11 Landing or dock facilities

3.12 Roads

3.13 Airstrips and associated facilities (markers, windsocks, hangars, tie-downs, etc.)

3.14 Helipads and associated facilities (markers, windsocks, hangars, tie-downs, etc.)
3.15 Nearby facilities (refuges, field huts, etc.)

4. Station Facilities – Fuel

4.1 Types, quantity and location of fuel (diesel, petrol, aviation fuel, etc.)
4.2 Type and condition of storage containers (drums, tanks, etc.)
4.3 Existence and condition of bunding and other spill containment facilities
4.4 Evidence of leaks and spills and their environmental impact

5. Station Facilities – Hazardous Substances

5.1 Types, quantities and location of hazardous substances (e.g., chemicals)
5.2 Type and condition of storage facilities buildings (drums, tanks, etc.)
5.3 Evidence of leaks and spills and their environmental impact

6. Station Facilities – Emergency Supplies (Do not break open supplies; if sealed contact National Programme)

6.1 List and location of emergency supplies
6.2 Capacity and condition of emergency accommodation
6.3 Types, quantities and condition of food supplies
6.4 Cooking equipment
6.5 Availability and quality of water supply
6.6 Heating and generating plant (heaters, stoves, etc.)
6.7 Sleeping bags and blankets
6.8 Communications (emergency radio, etc.)
6.9 Medical supplies
6.10. Clothing

7. Environmental Impact Assessment (EIA)

7.1 EIAs prepared for station (clean-up activity, removal of redundant structures, etc.)
7.2 Environmental monitoring of remedial activities undertaken at the station (e.g., hydrocarbon contamination of soils)

8. Conservation of Flora And Fauna

8.1 Areas of water (lakes, streams) which could be affected by the station (fuel spill, dispersion of waste, etc.)
8.2 Description of flora near the station (moss banks, etc.)
8.3 Description of fauna near the station (seabird colonies, seal haul out sites, etc.)
8.4 Scientific research carried out nearby which could be affected by the station (fuel spill, dispersion of waste, etc.)
8.5 Potential hazards to wildlife (loose wire, aerials / antennae, broken glass, leaking fuel drums, etc.)
8.6 Indications of impact of the station on local wildlife (animals entangled, etc.) and any remedial action taken
8.7 Colonisation of station site by wildlife (species, numbers, etc.)
8.8 Entry by wildlife into buildings

9. Waste

9.1 Types, quantities, condition and location of wastes (empty fuel drums, etc); If a waste disposal site is found then use the Waste Disposal Site Inspection Checklist.
9.2 Type and quantities of scattered debris
9.3 Evidence of measures to maintain the site and prevent dispersal of wastes
9.4 Evidence of clean-up activities or the removal of structures

10. Protected Areas

10.1 Protected areas including or near the station (type, name, site number)
10.2 Marking of protected area(s) in the vicinity of, or containing, the station
10.3 Evidence of monitoring or management of protected areas

10.4 Impact of station on protected areas

11. Tourist and Non-Governmental Activities

11.1 Evidence of visits to the station during the past year, and possible origin of those visits

11.2 Indications of environmental impact of visitors at the station or nearby

Checklist D: Waste Disposal Sites

1. General Information

1.1 Name of site (if any)

1.2 Location (geographical coordinates)

1.3 Map or sketch of site in relation to nearby landmarks

1.4 Description of waste disposal site (include general topography and area covered)

1.5 Estimate of total area and volume of the waste disposal site

1.6 Description of substrate of the waste disposal site

1.7 Nation responsible for site, if known

2. Inspection Details

2.1 Date

2.2 Time of visit

2.3 Duration of visit

2.4 Persons conducting inspection

2.5 Last inspection (nation(s), date)

3. Physical Description of Waste Disposal Site

3.1 Is the site marked? How?

3.2 Has the waste been covered by soil or rock?

3.3 Are there any unused or unusable buildings at the site?

3.4 Areas of water around waste disposal site, including distance of the site from sea and freshwater bodies and possible drainage into these areas

3.5 Distribution and description of flora near waste disposal site

3.6 Distribution and description of fauna near the waste disposal site (seabird colonies, skua and other scavengers' nests, seal haul-out sites)

3.7 Scientific research carried out near the waste disposal site

3.8 Means of containment, including means wind and run off

4. Contents of Waste Disposal Site

4.1 Estimate of contents

4.2 Age and state of contents

4.3 Types and quantities of:

(a) radioactive materials
(b) electrical batteries
(c) fuel (both liquid and solid) and lubricants
(d) fuel drums
(e) gas cylinders
(f) wastes containing heavy metals or toxic substances
(g) polyvinyl chloride (PVC), foam, polystyrene, rubber, plastics
(h) treated wood
(i) other hazardous materials (medical wastes, broken glass, wire, etc.)
(j) other solid non-combustible wastes
(k) organic wastes (bones, non-native plant material, etc.)
(l) sewage and domestic liquid wastes
(m) indications of soil from outside Antarctica

5. Any evidence of Environmental Impacts of Waste Disposal Site

5.1 Current impacts, e.g.:

(a) birds scavenging
(b) contamination of soil

(c) wind scattered debris
(d) run-off, seepage, oils slicks
(e) smell
(f) dead vegetation
(g) dead, injured, sick or contaminated native birds or other animals
(h) Potential for microbial contamination

5.2 Possible future impacts, e.g. oil seeping into the ground

5.3 Are there any sensitive sites nearby, that may be vulnerable to impacts? e.g. wildlife habitat

6. Evidence of Environmental Assessment and/or Corrective and Preventive Measures

6.1 Is the site included in a Waste Management Plan?

6.2 What measures have been taken to rehabilitate the site or prevent dispersal of wastes? Written or physical evidence of these measures.

6.3 Has a contaminated site assessment been done on the waste disposal site; Is the report available?

6.4 Has an EIA or EIAs been prepared on removal of the waste disposal site (clean-up, removal of toxic materials, etc.)

6.5 Is the waste disposal site and nearby areas being monitored to verify that no hazardous substances are being dispersed and its contents do not pose a hazard to human health or the environment (e.g. monitoring of hydrocarbon, heavy metal or microbial contamination of soil, ground water or melt water)?

7. Future plans

7.1 Future plans for the site, for cleaning up, analysing environmental effects and minimising environmental effects

7.2 Heritage historic considerations which might need to be taken into account before removal

7.3 Priority of action, that is, urgency of clean-up action

7.4 Recommendations for additional steps that should be taken to manage the impacts of the waste disposal site and protect adjacent areas

Resolution 8 (1995): New Historic Sites and Monuments: Suggested Guidelines for the Designation of Historic Sites

The Representatives of the Consultative Parties,

Recalling Recommendations I-IX, V-4, VI-14, VII-9, XII-7, XIII-16 and XIV-8;

Recommend that the following Guidelines for the Designation of Historic Sites, and/or Monuments should be used by the Governments of the Consultative Parties, in proposing sites for the "List of Historic Monuments Identified and Described by the proposing Government or Governments".

Guidelines

Proposals for Historic Sites and/or Monuments should address one or more of the following:

- A particular event of importance in the history of science or exploration of Antarctica occurred at the place;
- A particular association with a person who played an important role in the history of science or exploration of Antarctica;
- A particular association with a notable feat of endurance or achievement;
- Representative of, or forms part of, some wide-ranging activity that has been important in the development of knowledge of Antarctica;
- Particular technical or architectural value in its materials, design or method of construction;
- The potential, through study, to reveal information or has the potential to educate people about significant human activities in Antarctica;
- Symbolic or commemorative value for people of many nations.

Resolution 9 (1995): Uniform Model for Management Plans

The Representatives of the Consultative Parties,

Recalling the requests made by ATCM XVII and ATCM XVIII that SCAR should assist Parties in reviewing and revising Management Plans to conform with the provisions of Annex V of the Protocol on Environmental Protection to the Antarctic Treaty, and consider how a model could be developed to facilitate the preparation of new and revised Management Plans;

Recognising that a uniform model for such plans would eliminate repetition and would make them easier to use;

Recommend that:

The structure of the Management Plan for Specially Protected Area No. 13, adopted under Measure 1, be regarded as a model of all new and revised Management Plans for protected areas for the purposes of Annex V.

Resolution 2 (1996): Aesthetic Values of Antarctica

The Representatives,

Noting that Antarctica has been the subject of significant works of art, literature and music;

Recognising that the unique character of Antarctica itself represents an inspiration for protecting its values;

Recommend:

Promotion of understanding and appreciation of the values of Antarctica, in particular its scientific, aesthetic and wilderness values, including through:

(a) Educational opportunities, in particular for young persons, and
(b) The contribution of writers, artists and musicians.

Resolution 4 (1996): Effective Management and Conservation of Historic Sites and Monuments

The Representatives,

Noting the need to ensure the effective management and conservation of Historic Sites or Monuments;

Aware that those who originally created Historic Sites or Monuments are not necessarily the same as the designators for the Sites or the proposers of Management Plans for some sites;

Recognising the particular historic and cultural importance of such sites to originating Parties;

Recommend that:

During the preparations for the Listing of a Historic Site or Monument, or the writing of a Site Management Plan, adequate liaison is accorded by the proposing Party with the originator of the Historic Site or Monument and other Parties, as appropriate.

Resolution 2 (1997): Comprehensive Environmental Evaluation (CEE): Methodology for Reviewing Activities for which a CEE has been Prepared

The Representatives,

Recalling Annex I, Article 3 of the Protocol on Environmental Protection to the Antarctic Treaty;

Noting that further guidance is desirable for following up on the implementation of activities for which CEEs have been prepared under Annex I of the Protocol on Environmental Protection to the Antarctic Treaty;

Encourage Consultative Parties to:

1. Include in their procedures for assessing the environmental impacts of their activities in Antarctica, provision for review of the activities undertaken following the completion of a CEE.

2. Adopt the following process for CEE follow-up:

(a) Review activities carried out following completion of CEE, including analysis of whether the activities were conducted as proposed, whether applicable mitigation measures were implemented, and whether the impacts of the activity were as predicted in the assessment;

(b) Record any changes to the activities described in the CEE, the reasons for the changes, and the environmental consequences of those changes; and

(c) Report to the Parties on the outcomes of (a) and (b) above.

Decision 2 (2002): Emblem of the Antarctic Treaty

Desiring to provide a clear identity to the work of the ATCM and its Secretariat;

Conscious that there exists a design traditionally employed by the Antarctic Treaty parties to identify their work, but that the design has no formal status;

Believing that the adoption of such a design would enhance presentationally the work of the ATCM and its Secretariat when located in Buenos Aires;

Decide:

1. That the design annexed to this Decision shall constitute the formal emblem of the Antarctic Treaty.

2. That it may be used by:

- The Secretariat of the Antarctic Treaty;
- The host state of the ATCM or Special ATCM in the period of preparation for and during a Consultative Meeting;
- By any other Consultative Party when hosting other meetings under the auspices of the Antarctic Treaty of its Environmental Protocol;
- By others with the authority of the ATCM.

3. That the design shall be shown on the official Reports of the ATCM and may be employed at the premises of the Antarctic Treaty Secretariat, on its official means of transport, as well as on stationary, electronic communications, reports, flags, signs, etc.

Annex to the Decision 2 (2002): Emblem of the Antarctic

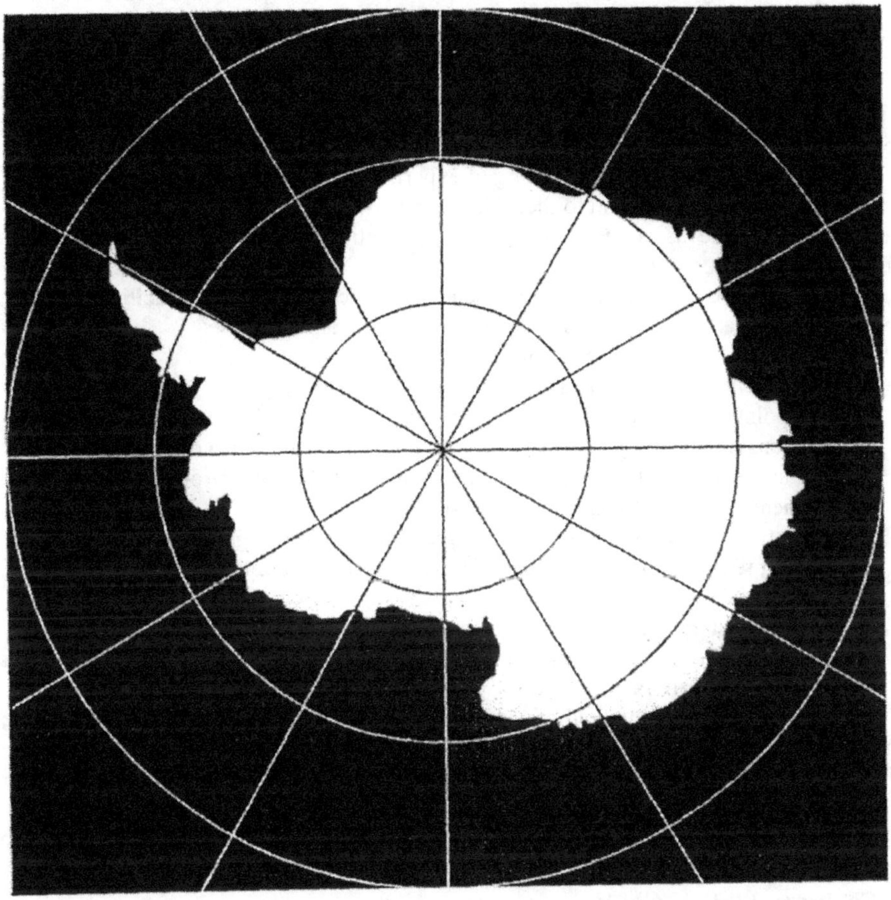

Decision 3 (2002): The Status of ATCM Recommendations

The Representatives,

Conscious of the significant number of measures[2] adopted by previous Antarctic Treaty Consultative Meetings;

Desiring to clarify which of these measures, whether approved or not, still require action by the Parties;

Recognising that some of these measures are spent as a result of the passing of a specific event, or of time;

Recognising also that the review of measures is an ongoing process required to maintain an accurate record of the instruments of the ATCM, and their content if relevant;

Decide that,

– the measures listed in Annex A are spent, and, as such, these measures will require no further action by the Parties; and

[2] Note: measures previously adopted under Article IX of the Antarctic Treaty were described as recommendations up to ATCM XIX (1995).

- the Parties will continue the review of measures adopted at ATCM I to XXIV, on an informal basis intersessionally so that further consideration can be undertaken at ATCM XXVI concerning which other measures may be considered spent, superseded or otherwise obsolete.

Appendix to Decision 3 (2002)
Spent recommendations

I-11 (Canberra, 1961)

Spent

Consultative Parties to convene a meeting of experts in Antarctic radio communications

The Representatives recommend to their Governments:

1. that they convene as soon as practicable a meeting of specialists in Antarctic radio communications;

2. that this meeting of specialists should discuss the telecommunications facilities needed for scientific, technical and other purposes in the Treaty Area, and their use;

3. that the meeting should take into consideration:

(a) the requirements of governments;

(b) the viewpoint of the United Nations Specialized Agencies and other international organizations having a scientific or technical interest in Antarctic communications;

(c) the relevant recommendations of the Communications Working Group of SCAR;

(d) the experience of the various Antarctic expeditions;

4. that the meeting should examine and make recommendations regarding such matters as:

(i) the routing required to meet demands of users most effectively;

(ii) the modes of transmission;

(iii) the power requirements for effective reception;

(iv) the rationalization of schedules and the evaluation of priorities for traffic in normal and post blackout conditions;

(v) new developments in the field of communications relevant to Antarctic requirements;

(vi) emergency radio procedures;

(vii) such other matters of an engineering or traffic nature as may be appropriate;

5. that the governments should consult regarding the date, place and definitive agenda of the meeting, and as to which Specialized Agencies and other internal organizations referred to in paragraph 3(b) should be informed of the meeting and be invited to send observers.

I-15 (Canberra, 1961) ATCM II

Spent

The Representatives recommend to their Governments that they accept the offer by the delegation of Argentina of the city of Buenos Aires as the seat of the second consultative meeting under Article IX of the Antarctic Treaty, to be held on a date mutually decided upon by the Participating Governments.

II-3 (Buenos Aires, 1962)

Spent

Meeting of Antarctic radio communications specialists to be held between 1 May and 31 August 1963The Representatives, taking into consideration Recommendation I-XI of the First Consultative Meeting concerning Antarctic radio communications, recommend to their Governments that the proposed meeting of specialists in Antarctic radio communications would take place between 1st May and 31st August 1963, on a date and at a place to be fixed.

II-5 (Buenos Aires, 1962)

Spent

Consultative Parties to hold an Expert Meeting on logistics

The Representatives recommend to their Governments that in view of Recommendation I-VII of the First Consultative Meeting designed to achieve one of the objectives of the Antarctic

Treaty, namely the creation of conditions necessary for carrying out scientific investigation, and in view of the logistic symposium organized by SCAR which is soon to take place:

(a) a meeting or symposium of experts should be held, to review the present state of knowledge acquired on the organization of expeditions, logistic support and transport, in order to evaluate such knowledge;

(b) consultations be held during the preparations for the next Consultative Meeting to fix a suitable date, place, organization and agenda for such meeting or symposium.

II-8 (Buenos Aires, 1962)

Spent

Consultative Parties to encourage cooperation with regard to the International Year of the Quiet Sun (1964/5)

The Representatives recommend to their Governments that they should encourage, by whatever means they consider appropriate, international cooperation and the exchange of scientific personnel, observations and results, in connection with their respective national programmes of Antarctic scientific investigation and research associated with the International Year of the Quiet Sun.

II-10 (Buenos Aires, 1962) ATCM III

Spent

The Representatives recommend that their Governments accept the offer made by the Delegation of Belgium, to the effect that the Third Consultative Meeting under Article IX of the Antarctic Treaty be held in Brussels. This Meeting will be held on a date to be decided upon by agreement among the participating governments.

III-3 (Brussels, 1964)

Spent

Arrangements for the Expert Meeting on logistics to be considered at the ATCM IV preparatory meeting.

In view of the Recommendations by the First and Second Consultative Meetings (I-VII and II-V) concerning logistics. Taking into consideration the Logistics Symposium which took place at Boulder, Colorado, USA, in August 1962, under the auspices of the Scientific Committee on Antarctic Research (SCAR), and the Report on this Symposium published in 1963.

The Representatives recommend to their Governments that the organization, agenda, date and place for the inter-governmental meeting of experts, on the present state of knowledge about useful aspects of logistic activities in the Antarctic to which the above recommendations refer, be considered during the preparatory meetings for the Fourth Consultative meeting.

III-4 (Brussels, 1964) ATCM IV

Spent

The Representatives recommend to their Governments that they accept the offer of the Chilean Delegation to hold the Fourth Consultative Meeting under Article IX of the Antarctic Treaty, in Santiago, Chile. The Meeting shall take place at a date which will be agreed upon by the participating Governments.

III-6 (Brussels, 1964)

Spent

Consultative Parties to examine questions concerning expert meetings and come back to it during ATCM IV.

The Representatives, recognizing the importance of the problem raised during the examination of Item 7 (that is, the Item entitled 'Questions concerning Meetings of Specialists'), recommend their governments to examine this question attentively before the Fourth Consultative Meeting and to consider including it on the Agenda of that Meeting.

III-9 (Brussels, 1964)

Spent

Agreed Measures to be used as guidelines until approved.

The Representatives recommend to their Governments that until such time as the Agreed Measures on the Conservation of Antarctic Fauna and Flora may become effective in accordance with Article IX of the Antarctic Treaty, these Agreed Measures as far as feasible be considered as guide lines in this interim period.

IV-20 (Santiago, 1966)

Spent

Consultative Parties to consider Recommendations IV-1 to IV-19 as guidelines until the Agreed Measures are approved.

The Representatives recommend to their Governments that until such time as the Agreed Measures on the Conservation of Antarctic Fauna and Flora may become effective in accordance with Article IX of the Antarctic Treaty, the following Recommendations as far as feasible be considered as guide lines in the interim period. Recommendations IV-1 to IV-19 inclusive.

IV-25 (Santiago, 1966)

Spent

Meeting in Japan on logistic cooperation.

The Representatives recommend to their Governments that they accept the offer made by the Government of Japan to hold a meeting on logistics in Japan in June 1968.

1. The meeting will be held in furtherance of principles and objectives of the Antarctic Treaty.

2. The meeting will be for a period of about one week and will be attended by experts in selected fields. The meeting will have the following terms of reference:

(i) to discuss problems in the fields of Antarctic logistics specified in paragraph 3 below;
(ii) to exchange views on possible solutions which have been tried recently;
(iii) to examine critically new solutions which may be proposed in papers submitted at the meeting.

3. The fields for discussion will include aspects of:

(i) design of buildings and building services, including waste disposal and water supply
(ii) oversnow transport
(iii) air transport, including airfields
(iv) sea transport
(v) safety measures
(vi) new and urgent problems which Governments agree require discussion.

IV-26 (Santiago, 1966)

Spent

Consultative Parties to include an item on telecommunications in the agenda of ATCM V
Considering the need to keep up to date the traffic system of Antarctic radio communications and to transmit observational data from the Treaty Area to the world system for the collection and transmission of meteorological information.

The Representatives recommend to their Governments that, before the Consultative Meeting scheduled to take place in Paris in 1968, they consider including in the Agenda an examination of the Recommendations made by the Washington Meeting on Telecommunications in 1963, in the light of conditions prevailing in 1968.

IV-28 (Santiago, 1966) ATCM V

Spent

The Representatives recommend to their Governments that they accept the offer of the French Delegation to hold a Consultative Meeting under Article IX of the Antarctic Treaty in Paris in 1968, on a date to be agreed upon by the Consultative Governments.

V-1 (Paris, 1968)

Spent

Consultative Parties to issue stamps to commemorate the Tenth Anniversary of the Antarctic Treaty.

The Representatives recommend to their Governments:

1. that, on the occasion of the Tenth Anniversary of the entry into force of the Antarctic Treaty, each Consultative Party should issue a commemorative postage stamp during 1971;
2. that this stamp should bear, in the language or languages of each issuing country, the following words: 'Antarctic Treaty 1961–71';
3. that the most prominent feature of the stamp should be the Antarctic Treaty emblem representing a map of Antarctica, which appears on the official documents of Consultative Meetings;
4. that any additional matter should be consonant with the provisions and the spirit of the Antarctic Treaty;
5. that the denominations of the stamp should remain at the discretion of each issuing country.

V-8 (Paris, 1968)

Spent

Consultative Parties to study draft CCAS before ATCM VI

The Representatives, Having had a preliminary exchange of views at the Fifth Consultative Meeting on the draft Convention for the Regulation of Antarctic Pelagic Sealing annexed to the Final Report of the Meeting [not reproduced];

Recognizing the need to study the preparation of such a Convention;

Recommend to their Governments that, before the next Consultative Meeting, they study the draft Convention with a view to its consideration at that Meeting.

V-9 (Paris, 1968) ATCM VI

Spent

The Representatives recommend to their governments that they accept the offer by the Delegation of Japan to hold the Sixth Consultative Meeting under Article IX of the Antarctic Treaty in Tokyo on a date in 1970 to be mutually decided upon by the Consultative Governments.

VI-15 (Tokyo, 1970) ATCM VII

Spent

The Representatives, Recommend to their Governments that they accept the offer by the Delegation of New Zealand to hold the Seventh Consultative Meeting under Article IX of the Antarctic Treaty in Wellington, on a date in 1972 to be mutually decided upon by the Consultative Governments.

IX-3 (London, 1977)

Spent

Consultative Parties to collect data on Antarctic telecommunications, to exchange these among themselves, to ask SCAR for advice and to arrange for another Expert Meeting.

The Representatives,

Considering that requirements in the field of telecommunications as regards collection and dissemination of meteorological data, and the need for scientific, administrative and operational traffic have developed substantially since the second telecommunications meeting of experts of the Consultative Parties held in Buenos Aires in 1969;

Considering that the implementation of Recommendation VI-I and VII-7, and participation in the programs of the World Meteorological Organisation, particularly the World Weather Watch, require a thorough review and improvement of the network operating in the Antarctic;

Recommend to their Governments that they:

1. Compile comprehensive data, each for its own part, on the types of traffic, modes of transmission, timing, frequencies of their telecommunications schedules and current equipment

of their telecommunications programmes in the Antarctic, as well as on projects in the process of implementation and proposed improvements, in particular by designating, where appropriate, stations capable of replacing others in the event of breakdown;

2. Forward all such data to each of the other Consultative parties via diplomatic channels on the one hand and on the other by direct dispatch to the departments concerned;

3. Arrange for a meeting of telecommunications experts to be held, on the initiative of the Government of the host country, before the Tenth Consultative Meeting, to analyze the data thus compiled, suggest desirable measures of harmonization and put forward recommendations on improvements to be made in the operation of the telecommunications network in the Antarctic;

4. Request SCAR through their National Antarctic Committees to undertake, at the earliest opportunity, a study of the most recent applications of science and technology to the specific problems of the Antarctic in the field of propagation of radio waves, and to pass on its conclusions to the Consultative Parties prior to their Tenth Meeting or if necessary to the next Consultative Meetings.

X-9 (Washington, 1979)

Spent

Consultative Parties to thank the Antarctic scientific community and to consider ways of commemorating the 20th anniversary of the Antarctic Treaty

The Representatives,

Noting that the Tenth Antarctic Treaty Consultative Meeting marks the twentieth anniversary of the signature in Washington of the Antarctic Treaty and that the Eleventh Consultative Meeting in Argentina will mark the twentieth anniversary of its entry into force;

Recalling the second preambular paragraph of the Antarctic Treaty in which it is recognized that is in the interest of all mankind that Antarctica shall continue forever to be used exclusively for peaceful purposes and shall not become the scene or object of international discord;

Conscious of:

(a) the responsibility assumed by the Consultative Parties for the Protection of the environment and the wise use of the Treaty area;

(b) the increased understanding of the Antarctic and of its relationship to the world as a whole that has resulted from the endeavours of the Antarctic scientific community;

(c) the benefits derived from the coordination of Antarctic scientific research through the Scientific Committee on Antarctic Research (SCAR), its subsidiary institutions and from its cooperation with other international organizations having a scientific or technical interest in the Antarctic; and

(d) the value of the scientific advice from SCAR, requested by their Governments through their respective National Antarctic Committees, in connection with the development of the Antarctic Treaty system;

Recommend to their Governments that:

I. Scientific research.

Through their respective National Antarctic Committees, or the offices administering their Antarctic research programmes, as appropriate, they express their gratitude to the members of the Antarctic scientific community, past and present, and to SCAR for the devoted service which they have given to the achievement of a better understanding of the Antarctic and to the development of the Antarctic Treaty System;

II. Commemoration of the twentieth anniversary of the entry into force of the Antarctic Treaty.

1. They consider suitable ways of commemorating the twentieth anniversary of the entry into force of the Antarctic Treaty, including the possibility of issuing a commemorative postage stamp during 1981 on the lines indicated in Recommendation V-1;

2. Any commemorative event should be consonant with the provisions and spirit of the Antarctic Treaty.

XI-2 (Buenos Aires, 1981)

Spent

Consultative Parties to seek the earliest possible entry into force of CAMLR and to facilitate early operation of bodies for which CCAMLR provides

The Representatives,

Recalling the responsibilities of the Consultative Parties regarding the conservation of Antarctic marine living resources;

Recalling further the history of actions taken by Consultative Parties concerning protection of the Antarctic ecosystem, including in particular, Recommendations III-VIII, VIII-10, VIII-13, IX-2, IX-5 and X-2;

Welcoming the conclusion of the Convention on the Conservation of Antarctic Marine Living Resources at a diplomatic conference held in Canberra, Australia in May 1980 and the signature of that convention, also in Canberra, Australia in September 1980;

Noting that a meeting is to be held later this year in Hobart, Tasmania to consider steps to facilitate the early operation of the Commission, the Scientific Committee and the Executive Secretariat to be established under the Convention on the Conservation of Antarctic Marine Living Resources,

Recommend to their Governments that:

1. They seek the earliest possible entry into force of the Convention on the Conservation of Antarctic Marine Living Resources; and

2. They take all possible steps to facilitate the early operation of the bodies to be established by the Convention on the Conservation of Antarctic Marine Living Resources upon entry into force.

XIV-9 (Rio de Janeiro, 1987)

Spent

Consultative Parties to convene an Expert Meeting on air safety.

The Representatives,

Recalling Recommendation 1-X;

Recognizing the importance of safe air operations in the Antarctic and:

(i) that there is a wide range of problems in air operations, which are becoming more important and urgent with increasing activity;

(ii) that the principal body of knowledge and experience of Antarctic air operations, and its current problems, lies with the operators of national Antarctic programmes;

Recommend to their Governments that:

1. Arrangements be made for a meeting of experts in accordance with Recommendation IV-24, to be held well in advance of the Fifteenth Consultative Meeting, at a time and place to be decided through diplomatic channels, and that the host Government for the XVth Consultative Meeting should initiate the necessary consultations. Delegations from Consultative Parties to the meeting should include experts with direct experience in Antarctic operations. In the course of preparing for the meeting, consideration shall be given to the invitation of ICAO and other experts to attend the meeting in accordance with paragraph I of Recommendation IV-24 (e.g. WMO, ITU);

2. The terms of reference for the meeting shall be to provide for:

(i) avoidance of inter-operator air-incidents;

(ii) mutual assistance in the course of Antarctic operations, including medical evacuations;

(iii) coordinated measures to improve search and rescue procedures;

3. In the fulfillment of these terms of reference, the meeting shall have regard to:

(i) existing systems for safe air operations;

(ii) means of mutually coordinating air traffic movements in Antarctica;

(iii) means of ensuring adequate communications between operators originating air traffic movements, between aircraft and stations in the vicinity of their operations and between aircraft, including consideration of the possible advantages of satellite communications and adoption of predetermined radio frequencies;

(iv) means of rapidly initiating search and rescue operations, including the advantages of using common dedicated calling frequencies and of coordinating subsequent operations;

(v) how best to ensure that all operators in the Antarctic are aware of air-operational safety requirements and search and rescue procedures;

(vi) air operations from ships.

4. In order to facilitate the work of the Meeting they provide relevant information to the host government, preferably 3 months in advance of the meeting, for circulation to other Consultative Parties. An indicative list of such information is set out in the Annex to this recommendation.

5. The report of the meeting be circulated to all Consultative Parties and be referred for consideration at the XVth Consultative Meeting in accordance with Paragraphs 3 and 4 of Recommendation IV-24.

Annex

The following information is an indicative list of the relevant information to be circulated to all Consultative Parties prior to the Meeting of Experts in Air Safety in Antarctica as recommended at the XIVth Consultative Meeting:

(i) current areas of air operation;

(ii) period and frequency of operation;

(iii) types of aircraft used and their navigation and communication equipment;

(iv) operating altitudes and ranges;

(v) other airborne devices (e.g. balloons, rockets) or other uses of air space in Antarctica

(vi) runway length, width, slope, orientation, surface type and condition, load capacity and markings;

(vii) Radio Direction Finding and Distance Measuring equipment;

(viii) navigation aids, including beacon power and frequencies and communications equipment;

(ix) features in the vicinity of landing facilities, which could be hazardous to aircraft;

(x) prevailing weather conditions of significance to air operations in the vicinity of landing facilities;

(xi) service facilities;

(xii) type and specification of fuel used;

(xiii) operating times of landing and communication facilities;

(xiv) available air navigation charts and published visual and instrument approach procedures;

(xv) medical facilities available, including medical personnel, and whether stations have trained search and rescue personnel.

XV-22 (Paris, 1989)

Spent

Consultative Parties to issue a commemorative stamp on the 30th anniversary of the Antarctic Treaty

The Representatives,

Recommend to their Governments that:

1. On the occasion of the Thirtieth Anniversary of the entry into force of the Antarctic Treaty. Each Consultative party should issue a commemorative stamp (or stamps) on a common date in 1991 (e.g. 23 June 1991).

2. The stamp (or stamps) should bear, in the language or languages of each issuing country, the following words: 'Antarctic Treaty 1961–1991'

3. Consideration be given to the themes of protecting the Antarctic environment and international cooperation in Antarctic scientific research for the most prominent features of the design.

4. There should be incorporated into the design of the stamp (or stamps), the Antarctic Treaty emblem representing a map of Antarctica which appears on the official documents of Consultative Meetings.

5. Any additional matter should be consonant with the provisions and the spirit of the Antarctic Treaty.

6. The number of stamps to be issued and the denominations of the stamp or stamps should remain at the discretion of the issuing country.

XVI-13 (Bonn, 1991)

Spent

Intersessional meeting to be held to make proposals on tourism and non-governmental activities to ATCM XVII

The Representatives,

Bearing in mind that the XVth Consultative Meeting agreed that a comprehensive review of tourism and non-governmental activities was required;

Noting that the Protocol on Environmental Protection to the Antarctic Treaty and its Annexes apply to tourist and non-governmental activities in Antarctica;

Recalling that the XIth Special Consultative Meeting asked the XVIth Consultative Meeting to address the issue of tourism and non-governmental activities;

Acknowledging that the Protocol constitutes the framework for further progress in Antarctic environmental protection;

Concerned about the possible effect of increased tourism and non-government activities in Antarctica;

Recommend to their Governments that:

1. An informal meeting of the Parties be convened with a view to making proposals to the XVIIth Consultative Meeting on the question of a comprehensive regulation of tourist and non-governmental activities in Antarctica in accordance with the Protocol and taking into account the proposals made at the present XVIth Consultative Meeting, including proposals for a future Annex to the Protocol on Environmental Protection;

2. Prior to the convening of that meeting and in order to ensure due preparation of its work, proposals should be prepared by them taking into account the list of issues stated below, which meeting should, inter alia, primarily address:

(a) environmental issues implementation of the Protocol on Environmental Protection to the Antarctic Treaty and its Annexes
   - number of tourists/carrying capacity
   - homologation of standards relating to vessels
   - permanent infrastructure for tourists
   - concentration/dispersal of tourist activities
   - access to unexplored areas

(b) operational issues
   - notification and expansion of information to be exchanged
   - system for granting permission to visit stations
   - self sufficiency
   - insurance, including search and rescue insurance
   - information obligation of Parties
   - preparation and training of tour guides, and visitors' guides
   - examination of the need for specific kinds of control and monitoring
   - requirements for organizational procedures

3. The meeting shall begin its work in Venice on 9 November 1992.

4. Representatives of the WTO, IUCN. IAATO, IMO, ASOC, PATA, SCAR and COMNAP be invited to attend the Meeting as observers.

Resolution 3 (2002): Support for CCAMLR and Action to Combat Illegal, Unreported and Unregulated Fishing in *Dissostichus spp* (toothfish)

The Representatives,

Recalling ATCM XXIII Resolution 3 (1999), SATCM XII Resolution 2 (2000) and ATCM XXIV Resolution 2 (2001) providing support for the Commission for the Conservation of Antarctic Marine Living resources (CCAMLR) in its continued efforts aimed at eliminating illegal, unreported and unregulated (IUU) fishing in the Convention Area;

Noting with appreciation the Report of CCAMLR to ATCM XXV; and

Recognising that illegal, unreported and unregulated fishing threatens the conservation objectives of the Convention on the Conservation of Antarctic Marine Living Resources and thus is undermining the integrity of the Antarctic Treaty System;

Recommend that:

All parties to the Antarctic Treaty which are Party to the Convention on the Conservation of Antarctic Marine living Resources, but not yet members of its Commission, take steps to implement all relevant Conservation Measures adopted by CCAMLR, in particular Measures relating to the Dissostichus Catch Documentation Scheme; and

Parties to the Antarctic Treaty which are not Party to the Convention on the Conservation of Antarctic Marine Living Resources but which nevertheless are involved in the harvesting and trade of tooth fish, consider acceding to the Convention and, in the meantime, agree voluntarily to implement the Dissostichus Catch Documentation Scheme.

Resolution 1 (2003): The inclusion of the Protocol on Environmental Protection to the Antarctic Treaty (1998) in Advices to Marines

The Representatives,

Conscious of the importance of ensuring that mariners and vessel operators are aware of, and comply with, the obligations set out in the Environmental Protocol and in particular its Annex IV (Prevention of Marine Pollution);

Desiring to provide clear and easily understood advice to those operating vessels and yachts in the Antarctic Treaty Area; and

Recalling discussions at ATCM XXV that a means to improve compliance with the Protocol's obligations by vessel and yacht operators would be to include details of the Protocol and its Annexes, as appropriate in the Antarctic navigational guides or pilots published by parties.

Recommend that:

– Those Parties that publish advice to marines in the form of, for example, Antarctic "Sailing Directions", "Marine Notices", or "Pilots", should ensure that appropriate detail of the Protocol on Environmental Protection to the Antarctic Treaty (1998) and in particular details of its Annex IV, are included in such publications.

Resolution 4 (2003): Support for the Conservation of Albatrosses and Petrels

The Representatives,

Recalling their responsibilities and the Article IX of the Antarctic Treaty in respect of the preservation and conservation of living resources in Antarctica;

Recognising that Annex II to the Environmental Protocol provides for protection to native birds including Albatrosses and Petrels;

Noting that a number of international instruments have been adopted to enhance the conservation of Albatrosses and Petrels;

Concerned nevertheless that populations of Albatrosses and Petrels are declining, due in large part to the unsustainable mortality of these birds from illegal, unregulated and unreported (IUU) fishing, to the extent that the status of many species of these birds is regarded as threaten, endangered or vulnerable by the IUCN in its Red Data list;

Recommend that:

1. Those Parties to the Antarctic Treaty that have signed, but not yet ratified the Albatross and Petrel Agreement (ACAP), do so as soon as possible; and

2. Furthermore, that other Parties to the Antarctic Treaty that are range states for, or have a particular interest in the conservation of, Albatrosses and Petrels in Antarctica consider acceding to and/or implementing international instruments contributing to the conservation of Albatrosses and Petrels, including the above Agreement.

Decision 4 (2004): Guidelines for Ships Operating in Arctic and Antarctic Ice-Covered Waters

The Representatives:

Noting the provisions of Article 10 of Annex IV to the Environmental Protocol relating to the design, construction, manning and equipment of ships engaged in or supporting Antarctic operations;

Conscious of the increasing levels of shipping, including tourist vessels, operating in the waters of the Antarctic Treaty Area;

Desiring to ensure the safety of life at sea and the protection of the environment in the Antarctic Treaty Area;

Noting the intersessional efforts of COM NAP to produce these Guidelines;

Noting the Guidelines should be interpreted as providing recommendations, rather than mandatory directions;

Noting the IMO Guidelines for ships operating in Arctic ice-covered waters and desiring that the IMO amend those Guidelines to apply them specifically to ships in ice-covered waters in the Antarctic Treaty Area.

Decide to:

- endorse the Guidelines annexed to this Decision;
- transmit the Guidelines through the Chair of ATCM XXV II to the Secretary General of the IMO with a request for them to be considered by the IMO at the earliest opportunity;
- urge their national representatives to take action at the IMO to secure the consideration of the Guidelines at the earliest opportunity.

Guidelines for Ships Operating in Arctic and Antarctic Ice-Covered Waters

PREAMBLE

P-1 Introduction

P-1.1 Ships operating in the Arctic and Antarctic environment are exposed to a number of unique risks. Poor weather conditions and the relative lack of good charts, communication systems and other navigational aids pose challenges for mariners. The remoteness of the areas makes rescue or clean-up operations difficult and costly. Cold temperatures may reduce the effectiveness of numerous components of the ship, ranging from deck machinery and emergency equipment to sea suctions. When ice is present, it can impose additional loads on the hull, propulsion system and appendages.

Whilst Arctic and Antarctic waters have a number of similarities, there are also significant differences. The Arctic is an ocean surrounded by continents while the Antarctic is a continent surrounded by water. The Antarctic sea ice retreats significantly during the summer season or is dispersed by permanent gyres in the two major seas of the Antarctic; the Weddell and the Ross. Thus there is relatively little multi-year ice in the Antarctic. Conversely, the Arctic sea ice survives many summer seasons and there is a significant amount of multi-year ice. Whilst the marine environments of both polar seas are similarly vulnerable, response to such challenge should duly take into account specific features of the legal and political regimes applicable to their respective marine species.

P-1.2 These Guidelines for ships operating in Arctic and Antarctic ice-covered waters (hereinafter called "the Guidelines") are intended to address those additional provisions deemed necessary for consideration beyond existing requirements of the SOLAS Convention, the Torremolinos Protocol and the MARPOL Convention, in order to take into account the climatic conditions of Arctic and Antarctic ice-covered waters and to meet appropriate standards of maritime safety and pollution prevention.

P-1.3 The Guidelines are recommendatory and their wording should be interpreted as providing recommendations rather than mandatory direction.

P-2 Principles

P-2.1 The Guidelines aim to promote the safety of navigation and to prevent pollution from ship operations in Arctic and Antarctic ice-covered waters.

P-2.2 The Guidelines recognise that this is best achieved by an integrated approach based on requirements in existing Conventions which cover the design, outfitting, crewing and operation of ships for the conditions which they will encounter.

P-2.3 The Guidelines take into account that Arctic and Antarctic conditions may include sea and glacial ice that can represent a serious structural hazard to all ships. This is the single most significant factor in the Arctic and Antarctic operations and is reflected in many of the Guidelines' provisions.

P-2.4 The Guidelines address the fact that the Arctic and Antarctic environment imposes additional demands on ship systems, including navigation, communications, life-saving, main and auxiliary machinery, etc. They emphasize the need to ensure that all ship systems are capable of functioning effectively under anticipated operating conditions and providing adequate levels of safety in accident and emergency situations.

P-2.5 In addition, the Guidelines recognize that safe operation in such conditions requires specific attention to human factors including training and operational procedures.

P-2.6 The basic requirements for structure, stability and subdivision, machinery, life-saving appliances, fire protection, ship routing, navigation systems and equipment, radiocommunication, pollution prevention equipment, liability and safety management systems, as applicable to the different types and sizes of ships which may undertake voyages in Arctic and Antarctic ice-covered waters, are obtained from the relevant conventions. The standards expressed in these Guidelines have been developed to mitigate the additional risk imposed on shipping due to the harsh environmental and climatic conditions existing in Arctic and Antarctic ice-covered waters.

P-2.7 Not all ships which enter the Arctic and Antarctic environment will be able to navigate safely in all areas at all times of the year. A system of Polar Classes has therefore been developed to designate different levels of capability. In parallel to the development of the Guidelines, the International Association of Classification Societies (IACS) has developed a set of Unified Requirements which, in addition to general classification society rules, address all essential aspects of construction for ships of Polar Class.

P-2.8 These Guidelines are not intended to infringe on national systems of shipping control.

GUIDE

G-1 Layout of the Guidelines

G-1.1 The Guidelines include general, construction, equipment and operational parts, presented in that order and subdivided into chapters.

G-1.2 This section provides definitions for important terms that are used exclusively within the Guidelines or where any term has more than one meaning in other applicable conventions. Otherwise, terms have the meanings defined in the convention(s) relevant to each chapter.

G-1.3 All parts and chapters of the Guidelines should be applied to Polar Class ships. All parts and chapters, with the exception of those dealing with purely construction guidelines (Part A), should be applied to non-Polar Class ships. Each chapter notes any additional differentiation of Guidelines between ship classes specific to that chapter.

G-1.4 Guidance provided in Part A of the Guidelines is only intended for new Polar Class ships.

G-1.5 Commonly accepted nominal equivalencies are shown in the following table:

Nominal ship equivalencies

Finnish/Swedish (Baltic) Class	ASPPR Class	Russian Register Class	Polar Class
IA Super	Type A	UL	PC6
IA	Type B	LI	PC7

*Note: Authorized classification society equivalents to Baltic classes should also be recognised. The classification society equivalents for the Finnish/Swedish ice classes have been issued in the Finnish Maritime Administrations' Bulletin No. 16/27.11.2002, which can he found in website vww.fma.fi.

G-2 Key provisions

G-2.1 The combination of hull structural design, material quality, subdivision and segregation measures prescribed in the Guide lines and supporting standards should be adequate to reduce the risk of human casualties, pollution incidents or ship losses to acceptably low levels of probability during prudent operations in Arctic and Antarctic ice-covered waters.

G-2.2 No pollutants should be carried directly against the shell in areas at significant risk of ice impact. Operational pollution of the environment should be minimized by equipment selection and operational practice.

G-2.3 Key safety-related, survival and pollution control equipment should be rated for the temperatures and other conditions which may be encountered in the service intended.

G-2.4 Navigation and communications equipment should be suitable to provide adequate performance in high latitudes, areas with limited infrastructure and unique information transfer requirements.

G-2.5 Sea suction(s) should be capable of being cleared of accumulation of slush ice.

G-3 Definitions

For the purpose or these Guidelines, unless expressly provided otherwise, the terms used have the meanings defined in the following paragraphs. Additional definitions are given in the various chapters as required. Terms used, but not defined in these Guidelines, are to be interpreted as they are defined in the relevant Conventions.

G-3.1 "Administration" means the Government of the State whose flag the ship is entitled to fly.

G-3.2 "Arctic and Antarctic ice-covered waters"

G-3.2.1 "Arctic Ice Covered Waters" – solely for the purposes of these Guidelines, means those waters which are both:

1. located north or a line from the southern lip of Greenland and thence by the southern shore of Greenland to Kape Hoppe and thence by a rhumb line to latitude 67"03'9 N, longitude 026"33'4 W and thence by a rhumb line to Sorkapp, Jan Mayen and by the southern shore of Jan Mayell to the Island of Bjørnøya, and thence by a great circle from the Island of Bjørnøya to Cap Konin Nos and thence by the northern shore of the Asian Continent eastward to the Bering Strait and thence from the Bering Strait westward to latitude 60° North as far as Il'pyrskiy and following the 60th North parallel eastward as far as and including Etolin Strait and thence by the northern shore or the North American continent as far south as latitude 60 ° North and thence eastward 10 the southern tip of Greenland (see figure 1); and
2. in which sea ice concentrations of 1/10 coverage or greater are present and which pose a structural risk to ships.

G-3.2.2 "Antarctic ice-covered waters" – solely for the purposes of these Guidelines, means those waters which are both:

1. South of 60°S and
2. In which sea ice concentrations of 1/10 coverage or greater are present and which pose a structural risk to shops.

G-3.3 "COLREG" means the International Regulations for Preventing Collisions at Sea, 1972, as amended.

G-3.4 "Company" means the owner of the ship or any other organization or person such as the manager, or the bareboat charterer, who has assumed the responsibility for operation of the ship from the ship owner.

G-3.5 "Conning position" means the stations in which the ship's control devices for ahead or astern operations are located.

G-3.6 "Escort" means any ship with superior ice capability in transit with another ship.

G-3.7 "Escorted operation" means any operation in which a ship's movement is facilitated through the intervention of an escort.

G-3.8 "Guidelines" means the IMO recommendatory Guidelines for ships operating in Arctic and Antarctic ice-covered waters.

G-3.9 "IACS" means the International Association of Classification Societies.

G-3.10 "Ice Navigator" means any individual who, in addition to being qualified under the STCW Convention, is specially trained and otherwise qualified to direct the movement of a ship in ice-covered waters.

G-3.11 "Icebreaker" means any ship whose operational profile may include escort or ice management functions, whose powering and dimensions allow it to undertake aggressive operations in ice-covered waters.

G-3.12 "International voyages" means voyages in international waters, as defined in chapter I of the SOLAS Convention.

G-3.13 "ISM Code" means the International Management Code for the Safe Operation of Ships and for Pollution Prevention, as amended.

G-3.14 "LL Convention" means the International Convention on Load Lines, 1966, as amended.

G-3.I5 "MARPOL Convention" means the International Convention for the Prevention of Pollution from Ships, 1973, as modified by the 1978 Protocol relating thereto (MARPOL 73/78), as amended.

G-3.16 "Organization" means the International Maritime Organization.

G-3.17 "Polar Class" means the class assigned to a ship based upon IACS Unified Requirements.

G-3.18 "Polar Class ship" means a ship for which a Polar Class has been assigned.

G-3.19 "Pollutant" means the substances defined as oil, oily mixture and oil fuel in Annex I; noxious liquid substances in Annex II; and solids when carried in bulk, which are also identified as harmful substances in Annex III of the MARPOL Convention.

~~G-3.20 "Port State" means a State whose area of jurisdiction includes any destination port of a ship where such port lies within Arctic ice-covered waters.~~

G-3.20 "Recognized organization" means an organization recognized by an Administration in accordance with IMO resolutions A.739(18) and A.789(19).

G-3.21 "Ship" means any vessel covered by the SOLAS Convention.

G-3.22 "SOLAS Convention" means the International Convention for the Safety of Life at Sea, 1974, as amended.

G-3.23 "STCW Convention" means the International Convention on Standards of Training, Certification and Watchkeeping for Seafarers, 1978/1995, as amended.

G-3.24 "Unified Requirements" means the IACS Unified Requirements for Polar Class ships[3].

G-3.25 "WMO" means the World Meteorological Organization.

G-3.26 "Working liquid" means any oil or oily substance used for the operation of the ship's machinery.

[Omitted: Arctic map]

CHAPTER I GENERAL

1.1 Application

1.1.1 These Guidelines provide guidance for ships while operating in Arctic and Antarctic ice-covered waters as defined in paragraph G-3.2 and while engaged in international voyages.

1.1.2 Part A of the Guidelines provides guidance for Polar Class ships as defined in paragraph G-3–18.

1.1.3 Parts B and C of these Guidelines provide guidance for Polar Class and Non-Polar Class ships.

Table 1.1 – Class descriptions

(It should be noted that the IACS Unified Requirements which these class descriptions are based on are not yet completed and are subject to change)

POLAR CLASS	GENERAL DESCRIPTION
PC 1	Year-round operation in all Arctic and Antarctic ice-covered waters
PC 2	Year-round operation in moderate multi-year ice conditions
PC 3	Year-round operation in second-year ice which may include multi-year ice inclusions
PC 4	Year-round operation in thick first-year ice which may include old ice inclusions

[3] Under development.

PC 5	Year-round operation in medium first-year ice which may include old ice inclusions
PC 6	Summer/autumn operation in medium first-year ice which may include old ice inclusions
PC 7	Summer/autumn operation in thin first-year ice with which may include old ice inclusions

Note: Ice descriptions follow WMO Sea Ice Nomenclature.

1.1.4 All Polar Class ships and the equipment to be carried in accordance with these Guidelines should be designed, constructed and maintained in compliance with applicable national standards of the Administration or the appropriate requirements of a recognized organization which provide an equivalent level of safety[4] for its intended service.

1.1.5 The structures, equipment and arrangements essential for the safety and operation of the ship should take account of the expected air temperatures.

1.1.6 The life-saving and fire-extinguishing equipment specified in part B of the Guidelines, when stored or located in an exposed position, should be of a type that is rated to perform its design functions at a minimum air temperature of -30°C, or at any appropriate lower temperature in accordance with paragraph 1.1.5. In particular, attention is drawn to the inflation of life-saving equipment and the starting of engines in lifeboats and rescue boats.

1.1.7 Operations in Arctic and Antarctic ice-covered waters should take due account of factors such as: ship class, environmental conditions, icebreaker escort, prepared tracks, short or local routes, crew experience, support technology and services such as ice-mapping, communications, safe ports, repair facilities and other ships in convoy.

1.1.8 The provisions of these Guidelines do not apply to any warship, naval auxiliary, other vessels or aircraft owned or operated by a State and used, for the time being, only on government non-commercial service. However, each State should ensure, by the adoption of appropriate measures not impairing operations or operational capabilities of such vessels or aircraft owned or operated by it, that such vessels or aircraft act in a manner consistent, so far as is reasonable and practicable, with these Guidelines.

1.2 Ice Navigator

1.2.1 All ships operating in Arctic and Antarctic ice-covered waters should carry at least one Ice Navigator qualified in accordance with chapter 14.

1.2.2 Continuous monitoring of ice conditions by an Ice Navigator should be available at all times while the ship is underway and making way in the presence of ice.

PART A – CONSTRUCTION PROVISIONS

CHAPTER 2 STRUCTURES

2.1 General

2.1.1 All ships should have structural arrangements adequate to resist the global and local ice loads characteristic of their Polar Class.[5]

2.1.2 Each area of the hull and all appendages should be strengthened to resist design structure/ice interaction scenarios applicable to each case.

2.1.3 Structural arrangements should aim to limit damage resulting from accidental overloads to local areas.

2.1.4 Polar Class ships may experience in-service structural degradation at an accelerated rate. Structural surveys should, therefore, cover areas identified as being at high risk of accelerated degradation, and areas where physical evidence such as coating breakdown indicates a potential for high wastage rates.

[4] Refer to SOLAS regulation 11-1/3-1 and to the proposed IACS Unified Requirements for Polar Ships.

[5] Refer to the proposed IACS Unified Requirements for Polar Ships.

2.2 Materials

2.2.1 Materials used in ice-strengthened and other areas of the hull should be suitable for operation in the environment that prevails at their location.

2.2.2 Materials used in ice-strengthened areas should have adequate ductility to match the selected structural design approach.

2.2.3 Abrasion and corrosion resistant coatings and claddings used in ice-strengthened areas should be matched to the anticipated loads and structural response.

CHAPTER 3 SUBDIVISION AND STABILITY

3.1 Intact stability in ice

3.1.1 Account should be taken of the effect of king in the stability calculations.[6]

3.1.2 Suitable calculations should be carried out and/or tests conducted to demonstrate the following:

.1 the ship, when operated in ice within approved limitations, during a disturbance causing roll, pitch, heave or heel due to turning or any other cause, should maintain sufficient positive stability; and

.2 ships of Polar Classes 1 to 3 and icebreakers of all classes, when riding up in ice and remaining momentarily poised at the lowest stem extremity, should maintain sufficient positive stability.

3.1.3 Sufficient positive stability in paragraphs 3.1.2.1 and 3.1.2.2 means that the ship is in a positive state of equilibrium with a positive metacentric height of at least 150mm, and a line 150 mm below the edge of the freeboard deck as defined in the applicable LL Convention, is not submerged.

3.1.4 For performing stability calculations on ships that ride up onto the ice, the ship should be assumed to remain momentarily poised at the lowest stem extremity as follows:

.1 for a regular stem profile, at the point at which the stem contour is tangent to the keel line;

.2 for a stem fitted with a structurally defined skeg, at the point at which the stem contour meets the top of the skeg;

.3 for a stem profile where the skeg is defined by shape alone, at the point at which the stem contour tangent intersects the tangent of the skeg; or

.4 for a stem profile of novel design, the position should be specially considered.

3.2 Stability in damaged conditions

3.2.1 All Polar Class ships should be able to withstand flooding resulting from hull penetration due to ice damage of the extent set out in paragraph 3.2.2 and location set out in paragraph 3.2.3, and should remain in a satisfactory condition of equilibrium after such damage, as defined by the IMO instruments applicable to the ship.

3.2.2 The dimensions of an ice damage penetration should be taken as:

.1 longitudinal extent 0.045 of deepest ice waterline length if centred forward of the point of maximum beam on the waterline. and 0.015 of waterline length otherwise;

.2 depth 760 mm measured normal to the shell over the full extent of the damage; and

.3 vertical extent the lesser of 0.2 of deepest ice draft, or of longitudinal extent.

3.2.3 The centre of the ice damage may be located at any point between the keel and 1.2 times the deepest ice draft. The vertical extent of damage may be assumed to be confined between the keel and 1.2 times the deepest ice draft. For ships of Polar Classes 5, 6 and 7 not carrying polluting or hazardous cargoes, damage may be assumed to be confined between watertight bulkheads, except where such bulkheads are spaced at less than the damage dimension.

3.3 Subdivision

3.3.1 Subject to paragraphs 3.3.2 and 3.3.3, no Polar Class ship should carry any pollutant directly against the outer shell. Any pollutant should be separated from the outer shell of the ship by double skin construction of at least 760 mm in width.

[6] Refer to resolution A.749(18), Code on Intact Stability for All Types of Ships Covered by IMO Instruments.

3.3.2 All Polar Class ships should have double bottoms over the breadth and the length between forepeak and afterpeak bulkheads. Double bottom height should be in accordance with the rules of the classification societies in force. Double bottoms should not be used for the carriage of pollutants except where a double skin construction complying with paragraph 3.3.1 is provided, or where working liquids, are carried in way of main machinery spaces in tanks not exceeding 20 m3 individual volume.

3.3.3 Double bottoms in ships of Polar Classes 6 and 7 may be used for the carriage of any working liquids where the tanks are aft of midships and within the flat of bottom.

3.3.4 All Polar Class ships with icebreaking bow forms and short forepeaks may dispense with double bottoms up to the forepeak bulkhead in the area of the inclined stem, provided that the watertight compartments between the forepeak bulkhead and the bulkhead at the junction between the stem and the keel are not used to carry pollutants.

CHAPTER 4 ACCOMMODATION AND ESCAPE MEASURES

4.1 General

4.1.1 All personnel accommodations should be designed and arranged to protect the occupants from unfavourable environmental conditions and minimize risk of injury during normal (including ice transiting or icebreaking) operations and emergency conditions.

4.1.2 All personnel accommodations, public spaces and the equipment installed in them should be designed so that each person making proper use of them will not suffer injury during normal open water operations, designed ice transiting modes of operation, and emergency manoeuvring conditions.

4.1.3 Ships of Polar Classes 1 to 5 inclusive should have sufficiently available and reliable facilities to maintain a life sustaining environment in the event of an emergency and/or of extended ice entrapment.

4.2 Public address systems and other safely items

4.2.1 The public address system and the general emergency alarm system should be audible over the loudest ambient noise level occurring during ice transiting, ice breaking or ramming.

4.2.2 Ships of Polar Classes 1 to 3 inclusive, icebreakers and ships intended to be used in the ramming mode should be designed with adequate provisions to ensure the safety of personnel using shower facilities. Such facilities should include non-slip decking, three rigid sides, handholds and insulation from exposed hot water pipes.

4.2.3 Galley facilities should be provided with grab rails projecting from the front on cooking equipment for use by the crew during ice operations.

4.2.4 Equipment designed to heat oil for cooking purposes such as deep fat fryers should be located in a position suitably separated from hotplates or other hot surfaces. Such appliances should also be secured to the deck or other fixed structure and provided with an oil tight lid or closure to prevent splashing or spillage during ice operations.

4.3 Escape measures

4.3.1 All means of escape from accommodation or interior working spaces should not be rendered inoperable by ice accretion or by malfunction due to low external ambient air temperatures.

4.3.2 All escape routes should be dimensioned so as not to hinder passage for persons wearing suitable Polar clothing.

4.3.3 Escape routes should be designed to minimize the distance between their exit to an open deck and the survival equipment to which they lead.

CHAPTER 5 DIRECTIONAL CONTROL SYSTEMS

General

5.1 All Polar Class ships should be provided with directional control systems of adequate strength and suitable design to enable efficient operation in Arctic and Antarctic ice-covered waters.

5.2 For the purpose of this chapter, a directional control system includes any device or devices intended either as a primary or auxiliary means of steering the ship. The directional control system includes all associated power sources, linkages, controls and actuating systems.

5.3 Attention is drawn to the possibility of interaction between directional control systems and propulsion systems. Where such interaction occurs or where dual-purpose components are fitted, the provisions of chapters 7 and 8 should also be complied with, as applicable.

CHAPTER 6 ANCHORING AND TOWING ARRANGEMENTS

6.1 General

All Polar Class ships navigating in Arctic and Antarctic ice-covered waters should be capable of anchoring and providing limited assistance in the case of debilitating damage or breakdown, towards the prevention of a catastrophic loss or pollution incident. The capability of ships to provide assistance should be considered of prime importance, having due regard to the lack of repair facilities, the limited number of dedicated towing ships available and the response time that may be required by a dedicated towing ship to be able to provide effective assistance in Arctic and Antarctic ice-covered waters.

6.2 Anchoring arrangements

6.2.1 Ships of Polar Classes 1 to 5 inclusive and icebreakers of all classes should, as far as practicable, be designed to protect the anchor from being dislodged from its stowed position and from jamming or damaging the hull by direct impact with ice.

6.2.2 Anchoring systems should be provided with an independent means of securing the anchor so that the anchor cable can be disconnected for use as an emergency-towing bridle.

6.3 Towing arrangements

6.3.1 All Polar Class ships designed to perform dedicated towing operations and all icebreakers should be equipped with line throwing apparatus in addition to that required for life saving. This apparatus should be capable of delivering messenger lines for the transfer of towing equipment. Such line throwing apparatus should not be of the powder/rocket type, in order that it may be surely used to make a transfer to a tanker.

6.3.2 All Polar Class ships designed to perform dedicated towing operations should be provided with a quick release system, operable from the conning position.

6.3.3 Where fitted, close coupled bow to stem towing arrangements should comprise strengthened bow plating on the towed ship, appropriate towing slings, non-interfering positioning of bower anchors and disallowance of bulbous bows. In this case, arrangements should be provided for securing the anchor in the stowed position.

6.4 Emergency towing arrangements

6.4.1 All Polar Class ships should be capable of receiving emergency towing assistance.

6.4.2 Where appropriate towing arrangements should facilitate connection and release of a towline and provide bollards, fairleads, and other components suitable for the size of ship on which they are fitted.

CHAPTER 7 MAIN MACHINERY

7.1 General

7.1.1 The design, rating, installation, operation and maintainability of shipboard engineering systems should be suitable for navigation in Arctic and Antarctic ice-covered waters.[7]

7.1.2 In the event of damage, malfunction or failure of any machinery component, means should be provided to control and limit any resulting emission of pollutants to within the confines of the ship's hull.

7.1.3 The layout and construction of machinery essential for the safe operation of the ship should be such that repairs which can be affected using the resources on board may be completed safely and effectively. Ventilation systems should provide sufficient air at an appropriate temperature for the operation of machinery.

[7] Refer to the proposed IACS Unified Requirements for Polar Ships.

7.1.4 For Polar Class ships which may be laid up in Arctic and Antarctic ice-covered waters, materials for all systems with the potential of polluting should be suitable for preventing pollution at the lowest ambient temperatures to which they may be subjected and should be suitable to avoid pollution and ensure safe operation on re-activation of the systems.

7.2 Main propulsion systems

7.2.1 The main propulsion machinery should be designed so that the effects of loads with the potential to damage the system are limited to those components which can be readily repaired, replaced or reset. The reliability and availability of the equipment and systems should be considered.

7.2.2 Main propulsion machinery and all auxiliary machinery essential to the propulsion system, should be:

.1 designed for loads and vibrations resulting from propeller/hull/rudder-ice interactions;

.2 located to provide protection from freezing spray, ice and snow; and

.3 designed to operate when the ship is inclined at any combined angle of heel or trim that may be expected during operations in ice.

7.2.3 Sterntube bearings, seals and main propulsion components located outside the hull should not leak pollutants. Non-toxic, biodegradable lubricants are not considered to be pollutants.

7.2.4 The installed propulsive power should be sufficient to ensure that the ship can navigate safely and without risk of pollution under the design ice, weather and operational conditions.

7.2.5 Piping and intake systems associated with the main propulsion plant should be designed so as not to be affected by the impact of the Arctic and Antarctic environment.

CHAPTER 8 AUXILIARY MACHINERY SYSTEMS

8.1 General

8.1.1 Equipment and systems should be designed so that personnel exposure to cold temperatures and other environmental hazards during normal operations including routine maintenance is minimized.

8.1.2 Ventilation systems should provide sufficient air for the operation of auxiliary machinery, air conditioning and heating purposes.

8.2 Materials

8.2.1 Materials used in equipment and systems should be suitable for operation in the environment which prevails at their location. In particular, equipment or systems which are essential for preventing pollution or for safe operation of the ship when:

.1 located outside and above the waterline in any ship operating condition; or

.2 in unheated locations inside;

should not be susceptible to brittle fracture within the range of operating conditions.

8.2.2 Essential equipment or systems required for the safe operation of the ship or systems required for preventing pollution, located within spaces which, upon failure of the primary heating system, could be subject to outside ambient air temperatures should be:

.1 provided with an independent source of heat; and

.2 fabricated from materials that will not be susceptible to brittle fracture under the anticipated loads and temperatures.

8.2.3 For Polar Class ships which may be laid up in Arctic and Antarctic ice-covered waters, materials for all systems with the potential of polluting should be suitable for preventing pollution at the lowest ambient temperatures to which they may be subjected and should be suitable to avoid pollution and ensure safe operation on re-activation of the systems.

CHAPTER 9 ELECTRICAL INSTALLATIONS

9.1 Electrical installations should be subject to the provisions listed in chapters 4, 7 and 8 regarding design for operation in Arctic and Antarctic ice-covered waters and for the provision of emergency heat and power.

9.2 Precautions should be taken to minimize risk of supplies to essential and emergency services being interrupted by the inadvertent or accidental opening of switches or circuit breakers due to vibrations or accelerations during icebreaking operations.

9.3 Emergency power for communications equipment provided by battery should be provided with a means whereby the batteries are protected from extreme low temperatures.

9.4 Emergency power batteries, including those stored in deck boxes, should be secured in a position where excessive movement is prevented during ice-transiting operations and explosive gas ventilation is not restricted by the accumulation of ice or snow.

9.5 Control systems based on computers and other electronic hardware installations necessary for the proper functioning of essential equipment should be designed for redundancy and resistance to vibration, dampness and low humidity.

PART B – EQUIPMENT

CHAPTER 10 FIRE SAFETY

10.1 Fuel and other flammable fluid tanks and systems

Refueling of ships should be carried out taking into account the special conditions imposed by low temperatures

10.2 Ventilation

Closing apparatus for ventilation inlets and outlets should be designed and located to protect them from ice or snow accumulation that could interfere with the effective closure of such systems.

10.3 Fire detection and extinguishing systems

10.3.1 Fire-extinguishing systems should be designed or located so that they are not made inaccessible or inoperable by ice or snow accumulation or low temperature such that:

.1 equipment, appliances, systems and extinguishing agents should be protected from freezing for minimum temperature for the intended voyage, as specified in paragraph 1.1.6;

.2 precautions should be taken to prevent nozzles, piping and valves of any fire-extinguishing system from becoming clogged by impurities, corrosion or ice build up; and

.3 exhaust gas outlets and pressure vacuum arrangements should be protected from ice build up that could interfere with effective operation.

10.3.2 Water or foam extinguishers should not be located in any position that is exposed to freezing temperatures. These locations should be provided with extinguishers capable of operation under such conditions.

10.4 Fire pumps and associated equipment (Polar Class ships)

10.4.1 Where a fixed fire-extinguishing system or alternative fire-extinguishing system situated in a space separate from the compartment containing the main fire pumps utilizes its own independent sea suction, this sea suction should be capable of being cleared of accumulations of slush ice.

10.4.2 Fire pump(s) including emergency fire pump(s) should, wherever reasonable and practicable, be installed in heated compartment(s) and in any event should be adequately protected from freezing for minimum temperature for the intended voyage, as specified in paragraph 1.1.6.

10.4.3 Isolating valves should be located so that they are accessible. Any isolating valves located in exposed positions should not be subject to icing from freezing spray. The fire main should be arranged so that external sections can be isolated and draining devices should be provided.

10.4.4 Hydrants should be positioned or designed to remain operable under all anticipated temperatures. Ice accumulation and freezing should be taken into account.

10.4.5 All hydrants should be equipped with an efficient two-handed valve handle.

10.5 Protection against ice build-up

Components of the fire-fighting system which may be exposed to icing which could interfere with the proper functioning of that component should be adequately protected.

10.6 Fire fighter's outfits

10.6.1 Sufficient fire fighter's outfits should be readily available to the accommodation area and elsewhere as appropriate. Such fire fighter's outfits should be stored in positions as widely separated as practical.

10.6.2 In addition to the fire fighter's outfits provided in accordance with paragraph 10.5.1, one spare fire fighter's outfit should be provided. The spare outfit should be stored in a warm location on the ship.

CHAPTER 11 LIFE-SAVING APPLIANCES AND SURVIVAL ARRANGEMENTS

11.1 General

11.1.1 Adequate supplies of protective clothing and thermal insulating materials should be provided in all ships operating in Arctic and Antarctic ice-covered waters for all persons on board at any time.

11.1.2 Training in the use of all emergency equipment should be included as an element of the operating procedures and drills described in chapter 13. Where appropriate, dedicated training equipment should be carried to avoid compromising the performance of the emergency equipment itself.

11.2 Categories of life-saving equipment

11.2.1 Ships operating in Arctic and Antarctic ice-covered waters should carry life-saving appliances and survival equipment according to their environmental conditions of operation, as indicated in paragraph 1.1.6.

11.2.2 Personal survival kits (PSKs) as described in section 11.3 should be carried whenever a voyage is expected to encounter mean daily temperatures below 0°C.

11.2.3 Group survival kits (GSKs) as described in section 11.4 should be carried whenever a voyage is expected to encounter ice conditions which may prevent the lowering and operation of survival craft.

11.2.4 Sufficient PSKs and GSKs (as applicable) should be carried to cover at least 110% of the rated complement of the ship.

11.2.5 Personal survival kits should be stored so that they may be easily retrieved in an emergency situation. Arrangements such as storage in cabins or in dedicated lockers near the assembly stations may be considered.

11.2.6 Group survival kits should be stored so that they may be easily retrieved in an emergency situation. The containers should be located adjacent to the survival craft and life rafts and be stowed on cradles. Containers should be designed so that they may be easily moved over the ice and be floatable.

11.3 Personal survival kits (PSK)

11.3.1 A Personal survival kit should consist of the items listed in table 11.1 or appropriate alternatives.

Table 11.1 Contents of the personal survival kits

Equipment	Quantity
Clothing	
Head protection (VP[1])	1
Neck and face protection (VP)	1
Hand protection – Mitts (VP)	1 pair
Hand protection – Gloves (VP)	1 pair
Foot protection – Socks (VP)	1 pair
Foot protection – Boots	1 pair
Insulated suit (VP)	1
Approved immersion suit	1
Thermal underwear (VP)	1 set
Miscellaneous	
Hand warmers	240 hours

Sunglasses	1 pair
Survival candle	1
Matches	2 boxes
Whistle	1
Drinking mug	1
Pen knife	1
Handbook (Arctic Survival)	1
Carrying bag	1

* VP means vacuum packed

11.3.2 The following notice should be displayed wherever personal survival kits are stored:

NOTICE

CREW MEMBERS AND PASSENGERS ARE REMINDED THAT THEIR PERSONAL SURVIVAL KIT IS FOR EMERGENCY SURVIVAL USE ONLY. NEVER REMOVE ITEMS OF SURVIVAL CLOTHING OR TOOLS FROM THE PERSONAL SURVIVAL KIT CARRYING BAG – YOUR LIFE MAY DEPEND ON IT.

11.3.3 Personal survival kits should not be opened for training purposes. Equipment for training purposes should be provided in accordance with paragraph 11.1.2.

11.4 Group survival kit (GSK)

11.4.1 The contents of the group survival kit should include those items defined in table 11.2 or appropriate alternatives.

Table 11.2 Contents of the group survival kits (GSK)

Equipment	Quantity
Group equipment	
Tents	1 per 6 persons
Air mattresses	1 per 2 persons
Sleeping bags (VP)[2]	1 per 2 persons
Stove	1 per tent
Stove fuel	0.5 litres per person
Fuel paste	2 tubes per stove
Matches	2 boxes per tent
Pan (with sealing lid)	1 per stove
Fortified health drinks	5 packets per person
Flashlights	1 per tent
Candles and holders	5 per tent
Snow shovel	1 per tent
Snow saw and snow knife	1 per tent
Tarpaulin	1 per tent
Foot protection – Booties	1 per person
GSK container	1
Spare personal equipment	(1 set per GSK container)
Head protection (VP)	1
Neck and face protection (VP)	1

Hand protection – Mitts (VP)	1 pair
Hand protection – Gloves (VP)	1 pair
Foot protection – Socks (VP)	1 pair
Foot protection – Boots	1 pair
Insulated suit (VP)	1
Thermal underwear (VP)	1 pair
Hand warmers	1 set
Sunglasses	1
Whistle	1
Drinking mug	1

* VP means vacuum packed

11.4.2 Where a shot gun or hunting rifle is provided to protect survivors from wildlife, it should be stored in a secure location readily available in an emergency.

11.5 Lifeboats

11.5.1 All lifeboats carried by Polar Class ships should be of the fully enclosed type to provide adequate shelter from the environment. Other ships which are equipped with open or partially enclosed boats should carry tarpaulins of sufficient size to provide complete coverage of the lifeboats, and suitable structure to support them.

11.5.2 The capacity of lifeboats should be evaluated with regard to operability, accessibility, seating capacity and overall space considering the needs of personnel wearing suitable Polar clothing.

11.5.3 Ice accretion should be regularly removed from the lifeboats and launching equipment to ensure ease of launching when required. An icing removal mallet should be available in the vicinity of the lifeboats.

11.5.4 All lifeboat engines should be equipped with a means to ensure they will start readily when required at the minimum anticipated operating temperature.

11.5.5 The lifeboat engine fuel oil should be suitable for operation in the minimum anticipated operating temperature.

11.5.6 Drinking water should be stored in containers that allow for expansion due to freezing.

11.5.7 Consideration should be given to the provision of additional emergency rations to account for high rates of energy expenditure under Arctic and Antarctic conditions.

11.6 Life rafts

11.6.1 Ice accretion should be regularly removed from the life rafts, cradles and launching equipment to ensure ease of launching and inflation when required. An icing removal mallet should be available in the vicinity of the life rafts.

11.6.2 Ships should carry in a warm space in the vicinity of the life rafts manual inflation pumps that are proven to be effective in the expected air temperatures.

11.6.3 Air or other proven cold temperature gas should be used for the inflation of lifesaving equipment according to their environmental conditions of operation, as indicated in paragraph 1.1.6.

11.6.4 Consideration should be given to the provision of additional emergency rations to account for high rates of energy expenditure under Arctic and Antarctic conditions.

CHAPTER 12 NAVIGATIONAL EQUIPMENT

12.1 Application

It should be noted that the provisions prescribed in this chapter are not to be considered in addition to the requirements of SOLAS chapter V. Rather, any equipment fitted or carried in compliance with the requirements of SOLAS chapter V may be considered as part of the recommended equipment complement detailed in this chapter. Unless specifically provided in this chapter, the performance standards and other applicable guidance for equipment and systems contained in this chapter should be applied *mutatis mutandis* as per SOLAS chapter V.

12.2 Compasses

12.2.1 Magnetic variations in high latitudes may lead to unreliable readings from magnetic compasses.

12.2.2 Gyro-compasses may become unstable in high latitudes and may need to be shut down.

12.2.3 Companies should ensure that their systems for providing reference headings are suitable for their intended areas and modes of operation, and that due consideration has been given to the potential effects noted in paragraphs 12.2.1 and 12.2.2. For operations in Arctic and Antarctic ice-covered waters, ships should be fitted with a total of at least two gyro-compasses.

12.3 Speed and distance measurement

12.3.1 All Polar Class ships should be fitted with a total of at least two speed and distance measuring devices.[8] Each device should operate on a different principle, and at least one device should be capable of being operated in both the sea and the ground stabilized mode.

12.3.2 Speed and distance measuring devices should provide each conning position with a speed indication at least once per second.

12.3.3 Speed and distance measurement device sensors should not project beyond the hull and should be installed to protect them from damage by ice.

12.4 Depth sounding device

All Polar Class ships should be fitted with a total of at least two independent echo-sounding devices which provide indication of the depth of water under the keel. Due account should be taken of the potential for ice interference or damage to any device designed to operate below the waterline.

12.5 Radar-installations

12.5.1 All Polar Class ships should be fitted with a total of at least two functionally independent radar systems. One of these should operate in the 3 GHz (10 cm, S-band) frequency range.

12.5.2 Radar plotting systems that may be installed should have the capability of operating in both the sea and the ground stabilized mode.

12.6 Electronic positioning and electronic chart systems

12.6.1 All Polar Class ships should be provided with an electronic position fixing system.

12.6.2 A satellite system (GPS or GLONASS or equivalent) should be fitted on any ship intending to navigate in areas outside of reliable coverage by a terrestrial hyperbolic system.

12.6.3 Systems described in paragraphs 12.6.1 and 12.6.2 should provide input to allow for continuous representation of the ship's speed provided by a speed and distance measuring device according to paragraph 12.3, and the ship's course provided by a compass according to paragraph 12.2.

12.6.4 Where fitted, electronic charting systems should be able to use position input from systems compliant with paragraphs 12.6.1 and 12.6.2.[9]

12.7 Automatic identification system (AIS)

All Polar Class ships should be provided with an automatic identification system (AIS)[10] for ships using the broadcast mode.

12.8 Rudder angle indicator

12.8.1 Separate rudder angle indicators should be provided for each rudder on ships with more than one rudder.

---

[8] Refer to resolution A824(19) on Recommendation on Performance Standards for Devices to Indicate Speed and Distance.

[9] Refer to the proposed Performance Standards for Course and Speed Indication for Electronic Positioning and Satellite Systems.

[10] Refer to guidelines on the operation of AIS on ships (to be developed).

12.8.2 In ships without a rudder, indication should be given of the direction of steering thrust.

12.9 Searchlights and visual signals

12.9.1 Ships of Polar Classes 1 to 5 inclusive and all ships intended to operate in periods of prolonged darkness should be equipped with at least two suitable searchlights which should be controllable from conning positions.

12.9.2 The searchlights described in paragraph 12.9.1 should be installed to provide, as far as is practicable, all-round illumination suitable for docking, astern manoeuvres or emergency towing.

12.9.3 The searchlights described in paragraph 12.9.1 should be fitted with an adequate means of de-icing to ensure proper directional movement.

12.9.4 Ships of Polar Classes 1 to 5 inclusive, all icebreakers and all ships that may be involved in an escort of more than one ship following in an ice track should be equipped with a manually operated flashing red light visible from astern to indicate when the ship is stopped. This should be capable of use from any location from which the ship can be manoeuvred.

The flashing light should have a range of visibility of at least two (2) nautical miles. The colour and frequency of the flashing light should be according to standards given in COLREG. The horizontal and vertical arcs of visibility of the flashing light should be as specified for stem lights in COLREG.

12.10 Vision enhancement equipment

12.10.1 All Polar Class ships should be fitted with a suitable means to de-ice sufficient conning position windows to provide unimpaired forward and astern vision from conning positions.

12.10.2 The windows described in paragraph 12.10.1 should be fitted with an efficient means of clearing melted ice, freezing rain, snow, mist and spray from outside and accumulated condensation from inside. A mechanical means to clear moisture from the outside face of a window should have operating mechanisms protected from freezing or the accumulation of ice that would impair effective operation.

12.10.3 All persons engaged in navigating the ship should be provided with adequate protection from direct and reflected glare from the sun.

12.10.4 All indicators providing information to the conning positions should be fitted with means of illumination control to ensure readability under all operating conditions.

12.11 Voyage data recorder

Ships of Polar Classes 1 to 5 inclusive should be fitted with a voyage data recorder.[11]

12.12 Ice routing equipment

12.12.1 All ships should be provided with equipment capable of receiving ice and weather information charts.

12.12.2 Ships of Polar Classes 1 to 3 inclusive should be fitted with equipment capable of receiving and displaying ice imagery.

PART C – OPERATIONAL

CHAPTER 13 OPERATIONAL GUIDELINES

13.1 Documentation

All ships operating in Arctic and Antarctic ice-covered waters should carry on board at all times an operating manual and training manual for all Ice Navigators on board the ship.

13.2 Ship operational control

The ship should not be operated outside the worst intended conditions and design limitations.

13.3 Operating and training manuals

13.3.1 The operating manual, or supplementary manual in the case of ships not normally operating in Arctic and Antarctic ice-covered waters, should contain at least the following information on issues directly related to operations in such waters. With respect to contingency

[11] Refer to resolution A.861(20) on Recommendation on Performance Standards for Voyage Data Recorders (VDRs).

planning in the event that the ship suffers ice damage, the manual should conform to guidelines developed by the Organization:[12]

Normal operation

.1 principal particulars of the ship;

.2 loading procedures and limitations including any applicable recommendations against carrying pollutants in tanks and compartments against the hull envelopment, maximum operational weight, position of centre of gravity and distribution of load necessary for operation in Arctic and Antarctic ice-covered waters;

.3 acknowledgment of changes in standard operating procedures for radio equipment and navigational aids applicable to Arctic and Antarctic operations;

.4 information regarding the handling of the ship as determined in accordance with chapter 16 of these Guidelines (Environmental protection and damage control);

.5 maximum towing speeds and towing loads where applicable;

Risk management

.6 procedures for checking the integrity of hull structure;

.7 description and operation of fire detention and fire-extinguishing equipment in an Arctic and Antarctic environment; and for Polar Class ships, the operating manual should include the following supplementary information, in clearly defined chapters specified by the Administration:

.8 operating limitations for the ship and essential systems in anticipated ice conditions and temperatures;

.9 details arising from the standards of chapter 3 of these Guidelines (Subdivision and stability) likely to be of direct practical use to the crew in an emergency;

.10 passage planning procedures accounting for anticipated ice conditions;

.11 deviations in standard operating procedures associated with operation of propulsion and auxiliary machinery systems, remote control and warning systems and electronic and electrical systems made necessary by operations in Arctic and Antarctic ice-covered waters;

.12 deviations in standard damage control procedures made necessary by operations in Arctic and Antarctic ice-covered waters; and

.13 evacuation procedures into water, onto ice, or into a combination of the two, with due regard to chapter 11 of these Guidelines

13.3.2 Regarding information on machinery or system failures, guidance should take into account the results of any risk or failure analysis reports developed during the ship design.

TRAINING MANUAL

13.3.3 The training manual should cover all aspects of ship operation in Arctic and Antarctic ice-covered waters listed below plus other related information considered necessary by the Administration:

.1 summary of the Guidelines for ships operating in Arctic and Antarctic ice-covered waters;

.2 ice recognition;

.3 navigation in ice; and

.4 escorted operation.

Instructions for drills and emergency instructions as detailed in section 13.4 should be incorporated as annexes to the manual.

13.3.4 The Company should ensure that any additional documentation referenced in the training manual and required to provide a full understanding of its contents is on board the ship for all operations in Arctic and Antarctic ice-covered waters.

[12] Refer to resolution A.852(20) on Guidelines for the Structure of an Integrated System of Contingent Planning for Shipboard Emergencies.

13.4 Drills and emergency instructions

13.4.1 On board instruction and operation of the ship's evacuation, fire and damage control appliances and systems should include appropriate cross training of crew members with appropriate emphasis to changes to standard procedure made necessary by operations in Arctic and Antarctic ice-covered waters.

13.4.2 Evacuation

13.4.2.1 Evacuation drill scenarios should be varied so that different emergency conditions are simulated, including abandonment into the water, onto the ice, or a combination of the two.

13.4.2.2 Each evacuation craft drill should include:

.1 exercises in passenger control in cold temperatures as appropriate;

.2 checking that all personnel are suitably dressed;

.3 donning of immersion suits or thermal protective clothing by appropriate crew members;

.4 testing of emergency lighting for assembling and abandonment; and

.5 giving instructions in the use of the ship's life-saving appliances and in survival at sea, on the ice or a combination of both.

13.4.2.3 Rescue boat drills should be conducted as follows:

.1 As far as is reasonable and practicable, rescue boats should be launched each month as part of the evacuation drill with their assigned crew aboard and manoeuvred in the water, with due consideration of the dangers of launching into Arctic and Antarctic ice-covered waters if applicable.

.2 If rescue boat launching drills are carried out with the ship making headway, such drills should be practiced in sheltered waters only and under the supervision of an officer experienced in such drills.[13]

13.4.2.4 Individual instructions may cover different parts of the ship's life-saving system, but all the ship's life-saving equipment and appliances should be covered within any period of one month on passenger ship and two months on cargo ship. Each member of the crew should be given instructions which should include but not necessarily be limited to:

.1 Problems of hypothermia, first-aid treatment of hypothermia and other appropriate first-aid procedures; and

.2 Special instructions necessary for use of the ship's life-saving appliances in severe weather and severe sea conditions on the ice or in a combination of water and ice cover.

13.4.3 Fire drills

13.4.3.1 Fire drill scenarios should vary each week so that emergency conditions are simulated for different ship compartments, with appropriate emphasis on those changes to standard procedure made necessary by operations in Arctic and Antarctic ice-covered waters and low temperatures.

13.4.3.2 Each fire drill should include elements required by the SOLAS Convention plus additional elements made necessary by operation in an Arctic and Antarctic environment.

13.4.4 Damage Control

Damage control drill scenarios should vary each week so that emergency conditions are simulated for different damage conditions with appropriate emphasis to those conditions resultant from operations in Arctic and Antarctic ice-covered waters.

13.4.5 Survival kits

13.4.5.1 Where fitted, the master should ensure that sufficient PSKs and GSKs are available, in full working order, and ready for immediate use, to meet the standards set forth in paragraph 11.2.4.

13.4.5.2 The master should keep spare personal survival equipment on board for the purpose of providing replacements for missing or damaged items of equipment in those personal survival

[13] Refer to resolution A.624(15) on Guidelines for Training Crews for the Purpose of Launching Lifeboats and Rescue Boats from Ships Making Headway Through the Water.

kits issued to the complement. In addition, a number of sewing kits and replacement parts (buttons, boot laces etc.) should be kept on board for the purpose of minor repair to personal survival kit items of clothing.

13.4.5.3 Group survival kit inspections should be carried out no less frequently than on an annual basis at the beginning of each operating season.

CHAPTER 14 CREWING

14.1 General

14.1.1 The crewing of all ships in Arctic and Antarctic ice-covered waters should take account of the provisions listed in this chapter, and also of the relative lack of shore and support infrastructure which may be available to assist in any operations.

14.1.2 Ice Navigators should be provided as noted in chapter 1.

14.1.3 All of the ship's officers and crew should be made familiar with cold weather survival by training or self-study of course material or publications addressing the measures set forth in section 13.4.

14.1.4 As many as possible of the ship's deck and engine officers should be trained in ship operations in ice-covered waters.

14.2 Ice Navigator qualifications and training

The Ice Navigator should have documentary evidence of having satisfactorily completed an approved training program in ice navigation; in the Antarctic, documentary evidence of having completed an on-the-job training programme is acceptable.

Such a training program should provide knowledge, understanding and proficiency required for operating a ship in Arctic and Antarctic ice-covered waters, including recognition of ice formation and characteristics; ice indications; ice manoeuvring; use of ice forecasts, atlases and codes; hull stress caused by ice; ice escort operations; ice-breaking operations and effect of ice accretion on vessel stability.

14.3 Supplementary provisions

14.3.1 Where firearms are carried in accordance with paragraph 11.4.2, a minimum of two crew members should be cognizant of current firearm regulations and guidelines and be trained in the use of shotguns or hunting rifles.

14.3.2 A minimum of two crew members should be trained in the use of low frequency radio equipment where fitted.

CHAPTER 15 EMERGENCY EQUIPMENT

15.1 Medical equipment

15.1.1 All ships should be provided with an adequate number of first-aid kits and equipment with contents suitable to the on board location and recognized provisions for personnel safety hazards of such locations.

15.1.2 With respect to the nature of the voyage, ship operations and the ability to communicate and obtain timely assistance of medical aid or medical evacuation, exemptions of certain medical equipment, medicaments and facilities may be considered unreasonable or unnecessary.

15.1.3 Crews operating in Arctic and Antarctic ice-covered waters should be provided with appropriate equipment and training to safely evacuate an individual in a medical emergency from the ship.

15.2 Reserve supplies

15.2.1 Special consideration should be given to the reserve supply of fuel and lubricants taking into account the effect of heavy ice on fuel consumption.

15.2.2 Single screw ships may require special consideration (redundancy) in remote areas where conditions impose a risk of damage to machinery components.

15.3 Damage control and repair equipment

15.3.1 All icebreakers should carry the following emergency equipment:

.1 portable gas welding equipment for welding and cutting with a reserve of electrodes; and

.2 portable electro-submersible pump of 100 t/h capacity with a set of hoses.

15.3.2 Where built-up propellers are used, consideration should be given to the carriage of spare blades and of equipment facilitating removal and replacement.

PART D – ENVIRONMENTAL PROTECTION AND DAMAGE CONTROL

CHAPTER 16 ENVIRONMENTAL PROTECTION AND DAMAGE CONTROL

16.1 General

16.1.1 The following provisions concerning environmental protection and damage control equipment are made with due regard to the lack of waste reception and repair facilities, communications limitations, unique navigational and environmental hazards and limited response capabilities of available assistance in Arctic and Antarctic ice-covered waters.

16.1.2 Procedures for the protection of the environment under normal operations should be included in the ship's operating manual as described in chapter 13, and those under accident conditions into the Shipboard Oil Pollution Emergency Plan (SOPLP) according to the MARPOL Convention.

16.1.3 Training and drills covering environmental protection and damage control procedures should be provided for crew members as specified in chapter 13.

16.2 Equipment and materials

16.2.1 All ships navigating in Arctic and Antarctic ice-covered waters should be adequately equipped and their crews properly trained to provide effective damage control and minor hull repair. All ships should have the capability to contain and clean up minor deck and over side spills.

16.2.2 Damage control equipment, provided in accordance with paragraph 16.2.1, should be sufficient to enable a ship, as far as practicable, to make temporary repairs to a minor hull breach or to take precautionary measures to prevent escalation of damage or flooding, so that the ship may proceed to a location where more substantial repairs can be affected.

16.2.3 Icebreakers and ships of Polar Classes 1 to 4 inclusive should be provided with material, tools and equipment capable of effecting more substantial repairs and damage control activities, as described in chapter 15.

16.2.4 Hoses and pipelines should be manufactured out of materials retaining adequate strength and elasticity characteristics at the minimum anticipated operating temperature.

16.2.5 All hoses used to transfer pollutant cargoes from the ship to another ship or to shore should have the connection between the hose and the hose couplings made in an efficient and strong fashion to minimize the possibility of pollution due to failure of this connection. Couplings between hose sections should be capable of being securely locked together to prevent inadvertent disconnection.

Resolution 1 (2004): Enhancing Prevention of Marine Pollution by Fishing Activities

The Representatives,

Aware of the need to enhance the conservations and preservation of the Antarctic environment as stated in the Protocol for Environmental Protection to the Antarctic Treaty;

Taking into account existing marine activities within the Antarctic Treaty area, including fishing activities

Aware the Annex IV of the Madrid Protocol includes provisions to be applied to the activities of vessels, including fishing vessels, in relation to the prevention of marine pollutions;

Noting the actions undertaken by other organisations such as CCAMLR in line with Article 10 of Annex IV of the Madrid Protocol, on Prevention of Marine Pollution;

Supporting the prevention of marine pollution by fishing activities;

Highly support:

The progress achieved by CCAMLR/XXII urging its Members, which are harvesting in high Antarctic latitudes,[14] to license only those fishing vessels with at least an ice classification standard of ICE-IC.[15]

Resolution 3 (2004): Tourism and Non-governmental Activities: Enhanced Co-Operation Amongst Parties

The Representatives.

Concerned about the increasing trend in Antarctic tourism and the need to ensure more rigorous monitoring and control of such activities;

Desiring to ensure that all such activities undertaken in Antarctica are strictly in accordance with the Antarctic Treaty and its Environmental Protocol;

Aware that some individuals may circumvent national legislation by seeking approval for their activities from more than one national authority;

Noting that the consultations described below would be without prejudice to any Party's implementation of its own national legislation.

Recommend that:

1. All Parties nominate to the Secretariat a single contact point for information about tourism and non-Governmental activities in Antarctica;
2. Parties exchange information about such activities as and when they are notified, particularly where there are potential implications for other Parties;
3. Where Parties are notified, or become aware, of an activity involving a vessel or aircraft flagged or registered with another Treaty Party; or where the organisers are nationals of another Treaty Party, that they consult those relevant Parties as appropriate during the process of evaluating such activities and, where applicable, prior to any decision to authorise the activity or permit to proceed.

Resolution 4 (2004): Guidelines on Contingency Planning, Insurance and Other Matters for Tourist and Other Non-governmental Activities in the Antarctic Treaty Area

The Representatives,

Concerned at the potential impacts, including the imposition of additional costs, that tourist or other non-governmental activities may have on national programmes, and the risks to the safety of those involved in search and rescue operations;

Desiring to ensure that tourist or other non-governmental activities undertaken in Antarctica are carried out in a safe and self sufficient manner;

Desiring further to ensure that the risks associated with tourist or other non-governmental activities are fully identified in advance, and minimised;

Recalling the "Procedures to be Followed by Organisers and Operators", as set out in the Attachment to Recommendation XVIII-I;

Noting Measure 4 (2004) on "Insurance and Contingency Planning for Tourism and Non-governmental Activities in the Antarctic Treaty Area", and desiring to take certain steps before it enters into effect to promote its objectives in addition to recommending further guidelines to be followed by those organising or conducting activities without the supervision or support in the field of another operator or a national programme;

[14] Waters south of 60° South and adjacent to the Antarctic continent.

[15] As defined in the Det Norske Veritas; (DNV) Rules for Classification of Ships or an equivalent standard of certification as defined by a recognized classification authority.

Recommend:

– That Parties should require those under their jurisdiction organising or conducting tourist or other non-governmental activities in the Antarctic Treaty Area, for which advance notification is required in accordance with Article VII (5) of the Antarctic Treaty, to follow the Guidelines annexed to this Resolution.

Annex I: Guidelines on contingency planning, insurance and other matters for tourist and other non-governmental activities in the Antarctic Treaty Area

Those organising or conducting tourist or other non-governmental activities in the Antarctic Treaty area should ensure:

1. that appropriate contingency plans and sufficient arrangements for health and safety, search and rescue (SAR), and medical care and evacuation have been drawn-up and are in place prior to the start of the activity. Such plans and arrangements should not be reliant on support from other operators or national programmes without their express written agreement; and

2. that adequate insurance or other arrangements are in place to cover any costs associated with search and rescue and medical care and evacuation.

And the following guidelines should also be observed in particular by those organising conducting activities without the supervision or support in the field of another operator or a national programme:

3. that participants have sufficient and demonstrable experience appropriate for the proposed activity operating in polar, or equivalent, environments. Such experience may include survival training in cold or remote areas, flying, sailing or operating other vehicles in conditions and over distances similar to those being proposed in the activity;

4. that all equipment, including clothing, communication, navigational, emergency and logistic equipment is in sound working order, with sufficient backup spares and suitable for effective operation under Antarctic conditions:

5. that all participants are proficient in the use of such equipment;

6. that all participants are medically, physically and psychologically fit to undertake the activity in Antarctica;

7. that adequate first-aid equipment is available during the activity and that at least one participant is proficient in advanced first-aid.

Decision 4 (2005): Consultative Party Status

The Representatives,

Recognising the need for a procedure of consultation in the event that another state, having acceded to the Antarctic Treaty, should notify the Depositary Government that it considers it is entitled to appoint Representatives to participate in Antarctic Treaty Consultative Meetings;

Recalling their obligation under Article X of the Antarctic Treaty to exert appropriate efforts, consistent with the Charter of the United Nations, to the end that no one engages in an activity in Antarctica contrary to the principles or purposes of the Treaty;

Recognising that the entitlement of an acceding state to appoint Representatives to participate in Antarctic Treaty Consultative Meetings (ATCM) under Article IX.2 of the Antarctic Treaty depends on such a state demonstrating its interest in Antarctica by conducting substantial scientific research activities there, such as the establishment of a scientific station or the dispatch of a scientific expedition;

Recalling their obligation under Article 22.4 of the Protocol on Environmental Protection to the Antarctic Treaty (the Protocol) not to act upon a notification regarding the entitlement of a Contracting Party to the Antarctic Treaty to appoint representatives to participate in the ATCM unless the Contracting Party has first ratified, accepted, approved or acceded to the Protocol;

Emphasising the importance of Contracting Parties to the Antarctic Treaty that are seeking consultative status approving all Annexes to the Protocol that have become effective;

Recalling the decision of the First Special Antarctic Treaty Consultative Meeting (1977) and the amendments made to that decision by Decision 2 (1997);

Recalling also the Guidelines on Notification with respect to Consultative Status agreed at the XIVth ATCM;

Conscious of the adoption, subsequent to the adoption of the Protocol, of Annex V to the Protocol on Area Protection and Management and Annex VI to the Protocol on Liability Arising from Environmental Emergencies;

Noting that Annex V to the Protocol has become effective;

Decide that:

1. An acceding state which considers itself entitled to appoint Representatives in accordance with Article IX.2 of the Antarctic Treaty shall notify the Depositary Government for the Antarctic Treaty of this view and shall provide information concerning its activities in the Antarctic, in particular the content and objectives of its scientific programme. The Depositary Government should forthwith communicate for evaluation the foregoing notification and information to all other Consultative Parties.

2. Consultative Parties, in exercising the obligation placed on them by Article X of the Treaty, shall examine the information about its activities supplied by such an acceding state, may conduct any appropriate enquiries (including the exercising of their right of inspection in accordance with Article VII of the Treaty) and may, through the Depositary Government, urge such a state to make a declaration of intent to approve the Recommendations and Measures adopted at ATCM in pursuance of the Treaty and subsequently approved by all the Contracting Parties whose Representatives were entitled to participate in those meetings. Consultative Parties may, through the Depositary Government, invite the acceding state to consider approval of the other Recommendations and Measures.

3. The Government which is to host the next ATCM shall, in the context of its preparation of the Provisional Agenda for the ATCM in accordance with Rule 38 of the Rules of Procedure, include an appropriate item in the Provisional Agenda for consideration of the notification.

4. The ATCM shall determine, on the basis of all information available to it, whether to acknowledge that the acceding state in question has met the requirements of Article IX.2 of the Antarctic Treaty and of Article 22.4 of the Protocol, including whether the acceding state has approved all Annexes to the Protocol that have become effective. The ATCM shall also take into account the Guidelines on Notification with respect to Consultative Status. If agreed by the Representatives of all the Consultative Parties, such acknowledgement shall be recorded in a Decision of the ATCM and be notified by the host Government to the acceding state.

5. The procedure set out in paragraphs 1 to 4 above may be modified only by a unanimous decision of Consultative Parties.

6. The decision of the First Special Consultative Meeting (1977) and Decision 2 (1997) shall cease to be operative.

7. The Guidelines on Notification with respect to Consultative Status agreed at the XIVth ATCM shall remain unchanged.

Resolution 7 (2005): Biological Prospecting in Antarctica

The Representatives,

Convinced of the benefits of scientific research in the field of biological prospecting for the progress of humankind;

Recalling Article III(1)(c) of the Antarctic Treaty, which provides that scientific observations and results from Antarctica shall be exchanged and made freely available;

Recalling the Protocol on Environmental Protection to the Antarctic Treaty, including Article 2, as well as Article 3, which provides for the regulation of activities in the Antarctic Treaty area to be planned and conducted so as to limit adverse impacts on the Antarctic environment and dependent and associated ecosystems;

Bearing in mind ongoing discussions in other international fora on aspects of biological prospecting, including efforts to develop and clarify the nature and definition of such activities;

Reaffirming the importance of Article III(1) of the Antarctic Treaty with regard to scientific activities relating to biological prospecting, in that, to the greatest extent feasible and practicable:

(a) information regarding plans for scientific programs in Antarctica shall be exchanged to permit maximum economy and efficiency of operations;

(b) scientific personnel shall be exchanged in Antarctica between expeditions and stations;

(c) scientific observations and results from Antarctica shall be exchanged and made freely available;

Recommend that:

1. their governments draw to the attention of their national Antarctic programmes and other research institutes engaged in Antarctic biological prospecting activities the provisions of Article III(1) of the Antarctic Treaty;

2. their governments continue to keep under review the question of biological prospecting in the Antarctic Treaty Area, and exchange on an annual basis information and views relating to that question as appropriate.

Resolution 1 (2006): CCAMLR in the Antarctic Treaty System

The Representatives,

Recalling the prime responsibilities of the Antarctic Treaty Consultative Parties for the protection and preservation of the Antarctic environment and, in particular, their responsibilities under Article IX, paragraph 1 (f) of the Antarctic Treaty in respect of the preservation and conservation of living resources in Antarctica;

Conscious that the Convention on the Conservation of Antarctic Marine Living Resources is an integral part of the Antarctic Treaty System;

Further recalling that the objective of the Convention is the conservation of Antarctic marine living resources, which includes rational use;

Noting the commitment of all Contracting Parties to the Convention on the Conservation of Antarctic Marine Living Resources that they will not engage in any activities in the Antarctic Treaty area contrary to the principles and purposes of the Treaty and their acceptance of the obligations contained in Articles I, IV, V and VI of the Treaty;

Further noting the desirability of ensuring representation by states at the Antarctic Treaty Consultative Meeting and meetings of the Commission for the Conservation of Antarctic Marine Living Resources that reflects appropriate expertise of the Antarctic Treaty System;

Welcoming the endorsement by the Commission for the Conservation of Antarctic Marine Living Resources at its 24th annual meeting of the Scientific Committee's advice arising from the 2005 Workshop on Marine Protected Areas;

Recalling also Decision 9 (2005);

Recommend that the Parties:

1. regularly at the Antarctic Treaty Consultative Meetings reflect upon the contribution made by the Commission for the Conservation of Antarctic Marine Living Resources to the Antarctic Treaty System, including in respect of the conservation and protection of the Antarctic environment;

2. encourage increased cooperation at the practical level between the Antarctic Treaty Consultative Meeting and the Commission for the Conservation of Antarctic Marine Living Resources.

Resolution 4 (2007): Ship-based Tourism in the Antarctic Treaty Area

The Representatives,

Concerned by the potential impacts that the increase of tourist activities may have on the Antarctic environment, including its wildlife, and on the conduct of scientific research;

Concerned also about recent incidents involving vessels in the Antarctic Treaty area;

Desiring to promote the safety of life at sea and the protection of the environment in the Antarctic Treaty area;

Desiring also to minimize the likelihood of marine oil spills due to incidents involving large tourist vessels in Antarctica;

Recommend that:

Parties, consistent with their national law,

1. discourage or decline to authorize tour operators that use vessels carrying more than 500 passengers from making any landings in Antarctica; and
2. encourage or require tour operators to:
   (a) coordinate with each other such that not more than one tourist vessel is at a landing site at any one time;
   (b) restrict the number of passengers on shore at any one time to 100 or fewer, unless otherwise specified in applicable ATCM Measures or Resolutions; and
   (c) maintain a minimum 1:20 guide-to-passenger ratio while ashore, unless otherwise specified in applicable ATCM Measures or Resolutions.

Resolution 5 (2007): Tourism in the Antarctic Treaty Area

The Representatives,

Conscious of the rapid expansion and diversification of tourism activities in the Antarctic Treaty area;

Recalling the Environmental Principles contained in Article 3 of the Protocol on Environmental Protection to the Antarctic Treaty;

Desiring to limit the potential impacts of tourism activities, including cumulative impacts, upon the Antarctic environment;

Recommend that the Parties discourage any tourism activities which may substantially contribute to the long-term degradation of the Antarctic environment and its dependent and associated ecosystems.

Resolution 6 (2008): Enhancing the Role of Maritime Rescue Coordination Centres with Search and Rescue Regions in the Antarctic Treaty Area

The Representatives,

Concerned at the risk of a serious humanitarian and environmental maritime incident in the Antarctic Treaty Area;

Recalling the work of the International Maritime Organisation in producing guidelines relating to maritime search and rescue issues;

Recognising the important role of the five Rescue Coordination Centres with Search and Rescue Regions in the Antarctic Treaty Area in coordinating responses to search and rescue incidents;

Recommend that:

Their Governments, in accordance with their national laws, encourage operators of tourist vessels to:

1. consider the International Maritime Organisation's *"Enhanced contingency planning guidance for passenger ships operating in areas remote from SAR facilities"* (MSC.1/ Circ/1184) in planning their activities; and
2. in particular, report their vessel positions on a regular basis to the relevant regional Maritime Rescue Coordination Centres while operating within the Antarctic Treaty Area.

Measure 15 (2009): Landing of Persons from Passenger Vessels in the Antarctic Treaty Area

The Representatives,

Noting the increasing trend in tourist activities in the Treaty area and the possible impacts of such activities on the Antarctic environment, including its wildlife, and on the conduct of scientific research;

Conscious of their responsibilities to ensure that tourism is conducted in a safe and environmentally responsible manner consistent with the objectives of the Antarctic Treaty;

Acknowledging the tourism industry's collaboration in efforts to ensure that its activities are sustainable and compatible with the objectives of the Antarctic Treaty;

Aware of hazards confronting passenger vessels operating in the Antarctic Treaty area and desiring to promote the safety of life at sea;

Wishing to minimize the likelihood of marine oil spills due to incidents involving large tourist vessels in Antarctica;

Recalling Resolution 4 (2007);

Recalling the existence of resolutions which set site-specific recommendations;

Recommend to their Governments the following Measure for approval in accordance with paragraph 4 of Article IX of the Antarctic Treaty:

That:

1. Parties shall require their operators organizing tourist or other non-governmental activities in the Antarctic Treaty area, for which advance notification is required in accordance with Article VII(5) of the Antarctic Treaty,
   a. to refrain from making any landings in Antarctica from vessels carrying more than 500 passengers unless a lower number is otherwise specified in applicable ATCM measures; and
   b. in the case of vessels carrying 500 or fewer passengers,
      i. to coordinate with each other with the objective that not more than one tourist vessel is at a landing site at any one time;
      ii. to restrict the number of passengers on shore at any one time to 100 or fewer, unless a lower number is otherwise specified in applicable ATCM Measures and to maintain a 1:20 guide-to-passenger ratio, unless a more restrictive ratio is otherwise specified in applicable ATCM measures.
2. nothing in this Measure shall derogate from the rights and obligations of any Party with respect to environmental impact assessments and restrictions on the activities of their nationals in accordance with Article 8 and other relevant provisions of the Protocol on Environmental Protection to the Antarctic Treaty.
3. this Measure, including the specific restrictions in paragraph 1 above, shall be subject to further discussion in future ATCMs to take account of possible changes in circumstance, including with respect to specific sites in Antarctica.

Resolution 2 (2009): Role and Place of COMNAP in the Antarctic Treaty System

The Representatives,

Noting that, in 1989, the Council of Managers of National Antarctic Programs (COMNAP) evolved from a permanent SCAR working group on Antarctic logistics as an important mechanism for cooperation of the Parties,

Further noting that Rules 2, 3 and 31 of the Rules of Procedure for meetings held pursuant to Article IX of the Antarctic Treaty provide that COMNAP attends these meetings as an observer,

Noting the adoption by COMNAP of its new Constitution at XX COMNAP Meeting (Saint Petersburg, Russia, July 2008),

Emphasizing the important contribution of COMNAP in establishing and developing effective collaboration among National Antarctic programs,

Recommend that the Parties continue to recognize the importance of COMNAP as a body supporting the Antarctic Treaty Parties and promoting close cooperation among the National Antarctic programs.

Resolution 7 (2009): General Principles of Antarctic Tourism

Considering the increase in visitation to Antarctica which has taken place since the adoption of the Environmental Protocol and the potential for further expansion;

Committed to the comprehensive protection of the Antarctic environment;

Aware of the responsibilities of the Antarctic Treaty Parties to ensure that all activities undertaken in Antarctica are pre-planned to minimise any impact on the Antarctic environment;

Committed also to ensuring that all activities undertaken in Antarctica are conducted as safely as possible;

Recalling a range of previous instruments in relation to tourism and non-Governmental activities in Antarctica, including *inter alia* Recommendation XVIII-1 *Tourism and Non-Governmental Activities*, Measure 4 (2004) *Insurance and Contingency Planning for Tourism and Non-Governmental Activities in the Antarctic Treaty Area*, Resolution 4 (2004) *Guidelines on Contingency Planning, Insurance and Other Matters for Tourist and Other Non-Governmental Activities in the Antarctic Treaty Area*, Resolution 4 (2007) *Ship-based Tourism in the Antarctic Treaty Area* and Resolution 5 (2007) *Tourism in the Antarctic Treaty Area*;

Recognising that properly managed tourism can enhance public appreciation of the intrinsic values of Antarctica;

The Representatives, on the occasion of the 50th Anniversary of the Antarctic Treaty,

Recommend that the following general principles be used to inform and guide further work in managing Antarctic tourism activities.

General Principles:

- All tourism activities undertaken in Antarctica will be conducted in accordance with the Antarctic Treaty, its Protocol on Environmental Protection, and relevant ATCM Measures and Resolutions;
- Tourism should not be allowed to contribute to the long-term degradation of the Antarctic environment and its dependent and associated ecosystems, or the intrinsic natural wilderness and historical values of Antarctica. In the absence of adequate information about potential impacts, decisions on tourism should be based on a pragmatic and precautionary approach, that also incorporates an evaluation of risks;
- Scientific research should be accorded priority in relation to all tourism activities in Antarctica;

- Antarctic Treaty Parties should implement all existing instruments relating to tourism and non-Governmental activities in Antarctica and aim to ensure, as far as practicable, that they continue to proactively develop regulations relating to tourism activities that should provide for a consistent framework for the management of tourism;
- All operators conducting tourism activities in Antarctica should be encouraged to cooperate with each other and with the Antarctic Treaty Parties to coordinate tourism activities and share best practice on environmental and safety management issues;
- All tourism organisations should be encouraged to provide a focus on the enrichment and education of visitors about the Antarctic environment and its protection.

Resolution 9 (2009): Collection and Use of Antarctic Biological Material

The Representatives,

Recalling Resolution 7 (2005) on Biological Prospecting in Antarctica;

Convinced of the benefits for the progress of humankind of scientific research in the Antarctic Treaty area;

Recalling also that the Antarctic Treaty at Article II provides for the freedom of scientific investigation in Antarctica, and at Article III(1)(c) provides that to the greatest extent feasible and practicable, scientific observations and results from Antarctica shall be exchanged and made freely available;

Recalling further that the Protocol on Environmental Protection to the Antarctic Treaty provides for the regulation of scientific activities relating to the collection of biological material, consistent with the overarching principles of Article 3, and the means to promote these principles including the environmental impact assessment process of Annex I, the provisions for the conservation of Antarctic fauna and flora set out in Annex II and the area protection and management arrangements of Annex V;

Noting the role of the Convention on the Conservation of Antarctic Marine Living Resources in the conservation, including rational use, of marine living resources south of the Antarctic Convergence, in particular the capacity to regulate harvesting of marine living resources;

Recommend that their Governments:

1. reaffirm that the Antarctic Treaty System is the appropriate framework for managing the collection of biological material in the Antarctic Treaty area and for considering its use;
2. emphasize that existing Antarctic Treaty system arrangements under the Protocol on Environmental Protection and the Convention on the Conservation of Antarctic Marine Living Resources address the environmental aspects of scientific research and the collection of biological material in the Antarctic region; and
3. keep matters raised under Antarctic Treaty Consultative Meeting Agenda Item 17 *Biological Prospecting in Antarctica* under active consideration within the Antarctic Treaty system, including in relation to obligations under Article III(1)(c) of the Treaty.

Resolution 6 (2010): Improving the Co-ordination of Maritime Search and Rescue in the Antarctic Treaty Area

The Representatives,

Aware of the increase in vessel traffic, in particular passenger vessel traffic, in the Antarctic Treaty area;

Concerned about the possible risk of accidents involving these ships and the resulting harm to both persons and the environment;

Recalling the work of the International Maritime Organization (IMO) in the field of maritime safety and rescue;

Recalling the key outcomes and recommendations from the COMNAP Antarctic SAR Workshop I (Valparaíso, 2008) and the COMNAP Antarctic SAR Workshop II (Buenos Aires, 2009);

Recalling the work of the Antarctic Treaty Meeting of Experts on Management of Ship-borne tourism (Wellington, 2009);

Recalling Measure 4 (2004) and Resolution 6 (2008);

Recognising the value and importance of the search and rescue systems and procedures established under the auspices of the IMO, in particular as regards the network of Search and Rescue Regions and the corresponding Maritime Rescue Coordination Centres (MRCC);

Noting that these MRCCs have systems able to maintain the confidentiality of information transmitted by vessels and collected by the Centres;

Wishing to improve the coordination of maritime search and rescue efforts in the Antarctic Treaty area;

Recommend:

That their Governments recognise the importance of ensuring the effectiveness of search and rescue efforts by:

1. placing on the Antarctic Treaty Secretariat ("the Secretariat") website regular and up-to-date search and rescue related information, using the most appropriate technical means (eg, through the Electronic Information Exchange System – EIES), of coastal stations facilities as well as the availability of sea and air assets in the Antarctic Treaty area;

2. making available in advance vessel schedules of national Antarctic programmes and tourist operators to the Secretariat (eg, through the EIES) which then would be available to all MRCC to access; and

3. encouraging national Antarctic programmes and operators of tourist vessels not participating in the COMNAP and IAATO vessel tracking schemes to report the positions of their vessels regularly to the relevant regional MRCC.

Resolution 7 (2010): Enhancement of Port State Control for Passenger Vessels Bound for the Antarctic Treaty Area

The Representatives,

Recalling Resolution 8 (2009) regarding a Mandatory shipping code for vessels operating in Antarctic waters;

Welcoming the start of work by the International Maritime Organization in February 2010 on a mandatory International Code of safety for ships operating in polar waters (Polar Code);

Acknowledging the duties of the flag State as set out in article 94 of the United Nations Convention on the Law of the Sea which include *inter alia* the taking of such measures for vessels flying its flag as are necessary to ensure safety at sea;

Noting articles 218 and 219 of the United Nations Convention on the Law of the Sea regarding Enforcement by port States and Measures relating to seaworthiness of vessels to avoid pollution;

Recalling the requirements of the International Convention on the Safety of Life at Sea (SOLAS) 1974; the International Convention for the Prevention of Pollution from Ships 1973, as modified by the Protocol of 1978 relating thereto (MARPOL); the International Convention on Standards of Training, Certification and Watchkeeping for Seafarers (STCW) 1978; and the Protocol on Environmental Protection to the Antarctic Treaty;

Conscious that many passenger vessels operating in the Antarctic Treaty area are not flagged to States which are Parties to the Antarctic Treaty or to its Protocol on Environmental Protection;

Concerned about recent incidents involving passenger vessels in the Antarctic Treaty area;

Recommend:

That the Parties proactively apply, through their national maritime authorities, the existing regime of port State control to passenger vessels bound for the Antarctic Treaty area.

Resolution 1 (2011): Strengthening Support for the Protocol on Environmental Protection to the Antarctic Treaty

The Representatives,

Recalling the Protocol on Environmental Protection to the Antarctic Treaty adopted on 4 October 1991 (the Protocol);

Convinced of the continuing need for comprehensive protection of the Antarctic environment and dependent and associated ecosystems;

Reaffirming their will to protect the Antarctic environment, in the interest of mankind as a whole and to preserve the value of Antarctica as an area for the conduct of scientific research;

Reaffirming the objectives and principles contained in the Antarctic Treaty and its Protocol, the Convention for the Conservation of Antarctic Marine Living Resources and the Convention for the Conservation of Antarctic Seals;

Convinced that the Protocol has, since its entry into force, contributed to ensuring a high level of protection of the Antarctic environment;

Welcoming the work of the Committee for Environmental Protection (the Committee), and noting that all Parties to the Protocol are entitled to participate in the Committee;

Convinced that the achievement of the objectives and principles of the Protocol will be better ensured if the Protocol is supported by a larger number of States;

Recommend that their Governments:

1. appeal to States that are Antarctic Treaty Parties but not yet Party to the Protocol on Environmental Protection to the Antarctic Treaty, to become Party to the Protocol;
2. accept the offer by France, Australia and Spain to coordinate with other Consultative Parties on representations to these States; and
3. invite France, Australia and Spain to report on the outcome of these representations at the Antarctic Treaty Consultative Meeting XXXV.

Decision 1 (2012): Measures on Operational Matters Designated as No Longer Current

The Representatives,

Recalling Decision 3 (2002), Decision 1 (2007) and Decision 1 (2011), which established lists of measures[16] that were designated as spent or no longer current;

Having reviewed a number of measures on the subject of operational matters;

Recognising that the measures listed in the Annex to this Decision are no longer current;

Decide:

1. that the measures listed in the Annex to this Decision require no further action by the Parties; and
2. to request the Secretariat of the Antarctic Treaty to post the text of the measures that appear in the Annex to this Decision on its website in a way that makes clear that these measures are no longer current and that the Parties do not need to take any further action with respect to them.

Annex: Measures on Operational Matters Designated as No Longer Current

1. Telecommunications

- Recommendation III-V
- Recommendation VI-2

2. Logistics

- Recommendation IX-4

[16] Note: measures previously adopted under Article IX of the Antarctic Treaty were described as Recommendations up to ATCM XIX (1995) and were divided into Measures, Decisions and Resolutions by Decision 1 (1995).

3. Shipping regulations
- Decision 2 (1999)
- Decision 8 (2005)
- Decision 2 (2006)
- Resolution 8 (2009)

Resolution 2 (2012): Cooperation on Questions Related to the Exercise of Jurisdiction in the Antarctic Treaty Area

The Representatives,

Recalling Article IX(1)(e) of the Antarctic Treaty, which provides that Contracting Parties consult on "questions relating to the exercise of jurisdiction in Antarctica";

Convinced of the necessity to consider such questions with respect to human activities and incidents occurring in the Antarctic Treaty area;

Noting the increase of human activities in the Antarctic Treaty area;

Acknowledging the need to promote compliance with law in the Antarctic Treaty area;

Recognising the unique challenges, both practical and legal, of law enforcement in the Antarctic Treaty area;

Recommend that:

the Parties cooperate to institute discussion on issues related to the exercise of jurisdiction in the Antarctic Treaty area.

Resolution 3 (2012): Improving Cooperation in Antarctica

The Representatives,

Recalling the centrality of scientific cooperation in the Antarctic Treaty and its Protocol on Environmental Protection;

Recognising, with appreciation, the contributions of the Scientific Committee on Antarctic Research and the Council of Managers of National Antarctic Programmes to scientific and logistical cooperation among the Antarctic Treaty Parties;

Convinced of the need to promote broader Antarctic cooperation beyond scientific and logistical cooperation to facilitate and strengthen the work of the Parties in the implementation of the Antarctic Treaty system;

Convinced that sharing of knowledge, experience and technical support will help Parties at an earlier stage in their Antarctic development to achieve a higher level of compliance with their obligations;

Acknowledging that further cooperation will better equip Parties to respond to the multiple challenges posed by Antarctic activities;

Recommend that:

the Parties and other Antarctic Treaty Consultative Meeting participants conduct a discussion on promoting broader Antarctic cooperation.

Resolution 7 (2012): Vessel Safety in the Antarctic Treaty Area

The Representatives,

Recalling the Protocol on Environmental Protection to the Antarctic Treaty and Resolution 1 (2004), which strongly supported "the progress achieved by CCAMLR Resolution 20/XXII urging its Members, which are harvesting in high Antarctic latitudes, to license only those fishing vessels with at least an ice classification standard of ICE-1C";

Convinced of the continuing need for comprehensive protection of the Antarctic environment and dependent and associated ecosystems;

Registering concern about the continued occurrence of incidents involving stricken fishing vessels licensed by Members of the Commission for the Conservation of Antarctic Marine Living Resources ("CCAMLR") in the Antarctic region;

Noting the role of the International Maritime Organization ("IMO") with regard to vessel safety internationally;

Further recalling actions taken by CCAMLR to support the IMO in relation to the activities of fishing vessels operating in the Southern Ocean;

Reaffirming the role of the Antarctic Treaty Consultative Meeting to promote the protection of the Antarctic environment in the Antarctic Treaty area;

Recommend that their Governments:

1. continue to work on the International Maritime Organization mandatory code for ships operating in Polar waters and participate in the forthcoming negotiations on the Agreement on the Torremolinos Protocol;
2. consider appropriate measures to enhance the safety standards of fishing vessels that are flagged to Parties and that operate in the Antarctic Treaty area;
3. report annually to the Committee for Environmental Protection on responses to environmental emergencies involving vessels that are flagged to Parties and that operate in the Antarctic Treaty area in accordance with Article 17 of the Protocol on Environmental Protection to the Antarctic Treaty;
4. remind the operators of their flagged fishing vessels of the IMO Global Search and Rescue Plan and, specifically, to urge Members of the Commission for the Conservation of Antarctic Marine Living Resources to provide or encourage fishing vessels under their flag to make available their contact details and other relevant information to the responsible Maritime Rescue Coordination Centre in advance of entering the Antarctic Treaty area in line with CCAMLR Resolution 33/XXX; and
5. encourage CCAMLR Members to implement CCAMLR Resolution 20/XXII, which calls on Members to license only those fishing vessels with a minimum ice classification standard ICE-1C to operate within the Antarctic Treaty area.

Resolution 9 (2012): The Assessment of Land-Based Expeditionary Activities

The Representatives,

Concerned that poorly planned and executed land-based activities, particularly those undertaken in remote areas of Antarctica, have the potential to present risks to safety of life;

Concerned also to ensure that activities in remote and less well-studied areas of Antarctica do not have any adverse impacts on unique environmental attributes;

Recalling the Environmental Principles contained in Article 3 of the Protocol on Environmental Protection to the Antarctic Treaty;

Recalling also Resolution 3 (2004), Resolution 4 (2004), Resolution 5 (2007) and Resolution 7 (2009);

Noting the increasing interest in land-based expeditionary activities, particularly as a result of the recent centenaries of Amundsen and Scott's expeditions to the South Pole of 1911/12;

Desiring to ensure that all such activities are assessed in a consistent and thorough way, in respect of their environmental, safety and operational procedures;

Recommend that:

the Parties, consistent with their national law and as they consider appropriate, utilise the attached *Questions to consider as part of the authorisation or comparable regulatory process for non-Governmental land-based activities in Antarctica* when assessing proposed land-based expeditionary activities to be undertaken in Antarctica.

Annex: Questions to Consider as Part of the Authorisation Process for Non-Governmental Land-Based Activities in Antarctica

In undertaking domestic procedures to assess potential non-Governmental land-based activities in Antarctica, Competent Authorities may find it helpful to consider the following list of questions. The overall aim of the list is to underpin the consideration of land-based activities to ensure full compliance with the Protocol on Environmental Protection and other relevant ATCM instruments, including Measure 4(2004), Resolution 4(2004), Resolution 7(2009) and Resolution 3(2011), as appropriate.

The list of questions is neither exhaustive nor prescriptive and is intended for guidance purposes only. Not all of the questions will be relevant to every land-based activity, and the requirements of those operating regularly in Antarctica will clearly be different to those conducting one-off activities. Each Party's Competent Authority will determine how it wishes to utilise this list of questions to consider in each case.

General Environmental Issues

Overarching issues, likely relevant to all land-based activities:

- Are the proposed activities, in terms of scale (eg, number of participants, duration and extent of operational area) and type (ie, what is specifically planned), consistent with the Environmental Principles set out in Article 3 of the Environmental Protocol?
- Has the Environmental Impact Assessment (EIA) been developed in accordance with the Guidelines appended to Resolution 4(2005) and does it cover all of the activities to be undertaken whilst in Antarctica, including those of any other operator contracted to, or working with, the organisers of the activities, where these other operators are not already authorised by another Treaty Party? Does the EIA include any alternative activities that may be offered because of weather restrictions etc? In all cases, have the environmental risks been identified and appropriate mitigation measures planned?
- Does the Environmental Impact Assessment specify clearly defined geographic boundaries within which all of the proposed activities will take place, taking into account contingency plans and potential alternative operating areas (including the location of any field camps, storage facilities or depots, or the route of any traverses)? Are the organisers (or the Competent Authority) aware of what other activities might also be planned to take place simultaneously in this area, and how will any potential cumulative effects be assessed and considered? Are activities known to have previously taken place in the area or is it, as far as known, a pristine area? Is the proposed activity a one-off event or is it likely to be repeated in the foreseeable future in the same location?
- Can the organisers of the proposed activities demonstrate a good understanding of the environmental conditions of the full area of proposed operation, for example, through prior experience, or through seeking the advice of relevant experts? Are there any Antarctic Specially Protected Areas (ASPAs), Antarctic Specially Managed Areas (ASMAs) and Historic Sites and Monuments (HSMs) in proximity to their intended activities?
- Have the proposed activities been planned in accordance with *Guidance for those organising and conducting tourism and non-Governmental activities in the Antarctic* (Recommendation XVIII-1(1994))? Are plans in place to ensure that those planning to undertake the activities in Antarctica are fully aware of the *General Guidelines for Visitors to the Antarctic* (Resolution 3(2011)); and *Non-native Species Manual* (Resolution 2(2011))?
- Are the proposed management practices for waste and sewage appropriate for the scale and location of the proposed activities; particularly plans for discarding waste from travelling activities (paying particular attention to the likelihood of temporary camps being dismantled quickly)?
- Do contingency plans include provision for the removal of all equipment in the case of accident or damage to equipment, or in the event of an emergency evacuation?

- Have appropriate measures been identified to avoid introductions of non-native species, both by the members of the expeditions, and by their logistical support operator, if different?

Specific issues, to be considered as relevant:

- Are detailed fuel handling, storage procedures, and spill avoidance measures in place, including any specific procedures where fuel is to be transported long distances, or where vehicles and aircraft are to be refuelled on the ice? (The COMNAP Fuel Manual 2008 may be useful in assessing such measures);
- If vehicle use is proposed, what measures have been taken to demonstrate its appropriateness for the proposed area of operation? Are vehicles proposed to be used in any areas not covered by snow or ice, and if so, what is the potential risk of more than minor or transitory impacts (eg, visible tracks remaining after the activity is completed)?

Contingency Plans (including Search and Rescue and Medical Evacuation)

Overarching issues, likely relevant to all land-based activities:

- Have the proposed activities been planned in accordance with Measure 4(2004) and/or paragraph 1 of Resolution 4(2004), such as to ensure that appropriate contingency plans and appropriate arrangements for health and safety, search and rescue, and medical care and evacuation are in place? Do these contingency plans cover, in particular, weather-related implications, medical emergencies, and equipment failures?
- Can the organisers demonstrate adequate insurance or other arrangements to cover the costs associated with search and rescue and medical care and evacuation, in line with Measure 4(2004) and paragraph 2 of Resolution 4(2004)? Do all insurance policies make specific reference to Antarctica and the types of activities for which the policy/arrangements cover – for both the organisers, and all participants?
- Have the organisers developed a sufficiently detailed risk assessment for the activities proposed, in terms of search and rescue and evacuation (ie, identification of possible scenarios requiring search and rescue and/or evacuation, and clear plans as to how this would be enacted under each scenario)?
- Has radio linkage between each component of the activity (vehicles, groups, medical and/or logistical staff etc), with base camp and with organisers outside Antarctica been prepared and successfully tested?

Specific issues, to be considered as relevant:

- Where activities are planned to take place away from a base camp, are clear agreed protocols in place for regular (eg, at least once per day) reporting to base camp or to a designated contact elsewhere (including whether all necessary communication and location equipment and back-ups will be provided for prior at the beginning of the activities)? Is there a maximum proximity between base camp and the activities to be supported, and is this appropriate? Will search and rescue operations be automatically commenced if no communication is received after an agreed period of time? For travelling activities, will a continuous record of the last known (and regular) location of participants be kept?

Health and Safety of those undertaking the activities

- Do the organisers, or appointed leaders of the activities in Antarctica if different, have previous experience of operating in Antarctica (or other similar environments, combined with a clear understanding of the different conditions and requirements of Antarctica)? What safety equipment will they have available and is this appropriate for the type and scale of the proposed operation?
- Have the organisers identified the potential health and safety risks arising from their activities in Antarctica, and, if appropriate, will all potential participants be medically assessed for their physical aptitude to carry out the planned activities?
- Have standard operating procedures been developed for accidents and emergencies, health and safety and the provision of medical first aid? What medical equipment will they have available?

- As appropriate: what will the ratio be of medically and specialist polar trained staff/instructors to novice, or less experienced participants – is this appropriate and does it provide for continuous cover throughout the duration of the proposed activity?; or for remote activities, what will the arrangements be for ensuring timely access to medical assistance?

Specific issues, to be considered as relevant:

- Can the organisers of any potential activities to be undertaken in Antarctica without the supervision or support of an experienced operator demonstrate full compliance with paragraphs 3–7 of the Guidelines appended as Annex 1 to Resolution 4(2004)?
- For supervised/supported group activities which will involve participants engaging in endurance or highly physical activities (assessed relative to the abilities of the participants), what specific prior training and preparation will be undertaken, and will this be for <u>all</u> participants (for example, in line with paragraphs 3, 5 and 6 of Annex I of Resolution 4(2004), even where there are also on-site guides present?
- For supervised/supported group activities which will involve participants engaging in endurance or highly physical activities (assessed relative to the abilities of the participants), what arrangements will be in place for regular monitoring of the well-being of participants (eg, for races, this might be at a series of checkpoints)? Are formal procedures in place for the withdrawal or removal of participants on medical grounds?
- For travelling activities, is there a general agreed pre-planned (fixed) route (with contingencies), and if so, has there been reconnaissance and mapping of these routes (with particular emphasis on the location of crevasses and other natural hazards)? Are the organisers aware of recent meteorological data across the proposed routes?
- Where vehicles (including all wheeled, tracked or skied machinery, both powered or unpowered, eg, cars, snow mobiles, quad bikes, 'tractor trains') are to be used, what modifications have been made for Antarctic conditions, for example, will they be fitted with ground radar and other navigational equipment, and are the vehicle operators appropriately trained in the use of such equipment? Is the number of vehicles sufficient to support the proposed activities and what appropriate spare parts will be carried?
- Has the loss of one or more vehicles been taken into account and would such an event endanger lives?

Liaison with other Competent Authorities and Treaty Parties

- In line with Resolution 3(2004), what contact has been made with other national authorities that may have an interest in the activities (eg, sub-contractors, participants etc)?
- Will the proposed activities be taking place in proximity to known scientific research locations, or scientific stations? What contact has been made with relevant National Antarctic Programmes?

Education and Outreach

- How will the activities focus on the enrichment and education of visitors, before and during the period in Antarctica, in line with Resolution 7(2009)?
- Have the organisers fully considered whether, and how, the activities will generate a wider interest in the protection of Antarctica, for example, through education and outreach etc?

Resolution 10 (2012): Yachting Guidelines

The Representatives,

Recalling Resolution 1 (2003) regarding the provision of advice to yacht and vessel operators about the Protocol on Environmental Protection to the Antarctic Treaty;

Recalling the work of the Antarctic Treaty Meeting of Experts on Management of Ship-borne tourism (Wellington, 2009);

Concerned about the safety of vessels in the Southern Ocean and the possible risk of accidents involving these vessels and the resulting harm to both persons and the environment;

Desiring to bring forward safety issues for yacht operators and private sailors, to promote good practices and to further protect the environment;

Recommend that:

1. consistent with their national law and as they consider appropriate, the Parties utilise the attached *Checklist of yacht specific items for preparing safe Antarctic voyages* when assessing proposed yacht visits to Antarctica;

2. the Antarctic Treaty Secretariat (the Secretariat) place *Yachting Guidelines for Antarctic Cruises,* as discussed by the Antarctic Treaty Consultative Meeting, on its website;

3. the Parties provide details to the Secretariat, to enable it to maintain on its website in conjunction with the *Yachting Guidelines for Antarctic Cruises*:

(a) contact details of national competent authorities; and

(b) details of relevant Maritime Rescue Co-ordination Centres; and

4. the Parties urge all those intending to undertake a yacht visit to Antarctica to take into account in planning their voyage the *Checklist of yacht specific items for preparing safe Antarctic voyages* and, as appropriate, the *Yachting Guidelines for Antarctic Cruises.*

Annex: Checklist of Yacht Specific Items for Preparing Safe Antarctic Voyages

Preamble

Antarctica is one of the most remote and demanding cruising areas in the world's oceans. Weather conditions can be extreme, ice can pose a danger at any time and limited external assistance is available should things go wrong. Any yacht expedition heading south of 60°S needs enhanced planning and preparations and should be crewed by experienced yachtsmen.

The intention of the checklist is to support those planning yacht operations, and to provide guidance as to appropriate standards for Antarctic yacht operation. The safety of a yacht and her crew is the sole and inescapable responsibility of the person in charge who must do his best to ensure that the yacht is fully equipped, thoroughly seaworthy and manned by an experienced crew who have undergone appropriate training and are physically fit to face bad weather and the general conditions of sailing in the Antarctic which can be subject to rapid change.

Yachts heading towards Antarctica must be completely self-sufficient for very extended periods of time, capable of withstanding heavy storms and prepared to meet serious emergencies without the expectation of outside assistance. The materials used in the relevant areas of the vessel structure should provide adequate toughness and ductility to minimise the risk of structure failure due to impact or crushing, brittle failure and other causes. Yachts should be prepared for being "knocked down" and also for encountering extreme weather and sea conditions.

These checklist items for use by stakeholders do not replace, but rather supplement, the requirements of governmental authority, flag states or international regulations. All yachts are to comply with all relevant IMO regulations under SOLAS and MARPOL and with all relevant provisions under the Environmental Protocol and ATCM Resolutions and also appropriate national requirements.

Personal preparation

- Ensure good knowledge and understanding of the appropriate environmental protocols and regulations in the Antarctic Treaty System
- Consideration should be given to visiting Antarctic waters during Austral summer months and preferably areas with low ice concentration to avoid hazards. Only experienced and highly prepared crews should consider voyages outside the Austral summer or to an area outside the more commonly visited areas
- Review appropriate web sites (of national governments, IAATO, IMO, Antarctic Treaty System recommended sites) and other sources of information about the Antarctic, eg, specialised technical publications
- Risk assessments for all planned activities should be provided beforehand
- Finding anchoring/mooring sites that offer shelter from wind, waves/tides, and moving ice

can be a challenge. Consult appropriate publications and Antarctic sailing experts to identify suitable locations within the area in which you intend to cruise

- Experience, training and knowledge are the basis for pre-expedition decisions:
  - Involve experienced yachtsmen particularly of sailing in high latitudes
  - Ensure absolute self sufficiency for at least two weeks in excess of planned trip duration when operating south of 60 degrees: This includes comprehensive spares, tools and, most importantly, the ability to fit/use them. Carry a reserve of enough food, drinking water and fuel
  - Consideration needs to be given to the fact that Antarctica is a large area remote from search and rescue services and that responders may take days or weeks to find the location
  - Don't rely only on maps and charts-based GPS positioning
  - Detailed study of the nautical charts of the area considered to be sailed
  - Update information on rescue coordination centre responsibilities and contact those early
  - First aid equipment training for crew members verified by necessary certifications
  - All crew and passengers should be comprehensively briefed on vessel operations, safety procedures, environmental considerations and bio-security
  - Specific training for crew members in ship and sailing techniques relevant for high latitude operations (eg, ISAF Sea Survival Course). Particularly courses including "Navigation in icy waters" and "Sailing with severe weather conditions" would be an advantage as well as personal experience
- Reports/ Information:
  - Appropriate procedures based on domestic legislations, including reporting to competent authorities, must be taken prior to the departure towards Antarctica
  - Provide to your authorising government agency the details they require for advance notification of your activity (dates and places of the planned expedition) to include that information in EIES
  - Inform the appropriate MRCC of your intended voyage route, vessel details, equipment carried, and personnel on board; provide, if possible, the vessel's position at 08:00 and 20:00 hours to a MRCC or, alternatively, to a ship located nearby that can relay this information to MRCC
  - Post visit report to permitting authorities afterwards
  - Weather and ice observations are encouraged to be reported regularly to the Voluntary Observation Programme

Technical preparation

- Vessel structure and general equipment:
  - All hull types should be strong. For yachts regularly visiting Antarctica, well-built and sturdy metal hulls should be favored. Remember that the hull should be accessible from inside for damage control purposes
  - The vessel should be stable and able to withstand extreme weather conditions and large seas. Consider the vessel's watertight integrity. Small vessels may have great difficulty in these conditions and could expect to be rolled over
  - All items onboard should be prepared for withstanding extraordinary conditions; keep them well protected not to cause damage by flying loosely around
  - Comprehensive tool kit and spare parts inventory
  - Decks should be fitted with safety harness jackstays and attachment points
  - Robust mast & rigging on sailing vessels
  - Heavy weather sails for sailing yachts (storm sails, including a tri-sail and storm jib)
  - Bolt cutters or other appropriate equipment (eg, hydraulic cutters) should be carried on sailboats in order to free a broken rig
- Antarctic specification:
  - Spotlight for ice identification at night

   - Radar
   - Multiple shore landing craft if possible
   - Means to combat icing of the vessel and rig necessary in case of freezing weather conditions
   - Cold weather treatment for fuel
   - Storm boards (storm shutters or blanking plates) with the ability to replace, cover or repair any hatch or opening
- Anchoring and mooring:
   - Multiple sets of anchoring equipment and cables should be carried, suitable for the size of vessel, the type of seabed and the depth of water likely to be encountered. Possibly consider having heavier anchor(s) and chains than it is required as standard for the size of the vessel
   - Shorelines and associated equipment/ good ground tackle are recommended where their use is possible
- Communication equipment (installed on the vessel <u>and</u> portable for carriage onto a lifeboat or liferaft):
   - Long-range communications systems: satellite (Iridium, Inmarsat) and/or HF/SSB radio
   - VHF marine radio to talk to other vessels and aircraft in the event of a rescue, including portable set(s) for use off the vessel
   - Suitable means to receive weather and ice information
   - Preferably two 406 EPIRB (Emergency Position Indicating Radio Beacon)
- Rescue equipment:
   - Comprehensive first aid equipment such as a Category A kit
   - Ocean-going man-overboard marking and retrieval equipment (eg, throwable horseshoe buoys)
   - Ocean-going grade life rafts (SOLAS rafts with a SOLAS A pack), lifejackets (cp. ISO12042 part 2 275N) and survival suits and safety harnesses for at least 100% capacity; Immersion or survival suits should be carried for all onboard which are compatible with the lifejackets
   - Search and rescue transponder (SART) or GPS EPIRB to ensure that in the event of an incident, efforts can be focused upon rescue rather than search
   - Automatic Identification System (AIS) is recommended for collision avoidance as well as detection by search aircraft or ships
   - Personal Locator Beacon (PLB) or related devices, such as a Man Overboard Beacon on larger vessels, may be helpful to ease rescue operations in relation to a single person
   - Fire extinguisher and blanket
   - Flares and other pyrotechnics
   - Collision mat or similar material to be hauled over a damaged part of the hull
   - Portable spotlight
   - Tapered plugs
   - A sturdy boarding ladder or platform is highly recommended
- Other necessary equipment:
   - availability of an appropriate, relevant and up-to-date nautical chart set covering the area planned to be sailed
   - navigation system with redundancy
   - Other critical boat systems (i.e. steering, autopilot) should be robust and where possible with backup system (i.e. with redundancy)

Resolution 11 (2012): Checklist for Visitors' In-Field Activities

The Representatives,

Recalling Article VII of the Antarctic Treaty, which provides for the designation of observers to carry out inspections, and Article 14 of the Protocol on Environmental Protection to the Antarctic Treaty (the Protocol), which provides that inspections shall be arranged to promote the protection of the Antarctic environment and dependent and associated ecosystems and to ensure compliance with the Protocol;

Taking into account Resolution 5 (1995) *(Antarctic inspection checklists),* Resolution 4 (2008) *(Checklist for inspections of Antarctic Specially Protected Areas and Antarctic Specially Managed Areas),* and Resolution 3 (2010) *(Revised Antarctic inspection Checklist "A"),* which propose a number of checklists to guide the planning and conduct of inspections under Article VII of the Antarctic Treaty;

Considering Resolution 7 (2009) *(General Principles of Antarctic Tourism),* which states that Antarctic Treaty Parties aim to ensure, as far as practicable, that they continue to proactively develop regulations relating to tourism activities that should provide for a consistent framework for the management of tourism;

Reaffirming that inspection checklists are useful as guidelines for those planning and conducting inspections under Article VII of the Antarctic Treaty and in assessing implementation of the provisions of the Protocol;

Noting that inspection checklists are not mandatory and are not to be used as a questionnaire;

Recommend that:

their Governments encourage the use of the attached Checklist for visitors' in field activities.

Annex: Checklist for Visitors' In-Field Activities

The following checklist is aimed to support inspections under Article VII of the Antarctic Treaty and Article 14 of the Madrid Protocol.

The issues included in this checklist are to supplement (but not be a substitute for) information obtained from environmental assessment processes, information exchange, reports by Parties and Experts to the ATCM and CEP, and from documented industry practices and procedures (where applicable). This checklist is neither exhaustive nor prescriptive and is intended for guidance purposes only.

Except where indicated, all the information needed to reply to these questions will be obtained from on site sources (eg, interviews + field observation).

Section A. Inspection Details

1. Location (name of the site inspected)
2. Date and time of inspection visit
3. Mode of transport to the site (by sea/by air/land)
4. Name and flag of vessel (if appropriate)
5. Does the vessel comply with agreed restrictions on the number of passengers carried onboard at the site in question (in relation to Measure 15, 2009 and applicable Site guidelines for Visitors)
6. Tour/ Non-Governmental Organisation/ other operator (name, nationality)
7. Any other company involved in the operation (eg, vessel operator, tour operator, sub-charterer, providers of other services)
8. Affiliation to IAATO (yes/no)
9. Name of Expedition leader (or person in charge of disembarking visitors)
10. Duration of visit
11. Persons conducting inspection (name, nationality)

Section B. Advance Notification and other Legislation Requirements

12. Has the activity undergone authorisation / permit / environmental assessment procedures, and is a copy of the EIA available?
13. Identify if it has been single-year or multiyear, and if it covers the activities of a single-ship or company, or multiple ships and companies
14. Which Party provided the authorisation / permit / or administered the environmental assessment procedures?
15. Was the activity notified in advance to the appropriate Treaty Party?

Section C. Site Management

16. Is the area subject to particular management requirements, like Site Guidelines for Visitors, ASPA/ASMA Management Plan/Codes of Conduct, Facility's internal policies, or similar?

This information should be collected prior to the deployment of the inspection team, from off site sources, such as the ATS, IAATO and National Programmes' websites.

Section D. Information Management

17. Did the expedition party (cruise ship/aircraft/other) contact the facility (station, refuge, hut, field camp) prior to arrival in order to coordinate the visit? (if appropriate)

18. Was the Expedition leader (or person in charge of disembarking visitors) aware of the general provisions of the Antarctic Treaty and its Protocol on Environmental Protection?

19. Did visitors receive, prior to their arrival at the site, information on:

- the values present in the area, and on ways to avoid their degradation?; and on
- the contents of relevant guidelines and management instruments on Antarctic tourism? (eg, Site Guidelines for Visitors, General Guidelines for Visitors of the Antarctic, behaviour rules and commitments of Rec. XVIII-I, or ASPA/ ASMA-Management Plan)

Describe ways on which this information was transmitted (board presentation, a briefing prior to landing, a briefing immediately after landing)

Section E. Visit Description

20. Total number of visitors landed during the visit

21. Was there more than one tourist vessel at the landing site at any one time?

22. For vessel landings, what was the maximum number of passengers landed ashore at any one time? (Noting that the limit should be 100, unless a lower number is otherwise specified in applicable ATCM Measures or Site Guidelines)

23. Was the minimum ratio staff: passenger of 1:20 (unless otherwise specified in applicable ATCM Measures or Site Guidelines) maintained during visit?

24. What types of activities were carried out by visitors during their visit to the site? (eg, walks ashore, sea baths, swimming, kayaking, diving, trekking, hiking, climbing, camping, marathons, races, snowboard, skiing, hand gliding, wildlife watching, etc.)

25. Provide details of any on-ground visitor management or environmental protection measures implemented during visit (eg, temporary area markers to guide visitors, additional guides)

26. Describe in situ safety measures implemented during the visit (for example, in the event that the vessel/aircraft is not able to collect the visitors at the expected time)?

27. Were the provisions set out in any applicable ASPA/ASMA Management Plan/ Codes of Conduct, Facilities internal policies, or similar, adhered to in full?

28. Were the provisions set out in any applicable Site Guidelines for Visitors (eg, preferred landing sites, zoning schemes, behaviour ashore, precautionary notes, etc.) adhered to in full?

Section F. On Site Impacts / Conduct of Visit

29. Was any incident or evidence of direct impacts identified that was caused by visitors on the:

- site's flora and fauna?
- the landscape and wilderness values present in the site? (eg, trampling on pristine surfaces, digging bathing pits, building a cairn, graffiti on rocks, etc.)

30. Describe in-situ waste management procedures implemented during visit

31. Where appropriate, and not otherwise covered in site specific guidelines or management plans, describe how visit was managed in order to avoid impacts on historic sites and monuments (including immobile and mobile historic features) present in the site?

32. Describe procedures implemented during visit to avoid causing any disturbance to science and/or logistic operations (only applicable to visits to, *inter alia,* stations, refuges, huts, field camps)

Section G. Additional Information on Practices and Procedures to Ensure Safety and/or Environmental Protection

33. Were industry standard practices or operating procedures used (specify if so)?

34. Were guides / expedition personnel accredited according to any specific training standards? (Please, specify)

Resolution 1 (2013): Air Safety in Antarctica

The Representatives,

Recalling Recommendation XV-20 (1989);

Noting, with appreciation, the Report of the Meeting of Experts on Air Safety in Antarctica, held in Paris from 2 to 5 May 1989;

Recognising the importance of ensuring safe air operations in the Antarctic, and that the principal body of knowledge and experience of Antarctic air operations, and its current challenges, lies with the operators of national Antarctic programmes;

Desiring to contribute to air safety in Antarctica through updated recommendations;

Recommend that:

1. for the purpose of ensuring that measures for improved air safety apply to all flights in Antarctica, measures to improve air safety set out in paragraphs 2–8 below should be elaborated on the basis of ICAO criteria, taking due account of the specific features of Antarctica as well as of existing practices and services;

2. for the purpose of ensuring the safety of air operations in the Antarctic Treaty area, Parties should exchange, preferably by 1 September and no later than 15 November each year, information about their planned air operations in accordance with the standardized format of the Electronic Information Exchange System (EIES);

3. for the purpose of improving air safety in Antarctica, national Antarctic programmes operating aircraft in Antarctica and their aircrews should be provided with a continuously updated compendium produced by the Council of Managers of National Antarctic Programs (COMNAP) and now known as the COMNAP Antarctic Flight Information Manual (AFIM) describing ground facilities, aircraft (including helicopters) and aircraft operating procedures and associated communications facilities operated by each national Antarctic programme (out of the use of which questions of liability will not arise) and, therefore, they should:

(a) facilitate the ongoing revision of AFIM by their national Antarctic programme operators by collective action through COMNAP;

(b) adopt a format in which information provided by each national operator is kept in a manner that facilitates updating of information; and

(c) request their national Antarctic operators to provide information for the purpose of maintaining the AFIM.

4. for the purpose of ensuring mutual awareness of current air operations and exchanging information about them, Parties should designate:

(a) Primary Air Information Stations (PAIS) which coordinate their own air information and information from their Secondary Air Information Stations (if any) for the purpose of notifying current air operations to other PAIS. These PAIS should have adequate communication facilities able to transmit "hard copy" information by appropriate and agreed means; and

(b) Secondary Air Information Stations (SAIS) which comprise stations/bases (including field bases and ships) which provide air information to their parent coordinating PAIS;

5. for the purpose of avoiding air incidents in areas beyond the range of VHF radio coverage of primary and secondary stations, aircraft outside the areas covered by primary and secondary stations should use a specific radio frequency to apply the "TIBA" procedure laid down in Annex 11 to the Convention on International Civil Aviation;

6. so as to ensure compliance with Article VII, paragraph 5 of the Antarctic Treaty and also Recommendation X-8, Part IV, Parties should keep one another informed about non-

governmental Flights and a reminder about the AFIM should be given to all pilots filing a flight plan for flights to Antarctica;

7. so as to provide for the improved collection from, and for the exchange within Antarctica of meteorological data and information of significance to the safety of Antarctic air operations, Parties should:

(a) encourage the World Meteorological Organisation in its work towards this end;

(b) take steps to improve meteorological services available in Antarctica, specifically to meet aviation requirements; and

(c) take account of The International Antarctic Weather Forecasting Handbook;

8. for the purpose of ensuring effective communications between PAIS, the Parties should ensure that their PAIS have adequate facilities for communicating with other PAIS; and

9. Parties consider Recommendation XV-20 (1989) as no longer current.

Resolution 4 (2013): Improved Collaboration on Search and Rescue (SAR) in Antarctica

The Representatives,

Recalling Resolutions 6 (2008), 6 (2010), 7 (2012) and 8 (2012) regarding search and rescue in Antarctica;

Concerned about the tragic loss of life in several vessel incidents in Antarctica in recent years;

Noting the commitment of all Antarctic Treaty Parties to promoting safety with regard to activities taking place within the Antarctic Treaty area;

Mindful that anticipated increases in human activity in the Antarctic including national program operations, shipping, fishing and tourism, will add to the challenges and risks associated with Antarctic search and rescue (SAR) operations;

Expressing appreciation to the Antarctic Treaty Consultative Parties that operate Rescue Coordination Centres ("RCCs") with Antarctic responsibilities for the benefit of all persons in distress in their respective SAR regions;

Recognising the high level of coordination that already exists with respect to SAR in Antarctica among the RCCs with Antarctic responsibilities, including through the Council of Managers of National Antarctic Programs (COMNAP), and between the RCCs and the national Antarctic programs operating within their areas of responsibility;

Recalling the commitment of relevant Parties to the 1979 International Convention on Maritime Search and Rescue and the Convention on International Civil Aviation, Annex 12 – Search and Rescue, to cooperate in the execution of SAR missions and activities;

Noting the importance of discussions among experts held at the ATCM XXXVI Special Working Group on Search and Rescue; and

Desiring to increase the success and efficiency of SAR operations in the Antarctic.

Recommend that the Parties:

1. continue to collaborate actively on search and rescue in the Antarctic Treaty area;

2. commit to share best practices related to SAR in Antarctica, taking advantage of expertise developed by each of the five RCCs with Antarctic responsibilities;

3. cooperate as appropriate at the International Maritime Organization (IMO), the International Civil Aviation Organization (ICAO) and other relevant fora to promote the implementation of SAR protocols and practices that would be beneficial in the Antarctic context;

4. request that the Executive Secretary provide a copy of this Resolution and the section on the Special Working Group on Search and Rescue from the Final Report of ATCM XXXVI to the Secretaries General of the IMO and ICAO for information;

5. invite the Commission for the Conservation of Antarctic Marine Living Resources (CCAMLR) to consider appropriate means within its jurisdiction to support SAR efforts and to

improve fishing vessel safety within the CCAMLR Convention Area;

6. urge their National Antarctic Programs to provide annually updated information on assets that could be used for SAR purposes to COMNAP;

7. support COMNAP to continue to foster collaborative discussions and vital sharing of information regarding SAR matters including through:

a. holding triennial workshops on search and rescue, that include representatives of the RCCs, National Antarctic Programs, relevant experts, private operators as well as commercial emergency notification service providers, and inform future ATCMs on the results of these workshops;

b. establishing a web portal that promotes information exchange between RCCs on shared SAR goals and best practices; and

c. ensuring that other information on National Antarctic Programs, including assets, that could be used for SAR purposes be available to RCCs through the COMNAP website, and linked to the Electronic Information Exchange System (EIES).

8. encourage RCCs with Antarctic responsibilities to conduct SAR exercises with each other, National Antarctic Programs, IAATO, and other relevant entities to continually improve SAR cooperation and response.

Resolution 5 (2013): International Cooperation in Cultural Projects about Antarctica

The Representatives,

Convinced that international cooperation is one of the fundamental principles of the Antarctic Treaty system;

Recognising the merit of promoting knowledge about Antarctica through art projects;

Recalling Resolution 2 (1996), promoting scientific, aesthetic and wildlife values in Antarctica, through inspiration of young people and contributions by writers, artists and musicians;

Recommend that:

Parties be encouraged to promote the dissemination of knowledge about Antarctica through the development of art projects about Antarctica on the basis of international cooperation, to reflect, in particular, scientific activity and the importance of the preservation of the Antarctic environment.

Resolution 6 (2013): Biological Prospecting in Antarctica

The Representatives,

Recalling Resolution 7 (2005) on Biological Prospecting in Antarctica and Resolution 9 (2009) on Collection and Use of Antarctic Biological Material;

Convinced of the benefits for the progress of humankind of scientific research in the Antarctic Treaty area;

Reaffirming in this regard Article III(1)(c) of the Antarctic Treaty, which provides that, to the greatest extent feasible and practicable, scientific observations and results from Antarctica shall be exchanged and made freely available;

Noting that biological prospecting continues to occur in the Antarctic Treaty area;

Noting the lack of a working definition of biological prospecting in the Antarctic context;

Noting also ongoing discussions in other international fora on biological prospecting and genetic resources;

Noting also the need for further research and analysis to be undertaken related to the status and trends of biological prospecting in the Antarctic Treaty area and the wish that results be presented at future Antarctic Treaty Consultative Meetings:

Reaffirm that the Antarctic Treaty System is the appropriate framework for managing the collection of biological material in the Antarctic Treaty area and for considering its use;

Recommend that their governments report, as appropriate, on biological prospecting carried out under their respective legal regimes, with a view to facilitating a better understanding and assessment of these types of activities; and

Encourage their governments to examine ways to improve information exchange in this regard and to consider whether to adapt the Electronic Information Exchange System for this purpose.

Decision 1 (2014): Measures on Operational Matters Designated as no Longer Current

The Representatives,

Recalling Decision 3 (2002), Decision 1 (2007), Decision 1 (2011) and Decision 1 (2012), which established lists of measures that were designated as spent or no longer current;

Noting Resolution 1 (2014), Resolution 2 (2014) and Resolution 5 (2014);

Having reviewed a number of measures on the subject of operational matters;

Recognising that the measures listed in the Annex to this Decision are no longer current;

Decide:

1. that the measures listed in the Annex to this Decision require no further action by the Parties; and

2. to request the Secretariat of the Antarctic Treaty to post the text of the measures that appear in the Annex to this Decision on its website in a way that makes clear that these measures are no longer current and that the Parties do not need to take any further action with respect to them.

Annex: Measures on Operational Matters Designated as No Longer Current

1. Strengthening Cooperation in Hydrographic Surveying and Charting of Antarctic Waters:

- Recommendation XV-19 (1989)
- Resolution 1 (1995)
- Resolution 3 (2003)
- Resolution 5 (2008)
- Resolution 2 (2010)

2. Cooperation, Facilitation, and Exchange of Meteorological and Related Oceanographic and Cryospheric Environmental Information:

- Recommendation V-2 (1968)
- Recommendation VI-1 (1970)
- Recommendation VI-3 (1970)
- Recommendation XII-1 (1983)
- Recommendation XIV-7 (1987)
- Recommendation XIV-10 (1987)
- Recommendation XV-18 (1989)

3. Fuel Storage and Handling:

- Resolution 6 (1998)
- Resolution 3 (2005)

4. Exchange of Information on Logistic Problems:

- Recommendation I-VII (1961)

Resolution 5 (2014): Strengthening Cooperation in Hydrographic Surveying and Charting of Antarctic Waters

The Representatives,

Considering that reliable hydrographic data and nautical charts are essential to safe maritime operations;

Noting the increase in marine traffic, particularly tourist vessels, in the Antarctic region;

Concerned about the increased risk of harm to ships, persons and the environment in inadequately charted waters in the region;

Noting that the collection of accurate survey data will improve navigational safety and support scientific research;

Recognising the role of the International Hydrographic Organization Hydrographic Commission on Antarctica (HCA) in the coordination of hydrographic surveying and nautical charting in the Antarctic region, and the value of cooperating with the Scientific Committee on Antarctic Research (SCAR) and other relevant expert bodies;

Recalling Recommendation XV-19 (1989), Resolution 1 (1995), Resolution 3 (2003), Resolution 5 (2008) and Resolution 2 (2010), which encouraged cooperation on hydrographic surveying and charting of Antarctic waters;

Recommend that the Parties:

1. support and promote contacts and liaison between national Antarctic programs and national hydrographic offices;

2. increase their mutual cooperation in the hydrographic surveying and charting of Antarctic waters in order to contribute to safety of navigation, safeguarding life at sea, protection of the Antarctic environment, support of scientific activities, and furtherance of responsible economic activity; collaborating within, as appropriate, the framework(s) of national Antarctic programs, national hydrographic offices, the HCA and the International Chart scheme;

3. co-ordinate their hydrographic surveying and charting activities through the HCA and cooperate with it to:

   a. clarify requirements for the collection of hydrographic data of sufficient quality and accuracy for use in the development of electronic and paper navigational charts, being cognisant of the emerging challenges and opportunities faced in the digital navigation era;
   b. identify priority areas for the collection of additional hydrographic and bathymetric data;
   c. complete their inventory of data holdings and give high importance to liaison between Parties on future planned hydrographic surveys in order to avoid duplication of effort; and

4. encourage national Antarctic program vessels and all other vessels operating in the Antarctic Treaty area to collect hydrographic and bathymetric data including passage soundings on all Antarctic voyages, as practicable; to forward any hydrographic and bathymetric data collected to the relevant international chart producer for charting action; and to endeavour to find additional resources to improve hydrographic surveying and charting in the Antarctic region.

Resolution 6 (2014): Toward a Risk-based Assessment of Tourism and Non-governmental Activities

The Representatives,

Understanding the need for Antarctic Treaty Parties to consider safety and environmental impacts from tourism and non-governmental activities;

Desiring to promote safety of tourism and non-governmental activities;

Desiring also that all tourism and non-governmental activities, no matter the specific platform or nature of the activity, be adequately planned and executed in order to promote environmental protection and to avoid risks to safety of life and potential negative effects on Parties' national Antarctic programs;

Recalling Measure 4 (2004) and Resolution 4 (2004);

Desiring to ensure that all such activities are assessed in a consistent and thorough way to address the above concerns;

Recommend that their Governments:

consistent with their national legislation and as appropriate for tourism and non-governmental activities in Antarctica:

1. encourage operators to utilise a risk-based assessment process as a planning tool; and
2. take into account a risk-based assessment developed by operators as part of the authorisation or comparable regulatory process.

OTHER ATCM MATERIALS

Scientific Commission on Antarctic Research (SCAR) Constitution (1958)

Introductory note

Article II of the Treaty provides for freedom of scientific investigation in Antarctica and cooperation toward that end. To promote scientific cooperation, the Scientific Committee on Antarctic Research (SCAR) was established. SCAR has a unique role under the Antarctic Treaty System, inter alia, to provide scientific advice to Parties at Antarctic Treaty Consultative Meetings.

Article III of the Antarctic Treaty provides that 'to the greatest extent feasible and practicable... scientific observations and results from Antarctica shall be exchanged and made freely available'. For the purposes of the International Geographical Year, World Data Centers were established for a number of disciplines where data from all over the world, including Antarctica, relevant to each discipline were deposited.

Constitution

SCAR is a scientific committee of the International Council for Science (ICSU) charged with the initiation, promotion, and coordination of scientific activity in the Antarctic, with a view to framing and reviewing scientific programmes of circumpolar scope and significance. In establishing programmes, SCAR will respect the autonomy of other existing international bodies.

Guidelines for the conduct of SCAR affairs

1. SCAR will encourage and assist in the acquisition and dissemination of scientific knowledge derived from research carried out in its area of interest.

2. In formulating its scientific programmes, SCAR will pay attention to their possible contributions to global programmes of ICSU bodies and other scientific organisations.

SCAR may establish liaison and cooperation with international organisations having scientific interests in the Antarctic.

3. SCAR will abstain from involvement in political and juridical matters, including the formulation of management measures for exploitable resources, except where SCAR accepts an invitation for specific advice. However, in formulating its scientific programmes SCAR will take note of the need for the acquisition of the scientific knowledge necessary for the judicious management of the resources of the region.

4. SCAR may provide scientific and technological advice to the Antarctic Treaty Consultative Meetings, or to other international organisations (both governmental and nongovernmental).

5. SCAR will keep under review scientific matters pertaining to the integrity of the Antarctic environment, including the conservation of its terrestrial and marine ecosystems.

Membership

The membership of SCAR is as follows:

l. Full members

National organisations adhering to ICSU, representing the scientific communities of countries with active and continuing independent programmes of research in the Antarctic that have formed National Committees to communicate with SCAR.

2. Associate members

National organisations adhering to ICSU, or nominated by national organisations adhering to ICSU, which desire to participate in SCAR for scientific reasons but which do not qualify for full membership.

3. Union members

ICSU Unions wishing to participate in SCAR on a continuing basis.

Delegates

• Full members: One permanent voting delegate and one non-voting alternate delegate representing the National Committee communicating with SCAR.

• Associate members: One non-voting delegate representing the national organization adhering to ICSU or its nominee.

• Union members: One permanent voting delegate.

Organization and administration

l. SCAR elects an Executive Committee from its full member delegates to consist of a President, Immediate Past President, two Vice Presidents and a Secretary, each elected for a term of four years. One Vice President shall be elected for a term coinciding with that of the President. The other Vice President and Secretary shall be elected for a term which begins at the SCAR meeting in which a President is not elected. Presidents and Vice Presidents hold office for one four-year term only, but the Secretary is eligible for reelection for one further term only.

2. The Executive Committee is responsible to ICSU for the coordination of the scientific programmes adopted by SCAR.

3. SCAR or its Executive Committee may appoint ad hoc groups for the examination of special matters.

Scientific Commission on Antarctic Research (SCAR) Memorandum of Association (2008)

The Companies Acts 1985 to 2006
Company Limited by Guarantee

1. The name of the Company is "Scientific Committee on Antarctic Research ("the Charity").

2. The Charity's registered office is to be situated in England and Wales.

3. The Charity's objects ("the Objects") are:

3.1 to advance and promote scientific knowledge, understanding and education on any aspect of the Antarctic region, on the role of the Antarctic region in the Earth system, and on the effect of global change on the Antarctic region; and

3.2 to initiate, facilitate, co-ordinate and encourage international scientific research activity in the Antarctic region, on the role of the Antarctic region in the Earth system, and on the effect of global change on the Antarctic region; and for the purpose of this clause 3, the Charity may further the Objects in particular but not exclusively by:

(a) providing objective and independent scientific advice to the Parties to the Antarctic Treaty and other organisations on issues of science and conservation affecting the management of the Antarctic region and the Southern Ocean;

(b) facilitating free and unrestricted access to scientific data and information regarding the Antarctic region;

(c) developing scientific capacity in the Members of the Charity and young scientists, and to promote the incorporation of Antarctic science in education at all levels, and

(d) communicating scientific information about the Antarctic region to the public, and for the purposes of this clause 3 the term "Antarctic region" shall include Antarctica, the offshore islands of Antarctica, the surrounding ocean including the Antarctic Circumpolar Current, the northern boundary of which is the Subantarctic Front, and the Subantarctic islands lying south of the Subantarctic Front as well as those which lie north of the Subantarctic Front but fall within the Charity's area of interest, namely Ile Amsterdam, Ile St Paul, Macquarie Island and Gough Island.

4. In addition to any other powers it may have, the Charity may exercise the following powers in promoting the Objects (but not for any other purpose):

4.1 to draw, make, accept, endorse, discount, execute and issue promissory notes, bills, cheques and other instruments, and to operate bank accounts in the name of the Charity;

4.2 to raise funds and to invite and receive contributions provided that in raising funds the Charity shall not undertake any substantial permanent trading activities and shall conform to any relevant statutory regulations;

4.3 to buy, take on lease or in exchange, hire or otherwise acquire any property, to alter or improve it and maintain and equip it for use and (subject to such consents as may be required by law) to sell, lease or otherwise dispose of all or any part of any property belonging to the Charity. In exercising this power, the Charity must comply as appropriate with sections 36 and 37 of the Charities Act 1993;

4.4 to borrow money and to charge the whole or any part of any property belonging to the Charity as security for repayment of the money borrowed. The Charity must comply as appropriate with sections 38 and 39 Charities Act 1993 if it wishes to mortgage land;

4.5 to employ and remunerate such staff as are necessary for carrying out the work of the Charity and to make all reasonable and necessary provision for the payment of pensions and superannuation to staff and their dependants. The Charity may not employ or remunerate a director of the Charity;

4.6 to establish or support any charitable trusts, associations or institutions formed for all or any of the charitable purposes included in the Objects;

4.7 to co-operate with other charities, voluntary bodies and statutory authorities operating in furtherance of the Objects or similar charitable purposes and to exchange information and advice with them;

4.8 to acquire, merge with or enter into any partnership or joint venture arrangement with any other charity formed for any of the Objects;

4.9 to set aside income as a reserve against future expenditure but only in accordance with a written policy about reserves;

4.10 to deposit or invest funds, employ a professional fund-manager and arrange for investments or other property of the Charity to be held in the name of a nominee, in each case in the same manner and subject to the same conditions as the trustees of a trust are permitted to do so by the Trustee Act 2000;

4.11 to provide indemnity insurance for the directors or any other officer of the Charity in relation to any such liability as is mentioned in clause 5, but subject to the restrictions specified in clauses 6 and 7;

4.12 to pay out of the funds of the Charity the costs of forming and registering the Charity, both as a company and as a charity;

4.13 to appoint a President, Vice President or such other honorary officer(s) for such period and subject to such privileges and conditions as may be thought fit subject to compliance with the following clauses hereof;

4.14 to procure and provide information;

4.15 to print, publish and make, issue, show, circulate, commission and support papers, periodicals, books, circulars, tapes, films recordings and other media of communication;

4.16 to arrange and provide for or join in arranging and providing for the holding of public exhibitions, meetings, workshops, conferences, lectures and classes;

4.17 to do all such other lawful things as are necessary for the achievement of the Objects.

5. The liabilities referred to in clause 4.11 are:

5.1 any liability that by virtue of any rule of law would otherwise attach to a director of a company in respect of any negligence, default, breach of duty or breach of trust of which he or she may be guilty in relation to the Charity;

5.2 the liability to make a contribution to the Charity's assets as specified in section 214 of the Insolvency Act 1986 (wrongful trading).

6. The following liabilities are excluded from clause 5.1:

6.1 fines;

6.2 costs of unsuccessfully defending criminal prosecutions for offences arising out of the fraud, dishonesty or wilful or reckless misconduct of the director or other officer;

6.3 liabilities to the Charity that result from conduct that the director or other officer knew or must be assumed to have known was not in the best interests of the Charity or about which the person concerned did not care whether it was in the best interests of the Charity or not.

7. There is excluded from clause 5.2 any liability to make such a contribution where the basis of the director's liability is his or her knowledge prior to the insolvent liquidation of the Charity (or reckless failure to acquire that knowledge) that there was no reasonable prospect that the Charity would avoid going into insolvent liquidation.

8. The income and property of the Charity shall be applied solely towards the promotion of the Objects.

9. A director of the Charity is entitled to be reimbursed from the property of the Charity or may pay out of such property reasonable expenses properly incurred by him or her when acting on behalf of the Charity.

10. Subject to the restrictions of clauses 5, 6 and 7, a director may benefit from trustee indemnity insurance cover purchased at the Charity's expense.

11. None of the income or property of the Charity may be paid or transferred, directly or indirectly, by way of dividend, bonus or otherwise by way of profit, to any member of the Charity.

12. No director of the Charity may:

12.1 buy goods or services from the Charity;

12.2 sell goods, services or any interest in land to the Charity;

12.3 be employed by, or receive any remuneration from the Charity; or

12.4 receive any other financial benefit from the Charity.

13. The liability of the members is limited.

14. Every member of the Charity undertakes, if the Charity is dissolved while he or she is a member or within twelve months after he or she ceases to be a member, to contribute such amount (not exceeding £1) as may be demanded of him or her towards the payment of the Charity's debts and liabilities incurred before he or she ceases to be a member, and of the costs, charges and expenses of winding up, and the adjustment of the rights of the contributories among themselves.

15. The members of the Charity may at any time before, and in expectation of, its dissolution resolve that any net assets of the Charity after all its debts and liabilities have been paid, or provision has been made for them, shall on or before the dissolution of the Charity be applied or transferred in any of the following ways:

15.1 directly for the Objects; or

15.2 by transfer to any charity or charities for purposes similar to the Objects; or

15.3 to any charity for use for particular purposes that fall within the Objects.

16. Subject to any such resolution of the members of the Charity referred to in clause 15 the directors of the Charity may at any time before, and in expectation of, its dissolution resolve

that any net assets of the Charity after all its debts and liabilities have been paid, or provision has been made for them, shall on dissolution of the Charity be applied or transferred in any of the following ways:

16.1 directly for the Objects; or

16.2 by transfer to any charity or charities for purposes similar to the Objects; or

16.3 to any charity for use for particular purposes that fall within the Objects.

17. In no circumstances shall the net assets of the Charity be paid to or distributed among the members of the Charity (except to a member that is itself a charity) and, if no such resolution is passed by the members or the directors of the Charity as referred to in clauses 15 and 16, the net assets of the Charity shall be applied for charitable purposes as directed by the court or the Charity Commission.

Scientific Commission on Antarctic Research (SCAR) Articles of Association (2008)

The Companies Acts 1985 to 2006

Company Limited by Guarantee

1. Interpretation

1.1 In these Articles:

"the Act" means the Companies Act 1985 including any statutory modification or re-enactment thereof for the time being in force and any provisions of the Companies Act 2006 for the time being in force;

"address" means the postal address or, for the purposes of electronic communication, a fax number, an e-mail address or a text message number in each case registered with the Charity;

"Associate Member" has the meaning provided by Article 3.1.2;

"Articles" means these Articles of Association of the Charity;

"the Board of Directors" means the board of directors for the time being of the Charity or the Directors present or deemed to be present at a duly convened meeting of Directors at which a quorum is present;

"the Charity" means the company intended to be regulated by these Articles;

"clear days" in relation to the period of a notice means the period excluding the day when the notice is given or deemed to be given and the day for which it is given or on which it is to take effect;

"the Charity Commission" means the Charity Commissioners for England and Wales;

"communication" means the same as in the Electronic Communications Act 2000;

"Delegates" has the meaning provided by Article 4.1;

"Directors" means the directors of the Charity, who are charity trustees as defined by section 97 Charities Act 1993 (and "Director" means any one of them);

"electronic communication" means the same as in the Electronic Communications Act 2000;

"Full Member" has the meaning provided by Article 3.1.1;

"Honorary Member" has the meaning provided by Article 3.1.4;

"ICSU" means the International Council for Science;

"Meeting of Delegates" means a meeting of the Members held in accordance with Article 6.2 or Article 6.3;

"Member" means a member of the Charity;

"Membership" means membership in accordance with these Articles;

"Memorandum" means the Memorandum of Association of the Charity;

"officers" includes the Directors and the secretary;

"Rules of Procedure" means such rules adopted by the Charity in accordance with Article 24 from time to time;

"the seal" means the common seal of the Charity if it has one;

"secretary" means the secretary of the Charity or any other person appointed to perform the duties of the secretary of the Charity, including a joint, assistant or deputy secretary;

"Union Member" has the meaning provided by Article 3.1.3;

"United Kingdom" means Great Britain and Northern Ireland.

1.2 Words importing the masculine gender only shall include the feminine gender, and the singular includes the plural and vice versa.

1.3 Words importing persons shall include corporations.

1.4 Bearing in mind the above clarifications, words or expressions contained in these Articles shall, unless the context requires otherwise, bear the same meaning as in the Act, but excluding any statutory modification not in force on the date when the Charity is formed or when these Articles are adopted by the Charity (if later). In all other cases a reference to an Act of Parliament includes any statutory modification or re-enactment of it for the time being in force.

2. Members

2.1 The subscribers to the memorandum are the first Members of the Charity.

2.2 Membership is open to other individuals or organisations who:

2.2.1 satisfy the requirements for Membership as set out in these Articles and the Rules of Procedure of the Charity;

2.2.2 apply to the Charity in the form required by the Rules of Procedure of the Charity; and

2.2.3 are approved at a Meeting of the Delegates.

2.3 For the purposes of registration the number of Members is declared to be unlimited. For the avoidance of doubt, each Member may only hold one Membership.

2.4 The Meeting of Delegates may only refuse an application for Membership which satisfies the requirement of Article 2.2.1 and 2.2.2 if, acting reasonably and properly, they consider it to be in the best interests of the Charity to refuse the application.

2.5 Membership is not transferable to anyone else and shall cease on death or, if the Member is a corporation or unincorporated association, when it ceases to exist.

2.6 The provisions of the Act shall be observed by the Company and every Member shall either sign a written consent to become a Member or sign the Register of Members on becoming a Member.

2.7 Any subscriptions payable by Members from time to time shall be determined by the voting Members at a general meeting on a motion from the Board of Directors. The subscriptions payable by Members may be different for different categories of Member.

3. Classes of Membership

3.1 The Charity shall have the following classes of Membership:

3.1.1 Full Member

A Full Member shall be a national organisation adhering to ICSU, or nominated by a national organisation adhering to ICSU, that represents the scientific community of that country. The country must maintain an active and continuing programme of research in the Antarctic Region and the national organisation must have formed a National Committee to communicate with the Charity.

3.1.2 Associate Member

An Associate Member shall be a national organisation adhering to ICSU, or nominated by a national organisation adhering to ICSU, that desires to participate in the work of the Charity for scientific reasons but does not qualify as a Full Member.

3.1.3 Union Member

A Union Member shall be an organisation which is a Scientific Union member of ICSU, whose activity is related to the objects of the Charity and which wishes to participate in the work of the Charity on a continuing basis.

3.1.4 Honorary Member

An Honorary Member shall be an individual who has rendered outstanding service to SCAR and has been so approved by the Meeting of Delegates.

3.2 The Meeting of Delegates may establish classes of Membership (including but not limited to those classes of Membership in Article 3.1) with different rights and obligations and shall record the rights and obligations in the register of members.

3.3 The Directors may not directly or indirectly alter the rights or obligations attached to a class of Membership.

3.4 The rights attached to a class of Membership may only be varied if:

3.4.1 three-quarters of the Members of that class consent in writing to the variation; or

3.4.2 a special resolution is passed at a separate general meeting of the Members of that class agreeing to the variation.

3.5 The provisions in these Articles about general meetings shall apply to any meeting relating to the variation of the rights of any class of Members.

4. Representation of Members

4.1 Any organisation that is a Member may nominate any person to act as its representative at any meeting of the Charity. A person appointed to represent the Member organisation shall be known as a "Delegate". No person shall be entitled to represent the Member organisation at any meeting unless the Charity has received notice of his appointment as the representative of the Member organisation. The representative may continue to represent the Member organisation at general meetings of the Charity until written notice to the contrary is received by the Charity from the Member organisation. Any notice given to the Charity by the Member organisation will be conclusive evidence of the representative's authority or the revocation of that authority. The Charity shall not be required to consider whether the nominee has been properly appointed by the Member organisation.

4.2 Members shall, save as otherwise approved by the Meeting of Delegates, be represented at general meetings as follows:

4.2.1 a Full Member shall be represented by two Delegates appointed by the national organisation through its national committee for SCAR; the first Delegate shall be referred to as the Delegate, the second Delegate shall be referred to as the "Alternate Delegate";

4.2.2 an Associate Member shall be represented by one Delegate designated by the Associate Member;

4.2.3 a Union Member shall be represented by one Delegate designated by the Union Member;

4.2.4 any other classes of Members shall have such representation as determined by a resolution of the Meeting of Delegates when the class of Membership was established.

4.3 The Delegate and Alternate Delegate appointed to represent the Full Member, and the Delegate representing the Associate Member, should preferably be scientists directly involved in Antarctic Science.

5. Termination of Membership

5.1 Membership is terminated if:

5.1.1 the Member dies or, if it is an organisation, ceases to exist;

5.1.2 the Member resigns by giving at least three months' notice in writing to the Charity and ensuring that all contributions due from the Member to the Charity have been paid;

5.1.3 in the case of a Full Member, that Member:

(i) has not been active in scientific research in the Antarctic region for four years;

(ii) has not been active in the work of the Charity for four years; or

(iii) has not paid its contribution within two years of such contribution becoming due and where this Article 5.1.3 applies, the Directors shall give the Member written notice giving the Member the opportunity to apply to the Charity to become an Associate Member or to resign as a Member, with immediate effect. The Member shall have the right to respond within three months of the date of the notice. If the Member does not respond within that period of time, Membership shall be terminated in accordance with Article 5.1.5;

5.1.4 in the case of an Associate Member, that Member has not paid its contribution within two years of such contribution becoming due. Where this Article 5.1.4 applies, Membership shall be terminated in accordance with Article 5.1.5;

5.1.5 the Member is removed from Membership by a resolution of the Meeting of Delegates that it is in the best interests of the Charity that his, her or its (as appropriate) Membership is terminated and, for the avoidance of doubt, where this Article 5.1.5 applies by reason of the provisions of Article 5.1.3 and 5.1.4 such removal shall be deemed to be in the best interests of the Charity. A resolution to remove a Member from Membership may only be passed if:

(i) the Member has been given at least three months' notice in writing of the Meeting of Delegates at which the resolution will be proposed and the reasons why it is to be proposed;

(ii) the Member or, at the option of the Member, the Member's representative (who need not be a Member of the Charity) has been allowed to make representations to the meeting.

6. General meetings

6.1 The Charity shall hold its first annual general meeting within eighteen months after the date of its incorporation. An annual general meeting shall be held in each subsequent year and not more than fifteen months shall elapse between successive annual general meetings. The annual general meeting shall be held at such times and places as the Directors shall appoint in consultation with the Members.

6.2 The Directors may call a general meeting at any time.

6.3 In circumstances in which the Charity has passed an elective resolution to dispense with holding an annual general meeting a general meeting shall be held at least once every thirty months.

7. Notice of general meetings

7.1 The minimum periods of notice required to hold a general meeting of the Charity are:

7.1.1 twenty-one clear days for an annual general meeting;

7.1.2 fourteen clear days for all other general meetings.

7.2 A general meeting may be called by shorter notice if it is so agreed:

7.2.1 in the case of an annual general meeting, by all the Members entitled to attend and vote; and

7.2.2 in the case of a general meeting, by a majority in number of Members having a right to attend and vote at the meeting who together hold not less than 95 percent of the total voting rights.

7.3 The notice shall specify the date time and place of the meeting and the general nature of the business to be transacted. If the meeting is to be an annual general meeting, the notice shall say so.

7.4 The notice shall be given to all the Members and auditors.

7.5 The proceedings at a meeting shall not be invalidated because a person who was entitled to receive notice of the meeting did not receive it because of an accidental omission by the Charity.

8. Proceedings at general meetings

8.1 No business shall be transacted at any general meeting unless a quorum is present.

8.2 A quorum is one half of the total voting Members at the time.

8.3 The Delegate of a Member organisation shall be counted in the quorum provided that in the case of a Full Member either, but not both, of the Delegate or Alternate Delegate shall be counted in the quorum.

8.4 If:

8.4.1 a quorum is not present within half an hour from the time appointed for the meeting; or

8.4.2 during a meeting a quorum ceases to be present; the meeting shall be adjourned to such time and place as the Directors may determine.

The Directors shall reconvene the meeting and shall give at least seven days' notice of the reconvened meeting stating the date, time and place of the meeting. If no quorum is present at the reconvened meeting within 15 minutes of the time specified for the start of the meeting the Members present at that time shall constitute the quorum for that meeting.

8.5 General meetings shall be chaired by the President of the Charity who is appointed in accordance with Article 12.1.1. If there is no such person or he or she is not present within fifteen minutes of the time appointed for the meeting, a Vice-President nominated by the Directors shall chair the meeting. If there is only one Director present and willing to act, he shall chair the meeting. If no Director is present and willing to chair the meeting within 15 minutes after the time appointed for holding it, the Members present and entitled to vote shall choose one of their number to chair the meeting.

8.6 The voting Members present at a meeting may resolve by a special resolution that the meeting be adjourned. The person who is chairing the meeting must decide the date, time and place at which the meeting is to be reconvened unless those details are specified in the resolution. No business shall be conducted at a reconvened meeting unless it could properly have been conducted at the meeting had adjournment not taken place. If a meeting is adjourned by a resolution of the Members for more than seven days, at least seven clear days' notice shall be given of the reconvened meeting stating the date, time and place of the meeting.

8.7 Save as provided otherwise in these Articles, the Rules of Procedure and/or as otherwise approved by the Members, all decisions taken by the Meeting of Delegates shall require unanimity of the voting Members duly present and taking part.

8.8 The Rules of Procedure may specify that certain matters shall only be passed if all of the voting Members of the Charity vote in favour of the resolution.

8.9 The Directors shall be entitled to invite observers from governmental and nongovernmental organisations to attend general meetings on such terms determined by the Rules of Procedure. An organisation invited to attend as an observer shall be represented by one Delegate appointed by the observer, who shall be notified to the Directors in accordance with the Rules of Procedure, and who shall be entitled to speak at the discretion of the Chairman of the meeting, but who shall not be entitled to vote.

9. Votes of Members

9.1 Subject to Articles 3, 4 and 9.2, Members shall have the following voting rights:

9.1.1 Full Members shall have one vote per Full Member notwithstanding that the Full Member is represented by one Delegate and one Alternate Delegate;

9.1.2 Associate Members shall not have a right to vote;

9.1.3 Union Members shall have a right to vote on all matters except those matters determined by the Directors (in their sole discretion) to constitute financial matters;

9.1.4 Honorary Members shall not have a right to vote;

9.1.5 any other classes of Members shall have such voting rights as determined by the Meeting of Delegates when the class of Membership was established.

9.2 No Member shall be entitled to vote at any general meeting or at any adjourned meeting if he owes any money to the Charity.

9.3 Any objection to the qualification of any voter shall be raised at the meeting at which the vote is tendered and the decision of the person who is chairing shall be final.

10. Directors

10.1 A Director shall be a natural person aged eighteen years or older. No-one may be appointed a Director if he or she would be disqualified from acting under the provisions of Article 14. The number of Directors shall be not less than three but (unless otherwise determined by the Members) shall not be subject to any maximum. The first Directors shall be those persons notified to Companies House as the first directors of the Charity.

10.2 A Director may not appoint an alternate director or anyone to act on his behalf at meetings of the Directors.

10.3 Directors shall be elected at the Meeting of Delegates, from the Delegates present at such meetings, in accordance with the Rules of Procedure.

11. Powers of Directors

11.1 Subject to the provisions of the Act, the Memorandum and these Articles and to any resolution of the Meeting of Delegates, the Directors shall manage on behalf of the Members the business of the Charity and may exercise all the powers of the Charity. No alteration of the Memorandum or these Articles and no resolution of the Meeting of Delegates shall have retrospective effect to invalidate any prior act of the Directors. Any meeting of the Directors at which a quorum is present at the time the relevant decision is made may exercise all the powers exercisable by the Directors.

12. Appointment of Directors

12.1 The Directors of the Charity shall be as follows:

12.1.1 a President who shall be appointed by the Meeting of Delegates for a term of four years and shall be chosen from the Delegates and Alternate Delegates of Full Members;

12.1.2 four Vice Presidents who shall be appointed by the Meeting of Delegates for a term of four years and shall be chosen from the Delegates and Alternate Delegates of Full Members, two Vice Presidents being appointed at each biennial Meeting of the Delegates;

12.1.3 the immediate past President of the Charity who shall be appointed for a term of two years provided that the Directors (including the immediate Past President of the Charity) shall be Delegates and Alternate Delegates of at least six different Full Members and shall be elected in accordance with the Rules of Procedure.

12.2 Re-appointment of a Director who retires at a general meeting will be subject to the Rules of Procedure regarding elections.

12.3 Where a Director ceases to hold office before their appointed term of office is completed, the remaining Directors shall be entitled, after consulting with the Full Members, to appoint a Director to serve until the next Meeting of Delegates at which time an election shall be held, in accordance with this Article 12, to appoint a replacement (who may or may not be the person appointed as a replacement by the Directors) to serve for the remainder of the unexpired term.

12.4 The appointment of a Director, by the Charity in a Meeting of Delegates or general meeting, must not cause the number of Directors to exceed any number fixed by a resolution of the Members as the maximum number of Directors.

13. Retirement of Directors

13.1 A Director shall, subject to 12.2, retire at the Meeting of Delegates which occurs at the end of the term for which the Director has been appointed in accordance with Article 12.1 and the retirement shall take effect at the end of the Meeting of Delegates at which he retires.

14. Disqualification and removal of Directors

14.1 A Director shall cease to hold office if he or she:

14.1.1 ceases to be a Director by virtue of any provision in the Act or is prohibited by law from being a Director;

14.1.2 is disqualified from acting as a charity trustee by virtue of section 72 Charities Act 1993 (or any statutory re-enactment or modification of that provision);

14.1.3 except in the case of a Director appointed in accordance with Article 12.1.3, ceases to be a Delegate or Alternate Delegate of any Full Member;

14.1.4 becomes incapable by reason of mental disorder, illness or injury of managing and administering his or her own affairs;

14.1.5 resigns as a Director by notice to the Charity (but only if at least two Directors will remain in office when the notice of resignation is to take effect);

14.1.6 is absent without the permission of the Directors from two consecutive meetings and the Directors resolve that his office be vacated; or

14.1.7 dies.

15. Directors' remuneration

15.1 The Directors must not be paid any remuneration.

16. Proceedings of Directors

16.1 The Directors may regulate their proceedings as they think fit, subject to the provisions of these Articles. The Directors shall hold a minimum of two meetings in any twelve month period. Any such meeting shall be referred to as the "Meeting of Directors". Any Director may call a Meeting of the Directors. The company secretary must call a Meeting of the Directors if requested to do so by a Director. Questions arising at a meeting shall be decided by a majority of votes. In the case of an equality of votes, the person who chairs the meeting shall have a second or casting vote.

16.2 No decision may be made by a meeting of the Directors unless a quorum is present at the time the decision is purported to be made. The quorum shall be one half of the total number of Directors or, if such number is not a whole number, the next whole number which is greater than one half, or such larger number as may be decided from time to time by the Directors. A Director shall not be counted in the quorum present when any decision is taken about a matter upon which that Director is not entitled to vote.

If:

16.2.1 a quorum is not present within half an hour from the time appointed for the meeting; or

16.2.2 during a meeting a quorum ceases to be present the meeting shall be adjourned to such time and place as the Directors may determine. The Directors shall reconvene the meeting and shall give at least seven clear days' notice of the reconvened meeting stating the date, time and place of the meeting. If no quorum is present at the reconvened meeting within thirty minutes of the time specified for the start of the meeting the Directors present at that time shall constitute a quorum for that meeting.

16.3 If the number of Directors is less than the number fixed as the quorum, the continuing Director(s) may act only for the purpose of filling vacancies or of calling a general meeting.

16.4 The President shall chair meetings of the Directors. If there is no such person, or if the person appointed is unwilling to preside or is not present within ten minutes after the time appointed for the meeting, the Directors present may appoint one of the Vice-Presidents to chair that meeting. The person appointed to chair meetings of the Directors shall have no functions or powers except those conferred by these Articles or delegated to him or her by the Directors.

16.5 A resolution in writing, signed by all the Directors entitled to receive notice of a Meeting of Directors or a committee of Directors and to vote upon the resolution, shall be as valid and effectual as if it had been passed at a Meeting of Directors or (as the case may be) a committee of Directors duly convened and held. The resolution in writing may comprise several documents containing the text of the resolution in like form, each signed by one or more Directors.

16.6 Any Director or a member of a committee of the Directors may participate in a Meeting of the Directors or such committee by means of conference, telephone or similar communications equipment whereby all persons participating in the meeting can hear each other and participation in a meeting in this manner shall be deemed to constitute presence in person at such a meeting.

17. Delegation and Working Groups

17.1 The Directors may delegate any of their powers or functions to a committee of two or more Directors but the terms of any delegation shall be recorded in the minute book.

17.2 The Directors may impose conditions when delegating, including the conditions that:

17.2.1 the relevant powers are to be exercised exclusively by the committee to whom they are delegated;

17.2.2 no expenditure may be incurred on behalf of the Charity except in accordance with a budget previously agreed with the Directors.

17.3 The Directors may revoke or alter such a delegation.

17.4 All acts and proceedings of any such committee must be fully and promptly reported to the Directors.

17.5 With the approval of the Directors, responsibility for a particular duty normally discharged by the President may be delegated to a Vice President.

17.6 A Director shall absent himself or herself from any discussions of the Directors in which it is possible that a conflict of interest may arise between his or her duty to act solely in the interests of the Charity and any personal interest (including but not limited to any personal financial interest.)

17.7 Subject to Article 17.8, all acts done by a Meeting of Directors, or of a committee of Directors, shall be valid notwithstanding the participation in any vote of a Director:

17.7.1 who was disqualified from holding office; or

17.7.2 who had previously retired or who had been obliged by the Articles to vacate office;

17.7.3 who was not entitled to vote on the matter, whether by reason of a conflict of interest or otherwise; if without:

(i) the vote of that Director; and

(ii) that Director being counted in the quorum;

the decision has been made by a majority of the Directors at a quorate meeting.

17.8 Article 17.7 does not permit a Director to keep any benefit that may be conferred upon him or her by a resolution of the Directors or of a committee of Directors if, but for Article 17.7, the resolution would have been void, or if the Director has not complied with Article 17.6.

17.9 The Meeting of Delegates may create working groups (the "Working Groups") to undertake certain aspects of the business of the Charity. The Working Groups shall consist of:

17.9.1 the Delegates Committee on Scientific Affairs, and the Delegates Committee on Outreach and Administration, which shall be formed and operate solely during the Meeting of the Delegates, each being chaired by a Director;

17.9.2 the Standing Committee on the Antarctic Treaty System;

17.9.3 the Standing Committee on Antarctic Geographic Information;

17.9.4 the Standing Committee on Finance;

17.9.5 the Standing Scientific Groups;

17.9.6 such other working groups as appear appropriate.

17.10 All of the Working Groups shall be formed and operate in accordance with the Working Group rules of procedure that shall form part of the Rules of Procedure from time to time. Any Working Group may, subject to the Rules of Procedure, be dissolved at any time.

18. Minutes

18.1 The Directors shall keep and communicate to Members minutes of all:

18.1.1 appointments of officers made by the Directors;

18.1.2 proceedings at meetings of the Charity;

18.1.3 Meetings of the Directors and of committees of Directors including:

(i) the names of the Directors present at the meeting

(ii) the decisions taken at the meeting; and

(iii) where appropriate the reasons for the decisions.

19. The Seal

19.1 If the Charity has a seal, it shall only be used by the authority of the Directors or of a committee of Directors authorised by the Directors. The Directors may determine who shall sign any instrument to which the seal is affixed and unless otherwise so determined it shall be signed by a Director and by the secretary or by a second Director.

20. Accounts

20.1 The Directors must prepare for each financial year accounts as required by the Act. The accounts must be prepared to show a true and fair view and follow accounting standards issued or adopted by the Accounting Standards Board or its successors and adhere to the recommendations of applicable Statements of Recommended Practice.

20.2 The Directors shall keep accounting records as required by the Act.

21. Annual Report and Return and Register of Charities

21.1 The Directors shall comply with the requirements of the Charities Act 1993 with regard to:

21.1.1 the transmission of the statements of account to the Charity Commission;

21.1.2 the preparation of an annual report and its transmission to the Charity Commission;

21.1.3 the preparation of an annual return and its transmission to the Charity Commission.

21.2 The Directors shall notify the Charity Commission promptly of any changes to the Charity's entry on the Central Register of Charities.

22. Notices

22.1 Any notice to be given to or by any person pursuant to these Articles shall be in writing or shall be given using electronic communications.

22.2 The Charity may give any notice to a Member either:

22.2.1 personally; or

22.2.2 by sending it by post in a prepaid envelope addressed to the Member at his address; or

22.2.3 by leaving it at the address of the Member; or

22.2.4 by giving it using electronic communications to the Member's address.

22.3 A Member who does not register a postal address with the Charity or who registers only a postal address that is not within the United Kingdom shall not be entitled to receive any notice from the Charity, unless he gives to the Charity an address to which notices may be sent using electronic communications.

22.4 A Member present in person at any meeting of the Charity shall be deemed to have received notice of the meeting and, where necessary, of the purposes for which it was called.

22.5 Proof that an envelope containing a notice was properly addressed, prepaid and posted shall be conclusive evidence that the notice was given. Proof that a notice contained in an electronic communication was sent in accordance with guidance issued by the Institute of Chartered Secretaries and Administrators shall be conclusive evidence that the notice was given. A notice shall be deemed to be given forty-eight hours after the envelope containing it was posted or, in the case of a notice contained in an electronic communication, forty-eight hours after it was sent.

23. Indemnity

23.1 The Charity shall, to the extent permitted by the Act, indemnify every Director or other officer of the Charity against any liability incurred by him or her in that capacity in defending any proceedings, whether civil or criminal, in which judgement is given in favour of the Director or in which the Director is acquitted or in connection with any application in which the Director is acquitted or in connection with any application in which relief is granted to the Director by the court from liability for negligence, default, breach of duty or breach of trust in relation to the affairs of the Charity.

24. Rules

24.1 The Directors may from time to time recommend to the Members of the Charity such reasonable and proper rules or bye laws as they may deem necessary or expedient for the proper conduct and management of the Charity. The rules or bye laws may regulate the following matters but are not restricted to them:

24.1.1 the admission of Members of the Charity (including the admission of organisations to Membership) and the rights and privileges of such Members, and the entrance fees, subscriptions and other fees or payments to be made by Members;

24.1.2 the conduct of Members of the Charity in relation to one another, and to the Charity's employees and volunteers;

24.1.3 the setting aside of the whole or any part or parts of the Charity's premises at any particular time or times or for any particular purpose or purposes;

24.1.4 the procedure at general meetings and meetings of the Directors and subcommittees of the Directors in so far as such procedure is not regulated by the Act or these Articles;

24.1.5 the procedure for appointing Directors in so far as such procedure is not regulated by the Act or these Articles;

24.1.6 generally, all such matters as are commonly the subject matter of company rules.

24.2 The Charity shall, subject to the approval of the Members in each case, have power to alter, add to or repeal the rules or bye laws.

24.3 The Directors shall adopt such means as they think sufficient to bring the rules and bye laws to the notice of Members of the Charity.

24.4 The rules or bye laws, shall be binding on all Members of the Charity. No rule or bye law shall be inconsistent with, or shall affect or repeal anything contained in, the Memorandum or these Articles.

National Membership of SCAR (with dates of accession)

Full members

Argentina	3 Feb 1958
Australia	3 Feb 1958
Belgium	3 Feb 1958
Chile	3 Feb 1958
France	3 Feb 1958
Japan	3 Feb 1958
New Zealand	3 Feb 1958
Norway	3 Feb 1958
South Africa	3 Feb 1958
Russia (former USSR)	3 Feb 1958
United Kingdom	3 Feb 1958
United States of America	3 Feb 1958
Germany	22 May 1978
Poland	22 May 1978
Brazil	1 Oct 1984
India	1 Oct 1984
China	23 Jun 1986
Sweden (24 Mar 1987)	12 Sep 1988
Italy (19 May 1987)	12 Sep 1988
Uruguay (29 Jul 1987)	12 Sep 1988
Spain (15 Jan 1987)	23 Jul 1990
Netherlands (20 May 1987)	23 Jul 1990
Korea, Rep. of (8 Dec 1987)	23 Jul 1990
Finland (1 Jul 1988)	23 Jul 1990
Ecuador (12 Sep 1988)	15 Jun 1992

(Dates in brackets are those of admission to associate membership)

Associate members

Peru (14 April 1987)
Switzerland (16 June 1987)
Pakistan (23 Jul 1990)
Estonia (15 Jun 1992)
Canada (5 Sep 1994)
Ukraine (5 Sep 1994)
Bulgaria (5 March 1995)

ICSU Union Members

International Union of Biological Sciences (IUBS)

International Geographical Union (IGU)
International Union of Geological Sciences (IUGS)
International Union of Geodesy and Geophysics (IUGG)
International Union of Physiological Sciences (IUPS)
International Union of Pure and Applied Chemistry (IUPAC)
Union Radio Scientifique Internationale (URSI)

List of Special Antarctic Treaty Consultative Meetings (SATCM)

Meetings	**Dates**	**Location**
SATCM I	25–29 July 1977	London, United Kingdom
SATCM II-1	27 February 1978 – 10 March 1978	Canberra, Australia
SATCM II-2	17–28 July 1978	Buenos Aires, Argentina
SATCM II-3	5–6 May 1980	Canberra, Australia
SATCM III	3 March 1981	Buenos Aires, Argentina
SATCM IV-1	14–25 June 1982	Wellington, New Zealand
SATCM IV-2	17–28 January 1983	Wellington, New Zealand
SATCM IV-3	11–22 July 1983	Bonn, Germany
SATCM V	12 September 1983	Canberra, Australia
SATCM IV-4	18–27 January 1984	Washington, United States
SATCM IV-5	23–31 May 1984	Tokyo, Japan
SATCM IV-6	26 February 1986 – 8 March 1985	Rio de Janeiro, Brazil
SATCM IV-7	23 September 1985 – 4 October 1985	Paris, France
SATCM VI	7 October 1985	Brussels, Belgium
SATCM IV-8	14–25 April 1986	Hobart, Australia
SATCM IV-9	27 October 1986 – 12 November 1986	Tokyo, Japan
SATCM IV-10	11–20 May 1987	Montevideo, Uruguay
SATCM VII	5 October 1987	Rio de Janeiro, Brazil
SATCM IV-11	19–29 January 1988	Wellington, New Zealand
SATCM IV-12	2 May 1988 – 2 June 1988	Wellington, New Zealand
SATCM VIII	20–21 September 1988	Paris, France
SATCM IX	9 October 1989	Paris, France
SATCM X	19 November 1990	Viña del Mar, Chile
SATCM XI-1	19 November 1990 – 6 December 1990	Viña del Mar, Chile
SATCM XI-2	22–30 April 1991	Madrid, Spain
SATCM XI-3	17–22 June 1991	Madrid, Spain
SATCM XI-4	3–4 October 1991	Madrid, Spain
SATCM XII – CEP III	11–15 September 2000	The Hague, Netherlands

List of Antarctic Treaty Meetings of Experts (ATME)

Meetings	Dates	Location
ME Telecom 1	24–28 June 1963	Washington, United States
ME Logistics	3–8 June 1968	Tokyo, Japan
ME Telecom 2	1–12 September 1969	Buenos Aires, Argentina
ME Telecom 3	11–15 September 1978	Washington, United States
ME Air Safety	2–5 May 1989	Paris, France
ME Environmental Monitoring	1–4 June 1992	Buenos Aires, Argentina
ME Shipping	17–19 April 2000	London, United Kingdom
ME Tourism	22–25 March 2004	Tromsø, Norway
ME Ship-borne Tourism	9–11 December 2009	Wellington, New Zealand
ME Climate Change	6–9 April 2010	Svolær, Norway

Washington Declaration on the International Polar Year and Police Science[17]

On the occasion of the conclusion of the fourth International Polar Year (IPY), the Member States of the Arctic Council and the Consultative Parties to the Antarctic Treaty,

Observing that the IPY occurred against a backdrop of rapid and significant climate and environmental change in the polar regions,

Acknowledging the unique scientific importance of the polar regions, both as actors and barometers of these changes, which are vital to the functioning of the earth's terrestrial, biological, climate, ocean and atmosphere systems,

Recognising the need to improve the modelling and prediction of change on a regional basis,

Recognising the significant work of the Intergovernmental Panel on Climate Change in assessing documented and predicted changes in polar regions and in relating them to larger global systems

Affirming the importance of the IPY's findings to the scientific community, Arctic residents, including indigenous peoples, and to humanity as a whole,

Observing the success of participants in forming IPY collaborations that integrate the human, physical, and biological aspects of their research to achieve system-scale knowledge,

Recognising the vital contributions toward understanding the characteristics and dynamics of polar regions and their roles for the world's ecosystems made by scientists and other participants from over sixty countries,

Noting the extensive efforts of the International Council for Science (ICSU), the World Meteorological Organisation (WMO), the many IPY National Committees, and the scientists and other participants around the globe whose research made IPY a great success,

Recalling the goals for the IPY set forth in the 2006 Edinburgh Antarctic Declaration on the International Polar Year 2007–2008, and the strong support for IPY expressed by the Arctic Council in the 2006 Salekhard Declaration,

Expecting that the legacy of the IPY will continue well beyond its formal conclusion,

Hereby:

1. Urge states, national and international scientific bodies, and other interested parties to cooperate to deliver a lasting legacy from the IPY, and to support appropriate infrastructures to achieve this;

[17] Adopted 6 April 2009.

2. Commit themselves to reviewing key issues related to scientific cooperation and recent scientific findings at the biennial Ministerial Meetings of the Arctic Council and annual Antarctic Treaty Consultative Meetings, and further commit to using science to help inform the cooperative development of measures to address the threats to the polar regions;

3. Call upon IPY participants to continue to make data collected under IPY 2007–2008 and its legacy programs available in an open and timely manner, recall the obligations related to exchange of scientific information to this effect in the Antarctic Treaty, and encourage the same spirit of scientific openness among Arctic researchers;

4. Endorse the goal of strengthening international cooperation at all levels in polar regions among States, scientists, Arctic residents, including indigenous peoples, and their institutions in areas such as educational outreach, human and ecosystem health, environmental protection, and scholarships for young scientists;

5. Encourage the development of coordinated research and scientific observations at both poles to compare the current dynamics of polar areas and their contributions to the Earth's processes and changes;

6. Recommend that governments continue their support for efforts initiated during IPY to create and link observational systems in order to improve the modelling and prediction of climate change on both regional and temporal scales;

7. Encourage states and international bodies to use the scientific understandings derived from IPY research to support the development of concrete steps to protect the environment in the polar regions;

8. Support the analysis and use of scientific data and information collected from the polar regions as a result of IPY to contribute to future assessments by the Intergovernmental Panel on Climate Change, as well as other efforts to address climate change, and future Arctic Council assessments;

9. Call upon states, organisations, scientists, and other stakeholders to continue to engage with young people to cultivate the next generation of polar scientists, and to communicate with the general public to develop an awareness of the importance of polar research for life in all regions of the world; and

10. Affirm the value of collaboration and coordination between states and Arctic residents, including indigenous peoples, for the benefit of polar research.

Adopted at Washington, April 6, 2009.

PART 4
COMMITTEE FOR ENVIRONMENTAL PROTECTION UNDER THE 1991 PROTOCOL (CEP)

List of All Measures, Decisions, Resolutions and Recommendations Related to Committee for Environmental Protection (CEP) Issues (1998–2013)

CEP I (1998)

Decision 2 (1998):	Rules of Procedure for the Committee for Environmental Protection
Decision 4 (1998):	Marine Protected Areas
Measure 1 (1998):	Redesignation of SSSI 1 (Cape Royds) as SPA 27 (Cape Royds), designation of SPA 28 (Hut Point) and 29 (Cape Adare)
Measure 2 (1998):	Historic Monument 74 (Elephant Island)
Resolution 1 (1998):	National responsibilities for revising management plans of Antarctic protected areas
Resolution 2 (1998):	Guide for ASPA management plans
Resolution 3 (1998):	International Code of Safety for Ships in Polar Waters

CEP II (1999)

Decision 1 (1999):	CEP web site
Decision 2 (1999):	Guidelines for Antarctic Shipping and Related Activities
Resolution 1 (1999):	EIA Guidelines
Resolution 2 (1999):	Review of Specially Protected Species
Resolution 6 (1999):	Adherence to the Environmental Protocol by Non-consultative Parties
Measure 1 (1999):	Revised management plan for SSSI 23 (Svarthamaren)

CEP III (2000)

Decision 1 (2000):	List of CEP observers
Measure 1 (2000):	Revised management plans for SPA 14 (Lynch Island), 19 (Lagotellerie Island), 20 (New College Valley) and SSSI 8 (Admiralty Bay), 17 (Clark Peninsula), 22 (Yukidori Valley), and 34 (Lions Rump)
Measure 2 (2000):	Extension of expiry dates for SSSI 1 (Cape Royds), 2 (Arrival Heights), 3 (Barwick Valley), 16 (Bailey Peninsula), 20 (Biscoe Point), 21 (Deception Island), 24 (Mount Melbourne), 25 (Marine Plain), 26 (Chile Bay), 27 (Port Foster), 28 (South Bay), 29 (Ablation Point), 31 (Mount Flora), 32 (Cape Shirreff)
Resolution 1 (2000):	Guidelines for Implementation of the Framework for Protected Areas

CEP IV (2001)

Decision 2 (2001):	Guidelines on Circulation and Handling of CEP Documents
Resolution 3 (2001):	Protection of Antarctic meteorites.
Resolution 4 (2001):	Review of Historic Sites and Monuments
Resolution 5 (2001):	Guidelines for handling pre-1958 historic remains
Measure 1 (2001):	Historic Monument 75 (A Hut of Scott Base)
Measure 2 (2001):	Historical Monument 76 (Ruins of Base Pedro Aguirre Cerda)

CEP V (2002)

Measure 1 (2002):	Revised Management Plans for ASPA 106 (Cape Hallett), 107 (Emperor Island), 108 (Green Island), 117 (Avian Island), 121 (Cape

	Royds, subject to CCAMLR approval), 123 (Barwick Valley), 124 (Cape Crozier), 126 (Byers Peninsula), 130 (Tramway Ridge), 137 (White Island), 147 (Ablation Point), 148 (Mount Flora), and 157 (Backdoor Bay)
Decision 1 (2002):	Adoption of naming and numbering system for ASPAs
Resolution 1 (2002):	Review of conservation status of Antarctic Species
Resolution 2 (2002):	Revision of ASPA Management Plans
CEP VI (2003)	
Measure 2 (2003):	Designation of ASPA 160 (Frazier Islands) and 161 (Terra Nova Bay); management plans for ASPA 105 (Beaufort Island), 114 (Coronation Island), 118 (Cryptogam Ridge), 135 (Bailey Peninsula), 143 (Marine Plain), 152 (Bransfield Strait), 153 (Dallmann Bay), 154 (Botany Bay) and 156 (Lewis Bay)
Measure 3 (2003):	Revised list of historic sites and monuments
CEP VII (2004)	
Measure 1 (2004):	Designation of ASMA 2 (McMurdo Dry Valleys) and 3 (Cape Denison)
Measure 2 (2004):	Designation of ASPA 162 (Mawson's Huts); management plans for ASPA 113 (Litchfield Island), ASPA 122 (Arrival Heights), 139 (Biscoe Point) and 142 (Svarthamaren)
Measure 3 (2004):	Designation of Historic Monuments 77 (Cape Denison) and 78 (India Point)
Resolution 2 (2004):	Guidelines for Aircraft near concentrations of birds
CEP VIII (2005)	
Measure 1 (2005):	Annex VI (Liability)
Measure 2 (2005):	Designation of ASPA 163 (Dakshin Gangotri) and 164 (Scullin and Murray Monoliths); revised management plans for ASPA 101 (Taylor Rookery), 102 (Rookery Islands), 103 (Ardery and Odbert Islands), 119 (Forlidas and Davis Valley Ponds), 120 (Pointe-Geologie), 132 (Potter Peninsula), 133 (Harmony Point), 149 (Cape Shirreff), 155 (Cape Evans), 157 (Backdoor Bay), 158 (Hut Point), 159 (Cape Adare)
Measure 3 (2005):	Designation of ASMA 4 (Deception Island), including ASPA 140 (Parts of Deception Island) and 145 (Port Foster)
Measure 4 (2005):	Extension of Expiry Dates for ASPA 125 (Fildes Peninsula), 127 (Haswell Island), 144 (Chile Bay), 146 (South Bay), 150 (Ardley Island)
Measure 5 (2005):	Historic Monuments Lillie Marleen Hut and Amundsen's Tent
Decision 8 (2005):	Use of Heavy Fuel Oil
Decision 9 (2005):	Marine Protected Areas
Resolution 1 (2005):	Environmental Impact Assessment: Circulation of Information
Resolution 2 (2005):	Guidelines for Environmental Monitoring
Resolution 3 (2005):	Fuel Storage and Handling
Resolution 4 (2005):	Revised EIA guidelines
Resolution 5 (2005):	Site Guidelines for Visitors

CEP IX (2006)

Measure 1 (2006):	Designation of ASPA 165 (Edmonson Point), 166 (Port-Martin) and 167 (Hawker Island); Management Plans for ASPA 116 (New College Valley), 127 (Haswell Island), 131 (Canada Glacier), 134 (Cierva Point) and 136 (Clark Peninsula)
Measure 2 (2006):	Designation of ASMA 1 (Admiralty Bay), including ASPA 128 (Admiralty Bay) and HSM 51 (Puchalski Grave)
Measure 3 (2006):	Historic Site 81 (Rocher du Débarquement)
Measure 4 (2006):	De-listing of Fur Seals as Specially Protected Species
Decision 2 (2006):	Ballast Water Exchange: Referral to IMO
Resolution 2 (2006):	Site Guidelines for Visitors
Resolution 3 (2006):	Ballast Water Exchange
Resolution 4 (2006):	Southern Giant Petrels

CEP X (2007)

Measure 1 (2007):	Antarctic Specially Protected Areas: Revised Management Plans
Measure 2 (2007):	Antarctic Specially Managed Areas: Designations and Management Plans
Measure 3 (2007):	Antarctic Historic Sites and Monuments: Monument to the Antarctic Treaty
Resolution 1 (2007):	Resolution on Site Guidelines for Visitors
Resolution 2 (2007):	Conservation of Southern Giant Petrel *Macronectes giganteus*
Resolution 3 (2007):	Long-term Scientific Monitoring and Sustained Environmental Observation in Antarctica

CEP XI (2008)

Measure 1 (2008):	Antarctic Specially Managed Area No 7: Southwest Anvers Island and Palmer Basin
Measure 2 (2008):	Antarctic Specially Protected Area No 168: Mount Harding, Grove Mountains, East Antarctica
Measure 3 (2008):	Antarctic Specially Protected Area No 169: Amanda Bay, Ingrid Christensen Coast, Princess Elizabeth Land, East Antarctica
Measure 4 (2008):	Antarctic Specially Protected Area No 170: Marion Nunataks, Charcot Island, Antarctic Peninsula
Measure 5 (2008):	Antarctic Specially Protected Area No 118 (Summit of Mount Melbourne, Victoria Land): Revised Management Plan
Measure 6 (2008):	Antarctic Specially Protected Area No 123 (Barwick and Balham Valleys, Southern Victoria Land): Revised Management Plan
Measure 7 (2008):	Antarctic Specially Protected Area No 124 (Cape Crozier, Ross Island): Revised Management Plan
Measure 8 (2008):	Antarctic Specially Protected Area No 135 (North-East Bailey Peninsula, Budd Coast, Wilkes Land): Revised Management Plan
Measure 9 (2008):	Antarctic Specially Protected Area No 137 (North west White Island, McMurdo Sound): Revised Management Plan
Measure 10 (2008):	Antarctic Specially Protected Area No 138 (Linnaeus Terrace, Asgard Range, Victoria Land): Revised Management Plan
Measure 11 (2008):	Antarctic Specially Protected Area No 154 (Botany Bay, Cape Geology, Victoria Land): Revised Management Plan
Measure 12 (2008):	Antarctic Specially Protected Area No 155 (Cape Evans, Ross Island): Revised Management Plan
Measure 13 (2008):	Antarctic Specially Protected Area No 160 (Frazier Islands, Windmill Islands, Wilkes Land, East Antarctica): Revised Management Plan

Measure 14 (2008): Antarctic Specially Protected Area No 161 (Terra Nova Bay, Ross Sea): Revised Management Plan
Decision 5 (2008): Electronic Information Exchange System
Resolution 1 (2008): Guide to the Presentation of Working Papers Containing Proposals for Antarctic Specially Protected Areas, Antarctic Specially Managed Areas or Historic Sites and Monuments
Resolution 2 (2008): Site Guidelines for Visitors
Resolution 3 (2008): Environmental Domains Analysis for the Antarctic continent as a dynamic model for a systematic environmental geographic framework
Resolution 4 (2008): Checklist to assist in the inspection of Antarctic Specially Protected Areas and Antarctic Specially Managed Areas

CEP XII (2009)

Measure 1 (2009): Antarctic Specially Managed Area No 3 (Cape Denison, Commonwealth Bay, George V Land, East Antarctica): Revised Management Plan
Measure 2 (2009): Antarctic Specially Managed Area No 7 (Southwest Anvers Island and Palmer Basin): Revised Management Plan
Measure 3 (2009): Antarctic Specially Protected Area No 104 (Sabrina Island, Balleny Islands): Management Plan
Measure 4 (2009): Antarctic Specially Protected Area No 113 (Litchfield Island, Arthur Harbor, Anvers Island, Palmer Archipelago): Revised Management Plan
Measure 5 (2009): Antarctic Specially Protected Area No 121 (Cape Royds, Ross Island): Revised Management Plan
Measure 6 (2009): Antarctic Specially Protected Area No 125 (Fildes Peninsula, King George Island, South Shetland Islands): Revised Management Plan
Measure 7 (2009): Antarctic Specially Protected Area No 136 (Clark Peninsula, Budd Coast, Wilkes Land): Revised Management Plan
Measure 8 (2009): Antarctic Specially Protected Area No 142 (Svarthamaren): Revised Management Plan
Measure 9 (2009): Antarctic Specially Protected Area No 150 (Ardley Island, Maxwell Bay, King George Island): Revised Management Plan
Measure 10 (2009): Antarctic Specially Protected Area No 152 (Western Bransfield Strait): Revised Management Plan
Measure 11 (2009): Antarctic Specially Protected Area No 153 (Eastern Dallmann Bay): Revised Management Plan
Measure 12 (2009): Antarctic Specially Protected Area No 162 (Mawson's Huts Commonwealth Bay, George V Land, East Antarctica): Revised Management Plan
Measure 13 (2009): Antarctic Specially Protected Area No 171 (Narebski Point, Barton Peninsula, King George Island): Management Plan
Measure 14 (2009): Antarctic Historic Sites and Monuments: Base "W" and Hut at Damoy Point
Measure 16 (2009): Amendment of Annex II to the Protocol on Environmental Protection to the Antarctic Treaty: Conservation of Antarctic Fauna and Flora
Decision 1 (2009): ATME on Climate Change
Decision 3 (2009): Revised Guidelines for the Submission, Translation and Distribution of Documents for the ATCM and the CEP
Decision 6 (2009): Revised Rules of Procedure for the CEP
Resolution 1 (2009): Urging Parties to Enhance Environmental Protection for the Antarctic Ecosystem Northward to the Antarctic Convergence
Resolution 3 (2009): Guidelines for the designation and protection of Historic Sites and Monuments

Resolution 4 (2009): Site Guidelines for Visitors
Resolution 5 (2009): Protection of the Southern Giant Petrel

CEP XIII (2010)

Measure 1 (2010): Antarctic Specially Protected Area No. 101 (Taylor Rookery, Mac. Robertson Land): Revised Management Plan
Measure 2 (2010): Antarctic Specially Protected Area No. 102 (Rookery Islands, Holme Bay, Mac.Robertson Land): Revised Management Plan
Measure 3 (2010): Antarctic Specially Protected Area No. 103 (Ardery Island and Odbert Island, Budd Coast, Wilkes Land): Revised Management Plan
Measure 4 (2010): Antarctic Specially Protected Area No. 105 (Beaufort Island, McMurdo Sound, Ross Sea): Revised Management Plan
Measure 5 (2010): Antarctic Specially Protected Area No. 106 (Cape Hallett, Northern Victoria Land, Ross Sea): Revised Management Plan
Measure 6 (2010): Antarctic Specially Protected Area No. 119 (Davis Valley and Forlidas Pond, Dufek Massif, Pensacola Mountains): Revised Management Plan
Measure 7 (2010): Antarctic Specially Protected Area No. 139 (Biscoe Point, Anvers Island, Palmer Archipelago): Revised Management Plan
Measure 8 (2010): Antarctic Specially Protected Area No. 155 (Cape Evans, Ross Island): Revised Management Plan
Measure 9 (2010): Antarctic Specially Protected Area No. 157 (Backdoor Bay, Cape Royds, Ross Island): Revised Management Plan
Measure 10 (2010): Antarctic Specially Protected Area No. 158 (Hut Point, Ross Island): Revised Management Plan
Measure 11 (2010): Antarctic Specially Protected Area No. 159 (Cape Adare, Borchgrevink Coast): Revised Management Plan
Measure 12 (2010): Antarctic Specially Protected Area No. 163 (Dakshin Gangotri Glacier, Dronning Maud Land): Revised Management Plan
Measure 13 (2010): Antarctic Specially Protected Area No. 164 (Scullin and Murray Monoliths, Mac.Robertson Land): Revised Management Plan
Measure 14 (2010): Antarctic Specially Managed Area No. 7 (Southwest Anvers Island and Palmer Basin): Revised Management Plan
Measure 15 (2010): Antarctic Historic Sites and Monuments: Plaque Commemorating the PM-3A
Decision 3 (2010): Revised Rules of Procedure for the Committee for Environmental Protection
Resolution 1 (2010): Site Guidelines for visitors
Resolution 3 (2010): Revised Antarctic inspection Checklist
Resolution 4 (2010): SCAR Antarctic Climate Change and the Environment Report

CEP XIV (2011)

Measure 1 (2011): Antarctic Specially Protected Area No 116 (New College Valley, Caughley Beach, Cape Bird, Ross Island): Revised Management Plan
Measure 2 (2011): Antarctic Specially Protected Area No 120 (Pointe-Géologie Archipelago, Terre Adélie): Revised Management Plan
Measure 3 (2011): Antarctic Specially Protected Area No 122 (Arrival Heights, Hut Point Peninsula, Ross Island): Revised Management Plan
Measure 4 (2011): Antarctic Specially Protected Area No 126 (Byers Peninsula, Livingston Island, South Shetland Islands): Revised Management Plan
Measure 5 (2011): Antarctic Specially Protected Area No 127 (Haswell Island): Revised Management Plan

Measure 6 (2011): Antarctic Specially Protected Area No 131 (Canada Glacier, Lake Fryxell, Taylor Valley, Victoria Land): Revised Management Plan

Measure 7 (2011): Antarctic Specially Protected Area No 149 (Cape Shirreff and San Telmo Island, Livingston Island, South Shetland Islands): Revised Management Plan

Measure 8 (2011): Antarctic Specially Protected Area No 165 (Edmonson Point, Wood Bay, Ross Sea): Revised Management Plan

Measure 9 (2011): Antarctic Specially Protected Area No 167 (Hawker Island, Vestfold Hills, Ingrid Christensen Coast, Princess Elizabeth Land, East Antarctica): Revised Management Plan

Measure 10 (2011): Antarctic Specially Managed Area No 2 (McMurdo Dry Valleys, Southern Victoria Land): Revised Management Plan

Measure 11 (2011): Antarctic Historic Sites and Monuments: Monument to the Antarctic Treaty and Plaque

Measure 12 (2011): Antarctic Historic Sites and Monuments: No.1 Building at Great Wall Station

Decision 2 (2011): Revised Rules of Procedure for the Antarctic Treaty Consultative Meeting (2011); Revised Rules of Procedure for the Committee for Environmental Protection (2011); Guidelines for the Submission, Translation and Distribution of Documents for the ATCM and the CEP

Resolution 2 (2011): Revised Guide to the Preparation of Management Plans for Antarctic Specially Protected Areas

Resolution 3 (2011): General Guidelines for Visitors to the Antarctic

Resolution 5 (2011): Revised Guide to the Presentation of Working Papers Containing Proposals for Antarctic Specially Protected Areas, Antarctic Specially Managed Areas or Historic Sites and Monuments

Resolution 6 (2011): Non-Native Species

CEP XV (2012)

Measure 1 (2012): Antarctic Specially Protected Area No 109 (Moe Island, South Orkney Islands): Revised Management Plan

Measure 2 (2012): Antarctic Specially Protected Area No 110 (Lynch Island, South Orkney Islands): Revised Management Plan

Measure 3 (2012): Antarctic Specially Protected Area No 111 (Southern Powell Island and adjacent islands, South Orkney Islands): Revised Management Plan

Measure 4 (2012): Antarctic Specially Protected Area No 112 (Coppermine Peninsula, Robert Island, South Shetland Islands): Revised Management Plan

Measure 5 (2012): Antarctic Specially Protected Area No 115 (Lagotellerie Island, Marguerite Bay, Graham Land): Revised Management Plan

Measure 6 (2012): Antarctic Specially Protected Area No 129 (Rothera Point, Adelaide Island): Revised Management Plan

Measure 7 (2012): Antarctic Specially Protected Area No 133 (Harmony Point, Nelson Island, South Shetland Islands): Revised Management Plan

Measure 8 (2012): Antarctic Specially Protected Area No 140 (Parts of Deception Island): Revised Management Plan

Measure 9 (2012): Antarctic Specially Protected Area No 172 (Lower Taylor Glacier and Blood Falls,Taylor Valley, McMurdo Dry Valleys, Victoria Land): Management Plan

Measure 10 (2012): Antarctic Specially Managed Area No 4 (Deception Island): Revised Management Plan

Measure 11 (2012): Antarctic Historic Sites and Monuments: No 4 Pole of Inaccessibility Station building; No 7 Ivan Khmara's Stone; No 8 Anatoly Shcheglov's

Monument; No 9 Buromsky Island Cemetery; No 10 Soviet Oasis Station Observatory; No 11 Vostok Station Tractor; No 37 O'Higgins Historic Site

Resolution 4 (2012): Site Guidelines for visitors

Resolution 5 (2012): Barrientos Island – Aitcho Islands visitor Site Guidelines

Resolution 6 (2012): Antarctic Conservation Biogeographic Regions

CEP XVI (2013)

Measure 1 (2013): Antarctic Specially Protected Area No 108 (Green Island, Berthelot Islands, Antarctic Peninsula): Revised Management Plan

Measure 2 (2013): Antarctic Specially Protected Area No 117 (Avian Island, Marguerite Bay, Antarctic Peninsula): Revised Management Plan

Measure 3 (2013): Antarctic Specially Protected Area No 123 (Barwick and Balham Valleys, Southern Victoria Land): Revised Management Plan

Measure 4 (2013): Antarctic Specially Protected Area No 132 (Potter Peninsula, King George Island (Isla 25 de Mayo), South Shetland Islands): Revised Management Plan

Measure 5 (2013): Antarctic Specially Protected Area No 134 (Cierva Point and offshore islands, Danco Coast, Antarctic Peninsula): Revised Management Plan

Measure 6 (2013): Antarctic Specially Protected Area No 135 (North-east Bailey Peninsula, Budd Coast, Wilkes Land): Revised Management Plan

Measure 7 (2013): Antarctic Specially Protected Area No 137 (Northwest White Island, McMurdo Sound): Revised Management Plan

Measure 8 (2013): Antarctic Specially Protected Area No 138 (Linnaeus Terrace, Asgard Range, Victoria Land): Revised Management Plan

Measure 9 (2013): Antarctic Specially Protected Area No 143 (Marine Plain, Mule Peninsula, Vestfold Hills, Princess Elizabeth Land): Revised Management Plan

Measure 10 (2013): Antarctic Specially Protected Area No 147 (Ablation Valley and Ganymede Heights, Alexander Island): Revised Management Plan

Measure 11 (2013): Antarctic Specially Protected Area No 151 (Lions Rump, King George Island, South Shetland Islands): Revised Management Plan

Measure 12 (2013): Antarctic Specially Protected Area No 154 (Botany Bay, Cape Geology, Victoria Land): Revised Management Plan

Measure 13 (2013): Antarctic Specially Protected Area No 156 (Lewis Bay, Mount Erebus, Ross Island): Revised Management Plan

Measure 14 (2013): Antarctic Specially Protected Area No 160 (Frazier Islands, Windmill Islands, Wilkes Land, East Antarctica): Revised Management Plan

Measure 15 (2013): Antarctic Specially Protected Area No 161 (Terra Nova Bay, Ross Sea): Revised Management Plan

Measure 16 (2013): Antarctic Specially Protected Area No 170 (Marion Nunataks, Charcot Island, Antarctic Peninsula): Revised Management Plan

Measure 17 (2013): Antarctic Specially Protected Area No 173 (Cape Washington and Silverfish Bay, Terra Nova Bay, Ross Sea): Management Plan

Measure 18 (2013): Antarctic Historic Sites and Monuments: Location of the first permanently occupied German Antarctic research station "Georg Forster" at the Schirmacher Oasis, Dronning Maud Land

Measure 19 (2013): Antarctic Historic Sites and Monuments: Professor Kudryashov's Drilling Complex Building, Vostok Station

Measure 20 (2013): Antarctic Historic Sites and Monuments: Upper "Summit Camp", Mount Erebus

Measure 21 (2013): Antarctic Historic Sites and Monuments: Lower "Camp E", Mount Erebus

Resolution 2 (2013): Antarctic Clean-up Manual

CEP XVII (2014)

Measure 1 (2014): Antarctic Specially Protected Area No 113 (Litchfield Island, Arthur Harbor, Anvers Island, Palmer Archipelago): Revised Management Plan

Measure 2 (2014): Antarctic Specially Protected Area No 121 (Cape Royds, Ross Island): Revised Management Plan

Measure 3 (2014): Antarctic Specially Protected Area No 124 (Cape Crozier, Ross Island): Revised Management Plan

Measure 4 (2014): Antarctic Specially Protected Area No 128 (Western shore of Admiralty Bay, King George Island, South Shetland Islands): Revised Management Plan

Measure 5 (2014): Antarctic Specially Protected Area No 136 (Clark Peninsula, Budd Coast, Wilkes Land, East Antarctica): Revised Management Plan

Measure 6 (2014): Antarctic Specially Protected Area No 139 (Biscoe Point, Anvers Island, Palmer Archipelago): Revised Management Plan

Measure 7 (2014): Antarctic Specially Protected Area No 141 (Yukidori Valley, Langhovde, Lützow-Holm Bay): Revised Management Plan

Measure 8 (2014): Antarctic Specially Protected Area No 142 (Svarthamaren): Revised Management Plan

Measure 9 (2014): Antarctic Specially Protected Area No 162 (Mawson's Huts, Cape Denison, Commonwealth Bay, George V Land, East Antarctica): Revised Management Plan

Measure 10 (2014): Antarctic Specially Protected Area No 169 (Amanda Bay, Ingrid Christensen Coast, Princess Elizabeth Land, East Antarctica): Revised Management Plan

Measure 11 (2014): Antarctic Specially Protected Area No 171 (Narębski Point, Barton Peninsula, King George Island): Revised Management Plan

Measure 12 (2014): Antarctic Specially Protected Area No 174 (Stornes, Larsemann Hills, Princess Elizabeth Land): Management Plan

Measure 13 (2014): Antarctic Specially Protected Area No 175 (High Altitude Geothermal sites of the Ross Sea region): Management Plan

Measure 14 (2014): Antarctic Specially Managed Area No 1 (Admiralty Bay, King George Island): Revised Management Plan

Measure 15 (2014): Antarctic Specially Managed Area No 6 (Larsemann Hills, East Antarctica): Revised Management Plan

Measure 16 (2014): Antarctic Specially Protected Area No 114 (Northern Coronation Island, South Orkney Islands): Revoked Management Plan

Resolution 1 (2014): Fuel Storage and Handling

Resolution 2 (2014) : Cooperation, Facilitation, and Exchange of Meteorological and Related Oceanographic and Cryospheric Environmental Information

Resolution 3 (2014) : Supporting the Polar Code

Resolution 4 (2014): Site Guidelines for Visitors

Thematic Index of All ATCM Measures, Decisions, and Resolutions Related to CEP Issues (1998–2014)

Scientific research (facilitation, cooperation)	**Resolutions**: 3 (2001); 3 (2007); 4 (2010); 3 (2008); 2 (2014)
Conservation of fauna and flora	**Resolutions**: 2 (1999); 1 (2002); 2 (2004); 4 (2006); 2 (2007); 5 (2009); 6 (2011); 6 (2012) **Measure** 4 (2006)

Historic sites and monuments	**Measures**: 2 (1998); 1 (2001); 2 (2001); 3 (2003); 3 (2004); 5 (2005); 3 (2006); 3 (2007); 14 (2009); 15 (2010); 11 (2011); 12 (2011); 11 (2012); 18 (2013); 19 (2013); 20 (2013); 21 (2013) **Resolutions**: 4 (2001); 5 (2001); 3 (2009)
Specially Protected Areas; the Antarctic Protected Area System (generally)	**Measures**: 1 (1998); 2 (2000); 1 (2002); 2 (2003); 1 (2004); 2 (2004); 2 (2005); 3 (2005); 4 (2005); 1 (2006); 2 (2006); 1 (2007); 2 (2007); 1 (2008); 2 (2008); 3 (2008); 4 (2008); 5 (2008); 6 (2008); 7 (2008); 8 (2008); 9 (2008); 10 (2008); 11 (2008); 12 (2008); 13 (2008); 14 (2008); 1 (2009); 2 (2009); 3 (2009); 4 (2009); 5 (2009); 6 (2009); 7 (2009); 8 (2009); 9 (2009); 10 (2009); 11 (2009); 12 (2009); 13 (2009); 1 (2010); 2 (2010); 3 (2010); 4 (2010); 5 (2010); 6 (2010); 7 (2010); 8 (2010); 9 (2010); 10 (2010); 11 (2010); 12 (2010); 13 (2010); 14 (2010); 1 (2011); 2 (2011); 3 (2011); 4 (2011); 5 (2011); 6 (2011); 7 (2011); 8 (2011); 9 (2011); 10 (2011); 1 (2012); 2 (2012); 3 (2012); 4 (2012); 5 (2012); 6 (2012); 7 (2012); 8 (2012); 9 (2012); 10 (2012); 1 (2013); 2 (2013); 3 (2013); 4 (2013); 5 (2013); 6 (2013); 7 (2013); 8 (2013); 9 (2013); 10 (2013); 11 (2013); 12 (2013); 13 (2013); 14 (2013); 15 (2013); 16 (2013); 17 (2013); 1 (2014); 2 (2014); 3 (2014); 4 (2014); 5 (2014); 6 (2014); 7 (2014); 8 (2014); 9 (2014); 10 (2014); 11 (2014); 12 (2014); 13 (2014); 14 (2014); 15 (2014); 16 (2014) **Resolutions**: 1 (1998); 2 (1998); 1 (2000); 2 (2002); 1 (2008); 4 (2008) 2 (2011) **Decision**: 1 (2002)
Site Visits	**Resolutions**: 5 (2005); 2 (2006); 1 (2007); 2 (2008); 4 (2009); 1 (2010); 5 (2011); 4 (2012); 5 (2012); 4 (2014)
The Antarctic environment (human impact on; protection of)	**Resolutions**: 1 (2009); 2 (2013)
Antarctic marine environment and resources	**Decisions**: 4 (1998); 9 (2005)
Fuel (use, storage and handling)	**Decision** 8 (2005) **Resolution** 3 (2005); 1 (2014)
Protocol on Environmental Protection	**Recommendation** XV-5 (1989) **Resolution** 6 (1999) **Measures:** 1 (2005); 16 (2009)
Environmental monitoring and data management; Environmental Impact Assessments	**Recommendation** XVII-1 **Resolutions**: 1 (1999); 1 (2005); 2 (2005); 4 (2005)
Ships and boats operating in Arctic and Antarctic Waters	**Resolutions**: 3 (1998); 3 (2006); 3 (2014) **Decisions:** 2 (1999); 2 (2006)
Rules of Procedure (amendments and revisions)	**Decisions**: 2 (1998); 6 (2009); 3 (2010); 2 (2011)
Circulation and Handling of CEP and ATCM Documents	**Decisions**: 2 (2001); 3 (2009)

Miscellaneous	**Measure** 1 (1999) (Sites of Specific Scientific Interest) **Decisions**: 1 (1999) (ATCM and CEP websites); 1 (2000) (CEP observers); 5 (2008) (Electronic Information Exchange System); 1 (2009) (meeting of experts on climate change) **Resolutions:** 3 (2010) (Antarctic Inspection Checklists); 3 (2011) (Visitors to the Antarctic)

Decision 2 (2011), Annex 2: Revised Rules of Procedure for the Committee for Environmental Protection

Rule 1

Where not otherwise specified the Rules of Procedure for the Antarctic Treaty Consultative Meeting shall be applicable.

Rule 2

For the purposes of these Rules of Procedure:

(a) the expression "Protocol" means the Protocol on Environmental Protection to the Antarctic Treaty, signed in Madrid on 4 October, 1991;
(b) the expression "the Parties" means the Parties to the Protocol;
(c) the expression "Committee" means the Committee for Environmental Protection as defined in Article 11 of the Protocol;
(d) the expression "Secretariat" means the Secretariat of the Antarctic Treaty.

Part I Representatives and Experts

Rule 3

Each Party to the Protocol is entitled to be a member of the Committee and to appoint a representative who may be accompanied by experts and advisers with suitable scientific, environmental or technical competence.

Before each meeting of the Committee each member of the Committee shall, as early as possible, notify the Host Government of that meeting of the name and designation of each representative, and before or at the beginning of the meeting, the name and designation of each expert and adviser.

Part II Observers and Consultation

Rule 4

Observer status in the Committee shall be open to:

(a) any Contracting Party to the Antarctic Treaty which is not a Party to the Protocol;
(b) the President of the Scientific Committee on Antarctic Research, the Chairman of the Scientific Committee for the Conservation of Antarctic Marine Living Resources and the Chairman of the Council of Managers of National Antarctic Programmes, or their nominated Representatives;
(c) subject to the specific approval of the Antarctic Treaty Consultative Meeting, other relevant scientific, environmental and technical organisations which can contribute to the work of the Committee.

Rule 5

Before each meeting of the Committee each observer shall, as early as possible, notify the Host Government of that meeting of the name and designation of its representative attending the meeting.

Rule 6

Observers may participate in the discussions, but shall not participate in the taking of decisions.

Rule 7

In carrying out its functions the Committee shall, as appropriate, consult with the Scientific Committee on Antarctic Research, the Scientific Committee for the Conservation of Antarctic

Marine Living Resources, the Council of Managers of National Antarctic Programmes and other relevant scientific, environmental and technical organisations.

Rule 8

The Committee may seek the advice of experts as required on an ad hoc basis.

Part III Meetings

Rule 9

The Committee shall meet once a year, generally and preferably in conjunction with the Antarctic Treaty Consultative Meeting and at the same location. With the agreement of the ATCM, and in order to fulfill its functions, the Committee may also meet between annual meetings.

The Committee may establish informal open-ended contact groups to examine specific issues and report back to the Committee.

Open-ended contact groups established to undertake work during intersessional periods shall operate as follows:

(a) where appropriate, the contact group coordinator shall be agreed by the Committee during its meeting and noted in its final report;

(b) where appropriate, the terms of reference for the contact group shall be agreed by the Committee and included in its final report;

(c) where appropriate, the modes of communication for the contact group, such as e-mail, the online discussion forum maintained by the Secretariat and informal meetings, shall be agreed by the Committee and included in its final report;

(d) representatives who wish to be involved in a contact group shall register their interest with the coordinator through the discussion forum, by e-mail or by other appropriate means;

(e) the coordinator shall use appropriate means to inform all group members of the composition of the contact group;

(f) all correspondence shall be made available to all members of the contact group in a timely manner; and

(g) when providing comments, members of the contact group shall state for whom they are speaking.

The Committee may also agree to establish other informal sub-groups or to consider other ways of working such as, but not limited to, workshops and video-conferences.

Rule 10

The Committee may establish, with the approval of the Antarctic Treaty Consultative Meeting, subsidiary bodies, as appropriate.

Such subsidiary bodies shall operate on the basis of the Rules of Procedure of the Committee as applicable.

Rule 11

The Rules of Procedure for the preparation of the Agenda of the Antarctic Treaty Consultative Meeting shall apply with necessary changes to Committee meetings.

Before each meeting of any subsidiary body the Secretariat, in consultation with the Chairperson of both the Committee and of the subsidiary body, shall prepare and distribute a preliminary annotated Agenda.

Part IV Submission of Documents

Rule 12

1. Working Papers shall refer to papers submitted by Members of the Committee that require discussion and action at a Meeting and papers submitted by Observers referred to in Rule 4(b).

2. Secretariat Papers shall refer to papers prepared by the Secretariat pursuant to a mandate established at a Meeting, or which would, in the view of the Executive Secretary, help inform the Meeting or assist in its operation.

3. Information Papers shall refer to:
   - Papers submitted by Members of the Committee or Observers referred to in Rule 4(b) that provide information in support of a Working Paper or that are relevant to discussions at a Meeting;
   - Papers submitted by Observers referred to in Rule 4(a) that are relevant to discussions at a Meeting; and
   - Papers submitted by Observers referred to in Rule 4(c) that are relevant to discussions at a Meeting.

4. Background Papers shall refer to papers submitted by any participant that will not be introduced in a Meeting, but that are submitted for the purpose of formally providing information.

5. Procedures for the submission, translation and distribution of documents are annexed to the ATCM Rules of Procedure.

Part V Advice and Recommendations

Rule 13

The Committee shall try to reach consensus on the recommendations and advice to be provided by it pursuant to the Protocol.

Where consensus cannot be achieved the Committee shall set out in its report all views advanced on the matter in question.

Part VI Decisions

Rule 14

Where decisions are necessary, decisions on matters of substance shall be taken by a consensus of the members of the Committee participating in the meeting. Decisions on matters of procedure shall be taken by a simple majority of the members of the Committee present and voting. Each member of the Committee shall have one vote. Any question as to whether an issue is a procedural one shall be decided by consensus.

Part VII Chairperson and Vice-chairs

Rule 15

The Committee shall elect a Chairperson and two Vice-chairs from among the Consultative Parties. The Chairperson and the Vice-chairs shall be elected for a period of two years and, where possible, their terms shall be staggered.

The Chairperson and the Vice-chairs shall not be re-elected to their post for more than one additional two-year term. The Chairperson and Vice-chairs shall not be representatives from the same Party.

The Vice-chair who has been a Vice-chair for the longer period of time (in total, counting any previous term of office) shall be first Vice-chair.

In the event that both Vice-chairs are appointed for the first time at the same meeting, the Committee shall determine which Vice-chair is elected as first Vice-chair.

Rule 16

Amongst other duties the Chairperson shall have the following powers and responsibilities:

(a) convene, open, preside at and close each meeting of the Committee;

(b) make rulings on points of order raised at each meeting of the Committee provided that each representative retains the right to request that any such decision be submitted to the Committee for approval;

(c) approve a provisional agenda for the meeting after consultation with Representatives;

(d) sign, on behalf of the Committee, the report of each meeting;

(e) present the report referred to in Rule 22 on each meeting of the Committee to the Antarctic Treaty Consultative Meeting;

(f) as required, initiate intersessional work; and

(g) as agreed by the Committee, represent the Committee in other forums.

Rule 17

Whenever the Chairperson is unable to act, the first Vice-chair shall assume the powers and responsibilities of the Chairperson.

Whenever both the Chair and first Vice-chair are unable to act, the second Vice-chair shall assume the powers and responsibilities of the Chairperson.

Rule 18

In the event of the office of the Chairperson falling vacant between meetings, the first Vice-chair shall exercise the powers and responsibilities of the Chairperson until a new Chairperson is elected.

If the offices of both the Chairperson and first Vice-chair fall vacant between meetings, the second Vice-chair shall exercise the powers and responsibilities of the Chairperson until a new Chairperson is elected.

Rule 19

The Chairperson and Vice-chairs shall begin to carry out their functions on the conclusion of the meeting of the Committee at which they have been elected.

Part VIII Administrative Facilities

Rule 20

As a general rule the Committee, and any subsidiary bodies, shall make use of the administrative facilities of the Government which agrees to host its meetings.

Part IX Languages

Rule 21

English, French, Russian and Spanish shall be the official languages of the Committee and, as applicable, the subsidiary bodies referred to in Rule 10.

Part X Records and Reports

Rule 22

The Committee shall present a report on each of its meetings to the Antarctic Treaty Consultative Meeting. The report shall cover all matters considered at the meeting of the Committee, including at its intersessional meetings and by its subsidiary bodies as appropriate, and shall reflect the views expressed. The report shall also include a comprehensive list of the officially circulated Working Papers, Information Papers and Background Papers. The report shall be presented to the Antarctic Treaty Consultative Meeting in the official languages. The report shall be circulated to the Parties, and to observers attending the meeting, and shall thereupon be made publicly available.

Part XI Amendments

Rule 23

The Committee may adopt amendments to these rules of procedure, which shall be subject to approval by the Antarctic Treaty Consultative Meeting.

SELECTED ATCM INSTRUMENTS RELATED TO CEP ISSUES

Decision 4 (1998): Marine Protected Areas

The Representatives,

Noting the requirements in Annex V, Article 6, paragraphs 1 and 2, of the Protocol on Environment Protection to the Antarctic Treaty (the Protocol) that the views of the Commission of the Convention on the Conservation of Antarctic Marine Living Resources (CCAMLR) must be sought on proposals for Antarctic Specially Protected Areas which contain marine areas;

Recalling the adoption at ATCM XXI of a draft text on marine areas;

Noting also the endorsement by CCAMLR at its XVIth Meeting of that draft text;

Decide:

1. To adopt the following:

For the purposes of implementation of Article 6(2) of the Environmental Protocol, draft management plans which require the approval of CCAMLR are those which include marine areas

- In which there is actual harvesting or potential capability for harvesting of marine living resources which might be affected by site designation, or
- For which there are provisions specified in a draft management plan which might prevent or restrict CCAMLR-related activities;

2. That the sites listed in the appendix to this Decision meet the above criteria;

3. Proposals for designations of Antarctic Specially Protected Areas or Antarctic Specially Managed Areas which might have implications for CCAMLR Ecosystem Monitoring Programme (CEMP). Sites shall be submitted to CCAMLR for its consideration before any decision is taken on the proposals;

4. That the above procedures should be followed pending entry into force of Annex V.

Appendix to Decision 4 (1998): List of SSSIs with Marine Areas of Interest to CCAMLR

SSSI 1: Cape Royds, Ross Island
SSSI 20: Biscoe Pont, Anvers Island
SSSI 26: 'Child Bay' (Discovery Bay), Greenwich Island, South Shetland Islands
SSSI 27: Port Foster, Deception Island, South Shetland Islands
SSSI 28: South Bay, Doumer Island, Palmer Archipelago
SSSI 32: Cape Shirreff, Livingstone Island, South Shetland Islands
SSSI 34: Lions Rump, King George Island, South Shetland Islands
SSSI 35: Western Bransfield Strait off Low Island, South Shetland Islands
SSSI 36: Eastern Dallmann Bay off Brabant Island, Palmer Archipelago

Resolution 1 (1998): National Responsibilities for Revising Management Plans of Antarctic Areas

The Representatives,

Welcoming the entry into force of the Environmental Protocol, including its Annexes I-IV;

Conscious that this situation does not extend to Annex V on Area Protection and Management which was adopted under Recommendation XVI-10;

Aware that, to become effective, that Recommendation requires approval under the procedures of Article IX (4) of the Treaty;

Recommend that:

Those Consultative Parties which have yet to approve Recommendation XVI-10 under the procedures of Article IX(4), take steps to do so as soon as possible.

The Consultative Parties identified in the Appendix to this Resolution have responsibility for the preparation or revision of Management Plans for those sites listed.

Those Consultative Parties identified in the Annex should prepare a timetable for the preparation or revision of Management Plans for those sites for which they have principal responsibility, and should submit the timetable for information to ATCM XXIII.

Appendix to Resolution 1 (1998): National Responsibilities for Revising Management Plans of Antarctic Protected Areas

Australia

Sites of Special Scientific Interest
16. North-eastern Bailey Peninsula
17. Clark Peninsula
25. Marine Plain, Vestfold Hills

Chile

Specially Protected Areas
16. Coppermine Peninsula
Sites of Special Scientific Interest
5. Fildes Peninsula
6. Byers Peninsula (joint with UK)
26. Chile Bay, Greenwich Island
27. Port Foster, Deception Island
28. South Bay, Doumer Island
32. Cape Shirreff (joint with USA)
24. Ardley Island

New Zealand

Specially Protected Areas
4. Sabrina Island
22. Cryptogram Ridge
Sites of Special Scientific Interest
10. Caughley Beach
24. Summit of Mount Melbourne

USA

Specially Protected Areas
7. Cape Hallett
17. Litchfield Islands
23. Forlidas Ponds
Sites of Special Scientific Interest
1. Cape Royds
2. Arrival Heights
3. Barwick Valley
4. Cape Crozier
18. North-western White Island
20. Biscoe Point
32. Cape Shirreff (joint with Chile)
35. Western Bransfield Strait
36. East Dallman Bay

Norway

Sites of Special Scientific Interest
23. Svarthamaren

Russia

Sites of Special Scientific Interest
7. Haswell Island

Poland

Sites of Special Scientific Interest
8. Western Shore, Admiralty Bay
34. Lions Rump, King George Island

Japan

Sites of Special Scientific Interest
22. Yukidori Valley

United Kingdom

Specially Protected Areas
8. Dion Island
9. Green Island
14. Lynch Island
18. North Coronation Island
19. Lagotellerie Island
21. Avian Island
Sites of Special Scientific Interest
6. Byers Peninsula (joint with Chile)
21. Parts of Deception Island
29. Ablation Point
31. Mount Flora

Resolution 3 (1998): International Code of Safety for Ships in Polar Waters

The Representatives,
Noting the draft International Code of Safety for Ships in Polar Waters (Polar Code), being developed by the International Maritime Organisation (IMO);

Recognising the benefits of having a Code of Practice for Ship Safety for vessels operating in Antarctic water;

Noting also that a Polar Code should meet the requirements of Article 10 of Annex IV to the Protocol on Environmental Protection to the Antarctic Treaty;

Recommend that:

Consultative Parties provide input to IMO, via their national maritime authorities, on the draft Polar Shipping Code as it relates to shipping operations within the Antarctic Treaty area.

Decision 2 (1999): Guidelines for Antarctic Shipping and Related Activities

The Representatives,

Recalling Resolution 3 (1998) on the draft Polar Shipping Code;

Noting the outcome of the 71st session of the International Maritime Organisation's Maritime Safety Committee regarding the development of a Polar Shipping Code in the form of non-mandatory guidelines, and the intention to exclude Antarctica from the application of these guidelines unless Antarctic Treaty Consultative Parties decide otherwise;

Recalling the provisions of Article 10 of Annex IV of the Protocol on Environmental Protection to the Antarctic Treaty;

Recognising the importance of maximising the safety of vessels operating in Antarctic waters;

Decide:

1. To give priority to the development of guidelines for Antarctic shipping and related activities pursuant to Article 10 of Annex IV to the Protocol;

2. To seek subsequent adoption of these guidelines by the International Maritime Organisation (IMO) as a means of extending their applicability to members of the IMO that are not Antarctic Treaty Consultative Parties;

3. To convene a Meeting of Experts under the provisions of Recommendation IV-24, with the aim of developing draft guidelines for Antarctic shipping and related activities;

4. To notify the IMO, through Peru as host Government of ATCM XXIII, of the provisions of paragraphs 1, 2 and 3 above;

5. Pursuant to paragraph 3 above, to request the Meeting of Experts:

(i) to examine the most recent version of the draft Polar Shipping guidelines being developed for the Arctic by the IMO, and decide which elements of those draft Arctic guidelines should form the basis of the Antarctic guidelines;

(ii) to consider other aspects of the design, construction, manning and equipment of vessels operating in Antarctic waters that might require elaboration in the Antarctic guidelines;

(iii) to take into account existing international instruments regulating shipping activities in Antarctica, including for example MARPOL, SOLAS, UNCLOS and the Environmental Protocol to the Antarctic Treaty;

(iv) to take into account existing guidelines adopted under the Antarctic Treaty, and in particular those adopted under Resolution 6 (1998);

(v) to ensure the guidelines adequately take account of the nature of Antarctic shipping, the environmental conditions of Antarctica and the system of international governance applying to the Antarctic Treaty area;

(vi) to report back to ATCM XXIV.

6. To encourage attendance at the Meeting by representatives from Consultative Parties, particularly their Antarctic and marine safety experts, and to invite experts from, Non-Consultative Parties, the Council of Managers of National Antarctic Programmes (COMNAP) and the Scientific Committee on Antarctic Research (SCAR).

7. To also invite experts from the following bodies: International Hydrographic Organisation (IHO), International Maritime Organisation (IMO), World Meteorological Organisation

(WMO), International Association of Classification Societies (IACS), International Association of Protection and Indemnity Clubs (P&I Clubs), International Association of Antarctic Tour Operators (IAATO) and the Antarctic and Southern Ocean Coalition (ASOC).

8. To accept the offer of the United Kingdom Government to host the Meeting of Experts in London, which should, as far as possible, be held in conjunction with a meeting of the appropriate IMO expert body.

9. That in accordance with Recommendation IV-24, the United Kingdom should submit a report of the Meeting of Experts to ATCM XXIV for consideration.

Resolution 6 (1999): Adherence to the Environmental Protocol by Non-Consultative Parties

The Representatives,

Considering the entry into force of the Protocol on Environmental Protection to the Antarctic Treaty;

Noting that certain non-Consultative Parties are not yet Parties to the Protocol and are therefore not bound by its provisions;

Aware that vessels carrying significant numbers of tourists are operating, or planning to operate, in Antarctic waters, and that some of these vessels are chartered by tourist companies organizing their expeditions in the territory of non-Consultative Parties;

Conscious of the potential for cumulative environmental impacts as a result of large numbers of tourists visiting sites in Antarctica;

Concerned that the presence of such vessels in Antarctic waters may result, in the event of a major maritime accident, in a serious risk to the safety of the crew and passengers involved, and significant adverse impact on the Antarctic environment and dependent and associated ecosystems, as well as major implications for search and rescue resources in Antarctica;

Urge:

Those non-Consultative Parties which have not yet become Parties to the Protocol on Environmental Protection to the Antarctic Treaty, particularly those with Antarctic tourist activities organised in their territory, to adhere to the Protocol as soon as possible.

Resolution 1 (2000): Guidelines for Implementation of the Framework for Protected Areas set forth in Article 3, Annex V of the Environmental Protocol

The Representatives,

Noting that Article 3 of Annex V of the Protocol provides a framework for the designation of Antarctic Specially Protected Areas;

Recognising that these Areas must conform to the requirements of Article 3 of Annex V;

Recalling Resolution 2(1998) *Guide to the Preparation of Management Plans for Antarctic Specially Protected Areas*;

Conscious of the need for general guidance in the assessment and definition of potential specially protected areas;

Recommend that the "Guidelines for Implementation of the Framework for Protected Areas set forth in Article 3, Annex V of the Environmental Protocol", attached to this Resolution, be used by those engaged in the development of proposals for specially protected areas in Antarctica.

Guidelines for Implementation of the Framework for Protected Areas Set Forth in Article 3, Annex V of the Environmental Protocol

CONTENTS

PART I: INTRODUCTION

1.1 The Antarctic Treaty System and Protected Areas

A variety of instruments have been developed within the Antarctic Treaty system to help protect special places such as important wildlife breeding areas, fragile plant communities, cold desert ecosystems and historic places. These instruments have included the Agreed Measures for the Conservation of Antarctic Fauna and Flora and numerous recommendations to Parties.

More recently Annex V of the Environmental Protocol was agreed. It defines the basic structure or framework for Antarctic Specially Protected Areas (ASPAs) with a list of values that may merit special protection (Article 3(1) and types or examples of area to be protected (Article 3(2)) (refer Appendix I). Article 3(2) of Annex V states that Parties shall seek to identify such areas within a systematic environmental-geographical framework. Such areas will then be included in the existing series of Antarctic Specially Protected Areas.

Antarctic Specially Protected Areas is the only category of protected area provided for under Annex V of the Environmental Protocol (refer Article 2). Another category of area, Antarctic Specially Managed Areas (ASMAs) are defined in Article 4 and are areas with special management requirements. ASMAs are not considered in these guidelines.

Protected areas provide a higher level of protection for specific values beyond that achieved by other forms of planning and management measures under the Protocol. These areas are designated within geographically defined limits and are managed to achieve specific protection aims and objectives.

1.2 Aim of the Guidelines

The aim of the guidelines is to assist the Parties, SCAR, CCAMLR, COMNAP and the CEP to apply Article 3 of Annex V of the Environmental Protocol for the designation of Antarctic Specially Protected Areas. The guidelines provide a set of tools to enable more systematic assessment, selection, definition and proposal of areas that might require greater protection in accordance with the provisions of Annex V of the Environmental Protocol. It is hoped that they will facilitate methodical assessment and designation of such areas.

1.3 Structure of the Guidelines

The guidelines are organised into three main parts representing a process for assessing, selecting, defining and proposing new protected areas.

Part I is an introductory section, which offers a brief explanation of the existing mechanisms to protect Antarctic areas within the Antarctic Treaty system. This section also establishes the aims of the guidelines and details the way they are structured.

Part II provides guidance for assessing the potential of an area or site for protection and includes checklists on the framework for protected areas provided in Article 3(1) and 3(2). The checklist provides guidance on the values to be protected and on how to determine what should be protected and why, i.e. the reasons for protection. The concept of quality, including quality criteria, is defined to provide a further means of assessing whether an area merits being specially protected. Finally, the concept of environmental risk is presented as a very important aid in assessing the area's need for enhanced protection.

Part III provides guidance for defining areas for protection under Article 3 of Annex V of the Protocol, including ways to apply the concept of feasibility.

Part IV briefly notes the steps for proposing areas for protection including drafting of management plans and refers readers to the "Guide to Preparing Management Plans for Antarctic Specially Protected Areas".

NOTE:

As these guidelines have no legal status, those wishing to establish new protected areas should also carefully examine the provisions of Annex V of the Environmental Protocol to the Antarctic Treaty and should seek advice from their national authority at an early stage.

PART II: ASSESSING THE PROTECTION POTENTIAL OF AN AREA

2.1 Assessing Values to be Protected (Article 3(1))

When seeking to assess whether an area merits protection, a clear understanding is needed of the values to be protected. Values are generally taken to mean something of worth, merit or importance. Table 1 offers a checklist of the values listed in Article 3(1) that could be used to help identify those values represented in possible specially protected areas.

Table 1. Checklist of the values listed in Article 3(1)

Environmental values	does the area contain physical, chemical or biological features e.g., glaciers, fresh water lakes, melt pools, rock outcrops, plant life or animal life that are particularly unique or representative components of the Antarctic environment?
Scientific values	does the area contain physical, chemical or biological features of special interest to scientific researchers where the principles and methods of science would be applicable?
Historic values	does the area contain features or objects that represent, connate or recall events, experiences, achievements, places or records that are important, significant or unusual in the course of human events and activity [1] in Antarctica?
Aesthetic values	does the area contain features or attributes e.g., beauty, pleasantness, inspirational qualities, scenic attraction and appeal [3] that contribute to people's appreciation and sense or perception of an area?
Wilderness values	does the area contain characteristics e.g., remoteness, few or no people, an absence of human-made objects, traces, sounds and smells, untravelled or infrequently visited terrain that are particularly unique or representative components of the Antarctic environment? [3]
Combination	does the area contain any combination of the above values?
Ongoing or planned scientific activities	does the area include ongoing or planned scientific projects or activities?

If it is considered that any examples of the values listed in Article 3(1) are contained or represented in a particular area then further investigation of the area for protected area status may be worthwhile.

2.2 Assessment of Potential Protection and Use Category (Article 3(2a-i))

Article 3(2a-i) provides a list of examples of areas that can be designated as ASPAs. It should be noted that the specific examples of areas identified are not exclusive and that other examples of protected area could potentially be included provided they aim to protect the values set out in Article 3(1). In addition, it should be noted that Article 3(2) does not provide a uniform series of values, features, objectives, categories or uses of potential ASPAs.

A conceptual methodology has been developed to help understand more systematically what should be protected and why (i.e. examples or categories of areas and reasons for their proposed designation). Table 2 provides a checklist of the potential types or categories of areas to be protected and their management or use objectives. The aim is to provide a tool that can be used for the clearer identification of the important components or attributes of possible protected areas once the values to be protected have been agreed (refer section 2.1).

The checklist may also help to ensure that possible protected areas are considered in a more standardised way and to aid further work in the designation process (e.g. assessment and subsequent development of management plans.

Table 2. Checklist for identifying and clarifying the type of area to be protected (protection category) as well as the use or reasons (use category).

Protection Categories (i.e. what is being protected)

Ecosystems	would the area be protected for its ecosystems? I.e. dynamic complexes of plant, animal and micro-organism communities and their non-living environment interacting as an ecological unit [4].
Habitats	would the area be protected for its habitats? I.e. the places or types of site where an organism or population naturally occurs [4].
Species assemblages	would the area be protected for its species assemblages? I.e. important or unusual groupings or populations of one or more species of fauna or flora (usual type of area protection of species in Antarctica).
Species (taxa)	would the area be protected for its species? I.e. special groups of organisms which resemble each other and sometimes are linked to a common habitat to a greater degree than members of other groups, and which commonly form reproductively isolated groups that will not normally breed with members of another group [5].
Geological, glaciological or geomorphological Features	would the area be protected for its geological, glaciological or geomorphological features? I.e. distinctive or special characteristics of the history, structure or components of the Earth's crust, rocks, fossils and cryosphere or a result of present or past processes beneath or at the Earth's surface in Antarctica
Landscapes	would the area be protected for its landscape? I.e. expanses of coastal or inland scenery, usually at a scale where they contain a mosaic of inter-related ecosystems and characterised by particular patterns of geometry, heterogeneity, patch dynamics and biophysical processes [6].
Aesthetic	would the area be protected for its aesthetic features? I.e. attributes concerned with beauty, appreciation, perception and inspiration [3].
Wilderness	would the area be protected for its wilderness features? I.e. attributes concerned with remoteness and a relative absence of both people and indications of past and present human presence or activity [3].

Historic	would the area be protected for its historic features? I.e. things which represent or recall events, experiences, places, achievements or records that are important, significant or unusual in the course of human events and activity in Antarctica.
Intrinsic	would the area be protected for its intrinsic features? (The real or inherent nature of a thing is worth protecting in its own right i.e. without requiring use).

Use Categories (why the area is being protected)

Scientific research	would the area be protected for scientific research?
Conservation	would the area be protected for its conservation purposes? (Conservation embraces both protection and judicious use, management of biodiversity, intrinsic value and importance in maintaining the life sustaining systems of the biosphere: distinguished from "sustainable use" and "sustainable management" [4])

2.3 Quality Criteria

Quality criteria can be applied as a checklist to evaluate further whether an area deserves special protection or not. The quality of a potential protected area can be thought of as an overall degree of excellence in terms of the values it contains. Table 3 provides a checklist of questions that can be used to assess the quality of a proposed protected area.

Table 3. Checklist for assessing quality aspects of proposed protected areas

Representativeness

- Is the potential area **representative** of other comparable parts of Antarctica?
- Does it contain ecosystems, species, habitats, physical, historic, aesthetic and wilderness or other values or features represented elsewhere?
- What contribution would the area make to an Antarctic Protected Area system with a full range of outstanding natural environmental, biological, geographic and geological values of the Antarctic region?
- In relation to Antarctica as a whole, what proportion of the values or types of protected area identified in Articles 3(1) and 3(2) are represented in the site being investigated?

E.g. an area containing representative examples of marine & terrestrial ecosystems & assemblages of species of seabird may be higher quality than one containing a single colony of a common species.

Diversity

- What **diversity** of species, habitats or other values or features does the area contain?

For example an area might be of higher quality if it contained a greater diversity of biological and/or geological features than a nearby area.

Distinctiveness

- Is the potential area **distinctive** from other areas? How different is it from other areas?
- Does it contain species, habitats or other values or features not duplicated elsewhere? Are they **unique**, **rare**, uncommon or common?
- Are there naturally uncommon taxa present, including *"sparse"* taxa which occur within typically small and widely scattered natural populations, *"range restricted"* taxa whose distribution is naturally confined to specific substrates (e.g a specific rock type), habitats (e.g. geothermally-heated soils) or geographic areas (e.g. nunataks), *"vagrant"* taxa which may appear for short periods without establishing long-term breeding populations, and *"seasonal"* taxa which migrate into the polar regions during summer?
- Are there naturally uncommon abiotic features present that have been formed or preserved through an unusual or infrequent set of geological, geomorphological or glaciological processes?

For example an area containing the only example of a terrestrial ecosystem or a unique fossil locality might be of higher quality than one that contained a common terrestrial ecosystem or type of fossil.

Ecological importance

- How important/critical is the area ecologically or numerically for key species, ecosystems or as a type locality?
- Do the number of individuals or groups occurring at the area include a high proportion of the global population? *For example, if 90% of the global population were present, this would represent a key population and a very important ecological site.*
- What contribution does the area make to maintenance of essential ecological processes or life-support systems or habitats?
- Does the area have any inherent vulnerability due to local endemism, rarity of species, biological vulnerability or for other reasons?

Degree of interference

- To what extent has the area been subject to human interference?
- Does the area lack signs of human activities (e.g. tracks, litters)?
- Is there minimal loss or addition of species, natural processes and abiotic material?
- What is the degree of visitation and alteration of the adjacent landscape?

E.g. an area that has not experienced local human-induced change and is protected from it because of isolation may have higher quality wilderness values and might be more valuable as an undisturbed reference area than a less natural area.

Scientific and monitoring uses

- What is the potential for the pursuit of science including gaining of knowledge by study and analysis?
- What is the potential of the area to be used as a reference area (e.g. for environmental monitoring)?

The reasons for area protection summarised in Tables 1 and 2 could be analysed together with the quality criteria in Table 3 using the matrix set out in Table 4 as a guide. This approach may provide a convenient and efficient method of evaluation and identification of a potential area. It could also help in the comparison of potential areas and for determining priorities for protection.

Table 4. Matrix of area values and categories from Tables 1 and 2 against quality criteria from Table 3.

	Quality Criteria					
Value/ category	Representativeness	Diversity	Distinctiveness	Ecological Importance	Degree of Interference	Science & monitoring
Ecosystems						
Habitats						
Assemblages						
Species						
Features						
Landscapes						
Aesthetics						
Wilderness						
Historic						
Science						
Conservation						
Intrinsic						

2.4 Environmental Risk Assessment

Environmental risk assessment can be used to further assess possible protected areas i.e. to help decide whether a particular area merits protection of its special characteristics (not as a means to modify or prohibit ongoing activities in or near the area). Risk assessment should assist in identifying what the actual and potential threats and risks are to an area containing outstanding values.

This step in the protected area process recognises that every area identified as having important values may not need to be formally designated as an ASPA. Most areas will not need additional protection because they are naturally robust or because the Antarctic Treaty system already provides sufficient protection. It should be noted that the degree of environmental risk to a potential area (e.g. as identified through application of the checklist in Table 5) is not a prerequisite for formal protection of an area under the Environmental Protocol. However, areas identified as subject to risks that threaten the identified values to an unacceptable or unmanageable level may need to be considered as a priority or more worthy of more formal protection.

Table 5 provides risk criteria in the form of a checklist for assessing environmental risk to a possible protected area

Table 5. Checklist for assessing environmental risk to a possible protected area

Human activities and impacts

- Are human activities regularly, infrequently or almost never carried out in the area?
- Are biological or abiotic components or processes of the area vulnerable to any existing or likely future human activities in the area itself or nearby?
- Could these activities directly, indirectly or in a cumulative way result in impacts on the values for which this area has been identified or modify them in any way?
- How likely, frequent and intensive might the impacts be and over what temporal and spatial scales?
- When disturbance occurs, what is the time taken to return to pre-disturbance or equilibrium levels?

Natural processes

- Are natural processes (e.g. atmospheric, climatic, marine, biological or glacial processes) likely to modify the area or its values?

Natural variability and viability

- What are the short and long term variations (e.g. seasonal changes) in populations of biota present in the area?
- Is the likely variation due to natural processes likely to be smaller, similar to or larger than impacts of human activities in the area?
- Are there any medium- or long-term indications that natural trends could result in significantly different characteristics of the area which could effect its future viability, require a reassessment of protected status or necessitate changes in management?
- To what extent does natural buffering protect the area from outside influences?

Non-Antarctic threats

- Would protection of the area be compromised by processes originating or driven from outside the Antarctic such as global change, ozone depletion or long-range transport of contaminants such as long-lived chemical pollutants and introduction of non-native species?

Urgency

- Do human activities pose imminent environmental risks?

Scientific uncertainty

- How well known are the natural values and other characteristics of the area and potential impacts of human activities on them?
- Could these uncertainties mask significant threats to the area and its values?

Potential areas that "score" highly in regard to the checklists in Tables 3 and 4 (e.g. meet many of the criteria listed) and that have been assessed as being at some risk environmentally (Table 5) may be considered for further investigation as a possible ASPA. Consideration should then be given to advancing the proposal further, in particular into the selection and proposal phases.

PART III: DEFINING AREAS FOR PROTECTION

3.1 Tools for Assisting in Selecting Protected Areas

Once potential areas have been assessed, further design and assessment is needed to ensure that they are suitable for eventual selection and proposal as ASPAs. Area design and feasibility criteria are two tools that can be used to assist in further defining of areas for protection.

3.2 Area Design

There is a wide body of literature on aspects of protected area design and selection relevant here which is beyond the scope of these guidelines. Important aspects of design include boundaries, size and shape, access, management tools, duration and relation to other protected areas (see Table 6). Proposers may wish to consult Lewis-Smith and others (1992), Thorsell (1997), IUCN (1998), FAO (1988) and Dingwall (1992).

3.3 Feasibility Criteria

The feasibility of a possible protected area is defined here *as how possible is it to implement proposed management objectives for a particular area under consideration.* The criteria defined in Table 6 could be used to assess feasibility. While the meaning of each of these criteria is generally clear, the implications or their application may not be. Therefore Table 6 is structured as a checklist with additional questions to highlight some of the issues involved and to offer further guidance.

Table 6. Checklist of feasibility criteria for assessment of possible protected areas

Boundaries

- Are the proposed boundaries consistent with management objectives? (E.g. do they protect foraging areas of birds in an important breeding area and/or do they enclose other ecosystem components required for continuity of species identified?).
- Can boundaries be easily defined for management purposes and identified by visitors? (E.g. can fixed natural boundaries such as mountain peaks, ridgelines, shorelines, or water depth be used?).
- Can management objectives be met regardless of the future use of areas adjacent to the protected area boundary, including conflicts between different values or management objectives, and acceptability to others?

What are the existing scientific or other uses of the area?

- Are there conflicting values (e.g. between environmental and scientific values in Article 3(1)) or between protection and use categories, or management objectives?

Size

- Is the area large enough to maximise the chance of management objectives being achieved?
- Is it large enough to contain all or most of the key elements identified, in their natural relationships, so that it will be self-perpetuating?
- What is the minimum size needed to achieve management objectives?
- Is the area small enough to minimise conflicts between different values or management objectives?
- Is the area large enough to accommodate future changes (e.g. due to climate change?)

Possible management tools

- Are there management tools available that could be used to help achieve management objectives and minimise conflicts? (E.g. would zoning be useful to facilitate recognition, protection and management including partitioning between objectives such as protection of vulnerable species in core breeding areas, provision of reference areas and capacity for human activity in suitable fringe areas?).

- Can management programmes be formulated to attain management objectives? (E.g. signage or boundary markers, survey and research, monitoring, any specific information needed for reporting).

Time period/duration

- Can the area be protected for a time period that allows full achievement of management objectives?
- Are there some seasonal periods when parts of the area or species in it are not vulnerable to human activity?

Accessibility/logistics

- Is the area sufficiently accessible for management operations?
- Might the logistics needed negatively impact on management objectives and are there alternative management options?
- Would inaccessibility help achieve management objectives by deterring potentially impacting activity?

Ability to protect more than one value and meet different management objectives (i.e. complementarity)

- Is there more than one value or objective in Article 3 (1) & 3(2) that can be protected in the area?
- Would the site add value to the Antarctic protected area system, in quality as well as quantity?
- Is there an appropriate balance between the costs and benefits of protecting the area, and appropriate equity in the distribution of it and adjacent protected and unprotected areas?

Therefore, if an area has been through an assessment process (Part II), and has satisfied feasibility criteria (Part III), it may be considered as a worthy candidate for further evaluation as a potential ASPA. The outcome of checking and analysis against criteria in Table 6 could also be used to help prepare the draft management plan for the area.

Figure 1 below provides a flowchart illustrating the assessment process from identifying the values and potential protection categories of a proposed area, to considering quality aspects, to identifying any environmental risks, to assessment of feasibility and finally to a decision on whether to develop a proposal for designation of the site as an ASPA.

Figure 1: The assessment process for potential protected areas as outlined in Part II and Part III of these guidelines.

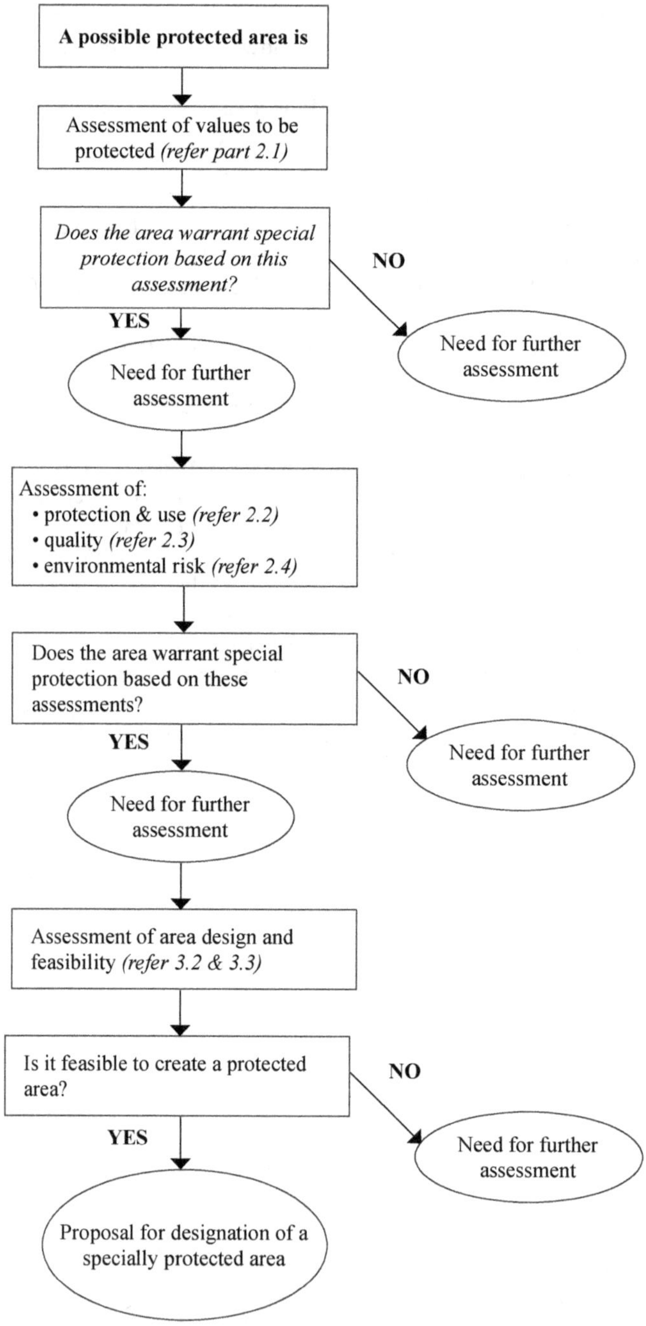

PART IV: PROPOSING AREAS FOR PROTECTION

4.1 Drafting Management Plans for Proposed ASPAs

Once a candidate area has been assessed, it is ready for the next stages in the process. A draft management plan is prepared as required by Article 5 of Annex V. The document "Guide to the Preparation of Management Plans for Protected Areas" was recommended by CEP 1 and adopted at ATCM XXII in 1998 to give some practical elaboration of Article 5. This document should be referred to when drafting management plans for ASPAs.

4.2 Further Steps in the Designation Process

The final stages in the designation process involve formal consideration (review) by the Antarctic Treaty Consultative Parties of a draft management plan following the outline in Article 6 of Annex V.

PART V: DOCUMENTATION

5.1 Articles 3(1) and 3(2) of the Environment Protocol

Article 3(1)

Any area, including any marine area, may be designated as an Antarctic Specially Protected Area to protect outstanding environmental, scientific, historic, aesthetic or wilderness values, any combination of those values, or ongoing or planned scientific research.

Article 3(2)

Parties shall seek to identify, within a systematic environmental-geographical framework, and to include in the series of Antarctic Specially Protected Areas:

(a) areas kept inviolate from human interference so that future comparisons may be possible with localities that have been affected by human activities;

(b) representative examples of major terrestrial, including glacial and aquatic, ecosystems and marine ecosystems;

(c) areas with important or unusual assemblages of species, including major colonies of breeding native birds or mammals;

(d) the type locality or only known habitat of any species;

(e) areas of interest to ongoing or planned scientific research;

(f) examples of outstanding geological, glaciological, or geomorphological features;

(g) areas of outstanding aesthetic and wilderness value;

(h) sites or monuments of recognised historic value; and

(i) such other areas as may be appropriate to protect the values set out in paragraph 1 above [Article 3(1)].

5.2 REFERENCES

(see bibliography for full citation where needed)

1. adapted from Geddes and Grosset 1996
2. Antarctic Heritage Trust
3. adapted from Porteous 1996 with reference to philosopher Kant.
4. Convention on Biological Diversity
5. Allaby 1977

BIBLIOGRAPHY

Allaby, M 1977. A dictionary of the environment. MacMillan Press, London.

Anon 1998. Guide to the Preparation of Management Plans for Protected Areas. Report of Antarctic Treaty Consultative Meeting XXII, Norway

Austin, MP and Margules CR 1986. Assessing representativeness. In "Wildlife conservation evaluation", (MB Usher, Editor) Chapman and Hall, London, pp 45–67.

Calow, P 1998. Handbook of environmental risk assessment & management. Blackwell Science, Oxford.

De Lange PJ and Norton DA 1998. Revisiting rarity: a botanical perspective on the meanings of rarity and the classification of New Zealand's uncommon plants. In "Ecosystems, entomology and plants", Royal Society of New Zealand Misc. Series 48, pp 145–160.

De Poorter, M and Dalziell, JC (Editors) 1996. Cumulative impacts in Antarctica. Proceedings of the Washington Workshop 18–21 September 1996. IUCN. 145 pages.

Dingwall, PR 1992. Design and delimitation of protected areas. In "Developing the Antarctic Protected Area System" (Lewis Smith and others, Editors). Proceedings of the SCAR/IUCN Workshop 29 June–2 July 1992. IUCN, Gland Switzerland and Cambridge UK, pp 49–52.

FAO 1988. National parks planning: a manual with annotated examples. Food and Agriculture Organisation of the United Nations, Rome. Conservation Guide 17, 105 pages.

Forey, PL, Humphries, CJ and Vane-Wright RI (Editors) 1994. Systematics and conservation evaluation. Clarendon Press, Oxford.

Geddes and Grosset 1996 English dictionary. Geddes and Grosset Ltd.

German Republic 1999. Factors influencing risk analysis in relation to human activities in Antarctica based on German experience with logistics during German Antarctic research. Information Paper 38, XXIII ATCM, Lima, Peru, 13 pages.

Harwell, MA, Cooper W and Flaak R 1992. Prioritising ecological and human welfare risks from environmental stresses. Environmental Management 16, pp 451–464.

IUCN 1994. Guidelines for protected area management categories. Commission on National Parks and Protected Areas, with the World Conservation Monitoring Centre. IUCN, Gland, Switzerland and Cambridge UK, 261 pages.

IUCN 1998. National system planning for protected areas (AG Davey, main author). World Commission on Protected Areas, Best Practice Protected Area Guidelines Series No. 1, 71 pages.

Lewis Smith, RI, Walton DWH and Dingwall PR (Editors) 1992. Developing the Antarctic Protected Area System. Proceedings of the SCAR/IUCN Workshop 29 June–2 July 1992. IUCN, Gland, Switzerland and Cambridge UK, 137 pages.

Mackinnon, J and K, Child, K and Thorsell J 1986.Managing protected areas in the tropics. IUCN, Gland, Switzerland.

Njaastad , B. 1998. Antarctic Protected Areas Workshop, Norwegian Polar Institute Report 110, 86 pages.

Norton, DA 1999. Forest reserves. In "Maintaining biodiversity in forest ecosystems" (M Hunter, Editor) Cambridge University Press , pp 525–555.

O'Conner, KF, Overmars FB and Ralston MM 1990. Land evaluation for nature conservation- a scientific review. Conservation Science Publication 3, Department of Conservation, Wellington.

Porteous, JD 1996. Environmental aesthetics. Routledge, London and New York, 290 pages.

Pressey, RL and Logan, VS 1994. Level of geographical subdivision and its effects on assessments of reserve coverage: a review of regional studies. Conservation Biology 8(4), pp 1037–1046

SCAR and COMNAP 1996. Monitoring of environmental impacts from science and operations in Antarctica. Report of the Oslo and Texas workshops in 1995 and 1996. Scientific Committee on Antarctic Research and Council of Managers of National Antarctic Programs. 43 pages plus annexes.

Thorsell, J 1997. Nature's hall of fame: IUCN and the World Heritage Convention. Parks 7 (2), pp 3–7

Udvardy, MDF 1975. A classification of the biogeographical provinces of the world. IUCN, Gland, Switzerland Occasional Paper 18.

Valencia, J. (Editor) 1999 Final report of the second workshop on Antarctic Protected Areas. Instituto Antarctico Chileno, Santiago, 37 pages

Resolution 3 (2001): Collection of Meteorites in Antarctica

The Representatives,

Concerned at the potential loss to scientific research because of unrestricted collection of meteorites in Antarctica;

Urge Parties to the Environmental Protocol to take such legal or administrative steps as are necessary to preserve Antarctic meteorites so that they are collected and curated according to accepted scientific standards, and are made available for scientific purposes.

Resolution 5 (2001): Guidelines for Handling of Pre-1958 Historic Remains Whose Existence or Present Location is Not Known

The Representatives,

Recalling Recommendation VII-9 which provides for Consultative Parties to adopt all adequate measures to preserve and protect from damage the historic monuments situated in the Antarctic Treaty area, and the provisions of Annex V to the Environmental Protocol,

Recalling also Resolution 8 (1995), which sets out criteria by which types of sites and artefacts that could be designated as historic sites and monuments,

Aware of the prohibition in Article 8 (4) of Annex V on the removal of listed historic monuments,

Recognizing the unique value of all the historic remains of early exploration of the Antarctic continent, and

Noting that increased activity in Antarctica has increased the pressure on historic sites and artefacts not protected by current measures,

Recommend that:

The Guidelines, appended to this Resolution, for handling of pre-1958 historic remains whose existence or present location is not known, be used by Parties as guidance on questions relating to protection of such historic remains in Antarctica.

Appendix to Resolution 5 (2001): Guidelines for Handling of Pre-1958 Historic Remains Whose Existence or Present Location is Not Known

1. These guidelines apply to pre-1958 historic artefacts/sites whose existence or location is not known.

2. These guidelines should be applied, as far as possible, to provide interim protection of pre-1958 historic artefacts/sites until the Parties have had due time to consider their inclusion into the protection system under Annex V to the Protocol on Environmental Protection. This interim protection should not extend beyond three years after the discovery of a new historic artefact/site has been brought to the attention of the Parties.

3. Historic artefacts/sites for the purpose of these Guidelines, include but are not necessarily limited to:

- Artefacts with a particular association with a person who played an important role in the history of science or exploration of Antarctica;
- Artefacts with a particular association with a notable feat of endurance achievement;
- Artefacts representative of, or which form part of, some wide-ranging activity that has been important in the development of knowledge of Antarctica;
- Artefacts with particular technical or architectural value in its materials, design or method of construction;
- Artefacts with the potential, through study, to reveal information or which have the potential to educate people about significant human activities in Antarctica;
- Artefacts with symbolic or commemorative value for people of many nations.

4. Any person/expedition who discovers pre-1958 historic remains should notify the appropriate authorities in their home country. The consequences of removing such remains should be

duly considered. If items nonetheless are removed from Antarctica, they should be delivered to the appropriate authorities in the home country of the discoverer.

5. If historic artefacts/sites are discovered during construction activities, all construction should be discontinued to the greatest extent practical until the artefacts have been appropriately recorded and evaluated.

6. The Party whose nationals have discovered pre-1958 historic artefacts/sites should notify the other Treaty Parties about the discovery, indicating what remains have been found, and where and when.

7. If there is uncertainty as to the age of a newly discovered historic artefact/site it should be treated as a pre-1958 artefact/site until its age has been established.

Decision 1 (2002): Naming and Numbering System for Antarctic Specially Protected Areas

The Representatives,

Noting the entry into force of Annex V to the Environmental Protocol on 24 May 2002;

Noting also the provision of Article 3(3) of Annex V that all SPAs and SSSIs designated as such by past Antarctic Treaty Consultative Meetings are hereby designated as Antarctic Specially Protected Areas (ASPAs) on the entry into force of Annex V, and shall be renamed and renumbered accordingly;

Recognising the naming and numbering system for ASPAs adopted by means of Resolution V (1996) and the need to update this system to include new protected areas adopted by subsequent ATCMs;

Decide:

1. That the naming and numbering system for ASPAs annexed to this Decision be adopted;
2. That all ASPAs adopted by the present, and any subsequent ATCM, be added to the list in consecutive order of adoption and be numbered accordingly.

Annex to the Decision 1(2002): Naming and Numbering System for Antarctic Specially Protected Areas

No.	Antarctic Specially Protected Area name	Previous site number	Year adopted in Annex V format
101	Taylor Rookery, Mac. Robertson Land	SPA No. 1	1992
102	Rookery Islands, Holme Bay, Mac. Robertson Land	SPA No. 2	1992
103	Ardery Island and Odbert Island, Budd Coast	SPA No. 3	1992
104	Sabrina Island, Balleny Islands	SPA No. 4	
105	Beaufort Island, Ross Sea	SPA No. 5	1997
	Cape Crozier, Ross Island	SPA No. 6 [redesignated SSSI No.4]	
106	Cape Hallett, Victoria Land	SPA No. 7	
107	Dion Islands, Marguerite Bay, Antarctic Peninsula	SPA No. 8	
108	Green Island, Berthelot Islands, Antarctic Peninsula	SPA No. 9	
	Byers Peninsula, Livingston Island, South Shetland Islands	SPA No. 10 [redesignated SSSI No. 6]	
	Cape Shirreff, Livingston Island, South Shetland Islands	SPA No. 11 [redesignated SSSI No. 32]	
	Fildes Peninsula, King George Island, South Shetland Islands	SPA No. 12 [redesignated SSSI No. 5]	

109	Moe Island, South Orkney Islands	SPA No. 13	1995
110	Lynch Island, South Orkney Islands	SPA No. 14	2000
111	Southern Powell Island and adjacent islands, South Orkney Islands	SPA No. 15	1995
112	Coppermine Peninsula, Robert Island, South Shetland Islands	SPA No. 16	
113	Litchfield Island, Arthur Harbour, Anvers Island, Palmer Archipelago	SPA No. 17	
114	Northern Coronation Island, South Orkney Islands	SPA No. 18	
115	Lagotellerie Island, Marguerite Bay, Antarctic Peninsula	SPA No. 19	1992 / 2000
116	New College Valley, Caughley Beach, Cape Bird, Ross Island	SPA No. 20	1992/ 2000
117	Avian Island, off Adelaide Island, Antarctic Peninsula	SPA No. 21 [formerly SSSI No. 30]	
118	'Cryptogam Ridge', Mount Melbourne, Victoria Land	SPA No. 22	
119	Forlidas Pond and Davis Valley ponds, Dufek Massif	SPA No. 23	
120	Pointe-Geologie Archipelago, Terre Adélie	SPA No. 24	1995
121	Cape Royds, Ross Island	SSSI No. 1	
122	Arrival Heights, Hut Point Peninsula, Ross Island	SSSI No. 2	
123	Barwick Valley, Victoria Land	SSSI No. 3	
124	Cape Crozier, Ross Island	SSSI No. 4 [formerly SPA No. 6]	
125	Fildes Peninsula, King George Island, South Shetland Islands	SSSI No. 5 [formerly SPA No. 12]	
126	Byers Peninsula, Livingston Island, South Shetland Islands	SSSI No. 6 [formerly SPA No. 10]	
127	Haswell Island	SSSI No. 7	
128	Western shore of Admiralty Bay, King George Island	SSSI No. 8	2000
129	Rothera Point, Adelaide Island	SSSI No. 9	1996
	Caughley Beach, Cape Bird, Ross Island	SSSI No. 10 [incorporated into SPA No. 20]	
130	'Tramway Ridge', Mount Erebus, Ross Island	SSSI No. 11	1995
131	Canada Glacier, Lake Fryxell, Taylor Valley, Victoria Land	SSSI No. 12	1997
132	Potter Peninsula, King George Island, South Shetland Islands	SSSI No. 13	1997
133	Harmony Point, Nelson Island, South Shetland Islands	SSSI No. 14	1997
134	Cierva Point and offshore islands, Danco Coast, Antarctic Peninsula	SSSI No. 15	1997
135	North-eastern Bailey Peninsula, Budd Coast, Wilkes Land	SSSI No. 16	
136	Clark Peninsula, Budd Coast, Wilkes Land	SSSI No. 17	2000
137	North-west White Island, McMurdo Sound	SSSI No. 18	
138	Linnaeus Terrace, Asgaard Range, Victoria Land	SSSI No. 19	1996
139	Biscoe Point, Anvers Island	SSSI No. 20	
140	Parts of Deception Island, South Shetland Islands	SSSI No. 21	
141	'Yukidori Valley', Langhovde, Lützow-Holmbukta	SSSI No. 22	2000
142	Svarthamaren, Mühlig-Hofmannfjella, Dronning Maud Land	SSSI No. 23	1999

118	Summit of Mount Melbourne, Victoria Land	SSSI No. 24	
143	Marine Plain, Mule Peninsula, Vestfold Hills, Princess Elizabeth Land	SSSI No. 25	
144	Chile Bay (Discovery Bay), Greenwich Island, South Shetland Islands	SSSI No. 26	
145	Port Foster, Deception Island, South Shetland Islands	SSSI No. 27	
146	South Bay, Doumer Island, Palmer Archipelago	SSSI No. 28	
147	Ablation Point-Ganymede Heights, Alexander Island	SSSI No. 29	
	Avian Island, off Adelaide Island, Antarctic Peninsula	SSSI No. 30 [redesignated SPA No. 21]	
148	Mount Flora, Hope Bay, Antarctic Peninsula	SSSI No. 31	
149	Cape Shirreff, Livingston Island, South Shetland Islands	SSSI No. 32 [formerly SPA No.11]	
150	Ardley Island, Maxwell Bay, King George Island	SSSI No. 33	
151	Lions Rump, King George Island, South Shetland Islands	SSSI No. 34	2000
152	Western Bransfield Strait off Low Island, South Shetland Islands	SSSI No. 35	
153	Eastern Dallmann Bay off Brabant Island, Palmer Archipelago	SSSI No. 36	
154	Botany Bay, Cape Geology, Victoria Land	SSSI No. 37 [includes HSM No.67]	1997
155	Cape Evans, Ross Island	SPA No. 25 [includes HSM Nos.16 & 17]	1997
156	Lewis Bay, Mount Erebus, Ross Island	SPA No. 26 [designated a Tomb in 1981]	1997
157	Backdoor Bay, Cape Royds, Ross Island	SPA No. 27 [includes HSM No.15]	1998
158	Hut Point, Ross Island	SPA No. 28 [includes HSM No. 18]	1998
159	Cape Adare, Borchgrevink Coast	SPA No. 29 [includes HSM No.22]	1998

Measure 3 (2003): Antarctic Protected Areas System: Revised List of Historic Sites and Monuments

The Representatives,

Recalling Recommendations I-IX, V-4, VI-14, VII-9, XII-7, XIII-16, XIV-8, XV-12, XVI-11, XVII-3 and Measures 4 (1995), 2 (1996), 4 (1997), 2 (1998), 1 (2001) and 2 (2001);

Noting the requirements of Article 8 of Annex V to the Protocol on Environmental Protection to the Antarctic Treaty to maintain a list of current Historic Sites and Monuments and that such sites shall not be damaged, removed or destroyed;

Desiring to update the descriptions of Historic Site and Monument numbers 5, 14, 15, 16, 17, 18, 19, 21, 22, 23, 27, 28, 30, 32, 33, 34, 35, 36, 37, 38, 39, 42, 43, 44, 48, 50, 53, 56, 57, 59, 61, 62, 63, 64, 65, 66, 67, 68, 69, 70, 71, 74;

Desiring also to remove from the list those Historic Sites and Monuments numbered 25, 31 and 58, which no longer exist;

Recommend that their Governments, in accordance with paragraph 2 of Article 8 of Annex V to the Protocol on Environmental Protection to the Antarctic Treaty, approve that the "List of Historic Monuments Identified and Described by the Proposing Government or Governments" (annexed to Recommendation VII-9 and modified by the Recommendations and Measures recalled above) be terminated and replaced by the revised and updated "List of Historic Sites and Monuments" annexed to this Measure.

Annex: List of Historic Sites and Monuments Approved by the Antarctic Treaty Consultative Meeting

Note: The Antarctic Treaty Consultative Meeting neither approves, nor disapproves of the place names used in the listing below.

No.	Description	Location
1.	Flag mast erected in December 1965 at the South Geographical Pole by the First Argentine Overland Polar Expedition. Original proposing Party: Argentina[1] Party undertaking management: Argentina	90°S
2.	Rock cairn and plaques at Syowa Station in memory of Shin Fukushima, a member of the 4th Japanese Antarctic Research Expedition, who died in October 1960 while performing official duties. The cairn was erected on 11 January 1961, by his colleagues. Some of his ashes repose in the cairn. Original proposing Party: Japan[1] Party undertaking management: Japan	69°00'S
3.	Rock cairn and plaque on Proclamation Island, Enderby Land, erected in January 1930 by Sir Douglas Mawson. The cairn and plaque commemorate the landing on Proclamation Island of Sir Douglas Mawson with a party from the British, Australian and New Zealand Antarctic Research Expedition of 1929–31. Original proposing Party: Australia[1] Party undertaking management: Australia	65°51'S 53°41'E
4	Station building to which a bust of V.I. Lenin is fixed, together with a plaque in memory of the conquest of the Pole of Inaccessibility by Soviet Antarctic explorers in 1958. Original proposing Party: Russia[1] Party undertaking management: Russia	83°06'S 54°58'E
5.	Rock cairn and plaque at Cape Bruce, Mac. Robertson Land, erected in February 1931 by Sir Douglas Mawson. The cairn and plaque commemorate the landing on Cape Bruce of Sir Douglas Mawson with a party from the British, Australian and New Zealand Antarctic Research Expedition of 1929–31. Original proposing Party: Australia[1] Party undertaking management: Australia	67°25'S 60°47'E
6.	Rock cairn at Walkabout Rocks, Vestfold Hills, Princess Elizabeth Land, erected in 1939 by Sir Hubert Wilkins. The cairn houses a canister containing a record of his visit. Original proposing Party: Australia[1] Party undertaking management: Australia	68°22'S 78°33'E
7.	Stone with inscribed plaque, erected at Mirny Observatory, Mabus Point, in memory of driver-mechanic Ivan Kharma who perished on fast ice in the performance of official duties in 1956. Original proposing Party: Russia[1] Party undertaking management: Russia	66°33'S 93°01'E
8.	Metal monument-sledge at Mirny Observatory, Mabus Point, with plaque in memory of driver-mechanic Anatoly Shcheglov who perished in the performance of official duties. Original proposing Party: Russia[1] Party undertaking management: Russia	66°33'S 93°01'E

9.	Cemetery on Buromskiy Island, near Mirny Observatory, in which are buried Soviet, Czechoslovakian and GDR citizens, members of Soviet Antarctic Expeditions, who perished in the performance of official duties on 3 August, 1960. Original proposing Party: Russia[1] Party undertaking management: Russia	66°32'S 93°01'E
10.	Building (magnetic observatory) at Dobrowolsky Station, Bunger Hills, with plaque in memory of the opening of Oasis Station in 1956. Original proposing Party: Russia[1] Party undertaking management: Russia	66°16'S 100°45'E
11.	Heavy tractor at Vostok Station with plaque in memory of the opening of the Station in 1957. Original proposing Party: Russia[1] Party undertaking management: Russia	78°28'S 106°48'E
12.	Cross and plaque at Cape Denison, George V Land, erected in 1913 by Sir Douglas Mawson on a hill situated 300 metres west by south from the main hut of the Australasian Antarctic Expedition of 1911–14. The cross and plaque commemorate Lieutenant B.E.S Ninnis and Dr X. Mertz, members of the expedition, who died in 1913 while engaged in the work of the expedition. Original proposing Party: Australia[1] Party undertaking management: Australia	67°00'S 142°42'E
13.	Hut at Cape Denison, George V Land, built in January 1912 by Sir Douglas Mawson for the Australasian Antarctic Expedition of 1911–14. This was the main base of the expedition. Original proposing Party: Australia[1] Party undertaking management: Australia	67°00'S 142°42'E
14.	Site of ice cave at Inexpressible Island, Terra Nova Bay, constructed in March 1912 by Victor Campbell's Northern Party, British Antarctic Expedition, 1910–13. The party spent the winter of 1912 in this ice cave. A wooden sign, plaque and seal bones remain at the site. Original proposing Party: New Zealand[1&2] Parties undertaking management: New Zealand/Italy/UK	74°54'S, 163°43'E
15.	Hut at Cape Royds, Ross Island, built in February 1908 by the British Antarctic Expedition of 1907–09, led by Sir Ernest Shackleton. Restored in January 1961 by the Antarctic Division of New Zealand Department of Scientific and Industrial Research. Site incorporated within ASPA 157 Original proposing Parties: New Zealand/UK[1] Parties undertaking management: New Zealand/UK	77°33'S, 166°10'E
16.	Hut at Cape Evans, Ross Island, built in January 1911 by the British Antarctic Expedition of 1910–1913, led by Captain Robert F. Scott. Restored in January 1961 by the Antarctic Division of New Zealand Department of Scientific and Industrial Research.	77°38'S, 166°24'E
	Site incorporated within ASPA 155 Original proposing Parties: New Zealand /UK[1] Parties undertaking management: New Zealand/UK	
17.	Cross on Wind Vane Hill, Cape Evans, Ross Island, erected by the Ross Sea Party, led by Captain Aeneas Mackintosh, of Sir Ernest Shackleton's Imperial Trans-Antarctic Expedition of 1914–1916, in memory of three members of the party who died in the vicinity in 1916. Site incorporated within ASPA 155 Original proposing Parties: New Zealand/UK[1] Parties undertaking management: New Zealand/UK	77°38'S, 166°24'E

18.	Hut at Hut Point, Ross Island, built in February 1902 by the British Antarctic Expedition of 1901–04, led by Captain Robert F. Scott. Partially restored in January 1964 by the New Zealand Antarctic Society, with assistance from the United States Government. Site incorporated within ASPA 158 Original proposing Parties: New Zealand/UK[1] Parties undertaking management: New Zealand/UK	77°50'S, 166°37'E
19.	Cross at Hut Point, Ross Island, erected in February 1904 by the British Antarctic Expedition of 1901–04, in memory of George Vince, a member of the expedition, who died in the vicinity. Original proposing Parties: New Zealand/UK[1] Parties undertaking management: New Zealand/UK	77°50'S, 166°37'E
20.	Cross on Observation Hill, Ross Island, erected in January 1913 by the British Antarctic Expedition of 1910–13, in memory of Captain Robert F. Scott's party which perished on the return journey from the South Pole in March 1912. Original proposing Parties: New Zealand/UK[1] Parties undertaking management: New Zealand/UK	77°51'S, 166°41'E
21.	Remains of stone hut at Cape Crozier, Ross Island, constructed in July 1911 by Edward Wilson's party of the British Antarctic Expedition (1910–13) during the winter journey to collect Emperor penguin eggs. Original proposing Party: New Zealand[1] Parties undertaking management: New Zealand/UK	77°31'S, 169°22'E
22.	Three huts and associated historic relics at Cape Adare. Two were built in February 1899 during the British Antarctic (*Southern Cross*) Expedition, 1898–1900, led by Carsten E. Borchgrevink. The third was built in February 1911 by Robert F. Scott's Northern Party, led by Victor L.A.Campbell. Scott's Northern Party hut has largely collapsed with only the porch standing in 2002. Site incorporated within ASPA 159. Original proposing Parties: New Zealand/UK[1] Parties undertaking management: New Zealand/UK	71°18'S, 170°12'E
23.	Grave at Cape Adare of Norwegian biologist Nicolai Hanson, a member of the British Antarctic (*Southern Cross*) Expedition, 1898–1900, led by Carsten E. Borchgrevink. A large boulder marks the head of the grave with the grave itself outlined in white quartz stones. A cross and plaque are attached to the boulder. Original proposing Parties: New Zealand/ UK[1] Parties undertaking management: New Zealand/Norway	71°17'S, 170°13'E
24.	Rock cairn, known as 'Amundsen's cairn', on Mount Betty, Queen Maud Range erected by Roald Amundsen on 6 January 1912, on his way back to *Framheim* from the South Pole. Original proposing Party: Norway[1] Party undertaking management: Norway	85°11'S, 163°45'W
25.	De-listed	
26.	Abandoned installations of Argentine Station 'General San Martin' on Barry Island, Debenham Islands, Marguerite Bay, with cross, flag mast, and monolith built in 1951. Original proposing Party: Argentina[1] Party undertaking management: Argentina	68°08'S, 67°08'W
27.	Cairn with a replica of a lead plaque erected on Megalestris Hill, Petermann Island, in 1909 by the second French expedition led by Jean-Baptiste E. A. Charcot. The original plaque is in the reserves of the Museum National d'Histoire Naturelle (Paris). Original proposing Parties: Argentina/France/UK[1] Parties undertaking management: France /UK	65°10'S, 64°09'W

28.	Rock cairn at Port Charcot, Booth Island, with wooden pillar and plaque inscribed with the names of the first French expedition led by Jean-Baptiste E. A. Charcot which wintered here in 1904 aboard *Le Français*. Original proposing Party: Argentina[1] Parties undertaking management: Argentina/France	65°03'S, 64°01'W
29.	Lighthouse named 'Primero de Mayo' erected on Lambda Island, Melchior Islands, by Argentina in 1942. This was the first Argentine lighthouse in the Antarctic. Original proposing Party: Argentina[1] Party undertaking management: Argentina	64°18'S, 62°59'W
30.	Shelter at Paradise Harbour erected in 1950 near the Chilean Base 'Gabriel Gonzalez Videla' to honour Gabriel Gonzalez Videla, the first Head of State to visit the Antarctic. The shelter is a representative example of pre-IGY activity and constitutes an important national commemoration. Original proposing Party: Chile[1] Party undertaking management: Chile	64°49'S, 62°51'W
31.	De-listed	
32.	Concrete monolith erected in 1947, near Capitán Arturo Prat Base on Greenwich Island, South Shetland Islands. Point of reference for Chilean Antarctic hydrographic surveys. The monolith is representative of an important pre-IGY activity and is currently preserved and maintained by personnel from Prat Base. Original proposing Party: Chile[1] Party undertaking management: Chile	62°28'S, 59°40'W
33.	Shelter and cross with plaque near Capitán Arturo Prat Base (Chile), Greenwich Island, South Shetland Islands. Named in memory of Lieutenant-Commander González Pacheco, who died in 1960 while in charge of the station. The monument commemorates events related to a person whose role and the circumstances of his death have a symbolic value and the potential to educate people about significant human activities in Antarctica. Original proposing Party: Chile[1] Party undertaking management: Chile	62°29'S, 59°40'W
34.	Bust at Capitán Arturo Prat Base (Chile), Greenwich Island, South Shetland Islands, of the Chilean naval hero Arturo Prat, erected in 1947. The monument is representative of pre-IGY activities and has symbolic value in the context of Chilean presence in Antarctica. Original proposing Party: Chile[1] Party undertaking management: Chile	62°50'S, 59°41'W
35.	Wooden cross and statue of the Virgin of Carmen erected in 1947 near Capitán Arturo Prat Base (Chile), Greenwich Island, South Shetland Islands. The monument is representative of pre-IGY activities and has a particularly symbolic and architectural value.	62°29'S, 59°40'W
	Original proposing Party: Chile[1] Party undertaking management: Chile	
36.	Replica of a metal plaque erected by Eduard Dallmann at Potter Cove, King George Island, to commemorate the visit of his German expedition on 1 March, 1874 on board *Grönland.* Original proposing Parties: Argentina/UK[1] Parties undertaking management: Argentina/Germany	62°14'S, 58°39'W
37.	Statue erected in 1948 at General Bernardo O'Higgins Base (Chile), Trinity Peninsula, of Bernardo O'Higgins, the first ruler of Chile to envisage the importance of Antarctica. This monument is representative of pre-IGY activities in Antarctica and has a symbolic meaning in the history of Antarctic exploration since it was	63°19'S, 57°54'W

	during O'Higgins' government that the vessel *Dragon* landed on the coast of the Antarctic Peninsula in 1820. Original proposing Party: Chile[1] Party undertaking management: Chile	
38.	Wooden hut on Snow Hill Island built in February 1902 by the main party of the Swedish South Polar Expedition led by Otto Nordenskjöld. Original proposing Parties: Argentina/ UK[1] Parties undertaking management: Argentina/Sweden	64°22'S, 56°59'W
39.	Stone hut at Hope Bay, Trinity Peninsula, built in January 1903 by a party of the Swedish South Polar Expedition. Original proposing Parties: Argentina/UK[1] Parties undertaking management: Argentina/Sweden	63°24'S, 56°59' W
40.	Bust of General San Martin, grotto with a statue of the Virgin of Lujan, and a flag mast at Base 'Esperanza', Hope Bay, erected by Argentina in 1955; together with a graveyard with stele in memory of members of Argentine expeditions who died in the area. Original proposing Party: Argentina[1] Party undertaking management: Argentina	63°24'S, 56°59'W
41.	Stone hut on Paulet Island built in February 1903 by survivors of the wrecked vessel *Antarctic* under Captain Carl A. Larsen, members of the Swedish South Polar Expedition led by Otto Nordenskjöld, together with a grave of a member of the expedition and the rock cairn built by the survivors of the wreck at the highest point of the island to draw the attention of rescue expeditions. Original proposing Parties: Argentina/UK[1&2] Parties undertaking management: Argentina/Sweden/Norway	63°34'S, 55°45'W
42.	Area of Scotia Bay, Laurie Island, South Orkney Island, in which are found: stone hut built in 1903 by the Scottish Antarctic Expedition led by William S. Bruce; the Argentine meteorological hut and magnetic observatory, built in 1905 and known as Moneta House; and a graveyard with twelve graves, the earliest of which dates from 1903. Original proposing Party: Argentina[1] Parties undertaking management: Argentina/UK	60°46'S, 44°40'W
43.	Cross erected in 1955, at a distance of 1,300 metres north-east of the Argentine General Belgrano I Station (Argentina) and subsequently moved to Belgrano II Station (Argentina), Nunatak Bertrab, Confin Coast, Coats Land in 1979. Original proposing Party: Argentina[1] Party undertaking management: Argentina	77°52'S, 34°37'W
44.	Plaque erected at the temporary Indian station 'Dakshin Gangotri', Princess Astrid Kyst, Dronning Maud Land, listing the names of the First Indian Antarctic Expedition which landed nearby on 9 January 1982.	70°45'S, 11°38'E
	Original proposing Party: India[3] Party undertaking management: India	
45.	Plaque on Brabant Island, on Metchnikoff Point, mounted at a height of 70 m on the crest of the moraine separating this point from the glacier and bearing the following inscription: This monument was built by François de Gerlache and other members of the Joint Services Expedition 1983–85 to commemorate the first landing on Brabant Island by the Belgian Antarctic Expedition, 1897–99: Adrien de Gerlache (Belgium) leader, Roald Amundsen (Norway), Henryk Arctowski (Poland), Frederick Cook (USA) and Emile Danco (Belgium) camped nearby from 30 January to 6 February 1898. Original proposing Party: Belgium[4] Party undertaking management: Belgium	64°02'S, 62°34'W

46.	All the buildings and installations of Port-Martin base, Terre Adélie constructed in 1950 by the 3rd French expedition in Terre Adélie and partly destroyed by fire during the night of 23 to 24 January 1952. Original proposing Party: France[3] Party undertaking management: France	66°49'S, 141°24'E
47.	Wooden building called 'Base Marret' on the Ile des Pétrels, Terre Adélie, where seven men under the command of Mario Marret overwintered in 1952 following the fire at Port Martin Base. Original proposing Party: France[3] Party undertaking management: France	66°40'S, 140°01'E
48.	Iron cross on the North-East headland of the Ile des Pétrels, Terre Adélie, dedicated as a memorial to André Prudhomme, head meteorologist in the 3rd International Geophysical Year expedition who disappeared during a blizzard on 7 January 1959. Original proposing Party: France[3] Party undertaking management: France	66°40'S, 140°01'E
49.	The concrete pillar erected by the First Polish Antarctic Expedition at Dobrolowski Station on the Bunger Hill to measure acceleration due to gravity g = 982,439.4 mgal ±0.4 mgal in relation to Warsaw, according to the Potsdam system, in January 1959. Original proposing Party: Poland Party undertaking management: Poland	66°16'S, 100°45'E
50.	A brass plaque bearing the Polish Eagle, the national emblem of Poland, the dates 1975 and 1976, and the following text in Polish, English and Russian: In memory of the landing of members of the first Polish Antarctic marine research expedition on the vessels 'Professor Siedlecki' and 'Tazar' in February 1976. This plaque, south-west of the Chilean and Soviet stations, is mounted on a cliff facing Maxwell Bay, Fildes Peninsula, King George Island. Original proposing Party: Poland[3] Party undertaking management: Poland	62°12'S, 59°01'W
51.	The grave of Wlodzimierz Puchalski, surmounted by an iron cross, on a hill to the south of Arctowski station on King George Island. W. Puchalski was an artist and a producer of documentary nature films, who died on 19 January 1979 whilst working at the station. Original proposing Party: Poland[3] Party undertaking management: Poland	62°13'S, 58°28'W
52.	Monolith erected to commemorate the establishment on 20 February 1985 by the Peoples Republic of China of the 'Great Wall Station' on Fildes Peninsula, King George Island, in the South Shetland Islands. Engraved on the monolith is the following inscription in Chinese: 'Great Wall Station, First Chinese Antarctic Research Expedition, 20 February 1985'.	62°13'S, 58°58'W
52.	Original proposing Party: China[5] Party undertaking management: China	
53.	Bust of Captain Luis Alberto Pardo, monolith and plaques on Point Wild, Elephant Island, south Shetland Islands, celebrating the rescue of the survivors of the British ship *Endurance* by the Chilean Navy cutter *Yelcho* displaying the following words: " Here on August 30th, 1916, the Chilean Navy cutter *Yelcho* commanded by Pilot Luis Pardo Villalón rescued the 22 men from the Shackleton Expedition who survived the wreck of the 'Endurance' living for four and one half months in this Island". The Monolith and the plaques have been placed on Elephant Island and their replicas on the Chilean bases Capitan Arturo Prat (62 ° 30'S, 59 ° 49'W) and President Eduardo Frei (62 ° 12'S, 62 ° 12'W). Bronze busts of the pilot Luis Pardo Villalon	61°03'S, 54°50'W

	were placed on the three above-mentioned monoliths during the XXIVth Chilean Antarctic Scientific Expedition in 1987–88. Original proposing Party: Chile[5] Party undertaking management: Chile	
54.	Richard E. Byrd Historic Monument, McMurdo Station, Antarctica. Bronze bust on black marble, 5ft high x 2ft square, on wood platform, bearing inscriptions describing the polar achievements of Richard Evelyn Byrd. Erected at McMurdo Station in 1965. Original proposing Party: USA[6]	77°51'S, 166°40'E
55.	East Base, Antarctica, Stonington Island. Buildings and artefacts at East Base, Stonington Island and their immediate environs. These structures were erected and used during two U.S. wintering expeditions: the Antarctic Service Expedition (1939–1941) and the Ronne Antarctic Research Expedition (1947–1948). The size of the historic area is approximately 1,000 metres in the north-south direction (from the beach to Northeast Glacier adjacent to Back Bay) and approximately 500 metres in the east-west direction. Original proposing Party: USA[5]	68°11'S, 67°00'W
56.	Waterboat Point, Danco Coast, Antarctic Peninsula. The remains and immediate environs of the Waterboat Point hut. It was occupied by the UK two-man expedition of Thomas W. Bagshawe and Maxime C. Lester in 1921–22. Only the base of the boat, foundations of doorposts and an outline of the hut and extension still exist. It is situated close to the Chilean station 'President Gabriel Gonzáles Videla'. Original proposing Party: Chile/UK[7] Parties undertaking management: Chile/UK	64°49'S, 62°51'W
57.	Commemorative plaque at 'Yankee Bay' (Yankee Harbour), MacFarlane Strait, Greenwich Island, South Shetland Islands. Near a Chilean refuge. Erected to the memory of Captain Andrew MacFarlane, who in 1820 explored the Antarctic Peninsula area in the brigantine *Dragon*. Original proposing Parties: Chile/UK[6] Parties undertaking management: Chile/UK	62°32'S, 59°45'W
58.	De-listed.	
59.	A cairn on Half Moon Beach, Cape Shirreff, Livingston Island, South Shetland Islands and a plaque on 'Cerro Gaviota' opposite San Telmo Islets commemorating the officers, soldiers and seamen aboard the Spanish vessel *San Telmo,* which sank in September 1819; possibly the first people to live and die in Antarctica. Site incorporated within ASPA 149. Original proposing Parties: Chile/Spain/Peru[6] Parties undertaking management: Chile/Spain/Peru	62°28'S, 60°46'W
60.	Wooden plaque and cairn located at Penguins Bay, southern coast of Seymour Island (Marambio), James Ross Archipelago. This plaque was placed on 10 November 1903 by the crew of a rescue mission of the Argentinian Corvette *Uruguay* in the site where they met the members of the Swedish expedition led by Dr Otto Nordenskjöld. The text of the wooden plaque reads as follows: "10.XI.1903 Uruguay (Argentine Navy) in its journey to give assistance to the Swedish Antarctic expedition." In January 1990, a rock cairn was erected by Argentina in memory of this event in the place where the plaque is located. Original proposing Party: Argentina[8] Parties undertaking management: Argentina/Sweden	64°16'S, 56°39'W

61.	'Base A' at Port Lockroy, Goudier Island, off Wiencke Island, Antarctic Peninsula. Of historic importance as an Operation Tabarin base from 1944 and for scientific research, including the first measurements of the ionosphere, and the first recording of an atmospheric whistler, from Antarctica. Port Lockroy was a key monitoring site during the International Geophysical Year of 1957/58. Original Proposing Party: UK[9] Party undertaking management: UK	64°49'S, 63°29'W
62.	'Base F (Wordie House)' on Winter Island, Argentine Islands. Of historic importance as an example of an early British scientific base. Original proposing Party: UK[9] Parties undertaking management: UK/Ukraine	65°15'S, 64°16'W
63.	'Base Y' on Horseshoe Island, Marguerite Bay, western Graham Land. Noteworthy as a relatively unaltered and completely equipped British scientific base of the late 1950s. 'Blaiklock', the refuge hut nearby, is considered an integral part of the base. Original proposing Party: UK[9] Party undertaking management: UK	67°48'S, 67°18'W
64.	'Base E' on Stonington Island, Marguerite Bay, western Graham Land. Of historical importance in the early period of exploration and later British Antarctic Survey (BAS) history of the 1960s and 1970s. Original proposing Party: UK[9] Party undertaking management: UK	68°11'S, 67°00'W
65.	Message post, Svend Foyn Island, Possession Islands. A pole with a box attached was placed on the island on 16 January 1895 during the whaling expedition of Henryk Bull and Captain Leonard Kristensen of the ship *Antarctic*. It was examined and found intact by the British Antarctic Expedition of 1898–1900 and then sighted from the beach by the USS *Edisto* in 1956 and USCGS *Glacier* in 1965. Original proposing Parties: New Zealand/Norway/UK[9] Parties undertaking management: New Zealand/ Norway	71°56'S, 171°05'W
66.	Prestrud's Cairn, Scott Nunataks, Alexandra Mountains, Edward VII Peninsula. The small rock cairn was erected at the foot of the main bluff on the north side of the nunataks by Lieutenant K. Prestrud on 3 December 1911 during the Norwegian Antarctic Expedition of 1910–1912. Original proposing Parties: New Zealand/ Norway/ UK[9] Parties undertaking management: New Zealand/Norway	77°11'S, 154°32'W
67.	Rock shelter, 'Granite House', Cape Geology, Granite Harbour. This shelter was constructed in 1911 for use as a field kitchen by Griffith Taylor's second geological excursion during the British Antarctic Expedition of 1910–1913. It was enclosed on three sides with granite boulder walls and used a sledge to support a seal-skin roof. The stone walls of the shelter have partially collapsed. The shelter contains corroded remnants of tins, a seal skin and some cord. The sledge is now located 50 m seaward of the shelter and consists of a few scattered pieces of wood, straps and buckles.	77°00'S, 162°32'E
	Site incorporated within ASPA 154. Original proposing Parties: New Zealand/Norway/UK[9] Parties undertaking management: New Zealand/UK	
68.	Site of depot at Hells Gate Moraine, Inexpressible Island, Terra Nova Bay. This emergency depot consisted of a sledge loaded with supplies and equipment which was placed on 25 January 1913 by the British Antarctic Expedition, 1910–1913. The sledge and supplies were removed in 1994 in order to stabilize their deteriorating condition. Original proposing Parties: New Zealand/Norway/UK[9] Parties undertaking management: New Zealand/UK	74°52'S, 163°50'E

69.	Message post at Cape Crozier, Ross Island, erected on 22 January 1902 by Captain Robert F. Scott's *Discovery* Expedition of 1901–04. It was to provide information for the expedition's relief ships, and held a metal message cylinder, which has since been removed. Site incorporated within ASPA 124 Original proposing Parties: New Zealand/Norway/UK[9] Parties undertaking management: New Zealand/UK	77°27'S, 169°16'E
70.	Message post at Cape Wadworth, Coulman Island. A metal cylinder nailed to a red pole 8 m above sea level placed by Captain Robert F. Scott on 15 January 1902. He painted the rocks behind the post red and white to make it more conspicuous. Original proposing Parties: New Zealand/Norway/UK[9] Parties undertaking management: New Zealand/UK	73°19'S, 169°47'E
71.	Whalers Bay, Deception Island, South Shetland Islands. The site comprises all pre-1970 remains on the shore of Whalers Bay, including those from the early whaling period (1906–12) initiated by Captain Adolfus Andresen of the Sociedad Ballenera de Magallanes, Chile; the remains of the Norwegian Hektor Whaling Station established in 1912 and all artefacts associated with its operation until 1931; the site of a cemetery with 35 burials and a memorial to ten men lost at sea; and the remains from the period of British scientific and mapping activity (1944–1969). The site also acknowledges and commemorates the historic value of other events that occurred there, from which nothing remains. Original proposing Parties: Chile/ Norway[9] Parties undertaking management: Chile/Norway/UK	62°59'S, 60°34'W
72.	Mikkelsen Cairn, Tryne Islands, Vestfold Hills. A rock cairn and a wooden mast erected by the landing party led by Captain Klarius Mikkelsen of the Norwegian whaling ship *Thorshavn* and including Caroline Mikkelsen, Captain Mikkelsen's wife, the first woman to set foot on East Antarctica. The cairn was discovered by Australian National Antarctic Research Expedition field parties in 1957 and again in 1995. Original proposing Parties: Australia/Norway[10] Parties undertaking management: Australia/Norway	68°22'S 78°24'E
73.	Memorial Cross for the 1979 Mount Erebus crash victims, Lewis Bay, Ross Island. A cross of stainless steel which was erected in January 1987 on a rocky promontory three kilometers from the Mount Erebus crash site in memory of the 257 people of different nationalities who lost their lives when the aircraft in which they were travelling crashed into the lower slopes of Mount Erebus, Ross Island. The cross was erected as a mark of respect and in remembrance of those who died in the tragedy. Original proposing Party: New Zealand[11] Party undertaking management: New Zealand	77°25'S, 167°27'E
74.	The un-named cove on the south-west coast of Elephant Island, including the foreshore and the intertidal area, in which the wreckage of a large wooden sailing vessel is located.	61°14'S, 55°22'W
74.	Original proposing Party: UK[12] Party undertaking management: UK	
75.	The A Hut of Scott Base, being the only existing Trans Antarctic Expedition 1956/1957 building in Antarctica sited at Pram Point, Ross Island, Ross Sea Region, Antarctica. Original proposing Party: New Zealand[13] Party undertaking management: New Zealand	77°51'S, 166°46'E

76.	The ruins of the Base Pedro Aguirre Cerda Station, being a Chilean meteorological and volcanological center situated at Pendulum Cove, Deception Island, Antarctica, that was destroyed by volcanic eruptions in 1967 and 1969. Original proposing Party: Chile[14] Party undertaking management: Chile	62°59'S, 60°40'W

[1] Adopted by means of Recommendation VII-9 (1972).
[2] Amended by means of Measure 5 (1995).
[3] Adopted by means of Recommendation XII-7 (1983).
[4] Adopted by means of Recommendation XIII-6 (1985).
[5] Adopted by means of Recommendation XIV-8 (1987).
[6] Adopted by means of Recommendation XV-12 (1989).
[7] Adopted by means of Recommendation XV-12 (1989).
[8] Adopted by means of Recommendation XVII-3 (1992).
[9] Adopted by means of Measure 4 (1995).
[10] Adopted by means of Measure 4 (1995).
[11] Adopted by means of Measure 4 (1997).
[12] Adopted by means of Measure 2 (1998).
[13] Adopted by means of Measure 1 (2001).
[14] Adopted by means of Measure 2 (2001).

Resolution 2 (2004): Guidelines for the Operation of Aircraft Near Concentrations of Birds in Antarctica

The Representatives,

Recalling Article 3 of the Environmental Protocol which requires that activities in the Antarctic Treaty area shall be planned and conducted so as to limit adverse impacts on the Antarctic environment,

Recalling also the requirements of Annex II of the Environmental Protocol on the Conservation of Antarctic Fauna and Flora,

Aware of the potential for harmful disturbance to concentrations of birds in Antarctica by the operation of aircraft,

Noting that specific standards for aircraft operations may be contained in Antarctic Specially Protected Area (ASPA) and Antarctic Specially Managed Area (ASMA) management plans,

Recognising that some Parties may already have in place more stringent guidelines for the operation of aircraft near wildlife,

Aware that the scientific data on the impact of aircraft operations on wildlife will continue to improve and that guidance on minimum standards should remain under review,

Conscious of the need for minimum guidance on the operation of aircraft near concentrations of birds in order to minimise the impacts of such activities,

Recommend that:

The Guidelines for the Operation of Aircraft Near Concentrations of Birds in Antarctica appended to this Resolution be used by those engaged in the operation of aircraft in the Antarctic.

Parties should be encouraged to adopt higher standards for the operation of aircraft near concentrations of birds to suit their particular needs and circumstances.

Guidelines for the Operation of Aircraft Near Concentrations of Birds in Antarctica

Fixed and rotary wing aircraft operations have the potential to cause disturbance leading to changes in the behaviour, physiology and the breeding success of wildlife. The level of impact will vary according to the intensity, duration and frequency of disturbance, the species involved and the phase in their breeding season. Most species are particularly sensitive to disturbance between late September and early May-the period when Antarctic helicopter and fixed wing operations usually occur.

There are many variables affecting noise levels received on the ground during aircraft operations, including: flight height; the type of aircraft and engine; the flight profile; the weather; and the geography of the location. Pilots have to make the final judgment regarding aircraft operations based on the aircraft type, task and safety considerations. Such judgments should also pay due consideration to potential wildlife impacts, noting that Annex II of the Protocol on Environmental Protection to the Antarctic Treaty defines that "harmful interference" means flying or landing helicopters or other aircraft in a manner that disturbs concentrations of birds and seals".

Minimum recommended separation distances for aircraft operations close to concentrations of birds are set out below. These recommended distances should be maintained to the greatest extent possible, unless greater separation distances are specified for the area of operation, for example by an ASPA or ASMA management plan or guidelines already developed by national operators to suit their own particular needs and circumstances. These distances are only a guide and if wildlife disturbance is observed at any separation distance, a greater distance should be maintained wherever practical:

- Penguin, albatross and other bird colonies are not to be over flown below 2000ft (~ 610 m) Above Ground Level, except when operationally necessary for scientific purposes.
- Landings within 1/2 nautical mile (~ 930 m) of penguin, albatross or other bird colonies should be avoided wherever possible.
- Never hover or make repeated passes over wildlife concentrations or fly lower than necessary.
- Maintain a vertical separation distance of 2000 ft (~ 610 m) AGL and a horizontal separation of 1/4 nautical mile (~ 460 m) from the coastline where possible.
- Cross the coastline at right angles and above 2000ft (~610 m) AGL where possible.

Location of aircraft operations (other considerations)

- Where practical, avoid overflying concentrations of birds.
- Be aware that concentrations of birds are most often found in coastal areas. Snow petrel and Antarctic petrel colonies are also frequently found inland on nunataks. Minimum vertical separation distances should be maintained in these areas.
- Where practical, landings near to concentrations of birds should be downwind and/or behind a prominent physical barrier (e.g. hill) to minimise disturbance.
- Avoid Antarctic Specially Protected Areas, unless authorised to over-fly and/or land by a permit issued by an appropriate national authority. For many ASPAs there are specific controls on aircraft operations, which are set out in the relevant Management Plans.
- Follow aircraft flight heights, preferred flight paths and approach paths contained in the Antarctic Flight Information Manual (AFIM), in station aircraft operation manuals and on relevant charts, maps and any Wild Life and Low Flying Avoidance Maps for the major airstrips in the Antarctic (e.g. Marsh, Marambio, Rothera, McMurdo).
- Particularly avoid flying toward concentrations of birds immediately after take-off and avoid steep banking turns in flight as these significantly increase the amount of noise generated.

Timing of aircraft operations

- Most native bird species breed at coastal locations in Antarctica between September and May each season. During the planning of aircraft operations near to concentrations of birds, consideration should be given to undertaking flying activities outside of the main breeding and/or moulting periods.
- Where aircraft operations are necessary close to concentrations of birds, then the duration of flights should be the minimum necessary.
- To minimise bird strikes, especially in coastal areas, avoid flying after dark between September and May. At this time of year, prions and petrels are active. These birds are nocturnal when breeding and are attracted by lights.

- Aircraft operations should be delayed or cancelled if weather conditions (e.g. cloud base, winds) are such that the suggested minimum vertical and horizontal separation distances given in these guidelines cannot be maintained.

Decision 9 (2005): Marine Protected Areas and Other Areas of Interest to CCAMLR

The Representatives,

Noting the requirements in Article 6(1) and 6(2) of Annex V to the Protocol of Environmental Protection to the Antarctic Treaty that the prior approval of the Commission of the Convention on the Conservation of Antarctic Marine Living Resources (CCAMLR) must be obtained on proposal for Antarctic Specially Protected Areas or Antarctic Specially Managed Areas which contain marine areas;

Recalling that ATCM XXI agreed to transmit a draft text addressing criteria for Marine Areas to CCAMLR for its consideration;

Recalling also the endorsement of that draft text by CCAMLR at its XVIth Meeting, and its adoption as Decision 4 (1998) of ATCM XXII;

Noting that Decision 4 (1998) set out procedures to be followed pending the entry into force of the Annex V, which is now in force;

Desiring to adopt updated procedures;

Decide:

1. That for the purpose of the implementation of Article 6.2 of the Environmental Protocol, draft management plans that contain marine areas which require a prior approval of CCAMLR are those:

(a) in which there is actual harvesting or potential capability of harvesting of marine living resources which might be affected by site designation; or

(b) for which there are provisions specified in a draft management plan which might prevent or restrict CCAMLR related activities.

2. That proposals for designations of Antarctic Specially Protected Areas or Antarctic Specially Managed Areas which meet the criteria of Paragraph 1 above shall be submitted to CCAMLR for its consideration before any decision is taken on the proposal relating to marine areas.

3. Furthermore that any other proposed designations which might have implications for CCAMLR Ecosystem Monitoring Programme (CEMP) sites shall also be submitted to CCAMLR for its consideration.

4. That this decision shall replace Decision 4 (1998), which shall cease to be operative.

Resolution 1 (2005): Environmental Impact Assessment: Circulation of Information

The Representatives,

Recalling Articles III and VII of the Antarctic Treaty and Articles 3, 6.2 and 17 of the Protocol on Environmental Protection to the Antarctic Treaty;

Noting that Annex I to the Protocol creates obligations to exchange information annually, including information on Initial Environmental Evaluations and Comprehensive Environmental Evaluations;

Noting that the requirements for the exchange of information have been further developed in numerous measures of the Antarctic Treaty Consultative Meetings;

Taking into account the establishment of the Secretariat of the Antarctic Treaty;

Conscious of Resolution 6 (1995), which states that the procedures on circulation of information should be reviewed following the establishment of a permanent Secretariat;

Desirous that such information should be easily accessible and in a comprehensive and uniform format so that the scale and trend of activities and developments in Antarctica can be readily monitored;

Recommend that:

1. Their Governments should provide the Secretariat of the Antarctic Treaty with a list of the Initial Environmental Evaluations and Comprehensive Environmental Evaluations prepared by or submitted to them during the period from April 1 of the previous year to March 31 prior to the ATCM.
2. The above list should, at a minimum, contain the following information: a short description of the development or activity; the type of environmental impact assessment undertaken (IEE or CEE); the location (name, latitude, and longitude) of the activity; the organisation responsible for the EIA; and any decision taken following consideration of the environmental impact assessment.
3. A copy in electronic format of these documents should also be submitted where possible.
4. The lists should be collated by the Secretariat, posted on the ATS website and circulated as an information paper to the ATCM and thereafter, if the ATCM so agrees, be published as an Annex to the final Report of the ATCM.

Resolution 2 (2005): Practical Guidelines for Developing and Designing Environmental Monitoring Programs in Antarctica

The Representatives,

Conscious that there has been an increased focus on the need for environmental monitoring among national Antarctic programs;

Noting the need of having standardized techniques to develop monitoring programs which are scientifically sound, practical and cost effective;

Noting also the need of a proper methodology to be followed when designing a monitoring program;

Considering that a unified approach to environmental monitoring will contribute to the continued protection of the Antarctic environment;

Recommend that:

1. the *Practical Guidelines for Developing and Designing Environmental Monitoring Programs in Antarctica* annexed to this Resolution be made available for use by those engaged in the preparation of monitoring Programs in Antarctica;
2. these guidelines be used in conjunction with the COMNAP/SCAR Antarctic Environmental Handbook.

Practical Guidelines for Developing and Designing Environmental Monitoring Programmes in Antarctica

January 2005

This document has been developed for the Council of Managers of National Antarctic Programs (COMNAP) by its Antarctic Environmental Officers Network (AEON). Up-to-date versions of this document can be found on the COMNAP web site at *http://www.comnap.aq*

FOREWORD

Environmental monitoring has been an important focus of the Council of Managers of National Antarctic Programmes' (COMNAP) work since the mid-1990s. Recent initiatives within the Antarctic Treaty system and within the Scientific Committee on Antarctic Research (SCAR) and COMNAP, as well as ongoing experience in the practical implementation of the Environmental Protocol to the Antarctic Treaty, have each advanced the understanding of the issues related to environmental monitoring in Antarctica.

During the 1999 meeting of COMNAP in Goa, India, the Antarctic Environmental Officers Network (AEON) arranged a workshop with the aim of following up and facilitating discussions on the issue of environmental monitoring of science and operational activities in Antarctica.

This workshop identified several steps in the process of developing, designing and implementing environmental monitoring programmes, and looked at areas where there may be gaps in the current documentation and information available to operators. Although information exists on these matters the workshop noted that much of it is not widely available, and is not written as practical guidelines that are readily understandable by operators.

Following the discussion, the workshop recommended that practical guidelines for developing and designing an environmental monitoring programme be prepared. Terms of Reference were then prepared, and the document developed reflects the intentions of these Terms of Reference.

The document has passed through several drafts in its development. The drafts have been circulated and reviewed by members of AEON. Comments have been incorporated to arrive at the final format and content.

This coordinated effort to provide practical monitoring guidelines should assist all national programmes, but particularly those with more limited resources and who do not currently have a systematic monitoring programme in place. Ultimately, a unified approach to environmental monitoring will assist the continued protection of resources and values, and in minimising human impacts on the Antarctic continent.

Gérard Jugie

Chair, Council of Managers of National Antarctic Programmes (COMNAP)

January 2005

LIST OF ACRONYMS

AEON	Antarctic Environmental Officers Network
ASMA	Antarctic Specially Managed Area
ASPA	Antarctic Specially Protected Area
ATCM	Antarctic Treaty Consultative Meeting
BOD	Biological Oxygen Demand
CEP	Committee for Environmental Protection
COD	Chemical Oxygen Demand
COMNAP	Council of Managers of National Antarctic Programmes
DO	Dissolved Oxygen
EIA	Environmental Impact Assessment
GIS	Geographical Information System
IAATO	International Association of Antarctica Tour Operators
PAH	Polycyclic Aromatic Hydrocarbon(s)
PCB	Polychlorinated Biphenyls
PM10	Particulate up to 10 microns in diameter
SCAR	Scientific Committee on Antarctic Research
SS	Suspended Solids
TOC	Total Organic Carbon
TSS	Total Suspended Solids
TPH	Total Petroleum Hydrocarbons

GLOSSARY OF TERMS

Action: Any step taken as part of an activity.

Activity: An event or process resulting from, or associated with, the presence of humans in Antarctica, and/or which may lead to the presence of humans in Antarctica.

Baseline monitoring: Collection of data and information from a particular site, ahead of an activity taking place that is predicted to have certain impacts on the site.

Cumulative Impact: The combined impact of past, present and reasonably foreseeable activities. These activities may occur over time and space and can be additive, interactive or synergistic.

Direct Impact: A change in environmental components that results from direct cause-effect consequences of interaction between the exposed environment and outputs.

Exposure: The process of interaction between an identified potential output and an environmental element or value.

Impact: A change in the values or resources attributable to a human activity. It is the consequence of an agent of change, not the agent itself.

Indicator: Indicators are measures of physical, chemical, biological or socio-economic factors which best represent the key elements of the environment. They capture, focus and condense information about complex environments for management, monitoring and reporting purposes. To be effective indicators must be scientifically credible.

Indirect indicator: Signs or symptoms of changes in features not directly related to the environmental feature, but which potentially may impact the environmental features. Output indicators indicate changes in outputs (emission, fuel spills, noise) that may impact the environment. Compliance indicators indicate changes in compliance with environmental legislation, which then indirectly may have consequences for the environment.

Indirect Impact: A change in environmental components that results from interactions between the environment and other impacts (direct or indirect).

Mitigation: The use of practice, procedure or technology to minimise or prevent impacts associated with proposed activities.

Monitoring: Consists of standardised measurements or observations of key parameters (outputs and environmental variables) over time, their statistical evaluation and reporting on the state of the environment in order to define quality and trends.

Output: A physical change or an entity imposed on or released to the environment as a result of an action or an activity.

Parameter: A measurable variable for an indicator.

Remediation: The steps taken after impacts have occurred to promote, as much as possible, the return of the environment to its original condition.

Unavoidable Impact: An impact for which no further mitigation is possible.

Value: The worth, merit or importance of something (**environmental value**: the worth, merit or importance of an environmental feature).

SECTION 1: Introduction to the Guidelines

1.1 Why Monitor in Antarctica?

The primary obligations for undertaking monitoring in Antarctica are set out in the Protocol on Environmental Protection to the Antarctic Treaty (the Protocol). These requirements are summarised in Appendix 1, and include the verification of predicted impacts linked to specific activities and monitoring for unforseen impacts and environmental change in Antarctica generally.

The issue of environmental monitoring was substantively discussed at ATCM XV (1989) and Recommendation XV-5 was the result (reproduced at Appendix 1). Further consideration of the issue at ATCM XVI (1991) led to the convening of a Meeting of Experts in Buenos Aires in June 1992. ATCM XVII considered the report of the Meeting of Experts and adopted Recommendation XVII-1 (reproduced at Appendix 1). ATCM XVII also proposed the convening of a workshop to pursue the issue of environmental monitoring further. In July 1996 the Scientific Committee on Antarctic Research (SCAR) and the Council of Managers of National Antarctic Programmes (COMNAP) published the results of two workshops entitled "Monitoring of Environmental Impacts from Science and Operations in Antarctica" (Kennicutt *et al*, 1996).

As a result of those workshops two further documents were proposed:

- a technical handbook of standardised monitoring methods, and
- a practical guide to monitoring in Antarctica.

The technical handbook was published by COMNAP and SCAR in May 2000 as the "COMNAP/SCAR Antarctic Environmental Monitoring Handbook".

The present "Practical Guidelines for Developing and Designing Environmental Monitoring Programmes in Antarctica" fulfil the second proposal of preparing a practical guide to monitoring in Antarctica. It is recommended that it be used in conjunction with the handbook.

1.2 **Objectives of these Guidelines**

The objective of these guidelines is to provide practical advice to national Antarctic operators in developing and designing environmental monitoring programmes, by:

(a) Setting out a practical approach to designing environmental monitoring programmes in Antarctica, with examples;
(b) Bringing together various sources of monitoring information into a single reference document; and
(c) Providing clear and understandable advice.

1.3 **How to use these Guidelines**

These Guidelines have been structured so as to provide a common approach to the design of monitoring programmes in Antarctica that can be used by national Antarctic operators that are:

- New signatories to the Environmental Protocol;
- Wishing to review existing or long-term monitoring programmes;
- Looking to establish new monitoring programmes for specific activities.

The guidelines can be used for a range of monitoring needs including:

- Meeting the monitoring requirements of the Environmental Protocol;
- Monitoring of activities in response to environmental impact assessment requirements;
- Reporting on the state of the Antarctic environment.

The guidelines have been prepared in a deliberately generic format to enable application to both simple and complex monitoring needs; though the basic process for designing monitoring programmes is likely to be the same in each case.

It is important to note that these guidelines have no mandatory status and are available for use by national Antarctic programmes at their own discretion.

SECTION 2: A Three-Step Approach to Environmental Monitoring

This section outlines a three-step approach to designing and developing an environmental monitoring programme in Antarctica. Figure 1 summarises these steps.

1.	**Scoping the Monitoring Programme**
•	Setting objectives
•	Undertaking background research
•	Allocating resources
•	Baseline monitoring

2.	**Defining the Monitoring Programme**
•	Deciding what to monitor
•	Sampling methods and statistical design
•	Consultation

3.	**Implementing the Monitoring Programme**
•	Undertaking a Pilot project
•	Collecting Baseline data
•	Data handling
•	Reporting and publishing
•	Programme review

Figure 1. A flow diagram summarising the three-step approach to designing a monitoring programme.

2.1 **STEP 1: Scoping the monitoring programme**

This section describes the preparatory work that is necessary prior to undertaking any monitoring programme. It is important to undertake this step in a thorough manner to ensure that an effective monitoring programme can be developed.

2.1.1 Setting objectives

All monitoring programmes should have clearly defined objectives, which must be agreed at the outset. Objectives should be meaningful, achievable, and concise. They need to identify what is to be achieved and over what time period. Objectives also need to make sense to those responsible for designing and implementing the monitoring programme, and to senior managers who may need to take action as a result of the findings of the monitoring programme.

Example of Setting Objectives

> *National Programme Alpha has decided to undertake an environmental monitoring programme for its Alpha Station. Having been assigned the task of developing and designing a monitoring programme, the Alpha Environmental Manager implemented the following process to set the objectives of the programme:*
>
> 1. *A review of all environmental policy documents and reports relevant to the Alpha National Programme was conducted.*
> 2. *A small brainstorming meeting of relevant personnel (managers and operators) was held to identify possible objectives of the environmental monitoring programme at Station Alpha.*
> 3. *Based on outcomes from the brainstorming meeting the Environmental Manager developed a set of draft objectives.*
> 4. *The draft objectives were reviewed and revised by relevant personnel (managers and operators) and were revised accordingly.*
> 5. *The following objectives were established for the environmental monitoring programme:*
>   - *To demonstrate compliance with the requirements of the Environmental Protocol*
>   - *To capture information that may show environmental changes/impacts around the Alpha Station that may result from station and related field activities*
>   - *To undertake the monitoring for a period of five years before conducting a major review of the programme*
>   - *To utilise existing equipment, station personnel and scientists as much as possible without appointing additional staff to minimise costs*
>   - *To amend the structure and processes in the organisation to ensure monitoring information is used as a part of management decisions*

2.1.2 Background Research

Having defined the objectives for monitoring it is essential to gather relevant information that will assist with the design of the monitoring programme. The following sets out the key issues that need to be addressed.

Existing data and research

A key issue will be to determine what is already known about the area to be monitored. The following questions may assist in meeting this need:

- Is there any scientific or environmental research being conducted in the area to be monitored that may provide useful data?
- What information and data has been, or is being collected at, or near to the area to be monitored?
- Are there any existing environmental monitoring programmes with similar aims being conducted by other national Antarctic programmes?
- Is there any data available prior to any human activity in the region that could be useful baseline data?
- What are the information gaps? What is not known about the area?
- Is there a need for baseline data collection to be undertaken? Will it be important to collect basic information about the site before implementing a larger-scale monitoring programme?

- Are there any environmental reports, or environmental impact assessments for the area to be monitored?

Environmental features within the monitoring area

When collecting background information about the area to be monitored it is particularly important to build up a picture of the key environmental features that are found in the area of interest. This information will be essential when considering what to monitor (Step 2 of these guidelines). Figure 2 highlights key environmental features that might typically be found either singularly or in combination.

Flora and Fauna (including marine species)

Consider if:

- there are species or species assemblages that are rare or unique in Antarctica.
- there are species or species assemblages that are rare or unique in the area.
- there are species or species assemblages that are important for on-going or planned science.
- the flora is particularly undisturbed.

Atmospheric, freshwater, marine or terrestrial environments including ice-shelves and ice free ground

Consider if:

- there are any unique or special physical, chemical or biological features related to these environments.
- the environment is important for on-going or planned science.
- the environment is undisturbed or pristine.
- the environment is protected as part of an Antarctic Specially Protected Area (ASPA) or Antarctic Specially Managed Area (ASMA).

Heritage.

Consider if:

- there are any historic sites listed on the Historic Site and Monument list or protected as part of an ASPA?
- there are any historic elements important for on-going or planned science?

Figure 2. Checklist of key environmental features that might typically be found in Antarctica.

2.1.3 Resources available

Sufficient resources are instrumental to the success of the monitoring programme. Required resources may include:

- A dedicated budget for the monitoring programme;
- A programme manager to oversee the implementation of the monitoring programme;
- The availability of expert scientists to take responsibility for sample collection and analysis;
- Specialist equipment, including field, laboratory and data management equipment;
- The availability of trained staff to assist with, for example, sample collection and analysis, or data handling and reporting;
- Collaborative opportunities with other national Antarctic operators and/or researchers.

Roles and responsibilities

At this point in the preparation of the monitoring programme it will also be important to clearly establish and record the roles and responsibilities for those people that will be needed to ensure effective implementation.

2.1.4 Baseline Monitoring

Baseline monitoring is undertaken ahead of a particular activity commencing. The primary purpose of baseline monitoring is to establish a data set of pre-impact conditions of the site or area in question.

Example for Baseline Monitoring:

> *National Programme Bravo wants to establish an ice runway near its existing station. The Environmental Impact Assessment for the runway has identified the need for an environmental monitoring programme for the life of the runway to ensure environmental impacts are monitored and mitigated. Baseline data for the runway site will need to be gathered on surface snow and ice quality prior to operation of the runway in order to compare future data during operation of the runway.*

2.2 STEP 2: Defining the programme

Completing the data and information gathering exercises highlighted in Step 1 should assist in providing a clear understanding of what is known about the site and what resources are available to implement a monitoring programme. The next step is to define the boundaries of the monitoring programme by identifying what needs to be monitored, and the techniques to be used.

2.2.1 Deciding what to monitor

Deciding what to monitor is an essential stage in the process, if the monitoring programme is to meet its stated objectives. Deciding what to monitor will be influenced by a number of factors. These include:

- The key environmental features of the area to be monitored (determined through Step 1);
- The predicted or known impacts of an activity for which monitoring may be required (for example as determined through an EIA);
- Practical and technical issues, such as the ease with which samples can be taken and/or analysed.

Prioritisation

Prioritisation or ranking will need to be undertaken particularly when values and impacts are of too large a number to be adequately monitored within available resources.

The prioritisation of values and impacts that are the most critical should be based on the work carried out in Step 1 using the judgement of relevant experts. Rank the findings, noting that the highest priority in terms of a monitoring programme should be those values that are the most sensitive, those most likely to be significantly impacted, those that are most important to protect, or a combination of these factors.

Choosing relevant indicators

An indicator is defined as: signs or symptoms of changes, potentially due to numerous factors, in an environmental feature or features. Some examples of indicators are shown in Table 1.

Choosing what parameters to measure to detect changes in the indicators

When the most appropriate indicators have been selected it is important to decide on the parameters to measure. There are usually numerous parameters that could be measured for each indicator chosen, and therefore these need to be carefully selected. There are several factors that may influence the choice of parameters, for example, the cost of sampling/analysis, and the level of expertise needed to sample. Consideration should also be given to ensuring comparability with monitoring programmes conducted elsewhere, especially if these are in the near vicinity. Table 1 also gives examples of parameters for the various indicators listed. The COMNAP/SCAR Antarctic Environmental Monitoring Handbook should be consulted as a primary reference.

SCAR/COMNAP 1996 have recommended that the following criteria be used when selecting parameters:

The parameters must:

- Have the potential to exhibit changes in excess of limits of detection;
- Be directly relatable to a testable hypothesis;
- Be known or measurable above natural variability (i.e. background levels);
- Give information from which management decisions can be made;

- Be able to sustain the monitoring activity;
- Be able to be sampled within logistical and time constraints;
- Be measurable on samples that can be transported without deterioration or be measurable on-site in the field;
- Be amenable to quality assurance procedures including demonstrable precision, accuracy and reproducibility.

It is also desirable that the parameters:

- Be measurable by cost effective, simple and standard procedures (if the procedures are non-standard intercalibrations are essential);
- Be strongly related by what is believed to be a causal link to a particular activity or process;
- Be a direct measure of change in a value of concern;
- Permit generalisations about causative agents;
- Be definable in terms of limits beyond which changes are judged to be deleterious; and
- Be measurable without conflicting with scientific activities.

Finally, make sure that the chosen indicators can be readily measured and are achievable within the available resources.

Table 1. An overview of some potential indicators and parameters for use in monitoring programmes in Antarctica.

Indicator	Parameter
"Footprint"	Area subject to human activity, e.g. spatial coverage of buildings and associated impact including roads, pipes etc; number and location of field expeditions
Air quality	SO_2, particulates
Soil quality	Erosion (e.g. footpaths), metals, TPH, PAH
Sea water quality	TSS, DO, BOD, COD, pH, conductivity
Fresh water quality	TSS, DO, BOD, COD, pH, conductivity
Snow and ice quality	Metals, TPH, particulates
Vegetation quality	Spatial extent, metals
Wildlife health	Population size, breeding success
Fuel handling	Amount consumed, number of spills, size and location of spills
Aircraft/vehicle	operations Distance travelled, number of landings, fuel consumed
Solid and liquid waste	Waste types (including hazard), volume / weight
Waste water	TSS, DO, BOD, COD, pH, conductivity, faecal coliforms, volume
Field activities	Number of person days in field, location of field camps
Introduced organisms	Species, distribution, population size
EIA/permit compliance	Number of breaches recorded

Examples for Deciding What to Monitor:

1st Example

National Programme Charlie has decided to undertake an environmental monitoring programme to monitor environmental change in an Antarctic Specially Protected Area (ASPA) near Charlie Station. The information will be used to assist in the preparation of a Management Plan for the ASPA.

The key environmental feature in the ASPA is vegetation, namely mosses and lichens. The only potential impact from nearby activities is through pollution.

2nd example

National Programme Delta is to undertake an environmental monitoring programme of its new summer station on the plateau. National Programme Delta has limited budget but is keen to meet Environmental Protocol requirements and ensure minimisation of environmental impacts.
It has initially developed a list of possible monitoring indicators from local environmental values and possible impacts but is unable to undertake monitoring of all of them due to resource constraints. The Environmental Manager uses the Impact Rating methodology already undertaken in the Environmental Impact Assessment for the new station to rank/prioritise the indicators:

Indicator	***Likelihood***	***Consequence***	***Resulting Impact Rating***
Station Footprint	*Certain*	*High*	*High*
Ice Pollution by Fuel	*Unlikely*	*High*	*High*
Air Quality – Emissions form state power plant	*Certain*	*Low*	*Medium*
Pollution from windblown debris	*Unlikely*	*Medium*	*Medium*
Introduced organisms on cargo	*Unlikely*	*Low (station is in a remote plateau location)*	*Low*

The Environmental Manager decides to only implement a monitoring programme on the indicators that score a high impact rating, which can also be undertaken within available resources.

2.2.2 Sampling methods and statistical design

It is important to ensure that the sampling methods and statistical design follow recognised scientific procedures. In this regard SCAR / COMNAP (1996) have recommended a series of basic tenets that need to be followed for the statistical design of monitoring programmes:

(i) *Have a clear question.* The thought process should be: question –>hypothesis –>indicators –>parameters –>model –>statistics and tests of hypothesis–>interpretation.
(ii) *Have controls.* These should be both spatial and temporal where appropriate.
(iii) *Have a balanced design,* e.g. the same number of replicate samples at each time and place.
(iv) *Have replicates randomly allocated.*
(v) *Conduct preliminary sampling (pilot study) in order to do the following (vi – ix):*
(vi) *Assess the sampling methods* to ensure they are efficient and do not introduce bias into the study. Adequate quality assurance must be applied from initial sample collection, through transport to the laboratory, and during the analysis.
(vii) *Estimate error variability* and necessary sampling effort to achieve the desired power.
(viii) *Determine natural environmental patterns* to be incorporated into the study design (e.g. stratification).
(ix) *If statistical analysis assumptions are not satisfied* (they probably will not be) then transform variable before analysis, use nonparametric methods or use simulation or randomisation methods.

Once specific parameters have been selected, technical requirements that need to be followed in order to measure the chosen parameters, need to be identified. The COMNAP/SCAR Antarctic Environmental Monitoring Handbook should be consulted when carrying out this step in the process.

2.2.3 Consultation

As a final step in the planning phase of the monitoring programme, it is important to consult with relevant stakeholders (scientists, logistics staff, managers, permitting authority etc) to ensure that the proposed monitoring programme meets the objectives identified in Step 1, and can effectively be resourced and implemented.

Example for Consultation

> *The Environmental Manager from National Programme Echo has prepared a draft monitoring programme for its shipping activities. The Environmental Manager undertakes widespread consultation with managers, maritime associations and the shipping companies to ensure the programme is realistic prior to implementation. As a result of consultation the Environmental Manager discovers that the maritime association already undertakes monitoring of one the indicators, and is pleased to provide data free of charge, saving thousands of dollars on the programme.*

2.3 STEP 3: Implementing the programme

2.3.1 Pilot project

If circumstances allow, consideration might be given to undertaking a pilot study to test the effectiveness of the indicators and parameters chosen. This could include taking a small set of samples for analysis to test both sampling and laboratory methodologies.

Example of a pilot study

> *National Programme Hotel undertakes the first year of its monitoring programme as a pilot study to ensure its effectiveness prior to full commitment and expenditure. As a result of the pilot study it discovers that it cannot retrieve sufficient water quality samples at one of the monitoring locations to achieve required statistical rigour due to unsafe sea ice conditions. National Programme Hotel amends its monitoring locations as a result of the pilot study to ensure reliable and continuous water quality data can be gathered.*

2.3.2 Baseline monitoring

It will be important to collect baseline data in circumstances where, for example, very little is known about the site to be monitored, or in those cases when some degree of impact is expected. Collection of baseline data may take some time (e.g. it may be necessary to collect baseline data over a full Antarctic season, or even over a full annual cycle. As such adequate time may need to be factored into the monitoring programme to ensure that sufficient baseline data can be collected.

2.3.3 Data handling (collection, storage and analysis)

The data collected through the monitoring programme must be analysed in order to assess whether the monitoring goals are being achieved. Relevant experts and scientists should be consulted in interpreting the data. It may be useful to establish a small group of relevant experts/scientists with responsibility for assessing and reporting on the monitoring information.

For more detailed assistance with data handling reference is made to Chapter 3 of the COMNAP/SCAR Antarctic Environmental Monitoring Handbook and to Section 11 of the SCAR report 1996.

It is also noted that in the future a State of the Environment Reporting system may be developed by the Committee for Environmental Protection (CEP) for centralised data management of key environmental indicators. As such standardised reporting and data handling methods will be important to ensure comparability of data collected from various sources.

In addition it is recommended that the expertise of the Joint Committee on Antarctic Data Management (JCADM – *www.jcadm.scar.org*) be considered for data management needs.

Example for Data Handling

> *Tourist Operator Foxtrot has decided to implement an environmental monitoring programme for all of its tours. It establishes a data handling system on its internet site, using password access to allow its Voyage Leaders to input data on a weekly basis*

2.3.4 Reporting and publishing

It is recommended that the results of environmental monitoring programmes in Antarctica should be made available to other operators and interested scientists for data comparison and knowledge sharing. Options include:

- Publishing in operational and environmental journals or peer-reviewed scientific journals;
- Informing the CEP by means of Information Papers;
- Making information available via COMNAP reporting procedures and website (refer to COMNAP database of environmental programmes);
- Publishing on national programme websites;
- Provision of data and information to the CEP's State of the environment reporting system.

Example for Reporting and Publishing

> *Tourist Operator Foxtrot stores its environmental management data on an internet site. It has developed a computer programme that automatically compiles and sends a monthly report to its national regulator. The Tourist Operator also uses the data to compile a yearly report that it forwards to IAATO for their information. In turn IAATO makes the information available to the CEP and the ATCM by means of annual reporting to the meetings.*

2.3.5 Programme review

Individual national programmes should periodically review any proposed monitoring programme, and, as noted above, the results of such reviews shared amongst national operators. It is recommended that review and critical evaluation focus on each of three phases of the monitoring activity: data collection, data analysis and use of the results in management decisions.

Data collection

The sampling process should be reviewed to ensure that:

- The original design of sampling location, frequency, replication and measured variables is being followed consistently. If costs, operational difficulties, changing technologies, etc. are limiting the intended design, appropriate changes must be put in place;
- The quality of the data is as originally specified.

Once analysis has begun, data collection should also be reviewed to ensure that the design is adequate and that the collected information is meeting the objectives of the monitoring programme.

It is also worth remembering that changes in the objectives/testable hypotheses may be required as new insights, or new activities, and/or technologies occur.

Data analysis and use

Data collection and analyses are intended to provide decision-makers with sound scientific information from which environmental management decisions are made. Therefore programme review should consider:

- If the data and the results of the monitoring are providing managers with the information that was envisaged in the original designs. If not adjustments must be made;
- Whether management's use of the data has resulted in a measurable decrease in human impact.

Review mechanism

For small scale monitoring programmes, review is likely to be conducted by the environmental manager or the monitoring programme supervisor. For larger scale or longer-term monitoring programmes programme evaluation/review is best undertaken by external peer review, which may include representatives from other national operators. Such peer review should be undertaken by individuals with relevant scientific, logistical or policy expertise.

Additional issues, which may also need to be factored into the programme review, include resource use and allocation, reporting procedures, and publication opportunities.

Example for Review of the Monitoring Programme

> *National Programme Golf undertakes its biannual review of its monitoring programme for its station. As part of its review it discovers that incineration is no longer undertaken on station, significantly improving air quality emissions. It revises its ranking/prioritisation of indicators and determines that air quality emissions is no longer a high ranking issue. It decides to cease all air quality monitoring, as the data no longer provides any management benefit.*

REFERENCES

AEON. 1999. "Environmental Monitoring and Environmental Impact Assessment". Workshop report. Available on *www.comnap.aq*.

Committee for Environmental Protection (CEP). 1999. "Guidelines for Environmental Impact Assessment in Antarctica". Available on *www.cep.aq*.

COMNAP. 1998. "Summary of Environmental Monitoring Activities in Antarctica". Available in archive version and updated version on *www.comnap.aq*.

COMNAP/SCAR. 2000. "Antarctic Environmental Monitoring Handbook". Available on *www.comnap.aq*.

SCAR/COMNAP. 1996. "Monitoring of Environmental Impacts from Science and Operations in Antarctica". Workshop reports. Available on *www.comnap.aq*. http://www.comnap.aq/comnap/comnap.nsf/P/Pages/About.Publications/?Open

The Protocol on Environmental Protection to the Antarctic Treaty (1991). Available on *www.cep.aq* and *www.ats.org.ar*.

The Antarctic Master Directory (AMD) has been established at *http://gcmd.nasa.gov/Data/portals/amd/* by the Joint Committee on Antarctic Data Management (JCADM) *www.jcadm.scar.org* for Antarctic Treaty nations to lodge metadata records.

APPENDICES

[Omitted: Appendix I: Monitoring requirements of the Environmental Protocol to the Antarctic Treaty; text of Recommendations XV-5 and XVII-1.]

Resolution 3 (2005): Fuel Storage and Handling

The Representatives,

Recalling Article 3 of the Environmental Protocol which requires that activities in the Antarctic Treaty area shall be planned and conducted so as to limit adverse impacts on the Antarctic environment;

Noting the importance which Article 14 of the Protocol attaches to inspections in accordance with Article VII of the Antarctic Treaty as a way to promote the protection of the Antarctic environment and dependent and associated ecosystems;

Noting also that the issue of fuel storage and handling has been raised in several reports of inspections under Article VII of the Antarctic Treaty and has been noted by the CEP on a number of occasions;

Conscious of the importance of bringing the issue of fuel storage and handling to the attention of the Treaty Parties;

Recommend:

1. That their Governments either replace bulk fuel facilities currently lacking secondary containment with double-skinned tanks or provide them with adequate bunding, and have adequate oil spill contingency plans in place;

2. That COMNAP consider undertaking a further assessment of fuel handling and storage facilities and procedures in Antarctica with a view to issuing a set of clear recommendations to operators.

Resolution 4 (2005): Updating of Guidelines for Environmental Impact Assessment in Antarctica

The Representatives,

Noting that under Resolution 1 (1999) the ATCM adopted Guidelines for Environmental Impact Assessment;

Conscious of the need for these guidelines to better address the possible cumulative impacts arising from multiple activities at multiple locations undertaken by one or more national or private operator;

Considering the revision by the Committee of Environmental Protection of these guidelines;

Recommend that the Guidelines for Environmental Impact Assessment adopted by Resolution 1 (1999) be replaced by the amended guidelines attached to this text.

Guidelines for Environmental Impact Assessment in Antarctica

1. Introduction

The Madrid Protocol, in Article 3, establishes a number of environmental principles which can be considered a guide to environmental protection in Antarctica and its dependent and associated ecosystems. Among such principles, those stated under paragraph C express the necessity of collecting sufficient information "to allow prior assessments of, and informed judgements about, their possible impacts on the Antarctic environment and dependent and associated ecosystems and on the value of Antarctica for the conduct of scientific research". In addition, it states that "such judgements shall take account of:

(i) the scope of the activity, including its area, duration and intensity;

(ii) the cumulative impacts of the activity, both by itself and in combination with other activities in the Antarctic Treaty Area;

(iii) whether the activity will detrimentally affect any other activity in the Antarctic Treaty Area;

(iv) whether technology and procedures are available to provide for environmentally safe operations;

(v) whether there exists the capacity to monitor key environmental parameters and ecosystem components so as to identify and provide early warning of any adverse effects of the activity and to provide for such modification of operating procedures as may be necessary in the light of the results of monitoring or increased knowledge of the Antarctic environment and dependent and associated ecosystems;

(vi) whether there exists the capacity to respond promptly and effectively to accidents, particularly those with potential environmental effects"

Article 8 of the Protocol introduces the term *Environmental Impact Assessment* and provides three categories of environmental impacts (*less than, equal to* and *more than minor or transitory*), according to their significance. The Article also requires that assessment of planned activities to be undertaken in Antarctica, subject to the procedures set out in Annex I.

Annex I of the Protocol provides a more comprehensive explanation of the different impact categories and establishes a set of basic principles to conduct an EIA for planned activities in Antarctica.

In addition, it sets up a preliminary stage for assessing the environmental impact of Antarctic activities, which is intended to determine if an impact produced by a certain activity is less than minor or transitory or not. Such determination must be accomplished through the appropriate national procedures.

According to the results of the preliminary stage, the activity can either:

- proceed (if the predicted impacts of the activity are likely to be less than minor or transitory); or
- be preceded by a an Initial Environmental Evaluation (IEE), if predicted impacts are likely to be minor or transitory; or

- be preceded by a Comprehensive Environmental Evaluation (CEE), if the predicted impacts are to be more than minor or transitory.

Although the key to decide whether an activity shall be preceded by an IEE or a CEE is the concept of "*minor or transitory impact*", no agreement on this term has so far been reached (contributions to this subject can be found in XX ATCM/IP 2, New Zealand; XXI ATCM/WP 35, New Zealand; XXI ATCM/IP 55, Argentina, XXII ATCM/IP 66, Russia and XXII ATCM/WP 19, Australia, among others). The difficulty with defining *"minor and transitory impact"* thus far appear to be due to the dependence of a number of variables associated with each activity and each environmental context.

Therefore the interpretation of this term will need to be made on a case by case site specific basis. As a consequence, this document does not focus on seeking a clear definition of "minor or transitory impact", but rather is an attempt to provide basic elements for the development of the EIA *process*.

Article 8 and Annex I of the Protocol on Environmental Protection to the Antarctic Treaty set out the requirements for Environmental Impact Assessments (EIAs) for proposed activities in Antarctica. These Guidelines to EIA in Antarctica do not amend, modify or interpret the requirements set out in Article 8 and Annex I of the Environmental Protocol, or the requirements of national legislation which may include procedures and guidelines for the preparation of EIAs in Antarctica. These Guidelines have been produced to assist those preparing EIAs for proposed activities in Antarctica.

2. Objectives

The general objective of these guidelines is to achieve transparency and effectiveness in assessing environmental impacts during the planning stages of possible activities in Antarctica, as well as consistency of approach in fulfilling the obligations of the Protocol.

Specifically, the guidelines aim to:

- assist proponents of activities who may have little experience of EIA in Antarctica;
- assist in determining the proper level of EIA document (according to the Protocol) to be prepared;
- facilitate co-operation and co-ordination in EIA for joint activities;
- facilitate comparison of EIAs for similar activities and/or environmental conditions;
- provide advice to operators other than ATCPs;
- assist in the retrospective analysis of cumulative impacts for specific sites;
- initiate a process of continuous improvement of EIA.

3. The EIA Process

The EIA is a process having the ultimate objective of providing decision makers with an indication of the likely environmental consequences of a proposed activity (figure 1).

The *process* of predicting the environmental impacts of an activity and assessing their significance is the same regardless of the apparent magnitude of the activity. Some activities require no more than a cursory examination to determine impacts, although it must be remembered that the level of assessment is relative to the significance of the environmental impacts, not to the scale or complexity of the activity. Thus, the picture that emerges with respect to the impacts of the activity will determine how much further the EIA process needs to be taken, and how complex it should be.

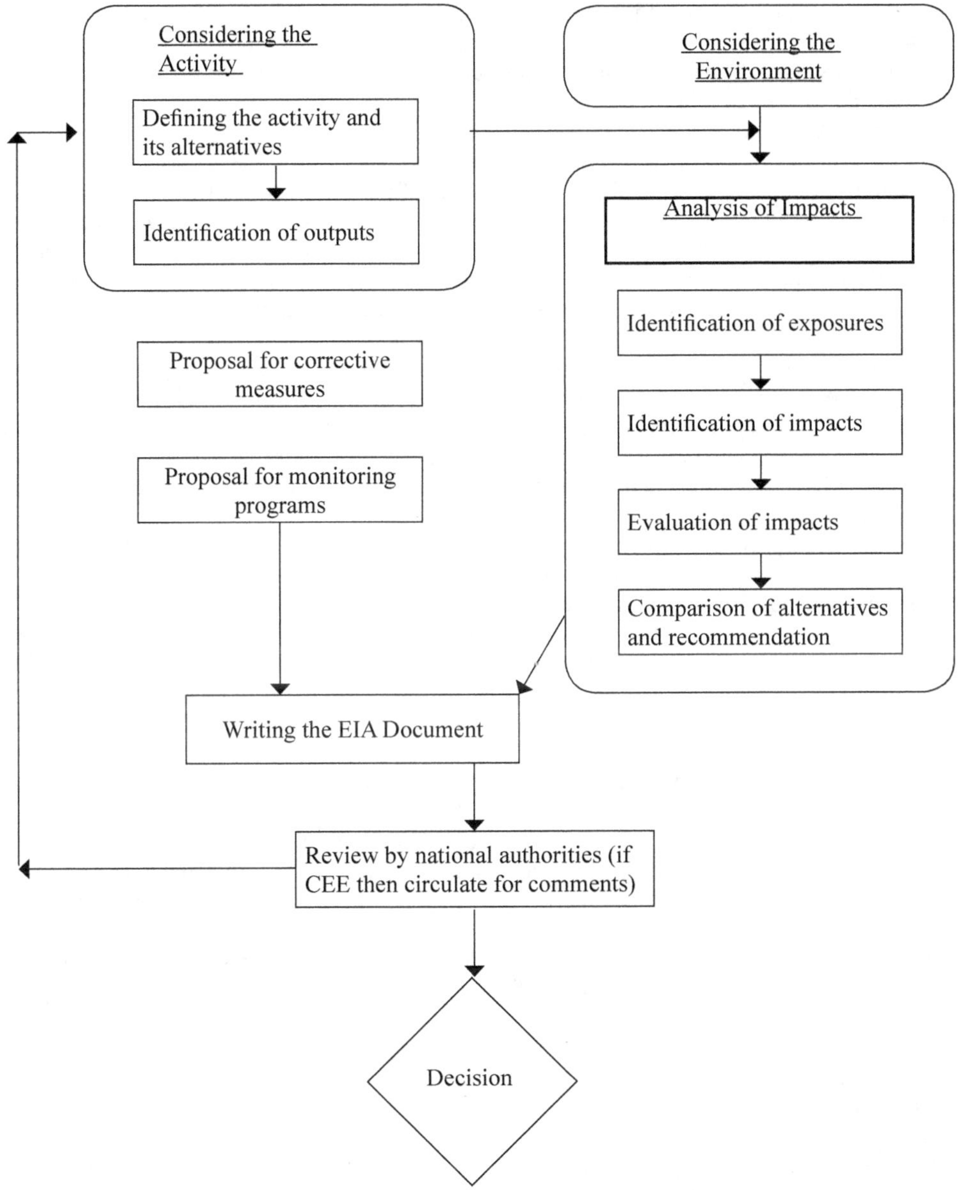

Figure 1: Steps of the EIA process for Antarctic activities

Those persons responsible for an Environmental Impact Assessment Process need to ensure that they consult as widely as is reasonably necessary and possible in order that the best available information and professional advice contribute to the outcome. A number of different participants may be involved throughout this process, ranging from those who are involved in the details of nearly all parts of the process (e.g. environmental officer, proponent of the activity) to those who are the technical experts who provide input in particular subjects of the process (e.g. researchers, logistic personnel, others with experience at the location or in a particular activity). In addition, EIAs undertaken in Antarctica for planned activities may represent a valuable source of information. At this respect, it should be pointed out that an updated list of EIAs is presented every ATCM, according to Resolution XIX-6. The Antarctic Data Directory System (ADDS) can also represent an helpful source of metadata.

3.1. Considering the activity

3.1.1. Defining the activity

An activity is an event or process resulting from (or associated with) the presence of humans in the Antarctic, and/or which may lead to the presence of humans in Antarctica. An activity may consist of several *actions*, e.g. an ice drilling *activity* may require *actions* such as the transport of equipment, establishment of a field camp, power generation for drilling, fuel management, drilling operation, waste management, etc. An activity should be analysed by considering all phases involved (e.g. construction, operation and potential dismantling or decommissioning phases).

The activity and the individual actions should be defined through a planning process which considers the physical, technical and economic aspects of the proposed project and its alternatives. Consultation with relevant experts to identify all these aspects is an important part of this initial scoping process. It is important to accurately define all aspects of the activity which could have environmental impacts. The rest of the EIA process relies on this initial description, which should occur during the planning process.

The following aspects of the proposed activity and its alternatives should be clearly identified:

- the purpose of and the need for the activity;
- the principal characteristics of the activity that might cause impact on the environment; for instance: design characteristics; construction requirements (types of material, technologies, energy, size of any installation, personnel, temporary constructions, etc.); transportation requirements (e.g. types, numbers and frequency of use of vehicles, fuel types); type (according to Annex III of the Protocol) and volume of wastes generated through different phases of the activity and their final disposition; dismantling of temporary constructions; decommissioning the activity if necessary; as well as those aspects that will result from the operational phase of the activity;
- the relationship of the proposed activity to relevant previous or current activities;
- a description of the activity's location and geographical area, indicating access roads, etc. Using maps will ease the evaluation process and, therefore, will be useful in the EIA documentation;
- timing of the activity (including range of calendar dates for construction time, as well as overall duration, periods of operation of the activity and decommissioning. This may be significant with respect to wildlife breeding cycles, for example.);
- location of the activity with regard to areas with special management requirements (SPA, SSSI, HSM, CCAMLR CEMP sites, already proposed ASPAs and/or ASMAs, etc.);
- precautionary measures that are integral to the project including during the construction, operational and decommissioning phases.

Careful consideration is required to determine the full scope of the activity so that the impacts can be properly assessed. This is necessary to avoid preparing a number of separate EIAs on actions which indicate an apparent low impact, when in fact, taken in its entirety, the activity actually has potential for impacts of much greater significance. This particularly common where a number of activities take place at the same site either spatially and/or temporally. Where activities are to be undertaken at sites which are visited repeatedly by one or more operators the cumulative effects of past, current and planned activities should be taken into consideration.

In identifying spatial and temporal boundaries for the EIA proponents should identify other activities occurring in the region within the EIA framework.

When defining an Antarctic activity, experience gained in similar projects undertaken within and outside the Antarctic Treaty System Area (e.g. the Arctic) may be an additional and valuable source of information.

Once the activity is defined, any subsequent changes to the activity must be clearly identified and addressed according to when they occur in the EIA process (e.g. if the change occurs once the EIA document is completed, then an amendment to the EIA or a rewrite of the document may be necessary depending on how significant the change is). In every case it is important that the change and its implications (in terms of impacts) is assessed in the same manner as other impacts previously identified in the EIA process.

3.1.2. Alternatives to the activity

Both the proposed activity and possible alternatives should be examined in concert so that a decision maker can more easily compare the potential impacts. Both the environmental and scientific consequences should be considered during the evaluation.

Examples of alternatives for consideration include:

- use of different locations or sites for the activity;
- use of different technologies, in order to reduce the outputs (or the intensity of the outputs) of the activity;
- use of pre-existing facilities; and
- different timing for the activity.

The alternative of not proceeding with the proposed activity (i.e. the "no-action" alternative) should always be included in any analysis of environmental impacts of the proposed activity.

3.1.3. Identification of outputs of the activity

An output is a physical change (e.g. movement of sediments by vehicle passage, noise) or an entity (e.g. emissions, an introduced species) imposed on or released to the environment as the result of an action or an activity. Outputs can also be defined as by-products of the activity (or action) and can include emissions, dust, mechanical action on substrate, fuel spills, noise, light, electromagnetic radiation, wastes, heat, introductions of alien species, etc.

Note that a single action may generate several different outputs (for example the use of vehicles may cause soil compaction, emissions, noise, visual interference etc.) and that the same type of output may be generated by different actions of a single activity, (for example in an ice drilling activity emissions may come from the use of vehicles, drilling operations, power generation, etc.).

When planning an activity the outputs of the proposed activity should be considered together with the outputs arising from past, present, and future activities. Therefore, potential for additive, synergistic or antagonistic interactions between outputs (thus resulting in possible significant environmental impacts) has to be considered.

It is also important to identify and consider outputs resulting from the activities of ractions of other proponents that can contribute to cumulative effects.

Systematising outputs and actions in a matrix format may be helpful in this process. The example below, taken from *"Monitoring of Environmental Impacts from Science and Operations in Antarctica"* (SCAR/COMNAP, 1996), illustrates a potential situation (e.g. actions and outputs associated with a station complex).

OUTPUTS						
ACTIONS	**Air emissions (incl. Dust)**	**Wastes**	**Noise**	**Fuel spills**	**Mechanical Action**	**Heat**
Vehicles	X	–	X	X	X	X
Power	X	–	X	X	–	X
generation						
Building	X	X	X	X	X	–
Fuel storage	–	–	–	X	–	–

Outputs may vary across different alternatives. That is there may not be a single set of outputs, but rather multiple sets if the alternatives are significantly different from one another.

The geographical spread of an output has to be accurately estimated in order to determine to what extent the environment is exposed.

3.2. Considering the environment

Consideration of the environment requires the characterisation of all relevant physical, biological, chemical and anthropic elements or values in a given area, where and when an activity is proposed. Relevant means all those aspects of the environment that the proposed activity might influence or which might influence the activity.

Such information should be quantitative (e.g., heavy metal concentration on organisms or on river flows, a bird population size) where available and appropriate. In many cases qualitative descriptions (e.g., aesthetic value of a landscape) may have to be used. Maps, publications, research results and researchers are different sources of information to be identified and taken into account.

Consideration of the existing environment should include:

- recognition of the special status accorded to Antarctica by the ATS, including its status as a natural reserve devoted to peace and science;
- the physical and biological features that could be affected directly or indirectly, including:
  - the physical characteristics (topography, bathymetry, geology, geomorphology, soils, hydrology, meteorology, glaciology etc.);
  - the biota (e.g. inventories of plant and animal species, populations and communities, and other important features such as the presence of breeding grounds.); and
  - any dependent and related populations (e.g. bird nesting areas related to feeding areas);
- natural variations in environmental conditions that could occur on a diurnal, seasonal, annual and/or interannual timescale;
- information about the spatial and temporal variability of the environmental sensitivity (e.g. differences in impacts when an area is snow covered compared to when it is not);
- current trends in natural processes such as population growth or spread of particular species, geological or hydrological phenomena;
- the reliability of the data (e.g. anecdotal, historical, scientific, etc.);
- aspects of the environment which have been changed, or may be changing as the result of other current or previous activities;
- recognition of management action taken/required to address or minimise the cumulative impacts of past and present activities;
- special values of the area (if previously identified);
- the existence of areas potentially subject to indirect and cumulative impacts;
- the influence that the activity may exert on dependent and associated ecosystems;
- existing activities being carried out in the area or at the site, particularly scientific activities, given their intrinsic importance as a value to be protected in Antarctica;
- specific parameters against which predicted changes are to be monitored, including:

A thorough consideration of the environment before starting the activity (baseline information) is essential to ensure a valid prediction of impacts and to define monitoring parameters, if required. If such a baseline information is not available, field research may be necessary to obtain reliable data about the state of the environment before beginning the activity.

It is also important to clearly identify gaps in knowledge and uncertainties encountered in compiling the information.

When an operator plans an activity which will be undertaken at several sites, each one of those sites should be described according to the methodology above.

3.3. Analysis of Impacts

3.3.1. Identification of exposures

Exposure is the process of interaction between an identified potential output and an environmental element or value. Identifying exposure means determining which component of the environment is susceptible to be affected by the outputs of an activity or action. Overlaying spatial information (e.g. use of a GIS) is a valuable tool to assist in this determination.

Determination of exposures may be summarised using a matrix of outputs and environmental elements or values, taking into account that matrices can only give information about the existence of exposures but not on their intensity.

The table below provides an example of the interaction of various outputs with environmental elements to identify relevant exposures resulting from the activity.

When the box is crossed (X) it means that the environmental element is exposed to the considered output. This is a random example for a given environment and may, therefore, vary in another context. For example, a noise may occur when a breeding site is unoccupied, or a breeding site may be protected from noise by a topographic feature. From the examples above it can be inferred that the occurrence of an output does not necessarily lead to exposure of environmental element or value and hence potential for environmental effects.

	ENVIRONMENTAL ELEMENTS OR VALUES				
OUTPUTS	**Flora**	**Fauna**	**Freshwater /Seawater**	**Soil**	**Air**
Emissions	X	X	X	X	X
Noise		X			
Fuel Spills	X	X	X	X	
Wastes	X	X	X	X	
Introduced species	X	X			

Correct identification of the intensity of exposure is a crucial step in making a reliable prediction of impacts. Some elements contributing to that identification are:

- Temporal variation. The exposure of an environmental element or value may change with the season in which the activity takes place, as climate cycles, breeding patterns, etc. may change over time.
- Cause-effect relationships between outputs and environmental elements or values must be determined, especially in cases where the relationships are indirect, or an element or value is exposed to outputs from numerous sources, or repeatedly from the same source.

3.3.2. Impact identification

An **impact** (synonym: **effect**) is a change in the values or resources attributable to a human activity.

It is the consequence (e.g. reduced plant cover) of an agent of change, not the agent itself (e.g. increase of trampling). Impact may also be defined as the result of the interaction between an output and an environmental value or resource.

The identification of environmental impacts consists of the characterisation of all changes in environmental elements or values exposed to the outputs of a given set of activities. The identification task requires that evaluators are able to determine the important cause-effect relationships between the activities and the environmental elements or values. Only when the impact is identified can an evaluation be made of its **significance**.

An impact may be identified by its nature, spatial extent, intensity, duration, reversibility and lag time.

***Nature**: type of change imposed on the environment due to the activity (e.g. contamination, erosion, mortality).*

***Spatial extent**: area or volume where changes are likely to be detectable.*

***Intensity**: a measure of the amount of change imposed on the environment due to the activity (it can be measured, or estimated, through, e.g. number of species or individuals effected, concentration of a given pollutant in a waterbody, rates of erosion, rates of mortality, etc.).*

***Duration**: period of time during which changes in the environment are likely to occur.*

***Reversibility**: possibility of the system to return to its initial environmental conditions once an impact is produced.*

***Lag time**: time span between the moment outputs are released to or imposed on the environment and the moment impacts occur.*

In addition, a proper impact identification should also enable a distinction between direct, indirect and cumulative impacts.

A ***direct impact*** is a change in environmental components that results from direct cause-effect consequences of interaction between the exposed environment and outputs (e.g. decrease of a limpet population due to an oil spill). An ***indirect impact*** is a change in environmental components that results from interactions between the environment and other impacts – direct or indirect – (e.g. alteration in seagull population due to a decrease in limpet population which, in turn, was caused by an oil spill).

A ***cumulative impact*** is the combined impact of past, present, and reasonably foreseeable activities. These activities may occur over time and space and can be additive or interactive/ synergistic (e.g. decrease of limpet population due to the combined effect of oil discharges by base and ship operations). Cumulative impacts can often be one of the hardest impact categories to adequately identify in the EIA process. When attempting to identify cumulative impacts it is important to consider both spatial and temporal aspects and to identify other activities which have and could occur at the same site or within the same area.

Several methods exist to identify impacts such as: overlay maps, checklists, matrices, etc. The choice of the methodology will depend on the character of the activity and the environment that is likely to be affected. Recognition should be given to relevant scientific data, where this exists, and to the results of monitoring programs.

3.3.3. Impact Evaluation

The purpose of impact evaluation is to assign relative significance to predicted impacts associated with an activity (and the various identified alternatives).

***Significance**: It is a value judgement about the severity and importance of a change in a given environment or environmental value.*

According to the Madrid Protocol, impacts shall be evaluated by taking into account three levels of significance:

- less than minor or transitory impact;
- minor or transitory impact; or
- more than minor or transitory impact.

The interpretation of these terms should be made on a case by case site specific basis. However it may be useful to consider how similar impacts have been judged in earlier EIAs at similar sites and/ or for similar types of activities.

An inherent consideration to judging significance is that it may have a rather subjective component and this fact should be acknowledged. Where an impact has the possibility of being significant, several experts should be consulted to achieve a view as objective as possible.. This is particularly important either if there is a reliance on incomplete data or if there are gaps in the knowledge.

Judging significance should not be based solely on direct impacts, but must also take account of possible indirect and cumulative impacts. This evaluation should determine the magnitude and significance of cumulative effects.

The significance of the unavoidable impacts (those impacts for which no further mitigation is possible) represents an important consideration for the decision maker in deciding whether, on balance, an activity is justified.

Some problems can arise when evaluating impacts, due to misunderstanding or overlooking some aspects of the process of evaluating impacts. These can include for example:

- confusing duration of the impact with duration of the activity;
- confusing outputs of activities with impacts;
- limiting the analysis to direct impacts, without consideration of indirect and cumulative impacts.

3.4. Comparison of impacts

When the project has been assessed with respect to environmental impacts it is necessary to summarise and aggregate the significant impacts for the various alternatives in a form suitable for communication to the decision makers. From such an aggregation of information a comparison among alternatives can be easily made.

3.5. Proposal for corrective measures

Corrective measures are composed of all steps conducted to decrease, avoid, or eliminate any of the components of an impact. It can be considered a process of feedback, and should occur throughout the EIA process, not simply as a final step. Corrective measures include mitigation and remediation actions.

Mitigation is the use of practice, procedure or technology to minimise or to prevent impacts associated with proposed activities. The modification of any aspect of the activity (and hence the consideration of outputs and the environmental exposure) as well as the establishment of supervision procedures represent effective ways of mitigation.

Mitigation measures will vary according to the activity and the characteristics of the environment, and may include:

- developing on site control procedures (e.g. recommended methods for waste disposal);
- establishing the best time for the activity (e.g. to avoid the breeding season of penguins);
- providing environmental education and training to personnel, or contractors, involved in the activity;
- ensuring adequate on site supervision of the activity by senior project staff or environmental specialists.

Remediation consists of the steps taken after impacts have occurred to promote, as much as possible, the return of the environment to its original condition.

The final version of the activity to be assessed must incorporate all corrective measures, including those associated with mitigation and remediation actions. Impact avoidance, as a form of mitigation, may contribute to minimising monitoring, reducing remediation costs and generally contribute also to maintaining the existing state of the environment.

When considering mitigation and remediation measures, the following issues should be addressed:

- making a clear distinction between mitigation and remediation measures;
- clearly defining the state of the environment that is being aimed for through such measures;
- considering that new, unforeseen impacts may appear as a result of inadequate implementation of proposed mitigation measures;
- noting that the environment may not always be capable of returning to its original condition, even when remediation actions are implemented;
- considering that a given corrective measure may interact antagonistically or synergically with other corrective measures.

3.6. Proposal for Monitoring Programs

Monitoring consists of standardised measurements or observations of key parameters (outputs and environmental variables) over time, their statistical evaluation and reporting on the state of the environment in order to define quality and trends. For the EIA process, monitoring should be oriented towards confirming the accuracy of predictions about environmental impacts of the activity, and to detect unforeseen impacts or impacts more significant than expected. Given this, it may be useful to set environmental thresholds or standards for an activity that monitoring results are assessed against. If these thresholds are exceeded, then a review or re-analysis would be required of assumptions made regarding the environmental impacts or of management systems related to the activity.

Monitoring may also include any other procedures that can be used to assess and verify the predicted impacts of the activity. Where measurement of specific parameters is not necessary or appropriate, assessment and verification procedures could include maintaining a log of the activity that actually occurred, and of changes in the nature of the activity where they were significantly different from those described in the EIA. This information can be useful for further minimising or mitigating impacts, and, where appropriate, for modifying, suspending or even cancelling all or part of the activity.

Monitoring is not about the measurement of everything in a haphazard approach to detect change but about precise measurement of a few target species, processes, or other indicators, carefully selected on the basis of scientifically sound predetermined criteria. Where a number of proponents are conducting activities at the same sites they should give consideration to establishing joint regional monitoring programs.

The process of selecting key indicators should be accomplished during the activity's planning stage, once outputs have been identified, the environment has been considered and associated impacts have been assessed, while monitoring environmental parameters generally should start before the commencement of the activity if adequate baseline information is not available.

Planning or undertaking monitoring activities may be hindered by a number of situations:

- leaving the planning of monitoring programs until the activity is in progress;
- monitoring activities can be costly, especially for multi-year projects and activities;
- some assumptions about the environmental impacts of an activity cannot be tested;
- failure to follow through with monitoring;
- failure to distinguish between natural and human-induced variability in environmental parameters.

4. Writing the EIA Document

The outcome of an EIA is a formal document, which presents all the relevant information about the EIA process. The EIA document represents a fundamental link between the EIA process and decision makers seeing that conclusions stemming from the EIA process will assist decision makers to consider the environmental aspects of the proposed activity.

Four bodies of information arise from an EIA process: *methodology, data, results* and *conclusions* derived from them. Since *results* and *conclusions* are of particular interest for decision makers, these chapters should be written in an accessible language, avoiding very technical terms. The use of graphical information, such as maps, tables and graphs, is an effective way of improving communication.

The size and level of detail in the document will depend on the significance of the environmental impacts that have been identified throughout the EIA process. Thus, Annex I to the Protocol establishes two formats to document it: Initial Environmental Evaluation (IEE) and Comprehensive Environmental Evaluation (CEE), for which the Protocol requires the presentation of different volumes of information (Annex 1, Articles 2 and 3).

Unless it has been determined that an activity will have less than a minor or transitory impact or it has already been determined that a Comprehensive Environmental Evaluation is needed, an Initial Environmental Evaluation (IEE) shall be prepared. If the EIA process indicates that a proposed activity is likely to have more than a minor or transitory impact a Comprehensive Environmental Evaluation must be prepared.

According to Annex I requirements a draft CEE shall be prepared first, which shall be circulated to all Parties as well as to CEP for comments. Once comments and suggestions have been incorporated, a final CEE is circulated to all Parties.

The following table summarises the steps to be considered throughout the EIA process (which are explained in Section 3 of the present guidelines). It also lists the requirements stemming from Annex I that should be included in an EIA document. In the case of IEE, some of the marked items are not specifically mentioned in Annex I, Article 2. However, their inclusion in the IEE document is often useful to communicate the results of the process in a transparent manner. These items were distinguished in the table with an X.

EIA Contents and Annex I Requirements	IEE	CEE
Description of the purpose and need of the activity	√	√
Description of the proposed activity and possible alternatives and the consequences of those alternatives	√	√
Alternative of not proceeding with the activity	X	√
Description of the initial environmental reference state and prediction of the environmental state in absence of the activity	X	√
Description of methods and data used to forecast impacts	X	√
Estimation of nature, extent, duration and intensity of direct impacts	√	√
Consideration of cumulative impacts	√	√
Consideration of possible indirect impacts	X	√
Monitoring programs	X	√
Mitigation and remediation measures	X	√
Identification of unavoidable impacts	X	√
Effects of the activity on scientific research and other uses or values	X	√
Identification of gaps in the knowledge	X	√
Preparers and advisors	X	√
References	X	X
Non-technical summary	X	√
Index	X	X
Glossary X		X
Cover sheet		X

√ Required by annex I.

X Often useful.

The following text focuses briefly on how the items listed above should be referred to in the text of any EIA. Further technical information is already described in previous chapters

Description of the purpose and need for the proposed activity

This section should include a brief description of the proposed activity and an explanation of the intent of the activity. It should include sufficient detail to make it clear why the activity is being proposed including the need for the activity to proceed. It should also provide details on the process by which the scope of the activity was defined. This will help ensure that the full scope of the activity has been included so that impacts can be properly assessed. If a formal process was used to accomplish this (a formal meeting or solicitation of input from the public or other groups), that process and its results should be discussed here.

Description of the proposed activity and possible alternatives and the consequences of those alternatives

This section should include a detailed description of the proposed activity as well as reasonable alternatives. The first alternative to be described would be the proposed activity. The description should be as comprehensive and detailed as possible (see section 3.1).

It may be useful to provide a comparison of alternatives in this section. For instance, for a new research station, alternatives might include differences in the size of the station and the number of persons that could be accommodated. These differences would mean different quantities of materials required, fuels consumed and emissions or wastes generated. Tables showing appropriate comparisons can be very helpful to the reader of the document.

Alternative of not proceeding with the activity

The alternative of not proceeding with the proposed activity (i.e. the "no-action" alternative) should be described to highlight the pros and cons of not conducting the activity. Although the Protocol only requires its inclusion in CEEs, it is useful to also include the "no-action" alternative in the text of IEEs in order to better justify the need for proceeding with the activity.

Description of the initial environmental reference state and prediction of the environmental state in absence of the activity

Such a description should not be limited to a characterisation of the relevant physical, biological, chemical and anthropic elements of the environment, but should also take into account the existence and behaviour of dynamic trends and processes in order to predict the state of the environment in absence of the activity. A proper description of the initial environmental reference state provides elements against which changes are to be compared.

Description of methods and data used to forecast the impacts

The purpose of this section is to explain and, if necessary, defend the design of the assessment and then provide enough detail that a further evaluator can understand and reproduce the procedure. Careful writing of the methodology is critically important because it determines that results can be reproducible and/or comparable.

Estimation of nature, extent, duration and intensity of impacts (including consideration of possible indirect and cumulative impacts).

This section contains the results of analyses of impacts, which includes a clear description of identified exposures as well as the identification of impact aspects, in terms of their nature, spatial extent, intensity, duration, reversibility and lag time. It must clearly establish the significance assigned to each impact and the justification for such assignment. In addition, and to summarise this section, the inclusion of a table showing the environmental impacts on each environmental component can be very helpful.

Special attention must be paid to the consideration of possible indirect and cumulative impacts, since cause-effect relationship determining the existence of such impacts usually exhibit a higher degree of complexity.

Monitoring programs

When necessary, this section should clearly define monitoring objectives, set testable hypotheses, choose key parameters to be monitored, assess data collection methods, design statistical sampling program, and decide on frequency and timing of data collection/recording. Implementation of such monitoring programs is a further step that may begin after the planning of the activity has been completed, even though the activity has not actually been initiated.

Mitigation and remediation measures

Since mitigation and remediation measures usually aim to correct some aspects of the activity, communication of these measures must be concrete, pointing out the proposed actions and their timing, as well as the benefits associated to each individual measure. It is often useful to include this section in the text of IEEs.

Identification of unavoidable impacts

Recognition of the existence of unavoidable impacts should be included within any impact analysis. Consideration of such impacts is of great importance given that the occurrence of unavoidable impacts may affect the decision on whether to proceed with the proposed activity.

Effects of the activity on scientific research and other uses or values

Taking into account that the Protocol designates Antarctica as an area devoted to peace and science, the effects of the proposed activity on ongoing scientific research, or on the potential of a site to future scientific research, must be a fundamental consideration when the impact analysis is carried out.

Identification of gaps in the knowledge

Existing bodies of knowledge (i.e. empirical, theoretical, or anecdotal data and information) are used to support the assessment process. Nonetheless, these bodies of knowledge may be incomplete or may be surrounded by varying degrees of uncertainty. It is critical to identify explicitly in the assessment where such incompleteness or uncertainty exists; and how this has been factored into the assessment process. This disclosure can be useful in assessment by clearly identifying where more knowledge is needed.

Preparers and advisors

This section provides a list of those experts who were consulted in preparing the assessment, their areas of expertise, and appropriate contact information. It should also list the persons who were responsible for the actual preparation of the document. This information is useful to reviewers and decision makers to ensure that the appropriate expertise was brought to bear on the analyses needed to assess the type and degree of impact from the proposed activity. It is also useful information for future assessments on similar activities or issues.

References

This section should list any references used in preparing the evaluation. They may include research or other scientific papers used in the analysis of impacts or monitoring data used to establish baseline conditions in the area where the activity is proposed. They may also include other environmental assessments of similar activities at other or similar locations.

Index

As an EIA document may be fairly large, an index is a very helpful aid to the reader.

Glossary

This section provides a list of terms and definitions as well as abbreviations that are helpful to the reader, especially if the terms are not commonly understood.

Cover sheet

The CEE should contain a title page or cover sheet that lists the name and address of the person or organization who prepared the CEE and the address to which comments should be sent (for the draft document only).

Non-technical summary

The CEE must contain a non-technical summary of the contents of the document. This summary should be written in an accessible language and include pertinent information on the purpose and need for the proposed activity, the issues and alternatives considered, the existing environment, and the impacts associated with each alternative. A non-technical summary might also be useful for an IEE.

Finally, in either case (IEE or CEE) a number of considerations about writing the EIA document should be taken into account, such as:

- avoidance of including irrelevant descriptive information;
- documenting all relevant steps of the process;
- clearly describing the impact identification methodology;
- clearly distinguishing between results (identification of impacts, mitigation measures, etc.) and final value judgement of significance;
- properly connecting results and conclusions.

5. Annex I Requirements for Circulation

5.1. Public circulation of an EIA

Under Annex I, public circulation is only required for CEEs. The draft CEE shall be made publicly available and shall be circulated to all Parties, which shall also make it publicly available, for comment. A period of 90 days shall be allowed for the receipt of comments. It shall be forwarded to the CEP at the same time as it is circulated to the Parties, and at least 120 days before the next ATCM, for consideration as appropriate.

5.2. Receipt and incorporation of comments

No final decision shall be taken to proceed with the proposed activity in the Antarctic Treaty area unless there has been an opportunity for consideration of the draft CEE by the ATCM on the advice of the CEP, provided that no decision to proceed with a proposed activity shall be delayed for longer than fifteen months from the day of circulation of the draft CEE. A final CEE shall address and shall include or summarise comments received on the draft CEE. The final CEE, notice of any decision relating thereto, and any evaluation of the significance of the predicted impacts in relation to the advantages of the proposed activity, shall be circulated to all Parties, which shall also make them publicly available, at least sixty days before the commencement of the proposed activity in the Antarctic Treaty area.

The following diagram illustrates this schedule for CEEs, as defined in Annex I.

Circulation of Draft CEE	Dealing for comments on Draft CEE	ATCM	Final decision to proceed	Circulation of Final CEE	Commencement of the Activity

6. Definition of terms in the EIA process

Action: any step taken as a part of an activity.

Activity: an event or process resulting from (or associated with) the presence of humans in the Antarctic, and/or which may lead to the presence of humans in Antarctica (adapted from *SCAR/COMNAP Monitoring Workshop*).

Comprehensive Environmental Evaluation (CEE): an environmental impact document required for proposed activities that may have more than a minor or transitory impact on the Antarctic environment (from *Madrid Protocol, Annex I, Article 3*).

Cumulative Impact: the combined impact of past, present, and reasonably foreseeable activities. These activities may occur over time and space and can be additive or interactive/synergistic (adapted from *IUCN Cumulative Impacts Workshop)*. These activities may involve visits by multiple operators or repeated visits to the same site by the same operator.

Direct Impact: a change in environmental components that results from direct cause-effect consequences of interaction between the exposed environment and outputs (from *Guidelines for EIA in the Arctic)*.

Environmental Impact Assessment (EIA): a process for identifying, predicting, evaluating and mitigating the biophysical, social and other relevant effects of proposed projects and physical activities prior to major decisions and commitments being made (from *Guidelines EIA in the Arctic*).

Exposure: the process of interaction between an identified potential output and an environmental element or value (adapted from *SCAR/COMNAP Monitoring Workshop*).

Impact: a change in the values or resources attributable to a human activity. It is the consequence (e.g. reduced plant cover) of an agent of change, not the agent itself (e.g. increase of trampling). Synonym: effect (from *SCAR/COMNAP Monitoring Workshop*).

Indirect Impact: a change in environmental components that results from interactions between the environment and other impacts (direct or indirect). (From *Guidelines for EIA in the Arctic.)*

Initial Environmental Evaluation (IEE): an environmental impact document required for proposed activities that may have a minor or transitory impact on the Antarctic environment (from *Madrid Protocol, Annex I, Article 2*).

Mitigation: the use of practice, procedure or technology to minimise or to prevent impacts associated with proposed activities. (*COMNAP Practical Guidelines.*)

Monitoring: consists of standardised measurements or observations of key parameters (outputs and environmental variables) over time, their statistical evaluation and reporting on the state of the environment in order to define quality and trends (adapted from *SCAR/COMNAP Monitoring Workshop*).

Operator: individuals or organisations undertaking activities from which impacts arise.

Output: a physical change (e.g. movement of sediments by vehicle passage, noise) or an entity (e.g. emissions, an introduced species) imposed on or released to the environment as the result of an *action* or an *activity*. (*SCAR/COMNAP Monitoring Workshop.*)

Preliminary Stage (PS): a process that considers the level of environmental impacts of proposed activities – before their commencement – referred to in Article 8 of the Protocol, in accordance with appropriate national procedures (from *Madrid Protocol, Annex I, Article 1*).

Proponent: an individual or a national program advocating the activity and responsible for the preparation of the EIA document.

Remediation: consists of the steps taken after impacts have occurred to promote, as much as possible, the return of the environment to its original condition.

Unavoidable Impact: an impact for which no further mitigation is possible.

7. References

ARCTIC ENVIRONMENTAL PROTECTION STRATEGY. 1997. Guidelines for Environmental Impacts Assessment (EIA) in the Arctic. Sustainable Development and Utilisation. Finnish Ministry of the Environment, Finland, 50 pp.

ATCPs. 1991. Protocol on Environmental Protection to the Antarctic Treaty (plus annexes). 11th Antarctic Treaty Special Consultative Meeting. Madrid, 22–30 April, 17–23 June 1991.

COMNAP. 1992. The Antarctic Environmental Assessment Process, Practical Guidelines. Bologna (Italy) June 20, 1991, revised Washington D.C. (USA), March 4, 1992.

FOREIGN AND COMMONWEALTH OFFICE. 1995. Guide to Environmental Impact Assessment of Activities in Antarctica. Polar Regions Section, South Atlantic and Antarctic Department, London.

IUCN – The World Conservation Union. 1996. Cumulative Environmental Impacts in Antarctica. Minimisation and Management. Edited by M. de Poorter and J.C. Dalziell. Washington, D.C., USA. 145 pp.

MINISTRY OF FOREIGN AFFAIRS AND TRADE. 1997. Guidelines and Procedures for Visitors to the Ross Sea Region. Ministry of Foreign Affairs and Trade. New Zealand.

SCAR/COMNAP. 1996. Monitoring of Environmental Impacts from Science and Operations in Antarctica. Workshop report. 43 pp and Annexes, 1996 Workshops.

XX ATCM/IP 2, Developing and Understanding of Minor or Transitory, submitted by New Zealand.

XXI ATCM/IP 55, Elementos para la Interpretación de los Procedimientos de Evaluación de Impacto Ambiental contenidos en el Anexo I del Protocolo de Madrid, submitted by Argentina.

XXI ATCM/WP 35, Further understanding of the term Minor or Transitory, submitted by New Zealand.

XXII ATCM/IP 66, Application of the "minor or transitory impacts" criterion of EIA in different regions of Antarctica, submitted by Russian Federation.

XXII ATCM/WP 19, Environmental Impact Assessment. The role of EIA Guidelines in understanding "Minor or Transitory", submitted by Australia.

8. Acronyms

ADDB: Antarctic Digital Database

ASMA: Antarctic Specially Managed Area

ASPA: Antarctic Specially Protected Area

ATCM: Antarctic Treaty Consultative Meeting
ATCP: Antarctic Treaty Consultative Party
ATS: Antarctic Treaty System
CCAMLR: Commission for the Conservation of Antarctic Marine Living Resources
CEE: Comprehensive Environmental Evaluation
CEMP: CCAMLR Ecosystem Monitoring Program
CEP: Committee of Environmental Protection
COMNAP: Council of Managers of National Antarctic Programmes
EIA: Environmental Impact Assessment
GIS: Geographical Information System
GOSEAC: SCAR Group of Specialists on Environmental Affairs and Conservation
HSM: Historic Sites and Monuments
IEE: Initial Environmental Evaluation
IUCN: International Union for the Conservation of Nature (World Conservation Union)
SCAR: Scientific Committee of Antarctic Research
SPA: Specially Protected Area
SSSI: Site of Special Scientific Interest

Measure 4 (2006): Specially Protected Species: Fur Seals

The Representatives,

Recalling Article 3 of Annex II to the Protocol on Environmental Protection to the Antarctic Treaty ("the Protocol"), providing for the designation of Specially Protected Species to be accorded special protection by the Parties;

Further recalling that the Committee for Environmental Protection ("CEP") adopted at CEP VIII guidelines for consideration of proposals for new and revised designations of Specially Protected Species, under which risk of extinction is to be assessed using criteria established by the IUCN;

Noting that SCAR has determined that the Antarctic Fur Seal (*Arctocephalus gazella*) and the Sub-antarctic Fur Seal (*Arctocephalus tropicalis*) are no longer at significant risk of extinction, and that as these are the only two species of the genus *Arctocephalus* in the Antarctic Treaty area, the genus *Arctocephalus* should be removed from the list of Specially Protected Species;

Further noting that the CEP has assessed the implications of removing these species from the list of Specially Protected Species, and has advised that they be removed;

Welcoming the recovery of the population and range of the Antarctic Fur Seal and the Sub-antarctic Fur Seal;

Believing that, in the light of the scientific advice from SCAR, the Antarctic Fur Seal and the Sub-antarctic Fur Seal should now be removed from the list of Specially Protected Species contained in Appendix A to Annex II to the Protocol;

Recognizing that the Antarctic Fur Seal and the Sub-antarctic Fur Seal will continue to receive comprehensive protection under the Protocol, and that their delisting will have no implications for the protection of those species of the genus *Arctocephalus* that occur only outside the Antarctic Treaty area;

Further noting that the Ross Seal *(Ommatophoca rossii)* remains a Specially Protected Species;

Bearing in mind the historical exploitation of fur seals in the region that made necessary the special protection of the Antarctic Fur Seal and the Sub-Antarctic Fur Seal, and the deep public interest in the protection and conservation of fur seals in Antarctica;

Resolving to keep under review the conservation status of fur seals in the Antarctic Treaty area;

Urging those Consultative Parties which are members of the Commission for the Conservation of Antarctic Marine Living Resources to continue to provide data on the amount of incidental seal mortality, potential impacts of krill harvesting on seal populations, and the development and effectiveness of mitigation measures in the krill fishery;

Recommend to their governments the following Measure for approval in accordance with Article 9 of Annex II to the Protocol on Environmental Protection to the Antarctic Treaty:

That:

In Appendix A to Annex II to the Protocol on Environmental Protection to the Antarctic Treaty, the words "All species of the genus *Arctocephalus*, Fur Seals." be deleted.

Resolution 2 (2006): Resolution on Site Guidelines for Visitors

The Representatives,

Recalling Resolution 5 (2005), which adopted a list of four sites subject to Site Guidelines;

Believing that Site Guidelines enhance the provisions set out in Recommendation XVIII-1 (Guidance for those organising and conducting Tourism and non-Governmental activities in the Antarctic);

Desiring to increase the number of Site Guidelines developed for visited sites;

Confirming that the term "visitors" does not include scientists conducting research within such sites, or individuals engaged in official governmental activities;

Noting that the Site Guidelines have been developed based on the current levels and types of visits at each specific site, and aware that the Site Guidelines would require review if there were any significant changes to the levels or types of visits to a site; and

Believing that the Site Guidelines for each site must be reviewed and revised promptly in response to changes in the levels and types of visits or in any demonstrable or likely environmental impacts;

Recommend that:

1. the list of Sites subject to Site Guidelines that have been adopted by the ATCM be extended to include a further eight new sites. The full list of Sites subject to Site Guidelines is annexed to this Resolution. This Annex lists the current Sites subject to Site Guidelines, and replaces the Annex to Resolution 5 (2005); and
2. the provisions of paragraphs 2 to 5 of Resolution 5 (2005) be implemented for all sites subject to Site Guidelines listed in the Annex to this Resolution.

Annex to Resolution 2 (2006)

List of Sites subject to Site Guidelines:

1. Penguin Island (Lat. 62° 06'S; Long. 57° 54'W);
2. Barrientos Island, Aitcho Islands (Lat. 62° 24'S; Long. 59° 47'W);
3. Cuverville Island (Lat. 64° 41'S; Long. 62° 38'W);
4. Jougla Point (Lat. 64° 49'S; Long. 63° 30'W);
5. Goudier Island, Port Lockroy (Lat. 64° 49'S; Long. 63° 29'W);
6. Hannah Point (Lat. 62° 39'S; Long. 60° 37'W);
7. Neko Harbour (Lat. 64° 50'S; Long. 62° 33'W);
8. Paulet Island (Lat. 63° 35'S; Long. 55° 47'W);
9. Petermann Island (Lat. 65° 10'S; Long. 64° 10'W);
10. Pleneau Island (Lat. 65° 06'S; Long. 64° 04'W);
11. Turret Point (Lat. 62° 05'S; Long. 57° 55'W); and
12. Yankee Harbour (Lat. 62° 32'S; Long. 59° 47'W);

Resolution 3 (2006): Ballast Water Exchange in the Antarctic Treaty Area

The Representatives,

Recalling the requirements of Annex II to the Protocol on Environmental Protection, on the Conservation of Antarctic Fauna and Flora, that precautions be taken to prevent the introduction of non-native species to the Antarctic Treaty area;

Aware of the potential for invasive marine organisms to be transported into or moved between biologically distinct regions within the Antarctic Treaty area by ships in their ballast water;

Conscious that the *International Convention for the Control and Management of Ships' Ballast Waters and Sediments*, 2004 (IMO Ballast Water Management Convention) has yet to enter into force;

Aware of the key principles of the IMO Ballast Water Management Convention, including that ballast water exchange be used as an interim measure until such time as ballast water treatment technologies have been developed, as set out in the Convention;

Noting the provision in the Convention which states that Parties with common interests bordering enclosed and semi-enclosed seas shall endeavour to seek co-operation with neighbouring Parties including through regional agreements to develop harmonised procedures (Article 13(3) of IMO Convention); and

Noting also that the Convention provides for a Party or Parties to put in place additional measures to require ships to meet a specified standard or requirement (Annex, Regulation C-1);

Desiring in the interim to put in place a Ballast Water Regional Management Plan for Antarctica;

Recommend that:

The Practical Guidelines for Ballast Water Exchange in the Antarctic Treaty area annexed to this Resolution be used by all ships in the Antarctic Treaty area except those referred to in Article 3, paragraph 2, of the *International Convention for the Control and Management of Ships' Ballast Waters and Sediments*, 2004 (IMO Ballast Water Management Convention).

Annex to Resolution 3 (2006) Practical Guidelines for Ballast Water Exchange in the Antarctic Treaty Area

1. The application of these Guidelines should apply to those vessels covered by Article 3 of the IMO's International Convention for the Control and Management of Ships' Ballast Water and Sediments (the Ballast Water Management Convention), taking into account the exceptions in Regulation A-3 of the Convention. These Guidelines do not replace the requirements of the Ballast Water Management Convention, but provide an interim Ballast Water Regional Management Plan for Antarctica under Article 13 (3).

2. If the safety of the ship is in any way jeopardised by a ballast exchange, it should not take place. Additionally, these guidelines do not apply to the uptake or discharge of ballast water and sediments for ensuring the safety of the ship in emergency situations or saving life at sea in Antarctic waters.

3. A Ballast Water Management Plan should be prepared for each vessel with ballast tanks entering Antarctic waters, specifically taking into account the problems of ballast water exchange in cold environments and in Antarctic conditions.

4. Each vessel entering Antarctic waters should keep a record of ballast water operations.

5. For vessels needing to discharge ballast water within the Antarctic Treaty area, ballast water should first be exchanged before arrival in Antarctic waters (preferably north of either the Antarctic Polar Frontal Zone or 60°S, whichever is the furthest north) and at least 200 nautical miles from the nearest land in water at least 200 metres deep. If this is not possible for operational reasons then such exchange should be undertaken in waters at least 50 nautical miles from the nearest land in waters of at least 200 metres depth.

6. Only those tanks that will be discharged in Antarctic waters would need to undergo ballast water exchange following the procedure in Paragraph 5. Ballast Water Exchange of all tanks is encouraged for all vessels that have the potential/capacity to load cargo in Antarctica, as changes in routes and planned activities are frequent during Antarctic voyages due to changing meteorological and sea conditions.

7. If a vessel has taken on ballast water in Antarctic waters and is intending to discharge ballast water in Arctic, sub-Arctic, or sub-Antarctic waters, it is recommended that ballast water should

be exchanged north of the Antarctic Polar Frontal Zone, and at least 200 nautical miles from the nearest land in water at least 200 metres deep. (If this is not possible for operational reasons then such exchange should be undertaken in waters at least 50 nautical miles from the nearest land in waters of at least 200 metres depth).

8. Release of sediments during the cleaning of ballast tanks should not take place in Antarctic waters.

9. For vessels that have spent significant time in the Arctic, ballast water sediment should preferably be discharged and tanks cleaned before entering Antarctic waters (south of 60°S). If this cannot be done then sediment accumulation in ballast tanks should be monitored and sediment should be disposed of in accordance with the ship's Ballast Water Management Plan. If sediments are disposed of at sea, then they should be disposed of in waters at least 200 nautical miles from the shoreline in waters at least 200 metres deep.

10. Treaty Parties are invited to exchange information (via the Council of Managers of National Antarctic Programs) on invasive marine species or anything that will change the perceived risk associated with ballast waters.

Resolution 4 (2006): Conservation of Southern Giant Petrels

The Representatives,

Noting that the Committee for Environmental Protection (CEP) is keeping under review the status of the southern giant petrel;

Recognising that the species, in its global distribution, is currently listed as "Vulnerable" by the IUCN;

Recalling SCAR's advice that the species meets the IUCN criteria for it to be listed as "Critically Endangered" in the Antarctic Treaty area;

Understanding that recent data indicating a larger global population may prompt a reappraisal of the IUCN status category of the species for its global distribution in the near future;

Recalling the *Guidelines for CEP Consideration of Proposals for New and Revised Designations of Antarctic Specially Protected Species under Annex II of the Protocol* adopted at CEP VIII, which provide, *inter alia*, for assessment of the status of species at a regional or local level;

Recommend that:

1. SCAR undertake a further review of the status of southern giant petrel using all available data and provide a report at CEP X, including, if appropriate, a proposal for inclusion of the species on the list of Specially Protected Species in Appendix A to Annex II to the Protocol on Environmental Protection, together with a draft Action Plan;

2. In the intervening period all Governmental and non-Governmental activities in Antarctica should be planned so as to avoid negative impacts on southern giant petrels, in particular on breeding colonies of this species

Resolution 2 (2007): Conservation of Southern Giant Petrel Macronectes giganteus

The Representatives,

Recalling Resolution 4 (2006) on the conservation of southern giant petrels;

Noting that the Committee for Environmental Protection (CEP) is keeping under review the possibility of designating the southern giant petrel as an Antarctic Specially Protected Species under Annex II to the Protocol on Environmental Protection;

Recalling that the *Guidelines for CEP Consideration of Proposals for New and Revised Designations of Antarctic Specially Protected Species under Annex II to the Protocol* adopted at CEP VIII, which provide, *inter alia,* for assessments of the status of species at a regional or local level;

Recognising that, while the southern giant petrel, in its global distribution, is currently being downlisted from *Vulnerable* to *Near Threatened* by the International Union for the Conservation of Nature, concern has been expressed that populations within the Antarctic Treaty area may fulfill the criteria for higher risk status;

Recognising that the life-history characteristics of the southern giant petrel may make it particularly sensitive to human disturbance;

Noting that the Agreement on the Conservation of Albatrosses and Petrels (ACAP) encourages the Antarctic Treaty system to further protect breeding sites of southern giant petrels;

Noting that many Parties support a precautionary approach to this matter;

Recommend that:

1. all Parties be encouraged to make available existing relevant scientific data and results to the Scientific Committee on Antarctic Research and to implement new research into the population biology of southern giant petrels;

2. SCAR, in collaboration with ACAP, the Commission for the Conservation of Antarctic Marine Living Resources (CCAMLR) and other relevant bodies as appropriate, complete a review as soon as practical of the population status and trends of the southern giant petrel in the Antarctic Treaty area including an assessment of

   1) whether this species fulfils the criteria for designation as a Specially Protected Species under Annex II of the Protocol at a regional scale (the Antarctic Treaty area), and;
   2) the demographic mechanisms underlying any changes in the population size;

3. the Chair of CEP contact the Secretariats of ACAP and CCAMLR to seek information on current conservation management measures for the southern giant petrel;

4. all Parties are encouraged to provide to the CEP website *http://cep.ats.aq* details of all existing national regulations, management plans or site guidelines for all areas with breeding colonies of southern giant petrels which may be at risk of disturbance that may serve as an example to develop an Action Plan for the Antarctic Treaty area under the *Guidelines for CEP Consideration of Proposals for New and Revised Designations of Antarctic Specially Protected Species under Annex II of the Protocol* and better inform local and regional measures to protect southern giant petrels in the Antarctic Treaty area;

5. in the intervening period, all Government and non-Governmental activities in Antarctica be planned so as to limit negative impacts on southern giant petrels.

Resolution 3 (2007): Long-term Scientific Monitoring and Sustained Environmental Observation in Antarctica

The Representatives,

Recalling the Edinburgh Antarctic Declaration on the International Polar Year 2007–2008 (IPY) that was agreed at ATCM XXIX, which supports the objective of delivering a lasting legacy for the International Polar Year, and promotes increasing collaboration and coordination of scientific studies within Antarctica;

Recalling that the Committee for Environmental Protection has a continuing commitment to environmental monitoring related to the implementation of the Protocol on Environmental Protection to the Antarctic Treaty;

Noting that the Arctic Council Ministerial Meeting of 26 October 2005 urged all member countries of the Arctic Council to maintain and extend long-term monitoring of change in all parts of the Arctic as well as to create a coordinated Arctic observing network;

Recalling the success of the CCAMLR Ecosystem Monitoring Programme in providing over two decades of circum-Antarctic data on the Antarctic marine ecosystem and biological environment;

Welcoming and supporting the proposal by the Scientific Committee for Antarctic Research to establish a multi-disciplinary pan-Antarctic observing system, which will, in collaboration with others, coordinate long-term monitoring and sustained observation in the Antarctic;

Recommend that the Parties:

1. urge national Antarctic programmes to maintain and extend long-term scientific monitoring and sustained observations of environmental change in the physical, chemical, geological and biological components of the Antarctic environment;
2. contribute to a coordinated Antarctic observing system network initiated during the IPY in cooperation with SCAR, CCAMLR, WMO, GEO and other appropriate international bodies;
3. support long-term monitoring and sustained observations of the Antarctic environment and the associated data management as a primary legacy of the IPY, to enable the detection, and underpin the understanding and forecasting of the impacts of environmental and climate change.

Resolution 3 (2008): Environmental Domains Analysis for the Antarctic Continent as a Dynamic Model for a Systematic Environmental Geographic Framework

The Representatives,

Noting that Article 3 of Annex V to the Protocol on Environmental Protection to the Antarctic Treaty provides a framework for the designation of Antarctic Specially Protected Areas;

Recognising that these Areas must conform to the requirements of Article 3 of Annex V;

Noting also that Article 3(2) of Annex V states that Parties shall seek to identify such areas within a systematic environmental geographical framework,

Desiring to give practical meaning to the phrase "systematic environmental-geographical framework";

Recalling Resolution 1 (2000) *Guidelines for Implementation of the Framework for Protected Areas*;

Recommend that:

The "*Environmental Domains Analysis for the Antarctic Continent*" annexed to this Resolution be used consistently and in conjunction with other tools agreed within the Antarctic Treaty System as a dynamic model for the identification of areas that could be designated as Antarctic Specially Protected Areas within the systematic environmental-geographical framework referred to in Article 3(2) of Annex V of the Protocol.

Annex: Environmental Domains Analysis for the Antarctic continent[1]

Environmental geographic frameworks are methods of classifying or organising subsets of environmental and geographic characteristics such as different types of ecosystem, habitat, geographic area, terrain, geology, and climate into environmental or geographic regions. Each region is distinctive or in some way different from other regions but some might have characteristics in common.

Environmental Domains Analysis (EDA) has been used, at the scale of the Antarctic continent, to classify a sub-sample of over 13 million 1000m pixels from eight underlying data layers, into 21 Environments (also known as "Environmental Domains"). The classification presented here is the best that can be achieved by this process using currently available climate, slope, land cover and geological data.

The 21 different Environments in Table 1 and Figure 1 represent 21 different environmental-geographic regions that fit together into a logical, integrated and complete system of regions representing Antarctica as a whole. This provides the fundamental scientific basis for the systematic environmental-geographic framework for protected areas as envisaged in, and consistent with, Article 3(2).

[1] Version 2.0, 2007.

A full description of these Environments, individual maps of them (as well as further details on the project background, data layers and the classification process itself) are contained in the technical report by Morgan and others (2007).

The spatial classification of Antarctica into 21 Environmental Domains is presented in the attached figure.

Reference

Morgan F, Barker G, Briggs C, Price R and Keys H. 2007. Environmental Domains of Antarctica Version 2.0 Final Report, Manaaki Whenua Landcare Research New Zealand Ltd, 89 pages.

Table 1 – Descriptions of Environments in Version 2.0 of Environmental Domains Analysis for the Antarctic continent, including type examples

Alphabet label	**EDA Type Environments and extended descriptors**
A	Antarctic Peninsula northern geologic
B	Antarctic Peninsula mid-northern latitudes geologic
C	Antarctic Peninsula southern geologic
D	East Antarctic coastal geologic (e.g. Vestfold, Bunger, Wilson hills)
E	Antarctic Peninsula, Alexander and other islands main ice fields and glaciers)
F	Larsen Ice Shelf (also includes Prince Gustav and other northern peninsula ice shelf remnants)
G	Antarctic Peninsula offshore islands (e.g. most of Deception Island)
H	East Antarctic low latitude glacier tongues (e.g. Mertz, Rennick)
I	East Antarctic ice shelves (e.g. Fimbulisen, Amery, Shackleton, Cook, Moubray Bay)
J	Southern latitude coastal fringe ice shelves and floating glaciers (e.g. Pine Island,Thwaites, Getz, Drygalski)
K	Northern latitude ice shelves (e.g. Wordie, George VI, Wilkins, Abbot, Riser-Larsenisen, Nansen)
L	Continental coastal-zone ice sheet
M	Continental mid-latitude sloping ice (e.g. Ellsworth & Coats lands, upper Lambert Gl, northern Berkner & Thurston islands)
N	East Antarctic inland ice sheet
O	West Antarctic Ice Sheet (also includes inland Coats Land, Taylor Dome, Ross Island ice cap)
P	Ross and Ronne-Filchner ice shelves
Q	East Antarctic high interior ice sheet
R	Transantarctic Mountains geologic (Shackleton Range to Cook Mountains)
S	McMurdo – South Victoria Land geologic (also includes Ellsworth, Werner etc mountains)
T	Inland continental geologic (Dronning Maud, MacRobertson, Victoria, Oates lands, Ford Range)
U	North Victoria Land geologic (also includes Executive Committee Range, Prince Charles & Jones mountains)

Omitted: Figure 1 – Map of Antarctica showing the classification layer with its 21 Environments

Resolution 4 (2008): Checklist to Assist in the Inspection of Antarctic Specially Protected Areas and Antarctic Specially Managed Areas

The Representatives,

Recalling Article VII of the Antarctic Treaty which provides for the designation of observers to carry out inspections and Article 14 of the Protocol on Environmental Protection to the Antarctic Treaty which provides that inspections shall be arranged to promote the protection of the Antarctic environment and dependent and associated ecosystems and to ensure compliance with the Protocol;

Further recalling Article 12 of the Protocol which sets out the functions of the Committee for Environmental Protection, including providing advice on inspection procedures, including formats for inspection reports and checklists for the conduct of inspections;

Considering that inspection checklists are useful as guidelines for those planning and conducting inspections;

Noting that checklists are not mandatory, exhaustive nor necessarily completely applicable to all areas and that they are not to be used as a questionnaire;

Recommend that:

Their Governments encourage the use of the attached *"Checklist to assist in the inspection of Antarctic Specially Protected and Managed Areas"*.

Annex: Checklist to assist in the inspection of Antarctic Specially Protected Areas and Antarctic Specially Managed Areas

This checklist is not intended to be exhaustive, but is designed to provide a guideline to observers conducting inspections in Antarctica in accordance with Article VII of the Antarctic Treaty and Article 14 of the Environment Protocol. Not all items in the checklist are necessarily applicable to the activity being inspected or directly related to Article VII of the Antarctic Treaty or the requirements of the Protocol on Environmental Protection to the Antarctic Treaty. It is recognised that some of the items could be addressed through the Antarctic Treaty Exchange of Information. It is also recognised that the purpose of an inspection is to verify through observation. Therefore, any inspection report should clearly identify which information was observed and which was taken from documents. It is recommended that observers seek out and examine all relevant documents prior to undertaking inspections.

1. General information

1.1 Name and number of Protected or Managed Area
1.2 Date of inspection visit
1.3 Name(s) of observers entering the Area
1.4 Mode of transport to/from the Area
1.5 Activities conducted by the observers in the Area
1.6 Authority issuing permit to observers to enter the Area

2. Nearby stations and visiting vessels (if any)

2.1 Nearest stations, bases and vessels
2.2 Are copies of the Area Management Plan held on the station or vessel?
2.3 Who is responsible for ensuring compliance with Management Plans at any nearby stations or vessels?
2.4 Entry by station or vessel personnel to the Area within the past year (issue of permits and reason for their issue)
2.5 Are there any problems with station or vessel personnel or visitors not observing the restrictions of the Area?
2.6 Are other Protected or Managed Areas in close proximity?

3. Assessment of Area Management Plan

3.1 Are the values for which the Area was designated still relevant?

3.2 Are the values of the Area being protected effectively?
3.3 Are the management aims and objectives appropriate?
3.4 Is the period of designation appropriate?
3.5 Do maps and photographs show the boundary of the Area clearly and the key features it contains?
3.6 Are the boundaries easy to locate?
3.7 Are maps and photographs easy to use and up to date?
3.8 What are the geographical coordinates of the Area? Are they correct (clearly state how this was checked in the field)?

4. Management activities

4.1 Are appropriate management activities being undertaken to protect the values of the Area?
4.2 Is any monitoring of the Area being undertaken?
4.3 What measures are in place to ensure that the aims and objectives of the Management Plan are being met? Do they need to be revised?

Resolution 1 (2009): Urging Parties to Enhance Environmental Protection for the Antarctic Ecosystem Northward to the Antarctic Convergence

The Representatives,

Reaffirming their commitment to the protection of the Antarctic environment and dependent and associated ecosystems;

Noting that the Antarctic Treaty, per its Article VI, provides that the Treaty applies to the area south of 60° south latitude;

Noting further that the Convention on the Conservation of Antarctic Marine Living Resources, per its Article I(1), applies to the Antarctic marine living resources of the area south of 60° south latitude and to the Antarctic marine living resources of the area between that latitude and the Antarctic Convergence;

Recalling that the "Antarctic area" Special Area defined in Annex I, regulation 1.11.7, and the "Antarctic Area" Special Area defined in Annex II, regulation 13.8.1, and the "Antarctic area" Special Area defined in Annex V, regulation 5(1) (g), of the International Convention for the Prevention of Pollution from Ships, 1973, as modified by its Protocol of 1978 (MARPOL 73/78), define this area (Antarctic Special Area) as the "sea area south of latitude 60° S" (MARPOL Special Areas);

Acknowledging the value of cooperation as among Parties and through the International Maritime Organization to prevent marine pollution;

Recommend that:

1. The Parties cooperate, consistent with the Protocol on Environmental Protection and in accordance with international law, to enhance environmental protection for the entire Antarctic marine ecosystem;

2. The Commission on the Conservation of Antarctic Marine Living Resources (CCAMLR) be asked by the Chairman of the ATCM XXXII to provide its views to the ATCM on the possibility of asking the International Maritime Organization (IMO) to amend the Antarctic Special Area to extend its boundary northward to the Antarctic Convergence; and

3. The Parties at ATCM XXXIII consider the views of CCAMLR and whether to recommend that further steps be taken within the IMO to extend northward the Antarctic Special Area to the Antarctic Convergence.

Resolution 3 (2009): Guidelines for the Designation and Protection of Historic Sites and Monuments

The Representatives,

Recalling the protection afforded to historical sites and monuments by Article 8 of Annex V to the Protocol on Environmental Protection to the Antarctic Treaty,

Recalling also Measure 3 (2003), as amended by subsequent Measures, which sets out the current list of Historic Sites and Monuments,

Recognizing the unique value of all the historic and cultural remains of early exploration of the Antarctic continent,

Considering that the cultural and historic heritage of Antarctica is susceptible to loss and decay over time through natural processes and increased human pressure through the placement of logistical and scientific facilities and increased human impacts from visitors and tourists,

Recalling Resolution 5 (2001), which provides guidelines for the handling of pre-1958 historic remains,

Recalling further Resolution 8 (1995), Resolution 4 (1996) and Resolution 4 (2001),

Aware that successive Antarctic Treaty Consultative Meetings have developed guidelines to ensure that the process for designating Historic Sites and Monuments under the Antarctic Treaty fully complies with the objective of identifying, protecting and preserving the historic and cultural values of Antarctica,

Recommend that the Guidelines for the designation and protection of Historic Sites and Monuments annexed to this Resolution be used by Parties as guidance on questions related to the designation, protection and preservation of historic sites, monuments, artefacts and other historic remains in Antarctica.

Guidelines for the designation and protection of Historic Sites and Monuments

1. Parties should make every effort to preserve and protect, in accordance with the Antarctic Treaty and its Protocol, including Annex V, the Historic Sites and Monuments situated in the Antarctic Treaty area. Whenever appropriate, they should consult together on their restoration or preservation and adopt all adequate measures to protect all artefacts, buildings, monuments, archaeological and cultural remains and sites endowed with historic significance, from damage or destruction.

2. Where appropriate, Parties should arrange for each of these historic monuments or sites to be appropriately marked with a notice indicating in the English, French, Russian and Spanish languages that the monument or site is designated as an Historic Site or Monument, in accordance with the provisions of the Protocol.

3. Parties who wish to nominate a particular Historic Site and or Monument should address in the proposal one or more of the following:

(a) a particular event of importance in the history of science or exploration of Antarctica occurred at the place;
(b) a particular association with a person who played an important role in the history of science or exploration in Antarctica;
(c) a particular association with a notable feat of endurance or achievement;
(d) representative of, or forms part of, some wide-ranging activity that has been important in the development and knowledge of Antarctica;
(e) particular technical, historical, cultural or architectural value in its materials, design or method of construction;
(f) the potential, through study, to reveal information or has the potential to educate people about significant human activities in Antarctica;
(g) symbolic or commemorative value for people of many nations.

4. The Party or Parties that nominated and/or are undertaking management of a Historic Site or Monument should keep the site or monument under review to assess whether:

(a) the site or monument still exists in whole or in part;
(b) the site or monument continues to meet the guidelines outlined in the previous paragraph;
(c) the description of the site or monument should be amended and updated when necessary;
(d) the location and if possible the limits of the site or monument are on its topographic maps, hydrographic charts and in other relevant publications;
(e) the site requires protection or management and, if so, whether it should be also designated as, or included in an Antarctic Specially Protected Area or as an Antarctic Specially Managed Area;
(f) in light of this review, the Historic Site or Monument should be de-listed.

5. During the preparations for a listing of a Historic Site or Monument, the proposing Party should ensure adequate liaison with the originator of the Historic Site or Monument and other Parties as appropriate. During the writing of a site management plan or conservation strategy, the proposing Party is encouraged to consider the adoption of further protective measures, including whenever appropriate:

(a) The development in a comprehensive manner of a conservation strategy, including the establishment when appropriate of buffer zones to guard buildings and monuments against damage;
(b) To the extent possible, seeking to achieve coherence through all the steps leading to historic commemoration such as the design of commemorative monuments, cairns or plaques, and any place-names attached to Historic Sites or areas of historical significance, including buffer zones.
(c) The requirement for environmental impact assessments of activities undertaken to erect a new historic monument or site. In the course of such assessment, the proponent should consider the most environmentally appropriate approach to achieving their objective of historic and cultural protection.
(d) The application of risk assessment in areas of intense human activity or otherwise in more remote and inaccessible areas where the vulnerable nature of historic sites and monuments may require that the protection include an area considered sufficient, compatible and adequate for preserving the historical values of the designated sites or monuments and avoid increased risk of damage arising out of human activity in Antarctica.
(e) The preparation of site guidelines, related to visitors and access by aircraft, vehicles or vessels, through visible marking, mapping and regular surveying, as well as issuing Historic Sites and Monuments Guidelines and other interpretive and educational material.
(f) The periodic undertaking of surveys or visits to the designated Historic Sites and Monuments and circulating reports thereafter on the condition of such Historic Sites and Monuments, including additional information on measures adopted to protect them from destruction or damage
(g) The inclusion of any relevant Historic Sites and Monuments in the checklists of Inspections undertaken under Article VII of the Antarctic Treaty and Article 14 of the Environmental Protocol.

6. Parties should observe the interim protection provided by Resolution 5 (2001) (Guidelines for handling of pre-1958 historic remains whose existence or present location is not yet known) during the three year period after the discovery of a new historic artefact or site has been brought to their attention by any person or expedition who discovers pre-1958 historic remains, and consider afterwards the formal incorporation of the artefact/site into the protected or managed areas designated under Annex V of the Protocol. If there is uncertainty as to the age of a newly discovered artefact/site it should be treated as a pre-1958 artefact/site until its age has been definitively established.

7. To that end, Parties should notify the other Parties of the discovery, indicating what remains have been found, and where and when. The consequences of removing such remains should be duly considered. If items nonetheless were removed from Antarctica, they should be delivered to the appropriate authorities or public institutions in the home country of the discoverer, and remain available upon request for research purposes.

8. Visitors to Antarctica should be informed of the importance of protecting the historic and cultural heritage of the Antarctic continent and its surrounding islands and of all restrictions applying to artefacts, sites and monuments listed under the Antarctic Treaty system or protected under Resolution 5 (2001). This may include by developing historic site information guidelines and incorporating information about cultural heritage into a range of public education and interpretive materials to be prepared by the Parties, reminding visitors to Antarctica that they must not engage in conduct that results in interference to any scientific stations or environmental protected areas, as well as buildings, historical monuments, sites, artefacts, relics, commemorative plaques or site markers. The conservation of these features differ from the protection of biological or environmental phenomena but are equally important to the understanding of the values of Antarctica.

Resolution 5 (2009): Protection of the Southern Giant Petrel

The Representatives,

Recalling Resolution 4 (2006) and Resolution 2 (2007) on the Conservation of southern giant petrels, and Resolution 4 (2003) on the Conservation of albatrosses and petrels;

Recalling that the *Guidelines for CEP Consideration of Proposals for New and Revised Designations of Antarctic Specially Protected Species under Annex II to the Protocol* adopted at CEP VIII provide, *inter alia*, for assessments of the status of species at a regional or local level;

Recalling further that CEP XI supported SCAR's assessment, on the basis of information made available to a workshop held on 19–20 May 2008 to consider the status of the southern giant petrel in the Antarctic region, that the regional status of the species was considered of "Least Concern" in accordance with IUCN criteria;

Recalling also the CEP's past work to compile existing measures for protection of Antarctic populations of southern giant petrels, and to prepare a draft Action Plan for the species as an example of possible protective measures;

Noting that ACAP has assessed the global status of the southern giant petrel to be "Near Threatened" and has advised that it does not have sufficient information to determine a population trend for Antarctic breeding sites;

Recalling the Parties' earlier recognition of the sensitivity of the southern giant petrel to human disturbance, particularly at breeding sites;

Welcoming advice from ACAP on a standardised methodology for population monitoring of southern giant petrels;

Desiring to ensure that further robust data are collected to inform future assessments of the Antarctic regional and global status of the species, and are made available to relevant other organisations with complementary conservation objectives;

Desiring also to take action to minimise disturbance of southern giant petrel breeding sites in the Antarctic region;

Recommend that the Parties:

1. Encourage regular population counts at Antarctic breeding locations, using standardised methodology prepared by ACAP, with priority given to those locations where the current population data are insufficient for trend analysis;

2. Encourage the submission of existing and any future southern giant petrel population data to ACAP;

3. Review the adequacy of existing site-specific measures, such as Management Plans or Site Guidelines, with a view to appropriately manage access and minimise disturbance to southern giant petrel breeding sites in the Antarctic Treaty area and, as required, develop and implement further measures; and

4. Monitor progress on the above actions and the conservation status of the southern giant petrel at a future meeting.

Resolution 3 (2010): Annex Checklist 'A' – Antarctic Stations and Subsidiary Installations

This checklist could also be used to help prepare for, and guide, inspections of remote camps and refuges that are not subsidiary facilities of a station. Some items on the checklist may not be relevant to the inspection of such remote camps and refuges. When planning inspections, the checklist should be examined and adapted for the particular facility to be inspected

INDEX

Section 1 – General information

1.1. Name of station visited

Off site sources

- ATS Electronic Information Exchange System (EIES), as agreed by Resolution 6 (2001), Appendix 4. Available at www.ats.aq, section "Information Exchange".
- COMNAP website (*www.comnap.aq*)

1.2. Operating nation(s)

Off site sources

- EIES – Permanent Information (Operational information-Stations)
- COMNAP website (*www.comnap.aq*)

1.3. Responsible agencies or ministries

Off site sources

- Contact National Authority for detailed information

On site sources

- Interview, if applicable

1.4. Location

Off site sources

- EIES – Permanent Information (Operational information-Stations)
- COMNAP website (*www.comnap.aq*)

1.5. Date established

Off site sources

- EIES – Permanent Information (Operational information-Stations)
- COMNAP website (*www.comnap.aq*)

On site sources

- Interview, if applicable

1.6. Station current and past status ("year-round", "seasonal", "temporarily closed", "closed", "no longer exists-clean up activities in progress")

Off site sources

- EIES – Permanent Information (Operational information-Stations)
- COMNAP website (*www.comnap.aq*)

On site sources

- Interview, if applicable

1.7. Operational language(s) of the station

On site sources

- Interview

1.8. Main uses of the station

Off site sources

- EIES

On site sources

- Interview

1.9. Plans for future use of the station

Off site sources

- Contact National Authority for detailed information

On site sources

- Interview (it should be born in mind that this is information that station staff may not always have exhaustive knowledge of. That is why such information should also be checked with the National Authority).

1.10. International logistic cooperation

Off site sources

- Contact National Authority for detailed information

On site sources

- Interview

Section 2 – Inspection details

2.1. Date

On site sources

- To be filled by the inspection team

2.2. Time of visit

On site sources

- To be filled by the inspection team

2.3. Duration of visit

On site sources

- To be filled by the inspection team

2.4. Last inspection (nation(s), date)

Off site sources

- ATS website (a list of past inspections and their reports, when available, can be found in *http://www.ats.aq/e/ats_governance_listinspections.htm*)

On site source

- Interview + document verification (copies of previous inspection reports available)

Section 3 – Station personnel

3.1. Name of person in charge of station

Off site sources

- EIES Pre-season information

On site sources

- Interview

3.2. Total number of personnel on station at the moment of the inspection. Average and maximum population on station

Off site sources

- COMNAP website (*www.comnap.aq*)

On site sources

- Interview

3.3. Number of science personnel on station at the moment of the inspection. Average and maximum number of science personnel on station

On site sources

- Interview

3.4. Number of over-wintering personnel, if applicable

On site sources

- Interview

3.5. Nominal/Optimal capacity of station

Off site sources

- EIES Permanent Information (Operational information-Stations)

On site sources

- Interview

3.6. General training - including on: fuel management, waste management, first aid, SAR activities, medical evacuation procedures, fire fighting, etc.

On site sources

- Interview

3.7. Training focused on the requirements of the Antarctic Treaty and the Environmental Protocol

On site sources

- Interview

Section 4 – Physical description of the station

- The National Program's website may contain additional details

4.1. Area covered by station (surface area of station footprint)

On site sources

- Interview

4.2. Number and type of buildings, including their purpose

On site sources

- Interview + field verification

4.3. Age and state/condition of buildings

On site sources

- Interview + field verification

4.4. Construction works currently in progress or recently completed

On site sources

- Interview + field verification

4.5. Map(s) of station showing buildings, services and other major structures and facilities

On site sources

- Interview + field verification

4.6. Description of major aerial systems (antennas)

On site sources

- Interview + field verification

4.7. Description of other major –on or under ground– services (power, water, sewage, etc.)

On site sources

- Interview + field verification

4.8. Port or dock facilities (wharf, craft landing site, anchorage)
Description and condition

On site sources

- Interview + field verification

4.9. Roads (length, type of surface, condition)

On site sources

- Interview + field verification

4.10. Airstrips. Status (active/not active), length, type of surface (snow, ice, gravel) and landing gear suitability (wheel, ski, both). Methods and frequence of maintenance. Period of operation

Off site sources

- COMNAP's Antarctic Flight Information Manual (AFIM).

On site sources

- Interview + field verification (inspectors should check, through observation on site, the information provided by AFIM to find out the degree of concordance and the need for likely update of AFIM's information).

4.11. Helipads (diameter, surface and condition)

Off site sources

- COMNAP's Antarctic Flight Information Manual (AFIM). Manuals and subscriptions to revisions of the AFIM are available through the COMNAP Secretariat

On site sources

- Interview + field verification (inspectors should check, through observation on site, the information provided by AFIM to find out the degree of concordance and the need for likely update of AFIM's information).

4.12. Subsidiary facilities (camps, refuges, depots, etc.). Status (active/not active), purpose, location and accessibility (by vehicle, by air, on foot).

Off site sources

- EIES Permanent Information (Operational information-Stations)

On site sources

- Interview

Section 5 – Scientific activities

5.1. Major scientific programmes supported by the station during the season in which the inspection takes place, and the following winter-over, if applicable

Off site sources

- Contact National Authority for detailed information

- EIES – Annual report (Scientific Information / Forward plans)

On site sources

- Interview

5.2. Dedicated permanent scientific facilities and other major scientific equipment on the station and subsidiary facilities

Off site sources

- EIES Permanent information (although EIES includes only information about "automatic recording stations/observatories")
- Contact National Authority for more detailed information

On site sources

- Interview

5.3. Number and nationality of science personnel from other National Antarctic Programs

On site sources

- Interview

5.4. Advance notice, use and control of radio-isotopes

Off site sources

- EIES (information exchange on the use of radio-isotopes is required by ATCM VI-6,Tokyo 1970)

On site sources

- Interview

Section 6 – Tourist and non-governmental activities

6.1. Visits to the station by tourists or non-governmental expeditions. Frequency, method (cruise ships, yachts, aircraft), numbers, availability of visit records (type of information included)

Off site sources

- EIES Pre-season information (Non-governmental expeditions) include data on proposed sites of tour operations)
- Contact National authority for more detailed information

On site sources

- Interview + document verification

6.2. Procedures developed to facilitate or control tourist and non-governmental activities (advance permission, maximum allowed length of the stay, restrictions on schedules, etc.)

On site sources

- Interview + document verification, if appropriate

6.3. Operational problems for the station caused by visitors (for example, unannounced visits, behaviour of visitors, etc.)

On site sources

- Interview

6.4. Environmental impact of visitors at the station or nearby

On site sources

- Interview (it was noted that inspectors should contact either the environmental officer or scientists at the station to properly answer this question).

6.5. Describe any other NGO activity carried out at the station.

Off site sources

- EIES Pre-season information (Non-governmental expeditions) can include information on NGO activities.

On site sources

- Interview

Section 7 – Logistics and operations

7.A. Communications

7.A.1. Communication facilities. Types of links (HF, VHF, Internet, satellite, other) and methods of communication (voice, fax, e-mail, web, video conferencing/telemedicine, etc.)

Off site sources

- EIES Permanent Information (Communication facilities and frequencies)
- COMNAP's AFIM and ATOM (Antarctic Telecommunications Operators Manual). Updated versions of COMNAP's ATOM can be downloaded from www.comnap.aq (Members only/password required)
- Contact National Authority for more detailed information

On site sources

- Interview + document verification

7.B. Transport

7.B.1. Number and type of ground vehicles

On site sources

- Interview + field verification

7.B.2. Number and type of small boats

On site sources

- Interview + field verification

7.B.3. Number and type of fixed and rotary wing aircraft

Off site sources

- EIES Pre-season information (Aircraft / Type of aircraft, planned number of flights, periods of flights or planned departure dates, routes and purpose)

On site sources

- Interview + field verification

7.B.4. Number of aircraft movements per year

Off site sources

- EIES Pre-season information (Aircraft / Type of aircraft, planned number of flights, periods of flights or planned departure dates, routes and purpose)
- Contact National Authority for more detailed information

On site sources

- Interview

7.B.5. Frequency and methods of resupply

Off site sources

- Contact National Authority for more detailed information

On site sources

- Interview

7.C. Fuel storage / usage

7.C.1. Fuel Contingency Plans / Fuel Management Plans. Availability and format

Off site sources

- EIES Permanent Information (Contingency Plans)

On site sources

- Interview + document verification

7.C.2. Types, amount and use of fuel (diesel, petrol, aviation fuel, etc.)

On site sources

- Interview + document verification

7.C.3. Types, number and capacity of station storage containers, including type of containment system(s) available

On site sources

- Interview + field verification

7.C.4. Monitoring of fuel pumping systems and storage tanks (method)
On site sources
- Interview + field verification + document verification

7.C.5. General description of fuel pipelines
On site sources
- Interview + field verification + document verification

7.C.6. Methods to transfer bulk fuel
On site sources
- Interview + document verification

7.C.7. Methods of emptying fuel pipelines (gravity, compressed air, etc.)
On site sources
- Interview

7.C.8. Field fuel depots (for example, quantity, type of fuel, type of containers, geographic location and distance to the station, and proximity to environmental values, such as freshwater systems, wildlife concentrations, etc.).
On site sources
- Interview

7.C.9. Responsibility for fuel management
On site sources
- Interview

7.C.10. Oil and other spills. Describe any spills over 200 litres (50 gallons) that have occurred during the past five years.
Off site sources
- COMNAP Accidents, Incidents and Near Misses Reporting System (AINMR)

On site sources
- Interview + document verification

7.D. Power generation and management

7.D.1. Electrical power and heat sources from fuel. Number, type and capacity of generation systems
On site sources
- Interview + field verification

7.D.2. Annual fuel consumption in generators and heaters (litres, m3 or metric tonnes)
On site sources
- Interview

7.D.3. Efficiency of the generation system. Average load (in kW) or output (in kW/h) of the station.
On site sources
- Interview

7.D.4. Methods of energy conservation (strategies, procedures, equipment and/or infrastructure to conserve energy at the station)
On site sources
- Interview + document verification

7.D.5. Renewable energy sources (eg, wind turbines, photovoltaic, solar hot water systems), purpose, and share of energy supplied.
On site sources
- Interview + field verification

7.D.6. Filtering and monitoring of emissions from generators and heaters (parameters measured, method, frequency and availability of records)
On site sources
- Interview + field verification + document verification

7.E. Water system

7.E.1. Availability and quality of water supply

On site sources

- Interview + document verification

7.E.2. Methods to supply and store water. Availability and quality of water supply.

On site sources

- Interview + field verification

7.E.3. Consumption of water per person/day. Distinguish between different water types, if appropriate

On site sources

- Interview

7.E.4. Methods of water conservation

On site sources

- Interview + field verification (if appropriate).

Section 8 – Management of dangerous elements

8.A. Hazardous chemicals

8.A.1. Types and quantities of chemicals

On site sources

- Interview + field verification

8.A.2. Storage and monitoring arrangements

On site sources

- Interview + field verification + document verification

8.A.3. Protection against leaks and spills

On site sources

- Interview + field verification

8.B. Firearms / explosives

8.B.1. Number, type and purpose of firearms and ammunition

Off site sources

- EIES Pre-season information (Military) includes an item on Armaments

On site sources

- Interview + field verification

8.B.2. Amount, type and use of explosives

On site sources

- Interview + field verification

8.B.3. Storage of explosives and method of disposal

On site sources

- Interview + field verification

Section 9 – Medical capabilities

9.1. Medical facilities (X ray, Anaesthetic equipment, surgery, dental suites, etc)

On site sources

- Interview + field verification

9.2. Medical personnel (general practitioner, nurse, paramedics, surgeon, dentist, other specialists) and specific training.

On site sources

- Interview + field verification

9.3. Number of patient beds

On site sources

- Interview + field verification

Section 10 – Emergency response capability

10.1. General – a) Search and rescue capability (SAR teams, vehicles, aircraft, positioning systems), including types of scenarios covered and undertaking of SAR drills (frequency and relevant records)

On site sources

- Interview + field verification + document verification

10.2. General – b) Accidents and incidents in the last year resulting in human death, significant injuries, significant damage to station facilities or to the environment

On site sources

- Interview

10.3. General – c) Method of reporting accidents, incidents or near-misses

Off site sources

- COMNAP Accident, Incident and Near-Miss Reporting –AINMR- system

On site sources

- Interview + document verification

10.4. Medical – a) Mobile medical emergency response capability

On site sources

- Interview + field verification

10.5. Medical – b) Evacuation plan for medical emergencies

On site sources

- Interview + document verification, if appropriate

10.6. Fire – a) Fire emergency plan. Latest update

On site sources

- Interview + document verification, if appropriate

10.7. Fire – b) Fire fighting equipment

On site sources

- Interview + field verification

10.8. Fire – c) Training of personnel for fire fighting

On site sources

- Interview

10.9. Fire – d) Fire fighting exercises (frequency, personnel involved, scenarios covered and relevant records available)

On site sources

- Interview + document verification

10.10. Pollution (oil and chemical spills) – a) Risk assessment for spills

On site sources

- Interview

10.11. Pollution (oil and chemical spills) – b) Training of personnel to deal with spills

On site sources

- Interview

10.12. Pollution (oil and chemical spills) – c) Spill response exercises (frequency, personnel involved, scenarios covered and relevant records available)

On site sources

- Interview + document verification

10.13. Pollution (oil and chemical spills) – d) Mobile spill response capability (boomers, adsorbent substances, pumps, centrifuge, other)

On site sources

- Interview + field verification

Section 11 – Matters related to the Madrid Protocol

11.A. Environmental Impact Assessment (EIA)

11.A.1. Degree of awareness of station management personnel of the requirement to conduct an EIA for all new activities

On site sources

• Interview

11.A.2. Availability of record/copies of EIAs for activities carried out in/by the station

Off site sources

• ATS website (note that only records of CEEs and IEEs are available at such a website)

On site sources

• Interview + document verification

11.A.3. Environmental monitoring of indicators of possible environmental impacts of the station or associated activities (parameters measured, method, frequency and availability of records)

Off site sources

• EIES annual report (Environmental Information-Monitoring activities report)

On site sources

• Interview + document verification

11.B. Conservation of flora and fauna

11.B.1. Methods of making station personnel aware of the rules relating to the conservation of Antarctic & flora and fauna

On site sources

• Interview

11.B.2. Wildlife or plant sites near the station

On site sources

• Interview + field verification

11.B.3. Activities undertaken in/through the station during the past year requiring taking and/ or harmful interference permits. Details of any damage or harm caused to & flora and fauna. Availability of permits on station.

Off site sources

• EIES Annual report (Permit information)

On site sources

• Interview + document verification

11.B.4. Non-native species. a) Measures taken to minimize introductions of non-native species (awareness programs, operational procedures, monitoring/surveillance programs), including relevant records; b) Are non-native species present?; c) If so, was the introduction managed in accordance with a permit?; d) For unintended introductions, what is known about the source and status and what actions have been / will be taken in response?

Off site sources

• EIES Annual report (Permit information)

On site sources

• Interview + document verification + field verification

11.B.5. Problems with station personnel or visitors not observing the provisions of Annex II.

On site sources

• Interview

11.B.6. Local guidelines controlling human activities close to concentrations of wildlife, including use of aircraft, vehicle operations, hiking, etc.

On site sources

• Interview + document verification

11.C. Waste management

11.C.1. Availability of a Waste management plan for the separation, reduction, collection, storage and disposal of wastes. Adequacy and compliance with Annex III provisions.

Off site sources

• EIES Annual report (Environmental information-Waste management plans)

On site sources

• Interview + document verification

11.C.2. Responsibility for waste management on the station.

On site sources

• Interview

11.C.3. Availability of waste production reports. Type of information included.

On site sources

• Interview + document verification

11.C.4. Waste classification system(s) at the station.

On site sources

• Interview + field verification

11.C.5. Methods of making station personnel aware of the provisions relating to waste management, including training and the need to minimize the impact of wastes on the environment.

On site sources

• Interview + field verification

11.C.6. Methods of treating and disposing of wastes at the station and subsidiary camps/refuges/depots, including use of landfill or ice pit.

On site sources

• Interview + field verification

11.C.7. Methods to store hazardous wastes until removal from the station.

On site sources

• Interview + field verification

11.C.8. Solid waste management facilities (eg, incinerator, containers, transportation, etc).

On site sources

• Interview + field verification

11.C.9. Use of incineration; Disposal of ash; Control and monitoring of emissions.

On site sources

• Interview + document verification

11.C.10. Treatment and disposal of sewage and domestic liquid wastes; Monitoring of effluent (parameters measured, method, frequency and availability of records).

On site sources

• Interview + document verification

11.C.11. Methods of waste recycling.

On site sources

• Interview + field verification

11.C.12. Measures taken to prevent wastes which are to be removed from the Treaty area being dispersed by wind or accessed by scavengers.

On site sources

• Interview + field verification

11.C.13. Inventory of past subsidiary facilities (abandoned camps or refuges, old fuel depots, etc.), including information reported and latest update.

Off site sources

• EIES (Permanent information) may contain data on non-active refuges

On site sources

• Interview + document verification

11.C.14. Clean-up of the effects of past activities and future plans, if applicable.

On site sources

• Interview

11.C.15. Problems with station personnel, station activities/infrastructure or visitors in relation to the provisions related to wastes. Measures taken in response (if applicable).

On site sources

- Interview

11.D. Management of protected areas (ASPAs, ASMAs and HSMs)

11.D.1. Methods of making station personnel aware of the provisions relating to ASPAs, ASMAs and Historic Sites and Monuments.

On site sources

- Interview

11.D.2. ASPAs, ASMAs and Historic Sites and Monuments in the vicinity of, or containing, the station (type, name, site number)

Off site sources

- An updated database on protected areas can be found at the AT Secretariat's website, under section "Environmental protection" (http://www.ats.aq/e/ep_protected.htm)

On site sources

- Interview

11.D.3. Relevant management plans and maps of protected areas held on the station.

On site sources

- Interview + document verification

11.D.4. Entry by station personnel to ASPAs within the past year; Issue of permits and reasons for their issue.

Off site sources

- EIES Annual report (Permit information)

On site sources

- Interview + document verification

11.D.5. Problems with station personnel or visitors not observing the provisions of protected areas.

On site sources

- Interview

11.D.6. Marking of the protected area(s) in the vicinity of, or containing, the station.

On site sources

- Field verification

11.D.7. Monitoring or management of protected areas

On site sources

- Interview

11.D.8. Additional steps that should be taken to protect the areas

On site sources

- Interview

Section 12 – Other matters

12.A. Military support activities

12.A.1. Describe any military support to the station

Off site sources

- EIES Pre-season information (Military) includes an item on Military equipment

On site sources

- Interview + field verification

12.A.2. Details of military equipment held at station

On site sources

- Interview + field verification

12.B. Antarctic Treaty legislation

12.B.1. Availability of Antarctic Treaty documentation on station

On site sources

- Interview + document verification

Resolution 4 (2010): SCAR Antarctic Climate Change and the Environment Report

The Representatives,

Recognising that the Antarctic region offers a unique environment for the study of climate change;

Recalling the Washington Ministerial Declaration on the fiftieth anniversary of the signing of the Antarctic Treaty, in which Ministers from all Antarctic Treaty Consultative Parties noted their concern over the implications of global environmental change, in particular climate change, for the Antarctic environment and dependent and associated ecosystems and confirmed their intention to work together to better understand changes to the Earth's climate and to actively seek ways to address the effects of climate and environmental change on the Antarctic environment and dependent and associated ecosystems;

Welcoming the report on Antarctic Climate Change and the Environment (ACCE) by the Scientific Committee on Antarctic Research (SCAR) as a first step in compiling a comprehensive assessment of scientific information on the climate system in the Antarctic region;

Concerned by the findings of the ACCE report that effects of climate change are already occurring in the Antarctic region;

Recommend that their Governments:

1. forward copies of the SCAR ACCE report to their respective departments and agencies engaged in climate change negotiations;
2. encourage dissemination of the findings of the SCAR ACCE report and of ongoing Antarctic climate change research to the general public and the media;
3. forward copies of the SCAR ACCE report to their national Antarctic science and research bodies, and encourage them to consider fully the findings and recommendations from the report; and
4. welcome regular updates by SCAR on Antarctic climate change and its implications.

Resolution 2 (2011): Revised Guide to the Preparation of Management Plans for Antarctic Specially Protected Areas

The Representatives,

Recalling the requirements under Article 5 of Annex V to the Protocol on Environmental Protection to the Antarctic Treaty (the Protocol) to prepare and revise Management Plans for Antarctic Specially Protected Areas;

Noting that under Resolution 2 (1998) the Antarctic Treaty Consultative Meeting (ATCM) adopted a Guide to the Preparation of Management Plans for Antarctic Specially Protected Areas;

Desiring to update the Guide to reflect current best practice in the preparation of Management Plans for Antarctic Specially Protected Areas;

Considering the revision of the Guide by the Committee for Environmental Protection and its Subsidiary Group on Management Plans;

Recommend that:

1. the Guide to the Preparation of Management Plans for Antarctic Specially Protected Areas annexed to this Resolution replace the Guide adopted by Resolution 2 (1998) and be used by those engaged in the preparation or revision of Management Plans; and
2. the Antarctic Treaty Secretariat post the text of Resolution 2 (1998) on its website in a way that makes clear that it is no longer current

Resolution 2 (2011) Annex: Guide to the Preparation of Management Plans for Antarctic Specially Protected Areas

Background

Purpose of the Guide

In 1991 the Antarctic Treaty Consultative Parties (ATCPs) adopted the Protocol on Environmental Protection to the Antarctic Treaty (Environment Protocol) to ensure comprehensive environmental protection in Antarctica. The Environment Protocol designates the whole of Antarctica as "a natural reserve" devoted to peace and science.

Annex V to the Environment Protocol, adopted subsequently at ATCM XVI under Recommendation XVI-10, provides a legal framework for the establishment of specially protected and managed areas within the overall "natural reserve". The text of Annex V is available on the ATS website at *http://www.ats.aq/documents/recatt/Att004fie.pdf.*

Annex V specifies that any area in the Antarctic Treaty area, including any marine area, may be designated as an Antarctic Specially Protected Area (ASPA) to protect outstanding environmental, scientific, historic, aesthetic or wilderness values, any combination of those values, or ongoing or planned scientific research (Article 3, Annex V).

The Annex further specifies that any Party to the Antarctic Treaty, the Committee for Environmental Protection (CEP), the Scientific Committee on Antarctic Research (SCAR) or the Commission for the Conservation of Antarctic Marine Living Resources (CCAMLR) *may propose an area for designation as an Antarctic Specially Protected Area by submitting a proposed Management Plan to the Antarctic Treaty Consultative Meeting* (Article 5, Annex V).

This Guide is a revision of the original version adopted by the Parties as an appendix to Resolution 2 (1998). It has been developed in order to assist any proponent in the process of proposing an Antarctic Specially Protected Area, with the following concrete aims:

- to assist Parties in their efforts to prepare Management Plans for proposed Antarctic Specially Protected Areas (ASPA) as required by the Protocol (Article 5, Annex V);
- to provide a framework which, when followed, enables Management Plans to meet the requirements of the Protocol; and
- to help achieve clear content, clarity, consistency (with other Management Plans) and effectiveness to expedite their review, adoption and implementation.

It is important to note that this guide is intended as no more than an aide-mémoire to the production of Management Plans for ASPAs. It has no legal status. Anyone intending to prepare a Management Plan should examine the provisions of Annex V to the Protocol carefully and seek advice from their national authority at an early stage.

Protected areas network

Annex V obliges Parties to seek to identify, within a *systematic environmental-geographical framework*, and to include in the series of Antarctic Specially Protected Areas:

- areas kept inviolate from human interference so that future comparisons may be possible with localities that have been affected by human activities;
- representative examples of major terrestrial, including glacial and aquatic, ecosystems and marine ecosystems;
- areas with important or unusual assemblages of species, including major colonies of breeding native birds or mammals;
- the type locality or only known habitat of any species;
- areas of particular interest to ongoing or planned scientific research;
- examples of outstanding geological, glaciological or geomorphological features;
- areas of outstanding aesthetic and wilderness value;
- sites or monuments of recognised historic value; and
- such other areas as may be appropriate to protect the outstanding environmental, scientific, historic, aesthetic or wilderness values, any combination of those values, or ongoing or planned scientific research.

This provision of the Environment Protocol provides the essential framework for an *Antarctic protected areas network*. The operationalization of what this framework entails has, however, been debated since the adoption of Annex V.

A number of analyses and evaluations of representation of the nine categories listed in Article 3(2) of Annex V have been conducted since the adoption of Annex V, first through a SCAR/IUCN Workshop on Protected Areas in 1992, then in two Protected Area workshops held in conjunction with CEP I and II in 1998 and 1999. In the analysis presented to CEP VIII in 2005 (ATCM XXVIII WP 11) it was noted that:

- there is an uneven distribution of ASPAs amongst the categories set out in Article 3(2) of Annex V, which is simply a product of history, in that a series of ad hoc designations have been made over time, rather than a systematic selection of sites within an overarching strategy or framework.
- in the absence of such a framework there is no means for assessing whether the current distribution is appropriate or not.
- in the absence of an holistic approach to management of the protected areas system (along the lines of a strategic environmental geographic framework as provided for in Article 3(2) of Annex V), the distribution of sites can be no more than simply noted.

The understanding of the term systematic environmental-geographic framework has evolved over time. However, the Environmental Domains Analysis prepared and presented in its final version to the CEP by New Zealand in 2005 constitutes the basis for our latest understanding of the concept. The Environmental Domains Analysis provides a classification of areas providing a data-derived, spatially explicit delineation of environmental variables in Antarctica, to be used for *inter alia* identification of priority sites for protection. The Domains Analysis provides a tool for an holistic and strategic designation of ASPAs, rather than assessing sites on their individual merits in isolation of other factors.

The ATCM has concurred that the Environmental Domains Analysis for the Antarctic Continent be used consistently and in conjunction with other tools agreed within the Antarctic Treaty System as a dynamic model for the identification of areas that could be designated as Antarctic Specially Protected Areas within the systematic environmental-geographical framework referred to in Article 33 of Annex V of the Protocol (Resolution 3 (2008)).

The Environmental Domains Analysis provides a useful and important measure of environmental variation across Antarctica that, in terms of the ice-free domains, can be considered essential as a first order assessment of likely systematic variation in biodiversity. For meaningful analysis at the finer spatial scales typically used in protected area designation, the EDA must nevertheless be supplemented with biodiversity data, which not only reflect current conditions but, importantly, historical processes that cannot in many instances be captured by modern environmental data.

Identifying areas for protection

The designation of an area as a protected area provides the area with a higher level of protection beyond that achieved by other forms of planning and management measures under the Protocol in order to achieve specific protection aims and objectives.

When seeking to assess whether an area in fact needs such protection, it is necessary to be clear as to what values the area would aim to protect and as to the actual need to protect these values beyond the general protection provided by the Environment Protocol. The CEP has adopted guidelines for implementation of the Framework for Protected Areas set forth in Article 3, Annex V of the Environment Protocol that will assist any proponent in the process of such an evaluation. In such a process it would also need to consider how the designation of an ASPA would complement the existing protected areas network within the systematic environmental-geographical framework provided by the Environmental Domains Analysis and other relevant data available. Ensuring a thorough and in-depth analysis along these lines will indicate to the proponent whether designation of the area as a protected area is in fact required.

Only when a candidate area has been through such an overall assessment is it correct to initiate the process of developing a Management Plan for the area, in line with the guidance provided by this document.

Relevant guidance material

- Annex V to the Environment Protocol (*http://www.ats.aq/documents/recatt/Att004fie.pdf*)
- Guidelines for implementation of the Framework for Protected Areas set forth in Article 3, Annex V of the Environmental Protocol (*http://www.ats.aq/documents/recatt/Att081fie.pdf*)
- Environmental Domains Analysis *(http://www.ats.aq/documents/recatt/Att408fie.pdf)*

Format of Management Plans for ASPAs

Article 5 of Annex V specifies matters that each ASPA Management Plan should address. The following sections of this Guide provide guidance in addressing those requirements (summarised in Table 1).

The CEP has highlighted the benefits of promoting consistency between protected area Management Plans. The Template for Antarctic Specially Protected Area Management Plans presented at Appendix 3 is intended as a standard framework into which proponents can insert content specific to the area in question when preparing a new or revised ASPA Management Plan.

The template includes cross-reference to the relevant sections of this Guide. References to the Guide are provided in *italicised text*, and should be deleted from the Management Plan.

The template is formatted in accordance with the *Manual for the submission of documents to the Antarctic Treaty Consultative Meeting and the Committee for Environmental Protection* prepared by the Secretariat of the Antarctic Treaty. Proponents should consult the Manual for guidance on specific formatting issues, such as for tables and figures incorporated in a Management Plan.

Table 1. Headings used in this Guide cross-referenced to Article 5 of Annex V

Management plan section / section of Guide	Article 5 reference
Introduction	
1. Description of values to be protected	3a
2. Aims and objectives	3b
3. Management activities	3c
4. Period of designation	3d
5. Maps	3g
6. Description of the Area	3 e (i – iv)
6(v) Special zones within the Area	3f
7. Terms and conditions for entry Permits	3 i (i – x)
8. Supporting documentation	3h

Guidance for the content of Management Plans

Since the development of Management Plans for ASPAs is an evolving process, preparers of Management Plans should be aware of current best practice and are strongly urged to consult examples agreed at past ATCMs. The current Management Plan for each ASPA can be accessed from the Protected Areas database on the website of the Secretariat of the Antarctic Treaty, at *http://www.ats.aq/devPH/apa/ep_protected.aspx.*

The template at Appendix 3 includes suggested standard wording for some sections. The availability of suggested standard wording is not intended to discourage proponents from developing and implementing site-specific or creative and innovative approaches to area protection and management. Suggested wording that relates directly to requirements arising from the Environment Protocol is identified with an asterisk (*). As appropriate, the suggested wording should be utilised, modified, or replaced with alternative text that adequately reflects site-specific considerations for the Area in question.

A Management Plan should provide sufficient details about the special features of the Area and any requirements for access and management to ensure that individuals planning to visit the Area and national authorities responsible for issuing permits are able to do so in a manner consistent with the purpose for designation. It should clearly identify why the Area is designated, and what additional measures (beyond the general provisions of the Environment Protocol and Annexes) apply to the Area as a result. The following sections provide guidance to proponents on the content addressed under each standard Management Plan heading.

Introduction

An introduction to the Management Plan is not a stated requirement of Article 5 of Annex V, but can provide a useful overview. Information might include a summary of the important features of the Area, its history (e.g. initial designation, modifications, earlier Management Plans), the scientific research and other activities that have been carried out there.

Reasons why special protection is deemed necessary or desirable should also be stated in the Management Plan, preferably in the introduction. In this respect, the *Guidelines for implementation of the Framework for Protected Areas set forth in Article 3, Annex V of the Environmental Protocol* appended to Resolution 1 (2000) (*http://www.ats.aq/documents/recatt/Att081fie.pdf*) are a useful reference. The CEP has agreed that Management Plans should include a clear statement about the primary reason for the Area's designation.[2] It is useful to include such a statement in the Introduction to the Management Plan, which serves as a summary of the Management Plan, as well as in the following section describing the values to be protected.

The CEP has also encouraged proponents to describe how the Area complements the Antarctic protected areas system as a whole.[3] For this purpose it should *inter alia* refer to the Environmental Domains Analysis of Antarctica (*http://www.ats.aq/documents/recatt/Att408fie.pdf*), appended to Resolution 3 (2008) and to the existing suite of ASPAs. If applicable, the Introduction might also usefully describe how the Area complements others in the local vicinity or region.

1. Description of values to be protected

Article 3 of Annex V of the Environment Protocol states that any area, including any marine area, may be designated as an ASPA so as to protect outstanding environmental, scientific, historic, aesthetic or wilderness values and sets out a series of such values which ATCPs shall seek to incorporate into ASPAs.

In considering any new proposal for an ASPA, thought needs to be given as to how protected area status would address the values identified in Article 3 of Annex V, and whether such values are already adequately represented by protected areas in Antarctica.

This section should include a statement about the primary reason for designation, but should also describe the full range of reasons for the Area's designation. The description of the value or values of the Area should state, clearly and in detail, why it is that the site deserves special protection and how ASPA designation will strengthen protection measures. This may include a description of the actual or potential risks the values are facing. For example, if the designation of the Area is intended to prevent interference with ongoing or planned scientific investigations this section should describe the nature and value of this research.

The Antarctic environment is subject not only to natural variability in factors such as climate, ice extent and the density and spatial extent of biological populations, but also the effects of rapid regional climate warming (particularly in the Antarctic Peninsula region). Therefore this section could also, where relevant, give a description of the potential environmental changes faced by the Area in light of such rapid warming (e.g. potential thinning of glaciers; rapid retreat

[2] CEP VIII Final Report, paragraph 187.

[3] CEP VIII Final Report, paragraph 187.

of ice-shelves and exposure of new ice-free terrain; impacts on sea ice-dependent penguin species by ocean warming and declining sea ice extent; the likelihood/risk of establishment of non-native species or natural colonists originating from more northerly (and therefore less climatically severe) latitudes etc.)

In cases where the intent is to protect the value of sites as reference areas or controls for long-term environmental monitoring programmes, the particular characteristics of the area relevant to long-term monitoring should be described. In cases where ASPA designation is being conferred to protect historic, geological, aesthetic, wilderness or other values, those values should be described in this section.

In all cases the description of values should provide sufficient detail to enable readers to understand precisely what the ASPA designation is intended to protect. It should not provide a full description of the Area, which is presented in Section 6.

2. Aims and objectives

This section should establish what is intended to be achieved by the Management Plan and how the Plan will address protection of the values described above. For example the aims of the Plan might highlight an intention to:

- avoid certain specified changes to the area;
- prevent any human interference with specified features or activities in the area;
- allow only certain types of research, management, or other activities that would not interfere with the reason for the site's designation; or
- minimise, to the maximum extent practicable, the introduction of non-native species, which could compromise the environmental and scientific values of an area.

It is important to note that the description of values and the objectives will be used by the national permitting authority to help decide activities that can, and cannot, be authorised to be conducted in the Area. Consequently the values to be protected and the objectives of the plan must be described specifically, not generally.

3. Management activities

Management activities outlined in this section should relate to the aims of the Management Plan and to the objectives for which the Area was designated.

There should be a clear indication of what is prohibited, what should be avoided or prevented as well as what is allowed. The Plan should make it clear when permitted activities can take place. For example some activities may only be allowed during periods that do not coincide with the breeding season of sensitive species.

This section should describe such actions as will be taken to protect the particular values of the Area (e.g. installation and maintenance of scientific instruments, establishment of marked routes or landing sites, erection of signs indicating that the site is an ASPA and that entry is prohibited except in accordance with a permit issued by an appropriate national authority, removal of abandoned equipment or materials). If the management activities require cooperative action by two or more Parties conducting or supporting research in the area, the arrangements for carrying out the required activities should be jointly developed, and described in the Management Plan.

It is important to remember and to note in the Management Plan that active management may require an environmental impact assessment, which should be undertaken in accordance with the requirements of Annex 1 of the Environment Protocol.

If no special management activities are required, this section of the Plan should state, "None required".

4. Period of designation

Designation of an ASPA is for an indefinite period unless the Management Plan provides otherwise. It is a requirement under Article 6(3) of Annex V that the Management Plan is reviewed at least every five years, and updated as necessary.

If the intent is to provide protection for a finite period, while a particular study or other activity is conducted, an expiry date should be included in this section.

5. Maps

Maps are a critical component of any Management Plan and should be clear and sufficiently detailed. If the area is particularly large a number of maps that vary in scale may be appropriate, but the minimum is likely to be two: one showing the general region in which the Area is situated, as well as the position of all nearby protected areas; and a second map illustrating the details of the Area itself.

It is essential that the maps clearly indicate the boundary of the Protected Area as described under section 6.1 below.

Guidelines for maps are given in Appendix 1 together with a checklist of features to be considered for inclusion.

6. Description of the Area

This section requires an accurate description of the Area and, where appropriate, its surroundings to ensure that individuals planning a visit and national authorities responsible for issuing permits are sufficiently appraised of the special features of the area.

It is important that this section describe adequately those features of the Area that are being protected, thus alerting users of the Management Plan to features of particular sensitivity. This section should preferably not duplicate the description of the values of the Area.

The section is divided into five subsections:

6(i) Geographical coordinates, boundary markers and natural features

The boundary of the Area should be delineated unambiguously and the important features clearly described, as the boundary delineation will form the basis of legal enforcement. The boundary of the Area should be carefully selected and described. It is preferable to describe a boundary that is identifiable at all times of the year. This is often difficult due to snow cover in winter, but at least in summer it should be possible for any visitor to determine the limits of the Area. For Areas near to sites frequented by tourists this is especially important. It is best to choose static boundary markers such as exposed rock features. Features that might be expected to vary in location throughout the year or during the five-year review period of the Management Plan, such as the edges of snow fields or wildlife colonies, are unlikely to be suitable. In some instances it may be advisable to install boundary markers where natural features are not sufficient.

Consideration should be given to the likely future impacts of climate change when determining or reviewing the boundaries of the Protected Area. Particular thought should be given to the designation of boundaries using features other than ice-free ground. For example, future climate change induced glacial retreat, ice shelf collapse and lake level change will have an impact on ASPAs whose boundary definitions follow these features.

Geographical coordinates included in the boundary description should be as accurate as possible. They should be given as latitude and longitude in degrees, minutes and seconds. If possible, reference should be made to published maps or charts to allow the Area boundaries to be delineated on the map. The survey and mapping methods employed should be stated if possible along with the name of the agency producing the maps or charts referred to.

The importance of GPS for fixing positions cannot be overstated. Over past years it has become clear that the original positioning of some protected areas is highly suspect. The opportunity to revise the plan for each ASPA is an opportunity to use GPS, to provide accurate locational information on boundaries. It is strongly recommended that plans are not submitted without such information.

When describing the physical features of the Area, only place names formally approved by a Consultative Party and included in the SCAR Composite Gazetteer of Antarctica should be used *(http://data.aad.gov.au/aadc/gaz/scar/)*. All names referred to in the text of the Plan should be shown on the maps. If a new place name is needed, approval will be required by the appropriate national committee and the place name submitted for inclusion in the SCAR Composite Gazetteer of Antarctica before using the new name on any maps and before submitting the plan.

The description of the natural features of the Area should include descriptions of, the local topography such as permanent snow/ice fields, the presence of any water bodies (lakes, streams, pools) and a brief summary of the local geology and geomorphology. An accurate, brief description of the biological features of the Area is also useful including notes on major plant communities; bird and seal colonies and numbers of individuals or breeding pairs of birds.

If the area contains a marine component the management plan may need to be submitted to CCAMLR for consideration – see the section below on "Approval process for ASPA Management Plans".

6(ii) Access to the area

This subsection should include descriptions of preferred access routes to the Area by land, sea or air. These should be clearly defined to prevent confusion and suitable alternatives provided if the preferred route is unavailable.

All access routes as well as marine anchorages and helicopter landing areas should be described and clearly marked on the accompanying map of the Area. Helicopter landing areas should usually be located well outside the ASPA boundary to ensure minimum interference with the integrity of the Area.

The subsection should also describe preferred walking and, when permitted, vehicle routes within the area.

6(iii) Location of structures within and adjacent to the Area

It is necessary to describe and accurately locate all structures within or adjacent to the Area. These include, for example, boundary markers, sign boards, cairns, field huts, depots and research facilities. Where possible the date the structures were erected and the country to whom they belong should be recorded, as well as the details of any HSMs in the area. If applicable the timing of the planned removal of any structures should also be noted (e.g. in the case of temporary scientific or other installations).

6(iv) Location of other protected areas in the vicinity

There is no specific radius to be used when describing other protected areas "in the vicinity", but a distance of approximately 50 km has been used in many plans adopted so far. All such protected areas (i.e. ASPAs, ASMAs, HSMs, CCAS Seal Reserves, CCAMLR CEMP sites etc.) in the vicinity should be given by name and, where appropriate, number. The coordinates and approximate distance and direction from the Area in question should also be provided.

6(v) Special zones within the Area

Article 5.3(f) of Annex V allows for the identification of zones within ASPAs and ASMAs "*in which activities are to be prohibited, restricted, or managed for the purpose of achieving the aims and objectives...*" of the management plan.

Those preparing management plans should consider whether the objectives of the plan could be achieved more effectively by designating one or more zones. Clearly demarcated zones help provide clear information to site visitors on where, when and why special management conditions apply. They can be useful to communicate the goals and requirements of management in a clear and simple manner. For example, special zones might include bird colonies to which access is restricted during the breeding season, or sites where scientific experiments should not be disturbed.

In order to help achieve greater consistency in the application of the zoning tool in Antarctica, a standard set of commonly used zones that should meet management needs in most situations has been identified and defined (Table 2).

As is the case with all guidelines, there may arise instances where exceptions are both needed and desirable. When this is the case, those preparing management plans might consider the application of alternative zones. It is important to keep in mind, however, that management plans should aim to use zones that are as simple and consistent as possible across all sites within Antarctica. This will help to ensure that plan conditions are understandable and easy to follow, and thereby assist in the practical protection and management of these special areas.

If no zones are designated within the Area, this should be specifically stated in the Management Plan.

Table 2. Zoning Guidelines for ASPAs

Zone	Specific Zone Objectives
Facilities Zone	To ensure that science support facilities and related human activities within the Area are contained and managed within designated areas
Access Zone	To provide guidance for approach and/or landing of aircraft, boats, vehicles or pedestrians accessing the Area and by doing so protect areas with sensitive assemblages of species or scientific equipment etc and/or provide for safety
Historic Zone	To ensure those who enter the Area are aware of the areas or features within that are sites, buildings and/or artefacts of historic importance and to manage them appropriately
Scientific Zone	To ensure those who enter the Area are aware of the areas within that are sites of current or long-term scientific investigation or have sensitive scientific equipment installed
Restricted Zone	To restrict access into a particular part of the Area and/or activities within it for a range of management or scientific reasons, e.g. owing to special scientific or ecological values, because of sensitivity, presence of hazards, or to restrict emissions or constructions at a particular site. Access into Restricted Zones should normally be for compelling reasons that cannot be served elsewhere within the Area
Prohibited Zone	To prohibit access into a particular part of the ASPA until such time it is agreed by the ATCM (and not individual Parties) that the Management Plan should be changed to allow access

7. Terms and conditions for entry permits

7(i) General permit conditions

Article 3 (4) of Annex V of the Environment Protocol specifies that entry into ASPAs is prohibited except in accordance with a permit issued by an appropriate national authority.

The Management Plan should set out the conditions under which a permit might be issued. When drafting Management Plans, authors should be aware that the authorities appointed to issue permits for entry into ASPAs will use the contents of this section to determine whether, and under what conditions, permits may be issued.

Article 7(3) of Annex V of the Environment Protocol directs that each Party must require the permit holder to carry a copy of the permit whilst in the ASPA. This section of the Management Plan should note that all permits should contain a condition requiring the permit holder to carry a copy of the permit whilst in the ASPA.

Article 5 of Annex V sets out 10 separate issues that need to be addressed when considering the terms and conditions that might be attached to permits. These are set out below:

7(ii) Access to, and movement within or over, the Area

This section of the Management Plan should set out restrictions on the means of transport, points of access, routes and movement within the Area. It should also address the direction of approach for aircraft and the minimum height for overflying the Area. Such information should state the type of aircraft (e.g. fixed or rotary wing) on which the restrictions are based, that should be included as conditions of permits that are issued.

Where appropriate, the Management Plan should make reference to relevant guidelines adopted by the CEP, such as the *Guidelines for the Operation of Aircraft near Concentrations of Birds (http://www.ats.aq/documents/recatt/Att224fie.pdf)* appended to Resolution 2 (2004).

7(iii) Activities which may be conducted in the Area

This should detail what may be undertaken within the protected area and the conditions under which such activities are allowed. For example, to avoid interference with wildlife, only certain types of activity might be permitted.

If the Management Plan proposes that active management within the Area may be necessary in the future, this should also be listed here.

7(iv) Installation, modification, or removal of structures

It is useful to identify what, if any, structures are permitted within the Area. For example, certain scientific research equipment, markers or other structures might be allowed to be installed within the Area.

To assist with tracking the purpose of such structures, the Management Plan should explain how structures are to be identifiable. General and/or specific guidance on relevant considerations to minimise the adverse effects of installations on the values of the Area may also be useful.

If any existing structures are present (e.g. refuges) the Management Plan should also indicate action which might be authorised to modify or remove the structures. Alternatively, if no structures are to be permitted within the Area the Management Plan should make this clear.

7(v) Location of field camps

It is likely that field camps would not usually be permitted within the boundaries of the Area. However, it may be permissible under certain conditions such as overriding reasons of safety. If so the conditions under which field camps may be permitted should be stated. It is possible that field camps would only be acceptable in certain parts of the Area. Such campsites should be identified and recorded on the supporting maps.

7(vi) Restrictions on materials and organisms which may be brought into the Area

This section should set out prohibitions and give guidance on the management of any materials that are to be used or stored in the Area

There is a complete prohibition on the deliberate introduction of non-native species and diseases to the Antarctic Treaty area under Article 4 of Annex II of the Environment Protocol, except in accordance with a separate permit issued under the Authority provided for in Annex II. Article 4 also states that (i) precautions are taken within the Treaty area to prevent accidental introductions of microorganisms, (ii) appropriate efforts are made to ensure poultry and avian products are free from contamination by diseases, (iii) deliberate introduction of non-sterile soil is prohibited and (iv) the unintentional importation of non-sterile soil is minimised to the maximum extent practicable. Therefore, recommended measures to reduce the risk of non-native species introductions applied throughout Antarctica should also apply to the Protected Area. The management should, as appropriate, include provisions relating to the cleaning of camping equipment, scientific equipment, vehicles and personal footwear and clothing to remove propagules before entering the ASPA. SCAR's "Environmental code of conduct for terrestrial scientific field research in Antarctica" may provide some useful biosecurity recommendations.

Careful consideration should be given to the risk of introducing non-native species to the Protected Area on or via foodstuffs or associated containers and packaging. Non-sterile soil, plant propagules, eggs and live insects could be introduced in association with fresh fruits and vegetables, while bird or marine mammal pathogens may be introduced to the area via poultry products. The Management Plan may state that such products should not be permitted in the area or specify measures to minimise the risk of pathogen release to the environment.

In some instances special precautions may need to be taken to prevent the introduction of non-native species. If, for example, the Area has been designated for its special microbial communities, it may be necessary to require more stringent biosecurity precautions to minimise shedding of human commensal microorganisms and redistribution of other environmental microorganism from outside the Area. The use of sterile protective over-clothing and thoroughly cleaned footwear may be appropriate.

It may be necessary, for example, to bring some chemicals into the Area for research or management purposes. If so guidance should be provided as to how they must be stored, handled and removed. It may also be necessary to bring food and fuel into the Area, and guidance about the use, storage and removal of such materials should be given. Radio isotope and/or stable isotopes should only be released into the environment within the ASPA after careful consideration of the long-term impacts of such activities on the future environmental and scientific values of the Area.

7(vii) Taking of, or harmful interference with, native flora and fauna

This is prohibited under Article 3 of Annex II of the Environment Protocol except in accordance with a permit issued under the provisions of Annex II; this should be stated in all permits authorising this activity in the area. The requirements under Article 3 of Annex II must be adhered to, and commonly applied guidelines such as the SCAR Code of Conduct for the Use of Animals for Scientific Purposes in Antarctica may be presented as the minimum standard.

7(viii) The collection or removal of materials not brought into the Area by the permit holder

It may be permissible to remove from the Area materials such as beach litter, dead or pathological fauna or flora or abandoned relics and artefacts from previous activities. What items or samples can be removed by the permit holder should be clearly stated.

7(ix) Disposal of waste

Annex III of the Environment Protocol deals with the management of wastes in Antarctica. This section of the plan should specify requirements for the disposal of wastes that should be included as conditions of permits. The requirements set out in Annex III must be used as the minimum standards for waste disposal in an ASPA.

As a general rule all wastes, including all human wastes, generated by visitors to an ASPA should be removed from the Area. Exceptions, which must accord with the provisions of the Environment Protocol, should be identified as appropriate in this section of the Management Plan. In particular, consideration should be given to the likely impacts of sewage waste disposal on birds and marine mammals within the Area.

7(x) Measures that may be necessary to continue to meet the aims of the Management Plan

When appropriate this section should establish the conditions under which the issue of a permit may be necessary so as to ensure continued protection of the Area. For example it may be necessary to issue permits to allow for monitoring of the Area; to allow for repair or replacement of boundary markers and signs; or to allow for some active management as set out in section 3 above.

Where a management plan provides that, for exceptional reasons, non-native species are introduced in accordance with a separate permit, this section should discuss the need for measures to contain the non-native species and contingency procedures to be followed should the non-native species be released unintentionally into the environment. For example, it might specify that adequate biosecurity materials should be taken into the field work location to fulfil the requirements of the biosecurity plan, and personnel undertaking the work should be trained in their use.

In Protected Areas where non-native species are known to have become established, the Management Plan may outline measures to minimise further distribution of the species or its propagules to other locations.

7(xi) Requirements for reports

This section should describe the requirement for reports that should be included as a condition in permits issued by an appropriate national authority. It should, as appropriate, specify the information that should be included in reports. An ASPA visit report form is presented in Appendix 2 of this guide, and is available for download from the ATS website, *www.ats.aq.*

It may be useful to give a deadline by which time reports of a visit to the Area must be made (e.g. within six months). To address instances where the Area may be visited by groups authorised by Parties other than the Party that proposed the Management Plan, it may be useful to indicate that visit reports should be exchanged to assist in managing the Area and reviewing the Management Plan.

Many reporting requirements will be generally applicable, but in some cases it may be appropriate to specify particular information that will be of assistance in managing the Area. For example, for Areas designated to protect bird colonies it may be appropriate to request visiting groups undertaking surveys to report detailed information on census data, and locations of any new colonies or nests not previously recorded.

8. Supporting documentation

This section should refer to any additional documents that may be relevant. These may include any scientific reports or papers describing the values of the Area in greater detail, although as a general rule the various components of the Area and the intended management activities should be explained in the various sections of the Management Plan itself. Any such papers or supporting documents should be fully cited.

Approval process for ASPA Management Plans

Article 5 of Annex V provides that any Party, the CEP, SCAR or CCAMLR may submit a draft Management Plan for consideration by the ATCM. In practice, draft Management Plans are generally submitted by one or more Parties to the CEP for consideration.

The process by which Management Plans are handled from drafting through to acceptance is summarised by the flow chart in Figure 1. This is based on the requirements of Article 6 of Annex V, the *Guidelines for CEP Consideration of New and Revised Draft ASPA and ASMA Management Plans* (Annex 1 of Appendix 3 to the CEP XI Final Report), and other related guidelines.

The approval process for an ASPA Management Plan has many critical stages, which can take a long time to complete. However, these stages are necessary as an ASPA Management Plan requires the agreement of all Antarctic Treaty Consultative Parties at an ATCM.

Preparing the draft Management Plan

In the initial stages of drafting the Management Plan, it is recommended that widespread consultation, both nationally and internationally, is undertaken on the scientific, environmental and logistical elements of the Plan as appropriate. This will aid the passage of the Plan through the more formal process at the ATCM.

Proponents of new Areas are strongly encouraged to consider relevant guidelines and references that will assist in assessing, selecting, defining and proposing areas that might require greater protection through designation as an ASPA, including:

- *Guidelines for Implementation of the Framework for Protected Areas set forth in Article 3, Annex V of the Environmental Protocol* – Resolution 1 (2000).
- *Environmental Domains Analysis for the Antarctic continent* – Resolution 3 (2008).

When considering the designation of a new ASPA, proponents are encouraged to inform the CEP at an early stage (e.g. even before detailing a management plan for the area) so that proposals can be discussed in the context of the protected areas system as a whole.

When revising an existing Management Plan, it may be informative to use the *Checklist to assist in the inspection of Antarctic Specially Protected Areas and Antarctic Specially Managed Areas* (Resolution 4 (2008)) as a tool to identify necessary changes and improvements.

Submitting the draft Management Plan for consideration

The draft Management Plan should be submitted to the CEP, as an attachment to a Working Paper prepared in accordance with Resolution 1 (2008) *Guide to the presentation of Working Papers containing proposals for Antarctic Specially Protected Areas, Antarctic Specially Managed Areas or Historic Sites and Monuments.*

If the Area contains a marine component that meets the criteria outlined in Decision 9 (2005) *Marine protected areas and other areas of interest to CCAMLR*, the draft Management Plan should also be submitted to CCAMLR for consideration. The proponents should make arrangements to ensure that any feedback from CCAMLR (which holds its annual meetings in October/November) is available before the proposal is considered by the CEP.

Consideration by the CEP and ATCM

The CEP will consider the Management Plan, if appropriate taking into account any comments from CCAMLR. The CEP may refer the Management Plan to the ATCM for consideration and adoption, or to the Subsidiary Group on Management Plans (SGMP) for intersessional review.

In accordance with its Terms of Reference (see Appendix 1 to the CEP XIII Final Report), the SGMP will consider each draft Management Plan referred to it, advise the proponent(s) on recommended changes, consider any revised version of the Management Plan prepared during the intersessional period, and report to the CEP on its review. The revised Management Plan and the CEP's report would then be considered by the CEP meeting and, if agreed, referred to the ATCM for consideration and adoption.

If the ATCM agrees on the management plan a Measure is adopted in accordance with Article IX(1) of the Antarctic Treaty. Unless the Measure specifies otherwise, the Plan is deemed to have been approved 90 days after the close of the ATCM at which it was adopted, unless one or more of the Consultative Parties notifies the Depository, within that time period, that it wishes an extension of that period or is unable to approve the Measure.

Review and revision of Management Plans

The Management Plan shall be reviewed every five years in accordance with Article 6(3) of Annex V of the Environment Protocol and updated as required. Updated Management Plans then follow the same course of agreement as before.

When undertaking Management Plan reviews, thought should be given to the need for further or continued site protection of species whose abundance or range has increased substantially. In contrast, site protection may be deemed unnecessary in an area where a protected species is no longer present and the environmental or scientific values for which the area was designated, no longer apply.

Figure 1. Flow chart showing the approval process for ASPA Management Plans

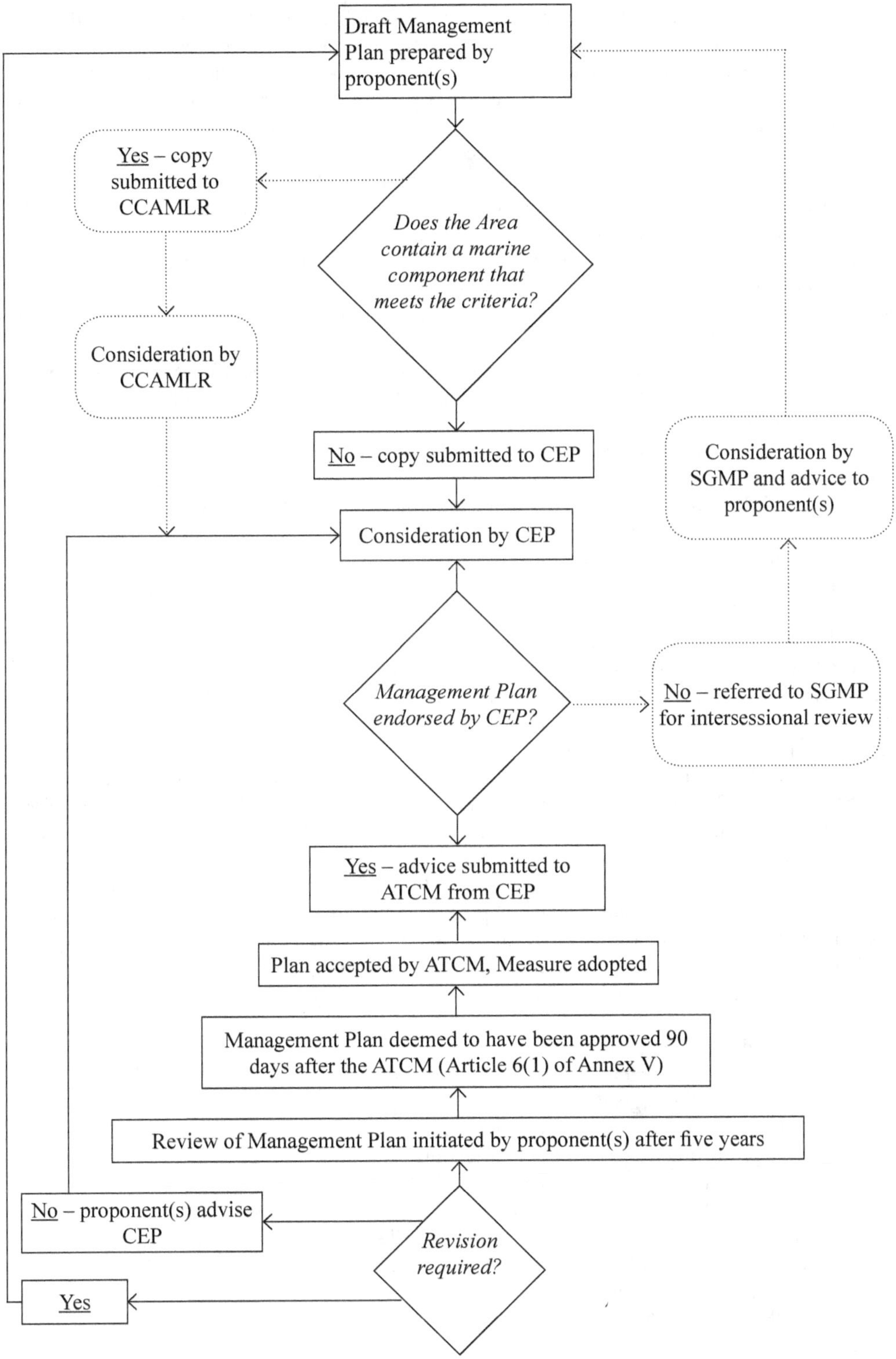

Appendix 1 Guidance notes for producing maps for inclusion in Management Plans

Management Plans should include a general location map to show the position of the Area and the location of any other protected areas in the vicinity, and at least one detailed map of the site showing those features essential for meeting the Management plan objectives.

1. Each map should include latitude and longitude as well as having a scale bar. Avoid statements of scale (e.g. 1:50000) because enlargement/reduction renders such statements useless. The map projection, and horizontal and vertical datums used should be indicated.
2. It is important to use up-to-date coastline data including features such as ice shelves, ice tongues and glaciers. Ice recession and advance continues to affect many areas with consequent changes to Area boundaries. If an ice feature is used as a boundary the date of the source from which the data was acquired (e.g. survey or satellite image) should be shown.
3. Maps should show the following features: any specified routes; any restricted zones; boat and/or helicopter landing sites and access points; campsites; installations and huts; major animal concentrations and breeding sites; any extensive areas of vegetation and should clearly delineate between ice/snow and ice-free ground. In many instances it is useful to include a geological map of the Area. It is suggested that, in most cases, it is helpful to have contouring at an appropriate interval on all maps of the Area. But contouring should not be too close as to mark other features or symbols on the map.
4. Contours should be included on maps at an interval appropriate to the scale of the map.
5. Be aware when preparing the map that it will be reduced to about 150 x 200 mm size to fit into the ATCM official report. This is of importance in selecting the size of symbols, the closeness of contouring and the use of shading. Reproduction is always monochrome so do not use colours to distinguish features in the original. There may well be other versions of an Area map available but as far as the legal status of the Management Plan is concerned it is the version published with the Final Report of the Antarctic Treaty Consultative Meeting that is the definitive version which will be included in national legislation.
6. If the Area will require evaluation by CCAMLR the location of nearby CEMP sites should be indicated. CCAMLR has requested that the location of bird and seal colonies and the access routes from the sea should be indicated on a map wherever possible.
7. Other figures can assist with using the Management Plan in the field:
   - For photographs, good contrast prints are essential for adequate reproduction. Screening or digitising of photograph will improve reproduction when the plan is photocopied. If an image such as an aerial photograph or satellite image is used in the map the source and date of acquisition of the image should be stated.
   - Some plans have already used 3-dimensional terrain models which again can provide important locational information when approaching an Area, especially by helicopter. Such drawings need careful design if they are not to become confusing when reduced.

A checklist of features to be considered for inclusion on maps

1. Essential features

1.1 Title
1.2 Latitude and longitude
1.3 Scale bar with numerical scale
1.4 Comprehensive legend
1.5 Adequate and approved place names
1.6 Map projection and spheroid modification
1.7 North arrow
1.8 Contour interval
1.9 If image data are included, date of image collection

2. Essential topographical features

2.1 Coastline, rock and ice
2.2 Peaks and ridge lines

- 2.3 Ice margins and other glacial features
- 2.4 Contours (labelled as necessary) survey points and spot heights

3. Natural Features

- 3.1 Lakes, ponds, streams
- 3.2 Moraines, screes, cliffs, beaches
- 3.3 Beach areas
- 3.4 Vegetation
- 3.5 Bird and seal colonies

4. Anthropogenic Features

- 4.1 Station
- 4.2 Field huts, refuges
- 4.3 Campsites
- 4.4 Roads and vehicle tracks, footpaths features overlap
- 4.5 Landing areas for fixed wing aeroplanes and helicopters
- 4.6 Wharf, jetties
- 4.7 Power supplies, cables
- 4.8 Aerials, antennae
- 4.9 Fuel storage areas
- 4.10 Water reservoirs and pipes
- 4.11 Emergency caches
- 4.12 Markers, signs
- 4.13 Historic sites or artefacts, archaeological sites
- 4.14 Scientific installations or sampling areas
- 4.15 Site contamination or modification

5. Boundaries

- 5.1 Boundary of Area
- 5.2 Boundaries of subsidiary zones areas. Boundaries of contained protected area
- 5.3 Boundary signs and markers (including cairns)
- 5.4 Boat/aircraft approach routes
- 5.5 Navigation markers or beacons
- 5.6 Survey points and markers

The same approach is obviously required of any inset maps.

At the conclusion of drafting a check should be made on cartographic quality to ensure:

- Balance between the elements.
- Appropriate shading to enhance features but which will not be confusing when photocopied and where degree should reflect importance.
- Correct and appropriate text with no features overlap.
- An appropriate legend using SCAR approved map symbols wherever possible.
- White text appropriately shadowed on all image data.

Appendix 2 Antarctic Specially Protected Area (ASPA) visit report form

(1) ASPA number:
(2) ASPA name:
(3) Permit number:
(4) Permit period From: To:
(5) National authority issuing Permit:
(6) Date Report filed:

(7) Contact details for Principal Permit Holder: Name: Job Title or Position: Phone number: Email:
(8) Number of people Permitted to enter the Area: That actually entered the Area:
(9) List of all persons who entered the Area under the current Permit:
(10) Objectives of the visit to the Area under the current Permit:
(11) Date(s) and duration of visit(s) under the current Permit:
(12) Mode of transport to/from and within the Area:
(13) Summary of activities conducted in the Area:
(14) Descriptions and locations of samples collected (type, quantity, and details of any Permits for sample collection):
(15) Descriptions and locations of markers, instrumentation or equipment installed or removed, or any material released into the environment (noting how new installations are intended to remain in the Area):
(16) Measures taken during this visit to ensure compliance with the Management Plan:
(17) On an attached photocopy of the map of the Area, please show (as applicable): camp site location(s), land/sea/air movements or routes, sampling sites, installations, deliberate release of materials, any impacts, and features of special significance not previously recorded. GPS coordinates should be provided for such locations wherever possible:
(18) Any other comment or information, such as: • Observations of human effects on the Area, distinguishing between those resulting from the visit and those due to previous visitors: • Evaluation of whether the values for which the Area was designated are being adequately protected: • Features of special significance that have not been previously recorded for the Area: • Recommendations on further management measures needed to protect the values of the Area, including location and appraisal of condition of structures, markers, etc.: • Any departures from the provisions of the Management Plan during this visit, noting dates, magnitudes and locations:

Appendix 3 Template for Antarctic Specially Protected Area Management Plans

Management Plan for Antarctic Specially Protected Area No. [XXX]
[INSERT NAME OF PROTECTED AREA]

Introduction

The Guide to the Preparation of Management Plans for Antarctic Specially Protected Areas (the Guide) provides guidance for this section of Management Plans. No suggested standard wording is provided here because the content of this section will be specific to the Area in question.

[Site-specific content should be inserted here]

1. Description of values to be protected

Section 1 of the Guide provides guidance for this section of Management Plans. No suggested standard wording is provided here because the content of this section will be specific to the Area in question.

[Site-specific content should be inserted here]

2. Aims and objectives

Many existing Management Plans share similar aims and objectives. A pool of suggested standard wording has been developed and can be used, amended or deleted as appropriate for the Area in question (see below). Proponents are encouraged to identify site-specific aims and objectives, and should consider the guidance for this section of Management Plans given in Section 2 of the Guide.

Management of [insert name of Area] aims to:

- avoid degradation of, or substantial risk to, the values of the Area by preventing unnecessary human disturbance to the Area;
- avoid degradation of, or substantial risk to, the values of the Area by preventing unnecessary human disturbance to the Area, its features and artefacts through managed access to [insert specific hut here];
- allow scientific research in the Area provided it is for compelling reasons which cannot be served elsewhere and which will not jeopardise the natural ecological system in that Area;
- prevent or minimise the introduction to the Area of alien plants, animals and microbes;
- minimise the possibility of the introduction of pathogens which may cause disease in fauna populations within the Area;
- preserve [a part of] the natural ecosystem of the Area as a reference area for future comparative studies;
- maintain the historic values of the Area through planned conservation and archaeological work programmes;
- [further site-specific content should be inserted here]

In the case of Areas to which educational and outreach visits are permitted, the following text might be considered:

- allow activities in the Area for educational and outreach purposes, provided that such activities are for compelling reasons which cannot be served elsewhere and which will not jeopardise the natural ecological system in that Area;
- [further site-specific content should be inserted here]

2. Management activities

Many existing Management Plans share similar wording in this section. A pool of suggested standard wording has been developed and can be used, amended or deleted as appropriate for the Area in question (see below). Proponents are encouraged to identify site-specific management activities, and should consider the guidance for this section of Management Plans given in Section 3 of the Guide.

None required.

[Insert type of information] on the location of the Area [stating special restrictions that apply] shall be displayed prominently, and a copy of this Management Plan shall be made available, at [insert location of information].

Copies of this Management Plan [and informative material] shall be made available to vessels [and aircraft] [insert: travelling/ planning to visit/visiting/operating in] the vicinity of the Area.

Signs illustrating the location and boundaries, with clear statements of entry restrictions, shall be placed at appropriate locations on the boundary of the Area [and Restricted Zone] to help avoid inadvertent entry.

Markers, signs or other structures (e.g. fences, cairns) erected within the Area for scientific or management purposes shall be secured and maintained in good condition and removed when no longer required.

In accordance with the requirements of Annex III of the Protocol on Environmental Protection to the Antarctic Treaty, abandoned equipment or materials shall be removed to the maximum extent possible provided doing so does not adversely impact on the environment and the values of the Area.*

The Area shall be visited as necessary[, and no less than once every five years,] to assess whether it continues to serve the purposes for which it was designated and to ensure that management [and maintenance] activities are adequate.

Visits shall be permitted as necessary in order to facilitate the study and monitoring of anthropogenic changes that could affect the protected values in the Area, in particular, [insert specific activity]. Impact study and monitoring should be conducted, to the maximum extent possible, by non-invasive methods.

National Antarctic Programmes operating in the Area shall consult together with a view to ensuring the above management activities are implemented.

The Management Plan shall be reviewed no less than once every five years and updated as required.*

Personnel [national programme staff, field expeditions, tourists and pilots] in the vicinity of, accessing or flying over the Area shall be specifically instructed, by their national programme [or appropriate national authority] as to the provisions and contents of the Management Plan.

All pilots operating in the region shall be informed of the location, boundaries and restrictions applying to entry and over-flight in the Area.

[Further site-specific content should be inserted here]

4. Period of designation

Many existing Management Plans share similar wording in this section. Suggested wording has been developed and can be utilised as appropriate (see below) Section 4 of the Guide provides guidance for this section of Management Plans.

Designated for an indefinite period. / Designated for a [x] year period.

5. Maps

Section 5 of the Guide provides guidance for this section of Management Plans. Guidance for producing the maps themselves is given in Appendix 1 of the Guide. No suggested standard wording is provided here because the content of this section will be specific to the Area in question. However, proponents could utilise the following suggested format:

- [Map X, Title of Map X
- Map Y, Title of Map Y
- Map Z, Title of Map Z]

6. Description of the Area

Section 6 of the Guide provides general guidance for this section of Management Plans. Content should be inserted under the following sub-section headings.

6(i) Geographical coordinates, boundary markers and natural features

Section 6(i) of the Guide provides guidance for this section of Management Plans. No suggested standard wording is provided here because the content of this section will be specific to the Area in question.

[Site-specific content should be inserted here]

6(ii) Access to the area

Section 6(ii) of the Guide provides guidance for this section of Management Plans. No suggested standard wording is provided here because the content of this section will be specific to the Area in question.

[Site-specific content should be inserted here]

6(iii) Location of structures within and adjacent to the Area

Section 6(iii) of the Guide provides guidance for this section of Management Plans. No suggested standard wording is provided here because the content of this section will be specific to the Area in question.

[Site-specific content should be inserted here]

6(iv) Location of other protected areas in the vicinity

Section 6(iii) of the Guide provides guidance for this section of Management Plans. No suggested standard wording is provided here because the content of this section will be specific to the Area in question. However, proponents could utilise the following suggested format (e.g. ASPA 167, Hawker Island, 68°35'S, 77°50'E, 22 km to the north-east):

Revised Guide to the Preparation of Management Plans for ASPAs

[Other protected areas in the vicinity include (see Map XX):

- ASPA XXX, Name of Protected Area, latitude, longitude, XX km to the [direction]
- ASPA YYY, Name of Protected Area, latitude, longitude, XX km to the [direction]
- etc]

6(v) Special zones within the Area

Section 6(v) of the Guide provides guidance for this section of Management Plans, if any such zones are present. If there are no special zones, the following standard wording could be used. No other suggested standard wording is provided here because the content of this section will be specific to the Area in question.

There are no special zones within the Area. / [Site-specific content should be inserted here]

7. Terms and conditions for entry permits

7(i) General permit conditions

Many existing Management Plans share similar wording in this section. A pool of suggested standard wording has been developed and can be used, amended or deleted as appropriate for the Area in question (see below). Proponents are encouraged to identify site-specific permit conditions, and should consider the guidance for this section of Management Plans given in Section 7(i) of the Guide.

Entry into the Area is prohibited except in accordance with a Permit issued by an appropriate national authority. Conditions for issuing a Permit to enter the Area are that:*

- it is issued for compelling scientific reasons which cannot be served elsewhere, or for reasons essential to the management of the Area;
- the actions permitted are in accordance with this Management Plan;*
- the activities permitted will give due consideration via the environmental impact assessment process to the continued protection of the [environmental, scientific, historic, aesthetic or wilderness] values of the Area;
- the Permit shall be issued for a finite period;
- the Permit shall be carried when in the Area;*
- [further site-specific content should be inserted here]

In the case of Areas to which educational and outreach visits are permitted, the following text might be considered:

- it is issued for compelling scientific, educational or outreach reasons which cannot be served elsewhere, or for reasons essential to the management of the Area;
- [further site-specific content should be inserted here]

7(ii) Access to, and movement within or over, the Area

Many existing Management Plans share similar wording in this section. A pool of suggested standard wording has been developed and can be used, amended or deleted as appropriate for the Area in question (see below). Proponents are encouraged to identify site-specific content, and should consider the guidance for this section of Management Plans given in Section 7(ii) of the Guide.

Vehicles are prohibited within the Area and all movement within the Area should be on foot.

Vehicle use in the Area should be kept to a minimum.

The operation of aircraft over the Area should be carried out, as a minimum requirement, in compliance with the "Guidelines for the Operation of Aircraft near Concentrations of Birds" contained in Resolution 2 (2004).

Pedestrian traffic should be kept to the minimum necessary to undertake permitted activities and every reasonable effort should be made to minimise trampling effects.

Movement within the Area by foot should be on designated tracks only.

Where no routes are identified, pedestrian traffic should be kept to the minimum necessary to undertake permitted activities and every reasonable effort should be made to minimise trampling effects.

Visitors should avoid areas of visible vegetation and care should be exercised walking in areas of moist ground, particularly the stream course beds, where foot traffic can easily damage sensitive soils, plant and algal communities, and degrade water quality.

[Further site-specific content should be inserted here]

7(iii) Activities which may be conducted within the Area

Many existing Management Plans share similar wording in this section. A pool of suggested standard wording has been developed and can be used, amended or deleted as appropriate for the Area in question (see below). Proponents are encouraged to identify site-specific content, and should consider the guidance for this section of Management Plans given in Section 7(iii) of the Guide.

Activities which may be conducted within the Area include:

- compelling scientific research which cannot be undertaken elsewhere;
- sampling, which should be the minimum required for approved research programmes;
- conservation and maintenance;
- essential management activities, including monitoring;
- operational activities in support of scientific research or management within or beyond the Area, including visits to assess the effectiveness of the Management Plan and management activities;
- [further site-specific content, including any requirements for active management within the site which may be necessary in the future, should be added here]

In the case of Areas to which tourist visits are permitted (e.g. Historic Sites and Monuments designated as ASPAs) or to which educational and outreach visits are permitted, the following text might be considered:

- tourist visits;
- activities for educational and outreach purposes;
- [further site-specific content should be inserted here]

7(iv) Installation, modification, or removal of structures

Many existing Management Plans share similar wording in this section. A pool of suggested standard wording has been developed and can be used, amended or deleted as appropriate for the Area in question (see below). Proponents are encouraged to identify site-specific content, and should consider the guidance for this section of Management Plans given in Section 7(iv) of the Guide.

No [new] structures are to be erected within the Area, or scientific equipment installed, except for compelling scientific or management reasons and for a pre-established period, as specified in a permit.

Permanent structures or installations are prohibited [with the exception of permanent survey markers and boundary signs].

No [new] structures are to be erected within the Area, or scientific equipment installed.

All markers, structures or scientific equipment installed in the Area must be clearly identified by country, name of the principal investigator or agency, year of installation and date of expected removal.

All such items should be free of organisms, propagules (e.g. seeds, eggs) and non-sterile soil, and be made of materials that can withstand the environmental conditions and pose minimal risk of contamination of the Area.

Installation (including site selection), maintenance, modification or removal of structures and equipment shall be undertaken in a manner that minimises disturbance to the values of the Area.

Existing structures must not be removed, except in accordance with a permit.

Structures and installations must be removed when they are no longer required, or on the expiry of the permit, whichever is the earlier.

Removal of specific structures or equipment for which the permit has expired shall be [the responsibility of the authority which granted the original permit and shall be] a condition of the Permit.

[Further site-specific content should be inserted here]

7(v) Location of field camps

In most cases the content of this section will be specific to the Area in question. Proponents are encouraged to identify site-specific content, and should consider the guidance for this section of Management Plans given in Section 7(v) of the Guide. In the case of Areas where camping is prohibited, or where there are existing campsites, the following text might be considered:

Camping is prohibited within the Area.

Existing campsites should be used where practicable.

[Further site-specific content should be inserted here]

7(vi) Restrictions on materials and organisms which may be brought into the Area

Many existing Management Plans share similar wording in this section. A pool of suggested standard wording has been developed and can be used, amended or deleted as appropriate for the Area in question (see below). Proponents are encouraged to identify site-specific content, and should consider the guidance for this section of Management Plans given in Section 7(vi) of the Guide.

In addition to the requirements of the Protocol on Environmental Protection to the Antarctic Treaty, restrictions on materials and organisms which may be brought into the area are:

- the deliberate introduction of animals, plant material, micro-organisms and non-sterile soil into the Area shall not be permitted. Precautions shall be taken to prevent the accidental introduction of animals, plant material, micro-organisms and non-sterile soil from other biologically distinct regions (within or beyond the Antarctic Treaty area).* Site-specific bio-security measures are listed below:
  – [site-specific measures should be inserted here];
- fuel or other chemicals shall not be stored in the Area unless specifically authorised by Permit condition. They shall be stored and handled in a way that minimises the risk of their accidental introduction into the environment;
- materials introduced into the Area shall be for a stated period only and shall be removed by the end of that stated period;
- [further site-specific conditions should be inserted here]

7(vii) Taking of, or harmful interference with, native flora and fauna

Many existing Management Plans share similar wording in this section. A pool of suggested standard wording has been developed and can be used, amended or deleted as appropriate for the Area in question (see below). Proponents are encouraged to identify site-specific content, and should consider the guidance for this section of Management Plans given in Section 7(vii) of the Guide.

Taking of, or harmful interference with, native flora and fauna is prohibited, except in accordance with a permit issued in accordance with Annex II of the Protocol on Environmental Protection to the Antarctic Treaty.*

Where taking or harmful interference with animals is involved this should, as a minimum standard, be in accordance with the SCAR Code of Conduct for the Use of Animals for Scientific Purposes in Antarctica.

[Further site-specific content should be inserted here]

7(viii) The collection or removal of materials not brought into the Area by the permit holder

Many existing Management Plans share similar wording in this section. A pool of suggested standard wording has been developed and can be used, amended or deleted as appropriate for the Area in question (see below). Proponents are encouraged to identify site-specific content, and should consider the guidance for this section of Management Plans given in Section 7(viii) of the Guide.

Unless specifically authorised by permit, visitors to the Area are prohibited from interfering with or from handling, taking or damaging any designated historic site or monument, or any anthropogenic material meeting the criteria in Resolution 5 (2001). Similarly, relocation or removal of artefacts for the purposes of preservation, protection or to re-establish historical accuracy is allowable only by permit. Any new or newly identified anthropogenic materials found should be notified to the appropriate national authority.

Other material of human origin likely to compromise the values of the Area, and which was not brought into the Area by the Permit Holder or otherwise authorised may be removed from the Area unless the environmental impact of the removal is likely to be greater than leaving the material in situ: if this is the case the appropriate national authority must be notified and approval obtained.

[Further site-specific content should be inserted here]

7(ix) Disposal of waste

Many existing Management Plans share similar wording in this section. A pool of suggested standard wording has been developed and can be used, amended or deleted as appropriate for the Area in question (see below). Proponents are encouraged to identify site-specific content, and should consider the guidance for this section of Management Plans given in Section 7(ix) of the Guide.

All wastes, including all human wastes, shall be removed from the Area.

All wastes, other than human wastes, shall be removed from the Area. [Although removal from the Area is preferable, human wastes may be disposed of into the sea]

Waste generated as a consequence of the activities developed in the Area shall be temporarily stored (insert site specific location details) in such a way as to prevent their dispersal into the environment and removed when activities have been concluded.

[Further site-specific content should be inserted here]

7(x) Measures that may be necessary to continue to meet the aims of the Management Plan

Many existing Management Plans share similar wording in this section. A pool of suggested standard wording has been developed and can be used, amended or deleted as appropriate for the Area in question (see below). Proponents are encouraged to identify site-specific content, and should consider the guidance for this section of Management Plans given in Section 7(x) of the Guide.

Permits may be granted to enter the Area to:

- carry out monitoring and Area inspection activities, which may involve the collection of a small number of samples or data for analysis or review;
- erect or maintain signposts, structures or scientific equipment;
- carry out protective measures;
- [further site-specific content should be inserted here]

Any specific sites of long-term monitoring shall be appropriately marked on site and on maps of the Area. A GPS position should be obtained for lodgement with the Antarctic Data Directory System through the appropriate national authority.

To help maintain the ecological and scientific values of the Area visitors shall take special precautions against introductions. Of particular concern are microbial, animal or vegetation introductions sourced from soils from other Antarctic sites, including stations, or from regions outside Antarctica. To the maximum extent practicable, visitors shall ensure that footwear, clothing and any equipment – particularly camping and sampling equipment – is thoroughly cleaned before entering the Area.

To avoid interference with long-term research and monitoring activities or duplication of effort, persons planning new projects within the Area should consult with established programmes and/or appropriate national authorities.

[Further site-specific content should be inserted here]

7(xi) Requirements for reports

Many existing Management Plans share similar wording in this section. A pool of suggested standard wording has been developed and can be used, amended or deleted as appropriate for the Area in question (see below). Proponents are encouraged to identify site-specific content, and should consider the guidance for this section of Management Plans given in Section 7(xi) of the Guide.

The principal permit holder for each visit to the Area shall submit a report to the appropriate national authority as soon as practicable, and no later than six months after the visit has been completed.*

Such reports should include, as appropriate, the information identified in the visit report form contained in the Guide to the Preparation of Management Plans for Antarctic Specially Protected Areas.

If appropriate, the national authority should also forward a copy of the visit report to the Party that proposed the Management Plan, to assist in managing the Area and reviewing the Management Plan.

Parties should, wherever possible, deposit originals or copies of such original visit reports in a publicly accessible archive to maintain a record of usage, for the purpose of any review of the Management Plan and in organising the scientific use of the Area.

[Further site-specific content should be inserted here]

8. Supporting documentation

Section 8 of the Guide provides guidance for this section of Management Plans. No suggested standard wording is provided here because the content of this section will be specific to the Area in question.

[Site-specific content should be inserted here]

Resolution 3 (2011): General Guidelines for Visitors to the Antarctic

The Representatives,

Recalling Resolution 5 (2005), Resolution 2 (2006), Resolution 1 (2007), Resolution 2 (2008), Resolution 4 (2009) and Resolution 1 (2010) which adopted lists of sites subject to Site Guidelines;

Acknowledging the benefits of focussing on site-specific information in Site Guidelines;

Recalling Recommendation XVIII-1(1994) *Guidance for those organising and conducting tourism and non-Governmental activities in the Antarctic*;

Noting that Recommendation XVIII-1(1994) provides guidance on both environmental and organisational matters;

Affirming the value of providing general environmental advice to visitors to complement site-specific information;

Acknowledging the work of the Committee for Environmental Protection since 1998 in enhancing the understanding of environmental impacts associated with visits to Antarctica;

Noting the desirability of providing contemporary advice to visitors to Antarctica to guide them in minimising their impacts at all sites;

Believing that the *General Guidelines for Visitors to the Antarctic* must be reviewed and revised as further information becomes available;

Confirming that the term "visitors" does not include scientists conducting research within such sites, or individuals engaged in official governmental activities;

Recommend that:

1. their Governments endorse the annexed *General Guidelines for Visitors to the Antarctic*;
2. the Guidelines be placed on the website of the Antarctic Treaty Secretariat;

3. their Governments urge all those intending to visit sites in Antarctica to ensure that they are fully conversant with and adhere to the advice in these *General Guidelines for Visitors to the Antarctic*; and

4. Parties work to make Recommendation XVIII-1 (1994) effective as soon as possible.

Resolution 3 (2011) Annex: General Guidelines for Visitors to the Antarctic

All visits to Antarctica should be conducted in accordance with the Antarctic Treaty, its Protocol on Environmental Protection, and relevant Measures and Resolutions adopted at Antarctic Treaty Consultative Meetings (ATCM). Visits may only occur after prior approval by a relevant national authority or if they have met all the requirements of their national authority.

These Guidelines provide general advice for visiting any location, with the aim of ensuring visits do not have adverse impacts on the Antarctic environment, or on its scientific and aesthetic values. ATCM Site Guidelines for Visitors provide additional site-specific advice for some locations. Read these Guidelines before you visit Antarctica and plan how to minimise your impact. If you are part of a guided visitor group, abide by these guidelines, pay attention to your guides, and follow their instructions.

If you have organised your own visit, you are responsible for abiding by these guidelines. You are also responsible for identifying the features of the sites you visit that may be vulnerable to visitor impacts, and for complying with any site specific requirements, including Site Guidelines, Antarctic Specially Protected Area (ASPA) and Antarctic Specially Managed Area (ASMA) management plans, or station visit guidelines. Guidelines for particular activities or risks (such as aircraft use, or avoiding the introduction of non-native species) may also apply. Management plans, a list of historic sites and monuments, and other relevant information can be found at *www.ats.aq/e/ep_protected.htm*. Site Guidelines can be found at *www.ats.aq/e/ats_other_siteguidelines.htm*.

PROTECT ANTARCTIC WILDLIFE

The taking of, or harmful interference with, Antarctic wildlife is prohibited except in accordance with a permit.	
WILDLIFE	• When in the vicinity of wildlife, walk slowly and carefully and keep noise to a minimum.
	• Maintain an appropriate distance from wildlife. While in many cases a greater distance may be appropriate, in general don't approach closer than 5m. Abide by any guidance on distances in site specific guidelines.
	• Observe wildlife behaviour. If wildlife changes its behaviour stop moving, or slowly increase your distance.
	• Animals are particularly sensitive to disturbance when they are breeding (including nesting) or moulting. Stay outside the margins of a colony and observe from a distance.
	• Every situation is different. Consider the topography and the individual circumstances of the site, as these may have an impact on the vulnerability of wildlife to disturbance.
	• Always give animals the right of way and do not block their access routes to the sea.
	• Do not feed wildlife or leave food or scraps lying around.
	• Do not use guns or explosives.
VEGETATION	• Vegetation, including mosses and lichens, is fragile and very slow growing. Do not damage the vegetation by walking, driving or landing on any moss beds or lichen covered rocks.

	• When travelling on foot, stay on established tracks whenever possible to minimise disturbance or damage to the soil and vegetated surfaces. Where a track does not exist, take the most direct route and avoid vegetation, fragile terrain, scree slopes and wildlife.
INTRODUCTION OF NON-NATIVE SPECIES	• Do not introduce any plants or animals into the Antarctic.
	• In order to prevent the introduction of non-native species and disease, carefully wash boots and clean all equipment including clothes, bags, tripods, tents and walking sticks before bringing them to Antarctica. Pay particular attention to boot treads, velcro fastenings and pockets which could contain soil or seeds. Vehicles and aircraft should also be cleaned.
	• The transfer of species and disease between locations in Antarctica is also a concern. Ensure all clothing and equipment is cleaned before moving between sites.

RESPECT PROTECTED AREAS

Activities in Antarctic Specially Protected Areas (ASPAs) or Antarctic Specially Managed Areas (ASMAs) must comply with the provisions of the relevant Management Plan. Many historic sites and monuments (HSMs) have been formally designated and protected.	
SPECIALLY MANAGED AND SPECIALLY PROTECTED AREAS	• A permit from a relevant national authority is required for entry into any ASPA. Carry the permit and obey any permit conditions at all times while visiting an ASPA.
	• Check the locations and boundaries of ASPAs and ASMAs in advance. Refer to the provisions of the Management Plan and abide by any restrictions regarding the conduct of activities in or near these areas.
HISTORIC SITES AND MONUMENTS AND OTHER STRUCTURES	• Historic huts and structures can in some cases be used for tourist, recreational and educational visits. Visitors should not use them for other purposes except in emergency circumstances.
	• Do not interfere with, deface or vandalise any historic site, monument, or artefact, or other building or emergency refuge (whether occupied or unoccupied).
	• If you come across an item that may be of historic value that authorities may not be aware of, do not disturb it. Notify your expedition leader or national authorities.
	Before entering any historic structure, clean your boots of snow and grit and remove snow and water from clothes, as these can cause damage to structures or artefacts.
	• Take care not to tread on any artefacts which may be obscured by snow when moving around historic sites.

RESPECT SCIENTIFIC RESEARCH

Do not interfere with scientific research, facilities or equipment
• Obtain permission before visiting Antarctic stations. • Reconfirm scheduled visits no less than 24–72 hours before arriving. • Comply with any site specific rules when visiting Antarctic stations. • Do not interfere with or remove scientific equipment or markers, and do not disturb experimental study sites, field camps or stored supplies

KEEP ANTARCTICA PRISTINE	
Antarctica remains relatively pristine. It is the largest wilderness area on earth. Please leave no trace of your visit.	
WASTE	• Do not deposit any litter or garbage on land nor discard it into the sea.

	• At stations or camps smoke only at designated areas, to avoid litter and risk of fire to structures. Collect ash and litter for disposal outside Antarctica.
	• Ensure that wastes are managed in accordance with Annexes III and IV of the Protocol on Environmental Protection to the Antarctic Treaty.
	• Ensure that all equipment and rubbish is secured at all times in such a way as to prevent dispersal into the environment through high winds or wildlife foraging.
WILDERNESS VALUES	• Do not disturb or pollute lakes, streams, rivers or other water bodies (e.g. by walking, washing yourself or your equipment, throwing stones, etc.)
	• Do not paint or engrave names or other graffiti on any man-made or natural surface in Antarctica.
	• Do not take souvenirs, whether man-made, biological or geological items, including feathers, bones, eggs, vegetation, soil, rocks, meteorites or fossils.
	• Place tents and equipment on snow or at previously used campsites where possible.

BE SAFE

Be prepared for severe and changeable weather. Ensure that your equipment and clothing meet Antarctic standards. Remember that the Antarctic environment is inhospitable, unpredictable and potentially dangerous.	
SAFETY PRECAUTIONS/ PREPARATIONS	• Know your capabilities, the dangers posed by the Antarctic environment, and act accordingly. Plan activities with safety in mind at all times.
	• Keep a safe distance from dangerous wildlife like fur seals, both on land and at sea. Keep at least 15m away, where practicable.
	• If you are travelling in a group, act on the advice and instructions of your leaders. Do not stray from your group.
	• Do not walk onto glaciers or large snow fields without proper equipment and experience. There is a real danger of falling into hidden crevasses.
	• Do not expect a rescue service. Self-sufficiency is increased and risks reduced by sound planning, quality equipment, and trained personnel.
	• Do not enter emergency refuges (except in emergencies). If you use equipment or food from a refuge, inform the nearest research station or national authority once the emergency is over.
	• Respect any smoking restrictions. Use of combustion style lanterns and naked flames in or around historic structures should be avoided. Take great care to safeguard against the danger of fire. This is a real hazard in the dry environment of Antarctica.

LANDING AND TRANSPORT REQUIREMENTS

Act in Antarctica in such a way so as to minimise potential impacts on the environment, wildlife and associated ecosystems, or the conduct of scientific research.	
TRANSPORT	• Do not use aircraft, vessels, small boats, hovercraft or other means of transport in ways that disturb wildlife, either at sea or on land. Avoid overflying concentrations of birds and mammals. Follow the advice in Resolution 2 (2004) *Guidelines for the operation of aircraft near concentrations of birds in Antarctica*, available from *www.ats.aq/devAS/info_measures_list.aspx?lang=e*.

	• Refilling of fuel tanks for small boats should take place in a way that ensures any spills can be contained, for example onboard a vessel.
	• Small boats must be free of any soil, plants, or animals and must be checked for the presence of any soil, plants, or animals prior to the commencement of any ship-to-shore operations.
	• Small boats must at all times regulate their course and speed so as to minimise disturbance to wildlife and to avoid any collisions with wildlife.
SHIPS*	• Only one ship may visit a site at any one time.
	• Vessels with more than 500 passengers shall not make landings in Antarctica.
LANDING OF PASSENGERS FROM VESSELS	• A maximum of 100 passengers may be ashore from a vessel at any one time, unless site specific advice requires fewer passengers.
	• During landings from vessels, maintain a 1:20 guide to passenger ratio at all sites, unless site specific advice requires more guides.

* A ship is defined as a vessel which carries more than 12 passengers

Resolution 5 (2011): Revised Guide to the Presentation of Working Papers Containing Proposals for Antarctic Specially Protected Areas, Antarctic Specially Managed Areas or Historic Sites and Monuments

The Representatives,

Noting that Annex V to the Protocol on Environmental Protection to the Antarctic Treaty (the Protocol) provides for the Antarctic Treaty Consultative Meeting ("ATCM") to adopt proposals to designate an Antarctic Specially Protected Area ("ASPA") or an Antarctic Specially Managed Area ("ASMA"), to adopt or amend a Management Plan for such an area, or to designate an Historic Site or Monument ("HSM"), by a Measure in accordance with Article IX(1) of the Antarctic Treaty;

Conscious of the need to ensure clarity concerning the current status of each ASPA and ASMA and its management plan, and each HSM;

Recalling Resolution 3 (2008), which recommended that the "Environmental Domains Analysis for the Antarctic Continent", annexed to it, be used consistently and in conjunction with other tools agreed within the Antarctic Treaty system as a dynamic model for the identification of areas that could be designated as Antarctic Specially Protected Areas within the systematic environmental-geographical framework referred to in Article 3(2) of Annex V of the Protocol;

Recalling also Resolution 1 (2008), which recommended that the Guide to the presentation of Working Papers containing a proposal for Antarctic Specially Protected Areas, Antarctic Specially Managed Areas or Historic Sites and Monuments, annexed to it, be used by those engaged in the preparation of such Working Papers;

Desiring to update the Guide appended to Resolution 1 (2008), to facilitate the collection of information to assist with the assessment and further development of the Antarctic protected areas system, specifically including the primary reason for designation of each ASPA and, where known, the main Environmental Domain represented by each ASPA and ASMA;

Recommend that:

1. the *Guide to the presentation of Working Papers containing proposals for Antarctic Specially Protected Areas, Antarctic Specially Managed Areas or Historic Sites and Monuments* annexed to this Resolution replace the version appended to Resolution 1 (2008) and the updated version of the Guide be used by those engaged in the preparation of such Working Papers; and
2. the Antarctic Treaty Secretariat post the text of Resolution 1 (2008) on its website in a way that makes clear that it is no longer current.

Resolution 5 (2011) Annex Guide to the presentation of Working Papers containing proposals for Antarctic Specially Protected Areas, Antarctic Specially Managed Areas or Historic Sites and Monuments

A. Working Papers on ASPA or ASMA

It is recommended that the Working Paper contain two parts:

(i) COVER SHEET explaining the intended effects of the proposal and the history of the ASPA/ASMA, using Template A as a guide. This cover sheet will NOT form part of the Measure adopted by the ATCM, so will not be published in the Final Report nor on the ATS website. Its sole purpose is to facilitate consideration of the proposal and the drafting of the Measures by the ATCM.

And

(ii) MANAGEMENT PLAN, written as a final version as it is intended to be published. This will be annexed to the Measure and published in the Final Report and on the ATS website.

It would be helpful if the plan is written *as final*, ready for publication. Of course, when it is first submitted to the CEP it is a draft and may be amended by the CEP or ATCM. However, the version adopted by the ATCM should be in final form for publication, and should not require further editing by the Secretariat, other than to insert cross-references to other instruments adopted at the same meeting.

For example, in its final form, the plan should not contain expressions such as:

- "this *proposed* area";
- "this *draft* plan";
- "this plan, *if adopted*, would…";
- accounts of discussions in the CEP or ATCM or details of intersessional work (unless this covers important information eg about the consultation process or activities that have occurred within the Area since the last review);
- views of individual delegations on the draft or intermediate versions of it;
- references to other protected areas using their pre-Annex V designations.

Please use the "Guide to the Preparation of Management Plans for Antarctic Specially Protected Areas" if the proposal concerns an ASPA. (The current version of this Guide is appended to Resolution 2 (1998) and is contained in the CEP Handbook).

There are several high quality management plans, including that for ASPA 109: Moe Island, that could be used as a model for the preparation of new and revised plans.

B. Working Papers on Historic Sites and Monuments (HSM)

HSMs do not have management plans, unless they are also designated as ASPAs or ASMAs. All essential information about the HSM is included in the Measure. The rest of the Working Paper will not be annexed to the Measure; if it is desired to keep any additional background information on the record, this material may be annexed to the report of the CEP for inclusion in the Final Report of the ATCM. To ensure that all the information required for inclusion in the Measure is provided, it is recommended that Template B below is used as a guide when drafting the Working Paper.

C. The tabling of draft Measures on ASPA, ASMA and HSM to the ATCM [•]

When a draft Measure to give effect to the advice of the CEP on an ASPA, ASMA or HSM is submitted to the Secretariat for tabling at the ATCM, the Secretariat is requested also to provide to the ATCM copies of the cover sheet from the original Working Paper setting out the proposal, subject to any revisions made by the CEP.

The sequence of events is as follows:

- A Working Paper consisting of a draft management plan and an explanatory cover sheet is prepared and submitted by the proponent;
- The Secretariat prepares a draft Measure before the ATCM;
- Draft Management Plan is discussed by the CEP and any revisions made (by the proponent in liaison with the Secretariat);

- If the CEP recommends adoption, the Management Plan (as agreed) plus the cover sheet (as agreed) are passed from the CEP Chair to the Chair of the Legal and Institutional Working Group;
- Legal and Institutional Working Group reviews the draft Measure;
- The Secretariat formally table the draft measure plus the agreed cover sheet;
- The ATCM considers and makes a decision.

TEMPLATE A: COVER SHEET FOR A WORKING PAPER ON AN ASPA OR ASMA

Please ensure that the following information is provided on the cover sheet:

(1) Is a new ASPA proposed? Yes/No

(2) Is a new ASMA proposed? Yes/No

(3) Does the proposal relate to an existing ASPA or ASMA?

If so, list all Recommendations, Measures, Resolutions and Decisions pertaining to this ASPA/ ASMA, including any previous designations of this area as an SPA, SSSI or other type of protected area:

In particular, please include the date and relevant Recommendation/Measure for the following:

- First designation:
- First adoption of management plan:
- Any revisions to management plan:
- Current management plan:
- Any extensions of expiry dates of management plan:
- Renaming and renumbering as ………... by Decision 1 (2002).

(Note: this information may be found on the ATS website in the Documents database by searching under the name of the area. While the ATS has made every effort to ensure the completeness and accuracy of the information in the database, occasional errors or omissions may occur. The proponents of any revision to a protected area are best placed to know the history of that area, and are kindly requested to contact the Secretariat if they notice any apparent discrepancy between the regulatory history as they understand it and that displayed on the ATS database.)

(1) If the proposal contains a revision of an existing management plan, please indicate the types of amendment:

   (i) Major or minor?

   (ii) any changes to the boundaries or coordinates?

   (iii) any changes to the maps? If yes, are the changes in the captions only or also in the graphics?

   (iv) any change to the description of the area that is relevant to identifying its location or its boundaries?

   (v) any changes that affect any other ASPA, ASMA or HSM within this area or adjacent to it? In particular, please explain any merger with, incorporation of or abolition of any existing area or site.

   (vi) Other – brief summary of other types of changes, indicating the paragraphs of the management plan in which these are located (especially helpful if the plan is long).

(2) If a new ASPA or ASMA is proposed, does it contain a marine area? Yes/No

(3) If yes, does the proposal require the prior approval of CCAMLR in accordance with Decision 9 (2005)? Yes/No

(4) If yes, has the prior approval of CCAMLR been obtained? Yes/No (If yes, the reference to the relevant paragraph of the relevant CCAMLR Final Report should be given).

(5) If the proposal relates to an ASPA, what is the primary reason for designation (i.e. which part under Article 3.2 of Annex V)?

(6) Have you identified the main Environmental Domain represented by the ASPA/ ASMA (refer to the 'Environmental Domains Analysis for the Antarctic Continent' appended to

Resolution 3 (2008))? Yes/No (If yes, the main Environmental Domain should be noted here).

The above format may be used as a template or as a checklist for the cover sheet, to ensure that all the requested information is provided.

TEMPLATE B: COVER SHEET FOR A WORKING PAPER ON A HISTORIC SITE OR MONUMENT

Please ensure that the following information is provided on the cover sheet:

(1) Has this site or monument been designated by a previous ATCM as a Historic Site or Monument? Yes/No (If yes, please list the relevant Recommendations and Measures).

(2) If the proposal is for a new Historic Site or Monument, please include the following information, worded for inclusion in the Measure:

- (i) Name of the proposed HSM, to be added to the list annexed to Measure 2 (2003);
- (ii) Description of the HSM to be included in the Measure, including sufficient identifying features to enable visitors to the area to recognise it;
- (iii) Coordinates, expressed in degrees, minutes and seconds;
- (iv) Original proposing Party;
- (v) Party undertaking management.

(3) If the proposal is to revise an existing designation of an HSM, please list the relevant past Recommendations and Measures.

The above format may be used as a template or as a checklist for the cover sheet, to ensure that all the requested information is provided

Resolution 6 (2011): Non-native Species

The Representatives,

Recognising that the introduction of non-native species to the Antarctic region, including the movement of species between locations in the region, presents a serious risk to biodiversity and to the intrinsic values of Antarctica

Recalling the valuable discussions held at the 2006 workshop in New Zealand on Non-native Species, and the subsequent agreement by the Committee for Environmental Protection ("CEP") IX that:

- the issue of non-native species in the Antarctic should be given the highest priority consistent with the high environmental standards set out in the Protocol on Environmental Protection to the Antarctic Treaty (the Protocol);
- a set of comprehensive and standardised guidance and / or procedures should be developed, aimed at all operators in the Antarctic;

Recalling also the 2010 Antarctic Treaty Meeting of Experts on Implications of Climate Change for Antarctic Management and Governance, which:

- acknowledged that the greatest effort should be placed on preventing the introduction of non-native species, and on minimising the risk of human assisted introductions;
- recommended that Parties be encouraged to comprehensively and consistently implement management measures to respond to the environmental implications of climate change, particularly measures to avoid introduction and translocation of non-native species, and to report on their effectiveness;

Welcoming the development by the CEP of a Non-native Species Manual that Parties can apply and use, as appropriate, to assist with meeting their obligations under Annex II of the Protocol;

Welcoming also the CEP's advice that it will continue to develop and refine the Manual to reflect improvements in the understanding of non-native species risks and in best practice measures for prevention, surveillance and response;

Recommend that Parties:

1. disseminate and encourage, as appropriate, the use of the Non-native Species Manual annexed to this Resolution; and

2. encourage the Committee for Environmental Protection to continue to develop the Non-native Species Manual with the input of the Scientific Committee on Antarctic Research and the Council of Managers of National Antarctic Programs on scientific and practical matters, respectively.

Resolution 6 (2011) Annex Non-native Species Manual July 2011

1. Introduction

a. Objective

The overall objective for Parties' actions to address risks posed by non native species is:

To conserve Antarctic biodiversity and intrinsic values by preventing the unintended introduction to the Antarctic region of species not native to that region, and the movement of species within Antarctica from one biogeographic zone to any other.

Preventing unintended introductions is an ambitious goal, consistent with the principles of the Protocol. In practice, measures should be put in place to minimise the risk of impacts from non-native species in the Antarctic, taking all possible steps towards prevention.

b. Purpose and background

The purpose of this manual is to provide guidance to Antarctic Treaty Parties in order to meet the objective (above), and minimise the risk of accidental or unintentional introduction of non-native species. This manual includes key guiding principles and links to recommended practical guidelines and resources that operators can apply and use, as appropriate, to assist with meeting their responsibilities under Annex II to the Protocol. The guidelines are recommendatory, not all guidelines will apply to all Parties' operations, and it is a 'living' document that will be updated and added to as new work, research and best practice develops to support further guidance. These measures are recommended as appropriate to assist Parties' efforts to prevent such accidental or unintended introductions and they should not be considered as mandatory.

This work is focussed on the unintended or accidental introduction of non-native species. The introduction of non-native species under permit (in accordance with Article 4 of Annex II to the Environmental Protocol) is not included. However, guidelines for response to unintentional introductions can be applied to responding to any dispersal of species intentionally introduced under permits. Consideration of natural pathways of introduction, human "ecosystems" (e.g. stomach flora) and human to human transfer of pathogens (e.g. illness) are also outside the scope of this work.

There is a limited understanding of the risks related to non-native species introductions and their impacts on the ecosystems. Another objective of this work is to support and encourage further work to fill in the gaps in our knowledge.

c. Context[4]

Biological invasions are amongst the most significant threats to biodiversity worldwide, threatening species survival and being responsible for major changes to ecosystem structure and functioning. Despite Antarctica's isolation and harsh climatic conditions, invasions are now recognised as a serious risk to the region: the ice-free areas of Antarctica and the surrounding Sub-Antarctic Islands support a large proportion of the world's seabird species, and their terrestrial biotas, though species poor, include a high proportion of endemic and well-adapted taxa. Species richness in the Southern Ocean is higher than in the Antarctic terrestrial environment, and there

[4] This section was written with the contribution of several scientists involved in the IPY "Aliens in Antarctica" project (D. Bergstrom, S. Chown, P. Convey, Y. Frenot, N. Gremmen, A. Huiskes, K. Hughes, S. Imura, M. Lebouvier, J. Lee, F. Steenhuisen, M.Tsujimoto, B. van de Vijver and J. Whinam) and adapted according to the ICG Members' comments.

is a high level of endemism. With rapid climate change occurring in some parts of Antarctica, increased numbers of introductions and enhanced success of colonisation by aliens are likely, with consequent increases in impacts on ecosystems, as is already visible in the Sub-Antarctic islands. In addition to introduction of species from outside Antarctica, cross-contamination between ice-free areas including isolated nunataks, or between different marine areas, also threatens the genetic diversity of the biogeographic zones and the risk must be addressed. Further development of human activity in these regions (including science, logistics, tourism, fisheries and recreation) will increase the risk of unintentional introductions of organisms which have a suite of life history traits that benefit them during transport, establishment and expansion phases of invasion, and are likely to be favored by warming conditions.

The vast majority of global alien species do not become invasive, but those that do are one of the main threats to global diversity. It is easier to fight invasiveness if the discovery of the alien species is made early. In addition, the presence of non-native species which are only "transient" or "persistent" but not yet "invasive" is also highly undesirable in terms of protecting the environmental and scientific values of Antarctica, especially as such species may become invasive. Therefore, prevention is the key. If not prevention, then early detection and rapid response will be very important.

The current environmental changes which occur in Antarctica, as in other parts of the world, will be very likely responsible for a natural alteration of the local biodiversity during the next decades or centuries. It is the responsibility of the Parties and others active in the region to minimise the chance of humans being a direct vector for change through introduction of non-native species and/or spread of diseases in the terrestrial and marine ecosystems of the Antarctic Treaty area.

The 2010 Antarctic Treaty Meeting of Experts on Implications of Climate Change for Antarctic Management emphasised the importance of preventing introductions, identifying species and environments at risk and developing measures to manage the issue. The meeting:

- Acknowledged that the greatest effort should be placed on preventing the introduction of non-native species, and on minimising the risk of human assisted introductions through national programmes and tourism activities. It stressed the importance of ensuring comprehensive implementation of new measures to address this risk (Para. 111, Co-chair's report).
- Recommended that the CEP 'consider using established methods of identifying
  (a) Antarctic environments at high risk from establishment by non-natives and
  (b) non-native species that present a high risk of establishment in Antarctica' (Recommendation 22).
- Recommended that Parties be encouraged to comprehensively and consistently implement management measures to respond to the environmental implications of climate change, particularly measures to avoid introduction and translocation of non-native species, and to report on their effectiveness (Recommendation 23).

d. Glossary

Terminology for non-native and invasive species has not been standardised internationally and some of the terms below are defined in the specific context of Antarctica.

• ***Non-native / alien species***: an organism occurring outside its natural past or present range and dispersal potential, whose presence and dispersal in any biogeographic zone of the Antarctic Treaty area is due to unintentional human action.

• ***Introduction / introduced***: direct or indirect movement by human agency, of an organism outside its natural range. This term may be applied to intercontinental or intracontinental movement of species.

• ***Transient***: non-native species that have survived in small populations for a short period in Antarctica, but which have either died out naturally or have been removed by human intervention.

• ***Persistent / established***: non-native species that have survived, established and reproduced for many years in a restricted locality in Antarctica, but which have not expanded their range from a specific location.

• ***Invasive / invasion***: non-native species that are extending their range in the colonised Antarctic region, displacing native species and causing significant harm to biological diversity or ecosystem functioning.

• ***Endemic***: Native species restricted to a specified region or locality in Antarctica.

2. Key Guiding Principles

In order to provide greater focus on the environmental risk related to the unintentional introduction of non-native species in Antarctica and to guide Parties' actions in accordance with the overall objective, 11 key guiding principles are proposed. They are categorised according to the three major components of a non-native species management framework: prevention, monitoring and response.

Prevention

Prevention is the most effective means of minimising the risks associated with the introduction of non-native species and their impacts.

Awareness

1. Raising awareness at multiple levels for different audiences is a critical component of management. All people travelling to the Antarctic should take appropriate steps to prevent the introduction of non-native species.

Operational procedures

2. The risk of non-native species introductions should be identified and addressed in the planning of all activities, including through the environmental impact assessment (EIA) process under Article 8 and Annex I to the Protocol.

3. In the absence of sound scientific baseline data, a precautionary approach should be applied to minimise the risk of human-mediated introduction of non-native species, as well as the risk of intra-regional and local transfer of propagules to pristine regions.

4. Preventive measures are most likely to be implemented and effective if they are:
   - focused on addressing activities and areas of highest risk;
   - developed to suit the particular circumstances of the activity or area in question, and at the appropriate scale;
   - technically and logistically simple;
   - easily applicable;
   - cost effective and not unnecessarily time consuming.

5. Prevention should focus on pre-departure measures within the logistics and supply chain,
   - at the point of origin outside Antarctica (e.g. cargo, personal gear, packages),
   - at gateways to Antarctica (ports, airports),
   - on means of transport (ships, aircraft),
   - at Antarctic stations and field camps that are departure points for activities within the continent.

6. Particularly close attention should be given to ensuring the cleanliness of items previously used in cold climates (e.g. Arctic, Sub-Antarctic, mountainous areas) which may be a means for transporting species 'pre-adapted' to the Antarctic environment.

Monitoring

Monitoring can be passive observation (i.e. waiting for non-native species to appear) or targeted (i.e. an active programme of identifying potential non-native species). Having good baseline data on native fauna and flora is important to support monitoring of non-native species.

7. Regular/periodic monitoring of high-risk sites (e.g. including, but not restricted to the area around research stations) should be encouraged.

8. Preventive measures should be periodically reviewed and revised.

9. Information and best practice related to non-native species should be exchanged between Parties and other stakeholders.

Response

The key factor will be to respond quickly and to assess the feasibility and desirability of eradicating non-native species. If eradication is not a feasible or desirable option then control and/or containment measures need to be considered.

10. To be effective, responses to introductions should be undertaken as a priority, to prevent an increase in the species' distribution range and to make eradication simpler, cost effective and more likely to succeed.

11. Efficacy of control or eradication programmes must be regularly assessed, including follow-up surveys.

3. Guidelines and resources to support prevention of the introduction of non-native species, including the transfer of species between sites in the Antarctic

In line with the objective for Parties' actions to address risks posed by non-natives species and the key guiding principles (sections 1 and 2), the following voluntary guidelines and resources have been developed that operators can apply and use, as appropriate, to assist with meeting their responsibilities under Annex II to the Protocol.

Prevention
1. Develop and deliver awareness programmes for all people travelling to and working in the Antarctic on the risks of inter- and intra-continental movements of non-native species and on the measures required to prevent their introduction, including a standard set of key messages for awareness programmes. Education and training programmes should be tailored to the activities and risks associated with the target audience, including: – managers of national programmes – logisticians /crew /contractors – tour operators – scientists – tourists – staff on fishing vessels – staff at suppliers /vendors /warehouses – other visitors
Guidelines: Checklists for supply chain managers (COMNAP, SCAR 2010). Link: *https://www.comnap.aq/nnsenvironment/* Environmental code of conduct for terrestrial scientific field research in Antarctica (SCAR, 2009). Link: *http://www.ats.aq/documents/ATCM32/ip/ATCM32_ip004_ie.doc* ***Resources:*** Preliminary Results from the International Polar Year Programme: Aliens in Antarctica (SCAR, 2010). Link: *http://www.ats.aq/documents/ATCM33/wp/ATCM33_wp004_ie.doc*
Instructional video on cleaning (Aliens in Antarctica Project, 2010). Link: *http://academic.sun.ac.za/cib/video/Aliens_cleaning_video%202010.wmv* 'Don't pack a pest' pamphlet (United States). Link: *http://www.usap.gov/usapgov/travelAndDeployment/documents/PackaPest_brochure_Final.pdf* 'Don't pack a pest' pamphlet (IAATO). Link: *http://www.iaato.org/do_not_pack_a_pest.html* Antarctic Pre-Arrival Biosecurity Declaration (IAATO) – available from IAATO. Boot washing guidelines (IAATO). Link: *http://www.iaato.org/docs/Boot_Washing07.pdf* 'Know before you go' pamphlet (ASOC). Link: *http://www.asoc.org/storage/documents/tourism/ASOC_Know_Before_You_Go_tourist_ pamphlet _2009_editionv2.pdf*

2. Include consideration of non-native species in future ASPA and ASMA Management Plans. ***Guidelines:*** Guide for the Preparation of Management Plans. Link: *http://www.ats.aq/documents/ATCM34/att/ATCM34_att004_e.doc*
3. Manage ballast water in accordance with the Practical Guidelines for Ballast Water Exchange in the Antarctic Treaty Area Resolution 3 (2006). ***Guidelines:*** Practical Guidelines for Ballast Water Exchange in the Antarctic Treaty Area Resolution 3 (2006). Link: *http://www.ats.aq/documents/recatt/Att345_e.pdf*
4. Clean vehicles in order to prevent transfer of non-native species into and around the Antarctic. ***Guidelines:*** Procedures for vehicle cleaning to prevent transfer of non-native species into and around Antarctica (United Kingdom 2010). Link: *http://www.ats.aq/documents/ATCM33/wp/ATCM33_wp008_e.doc*

Monitoring
5. Record non-native species introductions and submit records to the Aliens database managed by the Australian Antarctic Data Centre, as agreed by the CEP. ***Data base for entering records:*** Link: *http://data.aad.gov.au/aadc/biodiversity* ***Resource:*** Colonisation status of known non-native species in the Antarctic terrestrial environment (United Kingdom, 2010). Link: *http://www.ats.aq/documents/ATCM33/ip/ATCM33_ip042_e.doc*

Response
6. Develop or employ assessment metrics to help determine whether a newly discovered species is likely to have arrived through natural colonisation pathways or through human means. ***Guidelines:*** Guidance for visitors and environmental managers following the discovery of a suspected non-native species in the terrestrial and freshwater Antarctic environment (United Kingdom, 2010). Links: *http://www.ats.aq/documents/ATCM33/att/ATCM33_att010_e.doc http://www.ats.aq/documents/ATCM33/att/ATCM33_att011_e.doc* Suggested framework and considerations for scientists attempting to determine the colonisation status of newly discovered terrestrial or freshwater species within the Antarctic Treaty Area (United Kingdom, 2010). Link: *http://www.ats.aq/documents/ATCM33/ip/ATCM33_ip044_e.doc*

Appendix Guidelines and resources requiring further attention or development

In addition to the measures, guidelines and resources that have been developed (section 3) the following guidelines have been identified as appropriate for assisting Parties' work on non-native species. The use of these and the development of more detailed guidance under these items for inclusion in the Manual are encouraged.

Prevention
1. Revise EIA guidelines to include a special section on non-native species.
2. Improve understanding of risks and develop more specific guidelines for preventing introductions in the Antarctic marine environment.
3. Reduce non-native species risks for Antarctica, including identifying regions / activities / vectors / pathways of highest risk for introduction of non-native species, providing guidance on what will constitute a gateway between Antarctic biogeographical zones (according to organism types), and developing practical measures to address risks associated with the transport of personnel and equipment between locations in Antarctica. More generally, encourage Parties to develop baseline studies.

Resources: Current knowledge for reducing risks posed by terrestrial non-native species: towards an evidence-based approach (SCAR, Australia, 2010). Link: *http://www.ats.aq/documents/ATCM33/wp/ATCM33_wp006_e.doc* A framework for analysing and managing non-native species risks in Antarctica (New Zealand, 2009). Link: *http://www.ats.aq/documents/ATCM32/ip/ATCM32_ip036_e.doc*
4. Provide a list, with suitable descriptions, of the potential non-native species based on the experience of the Sub-Antarctic Islands (or other relevant environments) and the biological characteristics and adaptability of the "effective" colonisers. *Resources:* Information paper: Colonisation status of known non-native species in the Antarctic terrestrial environment (United Kingdom, 2010). Link: *http://www.ats.aq/documents/ATCM33/ip/ATCM33_ip042_e.doc*
5. Fresh foods and food wastes are strictly managed to prevent them entering the environment (secured from wildlife and removed from the Antarctic or incinerated)
6. Unless new, clothing supplied for use in Antarctica is cleaned using normal laundry procedures prior to sending to Antarctica. Pre-worn footwear is cleaned thoroughly before arrival in Antarctica or between sites in Antarctica. Specific cleaning requirements may be required if there is reason to think that people, clothing, equipment or vehicles have been in contact with diseased animals, disease causing agents or have been in an area of known disease risk.
7. Equip research stations with the means to clean and maintain clothing and equipment that is to be used in the field, particularly in distinct or multiple locations.
8. Check cargo to ensure it is clean of visible contamination before loading on board the aircraft or vessels.
9. Confirm vessels as being rodent-free before departure to the Antarctic.
10. Pack, store and load cargo in an area with a clean, sealed surface (e.g. bitumen, concrete free from weedy plants, soil, rodents and areas of waste ground). These areas should be regularly cleaned and inspected.
11. Containers, including ISO containers and boxes/crates, are not moved from one Antarctic site to another, except if cleaned before arrival at the new location.
12. Intercontinental aircraft are checked and treated as necessary, where applicable, to ensure they are insect free before departure to the Antarctic.
13. Preventive measures to diminish risks of introduction of diseases to Antarctic wildlife could include, for example, specific guidance for handling field and station waste to minimise introduction of non-native species.
Monitoring
14. Develop generally applicable monitoring guidelines, based on several workshops held on monitoring in the 1990s and in 2005, acknowledging that more detailed or site-specific monitoring may be required for particular locations; identify who will undertake the monitoring. A status report on established monitoring to be submitted regularly to the CEP.
Resources: Information paper: Summary of Environmental Monitoring and Reporting Discussions (Australia, 2008). Link: *http://www.ats.aq/documents/ATCM31/ip/ATCM31_ip007_e.doc*
15. Baseline biodiversity surveys and compilation of existing biodiversity data (terrestrial - including aquatic and marine) should be carried out to assist with identifying scale and scope of current and future introductions. Because it is not practical to conduct surveys everywhere, priority should be given to sites of high human activity (stations, most frequently visited scientific field sites and tourist sites), high value and/or high sensitivity. *Resources:* German experience with carrying out a terrestrial survey on soil fauna organisms on highly frequented visitor sites (German IP to CEP XIV). Existing methods from other environments, e.g. port surveys.

Response
16. Expert advice should be sought as quickly as possible when a non-native species (including diseases of wildlife) is detected. A network of experts (taxonomists and specialists of eradication or control of non-native species, should be identified, including a list of names, details and e-mail available on the ATS website) in order to react as quickly as possible when a non-native species or disease event is discovered. This network should primarily 1) provide advice and 2) facilitate action by Parties.
17. Consider a 'rapid response guideline', including possible guide with practical eradication tools / means. *Resources:* Eradication of a vascular plant species recently introduced to Whaler's Bay, Deception Island (United Kingdom, Spain 2010). Link: *http://www.ats.aq/documents/ATCM33/ip/ATCM33_ip043_e.doc* Mass animal mortality event response plan (British Antarctic Survey) – Available from BAS. Unusual mortality response plan (Australia). Link: referred to in: *http://www.ats.aq/documents/ATCM27/ip/ATCM27_ip071_e.doc* Procedures for reporting a high mortality event (IAATO) – Available from IAATO.
18. Develop (or formally adopt existing) guidance for responses to disease events. *Resources:* Report on the open-ended intersessional contact group on diseases of Antarctic wildlife. Report 2 – Practical measures to diminish risk (draft) (Australia, 2001). Link: *http://www.ats.aq/documents/ATCM24/wp/ATCM24_wp011_e.pdf* Health of Antarctic Wildlife: A Challenge for Science and Policy (Kerry and Riddle, 2009).

Resolution 6 (2012): Antarctic Conservation Biogeographic Regions

The Representatives,

Recalling Article 3 of Annex V to the Protocol on Environmental Protection to the Antarctic Treaty (the Protocol) which provides for the designation of Antarctic Specially Protected Areas;

Recalling further that Article 3(2) of Annex V states that Parties shall seek to identify such areas within a systematic environmental-geographic framework;

Recalling also that Resolution 3 (2008) recommended that the 'Environmental Domains Analysis of the Antarctic Continent' annexed to that Resolution be used consistently and in conjunction with other tools agreed within the Antarctic Treaty system as a dynamic model for the identification of areas that could be designated as Antarctic Specially Protected Areas within the systematic environmental-geographical framework referred to in Article 3(2) of Annex V of the Protocol;

Welcoming the classification of the ice-free areas of the Antarctic continent and close lying islands within the Antarctic Treaty area into 15 biologically distinct Antarctic Conservation Biogeographic Regions, based on analyses of spatially explicit biodiversity data available from the Scientific Committee on Antarctic Research (SCAR) Biodiversity Database;

Recommend that:

the Antarctic Conservation Biogeographic Regions annexed to this Resolution be used in conjunction with the Environmental Domains Analysis and other tools agreed within the Antarctic Treaty system to support activities relevant to the interests of the Parties, including as a dynamic model for the identification of areas that could be designated as Antarctic Specially Protected Areas within the systematic environmental-geographic framework referred to in Article 3(2) of Annex V to the Environmental Protocol.

Resolution 6 (2012) Annex: Antarctic Conservation Biogeographic Regions

The use of quantitative analyses to combine spatially explicit Antarctic terrestrial biodiversity data with other relevant spatial frameworks (a grid of 200 km x 200 km squares, the nine ice-free domains identified in the Environmental Domains Analysis for the Antarctic continent, and 22 bioregions identified by the SCAR Regional Sensitivity to Climate Change (RiSCC)

Programme) has identified 15 biologically distinct ice-free regions encompassing the Antarctic continent and close-lying islands within the Antarctic Treaty area (see Table 1). A full description of the methods employed is presented in Terauds *et al.* (2012). The Antarctic Conservation Biogeographic Regions illustrated in Figure 1 represent the best classification of Antarctic terrestrial biodiversity based on data currently available from the SCAR Biodiversity Database.

The spatial data layer representing the regions is publicly available for download from the Australian Antarctic Data Centre: *http://data.aad.gov.au/aadc/portal/download_file.cfm?_le_id=3420.*

Reference

Terauds, A., Chown, S., Morgan, F., Peat, H., Watts, D., Keys, H., Convey, P. & Bergstrom, D. (2012) Conservation biogeography of the Antarctic. *Diversity and Distributions*, 22 May 2012, DOI: 10.1111/j.1472-4642.2012.00925.x.

Table 1 – Descriptions of Antarctic Conservation Biogeographic Regions

Region	Name	Area (km^2)
1	North-east Antarctic Peninsula	1142
2	South Orkney Islands	148
3	North-west Antarctic Peninsula	5081
4	Central south Antarctic Peninsula	4959
5	Enderby Land	2152
6	Dronning Maud Land	5502
7	East Antarctica	1360
8	North Victoria Land	9522
9	South Victoria Land	10368
10	Transantarctic Mountains	19347
11	Ellsworth Mountains	2965
12	Marie Byrd Land	1158
13	Adelie Land	178
14	Ellsworth Land	220
15	South Antarctic Peninsula	2990

Omitted: Figure 1 – Map of Antarctica showing the 15 Antarctic Conservation Biogeographic Regions

Resolution 2 (2013): Antarctic Clean-Up Manual

The Representatives,

Reaffirming the commitment of Parties to the Protocol on Environmental Protection to the Antarctic Treaty (the Protocol) to reduce as far as practicable the amount of waste produced or disposed of in the Antarctic Treaty area, so as to minimise impact on the Antarctic environment and to minimise interference with the natural values of Antarctica, with scientific research and with other uses of Antarctica that are consistent with the Antarctic Treaty;

Recalling the requirement under Article 1(5) of Annex III to the Protocol that past and present waste disposal sites on land and abandoned work sites of Antarctic activities shall be cleaned up by the generator of such wastes and the user of such sites, provided that such actions shall not require the removal of any structure designated as a historic site or monument, or the removal of any structure or waste material in circumstances where the removal by any practical option would result in greater adverse environmental impact than leaving the structure or waste material in its existing location;

Recalling also the 2010 Antarctic Treaty Meeting of Experts on Implications of Climate Change for Antarctic Management and Governance, which noted that climate changes create the potential for localised release of contamination from past waste disposal sites and abandoned work sites through increased melting;

Noting the actions taken by Parties since the entry into force of the Protocol to effectively handle waste and to clean up past waste disposal sites on land and abandoned work sites;

Noting also the efforts of the Council of Managers of National Antarctic Programs to develop and formulate best practice procedures for waste management, including through the workshop on Waste Management in Antarctica held in Hobart in 2006;

Welcoming the development by the Committee for Environmental Protection of a Clean-Up Manual that Parties can apply and use, as appropriate, to assist with meeting their obligations under Article 1(5) of Annex III to the Protocol;

Recommend that Parties:

1. disseminate and encourage the use of the Clean-Up Manual annexed to this Resolution, as appropriate, to assist with addressing their obligations under Article 1(5) of Annex III to the Protocol on Environmental Protection to the Antarctic Treaty; and
2. encourage the Committee for Environmental Protection to continue to develop the Clean-Up Manual with the input of the Scientific Committee on Antarctic Research and the Council of Managers of National Antarctic Programs on scientific and practical matters, respectively.

Resolution 2 (2013) Annex: Committee for Environmental Protection Clean-Up Manual

1. Introduction

a) Background

In 1975 the Antarctic Treaty Parties adopted Recommendation VIII-11, which contained the first agreed guidance for the appropriate management and disposal of waste generated by expeditions and stations, with a view to minimising impacts on the Antarctic environment. As awareness of the potential environmental impacts of the disposal of waste in the Antarctic region increased, in parallel with improvements in logistics and technology, the Parties identified a need for improved on-site treatment of wastes and for the removal of some wastes from the Antarctic Treaty area.

Through Recommendation XV-3 (1989) the Parties adopted more stringent waste disposal and management practices, based on recommendations from a SCAR Panel of Experts on Waste Disposal in the Antarctic, with the aim of minimising impact on the Antarctic environment and minimising interference with scientific research or other legitimate uses of the Antarctic. These practices not only addressed requirements for the management of wastes associated with present and future activities, but also called for programs to clean up existing waste disposal sites and abandoned work sites, and for an inventory of locations of past activities.

Many elements of Recommendation XV-3 are closely reflected in the current provisions for waste disposal and management, contained in Annex III to the Environmental Protocol, on Waste Disposal and Waste Management. The Environmental Protocol as a whole sets the context in which the provisions of Annex III should be implemented.

Among other requirements Annex III provides, in Article 1.5, that:

"Past and present waste disposal sites on land and abandoned work sites of Antarctic activities shall be cleaned up by the generator of such wastes and the user of such sites. This obligation shall not be interpreted as requiring:

(a) the removal of any structure designated as a historic site or monument; or

(b) the removal of any structure or waste material in circumstances where the removal by any practical option would result in greater adverse environmental impact than leaving the structure or waste material in its existing location."

Prior to these instruments, waste management at Antarctic facilities often involved the open burning and disposal of waste in tips. Similarly, it was commonplace to abandon disused facilities and leave them to deteriorate. Many past waste disposal sites and abandoned work sites require ongoing management today. Such sites are frequently characterised by a mix of physical debris (e.g. building materials, machinery, vehicles, general rubbish) plus chemical contaminants, some of which may be in containers (which are subject to deterioration) and some of which may have been released into the environment. In some instances waste disposal sites extend into the near shore marine environment. Seepage and runoff from abandoned sites, and from more recent spill sites, can result in contamination spreading to other parts of the environment. In general such contaminants degrade very slowly in Antarctic conditions.

Based on extrapolation from a few well documented sites, it has been estimated that the volume of abandoned, unconfined tip materials in Antarctica may be greater than 1 million m^3 and that the volume of petroleum-contaminated sediment may be similar (Snape and others, 2001). Although this is a relatively small volume compared to the situation in other parts of the world, the significance of the associated environmental impacts is magnified due to the fact that many Antarctic contaminated sites are located in the relatively rare coastal ice-free areas that provide habitat for most of the terrestrial flora and fauna.

b) Overall Clean-Up objective

The overall objective for Parties' actions to address environmental risks posed by past waste disposal sites on land, abandoned works sites of Antarctic activities, and sites contaminated by spills of fuel or other hazardous substances is:

To minimise adverse impact on the Antarctic environment, and to minimise interference with the natural values of Antarctica, with scientific research and with other uses of Antarctica which are consistent with the Antarctic Treaty, by cleaning up past waste disposal sites on land, abandoned work sites of Antarctic activities, and sites contaminated by spills of fuel or other hazardous substances. Such clean-up actions shall not require the removal of any: structure designated as a historic site or monument: pre-1958 historic artefacts / sites subject to the provisions of Resolution 5 (2001); or structure or waste material in circumstances where the removal by any practical option would result in greater adverse environmental impact than leaving the structure or waste material in its existing location.

This objective reflects requirements outlined in Annex III (Waste Disposal and Waste Management) to the Protocol on Environmental Protection to the Antarctic Treaty (the Environmental Protocol).

c) Purpose of the Clean-Up Manual

The purpose of this manual is to provide guidance to Antarctic Treaty Parties in order to meet the objective above. The manual includes key guiding principles and links to practical guidelines and resources that operators can apply and use, as appropriate, to assist with addressing the requirements of the Environmental Protocol, in particular Annex III. The practical guidelines are recommendatory and not all guidelines will be appropriate to all operations, or to all sites. The manual is intended to be updated and added to as new work, research and best practice emerges.

The guidance provided here is focussed on the repair and remediation of past waste disposal sites on land, abandoned work sites of Antarctic activities, and sites contaminated by spills of fuel or other hazardous substances. Practical guidance for preventing, monitoring and responding to the introduction of non-native species is presented in the Committee for Environmental Protection (CEP) Non-Native Species Manual.

The Council of Managers of National Antarctic Programs (COMNAP) has developed a Fuel Manual, which outlines important measures for spill prevention and containment. This Clean-Up Manual complements the COMNAP Fuel Manual by providing guidance on appropriate clean-up and restoration actions, which the COMNAP Fuel Manual indicates should be addressed as part of the Operational Plans to be prepared for individual facilities or relevant geographic areas.

In practice, it will not be practicable to clean up all past waste disposal sites on land, abandoned work sites of Antarctic activities and contaminated sites immediately or concurrently, so the manual also aims to provide guidance on identifying priorities for clean-up activities, and on remediating or removing contaminated materials to a level where ongoing environmental risks are mitigated.

Reasons to undertake timely clean-up action, in accordance with the provisions of the Environmental Protocol, include:

- many abandoned waste disposal sites and abandoned work sites contain potential contaminants in containers (e.g. drums filled with fuel, oil, chemicals), and there is a limited time before they deteriorate, causing contamination and making clean-up much more difficult;
- as noted by the 2010 Antarctic Treaty Meeting of Experts on Climate Change and Implications for Antarctic Management and Governance, climate changes could accelerate localised release of contamination from past waste disposal sites and abandoned work sites through increased melting;
- the harmful effects of chemical contaminants on the environment and ecosystem can increase with increasing exposure time, and increase the chance of cumulative impacts from exposure to other environmental stressors;
- dispersion processes (e.g. entrainment with melt water) can cause the total area contaminated to increase with time, in some cases resulting in contamination of the marine environment;
- some sites may otherwise be lost to the ocean or covered by ice/snow where they may continue to have detrimental impacts but will be much more difficult and costly to manage; and
- possible risks to human health (e.g. hazardous chemicals or other substances, such as asbestos).

d) Glossary

The practice of environmental clean-up uses some technical terminology. Additionally, some words that are commonly used in everyday language have a specific meaning when used in the context of environmental clean-up. To help ensure a common understanding, this glossary will be expanded as part of the development of the manual. Definitions generally applicable to assessing, mitigating and monitoring the environmental impacts of activities are presented in the *Guidelines for Environmental Impact Assessment in Antarctica.*

CLEAN-UP: the removal and/or on-site remediation of past waste disposal sites on land, abandoned work sites and sites contaminated by spills of fuel or other hazardous substances.

2. Key Guiding Principles

Information management

Record keeping is important throughout the clean-up process and should commence well before any clean-up activities occur on site.

1. Record keeping should be designed so that information on individual sites is easily accessible and so that information on actions and events at each site can be added over time.

2. The record of information should be kept up to date and should include the precise location and status of contaminated sites, the clean-up actions that have occurred, the reasons why key decisions were made and the lessons learned.

3. The type of information to be recorded should reflect its intended use, including:

- site assessment and prioritisation;
- supporting operational decisions;
- ensuring compliance to environmental impact assessment / permit conditions;
- monitoring and evaluating the effectiveness of a clean–up process; and
- facilitating the exchange of information between Parties and with other stakeholders.

4. Record keeping should be designed so that it can also be used as the foundation for the Antarctic-wide inventory of locations of past activity, in accordance with Article 8.3 of Annex III.

Site assessment / characterisation

An assessment of the features of the site that will influence how contaminants behave, and the environmental values that may be impacted, should be undertaken before considering how best to clean-up a site.

5. The site assessment should consider:

- the nature and extent of physical debris and/or chemical contamination, and the landscape (e.g. geology, geomorphology, glaciology) of the site and surrounding area, with particular emphasis on slope, aspect and water flows;
- potential challenges for clean-up actions presented by the location, landscape, and surrounding area (e.g. accessibility and susceptibility to damage from machinery or recovery equipment);
- the environmental values of the site and surrounding area, including the range of values protected under the Environmental Protocol; and
- likely changes at the site including deterioration of containers (such as rusting fuel drums), changes in chemical compositions (e.g. through natural weathering processes) and transport of the contaminants (e.g. from wind or water flow).

6. All available information should be used to assess the current impact and potential future threat to the environment from the contamination.

Environmental risk assessment

Environmental risk assessment is the process of determining the inherent risks posed by the site to the environmental values.

7. The environmental risk assessment should use the information gained during site assessment, including uncertainties, and should inform the decisions taken throughout the clean-up process.

8. The environmental risk assessment should assist to prioritise which site(s) should be cleaned up first, to decide among the various clean-up options (see below) and to set realistic targets for clean-up (see below).

9. The environmental risk assessment should be regularly reviewed and confirmed or modified during the clean-up process.

Environmental quality targets for clean-up

In some cases, the complete removal of all traces of contamination would be impractical, or would result in greater adverse environmental impact. Environmental quality targets for clean-up are the concentration of contaminant that may remain within the environment without creating unacceptable impacts on the environmental values of the site.

10. Environmental quality targets for clean-up should be determined on a site specific basis taking into account the characteristics of the site and the environmental values present.

11. From the viewpoint of biodiversity conservation, environmental quality targets should be based on the sensitivity of relevant species to the specific contaminants (such as from ecotoxicology studies).

12. Environmental quality targets are just one factor when considering the options for clean-up (see below).

Consideration of clean-up options

At the highest level the range of possible clean-up options for sites contaminated by fuel and other hazardous substances may include: do nothing (which may result in natural attenuation); containment on site to reduce dispersion; *in situ* remediation to enhance attenuation processes; removal from the site with treatment in Antarctica (clean-up *ex situ*); and removal from the Antarctic Treaty area. Within each of these options there are further choices of possible clean-up actions (see below).

13. A risk assessment should be undertaken for all clean-up options being considered, with a focus on ensuring that greater adverse environmental impact does not occur as a result of the clean-up process.

14. Options analysis should consider the environmental quality targets and risk of additional adverse impacts arising from the clean-up activity. Given the practical realities of operating in Antarctica, other relevant considerations are likely to include feasibility, available technology, practicality, safety of personnel, and cost-effectiveness.

Clean-up actions

Clean-up actions are the operational activities that happen at the site and / or elsewhere on material that has been removed from the site.

15. Wherever appropriate, plans and environmental impact assessments for new activities in Antarctica should consider the nature and scale of any clean-up activity which will be subsequently required. Actions to clean-up sites of past activities should also be subject to environmental impact assessment in accordance with the provisions of the Protocol.

16. Clean-up techniques developed for contaminated sites in other regions of the world may have some value in Antarctica but are likely to require modification to make them suitable for local conditions.

17. All clean-up options, including the 'do nothing' option, may require some commitment of resources, such as monitoring (see below) to confirm the environmental risk assessment.

18. In some cases containment on site to reduce dispersion will be identified as the best means of protecting environmental values. Techniques for containment should be designed for:

(a) the types of contaminants present (the principal distinction being organic (e.g. fuel) or inorganic (e.g. metals from waste dumps); and

(b) the characteristics of the environment (principally the freeze/thaw process and the highly seasonal presence of free water).

19. In situ remediation to enhance attenuation processes (e.g. enhanced biodegradation by the adding of nutrients, increasing temperature and aerating soil) can be cost-effective and is likely to be less disturbing to the environment than options requiring extraction, but techniques must be appropriate for the types of contaminants and the characteristics of the environment (as above).

20. Removal from the site with treatment in Antarctica may create more disturbance at the site than in situ remediation but has the potential advantage of relocation to a site that is more easily managed such as close to a station. The receiving site should be controlled to ensure the safety of personnel and to prevent further environmental impact (e.g. clearly identifiable and known to station personnel, contained to prevent dispersal of contaminants).

21. In some cases the removal of contaminated materials from the Antarctic Treaty area may be the most appropriate option for addressing the requirements of the Environmental Protocol. As above, this may create more disturbance than in situ remediation and, in the case of ice-free sites, also has the disadvantage of removing rare soil from Antarctica. This option is also likely to be the most costly, is dependent on the availability and capacity of shipping, and may raise biosecurity or contaminated material concerns for the receiving country.

22. Monitoring and evaluation (see below) should be designed as an integral part of the clean-up process.

23. Clean-up should be considered complete only once the environmental quality targets have been met.

Monitoring and evaluation

Monitoring and evaluation are both used to characterise and record the quality of the environment but have specific and distinct roles before, during and/or after clean-up.

24. Monitoring should be undertaken to identify and provide early warning of any adverse effects of the clean-up activity that may require modifications of procedures, and to assess and verify predictions identified in the environmental impact assessment.

25. Evaluation refers to determining whether the clean-up activity has achieved the desired environmental quality targets.

26. Both monitoring and evaluation should focus on the vulnerable environmental values of the site and take into account the final use of the data.

3. Guidelines and resources to support clean-up

As the manual is developed, this section will be expanded to contain voluntary guidelines and resources to assist Parties to address their clean-up obligations under Annex III to the Protocol. Examples of desirable materials include:

- a standard approach and/or form for record keeping and reporting on clean-up activities;
- checklists and/or matrices for site assessment and environmental risk assessment;
- scientific information to inform the setting of appropriate environmental quality targets;
- techniques for preventing mobilisation of contaminants such as melt water diversion and containment barriers;
- techniques for in-situ and ex-situ remediation of sites contaminated by fuel spills or other hazardous substances;
- techniques for the clean-up of buildings or other structures at abandoned work sites;
- guidance for planning and undertaking monitoring and evaluation.

References

This list of references will be expanded to list further papers as the manual is developed.

ATCM XXXV/IP6 (Australia). 2012. Topic Summary: CEP Discussions on Clean-Up (contains links to electronic versions of papers on the subject of clean-up submitted to the Committee for Environmental Protection between 1998 and 2011)

Aronson, R.B., Thatje, S., McClintock, J.B., & Hughes, K.A. 2011. Anthropogenic impacts on marine ecosystems in Antarctica. *Annals of the New York Academy of Sciences*, 1223, 82–107.

Filler, D., Snape, I., & Barnes, D., Eds. 2008. *Bioremediation of Petroleum Hydrocarbons in Cold Regions*. Cambridge. 288 pp.

Poland, J.S., Riddle, M.J., & Zeeb, B.A. 2003. Contaminants in the Arctic and the Antarctic: a comparison of sources, impacts, and remediation options. *Polar Record*, 39(211), 369–383.

Riddle, M. 2000. Scientific studies of Antarctic life are still the essential basis for long-term conservation measures. In Davison, W., Howard-Williams, C., & Broady, P. Eds. *Antarctic Ecosystems: Models for Wider Ecological Understanding*. New Zealand Natural Sciences, Canterbury University, 497–302.

Snape, I., Riddle, M.J., Stark, S., Cole, C.M., King, C.K., Dubesque, S., & Gore, D.B. 2001. Management and Remediation of contaminated sites at Casey Station, Antarctica. *Polar Record*, 37(202), 199–214.

Stark, J.S., Snape, I., & Riddle, M.J. 2006. Abandoned Antarctic waste disposal sites: Monitoring remediation outcomes and limitations at Casey Station. *Ecological Management and Restoration*, 7(1), 21–31.

Tin, T., Fleming, Z.L., Hughes, K.A., Ainley, D.G., Convey, P., Moreno, C.A., Pfeiffer, S., Scott, J., & Snape, I. 2009. Impacts of local human activities on the Antarctic environment. *Antarctic Science*, 21, 3–33.

Resolution 1 (2014): Fuel Storage and Handling

The Representatives,

Recalling Article 3 of the Protocol on Environmental Protection to the Antarctic Treaty ("the Protocol") which requires that activities in the Antarctic Treaty area shall be planned and conducted so as to limit adverse impacts on the Antarctic environment;

Noting the provisions of Article 15 of the Protocol;

Conscious that implementation of the provisions requires actions by the Parties;

Recognising that the Council of Managers of National Antarctic Programs ("COMNAP") and the International Association of Antarctica Tour Operators ("IAATO") have undertaken initiatives on fuel storage and handling, and oil spill contingency planning;

Recalling Resolution 6 (1998) and Resolution 3 (2005);

Recommend that:

1. their Governments continue to implement measures for fuel spill prevention, oil spill contingency planning and response, and reporting, as incorporated in the COMNAP Fuel Manual guidelines. In particular:

a. that their Governments either replace bulk fuel facilities currently lacking secondary containment with double-skinned tanks or provide them with adequate bunding, and have adequate oil spill contingency plans in place;
b. that their Governments introduce and maintain oil spill contingency plans based on the COMNAP Fuel Manual guidelines and that to the extent possible they carry out regular contingency exercises, both theoretical and practical on land and at sea, to test and thereby refine their contingency plans, and report on results of the exercises to the Antarctic Treaty Consultative Meeting ("ATCM"); and

2. COMNAP be requested to keep under periodic review, and revise, as appropriate, the Fuel Manual guidelines.

Resolution 2 (2014): Cooperation, Facilitation, and Exchange of Meteorological and Related Oceanographic and Cryospheric Environmental Information

The Representatives,

Recognising the continuing importance of Antarctic meteorological data for support of operations within Antarctica and for weather forecasting and research, especially global climate research;

Desiring that risks to people and infrastructure in Antarctica from weather, climate, and weather-related oceanographic and cryospheric effects be minimised, and noting that mitigation strategies for such risks are most effective when informed by data;

Recognising the strong tradition of cooperation among the Antarctic Treaty Parties in the development and sharing of meteorological and related oceanographic and cryospheric environmental information;

Welcoming the strong cooperation between the Antarctic Treaty Consultative Meeting (ATCM) and the World Meteorological Organization (WMO);

Welcoming also the work of the WMO Executive Council Panel of Experts on Polar Observations, Research and Services, including but not limited to meteorological and marine (wave and sea ice) forecasting services over a range of time scales (such as described in WMO's Global Integrated Polar Prediction System (GIPPS) initiative) and the continued development and support of systems such as the Antarctic Observing Network (AntON), Global Cryosphere Watch (GCW), and the International Programme for Antarctic Buoys (IPAB);

Recalling Recommendation V-2 (1968), Recommendation VI-1 (1970), Recommendation VI-3 (1970), Recommendation X-3 (1979), Recommendation XII-1 (1983), Recommendation XIV-7 (1987), Recommendation XIV-10 (1987) and Recommendation XV-18 (1989), which together outlined a broad international effort at mitigating weather, climate, and marine-based (wave and sea ice) risks to Antarctic personnel and infrastructure;

Recommend that the Parties:

1. continue their cooperation to improve the system for the collection and timely distribution of Antarctic meteorological data with particular regard to increasing efficiency, reliability and economy of effort, and taking into account opportunities offered by new technology;
2. facilitate, where feasible, the development and use of systems and infrastructure to support robust Antarctic-related meteorological and marine (wave and sea ice) observations, research, and services; and
3. support and encourage the WMO in developing its service strategy in wide consultation with other relevant service developers and with service users.

Resolution 3 (2014): Supporting the Polar Code

The Representatives,

Welcoming the development of the draft International Code for Ships Operating in Polar Waters ("Polar Code") by the International Maritime Organization ("IMO");

Recognising that the IMO is the competent organisation to deal with shipping regulations;

Noting the progress of the important work on the Polar Code and the need for its completion to remain a priority;

Recalling Resolution 3 (1998) and Resolution 8 (2009);

Recognising the benefits of having a Polar Code pertaining to ship safety and environmental protection;

Recommend that their Governments:

1. encourage IMO Member States to continue as a matter of priority the important work of finalising the Polar Code pertaining to ship safety and environmental protection; and

2. further encourage IMO Member States to consider additional safety and environmental protection matters in a second step, as to be determined by the IMO.

Resolution 4 (2014): Site Guidelines for visitors

The Representatives,

Recalling Resolution 5 (2005), Resolution 2 (2006), Resolution 1 (2007), Resolution 2 (2008), Resolution 4 (2009), Resolution 1 (2010), Resolution 4 (2011), Resolution 2 (2012) and Resolution 3 (2013), which adopted lists of sites subject to Site Guidelines for visitors ("Site Guidelines");

Recalling Resolution 3 (2013), which provided that any proposed amendment to existing Site Guidelines be discussed by the Committee for Environmental Protection ("CEP"), which should advise the Antarctic Treaty Consultative Meeting ("ATCM") accordingly, and that if such advice is endorsed by the ATCM, the Secretariat of the Antarctic Treaty ("the Secretariat") should make the necessary changes to the texts of Site Guidelines on its website;

Believing that Site Guidelines enhance the provisions set out in Recommendation XVIII-1 (1994) (Guidance for those organising and conducting tourism and non-Governmental activities in the Antarctic);

Confirming that the term "visitors" does not include scientists conducting research within such sites, or individuals engaged in official governmental activities;

Noting that the Site Guidelines have been developed based on the current levels and types of visits at each specific site, and aware that the Site Guidelines would require review if there were any significant changes to the levels or types of visits to a site;

Believing that the Site Guidelines for each site must be reviewed and revised promptly in response to changes in the levels and types of visits, or in response to any demonstrable or likely environmental impacts;

Desiring to keep existing Site Guidelines up to date;

Recommend that:

1. the Site Guidelines for Horseshoe Island, Antarctic Peninsula, and Mawson's Huts and Cape Denison, East Antarctica be replaced by the modified Site Guidelines;

2. the Secretariat place the full list of sites subject to Site Guidelines, annexed to this Resolution, and the modified Site Guidelines, as adopted by the ATCM, on its website;

3. their Governments urge all potential visitors to ensure that they are fully conversant with and adhere to the advice in the relevant Site Guidelines, as published by the Secretariat;

4. any proposed amendment to existing Site Guidelines be discussed by the CEP, which should advise the ATCM accordingly, and that if such advice is endorsed by the ATCM, the Secretariat

should make the necessary changes to the texts of Site Guidelines on the website; and

5. the Secretariat post the text of Resolution 3 (2013) on its website in such a way that makes clear that it is no longer current.

Annex: List of sites subject to Site Guidelines

Site Guidelines	**First Adopted**	**Latest Version**
1. Penguin Island (Lat. 62° 06' S, Long. 57° 54' W)	2005	2005
2. Barrientos Island - Aitcho Islands (Lat. 62° 24' S, Long. 59° 47' W)	2005	2013
3. Cuverville Island (Lat. 64° 41' S, Long. 62° 38' W)	2005	2013
4. Jougla Point (Lat 64° 49' S, Long 63° 30' W)	2005	2013
5. Goudier Island, Port Lockroy (Lat 64° 49' S, Long 63° 29' W);	2006	2006
6. Hannah Point (Lat. 62° 39' S, Long. 60° 37' W)	2006	2013
7. Neko Harbour (Lat. 64° 50' S, Long. 62° 33' W)	2006	2013
8. Paulet Island (Lat. 63° 35' S, Long. 55° 47' W)	2006	2006
9. Petermann Island (Lat. 65° 10' S, Long. 64° 10' W)	2006	2013
10. Pleneau Island (Lat. 65° 06' S, Long. 64° 04' W)	2006	2013
11. Turret Point (Lat. 62° 05' S, Long. 57° 55' W)	2006	2006
12. Yankee Harbour (Lat. 62° 32' S, Long. 59° 47' W)	2006	2013
13. Brown Bluff, Tabarin Peninsula (Lat. 63° 32' S, Long. 56° 55' W)	2007	2013
14. Snow Hill (Lat. 64° 22' S, Long. 56° 59' W)	2007	2007
15. Shingle Cove, Coronation Island (Lat. 60° 39' S, Long. 45° 34' W)	2008	2008
16. Devil Island, Vega Island (Lat. 63° 48' S, Long. 57° 16.7' W)	2008	2008
17. Whalers Bay, Deception Island, South Shetland Islands (Lat. 62° 59' S, Long. 60° 34' W)	2008	2011
18. Half Moon Island, South Shetland Islands (Lat. 60° 36' S, Long. 59° 55' W)	2008	2013
19. Baily Head, Deception Island, South Shetland Islands (Lat. 62° 58' S, Long. 60° 30' W)	2009	2013
20. Telefon Bay, Deception Island, South Shetland Islands (Lat. 62° 55' S, Long. 60° 40' W)	2009	2009
21. Cape Royds, Ross Island (Lat. 77° 33' 10.7" S, Long. 166° 10' 6.5" E)	2009	2009
22. Wordie House, Winter Island, Argentine Islands (Lat. 65° 15' S, Long. 64° 16' W)	2009	2009
23. Stonington Island, Marguerite Bay, Antarctic Peninsula (Lat. 68° 11' S, Long. 67° 00' W)	2009	2009
24. Horseshoe Island, Antarctic Peninsula (Lat. 67° 49' S, Long. 67° 18' W)	2009	2014
25. Detaille Island, Antarctic Peninsula (Lat. 66° 52' S, Long. 66° 48' W)	2009	2009

26. Torgersen Island, Arthur Harbour, Southwest Anvers Island (Lat. 64° 46' S, Long. 64° 04' W)	2010	2013
27. Danco Island, Errera Channel, Antarctic Peninsula (Lat. 64° 43' S, Long. 62° 36' W)	2010	2013
28. Seabee Hook, Cape Hallett, Northern Victoria Land, Ross Sea, Visitor Site A and Visitor Site B (Lat. 72° 19' S, Long. 170° 13' E)	2010	2010
29. Damoy Point, Wiencke Island, Antarctic Peninsula (Lat. 64° 49' S, Long. 63° 31' W)	2010	2013
30. Taylor Valley Visitor Zone, Southern Victoria Land (Lat. 77° 37.59' S, Long. 163° 03.42' E)	2011	2011
31. North-east beach of Ardley Island (Lat. 62° 13' S; Long. 58° 54' W)	2011	2011
32. Mawson's Huts and Cape Denison, East Antarctica (Lat. 67° 01' S; Long. 142 ° 40' E)	2011	2014
33. D'Hainaut Island, Mikkelsen Harbour, Trinity Island (Lat. 63° 54' S, Long. 60° 47' W)	2012	2012
34. Port Charcot, Booth Island (Lat. 65° 04'S, Long. 64° 02'W)	2012	2012
35. Pendulum Cove, Deception Island, South Shetland Islands (Lat. 62°56'S, Long. 60°36' W)	2012	2012
36. Orne Harbour, Southern arm of Orne Harbour, Gerlache Strait (Lat 64° 38'S, Long. 62° 33'W)	2013	2013
37. Orne Islands, Gerlache Strait (Lat. 64° 40'S, Long. 62° 40'W)	2013	2013

PART 5
COMMISSION FOR THE CONSERVATION OF ANTARCTIC MARINE LIVING RESOURCES UNDER THE 1980 CONVENTION (CCAMLR)

Headquarters Agreement between the Commission for the Conservation of Antarctic Marine Living Resources and the Government of Australia 1986[1]

The Commission for the Conservation of Antarctic Marine Living Resources and the Government of Australia,

Having regard to Article XIII of the Convention on the Conservation of Antarctic Marine Living Resources drawn up at Canberra on 20 May 1980 which provides that the headquarters of the Commission for the Conservation of Antarctic Marine Living Resources shall be established at Hobart, Tasmania, Australia;

Desiring to define the legal capacity, privileges and immunities of the Commission and the privileges and immunities to be enjoyed by the staff of the Commission in Australia in accordance with Article VIII of the Convention on the Conservation of Antarctic Marine Living Resources; and

Wishing to provide for the privileges and immunities of certain other persons in the interests of facilitating the performance by the Commission of its functions under the Convention on the Conservation of Antarctic Marine Living Resources;

Have agreed as follows:

Article 1 Definitions

For the purpose of this Agreement:

(a) 'appropriate authorities' means the national, State, Territory or local authorities as the context may require, in accordance with the laws of Australia and its States and Territories;

(b) 'archives' includes all records, correspondence, documents, manuscripts, photographs, computer data storage, films and recordings belonging to or held by the Commission;

(c) 'Commission' means the Commission for the Conservation of Antarctic Marine Living Resources and, where the context so requires, includes the Scientific Committee for the Conservation of Antarctic Marine Living Resources, their subsidiary bodies and the Secretariat established by the Convention;

(d) 'Convention' means the Convention on the Conservation of Antarctic Marine Living Resources drawn up at Canberra on 20 May 1980, which entered into force on 7 April 1982;

(e) 'Envoy' means a diplomatic agent;

(f) 'Executive Secretary' means the Executive Secretary appointed under Article XVII of the Convention;

(g) 'Expert' means a person performing short term or temporary projects on behalf of the Commission and includes a person serving on the Scientific Committee or on another committee of the Commission or participating in the work of or performing a mission on behalf of the Commission or the Scientific Committee, without necessarily receiving remuneration from the Commission or the Scientific Committee, but does not include staff members;

(h) 'Government' means the Government of Australia;

[1] Signed on 8 September 1986 (CCAMLR-V, paragraph 9).

(i) 'Headquarters' means premises of the Commission including the buildings or parts of buildings and the land ancillary thereto, irrespective of ownership, occupied by the Commission for the performance of its official activities;
(j) 'Official activities' means all activities undertaken pursuant to the Convention, including the Commission's administrative activities;
(k) 'Parties' means Parties to the Convention;
(l) 'Representatives' means representatives of Parties to the Convention in attendance at Conferences or meetings convened by the Commission and includes delegates, alternates, advisers, technical experts and secretaries of delegations;
(m) 'Scientific Committee' means the Scientific Committee for the Conservation of Antarctic Marine Living Resources established by Article XIV of the Convention and includes any subsidiary body established by the Scientific Committee under Article XVI(3) of the Convention;
(n) 'Serious offence' means an offence under any law of Australia or of a State or Territory of Australia for which a person convicted would be liable on a first conviction to imprisonment for a period of five years or more according to the law applicable in the Australian Capital Territory if the offence had been committed in that Territory; and
(o) 'Staff member' means the Executive Secretary and all persons appointed or recruited for full-time employment with the Commission and subject to its staff regulations, but does not include:
  (i) experts; or
  (ii) persons recruited locally and assigned to hourly rates of pay.

Article 2 Interpretation

This Agreement shall be interpreted in the light of its primary objective of enabling the Commission to perform its functions in Australia.

Article 3 Legal Personality

The Commission has legal personality. It has, in particular, the capacity to contract, to acquire and dispose of movable and immovable property, and to institute and be a party to legal proceedings.

Article 4 Premises

1. The Headquarters of the Commission shall be inviolable and shall be under the full authority of the Commission.

2. The Government shall arrange for the provision at nominal rental to the Commission of suitable permanent premises in Hobart, Tasmania, Australia.

3. The Government shall take all appropriate steps to protect the Headquarters of the Commission against any intrusion or damage and to prevent any impairment of its dignity.

4. The Government shall arrange for the Headquarters to be supplied by the appropriate authorities with available public services, such as electricity, water, sewerage, gas, mail, telephone, telegraph, drainage, collection of refuse and fire protection, on terms no less favourable than those enjoyed by the Government.

5. The Commission shall make known to the Government the need for any changes to the location or extent of its permanent premises or archives and of any temporary occupation of premises for the performance of its official activities. Where any premises other than those arranged under Article 4(2) of this Agreement are used or occupied by the Commission for the performance of its official activities, such premises shall, with the concurrence of the Government, be accorded the status of premises of the Commission. Where any permanent or temporary changes are made to the premises of the Commission in accordance with this paragraph, any additional premises occupied by the Commission shall not necessarily be provided by the Government at nominal rental.

6. Without prejudice to the terms of this Agreement, the Commission shall not permit the Headquarters of the Commission to become a refuge from justice for persons avoiding arrest

or service of legal process or against whom an order of extradition or deportation has been issued.

7. The appropriate authorities may enter the Headquarters to carry out their duties only with the consent of the Executive Secretary and under the conditions agreed by him. The Executive Secretary's consent shall be deemed to have been given in the case of fire or other occurrence which may require immediate protective action.

Article 5 Immunities of the Commission

1. Except as otherwise provided in the Convention or in this Agreement, the activities of the Commission in Australia shall be governed by the laws of Australia.

2. Within the scope of its official activities the Commission and its property, premises and assets shall have immunity from suit and other legal process except:

(a) to the extent that the Commission expressly waives such immunity from such suit and other legal process in a particular case;

(b) in respect of any contract for the supply of goods or services and any loan or other transaction for the provision of finance and any guarantee or indemnity in respect of any such transaction or of any other financial obligation;

(c) in respect of a civil action by a third party for death, damage or personal injury arising from an accident caused by a motor vehicle belonging to, or operated on behalf of, the Commission;

(d) in respect of a motor vehicle offence involving a motor vehicle belonging to, or operated on behalf of, the Commission;

(e) in the event of the attachment, pursuant to the final order of a court of law, of the salaries, wages or other emoluments owed by the Commission to a staff member of the Commission or to an expert;

(f) in respect of a counter-claim directly connected with proceedings initiated by the Commission; and

(g) in respect of the enforcement of an arbitration award made under Articles 20(3) or 25 of this Agreement.

3. The Commission's property, premises and assets, wherever situated, shall have immunity from any form of restrictions or controls such as requisition, confiscation, expropriation or attachment. They shall also be immune from any form of administrative or judicial constraint provided that motor vehicles belonging to or operated on behalf of the Commission shall not be immune from administrative or judicial constraint when temporarily necessary in connection with the prevention of, and investigation into, accidents involving such motor vehicles. These immunities shall cease to apply in relation to property, premises and assets which have been abandoned by the Commission for a period in excess of twelve months.

Article 6 Archives

The archives of the Commission shall be inviolable wherever they are.

Article 7 Flag and Emblem

The Commission shall be entitled to display its flag and emblem on the premises and means of transport of the Commission and of the Executive Secretary.

Article 8 Exemption from Direct Taxes

1. Within the scope of its official activities, the Commission, its property, premises and assets, and its income, including contributions made to the Commission under the Convention, shall be exempt from all direct taxes including income tax, capital gains tax and corporation tax, and all State taxes. The Commission shall be exempt from municipal rates with the exception of those which constitute payment for specific services rendered in accordance with Article 4(4).

2. The exemption from taxation on income provided for in Article 8(1) and in Articles 16 and 17 shall be given on the understanding that no taxation shall be imposed on such income by other Parties.

Article 9 Exemption from Customs and Excise Duties and Sales Tax

1. Goods, including the Commission's publications, motor vehicles and items for official entertainment purposes that are intended for the official use of the Commission shall be exempt from all customs and excise duties including sales tax payable at the customs, except payment for services.

2. Sales tax shall not be payable in respect of goods, including publications and other information material, motor vehicles and items for official entertainment purposes, upon the sale of which to the Commission sales tax would otherwise be payable by the vendor, if the goods so purchased by the Commission are necessary for its official use.

Article 10 Exemption from Restrictions and Prohibitions

Goods imported or exported for the official activities of the Commission shall be exempt from prohibitions and restrictions applicable to such goods on grounds of national origin.

Article 11 Re-Sale

Goods which have been acquired or imported by the Commission to which exemptions under Article 9 of this Agreement apply and goods acquired or imported by the Executive Secretary under Article 16 of this Agreement shall not be given away, sold, lent, hired out or otherwise disposed of in Australia except under conditions agreed in advance with the Government.

Article 12 Currency and Exchange

The Commission shall be exempt from currency and exchange restrictions, including those in respect of funds, currency and securities received, acquired, held or disposed of. The Commission may also operate bank or other accounts for its official use in any currency, and have them transferred freely within Australia or to any other country.

Article 13 Communications

1. With regard to its official communications and the transfer of all its documents, the Commission shall enjoy treatment not less favourable than that generally accorded to equivalent inter-governmental organisations in the matter of priorities, rates and taxes on mails and all forms of telecommunications.

2. The Commission may employ all appropriate means of communication, including messages in code or cypher. The Government shall not impose any restriction on the official communications of the Commission or on the circulation of its publications.

3. The Commission may install and use a radio transmitter only with the consent of the Government.

4. Official correspondence and other official communications of the Commission are not subject to censorship.

Article 14 Publications

The importation and exportation of the Commission's publications and other information material imported or exported by the Commission within the scope of its official activities shall not be restricted in any way.

Article 15 Representatives in Attendance at Conferences Convened by the Commission

1. Representatives shall enjoy, while exercising their functions in Australia and while travelling in the exercise of their functions in Australia, the following privileges and immunities:

(a) immunity from arrest and detention and from attachment of personal luggage except when found committing, attempting to commit or just having committed a serious offence;

(b) inviolability of representatives' residences in Australia occupied during the course of their functions;

(c) immunity, which shall extend beyond the termination of their mission, from suit and other legal process in respect of acts and things done by them in the exercise of their official functions, including words written or spoken; this immunity shall not, however, apply in the case of civil or administrative proceedings arising out of death, damage or personal injury caused by a motor vehicle belonging to or driven by them;

(d) inviolability for all their official papers and documents;
(e) exemption (including exemption of the spouse of the representative) from the application of laws relating to the registration of aliens, the obligation to perform national service and any other national duty, and immigration;
(f) unless they are citizens of or permanently resident in Australia, the same exemption from currency and exchange restrictions as is accorded to a representative of a foreign government on a temporary mission to Australia on behalf of that government;
(g) the same exemptions in relation to inspection of their personal baggage as are accorded to envoys;
(h) the right to use codes and to send and receive correspondence and other papers and documents by couriers or in sealed bags;
(i) unless they are citizens of or permanently resident in Australia, the same exemption from taxes on income as is accorded an envoy in Australia; and
(j) similar repatriation facilities including such facilities in respect of a spouse and dependent relatives, in time of international crisis as are accorded to an envoy.

2. The provisions of the preceding paragraph shall be applicable irrespective of the relations existing between the governments which the persons referred to represent and the Government, and are without prejudice to any additional immunities to which such persons may be entitled.

3. In order to assist the Government to implement the provisions of this Article, the Commission shall, so far as possible, inform the Government of the names of representatives prior to their arrival in Australia.

4. The privileges and immunities described in paragraph 1 of this Article shall not be accorded to any representative of the Government or to any citizen or permanent resident of Australia.

5. Privileges and immunities are accorded to the representatives of Parties not for the personal benefit of individuals themselves, but in order to safeguard the independent exercise of their functions in connection with the Commission. Consequently, a Party not only has the right but is under a duty to waive the immunity of its representative in any case where in the opinion of the Party the immunity would impede the course of justice, and it can be waived without prejudice to the purpose for which the immunity is accorded. If the Party sending the representative does not waive the immunity of the representative, it shall make the strongest efforts to achieve an equitable solution of the matter.

6. The Government shall treat representatives with all due respect and shall take all necessary measures to prevent encroachment on their person, freedom and dignity. Where it appears that an offence may have been committed against a representative, steps shall be taken in accordance with Australian legal processes to investigate the matter and to ensure that appropriate action is taken with respect to the prosecution of the alleged offender.

Article 16 Executive Secretary

In addition to the privileges, immunities, exemptions and facilities provided for in Article 17 of this Agreement, the Executive Secretary, unless he is a citizen of or permanently resident in Australia, shall enjoy the privileges, immunities, exemptions and facilities to which an envoy in Australia is entitled, including privileges, immunities, exemptions and facilities in respect of a spouse and dependent children under the age of eighteen years.

Article 17 Staff Members

Staff members of the Commission:

(a) shall have, even after the termination of their service with the Commission, immunity from suit and other legal process in respect of acts and things done by them in the exercise of their official functions, including words written or spoken; this immunity shall not, however, apply in the case of a motor vehicle offence committed by such a staff member nor in the case of civil or administrative proceedings arising out of death, damage or personal injury caused by a motor vehicle belonging to or driven by him;

(b) shall be exempt from any obligations in respect of national service and all other kinds of mandatory service; staff members who are Australian citizens or permanent residents shall be accorded such exemption only if their names have been placed on a list compiled for that purpose by the Executive Secretary and approved by the Government;

(c) shall be exempt from the application of laws relating to the registration of aliens and immigration; the spouse and dependent children under the age of eighteen years of a staff member shall enjoy the same exemptions;

(d) unless they are citizens of or permanently resident in Australia, shall be accorded the same exemption from currency and exchange restrictions as is accorded to an official of comparable rank forming part of a diplomatic mission in Australia;

(e) unless they are citizens of or permanently resident in Australia shall, at the time of first taking up their post in Australia, be exempt from customs duties and other such charges (except payments for services) in respect of import of furniture and personal effects including motor vehicles in their ownership or possession or already ordered by them and intended for their personal use or for their establishment; such goods shall be imported within six months of a staff member's first entry into Australia but in exceptional circumstances an extension of this period shall be granted by the Government; goods which have been acquired or imported by staff members and to which exemptions under this sub-paragraph apply shall not be given away, sold, lent, hired out, or otherwise disposed of except under conditions agreed in advance with the Government; furniture and personal effects including motor vehicles may be exported free of duties when leaving Australia on the termination of the official functions of the staff member;

(f) shall be exempt from all taxes on income received from the Commission; exemption from taxation on income under this sub-paragraph shall not apply to staff members who are residents of Australia for services rendered in Australia, unless the staff member is not an Australian citizen and came to Australia solely for the purpose of performing his duties for the Commission; and

(g) shall have similar repatriation facilities, including such facilities in respect of a spouse and dependent relatives in time of international crisis as are accorded to an envoy.

Article 18 Experts

In the exercise of their functions experts shall enjoy the following privileges and immunities to the extent necessary for the carrying out of their functions, including during travel undertaken in Australia in carrying out their functions:

(a) immunity from suit and other legal process in respect of acts and things done in the exercise of their official functions, including words written or spoken; this immunity shall not, however, apply in the case of a motor vehicle offence committed by such an expert, nor in the case of civil or administrative proceedings arising out of death, damage or personal injury caused by a motor vehicle belonging to or driven by him; such immunity shall continue after the expert's function in relation to the Commission have ceased;

(b) inviolability for all their official papers and documents;

(c) unless they are citizens of or permanently resident in Australia, the same exemption from currency and exchange restrictions as is accorded to a representative of a foreign government on a temporary mission in Australia on behalf of that government; and

(d) unless they are citizens of or permanent residents of Australia, immunity from personal arrest and detention and from attachment of personal luggage except when found committing, attempting to commit or just having committed a serious offence.

Article 19 Visas

1. All persons having official business with the Commission, namely (a) representatives of Parties (and their spouses), (b) staff members of the Commission (and their spouses and

dependent relatives), and (c) experts and consultants on missions for the Commission, should have the right of entry into and exit from Australia.

2. The Government shall take all measures necessary to facilitate the entry into Australian territory, the sojourn on this territory and the exit therefrom of all persons mentioned in the preceding paragraph. Visas, where required, shall be granted without wait or delay, and without fee, on production of a certificate that the applicant is a person described in the preceding paragraph. In addition, the Australian Government will facilitate for such persons speedy travel within Australia.

Article 20 Object or Privileges and Immunities Accorded to Staff Members and Experts

1. Privileges and immunities are accorded to staff members and experts to ensure the independence of the persons to whom they are accorded in the exercise of their functions to achieve the purposes of the Convention.

2. The Executive Secretary has the right and duty after consultations with the Members of the Commission to waive any immunities, other than his own, and those of his spouse and dependent children under the age of eighteen years, when he considers that such immunities would impede the course of justice and they can be waived without prejudicing the purposes for which they were accorded. The immunities of the Executive Secretary and those of his spouse and dependent children under the age of eighteen years may be waived only by the Commission, in similar circumstances.

3. If such immunities are not waived, the Commission shall make the strongest efforts to achieve an equitable solution of the matter. Such a solution may include an arbitration procedure.

Article 21 Cooperation

The Commission shall cooperate fully at all times with the appropriate authorities in order to prevent any abuse of the privileges, immunities and facilities provided for in this Agreement. The Government reserves its sovereign right to take reasonable measures to preserve security. Nothing in this Agreement prevents the application of laws necessary for health and quarantine or, in respect of the Commission and its officials, laws relating to public order.

Article 22 Notification of Appointment Identity Cards

1. The Commission shall inform the Government when a staff member or expert takes up or relinquishes his post. Where possible, prior notice of arrival and final departure shall be given. If staff members are accompanied by a spouse or dependent children under the age of eighteen years, prior notice shall also be given, where possible, in respect of such persons.

2. The Commission shall twice each year send to the Government a list of all staff members, their spouses and dependent children under the age of eighteen years accompanying them in Australia, and experts. In each case the Commission shall indicate whether such persons are citizens or permanently resident in Australia.

3. The Government shall issue to all staff members and experts as soon as practicable after notification of their appointment, a card bearing the photograph of the holder and identifying him as a staff member or expert as the case may be. This card shall be accepted by the appropriate authorities as evidence of identity and appointment. The Commission shall return the card to the Government when the staff member or expert relinquishes his duties. The spouse and dependent children under the age of eighteen years of staff members shall also be issued with an identity card, which shall be returned to the Government when the staff member relinquishes his duties.

Article 23 Consultations

The Government and the Commission shall consult at the request of either of them concerning matters arising under this Agreement.

Article 24 Amendment

This Agreement may be amended by agreement between the Government and the Commission.

Article 25 Settlement of Disputes

Any dispute between the Government and the Commission concerning the interpretation or application of this Agreement or any question affecting the relations between the Government and the Commission which is not settled by consultation or negotiation or by some other mutually acceptable method shall be referred to an arbitral tribunal constituted *mutatis mutandis* as provided for in the Annex to the Convention.

Article 26 Entry into Force and Termination

1. This Agreement shall enter into force on signature.

2. Immediately on its entering into force, this Agreement shall terminate the Interim Agreement between the Government of Australia and the Commission for the Conservation of Antarctic Marine Living Resources concerning Privileges and Immunities of the Commission done at Canberra on 15 August 1983 as extended.

3. This Agreement may be terminated by a joint decision of the Government and the Commission. In the event of the Headquarters of the Commission being moved from Australia, this Agreement shall, after a period reasonably required for such transfer and the disposal of the property of the Commission in Australia, cease to be in force. In either event, the date on which the Agreement terminates shall be confirmed by an exchange of notes between the Government and the Commission.

Rules of Procedure of the Commission (1982)[2]

PART I REPRESENTATION

Rule 1[3]

Each Member of the Commission shall be represented by one representative who may be accompanied by alternate representatives and advisers.

Rule 2

Each Member of the Commission shall notify the Executive Secretary as far as possible in advance of any meeting of the name of its representative and before or at the beginning of the meeting the names of its alternate representatives and advisers.

Rule 3

Each Member of the Commission shall nominate a correspondent who shall have primary responsibility for liaison with the Executive Secretary between meetings.

PART II TAKING OF DECISIONS

Rule 4

The Chairman shall put to all Members of the Commission questions and proposals requiring decisions. Decisions shall be taken according to the following provisions:

(a) Decisions of the Commission on matters of substance shall be taken by consensus. The question of whether a matter is one of substance shall be treated as a matter of substance.

(b) Decisions on matters other than those referred to in paragraph (a) above shall be taken by a simple majority of the Members of the Commission present and voting.

(c) In Commission consideration of any item requiring a decision, it shall be made clear whether a regional economic integration organisation will participate in the taking of the decision and, if so, whether any of its Member States will also participate. The number of Contracting Parties so participating shall not exceed the number of Member States of the regional economic integration organisation which are Members of the Commission.

(d) In the taking of decisions pursuant to this rule, a regional economic integration organisation shall have only one vote.

Rule 5

At a meeting of the Commission, votes shall be taken by a show of hands. However, a roll call or a secret ballot vote shall be taken at the request of a Member of the Commission. In the case

[2] As adopted at CCAMLR-I (paragraph 13); amended at CCAMLR-VIII (paragraph 173); amended at CCAMLR-X (paragraph 17.2); amended at CCAMLR-XIII (paragraphs 13.10 and 13.11).

[3] Article V11(3) of the Convention on the Conservation of Antarctic Marine Living Resources.

of conflicting requests as between a roll call or a secret ballot vote, a secret ballot vote shall be used. A roll call vote shall be taken by calling the names of the Members of the Commission entitled to vote in alphabetical order of the language of the country in which the meeting is held, beginning with the Member which has been chosen by lot.

Rule 6

At a meeting of the Commission, unless it decides otherwise, the Commission shall not discuss or take a decision on any item which has not been included in the provisional agenda for the meeting in accordance with Part IV of these rules.

Rule 7

When necessary, the taking of decisions and votes on any proposal made during the period between meetings may be carried out by post or by other means of textual communication.

(a) The Chairman or a Member which request the application of the procedure laid down by this rule shall convey with the proposal a recommendation as to whether the decision should be taken in accordance with Rule 4(a) or Rule 4(b). Any disagreement on this matter shall be resolved in accordance with the provisions of Rule 4, and the following provisions.

(b) The Executive Secretary shall distribute copies of the proposal to all Members.

(c) The Executive Secretary shall enquire of a regional economic integration organisation whether it will participate in the taking of the decision. If such organisation intends to participate in the taking of the decision, in view of Rule 4(c), it and the member or members of that organisation not so participating shall inform the Executive Secretary accordingly.

(d) If the decision is to be taken in accordance with Rule 4(a):

(i) Members shall immediately acknowledge receipt of the Executive Secretary's communication and respond within 45 days of the date of acknowledgment of the proposal, indicating whether they wish to support it, reject it, abstain on it, refrain from participating in the taking of the decision, or whether they require additional time to consider it, or whether they consider that it is not necessary for the decision to be taken during the period between meetings. In the latter case the Chairman shall direct the Executive Secretary to inform all Members accordingly and the decision shall be remitted to the next meeting.

(ii) If there are no rejections and if no Member either seeks additional time or objects to the decision being taken between meetings, the Chairman shall direct the Executive Secretary to inform all Members that the proposal has been adopted.

(iii) If the responses include a rejection of the proposal, the Chairman shall direct the Executive Secretary to inform all Members that the proposal has been rejected, and provide them with a brief description of all individual responses.

(iv) If the initial responses do not include a rejection of the proposal or an objection to the decision being taken between meetings, but a Member requests additional time to consider it, a further 30 days shall be allowed. The Executive Secretary shall inform all Members of the final date by which responses must be lodged. Members who have not responded by that date shall be deemed to be in support of the proposal. After the final date, the Chairman shall direct the Executive Secretary to proceed in accordance with subparagraphs (ii) or (iii), as the case may be.

(v) The Executive Secretary shall distribute to each Member copies of all responses as they are received.

(e) If the decision is to be taken in accordance with Rule 4(b):

(i) Members shall immediately acknowledge receipt of the Executive Secretary's communication and respond within 45 days of the date of acknowledgment of the proposal, indicating whether they wish to support it, reject it, abstain on it or refrain from participating in the taking of the decision.

(ii) At the end of the 45-day period, the Chairman shall count the votes and direct the Executive Secretary to inform all Members of the result.
(iii) The Executive Secretary shall distribute to each Member copies of all responses as they are received.

(f) A proposal which has been rejected may not be reconsidered by way of postal voting until after the following meeting of the Commission, but may be considered at that meeting.

PART III CHAIRMAN, VICE-CHAIRMAN AND EXECUTIVE SECRETARY

Rule 8[4, 5]

The Commission shall elect from among its Members a Chairman and Vice-Chairman, each of whom shall serve for a term of two years and shall be eligible for re-election for one additional term. The first Chairman shall, however, be elected for an initial term of three years. The Chairman and Vice-Chairman shall not be representatives of the same Contracting Party.

Rule 9

A person representing a Member of the Commission as its Representative who is elected as Chairman shall cease to act as a Representative upon assuming office and, whilst holding this office, shall not act as Representative, Alternate Representative or Adviser at meeting of the Commission.

The Member of the Commission concerned shall appoint another person to replace the one who was hitherto its Representative.

Rule 10

The Chairman and Vice-Chairman shall take office at the conclusion of the meeting at which they have been elected, except for the first Chairman and Vice-Chairman who shall take office immediately upon their election.

Rule 11

The Chairman shall have the following powers and responsibilities:

(a) convene the regular and extraordinary meetings of the Commission;
(b) preside at each meeting of the Commission;
(c) open and close each meeting of the Commission;
(d) make rulings on points of order raised at meetings of the Commission, provided that each representative retains the right to request that any such decision be submitted to the Commission for approval;
(e) put questions and notify the Commission of the results of votes;
(f) approve a Provisional Agenda for the meeting after consultation with representatives and the Executive Secretary;
(g) sign, on behalf of the Commission, the reports of each meeting for transmission to its Members, Representatives and other interested persons as official documents of the proceedings; and

[4] Article XIII(4) of the Convention on the Conservation of Antarctic Marine Living Resources.

[5] Officers of the Commission.

Under paragraph 4 of Article XIII of the Convention, the Commission elected from among its Members Australia to be its first Chairman and Japan to be its first Vice-Chairman. In reaching these decisions the Commission noted the outstanding contribution made by Australia in bringing the Convention into effect, that Australia had acted as host government to the first Antarctic Treaty Consultative Meeting in 1961 and the precedent provided by other international organisations in which the first chairmanship had been accorded to the host government.

Regarding the election of the Chairman of the Commission in future, the Commission noted the benefits to be derived from an arrangement which would ensure an automatic election of all Members of the Commission to that office. Therefore it was decided that, after the Australian term, the Chairmen would in succession be the Members of the Commission in the order of their names arranged alphabetically in the English language.

Furthermore, the Commission agreed that, insofar as was feasible within the arrangement for staggered terms of office foreseen in paragraph 4 of Article XIII, the election as Chairman of a Member of the Commission not engaged in research or harvesting activities, should be balanced by the election to the Vice-Chairmanship of a Member of the Commission engaged in such activities.

(h) exercise other powers and responsibilities as provided in these rules and make such decisions and give such directions to the Executive Secretary as will ensure that the business of the Commission is carried out effectively and in accordance with its decisions.

Rule 12

Whenever the Chairman of the Commission is unable to act, the Vice-Chairman shall assume the powers and responsibilities of the Chairman. The Vice-Chairman shall act as Chairman until the Chairman resumes his duties. Whilst acting as Chairman, the Vice-Chairman will not act as Representative.

Rule 13

In the event of the office of Chairman falling vacant due to resignation or permanent inability to act, the Vice-Chairman shall act as Chairman until the Commission's next meeting on which occasion a new Chairman shall be elected. Until the election of a new Chairman, the Vice-Chairman will not act as Representative, Alternate Representative or Adviser.

Rule 14[6]

(a) The Commission shall appoint an Executive Secretary to serve the Commission and Scientific Committee according to such procedures and on such terms and conditions as the Commission may determine. His term of office shall be for four years and he shall be eligible for re-appointment.

(b) The Commission shall authorise such staff establishment for the Secretariat as may be necessary and the Executive Secretary shall appoint, direct and supervise such staff according to such rules, and procedures and on such terms and conditions as the Commission may determine.

(c) The Executive Secretary and Secretariat shall perform the functions entrusted to them by the Commission.

PART IV PREPARATION FOR MEETINGS

Rule 15

The Executive Secretary shall prepare, in consultation with the Chairman, a preliminary agenda for each meeting of the Commission and its subsidiary bodies. He shall transmit this preliminary agenda to all Members of the Commission no later than 100 days prior to the beginning of the meeting.

Rule 16

Members of the Commission proposing supplementary items for the preliminary agenda shall inform the Executive Secretary thereof no later than 65 days before the beginning of the meeting and accompany their proposal with an explanatory memorandum.

Rule 17

The Executive Secretary shall prepare, in consultation with the Chairman, a provisional agenda for each meeting of the Commission. The provisional agenda shall include:

(a) all items which the Commission has previously decided to include in the provisional agenda;

(b) all items the inclusion of which is requested by any Member of the Commission;

(c) proposed dates for the next regular annual meeting following the one to which the provisional agenda relates.

The Executive Secretary shall transmit to all Members of the Commission, at least 45 days in advance of the Commission's meeting, the provisional agenda and explanatory memoranda or reports related thereto.

Rule 18

The Executive Secretary shall:

(a) make all necessary arrangements for meetings of the Commission and its subsidiary bodies;

[6] Article XVII of the Convention on the Conservation of Antarctic Marine Living Resources.

(b) issue invitations to all such meetings to Members of the Commission and to such states and organisations as are to be invited in accordance with Rule 30;
(c) take all the necessary steps to carry out the instructions and directions given to him by the Chairman.

PART V CONDUCT OF BUSINESS AT MEETINGS

Rule 19

The Chairman shall exercise his powers of office in accordance with customary practice. He shall ensure the observance of the Rules of Procedure and the maintenance of proper order. The Chairman, in the exercise of his functions, shall remain under the authority of the meeting.

Rule 20

No representative may address the meeting without having previously obtained the permission of the Chairman. The Chairman shall call upon speakers in the order in which they signify their desire to speak. The Chairman may call a speaker to order if his remarks are not relevant to the subject under discussion.

Rule 21

The Chairman or Vice-Chairman of the Scientific Committee may attend all meetings of the Commission. They shall be entitled to present the report of the Scientific Committee to the Commission and to address the Commission with regard to it. The Commission shall take full account of the reports of the Scientific Committee.

Rule 22

Proposals and amendments shall normally be submitted in writing to the Executive Secretary, who shall circulate copies to all delegations. As a general rule, no proposal shall be discussed or put to the vote at any meeting of the Commission unless copies have been distributed to all delegations in all of the Commission's languages a reasonable time in advance. The Chairman may, however, permit the discussion and consideration of proposals even though such proposals have not been circulated.

Rule 23

As a general rule proposals which have been rejected may not be reconsidered until the next meeting of the Commission.

Rule 24

A representative may at any time make a point of order and the point of order shall be decided immediately by the Chairman in accordance with the Rules of Procedure. A representative may appeal against the ruling of the Chairman. The appeal shall be put to a vote immediately and the Chairman's ruling shall stand if upheld by a majority of the representatives present and voting. A representative making a point of order shall not speak on the substance of the matter under discussion. A point of order made during voting may concern only the conduct of the vote.

Rule 25

The Chairman may limit the time allotted to each speaker and the number of times he may speak on any subject.

In the event that a speaker has used his allotted time, the Chairman shall draw this to his attention and propose that he discontinue his speech.

Rule 26

A representative may at any time move the suspension or the adjournment of the session. Such motions shall not be debated, but shall be put to the vote immediately. The Chairman may limit the time to be allowed to each speaker putting such a motion.

Rule 27

A representative may at any time move the adjournment of the debate on the item under discussion. In addition to the proposer of the motion, two representatives may speak in favour of, and two against the motion, after which the motion shall be put to the vote immediately. The Chairman may limit the time to be allowed to speakers.

Rule 28

A representative may at any time move the closure of the debate on the item under discussion. In addition to the proposer of the motion, two representatives may speak against the motion, after which the motion shall be put to the vote immediately. If the meeting is in favour of the closure, the Chairman shall declare the closure of the debate and a decision shall be taken immediately on the item under discussion. The Chairman may limit the time to be allowed to speakers under this rule.

Rule 29

Subject to Rule 24 the following motions shall have precedence in the following order over all other proposals or motions before the session:

(a) to suspend the session;
(b) to adjourn the session;
(c) to adjourn the debate on the item under discussion;
(d) for the closure of the debate on the item under discussion.

PART VI OBSERVERS

Rule 30

Subject to Article XII of the Convention on the Conservation of Antarctic Marine Living Resources the Commission may:

(a) extend an invitation to any signatory of the Convention to participate, in accordance with Rules 32, 33 and 34 below, as Observers in meetings of the Commission;
(b)[7] extend an invitation to any State party to the Convention which is not a Member of the Commission to attend, in accordance with Rules 32, 33 and 34 below, as Observers in meetings of the Commission;
(c) invite as appropriate, any other state to attend, in accordance with Rules 32, 33 and 34 below, as Observers in the meetings of the Commission unless a Member of the Commission objects;
(d) invite, as appropriate, organisations named in Article XXIII(2) and (3) of the Convention to attend, in accordance with Rules 32, 33 and 34 below, as Observers in the meetings of the Commission;
(e) invite, as appropriate, other intergovernmental and non-governmental organisations, to which Article XXIII(3) of the Convention may apply, to attend in accordance with Rules 32, 33 and 34 below, as Observers in the meetings of the Commission unless a Member of the Commission objects.

Rule 31[8]

Each Observer invited in accordance with Rule 30 above shall notify the Executive Secretary as far as possible in advance of any meeting of the name of its representative and before or at the beginning of the meeting the names of its alternate representatives and advisers.

Rule 32

(a) The Executive Secretary may, when preparing with the Chairman the preliminary agenda for a meeting of the Commission, draw to the attention of Members of the Commission his view that the work of the Commission would be facilitated by the attendance at its next meeting of an observer referred to in Rule 30, an invitation to which was not considered at the previous meeting. The Executive Secretary shall so inform Members of the Commission when transmitting to them the preliminary agenda under Rule 15;

(b) The Chairman shall request the Commission to take a decision on the Executive Secretary's suggestion in accordance with Rule 7 and the Executive Secretary shall so inform Members of the Commission when transmitting to them the provisional agenda under Rule 17.

[7] Amended at CCAMLR-XIII (paragraph 13.11).

[8] Adopted at CCAMLR-XXIV (paragraph 20.6). Subsequent rules were renumbered accordingly.

Rule 33

(a) Observers may be present at public and private sessions of the Commission;

(b)[9] If a Member of the Commission so requests, sessions of the Commission at which a particular agenda item is under consideration shall be restricted to its Members and Observers referred to in Rule 30(a) and Rule 30(b). With respect to any session so restricted, the Commission may also agree to invite Observers referred to in Rule 30(c).

Rule 34

(a) The Chairman may invite observers to address the Commission unless a Member of the Commission objects;

(b) Observers are not entitled to participate in the taking of decisions.

Rule 35

(a) Observers may submit documents to the Secretariat for distribution to Membersof the Commission as information documents. Such documents shall be relevant to matters under consideration in the Commission;

(b) Unless a Member or Members of the Commission request otherwise such documents shall be available only in the language or languages and in the quantities in which they were submitted;

(c) Such documents shall only be considered as Commission documents if so decided by the Commission.

PART VII SUBSIDIARY BODIES

Rule 36

The Commission may determine the composition and terms of reference of any subsidiary body established by it. Insofar as they are applicable these Rules of Procedure shall apply to any subsidiary body of the Commission unless the Commission decides otherwise.

PART VIII LANGUAGES

Rule 37

The official and working languages of the Commission shall be English, French, Russian and Spanish.

PART IX REPORTS AND NOTIFICATIONS

Rule 38

Reports of meetings of the Commission shall be prepared by the Executive Secretary as required by the Commission before the end of each meeting. A draft report of such meetings shall be considered by the Commission before it is adopted at the end of the meeting. The Executive Secretary shall transmit reports of meetings of the Commission to all Members of the Commission, and to Observers which have attended the meeting, as soon as possible after the meeting.

Rule 39

The Executive Secretary shall:

(a) notify each Member of the Commission immediately after each meeting of all decisions, measures or recommendations made or adopted by the Commission;

(b) notify each Member of the Commission of any notification by a Member of the Commission pursuant to Article IX(6) of the Convention that it is unable to accept any conservation measure, in whole or in part, adopted by the Commission or of the withdrawal of any such notification.

[9] Amended at CCAMLR-XIII (paragraph 13.10) and CCAMLR-XVII (paragraph 16.2).

Rules of Procedure of the Scientific Committee (1983)[10*]

PART I REPRESENTATIVES AND INVITED SCIENTISTS AND EXPERTS

Rule 1

Each Member of the Commission shall be a Member of the Scientific Committee and shall appoint a representative with suitable scientific qualifications, who may be accompanied by other experts and advisers.

Each Member of the Commission shall notify the Executive Secretary as early as possible before each meeting of the Scientific Committee of the name of his representative and before or at the beginning of the meeting the names of his experts and advisers.

Rule 3

The Scientific Committee may seek the advice of other scientists and experts as may be required on an *ad hoc* basis.

Such scientists and experts may submit documents and participate in discussions on the questions for which they were invited, but do not participate in the taking of decisions.

In cases when an invitation to such scientists and experts has financial implications for the Commission not provided for in its budget, such an invitation should require approval of the Commission.

PART II CONDUCT OF BUSINESS

Rule 3

Scientific recommendations and advice to be provided by the Scientific Committee pursuant to the Convention shall normally be determined by consensus.

Where consensus cannot be achieved the Committee shall set out in its report all views advanced on the matter under consideration.

Reports of the Scientific Committee to the Commission shall reflect all the views expressed at the Committee on the matters discussed.

If a Member or group of Members in the Committee so wishes, additional views of that Member or group of Members on any particular questions may be submitted directly to the Commission.

Where the Committee takes decisions, it will do so in accordance with Article XII of the Convention.

PART III MEETINGS

Rule 4

The Committee shall meet as often as may be necessary to fulfil its functions.

Regular meetings of the Committee normally shall be held once a year at the Headquarters of the Commission, unless it decides otherwise.

Rule 5

The Chairman shall prepare in consultation with the Executive Secretary a preliminary agenda for each meeting of the Committee. The Executive Secretary shall distribute the preliminary agenda to all Members of the Committee no later than 100 days prior to the beginning of the meeting.

The Executive Secretary, in consultation with the Chairman of both the Scientific Committee and of the subsidiary body, shall prepare and distribute a preliminary agenda before each meeting of that body.

---

[10] As adopted at SC-CAMLR-II (paragraph 8) and approved at CCAMLR-II (paragraph 10); amended at SC-CAMLR-III (paragraph 4.3) and approved at CCAMLR-III (paragraph 65); amended at SC-CAMLR-X (paragraph 2.2) and approved at CCAMLR-X (paragraph 4.6); amended at SC-CAMLR-XXV (paragraph 15.18) in accordance with CCAMLR-XXIV, paragraph 20.6, and subject to the decision of SC-CAMLR-XXIV (paragraph 13.56).

Rule 6

Members of the Committee proposing supplementary items for the preliminary agenda shall inform the Executive Secretary thereof no later than 65 days before the beginning of the meeting and accompanying their proposal with an explanatory memorandum.

Rule 7

The Executive Secretary shall prepare, in consultation with the Chairman, a provisional agenda for each meeting of the Committee. The provisional agenda shall include:

(a) all items which the Committee has previously decided to include in the provisional agenda;

(b) all items the inclusion of which is requested by any Member of the Committee;

(c) proposed dates for the next regular annual meeting following the one to which the provisional agenda relates.

The Executive Secretary shall transmit to all Members of the Committee, at least 45 days in advance of the Committee's meeting, the provisional agenda and explanatory memoranda or reports related thereto.

PART IV CHAIRMAN AND VICE-CHAIRMEN

Rule 8

The Committee shall elect a Chairman and two or more Vice-Chairmen on the basis of procedures referred to in Rule 3 above. The Chairman and Vice-Chairmen shall be elected for a term which shall include two regular meetings, as defined in the second sentence of Rule 4, except in the case of the first Chairman who shall be elected for a term of office which shall include three regular meetings to ensure that the terms of office of the Chairman and Vice-Chairmen shall be staggered.

The Chairman and Vice-Chairmen shall not be re-elected to their post for more than one term. The Chairman and Vice-Chairmen shall not be representatives of the same Contracting Party.

Rule 9

Amongst other duties, the Chairman shall have the following powers and responsibilities:

(a) convene, open, preside at, and close each meeting of the Committee;

(b) make rulings on points of order raised at meetings of the Committee, provided that each representative retains the right to request that any such decision be submitted to the Committee for approval;

(c) put questions and notify the Committee of the results of votes;

(d) approve a provisional agenda for the meeting after consultation with representatives and the Executive Secretary;

(e) sign, on behalf of the Committee, the reports of each meeting for transmission to its Members, representatives and other interested persons as official documents of the proceedings;

(f) present the report of the Scientific Committee to the Commission; and

(g) exercise other powers and responsibilities as provided in these rules and make such decisions and give such directions to the Executive Secretary as will ensure that the business of the Committee is carried out effectively and in accordance with its decisions.

Rule 10

Whenever the Chairman is unable to act, the Vice-Chairmen shall assume the powers and responsibilities of the Chairman.

Rule 11

In the event of the office of the Chairman falling vacant between meetings, the Vice-Chairmen shall exercise the powers and perform the duties of the Chairman until a new Chairman is elected.

Rule 12

The Chairman and Vice-Chairmen shall commence the fulfilment of their obligations at the conclusion of the meeting of the Committee at which they have been elected, with the exception of the first Chairman and Vice-Chairmen who shall take office immediately upon their election.

PART V SUBSIDIARY BODIES

Rule 13

The Committee shall establish, with the approval of the Commission, such subsidiary bodies as it deems necessary for the performance of its functions and determine their composition and terms of reference.

Where applicable, subsidiary bodies shall operate on the basis of the Rules of Procedure of the Committee.

PART VI PROGRAM OF WORK

Rule 14

At each annual meeting the Scientific Committee shall submit to the Commission an estimate of the budget required for the work of the Scientific Committee for the forthcoming year with a forecast for the subsequent year.

PART VII SECRETARIAT

Rule 15

As a general rule, the Committee and its subsidiary bodies shall make use of the facilities of the Secretariat for the fulfilment of their functions.

PART VIII LANGUAGES

Rule 16

The official and working languages of the Committee shall be English, French, Russian and Spanish.

PART IX RECORDS AND REPORTS

Rule 17

At each meeting the Committee shall prepare, and immediately thereafter transmit, a report to the Commission in accordance with Rule 3. Such report shall summarise the discussions of the Committee. The report shall include and provide the rationale for all findings and recommendations and shall include any minority reports provided to the Chairman. A copy of the report shall be transmitted to Members of the Committee.

Rule 18

The Executive Secretary shall present as soon as possible to the Members of the Scientific Committee brief records of each plenary session, of every meeting of all subsidiary bodies, and of reports, resolutions, recommendations and other decisions taken.

PART X OBSERVERS

Rule 19

Subject to Article XII of the Convention on the Conservation of Antarctic Marine Living Resources, the Scientific Committee may:

(a) extend an invitation to any State party to the Convention which is not entitled to be a Member of the Commission under Article VII of the Convention to attend, in accordance with Rules 21, 22 and 23 below, as Observers in meetings of the Scientific Committee;

(b) invite, as appropriate, any other State to attend, in accordance with Rules 21, 22 and 23 below, as Observers in the meetings of the Scientific Committee unless a Member of the Scientific Committee objects;

(c) invite, as appropriate, organisations named in Article XXIII(2) and (3) of the Convention to attend, in accordance with Rules 21, 22 and 23 below, as Observers in the meetings of the Scientific Committee;

(d) invite, as appropriate, other intergovernmental and non-governmental organisations, to which Article XXIII(3) of the Convention may apply, to attend in accordance with Rules 21, 22 and 23 below, as observers in the meetings of the Scientific Committee unless a Member of the Scientific Committee objects;

(e) the Scientific Committee may also invite Observers, in accordance with Rules 19(a) to (d), to the meetings of any subsidiary body of the Committee.

Observers invited under this rule shall have appropriate scientific qualifications.

Rule 20

Each observer invited in accordance with Rule 19 above shall notify the Executive Secretary as early as possible before any meeting of the name of its representative and before or at the beginning of the meeting the names of its experts and advisers.

Rule 21[11]

(a) The Chairman may, when preparing with the Executive Secretary the preliminary agenda for a meeting of the Scientific Committee, draw to the attention of Members of the Scientific Committee his view that the work of the Scientific Committee would be facilitated by the attendance at its next meeting of an observer referred to in Rule 19, an invitation to which was not considered at the previous meeting. The Executive Secretary shall so inform Members of the Scientific Committee when transmitting to them the Preliminary Agenda under Rule 5;

(b) Unless a Member of the Committee objects to the participation of an observer no later than 65 days before the beginning of the next meeting, the Executive Secretary shall issue to that observer an invitation to the next meeting of the Scientific Committee. The Executive Secretary will so inform Members of the Scientific Committee when transmitting to them the Provisional Agenda under Rule 7. An objection by a Member of the Committee in accordance with this rule shall be considered at an early point during the next meeting of the Committee.

Rule 22

If a Member of the Committee so requests, sessions of the Committee at which a particular agenda item is under consideration shall be restricted to Members of the Committee.

Rule 23

(a) The Chairman may invite observers to address the Committee unless a Member of the Committee objects;

(b) Observers are not entitled to participate in the taking of decisions.

Rule 24

(a) Observers may submit documents to the Secretariat for distribution to Members of the Committee as information documents. Such documents shall be relevant to matters under consideration in the Committee;

(b) Unless a Member or Members of the Committee request otherwise such documents shall be available only in the language or languages and in the quantities in which they were submitted;

(c) Such documents shall only be considered as Committee documents if so decided by the Committee.

Establishment of the Standing Committee on Administration and Finance (SCAF) (1983)

The Standing Committee on Administration and Finance (SCAF) was established by the Commission as follows:[12]

1. The Commission for the Conservation of Antarctic Marine Living Resources hereby establishes in accordance with Article XIII(6) of the Convention a Standing Committee on Administration and Finance (SCAF).

2. The Commission shall elect from among its Members a Chairman of the Standing Committee who shall serve for a term of two years and shall be eligible for re-election for one additional term.

3. The Standing Committee shall advise the Commission on such matters of an administrative and financial character as are remitted to it by the Commission and shall annually:

(a) examine the audited financial statement of the Commission for the previous year;

(b) examine the operation of the budget for the current year; and

[11] Amended at SC-CAMLR-XXIX (paragraph 15.17).

[12] As adopted at CCAMLR-II (paragraph 13) and amended at CCAMLR-XI (paragraph 3.23).

(c) examine the draft budget for the ensuing year.

4. The Standing Committee may draw to the attention of the Commission any matter of an administrative or financial character.

5. The Standing Committee may appoint from amongst its members a smaller, informal group to give preliminary consideration, in consultation with the Executive Secretary, to matters before it.

6. The Standing Committee shall prepare a report of each meeting of the Committee for transmission to the Commission.

Financial Regulations of the CCAMLR (1982)[13]

Regulation 1 Applicability

1.1 These Regulations shall govern the financial administration of the Commission for the Conservation of Antarctic Marine Living Resources (hereinafter referred to as 'the Commission') and the Scientific Committee for the Conservation of Antarctic Marine Living Resources (hereinafter referred to as 'the Scientific Committee') established under Articles VII(1) and XIV(1) of the Convention on the Conservation of Antarctic Marine Living Resources (hereinafter referred to as 'the Convention').

Regulation 2 Financial Year

2.1 The financial year shall be for 12 months commencing 1 January and ending 31 December, both dates inclusive.

Regulation 3 The Budget

3.1 A draft budget comprising estimates of receipts by the Commission and of expenditures by the Commission and the Scientific Committee and any subsidiary bodies established pursuant to Articles XIII(6) and XVI(3) of the Convention shall be prepared by the Executive Secretary for the ensuing financial year.

3.2 The draft budget shall include a statement of the significant financial implications for subsequent financial years in respect of any proposed work programs presented in terms of administrative, recurrent and capital expenditure.

3.3 The draft budget shall be divided by functions into items and, where necessary or appropriate, into sub-items.

3.4 The draft budget shall be accompanied by details both of the appropriations made for the previous year and estimated expenditure against those appropriations, together with such information annexures as may be required by Members of the Commission or deemed necessary or desirable by the Executive Secretary. The precise form in which the draft budget is to be presented shall be prescribed by the Commission.

3.5 The Executive Secretary shall submit the draft budget to all Members of the Commission at least 60 days prior to the annual meeting of the Commission, as provided for in Article XIX(2) of the Convention. At the same time, and in the same form as the draft budget, he shall prepare and submit to all Members of the Commission a forecast budget for the subsequent financial year.

3.6 The draft budget and the forecast budget shall be presented in Australian dollars.

3.7[14] At each annual meeting, the Commission shall adopt by consensus its budget and the budget of the Scientific Committee.

---

[13] As adopted at CCAMLR-I (paragraph 23) and amended at CCAMLR-XIII (Annex 4, Appendix 1), CCAMLR-XVII (Annex 4, Appendix III), CCAMLR-XVIII (paragraph 3.5; Annex 4, paragraph 38), CCAMLR-XXI (Annex 4, paragraph 23) , CCAMLR-XXX (Annex 5, paragraph 22) and CCAMLR-XXXI, Annex 7, paragraph 4.15).

[14] Article XIX(1) of the Convention on the Conservation of Antarctic Marine Living Resources.

Regulation 4 Appropriations

4.1 The appropriations adopted by the Commission shall constitute an authorisation for the Executive Secretary to incur obligations and make payments for the purposes for which the appropriations were adopted.

4.2 Unless the Commission decides otherwise, the Executive Secretary may also incur obligations against future years before appropriations are adopted when such obligations are necessary for the continued effective functioning of the Commission, provided such obligations are restricted to administrative requirements of a continuing nature not exceeding the scale of such requirements as authorised in the budget of the current financial year. In other circumstances the Executive Secretary may incur obligations against future years only as authorised by the Commission.

4.3 Appropriations shall be available for the financial year to which they relate. At the end of the financial year all appropriations shall lapse. Commitments remaining undischarged against previous appropriations at the end of a financial year shall be carried over and be included in the budget for the next financial year, unless the Commission otherwise decides.

4.4 The Chairman may authorise the Executive Secretary to make transfers of up to 10 per cent of appropriations between items. The Chairman of the Standing Committee on Administration and Finance may authorise the Executive Secretary to make transfers of up to 10 per cent of appropriations between categories within expenditure items. The Executive Secretary may authorise the transfer of up to 10 per cent of appropriations between expenditure items. All transfers must be reported by the Executive Secretary to the next annual meeting of the Commission.

4.5 The conditions under which unforeseen and extraordinary expenses may be incurred, as agreed by the Commission, are provided in Annex 1 to the Financial Regulations.

Regulation 5 Provision of Funds

5.1 Each Member of the Commission shall contribute to the budget in accordance with Article XIX(3) of the Convention.

5.2 Staff Assessment Levy paid by an employee of the Commission shall be regarded by the Commission as payment towards the annual budget contribution for the year.

5.3 On approval of the budget for a financial year, the Executive Secretary shall send a copy of that budget to all Members of the Commission notifying them of their contributions and requesting them to remit their contributions due. A Member of the Commission that fails to pay its contributions for two consecutive years shall not, during the period of its default, have the right to participate in the taking of decisions in the Commission.

5.4 All contributions shall be made in Australian dollars.

5.5

(a) A new Member of the Commission whose membership becomes effective during the first six months of the financial year shall be liable to pay the full amount of the annual contribution which would have been payable had it been a Member of the Commission when assessments were made under Article XIX(3) of the Convention. A new Member whose membership becomes effective during the last six months of the financial year, shall be liable to pay half of the amount of the annual contribution referred to above;

(b) Where contributions are received from new Members the contributions of existing Members shall be adjusted in accordance with Regulation 6.1(d).

5.6 Contributions shall be due for payment on the first day of the financial year, 1 January (i.e. the due date). Contributions shall be paid not later than 31 May (extended period of payment), recognising that submission of payments later in the extended period of payment may impact the Secretariat's ability to meet its financial obligations. However, in the case referred to in Regulation 5.5(a), contributions by a new Member shall be made within 90 days following the date on which its membership becomes effective.

5.7 The Executive Secretary shall report to each meeting of the Commission on the receipt of the contributions and the position of arrears.

Regulation 6 Funds

6.1

(a) There shall be established a General Fund for the purpose of accounting for the income and expenditure of the Commission and Scientific Committee and any subsidiary bodies established pursuant to the Convention;

(b) Contributions paid by Members under Regulation 5.1 and miscellaneous income to finance general expenditure shall be credited to the General Fund;

(c) Any cash surplus in the General Fund at the close of a financial year that is not required to meet undischarged commitments in terms of Regulation 4.3 shall be divided in proportion to the contributions made by existing Members under Regulation 5.1 in the current financial year and used to offset such Members' contributions for the ensuing financial year;

(d) Where contributions are received from new Members after the commencement of the financial year and such funds have not been taken into account in formulating the budget, appropriate adjustment shall be made to the level of the assessed contributions of existing Members and such adjustments recorded as advances made by such Members;

(e) Advances made by Members shall be carried to the credit of the Members which have made such advances.

6.2 Trust and Special Funds may be established by the Commission for the purpose of receiving funds and making payments for purposes not covered by the regular budget of the Commission.

Regulation 7 Other Income

7.1 All income other than contributions to the budget under Regulation 5 and that referred to in Regulation 7.3 below, shall be classified as Miscellaneous Income and credited to the General Fund. The use of Miscellaneous Income shall be subject to the same financial controls as activities financed from regular budget appropriations.

7.2 Voluntary contributions above and beyond Members' budget contributions may be accepted by the Executive Secretary provided that the purposes for which the contributions are made are consistent with the policies, aims and activities of the Commission. Voluntary contributions offered by non-Members may be accepted, subject to agreement by the Commission that the purposes of the contribution are consistent with the policies, aims and activities of the Commission.

7.3 Voluntary contributions shall be treated as Trust or Special Funds under Regulation 6.2.

Regulation 8 Custody of Funds

8.1 The Executive Secretary shall designate institutions in Australia in which the funds of the Commission shall be kept and shall report the identity of the institutions so designated to the Commission.

8.2 The Executive Secretary may make investments of moneys not needed for the immediate requirements of the Commission. Such investments shall be in accordance with the Investment principles at Annex 2. Income derived from investments shall be reported in the documents supporting the budget.

8.3 Income derived from investments shall be credited to the Fund from which the investment was made.

Regulation 9 Internal Control

9.1 The Executive Secretary shall:

(a) establish detailed financial rules and procedures in accordance with the Investment Principles at Annex 2 to ensure effective financial administration and the exercise of economy in the use of funds;

(b) cause all payments to be made on the basis of supporting vouchers and other documents which ensure that the goods or services have been received and that payment has not previously been made;

(c) designate officers who may receive moneys, incur obligations and make payments on behalf of the Commission; and

(d) maintain and be responsible for internal financial control to ensure:

(i) the regularity of the receipt, custody and disposal of all funds and other financial resources of the Commission;

(ii) the conformity of obligations and expenditures with the appropriations adopted by the annual meeting; and

(iii) the economic use of the resources of the Commission.

9.2 No obligations shall be incurred until allotments or other appropriate authorisations have been made in writing under the authority of the Executive Secretary.

9.3 The Executive Secretary may propose to the Commission, after full investigation by him, the writing off of losses of assets, provided that a statement of all such amounts written off is submitted to the auditor with the accounts together with the justification for the writeoff. Such losses shall be included in the annual accounts.

9.4 Tenders in writing for equipment, supplies and other requirements shall be invited by advertisement, or by direct requests for quotation from at least three persons or firms able to supply the equipment, supplies, or other requirements, if such exist, in connection with all purchases or contracts, the amounts of which exceed $2 000 (Australian dollars). For amounts exceeding $100, but less than $2 000, competition shall be obtained either by the above means or by telephone or personal enquiry. The foregoing rules, shall, however, not apply in the following cases:

(a) where it has been ascertained that only a single supplier exists and that fact is so certified by the Executive Secretary;

(b) in case of emergency, or where, for any other reason, these rules would not be in the best financial interests of the Commission, and that fact is so certified by the Executive Secretary.

Regulation 10 The Accounts

10.1 The Executive Secretary shall ensure that appropriate records and accounts are kept of the transactions and affairs of the Commission and shall do all things necessary to ensure that all payments out of the Commission's moneys are correctly made and properly authorised and that adequate control is maintained over the assets of, or in the custody of, the Commission and over the incurring of liabilities by the Commission.

10.2 The Executive Secretary shall submit to the Members of the Commission, not later than 31 March immediately following the end of the financial year, annual financial statements showing, for the financial year to which they relate:

(a) the income and expenditure relating to all funds and accounts;

(b) the situation with regard to budget provisions, including:

(i) the original budget provisions;

(ii) the approved expenditure in excess of the original budget provisions;

(iii) any other income;

(iv) the amounts charged against these provisions and other income;

(c) the financial assets and liabilities of the Commission;

(d) details of investments;

(e) losses of assets proposed in accordance with Regulation 9.3.

The Executive Secretary shall also give such other information as may be appropriate to indicate the financial position of the Commission. These financial statements shall be prepared in a form approved by the Commission after consultation with the external auditor.

10.3 The Executive Secretary shall submit to all Members of the Commission, not later than 10 working days following the end of each financial quarter (being 31 March, 30 June, 30 September, 31 December), interim financial reports showing:

(a) income (including interest income) and expenditures relating to all funds and accounts;

(b) the status and performance of investments; and

(c) other advice or information the Executive Secretary considers relevant pertaining to the financial management of the Commission.

10.4 The Executive Secretary will inform Members of significant or unforseen financial events, particularly where such events may have substantial impact on the current or future financial position of the Commission, as soon as possible from when the Executive Secretary becomes aware of such events.

10.5 The accounting transactions of the Commission shall be recorded in the currency in which they took place but the annual financial statements shall record all transactions in Australian dollars.

10.6 Appropriate separate accounts shall be kept for all Special and Trust Funds.

10.7 The annual financial statements shall be submitted by the Executive Secretary to the external auditor in accordance with Article XIX(4) of the Convention at the same time as they are submitted to Members of the Commission under paragraph 2 of this Regulation.

Regulation 11 External Audit

11.1 The Commission shall appoint an external auditor who shall be the Auditor-General or equivalent statutory authority from a Member of the Commission and shall serve for a term of two years with the possibility of re-appointment. The Commission will ensure respect for the external auditor's independence of the Commission, the Scientific Committee, their subsidiary bodies and the Commission's staff, fix the terms of office, and appropriate funds to the external auditor to meet the costs of the audit.

11.2 The external auditor or a person or persons authorised by him shall be entitled at all reasonable times to full and free access to all accounts and records of the Commission relating directly or indirectly to the receipt or payment of moneys by the Commission or to the acquisition, receipt, custody or disposal of assets by the Commission. The external auditor or a person or persons authorised by him may make copies of or take extracts from any such accounts or records.

11.3 Full audits of the Commission's Financial Statement shall be conducted annually. In performing a full audit, the external auditor shall conduct his examination of the statements in conformity with generally accepted auditing standards and shall report to the Commission on all relevant matters, including:

(a) whether, in his opinion, the statements are based on proper accounts and records; and

(b) whether the statements are in agreement with the accounts and records.

11.4 The Commission may also seek of the auditor a separate report on other relevant matters, including:

(a) whether, in his opinion, the income, expenditure and investment of moneys and the acquisition and disposal of assets by the Commission during the year have been in accordance with these Regulations; and

(b) observations with respect to the efficiency and economy of the financial procedures and the conduct of business, the accounting system, internal financial controls and the administration and management of the Commission.

11.5 The Executive Secretary shall provide the external auditor with the facilities he may require in the performance of the audit.

11.6 The Executive Secretary shall provide to the Members of the Commission a copy of the audit report and the audited financial statements within 30 days of their receipt.

11.7 The Commission shall, if necessary, invite the external auditor to attend discussions on any item under scrutiny and consider recommendations arising out of his findings.

Regulation 12 Acceptance of Annual Financial Statements

12.1 The Commission shall, following consideration of the audited annual financial statements and audit report submitted to its Members under Regulation 11.5 of these Regulations, signify its acceptance of the audited annual financial statements or take such other action as it may consider appropriate.

Regulation 13 Insurance

13.1 The Commission may take out suitable insurances with a reputable financial institution against normal risks to its assets.

Regulation 14 General Provision

14.1 Subject to the provisions of the Convention, these Regulations may be amended by the Commission in accordance with its Rules of Procedure.

14.2 Where the Commission or the Scientific Committee is considering matters which may lead to a decision which has financial or administrative implications, it shall have before it an evaluation of those implications from the Executive Secretary.

Annex 1: Extract from CCAMLR-XXI, Annex 4, Paragraphs 20 and 21

Contingency Fund

20. At its 2001 meeting, the Commission established a Contingency Fund. Noting that this is intended to be used for necessary expenditure which has not yet been specifically authorised by the Commission, SCAF recommended that the following definitions be agreed by the Commission for unforeseen and extraordinary expenditure as envisaged in Financial Regulation 4.5:

> 'Unforeseen expenditure' is expenditure of which the Commission had been unaware at the time of its previous meeting, but which is necessary for the fulfilment of tasks required by the Commission to be performed, with the amount not being possible to subsume into the annual budget without inordinate disruption of the Commission's work.
>
> 'Extraordinary expenditure' is expenditure the nature of which was known by the Commission at its previous meeting, but the extent of which is far greater than had been anticipated at that time, with the extra amount not being possible to subsume into the annual budget without inordinate disruption of the Commission's work.

21. The Committee further recommended that the following procedures should be applied for any use of the Fund:

(i) As soon as the Executive Secretary believes that there is a reasonable expectation of unforseen or extraordinary expenditure, he/she will consult with the SCAF Chair and Vice-Chair to confirm that:
   - the nature of the expenditure complies with the above definitions;
   - the Contingency Fund has sufficient capacity to cover the expenditure; and
   - it is not possible to defer the decision on the use of the Fund until the next meeting of the Commission.

(ii) The Executive Secretary will advise all Members of any intended use of the Fund.

(iii) Any Member that considers such expenditure from the Fund to be inappropriate shall advise the Chair accordingly, including any proposal for alternative action.

(iv) The Commission Chair shall consult with the SCAF Chair and the Executive Secretary. If the three parties agree with the Member's advice, then this shall be acted upon and Members will be advised accordingly. If the parties fail to come to agreement on the Member's advice, and if time permits, then Members will be asked to decide on the issue in accordance with Rule 7. If there is insufficient time for such a decision, or if Members are unable to reach consensus, then the Executive Secretary, in consultation with the Commission Chair and the SCAF Chair and Vice-Chair, shall determine to what extent to use the Fund.

(v) Any actual expenditure from the Fund will be advised to Members immediately.

(vi) The Executive Secretary will report to the subsequent meeting of the Commission any expenditure from the Fund, including related expenditure from the current and future budgets of the General Fund, and proposals to re-establish the Contingency Fund at its former level.

Annex 2: Investment Principles

(i) The primary consideration in determining the investment strategy for the Commission shall be to safeguard the funds of the Commission. Funds shall be invested in such a way as to place primary emphasis on avoiding the erosion of principal funds while ensuring the liquidity necessary to meet the Commission's cash flow requirements.

(ii) Investment of moneys not needed for the immediate requirements of the Commission shall be conservative and low risk in nature. Investments shall be restricted to cash equivalents, term deposits and government bonds. Investments that attract a government guarantee shall be limited to terms of not more than 24 months unless otherwise agreed by the Commission. Investments that do not attract a government guarantee shall be restricted to those institutions assessed by the Australian Prudential Regulation Authority (APRA) as an Authorised Deposit-taking Institution (ADI) and shall be limited to terms of not more than 12 months unless otherwise agreed by the Commission.

(iii) To minimise risk, the investment portfolio of the Commission shall offer diversity across institutions, instruments and maturity dates. Where a government guarantee is available, investments in ADIs other than Australian-owned banks shall be limited to the amount guaranteed.

(iv) The Executive Secretary will provide quarterly interim financial reports of income (including interest income) and expenditure to Members. The quarterly reports will include a report on the status and performance of investments as well as providing Members with any other relevant advice or information pertaining to the financial management of the Commission.

(v) The Executive Secretary will inform Members of significant or unforseen financial events, particularly where such events may have a substantial impact on the current or future financial position of the Commission, as soon as possible from when the Executive Secretary becomes aware of such events.

(vi) Investments shall be recorded in an investment ledger held by the Secretariat, which shall show all relevant details for each investment, including face value, cost, date of maturity, interest rate, place of deposit, proceeds of sale, income earned and whether the investment attracts a government guarantee.

Staff Regulations of the CCAMLR (1982)[15]

PREAMBLE

1. These Staff Regulations establish the fundamental principles of employment, regulate the working relationships and establish the rights and responsibilities of formally appointed Employees who render their services in, and receive remuneration from, the Secretariat of the Commission for the Conservation of Antarctic Marine Living Resources (hereafter called 'the Commission').

2. These Regulations are to be applied giving due regard to the geographical distribution of the Members of the Commission.

3. These Staff Regulations are to be applied giving due regard to Article 5.1 of the Headquarters Agreement between the Commission for the Conservation of Antarctic Marine Living Resources and the Government of Australia, which states 'that except as provided in the Convention or this [Headquarters] Agreement, the activities of the Commission shall be governed by the laws of Australia'.

[15] As adopted at CCAMLR-XXXI (2012).

SECTION 1 – GENERAL TERMS AND CONDITION OF EMPLOYMENT FOR ALL STAFF

The following terms and conditions of employment apply to all CCAMLR staff unless otherwise specified.

Regulation 1.1 – Definitions

1.1.1 In these Staff Regulations, unless the context otherwise requires:

'APS System' means the Australian Public Service classification system established by the Australian Public Service Commission

'Award-free' means an employee is not covered by an applicable modern award

'Basic periodic rate of pay' means a rate of pay for a period worked that does not include incentive-based payments and bonuses, loadings, monetary allowances, penalty rate or any other similar separately identifiable entitlements

'CCAMLR Job Classification System' is the policy relating to the roles and responsibilities of staff posts at the CCAMLR Secretariat approved by the Commission

'CCAMLR Staffing and Salary Strategy' means the policies and procedures relating to the administration of staff arrangements at the CCAMLR Secretariat approved by the Commission

'Chair of the Commission' means Chair of the Commission

'Convention' means the Convention on the Conservation of Antarctic Marine Living Resources

'Deed of Employment' means the contract between a CCAMLR employee and the Commission describing the terms and conditions for their employment. As appropriate, the Staff Regulations are an integral element of the Deed of Employment

'Dependant' means:

(a) any unsalaried child, who is born of, or adopted by, a staff member, their spouse, or their children, who is below the age of eighteen years and who is dependent on a staff member or their spouse for main and continuing support

(b) any child fulfilling the conditions laid down in Clause (a) above, but who is between eighteen and twenty-five years of age and is receiving school or university education or vocational training

(c) any handicapped child who is dependent on a staff member or their spouse for main and continuing support

(d) any other child who is given a home by, and is dependent on, a staff member or their spouse for main and continuing support

(e) any person related by blood or marriage for whose main and continuing support a staff member or their spouse is legally responsible

'Employee' means, unless otherwise stipulated, a member of the Secretariat staff categorised under the Commission's Staff Regulations

'Employer' means the Commission for the Conservation of Antarctic Marine Living Resources

'Executive Secretary' means the Executive Secretary of the Commission

'Expiry date' means, where applicable, the date on which the agreed term for a Deed of Employment terminates

'*Fair Work Act 2009*' means the national legislation that regulates workplace relations in Australia

'Fair Work Australia' means the national workplace tribunal established under the *Fair Work Act 2009*

'General Services employee' means, unless otherwise stipulated, a member of the Secretariat staff as categorised and remunerated under the Commission's Staff Regulations and the CCAMLR Job Classification System, based on the Australian modern awards, which in the case of the Secretariat are, for the time being, the *Clerks – Private Sector Award 2010* and the *Professional Employees Award 2010*

'Headquarters Agreement' means the agreement between the Commission and the Government of Australia defining the legal capacity, privileges and immunities of the Commission and the privileges and immunities to be enjoyed by the staff of the Commission in Australia in accordance with Article VIII of the Convention

'Immediate family' means for the purpose of personal and compassionate leave only:

- spouse (including a former spouse, a de facto spouse and a former de facto spouse) of the employee. A de facto spouse means a person who lives with the employee as his or her partner on a bona fide domestic basis
- child or an adult child (including an adopted child, a step-child or an ex-nuptial child), parent, grandparent, grandchild or sibling of the employee or spouse of the employee

'International Professional employee' means, unless otherwise stipulated, a member of the Secretariat staff as categorised under the Commission's Staff Regulations and the CCAMLR Job Classification System, remunerated under the ICSC System

'ICSC System' means the system for classifying International Professional employees as established by the International Civil Service Commission (an expert body established by the United Nations General Assembly to regulate and coordinate the conditions of United Nations staff)

'Other officer' means an employee so designated by the Executive Secretary and whose duties carry responsibility for the supervision of staff

'Modern award' means a set of industry or occupation-based enforceable minimum employment standards

'National Employment Standards' means the National Employment Standards as contained in Sections 59 to 131 of the *Fair Work Act 2009*

'Pay step' means the pay step within each classification of Australian Public Service pay in force at 30 June 1998 in respect of a General Services employee or within each classification applicable to officials of the United Nations Secretariat employed in Australia in respect of a Professional Employee, or any other pay step as proposed by the Executive Secretary and agreed by the Commission

'Period of employment' means the number of years and days worked, commencing with the date when the employee took up employment as a staff member of the Secretariat

'Relevant industrial instrument' means an instrument that legally regulates the employment of an employee which may include a modern award, Deed of Employment or the *Fair Work Act 2009*

'Salary rate applicable' means, in relation to the General Services employee, the Australian Public Service pay rate applicable to the classification and pay step in force at 30 June 1998 and increased annually thereafter by the consumer price index announced by the Australian Bureau of Statistics, whereas in the case of the International Professional employee, the salary rate applicable means that which applies to officials of the United Nations Secretariat employed in Australia, or any other salary rate as agreed by the Commission

'Secretariat' means the Secretariat of the Commission

'Staff Assessment Levy' (SAL) means a levy in lieu of taxation, the rate set by the International Civil Service Commission of the United Nations, deducted from International Professional officers' gross fortnightly pay and retained by the Commission

'Staff member' means, unless otherwise stipulated, a member of the Secretariat staff categorised under the Commission's Staff Regulations

'Staff Regulations' means CCAMLR's policies and procedures relating to the employment terms and conditions for staff of the CCAMLR Secretariat, approved by the Commission. The Staff Regulations are implemented through the Deed of Employment.

Regulation 1.2 – Duties, obligations and privileges

1.2.1 Members of the staff of the Secretariat, and the Executive Secretary (hereafter called 'staff members or employees') are international civil servants. Upon accepting their appointments they pledge themselves to discharge their duties faithfully and to conduct themselves with the interests of the Commission in mind.

1.2.2 Staff members shall at all times conduct themselves in a manner in keeping with the international nature of the Commission. They shall always bear in mind the loyalty, discretion and tact imposed on them by their international responsibilities in the performance of their duties. They shall avoid all actions, statements or public activities which might be detrimental to the Commission and its aims.

1.2.3 Staff members are not required to renounce either their national feelings or their political or religious convictions.

1.2.4 In the performance of their duties, staff members may neither seek, nor accept, instructions from any government or authority other than the Commission.

1.2.5 Staff members shall observe maximum discretion regarding official matters and shall abstain from making private use of information they possess by reason of their position. Authorisation for the release of information for official purposes shall lie with the Commission or the Executive Secretary, as the case may require.

1.2.6 Staff members shall, in general, have no employment other than with the Commission. In special cases, staff members may accept other employment, provided that it does not interfere with their duties in the Commission, and that prior authorisation by the Executive Secretary has been obtained. The Commission's prior authorisation shall be obtained in respect of the Executive Secretary.

1.2.7 Staff members shall enjoy the privileges and immunities to which they are entitled under the Headquarters Agreement between the Government of Australia and the Commission, pursuant to Article VIII of the Convention.

1.2.8 Staff members shall not at any time, either directly or indirectly, deal with or employ the plant, equipment, stock, money, credit or other assets belonging or owing to the Commission for the employee's own gain.

1.2.9 Staff members will not do, or cause to be done, any act or thing whereby any property belonging to the Commission may be, or become liable to be, seized in execution, charged or affected or whereby the interest of the Commission may be prejudicially affected.

1.2.10 Staff members shall not at any time enter into any contract or arrangement on behalf of the Commission or bind the Commission without the prior consent of the Executive Secretary.

1.2.11 The employee shall not be engaged, concerned or interested in any capacity in any other trade, business or occupation whatsoever other than the business of the Commission:

(a) without the prior written consent of the Executive Secretary; or
(b) except where the interest, engagement or concern of the employee in such other trade, business or occupation does not, in the opinion of the Executive Secretary, interfere with the duties of the employee.

This provision shall not prohibit the holding of investments listed on any stock exchange. The employee shall notify the Executive Secretary in writing of any other trade, business or occupation in which the employee is, or proposes to be, engaged, concerned or interested, either before the commencement of the employee's employment or before becoming so engaged, concerned or interested, as the case may be.

Regulation 1.3 – Application and amendment of regulations

1.3.1 The Executive Secretary is responsible for the administration of these Staff Regulations on behalf of the Commission. Where they are applicable to the Executive Secretary, the Chair of the Commission shall determine the administration of the Staff Regulations.

1.3.2 Any doubts arising from application of these regulations shall be resolved by the Executive Secretary following consultation with the Chair of the Commission.

1.3.3 All matters not foreseen in these Staff Regulations shall be brought to the attention of the Commission by the Executive Secretary.

1.3.4 Subject to the provisions of the Convention, these regulations may be amended by the Commission in accordance with its Rules of Procedure.

Regulation 1.4 – Classification of staff

1.4.1 The CCAMLR Job Classification System describes two categories of staff that are supported at the CCAMLR Secretariat. One is recruited from within Australia from among citizens of Members of the Commission. This category is termed General Services. The terms and conditions for appointment to a post classified as General Services are governed by the Australian *Fair Work Act 2009*. Under the *Fair Work Act 2009*, two *Modern Award Classifications* currently apply to CCAMLR General Services staff: the *Clerks – Private Sector Award 2010* and the *Professional Employees Award 2010*.

1.4.2 The second category is recruited globally from among citizens of Members of the Commission. The terms and conditions for appointment to a post within this category are guided by the United Nations ICSC System. Except for the Executive Secretary, the posts within the CCAMLR Secretariat in this category are designated *International Professional*. The Executive Secretary post is designated *International Director*.

1.4.3 Staff members shall be classified in either of the following two categories:

(a) International Professional category: Positions of high responsibility of a managerial, professional or scientific nature. These posts will be filled by appropriately qualified professionals, preferably with university qualifications or the equivalent. Staff members in this category will be sourced internationally from citizens of Members of the Commission.

(b) General Services category: Managerial, auxiliary administrative, scientific and technical positions. Clerical, secretarial and other office personnel. Such staff members will be recruited in Australia from among citizens of Members of the Commission. Employees under the General Services category may be employed in accordance with a modern award or award-free.

1.4.4 Detailed classification information is located in CCAMLR's Job Classification System document. For those employees covered by a modern award, the table at Appendix 1 of the Staff Regulations provides a translation from the modern award classifications to CCAMLR's Job Classification System.

1.4.5 Persons employed under Section 5 of the Staff Regulations shall not be classified as ongoing staff members.

Regulation 1.5 – Salaries and other remuneration

1.5.1 The following clauses are only applicable to General Services category employees:

(a) staff members in the General Services category shall, in principle, be paid at rates equivalent to those paid in Hobart for staff of equivalent qualifications and experience in accordance with the CCAMLR Job Classification System

(b) General Services category employees shall receive an annual consumer price index adjustment to their salary in line with the 30 June figure for Hobart, published by the Australian Bureau of Statistics.

1.5.2 The following clauses are only applicable to International Professional category employees:

(a) additional salary conditions for International Professional category employees are as per Section 2 of the Staff Regulations

(b) the promotion of staff members from one salary scale to another requires the prior approval of the Commission.

1.5.3 The following clauses are applicable to all staff members:

(a) The salaries of staff members shall begin at Step 1 of the appropriate classification at which they are appointed. Staff members shall remain at that level for at least the first year of employment.

(b) During the continuation of the employee's employment by the Commission, subject to a satisfactory performance rating, the employee will advance by one pay step at each anniversary of their commencement date up to a maximum of the top pay step of the applicable classification in accordance with CCAMLR's Staffing and Salary Strategy.
(c) The remuneration payable by the Commission to the employee will occur in fortnightly payments (and proportionately for any lesser period), in arrears.
(d) In accordance with taxation arrangements entered into with the Australian Government through the Headquarters Agreement, and with the Australian Taxation Office, a SAL on the remuneration of the International Professional officers shall be deducted by the Commission from the remuneration of the International Professional officer and such deduction shall be retained by the Commission.
(e) General Service category employees shall be subject to Pay As You Go (PAYG) taxation in accordance with Australian tax rates in force. The deduction so withheld by the Commission is retained by the Commission in accordance with an agreement with the Australian Taxation Office. CCAMLR General Services staff shall be treated equally to other Australian taxpayers in respect of taxation matters.
(f) Only in very special cases, on the proposal of the Executive Secretary and with the approval of the Chair of the Commission, may staff members be appointed at a salary higher than Step 1 of the relevant category.

Regulation 1.6 – Additional hours – General Services category only

1.6.1 General Services employees shall not be entitled to receive any additional remuneration for additional hours performed outside the employee's normal working hours or for more than 37.5 hours per week unless such payment is for additional hours performed as authorised in advance by the Executive Secretary. Where this is the case, the General Services employee shall be entitled to be paid for such hours of work as exceed 37.5 for the week (except where a flexible working hours arrangement has been made in accordance with Regulation 1.7) at the following rates:

(a) where the hours worked by the employee exceed the contracted number of hours specified in the Deed of Employment but do not exceed 7.5 hours, the employee shall be entitled to receive 100% of the employee's usual hourly rate of pay for each hour so worked (and proportionately for any part of an hour)
(b) where the hours worked by the employee exceed 7.5 hours on any one day (other than on a Sunday or public holiday), or where any work is performed on a Saturday, the employee shall be entitled to receive 150% of the employee's usual hourly rate of pay for each hour so worked (and proportionately for any part of an hour)
(c) where any work is performed on a Sunday or public holiday, the employee shall be entitled to receive 200% of the employee's usual hourly rate of pay for each hour so worked (and proportionately for any part of an hour)
(d) where any work is performed over two consecutive days with a break of less than eight hours, the employee shall be entitled to receive 150% of the Employee's usual hourly rate for the work performed following the break for a period of up to 7.5 hours after the break, including such payment in conformity with that entitled under Clauses 1.6.1(a), 1.6.1(b) and 1.6.1(c)
(e) penalty rates are not cumulative. Where time worked is required to be paid at a penalty rate, that time must not be subject to more than one penalty, but will be subject to the penalty which is to the employee's greatest advantage.

Regulation 1.7 – Flexible working hours

1.7.1 By mutual agreement a General Services employee may work flexible working hours (flexitime) prescribed herein. Such agreement shall be recorded and filed with the relevant wage and time records.

1.7.2 Definitions

'Flexible working hours' (flexitime) means a system which allows employees to set their own patterns of attendance at work subject to the provisions of this agreement and the requirements of the workplace

'Standard day' means seven hours and thirty minutes per day worked in a continuous shift at any time within the ordinary hours of work as defined

'Bandwidth' means the span of any time on any day within which an employee may work as part of a flexible working hours arrangement subject to this agreement

'Core time' means the period during the day when all employees shall perform ordinary duties unless absent upon approved leave or core-time leave

'Core-time leave' means any approved absence during core time other than approved leave

'Approved leave' means any leave of absence other than core-time leave approved by the employer

'Flex credit' means the accumulated amount of time worked by an employee in excess of the standard days in the settlement period, including any carry-over, provided that any such time worked as overtime shall not be taken into account

'Flex debit' means the difference between the sum of the standard days in a settlement period and the aggregate amount of time worked by an employee where the total time worked is less than the sum of the standard days in the settlement period after any necessary adjustment has been made for an absence of approved paid leave and includes any carry-over

'Carry-over' means the aggregate of flex credit or flex debit which an employee has accumulated during a settlement period which, subject to these Staff Regulations, the employee may carry over to the next settlement period

'Settlement period' means the ordinary working days over which calculations are made to determine flex credit or flex debit carry-over and shall be a fixed period of 20 working days aligned with the fortnightly pay periods operating in the workplace.

(a) Under flexible working hours arrangements, the times of commencement and cessation of duty shall be subject to agreement between the employer and the employee.
(b) An employee's attendance outside the hours of a standard day shall be subject to the availability of work and the approval, which may be general or specific, of the employer.
(c) Where it is reasonable to do so because an employee has failed to comply with the provisions of flexible working hours (flexitime), the employer may, for a specified period, require that an employee shall revert to working an average 37.5 hour week.
(d) Unless otherwise agreed in a workplace, a bandwidth shall be between the ordinary hours of work as defined.
(e) Unless otherwise agreed in a workplace, core time shall be between the hours of 0900 h and 1200 h, and 1400 h and 1600 h.

1.7.3 Carry-over

(a) An employee may carry over a limit of 15 hours flex credit accumulated in any settlement period into the next settlement period.
(b) Where this limit is likely to be exceeded, the employer and employee shall arrange for sufficient core-time leave to be taken to bring the credits within the 15 hour limit as soon as is practicable before the limit is exceeded.

1.7.4 Core-time leave

(a) In any settlement period, and in addition to approved leave, an employee may, with the employer's prior approval, take core-time leave subject to the following requirements:
    (i) that core-time leave does not exceed the core time for a single day
    (ii) that the core-time leave does not result in the employee accruing more than a standard day flex debit by the end of the settlement period.

(b) Core-time leave may be used for a full day absence or part day absence during the settlement period.

Regulation 1.8 – Employee covenant

1.8.1 The employee shall not, except as authorised in writing by the Executive Secretary or as necessarily required by the employee's duties, reveal to any person any information concerning the organisation, business, finances, transactions or affairs of the Commission, its Members or the Secretariat which may come to the employee's knowledge during the employee's employment by the Commission and shall keep with complete secrecy all confidential information entrusted to the employee or of which the employee may become aware during the course of the employee's employment. These restrictions shall continue to apply after the termination of the employee's employment. These restrictions do not apply to the extent to which information comes into the public domain.

1.8.2 The employee shall conduct themselves in a manner in keeping with the international character of the Commission and shall:

(a) always bear in mind the loyalty, discretion and tact imposed by international responsibilities
(b) avoid all actions, statements or public activities which might be detrimental to the Commission and its aims
(c) not be required to renounce national feeling or political or religious convictions
(d) not seek, or accept, instructions from any government or authority other than the Commission
(e) observe maximum discretion involving official Commission matters.

Regulation 1.9 – Recruitment and appointment

1.9.1 In accordance with Article XVIII.1 of the Convention, the Commission shall appoint an Executive Secretary and shall establish the remuneration and such other entitlements as it deems appropriate. The Executive Secretary's term of office shall be for four years and the Executive Secretary shall be eligible for reappointment for one additional term. The total length of employment may not exceed eight years.

1.9.2 In accordance with Article XVII.2 of the Convention, the Executive Secretary shall appoint, direct and supervise staff. The paramount consideration in the appointment, transfer or promotion of the staff shall be the necessity for securing the highest standards of efficiency, competence and integrity.

1.9.3 Offers of appointment to the Secretariat are subject to the persons selected undergoing a medical examination and presenting a certificate stating that they have no medical condition which might prevent them from performing their duties, or which might endanger the health of others. The medical examination is at the expense of the Commission.

1.9.4 Upon selection, each staff member shall receive an offer of appointment stating:

(a) that the appointment is subject to the Staff Regulations applicable to the category of appointment in question, and to changes which may be duly made in such regulations
(b) the nature of the appointment
(c) the date on which the staff member is required to commence duty
(d) the period of appointment, the notice required to terminate it and the period of probation
(e) the category, level, commencing rate of salary and the scale of increments and the maximum salary attainable
(f) the allowances attached to the appointment
(g) any special terms and conditions which may be applicable.

1.9.5 Together with the offer of appointment, staff members shall be provided with a copy of these regulations. Upon acceptance of the offer, staff members shall state in writing that they are familiar with, and accept, the conditions set out in these regulations.

Regulation 1.10 – Separation from service

1.10.1 Staff members may resign at any time upon giving three months' notice or such lesser period as may be approved by the Executive Secretary or the Commission, as the case may require.

1.10.2 In the event of a staff member resigning without giving the required notice, the Executive Secretary reserves the right to decide whether repatriation expenses, or any other allowance, shall be paid.

1.10.3 In the event of separation from service with the Secretariat, a staff member shall receive one month's gross pay, less staff assessment levy, for each year of service or part thereof, including, but paid after completion of, the first year of service. If the appointment of a staff member is terminated for reasons of gross dereliction of duties or serious misconduct they will not receive a separation from service payment.

1.10.4 Appointment of staff members may be terminated upon prior written notice, at least three months in advance, by the Executive Secretary when he deems this to be for the benefit of the Commission due to restructuring of the Secretariat or if he considers that the staff member does not give satisfactory service, fails to comply with the duties and obligations set out in these Staff Regulations, or is incapacitated for service.

1.10.5 The separation from service payment in this clause is deemed to include all of the benefits and entitlements a staff member may have under any applicable legislation or industrial instrument. No additional payment will be made on termination of employment unless the quantum of the following payments exceeds the separation from service payment:

(a) notice of termination or payment in lieu of notice as per *Part 2-2, Division 11 of the Fair Work Act 2009*
(b) redundancy pay as per *Part 2-2, Division 11 of the Fair Work Act 2009*
(c) long-service leave as per *Part 2-2, Division 9 of the Fair Work Act 2009*
(d) any other benefit or entitlement that is applicable on termination in accordance with a relevant industrial instrument, excluding annual leave.

Regulation 1.11 – Higher duties

1.11.1 With the prior approval of the Executive Secretary, an employee who is required to perform the full duties and responsibilities of a higher classified employee for a period in excess of 10 working days shall be entitled to payment at the applicable classification rate for the period during which such duties are performed.

Regulation 1.12 – Annual leave

1.12.1 Entitlement

(a) Full-time and part-time employees shall be entitled to a minimum of 20 working days paid annual leave after 12 months continuous service. In addition, the Commission shall provide a further 10 working days of annual leave which must be taken within the year it accrues.
(b) The 20 days paid annual leave is cumulative and will accrue on a pro-rata basis. The additional 10 days shall not accrue from year to year if it is not taken within the applicable 12-month period.
(c) A period of annual leave does not break an employee's continuity of service.
(d) Staff members will be able to claim sick leave during a period of annual leave on the provision of a medical certificate from a recognised health professional.

1.12.2 Payment for leave

(a) The payment for annual leave is the staff member's basic periodic rate of pay immediately before the period begins.

1.12.3 Time of taking leave

(a) The taking of leave shall not cause undue disruption to normal Secretariat operations. In accordance with this principle, leave dates shall be subject to the needs of the Commission. Leave dates shall be approved by the Executive Secretary who shall, as far as possible, bear in mind the personal circumstances, needs and preferences of staff members.
(b) The staff member will endeavour to give the Executive Secretary four weeks' written notice of intention to take annual leave.

(c) The Executive Secretary will not unreasonably refuse to authorise an employee to take an amount of annual leave that is credited to the staff member, or revoke an authorisation enabling a staff member to take annual leave during a particular period.
(d) There is no maximum limit on the amount of annual leave that the Executive Secretary may authorise a staff member to take.

1.12.4 Payment of leave on termination of service

(a) A staff member is entitled to payment for untaken accumulated annual leave on termination of service.
(b) Where either party terminates the employment, the untaken accumulated annual leave is paid at the staff member's basic periodic rate of pay at the time of termination.

1.12.5 Annual leave exclusive of holidays with pay

(a) If any of the holidays prescribed in 'Holidays with pay' (Clause 1.13.6) falls within a staff member's period of annual leave, and is observed on a day which in the case of that staff member would have been an ordinary working day, there shall be added to that leave one day for each such holiday as occurring.

1.12.6 Continuity of service

(a) For the purposes of this subclause, service shall be deemed to be continuous notwithstanding:
    (i) any interruption or determination of the employment by the Executive Secretary if such interruption or determination has been made merely with the intention of avoiding obligations in respect of leave of absence
    (ii) any absence from work on account of personal sickness or accident and in calculating the period of twelve months' continuous service, absence on account of personal sickness or accident to the extent of 91 days in any 12 months shall be deemed to be part of the period of continuous service
    (iii) any absence with reasonable cause, proof of which shall be upon the employee, or leave lawfully granted by the employer, but such absence shall not be taken into account in calculating the period of 12 months' continuous service.

Regulation 1.13 – Personal leave

1.13.1 The provisions of this clause apply to full-time and part-time employees (on a prorate basis) but do not apply to casual employees, unless where expressly stated.

1.13.2 Conditions

(a) The entitlement to use personal leave for the purposes of carer's leave (see Clause 1.13.9) is subject to the person being a member of the staff member's immediate family.

1.13.3 Amount of paid personal leave

(a) Paid personal leave is available to a staff member, other than a casual employee, when they are absent:
    (i) due to personal illness or injury; or
    (ii) for the purposes of caring for an immediate family who is sick and requires the employee's care and support or who requires care due to an unexpected emergency.
(b) The amount of personal leave to which a full-time staff member is entitled depends on how long they have worked for the Commission and accrues as follows:
    (i) a full-time staff member is entitled to 10 days' paid leave a year
    (ii) pro-rata entitlement applies to part-time staff members.
(c) Staff members shall not be granted personal/sick leave for a period of more than three consecutive days and more than a total of seven working days in any calendar year without producing a medical certificate.

1.13.4 Accumulation of personal leave

(a) A staff member's entitlement to paid personal leave accrues progressively during a year of service according to the staff member's ordinary hours of work, and accumulates from year to year.

1.13.5 Payment for paid personal leave

(a) If a staff member takes a period of paid personal leave, the Commission must pay the staff member at the staff member's base rate of pay for the staff member's ordinary hours of work in the period.

1.13.6 Personal leave and holidays with pay

(a) If the period during which a staff member takes paid personal leave includes a day or part-day that is a public holiday in the place where the staff member is based for work purposes, the staff member is taken not to be on paid personal leave on that public holiday.

1.13.7 Effect of workers' compensation

(a) If a staff member is receiving workers' compensation payments, they are not entitled to personal leave.

1.13.8 Not payable on termination

(a) The Commission is not required to make a payment in respect of accumulated personal leave credits to an employee upon termination of employment.

1.13.9 Personal leave to care for an immediate family (personal/carer's leave)

(a) The entitlement is subject to the staff member being responsible for the care and support of the person concerned. In normal circumstances an employee is not entitled to take leave for this purpose where another person has taken leave to care for the same person.

1.13.10 Employee must give notice

(a) The staff member must, as soon as practicable prior to the commencement of work, inform the Executive Secretary of their inability to attend work and, as far as practicable, state the nature of the injury, illness or emergency and the estimated duration of the absence.

(b) When taking leave to care for members of their immediate family who are sick and require care and support, or who require care due to an unexpected emergency, the notice must include:

(i) the name of the person requiring care and support and their relationship to the employee

(ii) the reasons for taking such leave

(iii) the estimated length of absence.

1.13.11 Evidence supporting claim

(a) When taking leave to care for members of their immediate family who require care due to an unexpected emergency, the staff member must, if required by the Executive Secretary, establish by production of documentation acceptable to the Executive Secretary or a statutory declaration, the nature of the emergency and that such emergency resulted in the person concerned requiring care by the employee.

(b) An employee may provide a statutory declaration in lieu of a medical certificate.

1.13.12 Unpaid personal leave

(a) Where a staff member has exhausted all paid personal leave entitlements, they are entitled to take unpaid personal leave to care for members of their immediate family who are sick and require care and support or who require care due to an unexpected emergency. The Executive Secretary and the staff member shall agree on the period. In the absence of agreement, the staff member is entitled to take up to two days of unpaid leave per occasion, provided other requirements of these Staff Regulations are met.

Regulation 1.14 – Compassionate leave

1.14.1 An employee is entitled to two days' compassionate leave for each occasion when a member of the employee's immediate family:

(a) contracts or develops a personal illness that poses a serious threat to his or her life; or

(b) sustains a personal injury that poses a serious threat to his or her life; or

(c) dies.

1.14.2 An employee may take compassionate leave for a particular permissible occasion if the leave is taken:

(a) to spend time with the member of the employee's immediate family who has contracted or developed the personal illness, or sustained the personal injury; or

(b) after the death of the member of the employee's immediate family.

1.14.3 An employee may take compassionate leave for a particular permissible occasion as:

(a) a single continuous two-day period; or

(b) two separate periods of one day each; or

(c) any separate periods to which the employee and the Executive Secretary agree.

1.14.4 If the permissible occasion is the contraction or development of an illness, or the sustaining of an injury, the employee may take the compassionate leave for that occasion at any time while the illness or injury persists.

1.14.5 Proof of such death or illness or injury (in the form of a death notice or other written evidence) shall be the same evidence and notice requirements as personal/carer's leave.

1.14.6 An employee shall be paid at the base rate of pay for any period of compassionate leave.

1.14.7 The definition of immediate family for this clause shall be as per the 'personal/carer's leave' clause (Clause 1.13.9).

Regulation 1.15 – Leave without pay

1.15.1 Notwithstanding the absence of accrued annual holiday leave, and subject to the prior approval of the Executive Secretary, the employee may be absent for reasons other than those specified in these Staff Regulations but will not be entitled to any remuneration or accrual of benefits for the period of absence. Any leave without pay is at the discretion of the Executive Secretary.

Regulation 1.16 – Holidays with pay

1.16.1 All employees shall be allowed the following days as holidays with pay:

1 January	New Year's Day
26 January	Australia Day
	Regatta Day
	Eight Hours Day
	Good Friday
	Easter Monday
	Easter Tuesday
25 April	Anzac Day
	Queen's Birthday
	Show Day
25 December	Christmas Day
26 December	Boxing Day

1.16.2 Payment for holidays with pay mentioned in Clause 1.16.1 of this regulation which are taken and not worked, shall be at the normal rate of pay which would have applied to the employee concerned when, if it were not for such holiday, they would have been at work.

1.16.3 When staff are required to work on such holidays, they shall be compensated according to the award.

Regulation 1.17 – Jury service leave

1.17.1 An employee required to attend for jury duty shall be reimbursed by the Commission an amount equal to the difference between the amount the employee is able to claim from the court in respect of their attendance for such jury duty and the amount of wage they would have received in respect of the ordinary time they would have worked had they not been on jury duty, capped to a maximum period of 10 days.

1.17.2 An employee shall notify the Executive Secretary as soon as practicable of the date upon which they are required to attend for jury duty, and shall provide the Executive Secretary with proof of attendance, the duration of such attendance and the amount received in respect thereof.

Regulation 1.18 – Community service leave

1.18.1 An employee who engages in an eligible community service activity is entitled to be absent from their employment on unpaid leave of absence for a period if:

(a) The period consists of one or more of the following:
   (i) time when the employee engages in the activity
   (ii) reasonable travelling time associated with the activity
   (iii) reasonable rest time immediately following the activity.

(b) The employee's absence is reasonable in all the circumstances.

(c) An eligible community service activity is as defined in the *Fair Work Act 2009* and/or regulations.

1.18.2 Notice and evidence requirements

(a) An employee who wants an absence from their employment to be covered by this clause must give the Executive Secretary notice of the absence.

(b) The notice:
   (i) must be given to the Executive Secretary as soon as reasonably practicable (which may be a time after the absence has started)
   (ii) must advise the Executive Secretary of the period, or expected period, of the absence.

1.18.3 Evidence

(a) An employee who has given his or her employer notice of an absence under Clause 1.18.1(d) must, if required by the employer, give the Executive Secretary evidence that would satisfy a reasonable person that the absence is because the employee has been, or will be, engaging in an eligible community service activity.

1.18.4 Compliance

(a) An employee's absence from their employment is not covered by this clause unless the employee complies with its contents.

Regulation 1.19 – Parental leave

1.19.1 After 12 months' continuous service in the Secretariat, staff members shall be entitled to paid parental leave in relation to the birth of their child. On the basis of medical advice that the confinement will probably take place within six weeks, staff members shall be entitled to be absent from duty from that time until eight weeks after expected confinement. During this period staff members shall receive full pay and corresponding allowances.

1.19.2 After 12 months' continuous service, parents are entitled to a combined total of 52 weeks unpaid parental leave on a shared basis in relation to the birth, or adoption, of their child. An employee can choose to use some, or all, of their annual leave in addition to their parental leave. However, employees cannot access personal leave whilst on a period of unpaid parental leave.

1.19.3 Parental leave will be in accordance with the *Fair Work Act 2009*.

Regulation 1.20 – Superannuation

1.20.1 Staff members have the choice of the two superannuation options as outlined below:

(a) Option 1: Superannuation contributions shall be made by the Commission in accordance with the Superannuation Guarantee (Administration) Act 1992, the Superannuation Guarantee Charge Act 1992, the Superannuation Industry (Supervision) Act 1993 and the Superannuation (Resolution and Complaints) Act 1993. This legislation, as varied from time to time, shall govern the superannuation rights and obligations of the parties.

(b) Option 2: Where an employee wishes to contribute to an approved superannuation fund, the Commission shall pay two-thirds of the total contributions to the superannuation fund, up to the maximum applied in the United Nations Secretariat to the total of the staff member's salary and salary-related allowances.

Regulation 1.21 – Travel

1.21.1 All official travel shall be authorised by the Executive Secretary in advance within the limits of the budget, and the itinerary and travelling conditions shall be those best suited for maximum effectiveness in the fulfilment of duties assigned.

1.21.2 With regard to official travel, a travel allowance, generally consistent with United Nations practice, shall be paid in advance for fares, accommodation and daily living expenses.

1.21.3 Economy class shall be utilised, wherever feasible, for air travel.

1.21.4 First class may be utilised for land travel, but not for travel by sea or air.

1.21.5 Following completion of a duty journey, staff members shall repay any travel allowances to which, in the event, they were not entitled. Where staff members have incurred expenses above and beyond those for which travel allowances have been paid, they shall be reimbursed, against receipts and vouchers, as long as such expenses were necessarily incurred in pursuit of their official duties.

1.21.6 Staff members who, in the course of their duty, are required to use private motor vehicles for official travel purposes shall, with the prior authorisation of the Executive Secretary, be entitled to receive a reimbursement of the costs involved in line with that available to members of the Government Service in Australia but in no case will the employee receive payment at a rate less than the amount allowed as deduction by the Australian Taxation Office. The costs associated with normal daily travel to and from the place of work shall not be reimbursed.

SECTION 2 – INTERNATIONAL PROFESSIONAL CATEGORY TERMS AND CONDITIONS OF EMPLOYMENT

Regulation 2.1 – Salaries and other remuneration

2.1.1 The scale of salaries for staff members in the International Professional category shall be established in US dollars according to the corresponding scales of salaries which would apply to officials of the United Nations Secretariat employed in Australia and shall be paid in Australian dollars.

(a) The type of allowances available to staff members in the International Professional category shall, in principle, be those allowances in force in the United Nations. The scale of allowances shall be established in US dollars according to the corresponding scales of allowances which would apply to officials of the United Nations Secretariat in Australia and shall be paid in Australian dollars. However, education allowances for each dependent child shall not be paid:

   (i) in respect of children of Australian staff members

   (ii) in respect of attendance at an Australian public (state) school

   (iii) for attendance at a university in Australia

   (iv) for correspondence courses or private tuition

   (v) when schooling does not require regular attendance at an education institution

   (vi) in respect of education expenses covered from scholarship grants or subsidies from other sources.

(b) Except for the maximum figure for education allowance, changes in salaries and allowances applied in the United Nations Secretariat shall be applied to the salaries and allowances of staff members in the International Professional category.

(c) The Commission shall pay duly justified representation expenses incurred by the Executive Secretary in the performance of his duties within the limits prescribed annually in the budget.

(d) A SAL on the remuneration of staff members in the International Professional category shall be deducted by the Commission from the remuneration of the International Professional officer and such a deduction shall be retained by the Commission, in accordance with taxation arrangements entered into with the Australian Government through the Headquarters Agreement, and with the Australian Taxation Office.

Regulation 2.2 – United Nations common system of salaries, allowances and benefits

2.2.1 The Commission has adopted, where applicable, terms and conditions of employment from the *United Nations Common System of Salaries, Allowances and Benefits* within these Staff Regulations.

2.2.2 *The United Nations Common System of Salaries, Allowances and Benefits* has been used as a general reference for some Staff Regulations as appropriate, but the specific terms and conditions of employment are as per the Deed of Employment and the Staff Regulations ('the instruments') and any legal or administrative interpretations will be made on the basis of those instruments.

2.2.3 The annexes of the *United Nations Common System of Salaries, Allowances and Benefits* contain specific salary rates and allowances which are updated from time to time. Where applicable, the Commission will apply the appropriate variation of the annexes to the terms and conditions of employment within the Staff Regulations.

Regulation 2.3 – Hours of work

2.3.1 The normal working day shall be on average eight hours, Monday to Friday, for an average of 40 hours per week.

2.3.2 The Executive Secretary shall establish the working hours, and may alter them for the benefit of the Commission, as circumstances may require.

2.3.3 Staff members in the International Professional category are not entitled to overtime pay or compensatory leave for hours worked in excess of forty hours per week. Given the nature of the role, responsibilities and level of remuneration, any additional hours required are deemed to be reasonable.

Regulation 2.4 – Travel

2.4.1 On taking up an appointment in the International Professional category staff shall be eligible for:

(a) payment of economy class air fares (or equivalent) and travel allowance for themselves, their spouses and dependants to Hobart
(b) an installation grant calculated on the basis of the prevailing United Nations rate
(c) payment of removal costs, including the shipment of personal effects and household goods from the place of residence to Hobart, subject to a maximum volume of 30 cubic metres or one international standard shipping container
(d) payment or reimbursement of sundry other expenses related to relocation, including insurance of goods in transit and excess baggage charges subject to the prevailing relevant United Nations rules. Such payments shall be subject to prior approval by the Executive Secretary.

2.4.2 After 18 months of service, the Commission shall pay travel expenses to the staff member for travel to their home country on annual leave for the staff member and their dependants. Economy class shall be utilised, wherever feasible, for air travel and first class may be utilised for land travel, but not for travel by sea or air. Following this, home leave shall be granted at two-year intervals, provided that:

(a) dependants who benefit from this Commission grant have resided in Hobart for at least six months prior to travel
(b) staff members will return to the Secretariat to continue rendering their services for a minimum additional period of six months.

2.4.3 The possibility of combining travel to the home country on leave with official travel in Commission service may also be considered, provided the interests of the Commission are duly borne in mind.

Regulation 2.5 – Separation from service

2.5.1 In addition to the provisions provided in accordance with Regulation 1.10 on separation from service, an International Professional category employee shall, subject to Clause 2.5.2(b), be entitled to the following:

(a) payment of economy class air fares (or equivalent) to the staff member's country of origin or former residence, for the staff member and dependent members of his family
(b) payment of removal costs, including the shipment of personal effects and household goods from place of residence in Hobart to the country of origin or former residence, subject to a maximum volume of 30 cubic metres or one international shipping container
(c) a repatriation allowance generally consistent with United Nations practice.

2.5.2 At the discretion of the Executive Secretary, the right to the repatriation expenses provided for in Clause 2.5.1(a) may be cancelled or reduced appropriately if:

(a) less than one year has elapsed between the date of taking up the appointment and the date of separation from service
(b) the reason for separation from service was termination of employment due to gross dereliction of duty
(c) more than six months have elapsed between the staff member's separation from service and their return to their country of origin or former residence
(d) less than six months have elapsed since the staff member last visited his country of origin or former residence on home leave at the expense of the Commission; or
(e) the staff member has applied for, or received, status as a permanent resident of Australia.

Regulation 2.6 – Employee death

2.6.1 In the event of death of a staff member following illness or surgery not resulting from an accident covered by the appropriate insurance, the right to salary, allowances and other corresponding benefits shall cease on the day on which death occurs, unless the deceased leaves dependants, in which case these shall be entitled to mortality allowances and return travel and removal expenses to the country of origin or former residence at the expense of the Commission.

2.6.2 Eligibility of the dependants of a deceased staff member for the payment of return travel and removal expenses shall lapse if the travel is not undertaken within six months of the date of the staff member's death.

2.6.3 The above mortality allowance for death shall be calculated in accordance with the following scale:

Years of service	*Months of net base pay salary following death*
Less than 3 years	3 months
3 years and more, but less than 7 years	4 months
7 years and more, but less than 9 years	5 months
9 years and more	6 months

2.6.4 The Commission shall pay for shipment of the staff member's body from the place of death to the place designated by the next of kin.

SECTION 3 – GENERAL SERVICES CATEGORY EMPLOYEES (CLERICAL AWARD COVERED) TERMS AND CONDITIONS OF EMPLOYMENT

Regulation 3.1 – Hours of work

3.1.1 The normal working day shall be on average 7.5 hours, Monday to Friday, for an average of 37.5 hours per week over a four-week period.

3.1.2 The ordinary hours of work are to be worked between 0700 h to 1900 h Monday to Friday. The spread of hours may by altered by up to one hour at either end of the spread, by agreement between the employer and the majority of employees concerned or, in appropriate circumstances, between the employer and an individual employee.

3.1.3 Staff members in the General Services category required to work more than 37.5 hours during one week will be compensated in accordance with the 'Additional hours' clause in Section 1.

Regulation 3.2 – Annualised salaries

3.2.1 Staff members are remunerated under annualised salary arrangements. The annualised salary for those employees classified under the *Clerks – Private Sector Award 2010* comprises the following components:

(a) Clause 16 – minimum weekly wage
(b) Clause 19 – allowances (allowances included: clothing and footwear allowance, meal allowance, living away from home allowance, first-aid allowance and higher duties allowance)
(c) Clauses 27 and 28 – overtime and penalty rates (overtime incorporated is two additional hours per week in excess of 37.5 hours, any overtime in addition to this is to be paid as per applicable overtime rates) unless where specified in these Staff Regulations
(d) Clause 29.3 – annual leave loading.

3.2.2 General Service category employees shall be subject to PAYG taxation in accordance with Australian tax rates in force. The deduction so withheld by the Commission is retained by the Commission in accordance with an agreement with the Australian Taxation Office. CCAMLR General Services staff shall be treated equally to other Australian taxpayers in respect of taxation matters.

Regulation 3.3 – Breaks

3.3.1 Meal break

(a) A meal break of not less than 30 minutes must be taken by each employee. Such meal periods must be taken not later than five hours after commencing work and after the resumption of work from a previous meal break.

3.3.2 Rest break

(a) An employee must be allowed two 10-minute rest intervals to be counted as time worked on each day that the employee is required to work not less than 7.5 ordinary hours. Each rest interval should be taken at a time suitable to the employer, taking into account the needs of the CCAMLR Secretariat.

SECTION 4 – GENERAL SERVICES CATEGORY EMPLOYEES (PROFESSIONAL SERVICES AWARD COVERED) TERMS AND CONDITIONS OF EMPLOYMENT

Regulation 4.1 – Hours of work

4.1.1 The normal working day shall be on average 7.5 hours, Monday to Friday, for an average of 37.5 hours per week over a four-week period.

4.1.2 The ordinary hours of work are to be worked between 0700 h to 1900 h Monday to Friday. The spread of hours may by altered by up to one hour at either end of the spread, by agreement between the employer and the majority of employees concerned or, in appropriate circumstances, between the employer and an individual employee.

4.1.3 Staff members in the General Services category required to work more than 37.5 hours during one week will be compensated in accordance with the 'Additional hours' clause in Section 1.

Regulation 4.2 – Annualised salaries

4.2.1 All employees are remunerated under annualised salary arrangements. The annualised salary for those employees classified under the *Professional Employees Award 2010* includes the following components:

(a) Clause 15 – minimum weekly wage
(b) Clause 19.2 – annual leave loading
(c) reasonable additional hours as required, unless specified within these Staff Regulations.

4.2.2 General Service category employees shall be subject to PAYG taxation in accordance with Australian tax rates in force. The deduction so withheld by the Commission is retained by the Commission in accordance with an agreement with the Australian Taxation Office. CCAMLR General Services staff shall be treated equally to other Australian taxpayers in respect of taxation matters.

Regulation 4.3 – Breaks

4.3.1 Meal break

(a) A meal break of not less than 30 minutes must be taken by each employee. Such meal periods must be taken not later than five hours after commencing work and after the resumption of work from a previous meal break.

4.3.2 Rest break

(a) An employee must be allowed two 10-minute rest intervals to be counted as time worked on each day that the employee is required to work not less than 7.5 ordinary hours. Each rest interval should be taken at a time suitable to the employer, taking into account the needs of the CCAMLR Secretariat.

SECTION 5 – CASUAL/TEMPORARY TERMS AND CONDITIONS OF EMPLOYMENT

Persons in this category may include translators, interpreters, typists and other persons contracted for meetings, as well as those whom the Executive Secretary contracts for a specific task. Whenever possible, persons resident in Australia shall be utilised in such cases.

Regulation 5.1 – Hours of work

5.1.1 The normal working day shall be an average of 7.5 hours, Monday to Friday, for a total of 37.5 hours per week.

5.1.2 The ordinary hours of work are between 0700 h and 1900 h Monday to Friday and from 0700 h to 1230 h Saturday. The spread of hours may be altered by agreement between the employer and the majority of employees concerned or, in appropriate circumstances, between the employer and an individual employee.

Regulation 5.2 – Casual staff member

5.2.1 A casual staff member is an employee who is engaged on an irregular basis to perform specific duties for a specific period. The employee shall be engaged intermittently for work of an unexpected or casual nature.

(a) The minimum period of engagement for a casual employee shall be three hours.

(b) Casual employees shall be paid at the appropriate base hourly rate but shall receive an additional loading of 22% in lieu of annual leave, holidays with pay and sick leave.

(c) The casual loading at Clause 5.2.1(b) is effective from 1 January 2012. The Commission acknowledges that the loading provided in the relevant awards is 25% and that this is a transitional provision.

(d) In accordance with transitional provisions of the relevant awards, the difference between the loadings at Clauses 5.2.1(b) and 5.2.1(c) shall be known as the transitional percentage. From the following dates the employer must pay no less than the loading or penalty at Clause 5.2.1(c) minus the specified proportion of the transitional percentage:

First full pay period on or after

1 July 2012 40%

1 July 2013 20%.

APPENDIX 1 STAFF CLASSIFICATION TRANSLATION TABLE – GENERAL SERVICES EMPLOYEES

Translation table: Comparison of the CCAMLR Job Classification System and modern award classifications

There are two modern awards that are applicable to CCAMLR:

- *Clerks – Private Sector Award 2010*
- *Professional Employees Award 2010*

The following table compares the existing classifications used by CCAMLR to the relevant modern award classifications.

Classification	Classification Characteristics	Award	Award level
GS1 GS2	Basic understanding of guidelines Close or general supervision Achieve agreed tasks Limited decision-making Work within established guidelines and time frames	Clerks Award	Level 1 (years 1–3)
GS3	General understanding of guidelines General guidance Plan and coordinate tasks Limited decision-making Completion of tasks with accuracy and attention to detail	Clerks Award	Level 2 (years 1–2)
GS4	Moderate to complex work, often within area of speciality Good understanding of legislation, regulatory and compliance framework General guidance Development of team goals Decision-making within defined parameters Specialist advice and support Tertiary qualifications may be required	Clerks Award Professional Award	Level 3 Level 1
GS5	Moderate to complex work Well-developed knowledge of legislation, regulatory and compliance framework General or limited guidance Involvement in development of business plans, goals and performance monitoring Responsible for achievement of results Specialist knowledge and advice Tertiary qualifications may be required	Clerks Award Professional Award	Level 4 Level 2
GS6	Moderately complex to complex work Sound knowledge of legislation, regulatory and compliance framework Limited guidance Developing business plans, goals and change initiatives Taking responsibility for outcomes Representational responsibilities	Clerks Award Professional Award	Level 5 Level 3/4
M1	Only if the role requires a science or information technology qualification	Professional Award	Level 4

Standing Committee on Implementation and Compliance (SCIC) Terms of Reference and Organisation of Work (2002)

The Standing Committee on Implementation and Compliance (SCIC) was established by the Commission with the following terms of reference[16]:

[16] Based on the Commission's decision as adopted at CCAMLR-XXI (paragraph 5.16 and Annex 5, Appendix VII).

1. The Committee shall be tasked with providing the Commission with information, advice and recommendations necessary to give effect to Articles X, XXI, XXII and XXIV of the Convention.

2. The Committee shall:

(i) review and assess Contracting Parties' implementation of, and compliance with, conservation and management measures adopted by the Commission;

(ii) review and assess, as appropriate, the implementation of, and compliance with, conservation and management measures by those non-Contracting Parties which have agreed to apply such measures;

(iii) provide technical advice and recommendations on means to promote the effective implementation of, and compliance with, conservation and management measures;

(iv) review and analyse information pertaining to activities of Contracting Parties and non-Contracting Parties which undermine the objectives of the Convention, including in particular illegal, unregulated and unreported (IUU) fishing, and recommend actions to be taken by the Commission to prevent, deter and eliminate such activities;

(v) review the operation of, and recommend priorities of and improvements to, the System of Inspection and, in association with the Scientific Committee, as appropriate, the Scheme of International Scientific Observation;

(vi) exchange information with the Scientific Committee and its subsidiary bodies as well as the Standing Committee on Administration and Finance (SCAF), as appropriate, on matters of relevance for the exercise of their respective functions;

(vii) provide the Commission with recommendations on appropriate interaction with other fisheries or conservation management, technical or scientific organisations on matters of relevance to the effective implementation of, and compliance with, conservation and management measures;

(viii) perform such other functions consistent with its terms of reference as the Commission might decide; and

(ix) prepare a report on its activities and recommendations, as well as an agenda for its next meeting, for consideration by the Commission.

3. Organisation

(i) SCIC may establish working groups to address technical or other specific issues.

(ii) SCIC may propose terms of reference and agendas, and determine meeting frequency for such working groups.

(iii) Working groups will be supported by conveners/chairs, rapporteurs and the Secretariat, as appropriate.

(iv) Working groups will ordinarily meet preceding the annual meeting of the Commission, but may meet intersessionally if so required.

(v) Any funding for such an intersessional meeting of a working group shall be decided by the Commission.

Text of the CCAMLR System of Inspection (1988)[17]

I. Each Member of the Commission may designate Inspectors referred to in Article XXIV of the Convention.

(a) Designated Inspectors shall be familiar with the fishing and scientific research activities to be inspected, the provisions of the Convention and measures adopted under it.

[17] As adopted at CCAMLR-VII (paragraph 124) and amended at CCAMLR-XII (paragraphs 6.4 and 6.8), CCAMLR-XIII (paragraph 5.26), CCAMLR-XIV (paragraphs 7.22, 7.26 and 7.28), CCAMLR-XV (paragraph 7.24), CCAMLR-XVI (paragraph 8.14), CCAMLR-XVIII (paragraph 8.25), CCAMLR-XXV (paragraph 12.73) and CCAMLR-XXVI (paragraphs 13.79 to 13.83).

(b) Members shall certify the qualifications of each Inspector they designate.
(c) Inspectors shall be nationals of the Contracting Party which designates them and, while carrying out inspection activities, shall be subject solely to the jurisdiction of that Contracting Party.
(d) Inspectors shall be able to communicate in the language of the Flag State of the vessels on which they carry out their activities.
(e) Inspectors shall be accorded the status of ship's officer while on board such vessels.
(f) Names of Inspectors shall be communicated to the Secretariat within fourteen days of designation.

II. The Commission shall maintain a register of certified Inspectors designated by Members.
(a) The Commission shall communicate, each year, the register of Inspectors to each Contracting Party within a month of the last day of the Commission meeting.

III. In order to verify compliance with conservation measures adopted under the Convention, Inspectors designated by Members shall be entitled to board a fishing or fisheries research vessel in the area to which the Convention applies to determine whether the vessel is, or has been, engaged in scientific research, or harvesting, of marine living resources.[18]
(a) Inspection may be carried out by designated Inspectors from vessels of the Designating Member.
(b) Ships carrying Inspectors shall carry a special flag or pennant approved by the Commission to indicate that the Inspectors on board are carrying out inspection duties in accordance with this system.
(c) Such Inspectors may also be placed on board vessels, with the schedule of embarkation and disembarkation of Inspectors subject to arrangements to be concluded between the Designating Member and the Flag State.

IV. Each Contracting Party shall provide to the Secretariat:
(a) One month before the commencement of the research cruise and in accordance with Conservation Measure 24-01 'The Application of Conservation Measures to Scientific Research', the names of all vessels intending to conduct fishing for research purposes.
(b) Within seven days of the issuance of each permit or licence in accordance with Conservation Measure 10-02 'Licensing and Inspection Obligations of Contracting Parties with regard to their Flag Vessels Operating in the Convention Area', the following information about licences or permits issued by its authorities to its flag vessels authorising them to fish in the Convention Area:
   - name of the vessel;
   - time periods authorised for fishing (start and end dates);
   - area(s) of fishing;
   - species targeted; and
   - gear used.
(c) By 31 August, an annual report of steps it has taken to implement the inspection, investigation and sanction provisions of Conservation Measure 10-02 'Licensing and Inspection Obligations of Contracting Parties with regard to their Flag Vessels Operating in the Convention Area'.

V.
(a) Any vessel present in the Convention Area for the purpose of harvesting or conducting scientific research on marine living resources shall, when given the appropriate signal in the International Code of Signals by a ship carrying an Inspector (as signified by flying the flag or pennant referred to above), stop or take other such actions as necessary to facilitate the safe and prompt transfer of the Inspector to the vessel, unless the vessel is actively engaged in harvesting operations, in which case it shall do so as soon as practicable.

[18] The System of Inspection applies to flag vessels of all Members of the Commission and Contracting Parties.

(b) The Master of the vessel shall permit the Inspector, who may be accompanied by appropriate assistants, to board the vessel.

VI. Inspectors shall have the authority to inspect catch, nets and other fishing gear as well as harvesting and scientific research activities, and shall have access to records and reports of catch and location data insofar as necessary to carry out their functions.

(a) Each Inspector shall carry an identity document issued by the Designating Member in a form approved or provided by the Commission stating that the Inspector has been designated to carry out inspection in accordance with this system.

(b) On boarding a vessel, an Inspector shall present the document described in paragraph VI(a), above.

(c) The inspection shall be carried out so that the vessel is subject to the minimum interference and inconvenience. Inquiries shall be limited to the ascertainment of facts in relation to compliance with the Commission measures in effect for the Flag State concerned.

(d) Inspectors may take photographs and/or video footage as necessary to document any alleged violation of Commission measures in force.

(e) Inspectors shall affix an identification mark approved by the Commission to any net or other fishing gear which appears to have been used in contravention to conservation measures in effect and shall record this fact in the reports and notification referenced in paragraph VIII, below.

(f) Inspectors shall be provided appropriate assistance by the Master of the vessel in carrying out their duties, including access as necessary to communications equipment.

(g) Each Contracting Party, subject to and in accordance with their applicable laws and regulations, including rules governing the admissibility of evidence in domestic courts, shall consider and act on reports from Inspectors of Designating Members under this scheme on the same basis as reports from its own inspectors, and both Contracting Party and designating Member concerned shall cooperate in order to facilitate judicial or other proceedings arising from any such report.

VII. If a vessel refuses to stop or otherwise facilitate transfer of an Inspector, or if the Master or crew of a vessel interferes with the authorised activities of an Inspector, the Inspector involved shall prepare a detailed report, including a full description of all the circumstances and provide the report to the Designating Member to be transmitted in accordance with the relevant provisions of paragraph IX.

(a) Interference with an Inspector or failure to comply with reasonable requests made by an Inspector in the performance of his duties shall be treated by the Flag State as if the Inspector were an Inspector of that State.

(b) The Flag State shall report on actions taken under this paragraph in accordance with paragraph XI, below.

VIII. Inspectors shall complete the approved CCAMLR inspection report form.

(a) The Inspector shall provide a written explanation, on the inspection report form, of any alleged violation of Commission measures in force. The Inspector shall allow the Master of the vessel being inspected to comment, on the inspection report form, about any aspect of the inspection.

(b) The Inspector shall sign the inspection report form. The Master of the inspected vessel shall be invited to sign the inspection report form to acknowledge receipt of the report.

(c) Before leaving the vessel that has been inspected, the Inspector shall give the Master of that vessel a copy of the completed inspection form.

(d) The Inspector shall provide a copy of the completed inspection form along with photographs and video footage to the Designating Member not later than 15 days of his/her arrival to port.

(e) The Designating Member shall forward a copy of the inspection form not later than 15 days from its reception along with two copies of photographs and video footage to the CCAMLR Executive Secretary who shall forward one copy of this material to the Flag State of the inspected vessel not later than seven days from receipt.

(f) Fifteen days after the transmission of the completed inspection form to the Flag State, the CCAMLR Executive Secretary shall transmit that form to Members together with comments or observations, if any, received from the Flag State.

IX. Any supplementary reports or information, or any report prepared in accordance with paragraph VII, shall be provided by the Designating Member to the CCAMLR Executive Secretary. The latter shall provide such reports or information to the Flag State, which shall be then afforded the opportunity to comment. The CCAMLR Executive Secretary shall transmit the reports or information to Members within 15 days following their receipt from the Designating Member, and the observations or comments, if any, received from the Flag State.

X. A fishing vessel present in the area of application of the Convention shall be presumed to have been engaged in scientific research, or harvesting, of marine living resources (or to have been commencing such operations) if one or more of the following four indicators have been reported by an inspector, and there is no information to the contrary:

(a) fishing gear was in use, had recently been in use or was ready to be used, e.g.:
- nets, lines or pots were in the water;
- trawl nets and doors rigged;
- baited hooks, baited pots or traps or thawed bait were ready for use;
- log indicated recent fishing or fishing commencing;

(b) fish which occur in the Convention Area were being processed or had recently been processed, e.g.:
- fresh fish or fish waste were on board;
- fish were being frozen;
- from operational or product information;

(c) fishing gear from the vessel was in the water, e.g.:
- fishing gear bore the vessel's markings;
- fishing gear matched that on the vessel;
- log indicated gear in the water;

(d) fish (or their products) which occur in the Convention Area were stowed on board.

XI. If, as a result of inspection activities carried out in accordance with these provisions, there is evidence of violation of measures adopted under the Convention, the Flag State shall take steps to prosecute and, if necessary, impose sanctions.

XII. The Flag State shall, within fourteen days of the laying of charges or the initiation of proceedings relating to a prosecution, inform the Secretariat of this information, and shall continue thereafter to inform the Secretariat as the prosecution develops or is concluded. In addition, the Flag State shall at least once a year report to the Commission, in writing, about the results of such prosecutions and sanctions imposed. If a prosecution has not been completed, a progress report shall be made. When a prosecution has not been launched, or has been unsuccessful, the report shall contain an explanation.

XIII. Sanctions applied by Flag States in respect to infringements of CCAMLR provisions shall be sufficiently severe as to effectively ensure compliance with CCAMLR conservation measures and to discourage infringements and shall seek to deprive offenders of any economic benefit accruing from their illegal activities.

XIV. The Flag State shall ensure that any of its vessels which have been found to have contravened a CCAMLR conservation measure do not carry out fishing operations within the Convention Area until they have complied with the sanctions imposed.

Inspection Pennant

[*Omitted*]

Fishing Gear Identification Mark

A standard marker has been approved for identifying fishing gear that has been judged by an Inspector to be contrary to standards set by the Commission. It is in the form of a sealable plastic ribbon with an identifying number stamped into it. The identifying number is to be recorded in the appropriate space in the form for reporting the inspection.

[*Omitted*]

Identification Document

Inspectors are required to carry an identity document of the type shown below.

[*Omitted*]

Text of the CCAMLR Scheme of International Scientific Observation (1992)[19]

A. Each Member of the Commission may designate observers referred to in Article XXIV of the Convention.

(a) The Commission will specify activities of scientific observers on board vessels. These activities are described in Annex I and may be modified taking into account advice from the Scientific Committee. Additional scientific activities may be agreed between the Receiving and Designating Member States provided these do not conflict with, or detract from, the activities specified by the Commission.

(b) The Member wishing to place scientific observers on board a vessel of another Member shall be referred to as the 'Designating Member' and the Member who accepts a scientific observer on board its vessel shall be referred to as the 'Receiving Member'. Scientific observers in this scheme shall be nationals of the Designating Member and shall conduct themselves in accordance with the customs and order existing on the vessel on which they are operating.

(c) Members shall designate adequately qualified scientific observers who shall be familiar with the harvesting and scientific research activities to be observed, the provisions of the Convention and the measures adopted under it and who are adequately educated and trained to carry out competently the duties of scientific observers as required by the Commission.

(d) Scientific observers shall be able to communicate in the language of the Flag State of the vessels on which they carry out their activities.

(e) Scientific observers shall each carry a document issued by the Designating Member in a form approved by the Commission identifying them as CCAMLR scientific observers.

(f) Scientific Observers shall submit to the Commission through the Designating Member, not later than one month after the completion of the observer trip or after the return of the observer to his/her home country, all observer logbooks and reports of each observation assignment undertaken, using the observation formats approved by the Scientific Committee as they appear in the *Scientific Observers Manual*. The Secretariat shall send a copy of the scientific observer's report to the Receiving Member within 14 days of receipt. The language of the scientific observer's report shall be in one of the Commission's official languages, as agreed upon in the bilateral agreement between the Designating and Receiving Members.

(g) The Designating Member, in consultation with the scientific observer, shall be responsible for providing clarification about data collected, observations made, and incidents that may have occurred during deployment.

[19] As adopted at CCAMLR-XI (paragraph 6.11) and amended at CCAMLR-XVI (paragraph 8.21) and CCAMLR-XXVII (paragraph 13.68).

(h) Upon review of the observer's report, the Receiving Member shall advise the Secretariat and the Designating Member of any discrepancies as soon as they are identified. In the event of such notification, the Designating and Receiving Members will make every effort to resolve the issue. If the Designating and Receiving Members notify the Secretariat that they are unable to resolve such issues, the Secretariat will note any unresolved discrepancy.

B. In order to promote the objectives of the Convention, Members agree to take on board their vessels engaged in scientific research or harvesting of marine living resources designated scientific observers, who shall operate in accordance with bilateral arrangements concluded.

Such a bilateral arrangement shall include the following principles:

(a) The scientific observers shall be given the status of ship's officers. Accommodation and meals for scientific observers on board shall be of a standard commensurate with this status.

(b) Receiving Members shall ensure that their vessel operators cooperate fully with the scientific observers to enable them to carry out the tasks assigned to them by the Commission. This will include allowing scientific observers access to data, equipment and those operations of the vessel necessary to fulfil their duties as required by the Commission.

(c) Receiving Members shall ensure that their vessel operators cooperate fully with scientific observers to enable the observers to carry out their data collection duties as specified in the *Scientific Observers Manual* without impediment or influence. Arrangements shall be made for messages to be sent and received on behalf of scientific observers using the vessel's communication equipment and operator. Reasonable costs of such communications shall normally be borne by the Designating Member. After notifying the Master, scientific observers shall be allowed such access as is necessary to undertake observation duties, including the vessel's navigation equipment and personnel to determine the vessel's position, course and speed.

(d) Receiving Members shall take appropriate action with respect to their vessels to ensure safe working conditions, the protection, security and welfare of scientific observers in the performance of their duties, and to provide them with medical care and safeguard their freedom and dignity in adherence to all pertinent international maritime regulations.

(e) For transfers at sea, Members shall: (i) ensure that their vessel operators conduct transfers of observers under safe conditions and with the agreement of the observers, (ii) conduct the transfer in a manner which maximises the safety of observers and crew during the procedure, and (iii) provide experienced crew members to assist observers during any transfer which is made.

(f) Arrangements involving the transportation and boarding of scientific observers shall be organised so as to minimise interference with harvesting and research operations.

(g) Scientific observers shall provide to the relevant masters copies of such records, prepared by the scientific observers, as the masters may wish to retain.

(h) Designating Members shall ensure that their scientific observers carry insurance satisfactory to the Parties concerned.

(i) Transportation of scientific observers to and from boarding points shall be the responsibility of the Designating Member.

(j) Unless otherwise agreed, the equipment, clothing and salary and any related allowances of a scientific observer shall normally be borne by the Designating Member. The vessel of the Receiving Member shall bear the cost of on-board accommodation and meals of the scientific observer.

(k) The bilateral arrangement shall address such other matters as deemed appropriate by both the Designating and Receiving Members, such as liability and confidentiality.

C. For each observer deployed, the Designating Members shall provide the following information to the Secretariat prior to the deployment of the observer:

(a) date of signing the arrangement;
(b) name and flag of the vessel receiving the observer;
(c) Member designating the observer;
(d) area of fishing (CCAMLR statistical area, subarea, division);
(e) type of data to be collected by the observer and submitted to the Secretariat (e.g. by-catch, target species, biological data);
(f) expected dates of the start and end of the observation program;
(g) expected date of returning the observer to his/her home country.

D. In order to maintain the objectivity and scientific integrity of the data, Designating Members, Receiving Members, the vessels on which scientific observers are deployed and the scientific observers themselves, shall uphold and promote the following provisions:

(a) A scientific observer appointed in accordance with the CCAMLR Scheme of International Scientific Observation shall not:
   (i) contravene the requirements established in the laws and regulations of the Receiving Member or violate general rules of behaviour and safety that apply to all vessel personnel, provided such rules do not interfere with the duties of the observer under this Scheme, as stipulated in the bilateral arrangement between the Designating and the Receiving Members;
   (ii) inhibit the proper functioning and fishing activities of the vessel;
   (iii) solicit or accept, directly or indirectly, any gratuity, gift, favour, loan, or anything of monetary value from anyone who conducts fishing or fish processing activities that are regulated by CCAMLR, or who has interests that may be substantially affected by the performance or non-performance of the official duties of scientific observers, with the exception of meals, accommodations, or salary when provided by the vessel;
   (iv) have been convicted of a serious criminal offense for five years prior to appointment as an observer;
   (v) engage in any illegal actions or any other activities that would reflect negatively on his/her image as a professional scientist, on other scientific observers, on the integrity of data collection, or on CCAMLR as a whole;
   (vi) have any financial interest in, or relationship with, any vessel or business harvesting or processing products from a CCAMLR fishery.
(b) The owner, Master, agent, and crew of a vessel on which a scientific observer is deployed shall not:
   (i) offer a scientific observer, either directly or indirectly, any gratuity, gift, favour, loan, or anything of monetary value, except for meals, accommodations or salary when provided by the vessel;
   (ii) intimidate, or interfere with the duties of a scientific observer;
   (iii) interfere with or bias the sampling procedure employed by a scientific observer;
   (iv) tamper with, destroy, or discard a scientific observer's collected samples, equipment, records, photographic film, papers, or effects without the express consent of the observer;
   (v) prohibit, impede, threaten, or coerce, an observer from/into collecting samples, making observations, or otherwise performing the observer's duties; or
   (vi) harass a scientific observer.
(c) Deployment limitations. Designating Members shall seek, to the extent possible, to avoid having a scientific observer appointed in accordance with the CCAMLR Scheme of International Scientific Observation undertake multiple consecutive trips on the same vessel.
(d) Confidentiality. Designating Members shall require that a scientific observer appointed in accordance with the CCAMLR Scheme of International Scientific Observation shall not:

(i) disclose verbal, written, or other evidence or observations made on-board a vessel, or observations made in a processing facility, including data or commercially sensitive vessel-specific fishing, processing, and marketing information, to any person except to the Secretariat and as provided for in the bilateral arrangement;

(ii) take data or observer logbooks from one vessel onto another, except that if an observer is unable to submit data before being redeployed on another vessel, the scientific observer shall take reasonable steps to safeguard the data and observer logbooks.

E.

(a) When the Designating Member receives information regarding actions of the scientific observer that may contravene the provisions of this Scheme, the Designating Member shall take prompt and appropriate action, in accordance with its domestic law. The Designating Member will notify the Receiving Member and the Commission of any appropriate action taken.

(b) When the Receiving Member receives information regarding actions of the vessel owner, Master, agent, or crew that may contravene the provisions of this Scheme, the Receiving Member shall take prompt and appropriate action, in accordance with its domestic law. The Receiving Member will notify the Designating Member and the Commission of any appropriate action taken.

F. Members who have designated scientific observers will take the initiative in implementing assignments identified by the Commission.

G. The scope of functions and tasks described in Annex I should not be interpreted to suggest in any way the number of required observers which will be accepted on board a vessel.

Annex I: Functions and Tasks of International Scientific Observers On Board Vessels Engaged in Scientific Research or Harvesting of Marine Living Resources

1. The function of scientific observers on board vessels engaged in scientific research or harvesting of marine living resources is to observe and report on the operation of fishing activities in the Convention Area with the objectives and principles of the Convention for the Conservation of Antarctic Marine Living Resources in mind.

2. In fulfilling this function, scientific observers will undertake the following tasks, using the observation formats approved by the Scientific Committee:

(i) record details of the vessel's operation (e.g. partition of time between searching, fishing, transit etc., and details of hauls);

(ii) take samples of catches to determine biological characteristics;

(iii) record biological data by species caught;

(iv) record by-catches, their quantity and other biological data;

(v) record entanglement and incidental mortality of birds and mammals;

(vi) record the procedure by which declared catch weight is measured and collect data relating to the conversion factor between green weight and final product in the event that catch is recorded on the basis of weight of processed product;

(vii) prepare reports of their observations using the observation formats approved by the Scientific Committee and submit them to CCAMLR through the Designating Member;

(viii) assist, if requested, the captain of the vessel in the catch recording and reporting procedures;

(ix) undertake other tasks as may be decided by mutual agreement of the parties involved;

(x)[20] collect and report factual data on sightings of fishing vessels in the Convention Area, including vessel type identification, position and activity;

(xi)[21] collect information on fishing gear loss and garbage disposal by fishing vessels at sea.

[20] Added in accordance with CCAMLR-XVII (paragraph 8.16). The Commission decided to review the effectiveness and the need to continue this activity after a two-year trial period (CCAMLR-XVII, paragraph 8.17).

[21] Added in accordance with CCAMLR-XVIII (paragraph 8.21).

Rules for Access and Use of CCAMLR Data (2003)

The following Rules for Access and Use of CCAMLR Data were adopted by the Twenty-Second Meeting of the Commission (CCAMLR-XXII, paragraphs 12.1 to 12.6)[22]:

It is recognised that:

1. All data submitted to the CCAMLR Secretariat, and maintained by the CCAMLR Data Centre, shall be freely available to Members for analysis and preparation of documents for the Commission, Scientific Committee and their subsidiary bodies.

2. Such data may be analysed in respect of:

(a) work specifically outlined and endorsed by the Commission or Scientific Committee;

(b) work not specifically endorsed by the Commission or the Scientific Committee.

3. Inclusion of data, analyses or results from data held in the CCAMLR Data Centre into Working Papers, Background Papers, and any other documents tabled at meetings of the Commission, Scientific Committee or one of their subsidiary bodies does not constitute publication and therefore is not a release into the public domain.

4. Inclusion of data held in the CCAMLR Data Centre into the published reports of the Commission, Scientific Committee, Working Groups, CCAMLR Science, the Statistical Bulletin or any other CCAMLR publication constitutes release into the public domain.

5. Inclusion of data held in the CCAMLR Data Centre in any publication outside CCAMLR constitutes release into the public domain.

6. Subject to paragraphs (1) to (3), originators/owners of data have the right to:

(a) be consulted (including assignation of authorship) on the preparation, if necessary including publication, of documents describing analyses and interpretation of their data;

(b) approve the level of detail revealed in documents using their data;

(c) stipulate terms and/or levels of data security if necessary.

Accordingly,

7. Requests to the Secretariat for access and/or use of data maintained by the CCAMLR Data Centre by individual Member scientists/officials shall be approved in writing as appropriate by that Member's Commission Representative, Scientific Committee Representative, or CDS Officer in consultation with the Commission Representative. Members are responsible for informing individual scientists or individuals requesting data of the rules governing access and use of CCAMLR data and for obtaining agreement to comply with such rules.

8. Requests in support of analyses endorsed under (2)(a) above should include the type of data requested, the degree of data aggregation required, the spatial and temporal detail required, and the anticipated format to be used in presenting results of the analyses. For such requests, the Secretariat shall ensure that each request meets the conditions of the approval granted for the original endorsement, and, if so, release the data and inform the data owner(s)/originator(s) accordingly. Release of data by the Secretariat to the requestor does not constitute permission to publish or release data into the public domain. Such permission remains a matter to be determined between the requestor and the data originator(s).

9. Requests in support of non-endorsed analyses under (2)(b) above should include the information listed in (8) as well as details of the analytical procedures to be used and the opportunity for data owner(s)/originator(s) to be involved. For such requests, the Secretariat shall be satisfied that each request contains the required information before forwarding it to the data originator(s) for approval within a specified time period. Once approval has been received the Secretariat shall release the data. Release of data does not constitute permission to publish or

[22] These rules replace those adopted at the Eleventh Meeting of the Commission (CCAMLR-XI, paragraph 4.35). The current 'Rules for Access to CDS Data' (CCAMLR-XIX, paragraph 5.23) should remain in place alongside the new standard rules until such times as all aspects of CDS data handling are duly taken into account in the new standard rules (CCAMLR-XXII, paragraph 7.22).

for release into the public domain. Such permission remains a matter to be determined between the requestor and the data owner(s)/originator(s).

10. If approval for data release under (9) is not forthcoming within the specified period, the Secretariat shall initiate and facilitate consultation between the data requestor and data owner(s)/originator(s). The Secretariat shall not release data without the written approval of the data owner(s)/originator(s). Failure to achieve agreement shall be brought to the attention of the Scientific Committee and Commission.

11. The following statement shall be placed on the cover page of all Working Papers, Background Papers and any other papers tabled at meetings of the Commission, Scientific Committee or their subsidiary bodies:

'This paper is presented for consideration by CCAMLR and may contain unpublished data, analyses, and/or conclusions subject to change. Data in this paper shall not be cited or used for purposes other than the work of the CCAMLR Commission, Scientific Committee or their subsidiary bodies without the permission of the originators and/or owners of the data.'

Rules for Access to Catch Documentation Scheme Data (2000)

The following Rules for Access to the Catch Documentation Scheme for *Dissostichus* spp. (CDS) Data were adopted by the Nineteenth Meeting of the Commission (CCAMLR-XIX, paragraph 5.23)[23]:

Contracting Parties

1. Access to CDS data by Contracting Parties shall generally be managed in accordance with the Rules for Access and Use of CCAMLR Data (*Basic Documents*, Part 11). National CDS contact officers and other authorised persons will have access to all CDS data, including *Dissostichus* catch documents (DCDs) via the website and other means. Authorised CDS persons will have access to data from the DCDs needed for the purpose of implementing the CDS.

2. All data concerning the landing and trade details of individual companies shall be aggregated, or encrypted, as appropriate, to protect the confidentiality of such information before it is made available to working groups of the Commission or Scientific Committee.

Non-Contracting Parties

3. Non-Contracting Parties shall be given only limited access to data in order to validate individual shipments (both to that country, and from that country). Further access shall not be provided and password-protected access and other precautions shall be taken as appropriate. Non-Contracting Parties should advise the Secretariat of their national CDS contact point(s) before any access to CDS information is granted.

Policy to Enhance Cooperation between CCAMLR and Non-Contracting Parties (1999)

The Commission, in order to:

- ensure the effectiveness of CCAMLR conservation measures;
- enhance cooperation with non-Contracting Parties, including those implicated in fishing which undermines the effectiveness of those measures (hereafter referred to as illegal, unreported and unregulated fishing (IUU) fishing); and
- eliminate IUU fishing, including that by non-Contracting Parties,

hereby adopts the following policy:

[23] The Commission took into account the advice of the Standing Committee on Observation and Inspection (SCOI) that in considering the required Rules for Access of the Scientific Committee to CDS Data, the Commission should take into account the objectives of the data use, conditions for its release and its format (CCAMLR-XIX, Annex 5, paragraph 2.43).

I. The Executive Secretary is requested to develop a list of non-Contracting Parties implicated in IUU fishing and or trade either after the adoption of this policy or during the three years prior, which has undermined the effectiveness of CCAMLR conservation measures.

II. The Chairman of the Commission shall write to the Minister for Foreign Affairs of each non-Contracting Party included in the abovementioned list explaining how IUU fishing undermines the effectiveness of CCAMLR conservation measures. The letter, as appropriate, will:

(a) invite and encourage non-Contracting Parties to attend as observers at meetings of the Commission in order to improve their understanding of the work of the Commission and the effects of IUU fishing;
(b) encourage non-Contracting Parties to accede to the Convention;
(c) inform non-Contracting Parties of the development and implementation of the CCAMLR Catch Documentation Scheme for *Dissostichus* spp. and provide them with a copy of the conservation measure and the explanatory memorandum;
(d) encourage non-Contracting Parties to participate in the CCAMLR Catch Documentation Scheme and draw their attention to the consequences for them of not participating;
(e) request non-Contracting Parties to prevent their flag vessels from fishing in the Convention Area in a manner which undermines the effectiveness of measures adopted by CCAMLR to ensure conservation and sustainably managed fisheries;
(f) if their flag vessels are involved in IUU fishing, request non-Contracting Parties to provide information to the CCAMLR Secretariat on their vessels' activities, including catch and effort data;
(g) seek the assistance of non-Contracting Parties in investigating the activities of their flag vessels suspected of being involved in IUU fishing, including inspecting such vessels when they next reach port;
(h) request non-Contracting Parties to report to the CCAMLR Secretariat on landings and transhipments in their ports in accordance with the format specified in Attachment A; and
(i) request non-Contracting Parties to deny landing or transhipments in their ports for fish harvested in CCAMLR waters not taken in compliance with CCAMLR conservation measures and requirements under the Convention.

III. Parties shall individually and collectively take all appropriate efforts to implement or assist in the implementation of this policy; such efforts may include taking concerted action on joint demarches on non-Contracting Parties to complement correspondence from the Chairman.

IV. The Commission will annually review the effectiveness of the implementation of this policy.

V. The Executive Secretary will regularly inform non-Contracting Parties concerned of new conservation measures adopted by CCAMLR.

CONSERVATION MEASURES IN FORCE 2013–2014

Category 10 – Compliance

Conservation Measure 10-01 (1998):[24] Marking of Fishing Vessels and Fishing Gear

The Commission hereby adopts the following conservation measure in accordance with Article IX of the Convention:

[24] Except for waters adjacent to Kerguelen and Crozet Islands.

1. All Contracting Parties shall ensure that their fishing vessels licensed[25] in accordance with Conservation Measure 10-02 to operate in the Convention Area are marked in such a way that they can be readily identified in accordance with internationally recognised standards, such as the FAO Standard Specifications and Guidelines for the Marking and Identification of Fishing Vessels.

2. Marker buoys and similar objects floating on the surface and intended to indicate the location of fixed or set fishing gear shall be clearly marked at all times with the letter(s) and/or numbers of the vessels to which they belong.

Conservation Measure 10-02 (2013):[26,27] Licensing and Inspection Obligations of Contracting Parties with Regard to their Flag Vessels Operating in the Convention Area (Applicable to All Species, Areas, Seasons and Gear)

1. Each Contracting Party shall prohibit fishing by its flag vessels in the Convention Area except pursuant to a licence[28] that the Contracting Party has issued setting forth the specific areas, species and time periods for which such fishing is authorised and all other specific conditions to which the fishing is subject to give effect to CCAMLR conservation measures and requirements under the Convention.

2. A Contracting Party may only issue such a licence to fish in the Convention Area to a vessel flying its flag, if the vessel has an IMO number and if the Contracting Party is satisfied of the vessel's ability to exercise its responsibilities under the Convention and its conservation measures, by requiring from the vessel, *inter alia*, the following:

(i) timely notification by the vessel to its Flag State of exit from and entry into any port;

(ii) notification by the vessel to its Flag State of entry into the Convention Area and movement between areas, subareas/divisions;

(iii) reporting by the vessel of catch data in accordance with CCAMLR requirements;

(iv) reporting, where possible as set out in Annex 10-02/A by the vessel of sightings of fishing vessels[29] in the Convention Area;

(v) operation of a VMS system on board the vessel in accordance with Conservation Measure 10-04;

(vi) noting the International Management Code for the Safe Operation of Ships and for Pollution Prevention (International Safety Management Code), from 1 December 2009:

  (a) adequate communication equipment (including MF/HF radio and carriage of at least one 406MHz EPIRB) and trained operators on board. Wherever possible, vessels should be fitted with Global Maritime Distress and Safety System (GMDSS) equipment;

  (b) sufficient immersion survival suits for all on board;

  (c) adequate arrangements to handle medical emergencies that may arise in the course of the voyage;

  (d) reserves of food, fresh water, fuel and spare parts for critical equipment to provide for unforeseen delays and besetment;

  (e) an approved[30] Shipboard Oil Pollution Emergency Plan (SOPEP) outlining marine pollution mitigation arrangements (including insurance) in the event of a fuel or waste spill.

[25] Includes permitted.
[26] Except for waters adjacent to the Kerguelen and Crozet Islands.
[27] Except for waters adjacent to the Prince Edward Islands.
[28] Includes permit and authorisation.
[29] Including support vessels such as reefer vessels.
[30] Shipboard Oil Pollution Emergency Plan to be approved by the Maritime Safety Authority of the Flag State.

3. Each Contracting Party shall provide to the Secretariat within seven days of the issuance of each licence and prior to the vessel fishing in the Convention Area, the following information about licences issued:

(i) name of fishing vessel (any previous names if known)[31], registration number[32], IMO number, external markings and port of registry;
(ii) the nature of the authorisation to fish granted by the Flag State, specifying the date issued, time periods authorised for fishing (start and end dates), area(s), subareas or divisions of fishing, species targeted and gear used;
(iii) previous flag (if any)[6];
(iv) international radio call sign;
(v) vessel communication types and numbers (e.g. INMARSAT A, B and C numbers);
(vi) name and address of vessel's owner(s), and any beneficial owner(s) if known;
(vii) name and address of licence owner (if different from vessel owner(s));
(viii) type of vessel;
(ix) where and when built;
(x) length (m);
(xi) high-resolution colour photographs of the vessel of appropriate brightness and contrast[33] which shall consist of:
   - one photograph not smaller than 12 x 7 cm showing the starboard side of the vessel displaying its full overall length and complete structural features;
   - one photograph not smaller than 12 x 7 cm showing the port side of the vessel displaying its full overall length and complete structural features;
   - one photograph not smaller than 12 x 7 cm showing the stern taken directly from astern;
(xii) in accordance with Conservation Measure 10-04, details of the implementation of the tamper-proof requirements of the satellite monitoring device installed on board.

4. Each Contracting Party shall, to the extent practicable, also provide to the Secretariat at the same time as submitting information in accordance with paragraph 3, the following additional information in respect to each fishing vessel licensed:

(i) name and address of operator, if different from vessel owners;
(ii) names and nationality of master and, where relevant, of fishing master;
(iii) type of fishing method or methods;
(iv) beam (m);
(v) gross registered tonnage;
(vi) normal crew complement;
(vii) power of main engine or engines (kW);
(viii) carrying capacity (tonnes), number of fish holds and their capacity (m^3);
(ix) any other information in respect of each licensed vessel they consider appropriate (e.g. ice classification) for the purposes of the implementation of the conservation measures adopted by the Commission.

5. Contracting Parties shall communicate without delay to the Secretariat any change to any of the information submitted in accordance with paragraphs 3 and 4.

6. The Executive Secretary shall place a list of licensed vessels on the public section of the CCAMLR website.

7. The licence or an authorised copy of the licence must be carried by the fishing vessel and must be available for inspection at any time by a designated CCAMLR inspector in the Convention Area.

---

[31] In respect of any vessel reflagged within the previous 12 months, any information on the details of the process of (reasons for) previous deregistration of the vessel from other registries, if known.

[32] National registry number.

[33] All photographs shall be of sufficient quality to enable clear identification of the vessel.

8. Each Contracting Party shall verify, through inspections of all of its fishing vessels at the Party's departure and arrival ports, and where appropriate, in its Exclusive Economic Zone, its compliance with the conditions of the licence as described in paragraph 1 and with the CCAMLR conservation measures. In the event that there is evidence that the vessel has not fished in accordance with the conditions of its licence, the Contracting Party shall investigate the infringement and, if necessary, apply appropriate sanctions in accordance with its national legislation.

9. Each Contracting Party shall conduct an investigation into every very serious marine casualty in the CAMLR Convention Area involving a fishing vessel flying its flag. For the purposes of this conservation measure, a 'very serious marine casualty' means a marine casualty involving the total loss of the fishing vessel, loss of life, severe damage to the marine environment[34], serious injury to its own or another State's nationals, or serious damage[35] to its own or another State's vessels or installations. The Contracting Party shall forward its investigation report to the International Maritime Organization (IMO) and/or other relevant competent organisations, and also make available to CCAMLR Members a summary report of the findings and recommendations of relevance to CCAMLR. The Contracting Party shall notify CCAMLR of any findings made by the IMO and/or other organisations to which the investigation report was sent.

Annex 10-02/A: Reporting of Vessel Sightings (Applicable to All Species, Areas, Seasons and Gear)

1. In the event that the master of a licensed fishing vessel sights a fishing vessel[4] within the Convention Area, the master shall document as much information as possible on each such sighting, including:

(a) name and description of the vessel
(b) vessel call sign
(c) registration number and the Lloyds/IMO number of the vessel
(d) Flag State of the vessel
(e) photographs of the vessel to support the report
(f) any other relevant information regarding the observed activities of the sighted vessel.

2. The master shall forward a report containing the information referred to in paragraph 1 to their Flag State as soon as possible. The Flag State shall submit to the Secretariat any such reports that meet the criteria of paragraph 3 of Conservation Measure 10-06 or paragraph 8 of Conservation Measure 10-07.

3. The Secretariat shall use such reports for compiling estimates of IUU activities.

[34] For the purposes of this conservations measure, 'severe damage to the marine environment' refers to discharges of oil, hazardous substances, marine pollutants or noxious liquid substances (regardless of quantity) which produce a major deleterious effect upon the environment.

[35] For the purposes of this conservation measure, 'serious damage' includes fire, explosion, collision, grounding, severe heavy weather or ice damage, hull cracking, severe structural damage, or breakdown necessitating towage or shore assistance.

Conservation Measure 10-03 (2013):[36,37] Port Inspections of Fishing Vessels[38] Carrying Antarctic Marine Living Resources (Applicable to All Species, Areas, Seasons and Gear)

1. Contracting Parties shall undertake inspections of all fishing vessels carrying *Dissostichus* spp.[39] which enter their ports. The inspection shall be for the purpose of determining that if the vessel carried out harvesting activities in the Convention Area, these activities were carried out in accordance with CCAMLR conservation measures, and that if it intends to land or tranship *Dissostichus* spp. the catch to be unloaded or transhipped is accompanied by a *Dissostichus* catch document required by Conservation Measure 10-05 and that the catch agrees with the information recorded on the document.

2. Contracting Parties shall inspect at least 50% of fishing vessels that enter their ports carrying species other than *Dissostichus* spp., that were harvested in the Convention Area and that have not been previously landed or transhipped at a port. The purpose of the inspection will be to determine whether harvesting activities in the Convention Area were carried out in accordance with CCAMLR conservation measures.

3. In determining which fishing vessels carrying species other than *Dissostichus* spp. to inspect pursuant to paragraph 2, Contracting Parties shall take into account:

(i) whether a vessel has previously been denied entry or use of a port in accordance with this or any other conservation measure;

(ii) requests from other Contracting Parties that a particular vessel be inspected; and

(iii) whether clear grounds exist for suspecting that a vessel has engaged in illegal, unreported and unregulated (IUU) fishing[40], or fishing-related activities[41] in support of IUU fishing, including information derived from regional fisheries management organisations.

4. To facilitate the inspections referred to in paragraphs 1 and 2, Contracting Parties shall require vessels seeking entry to their ports to provide the information contained in the template in Annex 10-03/A and to convey a written declaration that they have not engaged in or supported IUU fishing in the Convention Area and have complied with relevant CCAMLR requirements. The Contracting Party shall require vessels seeking entry to their ports to provide the information contained in Annex 10-03/A at least 48 hours in advance to allow adequate time to examine the required information. Contracting Parties may designate ports to which fishing vessels may seek entry. Any such designations, and any subsequent changes, shall be notified to the Secretariat at least 30 days before they take effect. The Secretariat shall post information regarding designated ports on the CCAMLR website.

---

[36] Except for waters adjacent to the Kerguelen and Crozet Islands.

[37] Except for waters adjacent to the Prince Edward Islands.

[38] For the purposes of this conservation measure, 'fishing vessel' means any vessel of any size used for, equipped to be used for, or intended for use for the purposes of fishing or fishing related activities, including support ships, fish processing vessels, vessels engaged in transhipment and carrier vessels equipped for the transportation of fishery products except container vessels and excluding Members' marine science research vessels. In relation to only carrier vessels equipped for transportation of fishery products, Contracting Parties shall conduct a preliminary assessment of the relevant documentation. If that assessment raises concerns regarding compliance with CCAMLR conservation measures, an inspection according to the provisions of this conservation measure shall be required.

[39] Excluding by-catches of *Dissostichus* spp. By trawlers fishing outside the Convention Area. A by-catch shall be defined as no more than 5% of total catch of all species and no more than 50 tonnes for an entire fishing trip by a vessel.

[40] For the purposes of this conservation measure, IUU fishing refers to the activities described in paragraph 5 of the Conservation Measure 10-06 and paragraph 9 of Conservation Measure 10-07.

[41] For the purposes of this conservation measure, fishing-related activities mean any operation in support of, or in preparation for, fishing, including the landing, packaging, processing, transhipping or transporting of fish that have not previously been landed at a port, as well as the provisioning of personnel, fuel, gear and other supplies at sea.

5. Inspections shall be carried out in accordance with international law, and shall be conducted within 48 hours of port entry and shall be carried out in an expeditious fashion. The inspection shall impose no undue burdens on the vessel or its crew, and shall be guided by the relevant provisions of the CCAMLR System of Inspection. The collection of information during a port inspection shall be guided by the template provided in Annex 10-03/B.

6. Consistent with the provisions of Conservation Measures 10-06 and 10-07, except for the purposes of inspection, enforcement action or emergency, Contracting Parties shall take all necessary measures, subject to, and in accordance with, their applicable laws and regulations and international law, to deny port access to fishing vessels not entitled to fly their flag that:

(i) are included in a list of IUU vessels adopted by CCAMLR in accordance with Conservation Measure 10-06 or 10-07;

(ii) declare that they have been involved in IUU fishing; or

(iii) fail to make a declaration or provide advance notice as required under paragraph 4. Contracting Parties shall inspect any such fishing vessels that are granted port access for the purposes of inspection, enforcement action or emergency or that enter port without authorisation.

7. In the event that there is evidence that the vessel has fished in contravention of CCAMLR conservation measures, in particular when the fishing vessel is included in a list of IUU vessels adopted by CCAMLR in accordance with Conservation Measure 10-06 or 10-07, the Contracting Party shall prohibit the vessel from landing or transhipping the catch, or take other monitoring, control, surveillance or enforcement action of equivalent or greater severity in accordance with international law. The Contracting Party shall inform the Flag State of the vessel of its inspection findings and shall cooperate with the Flag State in taking such appropriate action as is required to investigate the alleged infringement and, if necessary, apply appropriate sanctions in accordance with national legislation.

8. Contracting Parties shall provide the Secretariat with a report on the outcome of each inspection conducted under this conservation measure within 30 days of the port inspection or as soon as possible where compliance issues have arisen[42]. The Secretariat shall promptly convey the report to the Flag State of the inspected vessel.

9. All port inspection reports shall consist of the completed template provided in Annex 10-03/A and, if it is determined that harvesting activities were conducted in the Convention Area, the port inspection report will include the completed template provided in Annex 10-03/B. The Secretariat shall promptly convey reports of any vessels denied port access or permission to land or tranship *Dissostichus* spp. or any other species harvested in the Convention Area, to all Contracting Parties and to any non-Contracting Party participating in the Catch Documentation Scheme for *Dissostichus* spp. (CDS) under Conservation Measure 10-05, Annex 10-05/C.

Conservation Measure 10-04 (2013): Automated Satellite-Linked Vessel Monitoring Systems (VMS) (Applicable to All Species, Areas, Seasons and Gear)

The Commission,

Recognising that in order to promote the objectives of the Convention and further improve compliance with the relevant conservation measures,

Convinced that illegal, unreported and unregulated (IUU) fishing compromises the objective of the Convention,

Recalling that Contracting Parties are required to cooperate in taking appropriate action to deter any fishing activities which are not consistent with the objective of the Convention,

[42] Contracting Parties may elect not to submit to the Secretariat reports of inspections of their vessels if they determine that all fishing activity occurred in waters under their jurisdiction.

Mindful of the rights and obligations of Flag States and Port States to promote the effectiveness of conservation measures,

Wanting to reinforce the conservation measures already adopted by the Commission,

Recognising the obligations and responsibilities of Contracting Parties under the Catch Documentation Scheme for *Dissostichus* spp. (CDS),

Recalling provisions as made under Article XXIV of the Convention,

Committed to take steps, consistent with international law, to identify the origins of *Dissostichus* spp. entering the markets of Contracting Parties and to determine whether *Dissostichus* spp. harvested in the Convention Area that is imported into their territories was caught in a manner consistent with CCAMLR conservation measures,

hereby adopts the following conservation measure in accordance with Article IX of the Convention:

1. Each Contracting Party shall ensure that its fishing vessels, licensed[43] in accordance with Conservation Measure 10-02, are equipped with a satellite-linked vessel monitoring device allowing for the continuous reporting of their position in the Convention Area for the duration of the licence issued by the Flag State. The vessel monitoring device shall automatically communicate at least every four hours to a land-based fisheries monitoring centre (FMC) of the Flag State of the vessel the following data:
   - (i) fishing vessel identification;
   - (ii) the current geographical position (latitude and longitude) of the vessel, with a position error which shall be less than 500 m, with a confidence interval of 99%; and
   - (iii) the date and time (expressed in UTC) of the fixing of the said position of the vessel.

2. Each Contracting Party as a Flag State shall ensure that the vessel monitoring device(s) on board its vessels are tamper proof, i.e. are of a type and configuration that prevent the input or output of false positions, and that are not capable of being over-ridden, whether manually, electronically or otherwise. To this end, the on-board satellite monitoring device must:
   - (i) be located within a sealed unit; and
   - (ii) be protected by official seals (or mechanisms) of a type that indicate whether the unit has been accessed or tampered with.

3. In the event that a Contracting Party has information to suspect that an on-board vessel monitoring device does not meet the requirements of paragraph 2, or has been tampered with, it shall immediately notify the Secretariat and the vessel's Flag State.

4. Each Contracting Party shall ensure that its FMC receives Vessel Monitoring System (VMS) reports and messages, and that the FMC is equipped with computer hardware and software enabling automatic data processing and electronic data transmission. Each Contracting Party shall provide for backup and recovery procedures in case of system failures.

5. Masters and owners/licensees of fishing vessels subject to VMS shall ensure that the vessel monitoring device on board their vessels within the Convention Area is at all times fully operational as per paragraph 1, and that the data are transmitted to the Flag State. Masters and owners/licensees shall in particular ensure that:
   - (i) VMS reports and messages are not altered in any way;
   - (ii) the antennae connected to the satellite monitoring device are not obstructed in any way;
   - (iii) the power supply of the satellite monitoring device is not interrupted in any way; and
   - (iv) the vessel monitoring device is not removed from the vessel.

6. A vessel monitoring device shall be active within the Convention Area. It may, however, be switched off when the fishing vessel is in port for a period of more than one week, subject to prior notification to the Flag State, and if the Flag State so desires also to the Secretariat, and providing that the first position report generated following the repowering (activating) shows that the fishing vessel has not changed position compared to the last report.

[43] Includes vessels licensed under French domestic law and vessels licensed under South African domestic law.

7. In the event of a technical failure or non-functioning of the vessel monitoring device on board the fishing vessel, the master or the owner of the vessel, or their representative, shall communicate to the Flag State every six hours, and if the Flag State so desires also to the Secretariat, starting at the time that the failure or the non-functioning was detected or notified in accordance with paragraph 11, the up-to-date geographical position of the vessel by electronic means (email, facsimile, telephone message, radio).

8. Vessels with a defective vessel monitoring device shall take immediate steps to have the device repaired or replaced as soon as possible and, in any event, within two months. If the vessel during that time returns to port, it shall not be allowed by the Flag State to commence a further fishing trip in the Convention Area without having the defective device repaired or replaced.

9. When the Flag State has not received for 12 hours data transmissions referred to in paragraphs 1 and 7, or has reasons to doubt the correctness of the data transmissions under paragraphs 1 and 7, it shall as soon as possible notify the master or the owner or the representative thereof. If this situation occurs more than two times within a period of one year in respect of a particular vessel, the Flag State of the vessel shall investigate the matter, including having an authorised official check the device in question, in order to establish whether the equipment has been tampered with. The outcome of this investigation shall be forwarded to the CCAMLR Secretariat within 30 days of its completion.

10.[44,45] Each Contracting Party shall forward VMS reports and messages received, pursuant to paragraph 1, to the CCAMLR Secretariat as soon as possible:

(i) but not later than four hours after receipt for those exploratory longline fisheries subject to conservation measures adopted at CCAMLR-XXIII; or

(ii) but not later than 10 working days following departure from the Convention Area for all other fisheries.

11. With regard to paragraphs 7 and 10(i), each Contracting Party shall, as soon as possible but no later than two working days following detection or notification of technical failure or non-functioning of the vessel monitoring device on board the fishing vessel, forward the geographical positions of the vessel to the Secretariat, or shall ensure that these positions are forwarded to the Secretariat by the master or the owner of the vessel, or their representative.

12. Each Flag State shall ensure that VMS reports and messages transmitted by the Contracting Party or its fishing vessels to the CCAMLR Secretariat, are in a computer-readable form in the data exchange format set out in Annex 10-04/A.

13. Each Flag State shall in addition separately notify by email or other means the CCAMLR Secretariat within 24 hours of each entry to, exit from and movement between subareas and divisions of the Convention Area by each of its fishing vessels in the format outlined in Annex 10-04/A. When a vessel intends to enter a closed area, or an area for which it is not licensed to fish, the Flag State shall provide prior notification to the Secretariat of the vessel's intentions. The Flag State may permit or direct that such notifications be provided by the vessel directly to the Secretariat.

14. Without prejudice to its responsibilities as a Flag State, if the Contracting Party so desires, it shall ensure that each of its vessels communicates the reports referred to in paragraphs 10 and 13 in parallel to the CCAMLR Secretariat.

15. Each Flag State shall notify to the CCAMLR Secretariat any changes without delay to the name, address, email, telephone and facsimile numbers, as well as the address of electronic communication of the relevant authorities of their FMC.

[44] This paragraph does not apply to vessels licensed under French domestic law in the EEZs surrounding Kerguelen and Crozet Islands.

[45] This paragraph does not apply to vessels licensed under South African domestic law in the EEZ surrounding Prince Edward Islands.

16. In the event that the CCAMLR Secretariat has not, for 48 consecutive hours, received the data transmissions referred to in paragraph 10(i), it shall promptly notify the Flag State of the vessel and require an explanation. The CCAMLR Secretariat shall promptly inform the Commission if the data transmissions at issue, or the Flag State explanation, are not received from the Contracting Party within a further five working days.

17. If VMS data received by the Secretariat indicate the presence of a vessel in an area or subarea for which no license details have been provided by the Flag State to the Secretariat as required by Conservation Measure 10-02, or in any area or subarea for which the Flag State or fishing vessel has not provided prior notification as required by paragraph 13, then the Secretariat shall notify the Flag State and require an explanation. The explanation shall be forwarded to the Secretariat for evaluation by the Commission at its next annual meeting.

18. The CCAMLR Secretariat and all Parties receiving data shall treat all VMS reports and messages received under paragraph 10 or paragraphs 19, 20, 21 or 22 in a confidential manner in accordance with the confidentiality rules established by the Commission as contained in Annex 10-04/B. Data from individual vessels shall be used for compliance and search and rescue purposes only, namely for:

(i) planning for active surveillance presence, and/or inspections by a Contracting Party in a specified CCAMLR subarea or division;

(ii) active surveillance presence, and/or inspections by a Contracting Party in a specified CCAMLR subarea or division;

(iii) the purposes of verifying the content of a *Dissostichus* catch document (DCD); or

(iv) supporting search and rescue activities undertaken by a competent Maritime Rescue Coordination Center (MRCC) subject to the terms of a Memorandum of Understanding (MOU) or Arrangement between the CCAMLR Secretariat and the competent MRCC[46].

19. The CCAMLR Secretariat shall place a list of vessels submitting VMS reports and messages pursuant to this conservation measure on a password-protected section of the CCAMLR website. This list shall be divided into subareas and divisions, without indicating the exact positions of vessels, and be updated when a vessel changes subarea or division. The list shall be posted daily by the Secretariat, establishing an electronic archive.

20. VMS data shall be provided by the Secretariat to a requesting Contracting Party other than the Flag State without the permission of the Flag State for the purposes of paragraph 18(i). Data shall only be provided by the Secretariat for surveillance and/or inspection planning where the requesting Contracting Party has designated inspectors, and has previously carried out active surveillance and/or inspection activity, in accordance with CCAMLR's System of Inspection. Contracting Parties requesting the data shall provide the geographic area[47] of the planned surveillance and/or inspection activity. In this case, the Secretariat shall provide current VMS data for the identified geographic area at a specified point in time no more than 48 hours prior to the commencement of each surveillance and/or inspection activity. In the event that planned surveillance and/or inspection activities do not proceed, the Contracting Party will notify the Secretariat and destroy the data, and confirm the data destruction to the Secretariat in writing, without delay. The Secretariat shall notify the Flag State(s) that the VMS data were provided to the Contracting Party and that they have received confirmation that the data have been destroyed.

21. VMS reports and messages (including vessel locations), for the purposes of paragraph 18(ii) above, shall be provided by the Secretariat to a requesting Contracting Party other than the Flag State without the permission of the Flag State only during active surveillance, and/or inspection, in accordance with the CCAMLR System of Inspection and subject to the time frames set out in paragraph 10. In this case, the Secretariat shall provide VMS reports and messages, including

[46] The draft MOU or Arrangement shall be submitted for the approval of the Commission.

[47] The area of planned surveillance and/or inspection activity shall be identified by CCAMLR subarea, division, or SSRU, whichever is the smallest geographical scale applicable to this area.

vessel locations over the previous 10 days, for vessels actually detected during surveillance, and/or inspection, by a Contracting Party, and VMS reports and messages (including vessel locations) for all vessels within 100 n miles of that same location. The Secretariat shall provide regular updates of positions to the Contracting Party for the duration of the active surveillance, and/or inspection, in accordance with the CCAMLR System of Inspection. The Flag State(s) concerned shall be provided by the Party conducting the active surveillance, and/or inspection, with a report including the name of the vessel or aircraft on active surveillance, and/or inspection under the CCAMLR System of Inspection, and the full name(s) of the CCAMLR inspector(s) and their ID number(s). The Contracting Parties conducting active surveillance, and/or inspection, shall make this information available to the Flag State(s) without undue delay after the surveillance and/or inspection activities are completed.

22. A Contracting Party may request the Secretariat to check VMS data from a vessel against the claims on a DCD in order to verify those claims. A Contracting Party may also request actual VMS reports and messages (including vessel locations) from the Secretariat for a vessel when verifying the claims on a DCD; the Secretariat shall provide that data only with Flag State permission.

23. Notwithstanding the requirements of paragraphs 1 and 4, Contracting Parties may request VMS data for their own flag vessels from the Secretariat.

24. The CCAMLR Secretariat shall annually, before 30 September, report on the implementation of, and compliance with, this conservation measure to the Commission.

Conservation Measure 10-06 (2008): Scheme to Promote Compliance by Contracting Party Vessels with CCAMLR Conservation Measures (Applicable to All Species, Areas, Seasons and Gear)

The Commission,

Convinced that illegal, unreported and unregulated (IUU) fishing compromises the objective of the Convention,

Aware that a number of vessels registered to Parties and non-Parties are engaged in activities which diminish the effectiveness of CCAMLR conservation measures,

Recalling that Contracting Parties are required to cooperate in taking appropriate action to deter any activities which are not consistent with the objective of the Convention,

Resolved to reinforce its integrated administrative and political measures aimed at eliminating IUU fishing in the Convention Area,

hereby adopts the following conservation measure in accordance with Article IX.2(i) of the Convention:

1. At each annual meeting, the Commission will identify those Contracting Parties whose vessels have engaged in fishing activities in the Convention Area in a manner which has diminished the effectiveness of CCAMLR conservation measures in force, and shall establish a list of such vessels (CP-IUU Vessel List), in accordance with the procedures and criteria set out hereafter.

2. This identification shall be documented, *inter alia*, on reports relating to the application of Conservation Measure 10-03, trade information obtained on the basis of the implementation of Conservation Measure 10-05 and relevant trade statistics such as Food and Agriculture Organization of the United Nations (FAO) and other national or international verifiable statistics, as well as any other information obtained from Port States and/or gathered from the fishing grounds which is suitably documented.

3. Where a Contracting Party obtains information that vessels flying the flag of another Contracting Party have engaged in activities set out in paragraph 5, it shall submit a report containing this information, within 30 days of having become aware of it, to the Executive Secretary and the

Contracting Party concerned. Contracting Parties shall indicate that the information is provided for the purposes of considering whether to include the vessel concerned in the CP-IUU Vessel List under Conservation Measure 10-06. The Executive Secretary shall within one business day circulate the report to the other Contracting Parties and to non-Contracting Parties cooperating with the Commission by participating in the Catch Documentation Scheme for *Dissostichus* spp. (CDS), and invite them to communicate any information available to them in respect of the vessels referred to above, including their ownership, operators and their trade activities.

4. For the purposes of this conservation measure, the Contracting Parties are considered as having carried out fishing activities that have diminished the effectiveness of the conservation measures adopted by the Commission if:

(i) the Parties do not ensure compliance by their vessels with the conservation measures adopted by the Commission and in force, in respect of the fisheries in which they participate that are placed under the competence of CCAMLR;

(ii) their vessels are repeatedly included in the CP-IUU Vessel List.

5. In order for a Contracting Party's vessel to be included in the CP-IUU Vessel List there must be evidence, gathered in accordance with paragraphs 2 and 3, that the vessel has:

(i) engaged in fishing activities in the CAMLR Convention Area without a licence issued in accordance with Conservation Measure 10-02, or in violation of the conditions under which such licence would have been issued in relation to authorised areas, species and time periods; or

(ii) not recorded or not declared its catches made in the CAMLR Convention Area in accordance with the reporting system applicable to the fisheries it engaged in, or made false declarations; or

(iii) fished during closed fishing periods or in closed areas in contravention of CCAMLR conservation measures; or

(iv) used prohibited gear in contravention of applicable CCAMLR conservation measures; or

(v) transhipped or participated in joint fishing operations with, supported or re-supplied other vessels identified by CCAMLR as carrying out IUU fishing activities (i.e. vessels on the CP-IUU Vessel List or the NCP-IUU Vessel List established under Conservation Measure 10-07); or

(vi) failed to provide, when required under Conservation Measure 10-05, a valid catch document for *Dissostichus* spp.; or

(vii) engaged in fishing activities in a manner that undermines the attainment of the objectives of the Convention in waters adjacent to islands within the area to which the Convention applies over which the existence of State sovereignty is recognised by all Contracting Parties, in the terms of the statement made by the Chairman on 19 May 1980; or

(viii) engaged in fishing activities contrary to any other CCAMLR conservation measures in a manner that undermines the attainment of the objectives of the Convention according to Article XXII of the Convention.

Draft CP-IUU Vessel List

6. The Executive Secretary shall, before 1 July of each year, draw up a draft list of Contracting Party vessels (the Draft CP-IUU Vessel List), listing all Contracting Party vessels that, on the basis of the information gathered in accordance with paragraphs 2 and 3, and any other information that the Executive Secretary might have obtained in relation thereto, and the criteria defined in paragraph 4, might be presumed to have engaged in any of the activities referred to in paragraph 5 during the period beginning 30 days before the start of the previous CCAMLR annual meeting. The Draft CP-IUU Vessel List shall be distributed immediately to the Contracting Parties concerned.

7. Contracting Parties whose vessels are included in the Draft CP-IUU Vessel List shall transmit their comments to the Executive Secretary before 1 September, including verifiable VMS data and other supporting information showing that the vessels listed have not engaged in the activities which led to their inclusion in the Draft CP-IUU Vessel List.

Provisional CP-IUU Vessel List

8. The Executive Secretary shall create a new list ('the Provisional CP-IUU Vessel List') which shall comprise the Draft CP-IUU Vessel List and all information received pursuant to paragraph 7. Before 1 October, the Executive Secretary shall transmit the Provisional CP-IUU Vessel List, the CP-IUU Vessel List agreed at the previous CCAMLR annual meeting, and any evidence or documented information received since that meeting regarding vessels on the Provisional CP-IUU Vessel List and CP-IUU Vessel List to all Contracting Parties and non-Contracting Parties cooperating with the Commission by participating in the CDS. The Executive Secretary shall at the same time:

(i) request non-Contracting Parties cooperating with the Commission by participating in the CDS that, to the extent possible in accordance with their applicable laws and regulations, they do not register or de-register vessels that have been placed on the Provisional CP-IUU Vessel List until such time as the Commission has had the opportunity to consider the List and has made its determination;

(ii) invite non-Contracting Parties cooperating with the Commission by participating in the CDS to submit any evidence or documented information regarding vessels on the Provisional CP-IUU Vessel List and CP-IUU Vessel List, at the latest 30 days before the start of the next CCAMLR annual meeting. Where the incident occurs within the month preceding the next CCAMLR annual meeting, evidence or documented information should be provided as soon as possible.

9. Contracting Parties shall take all necessary measures, to the extent possible in accordance with their applicable laws and regulations, in order that:

(i) they do not register or de-register vessels that have been placed on the Provisional CP-IUU List until such time as the Commission has had the opportunity to examine the List and has made its determination;

(ii) if they do de-register a vessel on the Provisional CP-IUU Vessel List they inform, where possible, the Executive Secretary of the proposed new Flag State of the vessel, whereupon the Executive Secretary shall inform that State that the vessel is on the Provisional CP-IUU Vessel List and urge that State not to register the vessel.

Proposed and Final CP-IUU Vessel List

10. Contracting Parties shall submit to the Executive Secretary any additional information which might be relevant for the establishment of the CP-IUU Vessel List within 30 days of having become aware of such information and at the latest 30 days before the start of the CCAMLR annual meeting. A report containing this information shall be submitted in the format set out in paragraph 16, and Contracting Parties shall indicate that the information is provided for the purposes of considering whether to include the vessel concerned in the CP-IUU Vessel List under Conservation Measure 10-06. The Secretariat shall collate all information received and, where this has not been provided in relation to a vessel, attempt to obtain the information in paragraphs 16(i) to (vii).

11. The Executive Secretary shall circulate to Contracting Parties, at the latest 30 days before the start of the CCAMLR annual meeting, all evidence or documented information received under paragraphs 8 and 9, together with any other evidence or documented information received in terms of paragraphs 2 and 3.

12. At each CCAMLR annual meeting, the Standing Committee on Implementation and Compliance (SCIC) shall, by consensus:

(i) adopt a Proposed CP-IUU Vessel List, following consideration of the Provisional CP-IUU Vessel List and information and evidence circulated under paragraph 10. The Proposed CP-IUU Vessel List shall be submitted to the Commission for approval;
(ii) recommend to the Commission which, if any, vessels should be removed from the CP-IUU Vessel List adopted at the previous CCAMLR annual meeting, following consideration of that List and information and evidence circulated under paragraph 10.

13. SCIC shall include a vessel on the Proposed CP-IUU Vessel List only if one or more of the criteria in paragraph 5 have been satisfied.

14. SCIC shall recommend that the Commission should remove a vessel from the CP-IUU Vessel List if the Contracting Party proves that:
(i) the vessel did not take part in the activities described in paragraph 1 which led to the inclusion of the vessel in the CP-IUU Vessel List; or
(ii) it has taken effective action in response to the activities in question, including prosecution and imposition of sanctions of adequate severity; or
(iii) the vessel has changed ownership, including beneficial ownership if known to be distinct from the registered ownership, and that the new owner can establish the previous owner no longer has any legal, financial, or real interests in the vessel, or exercises control over it and that the new owner has not participated in IUU fishing; or
(iv) it has taken measures considered sufficient to ensure the granting of the right to the vessel to fly its flag will not result in IUU fishing.

15. In order to facilitate the work of SCIC and the Commission, the Executive Secretary shall prepare a paper for each CCAMLR annual meeting, summarising and annexing all the information, evidence and comments submitted in respect of each vessel to be considered.

16. The Draft CP-IUU Vessel List, Provisional CP-IUU Vessel List, Proposed CP-IUU Vessel List and the CP-IUU Vessel List shall contain the following details:
(i) name of vessel and previous names, if any;
(ii) flag of vessel and previous flags, if any;
(iii) owner of vessel and previous owners, including beneficial owners, if any;
(iv) operator of vessel and previous operators, if any;
(v) call sign of vessel and previous call signs, if any;
(vi) Lloyds/IMO number;
(vii) photographs of the vessel, where available;
(viii) date vessel was first included on the CP-IUU Vessel List;
(ix) summary of activities which justify inclusion of the vessel on the List, together with references to all relevant documents informing of and evidencing those activities;
(x) date and location of subsequent sightings of the vessel in the Convention Area, if any, and of any other related activities performed by the vessel contrary to CCAMLR conservation measures.

17. On approval of the CP-IUU Vessel List, the Commission shall request Contracting Parties whose vessels appear thereon to take all necessary measures to address these activities, including if necessary, the withdrawal of the registration or of the fishing licences of these vessels, the nullification of the relevant catch documents and denial of further access to the CDS, and to inform the Commission of the measures taken in this respect.

18. Contracting Parties shall take all necessary measures, subject to and in accordance with their applicable laws and regulations and international law, in order that:
(i) the issuance of a licence to vessels on the CP-IUU Vessel List to fish in the Convention Area is prohibited;
(ii) the issuance of a licence to vessels on the CP-IUU Vessel List to fish in waters under their fisheries jurisdiction is prohibited;
(iii) fishing vessels, support vessels, refuel vessels, mother-ships and cargo vessels flying their flag do not in any way, in the Convention Area, assist vessels on the CP-IUU

Vessel List by participating in any transhipment or joint fishing operations, supporting or resupplying such vessels;

(iv) vessels on the CP-IUU Vessel List should be denied access to ports unless for the purpose of enforcement action or for reasons of *force majeure* or for rendering assistance to vessels, or persons on those vessels, in danger or distress. Vessels allowed entry to port are to be inspected in accordance with relevant conservation measures;

(v) where port access is granted to such vessels:

(a) documentation and other information, including DCDs where relevant are examined, with a view to verifying the area in which the catch was taken; and where the origin cannot be adequately verified, the catch is detained or any landing or transhipment of the catch is refused; and

(b) where possible

i. in the event catch is found to be taken in contravention of CCAMLR conservation measures, catch is confiscated;

ii. all support to such vessels, including non-emergency refuelling, resupplying and repairs is prohibited;

(vi) the chartering of vessels on the CP-IUU Vessel List is prohibited;

(vii) granting of their flag to vessels on the CP-IUU Vessel List is refused;

(viii) imports, exports and re-exports of *Dissostichus* spp. from vessels on the CP-IUU Vessel List are prohibited;

(ix) 'Export or Re-export Government Authority Validation' is not certified when the shipment (of *Dissostichus* spp.) is declared to have been caught by any vessel on the CP-IUU Vessel List;

(x) importers, transporters and other sectors concerned are encouraged to refrain from dealing with and from transhipping of fish caught by vessels on the CP-IUU Vessel List;

(xi) any appropriate information which is suitably documented is collected and submitted to the Executive Secretary, to be forwarded to Contracting Parties, and non-Contracting Parties, entities or fishing entities cooperating with the Commission by participating in the CDS, with the aim of detecting, controlling and preventing the importation or exportation of, and other trade-related activities relating to, catches from vessels on the CP-IUU Vessel List intended to circumvent this conservation measure.

19. The Executive Secretary shall place the CP-IUU Vessel List approved by the Commission on the public section of the CCAMLR website. Furthermore, the Executive Secretary shall communicate the CP-IUU Vessel List to the FAO and appropriate regional fisheries organisations to enhance cooperation between CCAMLR and these organisations for the purposes of preventing, deterring and eliminating IUU fishing.

20. The Executive Secretary shall circulate to non-Contracting Parties cooperating with the Commission by participating in the CDS the CP-IUU Vessel List, together with the request that, to the extent possible in accordance with their applicable laws and regulations, they do not register vessels that have been placed on the List unless they are removed from the List by the Commission.

21. If Contracting Parties obtain new or changed information for vessels on the CP-IUU Vessel List in relation to the details in paragraphs 16(i) to (vii), they shall notify the Executive Secretary who shall place a notification on the secure section of the CCAMLR website and advise all Contracting Parties of the notification. If there are no comments on the information within seven (7) days, the Executive Secretary will revise the CP-IUU Vessel List.

22. Without prejudice to their rights to take proper action consistent with international law, Contracting Parties should not take any trade measures or other sanctions which are inconsistent with their international obligations against vessels using as the basis for the action the fact that

the vessel or vessels have been included in the Draft CP-IUU Vessel List drawn up by the Executive Secretary, pursuant to paragraph 6.

23. The Chair of the Commission shall request the Contracting Parties identified pursuant to paragraph 1 to take all necessary measures to avoid diminishing the effectiveness of CCAMLR conservation measures resulting from their vessels' activities, and to advise the Commission of actions taken in that regard.

24. The Commission shall review, at subsequent CCAMLR annual meetings, as appropriate, action taken by those Contracting Parties to which requests have been made pursuant to paragraph 23, and identify those which have not rectified their activities.

25. The Commission shall decide appropriate measures to be taken in respect to *Dissostichus* spp. so as to address these issues with those identified Contracting Parties. In this respect, Contracting Parties may cooperate to adopt appropriate multilaterally agreed trade-related measures, consistent with their obligations as members of the World Trade Organization, that may be necessary to prevent, deter and eliminate the IUU activities identified by the Commission. Multilateral trade-related measures may be used to support cooperative efforts to ensure that trade in *Dissostichus* spp. and its products does not in any way encourage IUU fishing or otherwise diminish the effectiveness of CCAMLR's conservation measures which are consistent with the United Nations Convention on the Law of the Sea 1982.

Conservation Measure 10-07 (2009): Scheme to Promote Compliance by Non-Contracting Party Vessels with CCAMLR Conservation Measures (Applicable to All Species, Areas, Seasons and Gear)

The Commission,

Convinced that illegal, unreported and unregulated (IUU) fishing compromises the objective of the Convention,

Aware that a significant number of vessels registered to non-Contracting Parties are engaged in activities which diminish the effectiveness of CCAMLR conservation measures,

Recalling that Contracting Parties are required to cooperate in taking appropriate action to deter any activities which are not consistent with the objective of the Convention,

Resolved to reinforce its integrated administrative and political measures aimed at eliminating IUU fishing in the Convention Area,

hereby adopts the following conservation measure in accordance with Article IX.2(i) of the Convention:

1. The Contracting Parties request non-Contracting Parties to cooperate fully with the Commission with a view to ensuring that the effectiveness of CCAMLR conservation measures is not undermined.

2. At each annual meeting the Commission shall identify those non-Contracting Parties whose vessels are engaged in IUU fishing activities in the Convention Area that threaten to undermine the effectiveness of CCAMLR conservation measures, and shall establish a list of such vessels (NCP-IUU Vessel List), in accordance with the procedures and criteria set out hereafter.

3. This identification shall be documented, *inter alia*, on reports relating to the application of Conservation Measure 10-03, trade information obtained on the basis of the implementation of Conservation Measure 10-05 and relevant trade statistics such as Food and Agriculture Organization of the United Nations (FAO) and other national or international verifiable statistics, as well as any other information obtained from Port States and/or gathered from the fishing grounds which is suitably documented.

4. A non-Contracting Party vessel which has been sighted engaging in fishing activities in the Convention Area or which has been denied port access, landing or transhipment in accordance with Conservation Measure 10-03 is presumed to be undermining the effectiveness

of CCAMLR conservation measures. In the case of any transhipment activities involving a sighted non-Contracting Party vessel inside or outside the Convention Area, the presumption of undermining the effectiveness of CCAMLR conservation measures applies to any other non-Contracting Party vessel which has engaged in such activities with that vessel.

5. When a non-Contracting Party vessel referred to in paragraph 4 enters a port of any Contracting Party, it shall be inspected by authorised Contracting Party officials in accordance with Conservation Measure 10-03 and shall not be allowed to land or tranship any fish species subject to CCAMLR conservation measures it might be holding on board unless the vessel establishes that the fish were caught in compliance with all relevant CCAMLR conservation measures and requirements under this Convention.

6. A Contracting Party which sights a non-Contracting Party vessel engaging in fishing activities in the Convention Area or denies a non-Contracting Party port access, landing or transhipment under paragraph 5 shall attempt to inform the vessel that it is presumed to be undermining the effectiveness of CCAMLR conservation measures, and that this information will be distributed to the Executive Secretary, all Contracting Parties and the Flag State of the vessel.

7. Information regarding such sightings or denial of port access, landings or transhipments, and the result of all inspections conducted in the ports of Contracting Parties, and any subsequent action shall be transmitted within one business day to the Commission in accordance with Article XXII of the Convention. The Executive Secretary shall transmit this information to all Contracting Parties, within one business day of receiving it, and to the Flag State of the vessel concerned as soon as possible and to appropriate regional fisheries organisations. At this time, the Executive Secretary shall, in consultation with the Chair of the Commission, request the Flag State concerned that, where appropriate, measures be taken in accordance with its applicable laws and regulations to ensure that the vessel desists from any activities that undermine the effectiveness of CCAMLR conservation measures, and that the Flag State report back to CCAMLR on the results of such enquiries and/or on the measures it has taken in respect of the vessel. The other Contracting Parties and non-Contracting Parties cooperating with the Commission by participating in the Catch Documentation Scheme for *Dissostichus* spp. (CDS) shall be invited to communicate any information available to them in respect of the vessels referred to above, including their ownership, operators and their trade activities.

8. Where a Contracting Party obtains information that a non-Contracting Party vessel has engaged in activities set out in paragraph 9, it shall submit a report containing this information, within 30 days of having become aware of it, to the Executive Secretary (including where such information has already been transmitted under paragraph 7). Contracting Parties shall indicate that the information is provided for the purposes of considering whether to include the vessel concerned in the NCP-IUU Vessel List under Conservation Measure 10-07. In addition, the Contracting Party may also submit the report directly to the non-Contracting Party concerned. The Executive Secretary shall promptly forward the information to the non-Contracting Party concerned, indicating that it has been provided for the purposes of considering whether to include the vessel concerned in the NCP-IUU Vessel List under Conservation Measure 10-07. The Executive Secretary shall request that the Flag State take action to prevent the vessel undertaking any activities that undermine the effectiveness of CCAMLR conservation measures and that the Flag State report back to CCAMLR on the measures it has taken in respect of the vessel concerned. The Executive Secretary shall circulate the information and any report from the Flag State to all other Contracting Parties as soon as possible.

9. In order for a non-Contracting Party's vessel to be included in the NCP-IUU Vessel List, there must be evidence, gathered in accordance with paragraphs 3 and 8, that the vessel has:

(i) been sighted engaging in fishing activities in the CAMLR Convention Area; or

(ii) been denied port access, landing or transhipment in accordance with Conservation Measure 10-03; or

(iii) transhipped or participated in joint fishing operations with, supported or resupplied other vessels identified by CCAMLR as carrying out IUU fishing activities (i.e. vessels on the NCP-IUU Vessel List or the CP-IUU Vessel List established under Conservation Measure 10-06); or

(iv) failed to provide, when required under Conservation Measure 10-05, a valid catch document for *Dissostichus* spp.; or

(v) engaged in fishing activities in a manner that undermines the attainment of the objectives of the Convention in waters adjacent to islands within the area to which the Convention applies over which the existence of State sovereignty is recognised by all Contracting Parties, in the terms of the statement made by the Chairman on 19 May 1980; or

(vi) engaged in fishing activities contrary to any other CCAMLR conservation measures in a manner that undermines the attainment of the objectives of the Convention according to Article XXII of the Convention.

Draft NCP-IUU Vessel List

10. The Executive Secretary shall, before 1 July of each year, draw up a draft list ('the Draft NCP-IUU Vessel List'), listing all non-Contracting Party vessels that, on the basis of the information gathered in accordance with paragraphs 3 and 8 and any other information that the Executive Secretary might have obtained in relation thereto, might be presumed to have engaged in any of the activities referred to in paragraph 9 during the period beginning 30 days before the start of the previous CCAMLR annual meeting. The Draft NCP-IUU Vessel List shall be distributed immediately to the non-Contracting Parties concerned and to all Contracting Parties.

11. The Executive Secretary shall invite non-Contracting Parties whose vessels are included in the Draft NCP-IUU Vessel List to transmit their comments to the Executive Secretary before 1 September, including verifiable VMS data and other supporting information showing that the vessels listed have not engaged in the activities which led to their inclusion in the Draft NCP-IUU Vessel List.

Provisional NCP-IUU Vessel List

12. The Executive Secretary shall create a new list ('the Provisional NCP-IUU Vessel List') which shall comprise the Draft NCP-IUU Vessel List and all information received pursuant to paragraph 11. Before 1 October, the Executive Secretary shall transmit the Provisional NCP-IUU Vessel List, the NCP-IUU Vessel List agreed at the previous CCAMLR annual meeting, and any evidence or documented information received since that meeting regarding vessels on the Provisional NCP-IUU Vessel List or the NCP-IUU Vessel List to all Contracting Parties and non-Contracting Parties cooperating with the Commission by participating in the CDS. The Executive Secretary shall at the same time:

(i) request non-Contracting Parties cooperating with the Commission by participating in the CDS that, to the extent possible in accordance with their applicable laws and regulations, they do not register or de-register vessels that have been placed on the List until such time as the Commission has had the opportunity to consider the List and has made its determination;

(ii) invite non-Contracting Parties cooperating with the Commission by participating in the CDS to submit any evidence or documented information regarding vessels on the Provisional NCP-IUU Vessel List and NCP-IUU Vessel List, at the latest 30 days before the start of the next CCAMLR annual meeting. Where the incident occurs within the month preceding the next CCAMLR annual meeting, evidence or documented information should be provided as soon as possible;

(iii) transmit the Provisional NCP-IUU Vessel List and any evidence or documented information received regarding vessels on that List to all non-Contracting Parties whose vessels are included in the List and who are not non-Contracting Parties cooperating with the Commission by participating in the CDS.

13. Contracting Parties shall take all necessary measures, to the extent possible in accordance with their applicable laws and regulations, in order that:

(i) they do not register vessels that have been placed on the Provisional NCP-IUU Vessel List until such time as the Commission has had the opportunity to examine the List and has made its determination;

(ii) if they do de-register a vessel on the Provisional NCP-IUU Vessel List they inform, where possible, the Executive Secretary of the proposed new Flag State of the vessel, whereupon the Executive Secretary shall inform that State that the vessel is on the Provisional NCP-IUU Vessel List and urge that State not to register the vessel.

Proposed and Final NCP-IUU Vessel List

14. Contracting Parties shall submit to the Executive Secretary any additional information which might be relevant for the establishment of the NCP-IUU Vessel List within 30 days of having become aware of such information and at the latest 30 days before the start of the CCAMLR annual meeting. A report containing this information shall be submitted in the format set out in paragraph 20, and Contracting Parties shall indicate that the information is provided for the purposes of considering whether to include the vessel concerned in the NCP-IUU Vessel List under Conservation Measure 10-07. The Executive Secretary shall collate all information received and, where this has not been provided in relation to a vessel, attempt to obtain the information in paragraphs 20(i) to (vii).

15. The Executive Secretary shall circulate to Contracting Parties, at the latest 30 days before the start of the CCAMLR annual meeting, all evidence or documented information received under paragraphs 12 and 13, together with any other evidence or documented information received in terms of paragraphs 3 and 8.

16. At each CCAMLR annual meeting, the Standing Committee on Implementation and Compliance (SCIC) shall, by consensus:

(i) adopt a Proposed NCP-IUU Vessel List, following consideration of the Provisional NCP-IUU Vessel List and information and evidence circulated under paragraph 14. The Proposed NCP-IUU Vessel List shall be submitted to the Commission for approval;

(ii) recommend to the Commission which, if any, vessels should be removed from the NCP-IUU Vessel List adopted at the previous CCAMLR annual meeting, following consideration of that List and information and evidence circulated under paragraph 14.

17. SCIC shall include a vessel on the Proposed NCP-IUU Vessel List only if one or more of the criteria in paragraph 9 have been satisfied.

18. SCIC shall recommend that the Commission should remove a vessel from the NCP-IUU Vessel List if the non-Contracting Party proves that:

(i) the vessel did not take part in the activities described in paragraph 9 which led to the inclusion of the vessel in the NCP-IUU Vessel List; or

(ii) it has taken effective action in response to the activities in question, including prosecution and imposition of sanctions of adequate severity; or

(iii) the vessel has changed ownership including beneficial ownership if known to be distinct from the registered ownership and that the new owner can establish the previous owner no longer has any legal, financial, or real interests in the vessel, or exercises control over it and that the new owner has not participated in IUU fishing; or

(iv) it has taken measures considered sufficient to ensure the granting of the right to the vessel to fly its flag will not result in IUU fishing.

19. In order to facilitate the work of SCIC and the Commission, the Executive Secretary shall prepare a paper for each CCAMLR annual meeting, summarising and annexing all the information, evidence and comments submitted in respect of each vessel to be considered.

20. The Draft NCP-IUU Vessel List, Provisional NCP-IUU Vessel List, Proposed NCP-IUU Vessel List and the NCP-IUU Vessel List shall contain the following details:

(i) name of vessel and previous names, if any;
(ii) flag of vessel and previous flags, if any;
(iii) owner of vessel and previous owners including beneficial owners, if any;
(iv) operator of vessel and previous operators, if any;
(v) call sign of vessel and previous call signs, if any;
(vi) Lloyds/IMO number;
(vii) photographs of the vessel, where available;
(viii) date vessel was first included on the NCP-IUU Vessel List;
(ix) summary of activities which justify inclusion of the vessel in the List, together with references to all relevant documents informing of and evidencing those activities;
(x) date and location of subsequent sightings of the vessel in the Convention Area, if any, and of any other related activities performed by the vessel contrary to CCAMLR conservation measures;
(xi) an indication of whether the Flag State of the vessel has given permission to one or several Contracting parties to inspect the vessel.

21. On approval of the NCP-IUU Vessel List, the Commission shall request non-Contracting Parties whose vessels appear thereon to take all necessary measures to address these activities, including if necessary, the withdrawal of the registration or of the fishing licences of these vessels, the nullification of the relevant catch documents and denial of further access to the CDS, and to inform the Commission of the measures taken in this respect.

22. Contracting Parties shall take all necessary measures, subject to and in accordance with their applicable laws and regulations and international law, in order that:
(i) the issuance of a licence to vessels on the NCP-IUU Vessel List to fish in waters under their fisheries jurisdiction is prohibited;
(ii) fishing vessels, support vessels, refuel vessels, mother-ships and cargo vessels flying their flag do not in any way assist vessels on the NCP-IUU Vessel List by participating in any transhipment or joint fishing operations, supporting or resupplying such vessels;
(iii) vessels on the NCP-IUU Vessel List should be denied access to ports unless for the purpose of enforcement action or for reasons of *force majeure* or for rendering assistance to vessels, or persons on those vessels, in danger or distress. Vessels allowed entry to port are to be inspected in accordance with relevant conservation measures;
(iv) where port access is granted to such vessels:
  (a) documentation and other information, including DCDs where relevant are examined, with a view to verifying the area in which the catch was taken; and where the origin cannot be adequately verified, the catch is detained or any landing or transhipment of the catch is refused; and
  (b) where possible
    i. in the event catch is found to be taken in contravention of CCAMLR conservation measures, catch is confiscated;
    ii. all support to such vessels, including non-emergency refuelling, resupplying and repairs is prohibited;
(v) the chartering of vessels on the NCP-IUU Vessel List is prohibited;
(vi) granting of their flag to vessels on the NCP-IUU Vessel List is refused;
(vii) imports, exports and re-exports of *Dissostichus* spp. from vessels on the NCP-IUU Vessel List are prohibited;
(viii) 'Export or Re-export Government Authority Validation' is not certified when the shipment (of *Dissostichus* spp.) is declared to have been caught by any vessel on the NCP-IUU Vessel List;
(ix) importers, transporters and other sectors concerned are encouraged to refrain from dealing with and from transhipping of fish caught by vessels on the NCP-IUU Vessel List;

(x) any appropriate information which is suitably documented is collected and submitted to the Executive Secretary, to be forwarded to Contracting Parties and non-Contracting Parties, entities or fishing entities cooperating with the Commission by participating in the CDS, with the aim of detecting, controlling and preventing the importation or exportation of, and other trade-related activities relating to, catches from vessels on the NCP-IUU Vessel List intended to circumvent this conservation measure.

23. The Executive Secretary shall place the NCP-IUU Vessel List approved by the Commission on the public section of the CCAMLR website. Furthermore, the Executive Secretary shall communicate the NCP-IUU Vessel List to the FAO and appropriate regional fisheries organisations to enhance cooperation between CCAMLR and these organisations for the purposes of preventing, deterring and eliminating IUU fishing.

24. The Executive Secretary shall circulate to non-Contracting Parties cooperating with the Commission by participating in the CDS the NCP-IUU Vessel List, together with the request that, to the extent possible in accordance with their applicable laws and regulations, they do not register vessels that have been placed on the List unless they are removed from the List by the Commission.

25. If Contracting Parties obtain new or changed information for vessels on the NCP-IUU Vessel List in relation to the details in paragraphs 20(i) to (vii), they shall notify the Executive Secretary who shall place a notification on the secure section of the CCAMLR website and advise all Contracting Parties and the non-Contracting Party concerned of the notification. If there are no comments on the information within seven (7) days, the Executive Secretary will revise the NCP-IUU Vessel List.

26. Without prejudice to their rights to take proper action consistent with international law, Contracting Parties should not take any trade measures or other sanctions which are inconsistent with their international obligations against vessels using as the basis for the action the fact that the vessel or vessels have been included in the Draft NCP-IUU Vessel List drawn up by the Executive Secretary, pursuant to paragraph 10.

27. The Chair of the Commission shall request the non-Contracting Parties identified pursuant to paragraph 1 to take all necessary measures to avoid diminishing the effectiveness of CCAMLR conservation measures resulting from their vessels' activities, including, if necessary, withdrawal of a vessel's registration or fishing licence, nullification of the relevant CDS documents and denial of further access to the CDS, and to advise the Commission of actions taken in that regard.

28. Contracting Parties shall jointly and/or individually request non-Contracting Parties identified pursuant to paragraph 2 to cooperate fully with the Commission in order to avoid diminishing the effectiveness of conservation measures adopted by the Commission. Contracting Parties shall notify the CCAMLR Secretariat of any response received from non-Contracting Parties, particularly information on measures taken by non-Contracting Parties to improve the effectiveness of CCAMLR conservation measures. Such information shall be placed online in the password-protected section of the CCAMLR website, under the heading 'SCIC Information/Diplomatic actions undertaken with regard to IUU fishing'. A list of the non-Contracting Parties having authorised one or several Contracting Parties to inspect their vessel(s) in accordance with the CCAMLR System of Inspection, or having reported any other measure taken with regard to vessels flying their flag likely to facilitate their inspection within the CCAMLR Area, shall also be included.

29. The Commission shall review, at subsequent CCAMLR annual meetings, as appropriate, action taken by those non-Contracting Parties to which requests have been made pursuant to paragraph 26, and identify those which have not rectified their activities.

30. The Commission shall decide appropriate measures to be taken in respect to *Dissostichus* spp. so as to address these issues with those identified non-Contracting Parties. In this respect,

Contracting Parties may cooperate to adopt appropriate multilaterally agreed trade-related measures, consistent with their obligations as members of the World Trade Organization, that may be necessary to prevent, deter and eliminate the IUU activities identified by the Commission. Multilateral trade-related measures may be used to support cooperative efforts to ensure that trade in *Dissostichus* spp. and its products does not in any way encourage IUU fishing or otherwise diminish the effectiveness of CCAMLR's conservation measures which are consistent with the United Nations Convention on the Law of the Sea 1982.

Conservation Measure 10-08 (2009): Scheme to Promote Compliance by Contracting Party Nationals with CCAMLR Conservation Measures (Applicable to All Species, Areas, Seasons and Gear)

The Commission,

Convinced that illegal, unreported and unregulated (IUU) fishing undermines the objectives of the Convention,

Concerned that some Flag States do not comply with their obligations regarding jurisdiction and control according to international law in respect of fishing vessels entitled to fly their flag that carry out their activities in the Convention Area, and that as a result these vessels are not under the effective control of such Flag States,

Aware that the lack of effective control facilitates fishing by these vessels in the Convention Area in a manner that undermines the effectiveness of CCAMLR conservation measures, and can lead to IUU catches of fish and unacceptable levels of incidental mortality of seabirds,

Concerned that vessels that carry out activities in the Convention Area which do not comply with the CCAMLR conservation measures are benefiting from the support provided by persons subject to the jurisdiction of Contracting Parties, including through participation in transhipment, transport and trade of illegally harvested catches or engagement on board or in the management of these vessels,

Conscious that, without prejudice to the primacy of the responsibility of the Flag State, taking action in accordance with existing domestic law against individuals who engage in, or support, IUU fishing can be an effective way to confront IUU fishing,

Mindful of the fact that international corporate structures and financial arrangements are often employed by IUU operators to limit their liability and avoid legitimate acceptable codes of behaviour, Members undertake to encourage and support investigation of such practices,

Noting that the FAO International Plan of Action to Prevent, Deter and Eliminate Illegal, Unreported and Unregulated Fishing calls on States to take measures to discourage nationals subject to their jurisdiction from supporting and engaging in any activity that undermines the effectiveness of international conservation and management measures,

Recalling that Contracting Parties should cooperate in taking appropriate action to deter any activities which are not consistent with the objective of the Convention,

Resolved to reinforce its integrated administrative and political measures aimed at eliminating IUU fishing in the Convention Area,

hereby adopts the following conservation measure in accordance with Article IX.2(i) of the Convention:

1. Without prejudice to the primacy of the responsibility of the Flag State, the Contracting Parties shall take appropriate measures, subject to, and in accordance with, their applicable laws and regulations:

(i) to verify if any of their nationals or any natural or legal persons subject to their jurisdiction are engaged in the activities described in paragraphs 5(i) to (viii) of Conservation Measure 10-06 and 9(i) to (vi) of Conservation Measure 10-07;

(ii) to verify if any of their nationals or any natural or legal persons subject to their jurisdiction are responsible for or benefiting from the activities described above (e.g. as operators, effective beneficiaries, owners, logistics and service providers;

(iii) take appropriate action in response to any verified activities referred to in paragraphs 1(i) and 1(ii). Such action may include measures to effectively deprive any of the participants in such activities of the benefits obtained and effectively dissuade the actors of further illegal activities.

2. Contracting Parties shall cooperate, including by seeking reciprocal and cooperative arrangements for exchange of information, for the purpose of implementing this conservation measure. To this end, relevant agencies of Contracting Parties should designate a contact point through which information on reported activities described in paragraphs 1(i) and 1(ii), including information regarding vessel identification, ownership including beneficial ownership, crew and catch, as well as information regarding relevant domestic legislation and the results of actions taken with regard to the implementation of this conservation measure can be exchanged.

3. To assist with the implementation of this conservation measure, Contracting Parties shall submit reports to the CCAMLR Secretariat and the Contracting Parties and non-Contracting Parties cooperating with CCAMLR for the purpose of implementing the Catch Documentation Scheme for *Dissostichus* spp. on the actions and measures taken in accordance with paragraph 1, in a timely fashion. These reports shall be circulated to Parties by the Secretariat in an appropriate way.

4. These provisions shall be applicable from 1 July 2008. Contracting Parties may voluntarily decide to implement these provisions prior to this date.

Conservation Measure 10-09 (2011): Notification System for Transhipments within the Convention Area (Applicable to Various Species, Areas and Fisheries and All Seasons)

The Commission,

Desiring to improve knowledge within CCAMLR of all vessels operating within the Convention Area, and in particular those which offer support to harvesting vessels,

Noting that an increasing number of vessels are operating within the Convention Area, either engaged directly in harvesting activities or in providing support to those vessels,

Recognising the need to increase the control over transhipment operations which support the harvesting of species within the Convention Area,

Concerned that vessels involved in the support of illegal, unreported and unregulated (IUU) fishing may be operating inside the Convention Area,

Taking account of the need to combat IUU fishing activities because they undermine the effectiveness of the conservation measures already adopted by CCAMLR,

hereby adopts the following conservation measure in accordance with Article IX of the Convention:

1. This conservation measure applies to all CCAMLR new and exploratory fisheries as well as to those listed in Annex 10-09/A.

2. Each Contracting Party as a Flag State shall notify the Secretariat at least 72 hours in advance if any of its vessels intend to tranship[48] within the Convention Area. The Flag State may permit or direct that such notifications be provided by the vessel directly to the Secretariat.

3. Paragraph 2 does not apply to vessels licensed by CCAMLR Contracting Parties under Conservation Measure 10-02 within the Convention Area which propose to tranship items other than harvested marine living resources, bait or fuel. In this case, each Contracting Party shall

[48] Transhipment means the transfer of harvested marine living resources and any other goods or materials to or from fishing vessels.

notify the Secretariat at least 2 hours in advance of such transhipment. The Flag State may permit or direct that such notifications be provided by the vessel directly to the Secretariat.

4. Notifications of intended transhipment operations under paragraphs 2 or 3 above shall include the following information, for all vessels involved:

- name and registration number
- international radio call sign
- Flag State
- type of vessels, length, gross registered tonnage (GRT) and carrying capacity
- proposed time and position, in latitude and longitude, of transhipment.

The notification shall also include details of the type and amount of catches and/or other goods, such as food stores and fuel, involved in the transhipment.

5. The CCAMLR Secretariat shall maintain a list of all such notifications on the password-protected part of its website, in a manner consistent with confidentiality requirements notified by CCAMLR Contracting Parties for their vessels.

6. For fisheries not covered by the provisions of paragraph 1, CCAMLR Contracting Parties shall provide, as a background paper to the annual meeting of the Commission, a report including details set out in paragraph 4 of all transhipments activities in the Convention Area of the vessels flying their flag, during the previous year.

7. No vessel covered by paragraph 1 may tranship with any vessel, within the Convention Area for which prior notification, pursuant to paragraphs 2, 3 and 4 above, has not been given.

[Omitted: Annex 10-09A – Table of additional fisheries to which this conservation measure applies.]

Conservation Measure 10-10 (2012): CCAMLR Compliance Evaluation Procedure (Applicable to All Species, Areas, Seasons and Gear)

The Commission,

Recalling that the Commission has adopted a wide range of conservation measures to give effect to the objective of the Convention,

Noting Article XXI of the Convention which requires Contracting Parties to take appropriate measures within their competence to ensure compliance with the provisions of the Convention and with conservation measures adopted by the Commission,

Noting that, in accordance with Article X of the Convention, the Commission has undertaken to draw the attention of all Contracting Parties to any activity which, in the opinion of the Commission, affects the implementation by a Contracting Party of the objective of the Convention or the compliance by that Contracting Party with its obligations under the Convention,

Noting also that, in accordance with international law, as well as Conservation Measures 10-06 and 10-08, Contracting Parties have responsibilities to exercise effective control over their flagged vessels and with respect to their nationals,

Noting further that, in a responsible, open, transparent and non-discriminatory manner, the Commission should be made aware of all available information that may be relevant to the work of the Commission in identifying and addressing instances of non-compliance with conservation measures,

Recalling the obligation of Contracting Parties to notify and inform the Secretariat of possible instances of non-compliance and to respond to such instances in accordance with the requirements of existing conservation measures,

hereby adopts the following conservation measure in accordance with Article IX of the Convention:

1. Draft CCAMLR Compliance Reports

(i) The Secretariat shall compile a Draft CCAMLR Compliance Report using the template in Annex 10-10/A for each Member of the Commission. The Draft CCAMLR Compliance Report will cover the period 1 December–30 November[49] in the current fishing year. In compiling Draft CCAMLR Compliance Reports, the Secretariat shall take into account appropriate compliance data holdings, as well as data from other relevant sources.

(ii) The Secretariat shall circulate to each Member of the Commission its respective Draft CCAMLR Compliance Report no later than 75 days before the annual Commission meeting.

(iii) In considering its Draft CCAMLR Compliance Report, each Member of the Commission shall identify in the 'Additional Information' column in Annex 10-10/A, any information relevant to its implementation of each conservation measure. This may include, for example, a description of how the conservation measure is implemented and/or action taken to address any non-compliance.

(iv) Each Member of the Commission shall return its Draft CCAMLR Compliance Report incorporating any additional information to the Secretariat no later than 45 days before the annual Commission meeting. Where no response is received from a Member of the Commission under paragraph 1(iii), the Secretariat shall note nil response in the relevant Draft CCAMLR Compliance Report.

2. Summary CCAMLR Compliance Report

(i) The Secretariat shall prepare a Summary CCAMLR Compliance Report based on the Draft CCAMLR Compliance Reports. This report shall include, *inter alia*, a summary of Members' implementation of conservation measures. The Draft CCAMLR Compliance Reports shall be annexed to the Summary CCAMLR Compliance Report.

(ii) The Summary CCAMLR Compliance Report shall be made available on the secure CCAMLR website for consideration no later than 30 days before the annual Commission meeting. As soon as practicable after posting the Summary CCAMLR Compliance Report, the Secretariat shall notify Members of its availability.

3. Provisional CCAMLR Compliance Report

(i) At its annual meeting, the Standing Committee on Implementation and Compliance (SCIC) shall consider the Summary CCAMLR Compliance Report, taking into account any additional information received.

(ii) On the basis of the information considered in paragraph 3(i), SCIC shall adopt an annual Provisional CCAMLR Compliance Report, by consensus in which it shall record its findings of non-compliance. The Provisional CCAMLR Compliance Report shall include an assessment of compliance status, in accordance with Annex 10-10/B, 'Compliance Status Categories'. The Provisional CCAMLR Compliance Report shall also include recommendations to the Commission regarding:

(a) any remedial action taken, or proposed to be taken, by the Member;

(b) where appropriate, proposals to amend existing conservation measures;

(c) priority obligations to be monitored and reviewed; and

(d) other responsive action which may be considered by the Commission, as appropriate.

4. CCAMLR Compliance Report

(i) At its annual meeting, the Commission shall consider the Provisional CCAMLR Compliance Report.

(ii) The annual CCAMLR Compliance Report will outline the Commission's response to the recommendations of SCIC in the Provisional CCAMLR Compliance Report.

[49] Information for the period of fishing not covered in the report will be considered the following year.

5. Review of Conservation Measure

(i) At its annual meeting, SCIC will consider the effectiveness of this conservation measure in evaluating and addressing non-compliance, and will report to the Commission on its findings and recommendations for improving this conservation measure.

Resolution 10/XII (1993): Resolution on Harvesting of Stocks Occurring both Within and Outside the Convention Area (Applicable to All Species, Areas, Seasons and Gear)

The Commission,

Recalling the principles of conservation in Article II of the Convention and in particular that of the maintenance of the ecological relationships between harvested, dependent and related populations of Antarctic marine living resources,

Recalling the requirement under Article XI of the Convention for the Commission to seek to cooperate with Contracting Parties which may exercise jurisdiction in marine areas adjacent to the area to which the Convention applies in respect of the conservation of any stock or stocks of associated species which occur both within those areas and the area to which the Convention applies, with a view to harmonising the conservation measures adopted in respect of such stocks,

Emphasising the importance of further research on any stock or stocks of species which occur both within the area of the Convention and within adjacent areas,

Noting the concerns expressed by the Scientific Committee on the substantial exploitation of such stocks inside and outside the Convention Area, reaffirmed that Members should ensure that their flag vessels conduct harvesting of such stocks in areas adjacent to the Convention Area responsibly and with due respect for the conservation measures it has adopted under the Convention.

Resolution 19/XXI (2002): Flags of Non-compliance[50] (Applicable to All Species, Areas, Seasons and Gear)

The Commission,

Concerned that some Flag States, particularly certain non-Contracting Parties, do not comply with their obligations regarding jurisdiction and control according to international law in respect of fishing vessels entitled to fly their flag that carry out their activities in the Convention Area, and that as a result these vessels are not under the effective control of such Flag States,

Aware that the lack of effective control facilitates fishing by these vessels in the Convention Area in a manner that undermines the effectiveness of CCAMLR's conservation measures, leading to illegal, unreported and unregulated (IUU) catches of fish and unacceptable levels of incidental mortality of seabirds,

Considering therefore such fishing vessels to be flying Flags of Non-Compliance (FONC) in the context of CCAMLR (FONC vessels),

Noting that the FAO Agreement to Promote Compliance with International Conservation and Management Measures by Fishing Vessels on the High Seas emphasizes that the practice of flagging or reflagging fishing vessels as a means of avoiding compliance with international conservation and management measures for living marine resources and the failure of the States to fulfil their responsibilities with respect of fishing vessels entitled to fly their flag, are among the factors that seriously undermine the effectiveness of such measures,

Noting that the International Plan of Action to Prevent, Deter and Eliminate Illegal, Unreported and Unregulated Fishing calls on States to take measures to discourage nationals subject to their

[50] Many of the flags hereby called FONC are commonly referred to as 'flags of convenience'.

jurisdiction from supporting and engaging in any activity that undermines the effectiveness of international conservation and management measures,

urges all Contracting Parties and non-Contracting Parties cooperating with CCAMLR to:

1. Without prejudice to the primacy of the responsibility of the Flag State, to take measures or otherwise cooperate to ensure, to the greatest extent possible, that the nationals subject to their jurisdiction do not support or engage in IUU fishing, including engagement on board FONC vessels in the CAMLR Convention Area if this is consistent with their national law.
2. Ensure the full cooperation of their relevant national agencies and industries in implementing the measures adopted by CCAMLR.
3. Develop ways to ensure that the export or transfer of fishing vessels from their State to a FONC State is prohibited.
4. Prohibit the landings and transhipments of fish and fish products from FONC vessels.

Resolution 25/XXV (2006): Combating Illegal, Unreported and Unregulated Fishing in the Convention Area by the Flag Vessels of Non-Contracting Parties (Applicable to All Species, Areas, Seasons and Gear)

The Commission,

Concerned about the increasing number of vessels repeatedly fishing in the Convention Area in an illegal, unreported or unregulated (IUU) manner,

Recognising that such fishing is causing potentially irreversible damage to fish stocks and other marine species and preventing the Commission from achieving its objective of conservation of Antarctic marine living resources in the Convention Area,

Concerned that many of these vessels are flagged to non-Contracting Parties that have failed to respond to correspondence from the Commission and diplomatic and other representations by Commission Members, seeking that they cooperate with the Commission,

Acknowledging that many of the above non-Contracting Parties are Parties to the United Nations Convention on the Law of the Sea (UNCLOS),

Desiring to promote recognition that CCAMLR conservation measures constitute relevant standards needed to achieve conservation and rational use of Antarctic marine living resources,

Noting that the International Plan of Action to prevent, deter and eliminate IUU fishing (IPOA-IUU) urges States to ensure that fishing vessels entitled to fly their flag do not engage in or support IUU fishing and requires that a Flag State be in a position to exercise its responsibility to control any vessel it registers and ensure such vessels do not engage in or support IUU fishing,

Determined to pursue diplomatic and other action, in accordance with international law, with non-Contracting Parties that fail to cooperate with CCAMLR, including by failing to direct their flag vessels to cease IUU fishing and failing to take legal and other action against their flag vessels that disobey such directions,

Recognising the value of cooperation and joint diplomatic approaches by CCAMLR Contracting Parties in undertaking such action and exerting influence,

urges all Contracting Parties to individually and collectively, including in other relevant international fora such as the United Nations Food and Agriculture Organization and regional fisheries management organisations, to the extent possible in accordance with their applicable laws and regulations:

1. Pursue diplomatic and other action, in accordance with international law, with non-Contracting Party Flag States, seeking, as appropriate, that they:
   (i) recognise that CCAMLR conservation measures constitute relevant standards needed to achieve conservation and rational use of Antarctic marine living resources;

(ii) investigate the activities of vessels fishing under their flag in the Convention Area, in accordance with Article 94 of UNCLOS, and report findings of such investigations to the Commission;

(iii) accede to the Convention and cooperate with the Commission and, until such time as they do, direct their flag vessels not to fish in the Convention Area and take legal and other action against those vessels that disobey this directive;

(iv) grant permission for boarding and inspection by designated CCAMLR inspectors of their flag vessels suspected of, or found to be, fishing in an IUU manner in the Convention Area.

2. Seek the cooperation of non-Contracting Party Port States when IUU fishing vessels seek to use the ports of non-Contracting Parties, urging them to take the steps in accordance with Conservation Measure 10-07.

Resolution 28/XXVII (2008): Ballast Water Exchange in the Convention Area (Applicable to All Species, Areas, Seasons and Gear)

The Commission,

Affirming that CCAMLR was established to conserve the marine living resources of the Antarctic marine ecosystem,

Aware of the potential for invasive marine organisms to be transported into or moved between biologically distinct regions within the Convention Area by ships in their ballast water,

Recalling the requirements of Annex II to the Protocol on Environmental Protection to the Antarctic Treaty regarding conservation of Antarctic fauna and flora and in particular of the precautions taken to prevent the introduction of non-native species,

Conscious that the *International Convention for the Control and Management of Ships' Ballast Waters and Sediments*, 2004 (IMO Ballast Water Management Convention), has yet to enter into force, but noting in particular its Article 13, which provides that in order to further the objectives of the Convention, Parties with common interests to protect the environment... in a given geographical area...shall endeavour...to enhance regional cooperation, including through the conclusion of regional agreements consistent with the Ballast Water Management Convention,

Recalling also Resolution 3(2006) adopted by the Antarctic Treaty Consultative Meeting, and Resolution MEPC.163(56) adopted by the International Maritime Organisation, which adopted *Guidelines for Ballast Water Exchange in the Antarctic Treaty Area*,

Desiring to extend the application of the above mentioned guidelines to the whole of the CAMLR Convention Area,

1. Urges all Contracting Parties and non-Contracting Parties cooperating with CCAMLR to take particular measures to apply the existing IMO *Guidelines for Ballast Water Exchange in the Antarctic Treaty Area*, and also the *Guidelines for Ballast Water Exchange in the CAMLR Convention Area north of 60°S,* as set out in the annex to this resolution, as an interim measure to all ships engaged in harvesting and associated activities in the CAMLR Convention Area, before the Ballast Water Management Convention comes into force.

2. Furthermore, urges all Contracting Parties and non-Contracting Parties cooperating with CCAMLR to take action to develop effective treatment for ballast water.

Annex: Guidelines for Ballast Water Exchange in the CAMLR Convention Area North of 60°S[51]

1. The application of these Guidelines should apply to those vessels covered by Article 3 of the IMO's International Convention for the Control and Management of Ships' Ballast Water and

[51] ATCM Resolution 3(2006) and IMO Resolution MEPC.163(56) set out identical practical guidelines for all vessels operating in the Antarctic Treaty Area (i.e. south of 60°S).

Sediments (the Ballast Water Management Convention), taking into account the exceptions in Regulation A-3 of the Convention, which are engaged in harvesting and associated activities in the CAMLR Convention Area (as set out in Article II.3 of the Convention). These Guidelines do not replace the requirements of the Ballast Water Management Convention, but supplement the interim Ballast Water Regional Management Plan for Antarctica under Article 13(3), which has been adopted in ATCM Resolution 3(2006) and IMO Resolution MEPC.163(56).

2. If the safety of the ship is in any way jeopardised by a ballast exchange, it shall not take place. Additionally these guidelines shall not apply to the uptake or discharge of ballast water and sediments for ensuring the safety of the ship in emergency situations or saving life at sea in the CAMLR Convention Area.

3. A Ballast Water Management Plan should be prepared for each vessel with ballast tanks entering the Convention Area, specifically taking into account the problems of ballast water exchange in cold environments and in Antarctic conditions.

4. Each vessel entering the Convention Area should keep a record of ballast water operations.

5. Vessels are strongly encouraged to not discharge any ballast water in the Convention Area.

6. For vessels intending to discharge ballast water within the Convention Area, ballast water should first be exchanged before arrival in the Convention Area (preferably north of either the Antarctic Polar Frontal Zone or 60°S, whichever is the furthest north) and at least 200 n miles from the nearest land in water 200 m deep. (If this is not possible for operational reasons then such exchange should be undertaken in waters 50 n miles from the nearest land in waters of 200 m depth.)

7. Only those tanks that will be discharged in the Convention Area would need to undergo ballast water exchange following the procedure in paragraph 6. Ballast Water Exchange of all tanks is encouraged for all vessels that have the potential/capacity to load cargo in the Convention Area, as Antarctic voyages are renowned for their changes to planned routes and activities.

8. If a vessel has taken on ballast water in the Convention Area and is intending to discharge ballast water in Arctic, sub-Arctic, or sub-Antarctic waters, it is recommended that ballast water should be exchanged north of the Antarctic Polar Frontal Zone, and at least 200 n miles from the nearest land in water at least 200 m deep. (If this is not possible for operational reasons then such exchange should be undertaken in waters 50 n miles from the nearest land in waters of 200 m depth).

9. Release of sediments during the cleaning of ballast tanks should not take place in the Convention Area.

10. For vessels that have spent significant time in the Arctic, ballast water sediment should preferably be discharged and tanks cleaned before entering the Convention Area. If this cannot be done then sediment accumulation in ballast tanks should be monitored and sediment should be disposed of in accordance with the ship's Ballast Water Management Plan. If sediments are disposed of at sea, then they should be disposed of in waters greater than 200 n miles from the shoreline in waters 200 m deep.

11. CCAMLR Members are invited to exchange information on invasive marine species or anything that will change the perceived risk associated with ballast waters.

Resolution 32/XXIX (2010): Prevention, Deterrence and Elimination of IUU Fishing in the Convention Area

The Commission,

Convinced that illegal, unreported and unregulated (IUU) fishing undermines the objectives of the Convention,

Concerned about the increasing number of vessels repeatedly fishing in the Convention Area in an IUU manner,

Aware that a number of vessels registered to non-Contracting Parties are engaged in activities which diminish the effectiveness of CCAMLR conservation measures,

Noting that there have been sightings of IUU vessels fishing in the Convention Area using gillnetting,

Deeply concerned that deep-sea gillnetting in the Convention Area and the associated ghost-fishing by lost or discarded nets has serious detrimental effects on the marine environment and many species of marine living resources,

Recognising that IUU fishing is causing potentially irreversible damage to fish stocks and other marine species and preventing the Commission from achieving its objective of conservation of Antarctic marine living resources in the Convention Area,

Recalling that Contracting Parties should cooperate in taking appropriate action to deter any activities which are not consistent with the objective of the Convention,

Also aware that some Flag States do not comply with their obligations regarding jurisdiction and control according to international law in respect of fishing vessels entitled to fly their flag that carry out their activities in the Convention Area, and that as a result these vessels may not be under the effective control of such Flag States,

Deeply dismayed that vessels that carry out activities in the Convention Area which do not comply with CCAMLR conservation measures are benefitting from the support provided by persons subject to the jurisdiction of Contracting Parties, including through participation in transhipment, transport and trade of illegally harvested catches or engagement on board or in the management of these vessels,

Also conscious that, without prejudice to the primacy of the responsibility of the Flag State, taking action in accordance with existing domestic law against individuals who engage in, or support IUU fishing activities is one effective way to confront IUU fishing,

Also noting that Contracting Parties are required to undertake inspections of all fishing vessels carrying *Dissostichus* spp. which enter their ports, and where there is evidence that the vessel has fished in contravention of CCAMLR conservation measures not allow the catch to be landed or transhipped,

Further concerned that many of these vessels are flagged to non-Contracting Parties that have failed to respond to correspondence from the Commission and diplomatic and other representations by Commission Members seeking that they cooperate with the Commission,

Noting in addition that many non-Contracting Parties whose vessels are engaged in IUU fishing in the Convention Area are also Parties to the United Nations Convention on the Law of the Sea (UNCLOS) and other relevant international agreements,

Also recalling that Resolution 25/XXV on combating IUU fishing in the Convention Area by flag vessels of non-Contracting Parties referred to a range of action measures by which Contracting Parties should exert influence and seek the cooperation of non-Contracting Parties,

Further recognising the importance of enhancing cooperation with non-Contracting Parties to help prevent, deter and eliminate IUU fishing in the Convention Area,

Reaffirming its commitment to eliminate IUU fishing in the Convention Area,

urges all Contracting Parties, individually and collectively, and to the extent possible in accordance with their applicable laws and regulations, to:

1. Strengthen their efforts to address the problem of IUU fishing in the Convention Area through implementation of all relevant CCAMLR conservation measures, including in particular:
   - Conservation Measure 10-03 regarding port inspections of vessels carrying toothfish
   - Conservation Measure 10-05 regarding the Catch Documentation Scheme for *Dissostichus* spp.
   - Conservation Measure 10-06 regarding a scheme to promote compliance by Contracting Party vessels with CCAMLR conservation measures

- Conservation Measure 10-07 regarding a scheme to promote compliance by non-Contracting Party vessels with CCAMLR conservation measures
- Conservation Measure 10-08 regarding a scheme to promote compliance by Contracting Party nationals with CCAMLR conservation measures
- Conservation Measure 10-09 regarding a notification system for transhipments within the Convention Area.

2. Actively contribute, to the extent possible, to the CCAMLR System of Inspection in the Convention Area.

3. Pursue action in accordance with international law, with non-Contracting Party Flag States, seeking, as appropriate, that they:

(i) recognise that CCAMLR conservation measures constitute relevant standards needed to achieve conservation and rational use of Antarctic marine living resources;

(ii) investigate the activities of vessels fishing under their flag in the Convention Area, in accordance with Article 94 of UNCLOS, and report findings of such investigations to the Commission;

(iii) direct their flag vessels not to fish in the Convention Area and take legal action in accordance with their domestic legislation against those vessels that disobey this directive;

(iv) grant permission for boarding and inspection by CCAMLR-designated inspectors of their flag vessels suspected of, or found to be, carrying out IUU fishing activities in the Convention Area, in accordance with the CCAMLR System of Inspection and the procedures set out therein.

4. Seek the cooperation of non-Contracting Party Port States when IUU fishing vessels seek to use the ports of non-Contracting Parties, urging them to take the steps in accordance with Conservation Measure 10-07, and also to take similar port inspection steps as provided for Contracting Parties in Conservation Measure 10-03, including providing the CCAMLR Secretariat with reports of port inspections conducted.

5. Encourage the cooperation of non-Contracting Parties to take similar steps to implement CCAMLR's Catch Documentation Scheme for *Dissostichus* spp. at their ports in order to verify the origin of *Dissostichus* spp. imported and/or re-exported from its territory and that it was caught in a manner consistent with CCAMLR's conservation measures as provided for Contracting Parties in Conservation Measure 10-05.

Resolution 33/XXX (2011): Provision of Flag Vessel Information to Maritime Rescue Coordination Centres (Applicable to All Species, Areas, Seasons and Gear)

The Commission,

Recognising the difficult and dangerous conditions in which high-latitude fisheries operate in the Convention Area, and the challenges of search and rescue response,

Noting the duty to render assistance and to act as quickly as possible in order to rescue persons in distress, as enshrined in the United Nations Convention on the Law of the Sea, the International Convention for the Safety of Life at Sea and other international conventions,

Noting that many Contracting Parties have ratified the International Convention on Maritime Search and Rescue (SAR 1979),

Bearing in mind that designated Search and Rescue (SAR) Areas cover the Convention Area, with search and rescue responsibilities being carried out by relevant Maritime Rescue Coordination Centres (MRCCs) in accordance with the arrangements that each State has established with the International Maritime Organization (IMO) in particular in the Global SAR Plan, urges CCAMLR Members to provide, or encourage fishing vessels[52] under their flag to provide, contact details and other relevant information related to fishing vessels under their flag to the appropriate MRCC, in advance of vessels entering the Convention Area.

Category 11 – Notifications

Conservation Measure 21-01 (2010):[53,54] Notification that Members are Considering Initiating a New Fishery (Applicable to All Species, Areas, Seasons and Gear)

The Commission,

Recognising that in the past, Antarctic fisheries have been initiated in the Convention Area before sufficient information was available upon which to base management advice,

Noting that in recent years new fisheries have started without adequate information being available to evaluate either the fishery potential or the possible impacts on the target stocks or species dependent on them,

Believing that without prior notification of a new fishery, the Commission is unable to fulfil its function under Article IX,

hereby adopts the following conservation measure in accordance with Article IX of the Convention:

1. A new fishery, for the purposes of this conservation measure, is a fishery on a species using a particular fishing method in a statistical subarea or division for which:
   (i) information on distribution, abundance, demography, potential yield and stock identity from comprehensive research/surveys or exploratory fishing have not been submitted to CCAMLR; or
   (ii) catch and effort data have never been submitted to CCAMLR; or
   (iii) catch and effort data from the two most recent seasons in which fishing occurred have not been submitted to CCAMLR.

2. In addition to those fisheries identified according to paragraph 1, the use of fishing methods in high-seas areas of the Convention Area as specified in Annex 21-01/A will constitute new fisheries and will require approval of the Commission for specific areas before proceeding.

3. Any Member proposing to participate in a new fishery shall:
   (i) notify its intention to the Commission not less than three months in advance of the next regular meeting of the Commission. This notification shall include the information prescribed in paragraph 3 of Conservation Measure 10-02 in respect of vessels proposing to participate in the fishery, with the exception that the notification shall not be required to specify the information referred to in paragraph 3(ii) of Conservation Measure 10-02. Members shall, to the extent practicable, also provide in their notification the additional information detailed in paragraph 4 of Conservation Measure 10-02 in respect to each fishing vessel notified. Members are not hereby exempted from their obligations under Conservation Measure 10-02 to submit any necessary updates to vessel and licence details within the deadline established therein as of issuance of the licence to the vessel concerned;

[52] For the purposes of this resolution, 'fishing vessel' means any vessel of any size used for, equipped to be used for, or intended for use for the purposes of fishing or fishing related activities, including support ships, fish processing vessels, vessels engaged in transhipment and carrier vessels equipped for the transportation of fishery products except container vessels and excluding Members' marine science research vessels.

[53] Except for waters adjacent to the Kerguelen and Crozet Islands.

[54] Except for waters adjacent to the Prince Edward Islands.

(ii) prepare and submit to CCAMLR by a specified date a Fishery Operations Plan for the fishing season, for review by the Scientific Committee and the Commission. The Fishery Operations Plan shall include as much of the following information as the Member is able to provide, so as to assist the Scientific Committee in its preparation of the Data Collection Plan:
  (a) the nature of the new fishery, including target species, methods of fishing, proposed region and maximum catch levels proposed for the forthcoming season;
  (b) biological information on the target species from comprehensive research/survey cruises, such as distribution, abundance, demographic data and information on stock identity;
  (c) details of dependent and related species and the likelihood of their being affected by the proposed fishery;
  (d) information from other fisheries in the region or similar fisheries elsewhere that may assist in the evaluation of potential yield;
  (e) if the proposed fishery will be undertaken using bottom trawl gear, information on the known and anticipated impacts of this gear on vulnerable marine ecosystems, including benthos and benthic communities.

(iii) provide a commitment, in its proposal, to implement any Data Collection Plan developed by the Scientific Committee for the fishery.

4. The Member shall not initiate a new fishery pending the process specified in paragraphs 10 and 11 below.

5. If a Member proposing to participate in a new fishery fails to submit notification of this proposal to the Commission in accordance with the deadline specified in paragraph 3 above, the Commission shall not consider the proposal, and the Member shall not authorise, under Conservation Measure 10 02, vessels flying its flag to participate in the proposed fishing activities.

6. Where such a proposed new fishery includes bottom fishing activities, the Member shall not authorise, under Conservation Measure 10-02, vessels flying their flag to participate in the proposed bottom fishing activities if the procedures outlined in Conservation Measure 22-06, paragraph 7, have not been fully complied with.

7. To ensure that adequate information is made available to the Scientific Committee for evaluation, during the period when a fishery is classified as new, the Scientific Committee shall develop (and update annually as appropriate) a Data Collection Plan, which should include research proposals, as appropriate. This shall identify the data needed and describe any operational research actions necessary to obtain the relevant data from the new fishery to enable an assessment of the stock to be made.

8. The Data Collection Plan shall include, where appropriate:

(i) a description of the catch, effort and related biological, ecological and environmental data required to undertake the evaluations described in paragraph 1, and the date by which such data are to be reported annually to CCAMLR;

(ii) a plan for directing fishing effort during the initial phase to permit the acquisition of relevant data to evaluate the fishery potential and the ecological relationships among harvested, dependent and related populations and the likelihood of adverse impacts;

(iii) where appropriate, a plan for the acquisition of any other research data by fishing vessels, including activities that may require the cooperative activities of scientific observers and the vessel, as may be required for the Scientific Committee to evaluate the fishery potential and the ecological relationships among harvested, dependent and related populations and the likelihood of adverse impacts;

(iv) an evaluation of the time scales involved in determining the responses of harvested, dependent and related populations to fishing activities.

9. New fisheries shall be open only to those vessels that are equipped and configured so that they can comply with all relevant conservation measures. A vessel with a confirmed involvement in illegal, unreported or unregulated fishing in respect of Conservation Measures 10-06 and 10-07 shall not be permitted to participate in new fisheries.

10. The information provided in accordance with paragraphs 3 to 9, together with any other relevant information, shall be considered by the Scientific Committee, which shall then advise the Commission.

11. After its review of the information on the proposed new fishery, taking full account of the recommendations and the advice of the Scientific Committee, the Commission may then take such action as it deems necessary.

[Omitted: Annex 21-01/A – Additional Fishing Methods.]

Conservation Measure 21-02 (2013):[55,56] Exploratory Fisheries (Applicable to All Species, Areas, Seasons and Gear)

The Commission,

Recognising that in the past, some Antarctic fisheries had been initiated and subsequently expanded in the Convention Area before sufficient information was available upon which to base management advice,

Agreeing that exploratory fishing should not be allowed to expand faster than the acquisition of information necessary to ensure that the fishery can and will be conducted in accordance with the principles set forth in Article II,

hereby adopts the following conservation measure in accordance with Article IX of the Convention:

1. For the purposes of this conservation measure, exploratory fisheries are defined as follows:
   (i) an exploratory fishery shall be defined as a fishery that was previously classified as a 'new fishery', as defined by Conservation Measure 21-01;
   (ii) an exploratory fishery shall continue to be classified as such until sufficient information is available:
      (a) to evaluate the distribution, abundance and demography of the target species, leading to an estimate of the fishery's potential yield;
      (b) to review the fishery's potential impacts on dependent and related species;
      (c) to allow the Scientific Committee to formulate and provide advice to the Commission on appropriate harvest catch levels, as well as effort levels and fishing gear, where appropriate.

2. To ensure that adequate information is made available to the Scientific Committee for evaluation, during the period when a fishery is classified as exploratory, the Scientific Committee shall develop (and update annually as appropriate) a Data Collection Plan, which should include research proposals, as appropriate. This shall identify the data needed and describe any operational research actions necessary to obtain the relevant data from the exploratory fishery to enable an assessment of the stock to be made.

3. The Data Collection Plan shall include, where appropriate:
   (i) a description of the catch, effort, and related biological, ecological and environmental data required to undertake the evaluations described in paragraph 1(ii), and the date by which such data are to be reported annually to CCAMLR;
   (ii) a plan for directing fishing effort during the exploratory phase to permit the acquisition of relevant data to evaluate the fishery potential and the ecological relationships among harvested, dependent and related populations and the likelihood of adverse impacts;

[55] Except for waters adjacent to the Kerguelen and Crozet Islands.

[56] Except for waters adjacent to the Prince Edward Islands.

(iii) where appropriate, a plan for the acquisition of any other research data by fishing vessels, including activities that may require the cooperative activities of scientific observers and the vessel, as may be required for the Scientific Committee to evaluate the fishery potential and the ecological relationships among harvested, dependent and related populations and the likelihood of adverse impacts;

(iv) an evaluation of the timescales involved in determining the responses of harvested, dependent and related populations to fishing activities.

4. The Commission shall annually determine a precautionary catch limit at a level not substantially above that necessary to obtain the information specified in the Data Collection Plan and required to undertake the evaluations described in paragraph 1(ii).

5. A Member intending to fish pursuant to this conservation measure may only notify in respect to vessels flying its flag or that of another CCAMLR Member at the time of the notification[57].

6. Any Member proposing to participate in an exploratory fishery shall:

(i) notify its intention to the Commission by 1 June[58] prior to the next regular meeting of the Commission. This notification shall include the information prescribed in paragraph 3 of Conservation Measure 10-02 in respect of vessels proposing to participate in the fishery, with the exception that the notification shall not be required to specify the information referred to in paragraph 3(ii) of Conservation Measure 10-02. Members shall, to the extent practicable, also provide in their notification the additional information detailed in paragraph 4 of Conservation Measure 10-02 in respect to each fishing vessel notified. Members are not hereby exempted from their obligations under Conservation Measure 10-02 to submit any necessary updates to vessel and licence details within the deadline established therein as of issuance of the licence to the vessel concerned;

(ii) prepare and submit to CCAMLR by 1 June a Fishery Operations Plan for the fishing season, for review by the Scientific Committee and the Commission. The Fishery Operations Plan shall include as much of the following information as the Member is able to provide, so as to assist the Scientific Committee in its preparation of the Data Collection Plan:

(a) the nature of the exploratory fishery, including target species, methods of fishing, proposed region and maximum catch levels proposed for the forthcoming season;

(b) specification[59] and full description[60] of the types of fishing gear to be used;

(c) biological information on the target species from comprehensive research/survey cruises, such as distribution, abundance, demographic data and information on stock identity;

(d) details of dependent and related species and the likelihood of their being affected by the proposed fishery;

(e) information from other fisheries in the region or similar fisheries elsewhere that may assist in the evaluation of potential yield;

(f) if the proposed fishery will be undertaken using bottom trawl gear, information on the known and anticipated impacts of this gear on vulnerable marine ecosystems, including benthos and benthic communities;

[57] Consistent with Conservation Measure 10-02 any vessel notified would need to be flagged to the notifying Member before entering the fishery.

[58] This deadline allows notifications to be considered by the Scientific Committee's working groups as appropriate. The working groups will review notifications and advise whether notifications for exploratory fisheries meet the scientific requirements, and whether a notifying Member is required to submit additional information (e.g. further detail in the Research Plan) for consideration by the Scientific Committee.

[59] For example, integrated weight longline, Spanish longline, trotline, trawl, continuous trawl or pot.

[60] For example, snood length, hook spacing, number of hooks per cluster, cluster spacing, net dimensions, trawl-door type, size and weight, footrope dimensions and type, net opening, pumping volume, pot dimensions and any factors affecting gear selectivity.

(iii) for notifications for participation in exploratory fisheries for *Dissostichus* spp. in Divisions 58.4.1, 58.4.2 and 58.4.3a and Subarea 48.6, prepare and submit to CCAMLR by 1 June a Research Plan for review by the Scientific Committee and Commission. Research Plans shall be reported in accordance with the format of Conservation Measure 24-01, Annex 24-01/A, format 2;

(iv) provide a commitment, in its proposal, to implement any Data Collection Plan developed by the Scientific Committee for the fishery.

7. On the basis of the information submitted in accordance with paragraph 6, and taking into account the advice and evaluation provided by the Scientific Committee and the Standing Committee on Implementation and Compliance (SCIC), the Commission shall annually consider adoption of relevant conservation measures for each exploratory fishery.

8. The Commission shall not consider a notification by a Member unless the information required by paragraph 6 has been submitted by 1 June.

9. If a Member proposing to participate in an exploratory fishery fails to submit notification of this proposal to the Commission in accordance with the deadline specified in paragraph 6 above, the Member shall not authorise, under Conservation Measure 10-02, vessels flying its flag to participate in the proposed fishing activities.

10. Notwithstanding paragraph 8, Members shall be entitled under Conservation Measure 10-02 to authorise participation in an exploratory fishery by a vessel other than that identified by the Commission in accordance with paragraph 6 if the notified vessel is prevented from participation due to legitimate operational or *force majeure* reasons. In such circumstances the Member concerned shall immediately inform the Secretariat thereof providing:

(i) full details of the intended replacement vessel(s) as prescribed in paragraph 6(i);

(ii) a comprehensive account of the reasons justifying the replacement and any relevant supporting evidence or references;

(iii) specification and full description of the types of fishing gear to be used by the replacement vessel.

The Secretariat shall immediately circulate this information to all Members.

11. Where such a proposed exploratory fishery includes bottom fishing activities, the Member shall not authorise, under Conservation Measure 10-02, vessels flying their flag to participate in the proposed bottom fishing activities if the procedures outlined in Conservation Measure 22-06, paragraph 8, have not been fully complied with.

12. Members whose vessels participate in exploratory fisheries in accordance with paragraphs 6 and/or 10 shall:

(i) only use the types of fishing gear specified under paragraph 6(ii)(b) in the Fishery Operations Plan for the vessel notified, or under paragraph 10(iii) for any replacement vessel;

(ii) prohibit their vessel(s) from using fishing gear types other than those which were notified for a fishing season unless the gear change is required under research approved by the Scientific Committee for that vessel in that season;

(iii) ensure that their vessels are equipped and configured so that they can comply with all relevant conservation measures;

(iv) ensure that each vessel carries a CCAMLR-designated scientific observer to collect data in accordance with the Data Collection Plan, and to assist in collecting biological and other relevant data;

(v) annually (by the specified date) submit to CCAMLR the data specified by the Data Collection Plan;

(vi) be prohibited from continuing participation in the relevant exploratory fishing if the data specified in the Data Collection Plan have not been submitted to CCAMLR for the most recent season in which fishing occurred, until the relevant data have been submitted to CCAMLR and the Scientific Committee has been allowed an opportunity to review the data.

13. A vessel on either of the IUU Vessel Lists established under Conservation Measures 10-06 and 10-07 shall not be permitted to participate in exploratory fisheries.

14. Notifications for exploratory fisheries pursuant to the provisions above shall be subject to an administrative cost-recovery scheme and shall therefore be accompanied by a payment per vessel, the amount and refundable component of which shall be decided by the Commission, as well as the conditions and modalities according to which such payment shall be made.

Category 22 – Gear Regulations

Conservation Measure 22-01 (1986): Regulation on Mesh Size Measurement[61] (Applicable to All Species, Areas, Seasons and Trawl Gear)

Regulations on Mesh Size Measurement

Article 1 Description of Gauges

1. Gauges to be used for determining mesh sizes shall be 2 mm thick, flat, of durable material and capable of retaining their shape. They shall have either a series of parallel-edged sides connected by intermediate tapering edges with a taper of one to eight on each side, or only tapering edges with the taper defined above. They shall have a hole at the narrowest extremity.

2. Each gauge shall be inscribed on its face with the width in millimetres both on the parallel-sided section, if any, and on the tapering section. In the case of the latter the width shall be inscribed every 1 mm interval and the indication of the width shall appear at regular intervals.

Article 2 Use of the Gauge

1. The net shall be stretched in the direction of the long diagonal of the meshes.

2. A gauge as described in Article 1 shall be inserted by its narrowest extremity into the mesh opening in a direction perpendicular to the plane of the net.

3. The gauge shall be inserted into the mesh opening either with a manual force or using a weight or dynamometer, until it is stopped at the tapering edges by the resistance of the mesh.

Article 3 Selection of Meshes to be Measured

1. Meshes to be measured shall form a series of 20 consecutive meshes chosen in the direction of the long axis of the net.

2. Meshes less than 50 cm from lacings, ropes or codline shall not be measured. This distance shall be measured perpendicular to the lacings, ropes or codline with the net stretched in the direction of that measurement. Nor shall any mesh be measured which has been mended or broken or has attachments to the net fixed at that mesh.

3. By way of derogation from paragraph 1, the meshes to be measured need not be consecutive if the application of paragraph 2 prevents it.

4. Nets shall be measured only when wet and unfrozen.

Article 4 Measurement of Each Mesh

The size of each mesh shall be the width of the gauge at the point where the gauge is stopped, when using this gauge in accordance with Article 2.

Article 5 Determination of the Mesh Size of the Net

1. The mesh size of the net shall be the arithmetical mean in millimetres of the measurements of the total number of meshes selected and measured as provided for in Articles 3 and 4, the arithmetical mean being rounded up to the next millimetre.

2. The total number of meshes to be measured is provided for in Article 6.

Article 6 Sequence of Inspection Procedure

1. The inspector shall measure one series of 20 meshes, selected in accordance with Article 3, inserting the gauge manually without using a weight or dynamometer. The mesh size of the net shall then be determined in accordance with Article 5.

[61] This conservation measure supplements Conservation Measure 22-02.

If the calculation of the mesh size shows that the mesh size does not appear to comply with the rules in force, then two additional series of 20 meshes selected in accordance with Article 3 shall be measured. The mesh size shall then be recalculated in accordance with Article 5, taking into account the 60 meshes already measured. Without prejudice to paragraph 2, this shall be the mesh size of the net.

2. If the captain of the vessel contests the mesh size determined in accordance with paragraph 1, such measurement will not be considered for the determination of the mesh size and the net shall be remeasured.

A weight or dynamometer attached to the gauge shall be used for remeasurement. The choice of weight or dynamometer shall be at the discretion of the inspector.

The weight shall be fixed to the hole in the narrowest extremity of the gauge using a hook. The dynamometer may either be fixed to the hole in the narrowest extremity of the gauge or be applied at the largest extremity of the gauge.

The accuracy of the weight or dynamometer shall be certified by the appropriate national authority. For nets of a mesh size of 35 mm or less as determined in accordance with paragraph 1, a force of 19.61 newtons (equivalent to a mass of 2 kilograms) shall be applied and for other nets, a force of 49.03 newtons (equivalent to a mass of 5 kilograms).

For the purposes of determining the mesh size in accordance with Article 5 when using a weight or dynamometer, one series of 20 meshes only shall be measured.

Conservation Measure 22-04 (2010): Interim Prohibition of Deep-Sea Gillnetting (Applicable to All Species, Areas, Seasons and Gillnet Gear)

The Commission,

Concerned that there have been sightings of illegal, unreported and unregulated (IUU) vessels fishing in the Convention Area using gillnetting,

Also concerned that deep-sea gillnetting in the Convention Area and the associated ghost-fishing by lost or discarded nets has serious detrimental effects on the marine environment and many species of marine living resources,

Aware of the large quantities of non-target species, especially sharks and rays, that are killed by deep-sea gillnetting, and greatly concerned by the impacts on their populations,

Desiring to clearly indicate to the international community that the Commission considers deep-sea gillnetting to be a potentially destructive fishing method, and a practice which may undermine the ability of the Commission to achieve its conservation objective,

Noting that any application in respect of scientific research is subject to the requirements of Conservation Measure 24-01,

hereby adopts the following conservation measure in accordance with Article IX of the Convention:

1. The use of gillnets in the Convention Area, for purposes other than scientific research, is prohibited until such time as the Scientific Committee has investigated and reported on the potential impacts of this gear and the Commission has agreed on the basis of advice from the Scientific Committee that such a method may be used in the Convention Area.

2. The use of gillnets[62] for scientific research shall be permitted subject to the requirements of Conservation Measure 24-01.

[62] Gillnets are strings of single, double or triple netting walls, vertical, near the surface, in midwater or on the bottom, in which fish will gill, entangle or enmesh. Gillnets have floats on the upper line (headrope) and, in general, weights on the ground-line (footrope). Gillnets consist of single or, less commonly, double or triple netting (known as 'trammel net') mounted together on the same frame ropes. Several types of nets may be combined in one gear (for example, trammel net combined with gillnet). These nets can be used either alone or, as is more usual, in large numbers placed in line ('fleets' of nets). The gear can be set, anchored to the bottom or left drifting, free or connected with the vessel.

3. Any vessel seeking to transit the Convention Area carrying gillnets with a total cumulative area measuring greater than 100 m^2 must give advance notice of its intent, including the expected dates and route of its passage through the Convention Area, to the Secretariat. Any vessel in possession of gillnets with a total cumulative area measuring greater than 100 m^2 within the Convention Area which has not given such advance notice shall be in breach of this conservation measure.

Conservation Measure 22-05 (2008): Restrictions on the Use of Bottom Trawling Gear in High-Seas Areas of the Convention Area (Applicable to All Species, High Seas, All Seasons and Bottom Trawl Gear)

The Commission hereby adopts the following conservation measure in accordance with Article IX of the Convention:

1. The use of bottom trawling gear in the high-seas areas of the Convention Area is restricted to areas for which the Commission has conservation measures in force for bottom trawling gear.

2. This conservation measure does not apply to the use of bottom trawling gear in conducting scientific research in the Convention Area.

Conservation Measure 22-06 (2012):[63,64] Bottom Fishing in the Convention Area (Applicable to All Species, Specified Areas (see paragraphs 1 and 2), All Seasons and Bottom Fishing Gear)

The Commission,

Recognising the commitment made by Members to implement the CCAMLR precautionary and ecosystem approaches to fisheries management by embracing principles of conservation as stated in Article II of the Convention,

Conscious of the urgent need to protect vulnerable marine ecosystems (VMEs) from bottom fishing activities that have significant adverse impacts on such ecosystems,

Noting that United Nations General Assembly Resolution 61/105, adopted on 8 December 2006, calls on regional fisheries management organisations or arrangements with the competence to regulate bottom fisheries to adopt and implement measures to prevent significant adverse impacts of bottom fisheries on VMEs, and noting further that all CCAMLR Members joined in the consensus by which this resolution was adopted,

Noting also the importance of Article IX of the Convention, including the use of the best scientific evidence available,

Aware of the steps already taken by CCAMLR to address the impacts of deep-sea gillnetting and bottom trawling in the Convention Area, through the implementation of Conservation Measures 22-04 and 22-05 respectively,

Recognising that CCAMLR has responsibilities for the conservation of Antarctic marine living resources, part of which include the attributes of a regional fisheries management organisation,

Noting that all CCAMLR conservation measures are published on the CCAMLR website,

hereby adopts the following conservation measure in accordance with Article IX of the Convention:

Management of bottom fishing

1. This conservation measure applies to areas in the Convention Area south of 60°S, and to the rest of the Convention Area with the exception of subareas and divisions where an established fishery was in place in 2006/07 with a catch limit greater than zero.

[63] Except for waters adjacent to the Kerguelen and Crozet Islands.

[64] Except for waters adjacent to the Prince Edward Islands.

2. This conservation measure also applies to the area of Statistical Division 58.4.1 north of 60°S.

3. For the purposes of this measure, the term 'vulnerable marine ecosystems' in the context of CCAMLR includes seamounts, hydrothermal vents, cold water corals and sponge fields.

4. For the purposes of this measure, the term 'bottom fishing activities' includes the use of any gear that interacts with the bottom.

5. Contracting Parties whose vessels wish to engage in any bottom fishing activities shall follow the procedures described in paragraphs 7 to 11 below.

6. Contracting Parties shall not authorise vessels flying their flag to participate in bottom fishing activities, except in accordance with the provisions of this conservation measure and Conservation Measure 10-02. Specifically, notwithstanding a timely notification of intention to participate in a new fishery in accordance with Conservation Measure 21-01 or to participate in an exploratory fishery under Conservation Measure 21-02, Contracting Parties shall not authorise, under Conservation Measure 10-02, vessels flying their flag to participate in bottom fishing activities if:

(i) a preliminary assessment was not submitted to the Scientific Committee and the Commission at least three months prior to the annual meeting of the Commission, in accordance with paragraph 7(i); or

(ii) the Commission determines, based upon advice and recommendations from the Scientific Committee and pursuant to paragraph 7(ii), that the proposed bottom fishing activities should not proceed.

Assessment of bottom fishing

7. All bottom fishing activities shall be subject to assessment by the Scientific Committee, based on the best available scientific information, to determine if such activities, taking account of the history of bottom fishing in the areas proposed, would contribute to having significant adverse impacts on VMEs, and to ensure that if it is determined that these activities would make such contributions, that they are managed to prevent such impacts or are not authorised to proceed. The assessments shall include the following procedures:

(i) Each Contracting Party proposing to participate in bottom fishing activities shall submit to the Scientific Committee and Commission information and a preliminary assessment based on the pro forma in Annex 22-06/A, with the best available data, of the known and anticipated impacts of its bottom fishing activities on VMEs, including benthos and benthic communities, not less than three months prior to the annual meeting of the Commission. These submissions shall also include the mitigation measures proposed by the Contracting Party to prevent such impacts.

(ii) The Scientific Committee shall undertake an assessment, according to procedures and standards it develops, and provide advice to the Commission as to whether the proposed bottom fishing activities would contribute to having significant adverse impacts on VMEs and, if so, whether the proposed or additional mitigation measures would prevent such impacts. In its assessment, the Scientific Committee may use additional information available to it, including information from other fisheries in the region or similar fisheries elsewhere. The Scientific Committee will not consider, or provide advice on, preliminary assessments provided after the deadline for submission of preliminary assessments set forth in paragraph 7(i).

(iii) The Commission shall, taking account of advice and recommendations provided by the Scientific Committee concerning bottom fishing activities, including data and information arising from reports pursuant to paragraph 7, adopt conservation measures to prevent significant adverse impacts on VMEs, that as appropriate:

(a) allow, prohibit or restrict bottom fishing activities within particular areas;

(b) require specific mitigation measures for bottom fishing activities;

(c) allow, prohibit or restrict bottom fishing with certain gear types; and/or

(d) contain any other relevant requirements or restrictions to prevent significant adverse impacts to VMEs.

Encounters with VMEs

8. Annex 22-06/B provides guidelines specifying categories of information to be included in the notification to be submitted to the Secretariat by Contracting Parties when evidence of VMEs has been encountered, and has not otherwise been reported under Conservation Measure 22-07.

9. Contracting Parties, in the absence of site-specific or other conservation measures to prevent significant adverse impact on VMEs, shall require vessels flying their flag to cease bottom fishing activities in any location where evidence of a VME is encountered in the course of fishing activities, and to report the encounter to the Secretariat in accordance with the schedule of the Catch and Effort Reporting System (Conservation Measures 23-01, 23-02, 23-03 or 23-07, whichever is applicable), so that appropriate conservation measures can be adopted in respect of the relevant site.

10. The Scientific Committee shall provide advice to the Commission on the known and anticipated impacts of bottom fishing activities on VMEs and recommend practices, including ceasing fishing activities if needed, when evidence of a VME is encountered in the course of bottom fishing activities. Taking account of this advice, the Commission shall adopt conservation measures to be applied when evidence of a VME is encountered in the course of bottom fishing activities.

Monitoring and control of bottom fishing activities

11. Notwithstanding Members' obligations pursuant to Conservation Measure 21-02, all Contracting Parties whose vessels participate in bottom fishing activities shall:

(i) ensure that their vessels are equipped and configured so that they can comply with all relevant conservation measures;

(ii) ensure that each vessel carries at least one CCAMLR-designated scientific observer to collect data in accordance with this and other conservation measures;

(iii) submit data pursuant to Data Collection Plans for bottom fisheries to be developed by the Scientific Committee and included in conservation measures;

(iv) be prohibited from continuing participation in the relevant bottom fishery if data arising from conservation measures relevant to that bottom fishery have not been submitted to CCAMLR pursuant to paragraph 11(iii) for the most recent season in which fishing occurred, until the relevant data have been submitted to CCAMLR and the Scientific Committee has been allowed an opportunity to review the data.

12. The Secretariat shall annually compile a list of vessels authorised to fish pursuant to this conservation measure and shall make this list publicly available on CCAMLR's website.

Data collection and sharing and scientific research

13. The Scientific Committee shall, based on the best available scientific information, advise the Commission on where VMEs are known to occur or are likely to occur, and advise on potential mitigation measures. Contracting Parties shall provide the Scientific Committee with all relevant information to assist in this work. The Secretariat shall maintain an inventory including digital maps of all known VMEs in the Convention Area for circulation to all Contracting Parties and other relevant bodies.

14. Scientific bottom fishing research activities notified under Conservation Measure 24-01, paragraph 2, shall proceed according to Conservation Measure 24-01 and shall be undertaken with due regard to potential impacts on VMEs. Scientific bottom fishing research activities notified under Conservation Measure 24-01, paragraph 3, shall be treated in accordance with all aspects of paragraph 9 of this conservation measure, notwithstanding the procedures in Conservation Measure 24-01. Consistent with existing reporting requirements in Conservation Measure 24-01, paragraph 4, information regarding the location and the type of any VME

encountered, in the course of scientific bottom fishing research activities, shall be reported to the Secretariat.

Review

15. This conservation measure will be reviewed at the next regular meeting of the Commission, based on the findings of the Scientific Committee. In addition, beginning in 2009 and biennially thereafter, the Commission will examine the effectiveness of relevant conservation measures in protecting VMEs from significant adverse impacts, based on advice from the Scientific Committee.

Conservation Measure 22-07 (2013):[65,66] Interim Measure for Bottom Fishing Activities Subject to Conservation Measure 22-06 Encountering Potential Vulnerable Marine Ecosystems in the Convention Area (Applicable to All Species, Areas Specified in CM 22-06 and Bottom Fishing Gear)

The Commission,

Noting the commitment made by Members to avoid significant adverse impacts on vulnerable marine ecosystems (VMEs) from bottom fishing activities,

Acknowledging the current prohibitions on bottom trawling in Conservation Measure 22-05 and on deep-sea gillnetting in Conservation Measure 22-04 in the high-seas areas of the Convention Area,

Agreeing on the need to implement the precautionary approach for managing bottom fisheries with respect to VMEs due to the difficulty in acquiring data on their location, extent and risk of significant adverse impacts,

Further noting the need to acquire additional data to contribute to assessments and advice on a long-term precautionary approach to avoiding significant adverse impacts on VMEs,

hereby adopts the following conservation measure in accordance with Article IX of the Convention and Conservation Measure 22-06:

Area

1. This conservation measure applies to the same area as Conservation Measure 22-06.

Definitions

2. The following definitions apply to this conservation measure:
   (i) Those contained in paragraphs 3 and 4 in Conservation Measure 22-06 relating to 'vulnerable marine ecosystems' (VMEs) and 'bottom fishing activities'.
   (ii) 'VME indicator organism' means any benthic organism listed in the CCAMLR VME Taxa Classification Guide[67].
   (iii) 'VME indicator unit' means either one litre of those VME indicator organisms that can be placed in a 10-litre container, or one kilogram of those VME indicator organisms that do not fit into a 10-litre container.
   (iv) 'Line segment' means a 1 000-hook section of line or a 1 200 m section of line, whichever is the shorter, and for pot lines a 1 200 m section.
   (v) 'Risk Area' means an area where 10 or more VME indicator units are recovered within a single line segment. A Risk Area has a radius of 1 n mile from the midpoint[68] of the line segment from which the VME indicator units are recovered. However, Members may require their vessels to observe a larger Risk Area in accordance with their domestic laws.

[65] Except for waters adjacent to the Kerguelen and Crozet Islands.
[66] Except for waters adjacent to the Prince Edward Islands.
[67] Available from the CCAMLR Secretariat and on the CCAMLR website.
[68] In latitude and longitude.

Vessel requirements

3. Members shall require their vessels to clearly mark fishing lines into line segments and collect segment-specific data on the number of VME indicator units.

4. Members shall require their vessels, if 10 or more VME indicator units are recovered in one line segment, to complete hauling any lines intersecting with the Risk Area without delay and not to set any further lines intersecting with the Risk Area. The vessel shall immediately communicate to the Secretariat and to its Flag State the location of the midpoint of the line segment from which those VME indicator units were recovered along with the number of VME indicator units recovered.

5. Members shall require their vessels, if five or more VME indicator units are recovered within one line segment, to immediately communicate to the Secretariat[69] and to their Flag State the location of the midpoint of the line segment from which those VME indicator units were recovered along with the number of VME indicator units recovered.

Management

6. On receipt of a notification under paragraph 4, the Secretariat shall:

(i) record the location of the Risk Area;

(ii) within one working day of receipt, notify all fishing vessels in the relevant fishery and their Flag States that the Risk Area is closed; and that, as in paragraph 4, all vessels shall immediately cease setting any further lines intersecting with the Risk Area.

7. On receipt of five notifications under paragraph 5 within a single fine-scale rectangle[70], the Secretariat shall, within one working day of receiving the fifth notification, notify all fishing vessels in the relevant fishery and their Flag States of the coordinates of the fine-scale rectangle, indicating that VMEs may occur within that area. Vessels may continue to fish in the area consistent with paragraphs 4 and 5.

Data

8. Vessels shall report in accordance with Conservation Measure 23-07 total benthos recovered in a daily period. To the extent possible, VME indicator units for each line segment and the midpoint of each line segment on all lines, including zero catches, should be reported in the fine-scale data.

Review

9. A Risk Area shall remain closed for any fishery until reviewed by the Scientific Committee and management actions are determined by the Commission. Scientific research shall be allowed in Risk Areas as agreed by the Scientific Committee.

10. The Commission will review this conservation measure in 2012, in light of observer, vessel and other data collected, the results of the deliberations of the Working Group on Ecosystem Monitoring and Management (WG-EMM) and the Working Group on Fish Stock Assessment (WG-FSA), and in accordance with the advice of the Scientific Committee.

Conservation Measure 22-09 (2012): Protection of Registered Vulnerable Marine Ecosystems in Subareas, Divisions, Small-Scale Research Units, or Management Areas Open to Bottom Fishing (Applicable to Various Species and Areas, All Seasons and Bottom Fishing Gear)

The Commission,

Recognising CCAMLR's commitment to preventing significant adverse impacts to vulnerable marine ecosystems (VMEs),

[69] This may be through the Flag State or directly to the Secretariat, whichever is the most practicable.

[70] A fine-scale rectangle is defined as an area of 0.5° latitude by 1° longitude with respect to the northwest corner of the statistical subarea or division. The identification of each rectangle is by the latitude of its northernmost boundary and the longitude of the boundary closest to 0°.

Noting that the Scientific Committee has endeavoured to identify the location of VMEs within the Convention Area consistent with Conservation Measure 22-06,

hereby adopts the following conservation measure in accordance with Article II and article IX of the Convention:

Protection of registered VMEs in subareas, divisions, small-scale research units (SSRUs) and management areas open to bottom fishing:

1. This conservation measure applies to the same area as Conservation Measure 22-06.
2. The areas listed in Annex 22-09/A are identified as registered VMEs and afforded protection consistent with Conservation Measure 22-06.
3. To provide protection of the registered VMEs, bottom fishing shall be prohibited in the defined areas set out in Annex 22-09/A.
4. All bottom fishing activities shall be prohibited within the defined areas, with the exception of scientific research activities agreed by the Commission for monitoring or other purposes on advice from the Scientific Committee and in accordance with Conservation Measures 22-06 and 24-01.

[Omitted: Annex 22-09/A – Table of defined areas of registered vulnerable marine ecosystems in management areas open to bottom fishing.]

Resolution 7/IX (1990): Driftnet Fishing in the Convention Area (Applicable to All Species, Areas, Seasons and Gear)

1. The Commission endorsed the goals of the UN General Assembly Resolution 44/225 on large-scale pelagic driftnet fishing, which calls, *inter alia*, for a cessation of any further expansion of large-scale pelagic driftnet fishing on the high seas. Recognising the concentration of marine living resources present in Antarctic waters, it was noted that large-scale pelagic driftnet fishing can be a highly indiscriminate and wasteful fishing method that is widely considered to threaten the effective conservation of living marine resources. Although no Member is currently engaged in large-scale pelagic driftnet fishing in the Convention Area, the Commission expressed concern about the potential impact on marine living resources if large-scale pelagic driftnet fishing were to expand into the Convention Area.
2. To this end, the Commission agreed, in accordance with UN Resolution 44/225, that there will be no expansion of large-scale pelagic driftnet fishing into the Convention Area.
3. It was agreed that, in accordance with Article X, the Commission would draw this Resolution to the attention of any State that is not a Party to the Convention and whose nationals or vessels engage in large-scale pelagic driftnet fishing.

Category 23 – Data Reporting

Conservation Measure 23-01 (2005): Five-Day Catch and Effort Reporting System (Applicable to All Species and Seasons and Various Areas and Gear)

This conservation measure is adopted in accordance with Conservation Measure 31-01 where appropriate:

1. For the purposes of this Catch and Effort Reporting System the calendar month shall be divided into six reporting periods, viz: day 1 to day 5, day 6 to day 10, day 11 to day 15, day 16 to day 20, day 21 to day 25 and day 26 to the last day of the month. These reporting periods are hereinafter referred to as periods A, B, C, D, E and F.
2. At the end of each reporting period, each Contracting Party shall obtain from each of its vessels its total catch of all species, including by-catch species, and total days and hours fished

for that period and shall, by facsimile or email, transmit the aggregated catch and days and hours fished for its vessels. The catch and effort data shall reach the Executive Secretary not later than two (2) working days after the end of the reporting period. In the case of longline fisheries, the number of hooks shall also be reported. In the case of pot fisheries, the number of pots shall also be reported.

3. A report must be submitted by every Contracting Party taking part in the fishery for each reporting period for the duration of the fishery even if no catches are taken. A Contracting Party may authorise each of its vessels to report directly to the Secretariat.

4. Such reports shall specify the month and reporting period (A, B, C, D, E or F) to which each report refers.

5. Immediately after the deadline has passed for receipt of the reports for each period, the Executive Secretary shall notify all Contracting Parties engaged in fishing activities in the area, of the total catch taken during the reporting period, the total aggregate catch for the season to date together with an estimate of the date upon which the total allowable catch is likely to be reached for that season. In the case of exploratory fisheries, the Executive Secretary shall also notify the total aggregate catch for the season to date in each small-scale research unit (SSRU) together with an estimate of the date upon which the total allowable catch is likely to be reached in each SSRU for that season. Estimates shall be based on a projection forward of the trend in daily catch rates, obtained using linear regression techniques from a number of the most recent catch reports.

6. At the end of every six reporting periods, the Executive Secretary shall inform all Contracting Parties of the total catch taken during the six most recent reporting periods, the total aggregate catch for the season to date together with an estimate of the date upon which the total allowable catch is likely to be reached for that season.

7. If the estimated date of completion of the total allowable catch is within five days of the date on which the Secretariat received the report of the catches, the Executive Secretary shall inform all Contracting Parties that the fishery will close on that estimated day or on the day on which the report was received, whichever is the later. In the case of exploratory fisheries, if the estimated date of completion of the catch in any SSRU is within five days of the day on which the Secretariat received the report of catches, the Executive Secretary shall additionally inform all Contracting Parties, and their relevant fishing vessels if so authorised, that fishing in that SSRU will be prohibited from that calculated day, or on the day on which the report was received, whichever is the later.

8. Should a Contracting Party, or where a vessel is authorised to report directly to the Secretariat, the vessel, fail to transmit a report to the Executive Secretary in the appropriate form by the deadline specified in paragraph 2, the Executive Secretary shall issue a reminder to the Contracting Party. If at the end of a further two five-day periods, or, in the case of exploratory fisheries, a further one five-day period, those data have still not been provided, the Executive Secretary shall notify all Contracting Parties of the closure of the fishery to the vessel which has failed to supply the data as required and the Contracting Party concerned shall require the vessel to cease fishing. If the Executive Secretary is notified by the Contracting Party that the failure of the vessel to report is due to technical difficulties, the vessel may resume fishing once the report or explanation concerning the failure has been submitted.

Conservation Measure 23-02 (1993): Ten-Day Catch and Effort Reporting System (Applicable to All Species and Seasons and Various Areas and Gear)

This conservation measure is adopted in accordance with Conservation Measure 31-01 where appropriate:

1. For the purposes of this Catch and Effort Reporting System the calendar month shall be divided into three reporting periods, viz: day 1 to day 10, day 11 day 20, day 21 to the last day of the month. These reporting periods are hereinafter referred to as periods A, B and C.

2. At the end of each reporting period, each Contracting Party shall obtain from each of its vessels its total catch and total days and hours fished for that period and shall, by cable, telex or facsimile, transmit the aggregated catch and days and hours fished for its vessels so as to reach the Executive Secretary not later than the end of the next reporting period. In the case of longline fisheries, the number of hooks shall also be reported.

3. A report must be submitted by every Contracting Party taking part in the fishery for each reporting period for the duration of the fishery even if no catches are taken.

4. The retained catch of all species and by-catch species, must be reported.

5. Such reports shall specify the month and reporting period (A, B and C) to which each report refers.

6. Immediately after the deadline has passed for receipt of the reports for each period, the Executive Secretary shall notify all Contracting Parties engaged in fishing activities in the area, of the total catch taken during the reporting period, the total aggregate catch for the season to date together with an estimate of the date upon which the total allowable catch is likely to be reached for that season. The estimate shall be based on a projection forward of the trend in daily catch rates, obtained using linear regression techniques from a number of the most recent catch reports.

7. At the end of every three reporting periods, the Executive Secretary shall inform all Contracting Parties of the total catch taken during the three most recent reporting periods, the total aggregate catch for the season to date together with an estimate of the date upon which the total allowable catch is likely to be reached for that season.

8. If the estimated date of completion of the TAC is within ten days of the date on which the Secretariat received the report of the catches, the Executive Secretary shall inform all Contracting Parties that the fishery will close on that estimated day or on the day on which the report was received, whichever is the later.

Conservation Measure 23-03 (1991): Monthly Catch and Effort Reporting System (Applicable to All Species and Seasons and Various Areas and Gear)

This conservation measure is adopted in accordance with Conservation Measure 31-01 where appropriate:

1. For the purposes of this Catch and Effort Reporting System the reporting period shall be defined as one calendar month.

2. At the end of each reporting period, each Contracting Party shall obtain from each of its vessels its total catch and total days and hours fished for that period and shall, by cable or telex, transmit the aggregated catch and days and hours fished for its vessels so as to reach the Executive Secretary not later than the end of the next reporting period.

3. Such reports shall specify the month to which each report refers.

4. Immediately after the deadline has passed for receipt of the reports for each period, the Executive Secretary shall notify all Contracting Parties of the total catch taken during the reporting period, the total aggregate catch for the season to date together with an estimate of the date upon which the total allowable catch is likely to be reached for that season. The estimate shall be based on a projection forward of the trend in daily catch rates, obtained using linear regression techniques from a number of the most recent catch reports.

5. In the case of finfish, if the estimated date of completion of the TAC is within one reporting period of the date on which the Secretariat received the report of the catches, the Executive

Secretary shall inform all Contracting Parties that the fishery will close on that estimated day or on the day on which the report was received, whichever is the later.

Conservation Measure 23-04 (2000):[71,72] Monthly Fine-scale Catch and Effort Data Reporting System for Trawl, Longline and Pot Fisheries (Applicable to All Species Except Krill and All Areas, Seasons and Gear)

The Commission hereby adopts the following conservation measure in accordance with Conservation Measure 31-01, where appropriate.

This conservation measure is invoked by the conservation measures to which it is attached.

1. Specification of 'target species' and 'by-catch species' referred to in this conservation measure shall be made in the conservation measure to which it is attached.

2. At the end of each month each Contracting Party shall obtain from each of its vessels the data required to complete the CCAMLR fine-scale catch and effort data form (trawl fisheries Form C1, longline fisheries Form C2, or pot fisheries Form C5). It shall transmit those data in the specified format to the Executive Secretary not later than the end of the following month.

3. The catch of all target and by-catch species must be reported by species.

4. The numbers of seabirds and marine mammals of each species caught and released or killed must be reported.

5. Should a Contracting Party fail to transmit the fine-scale catch and effort data to the Executive Secretary in the appropriate form by the deadline specified in paragraph 2, the Executive Secretary shall issue a reminder to the Contracting Party. If at the end of a further two months those data have still not been provided, the Executive Secretary shall notify all Contracting Parties of the closure of the fishery to vessels of the Contracting Party which has failed to supply the data as required.

Conservation Measure 23-05 (2000):[73,74] Monthly Fine-scale Biological Data Reporting System for Trawl, Longline and Pot Fisheries (Applicable to All Species Except Krill and All Areas, Seasons and Gear)

The Commission hereby adopts the following conservation measure in accordance with Conservation Measure 31-01, where appropriate.

This conservation measure is invoked by the conservation measures to which it is attached.

1. Specification of 'target species' and 'by-catch species' referred to in this conservation measure shall be made in the conservation measure to which it is attached.

2. At the end of each month each Contracting Party shall obtain from each of its vessels representative samples of length composition measurements of the target species and by-catch species from the fishery (Form B2). It shall transmit those data in the specified form to the Executive Secretary not later than the end of the following month.

3. For the purpose of implementing this conservation measure:

(i) length measurements of fish should be of total length to the nearest centimetre below;

(ii) a representative sample of length composition should be taken from each single fine-scale grid rectangle (0.5° latitude by 1° longitude) in which fishing occurs. In the event that the vessel moves from one fine-scale grid rectangle to another during the course of a month, then a separate length composition should be submitted for each fine-scale grid rectangle.

[71] Except for waters adjacent to the Kerguelen and Crozet Islands.

[72] Except for waters adjacent to the Prince Edward Islands.

[73] Except for waters adjacent to the Kerguelen and Crozet Islands.

[74] Except for waters adjacent to the Prince Edward Islands.

4. Should a Contracting Party fail to transmit the fine-scale length composition data to the Executive Secretary in the appropriate form by the deadline specified in paragraph 2, the Executive Secretary shall issue a reminder to the Contracting Party. If at the end of a further two months those data have still not been provided, the Executive Secretary shall notify all Contracting Parties of the closure of the fishery to vessels of the Contracting Party which has failed to supply the data as required.

Conservation Measure 23-07 (2012): Daily Catch and Effort Reporting System for Exploratory Fisheries, with the Exception of Exploratory Krill Fisheries (Applicable to All Species Except Krill, Various Areas and All Seasons and Gear)

This conservation measure is adopted in addition to Conservation Measures 23-01 and 23-02.

1. All Contracting Parties with vessels operating in exploratory fisheries, with the exception of exploratory krill fisheries, shall provide a daily report to the Secretariat. A Contracting Party may authorise each of its vessels to report directly to the Secretariat.

2. The daily report shall include:
   (i) the total green weight, by vessel, of each target species and by-catch species caught for which there is a catch limit in that area;
   (ii) in the case of longline fisheries, the number of hooks in the water at the time of reporting shall also be included in the report;
   (iii) in the case of pot fisheries, the number of pots in the water at the time of reporting shall also be included in the report.

3. The Secretariat shall use the daily reports to assist fishery closure forecasts for an SSRU, division, subarea or any other area or unit with a specified catch limit.

4. The daily reporting period runs from 12 midnight to 12 midnight UTC.

5. Daily reports shall specify the day to which the report refers and shall reach the Executive Secretary not later than 0600h UTC of the following day.

6. The Executive Secretary shall inform all Contracting Parties at approximately five-day intervals of the total catch taken during the most recent reporting periods, the total aggregate catch for the season to date, and an estimate of the date upon which the catch limit is likely to be reached for that season.

7. Should a Contracting Party, or a vessel authorised to report directly to the Secretariat, fail to transmit a daily report to the Executive Secretary in the appropriate form by the deadline specified in paragraph 5:
   (i) the Executive Secretary shall issue a reminder to the Contracting Party and vessel where a vessel was reporting directly; and
   (ii) if, after five days, the outstanding report has still not been received, or if five reports are received later than the deadline specified in paragraph 5, the Executive Secretary shall notify all Contracting Parties of the closure of the fishery to the vessel which has failed to supply the data as required and the Contracting Party concerned shall require the vessel to cease fishing;
   (iii) if the Executive Secretary is notified by the Contracting Party that the failure of the vessel to report is due to technical difficulties, the vessel may resume fishing once the missing reports and the explanation of the failure have been submitted by the Contracting Party.

Category 24 – Research and Experiments

Conservation Measure 24-01 (2013):[75,76] The Application of Conservation Measures to Scientific Research (Applicable to All Species, Areas, Seasons and Gear)

This conservation measure governs the application of conservation measures to scientific research and is adopted in accordance with Article IX of the Convention.

1. General application:

(a) Catches taken by any vessel for research purposes will be considered as part of any catch limits in force for each species taken unless the catch limit in an area[77] is set at zero.

(b) In the event of research being undertaken in an area[3] with a zero catch limit, then the catches adopted under paragraphs 2 or 3 below shall be considered to be the catch limit for the season in that area. When such an area sits within a group of areas to which an overall catch limit applies, that overall catch limit shall not be exceeded, including any catch taken for research purposes.

2. Application to Members taking less than 50 tonnes of finfish in a season, including no more than the amounts specified for finfish taxa in Annex 24-01/B and less than 0.1% of a given catch limit for non-finfish taxa indicated in Annex 24-01/B:

(a) Any Member planning to use a vessel or vessels for research purposes when the estimated seasonal catch is as above shall notify the Secretariat of the Commission which in turn will notify all Members immediately, according to the format provided in Annex 24-01/A.

(b) Vessels to which the provisions of paragraph 2(a) above apply, shall be exempt from conservation measures relating to mesh size regulations, prohibition of types of gear, closed areas, fishing seasons and size limits, and reporting system requirements other than those specified in paragraph 4 below.

For krill and finfish, this paragraph does not apply for catches less than 1 tonne.

3. Application to Members taking more than 50 tonnes of finfish or more than the amounts specified for finfish taxa in Annex 24-01/B or more than 0.1% of a given catch limit for non-finfish taxa indicated in Annex 24-01/B:

(a) Any Member planning to use any type of vessel or vessels to conduct fishing for research purposes when the estimated seasonal catch is as above, shall notify the Commission and provide the opportunity for other Members to review and comment on its Research Plan. The plan shall be provided to the Secretariat for distribution to Members at least six months in advance of the planned starting date for the research. In the event of any request for a review of such plan being lodged within two months of its circulation, the Executive Secretary shall notify all Members and submit the plan to the Scientific Committee for review. Based on the submitted Research Plan and any advice provided by the appropriate working group, the Scientific Committee will provide advice to the Commission where the review process will be concluded. Until the review process is complete, the planned fishing for research purposes shall not proceed.

(b) Research Plans shall be reported in accordance with the standardised guidelines and formats adopted by the Scientific Committee, given in Annex 24-01/A.

(c) Each fishing vessel[78] conducting fishing for research purposes shall have at least two scientific observers, one of whom shall be an observer appointed in accordance with

[75] Except for waters adjacent to the Kerguelen and Crozet Islands.

[76] Except for waters adjacent to the Prince Edward Islands.

[77] Any management area including subarea, division or SSRU, whichever is designated as a zero catch limit.

[78] In the case of krill research undertaken by fishing vessels, the presence of qualified research scientist(s) on board is needed to conduct the notified Research Plan. In areas where there are no existing catch limits for krill, in

the CCAMLR Scheme of International Scientific Observation, on board throughout all fishing activities within the fishing period.

4. Reporting requirements for these research activities are:

(a) The CCAMLR within-season five-day reporting system shall apply, except for:
   (i) exploratory finfish fisheries, where the daily reporting system (Conservation Measure 23-07) shall apply;
   (ii) exploratory krill fisheries, where the reporting system in Conservation Measure 51-04 shall apply; and
   (iii) other krill fisheries with a catch limit greater than zero, where the reporting system in Conservation Measure 23-06 shall apply.

(a) All research catches shall be reported to CCAMLR as part of the annual STATLANT returns.

(b) A summary of the results of any research subject to the above provisions shall be provided to the Secretariat within 180 days of the completion of the research fishing. Members shall provide a full report to the Scientific Committee within 12 months for review and comment.

(c) Catch, effort and biological data resulting from research fishing should be reported to the Secretariat according to the following haul-by-haul reporting formats:
   (i) Fishing vessels conducting fishing for research purposes in accordance with this conservation measure or Conservation Measure 21-02 should report catch and effort data according to Conservation Measure 23-04 (trawl fisheries form C1, longline fisheries form C2, or pot fisheries form C5) and biological data as required in Conservation Measure 23-05.
   (ii) Vessels undertaking trawl surveys in accordance with this conservation measure should report catch, effort and biological data according to the reporting format for research vessels (C4) and would not be required to complete C1 data.

5. Other requirements for these research activities are:

(a) All vessels conducting research fishing under the research exemption, during a voyage that invokes any commercial fishing, shall be linked to an automated satellite-linked vessel monitoring system in accordance with Conservation Measure 10-04.

[Omitted: Annex 24-01/A – Formats for Notification of Research Vessel Activity]

Conservation Measure 24-02 (2008): Longline Weighting for Seabird Conservation (Applicable to Seabirds, Selected Areas, All Seasons and Longline Gear)

In respect of fisheries in Statistical Subareas 48.4, 48.6, 88.1 and 88.2 and Statistical Divisions 58.4.1, 58.4.2, 58.4.3a, 58.4.3b and 58.5.2, paragraph 5 of Conservation Measure 25-02 shall not apply only where a vessel can demonstrate its ability to fully comply with one of the following protocols.

Protocol A for vessels monitoring longline sink rate with Time-Depth Recorders (TDRs) and using longlines to which weights are manually attached

A1. Prior to entry into force of the licence for this fishery and once per fishing season, either prior to entering the Convention Area or at the first opportunity after entering the Convention Area and before commencing fishing, the vessel shall, under observation by a scientific observer:

---

accordance with Conservation Measure 51-04, one additional scientist who is a national of a Member other than the Member undertaking the research, shall be deemed to fulfil the requirements of paragraph 3(c). Where the krill research is to be conducted in areas where there are existing catch limits, the vessel must carry at least one scientific observer appointed in accordance with the CCAMLR Scheme of International Scientific Observation or at least one scientific observer appointed by the Contracting Party to fulfil the requirements of paragraph 3(c).

(i) set a minimum of two longlines, unbaited if set in the Convention Area, with a minimum of four TDRs on the middle one-third of each longline, where:
   (a) for vessels using the auto longline system, each longline shall be at least 6 000 m in length;
   (b) for vessels using the Spanish longline system, each longline shall be at least 16 000 m in length;
   (c) for vessels using the Spanish longline system, with longlines less than 16 000 m in length, each longline shall be of the maximum length to be used by the vessel in the Convention Area;
   (d) for vessels using a longline system other than an autoline or Spanish longline system, each longline shall be of the maximum length to be used by the vessel in the Convention Area;

(ii) randomise TDR placement on the longline, noting that, except for trotlines, all tests should be applied midway between weights. In the case of trotlines TDRs should be placed on droppers less than 1 m from the attachment position of the uppermost cluster of hooks (i.e. hooks most distant from line weight);

(iii) calculate an individual sink rate for each TDR when returned to the vessel, where:
   (a) the sink rate shall be measured as an average of the time taken for the longline to sink from the surface (0 m) to 15 m;
   (b) this sink rate shall be at a minimum rate of 0.3 m/s;

(iv) if the minimum sink rate is not achieved at all eight sample points (four tests on two longlines), continue the testing until such time as a total of eight tests with a minimum sink rate of 0.3 m/s are recorded;

(v) all equipment and fishing gear used in the tests is to be to the same specifications as that to be used in the Convention Area.

A2. During fishing, for a vessel to be allowed to maintain the exemption to night-time setting requirements (paragraph 5 of Conservation Measure 25-02), regular longline sink monitoring shall be undertaken by the CCAMLR scientific observer. The vessel shall cooperate with the CCAMLR observer who shall:

(i) attempt to conduct a TDR test on one longline set every twenty-four hour period;

(ii) every seven days place at least four TDRs on a single longline to determine any sink rate variation along the longline;

(iii) randomise TDR placement on the longline, noting that all tests should be applied halfway between weights;

(iv) calculate an individual longline sink rate for each TDR when returned to the vessel;

(v) measure the longline sink rate as an average of the time taken for the longline to sink from the surface (0 m) to 15 m.

A3. The vessel shall:

(i) ensure that all longlines are weighted to achieve a minimum longline sink rate of 0.3 m/s at all times whilst operating under this exemption;

(ii) report daily to its national agency on the achievement of this target whilst operating under this exemption;

(iii) ensure that data collected from longline sink rate tests and longline sink rate monitoring during fishing are recorded in the CCAMLR-approved format[79] and submitted to the relevant national agency and CCAMLR Data Manager within two months of the vessel departing a fishery to which this measure applies.

Protocol B for vessels monitoring longline sink rate with bottle tests and using longlines to which weights are manually attached

B1. Prior to entry into force of the licence for this fishery and once per fishing season either

[79] Included in the scientific observer electronic logbook.

prior to entering the Convention Area or at the first opportunity after entering the Convention Area and before commencing fishing, the vessel shall, under observation by a scientific observer:

(i) set a minimum of two longlines, unbaited if set in the Convention Area, with a minimum of four bottle tests (see paragraphs B5 to B9) on the middle one-third of each longline, where:

(a) for vessels using the auto longline system, each longline shall be at least 6 000 m in length;

(b) for vessels using the Spanish longline system, each longline shall be at least 16 000 m in length;

(c) for vessels using the Spanish longline system, with longlines less than 16 000 m in length, each longline shall be of the maximum length to be used by the vessel in the Convention Area;

(d) for vessels using a longline system other than an autoline or Spanish longline system, each longline shall be of the maximum length to be used by the vessel in the Convention Area;

(ii) randomise bottle test placement on the longline, noting that, except for trotlines, all tests should be applied midway between weights. In the case of trotlines TDRs should be placed on droppers less than 1 m from the attachment position of the uppermost cluster of hooks (i.e. hooks most distant from line weight);

(iii) calculate an individual sink rate for each bottle test at the time of the test, where:

(a) the sink rate shall be measured as the time taken for the longline to sink from the surface (0 m) to 10 m;

(b) this sink rate shall be at a minimum rate of 0.3 m/s;

(iv) if the minimum sink rate is not achieved at all eight sample points (four tests on two longlines), continue the testing until such time as a total of eight tests with a minimum sink rate of 0.3 m/s are recorded;

(v) all equipment and fishing gear used in the tests is to be to the same specifications as that to be used in the Convention Area.

B2. During fishing, for a vessel to be allowed to maintain the exemption to night-time setting requirements (paragraph 5 of Conservation Measure 25-02), regular longline sink rate monitoring shall be undertaken by the CCAMLR scientific observer. The vessel shall cooperate with the CCAMLR observer who shall:

(i) attempt to conduct a bottle test on one longline set every twenty-four hour period;

(ii) every seven days conduct at least four bottle tests on a single longline to determine any sink rate variation along the longline;

(iii) randomise bottle test placement on the longline, noting that all tests should be applied halfway between weights;

(iv) calculate an individual longline sink rate for each bottle test at the time of the test;

(v) measure the longline sink rate as the time taken for the longline to sink from the surface (0 m) to 10 m.

B3. The vessel shall:

(i) ensure that all longlines are weighted to achieve a minimum longline sink rate of 0.3 m/s at all times whilst operating under this exemption;

(ii) report daily to its national agency on the achievement of this target whilst operating under this exemption;

(iii) ensure that data collected from longline sink rate tests and longline sink rate monitoring during fishing are recorded in the CCAMLR-approved format[1] and submitted to the relevant national agency and CCAMLR Data Manager within two months of the vessel departing a fishery to which this measure applies.

B4. A bottle test is to be conducted as described below.

Bottle Set Up

B5. 10 m of 2 mm multifilament nylon snood twine, or equivalent, is securely attached to the neck of a 500–1 000 ml plastic bottle[80] with a longline clip attached to the other end. The length measurement is taken from the attachment point (terminal end of the clip) to the neck of the bottle, and should be checked by the observer every few days.

B6. Reflective tape should be wrapped around the bottle to allow it to be observed in low light conditions and at night.

Test

B7. The bottle is emptied of water, the stopper is left open and the twine is wrapped around the body of the bottle for setting. The bottle with the encircled twine is attached to the longline[81], midway between weights (the attachment point).

B8. The observer records the time at which the attachment point enters the water as $t1$ in seconds. The time at which the bottle is observed to be pulled completely under is recorded as $t2$ in seconds[82]. The result of the test is calculated as follows:

Longline sink rate = $10 / (t2 - t1)$.

B9. The result should be equal to or greater than 0.3 m/s. These data are to be recorded in the space provided in the electronic observer logbook.

Protocol C for vessels monitoring longline sink rate with either (TDR) or bottle tests, and using internally weighted longlines with integrated weight of at least 50 g/m and designed to sink instantly with a linear profile at greater than 0.2 m/s with no external weights attached

C1. Prior to entry into force of the licence for this fishery and once per fishing season either prior to entering the Convention Area or at the first opportunity after entering the Convention Area and before commencing fishing, the vessel shall, under observation by a scientific observer:

(i) set a minimum of two longlines, unbaited if set in the Convention Area, with either a minimum of four TDRs, or a minimum of four bottle tests (see paragraphs B5 to B9) on the middle one-third of each longline, where:
   - (a) for vessels using the auto longline system, each longline shall be at least 6 000 m in length;
   - (b) for vessels using the Spanish longline system, each longline shall be at least 16 000 m in length;
   - (c) for vessels using the Spanish longline system, with longlines less than 16 000 m in length, each longline shall be of the maximum length to be used by the vessel in the Convention Area;
   - (d) for vessels using a longline system other than an autoline or Spanish longline system, each longline shall be of the maximum length to be used by the vessel in the Convention Area;

(ii) randomise TDR or bottle test placement on the longline;

(iii) calculate an individual sink rate for each TDR when returned to the vessel, or for each bottle test at the time of the test, where:
   - (a) the sink rate shall be measured as an average of the time taken for the longline to sink from the surface (0 m) to 15 m for TDRs and the time taken for the longline to sink from the surface (0 m) to 10 m for bottle tests;
   - (b) this sink rate shall be at a minimum rate of 0.2 m/s;

[80] A plastic water bottle that has a 'stopper' is needed. The stopper of the bottle is left open so that the bottle will fill with water after being pulled under water. This allows the plastic bottle to be re-used rather than being crushed by water pressure.

[81] On autolines attach to the backbone; on the Spanish longline system attach to the hookline.

[82] Binoculars will make this process easier to view, especially in foul weather.

(iv) if the minimum sink rate is not achieved at all eight sample points (four tests on two longlines), continue the testing until such time as a total of eight tests with a minimum sink rate of 0.2 m/s are recorded;

(v) all equipment and fishing gear used in the tests is to be to the same specifications as that to be used in the Convention Area.

C2. During fishing, for a vessel to be allowed to maintain the exemption to night-time setting requirements (paragraph 5 of Conservation Measure 25-02), regular longline sink rate monitoring shall be undertaken by the CCAMLR scientific observer. The vessel shall cooperate with the CCAMLR observer who shall:

(i) attempt to conduct a TDR or bottle test on one longline set every twenty-four hour period;

(ii) every seven days conduct at least four TDR or bottle tests on a single longline to determine any sink rate variation along the longline;

(iii) randomise TDR or bottle test placement on the longline;

(iv) calculate an individual longline sink rate for each TDR when returned to the vessel or each bottle test at the time of the test;

(v) measure the longline sink rate for bottle tests as the time taken for the longline to sink from the surface (0 m) to 10 m, or for TDRs the average of the time taken for the longline to sink from the surface (0 m) to 15 m.

C3. The vessel shall:

(i) ensure that all longlines are set so as to achieve a minimum longline sink rate of 0.2 m/s at all times whilst operating under this exemption;

(ii) report daily to its national agency on the achievement of this target whilst operating under this exemption;

(iii) ensure that data collected from longline sink rate tests and longline sink rate monitoring during fishing are recorded in the CCAMLR-approved format[1] and submitted to the relevant national agency and CCAMLR Data Manager within two months of the vessel departing a fishery to which this measure applies.

Conservation Measure 24-03 (2003): Experimental Integrated Line-Weighting Trials in Statistical Subareas 88.1 and 88.2 in the 2003/04 Season

The Commission,

Noting the advice of the Scientific Committee and the desire to resolve line weighting issues for autoline vessels in the Convention Area, and the proposal to undertake a comprehensive trial to further resolve this issue from Australia and New Zealand in Statistical Subareas 88.1 and 88.2,

Accepting the need to have two specified vessels use longlines that will not meet the normal sink rate requirements during these trials,

Agrees to adopt the following conservation measure to allow the trials to occur only on the specified agreed vessels pursuant to the experimental design put forward by the Scientific Committee.

In respect of fishing in Statistical Subareas 88.1 and 88.2, paragraphs 1 and 2 of Conservation Measure 25-02, protocols A2, A3, B2, and B3 of Conservation Measure 24-02, paragraph 8 of Conservation Measure 41-09, and paragraph 7 of Conservation Measure 41-10 shall not apply to the FV *Janas*[83] and the FV *Avro Chieftain*[1] whilst these vessels comply with the following experimental protocol.

1. The CCAMLR Scientific Observer or the national observer shall observe all sets of longlines during the trial (100% coverage of sets).

[83] Subject to a licence being issued by the Flag State.

2. Vessels shall deploy two streamer lines on all sets of longlines during the trial. Streamer lines shall be deployed on either side of the longline. The windward streamer will be of the same specification as that detailed in the Appendix to Conservation Measure 25-02. The leeward streamer must be as close as possible to that specification, recognising that modifications will be needed to prevent entanglement of the two streamer lines and the vessels in the trial shall have operational discretion to avoid this.

3. The CCAMLR Scientific Observer shall provide a detailed description of the leeward streamer line use and construction in their cruise report.

4. One of the observers shall determine during every trial set whether seabirds of any species enter the 'risk zone' near vessels. The risk zone is defined as:

(i) up to 100 m astern of the vessel;

(ii) up to 10 m either side of the setting direction of the longline;

(iii) up to 10 m above the longline.

5. Whenever a seabird is sighted in the risk zone during a set, the observer shall immediately inform the officer in charge of the setting operation who shall immediately begin firing a bird scaring gas cannon until such time that the seabird(s) leave the prescribed area. The gas cannon shall be fired on a randomised cycle with a firing frequency of at least two times every three minutes.

6. If, on firing the gas cannon three times, seabirds remain in the risk zone:

(i) if the seabird(s) is/are an albatross (all species) or giant petrel (both species) the vessel shall immediately deploy external weights on unweighted longlines (but not on integrated weight longlines) at such a rate as to achieve a 0.3 m/s line sink rate (~5 kg per 50 m) until such time that the seabird(s) leaves the prescribed area; or, alternatively

(ii) if the seabird(s) is not a species of albatross or giant petrel, the vessel may continue the trial until such time as the seabird catch limits, for species other than in (i) above, prescribed in Annex 24-03/A are reached.

7. If either the second streamer line described in paragraph 2 above, or the gas cannon described in paragraph 6 above are not able to be operated, the trials shall cease immediately until such time as they are able to be deployed again.

8. If any one of the seabird by-catch limits in Annex 24-03/A is reached, the vessel shall revert to fishing under the requirements of Conservation Measure 41-09, Conservation Measure 41-10, Conservation Measure 25-02 and Conservation Measure 24-02.

Annex 24-03/A

The by-catch limits for seabirds caught[84] during these trials are:

(i) 50 Antarctic petrels; and/or

(ii) 20 individuals of all other non-albatross or non-giant petrel species; and/or

(iii) any one of either of the giant petrel species or any one of any albatross species.

Resolution 30/XXVIII (2009): Climate Change (Applicable to All Species, Areas and Seasons)

The Commission,

Recognising that global climate change is one of the greatest challenges facing the Southern Ocean,

Understanding that the Southern Ocean will continue to warm over this century and believing that the Southern Ocean will experience increased acidification with possible impacts on its marine ecosystems,

Concerned about the effects of climate change in Antarctica, on Antarctic marine living resources,

[84] Where the number of birds caught is defined in SC-CAMLR-XXII, Annex 5, paragraphs 6.124 to 6.127.

Recalling Article II of the Convention, which provides, *inter alia*, that any harvesting and associated activities shall be conducted in accordance with provisions of this Convention and with the following principles of conservation:

- prevention of decrease in the size of any harvested population to levels below those which ensure its stable recruitment;
- maintenance of the ecological relationships between harvested, dependent and related populations of Antarctic marine living resources;
- prevention of changes or minimisation of the risk of changes in the marine ecosystem which are not potentially reversible over two or three decades, taking into account the effects of environmental changes, with the aim of making possible the sustained conservation of Antarctic marine living resources,

Conscious of the need to safeguard the environment and protect the integrity of marine ecosystems in the seas surrounding Antarctica in the face of climate change effects,

Noting that management action can help build resilience and protect the unique Southern Ocean environment against potentially irreversible impacts of climate change, and ensure the continued conservation and rational use of the Antarctic marine living resources,

Recalling that the Commission has previously endorsed the work of the Scientific Committee (CCAMLR-XXVII, paragraph 4.61) in relation to the impacts of climate change,

1. Urges increased consideration of climate change impacts in the Southern Ocean to better inform CCAMLR management decisions.

2. Encourages the commitment of all CCAMLR Parties to actively contribute towards relevant science initiatives, such as the *Integrating Climate and Ecosystem Dynamics* science program, and the *Southern Ocean Sentinel* program, which will contribute information needed to improve CCAMLR management actions.

3. Encourages wide dissemination of the Scientific Committee on Antarctic Research's report on Antarctic Climate Change and the Environment when it is published at the end of November 2009, including among delegations to the United Nations Framework Convention on Climate Change (UNFCCC) 15th Conference of the Parties (CoP15) in Copenhagen in December 2009.

4. Requests that the Chairman of the Commission writes to the President of the Conference of the Parties of the UNFCCC, to express that the CAMLR Commission considers that an effective global response by the UNFCCC is urgently needed to address the challenge of climate change in order to protect and preserve the Southern Ocean ecosystems and their biodiversity.

Resolution 31/XXVIII (2009): Best Available Science (Applicable to All Species, Areas and Seasons)

The Commission,

Recognising the importance of sound scientific advice as the centerpiece of its ecosystem approach to the conservation and management of Antarctic marine living resources,

Aware that the availability of adequate scientific information is fundamental to carrying out the objectives of the Convention and, in particular, those in Article II,

Determined to preserve its leading position in the development of the precautionary approach and the ecosystem approach embodied in Article II,

Conscious that Article XIV establishes the Scientific Committee and that each Member of the Commission shall be a Member of the Scientific Committee and shall appoint a representative to the Committee with suitable scientific qualifications,

Emphasising the importance of the effective participation of the developing Member countries in the work of the Scientific Committee and its working groups,

Reminded that under Article XV, the Scientific Committee was established as a forum for consultation and cooperation concerning the collection, study and exchange of information and to provide to the Commission with assessments, analyses, reports and recommendations to implement the objectives of the Convention,

Reaffirming its commitment to Article IX.4 of the Convention, whereby the Commission shall take full account of the recommendations and advice of the Scientific Committee in the development of measures to implement the principles of conservation embodied in the Convention,

Determined to preserve its record as a global leader in science-based conservation, sustainable use and fisheries management,

Building on the deliberations and conclusions of the Working Group for the Development of Approaches to Conservation of Antarctic Marine Living Resources (WG-DAC) in 1990 (CCAMLR-IX, Annex 7, Appendix 2) regarding the ways in which scientific evidence is used by the Commission to aid its decision-making, and the Commission's conclusion that the Commission should regard the Scientific Committee as the source of the best scientific evidence available (CCAMLR-IX, paragraph 7.6),

Acknowledging the recommendations received from the independent Review Panel in 2008 regarding the collection and use of scientific information in the conservation and management of Antarctic marine living resources,

urges all Members to:

1. Take full account of the best scientific information available from the Scientific Committee in the formulation, adoption and revision of conservation measures.

2. Work together to ensure that scientific information is adequately collected, reviewed and applied in a transparent fashion in accordance with sound scientific principles.

3. Facilitate a coordinated and coherent approach to ecosystem monitoring, research and management that provides robust scientific advice to the Commission by:

(i) participating actively in the work of the Scientific Committee and its working groups, and becoming involved in the programs initiated by these bodies;

(ii) contributing to the scientific data and real-time information necessary to the work of the Scientific Committee and its working groups.

4. Contribute to, and enhance the quality of, the work of the Scientific Committee and its working groups as a means to promote rigorous science-based discussions. In particular, Members are encouraged to:

(i) regularly notify the Commission of potentially relevant research and monitoring being conducted within the Convention Area;

(ii) promote active dialogue, information exchange and scientific collaborations between Members' representatives to the Commission and the Scientific Committee, and the scientists in their respective Member countries;

(iii) ensure the participation of scientists with suitable scientific qualifications or experience at intersessional and sessional meetings of the Scientific Committee and its working groups;

(iv) contribute to the capacity-building of the developing Member countries and to enhance their effective participation in the work of the Scientific Committee and its working groups, by providing, *inter alia*, financial assistance and training programs;

(v) seek mechanisms for obtaining financial means to provide scientific analysis and support for the Scientific Committee and its working groups more equitably among all Members of the Commission without compromising the quality of the scientific input.

5. Promote the independence and excellence of the Scientific Committee and its working groups process by:

(i) enabling the presentation to the Commission of their scientists' best, independent, objective advice;
(ii) providing for transparent and effective decision-making;
(iii) providing clear expression of the contents and significance of scientific findings to the Commission.

6. Support and encourage the peer review, wide distribution and discussion of assessments and other significant outputs of the Scientific Committee and its working groups, within and outside of CCAMLR's organisational structure.

Category 25 – Minimisation of Incidental Mortality

Conservation Measure 25-02 (2012):[85,86] Minimisation of the Incidental Mortality of Seabirds in the Course of Longline Fishing or Longline Fishing Research in the Convention Area

The Commission,

Noting the need to reduce the incidental mortality of seabirds during longline fishing by minimising their attraction to fishing vessels and by preventing them from attempting to seize baited hooks, particularly during the period when the lines are set,

Recognising that in certain subareas and divisions of the Convention Area there is also a high risk that seabirds will be caught during line hauling,

Adopts the following measures to reduce the possibility of incidental mortality of seabirds during longline fishing:

1. Fishing operations shall be conducted in such a way that hooklines[87] sink beyond the reach of seabirds as soon as possible after they are put in the water.

2. Vessels using autoline systems should add weights to the hookline or use integrated weight (IW) hooklines while deploying longlines. IW longlines of a minimum of 50 g/m or attachment to non-IW longlines of 5 kg weights at 50 to 60 m intervals are recommended.

3. Vessels using the Spanish method of longline fishing should release weights before line tension occurs; traditional weights[88] of at least 8.5 kg mass shall be used, spaced at intervals of no more than 40 m, or traditional weights[4] of at least 6 kg mass shall be used, spaced at intervals of no more than 20 m, or solid steel weights[89] of at least 5 kg mass shall be used, spaced at intervals of no more than 40 m.

4. Vessels using the trotline system exclusively (not a mix of trotlines and the Spanish system within the same longline) shall deploy weights only at the distal end of the droppers in the trotline. Weights shall be traditional weights of at least 6 kg or solid steel weights of at least 5 kg. Vessels alternating between the use of the Spanish system and trotline method shall use: (i) for the Spanish system: line weighting shall conform to the provisions in paragraph 3; (ii) for the trotline method: line weighting shall be either 8.5 kg traditional weights or 5 kg steel weights attached on the hook-end of all droppers in the trotline at no more than 80 m intervals[90].

---

[85] Except for waters adjacent to the Kerguelen and Crozet Islands.

[86] Except for waters adjacent to the Prince Edward Islands.

[87] Hookline is defined as the groundline or mainline to which the baited hooks are attached by snoods.

[88] Traditional weights are those made from rocks or concrete.

[89] Solid steel weights shall not be made from chain links. They should be made in a hydrodynamic shape designed to sink rapidly.

[90] Recognising that Spanish system longlines with weights at 40 m intervals are typically configured with lines at 80 m intervals that connect hauling and hook lines (see diagram Annex 25-02/C). These connecting lines form the dropper lines of the trotline method.

5. Longlines shall be set at night only (i.e. during the hours of darkness between the times of nautical twilight[91])[92]. During longline fishing at night, only the minimum ship's lights necessary for safety shall be used.[93]

6. The dumping of offal[94] and discards[95] is prohibited while longlines are being set. The dumping of offal during the haul shall be avoided. Any such discharge shall take place only on the opposite side of the vessel to that where longlines are hauled. For vessels or fisheries where there is not a requirement to retain offal on board the vessel, a system shall be implemented to ensure the removal of all fish hooks from offal prior to discharge.

7. Vessels which are so configured that they lack on-board processing facilities or adequate capacity to retain offal on board, or the ability to discharge offal on the opposite side of the vessel to that where longlines are hauled, shall not be authorised to fish in the Convention Area.

8. A streamer line shall be deployed during longline setting to deter birds from approaching the hookline. Specifications of the streamer line and its method of deployment are given in Annex 25-02/A.

9. A bird exclusion device (BED) designed to discourage birds from accessing baits during the hauling of longlines shall be employed to the extent allowed by prevailing weather conditions in those areas defined by CCAMLR as average-to-high or high (Level of Risk 4 or 5) in terms of risk of seabird by-catch. These areas are currently Statistical Subareas 48.3, 58.6 and 58.7 and Statistical Divisions 58.5.1 and 58.5.2. Guidelines for a BED are given in Annex 25-02/B. Vessels operating in low- to medium-risk areas (Level of Risk 1 to 3) are encouraged to use BEDs during the haul of longlines.

10. Every effort should be made to ensure that birds captured alive during longlining are released alive and that, wherever possible, hooks are removed without jeopardising the life of the bird concerned.

11. Other variations in the design of mitigation measures may be tested on vessels carrying two observers, at least one appointed in accordance with the CCAMLR Scheme of International Scientific Observation, providing that all other elements of this conservation measure are complied with. Full proposals for any such testing must be notified to the Working Group on Fish Stock Assessment (WG-FSA) in advance of the fishing season in which the trials are proposed to be conducted.

[Omitted: Annex 25-02/A – Specifications of the streamer line and its method of deployment.]

Resolution 22/XXV (2006): International Actions to Reduce the Incidental Mortality of Seabirds Arising from Fishing (Applicable to Seabirds and All Areas, Seasons and Gear)

The Commission,

Recollecting that the greatest current threats to species and populations of Southern Ocean

[91] The exact times of nautical twilight are set forth in the Nautical Almanac tables for the relevant latitude, local time and date. A copy of the algorithm for calculating these times is available from the CCAMLR Secretariat. All times, whether for ship operations or observer reporting, shall be referenced to GMT.

[92] Wherever possible, setting of lines should be completed at least three hours before sunrise (to reduce loss of bait to/catches of white-chinned petrels).

[93] The mitigation measures under test should be constructed and operated taking full account of the principles set out in WG-FSA-03/22 (the published version of which is available from the CCAMLR Secretariat and website); testing should be carried out independently of actual commercial fishing and in a manner consistent with the spirit of Conservation Measure 21-02.

[94] 'Offal' is defined as bait and by-products from the processing of fish and other organisms, including parts or sections of fish or organisms which are by-products of processing.

[95] For the purpose of this conservation measure, 'discards' are defined as whole fish or other organisms, except elasmobranchs and invertebrates where the vessel is fishing north of 60°S, returned to the sea dead or with low expectation of survival, as described in the Observer Logbook L5 form.

seabirds breeding in the Convention Area are fishery-related incidental mortality and the potential impact of illegal, unreported and unregulated (IUU) fishing,

Noting the substantial reduction of incidental mortality of seabirds in the Convention Area as a result of conservation measures implemented by the Commission,

Concerned that, despite such measures, many populations of albatross and petrel species breeding in the Convention Area continue to decline and that such reductions in their populations are unsustainable,

Concerned at increasing evidence of fishery-related incidental mortality of seabirds that breed and forage in the Convention Area,

Noting that the seabirds caught are almost entirely albatross and petrel species which are threatened with global extinction,

Recognising that some populations of albatrosses and petrels will not stabilise until total incidental mortality levels are significantly reduced,

Recalling CCAMLR's collaborations with the Agreement on the Conservation of Albatrosses and Petrels (ACAP), a multilateral agreement that provides a focus for international cooperation and exchange of information and expertise towards the conservation of the declining populations of these seabirds,

Recalling repeated attempts to communicate these concerns to RFMOs,

1. Invites listed RFMOs (Appendix 1), consistent with the FAO's Code of Conduct for Responsible Fisheries and the IPOA-Seabirds, to implement or develop, as appropriate, mechanisms to require the collection, reporting and dissemination of annual data on seabird incidental mortality, particularly:

   (i) rates of incidental mortality of seabirds associated with each fishery, details of the seabird species involved, and estimates of total seabird mortality (at least at the scale of FAO area);

   (ii) measures to reduce or eliminate incidental mortality of seabirds that are in use in each fishery and the extent to which any of these are voluntary or mandatory, together with an assessment of their effectiveness;

   (iii) scientific observer programs that can provide comprehensive spatial and temporal coverage of fisheries to allow statistically robust estimation of incidental mortality associated with each fishery.

2. For high-seas areas within the range of seabirds that breed and forage in the Convention Area, where unregulated fishing takes place or where systematic data reporting has not yet been introduced by listed RFMOs, the Executive Secretary should contact Flag States which have vessels in these areas to:

   (i) express CCAMLR's interest in such seabird species,

   (ii) indicate the need to require such fishing vessels to collect and report the data specified in paragraph 1 above, and

   (iii) forward these data to the CCAMLR Secretariat to be made available to ad hoc WG-IMAF.

3. Encourages Contracting Parties to:

   (i) request that the topic of seabird incidental mortality be included on the agenda of meetings of pertinent RFMOs and, where possible and appropriate, to send relevant experts to these meetings;

   (ii) identify those areas and circumstances where incidental mortality of seabirds that breed and forage in the Convention Area occurs;

   (iii) identify and continue to develop those mitigation measures which would be most effective at reducing or eliminating such mortality and to require such measures to be implemented in the relevant fisheries.

4. Encourages Contracting Parties involved with new and developing RFMOs to request that incidental mortality of seabirds is adequately addressed and mitigated. Appropriate initiatives might include:
   (i) establishment or expansion of existing observer programs and adoption of appropriate data collection protocols on seabird incidental mortality;
   (ii) establishment of by-catch working groups that will address incidental mortality issues and make recommendations for practicable and effective mitigation measures, including evaluation of established and innovative technologies and techniques;
   (iii) evaluations of fishery impacts on the affected seabird populations;
   (iv) collaborations (e.g. on data exchange) with listed RFMOs.

5. Encourages Contracting Parties to:
   (i) implement, as appropriate, measures to reduce or eliminate seabird incidental mortality;
   (ii) require their flagged vessels to collect and report the data specified in paragraph 1 above;
   (iii) report to the CCAMLR Secretariat annually on the implementation of such measures, including their effectiveness in reducing seabird incidental mortality.

6. Requests ad hoc WG-IMAF, at its annual meeting, to collate and analyse reports relating to paragraphs 1, 2 and 5 above and advise the Commission, through the Scientific Committee, on the implementation and effectiveness of this resolution.

7. Further requests the Secretariat to bring this resolution to the attention of the RFMOs listed in Appendix 1 and seek their cooperation on its implementation.

Appendix 1: Regional Fisheries Management Organisations Identified for Contact with respect to Collaborations on the Mitigation of By-Catch of Southern Ocean Seabirds

Inter-American Tropical Tuna Commission (IATTC)

International Commission for the Conservation of Atlantic Tunas (ICCAT) South East Atlantic Fisheries Organisation (SEAFO)

Indian Ocean Tuna Commission (IOTC)

Commission for the Conservation of Southern Bluefin Tuna (CCSBT)

Agreement on the Organization of the Permanent Commission on the Exploitation and Conservation of the Marine Resources of the South Pacific, 1952 (CPPS) Southwest Indian Ocean Fisheries Commission (SWIOFC)

Commission for Conservation and Management of Highly Migratory Fish Stocks in the Western and Central Pacific WCPFC) Western Indian Ocean Tuna Organization Convention (WIOTO) The organization does not have regulatory power.

Southern Indian Ocean Fisheries Agreement (SIOFA)

Category 26 – Environmental Protection

Conservation Measure 26-01 (2009):[96,97] General Environmental Protection During Fishing

The Commission,

Concerned that certain activities associated with fishing may affect the Antarctic marine environment and that these activities have played a notable role in CCAMLR's efforts to minimise incidental mortality of non-target species such as seabirds and seals,

Noting that previous CCAMLR recommendations, and the provisions of the MARPOL 73/78 Convention and its annexes, prohibit the disposal of all plastics at sea in the CAMLR Convention Area,

[96] Except for waters adjacent to the Kerguelen and Crozet Islands.

[97] Except for waters adjacent to the Prince Edward Islands.

Noting various provisions of the Protocol on Environmental Protection to the Antarctic Treaty, in particular its annexes as well as related Recommendations and Measures of the Antarctic Treaty Consultative Meetings,

Recollecting that for many years advice from the Scientific Committee has indicated that significant numbers of Antarctic fur seals have been entangled and killed in plastic packaging bands in the Convention Area,

Noting the recommendations of CCAMLR and the provisions of the MARPOL Convention and its annexes which prohibit the jettisoning of all plastics at sea, and that entanglement of fur seals is still continuing,

Recognising that the bait boxes used on fishing vessels in particular, and other packages in general, need not be secured by plastic packaging bands because suitable alternatives exist,

Adopts the following conservation measure to minimise possible effects on the marine environment arising from fishing-related activities in the context of mitigating incidental mortality of non-target species and protecting the marine environment in accordance with Article IX of the Convention.

Disposal of Plastic Packaging Bands

1. The use on fishing vessels of plastic packaging bands to secure bait boxes shall be prohibited.
2. The use of other plastic packaging bands for other purposes on fishing vessels which do not use on-board incinerators (closed systems) shall be prohibited.
3. Any packaging bands, once removed from packages, shall be cut into approximately 30 cm sections, so that they do not form a continuous loop and at the earliest opportunity burned in the on-board incinerator.
4. Any plastic residue shall be stored on board the vessel until reaching port and in no case discarded at sea.

Prohibition of Discharge in High-Latitude Fisheries

5. Vessels fishing south of 60°S shall be prohibited from dumping or discharging:
   (i) oil or fuel products or oily residues into the sea, except as permitted under Annex I of MARPOL 73/78;
   (ii) garbage;
   (iii) food wastes not capable of passing through a screen with openings no greater than 25 mm;
   (iv) poultry or parts (including egg shells);
   (v) sewage within 12 n miles of land or ice shelves, or sewage while the ship is travelling at a speed of less than 4 knots;
   (vi) incineration ash.
6. Vessels fishing south of 60°S also shall be prohibited from dumping or discharging:
   (i) offal[98]
   (ii) discards[99].
7. Fish or other organisms taken during fishing operations with high expectation of survival[100], and other benthic organisms[101] may be returned to the sea, only after fulfilling the relevant requirements of Conservation Measure 22-07 and the relevant reporting requirements of other conservation measures.

Translocation of Poultry

8. Live poultry or other living birds shall not be brought into areas south of 60°S, and any dressed poultry not consumed shall be removed from those areas.

[98] 'Offal' is defined as bait and by-products from the processing of fish and other organisms, including parts or sections of fish or organisms which are by-products of processing.

[99] 'Discards' are defined as whole fish or other organisms returned to the sea dead or with low expectation of survival, as described in Observer Logbook L5 form.

[100] As described in Observer Logbook L5 form.

[101] For the purposes of this conservation measure, 'other benthic organisms' refers to benthic organisms as defined in the CCAMLR VME Taxa Classification Guide and other habitat forming taxa, which are not included in the definitions of offal and discards in footnotes 3 and 4 respectively.

Category 31 – General Measures

Conservation Measure 31-01 (1986): Regulation of Fishing around South Georgia (Statistical Subarea 48.3)

Without prejudice to other conservation measures adopted by the Commission, for species upon which fisheries are permitted around South Georgia (Statistical Subarea 48.3), the Commission shall, at its 1987 Meeting, adopt limitations on catch, or equivalent measures, binding for the 1987/88 season.

Such limitations of catch or equivalent measures shall be based upon the advice of the Scientific Committee, taking into account any data resulting from fishery surveys around South Georgia.

For each fishing season after 1987/88, the Commission shall establish such limitations or other measures, as necessary, around South Georgia on a similar basis at the meeting of the Commission immediately preceding that season.

Conservation Measure 31-02 (2007):[102,103] General Measure for the Closure of all Fisheries (Applicable to All Species, Areas, Seasons and Gear)

This conservation measure governs the closure of all fisheries and is adopted in accordance with Article IX of the Convention

General Application

1. Following notification by the Secretariat of the closure of a fishery (Conservation Measures 23-01, 23-02, 23-03 and 41-01 refer), all vessels in the area, management area, subarea, division, small-scale research unit or other management unit subject to the closure notice, shall remove all their fishing gear from the water by the notified closure date and time.

2. On receipt of such notification by the vessel, no further longlines may be set within 24 hours of the notified closure date and time. If such notification is received less than 24 hours before the closure date and time, no further longlines may be set following receipt of that notification.

3. All vessels should depart the closed fishery as soon as all fishing gear has been removed from the water.

4. Notwithstanding paragraph 1, should it appear likely that a vessel will be unable to remove all its fishing gear from the water by the notified closure date and time because of:

(i) consideration of the safety of the vessel and crew;
(ii) the limitations which may arise from adverse weather conditions;
(iii) sea-ice cover; or
(iv) the need to protect the Antarctic marine environment, the vessel shall notify the Flag State concerned of the situation. The Flag State or vessel shall also notify the Secretariat. The vessel shall nonetheless make all reasonable efforts to remove all its fishing gear from the water as soon as possible.

Other Relevant Considerations

5. In the event the vessel is unable to remove all of its fishing gear from the water by the notified closure date and time, the Flag State shall promptly inform the Secretariat. On receipt of such information the Secretariat shall promptly inform Members.

6. If paragraph 5 applies, the Flag State shall carry out an investigation of the vessel's actions and, according to its domestic procedures, report on its findings, including all relevant matters, to the Commission no later than the next meeting of the Commission. The final report should assess whether the vessel made all reasonable efforts to remove all its fishing gear from the water:

[102] Except for waters adjacent to the Kerguelen and Crozet Islands.
[103] Except for waters adjacent to the Prince Edward Islands.

(i) by the notified closure date and time; and

(ii) as soon as possible after the notification referred to in paragraph 4.

7. In the event that a vessel does not depart the closed fishery as soon as all fishing gear has been removed from the water, the Flag State or vessel should inform the Secretariat. On receipt of such information the Secretariat shall promptly inform Members.

Resolution 20/XXII (2003): Ice-Strengthening Standards in High-Latitude Fisheries[104] (Applicable to All Species, Areas South of 60°S and All Seasons and Gear)

The Commission,

Recognising the unique circumstances in high-latitude fisheries, especially the extensive ice coverage which can pose a risk to fishing vessels operating in those fisheries,

Recognising also that the safety of fishing vessels, crew and CCAMLR scientific observers is a significant concern of all Members,

Further recognising the difficulties of search and rescue response in high-latitude fisheries,

Concerned that collisions with ice could result in oil spills and other adverse consequences for Antarctic marine living resources and the pristine Antarctic environment,

Considering that vessels fishing in high-latitude fisheries should be suitable for ice conditions,

urges Members to licence to fish in high-latitude fisheries only those of their flag vessels with a minimum ice classification standard of ICE-1C[105] which will remain current for the duration of the planned fishing activity.

Resolution 23/XXIII (2004): Safety on Board Vessels Fishing in the Convention Area (Applicable to All Species, Areas, Seasons and Gear)

The Commission,

Recognising the difficult and dangerous conditions experienced in high-latitude fisheries in the Convention Area,

Further considering the remoteness of those waters and in consequence the difficulties of search and rescue response,

Desiring to ensure that the safety of fishing crews and CCAMLR scientific observers remains a priority concern of all Members,

urges Members to take particular measures through, *inter alia*, appropriate survival training and the provision and maintenance of appropriate equipment and clothing to promote the safety of all those on board vessels fishing in the Convention Area.

Resolution 29/XXVIII (2009): Ratification of the Salvage Convention by Members of CCAMLR (Applicable to All Species, Areas and Seasons)

The Commission,

Recognising the difficult and dangerous conditions experienced in high-latitude fisheries in the Convention Area,

Further considering the remoteness of those waters and in consequence the difficulties of search and rescue response,

Noting the duty to render assistance and to proceed with all possible speed to the rescue of persons in distress, as enshrined in the United Nations Convention on the Law of the Sea,

[104] Subareas and divisions south of 60°S and adjacent to the Antarctic Continent.

[105] As defined in the Det Norske Veritas (DNV) Rules for Classification of Ships or an equivalent standard of certification as defined by a recognised classification authority.

Conscious of the importance of intervention in maritime accidents to ensure the safety of fishing crews and CCAMLR scientific observers and to minimise damage to the marine environment and the surrounding ecosystems,

Aware of the potential costs associated with the rescue of fishing crews and CCAMLR scientific observers or the salvage of a vessel, its cargo or any other property,

Desiring swift intervention in the event of a maritime accident without undue delay due to concern about the process to recover costs,

recommends all Members of CCAMLR that have not yet ratified the International Convention on Salvage, 1989, to consider its ratification, or the adoption of other mechanisms that Members may deem appropriate, to facilitate recovery of expenses reasonably incurred to operators of vessels that assist a vessel or any other property in danger in the CAMLR Convention Area.

Resolution 34/XXXI (2012): Enhancing the Safety of Fishing Vessels in the Convention Area (Applicable to All Species, Areas, Seasons and Gear)

The Commission,

Concerned about the safety of life and potential environmental consequences of a maritime incident involving a fishing vessel operating in the CAMLR Convention Area,

Recognising the progress in the development at the International Maritime Organization (IMO) of a mandatory code for vessels operating in Polar waters,

Recalling Resolution 20/XXII on ice-strengthening standards in high-latitude fisheries and Resolution 23/XXIII on safety on board vessels fishing in the Convention Area,

Noting the Cape Town Agreement of 2012 on the Implementation of the Provisions of the 1993 Protocol relating to the Torremolinos International Convention for the Safety of Fishing Vessels, 1977 ('Cape Town Agreement'),

encourages Members:

1. To continue the work, through their delegations to the IMO, on the mandatory code for ships operating in Polar waters.
2. To consider ratifying the Cape Town Agreement as soon as practicable.
3. To consider and implement appropriate measures to enhance the safety standards of those fishing vessels which they license to operate in the Convention Area.

Category 32 – Fishing Seasons, Closed Areas and Prohibition of Fishing

Conservation Measure 32-01 (2001): Fishing Seasons (Applicable to All Species, Areas, Seasons and Gear)

The Commission hereby adopts the following conservation measure in accordance with Article IX of the Convention:

The fishing season for all Convention Area species is 1 December to 30 November of the following year, unless otherwise set in specific conservation measures.

Conservation Measure 32-02 (2012): Prohibition of Directed Fishing (Applicable to All Species, Areas, Seasons and Gear)

This conservation measure is adopted in accordance with Article IX of the Convention:

Directed fishing on taxa in areas specified in Annex 32-02/A is prohibited, subject to the conditions listed in that annex.

[Omitted: Annex 32-02/A – Table of areas subject to prohibition on directed fishing and conditions specific to those areas.]

Category 33 – By-catch Limits

Conservation Measure 33-02 (2013): Limitation of By-catch in Statistical Division 58.5.2 in the 2013/14 Season (Applicable to By-catch, Area 58.5.2, 2013/14 Season and All Gear)

1. There shall be no directed fishing for any species other than *Dissostichus eleginoides* and *Champsocephalus gunnari* in Statistical Division 58.5.2 in the 2013/14 fishing season.

2. In directed fisheries in Statistical Division 58.5.2 in the 2013/14 season, the by-catch of *Channichthys rhinoceratus* shall not exceed 150 tonnes, the by-catch of *Lepidonotothen squamifrons* shall not exceed 80 tonnes, the by-catch of *Macrourus* spp. shall not exceed 360 tonnes and the by-catch of skates and rays shall not exceed 120 tonnes. For the purposes of this measure, '*Macrourus* spp.' and 'skates and rays' should each be counted as a single species.

3. The by-catch of any fish species not mentioned in paragraph 2, and for which there is no other catch limit in force, shall not exceed 50 tonnes in Statistical Division 58.5.2.

4. If, in the course of a directed fishery, the by-catch in any one haul of *Channichthys rhinoceratus*, *Lepidonotothen squamifrons*, *Macrourus* spp., *Somniosus* spp. or skates and rays is equal to, or, or greater than, 2 tonnes, then the fishing vessel shall not fish using that method of fishing at any point within 5 n miles[106] of the location where the by-catch exceeded 2 tonnes for a period of at least five days[107]. The location where the by-catch exceeded 2 tonnes is defined as the path[108] followed by the fishing vessel.

5. If, in the course of a directed fishery, the by-catch in any one haul of any other by-catch species for which by-catch limitations apply under this conservation measure is equal to, or greater than, 1 tonne, then the fishing vessel shall not fish using that method of fishing at any point within 5 n miles[1] of the location where the by-catch exceeded 1 tonne for a period of at least five days[2]. The location where the by-catch exceeded 1 tonne is defined as the path[3] followed by the fishing vessel.

Conservation Measure 33-03 (2013):[109,110] Limitation of By-catch in New and Exploratory Fisheries in the 2013/14 Season (Applicable to By-catch, Various Areas, the 2013/14 Season and All Gear)

1. This conservation measure applies to new and exploratory fisheries in all areas containing small-scale research units (SSRUs) in the 2013/14 season, except where specific by-catch limits apply.

2. The catch limits for all by-catch species are set out in Annex 33-03/A. Within these catch limits, the total catch[111] of by-catch species in any SSRU or combination of SSRUs, as defined in relevant conservation measures shall not exceed the following limits:

- skates and rays 5% of the catch limit of *Dissostichus* spp. or 50 tonnes, whichever is greater;

[106] This provision concerning the minimum distance separating fishing locations is adopted pending the adoption of a more appropriate definition of a fishing location by the Commission.

[107] The specified period is adopted in accordance with the reporting period specified in Conservation Measure 23-01, pending the adoption of a more appropriate period by the Commission.

[108] For a trawl, the path is defined from the point at which the fishing gear was first deployed from the fishing vessel to the point at which the fishing gear was retrieved by the fishing vessel. For a longline or a pot, the path is defined from the point at which the first anchor of a set was deployed to the point at which the last anchor of that set was deployed.

[109] Except for waters adjacent to the Kerguelen and Crozet Islands.

[110] Except for waters adjacent to the Prince Edward Islands.

[111] Total green weight caught, excluding individuals released alive.

- *Macrourus* spp. 16% of the catch limit for *Dissostichus* spp. or 20 tonnes, whichever is greater;
- all other species combined 20 tonnes.

3. For the purposes of this measure '*Macrourus* spp.' and 'skates and rays' should each be counted as a single species.

4. On all vessels, all skates and rays must be brought on board or alongside the hauler to be checked for tags and for their condition to be assessed. Recaptured tagged skates and rays, as per Conservation Measure 41-01, Annex 41-01/C, paragraphs 2(v) and (vii), should not be re-released. Unless otherwise specified by scientific observers, all other skates and rays caught alive and with a high probability of survival should be released alive, by vessels, by cutting snoods, and when practical, removing the hooks, and the number should be recorded and reported to the Secretariat.

5. If the by-catch of any one species is equal to, or greater than, 1 tonne in any one haul or set, then the fishing vessel shall move to another location at least 5 n miles[112] distant. The fishing vessel shall not return to any point within 5 n miles of the location where the by-catch exceeded 1 tonne for a period of at least five days[113]. The location where the by-catch exceeded 1 tonne is defined as the path[114] followed by the fishing vessel.

6. If the catch of *Macrourus* spp. taken by a single vessel in any two 10-day periods[115] in a single SSRU exceeds 1 500 kg in each 10-day period and exceeds 16% of the catch of *Dissostichus* spp. by that vessel in that SSRU in those periods, the vessel shall cease fishing in that SSRU for the remainder of the season.

[*Omitted: Annex 33-03/A – Table of by-catch catch limits for new and exploratory fisheries in 2013/14.*]

Category 91 – Protected Areas

Conservation Measure 91-01 (2004): Procedure for According Protection to CEMP Sites (Applicable to All Species and General Areas)

The Commission,

Bearing in mind that the Scientific Committee has established a system of sites contributing data to the CCAMLR Ecosystem Monitoring Program (CEMP), and that additions may be made to this system in the future,

Recalling that it is not the purpose of the protection accorded to CEMP sites to restrict fishing activity in adjacent waters,

Recognising that studies being undertaken at CEMP sites may be vulnerable to accidental or wilful interference,

Concerned, therefore, to provide protection for CEMP sites, scientific investigations and the Antarctic marine living resources therein, in cases where a Member or Members of the Commission conducting or planning to conduct CEMP studies believes such protection to be desirable,

hereby adopts the following conservation measure in accordance with Article IX of the Convention:

[112] This provision concerning the minimum distance separating fishing locations is adopted pending the adoption of a more appropriate definition of a fishing location by the Commission.

[113] The specified period is adopted in accordance with the reporting period specified in Conservation Measure 23-01, pending the adoption of a more appropriate period by the Commission.

[114] For a trawl, the path is defined from the point at which the fishing gear was deployed from the fishing vessel to the point at which the fishing gear was retrieved by the fishing vessel. For a longline, the path is defined from the point at which the first anchor of a set was deployed to the point at which the last anchor of that set was deployed.

[115] A 10-day period is defined as day 1 to day 10, day 11 to day 20, or day 21 to the last day of the month.

1. In cases where a Member or Members of the Commission conducting, or planning to conduct, CEMP studies at a CEMP site believe it desirable that protection should be accorded to the site, it, or they, shall prepare a draft management plan in accordance with Annex A to this conservation measure.

2. Each such draft management plan shall be sent to the Executive Secretary for transmission to all Members of the Commission for their consideration at least three months before its consideration by WG-EMM.

3. The draft management plan shall be considered in turn by WG-EMM, the Scientific Committee and the Commission. In consultation with the Member or Members of the Commission which drew up the draft management plan, it may be amended by any of these bodies. If a draft management plan is amended by either WG-EMM or the Scientific Committee, it shall be passed on in its amended form either to the Scientific Committee or to the Commission as the case may be.

4. If, following completion of the procedures outlined in paragraphs 1 to 3 above, the Commission considers it appropriate to accord the desired protection to the CEMP site, the Commission shall adopt a Resolution calling on Members to comply, on a voluntary basis, with the provisions of the draft management plan, pending the conclusion of action in accordance with paragraphs 5 to 8 below.

5. The Executive Secretary shall communicate such a Resolution to SCAR, the Antarctic Treaty Consultative Parties and, if appropriate, the Contracting Parties to other components of the Antarctic Treaty System which are in force.

6. Unless, before the opening date of the next regular meeting of the Commission, the Executive Secretary has received:

(i) an indication from an Antarctic Treaty Consultative Party that it desires the resolution to be considered at a Consultative Meeting; or

(ii) an objection from any other quarter referred to in paragraph 5 above;

the Commission may, by means of a conservation measure, confirm its adoption of the management plan for the CEMP site and shall include the management plan in Annex 91-01/A of that conservation measure.

7. In the event that an Antarctic Treaty Consultative Party has indicated its desire for the Resolution to be considered at a Consultative Meeting, the Commission shall await the outcome of such consideration, and may then proceed accordingly.

8. If objection is received in accordance with paragraphs 6(ii) or 7 above, the Commission may institute such consultations as it may deem appropriate to achieve the necessary protection and to avoid interference with the achievement of the principles and purposes of, and measures approved under, the Antarctic Treaty and other components of the Antarctic Treaty System which are in force.

9. The management plan of any site may be amended by decision of the Commission. In such cases full account shall be taken of the advice of the Scientific Committee. Any amendment which increases the area of the site or adds to categories or types of activities that would jeopardise the objectives of the site shall be subject to the procedures set out in paragraphs 5 to 8 above.

10. Entry into a CEMP site described by a conservation measure shall be prohibited except for the purposes authorised in the relevant management plan for the site and in accordance with a permit issued under paragraph 11.

11. Each Contracting Party shall, as appropriate, issue permits authorising its nationals to carry out activities consistent with the provisions of the management plans for CEMP sites and shall take such other measures, within its competence, as may be necessary to ensure that its nationals comply with the management plans for such sites.

12. Copies of such permits shall be sent to the Executive Secretary as soon as practical after they are issued. Each year the Executive Secretary shall provide the Commission and the

Scientific Committee with a brief description of the permits that have been issued by the Parties. In cases where permits are issued for purposes not directly related to the conduct of CEMP studies at the site in question, the Executive Secretary shall forward a copy of the permit to the Member or Members of the Commission conducting CEMP studies at that site.

13. Each management plan shall be reviewed every five years by WG-EMM and the Scientific Committee to determine whether it requires revision and whether continued protection is necessary. The Commission may then act accordingly.

Annex 91-01/A: Information to be Included in Management Plans for CEMP Sites:

A Geographical Information

1. A description of the site, and any buffer zone within the site, including:
    - 1.1 geographical coordinates
    - 1.2 natural features, including those that define the site
    - 1.3 boundary markers
    - 1.4 access points (pedestrian, vehicular, airborne, sea-borne)
    - 1.5 pedestrian and vehicular routes
    - 1.6 preferred anchorages
    - 1.7 location of structures within the site
    - 1.8 restricted areas within the site
    - 1.9 location of nearby scientific stations or other facilities
    - 1.10 location of areas or sites, in or near the site, which have been accorded protected status in accordance with measures adopted under the Antarctic Treaty or other components of the Antarctic Treaty System that are in force.
2. Maps, including the following elements where appropriate:
    - 2.1 Essential features
        - 2.1.1 Title
        - 2.1.2 Latitude and longitude
        - 2.1.3 Scale bar with numerical scale
        - 2.1.4 Comprehensive legend
        - 2.1.5 Adequate and approved place names
        - 2.1.6 Map projection and spheroid modification (indicate beneath the scale bar)
        - 2.1.7 North arrow
        - 2.1.8 Contour interval
        - 2.1.9 Date of map preparation
        - 2.1.10 Map preparer
        - 2.1.11 Date of image collection (where applicable)
    - 2.2 Essential topographical features
        - 2.2.1 Coastline, rock, and ice
        - 2.2.2 Peaks and ridgelines
        - 2.2.3 Ice margins and other glacial features, clear delineation between ice/snow and ice-free ground; if glacial features are part of the boundary, date of survey should be indicated
        - 2.2.4 Contours (labelled as appropriate), survey points, and spot heights
        - 2.2.5 Bathymetric contours of marine areas, with relevant bottom features if known
    - 2.3 Natural features
        - 2.3.1 Lakes, ponds, and streams
        - 2.3.2 Moraines, screes, cliffs, beaches
        - 2.3.3 Beach areas
        - 2.3.4 Bird and seal concentrations or breeding colonies
        - 2.3.5 Extensive areas of vegetation
        - 2.3.6 Wildlife access areas to the sea

2.4 Anthropogenic features
- 2.4.1 Stations
- 2.4.2 Field huts, refuges
- 2.4.3 Campsites
- 2.4.4 Roads and vehicle tracks, footpaths, feature overlaps
- 2.4.5 Approach paths and landing areas for airplanes and helicopters
- 2.4.6 Approach paths and access points for boats (wharfs, jetties)
- 2.4.7 Power supplies, cables
- 2.4.8 Antennae
- 2.4.9 Fuel storage areas
- 2.4.10 Water reservoirs and pipes
- 2.4.11 Emergency caches
- 2.4.12 Markers, signs
- 2.4.13 Historic sites or artefacts, archaeological sites
- 2.4.14 Scientific installations or sampling areas
- 2.4.15 Site contamination or modification

2.5 Boundaries
- 2.5.1 Boundary of area
- 2.5.2 Boundaries of subsidiary zones and protected areas within the mapping area
- 2.5.3 Boundary signs and markers (including cairns)
- 2.5.4 Boat/aircraft approach routes
- 2.5.5 Navigation markers or beacons
- 2.5.6 Survey points and markers
- 2.6 Other mapping guidelines
- 2.6.1 Verify all features and boundaries by GPS if possible
- 2.6.2 Ensure visual balance among elements
- 2.6.3 Appropriate shading (shading should be distinguishable on a photocopy of the map)
- 2.6.4 Correct and appropriate text; no feature overlap
- 2.6.5 Appropriate legend; use SCAR approved map symbols when possible
- 2.6.6 Text appropriately shadowed on image data
- 2.6.7 Photographs may be used where appropriate
- 2.6.8 Official maps should be in black and white
- 2.6.9 Most likely two or more maps will be needed for a management plan, one showing the site and the vicinity, and one detailed map of the site showing features essential for the management plan objectives; other maps may be useful (i.e. geological map of the area, three dimensional terrain model).

B Biological Features

1. A description of the biological features of the site, in both space and time, which it is the purpose of the management plan to protect.

C CEMP Studies

1. A full description of the CEMP studies being conducted or planned to be conducted, including the species and parameters which are being or are to be studied.

D Protection Measures

1. Statements of prohibited activities:
   - 1.1 throughout the site at all times of the year
   - 1.2 throughout the site at defined parts of the year
   - 1.3 in parts of the site at all times of the year
   - 1.4 in parts of the site at defined parts of the year.
2. Prohibitions regarding access to and movement within or over the site.

3. Prohibitions regarding:
   3.1 the installation, modification, and/or removal of structures
   3.2 the disposal of waste.
4. Prohibitions for the purpose of ensuring that activity in the site does not prejudice the purposes for which protection status has been accorded to areas or sites, in or near the site, under the Antarctic Treaty or other components of the Antarctic Treaty System which are in force.

E Communications Information

1. The name, address, telephone and facsimile numbers, and email addresses, of:
   1.1 the organisation or organisations responsible for appointing national representative(s) to the Commission;
   1.2 the national organisation or organisations conducting CEMP studies at the site.

Notes:

1. A code of conduct. If it would help towards achieving the scientific objectives of the site, a code of conduct may be annexed to the management plan. Such a code should be written in hortatory rather than mandatory terms, and must be consistent with the prohibitions contained in Section D above.
2. Members of the Commission preparing draft management plans for submission in accordance with this conservation measure should bear in mind that the primary purpose of the management plan is to provide for the protection of CEMP studies at the site through the application of the prohibitions contained in Section D. To that end, the management plan is to be drafted in concise and unambiguous terms. Information which is intended to help scientists, or others, appreciate broader considerations regarding the site (e.g. historical and bibliographic information) should not be included in the management plan but may be annexed to it.

Conservation Measure 91-02 (2012): Protection of the Values of Antarctic Specially Managed and Protected Areas (Applicable to All Species, Areas, Seasons and Gear)

The Commission,

Recognising that the protection of the Antarctic marine environment and of Antarctic marine living resources, including through Marine Protected Areas, has long been recognised as desirable and valuable within the agreements and bodies that make up the Antarctic Treaty System,

Recalling that the commitment towards the designation of spatial protection is clearly defined both within the 1991 Protocol of Environmental Protection to the Antarctic Treaty and the 1980 CAMLR Convention,

Recalling that in accordance with the Protocol, any Antarctic area, including any marine area, may be designated as an Antarctic Specially Protected Area (ASPA) or an Antarctic Specially Managed Area (ASMA),

Recognising that activities in ASPAs and ASMAs may be prohibited, restricted or managed, in accordance with management plans adopted under the provisions of Annex V of the Protocol,

Noting that the Convention (Articles V and VIII) provides for close cooperation between CCAMLR and the Antarctic Treaty,

Recalling that the competences of, and relationships between the ATCM and CCAMLR have been clarified and affirmed in the Protocol itself and subsequently by Decision 4 (1998) – *Marine Protected Areas*, and Decision 9 (2005) – *Marine Protected Areas and Other Areas of Interest to CCAMLR*, respectively,

Noting that the 2011 CCAMLR MPA Workshop noted that a harmonised approach in the Antarctic Treaty System to spatial protection may result in having ASPAs and ASMAs designated by the ATCM within CCAMLR MPAs,

Understanding that such a multi-level hierarchical approach to area management could harmonise decisions made at the ATCM and CCAMLR, allowing for detailed consideration of activities not normally considered by CCAMLR,

Concerned that potential harvesting in ASPAs and ASMAs could jeopardise the high scientific value of the long-term ecosystem studies being carried out in these areas, undermining the goals established in the management plans of these areas,

Noting that the presence of fishing vessels in ASPAs and ASMAs might have occurred due to a lack of awareness of the existence of these designated areas among those responsible for fishing vessels,

Recognising the need for more informative and timely communications between the ATCM and CCAMLR with regard to the publication and availability of management plans of ASPAs and ASMAs containing marine areas,

Recalling that the Commission has previously endorsed the harmonised approach in the Antarctic Treaty System to spatial protection,

adopts the following Conservation Measure in accordance with Article III of the Convention:

1. Each Contracting Party shall ensure that their fishing vessels licensed[116] in accordance with Conservation Measure 10-02 are aware of the location and relevant management plan of all designated ASPAs and ASMAs which include marine areas listed in Annex 91-02/A.

Annex 91-02/A: List of ASPAs and ASMAs which have Marine Components and are Located Within the Convention Area[117]

The management plans for these areas can be found on the Antarctic Protected Areas (APA) database on the Antarctic Treaty Secretariat (ATS) website.

ASPAs which are marine or partly marine:

1. ASPA 144, Chile Bay, Greenwich Island, South Shetland Islands (Subarea 48.1)
2. ASPA 145, Port Foster, Deception Island, South Shetland Islands (Subarea 48.1)
3. ASPA 146, South Bay, Doumer Island, Palmer Archipelago (Subarea 48.1)
4. ASPA 152, Western Bransfield Strait, South Shetland Islands (Subarea 48.1)
5. ASPA 153, Eastern Dallmann Bay, Palmer Archipelago (Subarea 48.1)
6. ASPA 161, Terra Nova Bay, Ross Sea (Subarea 88.1)
7. ASPA 121, Cape Royds, Ross Sea (Subarea 88.1)
8. ASPA 149, Cape Shirreff, South Shetland Islands (Subarea 48.1)
9. ASPA 151, Lions Rump, South Shetland Islands (Subarea 48.1)
10. ASPA 165, Edmonson Point, Ross Sea (Subarea 88.1).

Partly marine ASMAs:

11. ASMA 1, Admiralty Bay, South Shetland Islands (Subarea 48.1)
12. ASMA 3, Deception Island, South Shetland Islands (Subarea 48.1)
13. ASMA 7, Southwest Anvers Island, Palmer Archipelago (Subarea 48.1).

Conservation Measure 91-03 (2009) Protection of the South Orkney Islands Southern Shelf (Applicable to All Species, Area 48.2 and All Seasons)

The Commission,

Recalling its endorsement of the work program of the Scientific Committee to develop a representative network of marine protected areas, based on scientific information and with the aim of conserving marine biodiversity (CCAMLR-XXVII, paragraphs 7.2 and 7.3),

[116] Includes permitted.

[117] The present list includes only those ASPAs and ASMAs for which management plans have previously been approved by CCAMLR in accordance with ATCM Decision 9 (2005). Additional ASPAs and ASMAs with small marine components are not included in this list, as they did not require CCAMLR approval under the ATCM Decision 9 'Criteria defining areas of interest to CCAMLR'.

Noting the results of analyses undertaken by the Scientific Committee to identify areas of conservation importance within Subarea 48.2, which have identified the area to the south of the South Orkney Islands as being of high conservation importance, and representative of key environmental and ecosystem characteristics in the region,

Conscious of the need to afford additional protection to this important area in order to provide a scientific reference area, and to conserve important predator foraging areas and representative examples of pelagic and benthic bioregions,

hereby adopts the following conservation measure in accordance with Article II and Article IX of the Convention:

Protection of the South Orkney Islands southern shelf

1. The area defined in Annex 91-03/A (the 'defined area') shall be designated as a marine protected area, to contribute towards the conservation of marine biodiversity in Subarea 48.2, and managed under this conservation measure.

2. All types of fishing activities shall be prohibited within the defined area, with the exception of scientific fishing research activities agreed by the Commission for monitoring or other purposes on advice from the Scientific Committee and in accordance with Conservation Measure 24-01.

3. No discharges and no dumping of any type of waste by any fishing vessel[118] shall take place within the defined area.

4. No transhipment activities that involve any fishing vessel shall take place within the defined area.

5. For the purpose of monitoring traffic within the protected area, fishing vessels transiting the area are encouraged to inform the CCAMLR Secretariat of their intended transit prior to entering the defined area, providing details of their Flag State, size, IMO number and intended course.

6. In the case of an emergency relating to safety of life at sea, the prohibitions in this conservation measure shall not apply.

7. In accordance with Article X, the Commission shall draw this conservation measure to the attention of any State that is not a Party to the Convention, whose nationals or vessels are present in the Convention Area.

8. Details of the South Orkney Islands southern shelf marine protected area shall be communicated to the Antarctic Treaty Consultative Meeting.

9. This conservation measure will be reviewed by the Commission, based on advice from the Scientific Committee, at its regular meeting in 2014 and at subsequent five-year periods.

[Omitted: Annex 91-03/A – Map and coordinates of boundary of the South Orkney Island southern shelf marine protected area.]

Conservation Measure 91-04 (2011): General Framework for the Establishment of CCAMLR Marine Protected Areas (Applicable to All Species, Various Areas and All Seasons and Gear)

The Commission,

Recalling its endorsement of the work program of the Scientific Committee to develop a representative system of Antarctic Marine Protected Areas (MPAs) with the aim of conserving marine biodiversity in the Convention Area, and in accordance with the decision at the World Summit on Sustainable Development (WSSD) in 2002 to achieve a representative network of MPAs by 2012,

[118] For the purposes of this conservation measure 'fishing vessel' means any vessel of any size used for, equipped to be used for, or intended for use for the purposes of fishing or fishing-related activities, including support ships, fish processing vessels, vessels engaged in transhipment and carrier vessels equipped for the transportation of fishery products except container vessels and excluding Members' marine science research vessels.

Desiring to implement Article IX.2(f) and 2(g) of the CAMLR Convention where conservation measures, formulated on the basis of the best scientific evidence available, may designate the opening and closing of areas, regions or sub-regions for the purposes of scientific study or conservation, including special areas for protection and scientific study,

Noting the establishment by CCAMLR of the South Orkney Islands southern shelf MPA as a first step towards a network of MPAs in the Convention Area,

Noting the importance of MPAs in facilitating research and monitoring of Antarctic marine living resources,

Appreciating that establishment of MPAs in the Convention Area (CCAMLR MPAs) may involve exchange of information between CCAMLR and the Antarctic Treaty Consultative Meeting,

Recognising that CCAMLR MPAs aim to contribute to sustaining ecosystem structure and function, including in areas outside the MPAs, maintain the ability to adapt in the face of climate change, and reduce the potential for invasion by alien species, as a result of human activity,

Noting the importance of establishing CCAMLR MPAs in the Convention Area in accordance with Article II of the CAMLR Convention, where conservation includes rational use,

Recognising that activities and management arrangements within CCAMLR MPAs should be consistent with the objectives of those MPAs,

Noting that individual MPAs alone will not be able to achieve all of the desired objectives for MPAs in the CAMLR Convention Area, but that together they should be able to do so,

Recalling the Scientific Committee's advice that the whole Convention Area is equivalent to an IUCN Category IV MPA, but there are areas within the Convention Area that require further special consideration in a representative system of MPAs,

hereby adopts the following conservation measure in accordance with Article IX of the Convention to provide a framework for the establishment of CCAMLR MPAs:

1. This conservation measure and any other CCAMLR conservation measures relevant to CCAMLR MPAs shall be adopted and implemented consistent with international law, including as reflected in the United Nations Convention on the Law of the Sea.

2. CCAMLR MPAs shall be established on the basis of the best available scientific evidence, and shall contribute, taking full consideration of Article II of the CAMLR Convention where conservation includes rational use, to the achievement of the following objectives:

- (i) the protection of representative examples of marine ecosystems, biodiversity and habitats at an appropriate scale to maintain their viability and integrity in the long term;
- (ii) the protection of key ecosystem processes, habitats and species, including populations and life-history stages;
- (iii) the establishment of scientific reference areas for monitoring natural variability and long-term change or for monitoring the effects of harvesting and other human activities on Antarctic marine living resources and on the ecosystems of which they form part;
- (iv) the protection of areas vulnerable to impact by human activities, including unique, rare or highly biodiverse habitats and features;
- (v) the protection of features critical to the function of local ecosystems;
- (vi) the protection of areas to maintain resilience or the ability to adapt to the effects of climate change.

3. The Commission shall establish CCAMLR MPAs following advice from the Scientific Committee by adopting conservation measures in accordance with this measure. These conservation measures shall include:

- (i) the specific objectives of the MPA, consistent with paragraph 2;
- (ii) spatial boundaries of the MPA, including as needed, the geographical coordinates, boundary markers (where feasible), and natural features that delineate the area;
- (iii) activities that are restricted, prohibited, or managed in the MPA or parts thereof, and any temporal (seasonal) or spatial limits on those activities;

(iv) unless otherwise agreed by the Commission, priority elements for a management plan, including administrative arrangements, and for a research and monitoring plan, and any interim management, research and monitoring arrangements required until those plans are adopted. These requirements shall include the date when plans would need to be introduced to the Commission;

(v) the period of designation, if any, which shall be consistent with the specific objectives of the MPA.

4. The management plan for an MPA, once developed and adopted by the Commission, will be annexed to the conservation measure and will include management and administrative arrangements for achieving the specific objectives of the MPA.

5. The Commission will, on the basis of the advice of the Scientific Committee, adopt a research and monitoring plan for an MPA.

(i) This plan shall specify, to the extent necessary, the scientific research to be undertaken in the MPA, including, *inter alia*:

(a) scientific research pursuant to the specific objectives of the MPA;

(b) other research consistent with the specific objectives of the MPA; and/or

(c) monitoring of the degree to which the specific objectives of the MPA are being met.

(ii) Research activities not in the research and monitoring plan shall be managed according to Conservation Measure 24-01 unless otherwise decided by the Commission.

(iii) All Members may undertake research and monitoring activities in accordance with this plan.

(iv) The data as specified in the research and monitoring plan will be submitted to the Secretariat and made available in accordance with the Rules for Access and Use of CCAMLR Data for analyses by Members pursuant to this plan.

(v) Unless otherwise agreed by the Commission, every five years, Members conducting activities according or related to the research and monitoring plan will compile a report on those activities, including any preliminary results for review by the Scientific Committee.

6. Vessels subject to CCAMLR conservation measures designating CCAMLR MPAs shall be vessels under the jurisdiction of Parties to the Convention, which are either fishing vessels[119] or vessels conducting scientific research activities on Antarctic marine living resources in accordance with CCAMLR conservation measures.

7. Notwithstanding paragraph 6, the CCAMLR conservation measures designating MPAs shall not apply to any warship, naval auxiliary or other ship owned or operated by a State and used, for the time being, only on government non-commercial service. However, each Party shall ensure by the adoption of appropriate measures not impairing the operations or operational capabilities of such ships owned or operated by it, that such ships act in a manner consistent, so far as is reasonable and practicable, with this conservation measure.

8. Unless otherwise provided in the relevant conservation measure to take appropriate account of specific objectives for the CCAMLR MPAs, conservation measures designating CCAMLR MPAs shall be reviewed every 10 years or as agreed by the Commission when advised by the Scientific Committee, including in order to evaluate if the specific objectives of the MPAs are still relevant or being achieved and the delivery of the research and monitoring plan.

9. In order to encourage cooperation in implementing CCAMLR MPAs, the Commission shall make available information on CCAMLR conservation measures establishing MPAs in the Convention Area, including to any relevant international or regional organisation and any State that is not a Party to the Convention, whose nationals or vessels may enter the Convention Area.

[119] For the purposes of this conservation measure, 'fishing vessel' means any vessel of any size used for, equipped to be used for, or intended for use for fishing or fishing-related activities, including support ships, fish processing vessels, vessels engaged in transhipment and carrier vessels equipped for the transportation of fishery products except container vessels and excluding Members' marine science research vessels.

10. When a new CCAMLR MPA is designated, the Commission shall endeavour to identify which actions by other elements of the Antarctic Treaty System, and other organisations, such as the International Maritime Organization, should be pursued to support the specific objectives of the MPA once established.

List of Species-Specific CCMALR Measures in Force 2013–14

1. Toothfish

Category 41 – Toothfish

Conservation Measure 41-01: General measures for exploratory fisheries for Dissostichus spp. in the Convention Area in the 2013/14 season

Conservation Measure 41-02: Limits on the fishery for Dissostichus eleginoides in Statistical Subarea 48.3 in the 2013/14 and 2014/15 seasons

Conservation Measure 41-03: Limits on the fishery for Dissostichus spp. in Statistical Subarea 48.4 in the 2013/14 season

Conservation Measure 41-04: Limits on the exploratory fishery for Dissostichus spp. in Statistical Subarea 48.6 in the 2013/14 season

Conservation Measure 41-05: Limits on the exploratory fishery for Dissostichus spp. in Statistical Division 58.4.2 in the 2013/14 season

Conservation Measure 41-06: Limits on the exploratory fishery for Dissostichus spp. on Elan Bank (Statistical Division 58.4.3a) outside areas of national jurisdiction in the 2013/14 season

Conservation Measure 41-07: Limits on the exploratory fishery for Dissostichus spp. on BANZARE Bank (Statistical Division 58.4.3b) outside areas of national jurisdiction in the 2013/14 season

Conservation Measure 41-08: Limits on the fishery for Dissostichus eleginoides in Statistical Division 58.5.2 in the 2013/14 season

Conservation Measure 41-09: Limits on the exploratory fishery for Dissostichus spp. in Statistical Subarea 88.1 in the 2013/14 season

Conservation Measure 41-10: Limits on the exploratory fishery for Dissostichus spp. in Statistical Subarea 88.2 in the 2013/14 season

Conservation Measure 41-11: Limits on the exploratory fishery for Dissostichus spp. in Statistical Division 58.4.1 in the 2013/14 season

See also:

Category 10 – Compliance

Conservation Measure 10-05: Catch Documentation Scheme for Dissostichus spp.

Resolution 14/XIX: Catch Documentation Scheme: implementation by Acceding States and non-Contracting Parties

Resolution 15/XXII: Use of ports not implementing the Catch Documentation Scheme for Dissostichus spp.

Resolution 16/XIX: Application of VMS in the Catch Documentation Scheme

Resolution 17/XX: Use of VMS and other measures for the verification of CDS catch data for areas outside the Convention Area, in particular, in FAO Statistical Area 51

Resolution 18/XXI: Harvesting of Dissostichus eleginoides in areas outside of Coastal State jurisdiction adjacent to the CCAMLR Area in FAO Statistical Areas 51 and 57

Category 22 – Gear regulations

Conservation Measure 22-02: Mesh size for Dissostichus eleginoides, Gobionotothen gibberifrons, Lepidonotothen squamifrons, Notothenia rossii

Conservation Measure 22-08: Prohibition on fishing for Dissostichus spp. in depths shallower than 550 m in exploratory fisheries

Category 32 – Fishing seasons, closed areas and prohibition of fishing

Conservation Measure 32-09: Prohibition of directed fishing for Dissostichus spp. except in accordance with specific conservation measures in the 2013/14 season

2. Icefish

Category 42 – Icefish

Conservation Measure 42-01: Limits on the fishery for Champsocephalus gunnari in Statistical Subarea 48.3 in the 2013/14 season

Conservation Measure 42-02: Limits on the fishery for Champsocephalus gunnari in Statistical Division 58.5.2 in the 2013/14 season

See also:

Category 22 – Gear regulations

Conservation Measure 22-03: Mesh size for Champsocephalus gunnari

3. Krill

Category 51 – Krill

Conservation Measure 51-01: Precautionary catch limitations on Euphausia superba in Statistical Subareas 48.1, 48.2, 48.3 and 48.4

Conservation Measure 51-02: Precautionary catch limitation on Euphausia superba in Statistical Division 58.4.1

Conservation Measure 51-03: Precautionary catch limitation on Euphausia superba in Statistical Division 58.4.2

Conservation Measure 51-04: General measure for exploratory fisheries for Euphausia superba in the Convention Area in the 2013/14 season

Conservation Measure 51-06: General measure for scientific observation in fisheries for Euphausia superba

Conservation Measure 51-07: Interim distribution of the trigger level in the fishery for Euphausia superba in Statistical Subareas 48.1, 48.2, 48.3 and 48.4

See also:

Category: 10 – Compliance

Resolution 27/XXVII: Use of a specific tariff classification for Antarctic krill

Category: 11 – Notifications

Conservation Measure 21-03: Notifications of intent to participate in a fishery for Euphausia superb

Category: 23 - Data reporting

Conservation Measure 23-06: Data Reporting System for Euphausia superba Fisheries

4. Other species-specific measures

Category 22 – Gear regulations

Conservation Measure 22-02: Mesh size for Dissostichus eleginoides, Gobionotothen gibberifrons, Lepidonotothen squamifrons, Notothenia rossii

Category 32 – Fishing seasons, closed areas and prohibition of fishing

Conservation Measure 32-18: Conservation of sharks

Category 33 – By-catch limits

Conservation Measure 33-01: Limitation of the by-catch of Gobionotothen gibberifrons, Chaenocephalus acseratus, Pseudochaenichthys georgianus, Notothenia rosii and Lepidonotothen squamifrons in Statistical Subarea 48.3

PART 6
COUNCIL OF MANAGERS OF NATIONAL ANTARCTIC PROGRAMS (COMNAP)

COMNAP Constitution (adopted 4 July 2008)

Preamble

Supporting Science

What member National Antarctic Programs have in common is their national responsibility to manage the support of scientific research in the Antarctic Treaty Area.

Consistent with this, COMNAP's primary mission is to develop and promote best practice in managing the support of scientific research in the Antarctic.

Supporting the Antarctic Treaty System

COMNAP is committed to serve its role in the Antarctic Treaty System and in the protection of the Antarctic environment by providing objective and practical, technical and nonpolitical advice drawn from the National Antarctic Programs' pool of expertise.

COMNAP Origins

The Council of Managers of National Antarctic Programs (COMNAP) was formally created on 15 September 1988 to bring together the *Managers of National Antarctic Programs*, the officials responsible for carrying out national activity in the Antarctic on behalf of their governments all Parties to the Antarctic Treaty.

Until then, Managers of National Antarctic Programs only met informally on the margins of other meetings that they attended: meetings of the Scientific Committee on Antarctic Research (SCAR – a nongovernmental organisation), and Antarctic Treaty Consultative Meetings (ATCMs).

Some of their staff members were members of the SCAR Working Group on Logistics, which was then transformed into the Standing Committee on Antarctic Logistics and Operations (SCALOP), a group that had a special status as it was under the authority of both COMNAP and SCAR.

COMNAP maintains a special, complementary relationship with SCAR. The Executives of both organisations meet annually and both organisations attempt to coordinate their biannual meetings so as to facilitate crossparticipation in both meetings.

COMNAP immediately started contributing positively to the Antarctic Treaty System and was very quickly formally recognised as a valuable member of the Treaty System. It was invited to provide a report to the ATCM as early as 1991 (XVI ATCM, Bonn, Germany, 07–18 Oct 1991). XVI ATCM *recognised the important role of COMNAP in examining and solving practical problems relating to the implementation of scientific activities and their associated logistics* (refer XVI ATCM final report, paragraph 23). Since then, COMNAP has had the status of observer at ATCMs.

COMNAP Constitution

1 General

1.1 Each signatory to the Antarctic Treaty normally establishes a "National Antarctic Program". The National Antarctic Program is defined as the entity with national responsibility for managing the support of scientific research in the Antarctic Treaty Area on behalf of its government and in the spirit of the Antarctic Treaty.

1.2 Those National Antarctic Programs can choose to become a member of the Council of Managers of National Antarctic Programs, hereafter referred to as COMNAP.

1.3 Ultimate decision power on COMNAP matters rests with the assembly of the "Managers of National Antarctic Programs" (MNAPs) which meets in an Annual General Meeting (AGM) at a location agreed at a previous AGM. Each member National Antarctic Program has one vote at the AGM.

1.4 Decision making at COMNAP generally follows the principle of consensus, in its meaning of an opinion or position reached by a group as a whole. It is not intended as a defacto right of veto given to every member.

1.5 MNAPs elect one COMNAP Chair and one or more COMNAP ViceChairs as specified in the Rules of Procedure.

1.6 A COMNAP Executive Committee (EXCOM) is constituted by the Chair and ViceChair(s), and any other persons as specified in the COMNAP Rules of Procedure. EXCOM members shall all be representatives from different member National Antarctic Programs, reflecting COMNAP's diversity and range of expertise.

1.7 The COMNAP Chair, with the support and advice of EXCOM, chairs the AGM and takes responsibility for COMNAP matters between AGMs.

1.8 COMNAP functions under the general principles of a notfor-profit organisation and, for all intents and purposes, subjects itself to normal international principles and standards for organisations like COMNAP.

1.9 COMNAP is domiciled at its Secretariat.

2 Purpose

The purpose of COMNAP is to develop and promote best practice in managing the support of scientific research in Antarctica, by

- Serving as a forum to develop practices that improve effectiveness of activities in an environmentally responsible manner;
- Facilitating and promoting international partnerships;
- Providing opportunities and systems for information exchange; and
- Providing the Antarctic Treaty System with objective and practical, technical and non-political advice drawn from the National Antarctic Programs' pool of expertise.

3 Membership

3.1 Membership of COMNAP is open to National Antarctic Programs, as defined in paragraph 1.1, not to individuals.

3.2 Membership of COMNAP is open to National Antarctic Programs from nations whose governments are signatories to the Antarctic Treaty and have ratified its Protocol on Environmental Protection. There can be only one member National Antarctic Program per nation.

3.3 Members must comply with this constitution and the Rules of Procedure.

3.4 While structures can differ widely from country to country, what characterises and unifies member National Antarctic Programs is their national responsibility to manage the support of scientific research in the Antarctic Treaty Area.

3.5 Each member National Antarctic Program is represented on COMNAP by a lead national agency.

3.6 Whenever this lead agency has a broader mission, only those parts of the organisation that have this national responsibility are considered part of the "National Antarctic Program" member of COMNAP.

3.7 Whenever this national responsibility is divided between several national organisations, the lead agency will, as appropriate, organise for relevant parts of the other national organisations to participate in the work of COMNAP under its authority and responsibility.

4 Secretariat

4.1 A COMNAP Secretariat serves and supports the functional needs of COMNAP and is accountable to the COMNAP Chair.

4.2 The COMNAP Secretariat is subject to the laws and regulations of the country it is domiciled in.

5 COMNAP Finances

5.1 The income of COMNAP is obtained from the following:

- an equal annual contribution ("membership fee") from each of its member National Antarctic Programs, as determined by the MNAPs at an AGM;
- any additional, voluntary contributions from member National Antarctic Programs;
- any grants from external bodies, as and if agreed by the MNAPs at an AGM.

5.2 COMNAP funds are intended to support the internal work of COMNAP to support its activities and purpose. The level of the annual contribution should be kept under regular review to ensure it best meets the needs of COMNAP and provides best value to members.

5.3 The COMNAP budget is approved by the MNAPs at each AGM.

6 Representation of COMNAP

6.1 The COMNAP Chair is the official representative of COMNAP. If unavailable one of the ViceChairs or another representative agreed by EXCOM will represent COMNAP.

7 Preamble and Rules of Procedure

7.1 A Preamble and Rules of Procedure complement this constitution but are not part of it.

Both are subject to the rules, principles and intent of this constitution, and can be separately amended by the MNAPS at an AGM as and when required. Any new version takes effect at the time it is approved and supersedes any previous version.

8 Modification of this COMNAP Constitution

8.1 This COMNAP Constitution may be modified by agreement of the MNAPs at an AGM.

COMNAP, Main Antarctic Facilities Operated by National Antarctic Programs in the Antarctic Treaty Area (South of 60° Latitude South), updated 15 May 2013

Facility	State	Latitude	Longitude	Opened	Status[1*]	Peak / (Winter) Population
Belgrano II	Argentina	77° 52.467' S	34° 37.617' W	1955	Y	12 (12)
Brown	Argentina	64° 53.722' S	62° 52.227' W	1951	S	18 (0)
Cámara	Argentina	62° 35.631' S	59° 55.161' W	1953	S	36 (0)
Decepcíon	Argentina	62° 58.606' S	60° 42.042' W	1948	S	65 (0)
Esperanza	Argentina	63° 23.818' S	56° 59.883' W	1952	Y	90 (55)
Carlini (Jubany)	Argentina	62° 14.274' S	58° 40.011' W	1982	Y	100 (20)
Marambio	Argentina	64° 14.506' S	56° 37.393' W	1969	Y	150 (55)
Matienzo	Argentina	64° 58.552' S	60° 4.257' W	1961	S	15 (0)
Melchior	Argentina	64° 19.542' S	62° 58.580' W	1947	S	36 (0)
Orcadas	Argentina	60° 44.256' S	44° 44.243' W	1904	Y	45 (14)
Petrel	Argentina	63° 28.698' S	56° 13.860' W	1967	S	55 (0)
Primavera	Argentina	64° 9.351' S	60° 57.255' W	1977	S	18 (0)
San Martín	Argentina	68° 7.818' S	67° 6.176' W	1951	Y	20 (20)
Edgeworth David	Australia	66° 14.996' S	100° 36.253' E		S	
Wilkins Aerodrome	Australia	66° 41.380' S	111° 29.074' E		S	
Casey	Australia	66° 16.941' S	110° 31.608' E	1969	Y	70 (20)
Davis	Australia	68° 34.556' S	77° 58.171' E	1957	Y	70 (22)
Mawson	Australia	67° 36.159' S	62° 52.382' E	1954	Y	60 (20)

[1] Y = open year-round; S = open seasonally

Beaver Lake	Australia	70°48.18'S	68°10.79'E			
Law - Racovita - Negoita	Australia & Romania	69° 23.298' S	76° 22.842' E	1987	S	13 (0)
Princess Elisabeth	Belgium	71° 56.991' S	23° 20.813' E	2009	S	20 (0)
Comandante Ferraz	Brazil	62° 5.077' S	58° 23.554' W	1984	Y	40 (12)
Ohridski	Bulgaria	62° 38.443' S	60° 21.914' W	1988	S	18 (0)
Lieutenant Arturo Parodi	Chile	80° 18.716' S	81° 21.994' W	1999	S	25 (0)
Lieutenant Rodolfo Marsh M. Aerodrome	Chile	62° 11.624' S	58° 58.798' W	1969	Y	15 (8)
Arturo Prat	Chile	62° 28.760' S	59° 39.811' W	1947	Y	15 (9)
Lieutenant Luis Carvajal Villarroel	Chile	67° 45.679' S	68° 54.889' W	1985	S	30 (0)
Julio Escudero	Chile	62° 12.082' S	58° 57.761' W	1994	Y	26 (2)
Eduardo Frei Montalva	Chile	62° 12.014' S	58° 57.758' W	1969	Y	120 (70)
Bernardo O'Higgins Riquelme	Chile	63° 19.257' S	57° 53.987' W	1948	Y	44 (16)
Ripamonti	Chile	62° 12.609' S	58° 56.084' W		S	
Risopatrón	Chile	62° 22.712' S	59° 42.043' W	1957	S	8 (0)
President Gabriel Gonzalez Videla	Chile	64° 49.432' S	62° 51.450' W	1951	S	9 (0)
Guillermo Mann	Chile	62° 28.001' S	60° 46.001' W	1991	S	6 (0)
Sub Base Yelcho	Chile	64° 52.551' S	63° 35.028' W	1962	S	
Great Wall	China	62° 13.051' S	58° 57.720' W	1985	Y	40 (14)
Kunlun	China	80° 25.031' S	77° 6.960' E	2009	S	20 (0)
Zhongshan	China	69° 22.392' S	76° 22.312' E	1989	Y	30 (15)
Johann Gregor Mendel	Czech Republic	63° 48.038' S	57° 52.956' W	2006	S	20 (0)
Refugio Ecuador	Ecuador	62° 7.259' S	58° 23.710' W	1990	S	4 (0)
Maldonado	Ecuador	62° 26.960' S	59° 44.458' W	1990	S	22 (0)
Aboa	Finland	73° 2.537' S	13° 24.441' W	1989	S	20 (0)
Cap Prud'homme	France	66° 41.256' S	139° 54.430' E		S	20 (0)
Dumont d'Urville	France	66° 39.770' S	140° 0.080' E	1956	Y	100 (26)
Concordia	France & Italy	75° 5.998' S	123° 19.956' E	1997	Y	60 (13)
Dallman Lab at Base Carlini	Germany	62° 14.257' S	58° 40.003' W	1994	S	12 (0)
Antarctic Receiving Station (GARS)	Germany	63° 19.266' S	57° 54.056' W		S	
Gondwana	Germany	74° 38.130' S	164° 13.273' E	1983	S	
Kohnen	Germany	75° 0.115' S	0° 4.004' E	2001	S	28 (0)
Neumayer III	Germany	70° 40.635' S	8° 16.296' W	1981	Y	50 (9)
Bharati	India	69° 24.000' S	76° 11.000' E	2012	Y	(15)
Dakshin Gangotri	India	70° 5.000' S	12° 0.000' E	1983	S	

Maitri	India	70° 46.010' S	11° 43.847' E	1989	Y	65 (25)
Browning Pass	Italy	74° 37.374' S	163° 54.910' E	1997	S	2 (0)
Enigma Lake	Italy	74° 43.150' S	164° 1.663' E	2005	S	
Mid Point	Italy	75° 32.502' S	145° 49.224' E	1998	S	
Sitry	Italy	71° 39.104' S	148° 39.284' E	2000	S	
Mario Zucchelli	Italy	74° 41.688' S	164° 6.796' E	1986	S	90 (0)
S17	Japan	69° 1.685' S	40° 5.547' E	2005	S	
Asuka	Japan	71° 31.576' S	24° 6.751' E	1984	S	
Dome Fuji	Japan	77° 19.025' S	39° 41.926' E	1995	S	15 (0)
Mizuho	Japan	70° 41.943' S	44° 16.669' E	1970	S	
Syowa	Japan	69° 0.247' S	39° 34.910' E	1957	Y	110 (28)
King Sejong	Korea	62° 13.394' S	58° 47.190' W	1988	Y	70 (18)
Dirck Gerritsz Laboratory	Netherlands & UK	67° 34.118' S	68° 7.463' W	2012	Seaonal	
Scott Base	NZ	77° 50.966' S	166° 46.037' E	1957	Y	85 (10)
Tor	Norway	71° 53.371' S	5° 9.594' E	1985	S	4 (0)
Troll	Norway	72° 0.717' S	2° 31.984' E	1990	Y	40 (7)
Machu Picchu	Peru	62° 5.496' S	58° 28.234' W	1989	S	28 (0)
Arctowski	Poland	62° 9.586' S	58° 28.399' W	1977	Y	40 (12)
Molodezhnaya Airfield	Russia	67° 40.184' S	45° 49.717' E		S	
Novolazarevskaya Airfield	Russia	70° 49.308' S	11° 38.392' E		S	
Bellingshausen	Russia	62° 11.891' S	58° 57.637' W	1968	Y	38 (25)
Druzhnaya-4	Russia	69° 44.870' S	73° 42.553' E	1987	S	50 (0)
Leningradskaya	Russia	69° 30.090' S	159° 23.469' E	1971	S	
Mirny	Russia	66° 33.494' S	93° 0.023' E	1956	Y	169 (60)
Molodezhnaya	Russia	67° 39.927' S	45° 50.522' E	1962	S	
Novolazarevskaya	Russia	70° 46.616' S	11° 49.420' E	1961	Y	70 (30)
Progress	Russia	69° 22.687' S	76° 23.268' E	1989	Y	77 (20)
Russkaya	Russia	74° 45.944' S	136° 48.004' W	1980	S	
Soyuz	Russia	70° 34.595' S	68° 47.696' E	1982	S	
Vostok	Russia	78° 27.850' S	106° 50.278' E	1957	Y	25 (13)
SANAE IV	South Africa	71° 40.372' S	2° 50.419' W	1962	Y	80 (10)
Gabriel de Castilla	Spain	62° 58.632' S	60° 40.545' W	1990	S	25 (0)
Juan Carlos I	Spain	62° 39.805' S	60° 23.289' W	1989	S	25 (0)
Svea	Sweden	74° 34.564' S	11° 13.492' W		S	
Wasa	Sweden	73° 2.568' S	13° 24.775' W	1989	S	20 (0)
Vernadsky	Ukraine	65° 14.745' S	64° 15.449' W	1996	Y	24 (12)
Fossil Bluff	UK	71° 19.405' S	68° 17.344' W	1961	S	6 (0)
Rothera Skiway	UK	67° 34.055' S	68° 7.631' W	1975	S	
Sky Blu	UK	74° 51.381' S	71° 35.112' W		S	6 (0)
Halley	UK	75° 34.789' S	26° 43.717' W	1956	Y	65 (15)

Rothera	UK	67° 34.118' S	68° 7.463' W	1975	Y	130 (22)
Signy	UK	60° 42.497' S	45° 35.723' W	1947	S	10 (0)
Artigas	Uruguay	62° 11.073' S	58° 54.147' W	1984	Y	60 (9)
Ruperto Elichiribehety	Uruguay	63° 24.142' S	56° 59.454' W	1997	S	
Marble Point Heliport	USA	77° 24.820' S	163° 40.750' E		S	
Odell Glacier Camp	USA	76° 39.607' S	159° 57.189' E		S	
Siple Dome	USA	81° 39.258' S	149° 0.308' W		S	
Amundsen-Scott South Pole Station	USA	89° 59.850' S	139° 16.370' E	1956	Y	250 (75)
McMurdo Station	USA	77° 50.893' S	166° 40.105' E	1955	Y	1000 (250)
Palmer Station	USA	64° 46.456' S	64° 3.200' W	1965	Y	43 (12)

Australian Antarctic Data Centre, Map of Stations in Antarctica (September 2009)

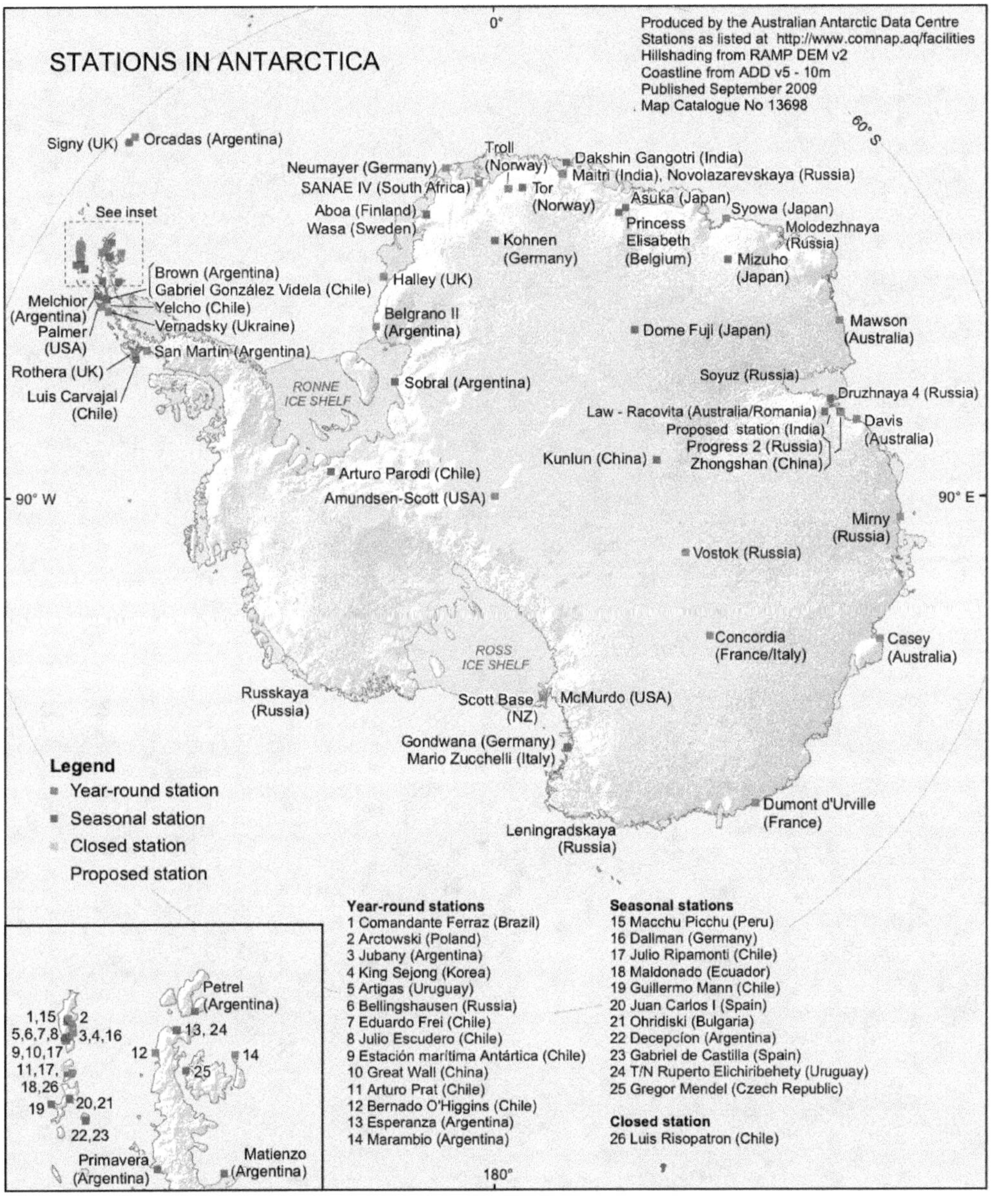

PART 7
OTHER INTERNATIONAL INSTRUMENTS RELEVANT TO ANTARCTICA

TREATIES

International Convention for the Regulation of Whaling and Schedule (Containing the Southern Ocean Whale Sanctuary)[1]

The Governments whose duly authorized representatives have subscribed hereto,

Recognizing the interest of the nations of the world in safeguarding for future generations the great natural resources represented by the whale stocks;

Considering that the history of whaling has seen overfishing of one area after another and of one species of whale after another to such a degree that it is essential to protect all species of whales from further overfishing;

Recognizing that the whale stocks are susceptible of natural increases if whaling is properly regulated, and that increases in the size of whale stocks will permit increases in the numbers of whales which may be captured without endangering these natural resources;

Recognizing that it is in the common interest to achieve the optimum level of whale stocks as rapidly as possible without causing wide-spread economic and nutritional distress;

Recognizing that in the course of achieving these objectives, whaling operations should be confined to those species best able to sustain exploitation in order to give an interval for recovery to certain species of whales now depleted in numbers;

Desiring to establish a system of international regulation for the whale fisheries to ensure proper and effective conservation and development of whale stocks on the basis of the principles embodied in the provisions of the International Agreement for the Regulation of Whaling signed in London on June 8, 1937[2] and the protocols to that Agreement signed in London on June 24, 1938[3] and November 26, 1945;[4] and

Having decided to conclude a convention to provide for the proper conservation of whale stocks and thus make possible the orderly development of the whaling industry;

Have agreed as follows:

Article I

1. This Convention includes the Schedule attached thereto which forms an integral part thereof. All references to "Convention" shall be understood as including the said Schedule either in its present terms or as amended in accordance with the provisions of Article V.

2. This Convention applies to factory ships, land stations, and whale catchers under the jurisdiction of the Contracting Governments, and to all waters in which whaling is prosecuted by such factory ships, land stations, and whale catchers.

Article II

As used in this Convention

1. "factory ship" means a ship in which or on which whales are treated whether wholly or in part;

2. "land station" means a factory on the land at which whales are treated whether wholly or in part;

[1] Adopted 2 December 1946, entered into force 10 November 1948, 161 UNTS 72.

[2] League of Nations, *Treaty Series*, Vol. CXC, p. 79; United Nations, *Treaty Series*, Vol. 32, p. 404, and Vol. 91, p. 388.

[3] League of Nations, *Treaty Series*, Vol. CXCVI, p. 131; United Nations, *Treaty Series*, Vol. 32, p. 405, and Vol. 92, p. 435.

[4] United Nations, *Treaty Series*, Vol. 11, p. 43, and Vol. 32, p. 396.

3. "whale catcher" means a ship used for the purpose of hunting, taking, towing, holding on to, or scouting for whales;

4. "Contracting Government" means any Government which has deposited an instrument of ratification or has given notice of adherence to this Convention.

Article III

1. The Contracting Governments agree to establish an International Whaling Commission, hereinafter referred to as the Commission, to be composed of one member from each Contracting Government. Each member shall have one vote and may be accompanied by one or more experts and advisers.

2. The Commission shall elect from its own members a Chairman and Vice Chairman and shall determine its own Rules of Procedure. Decisions of the Commission shall be taken by a simple majority of those members voting except that a three-fourths majority of those members voting shall be required for action in pursuance of Article V. The Rules of Procedure may provide for decisions otherwise than at meetings of the Commission.

3. The Commission may appoint its own Secretary and staff.

4. The Commission may set up, from among its own members and experts or advisers, such committees as it considers desirable to perform such functions as it may authorize.

5. The expenses of each member of the Commission and of his experts and advisers shall be determined and paid by his own Government.

6. Recognizing that specialized agencies related to the United Nations will be concerned with the conservation and development of whale fisheries and the products arising therefrom and desiring to avoid duplication of functions, the Contracting Governments will consult among themselves within two years after the coming into force of this Convention to decide whether the Commission shall be brought within the framework of a specialized agency related to the United Nations.

7. In the meantime the Government of the United Kingdom of Great Britain and Northern Ireland shall arrange, in consultation with the other Contracting Governments, to convene the first meeting of the Commission, and shall initiate the consultation referred to in paragraph 6 above.

8. Subsequent meetings of the Commission shall be convened as the Commission may determine.

Article IV

1. The Commission may either in collaboration with or through independent agencies of the Contracting Governments or other public or private agencies, establishments, or organizations, or independently

(a) encourage, recommend, or if necessary, organize studies and investigations relating to whales and whaling;

(b) collect and analyze statistical information concerning the current condition and trend of the whale stocks and the effects of whaling activities thereon;

(c) study, appraise, and disseminate information concerning methods of maintaining and increasing the populations of whale stocks.

2. The Commission shall arrange for the publication of reports of its activities, and it may publish independently or in collaboration with the International Bureau for Whaling Statistics at Sandefjord in Norway and other organizations and agencies such reports as it deems appropriate, as well as statistical, scientific, and other pertinent information relating to whales and whaling.

Article V

1. The Commission may amend from time to time the provisions of the Schedule by adopting regulations with respect to the conservation and utilization of whale resources, fixing (a) protected and unprotected species; (b) open and closed seasons; (c) open and closed

waters, including the designation of sanctuary areas; (d) size limits for each species; (e) time, methods, and intensity of whaling (including the maximum catch of whales to be taken in anyone season); (f) types and specifications of gear and apparatus and appliances which may be used; (g) methods of measurement; and (h) catch returns and other statistical and biological records.

2. These amendments of the Schedule (a) shall be such as are necessary to carry out the objectives and purposes of this Convention and to provide for the conservation, development, and optimum utilization of the whale resources; (b) shall be based on scientific findings; (c) shall not involve restrictions on the number or nationality of factory ships or land stations, nor allocate specific quotas to any factory ship or land station or to any group of factory ships or land stations; and (d) shall take into consideration the interests of the consumers of whale products and the whaling industry.

3. Each of such amendments shall become effective with respect to the Contracting Governments ninety days following notification of the amendment by the Commission to each of the Contracting Governments, except that (a) if any Government presents to the Commission objection to any amendment prior to the expiration of this ninety-day period, the amendment shall not become effective with respect to any of the Governments for an additional ninety days; (b) thereupon, any other Contracting Government may present objection to the amendment at any time prior to the expiration of the additional ninety-day period, or before the expiration of thirty days from the date of receipt of the last objection received during such additional ninety-day period, whichever date shall be the later; and (c) thereafter, the amendment shall become effective with respect to all Contracting Governments which have not presented objection but shall not become effective with respect to any Government which has so objected until such date as the objection is withdrawn. The Commission shall notify each Contracting Government immediately upon receipt of each objection and withdrawal and each Contracting Government shall acknowledge receipt of all notifications of amendments, objections, and withdrawals.

4. No amendments shall become effective before July 1, 1949.

Article VI

The Commission may from time to time make recommendations to any or all Contracting Governments on any matters which relate to whales or whaling and to the objectives and purposes of this Convention.

Article VII

The Contracting Governments shall ensure prompt transmission to the International Bureau for Whaling Statistics at Sandefjord in Norway, or to such other body as the Commission may designate, of notifications and statistical and other information required by this Convention in such form and manner as may be prescribed by the Commission.

Article VIII

1. Notwithstanding anything contained in this Convention, any Contracting Government may grant to any of its nationals a special permit authorizing that national to kill, take, and treat whales for purposes of scientific research subject to such restrictions as to number and subject to such other conditions as the Contracting Government thinks fit, and the killing, taking, and treating of whales in accordance with the provisions of this Article shall be exempt from the operation of this Convention. Each Contracting Government shall report at once to the Commission all such authorizations which it has granted. Each Contracting Government may at any time revoke any such special permit which it has granted.

2. Any whales taken under these special permits shall so far as practicable be processed and the proceeds shall be dealt with in accordance with directions issued by the Government by which the permit was granted.

3. Each Contracting Government shall transmit to such body as may be designated by the Commission, in so far as practicable, and at intervals of not more than one year, scientific

information available to that Government with respect to whales and whaling, including the results of research conducted pursuant to paragraph 1 of this Article and to Article IV.

4. Recognizing that continuous collection and analysis of biological data in connection with the operations of factory ships and land stations are indispensable to sound and constructive management of the whale fisheries, the Contracting Governments will take all practicable measures to obtain such data.

Article IX

1. Each Contracting Government shall take appropriate measures to ensure the application of the provisions of this Convention and the punishment of infractions against the said provisions in operations carried out by persons or by vessels under its jurisdiction.

2. No bonus or other remuneration calculated with relation to the results of their work shall be paid to the gunners and crews of whale catchers in respect of any whales the taking of which is forbidden by this Convention.

3. Prosecution for infractions against or contraventions of this Convention shall be instituted by the Government having jurisdiction over the offense.

4. Each Contracting Government shall transmit to the Commission full details of each infraction of the provisions of this Convention by persons or vessels under the jurisdiction of that Government as reported by its inspectors. This information shall include a statement of measures taken for dealing with the infraction and of penalties imposed.

Article X

1. This Convention shall be ratified and the instruments of ratification shall be deposited with the Government of the United States of America.

2. Any Government which has not signed this Convention may adhere thereto after it enters into force by a notification in writing to the Government of the United States of America.

3. The Government of the United States of America shall inform all other signatory Governments and all adhering Governments of all ratifications deposited and adherences received.

4. This Convention shall, when instruments of ratification have been deposited by at least six signatory Governments, which shall include the Governments of the Netherlands, Norway, the Union of Soviet Socialist Republics, the United Kingdom of Great Britain and Northern Ireland, and the United States of America, enter into force with respect to those Governments and shall enter into force with respect to each Government which subsequently ratifies or adheres on the date of the deposit of its instrument of ratification or the receipt of its notification of adherence.

5. The provisions of the Schedule shall not apply prior to July 1, 1948. Amendments to the Schedule adopted pursuant to Article V shall not apply prior to July 1, 1949.

Article XI

Any Contracting Government may withdraw from this Convention on June thirtieth of any year by giving notice on or before January first of the same year to the depositary Government, which upon receipt of such a notice shall at once communicate it to the other Contracting Governments. Any other Contracting Government may, in like manner, within one month of the receipt of a copy of such a notice from the depositary Government, give notice of withdrawal, so that the Convention shall cease to be in force on June thirtieth of the same year with respect to the Government giving such notice of withdrawal.

This Convention shall bear the date on which it is opened for signature and shall remain open for signature for a period of fourteen days thereafter.

In witness whereof the undersigned, being duly authorized, have signed this Convention.

Done in Washington this second day of December 1946, in the English language, the original of which shall be deposited in the archives of the Government of the United States of America. The Government of the United States of America shall transmit certified copies thereof to all the other signatory and adhering Governments.

[Signatories omitted]

Schedule

1.

(a) There shall be maintained on each factory ship at least two inspectors of whaling for the purpose of maintaining twenty-four hour inspection. These inspectors shall be appointed and paid by the Government having jurisdiction over the factory ship.

(b) Adequate inspection shall be maintained at each land station. The inspectors serving at each land station shall be appointed and paid by the Government having jurisdiction over the land station.

2. It is forbidden to take or kill gray whales or right whales, except when the meat and products of such whales are to be used exclusively for local consumption by the aborigines.

3. It is forbidden to take or kill calves or suckling whales or female whales which are accompanied by calves or suckling whales.

4. It is forbidden to use a factory ship or a whale catcher attached thereto for the purpose of taking or treating baleen whales in any of the following areas:

(a) in the waters north of 66° North Latitude except that from 150° East Longitude eastward as far as 140° West Longitude the taking or killing of baleen whales by a factory ship or whale catcher shall be permitted between 66° North Latitude and 72° North Latitude;

(b) in the Atlantic Ocean and its dependent waters north of 40° South Latitude;

(c) in the Pacific Ocean and its dependent waters east of 150° West Longitude between 40° South Latitude and 35° North Latitude;

(d) in the Pacific Ocean and its dependent waters west of 150° West Longitude between 40° South Latitude and 20° North Latitude;

(e) in the Indian Ocean and its dependent waters north of 40° South Latitude.

5. It is forbidden to use a factory ship or a whale catcher attached thereto for the purpose of taking or treating baleen whales in the waters south of 40° South Latitude from 70° West Longitude westward as far as 160° West Longitude.

6. It is forbidden to use a factory ship or a whale catcher attached thereto for the purpose of taking or treating humpback whales in any waters south of 40° South Latitude.

7.

(a) It is forbidden to use a factory ship or a whale catcher attached thereto for the purpose of taking or treating baleen whales in any waters south of 40° South Latitude, except during the period from December 15 to April 1 following, both days inclusive.

(b) Notwithstanding the above prohibition of treatment during a closed season, the treatment of whales which have been taken during the open season may be completed after the end of the open season.

8.

(a) The number of baleen whales taken during the open season caught in any waters south of 40° South Latitude by whale catchers attached to factory ships under the jurisdiction of the Contracting Governments shall not exceed sixteen thousand blue-whale units.

(b) For the purposes of subparagraph (a) of this paragraph, blue-whale units shall be calculated on the basis that one blue whale equals:

(1) two fin whales or

(2) two and a half humpback whales or

(3) six sei whales.

(c) Notification shall be given in accordance with the provisions of Article VII of the Convention, within two days after the end of each calendar week, of data on the number of blue-whale units taken in any waters south of 40° South Latitude by all whale catchers attached to factory ships under the jurisdiction of each Contracting Government.

(d) If it should appear that the maximum catch of whales permitted by subparagraph (a) of this paragraph may be reached before April 1 of any year, the Commission, or such other body as the Commission may designate, shall determine, on the basis of the data provided, the date on which the maximum catch of whales shall be deemed to have been reached and shall notify each Contracting Government of that date not less than two weeks in advance thereof. The taking of baleen whales by whale catchers attached to factory ships shall be illegal in any waters south of 40° South Latitude after the date so determined.

(e) Notification shall be given in accordance with the provisions of Article VII of the Convention of each factory ship intending to engage in whaling operations in any waters south of 40° South Latitude.

9. It is forbidden to take or kill any blue, fin, sei, humpback, or sperm whales below the following lengths:

(a) blue whales....................................70 feet (21.3 meters)
(b) fin whales.......................................55 feet (16.8 meters)
(c) sei whales.......................................40 feet (12.2 meters)
(d) humpback whales.............................35 feet (10.7 meters)
(e) sperm whales..................................35 feet (10.7 meters)

except that blue whales of not less than 65 feet (19.8 meters), fin whales of not less than 50 feet (15.2 meters), and sei whales of not less than 35 feet (10.7 meters) in length may be taken for delivery to land stations provided that the meat of such whales is to be used for local consumption as human or animal food.

Whales must be measured when at rest on deck or platform, as accurately as possible by means of a steel tape measure fitted at the zero end with a spiked handle which can be stuck into the deck planking abreast of one end of the whale. The tape measure shall be stretched in a straight line parallel with the whale's body and read abreast the other end of the whale. The ends of the whale, for measurement purposes, shall be the point of the upper jaw and the notch between the tail flukes. Measurements, after being accurately read on the tape measure, shall be logged to the nearest foot: that is to say, any whale between 75'6" and 76'6" shall be logged as 76', and any whale between 76'6" and 77'6" shall be logged as 77'. The measurement of any whale which falls on an exact half foot shall be logged at the next half foot, e.g. 76'6" precisely, shall be logged as 77'.

10. It is forbidden to use a land station or a whale catcher attached thereto for the purpose of taking or treating baleen whales in any area or in any waters for more than six months in any period of twelve months, such period of six months to be continuous.

11. It is forbidden to use a factory ship, which has been used during a season in any waters south of 40° South Latitude for the purpose of treating baleen whales, in any other area for the same purpose within a period of one year from the termination of that season.

12.

(a) All whales taken shall be delivered to the factory ship or land station and all parts of such whales shall be processed by boiling or otherwise, except the internal organs, whale bone and flippers of all whales, the meat of sperm whales and of parts of whales intended for human food or feeding animals.

(b) Complete treatment of the carcasses of "Dauhval" and of whales used as fenders will not be required in cases where the meat or bone of such whales is in bad condition.

13. The taking of whales for delivery to a factory ship shall be so regulated or restricted by the master or person in charge of the factory ship that no whale carcass (except of a whale used as a fender) shall remain in the sea for a longer period than thirty-three hours from the time of killing to the time when it is taken up on to the deck of the factory ship for treatment. All whale catchers engaged in taking whales must report by radio to the factory ship the time when each whale is caught.

14. Gunners and crews of factory ships, land stations, and whale catchers shall be engaged on such terms that their remuneration shall depend to a considerable extent upon such factors

as the species, size, and yield of whales taken, and not merely upon the number of the whales taken. No bonus or other remuneration shall be paid to the gunners or crews of whale catchers in respect of the taking of milk-filled or lactating whales.

15. Copies of all official laws and regulations relating to whales and whaling and changes in such laws and regulations shall be transmitted to the Commission.

16. Notification shall be given in accordance with the provisions of Article VII of the Convention with regard to all factory ships and land stations of statistical information (a) concerning the number of whales of each species taken, the number thereof lost, and the number treated at each factory ship or land station, and (b) as to the aggregate amounts of oil of each grade and quantities of meal, fertilizer (guano), and other products derived from them, together with (c) particulars with respect to each whale treated in the factory ship or land station as to the date and approximate latitude and longitude of taking, the species and sex of the whale, its length and, if it contains a fœtus, the length and sex, if ascertainable, of the fœtus.

The data referred to in (a) and (c) above shall be verified at the time of the tally and there shall also be notification to the Commission of any information which may be collected or obtained concerning the calving grounds and migration routes of whales.

In communicating this information there shall be specified:

(a) the name and gross tonnage of each factory ship;

(b) the number and aggregate gross tonnage of the whale catchers;

(c) a list of the land stations which were in operation during the period concerned.

17. Notwithstanding the definition of land station contained in Article II of the Convention, a factory ship operating under the jurisdiction of a Contracting Government, and the movements of which are confined solely to the territorial waters of that Government, shall be subject to the regulations governing the operation of land stations within the following areas:

(a) on the coast of Madagascar and its dependencies, and on the west coasts of French Africa;

(b) on the west coast of Australia in the area known as Shark Bay and northward to Northwest Cape and including Exmouth Gulf and King George's Sound, including the port of Albany; and on the east coast of Australia, in Twofold Bay and Jervis Bay.

18. The following expressions have the meanings respectively assigned to them, that is to say:

"baleen whale" means any whale other than a toothed whale;

"blue whale" means any whale known by the name of blue whale, Sibbald's rorqual, or sulphur bottom;

"fin whale" means any whale known by the name of common finback, common rorqual, finback, finner, fin whale, herring whale, razorback, or true fin whale;

"sei whale" means any whale known by the name of *Balaenoptera borealis*, sei whale, Rudolphi's rorqual, pollack whale, or coalfish whale, and shall be taken to include *Balaenoptera brydei*, Bryde's whale;

"gray whale" means any whale known by the name of gray whale, California gray, devil fish, hard head, mussel digger, gray back, rip sack;

"humpback whale" means any whale known by the name of bunch, humpback, humpback whale, hunchbacked whale, hump whale, or hunchbacked whale;

"right whale" means any whale known by the name of Atlantic right whale, Arctic right whale, Biscayan right whale, bowhead, great polar whale, Greenland right whale, Greenland whale, Nordkaper, North Atlantic right whale, North Cape whale, Pacific right whale, pigmy right whale, Southern pigmy right whale, or Southern right whale;

"sperm whale" means any whale known by the name of sperm whale, spermacet whale, cachalot, or pot whale;

"Dauhval" means any unclaimed dead whale found floating.

Torremolinos Protocol of 1993 relating to the Torremolinos International Convention for the Safety of Fishing Vessels 1977, Annex, Chapter III (Stability and Associated Seaworthiness), Regulation 8: Ice Accretion[5]

1. For vessels operating in areas where ice accretion is likely to occur the following icing allowance shall be made in the stability calculations:

(a) 30 kilogrammes per square metre on exposed weather decks and gangway;

(b) 7.5 kilogrammes per square metre for projected lateral area of each side of the vessel above the water plane;

(c) the projected lateral area of discontinuous surfaces of rail, spars (except masts) and rigging of vessels having no sails and the projected lateral area of other small objects shall be computed by increasing the total projected area of continuous surfaces by 5 per cent and the static moments of this area by 10 per cent.

2. Vessels intended for operation in areas where ice accretion is known to occur shall be:

(a) designed to minimize the accretion of ice; and

(b) equipped with such means for removing ice as the Administration may require.

Recommendation 2 of the Torremolinos Conference 1993: Guidance Relating to Ice Accretion (Regulation III/8)

In the application of regulation III/8 the following icing areas should apply:

1.

(a) The area north of latitude 65°30 - N, between longitude 28° W and the west coast of Iceland; north of the north coast of Iceland; north of the rhumb line running from latitude 66° N, longitude 15° W to latitude 73°30 - N, longitude 15° E, north of latitude 73°30 - N between longitude 15° E and 35° E, and east of longitude 35° E, as well as north of latitude 56° N in the Baltic Sea.

(b) The area north of latitude 43° N bounded in the west by the North American coast and the east by the rhumb line running from latitude 43° N longitude 4M to latitude 63° N longitude 2M and thence along longitude 2M.

(c) All sea areas north of the North American continent, west of the areas defined in subparagraphs (a) and (b) of this paragraph.

(d) The Bering and Okhotsk Seas and the Tartary Strait during the icing season.

(e) South of latitude 60° S.

A chart to illustrate the areas is attached.[6]

2. For vessels operating in areas where ice accretion may be expected:

(a) Within the areas defined in paragraph (1)(a), (c), (d) and (e) known to having icing conditions significantly different from those in regulation III/8(1), ice accretion requirements of one-half to twice the required allowance may be applied.

(b) Within the area defined in paragraph (1)(b) where ice accretion in excess of twice the allowance required by regulation III/8(1) may be expected, more severe requirements than those given in that paragraph may be applied.

[5] Note: The Torremolinos International Convention for the Safety of Fishing Vessels 1977 never entered into force. However, pursuant to Article 1(1)(b) of the Torremolinos Protocol 1993, the regulations annexed to the 1977 Convention are given effect, subject to the modifications set out in the annex to the Protocol. The annex inserts Regulation 34 of the 1977 Convention as Regulation 8 (Ice accretion) in Chapter III (Stability and Associated Seaworthiness) under the 1993 Protocol.

[6] Chart omitted.

International Convention for the Prevention of Pollution from Ships (MARPOL)[7]

The Parties to the Convention,

Being conscious of the need to preserve the human environment in general and the marine environment in particular,

Recognizing that deliberate, negligent or accidental release of oil and other harmful substances from ships constitutes a serious source of pollution,

Recognizing also the importance of the International Convention for the Prevention of Pollution of the Sea by Oil, 1954,[8] as being the first multilateral instrument to be concluded with the prime objective of protecting the environment, and appreciating the significant contribution which that Convention has made in preserving the seas and coastal environment from pollution,

Desiring to achieve the complete elimination of intentional pollution of the marine environment by oil and other harmful substances and the minimization of accidental discharge of such substances,

Considering that this object may best be achieved by establishing rules not limited to oil pollution having a universal purport,

Have agreed as follows:

Article 1 General Obligations under the Convention

1. The Parties to the Convention undertake to give effect to the provisions of the present Convention and those Annexes thereto by which they are bound, in order to prevent the pollution of the marine environment by the discharge of harmful substances or effluents containing such substances in contravention of the Convention.

2. Unless expressly provided otherwise, a reference to the present Convention constitutes at the same time a reference to its Protocols and to the Annexes.

Article 2 Definitions

For the purposes of the present Convention, unless expressly provided otherwise:

1. "Regulations" means the Regulations contained in the Annexes to the present Convention.

2. "Harmful substance" means any substance which, if introduced into the sea, is liable to create hazards to human health, to harm living resources and marine life, to damage amenities or to interfere with other legitimate uses of the sea, and includes any substance subject to control by the present Convention.

3.

(a) "Discharge", in relation to harmful substances or effluents containing such substances, means any release howsoever caused from a ship and includes any escape, disposal, spilling, leaking, pumping, emitting or emptying;

(b) "Discharge" does not include:

(i) Dumping within the meaning of the Convention on the Prevention of Marine Pollution by Dumping of Wastes and Other Matter, done at London on 13 November 1972;[9] or

(ii) Release of harmful substances directly arising from the exploration, exploitation and associated off-shore processing of sea-bed mineral resources; or

(iii) Release of harmful substances for purposes of legitimate scientific research into pollution abatement or control.

4. "Ship" means a vessel of any type whatsoever operating in the marine environment and includes hydrofoil boats, air-cushion vehicles, submersibles, floating craft and fixed or floating platforms.

---

[7] Adopted 2 November 1973, entered into force 2 October 1983, 1340 UNTS 184.

[8] United Nations, *Treaty Series*, vol. 327, p. 3.

[9] Should read 29 December 1972. For the text of the Convention, see United Nations, Treaty Series, vol. 1046, p. 120.

5. "Administration" means the Government of the State under whose authority the ship is operating. With respect to a ship entitled to fly a flag of any State, the Administration is the Government of that State. With respect to fixed or floating platforms engaged in exploration and exploitation of the sea-bed and subsoil thereof adjacent to the coast over which the coastal State exercises sovereign rights for the purposes of exploration and exploitation of their natural resources, the Administration is the Government of the coastal State concerned.

6. "Incident" means an event involving the actual or probable discharge into the sea of a harmful substance, or effluents containing such a substance.

7. "Organization" means the Inter-Governmental Maritime Consultative Organization.

Article 3 Application

1. The present Convention shall apply to:

(a) Ships entitled to fly the flag of a Party to the Convention; and

(b) Ships not entitled to fly the flag of a Party but which operate under the authority of a Party.

2. Nothing in the present Article shall be construed as derogating from or extending the sovereign rights of the Parties under international law over the sea bed and subsoil thereof adjacent to their coasts for the purposes of exploration and exploitation of their natural resources.

3. The present Convention shall not apply to any warship, naval auxiliary or other ship owned or operated by a State and used, for the time being, only on government non-commercial service. However, each Party shall ensure by the adoption of appropriate measures not impairing the operations or operational capabilities of such ships owned or operated by it, that such ships act in a manner consistent, so far as is reasonable and practicable, with the present Convention.

Article 4 Violation

1. Any violation of the requirements of the present Convention shall be prohibited and sanctions shall be established therefor under the law of the Administration of the ship concerned wherever the violation occurs. If the Administration is informed of such a violation and is satisfied that sufficient evidence is available to enable proceedings to be brought in respect of the alleged violation, it shall cause such proceedings to be taken as soon as possible, in accordance with its law.

2. Any violation of the requirements of the present Convention within the jurisdiction of any Party to the Convention shall be prohibited and sanctions shall be established therefor under the law of that Party. Whenever such a violation occurs, that Party shall either:

(a) Cause proceedings to be taken in accordance with its law; or

(b) Furnish to the Administration of the ship such information and evidence as may be in its possession that a violation has occurred.

3. Where information or evidence with respect to any violation of the present Convention by a ship is furnished to the Administration of that ship, the Administration shall promptly inform the Party which has furnished the information or evidence, and the Organization, of the action taken.

4. The penalties specified under the law of a Party pursuant to the present Article shall be adequate in severity to discourage violations of the present Convention and shall be equally severe irrespective of where the violations occur.

Article 5 Certificates and Special Rules on Inspection of Ships

1. Subject to the provisions of paragraph (2) of the present Article a certificate issued under the authority of a Party to the Convention in accordance with the provisions of the Regulations shall be accepted by the other Parties and regarded for all purposes covered by the present Convention as having the same validity as a certificate issued by them.

2. A ship required to hold a certificate in accordance with the provisions of the Regulations is subject, while in the ports or off-shore terminals under the jurisdiction of a Party, to inspection by officers duly authorized by that Party. Any such inspection shall be limited to verifying that there is on board a valid certificate, unless there are clear grounds for believing that the

condition of the ship or its equipment does not correspond substantially with the particulars of that certificate. In that case, or if the ship does not carry a valid certificate, the Party carrying out the inspection shall take such steps as will ensure that the ship shall not sail until it can proceed to sea without presenting an unreasonable threat of harm to the marine environment. That Party may, however, grant such a ship permission to leave the port or off-shore terminal for the purpose of proceeding to the nearest appropriate repair yard available.

3. If a Party denies a foreign ship entry to the ports or off-shore terminals under its jurisdiction or takes any action against such a ship for the reason that the ship does not comply with the provisions of the present Convention, the Party shall immediately inform the consul or diplomatic representative of the Party whose flag the ship is entitled to fly, or if this is not possible, the Administration of the ship concerned. Before denying entry or taking such action the Party may request consultation with the Administration of the ship concerned. Information shall also be given to the Administration when a ship does not carry a valid certificate in accordance with the provisions of the Regulations.

4. With respect to the ships of non-Parties to the Convention, Parties shall apply the requirements of the present Convention as may be necessary to ensure that no more favourable treatment is given to such ships.

Article 6 Detection of Violations and Enforcement of the Convention

1. Parties to the Convention shall co-operate in the detection of violations and the enforcement of the provisions of the present Convention, using all appropriate and practicable measures of detection and environmental monitoring, adequate procedures for reporting and accumulation of evidence.

2. A ship to which the present Convention applies may, in any port or off-shore terminal of a Party, be subject to inspection by officers appointed or authorized by that Party for the purpose of verifying whether the ship has discharged any harmful substances in violation of the provisions of the Regulations. If an inspection indicates a violation of the Convention, a report shall be forwarded to the Administration for any appropriate action.

3. Any Party shall furnish to the Administration evidence, if any, that the ship has discharged harmful substances or effluents containing such substances in violation of the provisions of the Regulations. If it is practicable to do so, the competent authority of the former Party shall notify the Master of the ship of the alleged violation.

4. Upon receiving such evidence, the Administration so informed shall investigate the matter, and may request the other Party to furnish further or better evidence of the alleged contravention. If the Administration is satisfied that sufficient evidence is available to enable proceedings to be brought in respect of the alleged violation, it shall cause such proceedings to be taken in accordance with its law as soon as possible. The Administration shall promptly inform the Party which has reported the alleged violation, as well as the Organization, of the action taken.

5. A Party may also inspect a ship to which the present Convention applies when it enters the ports or off-shore terminals under its jurisdiction, if a request for an investigation is received from any Party together with sufficient evidence that the ship has discharged harmful substances or effluents containing such substances in any place. The report of such investigation shall be sent to the Party requesting it and to the Administration so that the appropriate action may be taken under the present Convention.

Article 7 Undue Delay to Ships

1. All possible efforts shall be made to avoid a ship being unduly detained or delayed under Article 4, 5 or 6 of the present Convention.

2. When a ship is unduly detained or delayed under Article 4, 5 or 6 of the present Convention, it shall be entitled to compensation for any loss or damage suffered.

Article 8 Reports on Incidents Involving Harmful Substances

1. A report of an incident shall be made without delay to the fullest extent possible in accordance with the provisions of Protocol I to the present Convention.

2. Each Party to the Convention shall:

(a) Make all arrangements necessary for an appropriate officer or agency to receive and process all reports on incidents; and

(b) Notify the Organization with complete details of such arrangements for circulation to other Parties and Member States of the Organization.

3. Whenever a Party receives a report under the provisions of the present Article, that Party shall relay the report without delay to:

(a) The Administration of the ship involved; and

(b) Any other State which may be affected.

4. Each Party to the Convention undertakes to issue instructions to its maritime inspection vessels and aircraft and to other appropriate services, to report to its authorities any incident referred to in Protocol I to the present Convention. That Party shall, if it considers it appropriate, report accordingly to the Organization and to any other party concerned.

Article 9 Other Treaties and Interpretation

1. Upon its entry into force, the present Convention supersedes the International Convention for the Prevention of Pollution of the Sea by Oil, 1954, as amended, as between Parties to that Convention.

2. Nothing in the present Convention shall prejudice the codification and development of the law of the sea by the United Nations Conference on the Law of the Sea convened pursuant to Resolution 2750 C(XXV) of the General Assembly of the United Nations[10] nor the present or future claims and legal views of any State concerning the law of the sea and the nature and extent of coastal and flag State jurisdiction.

3. The term "jurisdiction" in the present Convention shall be construed in the light of international law in force at the time of application or interpretation of the present Convention.

Article 10 Settlement of Disputes

Any dispute between two or more Parties to the Convention concerning the interpretation or application of the present Convention shall, if settlement by negotiation between the Parties involved has not been possible, and if these Parties do not otherwise agree, be submitted upon request of any of them to arbitration as set out in Protocol II to the present Convention.

Article 11 Communication of Information

1. The Parties to the Convention undertake to communicate to the Organization:

(a) The text of laws, orders, decrees and regulations and other instruments which have been promulgated on the various matters within the scope of the present Convention;

(b) A list of non-governmental agencies which are authorized to act on their behalf in matters relating to the design, construction and equipment of ships carrying harmful substances in accordance with the provisions of the Regulations;

(c) A sufficient number of specimens of their certificates issued under the provisions of the Regulations;

(d) A list of reception facilities including their location, capacity and available facilities and other characteristics;

(e) Official reports or summaries of official reports in so far as they show the results of the application of the present Convention; and

(f) An annual statistical report, in a form standardized by the Organization, of penalties actually imposed for infringement of the present Convention.

2. The Organization shall notify Parties of the receipt of any communications under the present Article and circulate to all Parties any information communicated to it under sub-paragraphs (1) (b) to (f) of the present Article.

[10] United Nations, *Official Records of the General Assembly, Twenty-fifth Session, Supplement No. 28* (A/8028), p. 26.

Article 12 Casualties to Ships

1. Each Administration undertakes to conduct an investigation of any casualty occurring to any of its ships subject to the provisions of the Regulations if such casualty has produced a major deleterious effect upon the marine environment.

2. Each Party to the Convention undertakes to supply the Organization with information concerning the findings of such investigation, when it judges that such information may assist in determining what changes in the present Convention might be desirable.

Article 13 Signature, Ratification, Acceptance, Approval and Accession

1. The present Convention shall remain open for signature at the Headquarters of the Organization from 15 January 1974 until 31 December 1974 and shall thereafter remain open for accession. States may become Parties to the present Convention by:

(a) Signature without reservation as to ratification, acceptance or approval; or

(b) Signature subject to ratification, acceptance or approval, followed by ratification, acceptance or approval; or

(c) Accession.

2. Ratification, acceptance, approval or accession shall be effected by the deposit of an instrument to that effect with the Secretary-General of the Organization.

3. The Secretary-General of the Organization shall inform all States which have signed the present Convention or acceded to it of any signature or of the deposit of any new instrument of ratification, acceptance, approval or accession and the date of its deposit.

Article 14 Optional Annexes

1. A State may at the time of signing, ratifying, accepting, approving or acceding to the present Convention declare that it does not accept any one or all of Annexes III, IV and V (hereinafter referred to as "Optional Annexes") of the present Convention. Subject to the above, Parties to the Convention shall be bound by any Annex in its entirety.

2. A State which has declared that it is not bound by an Optional Annex may at any time accept such Annex by depositing with the Organization an instrument of the kind referred to in Article 13(2).

3. A State which makes a declaration under paragraph (1) of the present Article in respect of an Optional Annex and which has not subsequently accepted that Annex in accordance with paragraph (2) of the present Article shall not be under any obligation nor entitled to claim any privileges under the present Convention in respect of matters related to such Annex and all references to Parties in the present Convention shall not include that State in so far as matters related to such Annex are concerned.

4. The Organization shall inform the States which have signed or acceded to the present Convention of any declaration under the present Article as well as the receipt of any instrument deposited in accordance with the provisions of paragraph (2) of the present Article.

Article 15 Entry into Force[11]

1. The present Convention shall enter into force twelve months after the date on which not less than 15 States, the combined merchant fleets of which constitute not less than fifty per cent of the gross tonnage of the world's merchant shipping, have become parties to it in accordance with Article 13.

2. An Optional Annex shall enter into force twelve months after the date on which the conditions stipulated in paragraph (1) of the present Article have been satisfied in relation to that Annex.

[11] The International Conference on Tanker Safety and Pollution Prevention, 1978, which adopted the Protocol, envisaged that the International Convention for the Prevention of Pollution from Ships, 1973, should not be subject to independent application, in view of the modifications and additions set out in the 1978 Protocol. It is, therefore, the expectation of the Governments which adopted this policy, and of the depositary, that the 1973 Convention will be applied solely as it is incorporated in the 1978 Protocol, and subject to the aforementioned modifications and additions, but will never enter into force on its own. (Information provided by the International Maritime Organization.)

3. The Organization shall inform the States which have signed the present Convention or acceded to it of the date on which it enters into force and of the date on which an Optional Annex enters into force in accordance with paragraph (2) of the present Article.

4. For States which have deposited an instrument of ratification, acceptance, approval or accession in respect of the present Convention or any Optional Annex after the requirements for entry into force thereof have been met but prior to the date of entry into force, the ratification, acceptance, approval or accession shall take effect on the date of entry into force of the Convention or such Annex or three months after the date of deposit of the instrument whichever is the later date.

5. For States which have deposited an instrument of ratification, acceptance, approval or accession after the date on which the Convention or an Optional Annex entered into force, the Convention or the Optional Annex shall become effective three months after the date of deposit of the instrument.

6. After the date on which all the conditions required under Article 16 to bring an amendment to the present Convention or an Optional Annex into force have been fulfilled, any instrument of ratification, acceptance, approval or accession deposited shall apply to the Convention or Annex as amended.

Article 16 Amendments

1. The present Convention may be amended by any of the procedures specified in the following paragraphs.

2. Amendments after consideration by the Organization:

(a) Any amendment proposed by a Party to the Convention shall be submitted to the Organization and circulated by its Secretary-General to all Members of the Organization and all Parties at least six months prior to its consideration;

(b) Any amendment proposed and circulated as above shall be submitted to an appropriate body by the Organization for consideration;

(c) Parties to the Convention, whether or not Members of the Organization, shall be entitled to participate in the proceedings of the appropriate body;

(d) Amendments shall be adopted by a two-thirds majority of only the Parties to the Convention present and voting;

(e) If adopted in accordance with sub-paragraph (d) above, amendments shall be communicated by the Secretary-General of the Organization to all the Parties to the Convention for acceptance;

(f) An amendment shall be deemed to have been accepted in the following circumstances:

(i) An amendment to an Article of the Convention shall be deemed to have been accepted on the date on which it is accepted by two-thirds of the Parties, the combined merchant fleets of which constitute not less than fifty per cent of the gross tonnage of the word's merchant fleet;

(ii) An amendment to an Annex to the Convention shall be deemed to have been accepted in accordance with the procedure specified in sub-paragraph (f)(iii) unless the appropriate body, at the time of its adoption, determines that the amendment shall be deemed to have been accepted on the date on which it is accepted by two-thirds of the Parties, the combined merchant fleets of which constitute not less than fifty per cent of the gross tonnage of the world's merchant fleet. Nevertheless, at any time before the entry into force of an amendment to an Annex to the Convention, a Party may notify the Secretary-General of the Organization that its express approval will be necessary before the amendment enters into force for it. The latter shall bring such notification and the date of its receipt to the notice of Parties;

(iii) An amendment to an Appendix to an Annex to the Convention shall be deemed to have been accepted at the end of a period to be determined by the appropriate body at the time of its adoption, which period shall be not less than ten months, unless within that period an objection is communicated to the Organization by not less than one-third of the Parties or by the Parties the combined merchant fleets of which constitute not less than fifty per cent of the gross tonnage of the world's merchant fleet whichever condition is fulfilled;

(iv) An amendment to Protocol I to the Convention shall be subject to the same procedures as for the amendments to the Annexes to the Convention, as provided for in sub-paragraphs (f)(ii) or (f)(iii) above;

(v) An amendment to Protocol II to the Convention shall be subject to the same procedures as for the amendments to an Article of the Convention, as provided for in sub-paragraph (f)(i) above;

(g) The amendment shall enter into force under the following conditions:

(i) In the case of an amendment to an Article of the Convention, to Protocol II, or to Protocol I or to an Annex to the Convention not under the procedure specified in sub-paragraph (f)(iii), the amendment accepted in conformity with the foregoing provisions shall enter into force six months after the date of its acceptance with respect to the Parties which have declared that they have accepted it;

(ii) In the case of an amendment to Protocol I, to an Appendix to an Annex or to an Annex to the Convention under the procedure specified in subparagraph (f)(iii), the amendment deemed to have been accepted in accordance with the foregoing conditions shall enter into force six months after its acceptance for all the Parties with the exception of those which, before that date, have made a declaration that they do not accept it or a declaration under sub-paragraph (f)(ii), that their express approval is necessary.

3. Amendment by a Conference:

(a) Upon the request of a Party, concurred in by at least one-third of the Parties, the Organization shall convene a Conference of Parties to the Convention to consider amendments to the present Convention.

(b) Every amendment adopted by such a Conference by a two-thirds majority of those present and voting of the Parties shall be communicated by the Secretary-General of the Organization to all Contracting Parties for their acceptance.

(c) Unless the Conference decides otherwise, the amendment shall be deemed to have been accepted and to have entered into force in accordance with the procedures specified for that purpose in paragraph (2)(f) and (g) above.

4.

(a) In the case of an amendment to an Optional Annex, a reference in the present Article to a "Party to the Convention" shall be deemed to mean a reference to a Party bound by that Annex.

(b) Any Party which has declined to accept an amendment to an Annex shall be treated as a non-Party only for the purpose of application of that Amendment.

5. The adoption and entry into force of a new Annex shall be subject to the same procedures as for the adoption and entry into force of an amendment to an Article of the Convention.

6. Unless expressly provided otherwise, any amendment to the present Convention made under this Article, which relates to the structure of a ship, shall apply only to ships for which the building contract is placed, or in the absence of a building contract, the keel of which is laid, on or after the date on which the amendment comes into force.

7. Any amendment to a Protocol or to an Annex shall relate to the substance of that Protocol or Annex and shall be consistent with the Articles of the present Convention.

8. The Secretary-General of the Organization shall inform all Parties of any amendments which enter into force under the present Article, together with the date on which each such amendment enters into force.

9. Any declaration of acceptance or of objection to an amendment under the present Article shall be notified in writing to the Secretary-General of the Organization. The latter shall bring such notification and the date of its receipt to the notice of the Parties to the Convention.

Article 17 Promotion of Technical Co-operation

The Parties to the Convention shall promote, in consultation with the Organization and other international bodies, with assistance and co-ordination by the Executive Director of the United Nations Environment Programme, support for those Parties which request technical assistance for:

(a) The training of scientific and technical personnel;
(b) The supply of necessary equipment and facilities for reception and monitoring;
(c) The facilitation of other measures and arrangements to prevent or mitigate pollution of the marine environment by ships; and
(d) The encouragement of research;

preferably within the countries concerned, so furthering the aims and purposes of the present Convention.

Article 18 Denunciation

1. The present Convention or any Optional Annex may be denounced by any Parties to the Convention at any time after the expiry of five years from the date on which the Convention or such Annex enters into force for that Party.

2. Denunciation shall be effected by notification in writing to the Secretary-General of the Organization who shall inform all the other Parties of any such notification received and of the date of its receipt as well as the date on which such denunciation takes effect.

3. A denunciation shall take effect twelve months after receipt of the notification of denunciation by the Secretary-General of the Organization or after the expiry of any other longer period which may be indicated in the notification.

Article 19 Deposit and Registration

1. The present Convention shall be deposited with the Secretary-General of the Organization who shall transmit certified true copies thereof to all States which have signed the present Convention or acceded to it.

2. As soon as the present Convention enters into force, the text shall be transmitted by the Secretary-General of the Organization to the Secretary-General of the United Nations for registration and publication, in accordance with Article 102 of the Charter of the United Nations.

Article 20 Languages

The present Convention is established in a single copy in the English, French, Russian and Spanish languages, each text being equally authentic. Official translations in the Arabic, German, Italian and Japanese languages shall be prepared and deposited with the signed original.

In witness whereof the undersigned being duly authorized by their respective Governments for that purpose have signed the present Convention.

DONE at London this second day of November, one thousand nine hundred and seventy-three.

Amendments to the Annex of the MARPOL Protocol of 1978, adding Chapter 9: Special Requirements for the Use or Carriage of Oils in the Antarctic Area[12]

The Marine Environment Protection Committee,

Recalling Article 38(a) of the Convention on the International Maritime Organization concerning the functions of the Marine Environment Protection Committee (the Committee) conferred upon it by international conventions for the prevention and control of marine pollution,

[12] Adopted 26 March 2010 by resolution MPEC.189(60), entered into force 1 August 2011.

Noting Article 16 of the International Convention for the Prevention of Pollution from Ships, 1973 (hereinafter referred to as the "1973 Convention") and article VI of the Protocol of 1978 relating to the International Convention for the Prevention of Pollution from Ships, 1973 (hereinafter referred to as the "1978 Protocol") which together specify the amendment procedure of the 1978 Protocol and confer upon the appropriate body of the Organization the function of considering and adopting amendments to the 1973 Convention, as modified by the 1978 Protocol (MARPOL 73/78),

Having considered draft amendments to Annex I of MARPOL 73/78,

1. *Adopts*, in accordance with Article 16(2)(d) of the 1973 Convention, the amendments to Annex I of MARPOL 73/78 concerning the addition of a new chapter 9 on Special requirements for the use or carriage of oils in the Antarctic area;

2. *Determines*, in accordance with Article 16(2)(f)(iii) of the 1973 Convention, that the amendments shall be deemed to have been accepted on 1 February 2011 unless, prior to that date, not less than one third of the Parties or Parties the combined merchant fleets of which constitute not less than 50 per cent of the gross tonnage of the world's merchant fleet, have communicated to the Organization their objection to the amendments;

3. *Invites* the Parties to note that, in accordance with Article 16(2)(g)(ii) of the 1973 Convention, the said amendments shall enter into force on 1 August 2011 upon their acceptance in accordance with paragraph 2 above;

4. *Requests* the Secretary-General, in conformity with Article 16(2)(e) of the 1973 Convention, to transmit to all Parties to MARPOL 73/78 certified copies of the present resolution and the text of the amendments contained in the annex; and

5. *Requests further* the Secretary-General to transmit to the Members of the Organization which are not Parties to MARPOL 73/78 copies of the present resolution and its annex.

Annex: Amendments to MARPOL Annex I to Add Chapter 9 – Special Requirements for the Use or Carriage of Oils in the Antarctic Area

A new chapter 9 is added as follows:

"Chapter 9 – Special Requirements for the Use or Carriage of Oils in the Antarctic Area

Regulation 43

Special requirements for the use or carriage of oils in the Antarctic area

1. With the exception of vessels engaged in securing the safety of ships or in a search and rescue operation, the carriage in bulk as cargo or carriage and use as fuel of the following:

.1 crude oils having a density at 15°C higher than 900 kg/m3;

.2 oils, other than crude oils, having a density at 15°C higher than 900 kg/m3 or a kinematic viscosity at 50°C higher than 180 mm2/s; or

.3 bitumen, tar and their emulsions,

shall be prohibited in the Antarctic area, as defined in Annex I, regulation 1.11.7.

2. When prior operations have included the carriage or use of oils listed in paragraphs 1.1 to 1.3 of this regulation, the cleaning or flushing of tanks or pipelines is not required."

Convention for the Conservation of Southern Bluefin Tuna[13]

The Parties to this Convention:

Considering their mutual interest in southern bluefin tuna;

Recalling that Australia, Japan and New Zealand have already taken certain measures for the conservation and management of southern bluefin tuna;

Paying due regard to the rights and obligations of the Parties under relevant principles of international law;

Noting the adoption of the United Nations Convention on the Law of the Sea in 1982;

[13] Adopted 10 May 1993, entered into force 20 May 1994, 1819 UNTS 359.

Noting that States have established exclusive economic or fishery zones within which they exercise, in accordance with international law, sovereign rights or jurisdiction for the purpose of exploring and exploiting, conserving and managing the living resources;

Recognising that southern bluefin tuna is a highly migratory species which migrates through such zones;

Noting that the coastal States through whose exclusive economic or fishery zones southern bluefin tuna migrates exercise sovereign rights within such zones for the purpose of exploring and exploiting, conserving and managing the living resources including southern bluefin tuna;

Acknowledging the importance of scientific research for the conservation and management of southern bluefin tuna and the importance of collecting scientific information relating to southern bluefin tuna and ecologically related species;

Recognising that it is essential that they cooperate to ensure the conservation and optimum utilisation of southern bluefin tuna;

Have agreed as follows:

Article 1

This Convention shall apply to southern bluefin tuna (*Thunnus maccoyii*).

Article 2

For the purposes of this Convention:

(a) "ecologically related species" means living marine species which are associated with southern bluefin tuna, including but not restricted to both predators and prey of southern bluefin tuna;

(b) "fishing" means:

(i) the catching, taking or harvesting of fish, or any other activity which can reasonably be expected to result in the catching, taking or harvesting of fish; or

(ii) any operation at sea in preparation for or in direct support of any activity described in sub-paragraph (i) above.

Article 3

The objective of this Convention is to ensure, through appropriate management, the conservation and optimum utilisation of southern bluefin tuna.

Article 4

Nothing in this Convention nor any measures adopted pursuant to it shall be deemed to prejudice the positions or views of any Party with respect to its rights and obligations under treaties and other international agreements to which it is party or its positions or views with respect to the law of the sea.

Article 5

1. Each Party shall take all action necessary to ensure the enforcement of this Convention and compliance with measures which become binding under paragraph 7 of Article 8.

2. The Parties shall expeditiously provide to the Commission for the Conservation of Southern Bluefin Tuna scientific information, fishing catch and effort statistics and other data relevant to the conservation of southern bluefin tuna and, as appropriate, ecologically related species.

3. The Parties shall cooperate in collection and direct exchange, when appropriate, of fisheries data, biological samples and other information relevant for scientific research on southern bluefin tuna and ecologically related species.

4. The Parties shall cooperate in the exchange of information regarding any fishing for southern bluefin tuna by nationals, residents and vessels of any State or entity not party to this Convention.

Article 6

1. The Parties hereby establish and agree to maintain the Commission for the Conservation of Southern Bluefin Tuna (hereinafter referred to as "the Commission").

2. Each Party shall be represented on the Commission by not more than three delegates who may be accompanied by experts and advisers.

3. The Commission shall hold an annual meeting before 1 August each year or at such other time as it may determine.

4. At each annual meeting the Commission shall elect from among the delegates a Chair and a Vice-Chair. The Chair and the Vice-Chair shall be elected from different Parties and shall remain in office until the election of their successors at the next annual meeting. A delegate, when acting as Chair, shall not vote.

5. Special meetings of the Commission shall be convened by the Chair at the request of a Party supported by at least two other Parties.

6. A special meeting may consider any matter of relevance to this Convention.

7. Two-thirds of the Parties shall constitute a quorum.

8. The rules of procedure of the Commission and other internal administrative regulations as may be necessary to carry out its functions shall be decided upon at the first meeting of the Commission and may be amended by the Commission as occasion may require.

9. The Commission shall have legal personality and shall enjoy in its relations with other international organisations and in the territories of the Parties such legal capacity as may be necessary to perform its functions and achieve its ends. The immunities and privileges which the Commission and its officers shall enjoy in the territory of a Party shall be subject to agreement between the Commission and the Party concerned.

10. The Commission shall determine the location of its headquarters at such time as a Secretariat is established pursuant to paragraph 1 of Article 10.

11. The official languages of the Commission shall be Japanese and English. Proposals and data may be submitted to the Commission in either language.

Article 7

Each Party shall have one vote in the Commission. Decisions of the Commission shall be taken by a unanimous vote of the Parties present at the Commission meeting.

Article 8

1. The Commission shall collect and accumulate information described below:

(a) scientific information, statistical data and other information relating to southern bluefin tuna and ecologically related species;

(b) information relating to laws, regulations and administrative measures on southern bluefin tuna fisheries;

(c) any other information relating to southern bluefin tuna.

2. The Commission shall consider matters described below:

(a) interpretation or implementation of this Convention and measures adopted pursuant to it;

(b) regulatory measures for conservation, management and optimum utilisation of southern bluefin tuna;

(c) matters which shall be reported by the Scientific Committee prescribed in Article 9;

(d) matters which may be entrusted to the Scientific Committee prescribed in Article 9;

(e) matters which may be entrusted to the Secretariat prescribed in Article 10;

(f) other activities necessary to carry out the provisions of this Convention.

3. For the conservation, management and optimum utilisation of southern bluefin tuna:

(a) the Commission shall decide upon a total allowable catch and its allocation among the Parties unless the Commission decides upon other appropriate measures on the basis of the report and recommendations of the Scientific Committee referred to in paragraph 2(c) and (d) of Article 9; and

(b) the Commission may, if necessary, decide upon other additional measures.

4. In deciding upon allocations among the Parties under paragraph 3 above the Commission shall consider:

(a) relevant scientific evidence;

(b) the need for orderly and sustainable development of southern bluefin tuna fisheries;

(c) the interests of Parties through whose exclusive economic or fishery zones southern bluefin tuna migrates;
(d) the interests of Parties whose vessels engage in fishing for southern bluefin tuna including those which have historically engaged in such fishing and those which have southern bluefin tuna fisheries under development;
(e) the contribution of each Party to conservation and enhancement of, and scientific research on, southern bluefin tuna;
(f) any other factors which the Commission deems appropriate.

5. The Commission may decide upon recommendations to the Parties in order to further the attainment of the objective of this Convention.

6. In deciding upon measures under paragraph 3 above and recommendations under paragraph 5 above, the Commission shall take full account of the report and recommendations of the Scientific Committee under paragraph 2(c) and (d) of Article 9.

7. All measures decided upon under paragraph 3 above shall be binding on the Parties.

8. The Commission shall notify all Parties promptly of measures and recommendations decided upon by the Commission.

9. The Commission shall develop, at the earliest possible time and consistent with international law, systems to monitor all fishing activities related to southern bluefin tuna in order to enhance scientific knowledge necessary for conservation and management of southern bluefin tuna and in order to achieve effective implementation of this Convention and measures adopted pursuant to it.

10. The Commission may establish such subsidiary bodies as it considers desirable for the exercise of its duties and functions.

Article 9

1. The Parties hereby establish the Scientific Committee as an advisory body to the Commission.

2. The Scientific Committee shall:
(a) assess and analyse the status and trends of the population of southern bluefin tuna;
(b) coordinate research and studies of southern bluefin tuna;
(c) report to the Commission its findings or conclusions, including consensus, majority and minority views, on the status of the southern bluefin tuna stock and, where appropriate, of ecologically related species;
(d) make recommendations, as appropriate, to the Commission by consensus on matters concerning the conservation, management and optimum utilisation of southern bluefin tuna;
(e) consider any matter referred to it by the Commission.

3. A meeting of the Scientific Committee shall be held prior to the annual meeting of the Commission. A special meeting of the Scientific Committee shall be called at any time at the request of a Party provided that such request is supported by at least two other Parties.

4. The Scientific Committee shall adopt and amend as necessary its rules of procedure. The rules and any amendments thereto shall be approved by the Commission.

5.
(a) Each Party shall be a member of the Scientific Committee and shall appoint to the Committee a representative with suitable scientific qualifications who may be accompanied by alternates, experts and advisers.
(b) The Scientific Committee shall elect a Chair and a Vice-Chair. The Chair and the Vice-Chair shall be elected from different Parties.

Article 10

1. The Commission may establish a Secretariat consisting of an Executive Secretary to be appointed by the Commission and appropriate staff on conditions as may be determined by the Commission. The staff shall be appointed by the Executive Secretary.

2. Until such time as a Secretariat is established, the Chair of the Commission shall nominate from within his or her Government an official to act as Secretary to the Commission to perform the secretariat functions set out in paragraph 3 below for a term of one year. At each annual meeting of the Commission, the Chair shall advise the Parties of the name and address of the Secretary.

3. The Secretariat functions shall be prescribed by the Commission, and shall include the following:

(a) receiving and transmitting the Commission's official communications;

(b) facilitating the collection of data necessary to accomplish the objective of this Convention;

(c) preparing administrative and other reports for the Commission and the Scientific Committee.

Article 11

1. The Commission shall decide upon an annual budget.

2. The contributions to the annual budget from each Party shall be calculated on the following basis:

(a) 30% of the budget shall be divided equally among all the Parties; and

(b) 70% of the budget shall be divided in proportion to the nominal catches of southern bluefin tuna among all the Parties.

3. Notwithstanding the provisions of Article 7, any Party that has not paid its contributions for two consecutive years shall not enjoy the right to participate in the decision-making process in the Commission until it has fulfilled its obligations, unless the Commission decides otherwise.

4. The Commission shall decide upon, and amend as occasion may require, financial regulations for the conduct of the Commission and for the exercise of its functions.

5. Each Party shall meet its own expenses arising from attendance at meetings of the Commission and of the Scientific Committee.

Article 12

The Commission shall collaborate with other inter-governmental organisations which have related objectives, *inter alia*, to obtain the best available information including scientific information to further the attainment of the objective of this Convention and shall seek to avoid duplication with respect to their work. The Commission may make arrangements with such inter-governmental organisations to these ends.

Article 13

With a view to furthering the attainment of the objective of this Convention, the Parties shall cooperate with each other to encourage accession by any State to this Convention where the Commission considers this to be desirable.

Article 14

1. The Commission may invite any State or entity not party to this Convention, whose nationals, residents or fishing vessels harvest southern bluefin tuna, and any coastal State through whose exclusive economic or fishery zone southern bluefin tuna migrates, to send observers to meetings of the Commission and of the Scientific Committee.

2. The Commission may invite inter-governmental or, on request, non-governmental organisations having special competence concerning southern bluefin tuna to send observers to meetings of the Commission.

Article 15

1. The Parties agree to invite the attention of any State or entity not party to this Convention to any matter relating to the fishing activities of its nationals, residents or vessels which could affect the attainment of the objective of this Convention.

2. Each Party shall encourage its nationals not to associate with the southern bluefin tuna fishery of any State or entity not party to this Convention, where such association could affect adversely the attainment of the objective of this Convention.

3. Each Party shall take appropriate measures aimed at preventing vessels registered under its laws and regulations from transferring their registration for the purpose of avoiding compliance with the provisions of this Convention or measures adopted pursuant to it.

4. The Parties shall cooperate in taking appropriate action, consistent with international law and their respective domestic laws, to deter fishing activities for southern bluefin tuna by nationals, residents or vessels of any State or entity not party to this Convention where such activity could affect adversely the attainment of the objective of this Convention.

Article 16

1. If any dispute arises between two or more of the Parties concerning the interpretation or implementation of this Convention, those Parties shall consult among themselves with a view to having the dispute resolved by negotiation, inquiry, mediation, conciliation, arbitration, judicial settlement or other peaceful means of their own choice.

2. Any dispute of this character not so resolved shall, with the consent in each case of all parties to the dispute, be referred for settlement to the International Court of Justice or to arbitration; but failure to reach agreement on reference to the International Court of Justice or to arbitration shall not absolve parties to the dispute from the responsibility of continuing to seek to resolve it by any of the various peaceful means referred to in paragraph 1 above.

3. In cases where the dispute is referred to arbitration, the arbitral tribunal shall be constituted as provided in the Annex to this Convention. The Annex forms an integral part of this Convention.

Article 17

1. This Convention shall be open for signature by Australia, Japan and New Zealand.

2. This Convention is subject to ratification, acceptance or approval by these three States in accordance with their respective internal legal procedures, and will enter into force on the date of deposit of the third instrument of ratification, acceptance or approval.

Article 18

After the entry into force of this Convention, any other State, whose vessels engage in fishing for southern bluefin tuna, or any other coastal State through whose exclusive economic or fishery zone southern bluefin tuna migrates, may accede to it. This Convention shall become effective for any such other State on the date of deposit of that State's instrument of accession.

Article 19

Reservations may not be made with respect to any of the provisions of this Convention.

Article 20

Any Party may withdraw from this Convention twelve months after the date on which it formally notifies the Depositary of its intention to withdraw.

Article 21

1. Any Party may at any time propose an amendment to this Convention.

2. If one-third of the Parties request a meeting to discuss a proposed amendment the Depositary shall call such a meeting.

3. An amendment shall enter into force when the Depositary has received instruments of ratification, acceptance or approval thereof from all the Parties.

Article 22

1. The original of this Convention shall be deposited with the Government of Australia, which shall be the Depositary. The Depositary shall transmit certified copies thereof to all other Signatories and acceding States.

2. This Convention shall be registered by the Depositary pursuant to Article 102 of the Charter of the United Nations.

IN WITNESS WHEREOF the undersigned, being duly authorised thereto, have signed this Convention.

DONE at Canberra on the tenth day of May 1993, in a single original, in the English and Japanese languages, each text being equally authentic.

Annex for an Arbitral Tribunal

1. The arbitral tribunal referred to in paragraph 3 of Article 16 shall be composed of three arbitrators who shall be appointed as follows:

(a) The party commencing proceedings shall communicate the name of an arbitrator to the other party which, in turn, within a period of forty days following such notification, shall communicate the name of the second arbitrator. The parties shall, within a period of sixty days following the appointment of the second arbitrator, appoint the third arbitrator, who shall not be a national of either party and shall not be of the same nationality as either of the first two arbitrators. The third arbitrator shall preside over the tribunal.

(b) If the second arbitrator has not been appointed within the prescribed period, or if the parties have not reached agreement within the prescribed period on the appointment of the third arbitrator, that arbitrator shall be appointed, at the request of either party, by the Secretary-General of the Permanent Court of Arbitration, from among persons of international standing not having the nationality of a State which is a Party to this Convention.

2. The arbitral tribunal shall decide where its headquarters will be located and shall adopt its own rules of procedure.

3. The award of the arbitral tribunal shall be made by a majority of its members, who may not abstain from voting.

4. Any Party which is not a party to the dispute may intervene in the proceedings with the consent of the arbitral tribunal.

5. The award of the arbitral tribunal shall be final and binding on all parties to the dispute and on any party which intervenes in the proceedings and shall be complied with without delay. The arbitral tribunal shall interpret the award at the request of one of the parties to the dispute or of any intervening party.

6. Unless the arbitral tribunal determines otherwise because of the particular circumstances of the case, the expenses of the tribunal, including the remuneration of its members, shall be borne by the parties to the dispute in equal shares.

Framework Agreement for the Conservation of the Living Marine Resources of the High Seas of the South Pacific ('Galapagos Agreement')[14]

The coastal States of the Southeast Pacific, Members of the South Pacific Permanent Commission (SPPC) and other interested States,

Whereas:

The coastal States of the Southeast Pacific, through the 1952 Declaration of Santiago, proclaimed their sovereignty and exclusive jurisdiction within a 200-mile maritime zone, with the aim of ensuring the conservation and appropriate exploitation of the natural resources off their coasts, and laid the foundation for this zone's establishment and acceptance as one of the fundamental institutions of the new Law of the Sea;

The Declaration of Santiago also recognized that a coastal States' duty to prevent an excessive exploitation of natural resources outside the reach of their national jurisdiction, which could endanger those resources' existence, integrity and conservation, detrimental of the peoples that in their seas possess irreplaceable subsistence resources;

With these goals in mind, the coastal States in question agreed to establish the South Pacific Permanent Commission (SPPC), to coordinate their maritime policies and to promote the adoption of measures to preserve the environment and protect the integrity of the South Pacific's marine ecosystem;

In conformity with the relevant provisions of international law, all States have the right to allow their nationals to engage in fishing on the high seas, subject inter alia to the rights, duties

[14] Adopted 14 August 2000, not yet in force.

and interests of the coastal States with regard to the capture of straddling stocks and highly migratory species;

These provisions imply the recognition of a preferential status for the coastal States, justified by the relationship that exists between fish stocks of such species and the marine ecosystems of those States, as well as by the effects of fishing activities on certain coastal fish populations, associates or dependent of the same;

The uncontrolled exploitation of living marine resources in high seas areas adjacent to zones under national jurisdiction represents a threat to the conservation and sustainable use of said resources, as well as to fish populations dependent on or associated with them, and it may undermine the effectiveness of measures adopted by the coastal States with respect to the same species, within their 200-mile zones;

The provisions on these matters contained in recent instruments adopted within the United Nations Organization must be evaluated and adapted to the specific requirements of the South Pacific;

In light of the considerations set forth here, the coastal States of the Southeast Pacific have the right and duty to ensure the conservation and sustainable use of the living marine resources present in their subregion, including those which migrate from the zones under their national jurisdiction to the high seas and vice versa;

The countries have administered some of the world's biggest fishing grounds and have adopted effective measures to promote the long-term sustainability of the living marine resources there, and thus they have a special interest in ensuring that the measures applied on the adjacent high seas are no less strict than those in the zones under their jurisdiction;

Taking the above into account, at the Fifth Foreign Ministers' Summit of the SPPC Member States (Santafè de Bogotá, August 4, 1997), the decision was made to prepare a Framework Agreement for the Conservation of the Fishery Resources on the High Seas of the Southeast Pacific, the basic outlines of which were included in an attachment to the Ministerial Declaration emerging from that Summit;

According to those outlines, the Framework Agreement shall establish conditions and procedures allowing, after approval by the SPPC Member States, later accession by other States whose fishing fleets are active in the Agreement's area of application and which have an established interest in the living marine resources in question;

In conformity with the outlines mentioned, the Framework Agreement must also be general in nature and permit later development through the addition of complementary instruments establishing specific provisions to ensure the conservation and sustainable use of the living marine resources in question, in accordance with their nature, characteristics and area of distribution;

Before the permanent institutional mechanisms are put into place for the implementation of the Framework Agreement and its complementary instruments, the SPPC General Secretariat has indicated its willingness to act provisionally as Secretariat for the regional organization being established;

Agree to subscribe to the following Framework Agreement for the Conservation of Living Marine Resources on the High Seas of the Southeast Pacific:

Article 1 Definition of terms

1. For the purposes of this Framework Agreement, the following terms shall be defined as stated:

(1) "Coastal States": Chile, Colombia, Ecuador and Peru.

(2) "States Parties": the coastal States along with other interested States, which subscribe and ratify this Agreement or accede to it.

(3) "Other interested States": the States involved in distant-water fishing which have an established interest in specific fishery resources in this subregion, including qualified inter-governmental organization.

(4) "Established interest": the interest demonstrated by a State whose nationals habitually fish for one or more fish populations within this Agreement's area of application and whose participation may fall within the scope of this interest.

(5) "Concerned States": the States parties, whether coastal or otherwise, along with other interested States.

(6) "Qualified intergovernmental organizations": regional organizations constituted by States, which have had powers transferred to them in subjects covered by this Agreement, including the power to make decisions in relation to such subjects that are binding on member States.

(7) "Area of application of the Agreement": as established in Article 3.

(8) "Zones under national jurisdiction": those subject to the jurisdiction and sovereignty of the coastal States, up to the limit of 200 nautical miles measured from the baselines, including the jurisdictional zones established for island territories beyond the limit of the continental maritime zones.

(9) "SPPC": the South Pacific Permanent Commission.

(10) "General Secretariat": the General Secretariat of the SPPC.

(11) "Conservation measures": measures aimed at the sustainable exploitation of one or more fish populations, adopted in the Framework Agreement's area of application in a manner compatible with the relevant provisions of international law and in conformity with the provision of this Agreement. For the purposes of this Agreement, the term "conservation" shall henceforth include the concept of the sustainable exploitation of living marine resources.

(12) "Straddling and highly migratory fish populations": those defined in the United Nations Convention on the Law of the Sea, including fish and mollusks belonging to the same species regulated by the Agreement, in conformity with the provisions of Article 4.

(13) "Living marine resources": the straddling fish species or highly migratory and the other live marine resources associated or dependents of the same.

(14) "Relevant provisions of international law": those recognized in this subject in the United Nations Convention on the Law of the Sea and other international instruments currently in force for the States Parties, as well as the provisions incorporated into common law through the general practice of States.

(15) "Complementary instruments": those agreed upon by the States parties or concerned States, whichever the case may be, in conformity with the provisions of this Framework Agreement, through conventions, protocols or annexes, as appropriate, on specific matters where this is seen to be necessary, with the aim of developing or regulating the provisions of the Agreement, taking into account the nature of the species in question.

Article 2 Objective of the Agreement

The objective of this Framework Agreement is the conservation of living marine resources in the high seas zones of the Southeast Pacific, with special reference to straddling and highly migratory fish populations.

Article 3 Area of application

1. The Framework Agreement shall apply exclusively to the high seas of the Southeast Pacific, encompassed by the outer limits of the coastal States' national jurisdiction zones and a line traced along the complete length of the 120 west meridian of longitude, from the 5 north parallel of latitude to the 60 south parallel of latitude. It does not apply to the zones under national jurisdiction corresponding to oceanic islands belonging to any of the coastal States, but is shall also include the areas of high seas surrounding and adjacent to these oceanic islands, within the limits described.

2. The provisions of paragraph 1 notwithstanding, the complementary instruments may refer to other areas of application, according to the nature, characteristics, displacement and ecological relationships of the fish populations regulated by such instruments.

Article 4 Regulated species

1. Without prejudice to their later application to other living marine resources present in the area described in Article 3, conservation standards will first be adopted for particular species judged to be of high priority.

2. At the States Parties first meeting within the three-month period following this Agreement's entry into force, they must identify such high-priority species, considering those which require preferential treatment because of their commercial interest or special conservation requirements.

3. The specific species to be regulated, as well as later additions of species or exclusions of any of them, shall be established through an annex adopted by the States Parties.

4. The States Parties shall give due consideration to the provisions of existing multilateral instruments regarding one or more of such species, which may be applicable in conformity with the relevant provisions of international law.

5. In the determination of regulated species, the States parties shall also consider the need to preserve the ecological equilibrium that exists between fish stocks of those species and populations of associated or dependent fish species.

Article 5 Conservation principles

1. In the implementation of this Framework Agreement, the following principles, among others, shall be followed:

(a) The measures adopted shall be based on appropriate scientific and technical information, with the aim of ensuring the long-term conservation of the Southeast Pacific's living marine resources within the area of application.

(b) The scarcity or lack of available information shall not be construed as a reason to prevent or delay the adoption of precautionary measures, including points of reference for specific fish populations.

(c) In the establishment of conservation measures for regulated species, the effects of fishing for specific fish stocks on the populations of associated or dependent species, as well as on the marine ecosystem as a whole, shall be taken into account.

(d) The effects of environmental changes and other phenomena which might affect the marine ecosystem, along with the direct or indirect effects of capture, shall be taken into account, in order to reduce or prevent the risk of potentially irreversible alterations.

(e) The measures adopted shall not be less strict than those established for the same species in the zones under national jurisdiction adjacent to the Agreement's area of application, shall not undermine the effectiveness of the same, and shall be fully compatible with them in all cases.

(f) Appropriate measures shall be adopted to prevent incidental captures as well as excesses in fishing and fishing capacity.

2. In the application of these principles and in other provisions of the Framework Agreement, particularly in the decision-making process as described in Article 12, due account shall be taken of the fact that, in conformity with the relevant provisions of international law, the freedom of fishing on the high seas is subject inter alia to the rights, duties and interests of the coastal States and to the conservation and administration rules of the living resources of the high seas.

Article 6 Conservation and sustainable use measures

Measures for the conservation of regulated species may include the following elements, among others:

(a) The designation of subzones within the Framework Agreement's area of application, taking into account the nature, characteristics and distribution of the fish populations in question, as well as other geographical, ecological, scientific, statistical and operational criteria;

(b) The setting of catch limits for various fish populations in the area of application or in established subzones;

(c) The regulation of fishing effort to prevent its concentration on one particular species or zone;
(d) The establishment of appropriate open and closed seasons for fishing activities;
(e) The adoption of capture methods, including the selective use of fishing tackle and equipment and appropriate fishing methods;
(f) The regulation of minimum permissible sizes and/or ages for capture, and if applicable, the sex of regulated species, along with any other biological parameter which would assist in the conservation of those species; and
(g) Additional conservation measures that are deemed appropriate to ensure the fulfilment of this Agreement's objective.

Article 7 Obligations of the States Parties

With the aim of fulfilling this Agreement's objective, the States Parties assume the following obligations:

(a) To adopt necessary measures so that their national flag vessels comply with the conservation measures set forth in this Agreement and do not undertake activities that undermine the effectiveness of these measures.
(b) To grant fishing authorizations for the Agreement's area of application to vessels flying their national flag, maintain a registry of such vessels and exercise effective control over them to ensure the fulfilment of the measures adopted.
(c) To observe international norms regarding the identification and marking of fishing vessels and fishing equipment.
(d) To establish rules for the registry and communication, as appropriate, of data such as vessel location, captures of regulated fish species, by-catch, fishing effort, environmental conditions and other related data of interest, in conformity with international standards for the gathering of such data.
(e) To gather and make available scientific, technical and statistical information about the fish populations captured within the Agreement's area of application, and, as far as possible, about associated or dependent species, maintaining confidentiality, where appropriate, in the management of such information.
(f) To carry out and interchange studies on ecological, economic and social considerations related to the utilization of fishery resources.
(g) To carry out and support scientific studies and develop appropriate technologies related to the conservation of living marine resources.
(h) In the case of States possessing sufficient means, to cooperate in the support of technical assistance and training programs, aimed at contributing to the implementation of this Agreement; and
(i) In the case of the coastal States, to seek to harmonize the conservation measures in force in their national jurisdiction zones.

Article 8 Follow-up, monitoring, control and enforcement measures

1. The States Parties shall work together to ensure the fulfilment of the conservation measures adopted, through the establishment of follow-up, monitoring, control and enforcement systems, including the use of satellite data and positioning, and, where appropriate, the boarding and inspection of fishing vessels and the escorting of such vessels to port when infractions are discovered, in conformity with the relevant provisions of international law.

2. The States parties shall include provisions in their national laws to ensure the fulfilment by their nationals of the rules and measures agreed under this Agreement.

3. The States Parties shall hold consultations to determine the most effective measures to prevent illicit, unregulated and undeclared fishing, including boat-to-boat transfers to evade compliance with conservation measures, whether by vessels flying their national flags, those flying the flags of other States, those flying flags of convenience or those operating without a national flag.

Article 9 Measures to adopted by port States

In the exercise of their sovereignty in conformity with the relevant provisions of international law, the States Parties which are also port States shall adopt the following measures, among other:

(a) To inspect, when necessary, the documents, fishing equipment and catches of fishing vessels which voluntarily enter their ports and coastal installations;

(b) To prevent disembarkation and ship-to-ship transfers when reasonable grounds exist to believe that captures of fish in the Agreement's area of application have been carried out in the contravention of the rules and conservation measures adopted by the States Parties, or, in the absence of such measures, when such captures have served to undermine the effectiveness of the measures in force with respect to the same fish populations in the coastal States' national jurisdiction zones.

Article 10 Violations and penalties

1. The States Parties shall agree upon a list of violations and an adequate regimen of penalties, based on the principles of proportionality and adequate deterrence, for infringements of the measures adopted, including, as appropriate, the imposition of fines, the confiscation of catches and the suspension or revocation of authorizations to fish in the relevant area of the Agreement's application.

2. In addition, a system shall be put into place to inform concerned States of violations committed and the penalties imposed.

Article 11 Institutional mechanisms

1. The States parties shall establish an Organization for the conservation of living marine resources in the Southeast Pacific, which in principle shall include:

(a) Commission tasked with adopting the necessary decisions for the fulfilment of the Agreement's provisions;

(b) Scientific-Technical Committee, to serve as a consulting body for the Commission on these matters;

(c) Secretariat;

(d) any other subsidiary body that the States Parties, or the Commission once it has begun operation; decides to establish in support of the Agreement's implementation.

2. Until the institutional mechanisms have been put into place, the assembly of the States Parties shall carry out the functions of the Commission, and the General Secretariat those of the Organization's Secretariat.

3. In addition, the assembly of the States Parties shall designate a representative for the Scientific-Technical Committee from each State Party, who has adequate scientific capacity and who may be accompanied by experts and advisors.

4. The States Parties shall supply the necessary financial contributions to support these activities, assessed on a proportional scale similar to that used by the United Nations Organization.

5. The Agreement's complementary instruments shall also include provisions regarding the establishment and financing of those institutional mechanisms which may be considered appropriate by the States Parties.

Article 12 Decision-making process

1. The States Parties shall make all necessary efforts to ensure that decisions on issues considered to be substantive are reached by consensus. The determination of whether or not an issue is substantive shall also be considered a substantive question. If all efforts at conciliation are exhausted, however, and no consensus can be reached by the end of the day following the examination of the issue in question, the decision shall be made through the favourable vote of at least two-thirds of the representatives of the States present, including a majority of the coastal States. In the case of measures whose application may affect the conservation of fish stocks within the national jurisdiction zone of a coastal State, the adoption of such measures shall require that State's affirmative vote.

2. Decisions on non-substantive matters shall be adopted by a simple majority of the representatives of the States present. However, if a matter relates to a matter immediately adjacent to the national jurisdiction zone of a coastal State, and the measures to be adopted may affect the conservation of fishery resources in this zone, that State may declare the decision to be a substantive issue.

3. When the participation of the representative of a qualified inter-governmental organization is required in decision-making, it must be specified whether a representative of any of said organization's member States which is also a party to the Framework Agreement will also participate. If this is the case, the number of States Parties taking part in the vote shall not exceed the number of member States of the inter-governmental organization, and the representative of the latter shall have the right to only one vote.

Article 13 Non-Party States

The States Parties shall, individually or collectively, adopt appropriate measures, compatible with international law, to dissuade fishing vessels flying the flags of non-Party States from undertaking activities which undermine the effectiveness of the conservation measures adopted.

Article 14 Dispute settlement

1. Disagreements among the States Parties as to the interpretation or application of the provisions established in this Agreement, or in its complementary instruments, shall be resolved in the first instance through the dispute-settlement procedures set forth in Article 33 of the United Nations Charter, or in other international instruments in force for the States Parties.

2. If an agreement cannot be reached, disputes must be submitted either to a conciliation commission or a technical arbitration body, unless both parties have agreed upon a different procedure.

3. If the voluntary dispute-resolution measures are exhausted, or if agreement is not reached on recourse to other instances, such as the International Court of Justice or the International Law of the Sea Tribunal, either of the parties may solicit a binding arbitration procedure.

4. In no case, subject to the applicable provisions in conformity with international law, shall disputes concerning the exercise of the coastal States' sovereign rights within their respective national jurisdiction zones be submitted to the procedures set forth in paragraph 3.

Article 15 Safeguard clause

None of this Agreement's provisions shall be construed to infringe upon, affect or modify the positions of the States Parties with respect to the nature, limits or reach of their respective zones under national jurisdiction, nor their positions regarding the international instruments which address these issues.

Article 16 Signing, ratification and accession

1. The present Agreement shall be opened for signature by the four coastal States of the Southeast Pacific and ratified according to their respective constitutional procedures in force.

2. Once it enters into force, in accordance with the provisions of Article 19, the Agreement shall become open to the signature of other interested States for a twelve-month period. After this term has passed, any interested State may acceded to the Agreement.

Article 17 Deposit and registration

1. The original of this Agreement and the instruments of ratification or accession, as well as the texts of future amendments or withdrawals, shall be deposited with the General Secretariat of the SPPC, and as an alternative, with the Ministry of Foreign Relations of the State where the Organization's headquarters is established, in conformity with the provisions of Article 11.

2. The depository shall provide the States Parties with authenticated copies of each document.

3. Once the Agreement enters into force, it shall be registered with the General Secretariat of the United Nations Organization.

Article 18 Reservations and declarations

The Agreement shall not be the object of reservations. However, at the moment when any concerned State signs, ratifies or accedes to the Agreement, that State may formulate interpretative declarations, provided that such declarations do not have as their aim the nullification or modification of the legal effects of the Agreement's provisions in their application to that State.

Article 19 Entry into force

1. This Agreement shall enter into force on the thirtieth day following the date on which the four coastal States of the Southeast Pacific have deposited their instruments of ratification.

2. For each of the other interested States that ratify or accede to the Agreement, it shall enter into force on the thirtieth day following the date on which the instrument or accession is deposited.

Article 20 Amendments and revision

1. After one year has passed, counting from the date of the Agreement's entry into force, any State Party may propose amendments, through written communication to the institutional mechanism established in conformity with Article 11, or in its absence, to the General Secretariat.

2. Amendment proposals shall then be distributed to each of the States Parties, so they can be examined at a review conference for their decision.

3. Such proposals shall be required to receive the endorsement of at least a majority of the States Parties, including a majority of the coastal States, in order to proceed to convene the review conference.

4. The provisions set forth in Article 12 shall apply to the adoption of proposed amendments.

5. Approved amendments dealing with substantive issues shall be subject to ratification, and they shall enter into force on the thirtieth day following the date on which a majority of the States Parties have deposited their instruments of ratification. Other amendments shall enter into force on the thirtieth day following the date of their approval.

Article 21 Withdrawal

1. Any State Party may withdraw from the Agreement, by means of written notification addressed to the depository, after one year following its entry into force for the said State.

2. Withdrawal shall take effect one year after the date on which notification is received, unless a later date has been specified.

3. Withdrawal shall not release any State from financial or contractual obligations taken on while that State was a party to the Agreement, nor shall it affect any rights, obligations or legal situation of that State arising through the Agreement's execution before the State's withdrawal from it.

Article 22 Final provisions of complementary instruments

Complementary instruments, as appropriate, must contain final provisions that are similar, mutatis mutandi, to those established in this Agreement.

Article 23 Authentic texts

1. The original text of this Agreement, prepared in Spanish, and its translation into English are equally authentic.

2. In witness whereof, the duly authorized plenipotentiaries of the coastal States subscribe to the present Agreement, at Santiago, Chile, on the fourteenth day of the month of August of the year 2000.

Agreement on the Conservation of Albatrosses and Petrels[15]

The Contracting Parties,

Recalling that the Convention on the Conservation of Migratory Species of Wild Animals, 1979, (the Convention) encourages international cooperative action to conserve and manage migratory species, and that its Parties are encouraged to conclude Agreements on wild animals which periodically cross national jurisdictional boundaries;

Considering that the fifth meeting of the Conference of Parties to the Convention, held in Geneva in April 1997, listed all Southern Hemisphere albatross species on either Appendix I or II;

[15] Adopted 19 June 2001, entered into force 1 February 2004, 2258 UNTS 257.

Recalling that the sixth meeting of the Conference of Parties to the Convention, held in South Africa in November 1999, listed a number of petrel species on Appendix II, noted the threats posed by fisheries by-catch in general to a wide range of species, and in particular to albatrosses and petrels, and requested relevant Parties to develop an Agreement, under the Convention, for the conservation of Southern Hemisphere albatrosses;

Appreciating the work of the Group of Temperate Southern Hemisphere Countries on the Environment (known as the Valdivia Group) in considering the need to address the threats posed to Southern Hemisphere albatross populations, and the work of Australia in taking forward this need in the context of the Convention;

Recognising that albatrosses and petrels are an integral part of marine ecosystems which must be conserved for the benefit of present and future generations, and that their conservation is a matter of common concern, particularly in the Southern Hemisphere;

Aware that the conservation status of albatrosses and petrels can be adversely affected by factors such as degradation and disturbance of their habitats, pollution, reduction of food resources, use and abandonment of non-selective fishing gear, and specifically by incidental mortality as a result of commercial fishing activities;

Convinced that the vulnerability of Southern Hemisphere albatrosses and petrels to such threats warrants the implementation of specific conservation measures, where they do not already exist, by Range States;

Acknowledging that, notwithstanding past or ongoing scientific research, knowledge of the biology, ecology and population dynamics of albatrosses and petrels is limited, and that it is necessary to develop cooperative research and monitoring of these species in order to implement fully effective and efficient conservation measures;

Conscious of the cultural significance of albatrosses and petrels to some indigenous peoples;

Convinced that the conclusion of a multilateral agreement and its implementation through coordinated, concerted actions will contribute significantly to the conservation of Southern Hemisphere albatrosses and petrels and their habitats in the most effective and efficient manner;

Noting that Northern Hemisphere albatrosses and petrels may in future benefit from incorporation into this Agreement with a view to promoting co-ordinated conservation actions between Range States;

Recalling the obligation in the United Nations Convention on the Law of the Sea, 1982, to protect and preserve the marine environment;

Recognising the significance of the Antarctic Treaty, 1959, and the Convention on the Conservation of Antarctic Marine Living Resources, 1980, whose Commission has adopted conservation measures to reduce incidental catch within the area of application of that Convention, particularly of albatrosses and petrels;

Recognising further that the Convention for the Conservation of Southern Bluefin Tuna, 1992, enables its Commission to adopt conservation measures to reduce the incidental catch of seabirds;

Acknowledging that the Food and Agriculture Organization of the United Nations International Plan of Action for Reducing Incidental Catch of Seabirds in Longline Fisheries was adopted in 1999, and that a number of conventions relating to the conservation and management of marine living resources have the capacity to contribute positively to the conservation of albatrosses and petrels;

Recognising the Rio Declaration on Environment and Development, 1992, Principle 15, that, in order to protect the environment, the precautionary approach should be widely applied;

Recalling further that the Convention on Biological Diversity, 1992, obliges its Parties to cooperate with each other or through competent international organisations to conserve biological diversity,

Have agreed as follows:

Article I Scope, definitions and interpretation

1. This Agreement shall apply to the species of albatrosses and petrels listed in Annex I to this Agreement, and their range as defined in paragraph 2(i) of this Article.

2. For the purpose of this Agreement:

(a) "Albatross" and/or "petrel" means one of any species, subspecies or population of the albatrosses and/or, as the case may be, petrels listed in Annex I to this Agreement;

(b) "Secretariat" means the body established under Article VIII of this Agreement;

(c) "Convention" means the Convention on the Conservation of Migratory Species of Wild Animals, 1979;

(d) "UNCLOS" means the United Nations Convention on the Law of the Sea, 1982;

(e) "CCAMLR" means the Convention on the Conservation of Antarctic Marine Living Resources, 1980;

(f) "Convention Secretariat" means the body established under Article IX of the Convention;

(g) "Advisory Committee" means the body established under Article IX of this Agreement;

(h) "Party" means, unless the context otherwise indicates, a State or regional economic integration organisation that is a Party to this Agreement;

(i) "Range" means all the areas of land or water that any albatross or petrel inhabits, stays in temporarily, crosses, or over-flies at any time on its normal migration routes;

(j) "Habitat" means any area which contains suitable living conditions for albatrosses and or petrels;

(k) "Parties present and voting" means the Parties present and casting an affirmative or negative vote; those abstaining from voting shall not be counted amongst the Parties present and voting;

(l) "Migratory species" means the entire population or any geographically separate part of the population of any species or lower taxon of wild animals, a significant proportion of whose members cyclically and predictably cross one or more national boundaries;

(m) "Conservation status of a migratory species" means the sum of the influences acting on the migratory species that may affect its long-term distribution and abundance;

(n) Conservation status will be taken as "favourable" when all of the following conditions are met:

  (i) population dynamics data indicate that the migratory species is maintaining itself on a long-term basis;

  (ii) the range of the migratory species is neither currently being reduced, nor is likely to be reduced, on a long-term basis;

  (iii) there is, and will be in the foreseeable future, sufficient habitat to maintain the population of the migratory species on a long-term basis; and

  (iv) the distribution and abundance of the migratory species approach historic coverage and levels to the extent that potentially suitable ecosystems exist and to the extent consistent with wise wildlife management;

(o) Conservation status will be taken as "unfavourable" if any of the conditions set out in sub-paragraph (n) of this paragraph is not met;

(p) "Range State" means any State that exercises jurisdiction over any part of the range of albatrosses or petrels, or a State, flag vessels of which are engaged outside its national jurisdictional limits in taking, or which have the potential to take, albatrosses and petrels;

(q) "Taking" means taking, hunting, fishing, capturing, harassing, deliberate killing or attempting to engage in any such conduct; and

(r) "Regional economic integration organisation" means an organisation constituted by sovereign States of a given region which has competence in respect of matters governed by this Agreement and has been duly authorised, in accordance with its internal procedures, to sign, ratify, accept approve or accede to this Agreement.

3. Any regional economic integration organisation which becomes a Party to the Agreement without any of its member States being a Party to the Agreement shall be bound by all the obligations under the Agreement. Where one or more member States of such an organisation are also Party to the Agreement, the organisation and its member States shall decide on their respective responsibilities for the performance of their obligations under the Agreement. In such cases, the organisation and the member States shall not be entitled to exercise rights under the Agreement concurrently.

4. In their instruments of ratification, acceptance, approval or accession, regional economic integration organisations shall declare the extent of their competence with respect to the matters governed by the Agreement. They shall also promptly inform the Depository, who shall in turn inform the Parties, of any substantial modification in the extent of their competence.

5. This Agreement is an AGREEMENT within the meaning of Article IV (3) of the Convention.

6. The annexes to this Agreement form an integral part thereof. Any reference to the Agreement includes a reference to its annexes.

Article II Objective and Fundamental Principles

1. The objective of this Agreement is to achieve and maintain a favourable conservation status for albatrosses and petrels.

2. The Parties shall take measures, both individually and together, to achieve this objective.

3. In implementing such measures the Parties shall widely apply the precautionary approach. In particular, where there are threats of serious or irreversible adverse impacts or damage, lack of full scientific certainty shall not be used as a reason for postponing measures to enhance the conservation status of albatrosses and petrels.

Article III General Conservation Measures

1. In furtherance of their obligation to take measures to achieve and maintain a favourable conservation status for albatrosses and petrels, the Parties, having regard to Article XIII, shall:

(a) conserve and, where feasible and appropriate, restore those habitats which are of importance to albatrosses and petrels;
(b) eliminate or control non-native species detrimental to albatrosses and petrels;
(c) develop and implement measures to prevent, remove, minimize or mitigate the adverse effects of activities that may influence the conservation status of albatrosses and petrels;
(d) initiate or support research into the effective conservation of albatrosses and petrels;
(e) ensure the existence and appropriateness of training for, inter alia, the implementation of conservation measures;
(f) develop and maintain programmes to raise awareness and understanding of albatross and petrel conservation issues;
(g) exchange information and results from albatross and petrel, and other relevant, conservation programmes; and
(h) support the implementation of the actions elaborated in the FAO International Plan of Action for Reducing Incidental Catch of Seabirds in Longline Fisheries which complement the objectives of this Agreement.

2. The Parties shall, subject to paragraphs 3 to 5 of this Article, prohibit the deliberate taking of, or harmful interference with, albatrosses and petrels, their eggs, or their breeding sites.

3. Parties may grant an exemption to the prohibitions in paragraph 2 of this Article, but only if there is no other satisfactory course of action and the exemption is made for one of the following purposes:

(a) to enhance the propagation, re-establishment or survival of albatrosses or petrels;
(b) on a selective basis and to a limited extent for scientific, educational or similar purposes;
(c) to accommodate the traditional needs and practices of indigenous peoples; or
(d) in other exceptional circumstances, in which case, unless an exceptional circumstance is of the nature of a short-term emergency, a prior environmental impact assessment shall

be carried out and made publicly available in accordance with requirements in the Action Plan established by Article VI.

4. Any exemption under paragraph 3 of this Article, shall be precise, and limited in space and time, and shall not operate to the detriment of the conservation status of albatrosses or petrels. Any Parties granting such exemptions shall, as soon as possible, submit full details of them to the Secretariat.

5. Humane killing, by duly authorised persons, to end the suffering of seriously injured or moribund albatrosses or petrels shall not constitute deliberate taking or harmful interference.

6. In furtherance of their obligation to take measures to achieve and maintain a favourable conservation status for albatrosses or petrels, the Parties shall progressively implement the Action Plan.

Article IV Capacity Building

1. Effective implementation of this Agreement requires assistance to be provided to some Range States, including through research, training or monitoring for implementation of conservation measures for albatrosses and petrels and their habitats, for the management of those habitats as well as for the establishment or improvement of scientific and administrative institutions for the implementation of this Agreement.

2. The Parties shall give priority to capacity building, through funding, training, information and institutional support, for the implementation of the Agreement.

Article V Cooperation between Parties

The Parties shall cooperate, having regard to the Action Plan, to:

(a) develop systems for collecting and analysing data, and exchanging information;

(b) exchange information regarding adoption and enforcement of legislative and other management approaches to conservation of albatrosses and petrels;

(c) implement education and awareness programmes for users of areas where albatrosses and petrels may be encountered;

(d) design and implement comprehensive programmes for public information in relation to the conservation of albatrosses and petrels;

(e) develop and implement training programmes on conservation techniques and measures to mitigate threats affecting albatrosses and petrels; and

(f) undertake exchange of expertise, techniques and knowledge.

Article VI Action Plan

1. Annex 2 of this Agreement shall have effect as an Action Plan for the achievement and maintenance of a favourable conservation status for albatrosses and petrels.

2. With due consideration to the capabilities of Parties to implement such actions, and with specific reference to Article IV, the Action Plan shall at all times set out the actions that the Parties shall progressively undertake in relation to albatrosses and petrels, consistent with the general conservation measures specified in Article III, including:

(a) species conservation;

(b) habitat conservation and restoration;

(c) management of human activities;

(d) research and monitoring;

(e) collation of information;

(f) education and public awareness; and

(g) implementation.

3. Progress in implementing the Action Plan shall be assessed at each ordinary session of the Meeting of the Parties and the content of the Action Plan reviewed in light of that assessment.

4. The Meeting of Parties shall consider any proposed amendment to the Action Plan in the light of the provisions of Article III before deciding on its adoption in accordance with Article XII.

Article VII Implementation and Financing

1. Each Party shall:

(a) designate an Authority or Authorities to undertake, monitor and control all activities carried on with a view to the supervision, application and enforcement of this Agreement. Such Authority or Authorities shall, inter alia, monitor all activities that may have an impact on the conservation status of those albatross and petrel species for which the Party is a Range State;

(b) designate a Contact Point and communicate without delay its name and address to the Secretariat to be circulated forthwith to the other Parties; and

(c) in relation to each ordinary session of the Meeting of the Parties, beginning with the second session, provide information through the Secretariat to the Advisory Committee so that it may prepare a synthesised report on the implementation of the Agreement, with particular reference to the conservation measures undertaken, in accordance with Article IX (6).

Such an Authority or Authorities and Contact Point shall be the central Government Ministry or agency, as the case may be, responsible for the administration of this Agreement.

2.

(a) Decisions relating to the budget and any scale of contributions shall be adopted by the Meeting of the Parties by consensus, having regard to the differing resources of the different Parties.

(b) If consensus cannot be reached, the previously approved budget shall continue to apply until superseded by a new, agreed budget.

(c) Following the accession of any new Party, the Meeting of the Parties shall, at its next session, review and replace the scale of contributions unless it agrees such review and replacement to be inappropriate.

3. The Meeting of the Parties may establish a fund from voluntary contributions of Parties or from any other source for the purpose of work relating to the conservation of albatrosses and petrels, including monitoring, research, technical development, training, education and habitat management. No surcharge shall be levied on such voluntary contributions or on such a fund to meet administrative overheads of the Secretariat or any organisation providing services to it.

4. The Parties shall, in support of their obligations under Article IV, endeavour to provide training, technical and financial support to other Parties on a multilateral or bilateral basis to assist them in implementing the provisions of this Agreement. No surcharge shall be levied on the costs of such training, technical or financial support to meet administrative overheads of the Secretariat or any organisation providing services to it.

5. A fund may be used to meet expenses related to the participation of Party representatives in sessions of the Meeting of the Parties and the Advisory Committee. This shall not preclude such expenses being met by other arrangements, bilateral or otherwise.

Article VIII Meeting of the Parties

1. The Meeting of the Parties shall be the decision-making body of this Agreement.

2. The Depositary shall, in consultation with the Convention Secretariat, convene a session of the Meeting of the Parties not later than one year after the date of the entry into force of this Agreement. Ordinary sessions of the Meeting of the Parties shall be held at intervals of not more than three years, unless the Meeting of the Parties decides otherwise.

3. On the written request of at least one third of the Parties, the Secretariat shall convene an extraordinary session of the Meeting of the Parties.

4. The Meeting of the Parties shall make provision in its rules of procedure, adopted in accordance with paragraph 11 of this Article, for governing the attendance and participation of observers and to provide for transparency in the activities relating to the Agreement. Such rules

shall not be unduly restrictive in this respect and shall provide for timely access to the records and reports relating to the Agreement. The Meeting of the Parties shall adopt such rules of procedure, taking account of potential costs, as soon as possible.

5. Any State not a Party to the Agreement, the United Nations, any specialised Agency of the United Nations, any regional economic integration organisation, and any secretariat of relevant international conventions, particularly those concerned with the conservation and management of marine living resources or the conservation of albatrosses and petrels, may participate as observers in sessions of the Meeting of the Parties and its subsidiary bodies. Such participation shall be subject to the rules of procedure.

6. Any relevant scientific, environmental, cultural or technical body concerned with the conservation and management of marine living resources or the conservation of albatrosses and petrels, may participate as an observer in sessions of the Meeting of the Parties and its subsidiary bodies. Such participation shall be subject to the rules of procedure. Rules of procedure in relation to this paragraph, including provision for the attendance of observers, may include provision for voting different from that in paragraph 9 of this Article.

7. Each Party shall have one vote, but regional economic integration organisations which are Parties to this Agreement shall, in matters within their competence, exercise their right to vote with a number of votes equal to the number of their Member States which are Parties to the Agreement. A regional economic integration organisation shall not exercise its right to vote if its Member States exercise theirs, and vice versa.

8. The Meeting of the Parties shall establish and keep under review the financial regulations of this Agreement. The Meeting of the Parties shall, at each of its ordinary sessions, adopt a budget for the next financial period. Financial regulations, including the provisions of the budget and scale of contributions as well as their modifications, shall be adopted by consensus.

9. Unless provided otherwise in this Agreement, decisions of the Meeting of the Parties shall be adopted by consensus or, if consensus cannot be achieved, by a two-thirds majority of the Parties present and voting.

10. The Meeting of the Parties may require any information relevant to the effective functioning of this Agreement to be supplied to the Parties by way of the Secretariat, in addition to the information required by Article VII (I) (c).

11. At its first session, the Meeting of the Parties shall:

(a) adopt its rules of procedure by consensus;
(b) determine the financial arrangements, a scale of contributions and a budget by consensus;
(c) establish a Secretariat to perform the secretariat functions listed in Article X of this Agreement;
(d) establish the Advisory Committee provided for in Article IX of this Agreement; and
(e) adopt criteria to define emergency situations that require urgent conservation measures and determine the modalities for assigning responsibility for action to be taken.

12. At each of its ordinary sessions, the Meeting of the Parties shall:

(a) consider reports, advice and information from any of its subsidiary bodies;
(b) consider actual and potential changes in the conservation status of albatrosses and petrels, and the habitats important for their survival, as well as the factors that may affect them;
(c) review any difficulty encountered in the implementation of this Agreement;
(d) consider any matters relating to the financial arrangements for this Agreement and adopt a budget by consensus;
(e) deal with any matter relating to the Secretariat, and membership and funding of the Advisory Committee;
(f) adopt a report to be communicated to the Parties to this Agreement and to the Conference of the Parties of the Convention; and
(g) determine the time and venue of its next session.

13. At any of its sessions, the Meeting of the Parties may:
(a) amend the rules of procedure;
(b) make such recommendations as it deems necessary or appropriate;
(c) adopt measures to improve the effectiveness of this Agreement and, as the case may be, emergency measures as provided for in Article IX (7) of this Agreement;
(d) consider and decide upon proposals to amend this Agreement;
(e) amend Annex I;
(f) amend the Action Plan in accordance with Article VI (4) of this Agreement;
(g) establish such subsidiary bodies as it deems necessary to assist in the implementation of this Agreement, in particular for coordination with bodies established under other relevant international treaties;
(h) vary any time limits set in this Agreement for the submission of documents or otherwise; and
(i) decide on any other matter relating to the implementation of this Agreement.

14. At every third session of the Meeting of the Parties, it shall review the effectiveness of the Secretariat in facilitating the achievement of the objectives of this Agreement. The previous session of the Meeting of the Parties shall agree the Terms of Reference for the review.

15. The Meeting of the Parties may adopt by consensus provisions for the relationship to this Agreement by any member economy of the Asia Pacific Economic Co-operation forum whose vessels fish within the range of albatrosses and petrels. Those provisions, once adopted, shall enable the member economy to participate in the work of the Meeting of the Parties and its subsidiary bodies, including decision-making, and to comply with all obligations under this Agreement. For this purpose, references under those provisions to those participating in the Meeting of the Parties or its subsidiary bodies shall include such a member economy as well as Parties.

Article IX Advisory Committee

1. The Meeting of the Parties shall establish an Advisory Committee ("the Committee") to provide expert advice and information to Parties, the Secretariat and others.

2. Each Party shall be entitled to appoint one member to the Committee. Each Committee member may be accompanied by one or more advisers.

3. The Committee may invite other experts to attend its meetings. It may establish working groups.

4. The Parties shall seek to support the expenses of experts attending meetings of the Committee so as to optimise the contributions of all Parties to achieving the objective of the Agreement.

5. The Committee shall elect a Chair and Vice-chair and establish its own rules of procedure.

6. The Committee shall:
(a) provide scientific, technical and other advice and information to the Meeting of the Parties and, through the Secretariat, to the Parties;
(b) endorse a standard reference text listing the taxonomy and maintain a listing of taxonomic synonyms for all species covered by the Agreement;
(c) make recommendations to the Meeting of the Parties concerning the Action Plan, implementation of the Agreement and further research to be carried out;
(d) prepare a report to each ordinary Meeting of the Parties after the first on the implementation of the Agreement, with particular reference to the Action Plan and the conservation measures undertaken. Each such report shall include a synthesis of such information as Parties are required to submit to the Committee through the Secretariat under Article VII (I)(c), and an assessment of the status and trends of albatross and petrel populations, but:
    (i) the format of such reports from the Committee shall be determined by the first session of the Meeting of the Parties and reviewed as may be necessary at any subsequent session of the Meeting of the Parties; and the nature of the information to be provided

by the Parties shall be determined by the Committee at its first meeting, subject to any direction from the Meeting of the Parties, and reviewed as may be necessary at any subsequent meeting; and

(ii) each such report from the Committee shall be submitted to the Secretariat not less than one hundred and twenty days before the ordinary session of the Meeting of the Parties at which it is to be discussed; and, subject to any direction from the Meeting of the Parties, the Committee may set such prior time limits for the submission of information by Parties for this purpose as it may from time to time see fit;

(e) submit to the Secretariat for circulation to the Parties, not less than one hundred and twenty days before each ordinary session of the Meeting of the Parties, a report on its own activities;

(f) develop a system of indicators to measure the collective success of the Parties to the Agreement in addressing the objective set out in Article II (I), and subsequently apply it in the reports made under paragraph 6(d) of this Article; and

(g) carry out any other appropriate tasks referred to it by the Meeting of the Parties.

7. Where, in the opinion of the Committee, there has arisen an emergency that requires the adoption of immediate measures to avoid deterioration of the conservation status of one or more albatross or petrel species, the Committee may request the Secretariat to convene urgently a meeting of the Parties concerned. These Parties shall meet as soon as possible thereafter to establish a mechanism with a view to giving protection to the species identified as being subject to a threat. Where a recommendation has been adopted at such a meeting, the Parties concerned shall inform each other and the Secretariat of the measures they have taken to implement it, or of the reasons why the recommendation could not be implemented.

8. The Committee may incur such expenditure from the budget of the Agreement as may be authorised by the Meeting of the Parties under Article VIII (12) (e).

Article X Agreement Secretariat

The functions of the Secretariat shall be:

(a) to arrange and service the sessions of the Meeting of the Parties as well as the meetings of the Advisory Committee;

(b) to execute the decisions addressed to it by the Meeting of the Parties;

(c) to promote and coordinate activities under the Agreement, including the Action Plan, in accordance with decisions of the Meeting of the Parties;

(d) to liaise with non-Party Range States and regional economic integration organisations and to facilitate coordination between Parties and non-Party Range States, and international and national organisations and institutions whose activities are directly or indirectly relevant to the conservation, including the protection and management, of albatrosses and petrels;

(e) to invite the attention of the Meeting of the Parties to matters pertaining to the objectives of this Agreement;

(f) to provide to each ordinary session of the Meeting of the Parties a report on its work;

(g) to administer the budget for the Agreement and, if established, the fund provided for in Article VII (3);

(h) to provide information to the general public concerning the Agreement and its objectives, and promote the objectives of this Agreement;

(i) to develop a system of performance indicators to measure the effectiveness and efficiency of the Secretariat and report to each ordinary session of the Meeting of the Parties in terms of these;

(j) to collate as appropriate information provided by Parties through the Secretariat under Article VII (1)(c) and Article VIII (10); and

(k) to perform such other functions as may be entrusted to it by or under the Agreement.

Article XI Relations with Relevant International Bodies

1. The Parties shall promote the objectives of this Agreement and develop and maintain coordinated and complementary working relationships with all relevant international, regional and sub-regional bodies, including those concerned with the conservation and management of seabirds and their habitats and other marine living resources, particularly with the Commission of CCAMLR and the Food and Agriculture Organization of the United Nations, particularly in the context of the International Plan of Action for Reducing Incidental Catch of Seabirds in Longline Fisheries.

2. The Secretariat shall consult and cooperate, where appropriate, with:

(a) the Convention Secretariat, and the bodies responsible for secretariat functions under Agreements concluded pursuant to Article IV (3) and (4), of the Convention, that are relevant to albatrosses and petrels;

(b) the secretariats of other relevant conventions and international instruments in respect of matters of common interest; and

(c) other organisations or institutions with competence in the field of conservation of albatrosses and petrels and their habitats, as well as in the fields of research, education and awareness raising, including the Committee for Environmental Protection established under the Protocol for Environmental Protection to the Antarctic Treaty.

3. The Secretariat may enter into arrangements, with the approval of the Meeting of Parties, with other organisations and institutions as may be appropriate.

4. The Secretariat shall consult and cooperate with these bodies in exchanging information and data, and may, with the consent of the Chair of the Advisory Committee, invite these bodies to send observers to relevant meetings.

Article XII Amendment of the Agreement

1. This Agreement may be amended at any ordinary or extraordinary session of the Meeting of the Parties.

2. Any Party may make proposals for amendment.

3. The text of any proposed amendment and the reasons for it shall be communicated to the Secretariat not less than one hundred and fifty days before the opening of the session. The Secretariat shall transmit copies of any proposed amendment forthwith to the Parties. Any comments on a proposed amendment by the Parties shall be communicated to the Secretariat not less than sixty days before the opening of the session. The Secretariat shall, as soon as possible after the last day for submission of comments, communicate to the Parties all comments submitted by that day.

4. An amendment to the Agreement, other than an amendment to its annexes, shall be adopted by a two-thirds majority of the Parties present and voting. Parties accepting the amendment shall deposit their instruments of acceptance with the Depositary. Amendments enter into force for accepting Parties on the thirtieth day after the date on which two-thirds of the Parties to the Agreement on the date of the amendment's adoption have deposited their instruments of acceptance. For each Party that deposits an instrument of acceptance after the date on which two-thirds of the Parties have deposited their instruments of acceptance, the amendment shall enter into force on the thirtieth day after the date on which it deposits its instrument of acceptance.

5. Any additional annex or amendment to an annex shall be adopted by a two-thirds majority of the Parties present and voting and shall enter into force for all Parties on the ninetieth day after the date of its adoption by the Meeting of the Parties, except for Parties that have entered a reservation in accordance with paragraph 6 of this Article.

6. During the period of ninety days provided for in paragraph 5 of this Article, any Party may, by written notification to the Depositary, enter a reservation with respect to an additional annex or an amendment to an annex. Such reservation may be withdrawn at any time by written notification to the Depositary, and the additional annex or the amendment shall enter into force for that Party on the thirtieth day after the date of withdrawal of the reservation.

Article XIII Relationship between this Agreement and other Legislation and International Conventions

1. For the purposes of this Agreement:

(a) nothing in this Agreement shall derogate from the rights and obligations of any Party deriving from existing international treaties, particularly in relation to the United Nations Convention on the Law of the Sea (UNCLOS), and also to the Antarctic Treaty and CCAMLR and especially Article IV in both instruments;

(b) with respect to the Antarctic Treaty area, all Parties, whether or not they are Parties to the Antarctic Treaty, shall be bound by Articles IV and VI of the Antarctic Treaty in their relations with each other;

(c) nothing in this Agreement and no acts or activities taking place while the present Agreement is in force shall:

(i) be interpreted as a renunciation or diminution by any Party of, or as prejudicing, any right or claim or basis of claim to territorial sovereignty or to the exercise of coastal state jurisdiction under international law within the area to which this Agreement applies; or

(ii) be interpreted as prejudicing the position of any Party as regards its recognition or non-recognition of any such right, claim or basis of claim.

2. In relation to fishing activities under the auspices of a regional fisheries organisation, or other organisations managing marine living resources more generally, such as the Commission of CCAMLR, the Parties shall consider information and evaluations from that organisation, and shall adopt, in its area of competence, the measures agreed by that organisation for reducing the incidental taking of albatrosses and petrels. Notwithstanding this, and in conformity with paragraph 3 of this Article, the Parties may implement measures that are more strict than those measures, when such measures are within their competency, taking account of the provisions of Article I (3).

3. The provisions of this Agreement shall in no way affect the right of any Party to maintain or adopt stricter measures for the conservation of albatrosses and petrels and their habitats.

Article XIV Settlement of Disputes

1. Parties shall co-operate in order to avoid disputes.

2. Where a dispute between two or more Parties is agreed to be of a technical nature, the Parties shall confer with each other and the Chair of the Advisory Committee with a view to resolving the dispute amicably. Where the Parties are unable to resolve the dispute within twelve months of the Chair having been informed in writing of the dispute by one of the parties, and prolongation of the dispute could, in the view of the Chair, have an adverse effect on the conservation status of albatrosses and petrels listed in this Agreement, they shall refer the dispute to a technical arbitration panel.

3. The technical arbitration panel shall be established by the Chair of the Advisory Committee, in consultation with the Parties in dispute, and shall be drawn from members of the Advisory Committee, and such other experts as necessary. The panel shall confer with the Parties in dispute and endeavour to reach a final decision within five months of establishment of the panel. That decision shall be binding on the Parties in dispute.

4. The procedures relating to technical arbitration panels and other procedures to resolve disputes shall be determined by the Meeting of the Parties.

5. Any other dispute, that may arise between two or more Parties with respect specifically to the interpretation or application of this Agreement, shall be subject to the provisions of Article XIII of the Convention, which shall apply whether or not the Parties to the dispute are also Parties to the Convention.

6. This Article does not preclude the application of the dispute settlement provisions of any other treaty in force between the Parties in dispute in relation to disputes covered by those provisions.

Article XV Signature, Ratification, Acceptance, Approval, Accession

1. This Agreement shall be open for signature by any Range State or regional economic integration organisation, whether or not areas under its jurisdiction lie within the area of this Agreement, by:

(a) Signature without reservation in respect of ratification, acceptance or approval; or

(b) Signature with reservation in respect of ratification, acceptance or approval, followed by ratification, acceptance or approval.

2. This Agreement shall remain open for signature at Canberra until the date of its entry into force.

3. This Agreement shall be open for accession by any Range State or regional economic integration organisation on and after the date of its entry into force.

4. Instruments of ratification, acceptance, approval or accession shall be deposited with the Depositary.

Article XVI Entry into Force

l. This Agreement shall enter into force on the first day of the third month after at least five Range States or regional economic integration organisations have signed without reservation in respect of ratification, acceptance or approval, or have deposited their instruments of ratification, acceptance or approval in accordance with Article XV.

2. For any Range State or regional economic integration organisation which has:

(a) signed without reservation in respect of ratification, acceptance, or approval;

(b) ratified, accepted, or approved; or

(c) acceded to

this Agreement after the date on which the number of Range States or regional economic integration organisations necessary to enable entry into force have signed it without reservation or have ratified, accepted or approved it, this Agreement shall enter into force on the first day of the third month following the signature without reservation, or deposit, by that State or regional economic integration organisation of its instrument of ratification, acceptance, approval or accession.

Article XVII Reservations

1. The provisions of this Agreement shall not be subject to general reservations.

2. However, a specific reservation in respect of any species covered by the Agreement or any specific provision of the Action Plan may be entered by any Range State or regional economic integration organisation on signature without qualification in respect of ratification, acceptance or approval or, as the case may be, on depositing its instrument of ratification, acceptance, approval or accession.

3. Such a reservation may be withdrawn at any time by the Range State or regional economic integration organisation which had entered it, by notification in writing to the Depositary. Such a State or regional economic integration organisation shall not be bound by the provisions that are the object of the reservation until thirty days after the date on which the reservation has been withdrawn.

4. The provisions contained in paragraph I of this Article do not preclude a Party to this Agreement that is not a Party to the Convention from making declarations or statements to the effect of clarifying its status vis-à-vis each instrument, provided that such declarations or statements do not purport to exclude or to modify the legal effect of the provisions of this Agreement in their application to that Party.

Article XVIII Denunciation

A Party may denounce this Agreement by written notification to the Depositary at any time. The denunciation shall take effect twelve months after the date on which the Depositary has received the notification.

Article XIX Depositary

1. The original of this Agreement, in the English, French and Spanish languages, each version being equally authentic, shall be deposited with the Government of Australia, which shall be the Depositary. The Depositary shall transmit certified copies of these versions to all Range States and regional economic integration organisations referred to in Article XV(1) of this Agreement, and to the Secretariat after it has been established.

2. As soon as this Agreement enters into force, a certified copy thereof shall be transmitted by the Depositary to the Secretariat of the United Nations for registration and publication in accordance with Article 102 of the Charter of the United Nations.

3. The Depositary shall inform all Range States and regional economic integration organisations that have signed or acceded to the Agreement, and the Secretariat, of:

(a) any signature;
(b) any deposit of instruments of ratification, acceptance, approval or accession;
(c) the date of entry into force of this Agreement as well as of any amendment to the Agreement;
(d) any reservation with respect to the Agreement;
(e) any notification of withdrawal of a reservation; and
(f) any notification of denunciation of the Agreement.

4. The Depositary shall immediately transmit to all Range States and regional economic integration organisations that have signed or acceded to this Agreement, and to the Secretariat, the text of any reservation, any additional annex or amendment to the Agreement or to its annexes.

In witness whereof the undersigned, being duly authorised to that effect, have signed this Agreement.

Done at Canberra this nineteenth day of June 2001.

[Signatures not reproduced here]

Annex I –Albatross and Petrel Species to which this Agreement Applies

Existing Convention Appendices I and II	New Taxonomy*
Albatrosses	
Diomedea exulans (II)	Diomedea exulans
	Diomedea dabbenena
	Diomedea antipodensis
	Diomedea gibsoni
Diomedea amsterdamensis (I)	Diomedea amsterdamensis
Diomedea epomophora	Diomedea epomophora
	Diomedea sanfordi
Diomedea irrorata (II)	Diomedea irrorata
Diomedea cauta (II)	Thalassarche cauta
	Thalassarche steadi
	Thalassarche salvini
	Thalassarche eremita
Diomedea bulleri (II)	Thalassarche bulleri
	Thalassarche nov. sp. (platei)
Diomedea chrysotoma (II)	Thalassarche chrysotoma

Diomedea melanophris (II)	Thalassarche melanophris
	Thalassarche impavida
Diomedea chlororhynchos (II)	Thalassarche carteri
	Thalassarche chlororhynchos
Phoebetria fusca (II)	Phoebetria fusca
Phoebetria palpebrata (II)	Phoebetria palpebrata

Petrels

Macronectes giganteus (II)	Macronectes giganteus
Macronectes halli (II)	Macronectes halli
Procellaria aequinoctialis (II)	Procellaria aequinoctialis
Procellaria aequinoctialis conspicillata (II)	Procellaria conspicillata
Procellaria parkinsoni (II)	Procellaria parkinsoni
Procellaria westlandica (II)	Procellaria westlandica
Procellaria cinerea (II)	Procellaria cinerea

The lists above display the existing albatross and petrel taxonomy listed in Appendix I and II of the Convention (Column 1) and a new taxonomy (Column 2). In the event of the adoption by the Conference of Parties of the Convention of the taxonomy listed in Column 2, the taxonomy in Column 1 shall no longer form part of this Annex.

* New taxonomy follows:

Robertson, C.J.R. and Nunn, G.B. 1997. Toward a new taxonomy for albatrosses. Pp. 413–19 in Albatross biology and conservation, ed. by G. Robertson and R. Gales. Surrey Beatty & Sons, Chipping Norton; as modified by Croxall, J.P. and Gales, R. 1997. An assessment of the conservation status of albatrosses. Pp. 46–65 in Albatross biology and conservation, ed. by G. Robertson and R. Gales. Surrey Beatty & Sons, Chipping Norton; and

Ryan, P.G. 1998. The taxonomic and conservation status of the spectacled petrel Procellaria conspicillata. Bird Conservation International 8: 223–235.

Annex 2 – Action Plan

1. Species Conservation

1.1 Species Conservation

1.1.1 In addition to actions specified in Article III and without prejudice to any obligations they may have under the Convention on International Trade in Endangered Species of Wild Fauna and Flora (CITES), the Parties shall prohibit the use of, and trade in, albatrosses and petrels or their eggs, or any readily recognisable parts or derivatives thereof.

1.1.2 Except for provisions made for species listed under CITES, the Parties may grant exemptions to the prohibition in Paragraph 1.1.1 according to the circumstances provided for in Article III (3).

1.1.3 The Parties shall, where they consider it appropriate, co-operate to develop and implement conservation strategies for particular species or groups of species of albatrosses or petrels. The Secretariat shall co-ordinate the development, harmonisation and implementation of such conservation strategies.

1.2 Emergency measures

In the event of a request by the Advisory Committee for a meeting of Parties under the emergency provisions of Article IX (7), the Parties affected, in co-operation as appropriate with each other and with any others, shall develop and implement emergency measures.

1.3 Re-establishments and re-establishment schemes

The Parties shall take a precautionary approach when re-establishing albatrosses and petrels into parts of their traditional breeding range. In such cases, they shall develop and follow a detailed re-establishment scheme. Such schemes shall be based on best scientific evidence and should be publicly available. The Parties shall inform the Secretariat where possible in advance of all re-establishment schemes.

1.4 Non-native Taxa

1.4.1 The Parties shall take all feasible action to prevent the introduction to habitats, deliberately or otherwise, of non-native taxa of animals, plants or hybrids or disease-causing organisms that may be detrimental to populations of albatrosses and petrels.

1.4.2 The Parties shall take measures to the extent feasible to control and, where possible, eradicate non-native taxa of animals or plants, or hybrids thereof, that are, or may be, detrimental to populations of albatrosses or petrels. Such measures should satisfy to the extent feasible, humane and environmental considerations.

2. Habitat Conservation and Restoration

2.1 General Principles

So far as is appropriate and necessary, the Parties shall take such management action, and introduce such legislative and other controls, as will maintain populations of albatrosses and petrels at, or restore them to, favourable conservation status, and prevent the degradation of habitats.

2.2 Land-based conservation

2.2.1 Where feasible, the Parties shall give protection to the breeding sites of albatrosses and petrels, using existing mechanisms where available. For all such protected areas, the Parties shall endeavour to develop and implement management plans and take other actions which maintain and enhance the conservation status of the species, including inter alia the prevention of habitat degradation, the reduction of disturbance to habitats and the minimisation or elimination of damage by introduced non-native animals, plants, hybrids or disease-causing organisms.

2.2.2 The Parties shall, wherever possible and relevant, co-operate on habitat protection initiatives, especially to ensure the protection and restoration of as many as possible of the breeding sites of albatrosses and petrels that have unfavourable conservation status.

2.2.3 The Parties shall individually or collectively ensure that all breeding sites of international importance for albatrosses and petrels are given priority attention.

2.3 Conservation of marine habitats

2.3.1 The Parties shall endeavour individually and collectively to manage marine habitats so as to:

(a) ensure the sustainability of marine living resources that provide food for albatrosses and petrels; and

(b) avoid pollution that may harm albatrosses and petrels.

2.3.2 The Parties shall individually or collectively seek to develop management plans for the most important foraging and migratory habitats of albatrosses and petrels. Such plans shall seek to minimise risks in accordance with paragraph 2.3.1.

2.3.3 The Parties shall take special measures individually and collectively to conserve marine areas which they consider critical to the survival and/or restoration of species of albatrosses and petrels which have unfavourable conservation status.

3. Management of Human Activities

3.1 Impact Assessment

The Parties shall assess the potential impact on albatrosses and petrels of policies, plans, programmes and projects which they consider likely to affect the conservation of albatrosses and petrels before any decision on whether to adopt such policies, plans, programmes or projects, and shall make the results of these assessments publicly available.

3.2 Incidental mortality in fisheries

3.2.1 The Parties shall take appropriate operational, management and other measures to reduce or eliminate the mortality of albatrosses and petrels resulting incidentally from fishing activities. Where possible, the measures applied should follow best current practice.

3.2.2 In relation to fishing activities under the auspices of a regional fisheries organisation, or other organisations managing marine living resources more generally, such as the Commission of CCAMLR, the Parties shall consider information and evaluations from that organisation, and shall adopt, in its area of competence, the measures agreed by that organisation for reducing the incidental taking of albatrosses and petrels. Notwithstanding this, and in conformity with the provisions of Article XIII (3), the Parties may implement measures, that are more strict than those measures, when such measures are within their competency, taking account of the provisions of Article I (3).

3.2.3 The Parties which are also parties to other relevant treaties (such as CCAMLR), or members of relevant international organisations (such as FAO), shall encourage the institutions of, and other parties to, or members of, such treaties or organisations, to give effect to the objective of this Agreement.

3.2.4 The Parties shall endeavour, within the context of this Agreement, to adopt additional measures to combat illegal, unregulated and unreported fishing activities that may have an adverse effect on albatrosses and petrels.

3.3 Pollutants and marine debris

3.3.1 The Parties shall take appropriate measures, within environmental conventions and by other means, to minimise the discharge from land-based sources and from vessels, of pollutants which may have an adverse effect on albatrosses and petrels either on land or at sea.

3.3.2 The Parties shall seek to manage, in ways that are consistent with the aims of this Agreement, mineral exploration and exploitation in waters under their jurisdiction which are frequented by albatrosses and petrels.

3.4 Disturbance

3.4.1 In both marine and terrestrial habitats, the Parties shall seek to minimise disturbance of albatrosses and petrels, and to establish and maintain some areas that are kept free from disturbance.

3.4.2 The Parties shall seek to avoid or minimise disturbance caused by, inter alia, tourism, and in particular by controlling the proximity of approach to breeding birds.

3.4.3 In permitting access to breeding sites of albatrosses and petrels for purposes of scientific research, particularly where species are of unfavourable conservation status, the Parties shall require that such research is designed and carried out so as to avoid unnecessary disturbance to birds, or impact on their habitats.

4. Research and Monitoring

4.1 Parties shall seek to undertake research and monitoring in order to fulfil the requirements of Article III, both at sea and on land. Where appropriate, they shall do so cooperatively, and shall seek to facilitate the development of improved research and monitoring techniques.

4.2 The Parties shall, through the use of at-sea observers on fishing vessels or through other appropriate methods, collect reliable and, where possible, verifiable data to enable the accurate estimation of the nature and extent of albatross and petrel interactions with fisheries.

5. Collation of Information by the Advisory Committee

5.1 The reports of the Advisory Committee under Article IX (6)(c), should as appropriate include:

(a) assessments and reviews of the status of populations of albatrosses and petrels, including an assessment of population trends of the species, especially those in poorly known areas and of species for which few data are available;

(b) identification of internationally important breeding sites;

(c) reviews to characterise, on the basis of the best available evidence, the foraging range (and principal feeding areas within this) and migration routes and patterns, of populations of albatrosses and petrels;

(d) identification and assessment of known and suspected threats affecting albatrosses and petrels;

(e) identification of existing and new methods by which these threats may be avoided or mitigated;
(f) reviews, and updating on a regular basis, of data on the mortality of albatrosses and petrels in, inter alia, commercial, and other relevant fisheries;
(g) reviews of data on the distribution and seasonality of effort in fisheries which affect albatrosses and petrels;
(h) reviews of the status at breeding sites of introduced animals, plants and disease-causing organisms known or believed to be detrimental to albatrosses and petrels;
(i) reviews of the nature of, coverage by, and effectiveness of, protection arrangements for albatrosses and petrels;
(j) reviews of recent and current research on albatrosses and petrels with relevance to their conservation status;
(k) lists of authorities, research centres, scientists and non-governmental organisations concerned with albatrosses and petrels;
(l) a directory of legislation concerning albatrosses and petrels;
(m) reviews of education and information programmes aimed at conserving albatrosses and petrels; and
(n) reviews of current taxonomy in relation to albatrosses and petrels.

5.2 The Advisory Committee should identify gaps in information as part of the above reviews, with a view to addressing these in future priorities.

6. Education and Public Awareness

6.1 The Parties shall seek to make information on the conservation status of albatrosses and petrels, the threats facing them, and the activities taken under the Agreement, available to the scientific, fishing and conservation communities, as well as to relevant local authorities and other decision-makers, and to neighbouring states.

6.2 The Parties shall seek to make local communities and the public in general more aware of the status of albatrosses and petrels and the threats facing them.

6.3 The Parties shall cooperate with each other, the Secretariat and others with a view to developing training programmes and exchanging resource materials.

6.4 The Parties shall, where necessary, arrange for training programmes to ensure that personnel responsible for the implementation of this Action Plan have adequate knowledge to implement it effectively.

7. Implementation

7.1 The Advisory Committee shall develop conservation guidelines to assist the Parties in the implementation of this Action Plan. Where possible, these guidelines should be consistent with those developed under other international instruments.

7.2 The Parties shall collaborate with other countries and organisations involved with albatross and petrel research, monitoring and management for the purpose of exchanging knowledge, skills and techniques to ensure more effective implementation of this Action Plan.

7.3 The Parties shall urge parties of other relevant international instruments, in particular CCAMLR, to recognise as appropriate the objectives of this Action Plan.

7.4 The Secretariat shall regularly undertake a review of potential means for providing necessary resources (viz both funds and technical assistance) for the implementation of this Action Plan, and shall report on this to each ordinary session of the Meeting of the Parties.

7.5 The Parties shall, either individually or through the Secretariat, draw the attention of any state which is not a Party to this Agreement to any activity undertaken by its nationals or vessels which affects the implementation of the Action Plan.

Southern Indian Ocean Fisheries Agreement[16]

The Contracting Parties

Having a mutual interest in the proper management, long-term conservation and sustainable use of fishery resources in the Southern Indian Ocean, and desiring to further the attainment of their objectives through international cooperation;

Taking into consideration that the coastal States have waters under national jurisdiction in accordance with the United Nations Convention on the Law of the Sea of 10 December 1982 and general principles of international law, within which they exercise their sovereign rights for the purpose of exploring and exploiting, conserving and managing fishery resources and conserving living marine resources upon which fishing has an impact;

Recalling the relevant provisions of the United Nations Convention on the Law of the Sea of 10 December 1982, the Agreement for the Implementation of the Provisions of the United Nations Convention on the Law of the Sea of 10 December 1982 relating to the Conservation and Management of Straddling Fish Stocks and Highly Migratory Fish Stocks of 4 December 1995, and the Agreement to Promote Compliance with International Conservation and Management Measures by Fishing Vessels on the High Seas of 24 November 1993 and taking into account the Code of Conduct for Responsible Fisheries adopted by the 28th Session of the Conference of the Food and Agriculture Organization of the United Nations on 31 October 1995;

Recalling further Article 17 of the Agreement for the Implementation of the Provisions of the United Nations Convention on the Law of the Sea of 10 December 1982 relating to the Conservation and Management of Straddling Fish Stocks and Highly Migratory Fish Stocks 1995, and the need for non-Contracting Parties to this Southern Indian Ocean Fisheries Agreement to apply the conservation and management measures adopted hereunder and not to authorise vessels flying their flag to engage in fishing activities inconsistent with the conservation and sustainable use of the fishery resources to which this Agreement applies;

Recognizing economic and geographical considerations and the special requirements of developing States, in particular the least-developed among them and small island developing States and their coastal communities, for equitable benefit from fishery resources;

Desiring cooperation between coastal States and all other States, organizations and fishing entities having an interest in the fishery resources of the Southern Indian Ocean to ensure compatible conservation and management measures;

Bearing in mind that the achievement of the above will contribute to the realization of a just and equitable economic order in the interests of all humankind, and in particular the special interests and needs of developing States, in particular the least-developed among them and small island developing States;

Convinced that the conclusion of a multilateral agreement for the long-term conservation and sustainable use of fishery resources in waters beyond national jurisdiction in the Southern Indian Ocean would best serve these objectives;

Agree as follows:

Article 1 Definitions

For the purposes of this Agreement:

(a) "1982 Convention" means the United Nations Convention on the Law of the Sea of 10 December 1982;

(b) "1995 Agreement" means the Agreement for the Implementation of the Provisions of the United Nations Convention on the Law of the Sea of 10 December 1982 relating to the Conservation and Management of Straddling Fish Stocks and Highly Migratory Fish Stocks of 4 December 1995;

(c) "Area" means the area to which this Agreement applies, as prescribed in Article 3;

[16] Adopted 7 July 2006, entered into force 21 June 2012.

(d) "Code of Conduct" means the Code of Conduct for Responsible Fisheries adopted by the 28th Session of the Conference of the Food and Agriculture Organization of the United Nations on 31 October 1995;
(e) "Contracting Party" means any State or regional economic integration organization which has consented to be bound by this Agreement and for which the Agreement is in force;
(f) "fishery resources" means resources of fish, molluscs, crustaceans and other sedentary species within the Area, but excluding:
  (i) sedentary species subject to the fishery jurisdiction of coastal States pursuant to Article 77(4) of the 1982 Convention; and
  (ii) highly migratory species listed in Annex I of the 1982 Convention;
(g) "fishing" means
  (i) the actual or attempted searching for, catching, taking or harvesting of fishery resources;
  (ii) engaging in any activity which can reasonably be expected to result in the locating, catching, taking or harvesting of fishery resources for any purpose including scientific research;
  (iii) placing, searching for or recovering any aggregating device for fishery resources or associated equipment including radio beacons;
  (iv) any operation at sea in support of, or in preparation for, any activity described in this definition, except for any operation in emergencies involving the health or safety of crew members or the safety of a vessel; or
  (v) the use of an aircraft in relation to any activity described in this definition except for flights in emergencies involving the health or safety of crew members or the safety of a vessel;
(h) "fishing entity" means a fishing entity as referred to in Article 1(3) of the 1995 Agreement;
(i) "fishing vessel" means any vessel used or intended for fishing, including a mother ship, any other vessel directly engaged in fishing operations, and any vessel engaged in transhipment;
(j) "nationals" includes both natural and legal persons;
(k) "regional economic integration organization" means a regional economic integration organization to which its member States have transferred competence over matters covered by this Agreement, including the authority to make decisions binding on its member States in respect of those matters;
(l) "transhipment" means the unloading of all or any of the fishery resources on board a fishing vessel onto another vessel whether at sea or in port.

Article 2 Objectives

The objectives of this Agreement are to ensure the long-term conservation and sustainable use of the fishery resources in the Area through cooperation among the Contracting Parties, and to promote the sustainable development of fisheries in the Area, taking into account the needs of developing States bordering the Area that are Contracting Parties to this Agreement, and in particular the least-developed among them and small island developing States.

Article 3 Area of Application

1. This Agreement applies to the Area bounded by a line joining the following points along parallels of latitude and meridians of longitude, excluding waters under national jurisdiction: Commencing at the landfall on the continent of Africa of the parallel of 10° North; from there east along that parallel to its intersection with the meridian of 65° East; from there south along that meridian to its intersection with the equator; from there east along the equator to its intersection with the meridian of 80° East; from there south along that meridian to its intersection with the parallel of 20° South; from there east along that parallel to its landfall on the continent of Australia; from there south and then east along the coast of Australia to its intersection with the

meridian of 120° East; from there south along that meridian to its intersection with the parallel of 55° South; from there west along that parallel to its intersection with the meridian of 80° East; from there north along that meridian to its intersection with the parallel of 45° South; from there west along that parallel to its intersection with the meridian of 30° East; from there north along that meridian to its landfall on the continent of Africa.

2. Where for the purpose of this Agreement it is necessary to determine the position on the surface of the Earth of a point, line or area, that position shall be determined by reference to the International Terrestrial Reference System maintained by the International Earth Rotation Service, which for most practical purposes is equivalent to the World Geodetic System 1984 (WGS84).

Article 4 General Principles

In giving effect to the duty to cooperate in accordance with the 1982 Convention and international law, the Contracting Parties shall apply, in particular, the following principles:

(a) measures shall be adopted on the basis of the best scientific evidence available to ensure the long-term conservation of fishery resources, taking into account the sustainable use of such resources and implementing an ecosystem approach to their management;

(b) measures shall be taken to ensure that the level of fishing activity is commensurate with the sustainable use of the fishery resources;

(c) the precautionary approach shall be applied in accordance with the Code of Conduct and the 1995 Agreement, whereby the absence of adequate scientific information shall not be used as a reason for postponing or failing to take conservation and management measures;

(d) the fishery resources shall be managed so that they are maintained at levels that are capable of producing the maximum sustainable yield, and depleted stocks of fishery resources are rebuilt to the said levels;

(e) fishing practices and management measures shall take due account of the need to minimize the harmful impact that fishing activities may have on the marine environment;

(f) biodiversity in the marine environment shall be protected; and

(g) the special requirements of developing States bordering the Area that are Contracting Parties to this Agreement, and in particular the least-developed among them and small island developing States, shall be given full recognition.

Article 5 Meeting of the Parties

1. The Contracting Parties shall meet periodically to consider matters pertaining to the implementation of this Agreement and to make all decisions relevant thereto.

2. The ordinary Meeting of the Parties shall, unless the Meeting otherwise decides, take place at least once a year and, to the extent practicable, back-to-back with meetings of the South West Indian Ocean Fisheries Commission. The Contracting Parties may also hold extraordinary meetings when deemed necessary.

3. The Meeting of the Parties shall, by consensus, adopt and amend its own Rules of Procedure and those of its subsidiary bodies.

4. The Contracting Parties, at their first meeting, shall consider the adoption of a budget to fund the conduct of the Meeting of the Parties and the exercise of its functions and accompanying financial regulations. The financial regulations shall set out the criteria governing the determination of the amount of each Contracting Party's contribution to the budget, giving due consideration to the economic status of Contracting Parties which are developing States, and in particular the least-developed among them and small island developing States, and ensuring that an adequate share of the budget is borne by Contracting Parties that benefit from fishing in the Area.

Article 6 Functions of the Meeting of the Parties

1. The Meeting of the Parties shall:

(a) review the state of fishery resources, including their abundance and the level of their exploitation;

(b) promote and, as appropriate, co-ordinate research activities as required on the fishery resources and on straddling stocks occurring in waters under national jurisdiction adjacent to the Area, including discarded catch and the impact of fishing on the marine environment;
(c) evaluate the impact of fishing on the fishery resources and on the marine environment, taking into account the environmental and oceanographic characteristics of the Area, other human activities and environmental factors;
(d) formulate and adopt conservation and management measures necessary for ensuring the long-term sustainability of the fishery resources, taking into account the need to protect marine biodiversity, based on the best scientific evidence available;
(e) adopt generally recommended international minimum standards for the responsible conduct of fishing operations;
(f) develop rules for the collection and verification of scientific and statistical data, as well as for the submission, publication, dissemination and use of such data;
(g) promote cooperation and coordination among Contracting Parties to ensure that conservation and management measures for straddling stocks occurring in waters under national jurisdiction adjacent to the Area and measures adopted by the Meeting of the Parties for the fishery resources are compatible;
(h) develop rules and procedures for the monitoring, control and surveillance of fishing activities in order to ensure compliance with conservation and management measures adopted by the Meeting of the Parties including, where appropriate, a system of verification incorporating vessel monitoring and observation, and rules concerning the boarding and inspection of vessels operating in the Area;
(i) develop and monitor measures to prevent, deter and eliminate illegal, unreported and unregulated fishing;
(j) in accordance with international law and any applicable instruments, draw the attention of any non-Contracting Parties to any activities which undermine the attainment of the objectives of this Agreement;
(k) establish the criteria for and rules governing participation in fishing; and
(l) carry out any other tasks and functions necessary to achieve the objectives of this Agreement.

2. In determining criteria for participation in fishing, including allocation of total allowable catch or total level of fishing effort, the Contracting Parties shall take into account, *inter alia*, international principles such as those contained in the 1995 Agreement.

3. In applying the provisions of paragraph 2, the Contracting Parties may, inter alia:
(a) designate annual quota allocations or fishing effort limitations for Contracting Parties;
(b) allocate catch quantities for exploration and scientific research; and
(c) set aside fishing opportunities for non-Contracting Parties to this Agreement, if necessary.

4. The Meeting of Parties shall, subject to agreed rules, review quota allocations and fishing effort limitations of Contracting Parties and participation in fishing opportunities of non-Contracting Parties taking into account, *inter alia*, information on the implementation by Contracting and non-Contracting Parties of the conservation and management measures adopted by the Meeting of the Parties.

Article 7 Subsidiary Bodies

1. The Meeting of the Parties shall establish a permanent Scientific Committee, which shall meet, unless the Meeting of the Parties otherwise decides, at least once a year, and preferably prior to the Meeting of the Parties, in accordance with the following provisions:
(a) the functions of the Scientific Committee shall be:
   (i) to conduct the scientific assessment of the fishery resources and the impact of fishing on the marine environment, taking into account the environmental and oceanographic characteristics of the Area, and the results of relevant scientific research;

(ii) to encourage and promote cooperation in scientific research in order to improve knowledge of the state of the fishery resources;
(iii) to provide scientific advice and recommendations to the Meeting of the Parties for the formulation of the conservation and management measures referred to in Article 6(1)(d);
(iv) to provide scientific advice and recommendations to the Meeting of the Parties for the formulation of measures regarding the monitoring of fishing activities;
(v) to provide scientific advice and recommendations to the Meeting of the Parties on appropriate standards and format for fishery data collection and exchange; and
(vi) any other scientific function that the Meeting of the Parties may decide;

(b) in developing advice and recommendations the Scientific Committee shall take into consideration the work of the South West Indian Ocean Fisheries Commission as well as that of other relevant research organizations and regional fisheries management organizations.

2. Once the measures referred to in Article 6 are taken, the Meeting of the Parties shall establish a Compliance Committee, to verify the implementation of and compliance with such measures. The Compliance Committee shall meet, in conjunction with the Meeting of the Parties, as provided for in the Rules of Procedure and shall report, advise and make recommendations to the Meeting of the Parties.

3. The Meeting of the Parties may also establish such temporary, special or standing committees as may be required, to study and report on matters pertaining to the implementation of the objectives of this Agreement, and working groups to study, and submit recommendations on, specific technical problems.

Article 8 Decision Making

1. Unless otherwise provided in this Agreement, decisions of the Meeting of the Parties and its subsidiary bodies on matters of substance shall be taken by the consensus of the Contracting Parties present, where consensus means the absence of any formal objection made at the time a decision is taken. The question of whether a matter is one of substance shall be treated as a matter of substance.

2. Decisions on matters other than those referred to in paragraph 1 shall be taken by a simple majority of the Contracting Parties present and voting.

3. Decisions adopted by the Meeting of the Parties shall be binding on all Contracting Parties.

Article 9 Secretariat

The Meeting of the Parties shall decide on arrangements for the carrying out of secretariat services, or the establishment of a Secretariat, to perform the following functions:

(a) implementing and coordinating the administrative provisions of this Agreement, including the compilation and distribution of the official report of the Meeting of the Parties;
(b) maintaining a complete record of the proceedings of the Meeting of the Parties and its subsidiary bodies, as well as a complete archive of any other official documents pertaining to the implementation of this Agreement; and
(c) any other function that the Meeting of the Parties may decide.

Article 10 Contracting Party Duties

1. Each Contracting Party shall, in respect of its activities within the Area:

(a) promptly implement this Agreement and any conservation, management and other measures or matters which may be agreed by the Meeting of the Parties;
(b) take appropriate measures in order to ensure the effectiveness of the measures adopted by the Meeting of the Parties;
(c) collect and exchange scientific, technical and statistical data with respect to the fishery resources and ensure that:
    (i) data is collected in sufficient detail to facilitate effective stock assessment and are provided in a timely manner to fulfil the requirements set forth in the rules adopted by the Meeting of the Parties;

(ii) appropriate measures are taken to verify the accuracy of such data;
(iii) such statistical, biological and other data and information as the Meeting of the Parties may decide is provided annually; and
(iv) information on steps taken to implement the conservation and management measures adopted by the Meeting of the Parties is provided in a timely manner.

2. Each Contracting Party shall make available to the Meeting of the Parties a statement of implementing and compliance measures, including imposition of sanctions for any violations, it has taken in accordance with this Article and, in the case of coastal States that are Contracting Parties to this Agreement, as regards the conservation and management measures they have taken for straddling stocks occurring in waters under their jurisdiction adjacent to the Area.

3. Without prejudice to the primacy of the responsibility of the flag State, each Contracting Party shall, to the greatest extent possible, take measures, or cooperate, to ensure that its nationals and fishing vessels owned or operated by its nationals fishing in the Area comply with the provisions of this Agreement and with the conservation and management measures adopted by the Meeting of the Parties.

4. Each Contracting Party shall, to the greatest extent possible, at the request of any other Contracting Party, and when provided with the relevant information, investigate any alleged serious violation within the meaning of the 1995 Agreement by its nationals, or fishing vessels owned or operated by its nationals, of the provisions of this Agreement or any conservation and management measure adopted by the Meeting of the Parties. A reply, including details of any action taken or proposed to be taken in relation to the alleged violation, shall be provided to all Contracting Parties as soon as practicable and in any case within two (2) months of such request. A report on the outcome of the investigation shall be provided to the Meeting of the Parties when the investigation is completed.

Article 11 Flag State Duties

1. Each Contracting Party shall take such measures as may be necessary to ensure that:
(a) fishing vessels flying its flag operating in the Area comply with the provisions of this Agreement and the conservation and management measures adopted by the Meeting of the Parties and that such vessels do not engage in any activity which undermines the effectiveness of such measures;
(b) fishing vessels flying its flag do not conduct unauthorized fishing within waters under national jurisdiction adjacent to the Area; and
(c) it develops and implements a satellite vessel monitoring system for fishing vessels flying its flag and fishing in the Area.

2. No Contracting Party shall allow any fishing vessel entitled to fly its flag to be used for fishing in the Area unless it has been authorised to do so by the appropriate authority or authorities of that Contracting Party.

3. Each Contracting Party shall:
(a) authorize the use of vessels flying its flag for fishing in waters beyond national jurisdiction only where it is able to exercise effectively its responsibilities in respect of such vessels under this Agreement and in accordance with international law;
(b) maintain a record of fishing vessels entitled to fly its flag and authorized to fish for the fishery resources, and ensure that, for all such vessels, such information as may be specified by the Meeting of the Parties is entered in that record. Contracting Parties shall exchange this information in accordance with such procedures as may be agreed by the Meeting of the Parties;
(c) in conformity with the rules determined by the Meeting of the Parties, make available to each annual Meeting of the Parties a report on its fishing activities in the Area;
(d) collect and share in a timely manner, complete and accurate data concerning fishing activities by vessels flying its flag operating in the area, in particular on vessel position,

retained catch, discarded catch and fishing effort, where appropriate maintaining confidentiality of data as it relates to the application of relevant national legislation; and

(e) to the greatest extent possible, at the request of any other Contracting Party, and when provided with the relevant information, investigate any alleged serious violation within the meaning of the 1995 Agreement by fishing vessels flying its flag of the provisions of this Agreement or any conservation and management measure adopted by the Meeting of the Parties. A reply, including details of any action taken or proposed to be taken in relation to such alleged violation, shall be provided to all Contracting Parties as soon as practicable and in any case within two (2) months of such request. A report on the outcome of the investigation shall be provided to the Meeting of the Parties when the investigation is completed.

Article 12 Port State Duties

1. Measures taken by a port State Contracting Party in accordance with this Agreement shall take full account of the right and the duty of a port State to take measures, in accordance with international law, to promote the effectiveness of subregional, regional and global conservation and management measures. When taking such measures, a port State Contracting Party shall not discriminate in form or in fact against the fishing vessels of any State.

2. Each port State Contracting Party shall:

(a) in accordance with the conservation and management measures adopted by the Meeting of the Parties, inter alia, inspect documents, fishing gear and catch on board fishing vessels, when such vessels are voluntarily in its ports or at its offshore terminals;

(b) not permit landings, transhipment, or supply services in relation to fishing vessels unless they are satisfied that fish on board the vessel have been caught in a manner consistent with the conservation and management measures adopted by the Meeting of the Parties; and

(c) provide assistance to flag State Contracting Parties, as reasonably practical and in accordance with its national law and international law, when a fishing vessel is voluntarily in its ports or at its offshore terminals and the flag State of the vessel requests it to provide assistance in ensuring compliance with the provisions of this Agreement and with the conservation and management measures adopted by the Meeting of the Parties.

3. In the event that a port State Contracting Party considers that a vessel of another Contracting Party making use of its ports or offshore terminals has violated a provision of this Agreement or a conservation and management measure adopted by the Meeting of the Parties, it shall draw this to the attention of the flag State concerned and of the Meeting of the Parties. The port State Contracting Party shall provide the flag State and the Meeting of the Parties with full documentation of the matter, including any record of inspection.

4. Nothing in this Article affects the exercise by Contracting Parties of their sovereignty over ports in their territory in accordance with international law.

Article 13 Special Requirements of Developing States

1. The Contracting Parties shall give full recognition to the special requirements of developing States bordering the Area, in particular the least-developed among them and small island developing States, in relation to the conservation and management of fishery resources and the sustainable development of such resources.

2. The Contracting Parties recognize, in particular:

(a) the vulnerability of developing States bordering the Area, in particular the least-developed among them and small island developing States, that are dependent on the exploitation of fishery resources, including for meeting the nutritional requirements of their populations or parts thereof;

(b) the need to avoid adverse impacts on, and ensure access to fisheries by, subsistence, small-scale and artisanal fishers and fishworkers; and

(c) the need to ensure that conservation and management measures adopted by the Meeting of the Parties do not result in transferring, directly or indirectly, a disproportionate burden of conservation action onto developing States bordering the Area, in particular the least-developed among them and small island developing States.

3. Cooperation by the Contracting Parties under the provisions of this Agreement and through other subregional or regional organizations involved in the management of marine living resources should include action for the purposes of:

(a) enhancing the ability of developing States bordering the Area, in particular the least-developed among them and small island developing States, to conserve and manage fishery resources and to develop their own fisheries for such resources; and

(b) assisting developing States bordering the Area, in particular the least-developed among them and small island developing States, to enable them to participate in fisheries for such resources, including facilitating access in accordance with this Agreement.

4. Cooperation with developing States bordering the Area, in particular the least-developed among them and small island developing States, for the purposes set out in this Article should include the provision of financial assistance, assistance relating to human resources development, technical assistance, transfer of technology, and activities directed specifically towards:

(a) improved conservation and management of the fishery resources and of straddling stocks occurring in waters under national jurisdiction adjacent to the Area, which can include the collection, reporting, verification, exchange and analysis of fisheries data and related information;

(b) improved information collection and management of the impact of fishing activities on the marine environment;

(c) stock assessment and scientific research;

(d) monitoring, control, surveillance, compliance and enforcement, including training and capacity-building at the local level, development and funding of national and regional observer programmes and access to technology; and

(e) participation in the Meeting of the Parties and meetings of its subsidiary bodies as well as in the settlement of disputes.

Article 14 Transparency

1. The Contracting Parties shall promote transparency in decision making processes and other activities carried out under this Agreement.

2. Coastal States with waters under national jurisdiction adjacent to the Area that are not Contracting Parties to this Agreement shall be entitled to participate as observers in the Meeting of the Parties and meetings of its subsidiary bodies.

3. Non-Contracting Parties to this Agreement shall be entitled to participate as observers in the Meeting of the Parties and meetings of its subsidiary bodies.

4. Intergovernmental organizations concerned with matters relevant to the implementation of this Agreement, in particular the Food and Agriculture Organization of the United Nations, the South West Indian Ocean Fisheries Commission, and regional fisheries management organizations with competence over high seas waters adjacent to the Area, shall be entitled to participate as observers in the Meeting of the Parties and meetings of its subsidiary bodies.

5. Representatives from non-governmental organizations concerned with matters relevant to the implementation of this Agreement shall be afforded the opportunity to participate in the Meeting of the Parties and meetings of its subsidiary bodies as observers or otherwise as determined by the Meeting of the Parties. The Rules of Procedure of the Meeting of the Parties and its subsidiary bodies shall provide for such participation. The procedures shall not be unduly restrictive in this respect.

6. Observers shall be given timely access to pertinent information subject to the Rules of Procedure, including those concerning confidentiality requirements, which the Meeting of the Parties may adopt.

Article 15 Fishing Entities

1. After the entry into force of this Agreement any fishing entity whose vessels have fished or intend to fish for fishery resources in the Area may, by a written instrument delivered to the Chairperson of the Meeting of the Parties, in accordance with such procedures as may be established by the Meeting of the Parties, express its firm commitment to be bound by the terms of this Agreement. Such commitment shall become effective thirty (30) days from the date of receipt of the instrument. Any such fishing entity may withdraw such commitment by written notification addressed to the Chairperson of the Meeting of the Parties. Notice of withdrawal shall become effective ninety (90) days from the date of its receipt by the Chairperson of the Meeting of the Parties.

2. A fishing entity which has expressed its commitment to be bound by the terms of this Agreement may participate in the Meeting of the Parties and its subsidiary bodies, and partake in decision making, in accordance with the Rules of Procedure adopted by the Meeting of the Parties. Articles 1 to 18 and 20.2 apply, *mutatis mutandis*, to such a fishing entity.

Article 16 Cooperation with other Organizations

The Contracting Parties, acting jointly under this Agreement, shall cooperate closely with other international fisheries and related organizations in matters of mutual interest, in particular with the South West Indian Ocean Fisheries Commission and any other regional fisheries management organization with competence over high seas waters adjacent to the Area.

Article 17 Non-Contracting Parties

1. Contracting Parties shall take measures consistent with this Agreement, the 1995 Agreement and international law to deter the activities of vessels flying the flags of non-Contracting Parties to this Agreement which undermine the effectiveness of conservation and management measures adopted by the Meeting of the Parties or the attainment of the objectives of this Agreement.

2. Contracting Parties shall exchange information on the activities of fishing vessels flying the flags of non-Contracting Parties to this Agreement which are engaged in fishing operations in the Area.

3. Contracting Parties shall draw the attention of any non-Contracting Party to this Agreement to any activity undertaken by its nationals or vessels flying its flag which, in the opinion of the Contracting Party, undermines the effectiveness of conservation and management measures adopted by the Meeting of the Parties or the attainment of the objectives of this Agreement.

4. Contracting Parties shall, individually or jointly, request non-Contracting Parties to this Agreement whose vessels fish in the Area to cooperate fully in the implementation of conservation and management measures adopted by the Meeting of the Parties with a view to ensuring that such measures are applied to all fishing activities in the Area. Such cooperating non-Contracting Parties to this Agreement shall enjoy benefits from participation in the fishery commensurate with their commitment to comply with, and their record of compliance with, conservation and management measures in respect of the relevant stocks of fishery resources.

Article 18 Good Faith and Abuse of Right

Each Contracting Party shall fulfil in good faith the obligations assumed under this Agreement and shall exercise the rights recognized in this Agreement in a manner which would not constitute an abuse of right.

Article 19 Relation to other Agreements

Nothing in this Agreement shall prejudice the rights and obligations of States under the 1982 Convention or the 1995 Agreement.

Article 20 Interpretation and Settlement of Disputes

1. Contracting Parties shall use their best endeavours to resolve their disputes by amicable means. At the request of any Contracting Party a dispute may be submitted for binding decision in accordance with the procedures for the settlement of disputes provided in Section II of Part XV of the 1982 Convention or, where the dispute concerns one or more straddling stocks, the

procedures set out in Part VIII of the 1995 Agreement. The relevant part of the 1982 Convention and the 1995 Agreement shall apply whether or not the parties to the dispute are also parties to either of these instruments.

2. If a dispute involves a fishing entity which has expressed its commitment to be bound by the terms of this Agreement and cannot be settled by amicable means, the dispute shall, at the request of any party to the dispute, be submitted to final and binding arbitration in accordance with the relevant rules of the Permanent Court of Arbitration.

Article 21 Amendments

1. Any Contracting Party may propose an amendment to the Agreement by providing to the Depositary the text of a proposed amendment at least sixty (60) days in advance of an ordinary Meeting of the Parties. The Depositary shall circulate a copy of this text to all other Contracting Parties promptly.

2. Amendments to the Agreement shall be adopted by consensus of all Contracting Parties.

3. Amendments to the Agreement shall enter into force ninety (90) days after all Contracting Parties which held this status at the time the amendments were approved have deposited their instruments of ratification, acceptance, or approval of such amendments with the Depositary.

Article 22 Signature, Ratification, Acceptance and Approval

1. This Agreement shall be open for signature by:

(a) the States and regional economic integration organization participating in the Inter-Governmental Consultation on the Southern Indian Ocean Fisheries Agreement; and

(b) any other State having jurisdiction over waters adjacent to the Area;

and shall remain open for signature for twelve (12) months from 7 July 2006 (the date of opening for signature).

2. This Agreement is subject to ratification, acceptance or approval by the signatories.

3. The instruments of ratification, acceptance or approval shall be deposited with the Depositary.

Article 23 Accession

1. This Agreement shall be open for accession, after its closure for signature, by any State or regional economic integration organization referred to in Article 22.1, and by any other State or regional economic integration organization interested in fishing activities in relation to the fishery resources.

2. Instruments of accession shall be deposited with the Depositary.

Article 24 Entry into Force

1. This Agreement shall enter into force ninety (90) days from the date of receipt by the Depositary of the fourth instrument of ratification, acceptance or approval, at least two of which have been deposited by coastal States bordering the Area.

2. For each signatory which ratifies, accepts or approves this Agreement after its entry into force, this Agreement shall enter into force for that signatory thirty (30) days after the deposit of its instrument of ratification, acceptance or approval.

3. For each State or regional economic integration organization which accedes to this Agreement after its entry into force, this Agreement shall enter into force for that State or regional economic integration organization thirty (30) days after the deposit of its instrument of accession.

Article 25 The Depositary

1. The Director-General of the Food and Agriculture Organization of the United Nations shall be the Depositary of this Agreement and of any amendments thereto. The Depositary shall transmit certified copies of this Agreement to all signatories and shall register this Agreement with the Secretary-General of the United Nations pursuant to Article 102 of the Charter of the United Nations.

2. The Depositary shall inform all signatories of and Contracting Parties to this Agreement of signatures and of instruments of ratification, accession, acceptance or approval deposited under Articles 22 and 23 and of the date of entry into force of the Agreement under Article 24.

Article 26 Withdrawal

Any Contracting Party may withdraw from this Agreement at any time after the expiration of two years from the date upon which the Agreement entered into force with respect to that Contracting Party, by giving written notice of such withdrawal to the Depositary who shall immediately inform all the Contracting Parties of such withdrawal. Notice of withdrawal shall become effective ninety (90) days from the date of its receipt by the Depositary.

Article 27 Termination

This Agreement shall be automatically terminated if and when, as the result of withdrawals, the number of Contracting Parties drops below three.

Article 28 Reservations

1. Ratification, acceptance or approval of this Agreement may be made subject to reservations which shall become effective only upon unanimous acceptance by all Contracting Parties to this Agreement. The Depositary shall notify forthwith all Contracting Parties of any reservation. Contracting Parties not having replied within three (3) months from the date of notification shall be deemed to have accepted the reservation. Failing such acceptance, the State or regional economic integration organization making the reservation shall not become a Contracting Party to this Agreement.

2. Nothing in paragraph 1 shall prevent a State or a regional economic integration organization on behalf of a State from making a reservation with regard to membership acquired through territories and surrounding maritime areas over which the State asserts its rights to exercise sovereignty or territorial and maritime jurisdiction.

IN WITNESS WHEREOF, the undersigned Plenipotentiaries, having been duly authorized by their respective Governments, have signed this Agreement.

DONE in Rome on this Seventh day of July 2006 in English and French, both texts being equally authoritative.

Convention on the Conservation and Management of High Seas Fishery Resources in the South Pacific Ocean[17]

The Contracting Parties,

Committed to ensuring the long-term conservation and sustainable use of fishery resources in the South Pacific Ocean and in so doing safeguarding the marine ecosystems in which the resources occur;

Recalling relevant international law as reflected in the United Nations Convention on the Law of the Sea of 10 December 1982, the Agreement for the Implementation of the Provisions of the United Nations Convention on the Law of the Sea of 10 December 1982 relating to the Conservation and Management of Straddling Fish Stocks and Highly Migratory Fish Stocks of 4 December 1995 and the Agreement to Promote Compliance with International Conservation and Management Measures by Fishing Vessels on the High Seas of 24 November 1993 and taking into account the Code of Conduct for Responsible Fisheries adopted by the Conference of the Food and Agriculture Organisation of the United Nations at its twenty eighth session on 31 October 1995;

Recognising that under international law reflected in the relevant provisions of the above agreements, States have a duty to cooperate with each other in the conservation and management of living resources in the areas of the high seas and, as appropriate, to cooperate to establish subregional or regional fisheries organisations or arrangements with a view to taking the measures necessary for the conservation of such resources;

Taking into consideration that, under international law reflected in the relevant provisions of the United Nations Convention on the Law of the Sea of 10 December 1982, coastal States

[17] Adopted 14 November 2009, entered into force 24 August 2012.

have waters under national jurisdiction within which they exercise their sovereign rights for the purpose of exploring, exploiting, conserving and managing fishery resources and conserving living marine resources upon which fishing has an impact;

Recognising economic and geographical considerations and the special requirements of developing States, in particular the least developed among them, and small island developing States, and territories and possessions, and their coastal communities, in relation to the conservation, management and sustainable development of fishery resources and equitable benefit from those resources;

Noting the need for regional fisheries management organisations and arrangements to undertake performance reviews in order to assess the degree to which they are attaining their respective conservation and management objectives;

Determined to cooperate effectively to eliminate illegal, unreported and unregulated fishing and the adverse impact that it has on the state of the world fishery resources and the ecosystems in which they occur;

Conscious of the need to avoid adverse impacts on the marine environment, preserve biodiversity, maintain the integrity of marine ecosystems and minimise the risk of long-term or irreversible effects of fishing;

Mindful that effective conservation and management measures must be based on the best scientific information available and the application of the precautionary approach and an ecosystem approach to fisheries management;

Convinced that the long-term conservation and sustainable use of fishery resources in the South Pacific Ocean and the protection of the marine ecosystems in which those resources occur may best be achieved by the conclusion of an international convention for that purpose;

Have agreed as follows:

Article 1 Definitions

1. For the purposes of this Convention:

(a) '1982 Convention' means the United Nations Convention on the Law of the Sea of 10 December 1982;

(b) '1995 Agreement' means the Agreement for the Implementation of the Provisions of the United Nations Convention on the Law of the Sea of 10 December 1982 relating to the Conservation and Management of Straddling Fish Stocks and Highly Migratory Fish Stocks of 4 December 1995;

(c) 'Commission' means the Commission of the South Pacific Regional Fisheries Management Organisation established by Article 6;

(d) 'Convention Area' means the Area to which this Convention applies in accordance with Article 5;

(e) 'Code of Conduct' means the Code of Conduct for Responsible Fisheries adopted by the 28th session of the Conference of the Food and Agriculture Organisation of the United Nations (FAO) on 31 October 1995;

(f) 'fishery resources' means all fish within the Convention Area, including: molluscs; crustaceans; and other living marine resources as may be decided by the Commission; but excluding:

(i) sedentary species in so far as they are subject to the national jurisdiction of coastal States pursuant to Article 77 paragraph 4 of the 1982 Convention;

(ii) highly migratory species listed in Annex I of the 1982 Convention;

(iii) anadromous and catadromous species; and

(iv) marine mammals, marine reptiles and sea birds;

(g) 'fishing' means:

(i) the actual or attempted searching for, catching, taking or harvesting of fishery resources;

(ii) engaging in any activity which can reasonably be expected to result in the locating, catching, taking or harvesting of fishery resources for any purpose;
(iii) transhipment and any operation at sea in support of, or in preparation for, any activity described in this definition; and
(iv) the use of any vessel, vehicle, aircraft or hovercraft, in relation to any activity described in this definition;

but does not include any operation related to emergencies involving the health or safety of crew members or the safety of a vessel;

(h) 'fishing vessel' means any vessel used or intended for fishing, including fish processing vessels, support ships, carrier vessels and any other vessel directly engaged in fishing operations;

(i) 'flag State' means, unless otherwise indicated:
(i) a State whose fishing vessels are entitled to fly its flag; or
(ii) a regional economic integration organisation in which fishing vessels are entitled to fly the flag of a member State of that regional economic integration organisation;

(j) 'IUU fishing' means activities as referred to in paragraph 3 of the FAO International Plan of Action to Prevent, Deter and Eliminate Illegal, Unreported and Unregulated Fishing, and other activities as may be decided by the Commission;

(k) 'nationals' includes both natural and legal persons;

(l) 'port' includes offshore terminals and other installations for landing, transhipping, packaging, processing, refuelling or re-supplying;

(m) 'regional economic integration organisation' means a regional economic integration organisation to which its member States have transferred competence over matters covered by this Convention, including the authority to make decisions binding on its member States in respect of those matters;

(n) 'serious violation' has the same meaning as that set out in Article 21 paragraph 11 of the 1995 Agreement and such other violations as may be specified by the Commission; and

(o) 'transhipment' means the unloading of all or any of the fishery resources or fishery resource products derived from fishing in the Convention Area on board a fishing vessel to another fishing vessel either at sea or in port.

2.

(a) 'Contracting Party' means any State or regional economic integration organisation which has consented to be bound by this Convention and for which the Convention is in force.

(b) This Convention applies, *mutatis mutandis*, to any entity referred to in Article 305, paragraph 1 (c), (d) and (e), of the 1982 Convention which becomes a party to this Convention, and to that extent "Contracting Party" refers to any such entity.

Article 2 Objective

The objective of this Convention is, through the application of the precautionary approach and an ecosystem approach to fisheries management, to ensure the long-term conservation and sustainable use of fishery resources and, in so doing, to safeguard the marine ecosystems in which these resources occur.

Article 3 Conservation and Management Principles and Approaches

1. In giving effect to the objective of this Convention and carrying out decision making under this Convention, the Contracting Parties, the Commission and subsidiary bodies established under Article 6 paragraph 2 and Article 9 paragraph 1 shall:

(a) apply, in particular, the following principles;
(i) conservation and management of fishery resources shall be conducted in a transparent, accountable and inclusive manner, taking into account best international practices;
(ii) fishing shall be commensurate with the sustainable use of fishery resources taking into account the impacts on non-target and associated or dependent species and the general obligation to protect and preserve the marine environment;

(iii) overfishing and excess fishing capacity shall be prevented or eliminated;
(iv) full and accurate data on fishing, including information relating to impacts on the marine ecosystems in which fishery resources occur, shall be collected, verified, reported and shared in a timely and appropriate manner;
(v) decisions shall be based on the best scientific and technical information available and the advice of all relevant subsidiary bodies;
(vi) cooperation and coordination among Contracting Parties shall be promoted to ensure that conservation and management measures adopted by the Commission and conservation and management measures applied in respect of the same fishery resources in areas under national jurisdiction are compatible;
(vii) marine ecosystems shall be protected, in particular those ecosystems which have long recovery times following disturbance;
(viii) the interests of developing States, in particular the least developed among them and small island developing States, and of territories and possessions, and the needs of developing State coastal communities, shall be recognised;
(ix) effective compliance with conservation and management measures shall be ensured and sanctions for any violations shall be adequate in severity to discourage violations wherever they occur and in particular shall deprive offenders of the benefits accruing from their illegal activities; and
(x) pollution and waste originating from fishing vessels, discards, catch by lost or abandoned gear and impacts on other species and marine ecosystems shall be minimised; and

(b) apply the precautionary approach and an ecosystem approach in accordance with paragraph 2.

2.

(a) The precautionary approach as described in the 1995 Agreement and the Code of Conduct shall be applied widely to the conservation and management of fishery resources in order to protect those resources and to preserve the marine ecosystems in which they occur, and in particular the Contracting Parties, the Commission and subsidiary bodies shall:
(i) be more cautious when information is uncertain, unreliable, or inadequate;
(ii) not use the absence of adequate scientific information as a reason for postponing or failing to take conservation and management measures; and
(iii) take account of best international practices regarding the application of the precautionary approach, including Annex II of the 1995 Agreement and the Code of Conduct.

(b) An ecosystem approach shall be applied widely to the conservation and management of fishery resources through an integrated approach under which decisions in relation to the management of fishery resources are considered in the context of the functioning of the wider marine ecosystems in which they occur to ensure the long-term conservation and sustainable use of those resources and in so doing, safeguard those marine ecosystems.

Article 4 Compatibility of Conservation and Management Measures

1. The Contracting Parties recognise the need to ensure compatibility of conservation and management measures established for fishery resources that are identified as straddling areas under the national jurisdiction of a coastal State Contracting Party and the adjacent high seas of the Convention Area and acknowledge their duty to cooperate to this end.

2. Conservation and management measures established for the high seas and those adopted for areas under national jurisdiction shall be compatible in order to ensure conservation and management of straddling fishery resources in their entirety. In developing compatible conservation and management measures for straddling fishery resources Contracting Parties shall:

(a) take into account the biological unity and other biological characteristics of the fishery resources and the relationships between the distribution of the resources, the fishing activities for those resources and the geographical particularities of the region concerned, including the extent to which the fishery resources occur and are fished in areas under national jurisdiction;
(b) take into account the respective dependence of the coastal States and the States fishing on the high seas on the fishery resources concerned; and
(c) ensure that such measures do not result in harmful impact on the living marine resources as a whole in the Convention Area.

3. The Commission's initial conservation and management measures shall take due account of, and not undermine the effectiveness of, existing conservation and management measures established by relevant coastal State Contracting Parties in respect of areas under national jurisdiction and by Contracting Parties in respect of their flag vessels fishing in the adjacent high seas of the Convention Area.

Article 5 Area of Application

1. Except as otherwise provided, this Convention applies to waters of the Pacific Ocean beyond areas of national jurisdiction in accordance with international law:
(a) east of a line extending south along the 120° meridian of east longitude from the outer limit of the national jurisdiction of Australia off the south coast of Western Australia to the intersection with the 55° parallel of south latitude; then due east along the 55° parallel of south latitude to the intersection with the 150° meridian of east longitude; then due south along the 150° meridian of east longitude to the intersection with the 60° parallel of south latitude;
(b) north of a line extending east along the 60° parallel of south latitude from the 150° meridian of east longitude to the intersection with the 67°16' meridian of west longitude;
(c) west of a line extending north along the 67°16' meridian of west longitude from the 60° parallel of south latitude to its intersection with the outer limit of the national jurisdiction of Chile then along the outer limits of the national jurisdictions of Chile, Peru, Ecuador and Colombia to the intersection with the 2° parallel of north latitude; and
(d) south of a line extending west along the 2° parallel of north latitude (but not including the national jurisdiction of Ecuador (Galapagos Islands)) to the intersection with the 150° meridian of west longitude; then due north along the 150° meridian of west longitude to its intersection with 10° parallel of north latitude, then west along the 10° parallel of north latitude to its intersection with the outer limits of the national jurisdiction of the Marshall Islands, and then generally south and around the outer limits of the national jurisdictions of Pacific States and territories, New Zealand and Australia until it connects to the commencement of the line described in paragraph (a) above.

2. The Convention shall also apply to waters of the Pacific Ocean beyond areas of national jurisdiction bounded by the 10° parallel of north latitude and the 20° parallel of south latitude and by the 135° meridian of east longitude and the 150° meridian of west longitude.

3. Where for the purpose of this Convention it is necessary to determine the position on the surface of the earth of a point, line or area, that position shall be determined by reference to the International Terrestrial Reference System maintained by the International Earth Rotation Service, which for most practical purposes is equivalent to the World Geodetic System 1984 (WGS84).

4. Nothing in this Convention shall constitute recognition of the claims or positions of any of the Contracting Parties to this Convention concerning the legal status and extent of waters and zones claimed by any such Contracting Parties.

Article 6 The Organisation

1. The Contracting Parties hereby agree to establish, maintain and strengthen the South Pacific Regional Fisheries Management Organisation "the Organisation", which shall carry out its functions as set forth in this Convention in order to achieve the objective of this Convention.

2. The Organisation shall consist of:

(a) a Commission;
(b) a Scientific Committee;
(c) a Compliance and Technical Committee;
(d) an Eastern Sub-regional Management Committee;
(e) a Western Sub-regional Management Committee;
(f) a Finance and Administration Committee;
(g) a Secretariat,

and any other subsidiary bodies that the Commission may, from time to time, establish in accordance with Article 9 paragraph 1 to assist it in its work.

2. The Organisation shall have legal personality in accordance with international law and shall enjoy in its relations with other international organisations and in the territories of the Contracting Parties such legal capacity as may be necessary to perform its functions and achieve the objective of this Convention. The immunities and privileges which the Organisation and its officers shall enjoy in the territory of a Contracting Party shall be subject to an agreement between the Organisation and the Contracting Party including, in particular, an agreement between the Organisation and the Contracting Party hosting the Secretariat.

3. The Secretariat of the Organisation shall be in New Zealand or at such other place as may be decided by the Commission.

Article 7 The Commission

1. Each Contracting Party shall be a member of the Commission and shall appoint one representative to the Commission who may be accompanied by alternative representatives, experts and advisers.

2. The Commission shall elect a Chairperson and a Vice-Chairperson from among the Contracting Parties, each of whom shall serve for a term of two years and shall be eligible for re-election but shall not serve for more than two terms in succession in the same capacity. The Chairperson and Vice-Chairperson shall be representatives of different Contracting Parties.

3. The first meeting of the Commission shall take place no later than 12 months following the entry into force of this Convention. Thereafter the Chairperson of the Commission shall convene an annual meeting, unless the Commission decides otherwise, at a time and location to be decided by the Commission. The Commission shall hold such other meetings as may be necessary to carry out its functions under this Convention.

4. The principle of cost effectiveness shall apply to the frequency, duration and scheduling of meetings of the Commission and its subsidiary bodies.

Article 8 Functions of the Commission

The Commission shall, in accordance with the objective, principles and approaches, and specific provisions of this Convention, exercise the following functions:

(a) adopt conservation and management measures to achieve the objective of this Convention, including, as appropriate, conservation and management measures for particular fish stocks;
(b) determine the nature and extent of participation in fishing for fishery resources including, as appropriate, for particular fish stocks;
(c) develop rules for the collection, verification, reporting, storing and dissemination of data;
(d) promote the conduct of scientific research to improve knowledge of fishery resources and marine ecosystems in the Convention Area and of the same fishery resources in adjacent waters under national jurisdiction, and, in collaboration with the Scientific Committee,

establish procedures for the conduct of fishing for fishery resources for scientific purposes in the Convention Area;

(e) cooperate and exchange data with members of the Commission and with relevant organisations, coastal States, territories and possessions;

(f) promote compatibility of conservation and management measures in the Convention Area, adjacent areas under national jurisdiction and adjacent areas of high seas;

(g) develop and establish effective monitoring, control, surveillance, compliance and enforcement procedures, including non-discriminatory market-related and trade-related measures;

(h) develop processes in accordance with international law to assess flag State performance with respect to the implementation of their obligations under this Convention and adopt proposals, if appropriate, to promote implementation of such obligations;

(i) adopt measures to prevent, deter and eliminate IUU fishing;

(j) develop rules for cooperating non-Contracting Party status under this Convention;

(k) review the effectiveness of the provisions of this Convention and the conservation and management measures adopted by the Commission in meeting the objective of this Convention;

(l) supervise the organisational, administrative, financial and other internal affairs of the Organisation, including the relations among constituent bodies;

(m) guide the Commission's subsidiary bodies in their work;

(n) adopt by consensus the budget of the Organisation, the financial regulations of the Organisation and any amendments thereto, and its rules of procedure, which may include procedures for taking and recording decisions intersessionally;

(o) adopt and amend as necessary any other regulations necessary for the exercise of its functions and those of its subsidiary bodies; and

(p) exercise any other function and take any other decisions that may be necessary for achieving the objective of this Convention.

Article 9 Subsidiary Bodies

1. The Commission may establish other subsidiary bodies, additional to the Scientific Committee, the Compliance and Technical Committee, the Eastern Sub-regional Management Committee, the Western Sub-regional Management Committee and the Finance and Administration Committee as may be required. Such additional subsidiary bodies may be established on a permanent or temporary basis taking into account cost implications.

2. In establishing such additional subsidiary bodies the Commission shall provide specific terms of reference and methods of work, provided always that such specific terms of reference are consistent with the objective and the conservation and management principles and approaches of this Convention and with the 1982 Convention and the 1995 Agreement. Such terms of reference and methods of work may be reviewed and amended as appropriate by the Commission from time to time.

3. All subsidiary bodies shall report, advise and make recommendations to the Commission and contribute to regular reviews of the effectiveness of conservation and management measures adopted by the Commission.

4. In carrying out their functions, all subsidiary bodies shall take into consideration the relevant work of other subsidiary bodies established by the Commission, and as appropriate the work of other fisheries management organisations and the work of other relevant technical and scientific bodies.

5. All subsidiary bodies may establish working groups. Subsidiary bodies may also seek external advice as required in accordance with any general or specific guidance provided by the Commission.

6. All subsidiary bodies shall operate under the rules of procedure of the Commission unless otherwise decided by the Commission.

Article 10 Scientific Committee

1. Each member of the Commission shall be entitled to appoint one representative to the Scientific Committee who may be accompanied by alternate representatives and advisers.

2. The functions of the Scientific Committee shall be to:

(a) plan, conduct and review scientific assessments of the status of fishery resources including, in cooperation with the relevant coastal State Contracting Party or Parties, fishery resources that straddle the Convention Area and areas under national jurisdiction;

(b) provide advice and recommendations to the Commission and its subsidiary bodies based on such assessments including, as appropriate:

(i) reference points, including precautionary reference points as described in Annex II of the 1995 Agreement;

(ii) management strategies or plans for fishery resources based on such reference points; and

(iii) analyses of conservation and management alternatives, such as the establishment of total allowable catch or total allowable fishing effort at different levels, that estimate the extent to which each alternative would achieve the objective or objectives of any management strategy or plan adopted, or under consideration, by the Commission;

(c) provide advice and recommendations to the Commission and its subsidiary bodies on the impact of fishing on the marine ecosystems in the Convention Area including advice and recommendations on the identification and distribution of vulnerable marine ecosystems, the likely impacts of fishing on such vulnerable marine ecosystems and measures to prevent significant adverse impacts on them;

(d) encourage and promote cooperation in scientific research in order to improve knowledge of the state of fishery resources and the marine ecosystems in the Convention Area including knowledge in relation to fishery resources straddling the Convention Area and areas under national jurisdiction; and

(e) provide such other scientific advice to the Commission and its subsidiary bodies as it considers appropriate, or as may be requested by the Commission.

3. The rules of procedure of the Commission shall provide that where the Scientific Committee is unable to provide its advice by consensus, it shall set out in its report the different views of its members. The reports of the Scientific Committee shall be made publicly available.

4. The Commission, taking into account any recommendations from the Scientific Committee, may engage the services of scientific experts to provide information and advice on the fishery resources and marine ecosystems in the Convention Area and any related matters that may be relevant to the Commission's consideration of conservation and management measures.

5. The Commission shall make appropriate arrangements for the periodic independent peer review of the Scientific Committee's reports, advice and recommendations.

Article 11 Compliance and Technical Committee

1. Each member of the Commission shall be entitled to appoint one representative to the Compliance and Technical Committee who may be accompanied by alternate representatives and advisers.

2. The functions of the Compliance and Technical Committee shall be to:

(a) monitor and review the implementation of, and compliance with, conservation and management measures adopted under this Convention and provide advice and recommendations to the Commission;

(b) provide such other information, technical advice and recommendations as it considers appropriate or as may be requested by the Commission relating to the implementation of and compliance with the provisions of this Convention and the conservation and management measures adopted, or under consideration, by the Commission; and

(c) review the implementation of cooperative measures for monitoring, control, and surveillance and enforcement adopted by the Commission and provide advice and recommendations to the Commission.

Article 12 Eastern and Western Sub-Regional Management Committees

1. The Eastern and Western Sub-regional Management Committees shall, on their own initiative or at the request of the Commission, develop and make recommendations to the Commission on conservation and management measures, in accordance with Article 20, and on participation in fishing for fishery resources, in accordance with Article 21, for the parts of the Convention Area described in Annex I. Such recommendations shall be consistent with any measures of general application adopted by the Commission and shall require the consent of the coastal State Contracting Party or Parties concerned on the matters on which such consent is required under Article 20 paragraph 4 and Article 21 paragraph 2. Where appropriate the Committees shall make all efforts to coordinate their recommendations.

2. The Commission may by consensus amend Annex I at any time to adjust the geographic coordinates it contains. Such amendment shall take effect from the date of its adoption, or any other date specified in the amendment.

3. The Commission may decide to assign to one Sub-regional Management Committee primary responsibility for developing and making recommendations to the Commission in accordance with this Article for a specific fishery resource even if the range of that resource should extend beyond the part of the Convention Area for which that Committee has responsibilities in accordance with Annex I.

4. Each Committee shall develop its recommendations on the basis of the advice and recommendations of the Scientific Committee.

5.

(a) Members of the Commission situated adjacent to the part of the Convention Area for which a Committee has responsibility in accordance with this Article, or whose fishing vessels:
  (i) are currently fishing in that area; or
  (ii) have fished in that area within the past two years; or
  (iii) are fishing for a specific fishery resource assigned to that Committee pursuant to paragraph 3, including in areas under national jurisdiction adjacent to the Convention Area shall be members of that Committee.

(b) Any member of the Commission that is not a member of a Committee pursuant to subparagraph (a) that gives notice to the Secretariat of an intention to fish within two years of the notice in the part of the Convention Area for which a Committee has responsibility in accordance with this Article, shall become a member of that Committee. If the notifying member of the Commission does not fish in that part of the Convention Area within two years of the notice, it shall cease to be a member of that Committee.

(c) Any member of the Commission that is not a member of a Committee pursuant to subparagraph (a) or (b) may send a representative to participate in the work of that Committee.

(d) For the purposes of this paragraph, "fishing" includes only the activities described in Article 1 paragraph 1 (g) (i) and (ii).

6. The Eastern and Western Sub-regional Management Committees shall make all efforts to adopt their recommendations to the Commission by consensus. If all efforts to reach agreement on a recommendation by consensus have been exhausted, recommendations shall be adopted by a two-thirds majority of the members of the relevant Sub-regional Management Committee. Reports to the Commission may include majority and minority views.

7. The recommendations made in accordance with this Article will be the basis of conservation and management measures and decisions referred to in Articles 20 and 21, respectively, that shall be adopted by the Commission.

8. Any extraordinary costs incurred for the work of either of the Sub-regional Management Committees shall be borne by the members of the relevant Committee.

Article 13 Finance and Administration Committee

1. Each member of the Commission shall be entitled to appoint one representative to the Finance and Administration Committee who may be accompanied by alternate representatives and advisers.

2. The functions of the Finance and Administration Committee shall be to advise the Commission on the budget, on the time and place of meetings of the Commission, on publications of the Commission, on matters relating to the Executive Secretary and the staff of the Secretariat and on such other financial and administrative matters as may be referred to it by the Commission.

Article 14 Secretariat

1. The Secretariat shall perform the functions delegated to it by the Commission.

2. The chief administrative officer of the Secretariat shall be the Executive Secretary, who shall be appointed with the approval of the Contracting Parties on such terms as they may determine.

3. Any employees of the Secretariat shall be appointed by the Executive Secretary in accordance with such staff regulations as may be determined by the Commission.

4. The Executive Secretary shall ensure the effective functioning of the Secretariat.

5. The Secretariat to be established under this Convention shall be cost effective. The setting up and the functioning of the Secretariat shall, where appropriate, take into account the capacity of existing regional institutions to perform certain technical secretariat functions and more specifically the availability of services under contractual arrangement.

Article 15 Budget

1. The Commission, at its first meeting, shall adopt a budget to fund the Commission and its subsidiary bodies, and shall also adopt financial regulations. All decisions on the budget and financial regulations, including decisions relating to the contributions of members of the Commission and the formula for calculating such contributions, shall be taken by consensus.

2. Each member of the Commission shall contribute to the budget. The amount of the annual contributions due from each member of the Commission shall be a combination of a variable fee based on its total catch of such fishery resources as may be specified by the Commission and a basic fee and shall take account of its economic status. For a member of the Commission whose only catch in the Convention Area is that of its territory or territories adjoining the Convention Area the economic status shall be that of the territory concerned. The Commission shall adopt and may amend a formula for the calculation of these contributions which shall be set out in the financial regulations of the Commission.

3. The Commission may request and accept financial contributions and other forms of assistance from organisations, individuals and other sources for purposes connected with the fulfilment of its functions.

4. The Executive Secretary shall submit a draft of the annual budget for the two succeeding financial years to each member of the Commission together with a schedule of contributions, not less than 60 days before the meeting of the Finance and Administration Committee where the Committee will adopt its recommendations to the Commission. In preparing the draft budget the Secretariat shall take full account of the need for cost effectiveness together with the guidance of the Commission as to the meetings of the subsidiary bodies that may be required in the budget year. Each annual meeting of the Commission shall adopt a budget for the succeeding financial year.

5. If the Commission is unable to adopt a budget, the level of contributions to the administrative budget of the Commission shall be determined in accordance with the budget for the preceding year for the purposes of meeting the administrative expenses of the Commission for the following year until such time as a new budget can be adopted by consensus.

6. Following the annual meeting of the Commission, the Executive Secretary shall notify each member of the Commission of its contribution due as calculated under the formula adopted by

the Commission pursuant to paragraph 2 and as soon as possible thereafter each member of the Commission shall pay its contribution to the Organisation.

7. Contributions shall be payable in the currency of the country in which the Secretariat of the Organisation is located, except if otherwise authorised by the Commission.

8. A Contracting Party that becomes party to this Convention during the course of a financial year shall contribute in respect of that financial year a part of the contribution calculated in accordance with the provisions of this Article that is proportionate to the number of complete months remaining in the year from the date that the Convention enters into force for that Party.

9. Unless otherwise decided by the Commission, a member of the Commission that is in arrears with its payment of any monies owed to the Organisation by more than two years shall not participate in the taking of any decisions by the Commission until it has paid all monies owed by it to the Commission.

10. The financial activities of the Organisation shall be conducted in accordance with financial regulations adopted by the Commission and shall be subject to an annual audit by independent auditors appointed by the Commission.

Article 16 Decision Making

1. As a general rule, decisions by the Commission shall be taken by consensus. For the purpose of this Article, "consensus" means the absence of any formal objection made at the time the decision was taken.

2. Except where this Convention expressly provides that a decision shall be taken by consensus, if the Chairperson considers that all efforts to reach a decision by consensus have been exhausted:

(a) decisions of the Commission on questions of procedure shall be taken by a majority of the members of the Commission casting affirmative or negative votes; and

(b) decisions on questions of substance shall be taken by a three-fourths majority of the members of the Commission casting affirmative or negative votes.

3. When the issue arises as to whether a question is one of substance or not, that question shall be treated as one of substance.

Article 17 Implementation of Commission Decisions

1. Decisions on questions of substance adopted by the Commission shall become binding on the members of the Commission in the following manner:

(a) the Executive Secretary shall promptly notify each decision to all members of the Commission; and

(b) subject to paragraph 2, the decision shall become binding upon all members of the Commission 90 days after the date of transmittal specified in the notification pursuant to subparagraph (a) "the date of notification".

2.

(a) Any member of the Commission may present to the Executive Secretary an objection to a decision within 60 days of the date of notification "the objection period". In that event the decision shall not become binding on that member of the Commission to the extent of the objection, except in accordance with paragraph 3 and Annex II.

(b) A member of the Commission that presents an objection shall at the same time:

(i) specify in detail the grounds for its objection;

(ii) adopt alternative measures that are equivalent in effect to the decision to which it has objected and have the same date of application; and

(iii) advise the Executive Secretary of the terms of such alternative measures.

(c) The only admissible grounds for an objection are that the decision unjustifiably discriminates in form or in fact against the member of the Commission, or is inconsistent with the provisions of this Convention or other relevant international law as reflected in the 1982 Convention or the 1995 Agreement.

3. Any member of the Commission that has objected to a decision may at any time withdraw that objection. The decision shall then become binding on that member in accordance with paragraph 1(b) or on the date of the withdrawal of the objection whichever is the later.

4. The Executive Secretary shall promptly notify all members of the Commission of:

(a) the receipt and withdrawal of each objection; and

(b) the grounds for that objection and the alternative measures adopted, or proposed to be adopted, pursuant to paragraph 2.

5.

(a) When an objection is presented by a member of the Commission pursuant to paragraph 2, a Review Panel shall be established within 30 days after the end of the objection period. The Review Panel shall be established in accordance with the procedures in Annex II.

(b) The Executive Secretary shall promptly notify all members of the Commission of the establishment of the Review Panel.

(c) If two or more members of the Commission present objections based on the same grounds, those objections shall be dealt with by the same Review Panel, which shall have the membership specified in Annex II paragraph 2.

(d) If two or more members of the Commission present objections on different grounds, those objections may, with the consent of the members of the Commission concerned, be dealt with by the same Review Panel, which shall have the membership specified in Annex II paragraph 2. In the absence of such consent, objections on different grounds shall be dealt with by separate Review Panels.

(e) Within 45 days after its establishment, the Review Panel shall transmit to the Executive Secretary its findings and recommendations on whether the grounds specified for the objection presented by the member or members of the Commission are justified and whether the alternative measures adopted are equivalent in effect to the decision to which objection has been presented.

(f) The Executive Secretary shall promptly notify all members of the Commission of the findings and recommendations of the Review Panel. The findings and recommendations of the Review Panel shall be dealt with and have effect as set out in Annex II.

6. Nothing in this Article limits the right of a member of the Commission at any time to refer a dispute concerning the interpretation or application of this Convention for binding settlement in accordance with the provisions of this Convention relating to the settlement of disputes.

Article 18 Transparency

1. The Commission shall promote transparency in decision making processes and other activities carried out under this Convention.

2. All meetings of the Commission and its subsidiary bodies shall be open to all participants and observers registered in accordance with paragraph 4 unless otherwise decided by the Commission. The Commission shall publish its reports and conservation and management measures when adopted and shall maintain a public record of all reports and conservation and management measures in force in the Convention Area.

3. The Commission shall promote transparency in the implementation of this Convention through the public dissemination of non-commercially sensitive information and, as appropriate, facilitating consultations with, and the participation of, non-governmental organisations, representatives of the fishing industry, particularly the fishing fleet, and other interested bodies and individuals.

4. Representatives of non-Contracting Parties, relevant intergovernmental organisations and non-governmental organisations, including environmental organisations and fishing industry organisations with an interest in matters pertaining to the Commission shall be afforded the opportunity to take part in the meetings of the Commission and of its subsidiary bodies, as observers or otherwise as appropriate. The rules of procedure of the Commission shall provide

for such participation and shall not be unduly restrictive in this respect. The rules of procedure shall also provide for such representatives to have timely access to all relevant information.

Article 19 Recognition of the Special Requirements of Developing States

1. The Commission shall give full recognition to the special requirements of developing State Contracting Parties in the region, in particular the least developed among them and small island developing States, and of territories and possessions in the region, in relation to the conservation and management of fishery resources in the Convention Area and the sustainable use of such resources.

2. In giving effect to the duty to cooperate in the establishment of conservation and management measures for fishery resources covered by this Convention, the members of the Commission shall take into account the special requirements of developing State Contracting Parties in the region, in particular the least developed among them and small island developing States, and territories and possessions in the region, in particular:

(a) the vulnerability of such developing States and territories and possessions which are dependent on the exploitation of living marine resources, including for meeting the nutritional requirements of their populations or part thereof;

(b) the need to avoid adverse impacts on, and ensure access to fisheries by, subsistence, small-scale and artisanal fishers and women fish workers, as well as indigenous people in such developing States Parties, and territories and possessions; and

(c) the need to ensure that such measures do not result in transferring, directly or indirectly, a disproportionate burden of conservation action onto such developing State Contracting Parties, and territories and possessions.

3. The members of the Commission shall cooperate either directly or through the Commission and other regional or sub-regional organisations to:

(a) enhance the ability of developing State Contracting Parties in the region, in particular the least developed among them and small island developing States, and of territories and possessions in the region, to conserve and manage fishery resources and to develop their own fisheries for such resources;

(b) assist developing State Contracting Parties in the region, in particular the least developed among them and small island developing States, and territories and possessions in the region, to enable them to participate in fishing for fishery resources, including facilitating access to such fishery resources consistent with Article 3 and Article 21; and

(c) facilitate the participation of developing State Contracting Parties in the region, in particular the least developed among them and small island developing States, and of territories and possessions in the region, in the work of the Commission and its subsidiary bodies.

4. Cooperation for the purposes set out in this Article may include the provision of financial assistance, assistance relating to human resources development, technical assistance, transfer of technology, including through joint venture arrangements, and advisory and consultative services. Such assistance shall, *inter alia*, be directed towards:

(a) improved conservation and management of fishery resources through collection, reporting, verification, exchange and analysis of fisheries data and related information;

(b) stock assessment and scientific research; and

(c) monitoring, control, surveillance, compliance and enforcement, including training and capacity-building at the local level, development and funding of national and regional observer programmes and access to technology and equipment.

5. The Commission shall establish a fund to facilitate the effective participation of developing State Contracting Parties in the region, in particular the least developed among them and small island developing States, and, as appropriate, territories and possessions in the region, in the work of the Commission and its subsidiary bodies. The financial regulations of the Commission

shall include guidelines for the administration of the fund and criteria for eligibility for assistance.

Article 20 Conservation and Management Measures

1. The conservation and management measures adopted by the Commission shall include measures to:

(a) ensure the long-term sustainability of fishery resources and promote the objective of their responsible utilisation;

(b) prevent or eliminate over fishing and excess fishing capacity to ensure that levels of fishing effort do not exceed those commensurate with the sustainable use of fishery resources;

(c) maintain or restore populations of non-target and associated or dependent species to above levels at which their reproduction may become seriously threatened; and

(d) protect the habitats and marine ecosystems in which fishery resources and non-target and associated or dependent species occur from the impacts of fishing, including measures to prevent significant adverse impacts on vulnerable marine ecosystems and precautionary measures where it cannot adequately be determined whether vulnerable marine ecosystems are present or whether fishing would cause significant adverse impacts on vulnerable marine ecosystems.

2. The specific conservation and management measures adopted by the Commission shall, as appropriate, include the determination of:

(a) reference points, including precautionary reference points as described in Annex II of the 1995 Agreement;

(b) the actions to be taken if those reference points are approached or exceeded;

(c) the nature and extent of fishing for any fishery resource including the establishment of a total allowable catch or total allowable fishing effort;

(d) the general or specific locations in which fishing may or may not occur;

(e) the periods in which fishing may or may not occur;

(f) the size limits in respect of the catch which may be retained; and

(g) the types of fishing gear, fishing technology, or fishing practices which may be used when fishing.

3. In determining a total allowable catch or total allowable fishing effort for any fishery resource under paragraph 2 (c), the Commission shall take into account the following factors:

(a) the status and stage of development of the fishery resource;

(b) fishing patterns of the fishery resource;

(c) catch of the same fishery resource within areas under national jurisdiction where relevant;

(d) an allowance for discards and any other incidental mortality;

(e) catch of non-target and associated or dependent species and impacts on the marine ecosystems in which the fishery resource occurs;

(f) relevant ecological and biological factors limiting the nature of fishery resources that may be harvested;

(g) relevant environmental factors, including trophic interactions which may have an effect upon the fishery resource and non-target and associated or dependent species; and

(h) as appropriate, relevant conservation and management measures adopted by other intergovernmental organisations.

The Commission shall regularly review the total allowable catch or total allowable fishing effort established for any fishery resource.

4.

(a) For a fishery resource that straddles the Convention Area and an area under the national jurisdiction of a coastal State Contracting Party or Parties:

(i) the Commission shall establish a total allowable catch or total allowable fishing effort and other conservation and management measures, as appropriate, for the

Convention Area. The Commission and the coastal State Contracting Party or Parties concerned shall cooperate in the coordination of their respective conservation and management measures in accordance with Article 4 of this Convention;

(ii) with the express consent of the coastal State Contracting Party or Parties concerned, the Commission may establish, in accordance with Annex III of this Convention, and as appropriate, a total allowable catch or total allowable fishing effort that will apply throughout the range of the fishery resource; and

(iii) in the case where one or more of the coastal State Contracting Parties does not consent to a total allowable catch or total allowable fishing effort that will apply throughout the range of the fishery resource, the Commission may establish, as appropriate, a total allowable catch or total allowable fishing effort that will apply in the areas of national jurisdiction of the consenting coastal State Contracting Party or Parties and the Convention Area. Annex III will apply, *mutatis mutandis,* to the establishment of this total allowable catch or total allowable fishing effort by the Commission.

(b) In cases covered by subparagraph (a) (ii) or (a) (iii), other complementary conservation and management measures may be adopted so as to ensure sustainable conservation and management of the fishery resource throughout its range. To give effect to this paragraph, such measures may be adopted, in accordance with the principles of compatibility outlined in Article 4, by the Commission for the high seas and the coastal State Contracting Party or Parties concerned for the areas under national jurisdiction; and by the Commission, with the consent of the coastal State Contracting Party or Parties concerned, for measures that will apply throughout the range of the fishery resource.

(c) All conservation and management measures, including a total allowable catch or total allowable fishing effort, adopted by the

(d) Commission in accordance with subparagraphs (a) (ii), (a) (iii) and (b) are without prejudice to and do not affect the sovereign rights of coastal States for the purpose of exploring and exploiting, conserving and managing the living marine resources within areas under national jurisdiction in accordance with international law, as reflected in the relevant provisions of the 1982 Convention and the 1995 Agreement, and do not in any other respect affect the Area of application of this Convention established by Article 5.

5.

(a) The Commission shall adopt measures to be applied on an emergency basis, in accordance with Article 16, including intersessionally, if necessary, where fishing presents a serious threat to the sustainability of fishery resources or the marine ecosystem in which these fishery resources occur or when a natural phenomenon or human caused disaster has, or is likely to have, a significant adverse impact on the status of fishery resources to ensure that fishing does not exacerbate such threat or adverse impact.

(b) Measures taken on an emergency basis shall be based on the best scientific evidence available. Such measures shall be temporary and must be reconsidered for decision at the next meeting of the Commission following their adoption. The measures shall become binding on the members of the Commission in accordance with Article 17 paragraph 1. Such measures shall not be open to the objection procedure in Article 17 paragraph 2 but may be the subject of dispute settlement procedures under this Convention.

6. The conservation and management measures adopted by the Commission shall be progressively developed and integrated into management strategies or plans that set out the management objectives for each fishery resource, the reference points against which to measure progress in relation to those objectives, the indicators to be used in relation to those reference points and the measures to be taken in response to particular indicator levels.

Article 21 Participation in Fishing for Fishery Resources

1. When taking decisions regarding participation in fishing for any fishery resource, including the allocation of a total allowable catch or total allowable fishing effort, the Commission shall take into account the status of the fishery resource and the existing level of fishing effort for that resource and the following criteria to the extent relevant:

(a) historic catch and past and present fishing patterns and practices in the Convention Area;
(b) compliance with the conservation and management measures under this Convention;
(c) demonstrated capacity and willingness to exercise effective flag State control over fishing vessels;
(d) contribution to the conservation and management of fishery resources, including the provision of accurate data and effective monitoring, control, surveillance and enforcement;
(e) the fisheries development aspirations and interests of developing States in particular small island developing States and of territories and possessions in the region;
(f) the interests of coastal States, and in particular developing coastal States and territories and possessions, in a fishery resource that straddles areas of national jurisdiction of such States, territories and possessions and the Convention Area;
(g) the needs of coastal States and of territories and possessions whose economies are dependent mainly on the exploitation of and fishing for a fishery resource that straddles areas of national jurisdiction of such States, territories and possessions and the Convention Area;
(h) the extent to which a member of the Commission is utilising the catch for domestic consumption and the importance of the catch to its food security;
(i) contribution to the responsible development of new or exploratory fisheries in accordance with Article 22; and
(j) contribution to the conduct of scientific research with respect to fishery resources and the public dissemination of the results of such research.

2. When the Commission establishes a total allowable catch or total allowable fishing effort for any fishery resource pursuant to Article 20 paragraph 4 (a) (ii) or (iii), it may, with the express consent of the coastal State Contracting Party or Parties concerned, also take decisions regarding participation in fishing for that resource throughout its relevant range.

3. In taking decisions under paragraph 2, the Commission shall take into account the historic catch and past and present fishing patterns and practices throughout the relevant range of the fishery resource concerned and the criteria listed in paragraph 1(b) – (j).

4. When the consent of the coastal State Contracting Party or Parties concerned is not provided pursuant to paragraph 2:

(a) the Commission shall take decisions, in accordance with paragraph 1, regarding allocation of the portion of the total allowable catch or total allowable fishing effort established pursuant to Article 20 paragraph 4 (a) (i) that may be taken in the Convention Area; and
(b) the Commission and the coastal State Contracting Party or Parties concerned shall cooperate in accordance with Article 4.

5. In taking decisions under this Article, the Commission may also have regard, as appropriate, to performance with respect to other international fisheries management regimes.

6. The Commission shall, when appropriate, review decisions regarding participation in fishing for fishery resources, including the allocation of a total allowable catch or total allowable fishing effort, taking into account the provisions of this Article and the interests of new Contracting Parties.

Article 22 New or Exploratory Fisheries

1. A fishery that has not been subject to fishing or has not been subject to fishing with a particular gear type or technique for ten years or more shall be opened as a fishery or opened to fishing with such gear type or technique only when the Commission has adopted cautious preliminary

conservation and management measures in respect of that fishery, and, as appropriate, non-target and associated or dependent species, and appropriate measures to protect the marine ecosystem in which that fishery occurs from adverse impacts of fishing activities.

2. Such preliminary conservation and management measures, which may include requirements regarding notification of intention to fish, the establishment of a development plan, mitigation measures to prevent adverse impacts on marine ecosystems, use of particular fishing gear, the presence of observers, the collection of data, and the conduct of research or exploratory fishing, shall be consistent with the objective and the conservation and management principles and approaches of this Convention. The measures shall ensure that the new fishery resource is developed on a precautionary and gradual basis until sufficient information is acquired to enable the Commission to adopt appropriately detailed conservation and management measures.

3. The Commission may, from time to time, adopt standard minimum conservation and management measures that are to apply in respect of some or all new fisheries prior to the commencement of fishing for such new fisheries.

Article 23 Data Collection, Compilation and Exchange

1. To enhance the information base for the conservation and management of fishery resources, non-target and associated or dependent species and the protection of the marine ecosystems in which those resources occur; and to contribute to the elimination or reduction of IUU fishing and its negative impact on those resources, the Commission shall, taking full account of Annex I of the 1995 Agreement, develop standards, rules and procedures for, *inter alia*:

(a) the collection, verification and timely reporting to the Commission of all relevant data by members of the Commission;

(b) the compilation and management by the Commission of accurate and complete data to facilitate effective stock assessment and ensure that the provision of the best scientific advice is enabled;

(c) the security of, access to and dissemination of data while maintaining confidentiality where appropriate;

(d) the exchange of data among members of the Commission, and with other regional fisheries management organisations, and other relevant organisations including data concerning vessels engaged in IUU fishing, and, as appropriate, concerning the beneficial ownership of such vessels, with a view to consolidating such information into a centralised format for dissemination as appropriate;

(e) the facilitation of coordinated documentation and data sharing between regional fisheries management organisations, including procedures to exchange data on vessel registers, catch documentation and trade tracking schemes where applicable; and

(f) regular audits of Commission member compliance with data collection and exchange requirements, and for addressing any non-compliance identified in such audits.

2. The Commission shall ensure that data are publicly available concerning the number of vessels operating in the Convention Area, the status of fishery resources managed under this Convention, fishery resource assessments, research programmes in the Convention Area, and cooperative initiatives with regional and global organisations.

Article 24 Obligations of Members of the Commission

1. Each member of the Commission shall, in respect of its fishing activities within the Convention Area:

(a) implement this Convention and any conservation and management measures adopted by the Commission, and take all necessary measures to ensure their effectiveness;

(b) cooperate in furthering the objective of this Convention;

(c) take all necessary measures to support efforts to prevent, deter and eliminate IUU fishing; and

(d) collect, verify and report scientific, technical and statistical data pertaining to fishery resources and marine ecosystems in the Convention Area in conformity with the standards, rules and procedures established by the Commission.

2. Each member of the Commission shall report to the Commission on an annual basis indicating how it has implemented the conservation and management measures and compliance and enforcement procedures adopted by the Commission. In the case of coastal State Contracting Parties, the report shall include information regarding the conservation and management measures they have taken for straddling fishery resources occurring in waters under their jurisdiction adjacent to the Convention Area in accordance with Article 20 paragraph 4 and Article 4. Such reports shall be made publicly available.

3. Without prejudice to the primacy of the responsibility of the flag State, to the greatest extent possible, each member of the Commission shall take measures and cooperate to ensure compliance by its nationals, or fishing vessels owned, operated or controlled by its nationals, with the provisions of this Convention and any conservation and management measures adopted by the Commission, and immediately investigate any alleged violation of such provisions and measures. Members of the Commission shall provide reports on the progress of the investigation to the Commission and relevant members of the Commission at appropriate regular intervals, to the extent permitted by national law, as well as a final report on the outcome when the investigation is completed.

4. To the extent permitted by its national laws and regulations, each member of the Commission shall establish arrangements for making available to prosecuting authorities of other members of the Commission evidence related to alleged violations of the provisions of the Convention and any conservation and management measures adopted by the Commission, including information available on the beneficial ownership of vessels flying its flag.

5. Each member of the Commission shall fulfil in good faith the obligations assumed under this Convention and shall exercise the rights recognised in this Convention in a manner which would not constitute an abuse of right.

Article 25 Flag State Duties

1. Each member of the Commission shall take all necessary measures to ensure that fishing vessels flying its flag:

(a) comply with the provisions of this Convention and the conservation and management measures adopted by the Commission and that such vessels do not engage in any activity which undermines the effectiveness of such measures when operating in the Convention Area;

(b) do not conduct unauthorised fishing within waters under national jurisdiction adjacent to the Convention Area;

(c) carry and operate equipment sufficient to comply with vessel monitoring system standards and procedures adopted by the Commission; and

(d) land or tranship fishery resources caught in the Convention Area in accordance with standards and procedures adopted by the Commission.

2. No member of the Commission shall allow any fishing vessel entitled to fly its flag to be used for fishing in the Convention Area unless it has been authorised to do so by the appropriate authority or authorities of that member of the Commission.

3. Each member of the Commission shall:

(a) authorise the use of fishing vessels flying its flag for fishing in the Convention Area only where it is able to exercise effectively its responsibilities in respect of such vessels under this Convention and in accordance with international law;

(b) maintain a register of fishing vessels entitled to fly its flag and authorised to fish for fishery resources, and ensure that, for all such vessels, such information as may be specified by the Commission is entered in that register;

(c) in accordance with measures adopted by the Commission, investigate immediately and report fully on actions taken in response to any alleged violation by fishing vessels flying its flag of the provisions of this Convention or any conservation and management measure adopted by the Commission. Reporting shall include reports on the progress of the investigation to the Commission at appropriate regular intervals, to the extent permitted by national law, as well as a final report on the outcome when the investigation is completed;

(d) ensure that penalties applicable for such violations are of an appropriate severity, taking into account relevant factors including the value of the catch, to secure compliance, discourage further violations and deprive offenders of the benefits accruing from their illegal activities; and

(e) ensure in particular that, where it has been established, in accordance with its laws, that a fishing vessel flying its flag has been involved in the commission of a serious violation of the provisions of this Convention or of any conservation and management measures adopted by the Commission, the vessel concerned ceases fishing activities and does not engage in such activities in the Convention Area until it has complied with all outstanding sanctions imposed by the member of the Commission in respect of the violation.

4. Each member of the Commission is encouraged to ensure that fishing vessels flying its flag operate in the Convention Area in accordance with applicable international obligations, and with regard to relevant recommendations and guidelines, regarding safety at sea for vessels and their crews.

5. Each member of the Commission shall ensure that fishing vessels flying its flag engaged in or intending to engage in research into fishery resources comply with any procedures established by the Commission for the conduct of scientific research in the Convention Area.

Article 26 Port State Duties

1. A port State Contracting Party has the right and duty to take measures, in accordance with international law, to promote the effectiveness of sub-regional, regional and global conservation and management measures. When taking such measures, a port State Contracting Party shall not discriminate in form or in fact against the fishing vessels of any State.

2. Each member of the Commission shall:

(a) give effect to conservation and management measures adopted by the Commission in relation to the entry and use of its ports by fishing vessels that have engaged in fishing in the Convention Area including, *inter alia*, with respect to landing and transhipment of fishery resources, inspection of fishing vessels, documents, catch and gear on board, and use of port services; and

(b) provide assistance to flag States, as reasonably practical and in accordance with its national law and international law, when a fishing vessel is voluntarily in its ports and the flag State of the vessel requests it to provide assistance in ensuring compliance with the provisions of this Convention and with the conservation and management measures adopted by the Commission.

3. In the event that a member of the Commission considers that a fishing vessel making use of its ports has violated a provision of this Convention or a conservation and management measure adopted by the Commission, it shall notify the flag State concerned, the Commission and other relevant States and appropriate international organisations. The member of the Commission shall provide the flag State and, as appropriate the Commission with full documentation on the matter, including any record of inspection.

4. Nothing in this Article affects the exercise by Contracting Parties of their sovereignty over ports in their territory in accordance with international law.

Article 27 Monitoring, Compliance and Enforcement

1. The Commission shall establish appropriate cooperative procedures for effective monitoring, control and surveillance of fishing and to ensure compliance with this Convention and the conservation and management measures adopted by the Commission including, *inter alia*:

(a) the establishment and maintenance of a Commission record of vessels authorised to fish in the Convention Area, the marking of vessels and fishing gear, the recording of fishing activities, and the reporting of vessel movements and activities by a satellite vessel monitoring system that shall be designed to ensure the integrity and security of near real time transmissions, including through the possibility of direct and simultaneous transmissions, to the Commission and flag State;
(b) an inspection programme for Contracting Parties, both at sea and in port, including procedures for Contracting Parties to board and inspect each others' vessels in the Convention Area, and procedures for notification of inspection vessels and aircraft of Contracting Parties that may participate in the programme;
(c) regulation and supervision of transhipment;
(d) non discriminatory market-related measures, consistent with international law, to monitor transhipment, landings, and trade to prevent, deter and eliminate IUU fishing including, where appropriate, catch documentation schemes;
(e) reporting on violations detected, progress and outcomes of investigations, and enforcement actions taken; and
(f) addressing IUU fishing activities, including by identifying vessels engaging in IUU fishing activities, and by adopting appropriate measures to prevent, deter and eliminate IUU fishing, such as the development of an IUU vessels list, so that owners and operators of vessels engaging in such activities are deprived of the benefits accruing from those activities.

2. The Commission may adopt procedures that enable measures, including trade-related measures in relation to fishery resources, to be applied by members of the Commission to any state, member of the Commission, or entity whose fishing vessels engage in fishing activities that diminish the effectiveness of, or otherwise fail to comply with, the conservation and management measures adopted by the Commission. Such measures should include a range of possible responses so that account can be taken of the reason for and degree of non-compliance and should include, as appropriate, cooperative capacity-building initiatives. Any implementation of trade-related measures by a member of the Commission shall be consistent with that member's international obligations, including its obligations under the Agreement establishing the World Trade Organisation.

3. If, within three years of the entry into force of this Convention, the Commission has not adopted at sea inspection procedures as outlined in paragraph 1 (b), or an alternative mechanism which effectively discharges the obligations of the members of the Commission under the 1995 Agreement and this Convention to ensure compliance with the conservation and management measures adopted by the Commission, Articles 21 and 22 of the 1995 Agreement shall apply among Contracting Parties as if those Articles were part of this Convention, and boarding and inspection of fishing vessels in the Area, as well as any subsequent enforcement action, shall be conducted in accordance with Articles 21 and 22 of the 1995 Agreement and such additional practical procedures as the Commission may decide are necessary for the implementation of those Articles.

Article 28 Observer Programme

1. The Commission shall establish an observer programme, within three years of the entry into force of this Convention or such other period as the Commission may agree, to collect verified catch and effort data, other scientific data and additional information related to the fishing activity in the Convention Area, and its impacts on the marine environment. Information collected by the observer programme shall, as appropriate, also be used to support the functions of the Commission and its subsidiary bodies, including the Compliance and Technical Committee. The observer programme shall be coordinated by the Secretariat of the Commission, and shall be organised in a flexible manner which takes into account the nature of the fishery resources

and other relevant factors. In this regard, the Commission may enter into contracts for the provision of the observer programme.

2. The observer programme shall consist of independent and impartial observers that are sourced from programmes or service providers accredited by the Commission. The programme shall be coordinated, to the maximum extent possible, with other regional, sub-regional and national observer programmes.

3. The Commission shall develop the observer programme taking into account advice from the Scientific Committee and Compliance and Technical Committee. The programme shall be operated in accordance with standards, rules and procedures developed by the Commission including, *inter alia*:

(a) arrangements for the placing of observers by a member of the Commission on vessels flying the flag of another member of the Commission with the consent of that member;
(b) levels of coverage appropriate for different fishery resources to monitor and verify catch, effort, catch composition and other details of fishing operations;
(c) requirements for collection, validation and reporting of scientific data and information relevant to the implementation of the provisions of this Convention and the conservation and management measures adopted by the Commission; and
(d) requirements to ensure the safety and training of observers, for observer accommodation while on board the vessel, and to ensure observers have full access to and use of all relevant facilities and equipment on board the vessel in order to perform their duties effectively.

Article 29 Annual Report of the Commission

1. The Commission shall publish an annual report, which shall include details of decisions taken by the Commission to achieve the objective of this Convention. The report shall also provide information on actions taken by the Commission in response to any recommendations from the General Assembly of the United Nations or the FAO.

2. Copies of the report shall be publicly available and shall be provided to the Secretary-General of the United Nations and the Director-General of the FAO.

Article 30 Reviews

1. The Commission shall review the effectiveness of the conservation and management measures adopted by the Commission in meeting the objective of this Convention and the consistency of such measures with the principles and approaches in Article 3. Such reviews may include examination of the effectiveness of the provisions of the Convention itself and shall be undertaken at least every five years.

2. The Commission shall determine the terms of reference and methodology of such reviews which shall be carried out in accordance with criteria set by the Commission which shall be guided by best international practices and shall include contributions from the subsidiary bodies as appropriate and the participation of a person or persons of recognised competence who is independent of the Commission.

3. The Commission shall take account of the recommendations arising from any such review, including through the appropriate amendment of its conservation and management measures and the mechanisms for their implementation. Any proposals for amendment to the provisions of this Convention arising from any such review shall be dealt with in accordance with Article 35.

4. The results of any such review shall be made publicly available following its submission to the Commission.

Article 31 Cooperation with other Organisations

1. The Commission shall cooperate, as appropriate, with other regional fisheries management organisations, the FAO, with other specialised agencies of the United Nations, and with other relevant organisations on matters of mutual interest.

2. The Commission shall take account of the conservation and management measures or recommendations adopted by other regional fisheries management organisations and other

relevant intergovernmental organisations that have competency in relation to the Convention Area, or in relation to areas adjacent to the Convention Area or in respect of particular living marine resources including non-target and associated or dependent species, and that have objectives that are consistent with, and supportive of, the objective of this Convention. It shall endeavour to ensure that its own decisions are compatible with, and supportive of, such conservation and management measures or recommendations.

3. The Commission shall seek to make suitable arrangements for consultation, cooperation and collaboration with such other organisations. In particular it shall seek to cooperate with other relevant organisations with the aim of reducing and eventually eliminating IUU fishing.

Article 32 Non-Parties

1. Members of the Commission shall exchange information with respect to the activities of fishing vessels engaged in fishing in the Convention Area that are flying the flags of non-Contracting Parties to this Convention. Members of the Commission shall take measures, individually or collectively, consistent with this Convention and international law to deter activities of such vessels which undermine the effectiveness of conservation and management measures applicable in the Convention Area, and shall report to the Commission any action taken in response to fishing in the Convention Area by non-Contracting Parties.

2. Taking account of Articles 116 to 119 of the 1982 Convention, the members of the Commission, individually or collectively, may draw the attention of any State or fishing entity which is a non-Contracting Party to this Convention to any activity which in the opinion of the member or members of the Commission affects the implementation of the objective of this Convention.

3. Members of the Commission shall, individually or collectively, request non-Contracting Parties to this Convention whose vessels fish in the Convention Area to become party to this Convention or to agree to cooperate fully in the implementation of conservation and management measures adopted by the Commission.

4. Members of the Commission, individually or jointly, shall seek the cooperation of any non-Contracting Party that has been identified as a relevant port State or market State to ensure compliance with the objective of this Convention.

Article 33 Relation to other Agreements

1. Nothing in this Convention shall prejudice the rights, jurisdiction and duties of Contracting Parties under relevant provisions of international law as reflected in the 1982 Convention or the 1995 Agreement.

2. This Convention shall not alter the rights and obligations of Contracting Parties that arise from other agreements compatible with this Convention and that do not affect the enjoyment by other Contracting Parties of their rights or the performance of their obligations under this Convention.

Article 34 Settlement of Disputes

1. Contracting Parties shall cooperate in order to prevent disputes and shall use their best endeavours to resolve any disputes by amicable means which may include, where a dispute is of a technical nature, referring the dispute to an ad hoc expert panel.

2. In any case where a dispute is not resolved through the means set out in paragraph 1, the provisions relating to the settlement of disputes set out in Part VIII of the 1995 Agreement shall apply, *mutatis mutandis*, to any dispute between the Contracting Parties.

3. Paragraph 2 shall not affect the status of any Contracting Party in relation to the 1995 Agreement or the 1982 Convention.

Article 35 Amendments

1. The text of proposed amendments must be provided to the Executive Secretary at least 90 days in advance of a Commission meeting. The Executive Secretary shall promptly circulate a copy of this text to all members of the Commission.

2. Such proposals for amendment to this Convention shall be adopted by the Commission by a three-fourths majority of the Contracting Parties present and casting affirmative or negative votes. Adopted amendments shall be transmitted by the Depositary to all Contracting Parties without delay.

3. An amendment shall take effect for all Contracting Parties one hundred and twenty days following the date of transmittal specified in the notification by the Depositary of receipt of written notification of approval by three-fourths of all Contracting Parties unless any other Contracting Party notifies the Depositary that it objects to the amendment within ninety days of the date of transmittal specified in the notification by the Depositary of such receipt, in which case the amendment shall not take effect for any Contracting Party. Any Contracting Party which has objected to an amendment may at any time withdraw that objection. If all objections to an amendment are withdrawn, the amendment shall take effect for all Contracting Parties one hundred and twenty days following the date of transmittal specified in the notification by the Depositary of receipt of the last withdrawal.

4. Any State, regional economic integration organisation, or other entity referred to in Article 1 paragraph 2 (b) that becomes a Contracting Party after the adoption of an amendment in accordance with paragraph 2 shall be deemed to be bound by the Convention as amended once that amendment has entered into force in accordance with paragraph 3.

5. The Depositary shall promptly notify all Contracting Parties of the receipt of notifications of approval of amendments, the receipt of notifications of objection or withdrawal of objections, and the entry into force of amendments.

Article 36 Signature, Ratification, Acceptance and Approval

1. This Convention shall be open for signature by:

(a) States, the regional economic integration organisation and the other entities referred to in Article 1, paragraph 2 (b), that participated in the International Consultations on the Establishment of the South Pacific Regional Fisheries Management Organisation; and

(b) any other State or any other entity referred to in Article 1, paragraph 2 (b), that has jurisdiction over waters adjacent to the Convention Area;

and shall remain open for signature for 12 months from the first day of February 2010.

2. This Convention is subject to ratification, acceptance or approval by the signatories.

3. Instruments of ratification, acceptance or approval shall be deposited with the Depositary.

Article 37 Accession

1. This Convention shall be open for accession, after its closure for signature, by any State, regional economic integration organisation or other entity referred to in Article 36 paragraph 1, and by any other State or any other entity referred to in Article 1 paragraph 2 (b) having an interest in fishery resources.

2. Instruments of accession shall be deposited with the Depositary.

Article 38 Entry into Force

1. This Convention shall enter into force 30 days after the date of receipt by the Depositary of the eighth instrument of ratification, accession, acceptance or approval, which shall include ratification, accession, acceptance or approval by:

(a) at least three coastal States adjacent to the Convention Area, which must include representation from both the side of the Convention Area that is east of Meridian 120° West and the side of the Convention Area that is west of Meridian 120° West; and

(b) at least three States that are not coastal States adjacent to the Convention Area and whose fishing vessels are fishing in the Convention Area or have fished in the Convention Area.

2. If within three years of its adoption, this Convention has not entered into force in accordance with paragraph 1, it shall enter into force six months after the deposit of the tenth instrument of ratification, accession, acceptance or approval, or in accordance with paragraph 1, whichever is the earlier.

3. For each signatory which ratifies, accepts or approves this Convention after its entry into force, this Convention shall enter into force for that signatory 30 days after the deposit of its instrument of ratification, acceptance or approval.

4. For each State or regional economic integration organisation which accedes to this Convention after its entry into force, this Convention shall enter into force for that State or regional economic integration organisation 30 days after the deposit of its instrument of accession.

5. For the purposes of this Article, "fishing" includes only the activities described in Article 1 paragraph 1 (g) (i) and (ii).

Article 39 The Depositary

1. The Government of New Zealand shall be the Depositary of this Convention and any amendments thereto. The Depositary shall transmit certified copies of this Convention to all signatories and shall register this Convention with the Secretary-General of the United Nations pursuant to Article 102 of the Charter of the United Nations.

2. The Depositary shall inform all signatories of and Contracting Parties to this Convention of signatures and of instruments of ratification, accession, acceptance or approval deposited under Article 36 or 37 and of the date of entry into force of the Convention and of any amendments thereto.

Article 40 Participation by Territories

1. The Commission and its subsidiary bodies shall be open to participation, with the appropriate authorisation of the Contracting Party having responsibility for its international affairs, to territories in the region that have an interest in fishery resources.

2. The nature and extent of participation by territories shall be provided for by the Contracting Parties in separate rules of procedure of the Commission, taking into account international law, the distribution of competence on matters covered by this Convention and the evolution in the capacity of such territory to exercise rights and responsibilities under this Convention. These rules of procedure shall provide territories with the right to participate fully in the work of the Commission and its subsidiary bodies, except for the right to vote or block consensus on decisions, advice or recommendations.

3. Notwithstanding paragraph 2, all such territories shall be entitled to be present and to speak at the meetings of the Commission and its subsidiary bodies. In the performance of its functions, and in taking decisions, the Commission shall take into account the interests of all participants.

Article 41 Withdrawal

1. A Contracting Party may, by written notification addressed to the Depositary, withdraw from this Convention and may indicate its reasons. Failure to indicate reasons shall not affect the validity of the withdrawal. The withdrawal shall take effect 1 year after the date of receipt of the notification, unless the notification specifies a later date.

2. Withdrawal from this Convention by a Contracting Party shall not affect the financial obligations of such Contracting Party incurred prior to its withdrawal becoming effective.

3. Withdrawal from this Convention by a Contracting Party shall not in any way affect the duty of such Contracting Party to fulfil any obligation embodied in this Convention to which it would be subject under international law independently of this Convention.

Article 42 Termination

This Convention shall be automatically terminated if and when, as the result of withdrawals, the number of Contracting Parties drops below 4.

Article 43 Reservations

No reservations or exceptions may be made to this Convention.

Article 44 Declarations and Statements

Article 43 does not preclude a State, regional economic integration organisation or entity referred to in Article 1 paragraph 2 (b), when signing, ratifying or acceding to this Convention, from making declarations or statements, however phrased or named, with a view, *inter alia*, to the harmonisation of its laws and regulations with the provisions of this Convention, provided that such declarations or statements do not purport to exclude or to modify the legal effect of the provisions of this Convention in their application to that State, regional economic integration organisation or entity.

Article 45 Annexes

The Annexes form an integral part of this Convention and, unless expressly provided otherwise, a reference to this Convention includes a reference to the Annexes relating thereto.

IN WITNESS WHEREOF, the undersigned Plenipotentiaries, having been duly authorised by their respective Governments, have signed this Convention.

DONE at Auckland the fourteenth day of November, two thousand and nine, in a single original.

OPENED FOR SIGNATURE at Wellington this first day of February, two thousand and ten.

[*Signatories omitted.*]

Annex I: Parts of the Convention area for which the Eastern and Western Sub-regional Management Committees have responsibilities

1. The Eastern Sub-regional Management Committee shall be responsible for developing and recommending to the Commission conservation and management measures for that part of the Convention Area that lies east of Meridian 120° West.

2. The Western Sub-regional Management Committee shall be responsible for developing and recommending to the Commission conservation and management measures for that part of the Convention Area that lies west of Meridian 120° West.

Annex II: Review Panel – Establishment

1. A Review Panel to be established in accordance with Article 17 paragraph 5 shall be constituted as follows:

(a) It shall consist of three members appointed from the list of experts in the field of fisheries drawn up and maintained by the FAO pursuant to Annex VIII, Article 2 of the 1982 Convention or a similar list maintained by the Executive Secretary. The list maintained by the Executive Secretary shall be made up from experts whose competence in the legal, scientific or technical aspects of fisheries covered by this Convention is established and generally recognised and who enjoy the highest reputation for fairness and integrity. Each member of the Commission shall be entitled to nominate up to five experts and shall provide information on relevant qualifications and experience of each of its nominees.

(b) The Chairperson of the Commission and the member of the Commission that has presented objection to the decision shall each appoint one member. The name of the member appointed by the objecting member of the Commission shall be included in the notification of the objection to the Executive Secretary pursuant to Article 17 paragraph 2 (a). The name of the member appointed by the Chairperson of the Commission shall be notified to the objecting member of the Commission within 10 days of the expiry of the objection period.

(c) The third member shall be appointed within 20 days of the expiry of the objection period through agreement between the objecting member of the Commission and the Chairperson of the Commission and shall not be a national of the objecting member of the Commission. If there is no agreement within this time period on the appointment of the third member, the appointment shall be made by the Secretary General of the Permanent Court of Arbitration, unless it is agreed that the appointment be made by another person or third State.

(d) The Review Panel is considered to be established on the date that the third member is appointed, and this third member shall chair the Review Panel.

2. If more than one member of the Commission presents an objection to the decision on the same grounds, or where there is agreement pursuant to Article 17 paragraph 5 (d) that objections to the decision made on different grounds may be dealt with by the same Review Panel, the Review Panel shall consist of 5 members from the lists referred to in paragraph 1 (a) and shall be constituted as follows:

(a) One member shall be appointed, in accordance with paragraph 1 (b) by the member of the Commission that presented the first objection, two members shall be appointed by the Chairperson of the Commission within 10 days of the expiry of the objection period, one member shall be appointed by agreement between the subsequent objecting members of the Commission within 15 days of the expiry of the objection period and one member shall be appointed by agreement between all the objecting members of the Commission and the Chairperson of the Commission within 20 days of the expiry of the objection period. If within the latter two time periods as appropriate, agreement cannot be reached on either of the last two appointments, the appointment or appointments on which agreement has not been reached shall be made by the Secretary General of the Permanent Court of Arbitration unless there is agreement that the appointment or appointments be made by another person or third State.

(b) The Review Panel is considered to be established on the date that the final member is appointed. The Review Panel shall be chaired by the member appointed by agreement between all the objecting members of the Commission and the Chairperson of the Commission in accordance with subparagraph (a).

3. Any vacancy on a Review Panel shall be filled in the manner described for the initial appointment.

Functioning

4. The Review Panel shall determine its own rules of procedure.

5. A hearing shall be convened at a place and on a date to be determined by the Review Panel within 30 days following its establishment.

6. Any member of the Commission may submit a memorandum to the Review Panel concerning the objection under review and the Panel shall allow any such member of the Commission full opportunity to be heard.

7. Unless the Review Panel decides otherwise because of the particular circumstances of the case, the expenses of the Review Panel, including the remuneration of its members, shall be borne as follows:

(a) 70 per cent shall be borne by the objecting member of the Commission, or if there is more than one objecting member of the Commission, divided equally amongst them; and

(b) 30 per cent shall be borne by the Commission from its annual budget.

8. The findings and recommendations of the Review Panel shall be adopted by a majority of its members. Any member of the Panel may attach a separate or dissenting opinion. Any decisions on the procedure of the Review Panel shall also be taken by a majority of its members.

9. The Review Panel shall, within 45 days of its establishment, transmit its findings and recommendations to the Executive Secretary in accordance with Article 17 paragraph 5.

Findings and Recommendations

10. The findings and recommendations of the Review Panel shall be dealt with as follows:

Findings of Discrimination

(a) If the Review Panel finds that the decision to which objection has been presented discriminates in form or in fact against the objecting member or members of the Commission and the alternative measures have equivalent effect to the decision to which objection has been presented, the alternative measures shall be deemed to be equivalent to the decision and to be binding on the relevant member or members of the Commission in substitution for the decision.

(b) Subject to subparagraphs (d) and (e), if the Review Panel finds that the decision to which objection has been presented discriminates in form or in fact against the objecting member or members of the Commission and the alternative measures are equivalent in effect to the decision to which objection has been presented, subject to specific modifications, the Review Panel will recommend such modifications. On receipt of the findings and recommendations of the Review Panel the objecting member or members of the Commission shall, within 60 days, modify the relevant alternative measures as recommended by the Review Panel or institute dispute settlement proceedings under this Convention. The alternative measures shall be deemed to be equivalent to the decision to which an objection has been presented when they are modified as recommended by the Review Panel. Such alternative measures shall then be binding on the relevant member or members of the Commission in the modified form in substitution for the decision. If the objecting member or members of the Commission choose to institute dispute settlement proceedings under this Convention then neither the decision nor the modified alternative measures shall be binding on the objecting member or members of the Commission pending decisions made in those proceedings.

(c) Subject to subparagraphs (d) and (e), if the Review Panel finds that the decision to which objection has been presented unjustifiably discriminates in form or in fact against the objecting member or members of the Commission but the alternative measures do not have equivalent effect to the decision to which objection has been presented the objecting member or members of the Commission shall, within 60 days, adopt measures recommended by the Review Panel as equivalent in effect to the decision to which objection has been presented or institute dispute settlement proceedings under this Convention. If the objecting member or members of the Commission adopt the measures recommended by the Review Panel these measures shall be deemed to be binding on the objecting member or members of the Commission in substitution for the decision. If the objecting member or members of the Commission choose to institute dispute settlement proceedings under this Convention then neither the decision nor any measures recommended by the Review Panel shall be binding on the objecting member or members of the Commission pending decisions made in those proceedings.

(d) Where the Review Panel makes findings and recommendations under subparagraphs (b) or (c) the objecting member or members of the Commission may within 30 days from the date of the transmittal of the notification of those findings and recommendations request an extraordinary meeting of the Commission. The Extraordinary Meeting shall be convened by the Chairperson within 45 days of the receipt of any such request.

(e) If the Extraordinary Meeting convened under subparagraph (d) confirms or modifies the recommendations of the Review Panel, the 60 day period under subparagraphs (b) or (c) as appropriate, for the implementation of those findings and recommendations in original or modified form or the institution of dispute settlement proceedings, shall run from the date of the transmittal of the decision of the Extraordinary Meeting. If the Extraordinary Meeting of the Commission decides not to confirm or modify the recommendations of the Review Panel but to revoke the decision to which objection was presented and replace it with a new decision or a modified version of the original decision, the new or modified decision shall become binding on the members of the Commission in accordance with Article 17.

Findings of Inconsistency

(f) If the Review Panel finds that the decision to which objection has been presented is inconsistent with this Convention, or with relevant international law as reflected in the 1982 Convention or the 1995 Agreement, an Extraordinary Meeting of the Commission shall be convened by the Chairperson within 45 days of the notification of the Review Panel's findings and recommendations to reconsider the decision in the light of those findings and recommendations.

(g) If the Extraordinary Meeting of the Commission revokes the decision to which objection has been presented and replaces it with a new decision, or a modified version of the previous decision, the new or modified decision shall become binding on the members of the Commission in accordance with Article 17.

(h) If the Extraordinary Meeting of the Commission confirms its original decision, the objecting member or members of the Commission shall, within 45 days, implement the decision or institute dispute settlement proceedings under this Convention. If the objecting member or members of the Commission choose to institute dispute settlement proceedings under this Convention, the decision shall not be binding on the objecting member or members of the Commission pending decisions made in those proceedings.

Findings of Non-justification of Objection

(i) If the Review Panel finds that the decision to which objection has been presented does not discriminate in form or in fact against the objecting member or members of the Commission and is not inconsistent with this Convention or with relevant international law as reflected in the 1982 Convention or the 1995 Agreement, the objecting member or members of the Commission shall, subject to subparagraph (j), within 45 days implement the decision or institute dispute settlement proceedings under this Convention. If the objecting member or members of the Commission choose to institute dispute settlement proceedings under this Convention the decision shall not be binding on the objecting member or members of the Commission pending decisions made in those proceedings.

(j) If the Review Panel finds that the decision to which objection has been presented does not discriminate in form or in fact against the objecting member or members of the Commission and is not inconsistent with this Convention or with relevant international law as reflected in the 1982 Convention or the 1995 Agreement but that the alternative measures are equivalent in effect to the decision and should be accepted as such by the Commission, the alternative measures shall be binding on the objecting member or members of the Commission in substitution for the decision pending confirmation of their acceptance by the Commission at its next meeting.

Annex III: Procedures for the Establishment and Implementation of a Total Allowable Catch or Total Allowable Fishing Effort for a Straddling Fishery Resource when applied throughout its range

1. In accordance with Articles 23 and 24, coastal State Contracting Parties and members of the Commission whose vessels fish for the straddling fishery resource in areas under national jurisdiction or on the high seas in the adjacent Convention Area shall provide all relevant scientific, technical and statistical data with respect to such fishery resources to the Commission for consideration by the Scientific Committee and, as appropriate, the Compliance and Technical Committee.

2. In accordance with Article 10, the Scientific Committee shall assess the status of the straddling fishery resource throughout its range and provide advice to the Commission and the relevant Sub-regional Management Committee on an appropriate total allowable catch or total allowable fishing effort for the resource throughout its range. Such advice should include where possible estimates of the extent to which the establishment of a total allowable catch or a total allowable fishing effort at different levels would achieve the objective or objectives of any management strategy or plan adopted by the Commission.

3. In accordance with Article 12, and on the basis of the advice of the Scientific Committee and any relevant advice of the Compliance and Technical Committee, the relevant Sub-regional Management Committee shall make recommendations to the Commission on a total allowable catch or total allowable fishing effort for the fishery resource throughout its range and appropriate measures to ensure the total allowable catch or total allowable fishing effort is not exceeded.

4. In accordance with Articles 16 and 20, the Commission, on the basis of the recommendations

and advice from the Scientific Committee and the relevant Sub-regional Management Committee and any relevant advice of the Compliance and Technical Committee, shall establish a total allowable catch or total allowable fishing effort for the fishery resource throughout its range and adopt appropriate measures to ensure that the total allowable catch or total allowable fishing effort is not exceeded.

5. In relation to the conservation and management of *Trachurus murphyi* (jack mackerel), the Commission shall, in accordance with Article 20, and as appropriate, give primary consideration to establishing a total allowable catch, without prejudice to any other conservation and management measures which it considers appropriate to adopt to ensure the conservation and sustainable use of this fishery resource.

Annex IV Fishing Entities

1. After the entry into force of this Convention, any fishing entity whose vessels have fished or intend to fish for fishery resources may, by a written instrument delivered to the Depositary, express its firm commitment to abide by the terms of this Convention and comply with any conservation and management measures adopted pursuant to it. Such commitment shall become effective 30 days from the date of receipt of the instrument. Any such fishing entity may withdraw such commitment by written notification addressed to the Depositary. The withdrawal shall become effective 1 year after the date of its receipt, unless the notification specifies a later date.

2. Any fishing entity referred to in paragraph 1 above may by a written instrument delivered to the Depositary, express its firm commitment to abide by the terms of the Convention as it may be amended pursuant to Article 35(3). This commitment shall be effective from the dates referred to in Article 35(3) or on the date of receipt of the written communication referred to in this paragraph, whichever is later.

3. A fishing entity which has expressed its firm commitment to abide by the terms of this Convention and comply with conservation and management measures adopted pursuant to it in accordance with paragraph 1 must abide by the obligations of members of the Commission, and may participate in the work, including decision making, of the Commission in accordance with the provisions of this Convention. For the purposes of this Convention, references to the Commission or members of the Commission include such fishing entity.

4. If a dispute involves a fishing entity which has expressed its commitment to be bound by the terms of this Convention in accordance with this Annex and cannot be settled by amicable means, the dispute shall, at the request of any party to the dispute, be submitted to final and binding arbitration in accordance with the relevant rules of the Permanent Court of Arbitration.

5. The provisions of this Annex relating to the participation of a fishing entity are only for the purposes of this Convention.

OTHER INSTRUMENTS

IMO Code of Safety for Fishermen and Fishing Vessels 2005, Part A, Appendix 10: Recommendation for Skippers of Fishing Vessels on Ensuring a Vessel's Endurance in Conditions of Ice Formation[18]

(referred to in paragraphs 1.3.11 of section II and 1.2.11 of section III)

1 Brief Survey of the Causes of Ice Formation and its Influence upon the Seaworthiness of the Vessel

1.1 The skipper of a fishing vessel should bear in mind that ice formation is a complicated process which depends upon meteorological conditions, condition of loading and behaviour of the vessel in stormy weather as well as on the size and location of superstructures and rigging.

[18] Drawn from the annex of Assembly resolution A.269(VIII).

The most common cause of ice formation is the deposit of water droplets on the vessel's structure. These droplets come from spray driven from wave crests and from vessel-generated spray.

1.2 Ice formation may also occur in conditions of snowfall, sea fog including arctic sea smoke, a drastic fall in ambient temperature, as well as from the freezing of drops of rain on impact with the vessel's structure.

1.3 Ice formation may sometimes be caused or accentuated by water shipped on board and retained on deck.

1.4 Intensive ice formation generally occurs on stem, bulwark and bulwark rail, front walls of superstructures and deckhouses, hawse holes, anchors, deck gear, forecastle deck and upper deck, freeing ports, aerials, stays, shrouds, masts and spars.

1.5 It should be borne in mind that the most dangerous areas as far as ice formation is concerned are the following:

.1 The area north of latitude 65°30 N, between longitude 28°W and the west coast of Iceland; north of the north coast of Iceland; north of the rhumb line running from latitude 66°N, longitude l5°W to latitude 73°30 N, longitude l5°E, north of latitude 73°30 N between longitude l5°E and 35°E, and east of longitude 35°E, as well as north of latitude 56°N in the Baltic Sea .

.2 The area north of latitude 43°N bounded in the west by the North American coast and the east by the rhumb line running from latitude 43°N longitude 48°W to latitude 63°N longitude 28°W and thence along longitude 28°W.

.3 All sea areas north of the North American continent, west of the areas defined in .1 and .2 above.

.4 The Bering and Okhotsk Seas and the Tartary Strait during the icing season .

.5 South of latitude 60° S.

1.6 A chart to illustrate the areas of icing conditions is given below.

[*Chart omitted.*]

1.7 The most intensive ice formation takes place when wind and sea come from ahead. In beam and quartering winds, ice accumulates quicker on the windward side of the vessel, thus leading to a constant list which is extremely dangerous.

1.8 Listed below are meteorological conditions causing the most common type of ice formation due to spraying of a vessel. Examples of the weight of ice formation on a typical fishing vessel of displacement in the range 100 to 500 tons is also given. For larger vessels, the weight will be correspondingly greater.

1.9 Slow accumulations of ice take place:

.1 at ambient temperature from -1°C to -3°C and any wind force;

.2 at ambient temperature -4°C and lower and wind force from 0 to 9 m/s; and

.3 under the conditions of precipitation, fog or sea mist followed by a drastic fall of the ambient temperature.

Under all these conditions the intensity of ice accumulation may not exceed 1.5 t/h.

1.10 At ambient temperature of -4°C to -8°C and wind force 10–15 m/s, rapid accumulation of ice takes place. Under these conditions the intensity of ice accumulation can lie within the range1.5 to 4 t/h. Very fast accumulation of ice takes place:

.1 at ambient temperature of -4°C and lower and wind forces of 16 m/s and over; and

.2 at ambient temperature -9°C and lower and wind force 10 to 15 m/s.

Under these conditions the intensity of ice accumulation can exceed 4 t/h.

1.11 The skipper should bear in mind that ice formation adversely affects the seaworthiness of the vessel as ice formation leads to:

.1 an increase in the weight of the vessel due to accumulation of ice on the vessel's surfaces which causes the reduction of freeboard and buoyancy;

.2 a rise of the vessel's centre of gravity due to the high location of ice on the vessel's structures with corresponding reduction in the level of stability;
.3 an increase of windage area due to ice formation on the upper parts of the vessel and, hence, an increase in the heeling moment due to the action of the wind;
.4 a change of trim due to uneven distribution of ice along the vessel's length;
.5 the development of a constant list due to uneven distribution of ice across the breadth of the vessel; and
.6 impairment of the manoeuvrability and reduction of the speed of the vessel.

2 Recommendations for Skippers on Ensuring the Vessel's Endurance under Conditions of Ice Formation

2.1 Prior to departure

2.1.1 Firstly, the skipper should, as in the case of any voyages in any season, ensure that the vessel is generally in a seaworthy condition giving full attention to basic requirements, such as:
.1 loading of the vessel within the limits prescribed for the season (see 2.1.2.1);
.2 weathertightness and reliability of the devices for closing cargo and access hatches, outer doors and all other openings in the decks and superstructures of the vessel and the watertightness of the sidescuttles and of ports or similar openings in the sides below the freeboard deck to be checked;
.3 condition of the freeing ports and scuppers as well as operational reliability of their closures to be checked;
.4 emergency and life-saving appliances and their operational reliability;
.5 operational reliability of all external and internal communication equipment; and
.6 condition and operational reliability of the bilge and ballast pumping systems.

2.1.2 Further, with special regard to possible ice accretion, the skipper should:
.1 consider the most critical loading condition against approved stability documents with due regard to fuel and water consumption, distribution of supplies, cargoes and fishing gear and with allowance for possible ice accretion;
.2 be aware of the danger in having supplies and fishing gear stored on open weatherdeck spaces due to their large ice accretion surface and high centre of gravity;
.3 ensure that a complete set of warm clothing for all members of the crew is available on the vessel as well as a complete set of hand tools and other appliances for combating ice accretion, a typical list thereof is shown in 2.4 and 2.5;
.4 ensure that the crew is acquainted with the location of means for combating ice accretion, as well as the use of such means, and that drills are carried out so that members of the crew know their respective duties and have the necessary practical skills to ensure the vessel's endurance under conditions of ice accretion. When drills are carried out, it should be recorded in the vessel's log-book;
.5 acquaint himself with the meteorological conditions in the region of fishing grounds and en route to the place of destination; study the synoptical maps of this region and weather forecasts; be aware of warm currents in the vicinity of the fishing grounds, of the nearest coastline relief, of the existence of protected bays and of the location of ice fields and their boundaries; and
.6 acquaint himself with the timetable of the radio stations transmitting weather forecasts and warnings of the possibility of ice accretion in the area of the relevant fishing grounds.

2.2 At sea

2.2.1 During the voyage and when the vessel is on the fishing grounds, the skipper should keep himself informed on all long-term and short-term weather forecasts and should arrange for the following systematic meteorological observations to be systematically recorded:
.1 temperatures of the air and of the sea surface;
.2 wind direction and force;

.3 direction and height of waves and sea state;
.4 atmospheric pressure, air humidity; and
.5 frequency of splashing per minute and the intensity of ice accumulation on different parts of the vessel per hour.

All observed data should be recorded in the vessel's log-book. When the conditions suitable for ice accretion occur, the skipper should be informed. The skipper should compare the weather forecasts and icing charts with actual meteorological conditions, and should estimate the probability of ice formation and its intensity.

2.2.2 When the danger of ice formation arises, the following measures should be taken without delay:

.1 all the means of combating ice formation should be ready for use;
.2 all the fishing operations should be stopped, the fishing gear should be taken on board and placed in the underdeck spaces. If this cannot be done, all the gear should be fastened for storm conditions on its prescribed place;
It is particularly dangerous to leave the fishing gear suspended since its surface for ice formation is large and the point of suspension is generally located high;
.3 barrels and containers with fish, packing, all gear and supplies located on deck as well as portable mechanisms should be placed in closed spaces as low as possible and firmly lashed;
.4 all cargoes in holds and other compartments should be placed as low as possible and firmly lashed;
.5 the cargo booms should be lowered and fastened; and
.6 deck machinery, hawser reels and boats should be covered with deck covers;
.7 lifelines should be fastened on deck;
.8 freeing ports fitted with covers should be brought into operative condition, all objects located near scuppers and freeing ports and preventing water drainage from deck should be taken away;
.9 all cargo and companion hatches, manhole covers, weathertight outside doors in superstructures and deckhouses and portholes should be securely closed in order to ensure complete weathertightness of the vessel; access to the weather deck from inner compartments should be allowed only through the superstructure deck;
.10 a check should be carried out as to whether the amount of water ballast on board and its location is in accordance with that recommended in "Stability guidance to Skippers"; if there is sufficient freeboard, all the empty bottom tanks fitted with ballast piping should be filled with seawater;
.11 all fire-fighting, emergency and life-saving equipment should be ready for use;
.12 all drainage systems should be checked for their effectiveness;
.13 deck lighting and searchlights should be checked;
.14 a check should be carried out to make sure that each member of the crew has warm clothing; and
.15 reliable two-way radio communication with both shore stations and other vessels should be established; radio calls should be arranged for set times.

2.2.3 The skipper should seek to take the vessel away from the dangerous area keeping in mind that the lee edges of icefields, areas of warm currents and protected coastal areas are a good refuge for the vessel during weather when ice formation occurs.

2.2.4 Small fishing vessels on fishing grounds should keep nearer to each other and to larger vessels.

2.2.5 It should be remembered that the entry of the vessel into an icefield presents certain danger to the hull especially when there is a high sea swell. Therefore, the vessel should enter the icefield at a right angle to the icefield edge at low speed without inertia. It is less dangerous to enter an icefield bow to the wind. If a vessel must enter an icefield with the wind on the stern, the fact that the edge of the ice is more dense on the windward side should be taken into consideration. It is important to enter the icefield at the point where the ice floes are the smallest.

2.2.6 Additional lookouts should be posted when growlers are found to be in the vicinity of the vessel; it should be noted that growlers are not shown on radar.

2.3 During ice formation

2.3.1 If in spite of all measures taken the vessel is unable to leave the dangerous area, all means available for removal of ice should be used as long as it is subjected to ice formation.

2.3.2 Depending on the type of vessel, all or many of the following ways of combating ice formation may be used:

.1 removal of ice by means of cold water under pressure;

.2 removal of ice with hot water and steam; and

.3 breaking up of ice with ice crows, axes, picks, scrapers, wooden sledge hammers and clearing it with shovels.

2.3.3 When ice formation begins, the skipper should take into account recommendations listed below and ensure their strict fulfilment:

.1 report immediately ice formation to the owner and establish with him constant radio communication;

.2 establish radio communication with the nearest vessels and ensure that it is maintained;

.3 inform the owner about other vessels in the area;

.4 do not allow ice formation to accumulate on the vessel, immediately take steps to remove from the vessel's structures even the thinnest layer of ice and ice sludge from the upper deck;

.5 check constantly the vessel's stability by measuring the roll period of the vessel during ice formation. If the rolling period increases noticeably, immediately take all possible measures in order to increase the vessel's stability;

.6 ensure that each member of the crew working on the weather deck is warmly dressed and wears a safety helmet and a safety line securely attached to the guard rail;

.7 additional meals should be provided during extended working hours to reduce the effects of exposure to low temperatures. Supplies of warm drinks/soups should be available at all times;

.8 bear in mind that the work of the crew on ice clearing entails the danger of frost-bite. For this reason, it is necessary to make sure that the men working on deck are replaced periodically;

.9 keep the following structures and gears of the vessel free from ice:

  .1 aerials;

  .2 running and navigational lights;

  .3 freeing ports and scuppers;

  .4 life-saving craft;

  .5 stays, shrouds, masts and rigging;

  .6 doors of superstructures and deckhouses; and

  .7 windlass and hawse holes;

.10 remove the ice from large surfaces of the vessel, beginning with the upper structures (such as bridges, deckhouses, etc.), because even a small amount of ice on them causes a drastic worsening of the vessel's stability;

.11 when the distribution of ice is not symmetrical and a list develops, the ice should be cleared from the lower side first. Bear in mind that any correction of the list of the vessel by pumping fuel or water from one tank to another may reduce stability during the process when both tanks are slack;

.12 when a considerable amount of ice forms on the bow and a trim appears, ice should be quickly removed. Water ballast may be redistributed in order to decrease the trim;

.13 clear ice from the freeing ports and scuppers in due time in order to ensure free drainage of the water from the deck;
.14 check regularly for water accumulation inside the hull;
.15 avoid navigating in following seas since this may drastically worsen the vessel's stability;
.16 register in the vessel's log-book the duration, nature and intensity of ice formation, amount of ice on the vessel, measures taken to combat ice formation and their effectiveness; and
.17 if, in spite of all the measures taken to ensure the vessel's endurance in conditions of ice formation, the crew is forced to abandon the vessel and embark on life-saving craft (lifeboats, rafts), then, in order to preserve their lives, it is necessary to do all possible to provide all the crew with warm clothing or special bags as well as to have a sufficient number of lifelines and bailers for speedy bailing out of water from the life-saving craft.

2.4 Typical list of equipment and hand tools for combating ice formation on larger vessels

5 Ice crows or crowbars
5 Axes with long handles
5 Picks
5 Metal scrapers
5 Metal shovels
3 Wooden sledge hammers
3 Fore and aft lifelines to be rigged each side of the open deck fitted with travellers to which lizards can be attached
* Sufficient safety harnesses for all crew working on deck
* Search light operated directly from inside the wheelhouse

2.5 Typical list of personal protective clothing in addition to the normal working gear

1 Full balaclava, only eyes should be exposed
2 Full sets of thermal underwear
1 Thick woollen jersey
4 Sets of inner gloves
4 Sets of outer gloves
1 Pair of rubber soled working boots giving coverage above the ankle to the calf
4 Sets of inner liners for working boots
1 Padded working jacket

Notes:

1. Number of hand tools and life-saving appliances may be increased at the fishing vessel owners' discretion.
2. Hoses which may be used for ice combating should be readily available on board.
3. The lists can be used as a guide for smaller vessels.

IMO Enhanced Contingency Planning Guidance for Passenger Ships Operating in Areas Remote from Search and Rescue (SAR) Facilities[19]

1. The Maritime Safety Committee, at its eighty-first session (10 to 19 May 2006), with a view to providing enhanced guidance for passenger ships operating in areas remote from SAR facilities, approved the Enhanced contingency planning guidance for passenger ships operating in areas remote from SAR facilities, prepared by the Sub-Committee on Radiocommunications and Search and Rescue, at its tenth session (6 to 10 March 2006), as set out in the annex.

2. Member Governments and international organizations are invited to bring the annexed guidance to the attention of all concerned.

[19] MSC.1/Circ.1184, 31 May 2006.

Annex: Enhanced Contingency Planning Guidance for Passenger Ships Operating in Areas Remote from SAR Facilities

1. In accordance with the relevant provisions of the SOLAS and SAR Conventions and the ISM Code, contingency plans for passenger ships should be prepared for operating in areas considered to be remote from SAR facilities. Factors which may make an area remote from SAR services are set out in the Appendix and may include:

.1 the number of people potentially at risk as the result of an accident in the area;

.2 the total recovery capacity of SAR facilities available to reach the scene of the accident and recover those at risk within survival times (including all additional SAR facilities likely to be available, as well as designated SAR units); and

.3 whether there is any shortfall between the number to be recovered and the capacity of those SAR facilities available.

2. SAR co-operation planning arrangements should be enhanced for ships operating in areas remote from SAR facilities (see Appendix), as follows:

.1 the Company should give reasonable notice of the arrival of its ship in the remote area to the relevant RCC;

.2 if not already doing so, the Company should arrange direct exchange of the ship's SAR co-operation plan with the relevant SAR services;

.3 the relevant SAR services may request a copy of the relevant part of the Company's emergency plan, in addition to the basic SAR co-operation plan, in order to assist their own contingency planning; and

.4 the Company should keep the RCC informed as to the ship's position and intentions while the ship is operating in the remote area.

3. The risks of remote area operation should be assessed and planned for. The following enhancements should be among those considered:

.1 voyage 'pairing', i.e., mutual exchange of information that may be available to the SAR Authority or the vessel operator with reference to other passenger ships operating in the same area, so that, if two or more passenger ships are operating in the same general area at the same time, each can be used as a SAR facility in case of accident to another;

.2 the carriage of enhanced life-saving appliances;

.3 the provision of additional life-saving resources; and

.4 other sources of assistance that may be available in the area.

Appendix: Criteria for Determining What Constitutes an Area Remote from SAR Facilities

1. The following criteria are considered relevant in determining what constitutes an area remote from SAR facilities:

.1 the number of people at risk;

.2 the nature of the risk and whether containment strategies can mitigate its effects, in particular whether the effects of the incident can be so contained as to enable those at risk to remain on board until rescued, or for a period prior to eventual evacuation, thus extending the time to recover;

.3 the availability of SAR facilities and other resources which may be deployed in order to contain the incident and keep those at risk on board until rescued, or for a period prior to eventual evacuation, thus extending the time to recover;

.4 the total recovery capacity of SAR facilities available to reach the scene and recover those who have taken to survival craft within the five day "time to recover" parameter and/or within survival times;

.5 any shortfall between the number to be recovered and the capacity of those SAR facilities available;

.6 the distance (in time) between individual SAR facilities' start points and the scene of the emergency;

.7 the prevailing sea conditions, both on scene and encountered by SAR facilities proceeding;
.8 the prevailing weather conditions, both on scene and encountered by SAR facilities proceeding;
.9 any restrictions on SAR facility deployment which limit or remove their ability to respond even if theoretically within reach of the scene of the emergency;
.10 the ability of those at risk to survive in the prevailing weather and sea conditions until they can be recovered (that is, for a maximum of five days according to the "time to recover" parameter);
.11 the ability of available SAR facilities to recover those at risk in the prevailing weather and sea conditions;[20]
.12 any shortfall between the time taken to recover those at risk and the five day "time to recover" parameter and/or survival times in the prevailing conditions;
.13 availability and quality of communications; and
.14 effective co-ordination of search and rescue response.

IMO Guidelines on Voyage Planning for Passenger Ships Operating in Remote Areas[21]

The Assembly,

Recalling Article 15(j) of the Convention on the International Maritime Organization concerning the functions of the Assembly in relation to regulations and guidelines concerning maritime safety and the prevention and control of marine pollution from ships,

Recalling also regulation 6 of chapter V of the Inkternational Convention for the Safety of Life at Sea (SOLAS), 1974, as amended, on the Ice Patrol Service, including the Appendix to chapter V on Rules for the management, operation and financing of the North Atlantic Ice Patrol,

Recalling further resolution A.893(21) on *Guidelines for voyage planning*,

Noting that the Maritime Safety Committee, at its seventy-third session, agreed to enhance the safety of passenger ships from a holistic perspective, including consideration of concerns related to operations in remote areas,

Noting also that the Maritime Safety Committee, at its seventy-sixth session, and the Marine Environment Protection Committee, at its forty-eighth session, approved the "Guidelines for ships operating in Arctic ice-covered waters", which were subsequently issued as MSC/Circ.1056 – MEPC/Circ.399,

Recognizing the need to develop guidelines to supplement resolution A.893(21), particularly for passenger ships operating in remote areas, in order to prevent incidents of groundings and collisions, and thereby enhance safety of life at sea,

Having considered the recommendation made by the Maritime Safety Committee at its eighty-first session:

1. *Adopts* the "Guidelines on voyage planning for passenger ships operating in remote areas", set out in the annex to the present resolution;

2. *Invites* Governments to bring the annexed guidelines to the attention of masters of ships entitled to fly the flag of their States, shipowners, ship operators and managers, shipping companies, maritime pilots, training institutions, tour operators, ice-patrol and ice-breaking services and all other parties concerned, for information and action as appropriate;

3. *Requests* the Maritime Safety Committee to keep the above-mentioned guidelines under review and to amend them as appropriate.

[20] The continuing work on developing functional requirements for SOLAS ships on systems used to recover persons from survival craft and from the water should be noted in this regard. It is intended that SOLAS ships will, in future, be better able to recover people in such circumstances.

[21] IMO Assembly resolution A.999(25), adopted 29 November 2007 (Agenda item 9).

Annex: Guidelines on Voyage Planning for Passenger Ships Operating in Remote Areas

1 Introduction

1.1 The growing popularity of ocean travel for passengers and the desire for exotic destinations have led to increasing numbers of passenger ships operating in remote areas. When developing a plan for voyages to remote areas, special consideration should be given to the environmental nature of the area of operation, the limited resources, and navigational information.

1.2 Passenger ships operating in remote Arctic ice-covered waters should also refer to MSC/Circ.l056 – MEPC/Circ.399 for recommended construction provisions, equipment recommendations, and operational guidelines.

1.3 Guidance on voyage planning is given in resolution A.893(21). Passenger ships operating in remote areas should include the following additional factors in their voyage planning.

2 Appraisal

2.1 The detailed voyage and passage plan should include the following factors:

.1 the source, date and quality of the hydrographic data on which the charts to be used are based;

.2 limitations on available maritime safety information (MSI) data and Search and Rescue resources;

.3 availability or lack of aids to navigation; and

.4 places of refuge.

2.2 In addition, the detailed voyage and passage plan for ships operating in Arctic or Antarctic waters should include the following factors:

.1 knowledge of ice and ice formations, in order to be able to navigate in ice, and how environmental conditions relating to current, wind, calm weather, fog and different seasons affect the ice and navigation in ice;

.2 Current information on the extent and type of ice and icebergs in the vicinity of the intended route;

.3 statistical information on ice from former years;

.4 operational limitations in ice-covered waters; and

.5 availability and use of ice navigators.

3 Planning

3.1 The detailed voyage and passage plan should include the following factors:

.1 safe areas and no-go areas;

.2 surveyed marine corridors, if available; and

.3 contingency plans for emergencies in the event of limited support being available for assistance in areas remote from SAR facilities.[22]

3.2 In addition, the detailed voyage and passage plan for ships operating in Arctic or Antarctic waters should include the following factors:

.1 conditions when it is not safe to enter areas containing ice or icebergs because of darkness, swell, fog and pressure ice;

.2 safe distance to icebergs; and

.3 presence of ice and icebergs, and safe speed in such areas.

4 Execution

4.1 The detailed voyage and passage plan should report changes to a previously advised voyage and passage plan, to the relevant authorities.

4.2 In addition, the detailed voyage and passage plan for ships operating in Arctic or Antarctic waters should include the following factors:

.1 existing ice conditions; and

[22] Refer to "Enhanced contingency planning guidance for passenger ships operating in areas remote from SAR facilities" (MSC.1/Circ.1184).

.2 measures to be taken before entering waters where ice may be present, e.g., an abandon ship drill and preparation of special equipment.[23]

IMO International Code Intact Stability[24] under the SOLAS Convention and the 1988 Load Lines Protocol, Chapter 6: Icing Considerations

MSC 85/26/Add.1 Annex 2 Chapter 6 – Icing Considerations

6.1 General

6.1.1 For any ship operating in areas where ice accretion is likely to occur, adversely affecting a ship's stability, icing allowances should be included in the analysis of conditions of loading.

6.1.2 Administrations are advised to take icing into account and are permitted to apply national standards where environmental conditions are considered to warrant a higher standard than those recommended in the following sections.

6.2 Cargo ships carrying timber deck cargoes

6.2.1 The master should establish or verify the stability of his ship for the worst service condition, having regard to the increased weight of deck cargo due to water absorption and/or ice accretion and to variations in consumables.[25]

6.2.2 When timber deck cargoes are carried and it is anticipated that some formation of ice will take place, an allowance should be made in the arrival condition for the additional weight.

6.3 Fishing vessels

The calculations of loading conditions for fishing vessels (refer to 3.4.2.8) should, where appropriate, include allowance for ice accretion, in accordance with the following provisions.

6.3.1 Allowance for ice accretion[26]

For vessels operating in areas where ice accretion is likely to occur, the following icing allowance should be made in the stability calculations:

.1 30 kg per square metre on exposed weather decks and gangways;

.2 7.5 kg per square metre for projected lateral area of each side of the vessel above the water plane;

.3 the projected lateral area of discontinuous surfaces of rail, sundry booms, spars (except masts) and rigging of vessels having no sails and the projected lateral area of other small objects should be computed by increasing the total projected area of continuous surfaces by 5% and the static moments of this area by 10%.

Vessels intended for operation in areas where ice is known to occur should be:

.4 designed to minimize the accretion of ice; and

.5 equipped with such means for removing ice as the Administration may require; for example, electrical and pneumatic devices, and/or special tools such as axes or wooden clubs for removing ice from bulwarks, rails and erections.

6.3.2 Guidance relating to ice accretion

In the application of the above standards, the following icing areas should apply:

.1 the area north of latitude 65° 30' N, between longitude 28° W and the west coast of Iceland; north of the north coast of Iceland; north of the rhumb line running from latitude 66° N, longitude 15° W to latitude 73° 30' N, longitude 15° E, north of latitude 73° 30' N between longitude 15° E and 35° E, and east of longitude 35° E, as well as north of latitude 56° N in the Baltic Sea;

[23] Refer to "Guidelines for ships operating in Arctic ice covered waters" (MSC/Circ.1056 – MEPC/Circ.399).

[24] IMO Maritime Safety Committee resolution MSC.267(85), Annex, adopted 4 December 2008.

[25] Refer to regulation 44(10) of the 1966 Load Line Convention and regulation 44(7) of the 1988 Load Line Protocol as amended.

[26] Refer to regulation III/8 of the 1993 Torremolinos Protocol.

.2 the area north of latitude 43° N bounded in the west by the North American coast and the east by the rhumb line running from latitude 43° N, longitude 48° W to latitude 63° N, longitude 28° W and thence along longitude 28° W;

.3 all sea areas north of the North American Continent, west of the areas defined in 6.3.2.1 and 6.3.2.2;

.4 the Bering and Okhotsk Seas and the Tartary Strait during the icing season; and

.5 south of latitude 60° S.

A chart to illustrate the areas is attached at the end of this chapter.

[*chart omitted*]

For vessels operating in areas where ice accretion may be expected:

.6 within the areas defined in 6.3.2.1, 6.3.2.3, 6.3.2.4 and 6.3.2.5 known to having icing conditions significantly different from those described in 6.3.1, ice accretion requirements of one half to twice the required allowance may be applied; and

.7 within the area defined in 6.3.2.2, where ice accretion in excess of twice the allowance required by 6.3.1 may be expected, more severe requirements than those given in 6.3.1 may be applied.

6.3.3 Brief survey of the causes of ice formation and its influence upon the seaworthiness of the vessel

6.3.3.1 The skipper of a fishing vessel should bear in mind that ice formation is a complicated process which depends upon meteorological conditions, condition of loading and behaviour of the vessel in stormy weather as well as on the size and location of superstructures and rigging. The most common cause of ice formation is the deposit of water droplets on the vessel's structure. These droplets come from spray driven from wave crests and from ship-generated spray.

6.3.3.2 Ice formation may also occur in conditions of snowfall, sea fog (including arctic sea smoke), a drastic fall in ambient temperature, as well as from the freezing of drops of rain on impact with the vessel's structure.

6.3.3.3 Ice formation may sometimes be caused or accentuated by water shipped on board and retained on deck.

6.3.3.4 Intensive ice formation generally occurs on stem, bulwark and bulwark rail, front walls of superstructures and deck-houses, hawse holes, anchors, deck gear, forecastle deck and upper deck, freeing ports, aerials, stays, shrouds, masts and spars.

6.3.3.5 It should be borne in mind that the most dangerous areas as far as ice formation is concerned are the sub-Arctic regions.

6.3.3.6 The most intensive ice formation takes place when wind and sea come from ahead. In beam and quartering winds, ice accumulates quicker on the windward side of the vessel, thus leading to a constant list which is extremely dangerous.

6.3.3.7 Listed below are meteorological conditions causing the most common type of ice formation due to spraying of a vessel. Examples of the weight of ice formation on a typical fishing vessel of displacement in the range 100 t to 500 t are also given. For larger vessels the weight will be correspondingly greater.

6.3.3.8 Slow accumulations of ice take place:

.1 at ambient temperature from -1°C to -3 °C and any wind force;

.2 at ambient temperature -4°C and lower and wind force from 0 m/s to 9 m/s; and

.3 under the conditions of precipitation, fog or sea mist followed by a drastic fall of the ambient temperature.

Under all these conditions the intensity of ice accumulation may not exceed 1.5 t/h.

6.3.3.9 At ambient temperature of -4°C to -8°C and wind force 10 m/s to 15 m/s, rapid accumulation of ice takes place. Under these conditions the intensity of ice accumulation can lie within the range 1.5 t/h to 4 t/h.

6.3.3.10 Very fast accumulation of ice takes place:

.1 at ambient temperature of -4°C and lower and wind forces of 16 m/s and over; and

.2 at ambient temperature -9°C and lower and wind force 10 m/s to 15 m/s.

Under these conditions the intensity of ice accumulation can exceed 4 t/h.

6.3.3.11 The skipper should bear in mind that ice formation adversely affects the seaworthiness of the vessel as ice formation leads to:

.1 an increase in the weight of the vessel due to accumulation of ice on the vessel's surfaces which causes the reduction of freeboard and buoyancy;

.2 a rise of the vessel's centre of gravity due to the high location of ice on the vessel's structures with corresponding reduction in the level of stability;

.3 an increase of windage area due to ice formation on the upper parts of the vessel and hence an increase in the heeling moment due to the action of the wind;

.4 a change of trim due to uneven distribution of ice along the vessel's length;

.5 the development of a constant list due to uneven distribution of ice across the breadth of the vessel; and

.6 impairment of the manoeuvrability and reduction of the speed of the vessel.

6.3.4 Operational procedures related to ensuring a fishing vessel's endurance in conditions of ice formation are given in annex 2 (Recommendations for skippers of fishing vessels on ensuring a vessel's endurance in conditions of ice formation).

6.4 Offshore supply vessels 24 m to 100 m in length

For vessels operating in areas where ice accretion is likely to occur:

.1 no shutters should be fitted in the freeing ports; and

.2 with regard to operational precautions against capsizing, reference is made to the recommendations for skippers of fishing vessels on ensuring a vessel's endurance in conditions of ice formation, as given in paragraph 6.3.3 and in annex 2 (Recommendations for skippers of fishing vessels on ensuring a vessel's endurance in conditions of ice formation).

IMO Guidelines for Ships Operating in Polar Waters[27]

The Assembly,

Recalling Article 15(j) of the Convention on the International Maritime Organization concerning the functions of the Assembly in relation to regulations and guidelines concerning maritime safety and the prevention and control of marine pollution from ships,

Recalling also that, by circular MSCICirc.1056-MEPC/Circ.399, the Maritime Safety Committee and the Marine Environment Protection Committee, recognizing the need for recommendatory provisions applicable to ships operating in Arctic ice-covered waters, additional to the mandatory and recommendatory provisions contained in existing IMO instruments, approved Guidelines for ships operating in Arctic ice-covered waters (hereinafter referred to as "the Guidelines"),

Noting that the Maritime Safety Committee, at its seventy-ninth session, considered a request by the XXVIIth Antarctic Treaty Consultative Meeting (ATCM) to amend the Guidelines to render them applicable to ships operating in ice-covered waters in the Antarctic Treaty Area as well,

Acknowledging that the polar environment imposes additional demands on ship systems beyond the existing requirements of the International Convention for the Safety of Life at Sea (SOLAS), 1974 and the International Convention for the Prevention of Pollution from Ships, 1973, as modified by the 1978 Protocol relating thereto (MARPOL 73/78), as amended,

[27] IMO Assembly resolution A.1024(26), adopted 18 January 2010 (26th Session, Agenda item 10).

Recognizing the need to ensure that all such systems are capable of functioning effectively under anticipated operating conditions and provide an adequate level of maritime safety and pollution prevention, taking into account the challenges of polar operations,

Noting also the need for a general update of the Guidelines to take account of technical, technological and regulatory developments since their approval in 2002,

Conscious of the necessity to also give special consideration to all ships that only visit polar waters at certain times of the year,

Having considered the recommendations made by the Maritime Safety Committee at its eighty-sixth session and the Marine Environment Protection Committee at its fifty-ninth session,

1. *Adopts* the Guidelines for ships operating in polar waters, set out in the annex to the present resolution;

2. *Invites* all Governments concerned to take appropriate steps to give effect to the annexed Guidelines for ships constructed on or after I January 2011;

3. *Encourages* all Governments concerned to take appropriate steps to give effect to the annexed Guidelines for ships constructed before 1 January 2011 as far as is reasonable and practicable;

4. *Recommends* Governments to bring the annexed Guidelines to the attention of shipowners, ship operators, ship designers, shipbuilders, ship repairers, equipment manufacturers and installers and all other parties concerned with the operation of ships in polar waters;

5. *Authorizes* the Maritime Safety Committee and the Marine Environment Protection Committee to keep the annexed Guidelines under review and update them as necessary in light of experience gained in their application.

Annex: Guidelines for Ships Operating in Polar Waters

Preamble

Guide

Chapter 1– General

Part A – Construction Provisions

Chapter 2 – Structures

Chapter 3 – Subdivision and stability

Chapter 4 – Accommodation and escape measures

Chapter 5 – Directional control systems

Chapter 6 – Anchoring and towing arrangements

Chapter 7 – Main machinery

Chapter 8 – Auxiliary machinery systems

Chapter 9 – Electrical installations

Part B – Equipment

Chapter 10 – Fire safety

Chapter 11 – Life-saving appliances and survival arrangements

Chapter 12 – Navigational equipment

Part C – Operational

Chapter 13 – Operational arrangements

Chapter 14 – Crewing

Chapter 15 – Emergency equipment

Part D – Environmental Protection and Damage Control

Chapter 16 – Environmental protection and damage control

Preamble

P-l Introduction

P-1.1 Ships operating in the Arctic and Antarctic environments are exposed to a number of unique risks. Poor weather conditions and the relative lack of good charts, communication systems and other navigational aids pose challenges for mariners. The remoteness of the areas makes rescue or clean-up operations difficult and costly. Cold temperatures may reduce the effectiveness of numerous components of the ship, ranging from deck machinery and emergency equipment to sea suctions. When ice is present, it can impose additional loads on the hull, propulsion system and appendages.

P-1.2 Whilst Arctic and Antarctic waters have a number of similarities, there are also significant differences. The Arctic is an ocean surrounded by continents while the Antarctic is a continent surrounded by an ocean. The Antarctic sea ice retreats significantly during the summer season or is dispersed by permanent gyres in the two major seas of the Antarctic: the Weddell and the Ross. Thus there is relatively little multi-year ice in the Antarctic. Conversely, Arctic sea ice survives many summer seasons and there is a significant amount of multi-year ice. Whilst the marine environments of both Polar seas are similarly vulnerable, response to such challenge should duly take into account specific features of the legal and political regimes applicable to their respective marine spaces.

P-1.3 The Guidelines for ships operating in polar waters (hereinafter called "the Guidelines") are intended to address those additional provisions deemed necessity for consideration beyond existing requirements of the SOLAS and MAR POL Conventions, in order to take into account the climatic conditions of polar waters and to meet appropriate standards of maritime safety and pollution prevention.

P-l.4 The Guidelines are recommendatory and their wording should be interpreted as providing recommendations rather than mandatory direction.

P-2 Principles

P-2.1 The Guidelines aim to promote the safety of navigation and to prevent pollution from ship operations in polar waters.

P-2.2 The Guidelines recognize that this is best achieved by an integrated approach, based on requirements in existing Conventions which cover the design, outfitting, crewing and operation of ships for the conditions which they will encounter.

P-2.3 The Guidelines take into account that Arctic and Antarctic conditions may include sea and glacial ice that can represent a serious structural hazard to all ships. This is the single most significant factor in Arctic and Antarctic operations and is reflected in many of the Guidelines' provisions.

P-2.4 The Guidelines address the fact that the polar environment imposes additional demands on ship systems, including navigation, communications, life-saving, main and auxiliary machinery, environmental protection and damage control, etc. They emphasize the need to ensure that all ship systems are capable of functioning effectively under anticipated operating conditions and provide adequate levels of safety in accident and emergency situations.[28]

P-2.5 In addition, the Guidelines recognize that safe operation in such conditions requires specific attention to human factors including training and operational procedures.

P-2.6 The basic requirements for structure, stability and subdivision, machinery, life-saving appliances, fire protection, ship routing, navigation systems and equipment, radio communication, pollution prevention equipment, liability and safety management systems, as applicable to the different types and sizes of ships which may undertake voyages in polar waters, are obtained from the relevant Conventions.

P-2.7 The standards expressed in the Guidelines have been developed to mitigate the additional risk imposed on shipping due to the harsh environmental and climatic conditions existing in polar waters. The Guidelines should be applied taking into account the nature of the operations that are envisaged.

P-2.8 Not all ships which enter the Arctic and Antarctic environment will be able to navigate safely in all areas at all times of the year. A system of Polar Classes has therefore been developed

[28] Refer to the Enhanced contingency planning guidance for passenger ships operating in areas remote from SAR facilities (MSC.I/Circ.1184).

to designate different levels of capability. In parallel to the development of the Guidelines, the International Association of Classification Societies (IACS) has developed a set of Unified Requirements which, in addition to general classification society rules, address essential aspects of construction for ships of Polar Class.

P-2.9 The Guidelines are not intended to infringe on national systems of shipping control.

P-2.10 The Guidelines, recognizing the sensitive nature of polar waters, have the intention of providing high standards of environmental protection to address both accidents and normal operations.

Guide

G-l Layout of the Guidelines

G-l.1 The Guidelines include general, construction, equipment, operational and environmental protection and damage control parts, presented in that order and subdivided into chapters.

G-1.2 This section provides definitions for important terms that are used exclusively within the Guidelines or where any term has more than one meaning in other applicable Conventions. Otherwise, terms have the meanings defined in the Convention(s) relevant to each chapter.

G-1.3 All parts and chapters of the Guidelines should be applied to Polar Class ships. All parts and chapters, with the exception of those dealing with purely construction issues (Part A), should be applied to all ships in polar waters. Each chapter notes any additional differentiation of provisions between ship classes specific to that chapter.

G-1.4 Guidance provided in Part A of the Guidelines is only intended for new Polar Class ships.

G-2 Key provisions

G-2.1 Only those ships with a Polar Class designation or a comparable alternative standard of ice-strengthening appropriate to the anticipated ice conditions should operate in polar ice-covered waters.

G-2.2 The combination of hull structural design, material quality, subdivision and segregation measures prescribed in the Guidelines and supporting standards should be adequate to reduce the risk of human casualties, pollution incidents or ship losses to acceptably low levels of probability during prudent operations in polar waters.

G-2.3 No pollutants should be carried directly against the shell in hull areas at significant risk of ice impact. Operational pollution of the environment should be minimized by equipment selection and operational practice.

G-2.4 Key safety-related, survival and pollution control equipment should be rated for the temperatures and other conditions which may be encountered in the service intended.

G-2.5 Navigation and communications equipment should be suitable to provide adequate performance in high latitudes, areas with limited infrastructure and unique information transfer requirements.

G-2.6 Sea suction(s) should be capable of being cleared of accumulation of slush ice.

G-3 Definitions

For the purpose of the Guidelines, unless expressly provided otherwise, the terms used have the meanings defined in the following paragraphs. Terms used, but not defined in the Guidelines, are to be interpreted as they are defined in the relevant Conventions.

G-3.1 *Administration* means the Government of the State whose flag the ship is entitled to fly.

G-3.2 *Polar waters* includes both Arctic and Antarctic waters.

G-3.3 *Arctic waters* means those waters which are located north of a line extending from latitude 58°00'.0 N, longitude 042°00'.0 W 10 latitude 64°37'.0 N, longitude 035°27'.0 Wand thence by a rhumb line to latitude 67°03'.9 N, longitude 026°33'.4 Wand thence by a rhumb line to Sørkapp, Jan Mayen and by the southern shore of Jan Mayen to the Island of Bjørnøya and thence by a great circle line from the Island of Bjørnøya to Cap Kanin Nos and thence by the northern shore of the Asian continent eastward to the Bering Strait and thence from the

Bering Strait westward to latitude 60° N as far as Il'pyrskiy and following the 60th North parallel eastward as far as and including Etolin Strait and thence by the northern shore of the North American continent as far south as latitude 60° N and thence eastward along parallel of latitude 60°.N, to longitude 56°31'.1 Wand thence to the latitude 58°00'.0 N, longitude 042°00'.0 W (see figure 1).

G-3.4 *Antarctic waters* means those waters which are south of 60° S (see figure 2).

G-3.S *Ice-covered waters* means polar waters where local ice conditions present a structural risk to a ship.

G-3.6 *COLREG* means the International Regulations for Preventing Collisions at Sea, 1972, as amended.

G-3.7 *Company* means the owner of the ship or any other organization or person such as the manager, or the bareboat charterer, who has assumed the responsibility for operation of the ship from the shipowner.

G-3.8 *Conning position* means the stations in which the ship's steering control and devices for ahead or astern operations are located.

G-3.9 *Escort* means any ship with superior ice capability in transit with another ship.

G-3.10 *Escorted operation* means any operation in which a ship's movement is facilitated through the intervention of an escort.

G-3.11 *IACS* means the International Association of Classification Societies.

G-3.12 *Ice Navigator* means any individual who, in addition to being qualified under the STCW Convention, is specially trained and otherwise qualified to direct the movement of a ship in ice-covered waters.

G-3.13 *Icebreaker* means any ship whose operational profile may include escort or ice management functions, whose powering and dimensions allow it to undertake aggressive operations in ice-covered waters.

G-3.14 *International voyages* means voyages in international waters, as defined in chapter I of the 1974 SOLAS Convention, as amended.

G-3.1S *ISM Code* means the International Management Code for the Safe Operation of Ships and for Pollution Prevention, as amended.

G-3.16 *ICLL* means the International Convention on Load Lines, 1966.

G-3.17 *MARPOL* means the International Convention for the Prevention of Pollution from Ships, 1973, as modified by the 1978 Protocol relating thereto (MARPOL 73/78), as amended.

G-3.18 *Organization* means the International Maritime Organization.

G-3.19 *Polar Class* means the class assigned to a ship based upon IACS Unified Requirements.

G-3.20 *Polar Class ship* means a ship for which a Polar Class has been assigned.

G-3.21 *Pollutant* means any substance controlled by MARPOL which, if introduced into the sea, is liable to create hazards to human health, to harm1 living resources and marine life, to damage amenities or to interfere with other legitimate uses of the sea.

G-3.22 *Recognized organization* means an organization recognized by an Administration in accordance with IMO resolutions A.739(18) and A.789(19).

G-3.23 *Ship* means any vessel required to comply with the 1974 SOLAS Convention.

G-3.24 *SOLAS* means the International Convention for the Safety of Life at Sea, 1974, as amended.

G-3.2S *STCW* means the International Convention on Standards of Training, Certification and Watchkeeping for Seafarers, 1978, as amended.

G-3.26 *Unified Requirements* means IACS Unified Requirements for Polar Class Ships (UR-I).

G-3.27 *WMO* means the World Meteorological Organization.

G-3.28 *Working liquids* means any substances that are pollutants used for the operation of the ship's machinery.

G-3.29 *2008 IS Code* means the International Code on Intact Stability, 2008, as adopted by resolution MSC.267(85).

Figure 1 – Maximum extent of Arctic waters application (see paragraph G–3.3)

[*omitted.*]

Figure 2 - Maximum extent of Antarctic Waters application (see paragraph G-3.4)

[*omitted.*]

Chapter 1

General

1.1 Application

1.1.1 Except where specifically stated otherwise, these Guidelines provide guidance for ships operating in Antarctic waters or while engaged in international voyages in Arctic waters.

1.1.2 Part A of the Guidelines provides guidance for new Polar Class ships.

1.1.3 Parts B, C and D of the Guidelines provide guidance for Polar Class and all other ships.

Table 1.1 – Class descriptions

Polar Class	General Description
PC I	Year-round operation in all ice-covered waters
PC2	Year-round operation in moderate multi-year ice conditions
PC3	Year-round operation in second-year ice which may include multi-year ice inclusions
PC4	Year-round operation in thick first-year ice which may include old ice inclusions
PC 5	Year-round operation in medium first-year ice which may include old ice inclusions
PC 6	Summer/autumn operation in medium first-year ice which may include old ice inclusions
PC 7	Summer/autumn operation in thin first-year ice which may include old ice inclusions

Note: Ice descriptions follow the WMO Sea Ice Nomenclature.

1.1.4 All Polar Class ships and the equipment to be carried in accordance with the Guidelines should be designed, constructed and maintained in compliance with applicable national standards of the Administration or the appropriate requirements of a recognized organization which provide an equivalent level of safety[29] for its intended service. Special attention should be drawn to the need for winterization aspects. Ships intending to operate as an icebreaker are to receive special consideration.

1.1.5 The structures, equipment and arrangements essential for the safety and operation of the ship should take account of the anticipated temperatures.

1.1.6 Special attention should be given to essential operating equipment and systems and safety equipment and systems. For example, the potential for ice building up inside the ballast tanks and sea chests should be considered. The life-saving and fire extinguishing equipment specified in part B of the Guidelines, when stored or located in an exposed position, should be of a type that is rated to perform its design functions at the minimum anticipated air temperature. In particular, attention is drawn to the inflation of life-saving equipment and the starting of engines in lifeboats and rescue boats.

1.1.7 Operations in polar waters should take due account of factors such as: ship class, environmental conditions, icebreaker escort, prepared tracks, short or local routes, crew experience, support technology and services such as ice-mapping, availability of hydrographic information, communications, safe ports, repair facilities and other ships in convoy.

1.1.8 Equipment, fittings, materials, appliances and arrangements may deviate from the provisions of the Guidelines provided that their replacement is at least as effective as that specified in the Guidelines.

1.1.9 The provisions of the Guidelines do not apply to any warship, naval auxiliary, other vessels or aircraft owned or operated by a State and used, for the time being, only on government non-commercial service. However, each State should ensure, by the adoption of appropriate

[29] Refer to SOLAS chapter II-I and to the IACS Unified Requirements for Polar Class Ships.

measures not impairing operations or operational capabilities of such vessels or aircraft owned or operated by it, that such vessels or aircraft act in a manner consistent, so far as is reasonable and practicable, with the Guidelines.

1.2 Ice Navigator

1.2.1 All ships operating in polar ice-covered waters should can at least one Ice Navigator qualified in accordance with chapter 14. Consideration should also be given to carrying an Ice Navigator when planning voyages into polar waters.

1.2.2 Continuous monitoring of ice conditions by an Ice Navigator should be available at all times while the ship is underway and making way in the presence of ice.[30]

Part A: Construction Provisions

Chapter 2: Structures

2.1 General

2.1.1 All ships should have structural arrangements adequate to resist the global and local ice loads characteristic of their Polar Class.[31]

2.1.2 Each area of the hull and all appendages should be strengthened to resist design structure/ice interaction scenarios applicable to each case.

2.1.3 Structural arrangements should aim to limit damage resulting from accidental overloads to local areas.

2.1.4 Polar Class ships may experience in-service structural degradation at an accelerated rate. Structural surveys should, therefore, cover areas identified as being at high risk of accelerated degradation, and areas where physical evidence such as coating breakdown indicates a potential for high wastage rates.

2.2 Materials

2.2.1 Materials used in ice-strengthened and other areas of the hull should be suitable for operation in the environment that prevails at their location.

2.2.2 Materials used in ice-strengthened areas should have adequate ductility to match the selected structural design approach.

2.2.3 Abrasion and corrosion resistant coatings and claddings used in ice-strengthened areas should be matched to the anticipated loads and structural response.

Chapter 3: Subdivision and Stability

3.1 General

Account should be taken of the effect of icing in the stability calculations in accordance with the 2008 IS Code.

3.2 Intact stability in ice

3.2.1 Suitable calculations should be carried out and/or tests conducted to demonstrate the following:

.1 the ship, when operated in ice within approved limitations, during a disturbance causing roll, pitch, heave or heel due to turning or any other cause, should maintain sufficient positive stability; and

.2 ships of Polar Classes 1 to 3 and icebreakers of all classes, when riding up in ice and remaining momentarily poised at the lowest stem extremity, should maintain sufficient positive stability.

3.2.2 "Sufficient positive stability" in paragraphs 3.2.1.1 and 3.2.1.2 means that the ship is in a state of equilibrium with a positive metacentric height of at least 150 mm, and a line 150 mm below the edge of the freeboard deck as defined in the applicable ICLL, is not submerged.

3.2.3 For performing stability calculations on ships that ride up onto the ice, the ship should be assumed to remain momentarily poised at the lowest stem extremity as follows:

[30] Refer to the Guidelines on voyage planning, as adopted by resolution A.893(21), and the Guidelines on voyage planning for passenger ships operating in remote areas, as adopted by resolution A.999(25).

[31] Refer to the IACS Unified Requirements for Polar Class Ships.

.1 for a regular stem profile, at the point at which the stem contour is tangent to the keel line;
.2 for a stem fitted with a structurally defined skeg, at the point at which the stem contour meets the top of the skeg;
.3 for a stem profile where the skeg is defined by shape alone, at the point at which the stem contour tangent intersects the tangent of the skeg; or
.4 for a stem profile of novel design, the position should be specially considered.

3.3 Stability in damaged conditions

3.3.1 All Polar Class ships should be able to withstand flooding resulting from hull penetration due to ice impact. The residual stability following ice damage should be such that the factor s_i, as defined in SOLAS regulation II-1/7.2, has $s_i = 1$ for all loading conditions.

3.3.2 The ice damage extent to be assumed when demonstrating compliance with paragraph 3.3.1 should be such that:

.1 longitudinal extent 0.045 of deepest ice waterline length if centred forward of the point of maximum beam on the waterline, and 0.015 of waterline length otherwise;
.2 transverse extent is 760 mm measured normal to the shell over the full extent of the damage;
.3 vertical extent the lesser of 0.2 of draft at the upper waterline,[32] or of longitudinal extent;
.4 the centre of the ice damage may be located at any point between the keel and 1.2 times the deepest ice draft; and
.5 the vertical extent of damage may be assumed to be confined between the keel and 1.2 times the deepest ice draft.

3.3.3 Damage as defined in paragraph 3.3.2 is to be assumed at any position along the side shell.

3.3.4 For ships of Polar Classes 6 and 7 not carrying polluting or hazardous cargoes, damage as defined in paragraph 3.3.2 may be assumed to be continued between watertight bulkheads, except where such bulkheads are spaced at less than the damage dimension.

3.4 Subdivision

3.4.1 Subject to paragraphs 3.4.2 and 3.4.3, no Polar Class ship should carry any pollutant directly against the outer shell. Any pollutant should be separated from the outer shell of the ship by double skin construction of at least 760 mm in width.

3.4.2 All Polar Class ships should have double bottoms over the breadth and the length between forepeak and afterpeak bulkheads. Double bottom height should be in accordance with the rules of the classification societies in force. Double bottoms should not be used for the carriage of pollutants except where a double skin construction complying with paragraph 3.4.1 is provided, or where working liquids are carried in way of main machinery spaces in tanks not exceeding 20 m^3 individual volume.

3.4.3 Double bottoms in ships of Polar Classes 6 and 7 may be used for the carriage of any working liquids where the tanks are aft of midships and within the flat of bottom.

3.4.4 All Polar Class ships with icebreaking bow forms and short forepeaks may dispense with double bottoms up to the forepeak bulkhead in the area of the inclined stem, provided that the watertight compartments between the forepeak bulkhead and the bulkhead at the junction between the stem and the keel are not used to carry pollutants.

Chapter 4: Accommodation and Escape Measures

4.1 General

4.1.1 All personnel accommodation should be designed and arranged to protect the occupants from unfavourable environmental conditions and minimize risk of injury during normal (including ice transiting or icebreaking) operations and emergency conditions.

4.1.2 All personnel accommodation, public spaces and the equipment installed in them should be designed so that each person making proper use of them will not suffer injury during normal

[32] Refer to the IACS Unified Requirements for Polar Class Ships.

open water operations, designed ice transiting modes of operation, and emergency manoeuvring conditions.

4.1.3 Ships of Polar Classes 1 to 5 inclusive should have sufficiently available and reliable facilities to maintain a life sustaining environment in the event of an emergency and/or of extended ice entrapment.

4.2 Public address systems and other safety items

4.2.1 The public address system and the general emergency alarm system should be audible over the loudest ambient noise level occurring during ice transiting, icebreaking or ramming.

4.2.2 Ships of Polar Classes 1 to 3 inclusive, icebreakers and ships intended to be used in the ramming mode should be designed with adequate provisions to ensure the safety of personnel using shower facilities. Such facilities should include non-slip decking, three rigid sides, handholds and insulation from exposed hot water pipes.

4.2.3 Galley facilities should be provided with grab rails projecting from the front on cooking equipment for use by the crew during ice operations.

4.2.4 Equipment designed to heat oil for cooking purposes such as deep fat fryers should be located in a position suitably separated from hotplates or other hot surfaces. Such appliances should also be secured to the deck or other fixed structure and provided with an oil tight lid or closure to prevent splashing or spillage during ice operations.

4.3 Escape measures

4.3.1 All means of escape from accommodation or interior working spaces should not be rendered inoperable by ice accretion or by malfunction due to low external ambient air temperatures.

4.3.2 All escape routes should be dimensioned so as not to hinder passage for persons wearing suitable polar clothing.

4.3.3 Escape routes should be designed to minimize the distance between their exit to an open deck and the survival equipment to which they lead.

Chapter 5: Directional Control Systems

5.1 All Polar Class ships should be provided with directional control systems of adequate strength and suitable design to enable efficient operation in polar ice-covered waters.

5.2 For the purpose of this chapter, a directional control system includes any device or devices intended either as a primary or auxiliary means of steering the ship. The directional control system includes all associated power sources, linkages, controls and actuating systems.

5.3 Attention is drawn to the interaction between directional control systems and propulsion systems. Where such interaction occurs or where dual purpose components are fitted, the provisions of chapters 7 and 8 should also be complied with, as applicable.

Chapter 6: Anchoring and Towing Arrangements

6.1 General

All Polar Class ships should be capable of anchoring and providing limited assistance in the case of debilitating damage or breakdown, towards the prevention of a catastrophic loss or pollution incident. The capability of ships to provide assistance should be considered of prime importance, having due regard to the lack of repair facilities, the limited number of dedicated towing ships available and the response time that may be required by a dedicated towing ship to be able to provide effective assistance in polar ice-covered waters.

6.2 Anchoring arrangements

6.2.1 Ships of Polar Classes 1 to 5 inclusive and all icebreakers of all classes should, as far as is practicable, be designed to protect the anchor from being dislodged from its stowed position and from jamming or damaging the hull by direct impact with ice.

6.2.2 Anchoring systems should be provided with an independent means of securing the anchor so that the anchor cable can be disconnected for use as an emergency towing bridle.

6.3 Towing arrangements

6.3.1 All Polar Class ships designed to perform dedicated towing operations and all icebreakers should be equipped with line throwing apparatus in addition to that required for life-saving. This apparatus should be capable of delivering messenger lines for the transfer of towing equipment. Such line throwing apparatus should not be of the powder/rocket type, in order that it may be safely used to make a transfer to a tanker.

6.3.2 All Polar Class ships designed to perform dedicated towing operations should be provided with a quick release system, operable from the conning position.

6.3.3 Where fitted, close-coupled bow to stern towing arrangements should comprise strengthened bow plating on the towed ship, appropriate towing slings, non-interfering positioning of bower anchors and disallowance of bulbous bows. In this case, arrangements should be provided for securing the anchor in the stowed position.

6.4 Emergency towing arrangements[33]

6.4.1 All Polar Class ships should be capable of receiving emergency towing assistance.

6.4.2 Where appropriate, towing arrangements should facilitate connection and release of a towline and provide bollards, fairleads, and other components suitable for the size of ship on which they are fitted.

Chapter 7: Main Machinery

7.1 General

7.1.1 The design, rating, installation, operation and maintainability of shipboard engineering systems should be suitable for navigation in polar ice-covered waters.[34]

7.1.2 In the event of damage, malfunction or failure of any machinery component, means should be provided to control and limit any resulting emission of pollutants to within the confines of the ship's hull.

7.1.3 Special attention should be drawn to the fact that harsh weather conditions often occur in polar waters and that the propulsion effect plays a significant role in relation to the steering ability.

7.1.4 The layout and construction of machinery essential for the safe operation of the ship should be such that repairs which can be affected using the resources on board may be completed safely and effectively. Ventilation systems should provide sufficient air at an appropriate temperature for the operation of machinery.

7.1.5 For Polar Class ships which may be laid up in polar waters, materials for all systems with the potential of polluting should be suitable for preventing pollution at the lowest ambient temperatures to which they may be subjected and should be suitable to avoid pollution and ensure safe operation on re-activation of the systems.

7.2 Main propulsion systems

7.2.1 The main propulsion machinery should be designed so that the effects of loads with the potential to damage the system are limited to those components which can be readily repaired, replaced or reset. The reliability and availability of the equipment and systems should be considered.

7.2.2 Main propulsion machinery and all auxiliary machinery essential to the propulsion system, should be:

.1 designed for loads and vibrations resulting from propeller/hull/rudder-ice interactions;

.2 located to provide protection from freezing spray, ice and snow; and

.3 designed to operate when the ship is inclined at any combined angle of heel or trim that may be expected during operations in ice.

7.2.3 Stem tube bearings, seals and main propulsion components located outside the hull should not leak pollutants. Non-toxic biodegradable lubricants are not considered to be pollutants.

[33] Refer to the Guidelines for owners/operators on preparing emergency towing procedures (MSC.1/Circ.1255).

[34] Refer to the IACS Unified Requirements for Polar Class Ships.

7.2.4 The installed propulsive power should be sufficient to ensure that the ship can navigate safely and with effective icebreaking capability, as appropriate, without risk of structural damage or pollution under the design ice, weather and anticipated operational conditions.

7.2.5 Piping and intake systems associated with the main propulsion plant and auxiliary machinery essential to the propulsion system should be designed so as not to be affected by the impact of the polar environment.

Chapter 8: Auxiliary Machinery Systems

8.1 General

8.1.1 Equipment and systems should be designed so that personnel exposure to cold temperatures and other environmental hazards during normal operations including routine maintenance is minimized.

8.1.2 Ventilation systems should provide sufficient air for the operation of auxiliary machinery, air conditioning and heating purposes.

8.2 Materials

8.2.1 Materials used in equipment and systems should be suitable for operation in the environment which prevails at their location. In particular, equipment or systems which are essential for preventing pollution or for safe operation of the ship when:

.1 located outside and above the waterline in any ship operating condition; or

.2 in unheated locations inside,

should not be susceptible to brittle fracture within the range of operating conditions.

8.2.2 Essential equipment or systems required for the safe operation of the ship or systems required for preventing pollution, located within spaces which, upon failure of the primary heating system, could be subject to outside ambient air temperatures should be:

.1 provided with an independent source of heat; and

.2 fabricated from materials that will not be susceptible to brittle fracture under the anticipated loads and temperatures.

8.2.3 For Polar Class ships which may be laid up in polar waters, materials for all systems with the potential to pollute should be suitable for preventing pollution at the lowest ambient temperatures to which they may be subjected and should be suitable for avoiding pollution and ensuring safe operation on re-activation of the systems.

Chapter 9: Electrical Installations

9.1 Electrical installations should be subject to the provisions listed in chapters 4, 7 and 8 regarding design for operation in polar ice-covered waters and for the provision of emergency heat and power.

9.2 Precautions should be taken to minimize risk of supplies to essential and emergency services being interrupted by the inadvertent or accidental opening of switches or circuit breakers due to vibrations or accelerations during icebreaking operations.

9.3 Emergency power for communications equipment provided by batteries should be provided with a means whereby the batteries are protected from extreme low temperatures.

9.4 Emergency power batteries including the reserve source of energy for the radio installation, including those stored in deck boxes, should be secured in a position where excessive movement is prevented during ice-transiting operations and explosive gas ventilation is not restricted by the accumulation of ice or snow.

9.5 Control systems based on computers and other electronic hardware installations necessary for the proper functioning of essential equipment should be designed for redundancy and resistance to vibration, dampness and low humidity.[35]

[35] Such equipment should be approved in accordance with relevant international standards.

Part B: Equipment

Chapter 10: Fire Safety

10.1 Fuel and other flammable fluid tanks and systems

Refuelling of ships should be carried out while taking into account the special conditions imposed by low temperatures and ice conditions, where applicable.

10.2 Ventilation

Closing apparatus for ventilation inlets and outlets should be designed and located to protect them from ice or snow accumulation that could interfere with the effective closure of such systems.

10.3 Fire detection and extinguishing systems

10.3.1 Fire-extinguishing systems should be designed or located so that they are not made inaccessible or inoperable by ice or snow accumulation or low temperature such that:

.1 equipment, appliances, systems and extinguishing agents should be protected from freezing for minimum temperature for the intended voyage;

.2 precautions should be taken to prevent nozzles, piping and valves of any fire-extinguishing system from becoming clogged by impurities, corrosion or ice build-up; and

.3 exhaust gas outlets and pressure vacuum arrangements should be protected from ice build-up that could interfere with effective operation.

10.3.2 Water or foam extinguishers should not be located in any position that is exposed to freezing temperatures. These locations should be provided with extinguishers capable of operation under such conditions.

10.4 Fire pumps and associated equipment for Polar Class ships

10.4.1 Where a fixed fire-extinguishing system or alternative fire-extinguishing system situated in a space separate from the compartment containing the main fire pumps utilizes its own independent sea suction, this sea suction should be capable of being cleared of accumulations of slush ice.

10.4.2 Fire pump(s) including emergency fire pump(s) should, wherever reasonable and practicable, be installed in heated compartment(s) and in any event should be adequately protected from freezing for minimum temperature for the intended voyage.

10.4.3 Isolating valves should be located so that they are accessible. Any isolating valves located in exposed positions should not be subject to icing from freezing spray. The fire main should be arranged so that external sections can be isolated and draining devices should be provided.

10.4.4 Hydrants should be positioned or designed to remain operable under all anticipated temperatures. Ice accumulation and freezing should be taken into account.

10.4.5 All hydrants should be equipped with an efficient two-handed valve handle.

10.5 Protection against ice build-up

Components of the fire-fighting system which may be exposed to icing that could interfere with the proper functioning of that component should be adequately protected.

10.6 Firefighters' outfits

10.6.1 Sufficient firefighters' outfits should be readily available to the accommodation area and elsewhere as appropriate. Such firefighters' outfits should be stored in warm positions as widely separated as practical.

10.6.2 In addition to the firefighters' outfits provided in accordance with paragraph 10.6.1, one spare firefighter's outfit should be provided. The spare outfit should be stored in a warm location on the ship.

Chapter 11: Life-Saving Appliances and Survival Arrangements

11.1 General

11.1.1 Adequate supplies of protective clothing and thermal insulating materials should be provided, taking into account the intended voyage.

11.1.2 Training in the use of all emergency equipment, as appropriate, should be included as an element of the operating procedures and drills described in chapter 13. Where appropriate, dedicated training equipment should be carried to avoid compromising the performance of the emergency equipment itself.

11.2 Categories of life-saving equipment

11.2.1 Ships operating in polar waters should carry life-saving appliances and survival equipment according to their environmental conditions of operation.

11.2.2 Personal survival kits (PSKs) as described in section 11.3 should be carried whenever a voyage is anticipated to encounter mean daily temperatures below 0°C.

11.2.3 Group survival kits (GSKs) as described in section 11.4 should be carried whenever a voyage is anticipated to encounter ice conditions which may prevent the lowering and operation of survival craft.

11.2.4 Sufficient PSKs and GSKs (as applicable) should be carried to cover at least 110% of the persons on board the ship.

11.2.5 Personal survival kits should be stored so that they may be easily retrieved in an emergency situation. Arrangements such as storage in dedicated lockers near the assembly stations may be considered.

11.2.6 Group survival kits should be stored so that they may be easily retrieved and deployed in an emergency situation. Any containers should be located adjacent to the survival craft and liferafts. Containers should be designed so that they may be easily moved over the ice and be floatable.

11.3 Personal survival kit (PSK)

11.3.1 A sample of the contents of a personal survival kit is listed in the table below.

Table 11.1 Contents of the personal survival kits

Equipment	**Quantity**
Clothing	
Head protection (VP)[37]	1
Neck and face protection (VP)	1
Hand protection – Mitts (VP)	1 pair
Hand protection – Gloves (VP)	1 pair
Foot protection – Socks (VP)	1 pair
Foot protection – Boots	1 pair
Insulated suit (VP)	1
Approved immersion suit	1
Thermal underwear (VP)	1 set
Miscellaneous	
Handwarmers	240 hours
Sunglasses	1 pair
Survival candle	1
Matches	2 boxes
Whistle	1
Drinking mug	1
Penknife	1
Handbook (Polar Survival)	1
Carrying bag	1

[36] VP means "vacuum packed".

11.3.2 The following notice should be displayed wherever personal survival kits are stored:
Notice
Crew members and passengers are reminded that their personal survival kit is for emergency survival use only. Never remove items of survival clothing or tools from the personal survival kit carrying bag – your life may depend on it.

11.3.3 Personal survival kits should not be opened for training purposes. Equipment for training purposes should be provided in accordance with paragraph 11.1.2.

11.4 Group survival kit (GSK)

11.4.1 A sample of the contents of the group survival kit is listed in the table below.

Table 11.2 Contents of the group survival kits (GSK)

Equipment	**Quantity**
Group equipment	
Tents	1 per 6 persons
Air mattresses	1 per 2 persons
Sleeping bags (VP)[38]	1 per 2 persons
Stove	1 per tent
Stove fuel	0.5 litres per person
Fuel paste	2 tubes per stove
Matches	2 boxes per tent
Pan (with scaling lid)	1 per stove
Fortified health drinks	5 packets per person
Flashlights	1 per tent
Candles and holders	5 per tent
Snow shovel	1 per tent
Snow saw and snow knife	1 per tent
Tarpaulin	1 per tent
Foot protection – Booties	1 per person
GSK container	1
Spare personal equipment	(1 set per GSK container, which may be considered as part of the 110% as specified in paragraph 11.2.4)
Head protection (VP)	1
Neck and face protection (VP)	1
Hand protection Mitts (VP)	1 pair
Hand protection – Gloves (VP)	1 pair
Foot protection – Socks (VP)	1 pair
Foot protection – Boots (VP)	1 pair
Insulated suit (VP)	1
Thermal underwear	1 pair

[37] VP means "vacuum packed".

Handwarmers	1 set
Sunglasses	1
Whistle	1
Drinking mug	1

11.5 Lifeboats

11.5.1 All lifeboats should be either of the partially or totally enclosed type to provide adequate shelter from the anticipated operating environment.

11.5.2 The capacity of lifeboats should be evaluated with regard to operability, accessibility, seating capacity and overall space, considering the needs of personnel wearing suitable polar clothing.

11.5.3 Any ice accretion should be regularly removed from the lifeboats and launching equipment to ensure ease of launching when required. An icing removal mallet should be available in the vicinity of the lifeboats.

11.5.4 All lifeboat engines should be equipped with a means to ensure they will start readily when required at the minimum anticipated operating temperature.

11.5.5 The lifeboat engine fuel oil should be suitable for operation in the minimum anticipated operating temperature.

11.5.6 Drinking water should be stored in containers that allow for expansion due to freezing.

11.5.7 Consideration should be given to the provision of additional emergency rations to account for high rates of energy expenditure under polar conditions.

11.6 Liferafts

11.6.1 Any ice accretion should be regularly removed from the liferafts, cradles and launching equipment to ensure ease of launching and inflation when required. An icing removal mallet should be available in the vicinity of the liferafts.

11.6.2 Ships should carry in a warm space in the vicinity of the liferafts manual inflation pumps that are proven to be effective in the anticipated air temperatures.

11.6.3 Air or other proven cold temperature gas should be used for the inflation of life-saving equipment according to their environmental conditions of operation.

11.6.4 Consideration should be given to the provision of additional emergency rations to account for high rates of energy expenditure under polar conditions.

11.7 Protection from wildlife

Consideration should be given to protection from wildlife in areas where encounters are likely.

Chapter 12: Navigational Equipment

12.1 Application

It should be noted that the provisions prescribed in this chapter are not to be considered in addition to the requirements of SOLAS chapter V. Rather, any equipment fitted or carried in compliance with the requirements of SOLAS chapter V may be considered as part of the recommended equipment complement detailed in this chapter. Unless specifically provided in this chapter, the performance standards and other applicable guidance for equipment and systems contained in this chapter should be applied in accordance with SOLAS chapter V, as amended.

12.2 Compasses

12.2.1 Magnetic variations in high latitudes may lead to unreliable readings from magnetic compasses.

12.2.2 Gyro-compasses may become unstable in high latitudes and may need to be shut down.

12.2.3 Companies should ensure that their systems for providing reference headings are suitable for their intended areas and modes of operation, and that due consideration has been given to the potential effects noted in paragraphs 12.2.1 and 12.2.2. For operations in polar waters, ships should be fitted with at least one gyro-compass and should consider the need for installation of a satellite compass or alternative means.

12.3 Speed and distance measurement

12.3.1 All ships should be fitted with at least two speed and distance measuring devices. Each device should operate on a different principle in order to provide both speed through the water and speed over ground.

12.3.2 Speed and distance measuring devices should provide each conning position with a speed indication at least once per second.

12.3.3 Speed and distance measurement device sensors should not project beyond the hull and should be installed to protect them from damage by ice.

12.4 Depth sounding device

All ships should be fitted with at least two independent echo-sounding devices which provide indication of the depth of water under the keel. Due account should be taken of the potential for ice interference or damage to any device designed to operate below the waterline.

12.5 Radar installations

12.5.1 All ships should be fitted with a total of at least two functionally independent radar systems. One of these should operate in the 3 GHz (10 cm, S-band) frequency range.

12.5.2 Radar plotting systems that may be installed should have the capability of operating in both the sea and the ground stabilized mode.

12.6 Electronic positioning and electronic chart systems

12.6.1 All ships should be provided with an electronic position fixing system.

12.6.2 A satellite system (GPS or GLONASS or equivalent) should be fitted on any ship intending to navigate in areas outside of reliable coverage by a terrestrial hyperbolic system.

12.6.3 Systems described in paragraphs 12.6.1 and 12.6.2 should provide input to allow for continuous representation of the ship's speed provided by a speed and distance measuring device according to paragraph 12.3, and the ship's course provided by a compass according to paragraph 12.2.

12.6.4 Where fitted, electronic charting systems should be able to use position input from systems compliant with paragraphs 12.6.1 and 12.6.2.

12.7 Automatic identification system (AIS)

All ships should be provided with automatic identification system (AIS).

12.8 Rudder angle indicator

12.8.1 Separate rudder angle indicators should be provided for each rudder on ships with more than one independently operable rudder.

12.8.2 In ships without a rudder, indication should be given of the direction of steering thrust.

12.9 Searchlights and visual signals

12.9.1 All ships operating in polar waters should be equipped with at least two suitable searchlights which should be controllable from conning positions.

12.9.2 The searchlights described in paragraph 12.9.1 should be installed to provide, as far as is practicable, all-round illumination suitable for docking, astern manoeuvres or emergency towing.

12.9.3 The searchlights described in paragraph 12.9.1 should be fitted with an adequate means of de-icing to ensure proper directional movement.

12.9.4 All ships that may be involved in an escort of more than one ship following in an ice track should be equipped with a manually initiated flashing red light visible from astern to indicate when the ship is stopped. This should be capable of use from any conning position. The flashing light should have a range of visibility of at least two (2) nautical miles. The colour and frequency of the flashing light should be according to standards given in COLREG. The horizontal and vertical arcs of visibility of the flashing light should be as specified for stern lights in COLREG.

12.10 Vision enhancement equipment

12.10.1 All ships should be fitted with a suitable means to de-ice sufficient conning position windows to provide unimpaired forward and astern vision from conning positions.

12.10.2 The windows described in paragraph 12.10.1 should be fitted with an efficient means of clearing melted ice, freezing rain, snow, mist and spray from outside and accumulated condensation from inside. A mechanical means to clear moisture from the outside face of a window should have operating mechanisms protected from freezing or the accumulation of ice that would impair effective operation.

12.10.3 All persons engaged in navigating the ship should be provided with adequate protection from direct and reflected glare from the sun.

12.10.4 All indicators providing information to the conning positions should be fitted with means of illumination control to ensure readability under all operating conditions.[38]

12.11 Ice routeing equipment

12.11.1 All ships should be provided with equipment capable of receiving ice and weather information charts.

12.11.2 All ships operating in polar waters should be fitted with equipment capable of receiving and displaying ice imagery.

Part C: Operational

Chapter 13: Operational Arrangements

13.1 Documentation

All ships operating in polar waters should carry on board at all times a ship operating manual and training manual, as appropriate, for all Ice Navigators, as specified in paragraph 13.3.

13.2 Ship operational control

13.2.1 The ship should not be operated outside the worst intended conditions and design limitations which should be included in the operational guidelines.

13.2.2 All passenger vessels operating in polar waters should take account of the distance from search and rescue facilities and of the "Enhanced contingency planning guidance for passenger ships operating in areas remote from SAR facilities" (MSC.1/Circ.1184).

13.3 Operating and training manuals

Operating manual

13.3.1 The operating manual, or supplementary manual in the case of ships not normally operating in polar waters, should contain at least the following information on issues directly related to operations in such waters. With respect to contingency planning in the event that the ship suffers ice damage, the manual should conform to guidelines developed by the Organization:[39]

Normal operation

.1 principal particulars of the ship;

.2 loading procedures and limitations including any applicable recommendations against carrying pollutants in tanks and compartments against the hull envelope, maximum operational weight, position of centre of gravity and distribution of load necessary for operation in polar waters;

.3 acknowledgment of changes in standard operating procedures for radio equipment and navigational aids applicable to Arctic and Antarctic operations;

.4 operating limitations for the ship and essential systems in anticipated ice conditions and temperatures;

.5 passage planning procedures accounting for anticipated ice conditions;

.6 deviations in standard operating procedures associated with operation of propulsion and auxiliary machinery systems, remote control and warning systems and electronic and electrical systems made necessary by operations in polar waters;

[38] Refer to the Performance standards for the presentation of navigation-related information on shipborne navigational displays, as adopted by resolution MSC.191 (79).

[39] Refer to the Guidelines for the structure of an integrated system of contingency planning for shipboard emergencies, as adopted by resolution A.852(20).

Risk management

.7 deviations in standard damage control procedures made necessary by operations in polar ice-covered waters;

.8 evacuation procedures into water, onto ice, or into a combination of the two, with due regard to chapter 11 of these Guidelines;

.9 information regarding the handling of the ship as determined in accordance with chapter 16 of these Guidelines (Environmental protection and damage control);

.10 maximum towing speeds and towing loads where applicable;

.11 procedures for checking the integrity of hull structure;

.12 description and operation of fire detection and fire-extinguishing equipment in a polar environment;

.13 details arising from the standards of chapter 3 of the Guidelines (Subdivision and stability) likely to be of direct practical use to the crew in an emergency; and

.14 guidance taking into account the results of any risk or failure analysis reports developed during the ship's operational history and its design limits and redundancy features.

Training manual

13.3.2 The training manual should cover all aspects of ship operation in polar waters listed below plus other related information considered necessary by the Administration:

.1 the Guidelines for ships operating in polar waters;

.2 ice recognition;

.3 navigation in ice; and

.4 escorted operation.

Instructions for drills and emergency instructions as detailed in section 13.4 should be incorporated as annexes to the manual.

13.3.3 The Company should ensure that any additional documentation referenced in the training manual and required to provide a full understanding of its contents is on board the ship when operating in polar waters.

13.4 Drills and emergency instructions

13.4.1 Onboard instruction and operation of the ship's evacuation, fire and damage control appliances and systems should include appropriate cross training of crew members with appropriate emphasis to changes to standard procedure made necessary by operations in polar waters.

13.4.2 Evacuation

13.4.2.1 Evacuation drill scenarios for crew members should be varied so that different emergency conditions are simulated, including abandonment into the water, onto the ice if appropriate, or a combination of the two.

13.4.2.2 Each evacuation craft drill should include:

.1 exercises in passenger control in cold temperatures as appropriate;

.2 checking that all personnel are suitably dressed;

.3 donning of immersion suits or thermal protective clothing by appropriate crew members;

.4 testing of emergency lighting for assembling and abandonment; and

.5 giving instructions in the use of the ship's life-saving appliances and in survival at sea, on the ice or a combination of both, as appropriate.

13.4.2.3 Rescue boat drills should be conducted as far as is reasonable and practicable with due consideration of the dangers of launching into polar ice-covered waters, if applicable.

13.4.2.4 Individual instructions may cover different parts of the ship's life-saving system, but all the ship's life-saving equipment and appliances should be covered within any period of one month on passenger ships and two months on cargo ships. Each member of the crew should be given instructions which should include but not necessarily be limited to:

.1 problems of cold shock, hypothermia, first-aid treatment of hypothermia and other appropriate first-aid procedures;[40] and

.2 special instructions necessary for use of the ship's life-saving appliances in severe weather and severe sea conditions on the ice or in a combination of water and ice cover.

13.4.3 Fire drills

13.4.3.1 Fire drill scenarios should vary each week so that emergency conditions are simulated for different ship compartments, with appropriate emphasis on those changes to standard procedures made necessary by operations in polar waters and low temperatures.

13.4.3.2 Each fire drill should include elements required by SOLAS plus additional elements made necessary by operation in a polar environment.

13.4.4 Damage control

Damage control drill scenarios should vary each week so that emergency conditions are simulated for different damage conditions with appropriate emphasis to those conditions resultant from operations in polar waters.

13.4.5 Survival kits

13.4.5.1 Where PSK and/or GSK are fitted, additional kits for training and demonstration purposes should be provided in accordance with paragraph 11.3.3.

13.4.5.2 Training equipment should be maintained in good condition. A number of sewing kits and replacement parts (buttons, boot laces, etc.) should be kept on board for the purpose of minor repair to training kit items.

13.4.5.3 PSK and GSK inspections should be carried out no less frequently than on an annual basis.

Chapter 14: Crewing

14.1 General

14.1.1 The crewing of all ships in polar waters should take account of the provisions listed in this chapter, and also of the relative lack of shore and support infrastructure which may be available to assist in any operations.

14.1.2 Ice Navigators should be provided as noted in chapter 1.

14.1.3 All of the ship's officers and crew should be made familiar with cold weather survival by training or self-study of course material or publications addressing the measures set forth in section 13.4.

14.1.4 The ship's deck and engine officers should be trained in ship operations in ice-covered waters, as appropriate.

14.2 Ice Navigator qualifications and training

The Ice Navigator should have documentary evidence of having satisfactorily completed an approved training programme in ice navigation.[41] Such a training programme should provide knowledge, understanding and proficiency required for operating a ship in polar ice-covered waters, including recognition of ice formation and characteristics; ice indications; ice manoeuvring; use of ice forecasts, atlases and codes; hull stress caused by ice; ice escort operations; ice-breaking operations and effect of ice accretion on vessel stability. Qualifications of an Ice Navigator should include documentary evidence of having completed on-the-job training, as appropriate, and may include simulation training.

Chapter 15: Emergency Equipment

15.1 Medical equipment

15.1.1 All ships should be provided with an adequate number of first-aid kits and equipment with contents suitable to the onboard location and the recognized provisions for personnel safety hazards of such locations.

[40] Refer to the Guide to cold water survival (MSC. l/Circ.1185).

[41] Refer to the model course for Ice Navigation to be developed by the Organization.

15.1.2 With respect to the nature of the voyage, ship operations and the ability to communicate and obtain timely assistance of medical aid or medical evacuation, exemptions of certain medical equipment, medicines and facilities may be considered unreasonable or unnecessary.

15.1.3 Crews operating in polar waters should be provided with appropriate equipment and training to safely evacuate an individual in a medical emergency from the ship.

15.2 Reserve supplies

15.2.1 Special consideration should be given to the reserve supply of fuel and lubricants taking into account the effect of heavy ice on fuel consumption.

15.2.2 Single screw ships may require special consideration (redundancy) in remote areas where conditions impose a risk of damage to machinery components.

15.3 Damage control and repair equipment

15.3.1 All icebreakers and ships of Polar Classes 1 to 5 should carry the following emergency equipment:

.1 portable gas welding and cutting equipment with a reserve of consumables; and

.2 portable electro-submersible pump of 100 tonnes/h capacity with a set of hoses.

15.3.2 Where built-up propellers are used, consideration should be given to the carriage of spare blades and of equipment facilitating removal and replacement.

Part D: Environmental Protection and Damage Control

Chapter 16: Environmental Protection and Damage Control

16.1 General

16.1.1 The following provisions concerning environmental protection and damage control equipment are made with due regard to the lack of waste reception and repair facilities, communications limitations, unique navigational and environmental hazards and limited response capabilities of available assistance in polar waters.

16.1.2 Procedures for the protection of the environment under normal operations should be included in the ship's operating manual as described in chapter 13, and for those under accident conditions in the Shipboard Oil Pollution Emergency Plan (SO PEP), according to MARPOL. The procedures should be tailor-made to cover the remoteness and other environmental factors particular to Antarctic and Arctic waters.

16.1.3 Training and drills covering environmental protection and damage control procedures should be provided for crew members as specified in chapter 13.

16.2 Equipment and materials

16.2.1 All ships navigating in polar waters should be adequately equipped and their crews properly trained to provide effective damage control and minor hull repair.

16.2.2 All ships should have the capability to contain and clean up minor deck spills and contain minor over side spills. An inventory of such equipment should be included in the SOPEP, along with directions for safe use and guidelines to assist in determining when such use is warranted. The SOPEP should also establish personnel responsibilities for equipment deployment, oversight, maintenance and provide for crew training in equipment usage.

16.2.3 Damage control equipment, provided in accordance with paragraph 16.2.1, should be sufficient to enable a ship, as far as is practicable, to make temporary repairs to a minor hull breach or to take precautionary measures to prevent escalation of damage or flooding, so that the ship may proceed to a location where more substantial repairs can be effected.

16.2.4 Icebreakers and ships of Polar Classes I to 5 inclusive should be provided with material, tools and equipment capable of effecting more substantial repairs and damage control activities, as described in chapter 15.

16.2.5 Hoses and flexible pipes should be manufactured out of materials retaining adequate strength and elasticity characteristics at the minimum anticipated operating temperature.

16.2.6 All hoses used for transfer purposes from the ship to another ship or to shore should have the connection between the hose and the hose couplings made in an efficient and strong fashion to minimize the possibility of pollution due to failure of this connection. Couplings between hose sections should be capable of being securely locked together to prevent inadvertent disconnection.

16.3 Procedures for the protection of the environment under normal operations

Procedures for the protection of the environment under normal operations should take into account any applicable national and international rules and regulations and industry best practices related to operational discharges and emissions from ships, use of heavy grade oils, strategies for ballast water management, use of anti-fouling systems, and related measures.

PART 8
UNTED NATIONS GENERAL ASSEMBLY RESOLUTIONS[1]

UN General Assembly Resolution 38/77: Question of Antarctica (15 December 1983)

The General Assembly,

Having considered the item entitled "Question of Antarctica",

Conscious of the increasing international awareness of and interest in Antarctica,

Bearing in mind the Antarctic Treaty and the significance of the system it has developed,

Taking into account the debate on this item at its thirtyeighth session,

Convinced of the advantages of a better knowledge of Antarctica,

Affirming the conviction that, in the interest of all mankind, Antarctica should continue forever to be used exclusively for peaceful purposes and that it should not become the scene or object of international discord,

Recalling the relevant paragraphs of the Economic Declaration adopted by the Seventh Conference of Heads of State or Government of the Non-Aligned Countries, held at New Delhi from 7 to 12 March 1983,

1. *Requests* the Secretary-General to prepare a comprehensive, factual and objective study on all aspects of Antarctica, taking fully into account the Antarctic Treaty system and other relevant factors;

2. *Also requests* the Secretary-General to seek the views of all Member States in the preparation of the study;

3. *Requests* those States conducting scientific research in Antarctica, other interested States, the relevant specialized agencies, organs, organizations and bodies of the United Nations system and relevant international organizations having scientific or technical information on Antarctica to lend the Secretary-General whatever assistance he may request for the purpose of carrying out the study;

4. *Requests* the Secretary-General to report to the General Assembly at its thirty-ninth session;

5. *Decides* to include in the provisional agenda of its thirty-ninth session the item entitled "Question of Antarctica".

97th plenary meeting
15 December 1983

UN General Assembly Resolution 39/152: Question of Antarctica (17 December 1984)

The General Assembly,

Recalling its resolution 38/77 of 15 December 1983,

Having considered the item entitled "Question of Antarctica",

Taking note of the study on the question of Antarctica,

Conscious of the increasing international awareness of and interest in Antarctica,

Bearing in mind the Antarctic Treaty and the significance of the system it has developed,

Taking into account the debate on this item at its thirty-ninth session,

Convinced of the advantages of a better knowledge of Antarctica,

---

[1] Note: footnotes omitted from this Part.

Affirming the conviction that, in the interest of all mankind, Antarctica should continue forever to be used exclusively for peaceful purposes and that it should not become the scene or object of international discord,

Recalling the relevant paragraphs of the Economic Declaration adopted at the Seventh Conference of Heads of State or Government of Non-Aligned Countries, held at New Delhi from 7 to 12 March 1983,

1. *Expresses its appreciation* to the Secretary-General for the study on the question of Antarctica;

2. *Decides* to include in the provisional agenda of its fortieth session the item entitled "Question of Antarctica".

102nd plenary meeting
17 December 1984

UN General Assembly Resolution 40/156: Question of Antarctica (16 December 1985)

A

The General Assembly,

Recalling its resolutions 38/77 of 15 December 1983 and 39/152 of 17 December 1984,

Having considered the item entitled "Question of Antarctica",

Welcoming the increasing international awareness of and interest in Antarctica,

Bearing in mind the Antarctic Treaty and the significance of the system it has developed,

Taking into account the debate on this item at its fortieth session,

Convinced of the advantages of a better knowledge of Antarctica,

Affirming the conviction that, in the interest of all mankind, Antarctica should continue forever to be used exclusively for peaceful purposes and that it should not become the scene or object of international discord,

Recalling the relevant paragraphs of the Economic Declaration adopted by the Seventh Conference of Heads of State or Government of Non-Aligned Countries, held at New Delhi from 7 to 12 March 1983, and of the Final Political Declaration adopted by the Conference of Foreign Ministers of Non-Aligned Countries, held at Luanda from 4 to 7 September 1985, as well as the resolution on Antarctica adopted by the Council of Ministers of the Organization of African Unity at its forty-second ordinary session, held at Addis Ababa from 10 to 17 July 1985,

Conscious of the significance of Antarctica to the international community in terms, *inter alia*, of international peace and security, economy, environment, scientific research and meteorology,

Recognizing, therefore, the interest of mankind as a whole in Antarctica,

Bearing in mind the United Nations Convention on the Law of the Sea,

Noting once again with appreciation the study on the question of Antarctica,

Convinced that it would be desirable to examine further certain issues affecting Antarctica,

1. *Requests* the Secretary-General to update and expand the study on the question of Antarctica by addressing questions concerning the availability to the United Nations of information from the Antarctic Treaty Consultative Parties on their respective activities in and their deliberations regarding Antarctica, the involvement of the relevant specialized agencies and intergovernmental organizations in the Antarctic Treaty system and the significance of the United Nations Convention on the Law of the Sea in the southern ocean;

2. *Requests* the Secretary-General to seek the co-operation of all Member States and the relevant specialized agencies, organs, organizations and bodies of the United Nations system, as well as the relevant intergovernmental and non-governmental bodies, in the preparation of

the updated study by inviting them to transmit, as appropriate, their views and any information they may wish to provide;

3. *Requests* the Secretary-General to submit the study to the General Assembly at its forty-first session;

4. *Decides* to include in the provisional agenda of its forty-first session the item entitled "Question of Antarctica".

117th plenary meeting
16 December 1985

B

The General Assembly,

Recalling its resolutions 38/77 of 15 December 1983 and 39/152 of 17 December 1984,

Having considered the item entitled "Question of Antarctica",

Recalling the relevant paragraphs of the Economic Declaration adopted by the Seventh Conference of Heads of State or Government of Non-Aligned Countries, held at New Delhi from 7 to 12 March 1983, and of the Final Political Declaration adopted by the Conference of Foreign Ministers of Non-Aligned Countries held at Luanda from 4 to 7 September 1985, as well as the resolution on Antarctica adopted by the Council of Ministers of the Organization of African Unity at its forty-second ordinary session, held at Addis Ababa from 10 to 17 July 1985,

Recognizing that the management, exploration and use of Antarctica should be conducted in accordance with the purposes and principles of the Charter of the United Nations and in the interest of maintaining international peace and security and of promoting international cooperation for the benefit of mankind as a whole,

Aware that negotiations are in progress among the Antarctic Treaty Consultative Parties, with the non-Consultative Parties as observers, to which other States are not privy, with a view to establishing a régime regarding Antarctic minerals,

1. *Affirms* that any exploitation of the resources of Antarctica should ensure the maintenance of international peace and security in Antarctica, the protection of its environment, the non-appropriation and conservation of its resources and the international management and equitable sharing of the benefits of such exploitation;

2. *Invites* the Antarctic Treaty Consultative Parties to inform the Secretary-General of their negotiations to establish a régime regarding Antarctic minerals;

3. *Requests* the Secretary-General to submit to the General Assembly for consideration at its forty-first session a report containing the replies received from Consultative Parties;

4. *Decides* to include in the provisional agenda of its forty-first session the item entitled "Question of Antarctica".

117th plenary meeting
16 December 1985

C

The General Assembly,

Having considered the item entitled "Question of Antarctica",

Noting with regret that the racist *apartheid* régime of South Africa, which has been suspended from participation in the General Assembly of the United Nations, is a Consultative Party to the Antarctic Treaty,

Recalling the interest of African States in Antarctica as shown by the resolution adopted by the Council of Ministers of the Organization of African Unity at its forty-second ordinary session, held at Addis Ababa from 10 to 17 July 1985,

Recalling further that the Antarctic Treaty is, by its terms, intended to further the purposes and principles embodied in the Charter of the United Nations,

1. *Views with concern* the continued status of the *apartheid* régime of South Africa as a Consultative Party to the Antarctic Treaty;

2. *Urges* the Antarctic Treaty Consultative Parties to exclude the racist *apartheid* régime of South Africa from participation in the meetings of the Consultative Parties at the earliest possible date;

3. *Invites* the States parties to the Antarctic Treaty to inform the Secretary-General on the actions taken regarding the provisions of the present resolution.

117th plenary meeting
16 December 1985

UN General Assembly Resolution 41/88: Question of Antarctica (14 December 1986)

A

The General Assembly,

Recalling its resolutions 38/77 of 15 December 1983, 39/152 of 17 December 1984 and 40/156 A of 16 December 1985,

Having considered the item entitled "Question of Antarctica",

Welcoming the increasing international awareness of and interest in Antarctica,

Bearing in mind the Antarctic Treaty and the significance of the system it has developed,

Taking into account the debate on this item at its fortyfirst session,

Convinced of the advantages of a better knowledge of Antarctica,

Affirming the conviction that, in the interest of all mankind, Antarctica should continue forever to be used exclusively for peaceful purposes and that it should not become the scene or object of international discord,

Recalling the relevant paragraphs of the Political Declaration adopted by the Eighth Conference of Heads of State or Government of Non-Aligned Countries, held at Harare from I to 6 September 1986, and the resolution on Antarctica adopted by the Council of Ministers of the Organization of African Unity at its forty-second ordinary session, held at Addis Ababa from 10 to 17 July 1985, as well as the decision of the Council of Ministers of the League of Arab States held at Tunis on 17 and 18 September 1986,

Conscious of the significance of Antarctica to the international community in terms, *inter alia*, of international peace and security, economy, environment, scientific research and meteorology,

Recognizing, therefore, the interest of mankind as a whole in Antarctica.

Taking into account the provisions of the United Nations Convention on the Law of the Sea,

Noting with appreciation the expanded study on the question of Antarctica submitted by the Secretary-General,

Noting the increased flow of information from the Antarctic Treaty Consultative Parties, and expressing concern at the continuing non-availability of information to the Secretary-General on certain issues affecting the question of Antarctica,

1. *Requests* the Antarctic Treaty Consultative Parties to keep the Secretary-General fully informed on all aspects of the question of Antarctica so that the United Nations could function as the central repository of all such information;

2. *Requests* the Secretary-General to continue to follow all aspects of the question of Antarctica and to provide an updated report thereon to the General Assembly at its forty-second session;

3. *Decides* to include in the provisional agenda of its forty-second session the item entitled "Question of Antarctica".

96th plenary meeting
4 December 1986

B

The General Assembly,

Recalling its resolutions 38/77 of 15 December 1983, 39/152 of 17 December 1984 and 40/156 B of 16 December 1985,

Having considered the item entitled "Question of Antarctica",

Recalling the relevant paragraphs of the Political Declaration adopted by the Eighth Conference of Heads of State or Government of Non-Aligned Countries, held at Harare from 1 to 6 September 1986, and the resolution on Antarctica adopted by the Council of Ministers of the Organization of African Unity at its forty-second ordinary session, held at Addis Ababa from 10 to 17 July 1985, as well as the decision of the Council of Ministers of the League of Arab States held at Tunis on 17 and 18 September 1986,

Recognizing that the management, exploration and use of Antarctica should be conducted in accordance with the purposes and principles of the Charter of the United Nations and in the interest of maintaining international peace and security and of promoting international co-operation for the benefit of mankind as a whole,

Aware that negotiations are in progress among the Antarctic Treaty Consultative Parties, with the non-Consultative Parties as observers, to which other States are not privy, with a view to establishing a régime regarding Antarctica's minerals.

1. *Reaffirms* that any exploitation of the resources of Antarctica should ensure the maintenance of international peace and security in Antarctica, the protection of its environment, the non-appropriation and conservation of its resources and the international management and equitable sharing of the benefits of such exploitation;

2. *Calls upon* the Antarctic Treaty Consultative Parties to impose a moratorium on the negotiations to establish a minerals régime until such time as all members of the international community can participate fully in such negotiations;

3. *Decides* to include in the provisional agenda of its forty-second session the item entitled "Question of Antarctica".

96th plenary meeting
4 December 1986

C

The General Assembly,

Recalling its resolution 40/156 C of 16 December 1985,

Having considered the item entitled "Question of Antarctica",

Noting with regret that the racist *apartheid* régime of South Africa, which has been suspended from participation in the General Assembly of the United Nations, has continued to participate in the meetings of the Antarctic Treaty Consultative Parties.

Recalling the resolution adopted by the Council of Ministers of the Organization of African Unity at its fortysecond ordinary session, held at Addis Ababa from 10 to 17 July 1985,

Recalling also the relevant paragraphs of the Political Declaration adopted by the Eighth Conference of Heads of State or Government of Non-Aligned Countries, held at Harare from 1 to 6 September 1986,

Recalling further that the Antarctic Treaty is, by its terms, intended to further the purposes and principles embodied in the Charter of the United Nations,

Noting further that the policy of *apartheid* practised by the racist minority régime of South Africa, which has been universally condemned, constitutes a threat to regional and international peace and security,

1. *Views with concern* the continuing participation of the *apartheid* régime of South Africa in the meetings of the Antarctic Treaty Consultative Parties;

2. *Appeals once again* to the Antarctic Treaty Consultative Parties to take urgent measures to exclude the racist *apartheid* régime of South Africa from participation in the meetings of the Consultative Parties at the earliest possible date;

3. *Invites* the States parties to the Antarctic Treaty to inform the Secretary-General on the actions taken regarding the provisions of the present resolution;

4. *Requests* the Secretary-General to submit a report in this regard to the General Assembly at its forty-second session:

5. *Decides* to include in the provisional agenda of its forty-second session the item entitled "Question of Antarctica".

96th plenary meeting
4 December 1986

UN General Assembly Resolution 42/46: Question of Antarctica (30 November 1987)

A

The General Assembly,

Recalling its resolution 41/88 C of 4 December 1986,

Having considered the item entitled "Question of Antarctica",

Noting with regret that the racist *apartheid* régime of South Africa, which has been suspended from participation in the General Assembly of the United Nations, has continued to participate in the meetings of the Antarctic Treaty Consultative Parties,

Recalling the resolution adopted by the Council of Ministers of the Organization of African Unity at its forty-second ordinary session, held at Addis Ababa from 10 to 17 July 1985,

Recalling also the relevant paragraphs of the Political Declaration adopted by the Eighth Conference of Heads of State or Government of Non-Aligned Countries, held at Harare from 1 to 6 September 1986,

Recalling further that the Antarctic Treaty is, by its terms, intended to further the purposes and principles embodied in the Charter of the United Nations,

Noting further that the policy of *apartheid* practised by the racist minority régime of South Africa, which has been universally condemned, constitutes a threat to regional and international peace and security,

1. *Views with concern* the continuing participation of the *apartheid* régime of South Africa in the meetings of the Antarctic Treaty Consultative Parties;
2. *Appeals once again* to the Antarctic Treaty Consultative Parties to take urgent measures to exclude the racist *apartheid* régime of South Africa from participation in the meetings of the Consultative Parties at the earliest possible date,
3. *Invites* the States parties to the Antarctic Treaty to inform the Secretary-General on the actions taken regarding the provisions of the present resolution;
4. *Requests* the Secretary-General to submit a report in this regard to the General Assembly at its forty-third session;
5. *Decides* to include in the provisional agenda of its forty-third session the item entitled "Question of Antarctica".

85th plenary meeting
30 November 1987

B

The General Assembly,

Having considered the item entitled "Question of Antarctica",

Recalling its resolutions 38/77 of 15 December 1983, 39/152 of 17 December 1984, 40/156 A and B of 16 December 1985 and 41/88 A and B of 4 December 1986,

Recalling the relevant paragraphs of the Political Declaration adopted by the Eighth Conference of Heads of State or Government of Non-Aligned Countries, held at Harare from 1 to 6 September 1986, and the resolution on Antarctica adopted by the Council of Ministers of the Organization of African Unity at its forty-second ordinary session, held at Addis Ababa from 10 to 17 July 1985, as well as the decision of the Council of Ministers of the League of Arab States held at Tunis on 17 and 18 September 1986 and resolution 25/5-P(IS) adopted by the Fifth Islamic Summit Conference of the Organization of the Islamic Conference, held at Kuwait from 26 to 29 January 1987,

Welcoming the increasing awareness of and interest in Antarctica shown by the international community,

Taking into account the debates on this item held at its thirty-eighth, thirty-ninth, fortieth, forty-first and forty-second sessions,

Convinced of the advantages to the whole of mankind of a better knowledge of Antarctica,

Affirming its conviction that, in the interest of all mankind, Antarctica should continue for ever to be used exclusively for peaceful purposes and that it should not become the scene or object of international discord,

Conscious of the significance of Antarctica to the international community in terms, *inter alia*, of international peace and security, environment, economy, scientific research and meteorology,

Reaffirming that the management, exploration, exploitation and use of Antarctica should be conducted in accordance with the purposes and principles of the Charter of the United Nations and in the interest of maintaining international peace and security and of promoting international co-operation for the benefit of mankind as a whole,

Taking note with appreciation of the report of the Secretary-General on the question of Antarctica,

Also taking into account all aspects pertaining to all areas covered by the Antarctic Treaty system,

Reaffirming the principle that the international community is entitled to information covering all aspects of Antarctica and that the United Nations be made the repository for all such information in accordance with General Assembly resolution 41/88 A,

Reaffirming further that any eventual minerals régime on Antarctica should take fully into account the interests of the international community and that a moratorium on the negotiations to establish a minerals régime should be imposed until such time as all members of the international community can participate fully in such negotiations, in accordance with General Assembly resolution 41/88 B,

1. *Calls upon* the Antarctic Treaty Consultative Parties to invite the Secretary-General or his representative to all meetings of the Treaty parties, including their consultative meetings and the minerals régime negotiations;

2. *Requests* the Secretary-General to submit a report on his evaluations thereon to the General Assembly at its forty-third session;

3. *Also calls upon* the Antarctic Treaty Consultative Parties to impose a moratorium on the negotiations to establish a minerals régime until such time as all members of the international community can participate fully in such negotiations;

4. *Urges* all States Members of the United Nations to co-operate with the Secretary-General and to continue consultations on all aspects relating to Antarctica;

5. *Decides* to include in the provisional agenda of its forty-third session the item entitled "Question of Antarctica".

85th plenary meeting
30 November 1987

UN General Assembly Resolution 43/83: Question of Antarctica (7 December 1988)

A

The General Assembly,

Having considered the item entitled "Question of Antarctica",

Recalling its resolutions 38/77 of 15 December 1983, 39/152 of 17 December 1984, 40/156 A and B of 16 December 1985, 41/88 A and B of 4 December 1986 and 42/46 A and B of 30 November 1987,

Recalling also the relevant paragraphs of the Political Declaration adopted by the Eighth Conference of Heads of State or Government of Non-Aligned Countries, held at Harare from 1 to 6 September 1986, and the resolution on Antarctica adopted by the Council of Ministers of the Organization of African Unity at its forty-second ordinary session, held at Addis Ababa from 10 to 17 July 1985, as well as the decision of the Council of Ministers of the League of Arab States meeting at Tunis on 17 and 18 September 1986 and resolution 25/5-P(IS) adopted by the Fifth Islamic Summit Conference of the Organization of the Islamic Conference, held at Kuwait from 26 to 29 January 1987,

Taking into account the debates on this item held since its thirty-eighth session,

Welcoming the increasing awareness of and interest in Antarctica shown by the international community,

Convinced of the advantages to the whole of mankind of a better knowledge of Antarctica,

Affirming its conviction that, in the interest of all mankind, Antarctica should continue forever to be used exclusively for peaceful purposes and that it should not become the scene or object of international discord,

Reaffirming the principle that the international community is entitled to information covering all aspects of Antarctica and that the United Nations should be made the repository for all such information in accordance with General Assembly resolutions 41/88 A and 42/46 B,

Conscious of the particular significance of Antarctica to the international community in terms, *inter alia*, of international peace and security, environment, its effects on global climatic conditions, economy and scientific research,

Taking into account all aspects pertaining to all areas covered by the Antarctic Treaty system,

Taking note with appreciation of the reports of the Secretary-General on the question of Antarctica,

Reaffirming that the management, exploration, exploitation and use of Antarctica should be conducted in accordance with the purposes and principles of the Charter of the United Nations and in the interest of maintaining international peace and security and of promoting international co-operation for the benefit of mankind as a whole,

1. *Expresses its conviction* that any minerals régime on Antarctica, in order to be of benefit to all mankind, should be negotiated with the full participation of all members of the international community;

2. *Further expresses its deep regret* that the Antarctic Treaty Consultative Parties have proceeded with negotiations and adopted on 2 June 1988 a convention on the regulation of Antarctic mineral resource activities, notwithstanding General Assembly resolutions 41/88 B and 42/46 B, calling for the imposition of a moratorium on negotiations to establish a minerals régime until such time as all members of the international community can fully participate in such negotiations;

3. *Reiterates its call* upon the Antarctic Treaty Consultative Parties to invite the Secretary-General or his representative to all meetings of the Treaty parties, including their consultative meetings;

4. *Requests* the Secretary-General to submit a report on his evaluations thereon to the General Assembly at its forty-fourth session;

5. *Urges* all States Members of the United Nations to co-operate with the Secretary-General and to continue consultations on all aspects relating to Antarctica;

6. *Decides* to include in the provisional agenda of its forty-fourth session the item entitled "Question of Antarctica".

73rd plenary meeting
7 December 1988

B

The General Assembly,

Recalling its resolution 42/46 A of 30 November 1987,

Having considered the item entitled "Question of Antarctica",

Noting with regret that the racist *apartheid* régime of South Africa, which has been suspended from participation in the General Assembly of the United Nations, has continued to participate in the meetings of the Antarctic Treaty Consultative Parties,

Recalling the resolution on Antarctica adopted by the Council of Ministers of the Organization of African Unity at its forty-second ordinary session, held at Addis Ababa from 10 to 17 July 1985,

Recalling also the relevant paragraphs of the Political Declaration adopted by the Eighth Conference of Heads of State or Government of Non-Aligned Countries, held at Harare from 1 to 6 September 1986,

Recalling further that the Antarctic Treaty is, by its terms, intended to further the purposes and principles embodied in the Charter of the United Nations,

Noting that the policy of *apartheid* practised by the racist minority régime of South Africa, which has been universally condemned, constitutes a threat to regional and international peace and security,

1. *Views with concern* the continuing participation of the *apartheid* régime of South Africa in the meetings of the Antarctic Treaty Consultative Parties;

2. *Appeals once again* to the Antarctic Treaty Consultative Parties to take urgent measures to exclude the racist *apartheid* régime of South Africa from participation in the meetings of the Consultative Parties at the earliest possible date;

3. *Invites* the States parties to the Antarctic Treaty to inform the Secretary-General on the actions taken regarding the provisions of the present resolution;

4. *Requests* the Secretary-General to submit a report in this regard to the General Assembly at its forty-fourth session;

5. *Decides* to include in the provisional agenda of its forty-fourth session the item entitled "Question of Antarctica".

73rd plenary meeting
7 December 1988

UN General Assembly Resolution 44/124: Question of Antarctica (15 December 1989)

A

The General Assembly,

Recalling its resolution 43/83 B of 7 December 1988,

Having considered the item entitled "Question of Antarctica";

Noting with regret that the racist *apartheid* régime of South Africa, which has been suspended from participation in the General Assembly of the United Nations, has continued to participate in the meetings of the Antarctic Treaty Consultative Parties,

Recalling the resolution adopted by the Council of Ministers of the Organization of African Unity at its fiftieth ordinary session, held at Addis Ababa from 17 to 22 July 1989,

Recalling also the final document on Antarctica adopted by the Ninth Conference of Heads of State or Government of Non-Aligned Countries, held at Belgrade from 4 to 7 September 1989,

Recalling further that the Antarctic Treaty is, by its terms, intended to further the purposes and principles embodied in the Charter of the United Nations,

Noting that the policy of *apartheid* practised by the racist minority regime of South Africa, which has been universally condemned, constitutes a threat to regional and international peace and security,

1. *Views with concern* the continuing participation of the *apartheid* régime of South Africa in the meetings of the Antarctic Treaty Consultative Parties;

2. *Appeals once again* to the Antarctic Treaty Consultative Parties to take urgent measures to exclude the racist *apartheid* régime of South Africa from participation in the meetings of the Consultative Parties at the earliest possible date;

3. *Invites* the States parties to the Antarctic Treaty to inform the Secretary-General of the actions taken regarding the provisions of the present resolution;

4. *Requests* the Secretary-General to submit a report in this regard to the General Assembly at its forty-fifth session;

5. *Decides* to include in the provisional agenda of its forty-fifth session the item entitled "Question of Antarctica".

81st plenary meeting
15 December 1989

B

The General Assembly,

Having considered the item entitled "Question of Antarctica",

Recalling its resolutions 38/77 of 15 December 1983, 39/152 of 17 December 1984, 40/156 A and B of 16 December 1985, 41/88 A and B of 4 December 1986, 42/46 A and B of 30 November 1987 and 43/83 A and B of 7 December 1988,

Recalling also the relevant paragraphs of the Political Declaration adopted by the Eighth Conference of Heads of State or Government of Non-Aligned Countries, held at Harare from 1 to 6 September 1986, and the resolution on Antarctica adopted by the Council of Ministers of the Organization of African Unity at its forty-second ordinary session, held at Addis Ababa from 10 to 17 July 1985, as well as the relevant paragraphs of the decision of the Council of Ministers of the League of Arab States meeting at Tunis on 17 and 18 September 1986 and resolution 25/5-P(IS) adopted by the Fifth Islamic Summit Conference of the Organization of the Islamic Conference, held at Kuwait from 26 to 29 January 1987, the final document on Antarctica adopted by the Ninth Conference of Heads of State or Government of Non-Aligned Countries, held at Belgrade from 4 to 7 September 1989 and the communiqué issued by Commonwealth Heads of Government at Kuala Lumpur on 24 October 1989,

Taking into account the debates on this item held since its thirty-eighth session,

Welcoming the increasing awareness of and interest in Antarctica shown by the international community,

Convinced of the advantages to the whole of mankind of a better knowledge of Antarctica,

Affirming its conviction that, in the interest of all mankind, Antarctica should continue forever to be used exclusively for peaceful purposes and that it should not become the scene or object of international discord,

Reaffirming the principle that the international community is entitled to information covering all aspects of Antarctica and that the United Nations should be made the repository for all such information in accordance with General Assembly resolutions 41/88 A, 42/46 B and 43/83 A,

Conscious of the particular significance of Antarctica to the international community in terms, *inter alia*, of international peace and security, environment, its effects on global climatic conditions, economy and scientific research,

Conscious also of the interrelationship between Antarctica and the physical, chemical and biological processes that regulate the total Earth system,

Reaffirming that the management and use of Antarctica should be conducted in accordance with the purposes and principles of the Charter of the United Nations and in the interest of maintaining international peace and security and of promoting international co-operation for the benefit of mankind as a whole,

Affirming the necessity of ensuring, in the interest of all mankind, comprehensive environmental protection and conservation of the Antarctic environment and its dependent and associated ecosystems through negotiations with the full participation of all members of the international community,

Conscious of the environmental degradation that prospecting and mining in and around Antarctica would pose to the Antarctic and global environment and ecosystems.

Convinced of the need to prevent or minimize any impact of human activity resulting from the large number of scientific stations and expeditions in Antarctica on the environment and its dependent and associated ecosystems,

Taking into account all aspects pertaining to all areas covered by the Antarctic Treaty system,

Taking note with appreciation of the reports of the Secretary-General on the question of Antarctica,

1. *Expresses its regret* that, despite the numerous resolutions in which it has called upon the Antarctic Treaty Consultative Parties to invite the Secretary-General or his representative to their meetings, including their consultative meetings, the Secretary-General was not invited to the Preparatory Meeting of the XVth Antarctic Treaty Consultative Meeting or to the XVth Consultative Meeting, held in Paris from 9 to 13 May and from 9 to 20 October 1989, respectively;

2. *Reiterates its call* upon the Antarctic Treaty Consultative Parties to invite the Secretary-General or his representative to all meetings of the Treaty parties, including their consultative meetings;

3. *Requests* the Secretary-General to submit a report on his evaluations thereon to the General Assembly at its forty-fifth session;

4. *Expresses the conviction* that, in view of the significant impact that Antarctica exerts on the global environment and ecosystems, any régime to be established for the protection and conservation of the Antarctic environment and its dependent and associated ecosystems, in order to be for the benefit of mankind as a whole and in order to gain the universal acceptability necessary to ensure full compliance and enforcement, must be negotiated with the full participation of all members of the international community;

5. *Urges* all members of the international community to support all efforts to ban prospecting and mining in and around Antarctica and to ensure that all activities are carried out exclusively for the purpose of peaceful scientific investigation and that all such activities ensure the maintenance of international peace and security in Antarctica and the protection of its environment and are for the benefit of all mankind;

6. *Expresses its conviction* that the establishment, through negotiations with the full participation of all members of the international community, of Antarctica as a nature reserve or a world park would ensure the protection and conservation of its environment and its dependent and associated ecosystems for the benefit of all mankind;

7. *Also expresses its conviction*, in view of the large number of scientific stations and expeditions, that international scientific research should be enhanced through the establishment of international stations devoted to scientific investigations of global significance, regulated by stringent environmental safeguards, so as to avoid or minimize any adverse impact of human activities on the Antarctic environment and its dependent and associated systems;

8. *Urges* all States Members of the United Nations to co-operate with the Secretary-General and to continue consultations on all aspects relating to Antarctica;

9. *Decides* to include in the provisional agenda of its forty-fifth session the item entitled "Question of Antarctica".

81st plenary meeting
15 December 1989

UN General Assembly Resolution 45/78: Question of Antarctica (12 December 1990)

A

The General Assembly,

Having considered the item entitled "Question of Antarctica",

Recalling its resolutions 38/77 of 15 December 1983, 39/152 of 17 December 1984, 40/156

A and B of 16 December 1985, 41/88 A and B of 4 December 1986, 42/46 A and B of 30 November 1987, 43/83 A and B of 7 December 1988 and 44/124 A and B of 15 December 1989,

Recalling also the relevant paragraphs of the final documents adopted by the Ninth Conference of Heads of State or Government of Non-Aligned Countries, held at Belgrade from 4 to 7 September 1989, the second meeting of States of the Zone of Peace and Co-operation of the South Atlantic, held at Abuja, Nigeria, from 25 to 29 June 1990, and the Nineteenth Islamic Conference of Foreign Ministers, held at Cairo from 31 July to 5 August 1990,

Taking into account the debates on this item held since its thirty-eighth session,

Reaffirming the principle that the international community is entitled to information covering all aspects of Antarctica and that the United Nations should be made the repository for all such information in accordance with General Assembly resolutions 41/88 A, 42/46 B, 43/83 A and 44/124 B,

Conscious of the particular significance of Antarctica to the international community in terms, *inter alia*, of international peace and security, environment, its effects on global climatic conditions, economy and scientific research,

Conscious also of the interrelationship between Antarctica and the physical, chemical and biological processes that regulate the total Earth system,

Welcoming the increasing recognition of the significant impact that Antarctica exerts on the global environment and ecosystems and of the need for a comprehensive agreement on the protection and conservation of the Antarctic environment and its dependent and associated ecosystems,

Sharing the concern over the environmental degradation of Antarctica and its impact on global environment expressed at the first substantive session of the Preparatory Committee for the United Nations Conference on Environment and Development, held at Nairobi from 6 to 31 August 1990,

Welcoming also the increasing support for the establishment of Antarctica as a nature reserve or world park to ensure the protection and conservation of its environment and its dependent and associated ecosystems for the benefit of all mankind,

Welcoming further the increasing support within the international community for the banning of prospecting and mining in and around Antarctica,

Welcoming the initiative taken by some Antarctic Treaty Consultative Parties in promoting Antarctica as a nature reserve or world park and the banning of prospecting and mining in and around Antarctica,

Welcoming also the ongoing trend in acknowledging the need for internationally co-ordinated scientific research stations in Antarctica in order to minimize unnecessary duplication and logistical support facilities,

Welcoming further the increasing awareness of and interest in Antarctica shown by the international community, and convinced of the advantages to the whole of mankind of a better knowledge of Antarctica,

Affirming its conviction that, in the interest of all mankind, Antarctica should continue for ever to be used exclusively for peaceful purposes and that it should not become the scene or object of international discord,

Reaffirming that the management and use of Antarctica should be conducted in accordance with the purposes and principles of the Charter of the United Nations and in the interest of maintaining international peace and security and of promoting international cooperation for the benefit of mankind as a whole,

Convinced of the need to prevent or minimize any negative impact of human activity resulting from the large number of scientific stations and expeditions in Antarctica on the environment and its dependent and associated ecosystems,

Taking into account all aspects pertaining to all areas covered by the Antarctic Treaty,

Taking note with appreciation of the reports of the Secretary-General on the question of Antarctica of 6 September 1990 and 8 September 1990,

1. *Expresses its regret* that, despite the numerous resolutions adopted by the General Assembly, the Secretary-General or his representative has not been invited to the meetings of the Antarctic Treaty Consultative Parties, including the special session of the Antarctic Treaty Consultative Meeting at Santiago from 19 November to 7 December 1990, and urges once again the Consultative Parties to invite the Secretary-General or his representative to their future meetings;

2. *Calls upon* the Antarctic Treaty Consultative Parties to deposit information and documents covering all aspects of Antarctica with the Secretary-General of the United Nations, and requests the Secretary-General to submit a report on his evaluations thereon to the General Assembly at its forty-sixth session;

3. *Expresses the conviction* that any move to draw up a comprehensive environmental convention on the conservation and protection of Antarctica and its dependent and associated ecosystems as well as establishing a nature reserve or world park must be negotiated with the full participation of the international community, and in this regard stresses that this should be pursued within the context of the United Nations system, including the United Nations Conference on Environment and Development;

4. *Urges* all members of the international community to support all efforts to ban prospecting and mining in and around Antarctica and to ensure that all activities are carried out exclusively for the purpose of peaceful scientific investigation and that all such activities ensure the maintenance of international peace and security in Antarctica and the protection of its environment and are for the benefit of all mankind;

5. *Requests* the Secretary-General to undertake a comprehensive study with the help of relevant United Nations programmes and specialized agencies such as the World Meteorological Organization and the United Nations Environment Programme, using available data and resources, on the establishment of a United Nations-sponsored station in Antarctica with a view to promoting coordinated international co-operation in scientific research for the benefit of mankind, particularly the importance of Antarctica to the global environment and ecosystems, as well as to act as an early warning system on climate change and accidents, and submit a report thereon to the General Assembly at its forty-sixth session;

6. *Urges* all States Members of the United Nations to co-operate with the Secretary-General and to continue consultations on all aspects relating to Antarctica;

7. *Also requests* the Secretary-General to submit a report, using available data and resources, on the state of the environment in Antarctica and its impact on the global system to the General Assembly at its forty-sixth session;

8. *Decides* to include in the provisional agenda of its forty-sixth session the item entitled "Question of Antarctica".

66th plenary meeting
12 December 1990

B

The General Assembly,

Recalling its resolutions 43/83 B of 7 December 1988 and 44/124 A and B of 15 December 1989,

Having considered the item entitled "Question of Antarctica",

Noting with regret that the racist *apartheid* régime of South Africa, which has been suspended from participation in the General Assembly of the United Nations, has continued to participate in the meetings of the Antarctic Treaty Consultative Parties,

Recalling the resolution adopted by the Council of Ministers of the Organization of African Unity at its fiftieth ordinary session, held at Addis Ababa from 17 to 22 July 1989,

Recalling also the final document on Antarctica adopted by the Ninth Conference of Heads of State or Government of Non-Aligned Countries, held at Belgrade from 4 to 7 September 1989,

Recalling further that the Antarctic Treaty is, by its terms, intended to further the purposes and principles embodied in the Charter of the United Nations,

Noting that the policy of *apartheid* practised by the racist minority régime of South Africa, which has been universally condemned, constitutes a threat to regional and international peace and security,

1. *Takes note* of the report of the Secretary-General, and expresses deep concern that no concrete measures have been taken in accordance with paragraph 2 of resolution 44/124 A;
2. *Views with concern* the continuing participation of the *apartheid* régime of South Africa in the meetings of the Antarctic Treaty Consultative Parties;
3. *Appeals once again* to the Antarctic Treaty Consultative Parties to take urgent measures to exclude the racist *apartheid* régime from participation in the meetings of the Consultative Parties at the earliest possible date, and invites them to inform the Secretary-General of the measures taken regarding the provisions of the present resolution;
4. *Requests* the Secretary-General to submit a report in this regard to the General Assembly at its forty-sixth session, taking into account the concern expressed in paragraph 1 of the present resolution;
5. *Decides* to include in the provisional agenda of its forty-sixth session the item entitled "Question of Antarctica".

66th plenary meeting
12 December 1990

UN General Assembly Resolution 46/41: Question of Antarctica (6 December 1991)

A

The General Assembly,

Having considered the item entitled "Question of Antarctica",

Recalling its resolutions 38/77 of 15 December 1983, 39/152 of 17 December 1984, 40/156 A and B of 16 December 1985, 41/88 A and B of 4 December 1986, 42/46 A and B of 30 November 1987, 43/83 A and B of 7 December 1988, 44/124 A and B of 15 December 1989 and 45/78 A and B of 12 December 1990,

Recalling also the relevant paragraphs of the final documents adopted by the Ninth Conference of Heads of State or Government of Non-Aligned Countries, held at Belgrade from 4 to 7 September 1989, the second meeting of States of the Zone of Peace and Cooperation of the South Atlantic, held at Abuja from 25 to 29 June 1990, the Nineteenth Islamic Conference of Foreign Ministers, held at Cairo from 31 July to 5 August 1990, and the meeting of the Commonwealth Heads of Government, held at Harare from 16 to 22 October 1991,

Taking into account the debates on this item held since its thirty-eighth session,

Reaffirming the principle that the international community is entitled to information covering all aspects of Antarctica and that the United Nations should be made the repository for all such information in accordance with General Assembly resolutions 41/88 A, 42/46 B, 43/83 A, 44/124 B and 45/78 A,

Conscious of the particular significance of Antarctica to the international community in terms, *inter alia*, of international peace and security, environment, its effects on global climate conditions, economy and scientific research,

Conscious also of the interrelationship between Antarctica and the physical, chemical and biological processes that regulate the total Earth system,

Welcoming the increasing recognition of the significant impact that Antarctica exerts on the global environment and ecosystems and of the need for a comprehensive agreement to be negotiated by the international community on the protection and conservation of the Antarctic environment and its dependent and associated ecosystems,

Sharing the concern over the environmental degradation of Antarctica and its impact on the global environment expressed at the first, second and third substantive sessions of the Preparatory Committee for the United Nations Conference on Environment and Development,

Welcoming the increasing support, including by some Antarctic Treaty Consultative Parties, for the establishment of Antarctica as a nature reserve or world park to ensure the protection and conservation of its environment and its dependent and associated ecosystems for the benefit of all mankind,

Welcoming the signing of the Protocol on Environmental Protection by the Antarctic Treaty parties on 3 October 1991 at Madrid, which among other things banned prospecting and mining in and around Antarctica for the next fifty years,

Welcoming also the ongoing trend in acknowledging the need for internationally coordinated scientific research stations in Antarctica in order to minimize unnecessary duplication and logistical support facilities,

Welcoming further the increasing awareness of and interest in Antarctica shown by the international community, and convinced of the advantages to the whole of mankind of a better knowledge of Antarctica,

Affirming its conviction that, in the interest of all mankind, Antarctica should continue for ever to be used exclusively for peaceful purposes and that it should not become the scene or object of international discord,

Reaffirming that the management and use of Antarctica should be conducted in accordance with the purposes and principles of the Charter of the United Nations and in the interest of maintaining international peace and security and of promoting international cooperation for the benefit of mankind as a whole,

Convinced of the need to prevent or minimize any negative impact of human activity resulting from the large number of scientific stations and expeditions, including tourism, in Antarctica on the environment and its dependent and associated ecosystems,

1. *Takes note* of the report of the Secretary-General on a United Nations-sponsored station in Antarctica and decides to keep the matter under review;

2. *Takes note also* of the report of the Secretary-General on the state of the environment in Antarctica, and requests the Secretary-General to monitor and gather information within existing resources on the state of the environment in Antarctica and to submit an annual report to the General Assembly;

3. *Expresses its regret* that, despite the numerous resolutions adopted by the General Assembly, the Secretary-General or his representative has not been invited to the meetings of the Antarctic Treaty Consultative Parties, and urges once again the Consultative Parties to invite the Secretary-General or his representative to their future meetings;

4. *Reiterates its call* upon the Antarctic Treaty Consultative Parties to deposit information and documents covering all aspects of Antarctica with the Secretary-General of the United Nations, and requests the Secretary-General to submit a report on his evaluations thereof to the General Assembly at its forty-seventh session;

5. *Expresses its disappointment*, while welcoming the recent signing at Madrid of the Protocol on Environmental Protection by the Antarctic Treaty parties, that the Protocol was not negotiated with the full participation of the international community;

6. *Expresses its concern* that the Madrid Protocol on Environmental Protection lacks the monitoring and implementation mechanisms to comply with the provisions of the Protocol and has not taken into consideration the call of the international community to ban permanently prospecting and mining in Antarctica;

7. *Underlines its call* that any move at drawing up an international convention to establish a nature reserve or world park in Antarctica and its dependent and associated ecosystems must be negotiated with the full participation of the international community;

8. *Reaffirms* the need to promote public awareness of the importance of Antarctica to the ecosystem, and in this regard requests the Secretary-General to explore the possibility of providing the relevant materials on Antarctica through the Department of Public Information of the Secretariat;

9. *Calls upon* the Antarctic Treaty Consultative Parties to increase the level of cooperation and collaboration with a view to reducing the number of scientific stations in Antarctica;

10. *Urges* all members of the international community to ensure that all activities in Antarctica are carried out exclusively for the purpose of peaceful scientific investigation and that all such activities will ensure the maintenance of international peace and security and the protection of the Antarctic environment and are for the benefit of all mankind;

11. *Urges* all States Members of the United Nations to cooperate with the Secretary-General and to continue consultations on all aspects relating to Antarctica;

12. *Decides* to include in the provisional agenda of its forty-seventh session the item entitled "Question of Antarctica".

65th plenary meeting
6 December 1991

B

The General Assembly,

Recalling its resolutions 43/83 B of 7 December 1988, 44/124 B of 15 December 1989 and 45/78 B of 12 December 1990,

Having considered the item entitled "Question of Antarctica",

Noting with regret that the apartheid minority regime of South Africa, which has been suspended from participation in the General Assembly of the United Nations, has continued to participate in the meetings of the Antarctic Treaty Consultative Parties,

Recalling the resolution adopted by the Council of Ministers of the Organization of African Unity at its fiftieth ordinary session, held at Addis Ababa from 17 to 22 July 1989,

Recalling the relevant paragraphs of the final documents adopted by the Ninth Conference of Heads of State or Government of Non-Aligned Countries, held at Belgrade from 4 to 7 September 1989,

Recalling also declaration AHG/Decl.4 (XXVII) on South Africa adopted by the Assembly of Heads of State and Government of the Organization of African Unity at its twenty-seventh ordinary session, held at Abuja from 3 to 5 June 1991,

Recalling further that the Antarctic Treaty is, by its terms, intended to further the purposes and principles embodied in the Charter of the United Nations.

Noting that the system of apartheid existing in South Africa, which has been universally condemned, constitutes a threat to regional and international peace and security.

1. *Takes note* of the report of the Secretary-General;

2. *Views with concern* the continuing participation of the apartheid minority regime of South Africa in the meetings of the Antarctic Treaty Consultative Parties;

3. *Appeals once again* to the Antarctic Treaty Consultative Parties to take urgent measures to exclude the apartheid minority regime from participation in their meetings at the earliest possible date until such time that the abhorrent system and practices of apartheid minority domination are totally eliminated in South Africa;

4. *Requests* the Secretary-General to submit a report in this regard to the General Assembly at its forty-seventh session, taking into account the concern expressed in paragraph 2 above;

5. *Decides* to include in the provisional agenda of its forty-seventh session the item entitled "Question of Antarctica".

65th plenary meeting
6 December 1991

UN General Assembly Resolution 47/57: Question of Antarctica (6 December 1992)

The General Assembly,

Having considered the item entitled "Question of Antarctica",

Recalling its resolutions 38/77 of 15 December 1983, 39/152 of 17 December 1984, 40/156 A and B of 16 December 1985, 41/88 A and B of 4 December 1986, 42/46 A and B of 30 November 1987, 43/83 A and B of 7 December 1988, 44/124 A and B of 15 December 1989, 45/78 A and B of 12 December 1990 and 46/41 A and B of 6 December 1991,

Recalling also the relevant paragraphs of the final documents adopted by the second meeting of States of the Zone of Peace and Cooperation of the South Atlantic, held at Abuja from 25 to 29 June 1990, the Twentieth Islamic Conference of Foreign Ministers, held at Istanbul from 4 to 8 August 1991, the meeting of the Commonwealth Heads of Government, held at Harare from 16 to 22 October 1991 and the Tenth Conference of Heads of State or Government of Non-Aligned Countries, held at Jakarta from 1 to 6 September 1992,

Recalling further the Declaration on South Africa adopted by the Assembly of Heads of State and Government of the Organization of African Unity at its twenty-eighth ordinary session, held at Dakar from 29 June to 1 July 1992,

Taking into account the debates on this item held since its thirty-eighth session,

Reaffirming the principle that the international community is entitled to information covering all aspects of Antarctica and that the United Nations should be made the repository for all such information in accordance with General Assembly resolutions 41/88 A, 42/46 B, 43/83 A, 44/124 B, 45/78 A and 46/41 A,

Welcoming the decision of the Antarctic Treaty Consultative Parties to submit to the Secretary-General the final report of the Sixteenth Antarctic Treaty Consultative Meeting, which took place at Bonn from 7 to 18 October 1991,

Conscious of the particular significance of Antarctica to the international community in terms, *inter alia,* of international peace and security, environment, its effects on global climate conditions, economy and scientific research,

Conscious also of the interrelationship between Antarctica and the physical, chemical and biological processes that regulate the total Earth system,

Welcoming also the increasing recognition of the significant impact that Antarctica exerts on the global environment and ecosystems and of the need for a comprehensive agreement to be negotiated by the international community on the protection and conservation of the Antarctic environment and its dependent and associated ecosystems,

Reiterating the concern over the environmental degradation of Antarctica and its impact on the global environment,

Welcoming further the recognition by the United Nations Conference on Environment and Development, held at Rio de Janeiro from 3 to 14 June 1992, of the value of Antarctica as an area for the conduct of scientific research, in particular research essential to understanding the global environment,

Welcoming the increasing support, including by some Antarctic Treaty Consultative Parties, for the establishment of Antarctica as a nature reserve or world park to ensure the protection and conservation of its environment and its dependent and associated ecosystems for the benefit of all mankind,

Welcoming also the ongoing trend in acknowledging the need for internationally coordinated scientific research stations in Antarctica in order to minimize unnecessary duplication and logistical support facilities,

Welcoming further the increasing awareness of an interest in Antarctica shown by the international community, and convinced of the advantages to the whole of mankind of a better knowledge of Antarctica,

Affirming its conviction that, in the interest of all mankind, Antarctica should continue for ever to be used exclusively for peaceful purposes and that it should not become the scene or object of international discord,

Reaffirming that the management and use of Antarctica should be conducted in accordance with the purposes and principles of the Charter of the United Nations and in the interest of maintaining international peace and security and of promoting international cooperation for the benefit of mankind as a whole,

Convinced of the need for concerted international cooperation in order to protect and safeguard Antarctica and its dependent ecosystems from external environmental disturbances for future generations,

1. *Takes note* of the reports of the Secretary-General on the report of the Sixteenth Antarctic Treaty Consultative Meeting and on the participation of the apartheid minority regime of South Africa in meetings of the Antarctic Treaty Consultative Parties;

2. *Welcomes* the report of the Secretary-General on the state of the environment in Antarctica, and requests the Secretary-General to explore the possibilities of publishing, as official documents of the United Nations, extracts of data received from the various organizations in the preparation of future annual reports, within existing resources;

3. *Expresses its regret* – while noting the cooperation of some United Nations specialized agencies and programmes at the Sixteenth Antarctic Treaty Consultative Meeting – that, despite the numerous resolutions adopted by the General Assembly, the Secretary-General or his representative has not been invited to the meetings of the Antarctic Treaty Consultative Parties, and urges once again the Consultative Parties to invite the Secretary-General or his representative to their future meetings;

4. *Calls upon* – bearing in mind that the Antarctic Treaty is, by its terms, intended to further the purposes and principles embodied in the Charter of the United Nations, with which South Africa has yet to comply fully – the Antarctic Treaty Consultative Parties to prevent South Africa from participating fully in their meetings pending the attainment of a non-racial democratic government in that country;

5. *Encourages* – while welcoming the decision of the Antarctic Treaty Consultative Parties to provide information regarding the Sixteenth Antarctic Treaty Consultative Meeting – the Parties to provide to the Secretary-General, on a continuing basis, more information and documents covering all aspects of Antarctica, and requests the Secretary-General to submit a report on his evaluations thereof to the General Assembly at its forty-eighth session;

6. *Welcomes* the commitment made by the Antarctic Treaty Consultative Parties under chapter 17 of Agenda 21, adopted by the United Nations Conference on Environment and Development, as provided for in article III of the Antarctic Treaty, to continue:

(a) To ensure that data and information resulting from scientific research activities conducted in Antarctica are freely available to the international community;

(b) To enhance access of the international scientific community and specialized agencies of the United Nations to such data and information, including the encouragement of periodic seminars and symposia;

7. *Urges* the Antarctic Treaty Consultative Parties to build on the agreements achieved at the United Nations Conference on Environment and Development, particularly as noted in paragraph 6 of the present resolution, and, in this connection, actively to explore the possibility of organizing an annual seminar/symposium covering issues relating to the environment, commencing in 1993, with international participation as wide as possible, including that of international organizations such as the United Nations;

8. *Also urges* the Antarctic Treaty Consultative Parties to establish monitoring and implementation mechanisms to ensure compliance with the provisions of the 1991 Madrid Protocol on Environmental Protection;

9. *Reiterates its call*, in welcoming the ban on prospecting and mining in and around Antarctica

for the next fifty years by Antarctic Treaty Consultative Parties in accordance with the Madrid Protocol, for the ban to be made permanent;

10. *Also reiterates its call* that any move at drawing up an international convention to establish a nature reserve or world park in Antarctica and its dependent and associated ecosystems must be negotiated with the full participation of the international community;

11. *Reaffirms*, while welcoming the concrete steps taken by the Secretariat through the publication on Antarctica by the Department of Public Information, the need to promote further public awareness of the importance of Antarctica to the ecosystem, and in this regard requests the Secretary-General to continue to provide relevant materials on Antarctica through the Department of Public Information within existing resources;

12. *Encourages* the Antarctic Treaty Consultative Parties to increase the level of cooperation and collaboration with a view to reducing the number of scientific stations in Antarctica;

13. *Urges* the international community to ensure that all activities in Antarctica are carried out exclusively for the purpose of peaceful scientific investigation and that all such activities will ensure the maintenance of international peace and security and the protection of the Antarctic environment and are for the benefit of all mankind;

14. *Urges* all States Members of the United Nations to cooperate with the Secretary-General on matters pertaining to Antarctica and to continue consultations on all aspects relating to the continent;

15. *Decides* to include in the provisional agenda of its forty-eighth session the item entitled "Question of Antarctica".

81st plenary meeting
9 December 1992

UN General Assembly Resolution 48/80: Question of Antarctica (16 December 1993)

The General Assembly,

Having considered the item entitled "Question of Antarctica",

Recalling its resolutions 38/77 of 15 December 1983, 39/152 of 17 December 1984, 40/156 A and B of 16 December 1985, 41/88 A and B of 4 December 1986, 42/46 A and B of 30 November 1987, 43/83 A and B of 7 December 1988, 44/124 A and B of 15 December 1989, 45/78 A and B of 12 December 1990, 46/41 A and B of 6 December 1991 and 47/57 of 9 December 1992,

Recalling also the relevant paragraphs of the final documents adopted by the second meeting of States of the Zone of Peace and Cooperation of the South Atlantic, held at Abuja from 25 to 29 June 1990, the Twentieth Islamic Conference of Foreign Ministers, held at Istanbul from 4 to 8 August 1991, the meeting of the Commonwealth Heads of Government, held at Harare from 16 to 22 October 1991 and the Tenth Conference of Heads of State or Government of Non-Aligned Countries, held at Jakarta from 1 to 6 September 1992,

Taking into account the debates on this item held since its thirty-eighth session,

Reaffirming the principle that the international community is entitled to information covering all aspects of Antarctica and that the United Nations should be made the repository for all such information in accordance with General Assembly resolutions 41/88 A, 42/46 B, 43/83 A, 44/124 B, 45/78 A, 46/41 A and 47/57,

Welcoming the decision of the Antarctic Treaty Consultative Parties to submit to the Secretary-General the final report of the Seventeenth Antarctic Treaty Consultative Meeting, which took place at Venice, Italy, from 11 to 20 November 1992,

Conscious of the particular significance of Antarctica to the international community in terms, *inter alia*, of international peace and security, environment, its effects on global climate conditions, economy and scientific research,

Conscious also of the interrelationship between Antarctica and the physical, chemical and biological processes that regulate the total Earth system,

Welcoming the increasing recognition of the significant impact that Antarctica exerts on the global environment and ecosystems,

Welcoming also the recognition by the United Nations Conference on Environment and Development of the value of Antarctica as an area for the conduct of scientific research, in particular research essential to understanding the global environment,

Welcoming further the increasing support, including by some Antarctic Treaty Consultative Parties, for the establishment of Antarctica as a nature reserve or world park to ensure the protection and conservation of its environment and its dependent and associated ecosystems for the benefit of all mankind,

Welcoming the ongoing trend in acknowledging the need for internationally coordinated scientific research stations in Antarctica in order to minimize unnecessary duplication and logistical support facilities,

Welcoming also the increasing awareness of an interest in Antarctica shown by the international community, and convinced of the advantages to the whole of mankind of a better knowledge of Antarctica,

Reaffirming that the management and use of Antarctica should be conducted in accordance with the purposes and principles of the Charter of the United Nations and in the interest of maintaining international peace and security and of promoting international cooperation for the benefit of mankind as a whole,

Convinced of the need for concerted international cooperation in order to protect and safeguard Antarctica and its dependent ecosystems from external environmental disturbances for future generations,

1. *Takes note* of the report of the Secretary-General on the report of the Seventeenth Antarctic Treaty Consultative Meeting, which took place at Venice, Italy, from 11 to 20 November 1992;

2. *Welcomes* the report of the Secretary-General on the state of the environment in Antarctica, and requests the Secretary-General to explore the possibilities of publishing, as official documents of the United Nations, extracts of data received from the various organizations in the preparation of future annual reports, within existing resources;

3. *Reiterates* – while noting the cooperation of some United Nations specialized agencies and programmes at the Seventeenth Antarctic Treaty Consultative Meeting – the need for the Secretary-General or his representative to be invited to the meetings of the Antarctic Treaty Consultative Parties;

4. *Encourages* – while welcoming the decision of the Antarctic Treaty Consultative Parties to provide information regarding the Seventeenth Antarctic Treaty Consultative Meeting – the Parties to provide to the Secretary-General, on a continuing basis, more information and documents covering all aspects of Antarctica, and requests the Secretary-General to submit a report on his evaluations thereof to the General Assembly at its forty-ninth session;

5. *Welcomes* the commitment made by the Antarctic Treaty Consultative Parties under chapter 17 of Agenda 21, adopted by the United Nations Conference on Environment and Development, as provided for in article III of the Antarctic Treaty, to continue:

(a) To ensure that data and information resulting from scientific research activities conducted in Antarctica are freely available to the international community;

(b) To enhance access of the international scientific community and specialized agencies of the United Nations to such data and information, including the encouragement of periodic seminars and symposia;

6. *Urges* the Antarctic Treaty Consultative Parties to build on the agreements achieved at the United Nations Conference on Environment and Development, particularly as noted in paragraph 5 above, and, in this connection, actively to consider the possibility of organizing an

annual seminar/symposium covering issues relating to the environment, commencing in 1994, with international participation as wide as possible, including that of international organizations such as the United Nations;

7. *Also urges* the Antarctic Treaty Consultative Parties to establish monitoring and implementation mechanisms to ensure compliance with the provisions of the 1991 Madrid Protocol on Environmental Protection;

8. *Reiterates its call*, in welcoming the ban on prospecting and mining in and around Antarctica for the next fifty years by Antarctic Treaty Consultative Parties in accordance with the Madrid Protocol, for the ban to be made permanent;

9. *Also reiterates its call* that any move at drawing up an international convention to establish a nature reserve or world park in Antarctica and its dependent and associated ecosystems must be negotiated with the full participation of the international community;

10. *Reaffirms*, while welcoming the concrete steps taken by the Secretariat through the publication on Antarctica by the Department of Public Information, the need to promote further public awareness of the importance of Antarctica to the ecosystem, and in this regard requests the Secretary-General to continue to provide relevant materials on Antarctica through the Department of Public Information within existing resources;

11. *Encourages* the Antarctic Treaty Consultative Parties to increase the level of cooperation and collaboration with a view to reducing the number of scientific stations in Antarctica and to handle tourism effectively through transparent environmental impact assessment studies;

12. *Urges* the international community to ensure that all activities in Antarctica are carried out exclusively for the purpose of peaceful scientific investigation and that all such activities will ensure the maintenance of international peace and security and the protection of the Antarctic environment and are for the benefit of all mankind;

13. *Urges* all States Members of the United Nations to cooperate with the Secretary-General on matters pertaining to Antarctica;

14. *Decides* to include in the provisional agenda of its forty-ninth session the item entitled "Question of Antarctica".

81st plenary meeting
16 December 1993

UN General Assembly Resolution 49/80: Question of Antarctica (15 December 1994)

The General Assembly,

Having considered the item entitled "Question of Antarctica",

Taking into account the debates on this item held since its thirty-eighth session,

Reaffirming the interest of the international community in information on Antarctica,

Welcoming the provision by the Antarctic Treaty Consultative Parties to the Secretary-General of the final report of the Eighteenth Antarctic Treaty Consultative Meeting, held at Kyoto, Japan, from 11 to 22 April 1994,

Conscious of the particular significance of Antarctica to the international community, including for international peace and security, the global and regional environment, its effects on global and regional climate conditions, and scientific research,

Reaffirming that the management and use of Antarctica should be conducted in accordance with the purposes and principles of the Charter of the United Nations and in the interest of maintaining international peace and security and of promoting international cooperation for the benefit of mankind as a whole,

Recognizing that the Antarctic Treaty, which provides, *inter alia*, for the demilitarization of the continent, the prohibition of nuclear explosions and the disposal of nuclear wastes, the freedom of scientific research and the free exchange of scientific information, is in furtherance of the purposes and principles of the Charter,

Conscious also of the interrelationship between Antarctica and the physical, chemical and biological processes that regulate the total Earth system,

Taking into account the Protocol on Environmental Protection to the Antarctic Treaty, adopted by the Antarctic Treaty Parties at Madrid on 4 October 1991,

Welcoming the designation, in the Protocol, of Antarctica as a natural reserve devoted to peace and science and the procedures contained in the Protocol regarding the protection of the Antarctic environment and dependent and associated ecosystems in the planning and conduct of all activities in Antarctica,

Commending the prohibition on mineral resource activities contained in the Protocol,

Welcoming the recognition by the United Nations Conference on Environment and Development of the value of Antarctica as an area for the conduct of scientific research, in particular research essential to understanding the global environment,

Welcoming also the continuing cooperation among countries undertaking scientific research activities in Antarctica, which may help to minimize human impacts on the Antarctic environment,

Welcoming further the increasing awareness of an interest in Antarctica shown by the international community, and convinced of the advantages to the whole of mankind of a better knowledge of Antarctica,

Affirming its conviction that, in the interest of all mankind, Antarctica should continue forever to be used exclusively for peaceful purposes and that it should not become the scene or object of international discord,

1. *Takes note* of the report of the Secretary-General on Antarctica and on the report of the Eighteenth Antarctic Treaty Consultative Meeting, held at Kyoto, Japan, from 11 to 22 April 1994;

2. *Welcomes* the practice whereby the Antarctic Treaty Consultative Parties regularly provide the Secretary-General with information on their consultative meetings and on their activities in Antarctica, encourages the Parties to continue to provide to the Secretary-General and other interested States information on developments in relation to Antarctica, and requests the Secretary-General to submit that information in a report to the General Assembly at its fifty-first session;

3. *Notes* the role accorded by the Secretary-General to the United Nations Environment Programme in relation to Antarctic matters;

4. *Urges* the Antarctic Treaty Parties to extend invitations to the Executive Director of the United Nations Environment Programme to attend future consultative meetings in order to assist them in the substantive work;

5. *Welcomes* the statement under chapter 17 of Agenda 21, adopted by the United Nations Conference on Environment and Development, that States carrying out research activities in Antarctica should, as provided for in article III of the Antarctic Treaty, continue to:

(a) Ensure that data and information resulting from such research are freely available to the international community;

(b) Enhance access of the international scientific community and specialized agencies of the United Nations to such data and information, including the encouragement of periodic seminars and symposia;

6. *Urges* the Antarctic Treaty Consultative Parties to take into account in their deliberations the outcomes of the United Nations Conference on Environment and Development, particularly as noted in paragraph 5 above;

7. *Requests* the Antarctic Treaty Parties to continue to make available information on Antarctica as a means of promoting further public awareness of the importance of Antarctica to the global and regional environment;

8. *Urges* the Antarctic Treaty Parties to consider becoming parties as soon as possible to the Protocol on Environmental Protection to the Antarctic Treaty, and so bring the Protocol into

force, in order to ensure the implementation of strengthened measures for the protection of the Antarctic environment and dependent and associated ecosystems;

9. *Urges* countries whose nationals undertake activities in Antarctica to ensure that all such activities are carried out in a manner consistent with the principles of the Protocol;

10. *Decides* to include in the provisional agenda of its fifty-first session the item entitled "Question of Antarctica".

90th plenary meeting
15 December 1994

UN General Assembly Resolution 51/56: Question of Antarctica (10 December 1996)

The General Assembly,

Recalling its resolution 49/80 of 15 December 1994, in which it requested the Secretary-General to submit information provided by the Antarctic Treaty Consultative Parties on their consultative meetings and on their activities, and on developments in relation to Antarctica,

Taking into account the debates on the question of Antarctica held since its thirty-eighth session,

Conscious of the particular significance of Antarctica to the international community, including for international peace and security, the global and regional environment, its effects on global and regional climate conditions, and scientific research,

Reaffirming that the management and use of Antarctica should be conducted in accordance with the purposes and principles of the Charter of the United Nations and in the interest of maintaining international peace and security and of promoting international cooperation for the benefit of mankind as a whole,

Recognizing that the Antarctic Treaty, which provides, *inter alia*, for the demilitarization of the continent, the prohibition of nuclear explosions and the disposal of nuclear wastes, the freedom of scientific research and the free exchange of scientific information, is in furtherance of the purposes and principles of the Charter,

Recognizing also the designation, in the Protocol on Environmental Protection to the Antarctic Treaty, of Antarctica as a natural reserve devoted to peace and science and the provisions contained in the Protocol regarding the protection of the Antarctic environment and dependent and associated ecosystems, including for environmental assessment, in the planning and conduct of all activities in Antarctica,

Welcoming the continuing cooperation among countries undertaking scientific research activities in Antarctica, which may help to minimize human impacts on the Antarctic environment,

Welcoming also the increasing awareness of an interest in Antarctica shown by the international community, and convinced of the advantages to the whole of mankind of a better knowledge of Antarctica,

Reaffirming its conviction that, in the interest of all mankind, Antarctica should continue for ever to be used exclusively for peaceful purposes and that it should not become the scene or object of international discord,

1. *Takes note* of the report of the Secretary-General on the question of Antarctica and the role accorded by the Secretary-General to the United Nations Environment Programme in preparing his report, and also of the Nineteenth and Twentieth Antarctic Treaty Consultative Meetings, which took place at Seoul from 8 to 19 May 1995 and at Utrecht, the Netherlands, from 29 April to 10 May 1996, respectively;

2. *Recalls* the statement under chapter 17 of Agenda 21, adopted by the United Nations Conference on Environment and Development, that States carrying out research activities in Antarctica should, as provided for in article III of the Antarctic Treaty, continue:

(a) To ensure that data and information resulting from such research are freely available to the international community;

(b) To enhance the access of the international scientific community and the specialized agencies of the United Nations system to such data and information, including the encouragement of periodic seminars and symposia;

3. *Welcomes* the invitations to the Executive Director of the United Nations Environment Programme to attend Antarctic Treaty Consultative Meetings in order to assist such meetings in their substantive work, and urges the parties to continue to extend such invitations for future consultative meetings;

4. *Welcomes also* the practice whereby the Antarctic Treaty Consultative Parties regularly provide the Secretary-General with information on their consultative meetings and on their activities in Antarctica, and encourages the Parties to continue to provide the Secretary-General and other interested States with information on developments in relation to Antarctica, and requests the Secretary-General to submit a report which shall consist of that information to the General Assembly at its fifty-fourth session;

5. *Decides* to include in the provisional agenda of its fifty-fourth session the item entitled "Question of Antarctica".

79th plenary meeting
10 December 1996

UN General Assembly Resolution 54/45: Question of Antarctica (1 December 1999)

The General Assembly,

Recalling its resolution 51/56 of 10 December 1996, in which it requested the Secretary-General to submit a report consisting of the information provided by the Antarctic Treaty Consultative Parties on their consultative meetings and on their activities in Antarctica, and on developments in relation to Antarctica,

Taking into account the debates on the question of Antarctica held since its thirty-eighth session,

Conscious of the particular significance of Antarctica to the international community, including for international peace and security, the global and regional environment, its effects on global and regional climate conditions, and scientific research,

Reaffirming that the management and use of Antarctica should be conducted in accordance with the purposes and principles of the Charter of the United Nations and in the interest of maintaining international peace and security and of promoting international cooperation for the benefit of mankind as a whole,

Recognizing that the Antarctic Treaty, which provides, *inter alia*, for the demilitarization of the continent, the prohibition of nuclear explosions and the disposal of nuclear wastes, the freedom of scientific research and the free exchange of scientific information, is in furtherance of the purposes and principles of the Charter,

Welcoming the entry into force of the Protocol on Environmental Protection to the Antarctic Treaty on 14 January 1998, under which Antarctica has been designated as a natural reserve, devoted to peace and science, and the provisions contained in the Protocol regarding the protection of the Antarctic environment and dependent and associated ecosystems, including the need for environmental impact assessment in the planning and conduct of all relevant activities in Antarctica,

Welcoming also the continuing cooperation among countries undertaking scientific research activities in Antarctica, which may help to minimize human impact on the Antarctic environment,

Welcoming further the increasing awareness of an interest in Antarctica shown by the international community, and convinced of the advantages to the whole of mankind of a better knowledge of Antarctica,

Reaffirming its conviction that, in the interest of all mankind, Antarctica should continue for ever to be used exclusively for peaceful purposes and that it should not become the scene or object of international discord,

1. *Takes note* of the report of the Secretary-General on the question of Antarctica and the role accorded by the Secretary-General to the United Nations Environment Programme in preparing his report and also of the Twenty-first, Twenty-second and Twenty-third Antarctic Treaty Consultative Meetings, which were held at Christchurch, New Zealand, from 19 to 30 May 1997, at Tromso, Norway, from 25 May to 5 June 1998, and at Lima, from 24 May to 4 June 1999, respectively;

2. *Recalls* the statement under chapter 17 of Agenda 21, adopted by the United Nations Conference on Environment and Development, that States carrying out research activities in Antarctica should, as provided for in article III of the Antarctic Treaty, continue:

(a) To ensure that data and information resulting from such research are freely available to the international community;

(b) To enhance the access of the international scientific community and the specialized agencies of the United Nations system to such data and information, including the encouragement of periodic seminars and symposia;

3. *Welcomes* the invitations to the Executive Director of the United Nations Environment Programme to attend Antarctic Treaty Consultative Meetings in order to assist such meetings in their substantive work, and urges the parties to continue to do so for future consultative meetings;

4. *Welcomes also* the practice whereby the Antarctic Treaty Consultative Parties regularly provide the Secretary-General with information on their consultative meetings and on their activities in Antarctica, and encourages the parties to continue to provide the Secretary-General and interested States with information on developments in relation to Antarctica, and requests the Secretary-General to submit a report which shall consist of that information to the General Assembly at its fifty-seventh session;

5. *Decides* to include in the provisional agenda of its fifty-seventh session the item entitled "Question of Antarctica".

69th plenary meeting
1 December 1999

UN General Assembly Resolution 55/33: General and complete disarmament (12 January 2001)

…

I

Nuclear-Weapon-Free Southern Hemisphere and Adjacent Areas

The General Assembly,

Recalling its resolutions 51/45 B of 10 December 1996, 52/38 N of 9 December 1997, 53/77 Q of 4 December 1998 and 54/54 L of 1 December 1999,

Welcoming the adoption by the Disarmament Commission at its 1999 substantive session of a text entitled "Establishment of nuclear-weapon-free zones on the basis of arrangements freely arrived at among the States of the region concerned",

Determined to pursue the total elimination of nuclear weapons,

Determined also to continue to contribute to the prevention of the proliferation of nuclear weapons in all its aspects and to the process of general and complete disarmament under strict and effective international control, in particular in the field of nuclear weapons and other weapons of mass destruction, with a view to strengthening international peace and security, in accordance with the purposes and principles of the Charter of the United Nations,

Recalling the provisions on nuclear-weapon-free zones of the Final Document of the Tenth Special Session of the General Assembly, the first special session devoted to disarmament,

Stressing the importance of the treaties of Tlatelolco, Rarotonga, Bangkok and Pelindaba, establishing nuclear-weapon-free zones, as well as the Antarctic Treaty, to, inter alia, achieve a world entirely free of nuclear weapons,

Underlining the value of enhancing cooperation among the nuclear-weapon free zone treaty members by means of mechanisms such as joint meetings of States parties, signatories and observers to those treaties,

Recalling the applicable principles and rules of international law relating to the freedom of the high seas and the rights of passage through maritime space, including those of the United Nations Convention on the Law of the Sea,

1. *Welcomes* the continued contribution that the Antarctic and the treaties of Tlatelolco, Rarotonga, Bangkok and Pelindaba are making towards freeing the southern hemisphere and adjacent areas covered by those treaties from nuclear weapons;

2. *Calls* for the ratification of the treaties of Tlatelolco, Rarotonga, Bangkok and Pelindaba by all States of the region concerned, and calls upon all concerned States to continue to work together in order to facilitate adherence to the protocols to nuclear-weapon-free zone treaties by all relevant States that have not yet done so;

3. *Welcomes* the steps taken to conclude further nuclear-weapon-free zone treaties on the basis of arrangements freely arrived at among the States of the region concerned, and calls upon all States to consider all relevant proposals, including those reflected in its resolutions on the establishment of nuclear-weapon-free zones in the Middle East and South Asia;

4. *Convinced* of the important role of nuclear-weapon-free zones in strengthening the nuclear non-proliferation regime and in extending the areas of the world that are nuclear-weapon-free, and, with particular reference to the responsibilities of the nuclear-weapon States, calls upon all States to support the process of nuclear disarmament and to work for the total elimination of all nuclear weapons;

5. *Calls upon* the States parties and signatories to the treaties of Tlatelolco, Rarotonga, Bangkok and Pelindaba, in order to pursue the common goals envisaged in those treaties and to promote the nuclear-weapon-free status of the southern hemisphere and adjacent areas, to explore and implement further ways and means of cooperation among themselves and their treaty agencies;

6. *Welcomes* the vigorous efforts being made among States parties and signatories to those treaties to promote their common objectives, and considers that an international conference of States parties and signatories to the nuclear-weapon free zone treaties might be held to support the common goals envisaged in those treaties;

7. *Encourages* the competent authorities of the nuclear-weapon-free zone treaties to provide assistance to the States parties and signatories to such treaties so as to facilitate the accomplishment of these goals;

8. *Decides* to include in the provisional agenda of its fifty-sixth session the item entitled "Nuclear-weapon-free southern hemisphere and adjacent areas".

See similarly:

GA Resolution 58/49: Nuclear free southern hemisphere and adjacent areas (8 January 2004)

UN General Assembly Resolution 57/51: Question of Antarctica

The General Assembly,

Recalling its resolution 54/45 of 1 December 1999, in which it requested the Secretary-General to submit a report consisting of the information provided by the Antarctic Treaty Consultative Parties on their consultative meetings and on their activities in Antarctica, and on developments in relation to Antarctica,

Taking into account the debates on the question of Antarctica held since its thirty-eighth session,

Conscious of the particular significance of Antarctica to the international community, including for international peace and security, the global and regional environment, its effects on global and regional climate conditions, and scientific research,

Reaffirming that the management and use of Antarctica should be conducted in accordance with the purposes and principles of the Charter of the United Nations and in the interest of maintaining international peace and security and of promoting international cooperation for the benefit of mankind as a whole,

Recognizing that the Antarctic Treaty, which provides, inter alia, for the demilitarization of the continent, the prohibition of nuclear explosions and the disposal of nuclear wastes, the freedom of scientific research and the free exchange of scientific information, is in furtherance of the purposes and principles of the Charter,

Noting with satisfaction the entry into force of the Protocol on Environmental Protection to the Antarctic Treaty on 14 January 1998, under which Antarctica has been designated as a natural reserve, devoted to peace and science, and the provisions contained in the Protocol regarding the protection of the Antarctic environment and dependent and associated ecosystems, including the need for environmental impact assessment in the planning and conduct of all relevant activities in Antarctica,

Welcoming the continuing cooperation among countries undertaking scientific research activities in Antarctica, which may help to minimize human impact on the Antarctic environment,

Welcoming also the increasing awareness of and interest in Antarctica shown by the international community, and convinced of the advantages to the whole of mankind of a better knowledge of Antarctica,

Reaffirming its conviction that, in the interest of all mankind, Antarctica should continue for ever to be used exclusively for peaceful purposes and that it should not become the scene or object of international discord,

1. *Takes note* of the report of the Secretary-General on the question of Antarctica and the role accorded by the Secretary-General to the United Nations Environment Programme in preparing his report, and also of the Twelfth Special Antarctic Treaty Consultative Meeting, held in The Hague from 11 to 15 September 2000, the Twenty-fourth Antarctic Treaty Consultative Meeting, held in St. Petersburg, Russian Federation, from 9 to 20 July 2001, and the Twenty-fifth Antarctic Treaty Consultative Meeting, held in Warsaw from 10 to 20 September 2002;

2. *Recalls* the statement under chapter 17 of Agenda 21, adopted by the United Nations Conference on Environment and Development, that States carrying out research activities in Antarctica should, as provided for in article III of the Antarctic Treaty, continue:

(a) To ensure that data and information resulting from such research are freely available to the international community;

(b) To enhance the access of the international scientific community and the specialized agencies of the United Nations system to such data and information, including the encouragement of periodic seminars and symposia;

3. *Welcomes* the invitations to the Executive Director of the United Nations Environment Programme to attend Antarctic Treaty Consultative Meetings in order to assist such meetings

in their substantive work, and urges the parties to continue to do so for future consultative meetings;

4. *Welcomes also* the practice whereby the Antarctic Treaty Consultative Parties regularly provide the Secretary-General with information on their consultative meetings and on their activities in Antarctica, and encourages the parties to continue to provide the Secretary-General and interested States with information on developments in relation to Antarctica, and requests the Secretary-General to submit a report which shall consist of that information to the General Assembly at its sixtieth session;

5. *Decides* to include in the provisional agenda of its sixtieth session the item entitled "Question of Antarctica".

57th plenary meeting
22 November 2002

UN General Assembly Resolution 60/47: Question of Antarctica

The General Assembly,

Recalling its resolution 57/51 of 22 November 2002, in which it requested the Secretary-General to submit a report consisting of the information provided by the Antarctic Treaty Consultative Parties on their consultative meetings, on their activities in Antarctica and on developments in relation to Antarctica,

Taking into account the debates on the question of Antarctica held since its thirty-eighth session,

Conscious of the particular significance of Antarctica to the international community, including for international peace and security, the global and regional environment, its effects on global and regional climate conditions, and scientific research,

Reaffirming that the management and use of Antarctica should be conducted in accordance with the purposes and principles of the Charter of the United Nations and in the interest of maintaining international peace and security and of promoting international cooperation for the benefit of mankind as a whole,

Recognizing that the Antarctic Treaty, which provides, inter alia, for the demilitarization of the continent, the prohibition of nuclear explosions and the disposal of nuclear wastes, the freedom of scientific research and the free exchange of scientific information, is in furtherance of the purposes and principles of the Charter,

Noting with satisfaction the entry into force of the Protocol on Environmental Protection to the Antarctic Treaty on 14 January 1998, under which Antarctica has been designated as a natural reserve, devoted to peace and science, and the provisions contained in the Protocol regarding the protection of the Antarctic environment and dependent and associated ecosystems, including the need for environmental impact assessment in the planning and conduct of all relevant activities in Antarctica,

Welcoming the continuing cooperation among countries undertaking scientific research activities in Antarctica, which may help to minimize human impact on the Antarctic environment,

Welcoming also the increasing awareness of and interest in Antarctica shown by the international community, and convinced of the advantages to the whole of mankind of a better knowledge of Antarctica,

Welcoming further the secretariat of the Antarctic Treaty, established in Buenos Aires, which became operational as of 1 September 2004,

Reaffirming its conviction that, in the interest of all mankind, Antarctica should continue forever to be used exclusively for peaceful purposes and that it should not become the scene or object of international discord,

1. *Takes note* of the report of the Secretary-General on the question of Antarctica and the role

accorded by the Secretary-General to the United Nations Environment Programme in preparing his report, and also of the Twenty-sixth Antarctic Treaty Consultative Meeting, held in Madrid from 9 to 20 June 2003, the Twenty-seventh Antarctic Treaty Consultative Meeting, held in Cape Town, South Africa, from 24 May to 4 June 2004, and the Twenty-eighth Antarctic Treaty Consultative Meeting, held in Stockholm from 6 to 17 June 2005;

2. *Recalls* the statement under chapter 17 of Agenda 21, adopted by the United Nations Conference on Environment and Development, that States carrying out research activities in Antarctica should, as provided for in article III of the Antarctic Treaty, continue:

(a) To ensure that data and information resulting from such research are freely available to the international community;

(b) To enhance the access of the international scientific community and the specialized agencies of the United Nations system to such data and information, including the encouragement of periodic seminars and symposiums;

3. *Welcomes* the invitations to the Executive Director of the United Nations Environment Programme to attend Antarctic Treaty Consultative Meetings in order to assist such meetings in their substantive work, and urges the parties to continue to do so for future consultative meetings;

4. *Welcomes also* the practice whereby the Antarctic Treaty Consultative Parties regularly provide the Secretary-General with information on their consultative meetings and on their activities in Antarctica, and encourages the parties to continue to provide the Secretary-General and interested States with information on those meetings, activities and developments in relation to Antarctica;

5. *Decides* to remain seized of the matter.

61st plenary meeting
8 December 2005

PART 9
OTHER UNITED NATIONS DOCUMENTS

India, Explanatory Memorandum: Request for the Inclusion of an Item on Antarctica on the 11th Session of the UN General Assembly, 16 October 1956, UN Doc A/3118/Add.2

Antarctica, a region covering about six million square miles of territory, has considerable strategic, climatic and geophysical significance for the world as a whole. With the development of rapid communications, the area might shortly come to have further practical significance to the welfare and progress of nations. The mineral wealth of the land mass is believed to be considerable and its coastal waters contain important food resources.

The growing interest in Antarctica is manifesting itself in the face that a considerable number of recent expeditions sent by various nations have been or are at work in the area. Furthermore, these activities are to be intensified in the course of the International Geophysical Year, commencing July 1957 and in the preparations preceding it. One typical consequence will be that the number of observation posts in this area will be more than doubled by 1957.

Modern science is likely to reveal many possibilities for the peaceful utilization of a region hitherto regarded as unproductive. At the same time the influence of Antarctica on climatic and related conditions throughout the world, while obviously considerable, requires further study. Any disturbance of the equilibrium of natural forces in this area might lead to incalculable consequences for the rest of the world as a whole, involving the deterioration of the conditions for human and other forms of animal and plant life. In view of these facts and bearing in mind the size of the area, its international importance and the growing interest in it, the Government of India considers that in order to strengthen the universal peace it would be appropriate and timely for all nations to agree and to affirm that the area will be utilized entirely for peaceful purposes and for the general welfare. All nations should agree further to harmonize their actions to these ends and to ensure also that no activities in Antarctica will adversely affect climatic and other natural conditions.

The Government of India accordingly suggests that the General Assembly of the United Nations should call upon all States to agree to and affirm the peaceful utilization of Antarctica for the general welfare and in particular to agree that the area shall not be used in any manner that would create or accentuate world tensions, or extend to this area the influence and effects of existing tensions.

Chilean Memorandum Opposing the Indian Proposal, 4 October 1956[1]

Dated the 20th of February of this year, the Permanent Representative of India before the United Nations presented to the Secretary-General a note whereby his government requested the inclusion of the topic 'The Antarctic Question' in the provisional program of the XI ordinary period of sessions of the General Assembly. On the 13th of September, that Delegation officially requested the Secretary-General the title of the topic to be replaced with words that embraced the meaning 'Peaceful Use of the Antarctic', and, in accordance with Article 20 of the Rules of the General Assembly, his request was accompanied by the Explanatory Memorandum which reads as follows: ....

[1] Reproduced from W.M. Bush, Antarctica and International Law: A Collection of Inter-state and National Documents, vol. II (Oceana Publications, New York, 1991), 502–504 (translated from Spanish). By Permission of Oxford University Press, USA.

The Government of the Republic of Chile thinks highly of the humanitarian and altruistic sentiments which have guided the Government of India to propose the peaceful use of Antarctica, but is of the opinion that that request has the following implications: that it concerns the territorial sovereignty of Chile; that it accepts the jurisdiction of the United Nations, or of any other organisation, to examine and resolve the matter, and finally, that it has an impact on the international order of America, of which Antarctica is a natural prolongation.

Regarding the first point, the Government of Chile notes that in the year 1940, a Supreme Decree that specified the limits of the Chilean Antarctic Territory or Chilean Antarctic was issued through the Ministry of Foreign Affairs. This measure was adopted after a very comprehensive study of all the titles that Chile possesses and checking numerous documents about the historical, geographical, legal, diplomatic and administrative order, that are conserved in the Chilean Chancellery and in other offices of State. The text of Supreme Decree No 1747, dated 6 November 1940, reads as follows: …

The Ministry of Foreign Affairs would like to call the attention of the Member States of the United Nations towards the circumstance that Decree No 1747, does not create titles in favour of Chile above the aforesaid polar icecap, nor tried in another way to create them, but was issued only by virtue of existing titles. It was never the intent then to extend the dominion or to create a new right beyond those that Chile, from time immemorial, has possessed.

Consequently, the Government of Chile is not able to accept the Indian proposal which plainly and simply concerns territories which include the Antarctic sector, in which Chile exercises indisputable rights of possession, dominion and sovereignty.

As possessor of this territory, comprised between the meridians 53° and 90° east of Greenwich, and legitimate holder, supported by various authentic and incontestable titles, the Government of Chile has the right to exercise in it all its own acts of sovereignty and of dominion and, consequently, within the measures that a sovereign and independent country can adopt within its own territory, only the Government of Chile, in the region covered by its Antarctic sector, has the responsibility to ensure that the said territory will be used for peaceful ends, a humanitarian duty that, on the other hand, is implicit in the laws that should inform the international conduct of all nations that, calling themselves friends of peace, have adhered to the Charter of the Organisation.

In respect of the second point, it is worth expressing that the personality of States, their structure as well as their territoriality, are not subject to the domain of international affairs, the basis of which is precisely the due respect and intangibility of those elements. An international order would not be possible if the use and enjoyment of the territory of a state was able to be the object of examination by any organ or entity.

It is not possible, then, for the Government of India to invoke the peaceful sentiments of the Member States of the United Nations in order to obtain the acquiescence of Chile to raise the issue of the peaceful use of the Antarctic to an examination and decision on the part of the General Assembly, because this interference would affect a zone that forms part of the territory of the Republic of Chile and, for this reason, would fall into a matter that is essentially in the exclusive competence of States.

In the Charter of the United Nations, which binds both the Government of Chile and the Government of India, Article 2(7) of Chapter 1 states that 'Nothing contained in the present Charter shall authorize the United Nations to intervene in matters which are essentially within the domestic jurisdiction of any state…'.

The Government of Chile firmly believes that it is not possible to undervalue or exclude the basic principle of non-intervention, even for considerations as lofty as those put forward by the Government of India, without running the risk of affecting precisely the harmony and rationality that ought to reign among the countries of the United Nations, nor putting to the test the whole gradually-built moral, legal and political framework in which the world Organisation stands.

With respect to the international American order, the Government of the Republic of Chile points out that neither the spirit nor the letter of the Treaty of Reciprocal Assistance, signed in Rio de Janeiro in 1947, which sets a zone of security for our continent which includes the South American Antarctic, is able to be reconciled or harmonised with the Indian proposal, given that in order for it to take form it would presuppose making provisions that may affect an important treaty subscribed in accordance with Chapter VIII of the Charter.

On the other hand, the Government of Chile is fully convinced that, notwithstanding the good purposes that motivate India, there will always exist the possibility that even the mere examination of the topic concerning the peaceful use of Antarctica, will lead to possible inconvenient political diversions, that it is necessary to avoid.

The Government of Chile, while expressing its disagreement with the Indian proposal, is pleased to add that it is not part of its purposes the intent to oppose an agreement with other States in the sense that the Antarctic zone not be used in any manner that could begin, extend or deepen world tension. Indeed, as it was made known in an Official Declaration dated 29 October 1948, the Government of Chile, in keeping with its peaceful tradition that highlights reasons to be proud, stated that it is willing to consider a method that will aim to avoid any friction between friendly countries over the Antarctic continent. This possible solution would be based in direct agreement between States with legitimate interests in the region, outside of the framework of the international Organisations.

Finally, in light of the considerations that have been expressed in the present Memorandum, the Government of Chile trusts that the addition of the topic 'Peaceful use of the Antarctic' proposed by India will not be accepted in the program of the XI General Assembly of the United Nations.

Santiago, 4 October 1956.

Report of the Secretary-General, Question of Antarctica: Physical, Legal, Political, Economic and Scientific Aspects, Study Requested under General Assembly Resolution 38/77, UN Doc A/39/583 (Part I) (31 October 1984)[2]

Chapter II
Antarctica Legal and Political Aspects

A. Sovereignty Issue

11. The discoveries made by the explorers in Antarctica in the nineteenth century, who reached different parts of the continent and mapped them, opened the era of the scientific exploration in Antarctica and the commercial exploitation of its marine resources, mainly seals and whales, by United States, British, Russian, Norwegian, French and other vessels.

12. In the second half of the nineteenth century those activities increased the possibility of gaining access to some of the distant parts of the area and led States to consider seriously their national interests in Antarctica. Those national interests encouraged a number of countries to advance territorial claims in Antarctica. Since the beginning of the twentieth century, seven nations – Australia, Argentina, Chile, France, New Zealand, Norway and the United Kingdom of Great Britain and Northern Ireland – have made their respective formal, unilateral, territorial claims to parts of Antarctica in both national legislation and in international statements (figure 1).

13. Australia claims the largest area in Antarctica, approximately two fifths of the continent.[3] The claim comprises two sectors south of 60°S latitude, separated by the area claimed by France. The first is located between 45° and 136°E longitude and the second, between 142° and 160°E longitude.

[2] pp. 13–38 and 44–71.

[3] The United Kingdom ceded the rights to these territories to Australia on 7 February 1933 by an Order in Council. These rights were then confirmed by the Australian Antarctic Territory Acceptance Act of 13 June 1933. See British and Foreign State Papers, 1933, vol. CXXXVI, p. 293.

14. Argentina's claim in Antarctica encompasses the area between 25° and 74°W longitude, extending from the South Pole to the 60th parallel.[4]

15. Chile's claim in Antarctica, in accordance with Presidential Decree No. 1747 of 6 November 1940 marking the frontier lines for the area claimed, "is formed by all lands, islands, islets, reefs, pack-ice, etc., known and to be discovered, and their respective territorial sea, lying within the limit of the sector constituted by meridians of 53° am 90°W longitude".[5] [6]

16. France lays claim in Antarctica to Terre Adélie (Adelie Land), discovered by Dumont d'Urville in 1840. This area is located between 136° and 142°E longitude south of the 60° parallel.[7]

17. New Zealand's claim in Antarctica embraces the area between 160°E longitude and 150°W longitude south of the 60° parallel.[8]

18. Norway makes a claim in Antarctica over Dronning (Queen) Maud Land, situated between 20°W longitude and 45°E longitude.[9] It borders territories claimed by the United Kingdom in the west and by Australia in the east. The limits of the Norwegian claim to the north and to the south are not defined.

19. The claim of the United Kingdom in Antarctica encompasses "all islands and territories situated between longitudes 20° and 50° west, and south of latitude 50° south, and all islands and territories situated between longitudes 50° and 80° west, and south of latitude 58° south".[10]

20. All territorial claims in Antarctica are actually wedge-shaped. The claims of Argentina, Chile and the United Kingdom overlap at the Antarctic Peninsula. About 15 per cent of the Antarctic continent remains unclaimed.

21. The legal grounds on which the seven aforementioned States base their claims vary, being combinations of such arguments and principles as discovery, occupation, contiguity, inherited rights, geological affinity and geographical proximity, formal acts of taking possession, performance of administrative acts, the sector concept etc.[11]

22. Thus, the Government of the United Kingdom, for example, in submitting its application in 1955 to the International Court of Justice contended, *inter alia*, that the legal titles of the United Kingdom to relevant territories in Antarctica were superior to the claims of any other State:

---

[4] Decreto 8944 del 2 de septiembre de 1946, *Boletin Oficial* del 19 de noviembre de 1946; and Decreto 292191 del 28 febrero de 1957, *Boletin Oficial* del 19 de marzo de 1957.

[5] Pinochet de la Barra, *La Antarctica Chilena* (Santiago, 1944), pp. 23–24.

[6] See A/38/PV.3 and 16. See also M. M. Whiteman, *Digest of International Law* (Washington D.C., 1963), vol. 11, p. 1260.

[7] France laid claim to Adelie Land by a presidential Decree of 27 March 1924. The boundaries of the areas claimed by France were established by Decree of 1 April 1938. See part two of the present study, reply of the Government of France (A/39/583 (Part II), vol. II).

[8] The United Kingdom ceded to New Zealand the rights to this area, known as the Ross Dependency, on 30 July 1923 by an Order in Council. See *British and Foreign State Papers*, 1923, vol. XVIII, p. 91. The Order in Council vested in the New Zealand Governor-General executive and legislative power in respect of the Ross Dependency. Acting pursuant to this Order, the Governor, on 14 November 1923, made regulations respecting the Ross Dependency which had the effect of adopting as the law of the Ross Dependency all future enactments of the New Zealand Parliament Dependency. For more details, see part two of the present study, reply of the Government of New Zealand.

[9] "Proclamation of King Haakon of Norway", 14 January 1939. See *British and Foreign State Papers*, 1939, vol. CIVIII, p. 663. See also part two of the present study, reply of the Government of Norway (a/39/583) (Part II), volume III).

[10] International Court of Justice, "Antarctica Cases" (United Kingdom v. Argentina; United Kingdom v. Chile), Pleadings, Oral Arguments, Documents, 1956, pp. 15, 16, 39–41.

[11] See Russell W. MacKechnie, "Sovereignty in Antarctica: The Anglo-Argentine Dispute", *Syracuse Journal of International Law and Commerce*, vol. 5:119 (1977), pp. 119–148; Christopher C. Joyner, "The Exclusive Economic Zone and Antarctica", *Virginia Journal of International Law*, vol. 21:4 (1981), pp. 704–711; Barbara Mitchell and Richard Sandbrook "The Management of the Southern Ocean", (International Institute for Environment and Development, London, 1980), p. 6; and Evan Luard, "Who owns the Antarctic?", *Foreign Affairs*, vol. 62, No. 5, (1984), pp. 1177–1178. For the more precise information on the grounds put forward by each claimant country, see also part two of the present study, replies submitted by the Governments of Australia, Argentina, Chile, France, New Zealand, Norway and the United Kingdom.

"by reason of historic British discoveries of certain territories in the Antarctic and sub-Antarctic, by reason of the long-continued and peaceful display of British sovereignty from the date of those discoveries onwards in, and in regard to, the territories concerned, by reason of the incorporation of these territories in the dominions of the British Crown, by virtue of their formal constitution in the Royal Letters Patent of 1908 and 1917 as the British Possession".[12]

23. An official statement from Argentina on the issue dated 20 February 1953 asserted that:

"Argentine ... sovereignty [over Antarctica] is based ... in the aggregate of the historical antecedents of its titles – maintained firmly in all circumstances by the Argentine Government [and] spiritually identified with the feeling of the nation's entire population, in the insuperable geographical portion of the Republic, in the geological continuity of its land with the Antarctic lands, in the climatological influence that the neighboring polar zones exercise over its territories, in the rights of first occupancy; in the pertinent diplomatic measures; and, finally, in its uninterrupted activity in the same Antarctic terrain."[13]

24. The declaration of the Government of Chile made on 11 September 1950 states that:

"The Chilean Government has proclaimed repeatedly its right to a certain sector of the Antarctic continent, called the Chilean Antarctic. In that sector, the Republic exercises sovereignty by right and in fact with prior claim over any other power. This claim is supported by logical geographic continuity and contiguity, and furthermore there have been carried out, in addition to actual permanent occupation (of the territory), acts of government and administration that furnish evidence to the international community of the absolute validity of Chile's rights."[14]

25. The major political difficulty faced from the very beginning by the claimant States was that other States, in particular those active in the area, refused to recognize those claims.

26. For example, the United States of America and the Union of Soviet Socialist Republics at the outset categorically rejected the possibility of recognizing any territorial claim in Antarctica. Nevertheless, it should be noted that although neither State has ever made a formal claim to Antarctica, at the same time each has reserved its rights to Antarctic territories based on discoveries and explorations made by Russian and United States scientists and explorers.

27. Thus, when Norway annexed Queen Maud Land in Antarctica in 1939 the Soviet Union sent a note stating that "it would reserve its opinion as to the national status of territories discovered by Russian scientists".[15]

28. At a certain stage, members of the United States Antarctic Service were encouraged to take and record appropriate acts that might later assist the United States in supporting a sovereignty claim.

29. The instructions given in 1939 by President Roosevelt to the Commanding Officer of the United States Antarctic Service contained the following paragraphs:

"(f) The United States has never recognized any claims to sovereignty over territory in the Antarctic regions asserted by any foreign state. No member of the United States Antarctic Service shall take any action or make any statements tending to compromise this position.

"Members of the Service may take any appropriate steps such as dropping written claims from airplanes, depositing such writings in cairns, et cetera, which might assist in supporting a sovereignty claim by the United States Government. Careful record shall be kept of the circumstances surrounding each such act. No public announcement of the act shall, however, be made without specific authority in each case from the Secretary of State."[16]

[12] International Court of Justice, "Antarctic Cases", p. 37.

[13] Quoted in Joyner, "The Exclusive Economic Zone and Antarctica", p. 705.

[14] Quoted in Whiteman, *Digest of International Law*, pp. 1257–1258.

[15] See part two of the present study, reply of the Government of Soviet Socialist Republics (A/39/583 (Part II), vol. III). See also John Hanessian, "The Antarctic Treaty, 1959", *International and Comparative Law Quarterly*, vol. 9, p. 439. The Norwegian act met also with objection from Chile, Germany and the United States. See Finn Solle, "The Antarctic Treaty System: the Political Problem and Potential Resource Development", p. 11.

[16] Quoted in Whiteman, *Digest of International Law*, p. 1248.

30. The Acting United States Secretary of State, in a latter dated 14 December 1946 to the Secretary of the Navy, recommended that:

"In order that the maximum advantage in this regard may be gained for the United States from the activities of the Naval Antarctic Developments Project, I suggest that you authorize the expedition to take appropriate steps, such as depositing written claims in cairns, dropping from airplanes containers enclosing such written claims, etc., which might assist in supporting a claim of sovereignty by the United States Government and that you give instructions to the officers in charge of the expedition to keep a careful record of the circumstances surrounding each act. I suggest that no public announcement with respect to these activities should be made without prior specific authorization in each case from you after clearance with the Department of state."[17]

31. After the Second World War, both the United States and the Soviet Union supported, and in the case of the United States even initiated, discussions aimed at elaborating an international agreement for Antarctica with a view to establishing there some form of international régime. Nevertheless, on certain occasions both States felt it necessary to reiterate their reserved rights in Antarctica.

32. In a note dated 2 May 1958 from the Government of the United States, proposing the international conference on Antarctica that eventually resulted in the adoption of the Antarctic Treaty, it was reiterated that:

"The United States for many years had had, and at the present time continues to have, direct and substantial rights and interests in Antarctica. Throughout a period of many years, commencing in the early eighteen-hundreds, many areas of the Antarctic region have been discovered, sighted, explored and claimed on behalf of the United States by nationals of the United States and by expeditions carrying the flag of the United States. During this period, the Government of the United States and its nationals have engaged in well-known and extensive activities in Antarctica.

"In view of the activities of the United States and its nationals referred to above, my Government reserves all of the rights of the United States with respect to the Antarctic region, including the right to assert a territorial claim or claims."[18]

33. In reply to that note the Government of the Soviet Union stated:

"As to the question of territorial claims advanced by certain states in the Antarctic, the Soviet Government considers it necessary to state once again that it has not recognize and cannot recognize as legitimate any kind of separate solution for the problem of territorial possessions in [state sovereignty over] the Antarctic. In this connection it is appropriate to recall the outstanding merits of Russian explorers in discovering the Antarctic and, in particular, the generally recognized fact that it was the Russian navigators Bellingshausen and Lazarev who were the first to reach the shores of the Antarctic and circumnavigate this continent at the beginning of the 19th century.

"The Soviet Union reserves to itself all rights based on discoveries and explorations of Russian navigators and scientists, including the right to present corresponding territorial claims in the Antarctic."[19]

[17] Ibid, p. 1249.

[18] Ibid, p. 1250.

[19] See *Pravda*, 4 June 1958. The synthesis of the position of the Government of the Soviet Union was first fully presented in the memorandum dated 8 June 1950 to the United States Department of State, which stated that:

"... the Soviet Government deems it necessary to call to mind the outstanding services rendered by Russian navigators in discovering the Antarctic. It is a universally recognized fact that at the beginning of the nineteenth century the Russian voyagers Bellingshausen and Lazarev were the first to reach the shores of the Antarctic and circumnavigate this continent, thereby proving that the widespread view existing at that time to the effect that there was allegedly no land beyond the South Polar Circle was erroneous. This served rendered by the Russian navigators is no less important than the explorations conducted later on the continent itself and around its shores by expeditions of certain countries whose representatives now declare their interest in defining the regime in the Antarctic." See *Pravda*, 10 June 1950.

34. With regard to the position of Japan, once considered a potential claimant State,[20] it should be noted that, by the Treaty of Peace concluded in San Francisco on 8 September 1951, "Japan renounces all claim to any right or title to or interest in connection with any part of the Antarctic area, whether deriving from the activities of Japanese nationals or otherwise."[21]

35. Non-recognition of territorial claims inevitably led to tension. Confrontation in Antarctica between claimant States and States refusing to recognize these claims, supplemented by the conflict among the United Kingdom, Argentina and Chile over their overlapping claims, started sparking more and more political controversy after the end of the Second World War when the States concerned were able to pay more attention to their respective interests in Antarctica.

36. In the immediate post-war period, rivalry among three States with conflicting claims led to a number of serious incidents when flags were torn down, stations destroyed and rival expeditions sent to the same areas.[22]

37. In one incident, commemorative bronze plaques installed in 1942 on Deception and Wiencke islands by the expedition of the Argentinian ship *Primero de Mayo* were removed a year later by the members of the British warship H.M.S. *Carnavon Castle*. Crewmen of the British warship also removed the national colours of Argentina from the walls of the former whaling factory located on Deception Island.[23]

38. Each of the three countries, Argentina, Chile and the United Kingdom, actively proceeded in establishing or re-establishing stations and posts in the area under the dispute. That led to the mutual exchange of protests through diplomatic channels.

39. Despite their disagreement, Argentina and Chile succeeded in signing on 4 March 1948 the Joint Declaration on the Antarctic, stating that "until a friendly agreement is concluded concerning the common boundary line of the Antarctic territories of Chile and the Argentine Republic", both Governments "will act in common accord in the juridical protection and defense of their rights in the South American Antarctic, which is included between the 25th and 90th meridians of longitude west of Greenwich, and in these territories Chile and the Argentine Republic mutually recognize indisputable rights of sovereignty". The Parties to the Joint Declaration agreed that they would "continue their action of administration, exploitation, supervision and development in the undefined frontier region of their respective Antarctic zones"[24] and that they would continue negotiations with a view to arriving at agreement on the demarcation of boundaries in Antarctica.

40. In order to avoid the danger of an open military conflict in Antarctica, the United Kingdom, Argentina and Chile agreed on a Tripartee Naval Declaration, the substance of which was disclosed in the following statement made by the Foreign Office on 18 January 1949:

"Being anxious to avoid any misunderstanding in Antarctica which might affect the friendly relations between the United Kingdom, Argentina and Chile, the Governments of these three countries have informed each other that, in present circumstances, they foresee no need to send warships south of latitude 60 degrees during the 1948–49 Antarctic season, apart, of course, from routine movements such as have been customary for a number of years."[25]

Until 1957 the Declaration was renewed annually by the three countries.

---

[20] With respect to Chilean Decree No. 1747 marking frontier lines of the territories claimed by Chile in Antarctica, the Japanese note verbale dated 13 November 1940 stated that "Japan considers itself one of the countries which have an interest and rights in the said zone, for which reason it reserved the right to assert its point of view in this matter". See Whiteman, *Digest of International Law*, p. 1260.

[21] Quoted in Whiteman, *Digest of International Law*, p. 1261.

[22] Luard, "Who owns the Antarctic?", p. 1178.

[23] See International Court of Justice, "Antarctic Cases", p. 28; see also MacKechnie, "Sovereignty in Antarctica: The Anglo-Argentine Dispute", p. 138.

[24] Quoted in Whiteman, *Digest of International Law*, p. 1259.

[25] Ibid, p. 1238.

41. The aforementioned arrangements did not end the tension among the three countries caused by their overlapping claims in Antarctica. Continued expansion of activities by each of them in the area finally led to further confrontation.

42. In 1952, an Argentinian party in Hope Bay (South Orkney Islands), resorting to the use of gun fire, compelled a British scientific expedition, attempting to reoccupy a station, to withdraw from the Hope Bay area.[26]

43. A year later, British policemen dismantled huts constructed by Argentinian and Chilean nationals on Deception Island and arrested two Argentines.[27]

44. In 1955, the United Kingdom went to the International Court of Justice contending in its Application that the United Kingdom possessed, and at all material dates had possessed, legal titles to sovereignty over the claimed areas in Antarctica and that the pretensions of Argentina and Chile to any of these areas were illegal and invalid. The United Kingdom asked the Court to declare that Argentina and Chile were bound to respect the United Kingdom's sovereignty over those areas and, if called on by the United Kingdom, to withdraw from them their personnel and equipment.[28]

45. The case was dismissed after both Argentina and Chile declined to submit to the Court's jurisdiction.[29]

46. As already mentioned, relations between claimant States and those refusing to recognize such claims in Antarctica also give rise to difficulties. Exchanges of notes recording sharp divergencies of view were not uncommon.

47. Thus in an aide-mémoire dated 19 July 1955 from the Government of the United States to Argentina, the United States declared that

"The Government of the United States of America notes that legislation recently enacted by the Argentine Congress purports to incorporate into Argentine provincial administration those areas claimed by the Argentine in the Antarctic. The Government of the United States wishes to reiterate that it recognizes no claims advanced in the Antarctic and reserves all rights of the United States in the area."[30]

48. In its reply, the Government of Argentina stressed that reservation and declaration made by the United States did not in any way affect the legitimate and indispensable rights which Argentina exercised in the Antarctic in the sector of sovereignty.[31]

49. With respect to the note from the Government of Australia informing Governments about its decision to apply, by virtue of its membership, the Convention of the World Meteorological Organization to the Australian Antarctic Territory, the United States Secretary of State in a reply dated 30 January 1956 declared:

---

[26] See MacKechnie, "Sovereignty in Antarctica …", p. 138.

[27] See Whiteman, *Digest of International Law*, p. 1238. In explanation of actions taken, the Secretary of State for Foreign Affairs of the United Kingdom stated:

"No, we have not in any way infringed the arrangements under the Tripartite Naval Declaration. We adhere to those, and the presence of a British frigate south of that latitude is quite customary during the Antarctic summer. I ought to add, to make the position quite plain, that these men were expelled not as invaders but as illegal immigrants. They were dealt with under the civil law of the Dependencies themselves." Quoted in Whiteman, *Digest of International Law*, p. 1239.

[28] See International Court of Justice, "Antarctic Cases", pp. 38 and 75.

[29] International Court of Justice, "Antarctica Cases", Order of 16 March 1956. In a letter dated 1 August 1955 from the Government of Argentina to the Registrar of the Court it was stated:

"… the Argentine Government has several times had occasion to indicate in notes addressed to Her Britannic Majesty's Embassy in Buenos Aires that it cannot consent to the question of sovereignty over the Antarctic territories of Argentina which it is sought to raise being referred for decision to any International Court of Justice or Arbitration Tribunal. By this present note, my Government reaffirms its refusal in the most express way with regard to the jurisdiction of this Court and with regard to any possibility that it should be seised as such to deal with this case."

[30] Quoted in Whiteman, *Digest of International Law*, p. 1251.

[31] Whiteman, *Digest of International Law*, p. 1251.

"My Government wishes to point out, as it has on previous occasions, that it does not recognize any claims so far advanced in the Antarctic and reserves all rights accruing to the United States out of activities of nationals of the United States in the area."[32]

50. In response to a memorandum of 8 June 1950 on Antarctica from the Government of the Soviet Union,[33] the Government of Chile, in its Declaration of 11 September 1950, reaffirmed that "by virtue of geographical, historical, juridical, diplomatic and administrative rights, Chile exercises full sovereignty over the Chilean Antarctic Territory, and does not recognize within that territory the claims of any other powers".[34]

51. Diversity in the views on the sovereignty issue significantly complicated the work of the First International Geophysical Year (IGY) Antarctic Conference, held in Paris in 1955. The negotiations at the Conference were at one point halted until its president, M. Laclaver, finally succeeded in getting support for a statement saying that the objectives of the Conference were exclusively of a scientific nature. This statement was then reflected in a resolution adopted by the conference on 10 July 1955.[35]

52. In spite of the above-mentioned statement, difficulties persisted during the work of the Conference as a result of differing positions on the issue of sovereign claims in Antarctica.[36]

53. The complexities of the political and legal situation continued to persist and, during the IGY, problems arose caused by the activities of scientists of one State acting in the area claimed by another.[37] The claimant States started issuing declarations stating that they welcomed activities in their territories in Antarctica. Such statements were rejected by non-claimant States sending scientific expeditions to Antarctica as part of the IGY programme.

54. Thus, a note dated 2 August 1955 from the Government of Australia to the United States Secretary of State said:

"Following the recent meetings of scientists in Paris, the Australian Government understands that the Government of the United States is interested in the possibility of conducting scientific research in the Australian sector of the Antarctic.

"The Australian Government welcomes this interest on the part of the United States Government and will be happy to render any assistance in its power to this end."[38]

55. In reply to this note, the United States pointed out that offer of co-operation made by the Australian side in connection with the activities in the Antarctic during the IGY was appreciated, although the Government of the United States did not, of course, recognize any claims so far advanced in the Antarctic and reserved all rights accruing to the United States out of activities of its nationals in the Antarctic.[39]

56. A similar exchange of letters took place between the United States and New Zealand.[40]

57. By the time the Antarctic Treaty was concluded the situation surrounding territorial claims in Antarctica had reached a point at which some kind of solution assuring peace and stability in the area had become imperative. Differences on the sovereignty issue did not disappear with the signing of the Treaty but at least a forum had been provided through which situations arising from new activities could be addressed and solutions to emerging problems sought. The information provided in chapter III of the present study, devoted to the operation of the Antarctic Treaty system, will refer to the role of the Antarctic Treaty in dealing with issues raised by conflicting positions between the Parties on territorial claims. The views of some non-

[32] Ibid, p. 1252.

[33] See *Pravda*, 4 July 1958.

[34] Quoted in Whiteman, *Digest of International Law*, p. 1257.

[35] Whiteman, *Digest of International Law*, p. 1242.

[36] R. E. Guyer, "The Antarctic System", *Recueil des cours de L'Académie de droit international* (Leyden, 1974), vol. 139, p. 166.

[37] Ibid, p. 167.

[38] Quoted in Whiteman, *Digest of International Law*, p. 1243.

[39] Ibid, p. 1244.

[40] Ibid, pp. 1244 and 1245.

Treaty Parties on the sovereignty issue in Antarctica are reflected in section C of the present chapter devoted to the deliberations at the thirty-eighth session of the General Assembly.

B. Antarctic Treaty

58. Because of the generally unsatisfactory situation in Antarctica originating from the conflicting approaches of States to the sovereignty issue, which was aggravated by the outbreak of serious conflicts described above, attempts were made in the years immediately following the Second World War to initiate discussions aimed at establishing any international régime in Antarctica. These attempts failed. However, in the middle of the 1950s, the increase in tension around the sovereignty issue, accompanied by rapidly developing activities in Antarctica, proved that the Antarctic had dramatically entered into the world of politics. In the light of the position of the claimant States, the active involvement in the region of such non-claimant States, as the Soviet Union and the United States, the political difficulties arising from overlapping claims and other important factors including instances of military rivalry, it was felt that the need for an international agreement with respect to the Antarctic was increasingly urgent. It was also well understood by those concerned that unless an international solution for the Antarctic could be found, a confrontation on a world-wide scale might easily erupt in that area.[41]

59. Serious concern about the situation developing at that time in the Antarctic had prompted India twice, in 1956 and 1958, to make a formal proposal for inclusion in the agenda of the General Assembly of an item entitled "Question of Antarctica", but both times India withdrew the proposal.

60. In 1957, world attention was attracted to the enormous international scientific effort known as the International Geophysical Year (IGY), which culminated in 1958. Under the IGY, Antarctica was selected as one of the priority areas. Despite disagreement on the sovereignty issue and tension in east-west relations, the planning and implementation of the IGY programme in Antarctica were successful international co-operative efforts. A certain *modus vivendi* was achieved during the IGY between claimant and non-claimant States, allowing scientists from 12 interested States to participate in an unprecedented international venture that resulted in the establishment and expansion of scientific bases.[42]

61. The IGY activities in Antarctica not only made a significant contribution to mankind's scientific knowledge, but in addition prepared the basis for negotiations seeking to assure the establishment of Antarctica as an area of peace, to overcome conflicts resulting from the sovereignty issue and to assure freedom of scientific research in Antarctica.[43] In May 1958, the Government of the United States proposed to the Governments of Argentina, Australia, Belgium, Chile, France, Japan, New Zealand, Norway, South Africa, the Soviet Union and the United Kingdom to conclude a treaty designed to preserve the continent as an international laboratory for scientific research and to ensure that it be used only for peaceful purposes.

62. The selection of the countries invited to the Conference was evidently based on their participation in Antarctic research activities during the IGY. Since participation in the IGY was

---

[41] See Lawrence M. Gould, "Antarctica in World Affairs", *Headline Series*, Foreign Policy Association, March–April 1958, Number 128; S. V. Molodtsov, "Sovremennoye mejdunarodno – pravovoye polojeniye Antarctiki", Jurisdat, Moskva 1954; Report of the Secretary of State to the President of the Antarctic Treaty and the Final Act of the Conference, 4 February 1960 (United States Department of State, Pub. No. 7060); Bernard H. Oxman, "The Antarctic Régime: An Introduction", *University of Miami Law Review*, December 1978, vol. 33, No. 2, p. 296; David A. Colson, "The Antarctic Treaty System: The Mineral Issue", *Law and Policy in International Business*, vol. 12, No. 4 (1980), p. 845; and Roberto E. Guyer, "Comment", *Antarctic Challenge: Conflicting Interests, Co-operation, Environmental Protection, Economic Development – Proceedings of an Interdisciplinary Symposium*, Kiel, Federal Republic of Germany, 22–24 June 1983, pp. 52–57.

[42] Barbara Michell and Richard Sandbrook, *The Management of the Southern Ocean* (London, International Institute for Environment and Development, 1980), pp. 6–7.

[43] Finn Sollie, "The Antarctic Treaty System: The Political Problem of Potential Resource Development", pp. 15 and 16.

open to any interested State, by this approach none of those wishing to take part in conducting scientific research in Antarctica at that time was excluded.[44]

63. The initiative of the United States was accepted and efforts to elaborate an international agreement governing the situation in Antarctica resulted finally in the convocation in Washington, D.C. of the Conference which, on the first of December 1959, approved the Antarctic Treaty.[45]

64. The Antarctic Treaty entered into force on 23 June 1961 after all 12 Powers invited to the Washington Conference had ratified it. Thus, 12 States – Argentina, Australia, Belgium, Chile, France, Japan, New Zealand, Norway, South Africa, the Soviet Union, the United Kingdom and the United States – became the original Parties to the Treaty. Since then, 20 States have acceded to the Treaty; Brazil, Bulgaria, China, Czechoslovakia, Cuba, Denmark, Finland, German Democratic Republic, Germany, Federal Republic of, Hungary, India, Italy, Netherlands, Papua New Guinea, Peru, Poland, Romania, Spain, Sweden and Uruguay.

65. It is stipulated in the preamble of the Treaty that "it is in the interest of all mankind that Antarctica shall continue forever to be used exclusively for peaceful purposes and shall not become the scene or object of international discord" (second preambular paragraph). The preamble also emphasizes that, by ensuring "the use of Antarctica for peaceful purposes only and the continuance of international harmony in Antarctica", the Treaty "furthers the purposes and principles embodied in the Charter of the United Nations" (fifth preambular paragraph).

66. The Treaty proclaims in article I that it ensures that "Antarctica shall be used for peaceful purposes only" (para. 1). That objective is elaborated in the same paragraph where it is stated that the Treaty prohibits, *inter alia*, any measures of a military nature, such as establishment of military bases and fortifications, the carrying out of military manoeuvres, as well as the testing of any type of weapons. However, according to paragraph 2 of article I, the use of military personnel or equipment is not completely excluded, but is permitted only in support of scientific research or for any other peaceful purpose consistent with the principles of the Treaty.

67. By prohibiting any measure of a military nature, article I of the Treaty establishes in Antarctica a régime of demilitarization or, more precisely, a régime of non-militarization, since Antarctica has never been the scene of military installations. If any plans to involve Antarctica in the sphere of the arms race ever existed, they have not become reality.

68. For the purposes of further implementation of the objective proclaimed in the preamble and in article I, the Treaty, in paragraph 1 (a) of article IX, imposes on Contracting Parties participating in the work of the Consultative Meetings convened within the framework of the Treaty, an obligation to consider, formulate and recommend measures regarding the "use of Antarctica for peaceful purposes only".

69. The ban on military activities is complemented in the Treaty by the prohibition of any nuclear explosions in Antarctica and the disposal of radioactive waste material there (art. V, para. 1), making it the first international nuclear test-ban agreement. It should be noted that, in paragraph 2 of article V, the Treaty states that "in the event of the conclusion of international agreements concerning the use of nuclear energy, including nuclear explosions and the disposal of radioactive waste material, to which all the Contracting Parties whose representatives are entitled to participate in the meetings provided for under Article IX are parties, the rules established under such agreements shall apply in Antarctica".

70. When reviewing the situation with respect to the application of article V of the Treaty, it was decided at the Eighth Consultative Meeting that every appropriate effort should be exerted so that no one disposed of nuclear waste in the Antarctic Treaty area (recommendation VIII-12).

71. A powerful stimulus to the conclusion of the Treaty was provided by the general desire to maintain the international scientific co-operation built up during the IGY. Acknowledging in the preamble the substantial contributions to scientific knowledge resulting from international

[44] R. E. Guyer, "The Antarctic System", p. 177.

[45] United Nations, *Treaty Series*, vol. 402, No. 5778, p. 72.

co-operation in scientific investigation in Antarctica, the Treaty proclaims in article II the principles of the freedom of scientific investigation in Antarctica and co-operation toward that end. The Treaty emphasizes that the establishment of a firm foundation for the continuation and development of international co-operation on the basis of freedom of scientific investigation in Antarctica as applied during the IGY accords with the interests of science and the progress of all mankind (fourth preambular paragraph).

72. With a view to promoting further international co-operation in scientific investigation in Antarctica, the Treaty requires in subparagraph 1 (a) and (c) of article III the exchange of information regarding plans for scientific research and results of scientific observations. Another important form of international co-operation provided by the Treaty is the exchange of scientific personnel between expeditions and stations in Antarctica (art. III, subpara. 1 (b)). With reference to this provision of the Treaty, it was stressed at the First Consultative Meeting that Governments should make available such of their facilities as might be helpful in promoting the exchange of scientific personnel among their expeditions.

73. In the implementation of the provisions concerning scientific co-operation, the Treaty encourages in paragraph 2 of article III, the establishment of co-operative working relations with those specialized agencies of the United Nations and other international organizations having a scientific or technical interest in Antarctica.

74. Such working relations have been established with the World Meteorological Organization (WMO), the World Health Organization (WHO), the Food and Agriculture Organization of the United Nations (FAO), the International Maritime Organization (IMO), the International Telecommunication Union (ITU), the United Nations Environment Programme (UNEP), the Commission for the Conservation of Antarctic Marine Living Resources (CCAMLR), the Scientific Committee on Antarctic Research (SCAR), the Intergovernmental Oceanographic Commission (IOC) of the United Nations Educational, Scientific and Cultural Organization (UNESCO) and the Scientific Committee on Oceanic Research (SCOR) of the International Council of Scientific Unions (ICSU).[46]

75. One of the examples of co-operation between the Treaty Parties and other international organizations, on the basis of article III, was the invitation from the Fifth Consultative Meeting to experts from WMO, IOC, ITU and SCAR to attend a meeting of telecommunications experts (recommendation V-2).

76. The principal role in working relations is played by SCAR, which is regarded by the Treaty Parties as a vital source of scientific advice. To demonstrate the interrelation existing between SCAR and Treaty Parties one can mention the elaboration by SCAR of certain conservation principles later embodied at the Third Consultative Meeting into the Agreed Measures for the Conservation of Antarctic Fauna and Flora and submission by SCAR at the invitation of the Eighth Consultative Meeting of the report entitled "A preliminary Assessment of the Environmental Impact on Mineral Exploration or Exploitation in Antarctica". These close working relations have continued throughout the years of existence of the Antarctic Treaty.[47] One of the recent cases is the appeal in 1983 by the Twelfth Consultative Meeting to SCAR to examine issues relating to increased use of satellite communications, to examine the adequacy of the Antarctic telecommunications system to meet the demand arising from the expansion of shipping and aircraft activity in Antarctica and to suggest improvements where they might be desirable (recommendation XII-2).

---

[46] References to relations with these organizations are contained in the relevant recommendations of the Consultative Meetings. See *Handbook of Measures in Furtherance of the Principles and Objectives of the Antarctic Treaty*, Third Edition (Department of Foreign Affairs, Canberra, April 1983).

[47] For more detailed information on co-operation between SCAR and the Antarctic Treaty Parties, see Charles R. Bentley "International Science Programs in Antarctica", University of Rhode Island, Center for Ocean Management Studies, Eighty Annual Conference, 17–20 June 1984. The Twelfth Consultative Meeting adopted recommendation XII-8 entitled "SCAR Assistance to Consultative Parties".

77. In order to promote the objectives and ensure the observance of its provisions, the Treaty establishes a comprehensive system of on-site inspection by observers who have complete freedom of access at any time to any or all areas in Antarctica (art. VII, paras. 1 and 2). All stations, installations, equipment, ships and aircraft at points of discharging or embarking cargoes or personnel in Antarctica are open to inspection by observers designated in accordance with the provisions of article VII of the Treaty. Aerial observation may also be carried out over Antarctica at any time. Article VII states that each Contracting Party participating in the meetings organized under the provisions of article IX of the Treaty has the right to designate observers to carry out inspections provided they are its nationals. Other Contracting Parties should be informed of the names of the observers so designated, as well as of the termination of their appointment (para. 1).

78. Further provisions related to the question of inspection are contained in paragraph 5 of article VII, which were apparently included for the purpose of assisting the performance of inspections in Antarctica by giving the observers the necessary information on all activities in the area. This paragraph provides that each Contracting Party shall inform in advance other Parties to the Treaty of all expeditions to and within Antarctica, on the part of its ships or nationals, and of all expeditions to Antarctica organized in or proceeding from its territory, of all stations in Antarctica occupied by its nationals and of any military personnel or equipment intended to be introduced by it into Antarctica subject to the conditions prescribed in paragraph 2 of article I of the Treaty. In practice this has proved to be enormously helpful to those conducting scientific research in Antarctica, since it keeps scientists informed of where stations and expeditions are located and has made it easier to help stranded expeditions.[48]

79. The system of observation and inspection is one of the vital elements in the Treaty for assuring its operation in accordance with its terms. The Consultative Parties are convinced that it contributes significantly to the effectiveness of the Treaty and the realization of its Principles and objectives, the most important of which is preservation of peace in Antarctica. They believe that the practice of inspection has also served as the best way of assuring the absence of suspicion.

80. Under article VII, inspections of stations in Antarctica have been carried out by New Zealand, Australia, the United Kingdom, Argentina and the United States.[49]

81. The first inspections were carried out by a New Zealand team during November and December 1963. They inspected the United States stations at McMurdo, Byrd and the South Pole. Later in December 1963, teams from Australia and the United Kingdom inspected the same three United States stations and New Zealand's Scott Base. The United States provided these teams with some transportation and accommodation during their inspections.

82. None of the inspections carried out in Antarctica since 1963 has found evidence of activities contrary to the provisions of the Antarctic Treaty. Concrete detailed information of these inspections can be found in part two in the replies of the relevant Governments.

83. One of the most recent inspections was carried out in 1983 by a four-member United States observer team. Between 17 January and 20 March 1983, that team visited the following stations: Leningradskaya, Mirniy, Molodezhnaya and Novolazarevskaya of the Soviet Union; Dumont d'Urville of France; Casey, Davis and Mawson of Australia; Showa of Japan; Sanae III of South Africa; Georg von Neumayer of the Federal Republic of Germany; Halley of the United Kingdom; and General Belgrano II and Vicecomodoro Marambio of Argentina.[50]

84. In its report, the observer team concluded that, without exception, it had been warmly received at each of the stations visited during its tour around Antarctica. The operations of each

[48] Guyer, "The Antarctic System", p. 180.

[49] These facts are based on the Annual Exchange of Information under the Antarctic Treaty. See also Sollie, "The Political Experiment in Antarctica", *Bulletin of the Atomic Scientists*", (December 1970).

[50] See the Report of the United States Observer Team in Antarctica, 1983.

station had been explained and discussed. Although not every structure could be visited at each station in the time available, there was no doubt that all stations visited exemplified adherence to the peaceful purposes of the Antarctic Treaty. Moreover, each was seriously engaged in increasing man's knowledge of this remote frontier and the larger space environment for which Antarctica served as a window.

85. The report emphasized that what was most important was that at each station the co-operative spirit of Antarctica, as embodied in the Antarctic Treaty system, was alive and strongly affirmed. Frequently the wish had been expressed that the same spontaneous friendships based on shared goals and the same close co-operation founded in free scientific inquiry could exist without inhibition elsewhere in the world.[51]

86. The observer team found that all stations visited were complying with both the provisions and spirit of the Antarctic Treaty and its agreed measures.

87. The Treaty does not settle the issue of territorial sovereignty. It freezes the status quo in Antarctica by providing, in article IV, that nothing contained in it shall be interpreted as a renunciation of previously asserted rights of or claims to territorial sovereignty in Antarctica, as a renunciation or diminution of any basis of claim to territorial sovereignty in Antarctica which any Contracting Party may have whether as a result of its activities or those of its nationals in Antarctica, or otherwise, or as prejudicing the position of any Contracting Party as regards its recognition or non-recognition of any other State's right of or claim or basis of claim to territorial sovereignty in Antarctica (para. 1). In the same article, the Treaty emphasizes that no acts or activities taking place while it is in force shall constitute a basis for asserting, supporting or denying a claim to territorial sovereignty in Antarctica or create any rights of sovereignty in Antarctica. According to the Treaty, no new claim, or enlargement of an existing claim, to territorial sovereignty in Antarctica shall be asserted while it is in force (para. 2).

88. The Treaty addresses the questions likely to arise in the course of scientific activity in Antarctica, but neither article IV nor any other provision of the Treaty solves all potential jurisdictional problems, including those related to commercial exploration and exploitation of Antarctic resources.[52]

89. Article VIII of the Treaty, covering questions of jurisdiction in Antarctica, is closely related to the provisions of article IV on the sovereignty issue. Differences in the positions of principle between claimant and non-claimant States evidently prevented them in 1959 from finding a general solution on how to handle matters of jurisdiction in Antarctica. Nevertheless, they addressed such matters in the areas where the solution seemed to them most needed at that time, namely, with respect to jurisdiction over observers, scientific personnel exchanged under the Treaty and members of the staffs accompanying the first two categories.

90. The Treaty in article VIII, paragraph 1, states that "in order to facilitate the exercise of their functions under the present Treaty, and without prejudice to the respective positions of the Contracting Parties relating to jurisdiction over all other persons in Antarctica, observers designated under paragraph 1 of article VII and scientific personnel exchanged under subparagraph 1 (b) of article III of the Treaty, and members of the staffs accompanying any such persons, shall be subject only to the jurisdiction of the Contracting Party of which they are nationals in respect of all acts or omissions occurring while they are in Antarctica for the purpose of exercising their functions".

91. With a view toward possible future developments that might require common understanding in other areas, the drafters of the Treaty included in article VIII, paragraph 2, the following: "without prejudice to the provisions of paragraph 1 of this article, and pending the adoption of measures in pursuance of subparagraph 1 (e) of article IX, the Contracting Party concerned in

[51] Ibid, p. 48.

[52] Fernando Zegers Santa Cruz, "The Antarctic System and the Utilization of Resources", *University of Miami Law Review*, vol. 33, No. 2 (December 1978), pp. 456–461.

any case of dispute with regard to the exercise of jurisdiction in Antarctica shall immediately consult together with a view of reaching a mutually acceptable solution".

92. Elaboration in 1972 of the Convention for the Conservation of Antarctic Seals and, in 1980, of the Convention on the Conservation of Antarctic Marine Living Resources provides examples of mutually acceptable agreements on matters of jurisdiction in the areas not spelled out in the Treaty.

93. Article IV of the Treaty makes it clear that in the areas of activities not covered by the Treaty both the claimant and non-claimant States adhere to their own views.

94. It has been suggested that the claimants may maintain that, while the Treaty requires them to restrain themselves from exercising jurisdiction in certain express situations, they can act in full accord with their claims of territorial sovereignty as to any matter not expressly addressed by the Treaty. Therefore, since in their view the Antarctic Treaty is silent on the territorial sea, continental shelf or jurisdiction in maritime areas adjacent to the Antarctic continent, they are entitled to claim a territorial sea, a 200-mile economic zone and a continental shelf off the coast of their claimed territory in Antarctica.[53] The claimant States have clearly indicated that within these maritime areas, they would accept only those restrictions to which they have otherwise agreed.[54]

95. From the point of view of the non-claimant States, in the waters adjacent to the Antarctic continent (which they consider entirely as high seas) and corresponding sea-bed areas, there are no territorial seas, 200-mile zones or continental shelves and therefore they are free to conduct any activity not prohibited by the Treaty. Accordingly, their freedoms are restrained either by the requirement to have reasonable regard for the interests of others exercising the same rights and freedoms or by arrangements elaborated and approved with their consent.

96. Other views of some non-Treaty Parties on the status of maritime areas surrounding Antarctica are reflected in section C of the present chapter concerning deliberations at the thirty-eighth session of the General Assembly.

97. It should be noted that the 1982 United Nations Convention on the Law of Sea,[55] following upon the Declaration of Principles Governing the Sea-Bed and the Ocean Floor, and the Subsoil Thereon, beyond the Limits of National Jurisdiction (General Assembly resolution 2749 (XXV)), provides for a régime for the exploitation of the resources of the area, as defined in the Convention, beyond national jurisdiction. It further contains provisions on the relationship of the Law of the Sea Convention, which is not yet in force, to other Conventions.

98. Since article IV does not resolve the issue of sovereignty, the Treaty Parties, when starting negotiations for the purpose of elaborating measures regulating their activities not envisaged by the Treaty, have each time stressed that the basic non-prejudicial intent of article IV of the Treaty should be preserved.

99. Thus, while deciding to elaborate an international régime for the conservation of Antarctic marine living resources, the Ninth Consultative Meeting pointed out that the provisions of article IV of the Antarctic Treaty should not be affected by the régime, which should ensure that the principles embodied in article IV were safeguarded in application to the marine areas, south of 60°S latitude (recommendation IX-2).

100. Similar wording was used in the decisions of the Ninth, Tenth, and Eleventh Consultative Meetings concerning the elaboration of an international régime for Antarctic mineral resources.

---

[53] See Colson, "The Antarctic Treaty System, the Mineral Issue", p. 849; Zegers Santa Cruz, "The Antarctic System ...", pp. 459–460; Joyner, "The Exclusive Economic Zone and Antarctica"; and Ralph L. Harry "The Antarctic Régime and the Law of the Sea Convention: An Australian View", *Virginia Journal of International Law*, vol. 21:4 (1981).

[54] It appears that such agreed restrictions follow from the provisions of the Convention for the Conservation of Antarctic Seals and the Convention on the Conservation of Antarctic Marine Living Resources and would follow from the mineral resource regime as presently discussed. See chap. III, sect. F of the present study.

[55] Official Records of the Third United Nations Conference on the Law of the Sea, vol. XVII (United Nations publication, Sales No. E.84.V.2), document A/CONF.62/122.

The only difference was that the decisions referred to the need for the régime on mineral resources to safeguard the principles embodied in article IV in application to the whole area covered by the Antarctic Treaty (recommendations IX-I and XI-I).

101. A peculiarity of article IV is its application not only to the relations between Treaty Parties but also to relations between the parties of two other international multilateral agreements, namely, the Convention for the Conservation of Antarctic Seals and the Convention on the Conservation of Antarctic Marine Living Resources.

102. In paragraph 1 of article 1 of the Convention on Seals, the Contracting Parties affirm the provisions of article IV of the Antarctic Treaty in respect of the seas south of 60°S latitude. In accordance with paragraph 1 of article IV of the Convention on Living Resources, the Contracting Parties, whether or not they are Parties to the Antarctic Treaty, are also bound by article IV of the Treaty in their relations with each other. This article is considered by the Parties to be a pragmatic solution that became possible because the States concerned believed that some kind of mutual approach was better than the chaos of unilateral actions.

103. It follows from article VI of the Antarctic Treaty that it applies to the area south of 60°S latitude and that, subject to the objectives and principles of the Treaty, nothing in it shall prejudice or affect the rights of any State under international law with regard to the high seas within that area.

104. Article VI of the Treaty raises the problem of whether Antarctic ice forms, such as shelf ice and pack ice, should be included in the régime associated with land or with water. The juridical nature of shelf ice, pack ice and underlying waters is unclear and appears to be a very difficult issue to resolve.[56]

105. For the purpose of the exchange of information, consultations, consideration and formulation of measures in furtherance of the principles and objectives of the Treaty, the Treaty establishes in article IX a special mechanism in the form of Consultative Meetings. While the Treaty is open for accession by any Member State of the United Nations, full participation in the work of the Consultative Meetings is accorded to original Parties to the Treaty and those Contracting Parties which demonstrate their interest in Antarctica by conducting substantial scientific research activity there, such as the establishment of a scientific station or the despatch of a scientific expedition (art. IX, para.2)

106. Up to now, consultative status has been acquired, respectively, by Poland and the Federal Republic of Germany in 1977 and 1981, and by India and Brazil, in 1983.

107. Proof of interest in the form of substantial research activity may be regarded by some as a high entrance fee. This test would seem to be an outgrowth of the activities conducted during the IGY which established that the elaboration of measures further the principles and objectives of the Treaty required a degree of knowledge of the nature of the Antarctic environment that could be gained only from actual activity in the region. The Parties to the Treaty believe that the requirement that the acceding Parties must have a continuing research programme to maintain consultative status and to have a right to participate in the formulation of measures for Antarctica helps create a more professional approach, based on the knowledge and appreciation of the unique characteristics of the Antarctic region.[57] It is to be noted that the requirement does not apply to the original Parties to the Treaty, not all of which have continuing research programmes in Antarctica at this time.

108. Beginning with the Twelfth Consultative Meeting, the Consultative parties, have invited the acceding Treaty Parties without consultative status to participate as observers in the work of the regular Consultative Meetings as well as in preparatory meetings. In May 1984, in Tokyo,

[56] Frank C. Alexander, Jr., "Legal Aspects: Exploitation of Antarctic Resources", *University of Miami Law Review*, vol. 33, No. 2 (December 1978), pp. 382–387; and Joyner, "The Exclusive Economic Zone …", pp. 711–714.

[57] Sollie, "The Antarctic Treaty System …", pp. 6–10.

a decision was made to invite the non-Consultative Treaty Parties to attend also as observers negotiations on an Antarctic mineral resource régime.

109. In the joint statement at the Twelfth Consultative Meeting, the non-Consultative Parties recorded that their presence reflected the interest of their Governments in the development of the Antarctic system and their willingness to contribute to the maintenance and the further development of the principles and objectives of the Antarctic Treaty. It was pointed out in the statement that the non-Consultative Parties recognized the achievements of the Treaty, for example with regard to co-operation in the field of scientific research, the protection of the environment and demilitarization. The non-Consultative Parties emphasized that, in their view, their participation in the various activities of the Antarctic system was important for the strengthening of the system.[58]

110. The system of Consultative Meetings envisaged under the Treaty allows coverage of all aspects of the activities being carried out in Antarctica in accordance with the Treaty and is intended to provide facilities for the implementation of the Treaty's principles and objectives. The Meetings serve as some kind of mechanism for the discussion and elaboration of measures in furtherance of the principles and objectives of the Treaty, including those regarding,

(a) Use of Antarctica for peaceful purposes only;
(b) Facilitation of scientific research in Antarctica;
(c) Facilitation of international scientific co-operation in Antarctica;
(d) Facilitation of the exercise of the rights of inspection provided for in article VII of the Treaty;
(e) Questions relating to the exercise of jurisdiction in Antarctica;
(f) Preservation and conservation of living resources in Antarctica (art. IX, para. 1).

111. It has always been stated by the Consultative Parties that they understood the protection of the unique Antarctic environment to be one of the main objectives of the Antarctic Treaty and that the provisions of paragraph 1 of article IX should be understood in that sense (see recommendations VI-4, VII-1, VIII-1, VIII-13, IX-5 and XII-4).

112. Article IX, paragraph 4, of the Treaty states that such measures (or recommendations, as they are called in practice) "shall become effective when approved by all the Contracting Parties whose representatives were entitled to participate in the meetings held to consider those measures". Once approved, the recommended measures would become norms for conduct in Antarctica. In other words, the recommendation system represents a type of "legislative procedure" making it possible to implement new measures within the framework of the Treaty's principles and objectives.[59]

113. From the First through the Twelfth Consultative Meeting, the Consultative Parties have made 147 recommendations to their Governments. Those recommendations have focused on a wide range of scientific, environmental and operational matters.

114. The subjects covered by these recommendations can be grouped as follows: uses of the Antarctic, preservation and conservation of wildlife and living resources, facilitation of scientific research and scientific co-operation, implementation of Treaty provisions concerning exchanges of information, operation of the Treaty and Consultative Meetings and postal services.

115. The recommendations of the Consultative Meetings, which represent a considerable body of rules, are not automatically binding upon new parties to the Treaty, including those entitled to acquire consultative status. This situation was discussed by the Consultative Parties who found it necessary, in order to avoid a situation in which different Treaty Parties would be bound

[58] Report of the Twelfth Consultative Meeting, Canberra, 13–27 September 1094, annex C.

[59] Finn Sollie, "Jurisdictional Problems in Relation to Antarctic Mineral Resources in Political Perspective", Conference on Antarctic Resources Policy in Antarctic Station "Teniente Marsh", October 1982, in *Antarctic Resource Police, Scientific, Legal and Political Issues* (Cambridge University press, 1983), pp. 47–50; and Colson, "The Antarctic Treaty System ...", p. 851.

by different sets of rules, to appeal to other Contracting Parties, inviting them to approve the recommendations in force. In 1975, the Eighth Consultative Meeting, in its recommendation VIII-8 urged "the States that have or will become Parties to the Antarctic Treaty to approve the recommendations adopted at Consultative Meetings".

116. In 1977, the Consultative Parties adopted a stricter approach to this issue with respect to new members at their Meetings. The final report of the First Special Consultative Meeting emphasized that, because of their special obligations under the Treaty, the Consultative Parties might urge a State that considered itself entitled to appoint representatives to Consultative Meetings to make a declaration of intent to approve the recommendations in force and might also invite such an acceding State to consider approval of the other recommendations.

117. Consultative Meetings are held approximately every two years. To date there have been 12 such meetings, the last one being held at Canberra in September 1983. The next, the Thirteenth Consultative Meeting, will take place in 1985 in Belgium.

118. For consideration of matters requiring particular attention, there is a practice of convening Special Consultative Meetings. Thus, in accordance with recommendation IX-2, a Special Consultative Meeting was convened in 1977 in order to elaborate a draft definitive régime for the conservation of Antarctic marine living resources. Another Special Consultative Meeting was convened in 1981, in accordance with recommendation XI-1, to elaborate a régime on Antarctic mineral resources and to determine its form.

119. In accordance with article X of the Treaty, each of the Contracting Parties undertakes to exert appropriate efforts, consistent with the Charter of the United Nations, to the end that no one engages in any activity in Antarctica contrary to the principles and purposes of the Treaty.

120. As a result of thorough discussions of this issue, the Seventh, Eighth and Ninth Consultative Meetings urged the State or States concerned to accede to the Antarctic Treaty, pointing out the rights and benefits they would receive and also the responsibilities and obligations of parties to the Treaty.

121. In certain instances, in the light of article X, the Consultative Parties have felt it necessary to draw attention to the specific types of activities prescribing particular forms of conduct.

122. In recommendation VI-7, the Consultative Parties decided to exert appropriate efforts to ensure that no tourists or other visitors engaged in any activity in the Treaty area which was contrary to the principles and purposes of the Treaty or recommendations made under it.

123. Most important in this respect was the decision of the Ninth Consultative Meeting on mineral resources. Recommendation IX-l points to the responsibility of the Consultative Parties "to ensure that any activities in Antarctica, including commercial exploration and exploitation in the future, should they occur, should not become the cause of international discord, of danger to the unique Antarctic environment, of disruption to scientific investigation, or be otherwise contrary to the principles or purposes of the Antarctic Treaty". The Consultative Parties decided that, as a consequence of this responsibility, they would "endeavour to ensure that, pending the timely adoption of agreed solutions pertaining to exploration and exploitation of mineral resources, no activity should be conducted to explore or exploit such resources".

124. With regard to dispute settlement article XI, paragraph 1, of the Treaty provides that "if any dispute arises between two or more of the Contracting Parties concerning the interpretation or application of the present Treaty, those Contracting Parties shall consult among themselves with a view to having the dispute resolved by negotiation, inquiry, mediation, conciliation, arbitration, judicial settlement or other peaceful means of their own choice".

125. Paragraph 2 of article XI provides that any dispute over interpretation or application of the Treaty not resolved in accordance with the aforementioned procedures "shall, with the consent, in each case, of all parties to the dispute, be referred to the International Court of Justice for settlement, but failure to reach agreement on reference to the International Court shall not absolve parties to the dispute from the responsibility of continuing to seek to resolve it by any of the various peaceful means referred to in paragraph 1 of this Article".

126. Article XII of the Treaty contains the Treaty's rules on amendment to, revision of and withdrawal from the Treaty procedures. This article has the so-called 30-years clause, marking the dividing line between the amendment and withdrawal procedure, which may be called "normal" for the Treaty, and the special procedure that shall apply after 30 years in the event that a conference is summoned to review the operation of the Treaty.[60]

127. In accordance with the "normal" procedure provided in article XII, subparagraphs 1 (a) and (b), the Treaty may be modified or amended at any time by unanimous agreement of the Contracting Parties whose representatives are entitled to participate in the Consultative Meetings. Any such modification or amendment shall enter into force when the depositary Government has received notice from all such Contracting Parties that they have ratified it. These modifications or amendments shall thereafter enter into force as to any other Contracting Party when notice of ratification by it has been received by the depositary Government. If any non-Consultative Contracting Party fails to ratify the modifications or amendments within a period of two years, that Party shall be deemed to have withdrawn from the Treaty.

128. As stated in article XII, paragraph 2, of the Treaty, after the expiration of 30 years from the date of its entry into force, i.e., in 1991, any of the Contracting Parties entitled to participate in the Consultative Meetings may request the summoning of a conference of all parties to the Treaty in order to review its operation. According the Treaty, that conference shall be held as soon as practicable thereafter.

129. Such a conference may approve any modification or amendment to the Treaty. This should be done, according to subparagraph 2 (b) of article XII, by a majority of the Contracting Parties there represented, including a majority of those entitled to participate in the Consultative Meetings. The modifications or amendments would enter into force in accordance with the requirements of paragraph 1 of article XII, in other words, if ratified by all Treaty Parties with consultative status.

130. If any such modification or amendment has not entered into force within two years, any Contracting Party may withdraw from the Treaty at any time after the expiration of that period. Such withdrawal takes effect two years after receipt of the relevant notice by the depositary Government (art. XII, subpara. 2 (c)).

131. The 30-years clause in article XII is sometimes mistakenly interpreted as establishing a certain automatic time limit for the Treaty. However, the Treaty does not cease to be in force after 30 years. It remains effective whether or not a conference is summoned. The 30-years clause, making it possible to request a revision conference, actually represents an alternative amendment procedure. Therefore, the conference form does not supersede the "normal" amendment procedure of the Treaty, but represents an alternative procedure that may be followed after 30 years.[61]

132. Although it is more than 20 years since the Antarctic Treaty entered into force, no modification or amendment has been proposed to its text by the Contracting Parties.

133. The Antarctic Treaty is open for accession by any Member of the United Nations or by any other State invited to accede to the Treaty with the consent of all the Contracting Parties whose representatives are entitled to participate in the Consultative Meetings (art. XIII, para. 1). Therefore it gives any of those States an opportunity to join the Treaty and, under its provisions, to take part in scientific research and other activities within the framework of the Treaty.

134.The depositary Government to the Antarctic Treaty is the Government of the United States of America (art. XIII, para. 3).

[60] Finn Sollie, "The Duration of the Antarctic Treaty – An Analysis of the Amendment and Revision Procedures in a Political Perspective", the Fridtjof Nansen Foundation, Arctic/Antarctic Project Study 1973, pp. 8, 9 and 19–28.

[61] Sollie, "The Duration of the Antarctic Treaty …", pp. 28–38.

C. Deliberations on Antarctica at the thirty-eighth session of the General Assembly[62]

135. At their Seventh Summit Conference, held at New Delhi from 7 to 12 March 1983, the Heads of State or Government of the Non-Aligned Countries, while noting that relevant provisions of the Antarctic Treaty of 1959 related to international co-operation in the area, they also considered that, in view of the increasing international interest in the Antarctic, the United Nations should undertake a comprehensive study of the subject. The study was to take into account all relevant factors, including the Antarctic Treaty, with a view to widening international co-operation on the continent (A/39/132-S/15675 and Corr.1 and 2, annex, paras. 122 and 133).

136. On 11 August 1983, the representatives of Antigua and Barbuda and of Malaysia to the United Nations sent a letter to the Secretary-General requesting the inclusion in the agenda of the thirty-eighth session of the General Assembly of a supplementary item entitled "Question of Antarctica" (A/38/193 and Corr.1). On the recommendation of the General Committee, the General Assembly decided to include the item on its agenda and to allocate the item (agenda item 140) to the First Committee.

137. The First Committee held discussions on Antarctica at its 42nd to 46th meetings, from 28 to 30 November 1983 (see A/C.1/38/PV.42-46). The debate on Antarctica in the First Committee provided the first opportunity for Member States to express their views on the subject at the United Nations. The Committee heard statements from 41 delegations, including Consultative and non-Consultative parties to the Antarctic Treaty as well as countries not parties to the Treaty, some of whom intended to accede to the Treaty in the near future.

138. In the First Committee, statements were made on ways and means by which Antarctica could best be administered. Many delegations expressed the view that any international mechanism that administered Antarctica must, first, promote the purposes and principles of the Charter of the United Nations; second, ensure that Antarctica was used for peaceful purposes only, keeping it free from militarization of any kind, including nuclear weapons, and out of the arms race; third, ensure protection of its natural environment; and fourth, promote international co-operation and co-ordination in scientific research and other peaceful activities beneficial to man.

139. Some States were of the view that the Treaty not only satisfied those objectives, but also had served well the international community in all the aspects enumerated above, and that it would continue to do so in the future. Furthermore, the Treaty, in their view, had averted international strife and conflict over Antarctica and had removed the potential for disputes on sovereignty among those countries claiming territorial sovereignty over the area. They emphasized that the Antarctic Treaty was the best legal régime for that area that the present international community could ever agree upon, and they pointed out that the Treaty and other international agreements on Antarctica had proved to be successful, practical and dynamic in the sense that their agreements could accommodate needs that might arise in the future. For those reasons, they believed that the Antarctic Treaty and the existing international agreements on Antarctica must be preserved and that any attempt to revise or replace them would do more harm than good to the international community. Therefore, they had serious reservations about the initiative by the Governments of Antigua and Barbuda and of Malaysia which, in their view, inaccurately represented the Antarctic Treaty of 1959 and implied that there was a need for revision or replacement of the Antarctic Treaty system. They were of the view that revision of the Treaty, if there were any need for it, could be achieve only under international law by the Parties to the Treaty.

140. The States that had brought the question of Antarctica to the United Nations were of the view that Antarctica had considerable environmental, climatic, scientific and potential economic significance to the world, and that there was a need to examine the possibility for wider international co-operation in the region through the framework of the United Nations. In

[62] For earlier views regarding Antarctica, see in particular sect. F 2, chap. III.

their view, the present management of Antarctica within the framework of the Antarctic Treaty system did not reflect an international decision-making system needed to administer matter of universal concern such as those concerning Antarctica.

141. Several States expressed their appreciation that the Treaty has been successful in keeping Antarctica demilitarized, free from the arms race and from nuclear weapons. Furthermore, in their view, the Treaty had provided a framework for co-operation among those countries with an active interest in scientific research in Antarctica and had kept the continent free from conflicts by imposing a moratorium on competing claims for territorial sovereignty over the area. While recognizing the merits of the Antarctic Treaty and the achievements of the Parties to the Treaty, they nevertheless expressed certain views with regard to the Treaty.

142. Most importantly, they considered that major flaws in the Treaty consisted, on the one hand, of the composition of the parties and, on the other hand, of the exclusive character of the decision-making process which was restricted to the Consultative Parties. In their view, accession to the Treaty without the right of participation in the decision-making process was extremely difficult to accept, as it was beyond the means of most of the countries to meet the requirements for participation in decision-making, namely, a capacity to conduct substantial scientific research in the area. In addition, they felt that the determination of global interests and of ways to safeguard them could best be made by the entire community of nations. They also emphasized that the Parties could not be oblivious to the fact that the present world community had expanded radically since 1959, when a few countries established the current régime on Antarctica, and they stated that insisting on the preservation of this exclusive régime constituted an attempt to maintain a status quo advantageous only to the privileged few. This exclusive nature of the decision-making process in the Treaty was also referred to critically by a country that had recently acceded to the Treaty, but had not acquired the status of a Consultative Party.

143. Several States denied the alleged exclusiveness which some maintained was inherent in the Treaty structure. They noted that the Treaty was open to all countries that wished to accede to it. They further stated that, at the time of the deliberation in the First Committee during the thirty-eighth session of the General Assembly, in addition to the 12 original signatories, 16 countries had acceded to the Treaty since it had entered into force in 1961. (Since that time, four more States have acceded to the Treaty). Of the 20 countries, four – Poland, the Federal Republic of Germany, Brazil, and India – had acquired Consultative Status. They also denied the exclusive nature of the Treaty in so far as the composition of the Parties to the Treaty was concerned. In their view, the Parties to the Treaty represented a wide spectrum of interests: the industrialized countries with free market economies, socialist countries and developing countries in Asia and Latin America. They further stressed that, although a certain confidentiality was necessary in negotiations to reaching decisions on the management of Antarctica, those decisions and any other results of such negotiations were made public and were available to all countries interested in Antarctica. Moreover, they noted that non-Consultative parties to the Treaty had been invited to the Twelfth and Thirteenth regular Consultative Meetings as observers, and they expressed the view that representation of Consultative States in the decision-making mechanism of the Treaty was justifiable in view of their vested interest in scientific research in Antarctica and their contribution to the international community. They also felt that the responsibility to manage activities in Antarctica was more of a burden than a privilege, since the Antarctic Treaty system consisted of obligations and not of rights. They further stated that the fact that the Treaty had been successful in managing Antarctica for nearly two and a half decades proved that the Consultative States had provided good management,

144. It was, however, noted that no African State, except South Africa, was a party to the Antarctic Treaty. Moreover, some States found that one of the major flaws of the Treaty was the presence of South Africa among the signatory countries. They expressed serious doubts that a Treaty which provided tor the inclusion of a State that practiced the policy of apartheid could

be an ideal legal régime tor an area of global concern. They expressed the view that it would be in the interest of the international community to exclude South Africa from the Treaty and not allow it to participate in any future co-operative effort in the region, because, they argued, the apartheid régime of South Africa could not be relied upon to uphold the purposes and objectives of the present Treaty or any future treaty that might emerge.

145. Some States opposed the introduction of political elements into the discussion that, in their view, had nothing to do either with Antarctica or with the Antarctic Treaty.

146. Some States raised questions about the effectiveness of the Treaty in promoting and contributing to the interests of the international community at large, in particular in areas of information dissemination and environmental protection.

147. The States raising those questions pointed out that the flow of information about Antarctica was limited to the Consultative States and was not made available even to non-Consultative parties, let alone to the international community at large.

148. Other States noted that the bulk of documentation on treaties, agreements, research projects and a wide spectrum of other activities and problems concerning Antarctica was not only made public but also distributed through well-established and widely known channels by those States involved in Antarctic affairs.

149. Several States raised concerns about the present state of environmental management of Antarctica. They noted that the Treaty system lacked an international mechanism to ensure environmental review and that its enforcement was left to individual States.

150. Some States were of the view that Antarctic environmental management was one of the areas in which the Antarctic Treaty was most successful. Thanks to the consultative process provided by the Treaty, which made it possible to meet developing needs, the Parties to the Treaty had successfully met the requirements to preserve the delicate ecological and environmental balance of Antarctica through the adoption of separate legal instruments. These included the Agreed Measures for the Conservation of Antarctic Fauna and Flora (1964), the Convention for the Conservation of Antarctic Seals (1972) and the Convention on the Conservation of Antarctic Marine Living Resources (1982).

151. Some States pointed to the fact that the Treaty did not deal with the question of mineral resources and they expressed their concern about the future of Antarctica's environment, since they anticipated the likelihood of an emerging scramble to exploit the mineral resources in the region. Some of them stated that current negotiations among the Consultative Parties on a régime for exploiting mineral resources were being carried out in secrecy. In their view, the Consultative Parties, while holding the opinion that Antarctic mineral exploitation would not be technically and commercially feasible until the next century, were nonetheless pursuing seriously and secretly an exclusive mineral régime. They asked the question whether any group of countries should confer upon itself the moral or legal right to self-elected determination or management of Antarctica. They considered it unfair and unjust that only a handful of countries exclusively controlled access to the vast uninhabited continent of Antarctica.

152. Several States, while expressing the belief that the economic development of Antarctica still belonged to the future, stressed the fact that the primary concern of the present negotiations was to ensure the integrity of the Antarctic environment. They also pointed out the fact that, in keeping with the desire to protect the ecological balance and with the purpose and principles of the Treaty, the Consultative Parties had agreed in 1977 not to explore or exploit mineral resources of the area until a régime was established.

153. Some States referred to the absence of co-operation between the Antarctic Treaty system and the specialized agencies of the United Nations and other international organizations, despite the fact that the Treaty itself recommended such co-operation. They noted the absence of a formal mechanism to ensure that the international community at large was made aware of activities carried out under the Antarctic Treaty.

154. Other States, however, noted that the Antarctica Treaty system provided continuous working relations with those specialized agencies and other international organizations having a scientific and technical interest in Antarctica. These included WMO, WHO, UNEP, FAO, ITU, IOC of the UNESCO, SCAR and SCOR of ICSU.

155. Another major concern expressed by some States was the question of existing claims for territorial sovereignty over Antarctica. In their view, the Treaty did not provide sufficient guarantee that Antarctica would remain free from conflicts and competition because it did not provide for the resolution of the territorial claims but merely put a moratorium on them. They were also concerned that the Treaty would fail to keep the peace in Antarctica once the exploitation of mineral resources became feasible.

156. Several States explained that the moratorium on existing claims had been observed by a delicate agreement among claimant and non-claimant parties to the Treaty. They expressed their concerns that Antarctica might be turned into an arena for international competition and conflicts if and when this delicate agreement was tampered with. They further said that they were more aware than anyone else of the danger that the possibility of mineral exploitation would introduce into the delicate balance now maintained among the parties to the Treaty, whether claimant or non-claimant, and stressed the importance of the elaborating an agreement on a mining régime within the Treaty system designed to preserve the delicate moratorium.

157. Some States viewed Antarctica as the last frontier left for mankind as a whole. They considered Antarctica in the context of the new international economic order and stressed the applicability of the principle of the common heritage of mankind to the region. In their view, the application of that concept was a logical consequence of the established international trend in areas such as outer space and the international sea-bed area. They expressed the hope that the trend would be further enhanced through the establishment of a global régime for Antarctica based on the principle of the common heritage of mankind.

158. Several States considered that the principle of the common heritage of mankind was not relevant to Antarctica and that its application to the régime governing this area was inappropriate. They argued that there already existed an effective legal system in the region that was open to all States, and they saw no legal vacuum in the area. They further pointed to the fact that seven countries maintained national territorial claims in Antarctica. For those reasons, Antarctica was neither *res communis* nor *res nullius*, and the application of the principle of the common heritage of mankind was not acceptable.

159. The debate on Antarctica in the First Committee provided the opportunity to understand the issues, and in this regard many States expressed their view on the possible approaches in relation to the future development of the question. Some States said that they did not intend to disregard the valuable experience provided by the Antarctic Treaty system, not alter any of its major objectives. They expressed the hope that gaps and inadequacies in the Treaty would be remedied through a more general examination of the question in a forum that allowed for universal representation. Some other States maintained that the elimination of any flaws in the Treaty and changes and adjustments of the existing system should be of an evolutionary nature to be undertaken from within and not from outside with the aim of changing or replacing the system.

160. On 15 December 1983, the General Assembly adopted resolution 38/77 entitled "Question of Antarctica". For that resolution, the Assembly, affirming the conviction that, in the interest of all mankind, Antarctica should continue forever to be used exclusively for peaceful purposes and that it should not become the scene or object of international discord, requested the Secretary-General to prepare a comprehensive, factual and objective study on all aspects of Antarctica, taking fully into account the Antarctic Treaty system and other relevant factors. It also requested the Secretary-General to seek the views of all Member States in preparing the study; requested those States conducting scientific research in Antarctica, other interested States the relevant specialized agencies, organs, organizations and bodies of the United Nations

system and relevant international organizations having scientific or technical information on Antarctica to lend the Secretary-General whatever assistance he might request for the purpose of carrying out the study, and requested the Secretary-General to report to the General Assembly at its thirty-ninth session.

Chapter III
The Antarctic Treaty System in Practice

A. Peaceful uses of Antarctica

161. On 1 December 1959, all the countries involved in the Antarctic region, including the United States and the Soviet Union, signed the Antarctic Treaty and accepted the principle that it was in the interest of all mankind that Antarctic should continue to be used exclusively for peaceful purposes and should not become the scene of international discord. Since then, for nearly two and a half decades, Antarctica and its surrounding maritime areas have been free from militarization of any kind, including nuclear weapons. No armed conflict has taken place in the area. Peace on the continent has been maintained to a large extent through the agreements embodied in the Antarctic Treaty. The Treaty has provided a framework for the Parties to the Treaty to carry out peaceful activities related to scientific research, exploitation of marine resources and protection of the environment, and to promote co-operation among them in carrying out such activities in the region.

162. In order to prevent tension and political conflict on territorial claims, sovereign rights and jurisdiction, the Treaty formally set aside disputes between States claiming territorial sovereignty in Antarctica and disagreements between claimant States and States not recognizing such claims.

163. To secure the goals of scientific co-operation, the Treaty provided for the exchange of information on plans, programmes and results of investigations, as well as of scientific personnel.

164. The Treaty provided comprehensive disarmament measures for Antarctica. It not only prohibited the establishment of military bases in Antarctica, but it also prohibited the carrying out of military manoeuvres so that no military conflict would originate within the region. In fact, the Antarctic Treaty represented the only post-war international agreement for the complete demilitarization of a sizeable geographical region. At present, it includes all the countries involved in Antarctic issues as its Parties, among them the five permanent members of the Security Council and all the countries that maintained claims to territorial sovereignty over Antarctica. The conclusion of the Treaty has been invoked as a precedent for numerous initiatives and proposals for regional disarmament measures which have been made since the end of the Second World War.

165. The importance of maintaining Antarctica as demilitarized and free from nuclear weapons and strategic competition was clearly stressed by all the representatives that took the floor during the deliberations on Antarctica at the thirty-eighth session of the General Assembly. In particular, the representatives from the countries situated in geographic proximity to Antarctica emphasized the importance of peace in Antarctica in the context of their own national security. No one challenged the fact that two and a half decades of peace in Antarctica were attributable to the achievements of the Parties to the Treaty in implementing effectively the far-reaching disarmament measures of the Treaty. In this regard, several States emphasized the role of the consultative process which enabled active and continuous international co-operation despite various differences in the political relations among the Consultative Parties to the Treaty.

B. Antarctica as a nuclear-weapon-free zone

166. To date, Antarctica has been free from nuclear weapons and has been spared the threat of involvement in the global nuclear arms race. The complete absence of nuclear weapons in Antarctica has been ensured since 1959 by the Antarctic Treaty and, in fact, the Treaty was the first international agreement which, by establishing a demilitarized zone, contained

provisions ensuring that nuclear weapons would not be introduced into a specifically defined geographical area.

167. The Antarctic continent and its surrounding maritime areas south of 60°S latitude therefore became a forerunner of nuclear-weapon-free zones. Since then, several international agreements have been concluded and numerous proposals have been made with a view to securing the complete absence of nuclear weapons from various areas. The agreements are the Treaty on Principles Governing the Activities of States in the Exploration and Use of Outer Space, including the Moon and Other Celestial Bodies (General Assembly resolution 2222 (XXI), annex), the Treaty for the Prohibition of Nuclear Weapons in Latin America (Treaty of Tlatelolco)[63] and the Treaty on the Prohibition of the Emplacement of Nuclear Weapons and Other Weapons of Mass Destruction on the Sea-Bed and the Ocean Floor and in the Subsoil Thereof (Assembly resolution 2660 (XXV), annex). Furthermore, there are currently proposals to establish nuclear-weapon-free zones in Central Europe, the Balkans, the Mediterranean, Africa, Northern Europe, the Middle East, South Asia and the South Pacific.

168. Compared with subsequent international agreements establishing zones free of nuclear weapons, the Antarctic Treaty enjoys the concurring support of all five nuclear-weapon Powers of the world, including the United States and the Soviet Union. It was noted during the deliberations on Antarctica at the thirty-eighth session of the General Assembly that the Antarctic Treaty represented an important example of co-operation between the United States and the Soviet Union in the field of arms control, and that such an agreement between the two leading nuclear Powers would be extremely difficult to attain were it to be negotiated under the present international political climate. There was a clear consensus among all the delegations participating in the General Assembly's deliberations that maintaining Antarctica free from nuclear weapons and from involvement in the nuclear arms race was vitally important for the peace and security of the entire world.

169. The Antarctic Treaty, besides banning nuclear weapons, nuclear explosions and the dumping of nuclear waste, provides for a comprehensive verification system based on on-site inspection, for safeguards on future nuclear activities for peaceful purposes (by applying the rules established in international agreements concerning nuclear energy if and when all the Consultative Parties are parties to such agreements); and for the clear demarcation of the geographical area free from nuclear weapons agreed upon by all the Parties to the Treaty.

170. Since the signing of the Antarctic Treaty in 1959, Parties to the Treaty have assumed the obligations of the Treaty to keep Antarctica free from nuclear weapons. All nuclear-weapon Powers have refrained from carrying out nuclear explosions, dumping nuclear waste materials or installing nuclear weapons in Antarctica; in fact, no country, whether or not a Party to the Treaty, has attempted to violate the provisions that make Antarctica free of nuclear weapons. The successful implementation of the Antarctic Treaty in keeping Antarctica free from nuclear weapons is one of the significant post-war contributions toward averting nuclear weapon proliferation and halting the nuclear arms race.

C. Facilitation of international scientific co-operation

171. In article III, paragraph 2, the Antarctic Treaty encourages the establishment of co-operative working relations with the specialized agencies of the United Nations and other international organizations having scientific or technical interest in Antarctica.

172. By way of implementation of that provision of the Treaty, the Consultative Parties at their First Consultative Meeting decided that it should be an individual obligation of each of their Governments to encourage the work of such international organizations and to promote on a bilateral basis the establishment and development of co-operative relations with those organizations (recommendation I-5).

[63] United Nations, *Treaty Series*, vol. 634, No. 9068, p. 326.

173. Over the years, active co-operation has been promoted, with attention being focused on meteorology, telecommunications, oceanography (in particular, marine science) and protection of the environment. In this respect, close relations with WMO, ITU, IOC, and, in particular, SCAR deserve particular mention.

174. One example of this co-operation was the active support and participation of the Consultative Parties in the World Weather Watch Programme carried out under the auspices of WMO (see recommendations V-2, VI-J, IX-3 and X-3). The Consultative Parties recognized that their participation in the World Weather Watch required, on the one hand, a thorough review and improvement of the meteorological data collection and dissemination network operating in the Antarctic and, on the other hand, support of meteorological activities in Antarctica to the greatest extent feasible by transmission of processed data to the Antarctic from the World Weather Watch. In support of the World Weather Watch some of the Consultative Parties created Antarctic Meteorological Centres at their stations.

175. Telecommunications is an area of close co-operation between the Consultative Parties and interested international organizations. Experts from WMO, ITO and SCAR have been invited to be observers at the meetings of the Antarctic Treaty group of experts on telecommunications (see recommendations III-5 and V-2). Certain arrangements have been adopted by the Consultative Parties to facilitate transmission with minimum delay of meteorological information from Antarctica to the Global Telecommunications System (see recommendation X-3).

176. Of all international organizations, the closest relations maintained by the Antarctic Treaty Parties has been with SCAR. While there is no formal, direct link between SCAR and the Consultative Meetings, there is an effective interchange and SCAR is frequently invited to provide scientific advice to the Consultative Parties through recommendations of representatives at the Consultative Meetings to their Governments that, through their national committees for SCAR, they invite SCAR to undertake particular activities.[64] This mechanism is perhaps unusual but it has been reviewed from time to time and found to be satisfactory by the Consultative Parties and SCAR. It should also be noted that recommendations of the Consultative Meetings are made widely available through publication in the SCAR Bulletin.

D. Exchange of information

177. With a view to promoting international co-operation in scientific research, the Antarctic Treaty provides that information regarding plans for scientific programmes, observations and results "be exchanged and made freely available" (art. III, subpara. 1 (c)).

178. The Consultative Meetings are convened under the Treaty, *inter alia*, for the purpose of elaborating measures to facilitate scientific research in Antarctic, thus giving effect to the provisions of article III of the Antarctic Treaty. At an earlier stage of activity, those Meetings adopted numerous decisions on the question of the exchange of information (see recommendations I-1, I-3, I-5, I-7, I-13, II-1, II-8, IV-8, IV-27, VI-2, VI-3, VI-6, VI-7 and VI-12). Unfortunately, a lack of proper co-ordination resulted in the inclusion of sometimes conflicting or overlapping provisions in these decisions;[65] therefore, the exchange of scientific information at the initial stage had a somewhat unsystematic character.

179. It should be noted that, in addition to exchanging scientific information, Parties to the Antarctic Treaty, in accordance with its article on inspection and observation, are under the obligation to provide each other with extensive information on expeditions, stations, military personnel and equipment (art. VII, para. 5). A standard form for such information to be circulated under the Antarctic Treaty, drafted in very general terms, was adopted by the First Consultative

[64] See Charles R. Bentley, Statement, Eighth Annual Conference, Center for Ocean Management Studies, University of Rhode Island, 17–20 June 1981; and Tore Gjelsvik, "Scientific research and co-operation in Antarctica", *Antarctic Challenge – Proceedings of an Interdisciplinary Symposium*, 22–24 June 1983, Kiel, Federal Republic of Germany, pp. 41–51.

[65] See R. E. Guyer, "The Antarctic System", *Recueil des cours de L'Académie de droit international* (Leyden, 1974), vol. 139, p. 201.

Meeting in recommendation I-6. Additions to that form were later approved by the Third and Sixth Consultative Meetings in recommendations III-1 and VI-13.

180. For several years there was no single standard form for exchange of information on different activities in Antarctica. However, the Seventh Consultative Meeting decided that the whole subject needed to be examined with a view to consolidating all the various provisions into one recommendation.

181. This was done in 1975 at the Eighth Consultative Meeting in Oslo, where the Standard Format for the Annual Exchanges of Information was elaborated (annexed to the present chapter). It was decided that the report containing information described in the Standard Format should be exchanged through diplomatic channels not later than 30 November of each year. All extensions, reductions or other modifications in the development of activities, circulated before 30 November, should be reported prior to 30 June following the season of those activities (recommendation VIII-6).

182. The system of the exchange of information on activities in Antarctica existing under the Antarctic Treaty is being supplemented by a similar exchange of information exercised in accordance with the provisions of the Convention for the Conservation of Antarctic Seals, the Convention on the Conservation of Antarctic Marine Living Resources, and through existing channels of co-operative working relations established with such international organizations as SCAR, SCOR, WHO and ITU.

E. Protection of the environment

183. The Antarctic exerts a critical influence on oceanic and atmospheric circulation and thus on the global climate, most especially on the Southern Hemisphere. Although the effect that Antarctica has on the formation of the world's climate is complex and not fully understood, its role in the process of global heat circulation is evident. Most of the solar energy received in Antarctica is reflected back by its ice and snow cover, a process greatly facilitated by the thin and relatively unpolluted atmosphere. The Antarctic ice sheet stabilizes climate and is the principal factor controlling world sea levels. Because of its high albedo or reflectivity (proportion of solar light incident upon an element of the surface, which is again reflected by it), only a small proportion of the sun's radiant energy falling on the Antarctic is absorbed. Further, half of the bottom waters of the world's oceans are formed around Antarctica. Scientists speculate that the continent may play a major role in determining general climatic changes over periods as short as 10 to 100 years.

184. Antarctic ecosystems are extremely vulnerable to disturbance. A decrease in albedo of the Antarctic ice sheet, for example, because of industrial pollution, could result in an increase in heat input to the geosphere,[66] possibly leading to some melting of the ice sheet and to a rise in ocean levels and consequent climate changes.[67] Because of the extreme conditions there, Antarctic ecosystems are less able to withstand any change induced by human activities than other ecosystems. Areas of Antarctic land damaged by human activity cannot be rehabilitated in the fashion adopted in other areas, including the Arctic. The rehabilitation of disturbed ice sites does not appear feasible except by a slow natural process.[68]

185. Antarctica is now regarded as the best site for monitoring the world's pollution, because its environment so far has been kept virtually unspoiled. No commercial industrial activities

[66] See Ludger Kappen, "Ecological Aspects of an Exploitation of the Non-Living Resources of the Antarctic", *Proceedings of an Interdisciplinary Symposium*, p. 212.

[67] See Dick Laws, Earthscan Press Briefing Seminar on the Future of Antarctica, 25 July 1977, p. 2.

[68] See Report on the Group of Experts on Mineral Exploration and Exploitation, Report of the Ninth Consultative Meeting (London, 19 September–7 October 1977, pp. 69–72); see also "Preliminary Assessment of the Environmental Impact of Mineral Exploration/Exploitation in Antarctica (EAMREA) – Report of the SCARIS Group of Specialists", 1979; and Katherine H. Green, "Environmental Aspects of Potential Petroleum Exploration and Exploitation in Antarctica: Forecasting and Evaluating Risks", United States Marine Mammal Commission, Washington, D.C., February 1982.

have developed in the area, and the geographic isolation of the continent has kept Antarctica virtually unaffected by the major sources of pollution, both natural and "man-made". The purity of the Antarctic environment, as well as its unique physical characteristics, makes the region particularly suitable for wide-ranging scientific research activities.

186. In recent years, environmental concern has given rise to proposals, mainly from non-governmental organizations, to apply in Antarctica some conservationist concepts, including suggestions to declare the continent a World Park,[69] to place certain sites under the 1972 UNESCO Convention Concerning the Protection of the World Cultural and Natural Heritage,[70] and to set aside particular areas as biosphere reserves, established under the UNESCO Man and the Biosphere Programme.[71]

187. It would appear that no major damage has so far occurred to the Antarctic ecosystems.[72] Human activities in Antarctica remain very limited, are still confined to narrow areas around the scientific stations and are being carried out in accordance with the strict rules and regulations imposed on such activities by the Antarctic Treaty Consultative Parties.

188. Since 1961, environmental protection of Antarctic ecosystems has constituted a central issue on the agenda of the Consultative Meetings. It has been clearly understood by the Consultative Parties that the steadily increasing number of people working in Antarctica and the associated logistic support facilities would place more and more stress on Antarctic ecosystems. The Consultative Meetings have devoted their attention to this subject and have adopted very important measures aimed at protecting the unique and exceptionally vulnerable Antarctic environment.

189. Inspired by SCAR, the Consultative Parties first concentrated on the elaboration of measures for the conservation of Antarctic fauna and flora. At their First Consultative Meeting, in 1961, they set forth provisional guidelines on this subject (recommendation 1-8). The Third Consultative Meeting in 1964 approved the so-called mini-convention, Agreed Measures for the Conservation of Antarctic Fauna and Flora. That document became the first significant contribution by the Consultative Parties to the protection of the Antarctic environment.

190. The Agreed Measures proclaimed the Antarctic Treaty areas as a Special Conservation Area. It should be noted, however, that the Agreed Measures actually apply only to Antarctic land areas, since they do not affect the rights, or exercise of the rights, of States under international law with regard to the high seas within the Antarctic Treaty area (art. I, para. 2).

191. Under the Agreed Measures, Governments are required to take appropriate measures to minimize harmful interference with the normal living conditions of any native mammal or bird, or any attempt at such harmful interference. The following acts and activities are considered as harmful interference: allowing dogs to run free; flying helicopters or other aircraft in a manner that would unnecessarily disturb bird or seal concentrations, or landing close to such concentrations; driving vehicles unnecessarily close to the concentrations of birds and seals; use of explosives close to concentrations of birds and seals; discharge of firearms close to bird and seal concentrations; any disturbance of bird and seal colonies during the breeding period

[69] James N. Barnes, "Let's Save Antarctica", Richmond, Australia, 1982, p. 30.

[70] See "Protected Areas in the Antarctic", Antarctic and Southern Ocean Coalition (a workshop for delegates to the Antarctic Mineral Negotiations), Washington, D.C., 23 January 1984, pp. 4–5.

[71] A biosphere reserve is a protected area of land or coastal environment displaying one or more of the following characteristics: (a) representative examples of natural biomes; (b) unique communities or areas with unusual features of exceptional interest; (c) examples of harmonious landscape resulting from traditional patterns of land-use; (d) examples of modified or degraded ecosystems that are capable of being restored to more or less natural conditions. See "Looking at biosphere reserves – a 1983 Perspective", *Nature and Resources* (19(2) April–June 1983), UNESCO.

[72] See Boleslav A. Boczek, "The Protection of Antarctic Ecosystem", *Ocean Development and International Law, Journal of Marine Affairs*, vol. 13, No. 3 (January 1984), pp. 358–359; Report of the Group of Ecological, Technological and Other Related Experts on Mineral Exploration and Exploitation in Antarctica, Report of the Tenth Consultative Meeting, Washington, D.C. (17 September–5 October 1979), p. 111.

by persistent attention from persons on foot (art. VII, para. 2). However, the Agreed Measures envisage that some of the above activities may be exceptionally permitted to the minimum extent necessary for the establishment, supply and operation of the scientific stations.

192. The Agreed Measures prohibit bringing into the area of application of non-indigenous animal or plant species except by permit. Such a permit can be issued to allow importation only of the animals and plants listed in annex C to the Agreed Measures (art. IX). The Agreed Measures provide that Governments prohibit within the area of application the killing, wounding, capturing or molesting of any native mammal or native bird, or any attempt at any such act, except with a permit. Such a permit may be issued only for the following purposes: to provide indispensable food in limited quantities for men or dog; to provide specimens for scientific study or scientific information; and to provide specimens for museums, zoological gardens or other educational or cultural institutions or uses (art. VI).

193. In order to preserve the unique natural ecological systems of certain areas, the Consultative Parties agreed that such areas should be granted special status and designated as "Specially Protected Areas". In addition to the general restrictions listed in the Agreed Measures, in these areas Governments should prohibit the collection of any native plant, except with a permit, the driving of any vehicle and entry by their nationals, except with a permit (art. VIII).

194. In accordance with the above-mentioned provisions of the Agreed Measures, the subsequent Consultative Meetings have designated a large number of sites in Antarctica as "Specially Protected Areas", among them, the Rookery Islands, Cape Hallet, Lynch Island and Litchfield Island etc. (recommendations IV-2, IV-7, IV-14 and VIII-l and others).

195. For the purposes of having a single, systematic approach to the selection of Specially Protected Areas, the Consultative Parties, at their Seventh Meeting, approved in recommendation VII 2 the criteria to be met for designation of such areas. In accordance with that decision, the areas suggested for designation as specially protected should meet the following requirements:

(a) Represent examples of the major Antarctic land and freshwater ecological systems;
(b) Have unique complexes of species;
(c) Be the type locality or only known habitat of any plant or invertebrate species;
(d) Contain especially interesting breeding colonies of birds or mammals;
(e) Be kept inviolate so that in the future they may be used for purposes of comparison with localities that have been disturbed by man.

196. Article X of the Agreed Measures repeats almost exactly the text of article X of the Antarctic Treaty. It declares that each participating Government should undertake to exert appropriate efforts, consistent with the Charter of the United Nations, to the end that no one engages in any activity in the area of application contrary to the Principles or purposes of the Agreed Measures. By including this article, the Consultative Parties evidently wished to record that they would make every effort to assure effective application of the Agreed Measures by everyone exercising any activity in Antarctica.

197. The general policy of the Consultative Parties with respect to protection of the Antarctic environment was formulated at the Sixth Meeting, which, in recommendation VI-4, recognized the following principles:

(a) In the Antarctic Treaty area the ecosystem is particularly vulnerable to human interference;
(b) The Antarctic derives much of its scientific importance from its uncontaminated and undisturbed condition;
(c) There is an increasingly urgent need to protect the environment from human interference;
(d) The Consultative Parties should assume responsibility for the protection of the environment and the wise use of the Treaty Area.

198. By adopting those principles, the Consultative Parties institutionalized the protection of the Antarctic environment as a matter of common concern and agreed that responsibility

would be assumed jointly without regard to any party's status as a claimant or non-claimant.[73] In the same recommendation, the Consultative Parties invited SCAR to identify the types and assess the extent of human interference with the environment that had occurred as a result of human activities in Antarctica and to propose measures to minimize harmful interference (recommendations VI-4, para. 1).

199. On the basis of the response of SCAR, the Consultative Parties at their Eighth Meeting, in 1975, made further progress in protecting the Antarctic environment by approving the Code of Conduct for Antarctic Expeditions and Station Activities (recommendation VIII-11, annex). The Code recommended procedures for waste disposal, reaffirmed certain provisions of the Agreed Measures concerning the introduction of alien species and disturbance of breeding colonies of birds and mammals and, in an important step toward evaluating environmental impact, provided guidelines for organizations planning major Antarctic projects.

200. Noting the increase in the number of tourists visiting Antarctica, the Eighth Consultative Meeting restricted places where large numbers of tourists might land so that the ecological effects might be monitored. It was recommended that Governments request all organizers of tourist groups, except in an emergency, to visit only those Antarctic stations for which permission had been sought and granted and to land only within "Areas of Special Tourist Interest" to be designated by the Consultative Parties (recommendation VIII-9).

201. At the Eighth Consultative Meeting, the Parties stressed once again their responsibility, as State active in Antarctica, to protect the Antarctic environment. It was emphasized that their Governments, in exercising this responsibility, should act in a way to ensure that measures for the wise use and protection of the Antarctic environment were consistent with the interests of all mankind (recommendation VIII-13).

202. At their Ninth Consultative Meeting, in 1977, after thorough examination of the information and suggestions submitting by SCAR, the Consultative Parties elaborated some new environmental principles, thus extending the number of principles first formulated at the Sixth Meeting. Recommendation IX-5 declared:

"1. The Consultative Parties recognise their prime responsibility for the protection of the Antarctic environment from all forms of harmful human interference;

"2. They will ensure in planning future activities that the question of environmental effects and the possible impact of such activities on the relevant ecosystems are duly considered;

"3. They will refrain from activities having an inherent tendency to modify the Antarctic environment unless appropriate steps have been taken to foresee the probable modifications and to exercise appropriate controls with respect to harmful environmental effects;

"4. They will continue to monitor the Antarctic environment and to exercise their responsibility for informing the world community of any significant changes in the Antarctic Treaty Area caused by man's activities."

203. The Tenth Consultative Meeting concentrated on consideration of three concrete aspects related to protection of the Antarctic environment, namely, oil contamination of the Antarctic marine environment, effects of tourist and non-governmental expeditions in the Antarctic Treaty area and ecological aspects arising from discussions on the mineral resource régime.

204. The ecological aspects concerning mineral resource activities are dealt with in section F 2 of chapter III, "Antarctic mineral resources", of the present study. The Consultative Parties agreed at the Tenth Consultative Meeting that a future régime on mineral resources should provide strict guarantees for protection of the Antarctic environment and, moreover, should include means for determining whether mineral resource activities would be acceptable at all (recommendation X-1).

[73] See David A. Colson, "The Antarctic Treaty System: the Mineral Issue", *Law and Policy in International Business*, vol. 12, No. 4 (1980), p. 858.

205. On the question of oil contamination, it was concluded that for the time being, the most significant introduction of oil into the Antarctic marine ecosystem appeared to be from the operation of ships. It was decided to invite SCAR, in consultation with other appropriate international organizations, to keep under review the possibility of developing a programme for the determination of baseline measures of hydrocarbon content relevant to the needs for such determinations in the Antarctic marine environment. The Consultative Parties also agreed to review their respective obligations under existing international agreements which related to the reduction of contamination of the sea by oil, in the light of the particularly hazardous nature of Antarctic ship operations, and to consider whether their compliance with those obligations adequately minimized the risk of oil contamination of the Antarctic marine environment (recommendation X-7).

206. With reference to the effects of tourist and non-governmental expeditions, the Tenth Consultative Meeting approved the text of the Statement of Accepted Practices and the Relevant Provisions of the Antarctic Treaty, including Guidance for Visitors to the Antarctic (recommendation X-8). The main aim of that document is to assure that all visitors to Antarctica are aware of existing practices, rules and regulations in the Antarctic Treaty area and to provide them with guidance for proper conduct in Antarctica.

207. The most recent Consultative Meeting, the Twelfth, held at Canberra in September 1983, concentrated on the question of assessment procedures for determining whether the activities planned by the Consultative Parties in Antarctica were likely to have significant impact on the environment. The discussions proceeded from the assumption that those procedures should not prejudice one of the fundamental principles of the Antarctic Treaty, providing for freedom of scientific research, and that such procedures should not encroach upon or prejudice provisions for the protection of the environment and the conservation of living resources contained in instruments that had been or might be negotiated as parts of the Antarctic Treaty system. The conclusion was reached that if a preliminary determination indicated that a planned research or logistic activity could have potentially significant impacts on the environment, the relevant agencies of the Consultative Parties should undertake a detailed environmental assessment with a view to determining the factors likely to cause such impacts. If, as a result of such assessment, the seriousness of such impacts was determined, they should elaborate feasible research and logistic alternatives aimed at minimizing harmful effects on the environment (recommendation XII-3).

F. Antarctic resources

1. Conservation of Antarctic living resources

208. From the very beginning, the Consultative Parties to the Antarctic Treaty have shown their concern about the conservation of Antarctic living resources and have recognized the urgent need for measures to accomplish this goal. As stated in the decisions adopted by the Consultative Meetings, the participants feel themselves under obligation, deriving from the provisions of paragraph 1 (f) of article IX of the Treaty, to elaborate measures regarding preservation and conservation of living resources in Antarctica. The Consultative Parties have stressed on several occasions, that while proceeding in this matter, they are acting without prejudice to their positions of principle on the sovereignty issue (see recommendation III-B, IX-2, X-2 and XI-2).

209. Living resources of the Southern Ocean have attracted the interest of commercial enterprises since the early years of the nineteenth century, with seals and whales having become the object of wide-scale exploitation that has not been extended to other species.

210. In the periods from 1820 to 1830 and from 1870 to 1880, millions of seals were killed in Antarctica, to the extent that unrestricted harvesting of seals almost totally destroyed their population in the area. Since that time and because of the drastic depletion of seal herds, only a minor revival of seal harvesting occurred at the beginning of the twentieth century.

211. Starting from 1904, when the first whaling station was opened on one of the Antarctic islands, and for almost 60 years following, whales were the main object of commercial enterprises in Antarctic waters.[74] A decline in whale herds throughout the world and a growing understanding of the need for internationally agreed upon measures regulating their exploitation led to the conclusion in 1931 of the International Convention for the Regulation of Whaling, which entered into force in 1935.

212. After the Second World War, a new International Convention for the Regulation of Whaling was signed in 1946, establishing the International Whaling Commission which was given global responsibility for setting quotas on the catch of whales, including Antarctic waters. Management of the world's whale stocks by the Commission has been increasingly more conservative. Due to this policy, whaling in Antarctic waters has been drastically reduced.

213. Since whales are a highly migratory species, it is logical that the Convention on whaling has been applied world-wide and Antarctic waters are only one of the areas covered by it.

214. The first international agreement concluded solely for the purposes of the conservation and rational utilization of Antarctic living resources is the 1972 Convention for the Conservation of Antarctic Seals.

215. In accordance with modern international law, States have a duty to co-operate with each other in taking necessary measures for the conservation and management of living resources of the high seas. Those provisions of general international law were recently confirmed in the 1982 United Nations Convention on the Law of the Sea.[75] Article 118 of the Convention provides, *inter alia*, the following:

"States whose nationals exploit identical living resources, or different living resources in the same area, shall enter into negotiations with a view to taking the measures necessary for the conservation of the living resources concerned. They shall, as appropriate, co-operate to establish subregional or regional fisheries organizations to this end."

216. The various measures taken by the Consultative Parties for the conservation of Antarctic living resources have evidently aimed at fulfilling this goal.

217. There has been no commercial exploitation of Antarctic seals for many years, but the fear persists that growing populations of seals may attract the attention of commercial enterprises and that unrestricted harvesting could be resumed at some time in the future. In order to forestall a recurrence of destructive exploitation of seals, the Consultative Parties, in their efforts to protect the living resources of Antarctica, first focused attention on drafting an international régime for the conservation of Antarctic seals.

218. As an interim measure in the process of elaboration of that régime, they suggested, at the Third Consultative Meeting, held at Brussels in 1964, that Governments should voluntarily regulate pelagic sealing by their nationals in order to ensure that the natural ecological system was not seriously disturbed (recommendation III-11).

219. At the Fourth Consultative Meeting, held at Santiago in 1966, the Consultative Parties approved Interim Guidelines for Voluntary Regulations of Antarctic Pelagic Sealing. Those guidelines set limits on seals to be taken, sealing tones and seasons, prohibited killing certain species of seals and required that Governments exchange information on any steps taken in accordance with the guidelines (recommendation IV-21).

220. Finally, in 1972, at the initiative of the Consultative Parties, an international conference was convened in London during which the Convention for the Conservation of Antarctic Seals was negotiated. The Consultative Parties were motivated by a belief that a separate international agreement opened for accession by other States might better serve the purposes of effective

[74] See R. Tucker Scully, "The Marine Living Resources of the Southern Ocean", *University of Miami Law Review*, vol. 33, No. 2 (December 1978), p. 346; see also "Polar Regions Atlas", Central Intelligence Agency, United States of America, May 1978, pp. 52–53.

[75] See chap. II, note 53.

management of Antarctic sealing than would recommendations approved under article IX of the Antarctic Treaty.[76]

221. As in the case of the Antarctic Treaty, 60°S latitude was chosen for the northern boundary of the Convention for the Conservation of Antarctic Seals, which thus applies to the seas south of this latitude. The Convention reaffirms the Provisions of article IV of the Antarctic Treaty relating to the sovereignty issue with respect to these seas (art. 1, para. 1). That provision reflects the ability of claimant and non-claimant States, due to the existence of the Antarctic Treaty and despite their disagreement on the status of some of the marine areas, to reach an understanding on conservation measures applicable to these areas.

222. The Convention provides that a commission and a scientific advisory committee will be established if commercial sealing begins in Antarctica (art. 6, subparas. 1 (b) and 1 (c)). Until that time, SCAR was invited to assess information received from the Contracting Parties, to recommend programmes for scientific research and to recommend statistical and biological data to be collected by sealing expeditions. SCAR was also authorized to report on the basis of statistical, biological and other evidence available when the harvest of any species of seals was having a significantly harmful effect on the total stocks of such species or on the ecological system in any particular locality (art. 5, para. 4). Should SCAR estimate that the permissible catch limits for any species were likely to be exceeded, the Contracting Parties should then take appropriate measures to prevent further sealing by their nationals and vessels (art. 5, para. 5).

223. It was recorded in the preamble to the Convention that SCAR had agreed to carry out the tasks requested of it in the Convention.

224. The Convention provides for the establishment of an effective inspection system once commercial sealing begins (art. 6, subpara. 1 (a)).

225. Specific measures for the conservation of Antarctic seals are listed in the annex to the Convention, which forms an integral part thereof. Those measures forbid all sealing for six months of each year during the period between 1 March and 31 August. They restrict sealing to certain areas. The killing or capturing of three species of seals is completely forbidden and the total catch of three other species is limited to 192,000. SCAR for its part had a higher figure as a permissible catch in 1972.[77]

226. In accordance with article 3, paragraph 3, the conservation measures set out in the annex can be reviewed in the light of scientific assessments and in accordance with the procedures mentioned in article 9 of the Convention.

227. The Convention establishes a comprehensive system for exchanging information by imposing on each Contracting Party an obligation to provide to other Contracting Parties and to SCAR each year, before 31 October, a summary of statistical information on all seals killed or captured by their nationals and vessels (art. 5, para. 2, and annex).

228. Conservation measures and other provisions of the Convention are to be enforced through the adoption by each Contracting Party of such laws and regulations as may be necessary to implement the Convention (art. 2).

229. The Convention for the Conservation of Antarctic Seals came into force on 11 March 1978. It is open for accession by any State invited to accede by the Contracting Parties (art. 12). Since there is no commercial sealing now in Antarctica, the Convention plays a preventive rather than regulatory role.

230. In the early 19709, the potential for exploiting the living resources of the Antarctic region other than whales and seals began to attract interest. While it was realized at that time that some years of experimental fishery and technological development would be necessary before commercial large-scale exploitation would start in Antarctica, SCAR felt the need to

[76] Colson, "The Antarctic Treaty System: the Mineral Issue", p. 869.

[77] V. V. Golitsyn, "Antarctika-mejdunarodnopravovoy rejim", Mejdunarodniye atnosheniya, Moskva 1983 str. 109.

expand substantially the scientific understanding of Antarctic marine living resources and in particular the relationship between potentially exploitable species and other elements of the marine ecosystem.[78]

231. The efforts of SCAR to a certain extent were inspired by the Antarctic Treaty Consultative Parties. Being concerned with the inadequacy of the information available on stocks of the Antarctic marine living resources and being aware of the need to develop a good scientific foundation for appropriate conservation measures, they urged SCAR, at the Eighth Consultative Meeting, to consider convening a meeting to discuss current scientific work and report on programmes to study and conserve Antarctic marine living resources (recommendation VIII-10).

232. At the initiative of SCAR and with the co-sponsorship of the Scientific Committee on Oceanographic Research (SCOR), an international scientific conference on the living resources of the Southern Ocean was convened in August 1976 at Woods Hole, Massachusetts, United States. The major part of the conference, as well as the subsequent session of a group of specialists, was devoted to discussions on the finalization of an international programme for the Biological Investigation of Marine Antarctic Systems and Stocks (BIOMASS).

233. The BIOMASS proposal became the first major international effort to co-ordinate research for the development and proper management of the living resources of the Southern Ocean. Its principle objective was to gain a deeper understanding of the structure and dynamic functioning of the Antarctic marine ecosystem.[79] At the Ninth Consultative Meeting, the participants decided that their Governments should give sympathetic consideration to the provision of practical measures (such as ships, ship time, personnel and finance) in support of the implementation of the BIOMASS programme (recommendation IX-2).

234. The United Nations Development Programme (UNDP) in 1976 approved a $202,000 Southern Ocean Fisheries Survey Programme (GLO/75/006) executed by FAO. The major output of that project was three extensive reports, published in 1977, on the biology, harvesting and processing of living resources of the area.[80] From 1976 to 1978, FAO actively tested a proposal for a $45 million 10-year programme the goal of which was to assist in the exploration, exploitation and utilization of the living resources in the areas south of 45°S latitude. In the outcome, FAO did not pursue the idea because its members felt that Priority should be given to assisting developing countries in promoting development of their own economic zones.[81]

235. In light of the growing attention to the potential of living resources, the prospects of commercial harvesting, the unknown effects of such harvesting and the gaps in the data required for effective management of Antarctic marine living resources, the Antarctic Treaty Consultative Parties took steps for the preservation and conservation of those resources at the end of the 1970s in order to meet their responsibilities under article IX of the Treaty.

236. At the Ninth Consultative Meeting, in 1977, the Consultative Parties expressed their recognition of the urgency of ensuring that the Antarctic marine living resources be protected by the establishment of sound conservation measures that would prevent overfishing and protect the integrity of the Antarctic ecosystem. The Consultative Parties decided that three sets of steps should be taken to implement this aim (recommendation IX-2).

237. First, the Consultative Parties agreed to negotiate, as a matter of urgency, a definitive régime for the conservation of Antarctic marine living resources, and stated that such a régime should take into account, *inter alia*, the following key elements:

[78] *Biological Investigations of Marine Antarctic Systems and Stocks*, Volume I: *Research Proposals*, SCAR-SCOR Working Group 54 (August 1977), p. ix.

[79] Ibid., pp. ix and 5.

[80] I. Everson, "The Living Resources of the Southern Ocean", FAO GLC/SO/77/1; G. O. Eddie, "The Harvesting of Krill", FAO GLO/SO/77/2; see also Barbara Mitchell and Richard Sandbrook, "The Management of the Southern Ocean" (International Institute for Environment and Development Publication, London, 1980), p. 28.

[81] Mitchell and Sandbrook, "The Management of the Southern Ocean", pp. 28 and 29.

(a) The prime responsibility of the Consultative Parties for the protection and conservation of the environment in the Antarctic Treaty area;
(b) The provisions of article IV of the Antarctic Treaty on sovereignty issues;
(c) The need to provide effective conservation of the marine living resources of the Antarctic ecosystem as a whole;
(d) The régime should cover the area of specific competence of the Antarctic Treaty;
(e) The régime should, however, extend north to 60°S latitude where necessary for the effective conservation of species of the Antarctic ecosystem, without prejudice to coastal state jurisdiction in that area;
(f) The régime should not apply to species already regulated pursuant to existing international agreements but should take into account the relationship of such species to those species covered by the régime.

238. The report of the Ninth Consultative Meeting casts additional light on plans for the "definitive régime". It states that the term conservation, as used in the above-mentioned recommendation, includes rational use, in the sense that harvesting should not be prohibited but the régime would exclude catch allocation and other economic regulations of harvesting. The report also makes reference to the understanding that the word "resources" is not limited to commercially exploitable species.

239. Second, pending entry into force of a definitive régime, the Consultative Parties set up interim guidelines for conservation which consisted of co-operation in mutual exchange of statistics relating to catches of Antarctic marine living resources, agreement to show the greatest possible concern and care in harvesting so that it did not result in the depletion of stocks or in jeopardizing the Antarctic marine ecosystem as a whole, and an appeal to those Governments that were not parties to the Antarctic Treaty and that engaged in activities involving the use of Antarctic marine living resources to take account of the guidelines.

240. Third, they adopted several recommendations intended to intensify co-operation in scientific investigation of Antarctic marine living resources and in the exchange of information thereon. They also agreed in planning marine activities in Antarctica to have regard to the advantages that would accrue from the BIOMASS programme.

241. In accordance with the aforementioned recommendation IX-2, the elaboration of a "definitive régime" was entrusted to special Consultative Meetings, which succeeded in producing the text of a draft convention on the conservation of Antarctic marine living resources.

242. As in the case of seals, a decisive step in the elaboration of the régime for the Antarctic marine living resources was taken at a diplomatic conference. That international conference, called by the Government of Australia, was held at Canberra from 7 to 20 May 1980 and was attended by the 15 States actively engaged in research and exploration of Antarctic marine living resources as full participants with observers from the European Economic Community (EEC), FAO, SCAR, IOC, SCOR, the International Whaling Commission (IWC) and the International Union for the Conservation of Nature and Natural Resources (IUCN). The Conference adopted the Convention on the Conservation of Antarctic Marine Living Resources, which entered into force on 7 April 1982. As at 30 June 1984, the following States are parties to the Convention: Argentina, Australia, Belgium, Chile, France, German Democratic Republic, Germany, Federal Republic of, Japan, New Zealand, Norway, Poland, South Africa, Spain, Sweden, Union of Soviet Socialist Republics, United Kingdom and United States. EEC also acceded to the Convention.

243. The Convention provides that States whose nationals exploit identical living resources should, as appropriate, co-operate to establish regional fisheries organizations with a view to taking measures necessary for the conservation of the living resources concerned in the light of article 118 of the United Nations Convention on the Law of the Sea. The Convention can be characterized as a regional agreement for the conservation and management of the living

resources. It fits neatly into this general requirement of international law. At the same time, the Convention differs from other fishery agreements.

244. The traditional approach to management of living resources envisaged in most current fisheries agreements and reflected in the Law of the Sea Convention is the maximum sustainable yield concept, aiming for that level of harvesting that will maximize the catch of the species plotted over a time series of estimated species productivity.[82] It is based on the species-by-species approach and focuses largely on a single species in formulating standards for management.

245. The unique structure of the Antarctic ecosystem and the complex interactions between different species, all competing for food consisting mainly of krill, required different standards for the management of the Antarctic living resources. Therefore a new approach, based on the ecosystem, was chosen as the policy for the management of those resources. In light of its ecosystem conservation standard, as well as the fact that it was negotiated prior to heavy commercial pressure on the resources, the Convention on the Conservation of Antarctic Marine Living Resources represents an interesting development in international law.[83]

246. The preamble to the Convention recognizes the importance of safeguarding the environment and protecting the integrity of the ecosystem of the seas surrounding Antarctica. Article I, paragraph 3, defines the Antarctic marine ecosystem as the complex of relationships of Antarctic of marine living resources with each other and with their physical environment. Article II of the Convention sets forth its general objective, the conservation of Antarctic marine living resources (para. 1), which, by definition, includes rational use of the resources (para. 2). The Convention provides several means to achieve this objective, of which the main ones are the principles of conservation, extended area of application and the establishment of suitable international machinery.

247. The ecosystem approach envisaged by the Convention is laid down in the following principles of conservation contained in paragraph 3 of article II: prevention of decrease in the size of any harvested population to levels below those which ensure its stable replacement; maintenance of the ecological relationships between harvested, dependent and related populations and the restoration of depleted populations to the levels of their stable recruitment; and prevention of changes or minimization of the risk of changes in the marine ecosystem which are not potentially reversible over two or three decades.

248. The ecosystem approach is also reflected in the area of application of the Convention. As a geographic boundary of Antarctica and the natural boundary of its ecosystem, the Convention adopts the Antarctic Convergence – a strip of water lying somewhere between 47° and 63°S latitude, where the surface temperature of ocean waters changes sharply within a short distance as cold Antarctic waters mix with warmer sub-Antarctic waters.

249. For the purposes of achieving the objective of the Convention and implementation of its principles, the decision was made to apply the Convention to the Antarctic marine living resources of the area both south of 60°S latitude and between that latitude and the Antarctic Convergence which form part of the Antarctic marine ecosystem (art. I, para. 1). Although the Antarctic Convergence is a seasonally movable zone, for the purposes of the Convention it was decided to define a list of co-ordinates that were deemed to be the line of the Antarctic Convergence (art. I, para. 4).[84]

250. The ecosystem approach is also indicated in the very broad definition of marine living resources under the Convention, which includes "fin fish, molluscs, crustaceans and all other species of living organisms, including birds, found south of the Antarctic Convergence" (art. I, para. 2).

[82] Ronald F. Frank. "The Convention on the Conservation of Antarctic Marine Living Resources", *Journal of Marine Affairs*, vol. 13, No. 3 (January 1984), p. 303.

[83] Ibid., pp. 300–301.

[84] See David M. Edwards and John A. Heap, "Convention on the Conservation of Antarctic Marine Living Resources: A Commentary", *Polar Record*, vol. 20, No. 127 (1981), p. 354.

251. To give effect to its objectives and the principles of conservation the Convention, like the majority of other international fishery agreements, set up a Commission, with headquarters in Hobart, Tasmania, Australia, and a Scientific Committee.

252. The Commission for the Conservation of Antarctic Marine Living Resources is composed of the original signatories to the Convention, acceding States engaged in research or harvesting activities and acceding regional economic integration organizations whose States members are entitled to participate in the work of the Commission (art. VII, para. 2).

253. The Commission has a broad array of functions, which include, *inter alia*, facilitation of research, identification of conservation needs, formulation, adoption and revision of conservation measures, implementation of systems of observation to be elaborated by the Commission and such other activities as are necessary to fulfil the objectives of the Convention (art. IX, para. 1).

254. The illustrative list of the functions of the Commission does not include a provision on allocation of catches. This was done largely because of the desire to avoid matters that raised directly the sovereignty issue. It was felt that agreement on such allocations might prove impossible in the Commission without directly challenging the alleged rights of claimant States.[85]

255. Decisions of the Commission on matters of substance, including in particular conservation measures, are taken by consensus (art. XII, para. 1). The choice in favour of a consensus procedure, rather than the traditional majority voting, was influenced by the 20 years experience that had already been acquired by the Antarctic Treaty States.[86]

256. The conservation measures adopted by the Commission became binding upon members of the Commission in accordance with the procedures established in paragraph 6 of article IX, which are similar to the relevant provisions of other fisheries agreements.

257. The Commission is authorized to draw the attention of any State not a party to the Convention to any activity undertaken by its nationals or vessels which, in the opinion of the Commission, affects the implementation of the objectives of the Convention (art. X, para. 1).

258. The Convention establishes a Scientific Committee for the Conservation of Antarctic Marine Living Resources as a consultative body to the Commission. Its main functions include providing criteria and methods to be used for determinations concerning conservation measures, assessing the status and trends of the populations of the resources involved, formulating proposals for national and international scientific research programmes, and transmitting assessments, analyses, reports and recommendations to the Commission regarding measures and research to implement the objectives of the Convention (art. XIV, para. 1, and art. XV, para. 2).

259. Many articles of the Convention foresee very strong links between the Convention and the Antarctic Treaty. In a certain sense the Convention complements the Treaty. Article III of the Convention, for example, provides that all its Parties, "whether or not they are Parties to the Antarctic Treaty, agree that they will not engage in any activities in the Antarctic Treaty area contrary to the principles and purposes of that Treaty and that, in their relations with each other, they are bound by the obligations contained in Articles I and V of the Antarctic Treaty" concerning the use of Antarctica exclusively for peaceful purposes. According to article V of the Convention, its Contracting Parties also agree to pay due regard to the special responsibility of the Antarctic Treaty Consultative Parties for the protection of the Antarctic environment. The Commission, in its work pursuant to article IX of the Convention, is to take full account of any relevant measures or regulations of the Consultative Meetings. The Convention provides that Parties to it, in their relations with each other, are bound by articles IV and VI of the Antarctic Treaty.

[85] James N. Barnes, "The Emerging Convention on the Conservation of Antarctica Marine Living Resources: An Attempt to Meet the New Realities of Resource Exploitation in the Southern Ocean", MCRC, 20 April 1982, p. 263.

[86] Colson, "The Antarctic Treaty System", p. 876; Edwards and Heap, "Convention on the Conservation ...", p. 358.

260. In drafting the Convention the claimant and non-claimant States disagreed on the question of whether attempts to establish fishery or exclusive economic zones must be regarded as impermissible under article IV of the Antarctic Treaty as an enlargement of existing claims. The situation was in addition complicated by the existence, within the prospective area of application of the Convention, of certain islands over which individual States have undisputed sovereignty.[87]

261. The conferees decided to sidestep the sovereignty issue by adopting a pragmatic solution through the use of the so-called "bifocal" approach which permitted all interested States to participate in the Convention. The language of paragraph 2 of article IV of the Convention is analogous to article IV of the Antarctic Treaty, with the exception of subparagraph 2 (b). This subparagraph states that

> "2. Nothing in this Convention and no acts or activities taking place while the present Convention is in force shall:
>
> ...
>
> "(b) be interpreted as a renunciation or diminution by any contracting Party of, or as prejudicing, any right or claim or basis of claim to exercise coastal state jurisdiction under international law within the area to which this Convention applies;".

262. The key element which distinguishes the language of the Convention from the provisions of article IV of the Antarctic Treaty is the use in subparagraph 2 (b) of the words "to exercise coastal State jurisdiction under international law within the area to which the Convention applies". According to the opinions of some scholars, these words in the context of the "bifocal" approach mean that claimant States could interpret article IV, subparagraph 2 (b), as referring to both undisputed islands and disputed territorial claims. At the same time, non-claimant States could argue that a right to exercise coastal State jurisdiction under international law exists only as to undisputed islands north of 60°S latitude.[88]

263. Another difficulty which the drafters of the Convention had to resolve related to the rights of States to coastal jurisdiction in areas north of 60°S latitude. The problem was how to preserve the ecosystem approach, covering all Antarctic waters by the régime of the Convention, and at the same time accommodate the interests of States having the right to coastal jurisdiction in 200-mile areas around islands over which the existence of State sovereignty was generally recognized, for example, the French islands of Kerguelen and Crozet.

264. This matter was not resolved in the Convention since it was extremely difficult to satisfy the needs of those States without encroachment on the issue of territorial claims. The compromise solution was found through inclusion in the Final Act of the Conference of a statement by its Chairman regarding the application of the Convention to waters adjacent to the islands, within the Convention area, over which the existence of State sovereignty was recognized by all parties to the Convention. In accordance with the statement, each time the Commission undertakes examination of the conservation needs within these waters, it is left to the coastal State to decide whether the waters in question should be included in the area of application of any specific conservation measure or if they should be excluded. The Commission cannot proceed to the adoption of such a measure if the coastal State concerned raises an objection to it.

265. The Convention is open for accession by any State interested in research or harvesting activities in relation to the marine living resources to which it applies (art. XXIX, para. 1). The Convention is also open for accession by regional economic integration organizations, such as the European Economic Community, on which members of such organizations have conferred competence with regard to the matters covered by the Convention. The accession

[87] Frank, "The Convention on the Conservation ...", p. 304.

[88] Rainer Lagoni, "Convention on the Conservation of Marine Living Resources: A Model for the Use of a Common Good?", *Proceedings of an Interdisciplinary Symposium*, p. 97; Edwards and Heap, "Convention on the Conservation ...", pp. 359–361; and Barnes, "The Emerging Convention ...", pp. 265–266.

of those organizations is not automatic and is subject to consultations among members of the Commission (art. XXIX, para. 2). EEC has acceded to the Convention and become a member of the Commission in accordance with the provisions of article VIII of the Convention.

266. With other international organizations which do not have the right to accede to the Convention, the Commission and the Scientific Committee should, in accordance with the Convention, develop appropriate co-operative relations (art. XXIII). In this respect, it may be noted that observers from FAO, IOC, IUCN and IWC attended the second sessions of the Commission and of the Scientific Committee.

267. Dealing with a great many serious issues concerning legal, political and biological aspects of the conservation and rational utilization of the Antarctic marine living resources, the Convention, like many other similar international agreements, is a compromise that represents a practical solution for the parties to the Convention.

2. Antarctic mineral resources

268. The hidden mineral wealth of Antarctica has been a subject of interest for many years. It has still to be proved that there are mineral resources in Antarctica worth exploiting, and at the present time prospects for developing such resources appear to be remote.[89] However, in recent years, as a result of the scarcity of global resources coupled with technological advancements in resource exploration and exploitation, interest in the economic potential of the Antarctic region has increased substantially. As a result, concern for and tensions over the fate of the world's last unexploited continent are rising rapidly.

269. One of the major problems regarding exploration and exploitation of Antarctic mineral resources is that the environmental hazards attached to the use of these resources may be very serious. The Antarctic has a critical influence on oceanic and atmospheric circulation and thus on global climate. At the same time, Antarctic ecosystems are extremely vulnerable to disturbance. For example, a huge spill of crude oil altering the rate of formation and degradation of sea ice could conceivably affect planetary albedo (reflectivity),[90] with global climatic implications. In addition, the severity of local conditions, such as the cold and the presence of ice and icebergs, increases the likelihood of accidents and would complicate remedial measures.[91] At present only a number of preliminary studies have been conducted on the environmental impact of mineral resource exploration and exploitation in Antarctica but they indicate that measures for protection of the Antarctic environment should be worked out prior to any commercial exploration for or exploitation of mineral resources in Antarctica, should such activities ever begin there.[92]

270. The Antarctic mineral resource issue revives an old problem of claims for territorial sovereignty in Antarctica and non-recognition of such claims, because claimant States assert ownership over resources in their claims, while non-claimant States argue for freedom of access.[93] The possibility of unilateral actions by both sides, and therefore of conflicts, is quite real and should not be discounted. In this respect, the prospect of the use of Antarctic

[89] See Barbara Mitchell, "Frozen Stakes – The Future of Antarctic Minerals" (International Institute for Environment and Development, London, 1983), p. 7; James H. Zumberge, "Mineral Resources and Geopolitics in Antarctica, *American Scientist*, vol. 67 (January–February 1979); John A. Dugger, "Exploiting Antarctic Mineral Resources – Technology, Economics and the Environment", *University of Miami Law Review*, vol. 33, No. 2 (December 1978), pp. 315–340; and Franz Tessensohn, "Present Knowledge of the Non-Living Resources in the Antarctic, Possibilities for their Exploitation and Scientific Perspectives", *Proceedings of an Interdisciplinary Symposium*, pp. 189–210.

[90] See Ludger Kappen, "Ecological Aspects of an Exploitation of the Non-Living Resources of the Antarctic", p. 212; Boczek, "The Protection of the Antarctic Ecosystem", p. 363; and "The Future of the Antarctic", background for a United Nations debate, 1 October 1983, Greenpeace International publication, p. 5.

[91] Report of the Group of Experts on Mineral Exploration and Exploitation, annexed to the final report of the Ninth Consultative Meeting, London, 1977, pp. 69–72.

[92] Ibid, p. 67.

[93] Colson, "The Antarctic Treaty System: The Mineral Issue", p. 849.

mineral resources raises the question of the need for elaboration of an international régime for management of the exploration and exploitation of potential Antarctic mineral resources.

271. It should be noted that in light of the sovereignty issue it could prove to be much more difficult, in comparison with marine living resources, to approach the question of management of mineral resources, since they are non-renewable and are fixed in location. It should also be remembered that the development of mineral resources will involve problems and require regulation and control of a scale and nature different from the measures required in regard to marine living resources.[94]

272. Problems and conflicts raised by the emerging interest in the economic potential of Antarctic mineral resources revolve mainly around one issue, namely, how Antarctic mineral resources should be managed. There are two main approaches to the consideration of this issue, which reflect also to a certain extent, differences in attitudes towards management of resources.

273. The supporters of one approach insist on the discussion of the Antarctic mineral resource issue in a global international forum, preferably established by the United Nations. They consider the Antarctic Treaty mechanism too restrictive for the purposes of such discussions. As their objective, they claim to ensure that the exploration and exploitation of mineral resources should he carried out for the benefit of all mankind.[95]

274. Others, while also convinced of the need for an open international approach, favour the discussion of the questions of the management of Antarctic mineral resources within the framework of the Antarctic Treaty, which is, in their opinion, particularly designed for such discussions and can assure their meaningful and responsible character. They hold the view that, in such considerations, one should not ignore the realities of the Antarctic Treaty, including, *inter alia*, the provisions of article IV of the Treaty which puts at rest the sovereignty issue, and the long presence in Antarctica of certain countries which have invested large resources as well as the efforts and talents of their people in the scientific investigation and development of this continent.[96]

275. Both approaches are reflected in the debates on the Antarctic issue at the thirty-eighth session of the General Assembly. A summary of those debates is given in section C of chapter II of the present study. Below are listed some of the statements or summaries of such statements made by the advocates of these approaches prior to the thirty-eighth session. They may be helpful in a better understanding of the opinions advanced.

276. It can be assumed[97] that initiators of the discussion of the Antarctic mineral resource management issue in a wide international forum were inspired by the adoption, on 17 December 1970, by the General Assembly of the Declaration of Principles Governing the Sea-Bed and the Ocean Floor, and the Subsoil Thereof, beyond the Limits of National Jurisdiction and by the deliberations at the United Nations Conference on the Law of the Sea. The views set out below, some of which were made in a broader context, are nevertheless included because they are relevant to the mineral resource issue.

277. In 1975, in a speech before the General Assembly, Shirley Amerasinghe, who was then the President of the United Nations Conference on the Law of the Sea, stated,

[94] Sollie, "Jurisdictional Problems in Relation to Antarctic Mineral Resources in Political Perspective", p. 32.

[95] C. W. Pinto, "The International Community and Antarctica", *University of Miami Law Review*, vol. 33, No. 2 (December 1978), pp. 475–487; see also Pinto, "Comment on Professor Wolfrum's presentation 'The Use of Antarctic Non-Living Resources: The Search for a Trustee?'", *Proceedings of an Interdisciplinary Symposium*, pp. 164–168.

[96] Fernando Zegers Santa Cruz, "The Antarctic System and the Utilization of Resources", *University of Miami Law Review*, vol. 33, No. 2 (December 1978), p. 471; see also Wolfrum, "The Use of Antarctic Non-Living Resources …", p. 163.

[97] Mitchell, "Frozen Stakes …", p. 41; see also Ralph L. Harry, "The Antarctic Régime and the Law of the Sea Convention: An Australian View", *Virginia Journal of International Law*, vol. 21–4, pp. 727–728; and Scharnhorst Müller, "The Impact of UNCLOS III on the Antarctic Régime", *Proceedings of an Interdisciplinary Symposium*, pp. 169–176.

"There are still areas of this planet where opportunities remain for constructive and peaceful co-operation on the part of the international community for the common good of all rather than for the benefit of a few. Such an area is the Antarctic continent. ... there can be no doubt that there are vast possibilities for a new initiative that would rebound to the benefit of all mankind. Antarctica is an area where the now widely accepted ideas and concepts relating to international economic co-operation, with their special stress on the principle of equitable sharing of the world's resources, can find ample scope for application, given the co-operation and good-will of those who have so far been active in that area" (A/PV.2380, pp. 13–15).

278. Christopher Pinto, the delegate of Sri Lanka to the United Nations Conference on the Law of the Sea, vigorously advocated in his statement in 1977 to a press briefing seminar in London that Antarctica's resources should he made subject to a régime of rational management and utilization to secure optimum benefits for mankind as a whole and, in particular, for the developing countries, in accordance with appropriate global international arrangements and within the framework of the new international economic order.[98]

279. In 1979, Alvaro de Soto, the delegate of Peru to the Law of the Sea Conference and one of the co-ordinators of the Group of 77 at that Conference, warned that "a comprehensive political debate on the question of Antarctica is inevitable and it may well be desirable". Speaking at a press briefing seminar in Washington, he said that "the temptation to apply to Antarctica the same principles which are the basis for the régime of the sea-bed is very great, and some have not been able to resist it. ... Certainly there is no such thing as a perfect analogy. The sea-bed principles would probably require some adaptation in order to be applied to Antarctica".[99]

280. In 1982, the Prime Minister of Malaysia, Dr. Mahathir bin Mohamad, while congratulating the General Assembly on the successful conclusion of the United Nations Conference on the Law of the Sea, said that it was time now for the United Nations to focus its attention on the uninhabited lands of Antarctica. He added that, like the sea-beds, these uninhabited lands belong to the international community and "the United Nations must convene a meeting in order to define the problem of these uninhabited lands, whether claimed or unclaimed, and to determine the rights of all nations to these lands" (A/37/PV.10, p. 18).

281. The aforementioned approach is opposed by those who consider it questionable that the legal situation of Antarctica is really analogous to the deep sea-bed. They emphasize that, contrary to the deep sea-bed area, a legal system already exists with respect to the Antarctic area.[100]

282. Speaking in a personal capacity in 1977 at a press briefing seminar, Mr. Leigh Ratiner, administrator in the United States Ocean Mining Administration, stressed:

"Antarctica is not a no-man's-land, and a foundation upon which to build an alternative regime already exists and cannot in truth be ignored. For a very long time, this continent has been a sphere of political activity. Nations have, through forethought and initiative, developed substantial vested interests in Antarctica's future. ... The political difference between the deep seabed and Antarctica and between the moon and Antarctica is stated quite simply – territorial sovereignty, and a sovereignty claim, be it valid or dubious under international law, is nonetheless the grist of the international law mill."[101]

283. Mr. Fernando Zegers Santa Cruz, former head of the delegation of Chile to the Law of the Sea Conference in his 1978 article on "The Antarctic System and the Utilization of Resources" strongly argues against the comparison between Antarctica and, as he put it, other "human

[98] C. W. Pinto, Statement "Earthscan", Press Briefing Seminar on Antarctic Resources and Development, London, 25 July 1977.

[99] Alvaro de Soto, Statement, "Earthscan", Press Briefing Seminar on Antarctic Resources and Development, Washington, D.C., 14 September 1979.

[100] Wolfrum, "The Use of Antarctic Non-Living Resources ...", p. 145.

[101] Leigh Ratiner, Statement, "Earthscan", Press Briefing Seminar on the Future of Antarctica, London, 27 July 1977.

frontiers such as for example the ocean floor". While recognizing the existence of certain elements in common, he states that vast differences overshadow any possible similarities. He continues, saying that

> "Antarctica is not a territory without legal norms, remote to man and res nullius. To the contrary, there exists a real Antarctic system, which integrates perfectly with the general international system, conforms to the principles and objectives of the United Nations and has proven its efficiency in both time and place. Consequently it is through the Antarctic system, and in close cooperation with it, that the solution to the question of utilization of the resources of the area should be found."[102]

284. It is also argued that the common heritage concept cannot be applied to Antarctica by analogy, because the United Nations has not declared this concept to be a universal principle applicable to all spaces beyond generally recognized national sovereignty but has restricted it to two particular instances: the deep sea-bed and ocean floor and the subsoil thereof, beyond the limits of national jurisdiction, as well as its resources, and the moon and its resources.[103]

285. At the interdisciplinary symposium entitled Antarctic Challenge: Conflicting Interests, Cooperation, Environmental Protection, Economic Development, held at Kiel, Federal Republic of Germany in 1983, the opponents of the consideration of the mineral resource issue within the framework of the Antarctic Treaty were criticized for basing their approach solely on the suggestion of sharing profit and benefit while neglecting the consideration of burden and responsibility sharing. According to those views, they have not envisaged the need for a delicate balance between responsibilities and obligations, on one side, and rights, on the other. It was commented, in that regard, that some of those who most strongly advocated the possibilities of Antarctica as an area for international co-operation for the benefit of all mankind, rather than for a few rich States, were reluctant to use the opportunity to join the Antarctic Treaty and to take part in the research activities, to the extent that they were capable and willing within the Treaty's framework, for the benefit of all mankind.[104]

286. The Antarctic Treaty makes no special reference to Antarctic mineral resources. However, the Consultative Parties have recorded their view that it would be ironic not to allow them to address the question of exploration and exploitation of these resources once it became an urgent issue of public concern.

287. The specific character of the Antarctic Treaty and the system established by it are mentioned by some authors as one of the reasons why the claimant States seem more prepared to compromise in favour of a joint solution on the mineral resource issue within the framework of the Treaty.[105]

288. The issue of commercial activities related to exploitation of Antarctic resources was brought up during negotiation of the Antarctic Treaty in 1958–1959, but it became apparent that, at that time, the States concerned were not willing to accept provisions regulating such activities.[106]

289. In 1959, no urgent need was felt for negotiations on the mineral resource issue. Therefore, it was considered preferable to avoid them for fear that disagreement on the sovereignty problem might halt the conclusion of the Antarctic Treaty.[44] However, with the passage of time, the Consultative Parties concluded that the balance established by the Antarctic Treaty and

[102] Zegers Santa Cruz, "The Antarctic System ...", pp. 431, 470 and 471.

[103] Müller, "The Impact of UNCLOS III ...", p. 171.

[104] Sollie, Statement, "Earthscan", Press Briefing Seminar on the Future of Antarctica, London, 25 July 1977. See also statements of Croharé, sollie and Wolfrum, "The Use of Antarctic Non-Living Resources: The Search for a Trustee?", *Proceedings of an Interdisciplinary Symposium*, pp. 179, 184 and 187.

[105] Colson, "The Antarctic Treaty System ...", pp. 882–884. See also Zegers Santa Cruz, "The Antarctic System ...", pp. 470–472.

[106] Sollie, "Trends and Prospects for Régimes for Living and Mineral Resources in Antarctica", Statement at the Twelfth Annual Conference, *Law of the Sea Institute*, The Hague, October 1978, p. 12.

implementation of some of its principles, such as freedom of scientific research and protection of the environment, could be threatened by possible unilateral commercial development of Antarctic mineral resources by some States.[107] Thus, they felt that the need had emerged to take measures in order to assure implementation of the Antarctic Treaty principles and to meet the requirement of the Treaty that Antarctica should not become the scene or object of international discord.

290. The question of Antarctic mineral resources was first brought up informally in 1970, at the Sixth Consultative Meeting, held in Tokyo, where several representatives voiced concern about inquiries regarding Antarctic minerals that their Governments had received from private firms.[108]

291. Two years later, at the Seventh Consultative Meeting, its participants, "noting the technological developments in polar mineral exploration and the increasing interest in the possibility of there being exploitable minerals in the Antarctic Treaty area", decided to include in the agenda of that meeting the issue "Antarctic resources – effects of mineral exploitation". The Consultative Parties acted on the agreed assumption that mineral exploration is likely to raise problems of an environmental nature and that the Consultative Parties should assume responsibility for the protection of the environment and the wise use of resources" (recommendation VII-6).

292. The decision of the Seventh Consultative Meeting on the mineral resource issue, although a very general one, was a consensus between both claimant and non-claimant States to act collectively and address jointly the mineral resource issue within the framework of the system established by the Antarctic Treaty.

293. At the Eighth Consultative Meeting, held at Oslo in 1975, the Consultative Parties once again pointed out that mineral resource exploration and exploitation could adversely affect the unique environment of Antarctica and of other ecosystems dependent on the Antarctic environment, and reaffirmed that they bore a special responsibility for environmental protection in the Antarctic Treaty area. Since available scientific information on the possible impact of mineral resource exploration or exploitation on the environment of the Treaty area, if that was to occur there, was completely inadequate, SCAR was invited to prepare a study in that respect (recommendation VIII-14).

294. In that decision, the Consultative Parties emphasized that a close link between the operation of the Antarctic Treaty and an accommodation on the mineral issue should serve as a key-stone for any resolution of the Antarctic mineral resource issue. They stressed their intent "to seek to develop an approach to the problems raised by the possible presence of valuable mineral resources in the Antarctic Treaty area, bearing in mind the principles and purposes of the Antarctic Treaty" (preamble, recommendation VIII-14).

295. The Consultative Parties came to the joint conviction that there was a need to refrain from actions of commercial exploration and exploitation while they would also seek timely agreed solutions to the problems raised by the possible presence of valuable mineral resources in Antarctica. That conviction was expressed in the preamble of recommendation VIII-14 and in its report.

296. At the Ninth Consultative Meeting, held in London in 1977, the question of mineral resources was one of the major subjects. The decision taken by the Meeting on the issue (recommendation IX-1) reflects the substantial progress achieved by the Consultative Parties on fundamental issues relating to mineral resource development.

297. First, the Consultative Parties emphasized that the framework established by the Antarctic Treaty had proved effective in promoting international harmony in furtherance of the purposes and principles of the United Nations Charter, in ensuring the protection of the Antarctic environment and in promoting freedom of scientific research in Antarctica. They thus reiterated

[107] Sollie, "Jurisdictional Problems in Relation to Antarctic Mineral Resources in Political Perspective", p. 39; see also Mitchell and Kimball, "Conflict over the Cold Continent", *Foreign Policy*, No. 35 (1979), p. 140.

[108] Colson, "The Antarctic Treaty System ...", p. 884.

that Consultative Meetings could and should serve as a proper forum for consideration of the mineral resource issue.

298. Second, they gave an explicit definition of what they considered to be their responsibility under the Antarctic Treaty with respect to mineral resource development, in stating that "the special responsibilities of Consultative Parties are to ensure that any activities in Antarctica, including commercial exploration and exploitation in the future, should they occur, should not become the cause of international discord, of danger to the unique Antarctic environment, of disruption to scientific investigation, or be otherwise contrary to the principles or purposes of the Antarctic Treaty" (preamble, recommendation IX-1).

299. Third, the Consultative Parties established a set of principles on which to base the future régime for the Antarctic mineral resources. They endorsed the four following principles elaborated in 1976 in Paris at the meeting held in preparation for the Ninth Consultative Meeting:

"(i) the Consultative Parties will continue to play an active and responsible role in dealing with the question of the mineral resources of Antarctica;

"(ii) the Antarctic Treaty must be maintained in its entirety;

"(iii) protection of the unique Antarctic environment and of its dependent ecosystems should be a basic consideration;

"(iv) the Consultative Parties, in dealing with the question of mineral resources in Antarctica, should not prejudice the interests of all mankind in Antarctica" (recommendation IX-1, para. 4).

300. The aforementioned basic elements of the future régime were supplemented in the decision by one more principle assuring "that the provisions of Article IV of the Antarctic Treaty shall not be affected by the régime" and "that the principles embodied in Article IV of the Antarctic Treaty are safeguarded in application to the area covered by the Antarctic Treaty" (recommendation IX-1, para. 5).

301. Fourth, the Consultative Meeting transformed the appeal adopted at the previous meeting, of the need for restraint in commercial development of Antarctic mineral resources while a timely agreed solution was being sought, into a direct legal obligation on the Consultative Parties. The participants of the Ninth Consultative Meeting agreed to "urge their nationals and other States to refrain from all exploration and exploitation of Antarctic mineral resources while making progress towards the timely adoption of an agreed régime concerning Antarctic mineral resource activities" and by this to "endeavour to ensure that, pending the timely adoption of agreed solutions pertaining to exploration and exploitation of mineral resources, no activity shall be conducted to explore or exploit such resources" (recommendation IX-1, para. 8). The decision of the Meeting also mentions that these matters will be kept under continuing examination by the Consultative Parties.

302. The above-cited recommendation lacks any definition of what should be considered as timely progress toward the adoption of the régime. Therefore, it leaves the door open to different interpretations regarding the progress required.[109]

303. The mineral resource issue dominated the discussion at the Tenth Consultative Meeting, held in Washington D.C. in 1979. At the Meeting, emphasis was placed on consideration of the environmental aspects of the future régime. The Consultative Parties agreed that a régime for mineral resources should include means for assessing the possible impact of mineral resource activities on the Antarctic environment and for determining whether mineral resource activities would be acceptable. It was stated that rules relating to the protection of the Antarctic environment and the requirement that mineral resource activities be undertaken in compliance with such rules should constitute an important part of the régime (recommendation X-1, para. 4).

304. Objectives were defined in paragraph 6 of the recommendation for studies to improve "predictions of the environmental impacts of activities, events and technologies associated with mineral resource exploration and exploitation in the Antarctic, should such occur" there.

[109] Ibid, pp. 894–895.

305. At the Tenth Consultative Meeting the participants succeeded in progressing one step further in the elaboration of a joint understanding of the general scope of the régime on mineral resources. They decided that it should include "means for governing the ecological, technological, political, legal and economic aspects of the mineral resource activities in cases where they would be determined acceptable" (recommendation X-1, subpara. 4 (iii)).

306. The Eleventh Consultative Meeting, held at Buenos Aires in 1981, played a final and decisive role in identifying the goals of the Consultative Parties with respect to the régime on the Antarctic mineral resources. That Meeting marked the end of a preparatory stage during which the Consultative Parties had developed a joint general approach to the mineral resource issue and the start of negotiations on the substance of the concrete provisions of the régime.

307. In paragraph 2 of recommendation XI-1, the Consultative Parties concluded that the elaboration of the régime had become a matter of urgency. Therefore, to facilitate their work, they decided, as in the case of the marine living resources, to convene a Special Consultative Meeting "in order to elaborate a régime and to determine the form of the régime including the question as to whether an international instrument such as a convention is necessary" (para. 3) and endorsed guidelines for the Special Consultative Meeting.

308. It was reaffirmed that the régime should be based on the five principles approved at the Ninth Consultative Meeting and that it should include the agreements on requirements for the protection of the Antarctic environment, reached at the Tenth Consultative Meeting.

309. As in the past, when starting a round of negotiations on a new issue, the Consultative Parties felt it necessary to restate that the mineral resource régime should not prejudice their positions of principle on the question of sovereign rights claimed in Antarctica. Since a simple reaffirmation of the Antarctic Treaty, as suggested by the Ninth Consultative Meeting, was not found sufficient, the following formula was included in Paragraph 6 of the recommendation, specifying the meaning of the principle of the non-prejudicial approach:

> "Any agreement that may be reached on a régime for mineral exploration and exploitation in Antarctica elaborated by the Consultative Parties should be acceptable and be without prejudice to those States which have previously asserted rights of or claims to territorial sovereignty in Antarctica as well as to those States which neither recognize such rights of or claims to territorial sovereignty in Antarctica nor, under the provisions of the Antarctic Treaty, assert such rights or claims."

310. As to the question of protection of the environment, an additional requirement was included in subparagraphs 7(v) and (vii) of the recommendation, providing that the régime should also include the means:

(a) To promote the conduct of research necessary to make the environmental and resource management decisions required;

(b) To ensure that the special responsibilities of the Consultative Parties with respect to the environment in the Antarctic Treaty area were protected, taking into account responsibilities that might be exercised in the area by other international organizations.

311. With respect to the area of application of the mineral resource régime, the Consultative Parties appear to have proceeded from the assumption that the Antarctic continent and the surrounding islands and adjacent sea-bed areas constitute a single unity, and that the adjacent sea-bed areas constituting the natural prolongation of the Antarctic continent under the sea should be governed by the same régime as the continent. Using this concept of interrelation between the land mass and its natural prolongation undersea, the Consultative Parties concluded at the Eleventh Meeting that the régime for Antarctic mineral resources should "apply to all mineral resource activities taking place on the Antarctic continent and its adjacent offshore areas but without encroachment on the deep sea-bed" (subpara. 7 (iv)). The precise limits of the area of application of the régime were to be determined in the course of its elaboration.[110]

[110] V. V. Golitsyn, "Antarctika-mejdunarodnopravovoy rejim", Mejdunarodniue atnosheniya, Moskva 1983 str. 145–146.

312. That understanding among the Consultative Parties on the area of application of the régime apparently became possible because it allowed both claimant and non-claimant States to preserve their positions of principle states in article IV of the Antarctic Treaty.

313. Recommendation XI-1 contains a provision indicating that the participants were "mindful of the negotiations that were taking place at the Third United Nations Conference on the Law of the Sea" (preamble). In that regard, it could be concluded that the definition adopted of the area of application of the mineral resource régime was not considered by the Consultative Parties as contradictory in any way to the draft Convention on the Law of the Sea.

314. On the question of participation in the régime, the Consultative Parties agreed that the régime should include procedures for adherence by States other than the Consultative Parties, which would ensure that those States were bound by the basic provisions of the Antarctic Treaty and would make entities of those States eligible to participate in mineral resource activities (subpara. 7 (ii)).

315. With respect to the activities embraced by the mineral resource régime, the Consultative Parties decided that the régime should "cover commercial exploration (activities related to minerals involving, in general, retention of proprietary data and/or non-scientific exploratory drilling) and exploitation (commercial development and production); (subpara. 7 (vi)).

316. That definition of the term "exploration" may appear rather vague. Nevertheless, it could be helpful and should be considered a first step in drawing a precise distinction between "exploration", which is understood as a part of commercial activity and therefore subject to regulations under the mineral resource régime, and "scientific investigation", which can be conducted freely in accordance with the Antarctic Treaty. A clear understanding of that point is important in light of the restriction imposed in 1979 at the Ninth Consultative Meeting, namely, that "pending the timely adoption of agreed solutions pertaining to exploration and exploitation of mineral resources, no activity shall be conducted to explore or exploit such resources" (recommendation IX-1, para.8).

317. Since 1981, the Consultative Parties have continued negotiations on the mineral resource régime within the framework of the Special Consultative Meeting. Official sessions of it and informal consultations were held in June 1982 and January 1983 in New Zealand, in July 1983 in the Federal Republic of Germany, in January 1984 in the United States and in May 1984 in Japan. No official reports have been published on the deliberations which took place at these meetings. At the meeting in Tokyo, a decision was reached that the Antarctic Treaty Parties without consultative status should be invited to attend the next meeting on the Antarctic mineral resource negotiations as observers.

Report of the Secretary-General, Question of Antarctica, UN Doc A/41/88 (8 October 1986)

1. In its resolution 40/156 B of 16 December 1985, the General Assembly invited the Antarctic Treaty Consultative Parties to inform the Secretary-General of their negotiations to establish a régime regarding Antarctic minerals. The Assembly also requested the Secretary-General to submit to the General Assembly for consideration at its forty-first session a report containing the replies received from Consultative Parties.

2. In accordance with resolution 40/156 B, the Secretary-General, on 10 February 1986, addressed a note verbale to the Antarctic Treaty Consultative Parties[111] and requested them to submit as soon as possible, but not later than 1 May 1986, the replies that their respective Governments were prepared to provide pursuant to the relevant provisions of the resolution.

[111] Argentina, Australia, Belgium, Brazil, Chile, China, France, Germany, Federal Republic of, India, Japan, New Zealand, Norway, Poland, South Africa, Uruguay, Union of Soviet Socialist Republics, United Kingdom of Great Britain and Northern Ireland and United States of America.

3. On 30 April 1986, a communication was received from the Permanent Representative of Australia to the United Nations, acting on behalf of the Antarctic Treaty Consultative Parties with reference to the Secretary-General's note verbale.

4. In that communication, the Permanent Representative of Australia recalled that, before the voting on resolutions 40/156 A and 40/156 B in the First Committee at the fortieth session of the General Assembly "he made a statement on behalf of the Antarctic Treaty Consultative Parties. The statement noted that the insistence of some delegations in putting divisive resolutions to a vote had occasioned decisions by most of the Treaty Parties to take the unusual step of not participating in the voting. The statement also included the following observations:

> "It is a matter of great regret to members of the Antarctic Treaty that the tradition of consensus decision-making which has been followed since the question of Antarctica was first inscribed on the agenda of the United Nations at the thirty-eighth session has this year been broken.
>
> "the Antarctic Treaty Consultative Parties have been firm in their determination to proceed by consensus and have negotiated earnestly towards that end with Malaysia and some other delegations.
>
> "The Consultative Parties regret that the proponents of the draft resolution were not prepared to abide by the consensus traditions that had been established in the handling of this item in previous years. They are firmly of the view that consensus offers the only realistic basis for United Nations General Assembly consideration of Antarctica. Accordingly, they will be compelled to reconsider their further participation in this item unless consensus can be restored."

5. In his communication to the Secretary-General, the Permanent Representative of Australia further noted that, "consistent with this statement, the Antarctic Treaty Consultative Parties remain of the view that consideration of Antarctica in the United Nations should and can realistically proceed only on the basis of consensus. They are therefore not responding to resolutions 40/156 A and B, in the adoption of which they did not participate. They remain willing to provide information about Antarctica to the international community, as they have emphasized in their responses to previous General Assembly resolutions on this item, which were adopted by consensus."

Report of the Secretary-General, Question of Antarctica: Addendum, UN Doc A/41/688/Add.1 (27 October 1986)

At the request of the Permanent Mission of Australia to the United Nations, its note verbale, dated 30 April 1986, to the Secretary-General is being issued in its entirety as an addendum to A/41/688.

The Secretary-General's notes (of 10 February 1986) were issued pursuant to General Assembly resolutions 40/156 A and B. In this regard, the Permanent Representative of Australia has the honour to recall that, before the voting on these resolutions in the First Committee at the fortieth session, he made a statement on behalf of the Antarctic Treaty Consultative Parties.[112] The statement noted that the insistence of some delegations in putting divisive resolutions to a vote had occasioned decisions by most of the Treaty Parties to take the unusual step of not participating in the voting. The statement (see A/C.1/40/PV.55) also included the following observations:

> "It is a matter of great regret to members of the Antarctic Treaty that the tradition of consensus decision-making, which has been followed since the question of Antarctica was first inscribed on the agenda of the United Nations, at the thirty-eighth session, has this year for the first time been broken. The Antarctic Treaty Consultative Parties have been firm in their determination

[112] Argentina, Australia, Belgium, Brazil, Chile, China, France, Germany, Federal Republic of, India, Japan, New Zealand, Norway, Poland, South Africa, Uruguay, Union of Soviet Socialist Republics, United Kingdom of Great Britain and Northern Ireland and United States of America.

to proceed by consensus and have negotiated earnestly towards that end with Malaysia and some other delegations."

"... the Consultative Parties regret that the proponents of the draft resolutions were not prepared in the end to abide by the consensus traditions that have been established in the handling of this item in previous years. The Consultative Parties are firmly of the view that consensus offers the only realistic basis for consideration of Antarctica by the General Assembly. Accordingly, they will be compelled to reconsider their further participation in the consideration of this item unless consensus can be restored."

Consistent with this statement, the Antarctic Treaty Consultative Parties remain of the view that consideration of Antarctica in the United Nations should and can realistically proceed only on the basis of consensus. They are therefore not responding to resolutions 40/156 A and B, in the adoption of which they did not participate. They remain willing to provide information about Antarctica to the international community, as they have emphasized in their responses to previous General Assembly resolutions on this item, which were adopted by consensus.

In response to the Secretary-General's note issued pursuant to resolution 38/77, the Antarctic Treaty parties provided a very considerable volume of information about the Antarctic Treaty system and their activities in Antarctica. Some of this information was included in part two of the subsequent report of the Secretary-General (A/39/583), which announced also that the voluminous annexes, containing additional material provided by the parties, were available for consultation upon request to the Secretary-General.

In making that information available, the Antarctic Treaty parties proceeded from the conviction that the Antarctic Treaty system has furthered the purposes and principles of the United Nations Charter. It has preserved the peace and harmony in the Antarctic region; has established Antarctica as an effective, functioning nuclear-weapons-free zone; has excluded Antarctica from the arms race by prohibiting any measures of a military nature; and has enabled important scientific research and co-operation to take place in a manner which has benefited all mankind. In addition, it protects the natural environment of Antarctica; provides for a comprehensive system of on-site inspection by observers to promote the objectives and to ensure compliance with the provisions of the Treaty; has averted international stride and conflict over Antarctica, and has promoted active scientific co-operation with international organizations, particularly with WMO, ITU, IOC and the Scientific Committee on Antarctic Research (SCAR). The Antarctic Treaty is open to accession by any Member State of the United Nations, as are the other instruments already included within the Antarctic Treaty system. All Treaty Parties are able to participate in Antarctic Treaty meetings. Moreover, the Consultative Parties have reaffirmed that the Antarctic minerals régime would be open to all States, with all entitled to undertake minerals resource activities pursuant to it.

Based on these considerations, the responses of the Antarctic Treaty parties concluded that the operation of the Antarctic Treaty system since 1959 had demonstrated that the Treaty was a successful, practical and flexible instrument which has served important international objectives. These conclusions were acknowledged in the report of the Secretary-General (A/39/583).

Since publication of the Secretary-General's report, the Antarctic Treaty parties have shown a continuing willingness to provide information about Antarctica and the operation of the Antarctic Treaty system. In 1985, during debate at the fortieth session of the General Assembly, the Treaty Parties provided further information on their activities, including the ongoing negotiations on an Antarctic minerals régime.

In recognition of increased international interest in Antarctica, the Antarctic Treaty Consultative Parties decide at the Twelfth Consultative Meeting to forward to the Secretary-General copies of the final reports of their regular Consultative Meetings. The most recent report, on the Thirteenth Consultative Meeting in Brussels in October 1985, was forwarded to the Secretary-General in November 1985 (A/C.1/40/120). At the Twelfth and Thirteenth

Consultative Meetings, the Consultative Parties also took further decisions relating to: the establishment of National Contact Points to disseminate Consultative Meeting Reports, the Antarctic Treaty Handbook and annual exchanges of information, as well as to provide up-to-date information on the location of depositories of data and information sources relating to Antarctica; the public release of documents from earlier Consultative Meetings; and procedures to enable relevant matters of scientific or technical interest to be drawn to the attention of United Nations specialized agencies or other international organizations.

In summary, the Antarctic Treaty Consultative Parties are firmly of the view that the Antarctic Treaty system works in the interests of all mankind and furthers the principles of the United Nations Charter. They have shown their readiness to respond positively to indications of international interest in Antarctica and remain of the view that consensus offers the only realistic basis for consideration of Antarctica in the United Nations.

Report of the Secretary-General, Question of Antarctica, UN Doc A/41/722 (17 November 1986)[113]

...

II Involvement of the Relevant Specialized Agencies and Intergovernmental Organizations in the Antarctic Treaty System

A. Relationship of the Antarctic Treaty system with the specialized agencies of the United Nations and other international organizations

1. The Antarctic Treaty and Antarctic Treaty Consultative Meetings

(a) General principles on the relationship of the Antarctic Treaty system with the specialized agencies of the United Nations and other international organizations as established by the Antarctic Treaty and Antarctic Treaty Consultative Meetings

1. The involvement of the United Nations specialized agencies and other international organizations in the Antarctic Treaty system was first foreseen by the Antarctic Treaty itself. Article III of the Antarctic Treaty, *inter alia*, encourages the establishment of co-operative working relations with those specialized agencies of the United Nations and other international organizations having a scientific or technical interest in Antarctica.

2. In 1961, the First Antarctic Treaty Consultative Meeting recommended to the Governments of the Antarctic Treaty Consultative Parties that they should individually encourage the work of international organizations having a scientific or technical interest in Antarctica, including the specialized agencies of the United Nations, and should promote on a bilateral basis, the establishment and development of co-operative working relations with these organizations (recommendation I-V).

3. In recommendation XI-1 (1981), made with regard to the future régime on Antarctic mineral resources, the Consultative Meeting suggested that the régime should, *inter alia*, include provisions for co-operative arrangements between the régime and other relevant international organizations. It further suggested that responsibilities that may be exercised in the Antarctic Treaty area by other international organizations should be taken into account in the provisions to be included in the régime so as to ensure that the special responsibilities of the Consultative Parties in respect of the environment in the area are protected.

4. At the Twelfth Consultative Meeting in 1983, a specific responsibility concerning the interaction between the Antarctic Treaty system and the specialized agencies of the United Nations, or other international organizations having a scientific or technical interest in Antarctica, was suggested for the Government of the host country of each Consultative Meeting. According to recommendation XII-6, the Government of such country shall, as and when the representatives of the Consultative Parties consider it appropriate, draw the attention of any

[113] pp. 8–19 and 29–37.

of the above-mentioned bodies to any part of the report of the Consultative Meeting, or any information document submitted to the Meeting and made available to the public, relevant to the scientific or technical interest which that agency or organization has in Antarctica.

5. The Twelfth Consultative Meeting also came to the conclusion that, as part of the preparation for each regular Consultative Meeting, the Consultative Parties should consider whether they would be assisted in their discussion of any item of the agenda of the regular Consultative Meeting if a specialized agency of the United Nations or other international organization having a scientific or technical interest in Antarctica were to attend the meeting as an observer when that item was being discussed; and if so, whether the relevant organization should, with the agreement of all Consultative Parties, be invited by the host Government to attend the meeting on that basis.

(b) The relationship of the Antarctic Treaty system with the specialized agencies of the United Nations and other international organizations as demonstrated by the Antarctic Treaty Consultative Meetings

6. The Antarctic Treaty Consultative Meetings provide the forum where, over the years, a number of legally binding recommendations were adopted by the Consultative Parties in connection with the increasing involvement of the specialized agencies and international organizations in the Antarctic Treaty system.

7. In this regard, the following measures were recommended to the Governments of the Consultative Parties for approval and subsequent implementation:

(a) Invitation to an international organization to undertake new Antarctic research, to add new aspects to ongoing research, or to offer advice in specific scientific, technical or environmental fields (recommendations VI-4, VI-5, VII-3, VIII-7, VIII-14, IX-3, X-I, X-3, X-4, XII-2, XII-3, XIII-4, XIII-5);

(b) Encouragement of, and invitation to, an international organization to continue its interest and work in specific fields of Antarctic scientific investigation (recommendations I-IV, III-X, IV-22, VI-4, VI-9, VII-1, VII-2, VIII-10, VIII-11, VIII-14, IX-4, X-7);

(c) Taking into consideration viewpoints, recommendations, proposals of and measures by the United Nations specialized agencies and international organizations having scientific, technical or environmental interest in Antarctica (recommendations I-XI, II-I, II-II, V-7, VII-1, VII-7, XI-1, XII-l);

(d) Encouragement of, and invitation to appropriate international organizations to co-operate and consult with each other in specific areas of Antarctic research (recommendations V-3, VIII-11, VIII-13, X-7);

(e) Invitation to a specialized agency to provide help and advice in the exchange of meteorological data, and to give consideration to and undertake actions in specific aspects of the problem (recommendations VI-3, X-3, XII-1);

(f) Issuance and adoption as voluntary guidelines of the general rules; of conduct with regard to the conservation of Antarctic fauna and flora, as recommended by an international organization (recommendations I-VIII, VII-1);

(g) Invitation to observers from specialized agencies and appropriate international organizations to attend meetings on Antarctic telecommunications (recommendations I-XI, V-2);

(h) Providing an international organization with specific types of information on Antarctica (recommendations VIII-7, X-3);

(i) Facilitation of the exchange of information regarding plans for scientific programmes carried out through international organizations (recommendation I-I);

(j) Co-ordination of meetings and symposiums organized by the Governments of Consultative Parties on Antarctic logistic problems with similar action undertaken by an international organization (recommendation II-II);

(k) Adoption of specific measures for co-operation in transport in Antarctica, as recommended by an international organization (recommendation IX-4);

(l) Expression of gratitude to an international organization for the devoted service which it has given to the achievement of a better understanding of the Antarctic and to the development of the Antarctic Treaty system (recommendation X-9);

(m) Consideration of requests to meet costs incurred by an international organization when responding to requests for advice by the Antarctic Treaty Consultative Parties (recommendation XII-8);

(n) Invitation to an international organization to appoint its representative as an observer at the Consultative Meetings for the specific purpose of reporting on certain matters within its competence (recommendation XIII-2).

8. A number of the above-mentioned measures were recommended by the Consultative Meetings with reference to activities, viewpoints, recommendations and decisions of specialized agencies and international organizations concerned with Antarctic research (recommendations III-III, V-2, V-3, VII-2, VII-7, VIII-2, VIII-4, VIII-7, VIII-11, VIII-13, IX-l, IX-3, IX-4, IX-5, X-3, X-6, X-9, XII-l, XII-2, XII-5, XII-8, XIII-4, XIII-5, XIII-7, XIII-8).

9. According to article IX, paragraph 4, of the Antarctic Treaty, recommended measures "shall become effective when approved by all the Contracting Parties whose representatives were entitled to participate in the meetings held to consider those measures". Among the recommendations referred to in the above paragraphs, the following are not yet in effect:

(a) Recommendations of the thirteenth Consultative Meeting referred to in subparagraphs (a) and (n) of paragraph 7 and paragraph 8 above;

(b) Recommendations of the Twelfth Consultative Meeting referred to in paragraphs 4 and 8, and in subparagraphs (a), (c), (e), and (m) of paragraph 7 above;

(c) Recommendations XI-1 referred to in paragraph 3 and subparagraph (c) of paragraph 7 above;

(d) Recommendations of the Tenth Consultative Meeting referred to in subparagraphs (a), (b), (d), (h) and (l) of paragraph 7 and in paragraph 8 above.

2. Convention for the Conservation of Antarctic Seals

10. The purpose of this Convention, which was adopted in 1972 and came into force in 1978, is to forestall any recurrence of destructive exploitation of Antarctic seals.

11. The Convention provides that special advisory and regulatory bodies will be established within its framework should commercial sealing resume in Antarctica. Until that time, an international organization, the Scientific Committee for Antarctic Research (SCAR) of the International Council of Scientific Unions, was invited to assess available information, recommend programmes for research and report on potentially harmful effects of the harvesting of any species of seals.

12. SCAR agreed to carry out the tasks required of it in the Convention.

3. Convention on the Conservation of Antarctic Marine Living Resources

13. The Convention was adopted in 1980 at a diplomatic conference convened by the Antarctic Treaty Consultative Parties. Besides States, it was also attended by observers from an intergovernmental organization of regional economic integration (EEC) as well as a specialized agency of the United Nations (FAO) and intergovernmental and non-governmental international organizations (IOC, IUCN, IWC, SCAR and SCOR). Fifteen States and EEC became parties to this Convention, which entered into force in 1982.

14. The Convention established its functional bodies, namely the Commission for the Conservation of Antarctic Marine Living Resources (CCAMLR) and its Scientific Committee. The general principles for the interaction between the Commission and the Scientific Committee on the one hand, and international bodies on the other, are formulated in article XXIII of the Convention. This article provides that the Commission and the Scientific Committee:

(a) Shall co-operate, as appropriate, with the Food and Agriculture Organization of the United Nations and with other specialized agencies;
(b) Shall seek to develop co-operative working relationships, as appropriate, with intergovernmental and non-governmental organizations which could contribute to their work, including SCAR, SCOR, and IWC.

15. The Commission was given the right to enter into agreements with the organizations mentioned in article XXIII, as well as with other organizations. This article also provides for invitations to such organizations to send observers to meetings of the Commission and the Scientific Committee and their subsidiary organs.

16. At its third meeting in 1984, the Commission made a clarification regarding the general principles of its co-operation with other organizations. It was agreed that the Commission would not wish to conclude an agreement to accord observer status to an organization which was not willing to accord the same degree of support for the principles and objectives of the Convention as is inherent in membership of the Commission or accession to the Convention.

17. The first meetings of CCAMLR and its Scientific Committee in 1982 were attended by observers from FAO, IWC, IOC and IUCN. In addition to these organizations, SCAR and SCOR participated as observers in the second (1983) and subsequent meetings (1984 and 1985) of CCAMLR and its Committee.

18. At their second meetings and also at subsequent meetings, the Commission and the Scientific Committee discussed, among other things, their co-operation with other organizations in accordance with article XXIII of the Convention. At the meetings held in 1983, the Committee and the Commission confirmed their interest in further developing and maintaining non-formalized working, co-operative relations with FAO, SCAR, SCOR, IWC, IOC and the IUCN. It was noted at these sessions that the secretariat of the Commission had established direct links with the functional bodies of the above-mentioned organizations, including sending observers to their meetings.

19. At its second meeting in 1983, and also at subsequent meetings in 1984 and 1985, the Commission considered requests for observer status at the meetings of the Commission and the Scientific Committee by two non-governmental organizations, Greenpeace International and the Antarctic and Southern Ocean Coalition (ASOC). With regard to the ASOC, the question is still to be resolved by the Commission, pending further clarification from ASOC as to the adherence of the member organizations of ASOC to the principles and purposes of the Convention, in particular those contained in article II, and, in view of ASOC having no constitution, its durability as an organization, the relationship of its representatives with member organizations and, therefore, exactly how communication between the Commission and the member organizations of ASOC would work in practice. As to the request for observer status from Greenpeace International, the Commission noted in 1985 that Greenpeace International was a member organization of ASOC and was of the view that it was preferable for the time being to continue to investigate the possibility of establishing an appropriate channel for informal two-way communication between the Commission and interested non-governmental organizations through a representative umbrella organization.

B. Information provided by the relevant specialized agencies and bodies of the United Nations, as well as by the relevant intergovernmental and non-governmental bodies regarding their involvement in the Antarctic Treaty system

20. This part of the report is based on the responses received from organizations pursuant to General Assembly resolutions 38/77 and 40/156 A. It should be noted that some organizations did not respond to the Secretary-General's request for information while others sent insufficient material. Nevertheless, every effort was made to utilize all available sources of information on the question in the preparation of the present report.

1. World Meteorological Organization

21. International scientific co-operation in Antarctica during the International Geophysical Year (1957–1958) laid down the foundation for the involvement of the specialized agencies and other international organizations in the Antarctic Treaty system. Among the specialized agencies of the United Nations, WMO was the first to develop such co-operative relationships. Since the period of the International Geophysical Year, WMO has been closely involved in many ways in meteorological and related geophysical activities in the Antarctic, including research, as well as world-wide distribution of Antarctic meteorological data as they related to WMO programmes. In this connection, WMO was invited to participate in the meetings of the Antarctic Treaty Group of Experts on Telecommunications.

22. WMO has established close links with the Antarctic Treaty system through its Executive Council Working Group on Antarctic Meteorology. All recommendations of the Group are transmitted to all members who are parties to the Antarctic Treaty prior to their consideration by the Executive Council and prior to implementation by members.

23. WMO recommendations or resolutions on Antarctic meteorology are brought to the attention of the Consultative Meetings of the Antarctic Treaty through the permanent representatives of the members to WMO. Similarly, requests and recommendations of the Consultative Meetings of the Antarctic Treaty are conveyed to WMO through the permanent representatives of the parties signatory to the Treaty. This mechanism ensures that Antarctic meteorology is a full part of WMO programmes and that the conditions of the Antarctic Treaty are fully respected.

24. At the programme levels the activities of WMO in the Antarctic are closely co-ordinated with SCAR of ICSU and with IOC/UNESCO. In particular, WMO co-operates with the SCAR Working Group on Antarctic Meteorology in the planning of the SCAR Antarctic Climate Research Programme in support of the WMO/ISCU World Climate Research Programme; and it works with IOC on the Joint Integrated Global Ocean Station System Programme which is concerned with ocean data collection and ocean services in Antarctic waters. At the operational level, WMO co-operates also with ITU in carrying out its World Weather Watch (WWW) programme, which is the main programme of the first WMO long-term plan (1984–1993) and which has a global telecommunications system as one of its components.

25. At present, the extension of WMO activities into the Antarctic is regulated through a number of resolutions of the WMO Executive Council, which were endorsed by the Twelfth Consultative Meeting of the Antarctic Treaty (1983). These resolutions deal specifically with a meteorological observation network in the Antarctic, the collection and transmission of meteorological data in the Antarctic and adjacent areas, and meteorological data processing activities at stations on the continent.

2. Food and Agriculture Organization of the United Nations

26. One of the objectives of the Food and Agriculture Organization of the United Nations is to promote national and international action for the rational management and development of world fisheries both in fresh waters and in the oceans, including the Antarctic. The problem of the exploitation of Antarctic marine living resources was discussed by the FAO Conference in 1975 and 1977 and by the Committee on Fisheries in 1969, 1975, 1977 and 1978.

27. In 1976–1977, FAO was the executing agency of the preparatory phase of the Southern Ocean Fisheries Survey Programme funded by UNDP. The preparatory phase was approved by the UNDP Governing Council at its twenty-first session in January 1976. In authorizing the Administrator to make the appropriate arrangements for the execution of this phase, the UNDP Governing Council instructed that such arrangements should be made in consultation with the signatories of the Antarctic Treaty. Subsequently, notes verbale were received from the Governments of Argentina and Chile, and correspondence was exchanged with the Governments of the United Kingdom and Australia, all of which were concerned that the project's execution should be carried out with special regard to the rights and obligations of the Antarctic Treaty

Consultative Parties and in full recognition of the need to work in close co-operation with those countries. A proposal for a main phase project was discussed in several forums, but the drafting of a project document and a work plan for the main phase project was never undertaken in view of the uncertainties which surrounded the future of the programme at that time.

28. Through its Advisory Committee on Marine Resources (ACMR), FAO is co-sponsoring, together with SCOR and the International Association for Biological Oceanography (IABO), the "Group of Specialists on Southern Ocean Ecosystems and their Living Resources", which has been established by SCAR to co-ordinate the BIOMASS programme.

29. Since 1980, when FAO was invited to attend, as an observer, the Diplomatic Conference which adopted the Convention on the Conservation of Antarctic Marine Living Resources, it has been co-operating with CCAMLR on scientific and technical matters. FAO has been invited to attend meetings of CCAMLR and its Scientific Committee as an observer.

30. FAO invited CCAMLR to appoint experts as members of the FAO Co-ordinating Working Party on Atlantic Fishery Statistics (CWP). This co-operation resulted, *inter alia*, in the adoption of a CCAMLR/CWP statistical form which is now used by both FAO and CCAMLR member countries.

31. Another field of co-operation between FAO and CCAMLR is the preparation, at the request of CCANLR, of a set of FAO/CCAMLR identification sheets for southern ocean species that are considered to be of present or potential interest to fisheries or requiring special conservation measures. The project is implemented by the FAO regular programme in collaboration with experts on Antarctic resources and with financial support from CCAMLR.

3. International Civil Aviation Organization

32. As the air transport system in Antarctica developed over the years, ICAO became involved in Antarctica. Following the adoption by the Antarctic Treaty Consultative Parties of recommendation VII-7 (1975) on co-operation in transport, ICAO was approached by SCAR with a view to developing potential requirements for a co-operative air transport system in Antarctica.

33. In connection with the question of the application of ICAO standards to different aspects of Antarctic air traffic, in particular to the organization of search and rescue facilities, an expert from the Section on Rules of the Air, Air Traffic Services and Search and Rescue of ICAO participating at the meeting of the SCAR Working Group on Logistics during the last meeting of SCAR in June 1986, in San Diego, United States of America.

4. United Nations Environment Programme

34. UNEP collaborates with different international bodies with regard to Antarctica. The 1980 "World Conservation Strategy" which was prepared on behalf of UNEP and the WWF by IUCN in co-operation with FAO and UNESCO and endorsed by General Assembly resolution 35/74 of 5 December 1980, identifies Antarctica and the southern ocean among the priorities for international action to conserve living resources for sustainable development. The 1984 "Global Plan of Action for the Conservation, Management and Utilization of Marine Mammals" - which was prepared by UNEP and FAO in collaboration with IUCN, IWC and SCAR and endorsed by the UNEP Governing Council in its decision 12/12 (I) – has major implications for the conservation of living resources. It was reported in 1986 that UNEP was planning to issue a contract with SCAP Group of Specialists on Seals, on satellite-compatible telemetric data collection on Antarctic seals as a contribution to this programme.

35. Under the "System-Wide Medium-Term Environment Programme" of the United Nations system for 1984–1989, UNEP concentrates, among other things, on the promotion of the effective implementation of conservation conventions relevant to Antarctica, including the 1946 International Whaling Convention and the 1980 Convention on the Conservation of Antarctic Marine Living Resources.

5. Intergovernmental Oceanographic Commission of UNESCO

36. IOC has established links with the Antarctic Treaty system through its Programme Group for the Southern Ocean (IOCSOC). The Programme Group maintains working relations with CCAMLR. The two bodies exchange representatives at their meetings. At present, the Chairman of the Scientific Committee of CCAMLR is also the Chairman of IOCSOC. Working relationships are also established by IOCSOC with IWC, SCAR and SCOR.

37. At the last, fourth session of IOCSOC in 1983, IOC reiterated its interest in the southern ocean, first stated in 1967. At this session, the Programme Group addressed a number of issues concerning IOC involvement in international scientific programmes in the southern ocean such as WCRP, BIOMASS, IGOSS, PSMSL. The Group decided to form a task team on data management for the southern ocean to examine the data management requirements for the region. This study is to be carried out in close consultation with other international bodies, including SCOR and SCAR.

38. The Programme Group also stressed the necessity and vital importance of co-operation with all organizations concerned with research in the southern ocean. The Group felt that in particular, close co-operation and liaison was needed between IOCSOC and SCOR and ACMRR, as scientific advisory bodies of the Commission, and their relevant working groups, as well as with SCAR and its Group of Specialists on Southern Ocean Ecosystems and their Living Resources for the BIOMASS programme. The Programme Group further expressed its interest in the important work carried out by CCAMLR and IWC.

39. At present, IOC and CCAMLR are jointly organizing a scientific seminar on Antarctic Ocean variability and its influence on marine living resources, particularly krill, to be held in Paris, from 2 to 6 June 1987, immediately before the fifth session of the IOCSOC.

6. International Whaling Commission

40. The IWC attends CCAMLR meetings as observer since 1982. At the 35th annual meeting of the IWC held in Brighton, United Kingdom, in 1983, it was decided that it would be sufficient for IWC co-operation with CCAMLR if reciprocal representation at meetings could be by a delegate of a member country who would be attending anyway, together with an exchange of documents made available through the secretariat.

41. At its meetings, the IWC Scientific Committee accorded the CCAMLR observers the status of advisers to the Committee.

42. At present, the IWC is co-operating with CCAMLR by organizing a joint working group on the implications for whales of the management régimes for other marine resources, specifically to consider the role of whales in the Antarctic ecosystem. There are also plans for IWC and CCAMLR to consider jointly sponsoring a workshop on the feeding ecology and distribution of southern baleen whales.

7. Scientific Committee on Antarctic Research of the International Council of Scientific Unions

43. Since the inception of the Antarctic Treaty, SCAR has maintained its links with the Antarctic Treaty system by responding to specific requests addressed to it by the Antarctic Treaty Consultative Parties. Such requests have been made in the form of recommendations of the Antarctic Treaty Consultative Meetings (for example, see para. 6, subparas. (a) and (b)). Another type of involvement by SCAR in the Antarctic Treaty system is through its responsibilities under the Convention for the Conservation of Antarctic Seals (see above paras. 10–12). SCAR is represented as observer at meetings of CCAMLR and its Scientific Committee. By virtue of recommendation XIII-2 of the Thirteenth Antarctic Treaty Consultative Meeting (1985), SCAR will be invited, when this recommendations becomes effective, to the Antarctic Treaty Consultative Meetings as an observer for specific purposes of reporting on certain matters within its competence.

44. According to the SCAR Constitution, each country actively engaged in Antarctic research can be represented in SCAR by a scientific delegate. These countries adhere to SCAR through

a national academy of science, national research council, or comparable body which sends delegates to SCAR meetings held every two years. The countries that have declared an intention to undertake research in the region, or who are already active but have not yet sought full membership, are invited to send their representatives as observers to SCAR meetings or become associate members.

45. SCAR maintains links with other member of ICSU that have delegate status in SCAR. In addition, observers are invited to SCAR meetings from a number of other interested international organizations, notably from SCOR and COSPAR of ICSU; from the specialized agencies of the United Nations and intergovernmental organizations, such as WMO, FAO, and IOC; and from IUCN.

46. Much of the scientific work conducted by SCAR is undertaken through nine permanent discipline-oriented groups. For more multi-discipline scientific issues, SCAR forms groups of specialists, some of which are co-sponsored by SCOR, IABO and ACMRR.

47. SCAR, in collaboration with ACMRR, COSPAR, IABO, ICAR, SCOR, SCSTP and WMO, is involved in a number of international research programmes conducted in the Antarctic by different nations.

48. SCAR is also concerned with the question of an appropriate minerals régime for the Antarctic and surrounding seas and it submitted its reports on the subject to the Antarctic Treaty Parties in 1977 and 1983. Since 1964, SCAR has been responsible for setting up scientific guidelines for the conservation of Antarctic flora and fauna, which were later adopted by the Antarctic Treaty Parties and for developing concepts and designating a number of specially protected areas and sites of special scientific interest in Antarctica.

8. Scientific Committee on Oceanic Research of the International Council of Scientific Unions

49. With regard to the Antarctic, SCOR, within ICSU, provides the scientific focus for physical and chemical oceanography in the southern ocean.

50. SCOR maintains its direct link with the Antarctic Treaty system through its participation at the meetings of CCAMLR and its Scientific Committee with which SCOR has observer status.

51. Over the years, SCOR has also developed a very close relationship with SCAR and they both co-sponsor a number of joint scientific activities related to the Antarctic such as BIOMASS, sea ice studies and physical oceanography. The mechanism for their interaction is provided through the SCOR working group "General Circulation of the Southern Ocean", and through their joint working groups "Southern Ocean Ecosystems and their Living Resources" and "Antarctic Sea Ice".

9. Committee on Space Research of the International Council of Scientific Unions

52. Working contacts have been established recently between COSPAR and SCAR with a view to developing closer co-operation in COSPAR studies regarding weather, climate and earth sciences, etc., as they relate to Antarctica. For this purpose, a joint COSPAR/SCAR workshop on "Satellite Observations of the Antarctic: Past, Present and Future" was held during the 25th COSPAR plenary meeting in 1984 in Graz, Austria.

53. The significant scientific potential of satellite observations in Antarctica was emphasized at the workshop, and a more active role for COSPAR was suggested in Antarctica in such global programmes as the WMO/ICSU World Climate Research Programme and the International Solar-Terrestrial Physics Programme proposed for the 1990s.

54. At present, COSPAR maintains relationships with SCAR at the working level through the activities of individual scientists involved in both COSPAR and SCAR.

10. International Union for Conservation of Nature and Natural Resources

55. Since the entry into force of the Convention on the Conservation of Antarctic Marine Living Resources, IUCN has participated as an observer in the meetings of CCAMLR and its Scientific Committee. IUCN is concerned with the conservation of Antarctic resources, which

in the view of IUCN, involves ensuring that their exploration and exploitation have minimum environmentally adverse effects.

56. IUCN is currently working with SCAR to develop a programme for long-term conservation in Antarctica as a follow-up to the joint IUCN/SCAR symposium on scientific requirements for Antarctic conservation held in 1985. Thereafter, IUCN and SCAR have established a joint Working Group on Long-Term Conservation of Antarctica. The Group has now met twice in 1986 and has produced a draft framework document setting out the requirements for Antarctic conservation. A draft IUCN Antarctic programme is now under preparation by the IUCN Director General's Advisory Committee on Antarctica. It is intended that all activities of the Programme will be undertaken in collaboration and consultation with the Antarctic Treaty Parties, SCAR, the members of CCAMLR, and the IUCN members.

III. Availability to the United Nations of Information from the Antarctic Treaty Consultative Parties on their Respective Activities in and their Deliberations Regarding Antarctica

A. Sources and available of information about activities in Antarctica

1. Provisions of the Antarctic Treaty and recommendations of Antarctic Treaty Consultative Meetings

(a) Article III (I) and relevant recommendations

57. Article III, subparagraph 1 (a) of the Antarctic Treaty provides that "information regarding plans for scientific programmes in Antarctica be exchanged to permit maximum economy and efficiency of operations". Subparagraph (c) of the same article provides that information regarding plans for scientific programmes, observations and results "be exchanged and made freely available".

58. Article III has been further developed by a number of recommendations which have been approved by the Antarctic Treaty Consultative Parties. Recommendation I-I states that "the Representatives recommend to their Governments that they should facilitate the continuation of the exchange of information regarding plans for scientific programmes as now carried out through the Special Committee on Antarctic Research".

59. By recommendation I-III, the Antarctic Treaty Consultative Parties recommend to their Governments that they should promote the exchange and making available of observations and results from Antarctica through the recognized international data-gathering centres and by such other means as may be appropriate to ensure the exchange and free availability of this information. It is also important to note that recommendation XIII-5 calls for improving the comparability and accessibility of scientific data on Antarctica.

60. One of the ways in which scientific information is exchanged and made available is through publication in the scientific literature. Some measure of the magnitude of Antarctic scientific publications may be obtained by consulting the comprehensive Antarctic bibliographies published by the Antarctic Treaty Consultative Parties.

(b) Article VII (5) and relevant recommendations

61. In accordance with article VII (5) on inspection and observation, Parties to the Antarctic Treaty are under the obligation to provide each other with extensive information on expeditions, stations, military personnel and equipment. Information about inspections is available in national publications on the subject. In response to General Assembly resolution 38/77, requesting the Secretary-General to prepare a study on the question of Antarctica, the Consultative Party, the Government of the United States forwarded to the Secretary-General of the United Nations, as part of its submission on the question, inspection reports of its observer teams for the years 1964, 1971, 1975, 1977, 1980 and 1983.

62. The Eighth Consultative Meeting, held in 1975, consolidated various provisions into one recommendation elaborating the standard format for the annual exchanges of information (recommendation VIII-6) which brought uniformity to these exchanges. The standard format

for the annual exchanges of information between parties indicates the range of matters now covered, including telecommunication facilities, tourism matters, and measures dealing with living resources and logistic problems (A/39/583 (Part I), annex to chap. III).

63. Recommendation XIII-l encourages Consultative Parties to make these exchanges of information available upon request. Australia, Japan and New Zealand submitted such information as part of their reply in response to General Assembly resolution 38/77. Some of the other Antarctic Treaty Consultative Parties also make a practice of making these exchanges available.

2. Agreed Measures for the Conservation of Antarctic Fauna and Flora

64. These measures, approved under recommendation III-VIII in 1964, aim at protecting native mammals, birds and plants providing special protection for rare or vulnerable species, preventing the introduction of non-indigenous species, alleviating water pollution adjacent to the coast and ice shelves and providing for specially protected areas.

65. Article XII of the Agreed Measures for the Conservation of Antarctic Fauna and Flora deals with the exchange of general information concerning such matters as: the collection and exchange of records (including records of permits) and statistics concerning the number of each species of native mammal and bird killed or captured annually in the Treaty area, exchanging information as to the status of native mammals and birds in the Treaty area, and the extent to which any species needs protection, the number of native mammals or birds which should be permitted to be harvested for food, scientific study or other uses in the various regions, and the establishment of a common form in which this information shall he submitted by participating governments in accordance with paragraph 2 of this article.

66. According to paragraph 2 of the same article, each participating government shall inform the other Governments about steps taken and information relating to the implementation of these Agreed Measures. Governments exchanging information through the Annual Exchange of Information under paragraph 5 of article VII of the Antarctic Treaty transmit, at the same time, information relating to the implementation of these Agreed Measures (see para. 63).

3. Convention for the Conservation of Antarctic Seals

67. Under article 5 of the Convention, a comprehensive system for exchanging information is established, whereby each Contracting Party has an obligation to provide each year to other Contracting Parties and to the SCAR a summary of statistical information on all seals killed or captured by their nationals and vessels. This information is publicly available and may be obtained from SCAR headquarters. It is also published in the *SCAR Bulletin.*

4. Convention on the Conservation of Antarctic Marine Living Resources

68. Under article XX of the Convention, the Commission members shall provide annually to the Commission and to the Scientific Committee such statistical, biological and other data and information as the Commission and Scientific Committee may require in the exercise of their functions. Commission members shall also provide, in the manner and at such intervals as may be prescribed, information about their harvesting activities so as to enable reliable catch and effort statistics to be compiled. All data and catch statistics are submitted to CCAMLR for publication and are publicly available. Commission members shall also provide information on steps taken to implement the conservation measures adopted by the Commission and these are maintained as part of the available public record.

5. Scientific Committee on Antarctic Research

69. Whenever the Treaty Parties are in need of scientific advice or information about Antarctica, they have, through formal recommendations, turned to SCAR. The Antarctic Treaty Consultative Parties have called upon SCAR to render advice and information on a variety of subjects such as logistics, conservation, living resources of the southern ocean, telecommunications and the exploration and exploitation of mineral resources in Antarctica.

70. These subjects are dealt with by various reports of a special nature published by SCAR. These reports such as the Report of possible Environmental Effects of Mineral Exploration

and Exploitation in Antarctica published by SCAR in 1979 are *ad hoc* in nature. In the view of SCAR, such special reports should be made widely available. Other occasional publications by SCAR are issued from time to time. For example, SCAR has published the four volumes produced to date in the *BIOMASS Scientific Series.*

71. SCAR requires each member nation, through its national committee, to submit an annual report on its ongoing programmes of research and other activities in Antarctica. The national report must contain a list of the occupied stations with their latitudes and longitudes, plans for the following year for both summer and winter, and a bibliography on publications related to Antarctic research that have been published since the previous report. These reports become available to the United Nations system because the Secretary-General of WMO automatically receives a copy from the national committees.

72. Reports of the biennial meetings of SCAR as well as meetings of its Executive Committee, groups of specialists, working groups and sub-committees are included in the SCAR Bulletin, published in January, May and September of each year, and is publicly available. The Bulletin is published by the Scott Polar Research Institute of Cambridge, United Kingdom. Reports of the biennial meeting are also published in Spanish by the Instituto Antarctica Argentina in Buenos Aires.

B. Sources and availability of information about the Antarctic Treaty system

1. Regular Consultative Meetings

73. Recommendations and reports of the Antarctic Treaty Consultative Meetings have been publicly available in the national publications of each Consultative Party and in the national publications of the nation which serves as a host of a Consultative Meeting. In accordance with recommendation XII-6 (1983), the government of the host country shall, on behalf of the Consultative Parties, automatically send a certified copy of the final report and recommendations of regular Consultative Meetings to the Secretary-General of the United Nations. The Secretary-General has received both the reports of the Twelfth and Thirteenth Consultative Meetings and a letter transmitting these documents to the secretary-General is published as an official document of the united Nations. Conference and information documents of these meetings are not yet available. However, recommendations adopted at the Twelfth and Thirteenth Consultative Meetings have dealt with the need to increase the public availability of these documents (see paras. 85 to 89).

2. Special Consultative Meetings

74. Six Special Consultative Meetings have been convened so far. At the First (1977), Third (1981), Fifth (1983), and Sixth Special Consultative Meetings (1985), it was decided that certain countries were entitled to consultative status. In its recommendation IX-2, the Second Special Meeting held in 1977–1980, convened a series of meetings to conclude a regime for the conservation of marine living species and resulted in the Convention on the Conservation of Antarctic Marine Living Resources (CCAMLR) in 1980. Under Recommendation XI-I, the Fourth Special Meeting, which is ongoing, convened a series of meetings to conclude a regime to govern the possibility of Antarctic mineral resources development.

75. The reports of the First, Second (all formal sessions), Third, Fifth, and Sixth Special Consultative Meetings are publicly available. With respect to the Fourth Special Consultative Meeting on the question of Antarctic mineral resources, there have been eight meetings. The reports of the two formal sessions, which summarize the sessions, are publicly available. Reports were not prepared on the six informal sessions and the documentation from these meetings is not available. Press statements were prepared by the Chairman at the conclusion of each session (formal or informal) and these statements are publicly available.

3. Convention for the Conservation of Seals

76. Although the Convention, which entered into force in 1978, provides for the setting up of special advisory and regulatory bodies, there are no regular meetings under this Treaty due to

the absence of commercial sealing activity in the southern ocean. For this reason, the parties to the Treaty agreed that there was no need to meet in 1983 to review the operation of the Treaty every five years as called for in article 7. SCAR has been invited to perform special functions for the purposes of the Convention in the absence of commercial sealing.

77. Under article 5 of the Convention, the contracting parties have been providing information called for by the Convention to SCAR and this information is made publicly available by SCAR (see para. 67 above)

4. Convention on the Convention of Antarctic Marine Living Resources

78. The Convention established a Commission (CCAMLR) and a Scientific Committee which convene annually in August and September at the Commission's headquarters. These bodies produce information about the operation of the Convention (para. 68). Informal working groups may be convened during intersessional periods.

79. The Convention is the only Antarctic Treaty system forum which has invited United Nations specialized agencies to participate as observers. Under the rules of procedure of the Commission, observers receive reports of the meetings they have attended. Observers may attend public and private meetings although Commission members may request that meetings be restricted to Commission members and original signatories on any particular agenda item. FAO and the IOC/UNESCO attend meetings of the Commission and its Scientific Committee.

80. Five meetings of the Commission and the Scientific Committee have been held to date. All the reports of those meetings are publicly available from the Executive Secretary, CCAMLR, Hobart, Australia.

5. Information submitted in response to requests by the United Nations Secretariat in accordance with General Assembly resolutions

81. In response to General Assembly resolution A/38/77, a total of 16 ATCPs submitted information to the Secretary-General for his report on the question of Antarctica (A/39/583, part I and Corr.1 and 2, and part II, vols. I-III and III/Corr.1).

82. Included in these submissions are *inter alia*, general information about Antarctica, research activity reports, annual reports to SCAR, exchanges of information under article VII (5) of the Treaty and bibliographies on Antarctica.

83. This information is kept in the United Nations Secretariat and is available to all delegations.

C. Measures taken by the Antarctic Treaty Consultative Parties at the XII and XIII Consultative Meetings to increase the public availability of information about the Antarctic Treaty system

1. Consultative Meeting reports

84. As noted earlier, in accordance with recommendation XII-6, the Antarctic Consultative Parties agreed to send a copy of the final report of Consultative Meetings to the Secretary-General of the United Nations and, as appropriate, to draw the attention of other specialized agencies having a technical or scientific interest in Antarctica to portions of these reports or other information documents relevant to their interests.

2. Documentation of Consultative Meetings

85. Another matter of concern to the Consultative Parties has been the Question of whether the working documents of Consultative Meetings should be made available to the public. There are reportedly differing views among the Antarctic Consultative Parties on the sensitivity of negotiating documents as well as different national practices regarding them.

86. By recommendation XII-6, it was decided that starting with the Thirteenth regular Consultative Meeting, delegations should indicate, when submitting an information document, if they wish that document to be publicly available after closure of the meeting and provided no Consultative Party has objected, if any Consultative Party or non-Consultative Party which has been invited to that meeting may make such document publicly available on such terms as it may prescribe. No delegation at the Thirteenth Meeting designated documents they submitted as publicly available.

81. Recommendation XII-6 also stated that the Consultative Parties will consider in what circumstances conference and information documents, which have not been identified in accordance with the preceding paragraph as intended to be publicly available, may be made available. Because of the large number of documents submitted to the 12 preceding Consultative Meetings, the Thirteenth Meeting limited its consideration to the conference and information documents of the first three Consultative Meetings (1961, 1962, and 1964). The Meeting also decided that there was in principle no need for them to continue to be treated as confidential. The Meeting agreed that any Consultative Party that wished a conference and information document submitted to the First, Second or Third Consultative Meetings to remain confidential, should so notify Belgium, the host Government for the Meeting, by 31 December 1985. The Belgian Government would inform all other Parties of any such notification received by it, subject to such notification, the Conference and information documents of these three Consultative Meetings need no longer be treated as confidential after 31 December 1985. No Consultative Party chose to so inform the Government of Belgium of any objection on this matter.

88. The Meeting also agreed that it would be appropriate to carry forward the consideration of this matter at the Fourteenth Consultative Meeting, with particular reference to the conference and information documents of the Fourth to Seventh Consultative Meetings.

3. Handbook of the Antarctic Treaty

89. Recommendation XII-6 also deals with the *Handbook of the Antarctic Treaty*. The *Handbook* sets out the text of the Antarctic Treaty, the measures in furtherance of the principles and objectives of the Treaty recommended at Consultative Meetings held from 1961 to date and the relevant portions of the reports of the Antarctic meetings.

90. Interest was expressed by some delegations at the Thirteenth Meeting in preparing versions of the Handbook in other Treaty languages besides English, which would greatly assist in disseminating information about the Antarctic Treaty more widely.

4. The White Book

91. Also discussed at the Twelfth Consultative Meeting was the possibility of disseminating general knowledge of the Antarctic Treaty system through the future elaboration of an extensive report – a "White Book" – on the history and achievements of the Antarctic Treaty.

92. At the Thirteenth Meeting, the possibility of proceeding further with the elaboration of a "White Book" was further discussed. While delegations were favourably disposed to pursue the idea further, not all were yet prepared to commit themselves to it. Delegations agreed to consider the matter further at the Fourteenth Meeting.

5. Recommendation XIII-I: Ensuring and facilitating the availability of information

93. Recommendation XII-6 also invited the depositary government to examine the question of information about the Antarctic Treaty system, including publicly available documents arising from Consultative Meetings with a view to identifying the sources from which such information can be obtained.

94. The United States, as depositary government, reported to the Thirteenth Meeting and suggested steps to ensure and facilitate the availability of adequate and accurate information about the Antarctic Treaty system, This paper formed the basis for recommendation XIII-I.

95. Recommendation XIII-l decided that,

(a) Efforts be continued to ensure that final reports of Consultative Meetings provide full and accurate records of these meetings, including:

   (i) The general trends of discussion of the specific agenda items considered as well as steps or actions taken as a result of decisions or recommendations adopted at precious Consultative Meetings, and

   (ii) Appropriate additional documentation of the meeting,

(b) The *Antarctic Treaty Handbook* be regularly maintained as a current compilation of recommendations and other actions agreed by Consultative Meetings,

(c) To the greatest extent practicable and feasible and in accordance with national laws and regulations, the following be made available on request:
   (i) Final reports of Consultative Meetings;
   (ii) The *Antarctic Treaty Handbook*;
   (iii) Annual exchanges of information they provide under the Antarctic Treaty;
(d) Their national committees be encouraged to make available, on request and in accordance with national laws and regulations, annual activities reports that these committees submit to SCAR,[114]
(e) On request and in accordance with national laws and regulations, up-to-date information be made available to the greatest extent practicable and feasible, on:
   (i) The location of depositories of data, examples and collections resulting from scientific research in Antarctica, and
   (ii) The nature and location of bibliographies or other information sources concerning reports and published works related to Antarctic matters, including those related to scientific research activities in Antarctica,
(f) A national contact point, or contact points, be designated and charged with the functions referred to in subparagraph (c) above and maintaining the information referred to in subparagraph (e) above;
(g) The names and addresses of the institutions or entities designated as national contact points, pursuant to subparagraph (f) above, be published as an annex to the final report of each Consultative Meeting and the Antarctic Treaty Handbook and be otherwise publicly disseminated.

96. The Meeting agreed to keep this matter under continual review.

97. As noted earlier, recommended measures shall become effective when approved by all the Contracting Parties whose representatives were entitled to participate in the meetings held to consider those measures. Recommendations decided upon at the Twelfth Meeting have been approved by Argentina, Australia, the Federal Republic of Germany, Japan, New Zealand, Norway, South Africa, the Union of Soviet Socialist Republics and the United States. At present, none of the recommendations decided upon at the Thirteenth Meeting have been approved.

D. Information resulting from the interaction of the Antarctic Treaty system with United Nations specialized agencies and programmes and the Scientific Committee on Antarctic Research

1. United Nations agencies

98. The interaction between the Antarctic Treaty system and the United Nations, as described in the previous chapter, has resulted in the information becoming available to certain United Nations agencies and programmes such as, *inter alia*, the World Meteorological Organization, the Food and Agriculture Organization of the United Nations and the Intergovernmental Oceanographic Commission of UNESCO.

(a) World Meteorological Organization

99. The Antarctic Treaty Consultative Parties contribute information to the World Climate Research Programme (WCRP), which is co-ordinated jointly by WMO and ICSU. The co-operation of the ATCPs with WMO in the field of telecommunications results in the exchange of relevant information for both. Recommendation X-3 of the Tenth Antarctic Consultative Meeting described the telecommunications network for the exchange of meteorological data both within the Antarctic and between the Antarctic and the Global Telecommunications System (GTS) of the World Weather Watch (WWW).

(b) Intergovernmental Oceanographic Commission of UNESCO

[114] In response to General Assembly resolution 38/77, Australia, the German Democratic Republic, Japan, New Zealand and the United States submitted these reports to the United Nations Secretary-General for the preparation of his report on the question of Antarctica (A/39/583, Part I and Part I/Corr.1, Part II, vols. I-III and III/Corr.1).

100. Co-operation with the IOC has included contributions by the ATCPs to the IOC Programme Group for the Southern Oceans (IOCSOC).[115] For example, in 1983, the Programme Group noted the importance of co-ordinated activities in the southern ocean, and the need for sharing logistics, especially on research vessels, and that information transfer is essential to such sharing although it is often either incomplete or not disseminated sufficiently in advance of planned activities to ensure effective logistical co-ordination. The Programme Group recommended that the IOC secretariat and the relevant national offices make every attempt to improve the subscription of national oceanographic programmes and declared national oceanographic programmes. It also requested its Chairman to circulate information about national oceanographic programmes as it becomes available. The Programme Group also recommended that the IOC invite member States to identify national correspondents for such information so that it is properly distributed, and that the *UNESCO IMS Newsletter* include information on southern ocean programmes as it becomes available.

101. In a submission to the fourth session of the IOCSOC,[116] one ATCP suggested that IOCSOC should enhance its co-ordinating role in the execution of the IOC/WHO Programme on Climate Research and ensure the rapid exchange of information on national programmes in the southern ocean.

(c) Food and Agriculture Organization of the United Nations

102. FAO, as a result of its observer status at CCAMLR meetings, can gain information aimed at gaining a deeper understanding of the structure and functioning of the Antarctic marine ecosystem as a basis for the future management of Antarctic living resources.

103. Since the inception of CCAMLR, FAO has co-operated with that body on science and technical matters and this has resulted in an exchange of information on matters of mutual interest.

104. Co-operation between the Co-ordinating Working Party of FAO with CCAMLR on Atlantic Fishery Statistics (CWP) resulted, *inter alia*, in the adoption of a CCAMLR/CWP statistical form. The form is designed, reproduced, and distributed by FAO. Once completed by the statistical offices of CCAMLR member countries, the forms are returned both to FAO and CCAMLR, thus ensuring consistency in the data published by both organizations.

105. In another field of co-operation, FAO prepares, at the request of CCAMLR, a set of FAO/CCAMLR identification sheets for southern ocean species that are considered to be of present or potential interest to fisheries or requiring special conservation measures.

106. On the basis of data received from different States, including the ATCPs, FAO produces a yearly publication entitled Yearbook of Fishery Statistics which includes the waters included in the Antarctic region.

2. The special role of the Scientific Committee Antarctic Research

107. In discussing the availability of information from the Treaty system to the United Nations system of organizations, reference should be made to the special role of SCAR. Although indirect, relations between bodies such as SCAR and United Nations agencies and programmes are worth noting in that they often lead to a further source of information for the United Nations system.

108. The constitution of SCAR provides that it "may establish liaison and co-operate with any international organization concerned with research activities in the Antarctic. At the request of international organizations, SCAR may provide scientific and technological advice". It is through this type of co-operation that a source of information becomes available to United Nations agencies and programmes with a scientific or technical interest in Antarctica.

[115] IOC/SOC-IV/3-P; 9-10. Antarctic Treaty Consultative Parties participating in the work of this Group include: Argentina, Australia, Brazil, Chile, China, France, Germany, Federal Republic of, India, New Zealand, Norway, Poland, the Union of Soviet Socialist Republics, the United Kingdom, the United States of America and Uruguay.

[116] Appendices to document IOC/PG/IV/6 (1982) entitled "Scientific Investigations at the Southern Oceans: a Possible Role for the IOC".

109. The following are examples of co-operation between SCAR and specialized agencies of the United Nations: a representative of the SCAR Working Group on Biology is serving as liaison with a UNEP/FAO effort to implement a draft Global Plan of Action for Conservation Management and Utilization of Marine Mammals; WMO is represented on SCAR Working Group on Meteorology and as such its representative receives all the working group correspondence; the SCAR Group of Specialists on Antarctic Climate Research established in 1981 co-operates, *inter alia*, with WMO and IOC/UNESCO; the Group of Specialists on Antarctic Sea Ice established in 1983 co-operates with the IOC and other bodies; the SCAR Working Group on Logistics discusses with the International Civil Aviation Organization (ICAO) the application of ICAO standards for different aspects of Antarctic air traffic. In addition, SCAR is one of the co-sponsors of the 1976–1986 BIOMASS Programme along with the ACMRR of FAO and other bodies.

110. A *BIOMASS Newsletter* is published periodically by SCAR to facilitate communication among the BIOMASS community and those interested in Antarctic research. A BIOMASS data base is lodged with the British Antarctic Survey in Cambridge, United Kingdom. The IOC/UNESCO is on the distribution lists for information about the BIOMASS programme, in addition to which there is both formal and informal communication.

111. The SCAR Group of Specialists on Seals is in working contact with UNEP in connections with the FAO/UNEP Global Plan of Action for the Conservation, Management and Utilization of Marine Mammals, and with the ACMRR of FAO in connection with the BIOMASS programme.

112. According to SCAR, all the aforementioned agencies receive copies of the *SCAR Bulletin* and are welcome to ask for any further information they may require on any specific topic.

IV. Significance of the United Nations Convention on the Law of the Sea in the Southern Ocean

113. The General Assembly requested an additional study on, *inter alia*, the "*significance*" of the United Nations Convention on the Law of the Sea (referred to hereinafter in this section as the Convention) in the Southern Ocean. For the purposes of this study, this Southern Ocean is viewed as being the southern continuation of the Atlantic, Indian and Pacific Oceans. Its northern boundary is considered to be the Antarctic Convergence which generally lies between 45° and 60° south latitude.[117]

114. The Convention which was opened for signature on 10 December 1982, received a total of 159 signatures by 9 December 1984, the closing date for signatures. As at 30 September 1986, 32 instruments of ratification had been deposited with the Secretary-General. The Convention will enter into force 12 months after the date of deposit of the sixtieth instrument of ratification or accession. It is already having a stabilizing effect on the law of the sea at both national and international levels and the recent judgments of the International Court of Justice and arbitral awards have taken into consideration developments in the law of the sea as reflected in the Convention (see A/38/570, A/39/647 and A/40/923).

115. One of the main objectives of the Convention is to establish a new legal order for the seas and oceans, taking into account recent developments and the needs of the international community. It is a global convention applicable to all ocean space. No area of ocean space is excluded. It follows that the Convention must be of significance to the Southern Ocean in the sense that its provisions also apply to that ocean.

116. Examination of the significance of the Convention in the Southern Ocean involves the issue of the relationship of the Convention with other conventions and international agreements the Convention states, *inter alia*, that it "Shall not alter the rights and obligations of States Parties which arise from other agreements compatible with this Convention and which do not affect the enjoyment by other States Parties of their rights or the performance of their obligations under this Convention."[118]

[117] See report of the Secretary-General (A/39/583 (Part I)). The term Southern Ocean as used in resolution 40/156 is explained by Malaysia (see A/C.1/40/PV.55).

[118] United Nations Convention on the Law of the Sea, art. 311, para. 2.

117. Of particular importance in this respect is the Antarctic Treaty in force between 32 States (a majority of which have signed the Convention)[119] which sets forth principles and rules to be applied not only to the Antarctic continent, but also to the maritime space of the Antarctic. The Treaty is aimed at furthering the purposes and principles embodied in the Charter of the United Nations by ensuring the use of Antarctica for peaceful purposes only and the continuance of international harmony in Antarctica. It is open for accession by any Member of the United Nations or by any other State that may be invited to accede to it. A network of substantive agreements, including the Antarctic Treaty itself and a body of agreed recommendations, agreed measures and additional instruments have been adopted pursuant to the Antarctic Treaty – all of which constitute the Antarctic Treaty system.[120] For the purposes of the Antarctic Treaty, Antarctica is defined as an area south of 60° south latitude, which embraces a considerable extent of maritime space. Certain conventions of a global character dealing with aspects of the law of the sea also apply to the Southern Ocean.

A. Peaceful uses of the seas

118. One of the objectives laid down in the preamble of the 1982 Convention is the establishment of a legal order for the seas and oceans which will promote their peaceful uses. This theme is taken up in various parts of the Convention.[121] For instance the Convention states the "the high seas shall be reserved for peaceful purposes" and that the sea-bed and ocean floor and subsoil thereof beyond the limits of national jurisdiction (the Area) "shall be open to use exclusively for peaceful purposes". Installations constructed for carrying out activities in the International Sea-Bed Area (referred to hereafter as the Area) are to be used exclusively for peaceful purposes. The conference, which will be convened to review the operation of the system of exploration and exploitation of the Area, shall ensure, *inter alia*, that the principle of using the Area exclusively for peaceful purposes is maintained. In addition, marine scientific research is to be conducted exclusively for peaceful purposes.

119. The *leitmotiv* of the Antarctic Treaty is to ensure that Antarctica shall be used exclusively for peaceful purposes and shall not become the scene or object of international discord.[122] Any measures of a military nature, such as "the establishment of military bases and fortifications, the carrying out of military manoeuvres, as well as the testing of any types of weapons" are prohibited. Thus the Treaty bars all military activities in Antarctica. Furthermore it prohibits any nuclear explosions and the disposal of radioactive waste in Antarctica. To secure these ends the Treaty also provides for a system of observation and inspection.[123] However, the Treaty states that nothing in it shall prejudice or in any way affect the rights, or the exercise of the rights, of any State under international law with regard to the high seas within that area.[124]

B. Marine scientific research

120. Under the Convention all States have the right to conduct marine scientific research, subject to the rights and duties of other States as provided for in the Convention[125] and States and competent international organizations are enjoined to promote and facilitate the development and conduct of marine scientific research.

[119] The following parties to the Antarctic Treaty (Consultative and Non-Consultative) have signed the Convention: Argentina, Australia, Belgium, Brazil, Bulgaria, Cuba, Czechoslovakia, Chile, Denmark, Finland, France, German Democratic Republic, Hungary, India, Italy, Japan, Netherlands, New Zealand, Norway, Papua New Guinea, People's Republic of China, Poland, Romania, South Africa, Spain, Sweden, Uruguay and Union of Soviet Socialist Republics, Cuba ratified it. Germany, Federal Republic of, Peru, United Kingdom and the United States of America did not sign it.

[120] See A/C.1/40/PV.48 (Australia).

[121] United Nations Convention on the Law of the Sea, arts. 88; 141; 147, para. 2(d); 155, para. 2; 143, para. 1; 24-(a); 242, para. 1 and 246, para. 3.

[122] Antarctic Treaty, Preamble and art. I. See A/39/583 (Part I), paras. 66 to 70 and 161 to 170.

[123] Antarctic Treaty, art. VII.

[124] Ibid, art. VI.

[125] United Nations Convention on the Law of the Sea, arts. 238; 239; 87; 143; 245 and 246.

121. The Convention expressly makes freedom of scientific research a freedom of the high seas. States Parties to the Convention have the right to carry out marine scientific research in the Area, exclusively for peaceful purposes and for the benefit of mankind as a whole. The rules of the Convention governing marine scientific research indluving the powers granted the International Sea-Bed Authority in article 143, apply to the high seas and the international sea-bed area extending south of 60° south latitude.

122. The Convention has established special régimes for marine scientific research for areas falling under the sovereignty and jurisdiction of coastal States. Coastal States have the exclusive right to regulate, authorize and conduct scientific research in their territorial sea. Marine scientific research in the exclusive economic zone and on the continental shelf is subject to the consent régime embodied in the Convention. These special régimes are applicable to the Southern Ocean in so far as such areas exist (see below, para. 139 and ff).

123. The Antarctic Treaty, embracing a significant part of the Southern Ocean, provides for the freedom of scientific investigation and co-operation towards that end as basic principles, particularly geared to the conditions of Antarctica. It establishes a mechanism for promoting international co-operation in scientific investigation in Antarctica and encourages the establishment of co-operative relations with those specialized agencies of the United Nations and other international organizations having a scientific or technical interest in Antarctica.[126] To this end, the Consultative Meetings of the Antarctic Treaty have provided a number of recommendations which are binding upon the Treaty Parties if approved by them.

124. The provisions of the Convention relating to marine scientific research in the high seas apply to those parts of the Southern Ocean which constitute the high seas. However, the position with regard to States not parties to the Antarctic Treaty conducting maritime scientific investigation in maritime areas adjacent to claimed territories is not clear.

C. Protection and preservation of the marine environment

125. The Convention imposes a general obligation on States to protect and preserve the marine environment,[127] with respect to: (a) pollution from land-based sources; (b) pollution from sea-bed activities subject to national jurisdiction; (c) pollution from sea-bed activities beyond national jurisdiction; (d) pollution from activities in the Area; (e) pollution from dumping; (f) pollution from vessels; and (g) pollution from or through the atmosphere.[128]

126. The measures that States shall take to combat pollution of the marine environment significantly include those necessary to protect and preserve rare or fragile ecosystems as well as the habitat of depleted, threatened or endangered species and other forms of marine life. States are also obliged to take all measures necessary to prevent, reduce and control pollution of the marine environment resulting from the use of technologies under their jurisdiction and control and to avoid introducing alien or new species to a particular part of the marine environment which may cause significant and harmful changes to that environment.

127. With respect to activities in the Area, appropriate rules, regulations and procedures are required to be adopted, *inter alia*, to prevent, reduce and control pollution, paying particular attention to the need for protection from the harmful effects of such activities as drilling, dredging, excavation, disposal of waste, construction and operation or maintenance of installations, pipelines and other devices related to such activities. Measures should also be adopted to protect and conserve the natural resources of this area and to prevent damage to the flora and fauna of the marine environment.

128. The Convention deals expressly with the relationship between its part XII (Protection and Preservation of the Marine Environment) and other conventions and agreements relating to the protection and preservation of the marine environment. Specific obligations assumed

[126] Antarctic Treaty, art. III, para. 2.
[127] United Nations Convention on the Law of the Sea, art. 192.
[128] Ibid, part XIII.

by States under these conventions and agreements are not prejudiced by the provisions of part XII. However, these obligations should be carried out in a manner consistent with the general principles and objectives of the Convention.[129]

129. There are measures and regulations concerning protection and preservation of the marine environment applicable to the Southern Ocean that have been approved on the global level under the auspices of the International Maritime Organization, the United Nations Environment Programme etc. On the regional level such measures have been elaborated within the framework of the Antarctic Treaty (see A/39/583 (Part I), para. 3, sect. III). These rules and regulations are generally compatible with the Convention.

D. Conservation and management of marine living resources

130. The Convention provides that coastal States have sovereign rights, over all the natural resources to be found in their exclusive economic zones, as well as the specific rights and obligations with respect to the conservation and management of living resources.[130] All States have the right to fish on the high seas – a right which flows from the freedom of the high seas. This right, however, is subject, among other things, to any treaty obligations and to the rights and duties as well as the interests of coastal States provided for, *inter alia*, in article 63, paragraph 2, and articles 64 to 67. These provisions relate to straddling stocks, highly migratory species, marine mammals, anadromous stocks and catadromous species; they all have effect to a greater or lesser extent on the legal régime of the high seas.

131. All States have the general duty to co-operate in the conservation and management of the living resources of the high seas.[131] In particular they have a duty, where their "national exploit identical living resources or different living resources in the same area", to enter into negotiations with a view to taking the necessary conservation measures and as appropriate establish subregional or regional organizations. In establishing conservation measures it is the duty of States under the Convention to take measures which are designed, on the best scientific evidence available to the States concerned, to maintain or restore populations of harvested species at levels which can produce the maximum sustainable yield, as qualified by relevant environmental and economic factors, including the special requirements of developing States, and taking into account fishing patterns, the interdependence of stocks and any generally recommended international minimum standards, whether subregional, regional or global. The Convention further provides that States shall take into consideration the effects on species associated with or dependent upon harvested species with a view to maintaining or restoring populations of such associated or dependent species above levels at which their reproduction may become seriously threatened. With respect to fishing on the high seas the Convention expressly declares that States must ensure that the conservation measures and their implementation do not discriminate in form or in fact against the fishermen of any State.

132. On the initiative of the Antarctic Treaty Consultative Parties two instruments have been adopted for the conservation of Antarctic marine living resources in the Convention for the Conservation of Antarctic Seals (1972) and the Convention on the Conservation of Antarctic Marine Living Resources (CCAMLR, 1980).[132] Neither of these two treaties makes any distinction within the waters of the Antarctic area, but both are specific with regard to the outer limits of the area of application: the Convention for the Conservation of Antarctic Seals applies to areas situated south of 60° south latitude; the area of application of the CCAMLR is the Antarctic Convergence. The application area of the two instruments respectively include all ocean space comprised between each of those limits and the Antarctic coastline.

---

[129] Ibid, art. 237.

[130] United Nations Convention on the Law of the Sea, arts. 55 to 57 and 61 to 73.

[131] Ibid, arts 87 and 116 to 119.

[132] See also Agreed Measures for the Conservation of Antarctic Fauna and Flora adopted at the 3rd Consultative Meeting (1964). Further see Report of the Secretary-General A/39/583 (Part I), sects. II.B, III.F.

133. The CCAMLR states that the term "conservation" includes rational use and it adopts the ecosystem-oriented approach with respect to the conservation of marine living resources. This approach is somewhat different from the notion of "maximum sustainable yield" adopted in the Convention.

134. The CCAMLR has established a Commission for the Conservation of the Antarctic Marine Living Resources to give effect to its objectives and principles. The Commission shall take into account regulations or measures adopted by existing fisheries commissions responsible for species which may enter the area to which the CCAMLR applies.[133] The Commission must also seek to co-operate with contracting parties exercising jurisdiction in marine areas adjacent to the area of application of the CCAMLR in respect of the conservation of any stock or stocks of associated species which occur both within those areas and the area of application of the CCAMLR.[134]

135. Any State interested in research or harvesting activities in relation to Antarctic marine living resources can accede to the CCAMLR. Contracting Parties to CCAMLR not parties to the Antarctic Treaty acknowledge "the special obligations and responsibilities of the Antarctic Treaty Consultative Parties for the protection and preservation of the marine environment of the Antarctic Treaty area".[135] Such States are bound by articles I to VI of this instrument which concerns, *inter alia*, the issues of peaceful purposes and sovereignty.[136] Any acceding State is entitled to membership in the Commission for the Conservation of Antarctic Marine Living Resources as long as it is engaged in research or harvesting activities in relation to the Antarctic marine living resources.[137]

136. The Convention on the Conservation of Antarctic Seals is designed to promote and achieve the objectives of protection, scientific study and rational use of Antarctic seals, and to maintain a satisfactory balance within the ecological system. It establishes measures which are subject to review in the light of scientific assessment and envisages the establishment of a system of inspection. Since there is no commercial sealing in the area, the Convention plays mostly a preventive role.

137. The above-mentioned Conventions as well as the International Convention for the Regulation of Whaling (1946), which also applies to the waters of the Southern Ocean, are in accord with the requirements of the Convention.

V. Issues of Sovereignty and Jurisdiction

138. The Convention can be viewed as dividing ocean space into two categories of areas: areas falling under the sovereignty and jurisdiction of coastal States and areas beyond the limits of national jurisdiction. The former includes the internal waters, the territorial sea, the contiguous zone, the exclusive economic zone and the continental shelf. To these may be added the special régimes for islands.[138] The high seas and the international sea-bed area are maritime areas beyond the limits of national jurisdiction.

A. Areas falling within the sovereignty and jurisdiction of States

139. The question whether the régime embodied in the Convention relating to maritime areas falling under national sovereignty or jurisdiction applies to Antarctica is linked to the legal status of the land masses in Antarctica. Within the Southern Ocean there are islands that are subject to the undisputed sovereignty of various States. The régime of the Convention applies to such islands. Legislative acts concerning the territorial seas and the continental shelves around these islands have to a large extent been enacted by coastal States, and in certain instances declarations on 200 miles exclusive economic or fishery zones have been made.

---

[133] Ibid, art. IX, para. 5.

[134] Ibid, art. XI.

[135] Ibid, art. V.

[136] Ibid, articles III and IV.

[137] Ibid, art. VII, para. 2 (b).

[138] United Nations Convention on the Law of the Sea, arts. 8; 2; 3; 33; 55 to 58; 76 and 121.

140. With respect to Antarctica, seven States parties to the Antarctic Treaty have claimed sovereignty over territories and some of these claims overlap. Two States, while not recognizing any territorial claims in Antarctica, maintain a basis of claims in respect of Antarctic territories. Other States within the system have not made any claims nor do they recognize claims to sovereignty. A part of the Antarctic continent remains free from claims of national sovereignty.

141. The Antarctic Treaty has devised a mechanism for dealing with these conflicting positions. This is embodied in article IV which states:

"1. Nothing contained in the present Treaty shall be interpreted as:

"(a) a renunciation by any Contracting Party of previously asserted rights of or claims to territorial sovereignty in Antarctica;"

"(b) a renunciation or diminution by any Contracting Parties of any basis of claim to territorial sovereignty in Antarctica which it may have whether as a result of its activities or those of its nationals in Antarctica, or otherwise;"

"(c) prejudicing the position of any Contracting Party as regards the recognition or non-recognition of any other State's right of or claim or basis of claim to territorial sovereignty in Antarctica."

"2. No acts or activities taking place while the present Treaty is in force shall constitute a basic for asserting, supporting or denying a claim to territorial sovereignty in Antarctica or create any rights of sovereignty in Antarctica. No new claims or enlargement of an existing claim, to territorial sovereignty in Antarctica shall be asserted while the present Treaty is in force."

From the perspective of the Parties to the Antarctic Treaty, the extent to which the various types of maritime jurisdiction can be exercised by claimant States in the Antarctica depends on how article IV of the Antarctic Treaty is interpreted. The Antarctic Treaty Consultative Parties themselves are not in agreement on this question (see also A/39/583 (Part I), sect. II.B, III. F). States which have claimed territorial sovereignty in Antarctica have not renounced their rights. They assert claims to maritime jurisdiction over adjacent waters on the basis that title to territory automatically involves jurisdiction over appurtenant waters and continental shelves. Such rights, in their view, are merely an attribute of their sovereignty. On the other hand non-claimant States do not recognize any claims to territorial sovereignty in the Antarctic area. A number of these States also argue that certain assertions of sovereign rights over resources constitute a new claim or the extension of an existing claim to territorial sovereignty and therefore prohibited by article IV (2) of the Antarctic Treaty.[139] The validity of maritime claims is a broader question than that addressed in the present paragraph. It is not merely dependent on an interpretation of article IV, which is only binding upon the Parties.

143. The non-recognition of territorial sovereignty in Antarctica by some of the States parties to the Treaty is shared by a number of States not parties to the Antarctic Treaty. Some of these latter States contend that Antarctica should be the common heritage of mankind.[140]

144. This issue was also dealt with in the CCAMLR. The area of application of this instrument, extended north of 60° south latitude up to a point where the Antarctic Convergence begins covering certain islands over which there was generally undisputed sovereignty. In order to deal with certain problems arising from this extension the mechanism utilized in the Antarctic Treaty was somewhat modified. Article IV of the CCAMLR includes an analogous provision to that of article IV of the Antarctic Treaty with the exception of paragraph 2 (b) which states:

"Nothing in this Convention and no acts or activities taking place while the Convention is in force shall:

"...

[139] See Bush, Antarctica and International Law, A Collection of Inter-State and National Documents, vol. I, p. 62.

[140] See A/C.1/40/PV.48 (Malaysia); A/C.1/40/PV.50 (Bangladesh); Ibid (Sudan); Ibid. (Libya); Ibid. (Pakistan); Ibid (Thailand); A/C.1/40/PV.53 (Nepal); Ibid. (Cape Verde); Ibid (Algeria); Ibid. (Kenya). See the Declaration of the Organization of African Unity (OAU), at its forty-second ordinary session, held in Addis Ababa from 10 to 17 July 1985.

"(b) be interpreted as a renunciation or diminution by any Contracting Party, of, or as prejudicing, any right or claim or basis of claim to exercise coastal State jurisdiction under international law within the area to which this Convention applies;".

This provision enabled both claimant and non-claimant States to maintain their respective positions with respect to the question of whether attempts to establish fishing or exclusive economic zones were permissible under article IV of the Antarctic Treaty or constituted an enlargement of existing claim. With respect to the right of States to coastal jurisdiction in areas north of 60° south latitude a compromise solution was found through a statement by the Chairman of the Conference regarding the application of the CCAMLR régime to waters adjacent to the islands over which the existence of State sovereignty was recognized by all parties to the Treaty.

145. In the light of the differences referred to above, the extent to which the provisions of the Convention relating to national sovereignty and jurisdiction apply to the area of application of the Antarctic Treaty, and hence their significance thereto, remains unclear. The application area of the Treaty (the waters south of the 60° south latitude) indicates the limits of the areas within which the parties undertake to regulate their conduct and is not based on any claim of sovereignty or jurisdiction. The manner in which the instruments of the Antarctic Treaty system are applied by the Antarctic Treaty Parties supports this.

146. With respect to the delineation of baselines, it should be noted that there are unique geophysical conditions prevailing in the Antarctic region which neither the Convention nor any other rule of international law has dealt with. In the case of the Antarctic continent, the low waterline along the coast varies considerably because the ice layer permanently covering the land mass flows outwards and its extension changes depending upon the season.

B. Areas beyond the national jurisdiction of States

1. High seas

147. The provisions of the Convention relating to the high seas apply to all parts of the sea that are not included in the exclusive economic zone, in the territorial sea or in the internal waters of a State or in the archipelagic waters of an archipelagic State. In the high seas all States enjoy, *inter alia*, the freedom of navigation; of overflight; freedom to lay submarine cables and pipelines; to construct artificial islands and other installations; and the freedom of fishing and of scientific research.[141] The general rules relating to the high seas apply to the Southern Ocean.

2. The International Sea-Bed Area

148. The international régime under the Convention includes principles and rules governing the exploration and exploitation of the resources of the Area. It establishes an International Sea-Bed Authority – an organization designed to give effect to the principle that "The Area and its resources are the common heritage of mankind".[142] No State may claim or exercise sovereign rights over any part of the Area or its resources or appropriate any part thereof.[143] Activities in the Area shall be organized, carried out and controlled by the Authority acting on behalf of mankind as a whole and for its benefit.[144]

149. The area over which the international régime established in part XI of the Convention will apply is defined as the "sea-bed and ocean floor and subsoil thereof beyond the limits of national jurisdiction".[145]

150. Since neither the parallel 60° south not the Antarctic Convergence are limits of national jurisdiction, the Area would extend beyond those lines into the Southern Ocean. This is

[141] United Nations Convention on the Law of the Sea, arts. 86 and 87.

[142] United Nations Convention on the Law of the Sea, art. 136. See also the Declaration of principles governing the sea-bed and the ocean floor, and the subsoil thereof, beyond the limits of national jurisdiction General Assembly resolution 2749 (XXV) adopted by 108 votes to none, with 14 abstentions.

[143] Ibid, art. 137.

[144] Ibid, art. 140.

[145] Ibid, art. 1, para. 1 (i).

acknowledge by the Antarctic Treaty parties. At the eleventh Consultative Meeting, the Antarctic Treaty Consultative Parties, a majority of whom are signatories to the Convention, adopted a decision with respect to the régime of Antarctic Mineral Resources which stated that the régime should apply to all mineral resource activities taking place on the Antarctic continent and its adjacent off-shore areas "but without encroachment on the deep sea-bed". They further decided that the precise limits of the area of application would be determined by the Antarctic Treaty Consultative Parties in the elaboration of the régime.[146] As the Antarctic mineral resources régime is still under negotiation among the Antarctic Treaty Consultative Parties, it is not possible to analyse at this stage its scope and content nor to consider its relationship with the principles on which the international régime for the Area is based.

151. On the basis of the definition of the Area the sea-bed and ocean floor and subsoil thereof which lie beyond national jurisdiction are regulated by the international sea-bed régime embodied in the Convention. The precise determination of the limits of the Area in the Southern Ocean presents complex problems. First, there are claimed areas and unclaimed areas in Antarctica. Second, there is the position of claimant and non-claimant States within the Antarctic Treaty system. Third, there is the position of the Antarctic Treaty Consultative Parties referred to in paragraph 150. Fourth, there is the position of a number of States not parties to the Antarctic Treaty which do not recognize claims in Antarctica. And fifth, there is the position of those among the latter which contend that Antarctica should be proclaimed as the common heritage of mankind. As in the case referred to in paragraph 145, therefore, the question of the applicability of the international régime for the sea-bed and ocean floor beyond national jurisdiction to the sea-bed in the Antarctica region, and hence the significance thereto, remains unclear.

Report of the Secretary-General, Question of Antarctica, UN Doc A/42/587 (30 September 1987)

1. In its resolution 41/88 C of 4 December 1986, the General Assembly viewed with concern the continuing participation of the apartheid régime of South Africa in the meetings of the Antarctic Treaty Consultative Parties; appealed once again to the Consultative Parties to take urgent measures to exclude the racist apartheid régime of South Africa from participation in the meetings of the Consultative Parties at the earliest possible date; invited the States Parties to the Antarctic Treaty to inform the Secretary-General on the actions taken regarding the provisions of the resolution; and also requested the Secretary-General to submit a report in this regard to the Assembly at its forty-second session.

2. In accordance with resolution 41/88 C, the Secretary-General, on 10 February 1987, addressed a note verbale to the States Parties to the Atlantic Treaty[147] and requested them to submit as soon as possible, but not later than 30 April 1987, the replies that their respective Governments were prepared to provide pursuant to the provisions of the resolution.

3. On 2 July 1987, a communication was received from the Permanent Representative of Australia to the United Nations, acting on behalf of States Parties to the Antarctic Treaty, with reference to the Secretary-General's note verbale. The communication dated 1 July 1987 reads as follows:

[146] Eleventh Meeting of the Antarctic Treaty Consultative Parties, Recommendation XI-1, para. 7, IV.

[147] Argentina, Australia, Belgium, Brazil, Bulgaria, Chile, China, Cuba, Czechoslovakia, Democratic People's Republic of Korea, Denmark, Finland, France, German Democratic Republic, Federal Republic of Germany, Greece, Hungary, India, Italy, Japan, Netherlands, New Zealand, Norway, Papua New Guinea, Peru, Poland, Republic of Korea, Romania, South Africa, Spain, Sweden, Union of Soviet Socialist Republics, United Kingdom of Great Britain and Northern Ireland, United States of America and Uruguay.

"The Permanent Representative of Australia to the United Nations, acting on behalf of States Parties to the Antarctic Treaty,[148] has the honour to refer to the Secretary-General's note of 10 February 1987 relating to the question of Antarctica."

"The Permanent Representative of Australia has the honour to recall that, before the voting on resolution 41/88 C in the First Committee at the forty-first session of the General Assembly, he made a statement on behalf of Antarctic Treaty Parties. The statement expressed continuing disappointment at the lack of consensus in the General Assembly's consideration of Antarctica."

"In the case of two of the draft resolutions before the Assembly, this disappointment occasioned decisions by most Treaty Parties not to participate in the voting. In the case of the draft resolution subsequently adopted as resolution 41/88 C, the statement noted that Treaty Parties had decided to reflect their views in ways that did not affect their position on the successful functioning of the Antarctic Treaty. Treaty Parties reiterated their belief that the General Assembly's consideration of Antarctica could proceed usefully and realistically only on the basis of consensus. This remains the view of Treaty Parties."

"Based on their condemnation and abhorrence of the system of apartheid practised by the Government of South Africa, a number of Treaty Parties decided to vote for resolution 41/88 C, which called for urgent measures to exclude South Africa from participation in the meetings of the Consultative Parties to the Antarctic Treaty. The decision of these Parties should be seen as being without prejudice to their views on the merits of a consensus approach to Antarctica and on the successful functioning of the Antarctic Treaty."

"Other Treaty Parties, who likewise abhor and condemn the system of apartheid, decided not to participate in the voting on resolution 41/88 C. The decision of these Parties was based on their support for the principle of universality in the United Nations; on the importance they attach to the view that there is no valid basis under international law for limiting the exercise of a Party's right under the Antarctic Treaty; and that it is essential that all States Parties that undertake activities in Antarctica be bound by and carry out their obligation under the Treaty."

"Countries who host meetings under the aegis of the Antarctic Treaty make the necessary arrangements strictly in compliance with the relevant obligations that apply to such meetings. This will be the case with meetings held in 1987 and cannot in any way be interpreted as having a bearing upon broader foreign policy objectives."

"Treaty Parties are united in their determination to safeguard effective functioning of the Antarctic Treaty system. They believe that the consensus necessary to productive international consideration of Antarctica can be based only on resolutions that give full regard to the Antarctic Treaty and the continuing operation of the Treaty system."

Report of the Secretary-General, Question of Antarctica, UN Doc A/43/564 (31 August 1988)

1. On 30 November 1987, the General Assembly adopted resolution 42/46 B on the question of Antarctica.

2. While reaffirming, *inter alia*, that any eventual minerals régime on Antarctica should take fully into account the interests of the international community, the General Assembly, in paragraph 3 of the resolution called upon the Antarctic Treaty Consultative Parties[149] to

[148] Argentina, Australia, Belgium, Brazil, Bulgaria, Chile, China, Cuba, Czechoslovakia, Democratic People's Republic of Korea, Denmark, Finland, France, German Democratic Republic, Federal Republic of Germany, Greece, Hungary, India, Italy, Japan, Netherlands, New Zealand, Norway, Papua New Guinea, Peru, Poland, Republic of Korea, Spain, Sweden, Union of Soviet Socialist Republics, United Kingdom of Great Britain and Northern Ireland, United States of America and Uruguay.

[149] Argentina, Australia, Belgium, Brazil, China, France, German Democratic Republic, Germany, Federal Republic of, India, Italy, Japan, New Zealand, Norway, Poland, South Africa, the Union of Soviet Socialist Republics, the United Kingdom of Great Britain and Northern Ireland, the United States of America and Uruguay.

impose a moratorium on the negotiations to establish a minerals régime until all members of the international community could participate fully in such negotiations.

3. On 30 June 1988, the Secretary-General received a letter for Chargé d'affaires a.i. of the Permanent Mission of Australia to the United Nations conveying a statement of Mr. C. D. Beeby, Chairman of the Antarctic Treaty Special Consultative Meeting on Antarctic Mineral Resources, regarding the adoption on 2 June 1988 of a Convention on the regulation of mineral resource activities in Antarctica. The letter and the statement attached to it were circulated as an official document of the General Assembly (A/43/434).

4. On August 1988, the Secretary-General received a letter for the Chargé d'affaires a.i. of the Permanent Mission of New Zealand to the United Nations conveying an authenticated copy of the Final Act if the Fourth Antarctic Treaty Special Consultative Meeting on Antarctic Mineral Resources.

5. On 8 June 1988, the Secretary-General received a letter from the Chargé d'affaires a.i. of the Permanent Mission of Malaysia to the United Nations on behalf of the representatives of Antigua and Barbuda, Bangladesh, Brunei Darussalam, Cameroon, the Congo, Ghana, Indonesia, Kenya, Malaysia, Nepal Nigeria, Oman, Pakistan, Rwanda, Sri Lanka, the Sudan, Uganda, Zambia and Zimbabwe. This letter expressed the utmost regret and deep concern about the adoption of the aforementioned Convention. The letter was circulated as an official document of the General Assembly (A/43/396).

6. In its resolution 42/46 B, the General Assembly also called upon the Antarctic Treaty Consultative Parties to invite the Secretary-General or his representative to all meetings of the Treaty Parties, including their Consultative Meetings and the minerals régime negotiations, and requested the Secretary-General to submit a report on his evaluations thereon to the Assembly at its forty-third session.

7. The Secretary-General was not in receipt of an invitation to meetings of the Antarctic Treaty Consultative Parties, and therefore is not in a position to provide any evaluations thereon.

Report of the Secretary-General, Question of Antarctica, UN A/44/586 (3 October 1989)

In its resolution 43/83 A of 7 December 1988, the General Assembly, *inter alia*, expressed its conviction that any minerals régime on Antarctica, in order to be of benefit to all mankind, should be negotiated with the full participation of all members of the international community.

2. The Assembly further expressed its deep regret that the Antarctic Treaty Consultative Parties[150] had proceeded with negotiations and had adopted on 2 June 1988 a convention on the regulation of Antarctic mineral resource activities, notwithstanding Assembly resolutions 41/88 B of 4 December 1986 and 42/46 B of 30 November 1987, calling for the imposition of a moratorium on negotiations to establish a minerals régime until such time as all members of the international community could fully participate in such negotiations.

3. In response to a note verbale from the Secretary-General to the Antarctic Treaty Consultative Parties on the above issue, a note was received on 19 April 1989 from the Permanent Representative of Australia to the United Nations, responding on behalf of the States parties to the Antarctic Treaty. This note reads as follows:

"The Permanent Representative of Australia to the United Nations, acting on behalf of the States Consultative Parties to the Antarctic Treaty, presents his compliments to the Secretary-General of the United Nations and has the honour to refer to the Secretary-General's note with

[150] Argentina, Australia, Belgium, Brazil, Chile, China, France, German Democratic Republic, Germany, Federal Republic of, India, Italy, Japan, New Zealand, Norway, Poland, South Africa, Spain, Sweden, the Union of Soviet Socialist Republics, the United Kingdom of Great Britain and Northern Ireland, the United States of America and Uruguay.

reference to General Assembly resolution 43/83 A of 7 December 1988 with respect to the question of Antarctica.

"The Permanent Representative of Australia has the honour to recall that before the voting on resolution 43/83 A in the First Committee at the forty-third session of the General Assembly, Australia made a statement reflecting the views of Antarctic Treaty Parties. The statement noted that Treaty Parties continued to believe that consideration of Antarctica by the General Assembly should proceed only on the basis of consensus. That remains the conviction of the Antarctic Treaty Consultative Parties."

4. In paragraph 3 of its resolution 43/83 A, the General Assembly also reiterated its call upon the Antarctic Treaty Consultative Parties to invite the Secretary-General or his representative to all meetings of the Treaty Parties, including their Consultative Meetings. Moreover, the Secretary-General was requested to submit a report on his evaluations thereon to the Assembly at its forty-fourth session.

5. In a letter to the Secretary-General dated 6 July 1989, the Permanent Representative of France to the United Nations conveyed a press release issued by the President of the Preparatory Meeting of the XVth Antarctic Treaty Consultative Meeting, which was held in Paris from 9 to 13 May 1989. This letter and the attached press release were circulated as a document of the General Assembly on 11 July 1989 (A/44/383).

6. The Secretary-General was not in receipt of an invitation to meetings of the Antarctic Treaty Consultative Parties, and therefore is not in a position to provide any evaluations thereon.

Report of the Secretary-General, Question of Antarctica, UN Doc A/45/459 (8 September 1990)

1. In its resolution 44/124 B of 15 December 1989, the General Assembly, *inter alia*, expressed its conviction that, in view of the significant impact that Antarctica exerts on the global environment and ecosystem, any régime to be established for the protection and conservation of the Antarctic environment and its dependent and associated ecosystems, in order to be for the benefit of mankind as a whole and in order to gain the universal acceptability necessary to ensure full compliance and enforcement, must be negotiation with the full participation of all members of the international community.

2. The General Assembly urged all members of the international community to support all efforts to ban prospecting and mining in and around Antarctica and to ensure that all activities are exclusively used for the purpose of peaceful scientific investigation and that all such activities ensure the maintenance of international peace and security in Antarctica and the protection of its environment and are for the benefit of all mankind.

3. The General Assembly also expressed its conviction that the establishment, through negotiations with the full participation of all members of the international community, of Antarctica as a nature reserve or a world park would ensure the protection and conservation of its environment and its dependent and associated ecosystems for the benefit of all mankind.

4. In response to a note verbale from the Secretary-General to the Antarctic Treaty Consultative Parties[151] with regard to the resolution, a note dated 30 April was received from the Permanent Representative of Australia to the United Nations responding on behalf of the Consultative Parties to the Antarctic Treat. The note reads as follows:

"The Permanent Representative of Australia to the United Nations, acting on behalf of the States Consultative Parties to the Antarctic Treaty … has the honour to refer to the Secretary-

[151] Argentina, Australia. Belgium, Brazil, Chile, China, Finland, France, German Democratic Republic, Germany, Federal Republic of, India, Italy, Japan, New Zealand, Norway, Peru, Poland, Republic of Korea, South Africa, Spain, Sweden, Union of Soviet Socialist Republics, United Kingdom of Great Britain and Northern Ireland, United States of America, and Uruguay.

General's note of 19 March 1990 with reference to General Assembly resolution 44/124 B of 15 December 1989 with respect to the question of Antarctica."

"The resolution refers to the significant impact that Antarctica exerts on the global environment and ecosystems. The Antarctic Treaty Parties are aware of the need for concerted international action to protect the Antarctic environment from external environmental disturbances which could accelerate serious global environmental change. For their part, the Antarctic Treaty Parties as the countries active in the region will continue to develop measures to protect the fragile Antarctic environment and dependent associated ecosystems from the impact of human activity within the region. Given the indispensable contribution of Antarctic scientific research to the global effort to predict and understand climate change, the Antarctic Treaty Parties will also continue to make freely available the results of their Antarctic research bearing upon the global environment as well as all other subjects. Any State Member of the United Nations can participate in this work by acceding to the Antarctic Treaty."

"The Permanent Representative of Australia has the honour to recall that before the voting on resolution 44/124 B in the First Committee at the forty-fourth session of the General Assembly, Australia made a statement reflecting the views of Antarctic Treaty Parties. The statement noted, *inter alia*, that Treaty Parties had not participated in the voting as they continued to believe that consideration of Antarctica by the General Assembly should proceed only on the basis of consensus. That remains the conviction of the Antarctic Treaty Parties."

5. In the resolution, the General Assembly also reiterated its call upon the Antarctic Treaty Consultative Parties to invite the Secretary-General or his representative to all meetings of the Treaty parties, and requested the Secretary-General to submit a report on his evaluations thereon at its forty-fifth session.

6. The Secretary-General was not in receipt of an invitation to meetings of the Antarctic Treaty Consultative Parties, and therefore is not in a position to provide any evaluations thereon.

List of Further United Nations Documents

Report of the Secretary-General, Question of Antarctica: Views of States (vol 1), UN Doc A/39/583 (Part II) (29 October 1984)

Report of the Secretary-General, Question of Antarctica: Views of States (vol 2), UN Doc A/39/583 (Part II) (2 November 1984)

Report of the Secretary-General, Question of Antarctica: Views of States (vol 3), UN Doc A/39/583 (Part II) (9 November 1984)

Report of the Secretary-General, Question of Antarctica: Corrigendum, UN Doc A/39/583 (Part I)/Corr.1 (26 November 1984)

Report of the Secretary-General, Question of Antarctica: Corrigendum, UN Doc A/39/583 (Part II)/Corr.1 (3 December 1984)

Report of the Secretary-General, Question of Antarctica: Corrigendum, UN Doc A/39/583 (Part I)/Corr.2 (24 April 1985)

Report of the Secretary-General, Question of Antarctica: Corrigendum, UN Doc A/39/583 (Part I)/Corr.3 (18 July 1985)

Report of the First Committee, Question of Antarctica, UN Doc A/41/902 (26 November 1986)

Report of the Secretary-General, Question of Antarctica, UN Doc A/42/586 (30 September 1987)

Report of the Secretary-General, Question of Antarctica: Corrigendum, UN Doc A/42/586/Corr.1 (21 October 1987)

Report of the First Committee, Question of Antarctica, UN Doc A/42/758 (24 November 1987)

Report of the Secretary-General, Question of Antarctica, UN Doc A/43/565 (31 August 1988)

Report of the First Committee, Question of Antarctica, UN Doc A/43/911 (5 December 1988)

Report of the Secretary-General, Question of Antarctica, UN Doc A/44/518 (19 September 1989)
Report of the First Committee, Question of Antarctica, UN Doc A/44/819 (1 December 1989)
Report of the Secretary-General, Question of Antarctica, UN Doc A/45/458 (6 September 1990)
Report of the First Committee, Question of Antarctica, UN Doc A/45/789 (7 December 1990)
Report of the Secretary-General, Question of Antarctica, UN Doc A/46/512 (30 September 1991)
Report of the Secretary-General, Question of Antarctica: State of the Environment in Antarctica and its Impact on the Global System, UN Doc A/46/590 (25 October 1991)
Report of the Secretary-General, Question of Antarctica: Study on the Establishment of a United Nations-sponsored Station in Antarctica, UN Doc A/46/583 (25 October 1991)
Report of the First Committee, Question of Antarctica, UN Doc A/46/679 (2 December 1991)
Report of the Secretary-General, Question of Antarctica, UN Doc A/47/541 (20 October 1992)
Report of the Secretary-General, Question of Antarctica, UN Doc A/47/542 (20 October 1992)
Report of the Secretary-General: Question of Antarctica: State of the Environment in Antarctica, UN Doc A/47/624 (11 November 1992)
Report of the First Committee, Question of Antarctica, UN Doc A/47/696 (4 December 1992)
Report of the Secretary-General, Question of Antarctica: State of the Environment in Antarctica, UN Doc A/48/449 (18 October 1993)
Report of the Secretary-General, Question of Antarctica, UN Doc A/48/482 (18 October 1993)
Report of the First Committee, Question of Antarctica, UN Doc A/48/681 (9 December 1993)
Report of the Secretary-General, Question of Antarctica, UN Doc A/49/370 (13 September 1994)
Report of the First Committee, Question of Antarctica, UN Doc A/49/704 (28 November 1994)
Report of the Secretary-General, Question of Antarctica: State of the Environment in Antarctica, UN Doc A/51/390 (20 September 1996)
Report of the First Committee, Question of Antarctica, UN Doc A/51/567 (29 November 1996)
Report of the Secretary-General, Question of Antarctica, UN Doc A/54/339 (10 September 1999)
Report of the First Committee, Question of Antarctica, UN Doc A/54/553 (12 November 1999)
Report of the Secretary-General, Question of Antarctica, UN Doc A/57/346 (26 August 2002)
Report of the First Committee, Question of Antarctica, UN Doc A/57/503 (7 November 2002)
Report of the Secretary-General, Question of Antarctica, UN Doc A/60/222 (11 August 2005)
Report of the First Committee, Question of Antarctica, UN Doc A/60/454 (16 November 2005)

Draft Agreement on Antarctica (United Nations Trusteeship) Prepared by the US Department of State, 9 June 1948 (US Department of State, *Foreign Relations of the United States*, 1948, vol. I, part 2, pp. 984-987)

WHEREAS explorers and scientists of the signatory states have explored, investigated and charted extensive regions in Antarctica;

WHEREAS vast areas have not yet been seen by man, and large portions of the coasts are inaccessible by ship at all times because of ice conditions in contiguous seas;

WHEREAS scientific data that may be obtained only in the Antarctic regions are urgently needed because of their planetary significance in many fields of knowledge, including meteorology, terrestrial magnetism, studies of cosmic rays, geology, and biology, some of the results of which may prove to be of great practical value in relation to navigation by sea and air, telecommunications, agriculture and other human activities in many parts of the world;

WHEREAS facilitation of comprehensive scientific exploration and observation is of prime importance in the Antarctic regions, requiring encouragement in the establishment of fixed stations for scientific observations wherever it is physically feasible and advisable to locate and support them, and likewise requiring unhindered mobility of parties penetrating very large interior regions of continental ice-cap by air and surface transport;

WHEREAS Article 75 of the Charter of the United Nations provides for the establishment of an international trusteeship system for the administration and supervision of such territories as may be placed thereunder by subsequent agreements;

WHEREAS under Article 77 of the Charter the trusteeship system may be applied to territories voluntarily placed under the system by states responsible for their administration;

WHEREAS Argentina, Australia, Chile, France, the Kingdom of Norway, New Zealand, the United Kingdom of Great Britain and Northern Ireland, and the United States of America are for the purposes of Article 77 of the Charter responsible for the administration of Antarctica;

WHEREAS the aforesaid states, being the states responsible for Antarctica, have agreed in accordance with Article 79 of the Charter upon terms of trusteeship for Antarctica and jointly submit those terms to the General Assembly of the United Nations for approval;

Now, THEREFORE, Argentina, Australia, Chile, France, the Kingdom of Norway, New Zealand, the United Kingdom of Great Britain and Northern Ireland, and the United States of America have entered this agreement and the General Assembly of the United Nations, having satisfied itself that the relevant articles of the Charter have been complied with, hereby resolves to approve the following terms of trusteeship for Antarctica.

ARTICLE I

The territorial scope of the trusteeship established by this agreement shall be the following: the Antarctic continent and all islands south of 60° south latitude except the South Shetland and South Orkney groups.

ARTICLE II

By the conclusion of the present agreement, the parties hereto merge and join their claims to, and interests in, specific portions of the area covered by this agreement and vest such individual claims and interests in the special regime hereby established, each agreeing not to seek a division of the territory in the area, but to join with the others for the purposes embodied in this agreement.

ARTICLE III

1. Argentina, Australia, Chile, France, the Kingdom of Norway, New Zealand, the United Kingdom of Great Britain and Northern Ireland, and the United States of America are designated jointly as the administering authority of the trust territory.

2. For the purposes of Article 86(1) *(a)* of the Charter, the member administering the trust territory shall be understood to be one of the aforesaid states which comprise the administering authority. Each of those states shall serve successively in the English alphabetical order, beginning on January 1, 1949, as a member of the Trusteeship Council administering the trust territory for a three-year period.

3. At the regular session of the General Assembly immediately preceding the date on which one of the aforesaid states, not then a member of the Trusteeship Council, begins its period of membership by virtue of this Article, another member shall be elected to the Council in fulfillment of the terms of Article 86 *(G)* of the Charter.

ARTICLE IV

1. The aforesaid states which comprise the administering authority shall create a Commission, composed of one representative of each of these states to exercise the powers and carry out the responsibilities of the present agreement.

2. The Commission shall meet at such place as it deems appropriate and at such times as it may deem necessary. It shall adopt its own rules of procedure. Decisions of the Commission on substantive matters shall be made by a two-thirds majority of the members present and voting.

3. The Commission shall appoint a Secretary and authorize the appointment by the Secretary of such staff as it shall deem necessary. The Commission shall prescribe the conditions of employment of the Secretary and staff.

4. The Secretary shall maintain offices at such place and perform such functions as the Commission shall direct.

5. The cost of administering the special regime, including the expenses of the Commission and Secretary, shall be borne in equal shares by the parties hereto.

ARTICLE V

The Commission shall cooperate with appropriate specialized agencies of the United Nations and with international scientific bodies on matters of mutual concern.

ARTICLE VI

1. The Commission shall, through a scientific board or other appropriate agency, draw up plans for exploration, investigation, and ·scientific and technical development which may be carried out jointly by some or all of the signatories of this agreement, and into which projects of individual member states may be fitted. The parties hereto also undertake, through the Commission, to prescribe appropriate procedures and conditions under which states, and privately supported expeditions, may be granted permission to conduct scientific investigations, develop resources and carry on other activities consistent with the purposes of this agreement.

2. The parties hereto agree, upon approval of any such plans by the Commission, to insure that undertakings in the area shall be consistent with these plans. They agree also to foster individually and jointly the establishment of facilities and the conduct of scientific investigations.

3. The parties hereto likewise agree to foster, under such rules as the Commission may prescribe, tree access to, and freedom of transit through or over the area. The Commission may prescribe that expeditions and stations within the area display an emblem representing the international commission as well as any national emblem or flag which they may display.

ARTICLE VII

The administering authority may take all necessary measures in the trust territory, within the terms of Article 84 of the Charter, for the maintenance of international peace and security.

ARTICLE VIII

The administering authority shall carry out in the trust territory the basic objectives of the trusteeship system as set forth in Article 76 of the Charter, so far as they may be applicable to the trust territory.

ARTICLE IX

1. States other than those aforementioned may adhere to the present agreement with full rights, thereunder upon approval by the original signatories and with the approval of the General Assembly of the United Nations.

2. Antarctic and sub-Antarctic islands not included in the area of the present agreement may be included subsequently upon the request of the owning country or upon agreed request by claimant countries and with the approval of two-thirds of the signatories.

ARTICLE X

The terms of the present agreement shall not be altered or amended without the consent of the aforementioned states which comprise the administering authority.

ARTICLE XI

This agreement shall enter into force as between the aforementioned countries when all of them shall have become parties thereto by due constitutional process and as between those countries and the United Nations upon approval by the General Assembly of the United Nations.

Draft Agreement on Antarctica (International Administration) Prepared by the US Department of State, 9 August 1948 (US Department of State, *Foreign Relations of the United States*, 1948, vol. I, part 2, pp. 997–1000)

WHEREAS explorers and scientists of the signatory states have occupied a leading position in the exploration and investigation of the Antarctic regions and have explored and charted extensive areas thereof;

WHEREAS vast areas have not yet been explored and charted, and large portions of the coasts are inaccessible by ship at all times because of ice conditions in contiguous seas;

WHEREAS scientific data that may be obtained only in the Antarctic regions are urgently needed because of their planetary significance in many fields of knowledge, including meteorology, terrestrial magnetism, studies of cosmic rays, geology, and biology, some of the results of which may prove to be of great practical value in relation to navigation by sea and air, telecommunications, agriculture and other human activities in many parts of the world;

WHEREAS facilitation of comprehensive scientific exploration and observation is of prime importance in the Antarctic regions, requiring encouragement in the establishment of fixed stations for scientific observations wherever it is physically feasible and advisable to locate and support them, and likewise requiring unhindered mobility of parties penetrating very large interior regions of the continental icecap by air and surface transport;

WHEREAS Argentina, Australia, Chile, France, New Zealand, the Kingdom of Norway, the United Kingdom of Great Britain and Northern Ireland and the United States of America claim portions of Antarctica; and

WHEREAS these states have consulted as to the best means of facilitating and expediting scientific operations in the Antarctic regions, and recognize that the historic pattern of establishing mutually exclusive territorial claims manifested in other parts of the world is practically inapplicable in the Antarctic regions and that it would tend to impede scientific work in which they are all interested,

Now, THEREFORE, these states have agreed to establish a special regime in the Antarctic regions under the following terms:

ARTICLE I

The territorial scope of the special regime established by this agreement shall be the following: the Antarctic continent and all islands south of 60 degrees south latitude, except the South Shetland and South Orkney Groups.

ARTICLE II

By the conclusion of the present agreement, the parties hereto merge and join their claims to, and interests in, specific portions of the area covered by this agreement and vest such individual claims and interests in the special regime hereby established, each agreeing not to seek a division of the territory in the area, but to join with the others for the purposes embodied in this agreement.

ARTICLE III

1. There is hereby created an Antarctic Commission which shall constitute the actual government of the territories under its charge with full executive and administrative powers. The Commission shall be comprised of one representative of each participating state.

2. The Commission shall meet at such place as it deems appropriate and at such times as it may deem necessary. It shall adopt its own rules of procedure. Decisions of the Commission on substantive matters shall be made by a two-thirds majority of the members present and voting.

3. The Commission shall appoint a Secretary and authorize the appointment by the Secretary of such staff as it shall deem necessary. The Commission shall prescribe the conditions of employment of the Secretary and staff.

4. The Secretary shall maintain offices at such place and perform such functions as the Commission shall direct.

5. The cost of administering the special regime, including the expenses of the Commission and Secretary, shall be borne in equal shares by the parties hereto.

ARTICLE IV

The Commission shall cooperate with appropriate organs and specialized agencies of the United Nations and with international scientific bodies on matters of mutual concern.

ARTICLE V

1. The Commission shall, through a scientific board or other appropriate agency, draw up plans for exploration, investigation, and scientific and technical development which may be carried out jointly by some or all of the signatories of this agreement, and into which projects of individual member states may be fitted. The Commission shall prescribe appropriate procedures and conditions under which states, and privately supported expeditions, may conduct scientific investigations, develop resources and carry on other activities consistent with the purposes of this agreement.

2. The parties hereto agree, upon approval of plans by the Commission, to insure that undertakings in the area shall be consistent with these plans. They agree also to foster individually and jointly the establishment of facilities and the conduct of scientific investigations.

3. The parties hereto likewise agree to foster, under such rules as the Commission may prescribe, free access to, and freedom of transit through or over the area. The Commission may prescribe that expeditions and stations within the area display an emblem representing the international commission as well as any national emblem or flag which they may display.

ARTICLE VI

The signatory states, as authorized by the Commission, may take all necessary measures in the territory for the maintenance of international peace and security.

ARTICLE VII

The terms of the present agreement shall not be altered or amended without the consent of the aforementioned states.

ARTICLE VIII

This agreement shall enter into force when all of the aforesaid states shall have become parties thereto by due constitutional process.

PART 10
JUDICIAL PROCEEDINGS

A. INTERNATIONAL CASES

Antarctica (United Kingdom v Argentina) (Application Instituting Proceedings against the Argentine Republic) (1956) ICJ Reports 8 (May 1955)

Part I: Application Instituting Proceedings and Pleadings

Section A: Applications Instituting Proceedings

1. Application Instituting Proceedings against the Argentine Republic

The Agent for the Government of the United Kingdom to the Registrar of the International Court of Justice at The Hague

Foreign Office,

London. S.W.1. (May, 1955)

Sir,

I have the honour to refer to Article 40 (1) of the Statute of the International Court of Justice and Article 32 (2) of the Rules of Court and, by direction of Her Majesty's Principal Secretary of State for Foreign Affairs, to submit an Application instituting proceedings in the name of the United Kingdom of Great Britain and Northern Ireland against the Republic of Argentina in the following case.[1]

2. Differences have existed between the Governments of the United Kingdom and of the Republic of Argentina for a number of years, concerning pretensions advanced by the Republic in 1925, and at various dates thereafter, to the sovereignty of certain Antarctic and sub-Antarctic territories which belong to the United Kingdom under prior, long-standing, and well-established legal titles, dating from, at latest, the period 1775–1843. The territories in dispute between the two countries form part of the Falkland Islands Dependencies, consisting of already existing British possessions, which (following on a long series of analogous enactments—see paragraph 13 below) were proclaimed as such and formally placed under the administration of the Government of the Colony of the Falkland Islands by Royal Letters Patent of July 21, 1908. These Letters Patent, the full text of which is set out in Annex 1 (No. 1) to the present Application, specified as the principal territories included within the Dependencies the territories known as South Georgia, the South Orkneys, the South Shetlands and the Sandwich Islands, and the territory known as Graham Land. There were also other territories, such as Coats Land. Further Letters Patent of March 28, 1917 (Annex 1, No. 2), were issued for the purpose of clarifying the extent of the Antarctic mainland together with its coastal archipelagos which were comprised within the designation "territory of Graham Land" used in the earlier Letters Patent. Under the supplemental Letters Patent of 1917, the Dependencies were finally defined to include—

"all islands and territories whatsoever between the 20th degree of West longitude and the 50th degree of West longitude which are situated south of the 50th parallel of South latitude; and all islands and territories whatsoever between the 50th degree West longitude and the 80th degree of West longitude which are situated south of the 58th parallel of South latitude".

The territories of the Dependencies, as so defined in the Letters Patent of 1908 and 1917, which had long been British possessions, have for many years been utilised and administered

[1] It results from the present Application that the United Kingdom Government accepts the jurisdiction of the Court in respect of the questions hereby submitted to it, and in particular that of the title to sovereignty over the islands and lands of the Falkland Islands Dependencies. The present Application does not constitute a submission to the jurisdiction of the Court in any other respect, or as regards the title to sovereignty over any territory outside the Dependencies.

by the Falkland Islands Government effectively, openly and, until modern times, without any objection from the Republic of Argentina, which facts are conclusively shown in paragraphs 6 to 25 below.[2]

3. Notwithstanding the United Kingdom's open assumption, and long-standing and peaceful exercise of sovereignty over the territories concerned, and the clear and precise delimitation of the Falkland Islands Dependencies in the above-mentioned Letters Patent, the Government of the Republic of Argentina formulated pretensions in 1925 to the South Orkneys, in 1927 to South Georgia as well as to the South Orkneys, and in or about 1937 to *all* the territories of the Falkland Islands Dependencies. Subsequently, the Republic of Argentina, in a notice of claim deposited on Deception Island (South Shetlands) in January, 1942, and in a Note addressed to the United Kingdom Government on February 15, 1943, defined her pretensions in the area south of latitude 60° South as covering all Antarctic lands and dependencies between longitudes 25° and 68° 34' West. This westerly limit was later extended by a decree of September 2, 1946, to longitude 74° West. Thus, the pretensions which Argentina has from time to time formulated to territories in the Falkland Islands Dependencies appear to cover South Georgia and the South Sandwich Islands as well as the islands and lands situated between 25° and 68° 34' West and south of latitude 60° South.

4. South of latitude 60° South, the western limit of Argentina's pretensions, as given in the above-mentioned decree of September 2, 1946, is longitude 74° West; whereas the western limit of the Falkland Islands Dependencies is 6° further to the west at longitude 80° West. The United Kingdom's present Application does not, therefore, relate to the areas of the Falkland Islands Dependencies between longitudes 74° and 80° West, which lie outside the declared limits of Argentina's pretensions. Similarly, the eastern limit of Argentina's pretensions, as stated in Argentina's above-mentioned notice of claim, and diplomatic Note of February 15, 1943, is longitude 25° West, whereas the eastern limit of the Falkland Islands Dependencies is 5° further to the East at longitude 20° West. The United Kingdom's present Application does not, therefore, relate to the areas of the Falkland Islands Dependencies between 25° and 20° West, which lie outside the declared limits of Argentina's pretensions. It follows that the United Kingdom's complaint in the present Application relates to the pretensions of Argentina to the sovereignty of the islands and lands of the Falkland Islands Dependencies which lie between longitudes 25° and 74° West and to the southwards of latitude 60° South. A map depicting the territories to which the United Kingdom's present Application relates is attached as Annex 2. As this map shows, the principal territories in dispute between the United Kingdom and Argentina in the present case are the South Sandwich Islands, South Georgia, the South Orkneys, South Shetlands, and Graham Land together with its coastal archipelagos. There is also Coats Land, to which (at Vahsel Bay) the Argentine Government has, during the last few weeks, sent an expedition.

5. The main facts relative to the United Kingdom's titles to the sovereignty of the Falkland Islands Dependencies and the territories comprised in it, and to the violation of her sovereignty by the Republic of Argentina, are set out in paragraphs 6–33 below[3]. The United Kingdom Government considers that the facts stated in the present Application suffice to establish conclusively both the United Kingdom's title to sovereignty, and the violation of that sovereignty

[2] It will be understood that although, for reason of convenience, the territories to which the present Application relates were constituted Dependencies of the Falkland Islands for administrative purposes, the British title to them is a separate and independent one, which in no way derives from or depends on the title to the Falkland Islands themselves.

[3] The description of the origin of the British titles and of their subsequent consolidation by occupation, user, administration and other means appropriate to the circumstances of the territories, as contained in paragraphs 6–25 and 30–31 hereof, are substantially identical with the corresponding passages in the Application which the United Kingdom Government is making concurrently with the present one, complaining of violations of its sovereignty over the same area, on the part of the Republic of Chile.

by the Republic of Argentina. The United Kingdom Government reserves the right, however, to amplify in its pleadings its exposition of the relevant facts, and to furnish further proof of both these matters.

Origins of the British Titles, Historic Discoveries and Acts of Annexation by British Nationals in the Period 1675–1843

6. The British title to the territories concerned goes back to a number of dates varying from, at latest, 1775 to 1843. The first discovery of any of the islands or lands of the Falkland Islands Dependencies may well have been that of *South Georgia* in 1675 by the British merchant Anthony de la Roche. This group of islands was rediscovered in 1775 by the great English navigator Captain James Cook, R.N. On January 17 of that year he landed at three places on the island, took possession of it formally in the name of King George III and called it South Georgia in honour of the King.

7. Captain Cook also discovered the *South Sandwich Islands* in 1775. Sailing eastwards from South Georgia, he sighted first a small group of islands which he called the Clerke Rocks after the name of his lieutenant, and then, on January 31, a larger group which he called the Sandwich Land after the First Lord of the British Admiralty of that date.

8. The *South Shetland Islands* were discovered by the English sea captain William Smith on February 18, 1819. Revisiting the islands in October of the same year, he landed, planted the British flag and formally took possession of the group in the name of King George III, calling it New South Britain—(this was afterwards changed to South Shetlands, named after the Shetlands Islands, north of Scotland). A few months later, Edwards Bransfield, R.N., accompanied by William Smith, proceeded again to the islands and made a survey of the whole group. On January 16, 1820, he landed on the largest island (King George Island) in the centre of the group and took possession formally in the name of King George IV. After a voyage south-westwards between the South Shetlands and Graham Land, to which further reference is made in paragraph 10 below, he returned to the South Shetland Islands. On February 4 he landed on the most easterly island of the group, taking possession formally in the King's name and calling the island Clarence Island in honour of the Duke of Clarence, the brother of the King.

9. The *South Orkney Islands* (named after another Scottish group) were discovered by the British sealing captain, George Powell, on December 6, 1821. On the following day he landed on the largest of the islands, took possession of it formally in the name of King George IV and called it Coronation Island in honour of the King's Coronation.

10. *Graham Land,* the northern extremity of the Antarctic continent, was first discovered on January 30, 1820, by E. Bransfield, R.N., in the course of the voyage of exploration south-westwards from the South Shetlands which was mentioned in paragraph 8 above. He sighted, in hazy weather, the outline of parts of the Antarctic mainland and one or two coastal islands. He named the land Trinity Land in compliment to the Board of Trinity House (the British institution responsible for pilotage and maritime lights), and he named two of the coastal islands, Hope Island and Tower Island, respectively. He also traced the outline of the Antarctic mainland and coastal islands, as he had seen them, on the chart which he drew of the South Shetlands and forwarded to the British Admiralty. Soon afterwards, further sightings of the Antarctic peninsula or its coastal islands were reported by British and American sealers, by the Russian navigator Admiral Bellinghausen, and by the French navigator, Captain D'Urville, but the first sighting was that of E. Bransfield, R.N. In 1829, Captain H. Foster, R.N., in H.M.S. *Chanticleer,* effected a landing on one of the coastal islands, Hoseason Island off West Graham Land, and deposited there a copper cylinder in which was a document taking possession in the name of King George IV. On February 21, 1832, the British sealing captain, John Biscoe, landed on an island of the Palmer Archipelago, believing it to be part of the mainland, and took possession formally in the name of King William IV, calling the territory Graham Land, by which name the peninsula is known to-day, in honour of Sir James Graham, then First Lord of the British Admiralty. On

January 6, 1843, Captain J. C. Ross, R.N., commanding H.M.S. *Erebus* and H.M.S. *Terror*, penetrated into a gulf on the eastern side of the peninsula and landed on a coastal island. He named the gulf Erebus and Terror Gulf, and the island James Ross Island, and took possession of the island together with its "contiguous lands" for the British Crown.

11. The first discoveries of South Georgia, the South Sandwich Islands, the South Orkneys, the South Shetlands, and Graham Land were thus all made by British nationals—a fact reflected in the names given to these territories by which they have been known, and have figured in maps and charts, ever since. The same applies to Coats Land, as to which see paragraph 14 below. Some discoveries of particular parts of these principal groups of territory were made by explorers or seamen of other nationalities; but the initial discoveries of all five principal groups were British. There were no Spanish or Argentine discoveries. Furthermore, during this early period in Antarctic history from 1678 to 1843, acts of annexation were performed in the name of the British Crown at places ashore within all the principal groups except the South Sandwich Islands, where, frequently, the local conditions render landing impossible. On the other hand, during this period no acts of annexation were performed in any of the territories concerned on behalf of any other State.

12. The facts stated in paragraphs 6 to 11 above show that from very early dates varying between 1775 and 1843, Great Britain possessed, on the basis of discovery, accompanied by a formal claim in the name of the British Crown, an original root of title to all the territories concerned.

Display of British Sovereignty in or in regard to the Falkland Islands Dependencies in the Period 1843 to July 21, 1908

13. In pursuance of a British Act of Parliament (6 Victoria, Chapter 13—British and Foreign State Papers, Volume 31, page 1211), Royal Letters Patent were issued on June 23, 1843, making provision for the government of the "Settlements in the Falkland Islands and their Dependencies" (Annex 1 hereto, No. 3). Supplemental Letters Patent were issued on April 28, 1876, making further provision for the government of the "Settlements in the Falkland Islands and their Dependencies". On February 25, 1892, fresh Letters Patent were issued by which the Government of the "Settlements in the Falkland Islands and their Dependencies" was designated as the Government of a Crown Colony (British and Foreign State Papers, Volume 84, page 262). Similarly, the Commission issued to the new Governor in November, 1847 (Annex 1 hereto, No. 4) and the ten succeeding Commissions to Governors issued between that date and 1908, were in the form of an appointment covering "the Falkland Islands and their Dependencies". Again, numerous laws passed by the Falkland Islands Government during the period 1843–July 21, 1908, were made for "the Falkland Islands and their Dependencies"[4]. The particular territories comprised in the "Dependencies of the Falkland Islands" were not named in the various Letters Patent, Governor's Commissions, or laws of the Falkland Islands Government. The Colonial Office Year Book, however, began in 1887 to specify South Georgia as one of the Dependencies. There had been comparatively little whaling and similar activity in the Antarctic in the middle of the nineteenth century, but from 1892 onwards whaling, sealing and scientific exploration began to revive. This renewed activity called for a corresponding exercise of State authority in the Antarctic and led very soon to special provision being made by Great Britain for the government of the five principal territories as Dependencies of the Falkland Islands and to their formal constitution as the Falkland Islands Dependencies.

14. The Antarctic revival in the area now in dispute began with the voyage of four Scottish vessels in 1892 to the eastern side of Graham Land and the Weddell Sea for whaling and sealing. In the same year a Norwegian whaling expedition which went to the Weddell Sea, called at the South Orkneys, and further Norwegian expeditions in 1893 and 1894 visited the South Shetlands and Graham Land. In 1897 and 1901 respectively, Belgian and Swedish scientific

[4] As regards the nature of the connexion between the Falklands Islands and the Dependencies, see footnote 2 to paragraph 2 above.

expeditions went to the South Shetlands-Graham Land area, and in 1902 they were followed by a Scottish scientific expedition under Dr. W. S. Bruce in the s.s. *Scotia.* Dr. Bruce established a meteorological station at Laurie Island in the South Orkneys in 1903, the working of which was entrusted to the Argentine meteorological office in the following year. He spent the Antarctic winter of 1903 at Laurie Island and in 1904, after revisiting Laurie Island to land the Argentine meteorologists, he penetrated deep into the Weddell Sea, discovering *Coats Land* (named after a Scottish supporter of the expedition) which is now the eastern frontier of the Falkland Islands Dependencies on the Antarctic continent.

15. In 1904 the Norwegian whaling expert, Captain Larsen, formed a company in Buenos Aires, the Compania Argentina de Pesca, for the purpose of whaling in the Antarctic and established a shore whaling station at South Georgia. In 1905, a Chilean company, the South Georgia Exploration Company, financed by British subjects in Chile, was granted a mining and grazing lease of South Georgia by the Governor of the Falkland Islands and proceeded there, only to find Captain Larsen's Compania Argentina de Pesca already in occupation of the best site for a base. Meanwhile, the Captain had applied through the British Legation in Buenos Aires to the British Government in London for a whaling licence for South Georgia. The British Government, learning that another licence had previously been granted by the Governor, despatched H.M.S. *Sappho* to South Georgia to investigate the situation on the spot. The result was that a whaling licence was granted by the Governor to the Argentine company, and the Chilean company then abandoned its project. In the same year, 1905, Norwegian whalers visited South Georgia and the South Shetlands, taking with them the first whale-factory ship employed in the Antarctic. In connexion with this enterprise, the Norwegian Government addressed an inquiry to the British Government concerning the sovereignty of territories in the area between longitude 35° and 80° West and latitudes 45° and 65° South, *i.e.,* in the area covering South Georgia, the South Shetlands, the South Orkneys and the northern part of Graham Land. The British Government replied that the South Shetlands were not international but were British possessions as were also South Georgia, the South Orkneys and Graham Land (the South Sandwich Islands lie outside the area of the Norwegian inquiry) and that Norwegian whalers should apply to the Governor of the Falkland Islands for any facilities that they might need.

16. In view of these developments, the Falkland Islands Government promulgated a whaling ordinance in 1906 (Ordinance No. 3 of 1906) by which the taking of whales without licence was made unlawful, and a royalty was made payable in respect of each whale caught under licence from that Government. It was further considered desirable, in view of the increasing importance of the five principal territories as whaling and sealing bases, to make specific provision for their government and to make more specific provision for their government as dependencies of the Falkland Islands. Accordingly, on July 21, 1908, as recited in paragraph 2 above, South Georgia, the South Orkneys, the South Shetlands, the Sandwich Islands and the territory of Graham Land were by Royal Letters Patent formally constituted Dependencies of the Colony of the Falkland Islands and placed under its government. Under these Letters Patent (Annex 1 hereto, No. 1) it was provided that:—

(a) the Governor of the Colony should be the Governor also of the Dependencies and be invested with the same powers of government and legislation in respect of them as he should from time to time possess in the Colony;

(b) the Executive Council of the Colony should act also as the Executive Council of the Dependencies;

(c) the Governor should have, and be deemed always to have had, power by and with the advice and consent of the Legislative Council of the Colony, to make laws for the peace, order and good government of the Dependencies;

(d) the Governor should have, and be deemed always to have had, power to make grants and dispositions of land within the Dependencies in the name of the Crown.

The definition of the lands comprised in the Falkland Islands Dependencies, as mentioned in paragraph 2 above, was afterwards amended by Letters Patent of March 28, 1917, so as to include explicitly all islands and territories situated between longitudes 20° and 50° West, and south of latitude 50° South; and all islands and territories situated between longitudes 50° and 80° West, and south of latitude 58° South. The lines of longitude and latitude laid down in these Letters Patent as defining the territories comprised within the Falkland Islands Dependencies are indicated in red on the map exhibited as Annex 2 of this Application[5].

Display of British Sovereignty in or in Regard to the Dependencies in the Period July 21, 1908–September 22, 1938

17. Great Britain's title to the islands and territories of the Dependencies was thus formally confirmed and defined by the issue of the Letters Patent of 1908 and 1917, but, as has been shown, it did not originate in or depend on these Letters Patent, and had been in existence for many decades previously. This title was now consolidated and maintained by a further effective display and exercise of British sovereignty. In pursuance of the authority contained in the Letters Patent of 1908, a Falkland Islands Ordinance was promulgated in that year under which the Governor in Council was empowered to declare any law passed for the Colony to be applicable also in the Dependencies so far as might be appropriate to their circumstances. Under this principal Ordinance numerous laws were either made or made applicable to the Dependencies by the Governor in Council, covering *inter alia* the administration of civil and criminal justice, marriage, testacy and intestacy, &c., and constituting a full and sufficient corpus of laws for those territories, having regard to their particular circumstances.

18. Especially important are the laws made by the Falkland Islands Government for whaling and sealing, which provide convincing proof of the effectiveness of Great Britain's display and exercise of sovereignty in the Dependencies. In 1908 the whaling Ordinance of 1906 referred to in paragraph 16 above was repealed, and replaced by a new Ordinance. This principal whaling Ordinance of 1908, as amended by later Ordinances, together with the Regulations made under it, established a detailed and comprehensive code of whaling law for the Dependencies, as can be seen from the summary of the whaling laws in force in the Dependencies in 1920 which is contained in the report of an official committee presented to the British Parliament in that year (Command Paper No. 657). The relevant extract from this report is annexed to this Application (Annex 1 hereto, No. 5). It shows that one of the chief objects of the legislation was the conservation of stocks by regulating the number and tonnage of whaling vessels, the number of whaling licences, the number of whales to be taken by each licence-holder, by protecting whale calves and by other measures. Analogous, if somewhat less elaborate, laws were introduced in 1909 for the regulation of sealing in the Dependencies. These laws made it unlawful to take seals in the Dependencies without a licence, gave authority for the issue of licences, and provided for the creation of a close season and of seal reserves.

19. The above-mentioned whaling and sealing laws were actively and extensively applied in the Dependencies. For whaling-licence purposes, as appears from the summary of laws given in Annex 1, No. 5, the Dependencies were divided into four units—South Georgia, the South Shetlands together with Graham Land, the South Orkneys and South Sandwich Islands.

(1) *In the case of South Georgia*, the Buenos Aires company mentioned in paragraph 15 above, the Compania Argentina de Pesca, was granted a lease of 500 acres of land at an annual rent of £250 for 21 years from January 1, 1906, and obtained an additional lease of land in 1909. Seven other companies, four Norwegian and three British, were granted whaling leases between 1908 and 1911 on terms similar to those given to the Argentine company. Applications for further leases in South Georgia were refused in order to conserve whale stocks. The whaling companies concerned, in addition to their leases, were required to take out whaling licences for South Georgia which were renewable annually. In 1910 the Argentine Company took out,

[5] Reference is again made to footnote 2 to paragraph 2.

in addition, a sealing licence, and after that year South Georgia was divided into four areas for sealing purposes, three being let out on licence each year and the fourth being left vacant as a seal reserve. An additional place was made into a seal reserve in 1918.

(2) *In the case of the South Shetlands and Graham Land*, a licence to take whales in their territorial waters was granted to a Chilean company in 1907, and a similar licence was granted in 1908 to a Newfoundland company. By the season of 1912–13, there were 12 factory ships and 32 catchers of various companies working in the South Shetlands area, all holding licences from the Falkland Islands Government. In 1912 a Norwegian company, the Hektor Whaling Company, was granted a 21 years' lease of a site on Deception Island for a whaling station but, in the absence of other suitable sites, the remaining companies operated with factory ships moored at Deception Island or, occasionally, at King George Island. From that date, whaling companies operated in the territorial waters of the South Shetlands and Graham Land under licence from the Falkland Islands Government every year without interruption, even during the first world war, until 1930, when developments in pelagic whaling led them to conduct their operations on the high seas. Activity in these two territories has been practically confined to whaling, although one sealing licence was issued in 1913 with respect to Graham Land.

(3) *In the case of the South Orkneys*, the first whaling licence was granted in 1908 to the Newfoundland Steam Whaling Company. Other companies applied for licences, and in the 1914–15 season four Norwegian companies were granted licences. Whaling ceased during the remainder of the first world war, but in 1920 a Norwegian company, the A/S Tönsberg Hvalfangeri, was granted a lease of 500 acres on Signy Island for a shore whaling station. A further whaling lease for the South Orkneys was granted in 1925 but by 1930 pelagic whaling had made it unnecessary for whalers to conduct their operations in territorial waters, and applications for licences ceased. One sealing licence was also issued for the South Orkneys in 1913.

(4) *In the case of the South Sandwich Islands*, where access to the land is extremely difficult, whaling activity has been less frequent. In 1912, six Norwegian companies took out licences from the Falkland Islands Government, and in 1927 the Tönsberg Company applied for and obtained a licence. In addition, a sealing licence was granted in 1910 for the South Sandwich Islands to the Argentine company, the Compania Argentina de Pesca.

20. British sovereignty has also been displayed and exercised in the Dependencies through magistrates commissioned by the Falkland Islands Government.

(i) As early as 1909, a resident magistrate was sent to *South Georgia*, and there has been a British administration in that group continuously since that date. Customs and police officers were added to the magistrate's staff, and in 1912 a post office was established at Grytviken. By 1925, the Government buildings included offices, a wireless station and a marine laboratory in addition to dwelling houses.

(ii) The *South Shetlands* and *Graham Land*, as mentioned in paragraph 18 above, have been treated as a single unit for the purpose of the whale fishery, a single licence being granted to cover both these territories. The whaling companies normally made their base first at Deception Island in the South Shetlands. If the season was favourable, they moved southwards through the Bransfield Strait and established a forward base in the Palmer Archipelago either in the Melchior Islands or at Port Lockroy. But Port Foster at Deception Island is the most convenient starting point for operations in the Bransfield Strait and off Graham Land, and it was accordingly made by law a "port of entry" for shipping visiting the area. A resident British magistrate was sent to Port Foster every summer season from 1910 to 1930, and this official exercised jurisdiction over all whaling vessels operating in the waters either of the South Shetlands or of Graham Land and its coastal islands. From 1912 to 1930 a post office was maintained by the magistrate at Port Foster.

(iii) At the *South Orkneys* whaling activity was somewhat less frequent than at South Georgia and the South Shetlands, with the result that the visits of British magistrates were correspondingly less regular. But in 1913 a Customs Officer spent two months in the islands supervising the observance of the whaling laws, while a special Whaling Officer spent about three months there both in 1914 and 1915. Next, the South Georgia magistrate went to Signy Island in 1921 to inspect the site which the Tönsberg Hvalfangeri Company proposed to lease, and in the following year a Whaling Officer spent three months at Signy to ensure that the terms of the lease and the whaling laws were carried out by the company. In the three seasons 1925–26, 1926–27 and 1927–28, a Whaling Officer again spent three months in the South Orkneys. In 1928 the Governor of the Falkland Islands himself visited Signy Island to inspect the area leased to the Tönsberg Hvalfangeri Company.

(iv) The comparatively slight whaling activity at the almost inaccessible *South Sandwich Islands* has called for very little exercise of administrative authority at the islands themselves[6].

21. The cessation of certain facilities and activities after 1930 came about as follows. The introduction between 1925 and 1930 of pelagic whaling with large whale factory ships, enabled the whaling companies to conduct their operations on the high seas without the use of bases ashore or in coastal waters. The result was that after 1930 the companies, in order to avoid payment of the licence fees imposed by the Falkland Islands Government, ceased to take out licences for operating from bases in the various Dependencies—(licences continued to be taken out by the companies with permanent bases in South Georgia). But, although in consequence there was some diminution in the administrative activity of the Falkland Islands Government with regard to the whaling vessels themselves, British State activity in the Dependencies continued in full force and without interruption in the period between 1930 and the outbreak of the second world war. During this period, the Dependencies were extensively visited and surveyed by the vessels of the *Discovery Committee,* an official body responsible to the Secretary of State for the Colonies. As early as 1917, proposals had been made for a thorough investigation into the economic resources of the Dependencies, and a Committee had been set up to report on the preservation of the whaling industry, the possibilities of developing other industries, and the needs of scientific research. Following the presentation of this Committee's report to the United Kingdom Parliament in 1920, a permanent Committee known as the *Discovery Committee* was established in 1923 under the direction of the Secretary of State for the Colonies. The principal function of this Committee, under its terms of reference, was to conduct research into the economic resources of the Antarctic and sub-Antarctic regions, with special reference to the Falkland Islands Dependencies. But its functions also included coastal surveys and general scientific research into the oceanography, weather and ice conditions and flora and fauna of the Antarctic and sub-Antarctic regions. Between 1925 and 1939 the Committee's research ships, *Discovery I* (one commission), *Discovery II* (five commissions) and *William Scoresby* (seven commissions) made very extensive investigations of the Dependencies. Numerous voyages among the principal territories of the Dependencies were made by these ships on each commission, and detailed surveys were made of their coasts and coastal waters. As a result, the Dependencies during this period were covered literally by a network of patrols undertaken by the Discovery Committee. The main focus of the Committee's research was on the natural history of whales, the most important economic resource of the Dependencies, and especially intensive observations were made on the whaling grounds of South Georgia, the South Shetlands and Graham Land. But the Committee also collected very extensive information on the hydrography and biology of the Dependencies, on the navigation and charting of their waters, and on Antarctic ice and ice-navigation. A large and important body of scientific material has been published by the Committee in the 27 volumes of *"Discovery Reports",* and its research on the natural history of whales is admitted by expert opinion to have made a vital contribution towards the effective solving of the international problem of the conservation of whale fisheries.

[6] Coats Land (see paragraphs 14 and 15 above) is also not discussed here in any further detail, only very recent Argentine action having brought this territory into question (see paragraph 4 above).

22. In addition, a large-scale expedition, the *British Graham Land Expedition*, visited the southern parts of the Falkland Islands Dependencies in 1934–37 to make land investigations. Reaching Deception Island late in 1934, the expedition proceeded to Port Lockroy in the Palmer Archipelago in January 1935. Shortly afterwards, a base was established and occupied further south, and from there various sledge and plane journeys were made which threw much fresh light on the geography of the area. In February, 1936, the expedition moved still further to the south to Marguerite Bay and established a base on the Debenham Islands. From there, important sledge journeys were made across Graham Land to the east coast and far southwards into King George VI Sound. Numerous reconnaissance flights were carried out, and the expedition ascertained conclusively for the first time that Graham Land is attached to the Antarctic mainland.

23. Other examples of the display of British sovereignty in or in regard to the Dependencies during the period July 21, 1908–September 22, 1938, are mentioned in the three next succeeding paragraphs of this Application dealing with the recognition of the British claims by Norway, Argentina and Chile. Still further examples could be cited. The facts given in paragraphs 16–22 above and in paragraph 24 below, however, are by themselves sufficient to establish conclusively a continuous and peaceful display of British sovereignty in and in regard to the territories of the Dependencies during the period July 21, 1908–September 22, 1938, which is that reviewed in the present section.

Recognition of the British Claims by Norway, Argentina and Chile after the Issue of the Letters Patent of July 21, 1908

24.

(1) The existence of British claims, not only to South Georgia but to other territories in Antarctic and sub-Antarctic regions was known in *Norway* before the formal constitution of the five principal territories as Dependencies of the Falkland Islands by the Letters Patent of 1908. The Norwegian Government, as stated in paragraph 15 above, addressed an enquiry to Great Britain in 1905 concerning the sovereignty of the territories situated between 35° and 80° West, and was informed in reply that South Georgia, the South Orkneys, the South Shetlands and Graham Land were British possessions. When Norway made a further enquiry in 1907, Great Britain reasserted her claim. Norway, neither then nor after the issue of the Letters Patent of 1908, made any protest or reservation against the assertion and exercise of British sovereignty over the Dependencies. At the same time numerous Norwegian whaling companies took out British licences and otherwise complied with the laws of the Falkland Islands Government. These facts establish by implication Norway's recognition of British sovereignty over the Dependencies in or about 1908. This implication is completely confirmed by the Norwegian Proclamation of January 14, 1939, in which the western boundary of Norway's own Antarctic claim was defined by a line coinciding with the eastern boundary of the Falkland Islands Dependencies. It was further expressly stated in the Proclamation that the area named the Falkland Islands Dependencies had been brought under Great Britain's dominion in 1908.

(2) The existence of British claims to at least some of the Dependencies was also well known in *Argentina* before the issue of the Letters Patent of 1908. It has been mentioned above (paragraph 15) that as early as 1906 an Argentine company, the Compania Argentina de Pesca, took out a British lease of land in South Georgia for 21 years. *Indeed, it was the then Director at Armaments at the Argentine Ministry of Marine who, in his capacity as technical adviser to the company, visited the British Legation in Buenos Aires to apply for the lease.* In the same year Great Britain, in order to remove any possible misconception as to the legal basis on which operation of the meteorological station on Laurie Island in the South Orkneys had been transferred to the Argentine Meteorological Office (see paragraph 14 above), addressed a note to the Argentine Government emphasising that the islands were a British possession. This reservation of the British sovereignty over the South Orkneys was repeated to Argentina in January, 1907. Shortly afterwards, when Chile proposed to Argentina the negotiation of a treaty

dividing between the two countries "the islands and the American Antarctic continents", the Argentine Foreign Minister, in rejecting the proposal, said expressly that "Chile ought to know that England claimed all these lands". In 1908, after the issue of the Letters Patent formally constituting the Falkland Islands Dependencies, the Argentine Foreign Minister asked to be informed of the terms of the British "declaration". Accordingly, the British Minister in Buenos Aires in a note of February 20, 1909, transmitted to the Argentine Foreign Minister a copy of the *Falkland Islands Gazette* containing the text of the Letters Patent. The Argentine Foreign Minister replied in a note of March 18, 1909:—

> "I have the pleasure of acknowledging the receipt of your Note dated the 20th of February last with which you were good enough to forward a publication called *Falkland Islands Gazette* containing a Decree by which the 'South Orkneys' are declared a dependency of the 'Falkland Islands'.
>
> While thanking you for this attention, I am happy to renew to you the assurances of my high consideration."

The British Minister, in communicating this reply to the British Foreign Office, commented that he concluded from its terms that "Argentine Government do not dispute the rights of Great Britain over the South Orkneys". *A fortiori* it is to be concluded from the terms of her reply that in 1909 Argentina did not dispute the British title to South Georgia, the South Sandwich Islands, the South Shetlands and Graham Land, which territories were also covered by the communication sent to the Argentine Government, but were not mentioned in the Argentine reply[7]. Three years later, negotiations were begun for the cession by Great Britain to Argentina, of the South Orkneys in return for a Legation site in Buenos Aires and on condition of respecting any existing British whaling rights. By 1914, the final text of a treaty of cession had been agreed between the two countries but, on a change of Government in Argentina, the new Government declined on financial grounds to complete the transaction. The terms of this draft treaty provide further evidence of Argentina's recognition of the British title of the South Orkneys at this time, *notwithstanding the presence of the Argentine meteorological station on Laurie Island.* Again, Argentina made no protests or reservations against the issue of the British Letters Patent of 1917. Nor did she make any protests or reservations against the promulgation of British Laws for the Dependencies, nor against the application of those laws to the Argentine company, the Compania Argentina de Pesca, and to other foreign companies. Nor did she make any protests or reservations against the exercise of authority by British magistrates in the several territories of the Falkland Islands Dependencies and, in particular, in the South Orkneys, South Shetlands and Graham Land. These facts establish beyond question that at this period Argentina recognised British sovereignty over the Dependencies.

(3) The existence of British claims at least to some of the Dependencies was equally known in *Chile,* even before the issue of the Letters Patent of 1908. Three years earlier, in 1905, a Chilean company, as stated in paragraph 15 above, applied for a British lease of land in South Georgia from the Falkland Islands Government. In 1907, another Chilean company, the Sociedad Ballenera de Magallanes of Punta Arenas, took out a British whaling licence of the South Shetlands and Graham Land. In the same year, when Chile invited Argentina to negotiate a division of "the islands and American Antarctic continents", she was expressly warned by Argentina that "England claimed all these lands". Neither then nor after the issue of the Letters Patent of 1908 or of 1917 did Chile make any protest or reservation against the assertion and exercise of British sovereignty over the Dependencies. She maintained a Consular Officer in the Falkland Islands, but at no time did she make any representations either to the Government of Great Britain or to the Falkland Islands Government in regard to the Letters Patent, or to the promulgation of British laws for the Dependencies, or to the application of those laws to the

[7] It seems clear in fact that Argentine interest at that date hardly extended beyond the South Orkneys, where the Argentine meteorological station was situated.

Chilean company, the Sociedad Ballenera de Magallanes, and to other foreign companies. Nor did she make any protests or reservations against the exercise of authority by British magistrates in the several territories of the Falkland Islands Dependencies and, in particular, in the South Shetlands and Graham Land. All these facts establish beyond question that at this period Chile recognised British sovereignty over the Dependencies.

25. The facts recited in the three immediately preceding subparagraphs show conclusively that, during the years at the beginning of the present century, when Great Britain was confirming and consolidating her ancient titles to the Dependencies, Norway, the State principally interested in Antarctic whaling, and Argentine and Chile, made no reservations in regard to Great Britain's display and exercise of State activity in those territories. They further show that these three States in fact recognised Great Britain's sovereignty over the Dependencies. Nor did any other State during this period make any reservations or enter any protests against the British claims.

Origin and Development of Argentina's Pretensions to the Islands and Lands of the Falkland Islands Dependencies and Attempted Usurpation of British Sovereignty over these Territories

26. Argentina, as related in paragraph 24 (2) above, was left in no doubt by Great Britain that the transfer to the Argentine Meteorological Office in 1903 of the meteorological station previously established on Laurie Island in the South Orkneys by a British expedition did not also involve the transfer to Argentina of the sovereignty either of the South Orkneys group or of Laurie Island itself. Argentina, as was also related in paragraph 24 (2), was fully aware in 1908 of the British claims to the several territories of the Falkland Islands Dependencies, and during the first part of the present century showed by her acts that she recognised Great Britain's sovereignty.

27. Notwithstanding this, the Argentine Government in 1925 embarked upon a course of action by which it has progressively, and it would seem deliberately, sought to encroach upon the Falkland Islands Dependencies, with a view to ousting the British Crown from its sovereignty, and to replacing it by a pretended Argentine sovereignty. In that year, on the erection by Argentina of a wireless station at the observatory on Laurie Island, a Note was addressed to the Argentine Government drawing its attention to the fact that under the relevant International Telegraph Conventions, the call sign would have to be applied for through the British Government. The Argentine Government replied that, with regard to wireless stations constructed on Argentine territory, it would act in accordance with the Conventions. In view of the equivocal nature of this reply, a further Note was addressed to the Argentine Government on April 14, 1926, emphasising Great Britain's undoubted rights to the sovereignty of the islands and pointing out the absence of any previous notice of claim on the part of Argentina. No answer was returned by Argentina and, on the wireless station being put into operation in 1927 without reference to the British Government, the latter learned from the International Telegraph Bureau at Berne that the call signal had been applied for by Argentina in terms implying an assumption of Argentine sovereignty over the South Orkneys. Great Britain having objected to this action in a Note of September 8, 1927, Argentina replied in a Note of January 20, 1928, that she herself laid claim to the South Orkneys on the ground, apart from pretended "inalienable rights", of an alleged first occupation constantly maintained. (This may be contrasted with the Argentine attitude about the South Orkneys in 1909, described in paragraph 24 (2) above—and as regards the pretended Argentine "first occupation", see paragraph 14 above.) At the same time, however, the Argentine Government in an accompanying memorandum showed itself conscious of the weakness of its position by suggesting the reopening of the negotiations for the exchange of the islands against the grant of a Legation site in Buenos Aires (see paragraph 24 (2) above). Meanwhile, the Argentine Government in 1927 had also represented to the International Postal Bureau at Berne that Argentine territorial jurisdiction extended *de jure* and *de facto* over both the South Orkneys *and South Georgia.* On this statement being contested by Great Britain in

an aide-mémoire of December 17, 1927, the Argentine Government replied that, as regards the South Orkneys, it formally reaffirmed its previous claim. Accordingly, Great Britain took steps in 1928 to notify the International Postal Bureau that both the South Orkneys and South Georgia were included in the Falkland Islands Dependencies and were represented in Postal Union matters by the British Postmaster-General.

28. On June 1, 1937, the Argentine Ambassador in London drew the attention of the Foreign Office to a statement by the British Minister of Agriculture and Fisheries at the inaugural session of the Whaling Conference, to the effect that the Dependencies were under the jurisdiction of the Falkland Islands Government, and he reserved the rights claimed by Argentina over them. The Ambassador's *démarche* was the first intimation of an Argentine claim not merely to South Georgia and the South Orkneys *but to all the territories of the Falkland Islands Dependencies.* The progressive and deliberate character of the Argentine invasion of British rights is thus evident. The British Foreign Secretary, while joining in an agreed statement that the character and purpose of the Whaling Conference had nothing to do with questions of jurisdiction, made an express declaration that the Argentine reservation could not in any way affect British rights to the Falkland Islands Dependencies. That Argentina had now enlarged her pretensions to include all the Dependencies was, however, confirmed by an express reservation to that effect on September 22, 1938, made by the Argentine President when promulgating Argentina's ratification of the various postal conventions concluded at Cairo on March 20, 1934, which the United Kingdom had signed on behalf of the Falkland Islands and their Dependencies.

Rejection of the Argentine Pretensions by the United Kingdom and Continued Display of British Sovereignty up to the Present Time

29. The methods (of which some account has just been given) by which Argentina sought between 1925 and 1938 to advance pretensions to the sovereignty of the Falkland Islands Dependencies were not those to be expected of a State already having sovereignty, and relying upon prior and well-established legal titles. They were rather those of a State seeking gradually to manoeuvre another State out of its possession and rights. Instead of actively displaying and exercising its authority in and in regard to the territories of the Dependencies in accordance with their circumstances, the Argentine Government merely attempted by diplomatic moves to throw doubt upon the existing British titles. Thus, in the first quarter of the present century, when the territorial waters of the Dependencies were the base of operations of several whaling companies of different nationalities, Argentina took no measures (as a prudent *sovereign* would have done, or sought to do) to regulate these activities, or to conserve the stocks of the principal economic resource of the territories concerned. Nor in 1927, although she was a Member of the League of Nations and had recently formulated pretensions to the South Orkneys and South Georgia, did Argentina take any part in the Whaling Conference convened at Geneva in that year under the auspices of the League, which, if she had had sovereignty over these territories, she might be expected to have done. Nor did she voice any objection to the fact that the United Kingdom took a leading part in that conference in its capacity as the State responsible for the regulation of whaling in the Falkland Islands Dependencies. It was only in 1937 that Argentina first participated in an international whaling conference and contested the United Kingdom's right to represent the whaling interests of the Dependencies. During the whole period up to 1938 Argentine interests in the Dependencies consisted in actual practice of a meteorological station in the South Orkneys, taken over (but not on a basis of sovereignty) by the permission and at the invitation of the British Government (see paragraphs 14 and 24 (2) above), and an Argentine whaling company operating in South Georgia continuously under leases and licences issued by the British Crown as sovereign of the Dependencies (see paragraphs 15 and 19 (1) above). On the other hand, Great Britain during this period, as related in paragraphs 13–25 above, displayed and exercised her authority in and in regard to the Dependencies according

to their circumstances. During all this period, up to 1938, Great Britain alone undertook the responsibilities of sovereignty and performed the functions of a State in and in regard to the several territories of the Dependencies. It is not, therefore, to be wondered at that, as indicated above, the British Government rejected all Argentina's pretensions to the territories of the Dependencies and continued to assert its own titles to them.

30. After the outbreak of the second world war, in 1939, the United Kingdom Government was occupied in the North and South Atlantic in dealing with attacks by Axis naval forces on Allied and Neutral sea-borne trade; and in March, 1941, dispatched H.M.S. *Queen of Bermuda* to the South Shetlands to destroy oil tanks and stocks of oil left on Deception Island by the Hektor Whaling Company, one of the companies holding a lease of land on that island from the British Crown. This measure, which was taken to deny the use of the oil tanks and fuel stocks to Axis raiders, constituted a most significant display and exercise of British sovereignty over the South Shetlands. In January, 1943, another British warship, H.M.S. *Carnarvon Castle,* was dispatched to the South Orkneys and South Shetlands, to examine the anchorages in those territories for any signs of use by enemy raiders, and to investigate Press reports of purported acts of sovereignty at Deception Island by the Argentine naval transport *Primero de Mayo.* H.M.S. *Carnarvon Castle* landed a party at Deception Island in the South Shetlands on January 8, and there obliterated from the walls of the Hektor Whaling Company's factory the national colours of Argentina, which appeared to have been painted on them recently by the *Primero de Mayo,* and also removed the Argentine notice of claim mentioned in paragraph 3 above. A writ was at the same time affixed to the building proclaiming that the company's lease had lapsed and that the building was the property of the British Government. The warship then proceeded to the South Orkneys, and on February 8 landed a party on Signy Island, which erected flagstaffs carrying the Union Jack. The following day the vessel called at the meteorological station on Laurie Island and exchanged courtesies with the Argentine staff. Meanwhile the Argentine Government was notified of the visit of H.M.S. *Carnarvon Castle* to Deception Island, and was informed that the United Kingdom Government had no intention of allowing the British title to the island to be usurped by Argentina. Soon afterwards the *Primero de Mayo* was reported to be departing again for the Falkland Islands Dependencies, and to have two Chilean naval officers on board. The Republic of Chile having also formulated pretensions to the South Shetlands and Graham Land, the British Ambassador in Santiago made representations to the Chilean Government in regard to these officers. He was informed that they were sailing in the Argentine ship merely as observers, and that the Chilean Government had itself protested against Argentine attempts to establish a claim to Deception Island[8].

31. The United Kingdom Government, in view of the apparent intention of Argentina and Chile to disregard British territorial rights in the South Orkneys, South Shetlands and Graham Land, dispatched H.M.S. *William Scoresby* and S.S. *Fitzroy* to those territories at the end of January, 1944. These ships visited the mainland and coastal islands of Graham Land, Deception Island in the South Shetlands, and Signy Island in the South Orkneys. A permanent shore base was established at Deception Island and another at Port Lockroy in the Palmer Archipelago off the west coast of Graham Land, meteorological stations being attached to both bases. Further visits were paid by H.M.S. *William Scoresby* to these two bases in March and, again, in April, 1944. Magistrates were sworn in for the South Orkneys, South Shetlands and Graham Land, and a special series of postage stamps was issued for the use of British establishments in those territories and in South Georgia. Since 1944 the United Kingdom has maintained a number of British bases in the Dependencies, the following being the bases (either constructed or re-established) in the territories on which Argentina has made encroachments—

[8] It will be observed that both these States had now started to lay claim to the same British territories (see separate Application respecting Chile)—a circumstance that can hardly fail to reflect adversely both on the motives and the validity of both sets of claims.

South Orkneys—
Sandefjord Bay, Coronation Island (1945).
Cape Geddes, Laurie Island (1946).
Signy Island (1947).
South Shetlands—
Port Foster, Deception Island (1944)[9].
Admiralty Bay, King George Island (1947).
Graham Land and its Archipelagos—
Port Lockroy, Palmer Archipelago (1944).
Hope Bay, Trinity Peninsula (1945).
Stonington Island, Marguerite Bay (1946).
Barry Island, Debenham Islands (1946)[10].
Argentine Islands (1947)[10].
Duse Bay, Trinity Peninsula (1953).

The United Kingdom Government has sent ships to the South Shetlands-Graham Land area every Antarctic summer since 1944; and all the above bases, with the exception of those in Laurie Island and in the Debenham Islands, have been occupied either continuously or intermittently by British parties. A special organisation, the *Falkland Islands Dependencies Survey*, was set up in 1945 to administer these bases, together with three others in the South Orkneys, and to supervise their work. Under its direction extensive surveys and explorations were carried out in the Dependencies, including ground surveys, over large stretches of the Graham Land peninsula, and meteorological stations were established. Sovereignty was also displayed in other ways as, for example, by the appointment of magistrates, the issue of postage stamps, and the lodging of protests both locally and through the diplomatic channel against encroachments by Chilean and Argentine parties. Thus, the United Kingdom Government has at all times taken all such steps as were open to it in the circumstances to assert and maintain its title.

Argentina's Persistence in Her Pretensions to the Falkland Islands Dependencies and in Her Physical Encroachments on the South Orkneys, South Shetlands and Graham Land[11]

32. In 1941 Argentina, which in the period 1925–38 had put forward mainly paper claims, embarked upon a definite policy of encroachment in the South Orkneys, South Shetlands and Graham Land. In that year the meteorological station on Laurie Island in the South Orkneys was manned by Argentine *naval* personnel, and the opening of a permanent post office in the South Orkneys was ennounced in Argentina and notified through the International Postal Union. The following year the naval transport *Primero de Mayo* was sent to Deception Island in the South Shetlands where, as has already been stated, it painted the Argentine colours on the walls of the Hektor Whaling Company's factory and deposited the notice claiming all lands and dependencies between 25° and 68° 34' West, which is mentioned in paragraph 3 above. The ship then proceeded to Lambda Island (Melchior Group) in the Palmer Archipelago and erected a flag and beacon there. A year later, the Argentine colours on Deception Island were obliterated by H.M.S. *Carnarvon Castle*, and the Argentine act of possession was removed (paragraph 30 above). On being so informed, the Argentine Foreign Minister replied that the Argentine Government considered its claims, "inherited from Spain[12]", to be justified. In a memorandum

[9] Headquarters of British Magistrates, 1910–30.

[10] Built and occupied by the British Graham Land Expedition, 1935–37.

[11] As has already been mentioned (paragraphs 3 and 26–28 above), Argentina has made a *paper* claim to *all* the territories in the Falkland Islands Dependencies. She has not, however, attempted to assert this claim in any overt way with reference to the South Sandwich Islands or South Georgia. These territories are not therefore further mentioned herein, except in the Conclusions.

[12] The territories concerned were barely discovered in Spain's day, and then not by Spain (see paragraphs 6–11 above). They were never part of any Spanish dominion.

of February 15, 1943, the Argentine Government reaffirmed its pretensions to all Antarctic lands and dependencies south of latitude 60° South and between longitudes 25° and 68° 34' West. It also purported to "protest" against jurisdictional acts carried out by British officials. The United Kingdom Government, in a memorandum of April 7, 1943, replied reasserting the British titles. Meanwhile, the *Primero de Mayo* was engaged on a second expedition to the Antarctic, during which it visited the Melchior Islands and Port Lockroy in the Palmer Archipelago, and Marguerite Bay further to the South. The ship then returned to Deception Island in the South Shetlands, and there repainted the Argentine colours on the walls of the Whale factory. It was after this expedition that the United Kingdom, despite its heavy commitments in the second world war, initiated in 1944 the programme of maintaining British bases in the South Orkneys, South Shetlands and Graham Land described in paragraph 31 above.

33. In 1947, some three years after the renewal of the British programme of bases, the Argentine Government began a course of systematic encroachment on the British territories of the South Shetlands and Graham Land. While continuing its meteorological station at Laurie Island in the South Orkneys, it proceeded to establish, as well as a few emergency huts, the following Argentine Posts[13]:

South Shetlands—

Port Foster, Deception Island (1947).
Half Moon Island, Livingstone Island (1952).
Potter Cove, King George Island (1953).
Harmony Cove, Nelson Island (1954).
Ardley Peninsula, King George Island (1954).

Graham Land and its Archipelagos—

Gamma Island, Palmer Archipelago (1947).
Paradise Harbour, Danco Coast (1951).
Barry Island, Debenham Islands (1951).
Hope Bay, Trinity Peninsula (1951).
Dundee Island (1952).
Brialmont Cove (1954).
Petermann Island (1955).

Coats Land—

In the neighbourhood of Vahsel Bay (1955).

These posts are all within the Falkland Islands Dependencies and in areas covered by British activity as already described. The recent or very recent establishment of these Argentine posts appears to foreshadow a rapid expansion of the present Argentine encroachments and violations of British sovereignty. Protests against these violations and encroachments have been lodged at various dates by the United Kingdom through the diplomatic channel, and locally by officials of the British Administration in the Falkland Islands Dependencies. The Argentine Government has nevertheless persisted in its policy of encroachment, maintaining the above-mentioned posts, and repeatedly manifesting its intention to continue to disregard the United Kingdom's prior and well-established legal titles.

34. In the opinion of the United Kingdom Government, these Argentine acts taken together, and related to the complete absence of any Argentine claim prior to 1925 or 1937, as the case may be (depending on the territory concerned), and to the previous complete Argentine indifference to, and even recognition of, the British claim, are evidence of a quite recent, deliberate, and considered policy of infiltration on the part of the Argentine Government, directed to creating a semblance or fiction of Argentine sovereignty, and to placing that Government in a position,

[13] The United Kingdom Government are still engaged in investigating the most recent Argentine encroachment at Vahsel Bay in Coats Land (see paragraphs 4, 14 and 15 above) where an Argentine post may have been established.

after a sufficient lapse of time, to argue that any previous British sovereignty was now replaced or overlaid by Argentine sovereignty. In effect, this is a policy of usurpation.

Limited Relevance in Point of Law of Events after 1925 in the Case of the South Orkneys and after 1937 in the Case of the South Shetlands and Graham Land

35. The acts of the Parties after 1925 in the case of the South Orkneys and after 1937, in the case of the South Shetlands and Graham Land, are of limited juridical relevance, for two reasons. First, the dispute crystallised when Argentine first asserted her claims, namely in or about 1926 in the case of the South Orkneys and in or about 1937 in the case of the other two territories; and according to well-established principles of law, it is at the date of crystallisation that the rights of the Parties are to be adjudged. The subsequent acts of the Argentine Government were clearly undertaken, not as a genuine manifestation of an existing title, but with a view to trying to create one, and in order to improve Argentina's legal position. They are not, therefore, to be taken into consideration *(Minquiers and Ecrehos* Case, I.C.J. Reports, 1953, page 59). Secondly, even if the United Kingdom had not previously acquired a good title, it undoubtedly displayed and exercised its sovereignty in and in regard to the South Orkneys, South Shetlands and Graham Land during (at the latest) a period running—in the case of the first-named territory—from July 21, 1908, to 1925 and after; and—in the case of the other two territories—from July 21, 1908, to 1937 and after. Therefore, quite independently of its earlier titles, the United Kingdom had already in these periods established as against Argentina, an unimpeachable title to the sovereignty of these three territories. Accordingly, Argentina's assertions of title to the South Orkneys in 1925 and thereafter, and to the South Shetlands and Graham Land in 1937 and thereafter, were, and always have been, illegal and invalid *(Eastern Greenland* Case (1953), Series A/B 53, page 64). Events subsequent to 1925 or 1937, as the case may be, are thus primarily relevant for the purpose of showing that, in face of the Argentine pretensions, the United Kingdom did not abandon, but actively maintained, its titles to the territories in question. This is conclusively demonstrated in paragraphs 26–31 above. The United Kingdom, by its continued display of State activity; by protests or counter-measures, which were always prompt, and evidence of the exercise of due vigilance; by attempts to settle the dispute through diplomatic negotiations; by actively seeking to bring the dispute to arbitration or judicial settlement (see paragraph 40 below); and by submitting the present Application to the Court, had energetically prosecuted its case, upheld its sovereignty, and maintained its rights and titles.

The Jurisprudence of International Tribunals Negatives the Argentine Claims and Supports the United Kingdom's Titles.

36. The jurisprudence of international tribunals both negatives the Argentine claims and supports the legal titles of the United Kingdom, more especially the awards and judgments in the following well-known cases:

- The Island of Palmas (1928), 2 Reports of International Arbitral Awards, 831;
- Clipperton Island (1931), 2 Reports of International Arbitral Awards, 1105;
- Legal Status of Eastern Greenland (1933), Series A/B 53;
- Minquiers and Ecrehos, I.C.J. Reports, 1953, p. 47.

37. These modern cases of high authority, negative completely any Argentine claim based on alleged historic grounds of title deriving from succession to supposed titles acquired by Spain. Apart from the fact that, on the evidence, no original Spanish titles can be established at all (see footnote 12 to paragraph 32 above), the *Island of Palmas* Case (page 846) and the *Clipperton Island* Case (page 1109) clearly show that any such early Spanish titles could not prevail to-day against long-continued British display and exercise of sovereignty. Again, even if it were possible to apply the doctrine of geographical contiguity to islands distant some 400 miles, or to a separate continent distant some 500 miles, from Argentine territory, the *Island of Palmas* Case (pages 854–855, 869 and 870) negatives completely any Argentine claim based on so-called geographical grounds of title, and clearly lays down that they could not prevail against actual

display and exercise of sovereignty. It has also been suggested on behalf of Argentina that she never recognised British sovereignty over the Dependencies. Ignoring for present purposes the question whether recognition by other States is necessary for the acquisition of title, and if so in what circumstances, it suffices here to recall the facts related in paragraph 24 (2) above, which establish Argentina's acquiescence in and recognition of the British claims to those territories. But in any event the *Eastern Greenland* Case (page 62) and the *Minquiers and Ecrehos* Case (page 66) clearly show that any failure by Argentina to recognise the British claims would not have altered the character and legal effects of the British Letters Patent, or of the other British legislative and administrative acts, as manifestations of British sovereignty.

38. At the same time, the above-mentioned leading cases show conclusively that all recognised juridical grounds strongly support the claims of the United Kingdom, and not those of Argentina. Thus the *Island of Palmas* Case (page 870) and the *Clipperton Island* Case (page 1110) indicate that the British takings of possession described in paragraphs 6–11 of the present Application created initial British titles superior to any of Argentina's pretended historical or geographical titles. The *Island of Palmas* Case (pages 838–840 and 867), *Eastern Greenland* Case (pages 52, 54 and 63) and *Minquiers and Ecrehos* Case (at page 65) conclusively show that to-day, in case of dispute, the primary test of sovereignty is the actual display and exercise of the functions of a State in and in regard to the disputed territories during the relevant periods. In the present case, it is evident from the facts set out in the present Application that it is the United Kingdom, not Argentina, that has displayed and exercised the function of a State in regard to the South Orkneys, South Shetlands and Graham Land, and especially during the decisive periods immediately preceding the critical dates, that is the period up to 1925 in the case of the South Orkneys, and up to 1937 in the case of the other two territories, as well as earlier.

39. The United Kingdom, in its pleadings, will refer with greater particularity to the numerous passages in the four above-mentioned leading cases and in other authorities which support its titles to sovereignty over the Falkland Islands Dependencies. Although the present Application is necessarily preliminary in character, the special circumstances appear to justify drawing attention to the jurisprudence of the four leading cases, as an indication of how solid are the legal bases of the British titles and how devoid of any foundation the Argentine pretensions.

Acceptance of the Court's Jurisdiction in the Case

40. The United Kingdom, having regard to the long period during which British sovereignty has been effectively exercised in and in regard to the territories of the Falkland Islands, would be justified in taking strong measures to put an end to Argentina's encroachments on the South Orkneys, South Shetlands and Graham Land[14]. Firmly believing in the pacific settlement of disputes among nations by judicial procedures and on the basis of law, it has preferred, when negotiations proved fruitless, to seek to have its dispute with the Republic of Argentina regarding these territories submitted to the International Court or other judicial or arbitral tribunal. Thus, in Notes of December 17, 1947, the United Kingdom Government invited Argentina, and Chile to whom a separate invitation was sent, to challenge the British titles to sovereignty by invoking the jurisdiction of the International Court of Justice, which the United Kingdom would then accept. Argentina, in a Note of January 28, 1948, replied to the effect that she was convinced of the unquestionable rights of herself and Chile over the disputed areas[15], and that it would be wrong for her to appear before the Court in the position of a State requesting what already belonged to her. The United Kingdom renewed its offer to go before the Court in Notes of April 30, 1951, and February 16, 1953, without, however, obtaining a favourable response from the Republic of Argentina. As the continuance of the dispute concerning the sovereignty of the

[14] Forcible action had in fact to be taken in one case (namely at Deception Island in February 1953), when a particularly flagrant attempt was made to erect an Argentine hut actually within the precincts of the existing (and occupied) British base on that island.

[15] This can only increase the dubious character of the Argentine pretensions, since the Argentine and Chilean claims conflict over the most important part of the ground. Both could not be valid even if either were.

territories of the Falkland Islands Dependencies necessarily threatens to impair the existing friendly relations between the two countries, the United Kingdom addressed a further Note to Argentina on December 21, 1954, inviting her, jointly with the United Kingdom, to refer the dispute to an independent *ad hoc* arbitral tribunal. On the same date, the United Kingdom addressed an identical Note to Chile. Neither of these countries[16], however, has thought fit to accept the United Kingdom's proposal, and the Argentine Government has in the meantime sent an expedition to Vahsel Bay in Coats Land—a factor so recent that the United Kingdom Government has not yet had time to investigate it.

41. The United Kingdom, in its Notes of December 21 last stated that, in the event of Argentina (or equally Chile) failing to accept its offer of arbitration, it reserved the right to take such steps as might be open to it to obtain an adjudication of its legal rights. One of the steps open to the United Kingdom is to bring the dispute before the Court by a unilateral Application under Article 40 (1) of the Statute and Article 32 (2) of the Rules, and, as indicated in paragraph 1 above, it is this procedure which the United Kingdom has elected to adopt.

42. The United Kingdom Government, therefore, declares that it hereby submits to the jurisdiction of the Court for the purposes of the case referred to the Court in the present Application—(for the precise scope of this submission, see footnote 1 to paragraph 1 above). The Argentine Government has not, so far as the United Kingdom Government is aware, yet filed any declaration accepting the Court's jurisdiction, either generally under Article 36 (2) of the Statute or specially in the present case. The Argentine Government, which has frequently expressed its adherence to the principle of judicial settlement of international disputes, is, however, legally qualified to submit to the jurisdiction of the Court in this case. Consequently, upon notification of the present Application to the Republic of Argentina by the Registrar in accordance with the Rules of Court, the Argentine Government, under the settled jurisprudence of the Court, can take the necessary steps to that end, and thereby cause the Court's jurisdiction in the case to be constituted in respect of both Parties.

43. The United Kingdom Government founds the jurisdiction of the Court on the foregoing considerations and on Article 36 (1) of the Court's Statute; and asks that a copy of the present Application be transmitted to the Government of Argentina in accordance with Article 33 of the Rules of the Court, and to all members of the United Nations and other States entitled to appear before the Court, under Article 34 of the said Rules.

44. The attitude of the Argentine Government in this case has compelled the United Kingdom to take the initiative in placing the matter before the Court, and therefore in effect to appear as applicant. The United Kingdom Government nevertheless wishes to make the fullest reservations on the question of the onus of proof of title. It considers that the manifest priority in time of the British possession of the territories, dating back to periods varying between 110 and 180 years ago, and the complete absence during virtually the whole of those periods, until a quite recent date, of any activities of a sovereign character, other than British, in the territories, is indicative of a self-evident British title, which it is for any country challenging that title to rebut.

The Contentions and Claims of the United Kingdom Government in the Case

45. The Government of the United Kingdom, in submitting this application to the Court, accordingly contends:—

(1) that by reason of historic British discoveries of certain territories in the Antarctic and sub-Antarctic; by reason of the long-continued and peaceful display of British sovereignty from the date of those discoveries onwards in, and in regard to, the territories concerned; by reason of the incorporation of these territories in the dominions of the British Crown; by virtue of their

[16] While the present Application is of course, formally, quite separate from the concurrent application in respect of Chile, the fact that there are also Chilean pretensions relating to the South Shetlands-Graham Land area, and of equally or even more recent date, has a significance that cannot be overlooked. It is a clear case of two rival and incompatible attempts to oust and usurp the legitimate sovereignty of the United Kingdom.

formal constitution in the Royal Letters Patent of 1908 and 1917 as the British Possession called the Falkland Islands Dependencies: the United Kingdom possesses, and at all material dates has possessed, the sovereignty over the territories of the Falkland Islands Dependencies, and in particular the South Sandwich Islands, South Georgia, the South Orkneys, South Shetlands, Graham Land and Coats Land;

(2) that the legal titles of the United Kingdom to the Falkland Islands Dependencies, and in particular to the South Sandwich Islands, South Georgia, the South Orkneys, South Shetlands, Graham Land and Coats Land, are, and at all material dates have been, superior to the claims of any other State, and in particular to those of the Republic of Argentina;

(3) that, in consequence, the pretensions of the Republic of Argentina to the South Sandwich Islands, South Georgia, the South Orkneys, South Shetlands, Graham Land and Coats Land, and her encroachments and pretended acts of sovereignty in those territories are, under international law, illegal and invalid.

46. The Government of the United Kingdom, therefore, asks the Court to declare—

(1) that the United Kingdom, as against the Republic of Argentina, possesses, and at all material dates has possessed, valid and subsisting legal titles to the sovereignty over all the territories comprised in the Falkland Islands Dependencies, and in particular South Sandwich Islands, South Georgia, the South Orkneys, South Shetlands, Graham Land and Coats Land;

(2) that the pretensions of the Republic of Argentina to the territories comprised in the Falkland Islands Dependencies, and in particular South Sandwich Islands, South Georgia, the South Orkneys, South Shetlands, Graham Land and Coats Land, and her encroachments and pretended acts of sovereignty in or relative to any of those territories are, under international law, illegal and invalid;

(3) that the Republic of Argentina is bound to respect the United Kingdom's sovereignty over the territories comprised in the Falkland Islands Dependencies, and in particular South Sandwich Islands, South Georgia, the South Orkneys, South Shetlands, Graham Land and Coats Land, to cease her pretensions to exercise sovereignty in or relative to those territories and, if called on by the United Kingdom, to withdraw from them all or any Argentine personnel and equipment.

I have the honour to be, Sir, Your obedient Servant, *(Signed)* G. G. FITZMAURICE, Agent for the Government of the United Kingdom.

Annex I

(1) Letters Patent of July 21, 1908. Extract from *British and Foreign State Papers, 1907–08,* Vol. 101 (London, 1912), pp. 76–77.

BRITISH LETTERS PATENT appointing the Governor of the Colony of the Falkland Islands to be Governor of South Georgia, the South Orkneys, the South Shetlands, the Sandwich Islands, and Graham's Land, and providing for the Government thereof as Dependencies of the Colony.—Westminster, July 21, 1908[17].

Edward the Seventh, by the Grace of God of the United Kingdom of Great Britain and Ireland and of the British Dominions beyond the Seas King, Defender of the Faith, Emperor of India: To all to whom these Presents shall come, Greeting.

Whereas the group of islands known as South Georgia, the South Orkneys, the South Shetlands, and the Sandwich Islands, and the territory known as Graham's Land, situated in the South Atlantic Ocean to the south of the 50th parallel of south latitude, and lying between the 20th and the 80th degrees of west longitude, are part of our Dominions, and it is expedient that provision should be made for their government as Dependencies of our Colony of the Falklands;

1. Now we do hereby declare that from and after the publication of these our Letters Patent in the Government *Gazette* of our Colony of the Falkland Islands the said group of islands known as South Georgia, the South Orkneys, the South Shetlands, and the Sandwich Islands, and the

[17] *Falkland Islands Gazette,* No. 9, vol. xviii, September 1, 1908.

said territory of Graham's Land shall become Dependencies of our said Colony of the Falkland Islands.

2. And we do hereby further declare that from and after such publication as aforesaid the Governor and Commander-in-Chief of our Colony of the Falkland Islands for the time being (hereinafter called the Governor) shall be the Governor of South Georgia, the South Orkneys, the South Shetlands, and the Sandwich Islands, and the territory of Graham's Land (all of which are hereinafter called the Dependencies); and we do hereby vest in him all such powers of government and legislation in and over the Dependencies as are from time to time vested in our said Governor in and over our Colony of the Falkland Islands, subject, nevertheless, to any instructions which may from time to time be hereafter given him under our Sign Manual and Signet, or through one of our Principal Secretaries of State, and to such laws as are now or shall hereafter be in force in the said Dependencies.

3. In the event of the death or incapacity of the Governor, or in the event of his absence from our Colony of the Falkland Islands otherwise than for the purpose of visiting the Dependencies, the officer for the time being administering the government of our said Colony shall be Governor for the time being of the Dependencies.

4. There shall be an Executive Council for the Dependencies, and the said Council shall consist of such persons as shall from time to time constitute the Executive Council of our Colony of the Falkland Islands; and the said Council shall exercise the same functions in regard to all matters arising in connection with the Dependencies as are exercised by the Executive Council of our Colony of the Falkland Islands in regard to matters arising in connection with our said Colony.

5. It shall be, and shall be deemed always to have been, competent for the Governor, by and with the advice and consent of the Legislative Council of our Colony of the Falkland Islands, to make laws for the peace, order, and good government of the Dependencies.

6. The Governor is, and shall be deemed always to have been, authorised and empowered to make and execute, in our name and on our behalf, grants and dispositions of any lands which may lawfully be granted or disposed of by us within the Dependencies, either in conformity with instructions under our Sign Manual and Signet, or through one of our Principal Secretaries of State, or in conformity with such laws as may from time to time be in force in the Dependencies.

7. We do hereby reserve to us, our heirs and successors, full power and authority from time to time to revoke, alter, or amend these our Letters Patent as to us or them shall seem meet.

8. The Governor shall cause these our Letters Patent to be published in the Government *Gazette* of our Colony of the Falkland Islands, and the same shall thereupon come into force.

In witness whereof we have caused these our Letters to be made Patent. Witness ourself at Westminster, this 21st day of July, in the eighth year of our reign.

By warrant under the King's Sign Manual.

MUIR MACKENZIE.

(2) Letters Patent of March 28, 1917. Extract from *Falkland Islands Gazette,* July 2nd 1917; published in *British and Foreign State Papers,* 1917–18. Vol. III (London, 1921), pp. 16–17.

Falkland Islands (Dependencies)

Letters Patent, passed under the Great Seal of the United Kingdom, providing for the further Definition and Administration of certain Islands and Territories as Dependencies of the Colony of the Falkland Islands.

Dated March 28, 1917. George the Fifth by the Grace of God of the United Kingdom of Great Britain and Ireland and of the British Dominions beyond the Seas King, Defender of the Faith, Emperor of India: To all to whom these Presents shall come, Greeting.

Whereas doubts have arisen as to the limits of the groups of islands known as South Georgia, the South Orkneys, the South Shetlands, and the Sandwich Islands, and the territory of Graham Land otherwise known as Graham's Land; and whereas it is expedient that provision should be made for the government, not only of these islands and territory but also of certain other Our islands and territories adjacent thereto as Dependencies of Our Colony of the Falkland Islands:

I. Now We do hereby declare that from and after the publication of these Our Letters Patent in the Government Gazette of Our Colony of the Falkland Islands, the Dependencies of Our said Colony shall be deemed to include and to have included all islands and territories whatsoever between the 20th degree of West longitude and the 50th degree of West longitude which are situated south of the 50th parallel of South latitude; and all islands and territories whatsoever between the 50th degree of West longitude and the 80th degree of West longitude which are situated south of the 58th parallel of South latitude.

II. And We do hereby vest in the Governor and Commander-in-Chief of Our Colony of the Falkland Islands all such powers and authorities in and over the lands hereby included in the Dependencies of Our said Colony as are exercised by him over the Dependencies in virtue of certain Letters Patent bearing date at Westminster the Twenty-first day of July 1908.

III. We do hereby reserve to Ourselves, Our heirs and successors, full power and authority from time to time to revoke, alter or amend these Our Letters Patent as to Us or them shall seem meet.

IV. The Governor shall cause these Our Letters Patent to be published in the Government Gazette of Our Colony of the Falkland Islands and the same shall thereupon come into force.

In witness whereof We have caused these Our Letters to be made Patent. Witness Ourself at Westminster the Twenty-eighth day of March in the Seventh Year of Our Reign.

By Warrant under the King's Sign Manual.

(Signed) SCHUSTER.

(3) Letters Patent (Charter) of June 23, 1843. (Patent Roll 7 Vict. Part I, C.66/4690.)

Falkland Islands

Charter for the Government of the Falkland Islands

Victoria, by the Grace of God of the United Kingdom of Great Britain and Ireland, Queen, Defender of the Faith, to all whom these presents shall come, Greeting:

Whereas by an act of Parliament made and passed in the sixth year of our Reign, intituled "An Act to enable Her Majesty to provide for the Government of Her Settlements on the Coast of Africa, and in the Falkland Islands", after reciting that divers of Our subjects have resorted to and taken up their abode, and may hereafter resort to and take up their abode, at divers places on the Falkland Islands, and that it is necessary that We should be enabled to make further and better provision for the Civil Government of the said Settlement; it is enacted that it shall be lawful for Us, by any Order or Orders to be by Us made with the advice of Our Privy Council, to establish all such Laws, Institutions, and Ordinances, and to constitute such Courts and Officers, and to make such provisions and regulations for the proceedings in such Courts and for the Administration of Justice as may be necessary for the peace, order, and good government of Our subjects and others within the said present or future settlements respectively, or any of them, any law, statute, or usage to the contrary, in any wise notwithstanding:

And whereas by the said recited Act of Parliament it is further enacted that it shall be lawful for Us, by any Commission or Commissions under the Great Seal of the United Kingdom, or by any Instructions under Our Signet and Sign Manual accompanying and referred to in any such Commission or Commissions, to delegate to any three or more persons within any of the Settlements aforesaid respectively, the powers and authorities so vested in Us in Our Privy Council as aforesaid, either in whole or in part, and upon, under, and subject to all such conditions, provisoes, and limitations as by any such Commission, or Commissions or Instructions, as aforesaid, We shall see fit to prescribe: Provided always, that notwithstanding any such delegation of authority as aforesaid, it shall still be competent to Us in Our Privy Council, in manner aforesaid, to exercise all the powers and authorities so vested as aforesaid in Us in Our Privy Council:

Now therefore, in pursuance and exercise of the powers so vested in Us as aforesaid by the said recited Act of Parliament, We, of Our special Grace, certain knowledge and mere motion, by this Commission under the Great Seal of the United Kingdom aforesaid, delegate to the persons hereinafter named within the said Falkland Islands, the powers and authorities so vested in Us in Our Privy Council as aforesaid; but upon, under and subject to all such conditions, provisoes, and limitations as by this Our Commission, or by the Instructions under our Signet and Sign Manual accompanying the same, are prescribed. And We do declare Our Pleasure to be, and do hereby declare and grant, that the Governor for the time being of the said Falkland Islands, and such other persons, not being less than two, as are hereinafter designated, shall constitute and be a Legislative Council for the said Islands. And We do hereby direct and appoint that the persons other than the said Governor constituting the said Legislative Council shall be such Public Officers within the said Islands as shall be designated, or such other persons within the same as shall from time be named for that purpose by Us by any Instruction or Instructions, or Warrant or Warrants, to be by Us for that purpose issued under Our Signet and Sign Manual, and with the advice of Our Privy Council, all of which Councillors shall hold their places in the said Council at our pleasure.

And We do hereby authorise, empower, and enjoin such Legislative Council to make and establish all such Laws, Institutions, and Ordinances as may from time to time be necessary for the peace, order, and good government of Our subjects and others within the said present or future Settlements in the said Falkland Islands and in their Dependencies; and Our pleasure is that in the making and establishing all such Laws, Institutions, and Ordinances, the said Legislative Council shall conform to and observe all such rules and regulations as shall be given and prescribed in and by such Instructions as We, with the advice of Our Privy Council, shall from time to time make for their guidance therein: Provided nevertheless, and We do hereby reserve to Ourselves, Our Heirs and Successors, Our and Their right and authority to disallow any such Ordinances in the whole or in part; and to make and establish from time to time, with the advice and consent of Parliament, or with the advice of Our or Their Privy Council, all such Laws as may to Us or them appear necessary for the order, peace, and good government of Our said Settlements and their Dependencies as fully as if these Presents had not been made.

And whereas it is expedient that an Executive Council should be appointed to advise and assist the Governor of Our said Settlements in the Falkland Islands and in their Dependencies, for the time being, in the administration of the Government thereof, We do therefore, by these Our Letters Patent, authorise the Governor of Our said Settlements for the time being, to summon as an Executive Council such persons as may, from time to time, be named or designated by Us in any Instructions under Our Signet and Sign Manual addressed to him in that behalf.

And We do hereby authorise and empower the Governor of Our said Settlements in the Falkland Islands and in their Dependencies, for the time being, to keep and use the Public Seal appointed for the sealing of all things whatsoever that shall pass the Seal of Our said Settlements.

And We do hereby give and grant to the Governor of Our said Settlements in the Falkland Islands and in their Dependencies, for the time being, full power and authority, with the advice and consent of Our said Executive Council, to issue a Proclamation, or Proclamations dividing Our said Settlements into districts, counties, hundreds, towns, townships, and parishes, and to appoint the limits thereof respectively.

And We do hereby give and grant to the Governor of Our said Settlements in the Falkland Islands and in their Dependencies, for the time being, full power and authority, in Our name and on Our behalf, but subject nevertheless to such provisions as may be in that respect contained in any Instructions which may from time to time be addressed to him by Us for that purpose, to make and execute in Our name and on Our behalf, under the Public Seal of Our said Settlements, grants of waste land to Us belonging within the same, to private persons for their own use and benefit, or to any persons, bodies politic or corporate, in trust for the public uses of Our subjects there resident, or any of them.

And We do hereby authorise and empower the Governor of Our said Settlements in the Falkland Islands and in their Dependencies, for the time being, to constitute and appoint Judges, and, in cases requisite, Commissioners of Oyer and Terminer, Justices of the Peace, and other necessary Officers and Ministers in Our said Settlements, for the due and impartial administration of justice, and for putting the laws into execution, and to administer or cause to be administered unto them such oath or oaths as are usually given for the due execution and performance of offices and places, and for the clearing of truth in judicial matters:

And We do hereby give and grant unto the Governor of Our said Settlements in the Falkland Islands and in their Dependencies, for the time being, full power and authority, as he shall see occasion, in Our name and on Our behalf, to remit any fines, penalties, or forfeitures which may accrue or become payable to Us, provided the same do not exceed the sum of fifty pounds sterling in any one case, and to respite and suspend the payment of any such fine, penalty, or forfeiture, exceeding the said sum of fifty pounds, until Our pleasure thereon shall be made known and signified to such Governor.

And We do hereby give and grant unto the Governor of the said Settlements in the Falkland Islands and in their Dependencies, for the time being, full power and authority, as he shall see occasion, in Our name and on Our behalf, to grant to any offender convicted of any crime, in any Court, or before any Judge, Justice, or Magistrate within Our said Settlements, a free and unconditional pardon, or a pardon subject to such conditions as by any Law or Ordinance hereafter to be in force in Our said Settlements may be thereunto annexed, or any respite of the execution of the sentence of any such offender for such period as to such Governor may seem fit.

And We do hereby give and grant unto the Governor of Our said Settlements, for the time being, full power and authority, upon sufficient cause to him appearing, to suspend from the exercise of his office within Our said Settlements any person exercising any office or place under or by virtue of any Commission or Warrant granted, or which may be granted, by Us, or in Our name, or under Our authority; which suspension shall continue and have effect only until Our pleasure therein shall be made known and signified to such Governor. And We do hereby strictly require and enjoin the Governor of Our said Settlements, for the time being, in proceeding to any such suspension, to observe the directions in that behalf given to him by Our Instructions under Our Signet and Sign Manual, accompanying his Commission of appointment as Governor of the said Settlements.

And in the event of the death or absence out of Our said Settlements in the Falkland Islands and in their Dependencies, of such person as may be commissioned and appointed by Us to be the Governor thereof, We do hereby provide and declare Our pleasure to be, that all and every the powers and authorities herein granted to the Governor of Our said Settlements in the Falkland Islands and in their Dependencies for the time being, shall be and the same are hereby vested in such person as may be appointed by Us by Warrant under Our Signet and Sign Manual to be the Lieutenant-Governor of Our said Settlements; or in the event of there being no person within Our said Settlements commissioned

and appointed by Us to be Lieutenant-Governor thereof, then Our pleasure is and We do hereby provide and declare, that in such contingency all the powers and authorities herein granted to the Governor or Lieutenant-Governor of Our said Settlements, shall be and the same are hereby granted to the Justice of the Peace whose name shall be standing first in order in any general Commission of the Peace, issued by the Governor or Officer administering the Government of Our Settlements in the Falkland Islands and of their Dependencies, such Commission of the Peace being revocable and renewable from time to time by such Governor or Administrator of the Government, as he may find occasion; and such Lieutenant-Governor or such Justice of the Peace, as may be, shall execute all and every the powers and authorities herein granted until Our further pleasure shall be signified therein.

And We do hereby require and command all Our Officers and Ministers, civil and military, and all other the inhabitants of Our said Settlements in the Falkland Islands and their Dependencies, to be obedient, aiding and assisting to such person as may be commissioned and appointed by Us to be the Governor of Our said Settlements, or in the event of his death Of absence to such person as may, under the provisions of these Our Letters Patent, assume and exercise the functions of such Governor.

And We do hereby reserve to Us, Our Heirs and Successors, full power and authority, from time to time, to revoke, alter, or amend these Our Letters Patent, as to Us or Them shall seem meet.

In Witness, &c.

(4) Commission issued to the Governor of the Falkland Islands in November, 1847. Extract from *London Gazette*, No. 2080l, November 30, 1847, p. 4435.

Downing Street,
November 27, 1847.

… Her Majesty has further been pleased to appoint George Rennie, Esq., to be Governor and Commander in Chief in and over Her Majesty's settlements in the Falkland Islands and their dependencies.

(5) Summary of the Whaling Laws in Force in the Falkland Islands Dependencies in 1920. Annexure III to Appendix V of the Report of the Interdepartmental Committee on Research and Development in the Dependencies of the Falkland Islands. (Cmd. 657, April 1920, pp. 59–60.)

(A) Laws

Ordinance No. 5 of 1908 (as amended by subsequent Ordinances No. 5 of 1912, No. 5 of 1915, and No. 9 of 1915) forbids the killing, taking, or hunting of whales in Colonial waters without a licence. Subject to any regulations made by the Governor in Council the Governor is empowered to settle in regard to each licence:—

(a) The period;
(b) The number and tonnage of vessels to be employed in the taking of whales;
(c) The limits of Colonial waters within which whales may be taken;
(d) In which of the Dependencies the licensee may use the harbours by virtue of his licence.

The Colonial Secretary, or such other officer as the Government may appoint, is empowered to grant whaling licences and licences to utilise whale carcasses by means of a floating factory. The fees payable are:

(1) For a whaling licence, £100;
(2) For a floating factory: not less than £100, and not more than £200, as the Governor in Council may approve.

The penalty for taking whales without a licence is £300 for each offence in the case of the master or owner, and £100 in the case of other offenders. The penalty payable by an owner or master may be recovered by the arrest and sale of the vessel.

The Ordinance also makes it an offence, subject to a penalty of £100,

(a) to have unlawful possession of whale oil or whalebone;
(b) to employ, without authority, any vessel for manufacturing, towing, or buoying whale carcasses within Colonial waters;
(c) to employ any licensed vessel to tow, buoy, or manufacture in Colonial waters whale carcasses taken outside Colonial waters by any unauthorised vessel.

The Governor in Council may make regulations for:—

(a) Fixing the conditions of licences;
(b) Regulating the number of licences to be granted in any one year;
(c) Defining the limits within which a licence-holder may take whales;
(d) Regulating the number of whales to be taken;
(e) Regulating the disposal for forfeited whales, oil, &c.; and
(f) Generally for carrying out the provisions of the Ordinance.

The owner or lessee of any land may take possession of a derelict whale with permission of the Governor in Council and on payment of a royalty. Provision is made for taking whales for scientific purposes.

During the War Ordinances were passed requiring the products of the whaling industry to be brought to, and sold in, the United Kingdom.

(B) Regulations

(a) *South Georgia*.—The regulations

(1) Prohibit leaseholders from killing or shooting any whale calf or any female whale which is accompanied by a calf;

(2) Reserve to the Crown any dead whale abandoned or thrown up on the seashore;

(3) Prescribe penalties for breaches of the regulations.

(b) *Other Dependencies*.—The regulations

(1) Provide for the issue of annual licences (October to September);

(2) Prohibit licensed vessels from catching whales for a Company other than that mentioned in the licence;

(3) Authorise the use of *(a)* two floating factories, in conjunction with two whale catchers—fee £200; and *(b)* a third whale catcher—fee £100;

(4) Require the provision of pressure boilers for dealing with the residue of the carcass;

(5) Prescribe that separate licences shall be issued for:—

(a) The South Shetlands and Graham Land;

(b) The South Orkneys;

(c) The Falkland Islands;

(d) The South Sandwich Islands;

but that no further licence or lease for whaling purposes shall be issued, with the exception of renewals of existing annual licences for two floating factories and two whale catchers, or of a third whale catcher, without the permission of the Governor in Council;

(6) Require every licensed vessel at the end of the season to proceed direct to a port of entry and to report full particulars of the catch, including the number of barrels of oil and the quantity of baleen and guano obtained;

(7) Prohibit licensees from killing or shooting any whale calf or any female whale which is accompanied by a calf;

(8) Reserve to the Crown any dead whale abandoned or thrown up on the seashore;

(9) Prescribe penalties for breach of the regulations.

(c) In consequence of the War and the necessity for obtaining a maximum output of oil, the Governor was empowered by regulations made on September 13, 1916, to authorise, during the continuance of the War, the departure from any or all of the provisions of the abovementioned regulations as to him may seem fit and expedient.

(C) Leases and Licences

(a) *Form of Lease*.—Some particulars of the whaling leases already granted in South Georgia will be found in Annexure I. In addition, the lessees are prohibited from taking, removing, appropriating, killing, or in any way using for their own benefit or for the benefit of any other person or persons, any product or animal whatsoever on the island of South Georgia or any island adjacent thereto. The right to win and take mineral oil is reserved to the Crown. The lease also specifies the number of vessels which may be employed, and, in the case of the later leases, requires the utilisation, without waste, of the whole carcass of all whales taken. The lessees are required *(a)* to keep an accurate record of meteorological observations and to furnish full particulars of such observations to the Governor of the Falkland Islands; *(b)* to keep in stock a reasonable quantity of coal and provisions to be supplied at cost price to any ship requiring coal or provisions; *(c)* to establish and maintain and exhibit two leading beacon lights as guides to shipping; *(d)* to give certain facilities of access to the shore on which the site leased is situate; and *(e)* to furnish to the Governor of the Falkland Islands an annual report respecting their operations.

(b) *Form of Licence.*—The licences issued under the Ordinance provide for the payment of the fee either at the Colonial Treasury or to the Crown Agents. It specifies the names of the vessels to be employed in taking whales; the limits within which they may be taken (*i.e.*, in the territorial waters of a specified Dependency) and the harbours to be used; and it requires the licensee to render an accurate account of the number and description of the whales taken and the quantity of oil, bone, and guano obtained.

Annex II

Map of the Falkland Islands Dependencies [omitted]

Argentine Letter to the International Court of Justice Embodying a Note Declining to Accept the Jurisdiction of the Court in Respect of the British Application (1 August 1955)

Argentine Ambassador, The Hague (N. Carvajal Palacios) to the Registrar of the International Court of Justice (Julio López Oliván)

Translation:

Embassy of the Republic of Argentina

V. No. 93

The Hague, 1 August 1955

Sir,

With reference to your communication No. 22078 bis of May 6th last, relating to the claim presented by the United Kingdom Government concerning its pretensions to certain Antarctic territories, I have the honour to inform you that I have been authorised by the Argentine Government to furnish as a reply to the said claim the following Note which I set out hereunder:

Ministry for Foreign Affairs and Public Worship

Buenos Aires,

July, 1955

Sir,

With reference to your letter of May 6th, 1955, in which you informed me that the Government of the United Kingdom of Great Britain and Northern Ireland had submitted an Application to the International Court of Justice on the fourth day of the same month and year against my country, with regard to certain Antarctic territories, I have the honour to state the following.

As is recalled in the Application of the United Kingdom Government itself, to which reference is made, the Argentine Government has several times had occasion to indicate in notes addressed to Her Britannic Majesty's Embassy in Buenos Aires that it cannot consent to the question of sovereignty over the Antarctic territories of Argentina which it is sought to raise being referred for decision to any international Court of Justice or Arbitration Tribunal. By this present Note, my Government reaffirms its refusal in the most express way with regard to the jurisdiction of this Court and with regard to any possibility that it should be seised as such to deal with this case.

The Argentine Government feels itself obliged to make this declaration, by virtue of the fundamental principle in accordance with which territorial sovereignty cannot be submitted for discussion or be put in issue, especially when, as in the case of the Argentine Republic with regard to its Antarctic sector, that sovereignty is based on unquestionable rights and on titles derived from and based on legitimate methods of acquiring territorial domain, and effective, notorious and peaceful possession.

There are, moreover, equally decisive further reasons which prevent the Argentine Republic from accepting the means of settlement proposed by the United Kingdom. These reasons, like those previously referred to, have at the proper time been made clear on a number of occasions to that country in the diplomatic Notes to which I have referred and especially in that dated May 4th, 1955, which was handed in to the British Embassy in Buenos Aires on the same day as the United

Kingdom Government submitted its Application to the International Court of Justice. I append as an Annex a true copy of that Note. The Argentine Government therefore considers that the United Kingdom Government's claim to be entitled to raise this question as one capable of being resolved by the Court is unfounded. It accordingly reaffirms what it has said before, to the effect that there are no reasons which would justify any decision by the Court with regard to this matter.

I avail myself, &c.

(Signed) Jeronimo Remorino

I have, &c.

(Signed) Natalio Carvajal Palacios

Antarctica Case (United Kingdom v Argentina) (Order to Remove Case from the List) (1956) ICJ Reports 12 (16 March 1956)

Present: President Hackworth; *Vice-President* Badawi; *Judges* Basdevant, Winiarski, Klaestad, Read, Hsu Mo, Armand-Ugon, Kojevnikov, Sir Muhammad Zafrulla Khan, Sir Hersch Lauterpacht, Moreno Quintana, Córdova; *Registrar* López Oliván.

The International Court of Justice,

composed as above,

after deliberation,

having regard to Articles 36 and 48 of the Statute of the Court,

Makes the following Order:

Whereas, on May 4th, 1955, there was filed in the Registry an Application by the Government of the United Kingdom of Great Britain and Northern Ireland instituting proceedings before the Court against the Republic of Argentina concerning a dispute relating to the sovereignty over certain islands and lands in the Antarctic which lie between longitudes 25° and 74° West and to the southwards of latitude 60° South;

Whereas the Application was duly communicated by the Registry on May 6th, 1955, to the Minister for Foreign Affairs and Public Worship of the Argentine Republic;

Whereas the Application was also duly communicated by the Registry to the Members of the United Nations through the Secretary-General of the United Nations, and to the other States entitled to appear before the Court;

Whereas the Application contains the following:

"42. The United Kingdom Government... declares that it hereby submits to the jurisdiction of the Court for the purposes of the case referred to the Court in the present Application... The Argentine Government has not, so far as the United Kingdom Government is aware, yet filed any declaration accepting the Court's jurisdiction, either generally under Article 36 (2) of the Statute or specially in the present case. The Argentine Government, which has frequently expressed its adherence to the principle of judicial settlement of international disputes, is, however, legally qualified to submit to the jurisdiction of the Court in this case. Consequently, upon notification of the present Application to the Republic of Argentina by the Registrar in accordance with the Rules of Court, the Argentine Government, under the settled jurisprudence of the Court, can take the necessary steps to that end, and thereby cause the Court's jurisdiction in the case to be constituted in respect of both Parties.

43. The United Kingdom Government founds the jurisdiction of the Court on the foregoing considerations and on Article 36 (1) of the Court's Statute: ..."

Whereas, in a communication from the Minister for Foreign Affairs and Public Worship of Argentina to the Registrar, set out in a letter to the Registrar of August 1st, 1955, from the Ambassador of Argentina to the Netherlands, it is stated:

"... the Argentine Government has several times had occasion to indicate in notes addressed to Her Britannic Majesty's Embassy in Buenos Aires that it cannot consent to the question of sovereignty over the Antarctic territories of Argentina which it is sought to raise being referred for decision to any international Court of Justice or Arbitration Tribunal. By this present note, my Government reaffirms its refusal in the most express way with regard to the jurisdiction of this Court and with regard to any possibility that it should be seised as such to deal with this case."

Whereas a copy of the above-mentioned letter was communicated by the Registrar to the Agent for the Government of the United Kingdom by a letter dated August 3rd, 1955;

Whereas, in a letter dated August 31st, 1955, addressed to the Registrar, the Agent for the Government of the United Kingdom stated that it regarded the letter of August 1st, 1955, from the Argentine Ambassador to the Netherlands as amounting to a rejection of the jurisdiction of the International Court of Justice for the purposes of the present case;

Whereas, in these circumstances, the Court finds that it has not before it any acceptance by the Government of Argentina of the jurisdiction of the Court to deal with the dispute which is the subject of the Application submitted to it by the United Kingdom Government and that therefore it can take no further steps upon this Application;

The Court

orders that the case shall be removed from the list.

Done in English and French, the English text being authoritative, at the Peace Palace, The Hague, this sixteenth day of March, one thousand nine hundred and fifty-six, in three copies, one of which will be placed in the archives of the Court and the others transmitted to the Government of the United Kingdom of Great Britain and Northern Ireland and to the Government of the Republic of Argentina, respectively.

(Signed) GREEN H. HACKWORTH, President.

(Signed) J. LÓPEZ OLIVÁN, Registrar.

Antarctica Case (United Kingdom v Chile) (Order to Remove the Case from the List) (1956) ICJ Reports 15 (16 March 1956)

Present: President Hackworth; *Vice-President* Badawi; *Judges* Basdevant, Winiarski, Klaestad, Read, Hsu Mo, Armand-Ugon, Kojevnikov, Sir Muhammad Zafrulla Khan, Sir Hersch Lauterpacht, Moreno Quintana, Córdova; *Registrar* López Oliván.

The International Court of Justice,

composed as above,

after deliberation,

having regard to Articles 36 and 48 of the Statute of the Court,

Makes the following Order:

Whereas, on May 4th, 1955, there was filed in the Registry an Application by the Government of the United Kingdom of Great Britain and Northern Ireland instituting proceedings before the Court against the Republic of Chile concerning a dispute relating to the sovereignty over certain islands and lands in the Antarctic which lie between longitudes 53° and 80° West and to the southwards of latitude 58° South:

Whereas the Application was duly communicated by the Registry on May 6th, 1955, to the Minister for Foreign Affairs of the Republic of Chile;

Whereas the Application was also duly communicated by the Registry to the Members of the United Nations through the Secretary-General of the United Nations, and to the other States entitled to appear before the Court;

Whereas the Application contains the following:

"40. The United Kingdom Government ... declares that it hereby submits to the jurisdiction of the Court for the purposes of the case referred to the Court in the present Application... The Chilean Government has not, so far as the United Kingdom Government is aware, yet filed any declaration accepting the Court's jurisdiction either generally under Article 36 (2) of the Statute or specially in the present case. The Chilean Government, which has frequently expressed its adherence to the principle of judicial settlement of international disputes, is, however, legally qualified to submit to the jurisdiction of the Court in this case. Consequently, upon notification of the present Application to the Republic of Chile by the Registrar in accordance with the Rules of Court, the Chilean Government, under the settled jurisprudence of the Court, can take the necessary steps to that end, and thereby cause the Court's jurisdiction in the case to be constituted in respect of Parties.

41. The United Kingdom Government founds the jurisdiction of the Court on the foregoing considerations and on Article 36 (1) of the Court's Statute; ..."

Whereas, in a letter dated July 15th, 1955, addressed to the Registrar, and handed to him on August 2nd, 1955, the Chilean Minister to the Netherlands, on the instructions of his Government, recalled that on various occasions in the past his Government had "indicated to the Government of the United Kingdom that recourse to the International Court of Justice cannot be applicable in the case of the Chilean Antarctic", and after setting forth the text of a note addressed by the Ministry of Foreign Affairs of the Republic of Chile to the British Embassy in Santiago on May 4th, 1955, in which recourse to the Court for the settlement of the controversy was declined, the Minister concluded:

"My Government consequently will confine itself on this occasion to stating that the application of the Government of the United Kingdom is unfounded and that it is not open to the International Court of Justice to exercise jurisdiction in this case."

Whereas a copy of the above-mentioned letter was communicated to the Agent for the Government of the United Kingdom on August 3rd, 1955;

Whereas, in a letter dated August 31st, 1955, addressed to the Registrar, the Agent for the Government of the United Kingdom stated that it regarded the letter of July 15th, 1955, from the Chilean Minister to the Netherlands as amounting to a rejection of the jurisdiction of the International Court of Justice for the purposes of the present case;

Whereas, in these circumstances, the Court finds that it has not before it any acceptance by the Government of Chile of the jurisdiction of the Court to deal with the dispute which is the subject of the Application submitted to it by the United Kingdom Government and that therefore it can take no further steps upon this Application;

The Court

orders that the case shall be removed from the list.

Done in English and French, the English text being authoritative, at the Peace Palace, The Hague, this sixteenth day of March, one thousand nine hundred and fifty-six, in three copies, one of which will be placed in the archives of the Court and the others transmitted to the Government of the United Kingdom of Great Britain and Northern Ireland and to the Government of the Republic of Chile, respectively.

(Signed) GREEN H. HACKWORTH, President.

(Signed) J. LÓPEZ OLIVÁN, Registrar.

Whaling in the Antarctic (Australia v Japan, New Zealand intervening) ICJ, Judgment, 31 March 2014

[*Headnote omitted.*]

[Issue: alleged violations of the International Convention for the Regulation of Whaling by Japan]

JUDGMENT

Present: *President* TOMKA; *Vice-President* SEPÚLVEDA-AMOR; *Judges* OWADA, ABRAHAM, KEITH, BENNOUNA, SKOTNIKOV, CANÇADO TRINDADE, YUSUF, GREENWOOD, XUE, DONOGHUE, GAJA, SEBUTINDE, BHANDARI; *Judge* ad hoc

CHARLESWORTH; *Registrar* COUVREUR.

In the case concerning whaling in the Antarctic,

between

Australia,

represented by [*names of legal representatives omitted*] ...

and

Japan,

represented by [*names of legal representatives omitted*] ...

with New Zealand,

as a State whose Declaration of Intervention has been admitted by the Court,

represented by [*names of legal representatives omitted*] ...

THE COURT,

composed as above,

after deliberation,

delivers the following Judgment:

1. On 31 May 2010, Australia filed in the Registry of the Court an Application instituting proceedings against Japan in respect of a dispute concerning

> "Japan's continued pursuit of a large-scale program of whaling under the Second Phase of its Japanese Whale Research Program under Special Permit in the Antarctic ('JARPA II'), in breach of obligations assumed by Japan under the International Convention for the Regulation of Whaling . . . , as well as its other international obligations for the preservation of marine mammals and the marine environment".

In its Application, Australia invoked as the basis for the jurisdiction of the Court the declarations made, pursuant to Article 36, paragraph 2, of the Statute of the Court, by Australia on 22 March 2002 and by Japan on 9 July 2007.

2. In accordance with Article 40, paragraph 2, of the Statute, the Registrar communicated the Application forthwith to the Government of Japan; and, pursuant to paragraph 3 of that Article, all other States entitled to appear before the Court were notified of the Application.

3. On the directions of the Court under Article 43 of the Rules of Court, the Registrar addressed to States parties to the International Convention for the Regulation of Whaling (hereinafter the "ICRW" or the "Convention") the notification provided for in Article 63, paragraph 1, of the Statute. In accordance with the provisions of Article 69, paragraph 3, of the Rules of Court, the Registrar also addressed to the International Whaling Commission (hereinafter the "IWC" or the "Commission") the notification provided for in Article 34, paragraph 3, of the Statute. The Commission indicated that it did not intend to submit any observations in writing under Article 69, paragraph 3, of the Rules of Court.

4. Since the Court included upon the Bench no judge of Australian nationality, Australia proceeded to exercise its right conferred by Article 31, paragraph 2, of the Statute to choose a judge *ad hoc* to sit in the case; it chose Ms Hilary Charlesworth.

5. By an Order of 13 July 2010, the Court fixed 9 May 2011 and 9 March 2012 as the respective time-limits for the filing of the Memorial of Australia and the Counter-Memorial of Japan; those pleadings were duly filed within the time-limits thus prescribed.

6. On 23 April 2012, the President of the Court met with the Agents of the Parties in order to ascertain their views with regard to the organization of the oral proceedings. At this meeting, the Agent of Australia stated that his Government did not consider it necessary to organize a second round of written pleadings; the Agent of Japan, for his part, requested a second round of written pleadings.

The Court, having regard to Article 45, paragraph 2, of the Rules of Court, decided that a second round of written pleadings was not necessary. By letters dated 2 May 2012, the Registrar informed the Parties accordingly.

7. On 19 September 2012, the Government of New Zealand, referring to Article 53, paragraph 1, of the Rules of Court, requested the Court to furnish it with copies of the pleadings and documents annexed in the case. Having ascertained the views of the Parties pursuant to that same provision, the Court decided to grant this request. The documents in question were duly transmitted to New Zealand.

8. On 20 November 2012, New Zealand, pursuant to Article 63, paragraph 2, of the Statute, filed in the Registry of the Court a Declaration of Intervention in the case. In its Declaration, New Zealand stated that it "avail[ed] itself of the right . . . to intervene as a non-party in the proceedings brought by Australia against Japan in this case".

9. In accordance with Article 83, paragraph 1, of the Rules of Court, the Registrar, by letters dated 20 November 2012, transmitted certified copies of the Declaration of Intervention to the Governments of Australia and Japan, which were informed that the Court had fixed 21 December 2012 as the time-limit for the submission of written observations on that Declaration. In accordance with paragraph 2 of the same Article, the Registrar also transmitted a copy of the Declaration to the Secretary-General of the United Nations, as well as to States entitled to appear before the Court.

10. Australia and Japan each submitted written observations on New Zealand's Declaration of Intervention within the time-limit thus fixed. The Registrar transmitted to each Party a copy of the other's observations, and copies of the observations of both Parties to New Zealand.

11. In the light of Article 84, paragraph 2, of the Rules of Court, and considering the absence of objections from the Parties, the Court took the view that it was not necessary to hold hearings on the question of the admissibility of New Zealand's Declaration of Intervention.

12. By an Order of 6 February 2013, the Court decided that the Declaration of Intervention filed by New Zealand pursuant to Article 63, paragraph 2, of the Statute was admissible. The Court also fixed 4 April 2013 as the time-limit for the filing by New Zealand of the written observations referred to in Article 86, paragraph 1, of the Rules of Court; moreover, it authorized the filing by Australia and Japan of written observations on those submitted by New Zealand, and fixed 31 May 2013 as the time-limit for such filing.

13. New Zealand duly filed its written observations within the time-limit thus fixed. The Registrar transmitted copies of New Zealand's written observations to the Parties.

Japan then filed, within the time-limit prescribed by the Court in its Order of 6 February 2013, its observations on those filed by New Zealand. The Registrar transmitted copies of Japan's written observations to Australia and to New Zealand.

Australia, for its part, notified the Court, by letter dated 31 May 2013, that it would not submit such observations, but that it "reserve[d] its right to address certain points raised in the written observations of New Zealand in the course of oral argument". The Registrar communicated copies of this letter to Japan and to New Zealand.

*

14. By letters dated 17 October 2012, the Registrar informed the Parties that the Court had requested that they provide, by 28 December 2012, information regarding expert evidence which they intended to produce, including the details referred to in Article 57 of the Rules of Court. The Registrar informed the Parties, moreover, that each Party would then be given an opportunity to comment on the other's communication, and if necessary to amend the information it had given, including the list of experts to be called at the hearing, by 28 January 2013. Finally, the Registrar informed the Parties that the Court had decided that each Party should communicate to it, by 15 April 2013, the full texts of the statements of the experts whom the Parties intended to call at the hearings.

15. By letters dated 18 December 2012 and 26 December 2012, respectively, the Agents of Australia and Japan each communicated information concerning one expert to be called at the

hearing. By a letter dated 25 January 2013, the Co-Agent of Australia communicated such information regarding a second expert.

16. By letters dated 15 April 2013, the Parties communicated the full texts of the statements of the experts whom the Parties intended to call at the hearings. These texts were exchanged between the Parties and transmitted to New Zealand.

17. By letters dated 23 April 2013, the Registrar informed the Parties that the Court had decided that they could submit written statements in response to the statement submitted by each of the other Party's experts, and had fixed 31 May 2013 as the time-limit for such submission. Within the time-limit thus fixed, Australia submitted such statements in response from the two experts it would call at the hearing, and Japan submitted certain observations in response on the statements by the two experts to be called by Australia.

*

18. In accordance with Article 53, paragraph 2, of the Rules of Court, the Court, after ascertaining the views of the Parties, decided that copies of the pleadings and documents annexed would be made accessible to the public on the opening of the oral proceedings. After consulting the Parties and New Zealand, the Court decided that the same should apply to the written observations of the intervening State and of the Parties on the subject-matter of the intervention, as well as to the written statements of experts called to give evidence in the case, and the written statements and observations in response.

19. Public hearings were held between 26 June and 16 July 2013, at which the Court heard the oral arguments and replies of: [names of representatives of Australia, Japan and New Zealand omitted] …

20. During the public hearings of 27 June 2013, Australia called the following experts: Mr. Marc Mangel, Distinguished Research Professor of Mathematical Biology and Director of the Center for Stock Assessment Research, University of California, Santa Cruz; and Mr. Nick Gales, Chief Scientist of the Australian Antarctic Program. Mr. Mangel was examined by Mr. Philippe Sands, counsel for Australia, and cross-examined by Mr. Vaughan Lowe, counsel for Japan. Mr. Gales was examined by Mr. Justin Gleeson, counsel for Australia, and cross-examined by Mr. Vaughan Lowe, counsel for Japan. He was then re-examined by Mr. Gleeson. Several judges put questions to Mr. Mangel and to Mr. Gales, to which they replied orally.

21. During the public hearing on the afternoon of 3 July 2013, Japan called Mr. Lars Walløe, Professor Emeritus of the University of Oslo and Scientific Adviser to the Norwegian Government on Marine Mammals. He was examined by Mr. Vaughan Lowe, counsel for Japan, and cross-examined by Mr. Justin Gleeson, counsel for Australia. Several judges put questions to Mr. Walløe, to which he replied orally.

22. At the hearings, some judges put questions to the Parties, and to New Zealand as intervening State, to which replies were given orally and in writing. The Parties and New Zealand presented their comments on those replies.

*

23. In its Application, Australia made the following claims:

"For [the] reasons [set forth in its Application], and reserving the right to supplement, amplify or amend the present Application, Australia requests the Court to adjudge and declare that Japan is in breach of its international obligations in implementing the JARPA II program in the Southern Ocean.

In addition, Australia requests the Court to order that Japan:

(a) cease implementation of JARPA II;

(b) revoke any authorizations, permits or licences allowing the activities which are the subject of this application to be undertaken; and

(c) provide assurances and guarantees that it will not take any further action under the JARPA II or any similar program until such program has been brought into conformity with its obligations under international law."

24. In the course of the written proceedings, the following submissions were presented by the Parties:

On behalf of the Government of Australia,

in the Memorial:

"1. For the reasons given in this Memorial, and reserving the right to supplement, amplify or amend the present submissions, Australia requests the Court to adjudge and declare that Japan is in breach of its international obligations in authorising and implementing JARPA II in the Southern Ocean.

2. In particular, the Court is requested to adjudge and declare that, by its conduct, Japan has violated its international obligations to:

(a) observe the zero catch limit in relation to the killing of whales for commercial purposes;

(b) refrain from undertaking commercial whaling of fin whales in the Southern Ocean Sanctuary; and

(c) observe the moratorium on taking, killing or treating of whales, except minke whales, by factory ships or whale catchers attached to factory ships.

3. Further, the Court is requested to adjudge and declare that JARPA II is not a program for purposes of scientific research within the meaning of Article VIII of the International Convention for the Regulation of Whaling.

4. Further, the Court is requested to adjudge and declare that Japan shall:

(a) refrain from authorising or implementing any special permit whaling which is not for purposes of scientific research within the meaning of Article VIII;

(b) cease with immediate effect the implementation of JARPA II; and

(c) revoke any authorisation, permit or licence that allows the implementation of JARPA II."

On behalf of the Government of Japan,

in the Counter-Memorial:

"On the basis of the facts and arguments set out [in its Counter-Memorial], and reserving its right to supplement or amend these Submissions, Japan requests that the Court adjudge and declare:

- that it lacks jurisdiction over the claims brought against Japan by Australia, referred to it by the Application of Australia of 31 May 2010;
- in the alternative, that the claims of Australia are rejected."

25. At the oral proceedings, the following submissions were presented by the Parties:

On behalf of the Government of Australia,

"1. Australia requests the Court to adjudge and declare that the Court has jurisdiction to hear the claims presented by Australia.

2. Australia requests the Court to adjudge and declare that Japan is in breach of its international obligations in authorizing and implementing the *Japanese Whale Research Program under Special Permit in the Antarctic Phase II* (JARPA II) in the Southern Ocean.

3. In particular, the Court is requested to adjudge and declare that, by its conduct, Japan has violated its international obligations pursuant to the International Convention for the Regulation of Whaling to:

(a) observe the zero catch limit in relation to the killing of whales for commercial purposes in paragraph 10 *(e)* of the Schedule;

(b) refrain from undertaking commercial whaling of fin whales in the Southern Ocean Sanctuary in paragraph 7 *(b)* of the Schedule;

(c) observe the moratorium on taking, killing or treating of whales, except minke whales, by factory ships or whale catchers attached to factory ships in paragraph 10 *(d)* of the Schedule; and

(d) comply with the requirements of paragraph 30 of the Schedule.

4. Further, the Court is requested to adjudge and declare that JARPA II is not a program for purposes of scientific research within the meaning of Article VIII of the International Convention for the Regulation of Whaling.

5. Further, the Court is requested to adjudge and declare that Japan shall:
(a) refrain from authorizing or implementing any special permit whaling which is not for purposes of scientific research within the meaning of Article VIII;
(b) cease with immediate effect the implementation of JARPA II; and
(c) revoke any authorization, permit or licence that allows the implementation of JARPA II."
On behalf of the Government of Japan,
"Japan requests that the Court adjudge and declare:
1. — that it lacks jurisdiction over the claims brought against Japan by Australia, referred to it by the Application of Australia of 31 May 2010; and
— that, consequently, the Application of New Zealand for permission to intervene in the proceedings instituted by Australia against Japan lapses;
2. in the alternative, that the claims of Australia are rejected."

*

26. At the end of the written observations submitted by it in accordance with Article 86, paragraph 1, of the Rules of Court, New Zealand stated:

"In summary, the provisions of Article VIII must be interpreted in good faith in their context and in light of the object and purpose of the Convention, taking account of subsequent practice of the parties and applicable rules of international law, as confirmed by supplementary means of interpretation. On the basis of those considerations, Article VIII is properly to be interpreted as follows:
(a) Article VIII forms an integral part of the system of collective regulation established by the Convention, not an exemption from it. As such, it cannot be applied to permit whaling where the effect of that whaling would be to circumvent the other obligations of the Convention or to undermine its object and purpose.
(b) Only whaling that is conducted 'in accordance with' Article VIII is exempt from the operation of the Convention.
(c) Article VIII only permits a Contracting Government to issue a Special Permit for the exclusive 'purposes of scientific research'. The purpose for which a Special Permit has been issued is a matter for objective determination, taking account of the programme's methodology, design and characteristics, including: the scale of the programme; its structure; the manner in which it is conducted; and its results.
(d) Article VIII requires a Contracting Government issuing a Special Permit to limit the number of whales to be killed under that permit to a level that is the lowest necessary for and proportionate to the objectives of that research, and that can be demonstrated will have no adverse effect on the conservation of stocks.
(e) A Contracting Government issuing a Special Permit must discharge its duty of meaningful cooperation, and demonstrate that it has taken proper account of the views of the Scientific Committee and the Commission.
(f) Only whaling under Special Permit that meets all three of the requirements of Article VIII outlined above is permitted under Article VIII."

27. In the written observations which the Court, by its Order of 6 February 2013, authorized the Parties to submit on those filed by New Zealand, Japan stated *inter alia*:
— "Japan submits that the Court should defer its consideration of New Zealand's request until it has decided whether it has jurisdiction to examine Australia's Application"; and
— "New Zealand reaches erroneous conclusions on a number of points that are pertinent to the present case. New Zealand . . . misstates the scope of the discretion expressly reserved to the Contracting Governments by Article VIII of the ICRW, particularly in relation to research methods and sample sizes as well as to the duty of cooperation. New Zealand also attempts to reverse the burden of proof with regard to the precautionary approach, to the procedural duties incumbent upon Contracting Governments issuing special permits, and to the determination of

what constitutes 'scientific purposes' under Article VIII of the ICRW. Japan submits that New Zealand's characterization of each of these points is incorrect.

New Zealand implicitly requests the Court to substitute its own judgment for that of the Government of Japan as to the character of the special permits granted by Japan. It is respectfully submitted that the Court does not have such a power and cannot substitute its own appreciation for that of a Contracting Government granting a special permit."

28. Australia, for its part, did not submit any written observations (see paragraph 13 above).

29. At the end of the oral observations which it presented with respect to the subject-matter of its intervention, in accordance with Article 86, paragraph 2, of the Rules of Court, New Zealand stated *inter alia*:

"[T]he Convention establishes a system of collective regulation for the conservation and management of whale stocks. Article VIII must be interpreted in light of that object and purpose. Article VIII permits the grant of special permits only to take whales 'for purposes of scientific research'. Japan has sought to mystify the determination of what is scientific research, and to accord for itself the right to decide whether a programme of whaling is for that purpose . . .

Even where a Contracting Government issues a special permit 'for purposes of scientific research', it is still required to ensure that the number of whales to be killed under that permit is the lowest necessary for, and proportionate to, the scientific purpose, and takes into account the collective interests of the parties. This is a matter for objective determination in light of the facts, as evidenced through the Guidelines and Resolutions of the Scientific Committee and the Commission.

There is, in any case, a substantive duty of meaningful co-operation on a Contracting Government which proposes to issue a special permit. This requires it to show that it has taken into account the legitimate interests of the other parties to the Convention; that it has balanced the interests of all the parties in the conservation and management of whale stocks."

* * *

I. JURISDICTION OF THE COURT

30. In the present case Australia contends that Japan has breached certain obligations under the ICRW to which both States are parties by issuing special permits to take whales within the framework of JARPA II. Japan maintains that its activities are lawful because the special permits are issued for "purposes of scientific research", as provided by Article VIII of the ICRW. The Court will first examine whether it has jurisdiction over the dispute.

31. Australia invokes as the basis of the Court's jurisdiction the declarations made by both Parties under Article 36, paragraph 2, of the Court's Statute. Australia's declaration of 22 March 2002 reads in relevant part as follows:

"The Government of Australia declares that it recognizes as compulsory *ipso facto* and without special agreement, in relation to any other State accepting the same obligation, the jurisdiction of the International Court of Justice in conformity with paragraph 2 of Article 36 of the Statute of the Court, until such time as notice may be given to the Secretary-General of the United Nations withdrawing this declaration. This declaration is effective immediately.

This declaration does not apply to:

....

(b) any dispute concerning or relating to the delimitation of maritime zones, including the territorial sea, the exclusive economic zone and the continental shelf, or arising out of, concerning, or relating to the exploitation of any disputed area of or adjacent to any such maritime zone pending its delimitation."

Japan's declaration of 9 July 2007 reads in relevant part as follows:

"Japan recognizes as compulsory *ipso facto* and without special agreement, in relation to any other State accepting the same obligation and on condition of reciprocity, the jurisdiction of the International Court of Justice, over all disputes arising on and after 15 September 1958 with regard to situations or facts subsequent to the same date and being not settled by other means of peaceful settlement."

32. Japan contests the jurisdiction of the Court over the dispute submitted by Australia with regard to JARPA II, arguing that it falls within Australia's reservation *(b)*, which it invokes on the basis of reciprocity. While acknowledging that this dispute does not concern or relate to the delimitation of maritime zones, Japan maintains that it is a dispute "arising out of, concerning, or relating to the exploitation of any disputed area of or adjacent to any such maritime zone pending its delimitation".

In Japan's view, the latter part of Australia's reservation, introduced by the second conjunction "or", is separate from the first part, with the consequence that the reservation applies both to disputes on delimitation and to other kinds of disputes involving the exploitation of maritime zones or adjacent areas pending delimitation. Japan adds that this interpretation is in conformity with Australia's intention when making the declaration. According to Japan, the phrase "pending its delimitation" merely describes a point in time, but not the subject-matter of the dispute excluded from the Court's jurisdiction.

Japan maintains that the present dispute "relates to the exploitation" of a maritime zone claimed by Australia or of an area adjacent to such a zone. Japan argues that this would be the case under Australia's characterization of JARPA II as a programme for the commercial exploitation of whales, as well as under Japan's own characterization of JARPA II as a scientific research programme, given that the research conducted under JARPA II is "an element of the process leading to exploitation".

33. Japan further contends that the dispute between the Parties relates to a disputed area in the sense of the reservation, given that "the JARPA II programme is taking place in or around maritime areas Australia claims to be part of its exclusive economic zone (EEZ), the rights of which are generated, according to Australia's claims, by its purported sovereignty over a large part of the Antarctic continent". In Japan's view, these maritime areas are disputed since it does not recognize Australia's claims and considers the areas in question to be part of the high seas. Conceding that the area of operation of JARPA II and the areas of the Southern Ocean claimed by Australia do not overlap precisely, Japan argues that this is irrelevant because the Australian reservation also includes the waters that are "adjacent" to the area in dispute, the term being understood broadly by Australia.

34. Australia rejects Japan's interpretation of its reservation, maintaining that

"the reservation only operates in relation to disputes between Australia and another country with a maritime claim that overlaps with that of Australia that is, a situation of delimitation. Australia has no delimitation [dispute] with Japan and hence the paragraph *(b)* reservation can have no operation."

It adds that "[i]n particular, the reservation does not cover a dispute concerning the validity, or otherwise, under the 1946 Convention, of Japan's JARPA II programme, a dispute entirely unconnected with any delimitation situation".

According to Australia, the intent underlying the reservation was to give effect to its "belief that its overlapping maritime claims are best resolved by negotiations", especially the complex maritime boundary delimitations with New Zealand and Timor-Leste that were ongoing at the time the declaration was made. Australia maintains that the wording of the reservation is to be understood against this background. Thus, the purpose of the second part of the reservation "is to make clear [that] the reservation extends beyond disputes over delimitation of maritime zones per se, to associated disputes concerning [the] exploitation of resources that may arise between the States with overlapping maritime claims pending delimitation".

Australia also contests Japan's view that the dispute over JARPA II is about "exploitation" in the sense of its reservation, arguing that the exploitation contemplated by the reservation is "exploitation of resources covered by a potential delimitation arrangement and not any exploitation unrelated to that delimitation situation that happens to occur in the relevant geographic area".

35. Australia furthermore contends that the geographic area of operation of JARPA II, which in any event extends well outside any waters claimed by it, cannot determine the Court's jurisdiction over a treaty dispute that is unrelated to the status of the waters in which the activity occurs. According to Australia, "[t]he dispute before the Court concerning compliance of JARPA II with the whaling Convention exists whether or not Australia asserts maritime zones adjacent to Antarctica and irrespective of any delimitation with adjacent claimants". Australia emphasizes that, in the maritime context, the word "delimitation" has a specific meaning, referring solely to "the fixing of boundaries between neighbouring States, whether adjacent or opposite".

36. The Court recalls that, when interpreting a declaration accepting its compulsory jurisdiction, it "must seek the interpretation which is in harmony with a natural and reasonable way of reading the text, having due regard to the intention" of the declaring State (*Anglo-Iranian Oil Co. (United Kingdom v. Iran), Preliminary Objection, Judgment, I.C.J. Reports 1952*, p. 104). The Court noted in the *Fisheries Jurisdiction* case that it had "not hesitated to place a certain emphasis on the intention of the depositing State" (*Fisheries Jurisdiction (Spain v. Canada), Jurisdiction of the Court, Judgment, I.C.J. Reports 1998*, p. 454, para. 48). The Court further observed that "[t]he intention of a reserving State may be deduced not only from the text of the relevant clause, but also from the context in which the clause is to be read, and an examination of evidence regarding the circumstances of its preparation and the purposes intended to be served" (*ibid.*, p. 454, para. 49).

37. Reservation *(b)* contained in Australia's declaration (see paragraph 31 above) refers to disputes concerning "the delimitation of maritime zones" or to those "arising out of, concerning, or relating to the exploitation of any disputed area of or adjacent to any such maritime zone pending its delimitation". The wording of the second part of the reservation is closely linked to that of the first part. The reservation thus has to be read as a unity. The disputes to which the reservation refers must either concern maritime delimitation in an area where there are overlapping claims or the exploitation of such an area or of an area adjacent thereto. The existence of a dispute concerning maritime delimitation between the Parties is required according to both parts of the reservation.

38. The meaning which results from the text of the reservation is confirmed by the intention stated by Australia when it made its declaration accepting the compulsory jurisdiction of the Court. According to a press release issued by the Attorney-General and the Minister for Foreign Affairs of Australia on 25 March 2002, the reservation excluded "disputes involv[ing] maritime boundary delimitation or disputes concerning the exploitation of an area in dispute or adjacent to an area in dispute". The same statement is contained in the National Interest Analysis submitted by the Attorney-General to Parliament on 18 June 2002, which referred to "maritime boundary disputes" as the object of the reservation. Thus, the reservation was intended to cover, apart from disputes concerning the delimitation of maritime zones, those relating to the exploitation of an area in respect of which a dispute on delimitation exists, or of a maritime area adjacent to such an area. The condition of a dispute between the parties to the case concerning delimitation of the maritime zones in question was clearly implied.

39. Both Parties acknowledge that the dispute before the Court is not a dispute about maritime delimitation. The question remains whether JARPA II involves the exploitation of an area which is the subject of a dispute relating to delimitation or of an area adjacent to it.

Part of the whaling activities envisaged in JARPA II take place in the maritime zone claimed by Australia as relating to the asserted Australian Antarctic Territory or in an adjacent area. Moreover, the taking of whales, especially in considerable numbers, could be viewed as a form of exploitation of a maritime area even if this occurs according to a programme for scientific research. However, while Japan has contested Australia's maritime claims generated by the asserted Australian Antarctic Territory, it does not claim to have any sovereign rights in those areas. The fact that Japan questions those maritime entitlements does not render the delimitation of these maritime areas under dispute as between the Parties. As the Court stated in the *Territorial and Maritime Dispute* case, "the task of delimitation consists in resolving the overlapping claims by drawing a line of separation between the maritime areas concerned" (*Territorial and Maritime Dispute (Nicaragua v. Colombia), Judgment, I.C.J. Reports 2012 (II)*, pp. 674–675, para. 141). There are no overlapping claims of the Parties to the present proceedings which may render reservation *(b)* applicable.

40. Moreover, it is significant that Australia alleges that Japan has breached certain obligations under the ICRW and does not contend that JARPA II is unlawful because the whaling activities envisaged in the programme take place in the maritime zones over which Australia asserts sovereign rights or in adjacent areas. The nature and extent of the claimed maritime zones are therefore immaterial to the present dispute, which is about whether or not Japan's activities are compatible with its obligations under the ICRW.

41. The Court therefore concludes that Japan's objection to the Court's jurisdiction cannot be upheld.

II. ALLEGED VIOLATIONS OF INTERNATIONAL OBLIGATIONS UNDER THE CONVENTION

1. Introduction

A. General overview of the Convention

42. The present proceedings concern the interpretation of the International Convention for the Regulation of Whaling and the question whether special permits granted for JARPA II are for purposes of scientific research within the meaning of Article VIII, paragraph 1, of the Convention. Before examining the relevant issues, the Court finds it useful to provide a general overview of the Convention and its origins.

43. The ICRW was preceded by two multilateral treaties relating to whaling. The Convention for the Regulation of Whaling, adopted in 1931, was prompted by concerns over the sustainability of the whaling industry. This industry had increased dramatically following the advent of factory ships and other technological innovations that made it possible to conduct extensive whaling in areas far from land stations, including in the waters off Antarctica. The 1931 Convention prohibited the killing of certain categories of whales and required whaling operations by vessels of States parties to be licensed, but failed to address the increase in overall catch levels.

This increase in catch levels and a concurrent decline in the price of whale oil led to the adoption of the 1937 International Agreement for the Regulation of Whaling. The preamble of this Agreement expressed the desire of the States parties "to secure the prosperity of the whaling industry and, for that purpose, to maintain the stock of whales". The treaty prohibited the taking of certain categories of whales, designated seasons for different types of whaling, closed certain geographic areas to whaling and imposed further regulations on the industry. As had already been the case under the 1931 Convention, States parties were required to collect from all the whales taken certain biological information which, together with other statistical data, was to be transmitted to the International Bureau for Whaling Statistics in Norway. The Agreement also provided for the issuance by a "Contracting Government . . . to any of its nationals [of] a special permit authorising that national to kill, take and treat whales for purposes of scientific research". Three Protocols to the 1937 Agreement subsequently placed some additional restrictions on whaling activities.

44. In 1946, an international conference on whaling was convened on the initiative of the United States. The aims of the conference, as described by Mr. Dean Acheson, then Acting Secretary of State of the United States, in his opening address, were "to provide for the coordination and codification of existant regulations" and to establish an "effective administrative machinery for the modification of these regulations from time to time in the future as conditions may require".

The conference adopted, on 2 December 1946, the International Convention for the Regulation of Whaling, the only authentic text of which is in the English language. The Convention entered into force for Australia on 10 November 1948 and for Japan on 21 April 1951. New Zealand deposited its instrument of ratification on 2 August 1949, but gave notice of withdrawal on 3 October 1968; it adhered again to the Convention with effect from 15 June 1976.

45. In contrast to the 1931 and 1937 treaties, the text of the ICRW does not contain substantive provisions regulating the conservation of whale stocks or the management of the whaling industry. These are to be found in the Schedule, which "forms an integral part" of the Convention, as is stated in Article I, paragraph 1, of the latter. The Schedule is subject to amendments, to be adopted by the IWC. This Commission, established under Article III, paragraph 1, of the Convention, is given a significant role in the regulation of whaling. It is "composed of one member from each Contracting Government". The adoption by the Commission of amendments to the Schedule requires a three-fourths majority of votes cast (Art. III, para. 2). An amendment becomes binding on a State party unless it presents an objection, in which case the amendment does not become effective in respect of that State until the objection is withdrawn. The Commission has amended the Schedule many times. The functions conferred on the Commission have made the Convention an evolving instrument.

Among the objects of possible amendments, Article V, paragraph 1, of the Convention lists

> "fixing *(a)* protected and unprotected species . . . *(c)* open and closed waters, including the designation of sanctuary areas . . . *(e)* time, methods, and intensity of whaling (including the maximum catch of whales to be taken in any one season), *(f)* types and specifications of gear and apparatus and appliances which may be used". Amendments to the Schedule "shall be such as are necessary to carry out the objectives and purposes of this Convention and to provide for the conservation, development, and optimum utilization of the whale resources" and "shall be based on scientific findings" (Art. V, para. 2).

46. Article VI of the Convention states that "[t]he Commission may from time to time make recommendations to any or all Contracting Governments on any matters which relate to whales or whaling and to the objectives and purposes of this Convention". These recommendations, which take the form of resolutions, are not binding. However, when they are adopted by consensus or by a unanimous vote, they may be relevant for the interpretation of the Convention or its Schedule.

47. In 1950, the Commission established a Scientific Committee (hereinafter the "Scientific Committee" or "Committee"). The Committee is composed primarily of scientists nominated by the States parties. However, advisers from intergovernmental organizations and scientists who have not been nominated by States parties may be invited to participate in a non-voting capacity.

The Scientific Committee assists the Commission in discharging its functions, in particular those relating to "studies and investigations relating to whales and whaling" (Article IV of the Convention). It analyses information available to States parties "with respect to whales and whaling" and submitted by them in compliance with their obligations under Article VIII, paragraph 3, of the Convention. It contributes to making "scientific findings" on the basis of which amendments to the Schedule may be adopted by the Commission (Art. V, para. 2 *(b)*). According to paragraph 30 of the Schedule, adopted in 1979, the Scientific Committee reviews and comments on special permits before they are issued by States parties to their nationals for purposes of scientific research under Article VIII, paragraph 1, of the Convention. The Scientific Committee has not been empowered to make any binding assessment in this regard. It communicates to the Commission its views on programmes for scientific research, including the views of individual members, in the form of reports or recommendations. However, when there is a division of opinion, the Committee generally refrains from formally adopting the majority view.

Since the mid-1980s, the Scientific Committee has conducted its review of special permits on the basis of "Guidelines" issued or endorsed by the Commission. At the time that JARPA II was proposed in 2005, the applicable Guidelines had been collected in a document entitled "Annex Y: Guidelines for the Review of Scientific Permit Proposals" (hereinafter "Annex Y"). The current Guidelines, which were elaborated by the Scientific Committee and endorsed by the Commission in 2008 (and then further revised in 2012), are set forth in a document entitled "Annex P: Process for the Review of Special Permit Proposals and Research Results from Existing and Completed Permits" (hereinafter "Annex P").

B. Claims by Australia and response by Japan

48. Australia alleges that JARPA II is not a programme for purposes of scientific research within the meaning of Article VIII of the Convention. In Australia's view, it follows from this that Japan has breached and continues to breach certain of its obligations under the Schedule to the ICRW. Australia's claims concern compliance with the following substantive obligations: (1) the obligation to respect the moratorium setting zero catch limits for the killing of whales from all stocks for commercial purposes (para. 10 *(e)*); (2) the obligation not to undertake commercial whaling of fin whales in the Southern Ocean Sanctuary (para. 7 *(b)*); and (3) the obligation to observe the moratorium on the taking, killing or treating of whales, except minke whales, by factory ships or whale catchers attached to factory ships (para. 10 *(d)*). Moreover, according to Australia's final submissions, when authorizing JARPA II, Japan also failed to comply with the procedural requirements set out in paragraph 30 of the Schedule for proposed scientific permits.

49. Japan contests all the alleged breaches. With regard to the substantive obligations under the Schedule, Japan argues that none of the obligations invoked by Australia applies to JARPA II, because this programme has been undertaken for purposes of scientific research and is therefore covered by the exemption provided for in Article VIII, paragraph 1, of the Convention. Japan also contends that there has been no breach of the procedural requirements stated in paragraph 30 of the Schedule.

50. The issues concerning the interpretation and application of Article VIII of the Convention are central to the present case and will be examined first.

2. Interpretation of Article VIII, paragraph 1, of the Convention

A. The function of Article VIII

51. Article VIII, paragraph 1, of the Convention reads as follows:

> "Notwithstanding anything contained in this Convention any Contracting Government may grant to any of its nationals a special permit authorizing that national to kill, take and treat whales for purposes of scientific research subject to such restrictions as to number and subject to such other conditions as the Contracting Government thinks fit, and the killing, taking, and treating of whales in accordance with the provisions of this Article shall be exempt from the operation of this Convention. Each Contracting Government shall report at once to the Commission all such authorizations which it has granted. Each Contracting Government may at any time revoke any such special permit which it has granted."

52. Japan initially argued that "special permit whaling under Article VIII is entirely outside the scope of the ICRW". Article VIII, paragraph 1, it contended, was to be regarded as "free-standing" and would have to be read in isolation from the other provisions of the Convention. Japan later acknowledged that Article VIII "must . . . be interpreted and applied consistently with the Convention's other provisions", but emphasized that a consistent reading would consider Article VIII, paragraph 1, as providing an exemption from the Convention.

53. According to Australia, Article VIII needs to be read in the context of the other provisions of the Convention, to which it provides a limited exception. In particular, Australia maintained that conservation measures adopted in pursuance of the objectives of the Convention, "including the Moratorium and the Sanctuary", are relevant also for whaling for scientific purposes, given that

the reliance on Article VIII, paragraph 1, cannot have the effect of undermining the effectiveness of the regulatory régime as a whole.

54. New Zealand observed that the phrase "notwithstanding anything contained in this Convention", which opens paragraph 1 of Article VIII, "provide[s] a limited discretion for Contracting Governments to issue special permits for the specific articulated purpose of scientific research". It "do[es] not constitute a blanket exemption for Special Permit whaling from all aspects of the Convention". New Zealand pointed out that the provision in paragraph 1 setting out that the taking of whales in accordance with Article VIII is "exempt from the operation of this Convention" "would have been unnecessary if the opening words of the paragraph, 'notwithstanding anything in the Convention', were intended to cover all aspects of Special Permit whaling".

55. The Court notes that Article VIII is an integral part of the Convention. It therefore has to be interpreted in light of the object and purpose of the Convention and taking into account other provisions of the Convention, including the Schedule. However, since Article VIII, paragraph 1, specifies that "the killing, taking, and treating of whales in accordance with the provisions of this Article shall be exempt from the operation of this Convention", whaling conducted under a special permit which meets the conditions of Article VIII is not subject to the obligations under the Schedule concerning the moratorium on the catching of whales for commercial purposes, the prohibition of commercial whaling in the Southern Ocean Sanctuary and the moratorium relating to factory ships.

B. The relationship between Article VIII and the object and purpose of the Convention

56. The preamble of the ICRW indicates that the Convention pursues the purpose of ensuring the conservation of all species of whales while allowing for their sustainable exploitation. Thus, the first preambular paragraph recognizes "the interest of the nations of the world in safeguarding for future generations the great natural resources represented by the whale stocks". In the same vein, the second paragraph of the preamble expresses the desire "to protect all species of whales from further over-fishing", and the fifth paragraph stresses the need "to give an interval for recovery to certain species now depleted in numbers". However, the preamble also refers to the exploitation of whales, noting in the third paragraph that "increases in the size of whale stocks will permit increases in the number of whales which may be captured without endangering these natural resources", and adding in the fourth paragraph that "it is in the common interest to achieve the optimum level of whale stocks as rapidly as possible without causing widespread economic and nutritional distress" and in the fifth that "whaling operations should be confined to those species best able to sustain exploitation". The objectives of the ICRW are further indicated in the final paragraph of the preamble, which states that the Contracting Parties "decided to conclude a convention to provide for the proper conservation of whale stocks and thus make possible the orderly development of the whaling industry". Amendments to the Schedule and recommendations by the IWC may put an emphasis on one or the other objective pursued by the Convention, but cannot alter its object and purpose.

57. In order to buttress their arguments concerning the interpretation of Article VIII, paragraph 1, Australia and Japan have respectively emphasized conservation and sustainable exploitation as the object and purpose of the Convention in the light of which the provision should be interpreted. According to Australia, Article VIII, paragraph 1, should be interpreted restrictively because it allows the taking of whales, thus providing an exception to the general rules of the Convention which give effect to its object and purpose of conservation. New Zealand also calls for "a restrictive rather than an expansive interpretation of the conditions in which a Contracting Government may issue a Special Permit under Article VIII", in order not to undermine "the system of collective regulation under the Convention". This approach is contested by Japan, which argues in particular that the power to authorize the taking of whales for purposes of scientific research should be viewed in the context of the freedom to engage in whaling enjoyed

by States under customary international law.

58. Taking into account the preamble and other relevant provisions of the Convention referred to above, the Court observes that neither a restrictive nor an expansive interpretation of Article VIII is justified. The Court notes that programmes for purposes of scientific research should foster scientific knowledge; they may pursue an aim other than either conservation or sustainable exploitation of whale stocks. This is also reflected in the Guidelines issued by the IWC for the review of scientific permit proposals by the Scientific Committee. In particular, the Guidelines initially applicable to JARPA II, Annex Y, referred not only to programmes that "contribute information essential for rational management of the stock" or those that are relevant for "conduct[ing] the comprehensive assessment" of the moratorium on commercial whaling, but also those responding to "other critically important research needs". The current Guidelines, Annex P, list three broad categories of objectives. Besides programmes aimed at "improv[ing] the conservation and management of whale stocks", they envisage programmes which have as an objective to "improve the conservation and management of other living marine resources or the ecosystem of which the whale stocks are an integral part" and those directed at "test[ing] hypotheses not directly related to the management of living marine resources".

C. The issuance of special permits

59. Japan notes that, according to Article VIII, paragraph 1, the State of nationality of the person or entity requesting a special permit for purposes of scientific research is the only State that is competent under the Convention to issue the permit. According to Japan, that State is in the best position to evaluate a programme intended for purposes of scientific research submitted by one of its nationals. In this regard it enjoys discretion, which could be defined as a "margin of appreciation". Japan argues that this discretion is emphasized by the part of the paragraph which specifies that the State of nationality may grant a permit "subject to such restrictions as to number and subject to such other conditions as the Contracting Government thinks fit".

60. According to Australia, while the State of nationality of the requesting entity has been given the power to authorize whaling for purposes of scientific research under Article VIII, this does not imply that the authorizing State has the discretion to determine whether a special permit for the killing, taking and treating of whales falls within the scope of Article VIII, paragraph 1. The requirements for granting a special permit set out in the Convention provide a standard of an objective nature to which the State of nationality has to conform. New Zealand also considers that Article VIII states "an objective requirement", not "something to be determined by the granting Contracting Government".

61. The Court considers that Article VIII gives discretion to a State party to the ICRW to reject the request for a special permit or to specify the conditions under which a permit will be granted. However, whether the killing, taking and treating of whales pursuant to a requested special permit is for purposes of scientific research cannot depend simply on that State's perception.

D. The standard of review

62. The Court now turns to the standard that it will apply in reviewing the grant of a special permit authorizing the killing, taking and treating of whales on the basis of Article VIII, paragraph 1, of the Convention.

63. Australia maintains that the task before the Court in the present case is to determine whether Japan's actions are consistent with the ICRW and the decisions taken under it. According to Australia, the Court's power of review should not be limited to scrutiny for good faith, with a strong presumption in favour of the authorizing State, as this would render the multilateral régime for the collective management of a common resource established by the ICRW ineffective. Australia urges the Court to have regard to objective elements in evaluating whether a special permit has been granted for purposes of scientific research, referring in particular to the "design and implementation of the whaling programme, as well as any results obtained".

64. New Zealand maintains that the interpretation and application of Article VIII entail the "simple question of compliance" by Contracting Governments with their treaty obligations, a

question which is to be decided by the Court. New Zealand also emphasizes objective elements, stating that the question whether a programme is for purposes of scientific research can be evaluated with reference to its "methodology, design and characteristics".

65. Japan accepts that the Court may review the determination by a State party to the ICRW that the whaling for which a special permit has been granted is "for purposes of scientific research". In the course of the written and oral proceedings, Japan emphasized that the Court is limited, when exercising its power of review, to ascertaining whether the determination was "arbitrary or capricious", "manifestly unreasonable" or made in bad faith. Japan also stressed that matters of scientific policy cannot be properly appraised by the Court. It added that the role of the Court therefore is "to secure the integrity of the process by which the decision is made, [but] not to review the decision itself".

66. Near the close of the oral proceedings, however, Japan refined its position regarding the standard of review to be applied in this case as follows:

> "Japan agrees with Australia and New Zealand in regarding the test as being whether a State's decision is objectively reasonable, or 'supported by coherent reasoning and respectable scientific evidence and . . . , in this sense, objectively justifiable'".

67. When reviewing the grant of a special permit authorizing the killing, taking and treating of whales, the Court will assess, first, whether the programme under which these activities occur involves scientific research. Secondly, the Court will consider if the killing, taking and treating of whales is "for purposes of" scientific research by examining whether, in the use of lethal methods, the programme's design and implementation are reasonable in relation to achieving its stated objectives. This standard of review is an objective one. Relevant elements of a programme's design and implementation are set forth below (see paragraph 88).

68. In this regard, the Court notes that the dispute before it arises from a decision by a State party to the ICRW to grant special permits under Article VIII of that treaty. Inherent in such a decision is the determination by the State party that the programme's use of lethal methods is for purposes of scientific research. It follows that the Court will look to the authorizing State, which has granted special permits, to explain the objective basis for its determination.

69. The Court observes that, in applying the above standard of review, it is not called upon to resolve matters of scientific or whaling policy. The Court is aware that members of the international community hold divergent views about the appropriate policy towards whales and whaling, but it is not for the Court to settle these differences. The Court's task is only to ascertain whether the special permits granted in relation to JARPA II fall within the scope of Article VIII, paragraph 1, of the ICRW.

E. Meaning of the phrase "for purposes of scientific research"

70. The Parties address two closely related aspects of the interpretation of Article VIII the meaning of the terms "scientific research" and "for purposes of" in the phrase "for purposes of scientific research". Australia analysed the meaning of these terms separately and observed that these two elements are cumulative. Japan did not contest this approach to the analysis of the provision.

71. In the view of the Court, the two elements of the phrase "for purposes of scientific research" are cumulative. As a result, even if a whaling programme involves scientific research, the killing, taking and treating of whales pursuant to such a programme does not fall within Article VIII unless these activities are "for purposes of" scientific research.

72. The Court first considers the arguments of the Parties and the intervening State regarding the meaning of the term "scientific research" and then turns to their arguments regarding the meaning of the term "for purposes of" in the phrase "for purposes of scientific research".

(a) *The term "scientific research"*

73. At the outset, the Court notes that the term "scientific research" is not defined in the Convention.

74. Australia, relying primarily on the views of one of the scientific experts that it called, Mr. Mangel, maintains that scientific research (in the context of the Convention) has four essential characteristics: defined and achievable objectives (questions or hypotheses) that aim to contribute to knowledge important to the conservation and management of stocks; "appropriate methods", including the use of lethal methods only where the objectives of the research cannot be achieved by any other means; peer review; and the avoidance of adverse effects on stock. In support of these criteria, Australia also draws on resolutions of the Commission and the Guidelines related to the review of special permits by the Scientific Committee (see paragraph 47 above).

75. Japan does not offer an alternative interpretation of the term "scientific research", and stresses that the views of an expert cannot determine the interpretation of a treaty provision. As a matter of scientific opinion, the expert called by Japan, Mr. Walløe, agreed in certain respects with the criteria advanced by Mr. Mangel, while differing on certain important details. Japan disputes the weight that Australia assigns to resolutions of the Commission that were adopted without Japan's support, and notes that resolutions are recommendatory in nature.

76. The Court makes the following observations on the criteria advanced by Australia with regard to the meaning of the term "scientific research".

77. As to the question whether a testable or defined hypothesis is essential, the Court observes that the experts called by both Parties agreed that scientific research should proceed on the basis of particular questions, which could take the form of a hypothesis, although they disagreed about the level of specificity required of such a hypothesis. In short, the opinions of the experts reveal some degree of agreement, albeit with important nuances, regarding the role of hypotheses in scientific research generally.

78. As to the use of lethal methods, Australia asserts that Article VIII, paragraph 1, authorizes the granting of special permits to kill, take and treat whales only when non-lethal methods are not available, invoking the views of the experts it called, as well as certain IWC resolutions and Guidelines. For example, Australia refers to Resolution 1986–2 (which recommends that when considering a proposed special permit, a State party should take into account whether "the objectives of the research are not practically and scientifically feasible through non-lethal research techniques") and to Annex P (which provides that special permit proposals should assess why non-lethal methods or analyses of existing data "have been considered to be insufficient"). Both of these instruments were approved by consensus. Australia also points to Resolution 1995–9, which was not adopted by consensus, and which recommends that the killing of whales "should only be permitted in exceptional circumstances where the questions address critically important issues which cannot be answered by the analysis of existing data and/or use of non-lethal research techniques".

79. Australia claims that IWC resolutions must inform the Court's interpretation of Article VIII because they comprise "subsequent agreement between the parties regarding the interpretation of the treaty" and "subsequent practice in the application of the treaty which establishes the agreement of the parties regarding its interpretation", within the meaning of subparagraphs *(a)* and *(b)*, respectively, of paragraph 3 of Article 31 of the Vienna Convention on the Law of Treaties.

80. Japan disagrees with the assertion that special permits authorizing lethal methods may be issued under Article VIII only if non-lethal methods are not available, calling attention to the fact that Article VIII authorizes the granting of permits for the killing of whales and thus expressly contemplates lethal methods. Japan states that it does not use lethal methods "more than it considers necessary" in conducting scientific research, but notes that this restraint results not from a legal limitation found in the ICRW, but rather from "reasons of scientific policy". Japan notes that the resolutions cited by Australia were adopted pursuant to the Commission's power to make recommendations. Japan accepts that it has a duty to give due consideration to these recommendations, but emphasizes that they are not binding.

81. New Zealand asserts that special permits must be granted in a "reasonable and precautionary way", which requires that "whales may be killed only where that is necessary for scientific research and it is not possible to achieve the equivalent objectives of that research by non-lethal means". Like Australia, New Zealand refers to IWC resolutions and Guidelines to support this assertion.

82. The Court observes that, as a matter of scientific opinion, the experts called by the Parties agreed that lethal methods can have a place in scientific research, while not necessarily agreeing on the conditions for their use. Their conclusions as scientists, however, must be distinguished from the interpretation of the Convention, which is the task of this Court.

83. Article VIII expressly contemplates the use of lethal methods, and the Court is of the view that Australia and New Zealand overstate the legal significance of the recommendatory resolutions and Guidelines on which they rely. First, many IWC resolutions were adopted without the support of all States parties to the Convention and, in particular, without the concurrence of Japan. Thus, such instruments cannot be regarded as subsequent agreement to an interpretation of Article VIII, nor as subsequent practice establishing an agreement of the parties regarding the interpretation of the treaty within the meaning of subparagraphs *(a)* and *(b)*, respectively, of paragraph (3) of Article 31 of the Vienna Convention on the Law of Treaties.

Secondly, as a matter of substance, the relevant resolutions and Guidelines that have been approved by consensus call upon States parties to take into account whether research objectives can practically and scientifically be achieved by using non-lethal research methods, but they do not establish a requirement that lethal methods be used only when other methods are not available.

The Court however observes that the States parties to the ICRW have a duty to co-operate with the IWC and the Scientific Committee and thus should give due regard to recommendations calling for an assessment of the feasibility of non-lethal alternatives. The Court will return to this point when it considers the Parties' arguments regarding JARPA II (see paragraph 137).

84. As to the criterion of peer review advanced by Australia, even if peer review of proposals and results is common practice in the scientific community, it does not follow that a programme can be said to involve scientific research only if the proposals and the results are subjected to peer review. The Convention takes a different approach (while certainly not precluding peer review). Paragraph 30 of the Schedule requires prior review of proposed permits by the Scientific Committee and the current Guidelines (Annex P) also contemplate Scientific Committee review of ongoing and completed programmes.

85. Regarding the fourth criterion advanced by Australia, Japan and New Zealand agree with Australia that scientific research must avoid an adverse effect on whale stocks.

Thus, the Parties and the intervening State appear to be in agreement in respect of this criterion. In the particular context of JARPA II, however, Australia does not maintain that meeting the target sample sizes would have an adverse effect on the relevant stocks, so this criterion does not appear to be of particular significance in this case.

86. Taking into account these observations, the Court is not persuaded that activities must satisfy the four criteria advanced by Australia in order to constitute "scientific research" in the context of Article VIII. As formulated by Australia, these criteria appear largely to reflect what one of the experts that it called regards as well-conceived scientific research, rather than serving as an interpretation of the term as used in the Convention. Nor does the Court consider it necessary to devise alternative criteria or to offer a general definition of "scientific research".

(b) *The meaning of the term "for purposes of" in Article VIII, paragraph 1*

87. The Court turns next to the second element of the phrase "for purposes of scientific research", namely the meaning of the term "for purposes of".

88. The stated research objectives of a programme are the foundation of a programme's design, but the Court need not pass judgment on the scientific merit or importance of those objectives in order to assess the purpose of the killing of whales under such a programme. Nor is it for the

Court to decide whether the design and implementation of a programme are the best possible means of achieving its stated objectives.

In order to ascertain whether a programme's use of lethal methods is for purposes of scientific research, the Court will consider whether the elements of a programme's design and implementation are reasonable in relation to its stated scientific objectives (see paragraph 67 above). As shown by the arguments of the Parties, such elements may include: decisions regarding the use of lethal methods; the scale of the programme's use of lethal sampling; the methodology used to select sample sizes; a comparison of the target sample sizes and the actual take; the time frame associated with a programme; the programme's scientific output; and the degree to which a programme co-ordinates its activities with related research projects (see paragraphs 129–132; 149; 158–159; 203–205; 214–222 below).

89. The Parties agree that the design and implementation of a programme for purposes of scientific research differ in key respects from commercial whaling. The evidence regarding the programme's design and implementation must be considered in light of this distinction. For example, according to Japan, in commercial whaling, only species of high commercial value are taken and larger animals make up the majority of the catch, whereas in scientific whaling "species of less or no commercial value" may be targeted and individual animals are taken based on random sampling procedures.

90. Australia raises two features of a programme that, in its view, bear on the distinction between the grant of a special permit that authorizes whaling "for purposes of" scientific research and whaling activities that do not fit within Article VIII and thus, in Australia's view, violate paragraphs 7 *(b)*, 10 *(d)* and 10 *(e)* of the Schedule.

91. First, Australia acknowledges that Article VIII, paragraph 2, of the Convention allows the sale of whale meat that is the by-product of whaling for purposes of scientific research. That provision states:

> "Any whales taken under these special permits shall so far as practicable be processed and the proceeds shall be dealt with in accordance with directions issued by the Government by which the permit was granted."

However, Australia considers that the quantity of whale meat generated in the course of a programme for which a permit has been granted under Article VIII, paragraph 1, and the sale of that meat, can cast doubt on whether the killing, taking and treating of whales is for purposes of scientific research.

92. Japan states in response that the sale of meat as a means to fund research is allowed by Article VIII, paragraph 2, and is commonplace in respect of fisheries research.

93. On this point, New Zealand asserts that Article VIII, paragraph 2, can be read to permit the sale of whale meat, but that such sale is not required.

94. As the Parties and the intervening State accept, Article VIII, paragraph 2, permits the processing and sale of whale meat incidental to the killing of whales pursuant to the grant of a special permit under Article VIII, paragraph 1.

In the Court's view, the fact that a programme involves the sale of whale meat and the use of proceeds to fund research is not sufficient, taken alone, to cause a special permit to fall outside Article VIII. Other elements would have to be examined, such as the scale of a programme's use of lethal sampling, which might suggest that the whaling is for purposes other than scientific research. In particular, a State party may not, in order to fund the research for which a special permit has been granted, use lethal sampling on a greater scale than is otherwise reasonable in relation to achieving the programme's stated objectives.

95. Secondly, Australia asserts that a State's pursuit of goals that extend beyond scientific objectives would demonstrate that a special permit granted in respect of such a programme does not fall within Article VIII. In Australia's view, for example, the pursuit of policy goals such as providing employment or maintaining a whaling infrastructure would indicate that the killing of whales is not for purposes of scientific research.

96. Japan accepts that "special permits may be granted only for whaling that has scientific purposes, and not for commercial purposes". Japan points to the fact that the Schedule provision establishing the moratorium on commercial whaling, paragraph 10 *(e)*, calls for the "best scientific advice" in order for the moratorium to be reviewed and potentially lifted. Japan further asserts that a State party is within its rights to conduct a programme of scientific research that aims to advance its objective of resuming commercial whaling on a sustainable basis.

97. The Court observes that a State often seeks to accomplish more than one goal when it pursues a particular policy. Moreover, an objective test of whether a programme is for purposes of scientific research does not turn on the intentions of individual government officials, but rather on whether the design and implementation of a programme are reasonable in relation to achieving the stated research objectives. Accordingly, the Court considers that whether particular government officials may have motivations that go beyond scientific research does not preclude a conclusion that a programme is for purposes of scientific research within the meaning of Article VIII. At the same time, such motivations cannot justify the granting of a special permit for a programme that uses lethal sampling on a larger scale than is reasonable in relation to achieving the programme's stated research objectives. The research objectives alone must be sufficient to justify the programme as designed and implemented.

3. JARPA II in light of Article VIII of the Convention

98. The Court will now apply the approach set forth in the preceding section to enquire into whether, based on the evidence, the design and implementation of JARPA II are reasonable in relation to achieving its stated objectives.

99. JARPA II was preceded by the Japanese Whale Research Program under Special Permit in the Antarctic (JARPA). The legality of JARPA is not at issue in this case. In the course of presenting their views about JARPA II, however, the Parties draw a variety of comparisons between JARPA II and the predecessor programme. Therefore, the Court begins with a description of JARPA.

A. Description of the programmes

(a) *JARPA*

100. In 1982, the IWC amended the Schedule to adopt a moratorium on commercial whaling. Japan made a timely objection to the amendment, which it withdrew in 1986. Australia asserts that Japan withdrew that objection under pressure from other countries, and, in particular, in light of the prospect of trade sanctions being imposed against Japan by the United States. Following withdrawal of the objection, the moratorium entered into force for Japan after the 1986–1987 whaling season. Japan commenced JARPA in the next season. Like JARPA II, JARPA was a programme for which Japan issued special permits pursuant to Article VIII, paragraph 1, of the Convention.

101. Australia takes the position that JARPA was conceived in order to continue commercial whaling under the "guise" of scientific research. It points to various statements that Japanese authorities made after the adoption of the commercial whaling moratorium. For example, in 1983 a Japanese official stated that the Government's goal in the face of the adoption of the commercial whaling moratorium was "to ensure that our whaling can continue in some form or another". In 1984, a study group commissioned by the Government of Japan recommended that Japan pursue scientific whaling "in order to continue whaling in the Southern Ocean".

102. Japan rejects Australia's characterization of the factors that led to the establishment of JARPA and asserts that Australia has taken the statements by Japanese authorities out of context. It explains that JARPA was started following Japan's acceptance of the commercial whaling moratorium because "the justification for the moratorium was that data on whale stocks was inadequate to manage commercial whaling properly" and it was therefore "best to start the research program as soon as possible".

103. JARPA commenced during the 1987–1988 season and ran until the 2004–2005 season, after which it was followed immediately by JARPA II in the 2005–2006 season. Japan explains that JARPA was launched "for the purpose of collecting scientific data to contribute to the 'review' and 'comprehensive assessment'" of the moratorium on commercial whaling, as envisaged by paragraph 10 *(e)* of the Schedule. It was designed to be an 18-year research programme, "after which the necessity for further research would be reviewed".

104. The 1987 JARPA Research Plan described JARPA as, *inter alia*, "a program for research on the southern hemisphere minke whale and for preliminary research on the marine ecosystem in the Antarctic". It was "designed to estimate the stock size" of southern hemisphere minke whales in order to provide a "scientific basis for resolving problems facing the IWC" relating to "the divergent views on the moratorium". To those ends, it proposed annual lethal sample sizes of 825 Antarctic minke whales and 50 sperm whales from two "management areas" in the Southern Ocean. Later, the proposal to sample sperm whales by lethal methods was dropped from the programme and the sample size for Antarctic minke whales was reduced to 300 for JARPA's first seven seasons (1987–1988 to 1993–1994). Japan explains that the decision to reduce the sample size from 825 to 300 resulted in the extension of the research period, which made it possible to obtain accurate results with smaller sample sizes. Beginning in the 1995–1996 season, the maximum annual sample size for Antarctic minke whales was increased to 400, plus or minus 10 per cent. More than 6,700 Antarctic minke whales were killed over the course of JARPA's 18-year history.

105. In January 2005, during JARPA's final season, Japan independently convened a meeting, outside the auspices of the IWC, to review the then-available data and results from the programme. In December 2006, the Scientific Committee held a "final review" workshop to review the entirety of JARPA's data and results and to assess the extent to which JARPA had accomplished or made progress towards its stated objectives; several recommendations were made for the further study and analysis of the data collected under JARPA. Japan submitted its Research Plan for JARPA II to the IWC in March 2005, and launched JARPA II, in November 2005, after the January 2005 meeting convened by Japan but prior to the December 2006 final review of JARPA by the Scientific Committee.

106. Australia describes the "primary purpose" of JARPA as the estimation of the natural mortality rate of Antarctic minke whales (i.e., the chance that a whale will die from natural causes in any particular year). Australia also maintains that Japan purported to be collecting biological data that it viewed as relevant to the New Management Procedure (the "NMP") the model in use by the Commission to regulate whaling activity at the time of JARPA's launch but abandoned its initial approach after five years. According to Australia, the goal to estimate natural mortality was "practically unachievable" and the "irrelevance" of JARPA was confirmed in 1994 when the Commission agreed to replace the NMP with another management tool, the Revised Management Procedure (the "RMP"), which did not require the type of information that JARPA obtained by lethal sampling.

107. The RMP requires a brief explanation. The Parties agree that the RMP is a conservative and precautionary management tool and that it remains the applicable management procedure of the IWC, although its implementation has not been completed. Australia maintains that the RMP "overcomes the difficulties faced by the NMP" the mechanism that the Commission previously developed to set catch limits because it takes uncertainty in abundance estimates into account and "does not rely on biological parameters that are difficult to estimate". Japan disputes this characterization of the RMP and argues that its implementation requires "a huge amount of scientific data" at each step. Thus, the Parties disagree on whether data collected by JARPA and JARPA II contribute to the RMP.

108. With regard to JARPA, Australia asserts that the Scientific Committee was unable to conclude at the final review workshop held in 2006 that any of JARPA's stated objectives had

been met, including an adequately precise estimate of natural mortality rate. Japan maintains that recommendations made in the course of JARPA's final review led to further analysis of the JARPA data and that in 2010 the Scientific Committee accepted an estimate of natural mortality rate based on those data. Overall, the Parties disagree whether JARPA made a scientific contribution to the conservation and management of whales. The Court is not called upon to address that disagreement.

(b) *JARPA II*

109. In March 2005, Japan submitted to the Scientific Committee a document entitled "Plan for the Second Phase of the Japanese Whale Research Program under Special Permit in the Antarctic (JARPA II) Monitoring of the Antarctic Ecosystem and Development of New Management Objectives for Whale Resources" (hereinafter the "JARPA II Research Plan"). Following review of the JARPA II Research Plan by the Scientific Committee, Japan granted the first set of annual special permits for JARPA II in November 2005, after which JARPA II became operational. As was the case under JARPA, the special permits for JARPA II are issued by Japan to the Institute of Cetacean Research, a foundation established in 1987 as a "public-benefit corporation" under Japan's Civil Code. The evidence indicates that the Institute of Cetacean Research has historically been subsidized by Japan and that Japan exercises a supervisory role over the institute's activities. Japan has granted special permits to that institute for JARPA II for each season since 2005–2006.

110. The JARPA II Research Plan describes key elements of the programme's design: the research objectives, research period and area, research methods, sample sizes, and the expected effect on whale stocks. As further discussed below, the programme contemplates the lethal sampling of three whale species: Antarctic minke whales, fin whales and humpback whales (see paragraph 123). This Judgment uses the terms "Antarctic minke whales" and "minke whales" interchangeably.

111. Minke whales, fin whales and humpback whales are all baleen whales, meaning they have no teeth; baleen whales instead use baleen plates in the mouth to filter their food from sea water. Antarctic minke whales are among the smallest baleen whales: an average adult is between 10 and 11 metres long and weighs between 8 and 10 tons. The fin whale is the second largest whale species (after the blue whale): an average adult is between 25 and 26 metres long and its body mass is between 60 and 80 tons. Humpback whales are larger than minke whales but smaller than fin whales: adults are between 14 and 17 metres long.

112. The Court will now outline the key elements of JARPA II, as set forth in the Research Plan and further explained by Japan in these proceedings.

(i) Research objectives

113. The JARPA II Research Plan identifies four research objectives: (1) Monitoring of the Antarctic ecosystem; (2) Modelling competition among whale species and future management objectives; (3) Elucidation of temporal and spatial changes in stock structure; and (4) Improving the management procedure for Antarctic minke whale stocks.

114. *Objective No. 1.* The JARPA II Research Plan states that JARPA II will monitor changes relating to whale abundance and biological parameters, prey density and abundance, and the effects of contaminants on cetaceans, and the cetaceans' habitat, in three whale species Antarctic minke whales, humpback whales and fin whales and that "[t]he obtained data will be indicators of changes in the Antarctic ecosystem". The Research Plan stresses the importance of detecting changes in the whale populations and their habitat "as soon as possible" in order "to predict their effects on the stocks, and to provide information necessary for the development of appropriate management policies". Specifically, JARPA II will monitor "changes in recruitment, pregnancy rate, age at maturity and other biological parameters by sampling survey", while "abundance" will be monitored through "sighting surveys". JARPA II will also monitor prey consumption and changes in blubber thickness over time, as well as contaminant accumulation and the effects of toxins on cetaceans.

115. *Objective No. 2.* The second objective refers to "modelling competition among whale species and future management objectives". The JARPA II Research Plan states that "[t]here is a strong indication of competition among whale species in the research area" and that JARPA II therefore seeks to explore "hypotheses related to this competition". The Research Plan refers to the "krill surplus hypothesis". As presented to the Court, this hypothesis refers to two interrelated ideas: first, that the previous overhunting of certain whale species (including fin and humpback whales) created a surplus of krill (a shared food source) for other predators, including the smaller minke whale, which led to an increase in the abundance of that species; and, secondly, that a subsequent recovery in the humpback and fin whale populations (since the commercial catch of those species was banned in 1963 and 1976, respectively) has resulted in increased competition among these larger whales and minke whales for krill. The JARPA II Research Plan suggests that Antarctic minke whale stocks may decrease as a result of current conditions.

116. Japan explains that "JARPA II . . . does not purport to verify the validity of the krill surplus hypothesis" but instead seeks "to incorporate data on other animals/fish that prey on krill in order to develop a 'model of competition among whale species'" that may help to explain changes in the abundance levels of different whale species. In Japan's view, the "krill surplus hypothesis" is just one of several ideas (in addition to, for example, the effects of climate change) that JARPA II is designed to explore in connection with its construction of "an ecosystem model" for the Antarctic. The JARPA II Research Plan further explains that such a model may contribute to establishing "new management objectives" for the IWC, such as finding ways to accelerate the recovery of blue and fin whales, and will examine "the possible effects of the resumption of commercial whaling on the relative numbers of the various species and stocks". Mr. Mangel, the expert called by Australia, referred to the "krill surplus hypothesis" as the "only clearly identifiable hypothesis" in JARPA II.

117. *Objective No. 3.* The third objective concerns stock structure. With regard to fin whales, the programme's objective is to compare current stock structure to historic information on that species. With regard to humpback whales and Antarctic minke whales, the plan describes a need "to investigate shifts in stock boundaries" on a yearly basis.

118. *Objective No. 4.* The fourth objective concerns the management procedure for Antarctic minke whale stocks and builds upon the other three objectives. The JARPA II Research Plan states that the first objective will provide information on biological parameters "necessary for managing the stocks more efficiently under a revised RMP", the second objective "will lead to examining a multi-species management model for the future", and the third "will supply information for establishing management areas in the Antarctic Ocean". According to the Research Plan, the information relating to the "effects arising from inter-species relationships among the whale species" could demonstrate that the determination of a catch quota for Antarctic minke whales under the RMP would be too low, perhaps even set unnecessarily at zero. As noted above (see paragraph 107), the Parties disagree about the type of information necessary to implement the RMP.

(ii) Research period and area

119. Japan explains that JARPA II is "a long-term research programme and has no specified termination date because its primary objective (i.e., monitoring the Antarctic ecosystem) requires a continuing programme of research". JARPA II is structured in six-year phases. After each six-year phase, a review will be held to consider revisions to the programme. The first such six-year phase was completed after the 2010–2011 season. Following some delay, the first periodic review of JARPA II by the Scientific Committee is scheduled to take place in 2014.

120. The JARPA II Research Plan operates in an area that is located within the Southern Ocean Sanctuary established in paragraph 7 *(b)* of the Schedule to the Convention.

(iii) Research methods and sample size

121. The Research Plan indicates that JARPA II is designed to use a mix of lethal and non-lethal methods to pursue the research objectives, a point that Japan also made in these proceedings.

122. Japan asserts that lethal sampling is "indispensable" to JARPA II's first two objectives, relating to ecosystem monitoring and multi-species competition modelling. The JARPA II Research Plan explains that the third objective will rely on "genetic and biological markers" taken from whales that have been lethally sampled in connection with the first two objectives, as well as non-lethal methods, namely biopsy sampling from blue, fin and humpback whales.

123. The Research Plan provides that in each season the sample sizes for fin and humpback whales will be 50 and the sample size for Antarctic minke whales will be 850, plus or minus 10 per cent (i.e., a maximum of 935 per season). These target sample sizes are discussed in greater detail below (see paragraphs 157–198).

124. With regard to non-lethal methods, the JARPA II Research Plan describes the intended use of biopsy sampling and satellite tagging in addition to whale sighting surveys. According to Japan, it makes extensive use of non-lethal methods to obtain data and information to the extent practicable.

125. As to JARPA II's operation, Japan explains that JARPA II vessels follow "scientifically determined tracklines", including in areas "where the density of the target species is low", to obtain a proper distribution of samples and observations. Whales from the targeted species are taken if they are encountered within 3 nautical miles of the predetermined trackline being followed by a JARPA II vessel. If a lone whale is encountered, it will be taken; if a school of whales is encountered, two whales will be taken at random.

(iv) Effect on whale stocks

126. The JARPA II Research Plan sets out the bases for Japan's conclusion that the lethal sample sizes described above are designed to avoid having any adverse effect on the targeted whale stocks. The Research Plan states that, based on current abundance estimates, the planned take of each species is too small to have any negative effect. Japan also explains that the JARPA II Research Plan used conservative estimates of Antarctic minke whale abundance to assess the effects of the target sample size for that species.

B. Whether the design and implementation of JARPA II are reasonable in relation to achieving the programme's stated research objectives

127. The Court observes that the JARPA II Research Plan describes areas of inquiry that correspond to four research objectives and presents a programme of activities that involves the systematic collection and analysis of data by scientific personnel. The research objectives come within the research categories identified by the Scientific Committee in Annexes Y and P (see paragraph 58 above). Based on the information before it, the Court thus finds that the JARPA II activities involving the lethal sampling of whales can broadly be characterized as "scientific research". There is no need therefore, in the context of this case, to examine generally the concept of "scientific research". Accordingly, the Court's examination of the evidence with respect to JARPA II will focus on whether the killing, taking and treating of whales in pursuance of JARPA II is *for purposes of* scientific research and thus may be authorized by special permits granted under Article VIII, paragraph 1, of the Convention. To this end and in light of the applicable standard of review (see paragraph 67 above), the Court will examine whether the design and implementation of JARPA II are reasonable in relation to achieving the programme's stated research objectives, taking into account the elements identified above (see paragraph 88).

(a) *Japan's decisions regarding the use of lethal methods*

128. Lethal methods are central to the design of JARPA II. However, it should be noted that the Parties disagree as to the reasons for that.

129. Japan states that it does not use lethal methods more than it considers necessary to meet research objectives and that lethal methods are "indispensable" in JARPA II because the programme's first two objectives require data that can only realistically be obtained from internal organs and stomach contents. Japan accepts that non-lethal biopsies and satellite tagging have been used for certain larger species of whales but states that these methods are not practical

for minke whales. Japan also points out that, while certain relevant data may be obtainable by non-lethal means, such data would be of lesser quality or reliability, and, in some cases, would involve "unrealistic" amounts of time and expense.

130. By contrast, Australia maintains that Japan has an "unbending commitment to lethal take" and that "JARPA II is premised on the killing of whales". According to Australia, JARPA II, like JARPA before it, is "merely a guise" under which to continue commercial whaling. One of the experts called by Australia, Mr. Mangel, stated that JARPA II "simply assert[s] but [does] not demonstrate that lethal take is required". Australia further contends that a variety of non-lethal research methods, including satellite tagging, biopsy sampling and sighting surveys, are more effective ways to gather information for whale research and that the available technology has improved dramatically over the past quarter century since JARPA was first launched.

131. As previously noted, Australia does not challenge the use of lethal research methods per se. Australia accepts that there may be situations in which research objectives can, in fact, require lethal methods, a view also taken by the two experts that it called. However, it maintains that lethal methods must be used in a research programme under Article VIII only when "no other means are available" and the use of lethal methods is thus "essential" to the stated objectives of a programme.

132. In support of their respective contentions about the use of lethal methods in JARPA II, the Parties address three points: first, whether non-lethal methods are feasible as a means to obtain data relevant to the JARPA II research objectives; secondly, whether the data that JARPA II collects through lethal methods are reliable or valuable; and thirdly, whether before launching JARPA II Japan considered the possibility of making more extensive use of non-lethal methods. The Court considers these points in turn.

133. The Court notes that the Parties agree that non-lethal methods are not a feasible means to examine internal organs and stomach contents. The Court therefore considers that the evidence shows that, at least for some of the data sought by JARPA II researchers, non-lethal methods are not feasible.

134. Turning to the reliability and value of data collected in JARPA II, the Court heard conflicting evidence. For example, the experts called by Australia questioned the reliability of age data obtained from ear plugs and the scientific value of the examination of stomach contents, given pre-existing knowledge of the diet of the target species. The expert called by Japan disputed Australia's contentions regarding the reliability and value of data collected in JARPA II. This disagreement appears to be about a matter of scientific opinion.

135. Taking into account the evidence indicating that non-lethal alternatives are not feasible, at least for the collection of certain data, and given that the value and reliability of such data are a matter of scientific opinion, the Court finds no basis to conclude that the use of lethal methods is per se unreasonable in the context of JARPA II. Instead, it is necessary to look more closely at the details of Japan's decisions regarding the use of lethal methods in JARPA II, discussed immediately below, and the scale of their use in the programme, to which the Court will turn at paragraph 145 below.

136. The Court next examines a third aspect of the use of lethal methods in JARPA II, which is the extent to which Japan has considered whether the stated objectives of JARPA II could be achieved by making greater use of non-lethal methods, rather than by lethal sampling. The Court recalls that the JARPA II Research Plan sets lethal sample sizes at 850 minke whales (plus or minus 10 per cent), 50 fin whales and 50 humpback whales (see paragraph 123 above), as compared to a lethal sample size in JARPA of 400 minke whales (plus or minus 10 per cent) and no whales of the other two species (see paragraph 104 above).

137. As previously indicated, the fact that a programme uses lethal methods despite the availability of non-lethal alternatives does not mean that a special permit granted for such a programme necessarily falls outside Article VIII, paragraph 1 (see paragraph 83). There are,

however, three reasons why the JARPA II Research Plan should have included some analysis of the feasibility of non-lethal methods as a means of reducing the planned scale of lethal sampling in the new programme. First, IWC resolutions and Guidelines call upon States parties to take into account whether research objectives can be achieved using non-lethal methods. Japan has accepted that it is under an obligation to give due regard to such recommendations. Secondly, as noted above (see paragraphs 80 and 129), Japan states that, for reasons of scientific policy, "[i]t does not . . . use lethal means more than it considers necessary" and that non-lethal alternatives are not practical or feasible in all cases. This implies the undertaking of some type of analysis in order to ascertain that lethal sampling is not being used to a greater extent than is necessary in relation to achieving a programme's stated research objectives. Thirdly, the two experts called by Australia referred to significant advances in a wide range of non-lethal research techniques over the past 20 years and described some of those developments and their potential application with regard to JARPA II's stated objectives. It stands to reason that a research proposal that contemplates extensive lethal sampling would need to analyse the potential applicability of these advances in relation to a programme's design.

138. The Court did not hear directly from Japanese scientists involved in designing JARPA II. During the oral proceedings, however, a Member of the Court asked Japan what analysis it had conducted of the feasibility of non-lethal methods prior to setting the sample sizes for each year of JARPA II, and what bearing, if any, such analysis had had on the target sample sizes. In response, Japan referred to two documents: (1) Annex H to the 1997 interim review of JARPA by the Scientific Committee and (2) an unpublished paper that Japan submitted to the Scientific Committee in 2007.

139. The first of these documents is not an analysis of JARPA II and is not a study by Japan. It is a one-page summary by the Scientific Committee of opposing views within the Committee on the need to use lethal methods to collect information relating to stock structure. Japan stated that this document "formed the basis of section IX of the 2005 JARPA II Research Plan". Section IX, entitled "Necessity of Lethal Methods", comprises two short paragraphs that contain no reference to feasibility studies by Japan or to any consideration by Japan of developments in non-lethal research methods since the 1997 JARPA review. Japan identified no other analysis that was included in, or was contemporaneous with, the JARPA II Research Plan.

140. The 2007 document to which Japan refers the Court discusses the necessity of lethal methods in JARPA, not JARPA II. It states in summary format the authors' conclusions as to why certain biological parameters (listed in relation to particular JARPA objectives) required (or did not require) lethal sampling, without any analysis and without reference to the JARPA II objectives.

141. Thus, there is no evidence of studies of the feasibility or practicability of non-lethal methods, either in setting the JARPA II sample sizes or in later years in which the programme has maintained the same sample size targets. There is no evidence that Japan has examined whether it would be feasible to combine a smaller lethal take (in particular, of minke whales) and an increase in non-lethal sampling as a means to achieve JARPA II's research objectives. The absence of any evidence pointing to consideration of the feasibility of non-lethal methods was not explained.

142. Decisions about the use of lethal methods in JARPA II must also be evaluated in light of the Court's previous conclusion that a programme for purposes of scientific research may not use lethal methods on a larger scale than is reasonable in relation to achieving its stated objectives in order to fund that research (see paragraph 94 above).

143. The 2007 paper that Japan called to the Court's attention (see paragraphs 138 and 140 above) states that JARPA's research objectives, which required the examination of internal organs and a large number of samples, meant that non-lethal methods were "impractical, cost ineffective and prohibitively expensive". It also states that "whale research is costly and

therefore lethal methods which could recover the cost for research [are] more desirable". No analysis is included in support of these conclusions. There is no explanation of the relative costs of any methods or a comparison of how the expense of lethal sampling, as conducted under JARPA (or under JARPA II, which by 2007 was already operational), might be measured against the cost of a research programme that more extensively uses non-lethal alternatives.

144. The Court concludes that the papers to which Japan directed it reveal little analysis of the feasibility of using non-lethal methods to achieve the JARPA II research objectives. Nor do they point to consideration of the possibility of making more extensive use of non-lethal methods in order to reduce or eliminate the need for lethal sampling, either when JARPA II was proposed or in subsequent years. Given the expanded use of lethal methods in JARPA II, as compared to JARPA, this is difficult to reconcile with Japan's obligation to give due regard to IWC resolutions and Guidelines and its statement that JARPA II uses lethal methods only to the extent necessary to meet its scientific objectives. In addition, the 2007 paper to which Japan refers the Court suggests a preference for lethal sampling because it provides a source of funding to offset the cost of the research.

(b) *The scale of the use of lethal methods in JARPA II*

145. The scale of lethal methods used in JARPA II is determined by sample sizes, that is, the number of whales of each species to be killed each year. The Parties introduced extensive evidence on this topic, relying in particular on the JARPA II Research Plan, the actions taken under it in its implementation, and the opinions of the experts that each Party called.

146. Taking into account the Parties' arguments and the evidence presented, the Court will begin by comparing the JARPA II sample sizes to the sample sizes set in JARPA. It will then describe how sample sizes were determined in the JARPA II Research Plan and present the Parties' views on the sample sizes set for each of the three species. Finally, the Court will compare the target sample sizes set in the JARPA II Research Plan with the actual take of each species during the programme. Each of these aspects of the sample sizes selected for JARPA II was the subject of extensive argument by Australia, to which Japan responded in turn.

(i) A comparison of JARPA II sample sizes to JARPA sample sizes

147. The question whether the lethal sampling of whales under JARPA was "for purposes of scientific research" under Article VIII, paragraph 1, of the Convention is not before the Court. The Court draws no legal conclusions about any aspect of JARPA, including the sample sizes used in that programme. However, the Court notes that Japan has drawn comparisons between JARPA and JARPA II in addressing the latter programme and, in particular, the sample sizes that were chosen for JARPA II.

148. As noted above (see paragraph 104), JARPA originally proposed an annual sample size of 825 minke whales per season. This was reduced to 300 at JARPA's launch, and after a number of years was increased to 400 (plus or minus 10 per cent). Thus, the JARPA II sample size for minke whales of 850 (plus or minus 10 per cent) is approximately double the minke whale sample size for the last years of JARPA. As also noted above (see paragraph 110), JARPA II also sets sample sizes for two additional species fin and humpback whales that were not the target of lethal sampling under JARPA.

149. To explain the larger minke whale sample size and the addition of sample sizes for fin and humpback whales in JARPA II generally, Japan stresses that the programme's research objectives are "different and more sophisticated" than those of JARPA. Japan also asserts that the emergence of "a growing concern about climate change, including global warming, necessitated research whaling of a different kind from JARPA". In particular, Japan argues that "JARPA was focused on a one-time estimation of different biological parameters for minke whales, but JARPA II is a much more ambitious programme which tries to model competition among whale species and to detect changes in various biological parameters and the ecosystem". It is on this basis, Japan asserts, that the "new objectives" of JARPA II "notably ecosystem

research" dictate the larger sample size for minke whales and the addition of sample size targets for fin and humpback whales.

150. Given Japan's emphasis on the new JARPA II objectives particularly ecosystem research and constructing a model of multi-species competition to explain the larger JARPA II sample size for minke whales and the addition of two new species, the comparison between JARPA and JARPA II deserves close attention.

151. At the outset, the Court observes that a comparison of the two research plans reveals considerable overlap between the subjects, objectives, and methods of the two programmes, rather than dissimilarity. For example, the research proposals for both programmes describe research broadly aimed at elucidating the role of minke whales in the Antarctic ecosystem. One of the experts called by Australia, Mr. Mangel, stated that JARPA II "almost exclusively focuses data collection on minke whales", which, the Court notes, was also true of JARPA. Specifically, both programmes are focused on the collection of data through lethal sampling to monitor various biological parameters in minke whales, including, in particular, data relevant to population trends as well as data relating to feeding and nutrition (involving the examination of stomach contents and blubber thickness). JARPA included both the study of stock structure to improve stock management and research on the effect of environmental change on whales (objectives that were not included in the original research proposal for JARPA, but were added later), and JARPA II also includes the study of these issues.

152. The Court notes that Japan states that "the research items and methods" of JARPA II are "basically the same as those employed for JARPA", which is why "the explanation for the necessity of lethal sampling provided regarding JARPA also applies to JARPA II". Australia makes the point that "in practice Japan collects the same data" under JARPA II "that it collected under JARPA". Japan also asserts broadly that both programmes "are designed to further proper and effective management of whale stocks and their conservation and sustainable use".

153. Taken together, the overall research objectives of JARPA and JARPA II, as well as the subjects of study and methods used (i.e., extensive lethal sampling of minke whales) thus appear to have much in common, even if certain aspects differ. These similarities cast doubt on Japan's argument that the JARPA II objectives relating to ecosystem monitoring and multi-species competition are distinguishing features of the latter programme that call for a significant increase in the minke whale sample size and the lethal sampling of two additional species.

154. There is another reason to question whether the increased minke whale sample size in the JARPA II Research Plan is accounted for by differences between the two programmes. As previously noted, Japan launched JARPA II without waiting for the results of the Scientific Committee's final review of JARPA. Japan's explanation to the Court was that "it was important to keep the consistency and continuity in data obtained in the research area" and that waiting to commence JARPA II only following the final review of JARPA would have meant "no survey in one or two years". The JARPA II Research Plan also frames the monitoring of whale abundance trends and biological parameters as designed "to secure continuity with the data collected in JARPA".

155. This emphasis on the importance of continuity confirms the overlap in the focus of the two programmes and further undermines Japan's reliance on JARPA II's objectives to explain the larger minke whale sample size in JARPA II. Japan does not explain, for example, why it would not have been sufficient to limit the lethal take of minke whales during the "feasibility" phase of JARPA II (its first two years) to 440 minke whales, the maximum number of minke whales that were targeted during the final season of JARPA. Instead, 853 minke whales were taken during the first year of JARPA II, in addition to ten fin whales. This also meant that JARPA II began using the higher sample size for minke whales, and similar research methods (e.g., the examination of ear plugs to obtain age data and the examination of blubber thickness

to assess nutritional conditions) without having yet received the benefit of any feedback from the final review of JARPA by the Scientific Committee.

156. These weaknesses in Japan's explanation for the decision to proceed with the JARPA II sample sizes prior to the final review of JARPA lend support to the view that those sample sizes and the launch date for JARPA II were not driven by strictly scientific considerations. These weaknesses also give weight to the contrary theory advanced by Australia that Japan's priority was to maintain whaling operations without any pause, just as it had done previously by commencing JARPA in the first year after the commercial whaling moratorium had come into effect for it.

(ii) Determination of species-specific sample sizes

157. Bearing in mind these observations regarding Japan's general explanation for the difference between the JARPA and JARPA II sample sizes, the Court turns next to the evidence regarding the way that Japan determined the specific target sample sizes for each of the three species in JARPA II.

158. As a general matter, Australia asserts that Japan has failed to provide "a coherent scientific rationale" for the JARPA II sample sizes. One of the experts called by Australia, Mr. Mangel, took the view that "[i]t is very difficult to understand the statistical basis for setting the level of lethal take" in JARPA II. He focused in particular on the determination of the particular sample sizes that would be required to study different parameters, stating that "a range is given and then a particular number is picked without any explanation for that number". In Australia's view, the JARPA II Research Plan fails adequately to provide the rationales for the choices made therein and employs inconsistent methodologies. In essence, Australia's contention is that Japan decided that it wished to take approximately 850 minke whales for purposes other than scientific research and then "retro-fitted" individual sample sizes to justify the overall sample size.

159. Japan asserts that, contrary to Australia's characterization of the programme, the JARPA II sample sizes "were calculated on the basis of carefully selected parameters, using a standard scientific formula, whilst also taking into account the potential effects of research on whale populations". Japan also argues that the sample sizes are based on "norms used by the Scientific Committee", which has never expressed "any specific concern about the JARPA II sample size".

The expert called by Japan, Mr. Walløe, also addressed the setting of sample sizes in JARPA II. He stated that "Japanese scientists have not always given completely transparent and clear explanations of how sample sizes were calculated or determined". He indicated, however, that the minke whale sample size seemed to be "of the right magnitude" on the basis of his own calculations (which were not provided to the Court). In addition, Professor Walløe stated his impression that JARPA II sample sizes had been "influenced by funding considerations", although he found this unobjectionable.

160. Based on Japan's arguments and the evidence that it has presented, including, in particular, the JARPA II Research Plan, the Court discerns five steps to this process of sample size determination.

161. The first step is to identify the types of information that are relevant to the broader objectives of the research. Japan refers to these as "research items". For example, the research items of interest in JARPA II include pregnancy rate, the age at which whales reach sexual maturity and feeding patterns.

162. The second step is to identify a means to obtain the data relevant to a given research item. For example, Japan maintains that it is necessary to collect ear plugs from whales in order to determine age, that stomach contents can be examined to evaluate eating habits, and that measuring blubber thickness is a means to study changes in prey conditions (e.g., the availability of krill as a food source).

163. After it has been determined that information relevant to a research item is to be obtained from lethal sampling, the third step is to determine how many whales are necessary in order to

have a sufficiently large number of samples to detect changes relevant to the particular research item. For several research items, the determination of this number takes into account at least three variables: (i) the level of accuracy sought; (ii) the change to be measured; and (iii) the research period (i.e., the time within which a change is to be detected). This means that the number of whales needed for a particular research item depends, for example, on how accurate the results are required to be, on whether the change to be measured is large or small, and on the period over which one seeks to detect that change.

164. For a given research item, a standard equation is used to perform a calculation that shows the effect that differences in these variables would have on sample size. Australia did not challenge Japan's use of that equation.

165. To illustrate this third step, the Court calls attention to one example from the JARPA II Research Plan that shows how the researchers approached the selection of a sample size for a particular research item: the change in the proportion of pregnant minke whales in the populationof mature female whales. The relevant table from the Research Plan, which appears as Table 2 to Appendix 6 ("Sample sizes of Antarctic minke, humpback and fin whales required for statistical examination of yearly trend in biological parameters") to that document, is reproduced below. The far-left column shows that the JARPA II researchers considered using either a six-year or a 12-year research period and the second column shows that they considered using either of two estimates of the "initial rate" (i.e., whether the proportion of pregnant minke whales in the population of mature female whales at the start of the research was 80 or 90 per cent). The researchers then calculated how many whales would be required depending on the research period and the estimated "initial rate" to detect different rates of change in the proportion of pregnant minke whales (shown in percentages in the top row of the chart). The table is set forth below:

Table 2. Total sample size of Antarctic minke whales required for statistical examination of yearly trend [in the proportion of pregnant minke whales in the population of mature female whales]											
Research Period	Initial rate (%)	Rate of Change									
		+1%	-1%	+1.5%	-1.5%	+2%	-2%	+2.5%	-2.5%	+3%	-3%
6 years	80%	2022	2544	984	1089	618	591	462	369	402	249
	90%	912	1617	609	663	–	348	–	210	–	138
12 years	80%	189	312	129	132	–	72	–	45	–	30
	90%	–	213	–	87	–	45	–	27	–	18

(*Source:* Counter-Memorial of Japan, Vol. IV, Ann. 150, App. 6.)

166. This table illustrates how the selection of a particular value for each variable affects the sample size. For example, the decision to use a particular research period has a pronounced effect on the sample size. In order to detect a rate of change of minus 1.5 per cent and assuming an initial rate of 90 per cent (which were the criteria ultimately chosen by JARPA II researchers), a six-year period requires an annual sample size of 663 whales while the 12-year period requires an annual sample size of 87 whales. The table also illustrates that small differences in the rate of change to detect can have a considerable effect on sample size. For example, in order to detect a change of minus 1 per cent over a six-year period (assuming an initial rate of 90 per cent), the required yearly sample size is 1,617 whales. To detect a change of minus 2 per cent under the same circumstances, the required yearly sample size is 348 whales.

167. The fourth step is the selection of a particular sample size for each research item from the range of sample sizes that have been calculated depending on these different underlying decisions relating to level of accuracy, rate of change and research period. With respect to the above example, the JARPA II researchers recommended a sample size in the range of 663 to 1,617 whales in order to detect a rate of change from minus 1 to minus 1.5 per cent within a six-year period.

168. Based on the evidence presented by Japan, after the JARPA II researchers select a particular sample size for each research item, the fifth and final step in the calculation of sample

size is to choose an overall sample size in light of the different sample sizes (or ranges of sample sizes, as in the above example) required for different aspects of the study. Because different research items require different sample sizes, it is necessary to select an overall sample size for each species that takes into account these different research requirements.

169. To determine the overall sample size for Antarctic minke whales in JARPA II, for example, Japan asserts that it looked at the possible sample size ranges for each research item and selected the sample size of 850 (plus or minus 10 per cent) because that number of whales can provide sufficient data on most research items with "a reasonable level of statistical accuracy overall", but "will causeno harm to the stock".

170. It is important to clarify which steps in the above-described process give rise to disagreement between the Parties, in order to bring into focus the reasons for the Parties' detailed arguments in relation to sample sizes. As discussed above, there is disagreement about whether lethal methods are warranted and whether the information being gathered through the use of lethal methods is reliable and valuable (the first and second steps), but that disagreement is addressed elsewhere in this Judgment (see paragraphs 128–144). The proceedings revealed some areas of methodological agreement in respect of the third step. For example, the equation and the calculations used to create tables like the one shown above are not in dispute. There is also agreement that researchers need to make choices about variables such as the rate of change to detect or the length of a research period as part of the design of a scientific programme.

171. For present purposes, the critical differences between the Parties emerge at the fourth and fifth steps of the process of setting sample sizes. These differences are reflected in the arguments of the Parties summarized above (see paragraphs 157–159).

172. In considering these contentions by the Parties, the Court reiterates that it does not seek here to pass judgment on the scientific merit of the JARPA II objectives and that the activities of JARPA II can broadly be characterized as "scientific research" (see paragraphs 88 and 127 above). With regard to the setting of sample sizes, the Court is also not in a position to conclude whether a particular value for a given variable (e.g., the research period or rate of change to detect) has scientific advantages over another. Rather, the Court seeks here only to evaluate whether the evidence supports a conclusion that the sample sizes are reasonable in relation to achieving JARPA II's stated objectives.

173. The Court begins by considering the way that Japan set the target sample sizes for fin and humpback whales.

(1) *Fin and humpback whales*

174. For fin whales and humpback whales, the annual JARPA II lethal sample size is 50 per species. The JARPA II Research Plan states that the same conditions and criteria were used to set sample sizes for the two species, so the Court considers them together.

175. Sample sizes for both species were calculated on the basis of two "research items": apparent pregnancy rate and age at sexual maturity. The JARPA II Research Plan describes these research items, which according to Japan involve the examination of ear plugs and reproductive organs, as essential to the objectives of the programme. The Research Plan does not indicate the reason for using only two parameters to establish the sample sizes for these two species, as compared to the larger number of parameters used to calculate the minke whale sample size (see paragraph 182 below). As noted above, however (see paragraphs 165–166), a review of the JARPA II Research Plan establishes that decisions concerning, for example, the particular rate of change to detect, among other relevant variables, have a pronounced impact on the resulting sample size.

176. Although the JARPA II Research Plan sets forth possible sample sizes for fin and humpback whales that contemplate both six-year and 12-year research periods, the plan explains that researchers chose to use the 12-year research period for both species. It states that a six-year period would be "preferable since the research programme will be reviewed every six years" but would require "large" sample sizes. The Research Plan states that a 12-year

period was thus chosen as a "precautionary approach". In the oral proceedings, Japan offered an additional reason for the choice of a 12-year period: that a shorter period is unnecessary for these two species because implementation of the RMP for fin and humpback whales is not yet under consideration.

177. The Court does not need to decide whether a particular research period, taken in isolation, is more or less appropriate for a given species of whales. The selection of a 12-year period for two of three species, however, must be considered in light of other aspects of the design of JARPA II, including the selection of a six-year research period for detecting various changes in minke whales. In particular, Japan emphasizes multi-species competition and ecosystem research as explanations for the minke whale sample size of 850, as well as for including fin and humpback whales in the programme. JARPA II was designed with a six-year "research phase" after which a review will be held and revisions may be made. It is difficult to see how there could be a meaningful review of JARPA II in respect of these two critical objectives after six years if the research period for two of three species is 12 years.

178. Thus, the selection of a 12-year research period for fin whales and humpback whales is one factor that casts doubt on the centrality of the objectives that Japan highlights to justify the minke whale sample size of 850 (plus or minus 10 per cent).

179. Another factor casts doubt on whether the design of JARPA II is reasonable in relation to achieving the programme's stated objectives. The overall sample sizes selected for fin and humpback whales 50 whales of each species per year are not large enough to allow for the measurement of all the trends that the programme seeks to measure. Specifically, the JARPA II Research Plan states that at least 131 whales of each species should be taken annually to detect a particular rate of change in age at sexual maturity. The Research Plan does not indicate whether the researchers decided to accept a lower level of accuracy or instead adjusted the rate of change that they sought to detect by targeting fewer whales, nor did Japan explain this in the present proceedings. In light of the calculations of its own scientists, JARPA II does not appear designed to produce statistically relevant information on at least one central research item to which the JARPA II Research Plan gives particular importance.

180. The Court also notes that the expert called by Japan, Mr. Walløe, raised concerns about the fin whale component of JARPA II that go beyond the sample size. Mr. Walløe testified that the fin whale proposal was "not very well conceived" for two reasons. He stated that random sampling of fin whales within the JARPA II research area is not possible, first, because the main fin whale population is beyond the JARPA II research area further to the north and, secondly, because the JARPA II vessels can only accommodate the lethal take of smaller fin whales (a point also raised by Australia). The Court recalls that Japan identified random sampling as an element of a programme for purposes of scientific research.

181. The Court finds that the JARPA II Research Plan overall provides only limited information regarding the basis for the decisions used to calculate the fin and humpback whale sample size. These sample sizes were set using a 12-year period, despite the fact that a shorter six-year period is used to set the minke whale sample size and that JARPA II is to be reviewed after each six-year research phase. Based on Japan's own calculations, the sample sizes for fin and humpback whales are too small to produce statistically useful results. These shortcomings, in addition to the problems specific to the decision to take fin whales, as noted in the preceding paragraph, are important to the Court's assessment of whether the overall design of JARPA II is reasonable in relation to the programme's objectives, because Japan connects the minke whale sample size (discussed below) to the ecosystem research and multi-species competition objectives that, in turn, are premised on the lethal sampling of fin and humpback whales.

(2) *Antarctic minke whales*

182. The Court turns next to the design of the sample size for Antarctic minke whales in JARPA II. The JARPA II Research Plan indicates that the overall sample size for minke whales

was chosen following Japan's calculation of the minimum sample size for a number of different research items, including age at sexual maturity, apparent pregnancy rate, blubber thickness, contaminant levels, mixing patterns between different stocks, and population trends. The plan further states that for most parameters "the sample sizes calculated were in a range of 800–1,000 animals with more than 800 being desirable". Japan describes the process that it followed to determine the overall sample size for minke whales with reference to the following illustration that appears as Figure 5-4 in its Counter-Memorial:

— Figure 5-4: "Necessary annual sample sizes for respective research items under JARPA II, which was calculated by the established statistical procedures (*source:* Institute of Cetacean Research)."

[Omitted.]

183. As depicted in this illustration, the overall sample size falls within a range that corresponds to what the JARPA II Research Plan sets forth as the minimum requirements for most of the research that JARPA II is designed to undertake. Japan asserts that for this reason, the overall annual lethal sample size was set at 850 (plus or minus 10 per cent, which allows for a maximum of 935 minke whales per year). As noted above (see paragraphs 159 and 169), Japan considered this number of whales to be sufficient for purposes of research, taking into account the need to avoid causing harm to the stocks.

184. In contrast, in Australia's view, Japan started with the goal of establishing a sample size of approximately 850 minke whales per year and then "retro-fitted" the programme's design by selecting values designed to generate sample sizes for particular research items that corresponded to Japan's desired overall sample size. Australia emphasizes that the JARPA II Research Plan is not clear in stating the reasons for the selection of the particular sample size appertaining to each research item. Australia also notes that different choices as to values for certain variables would have led to dramatically smaller sample sizes, but that, in general, the JARPA II Research Plan provides no explanation for the underlying decisions to use values that generate larger sample sizes. These shortcomings, in Australia's view, support its conclusion that the minke whale sample size was set not for purposes of scientific research, but instead to meet Japan's funding requirements and commercial objectives.

185. In light of these divergent views, the Court will consider the evidence regarding Japan's selection of the various minimum sample sizes that it chose for different individual research items, which form the basis for the overall sample size for minke whales. As noted above (see paragraph 172), the purpose of such an inquiry is not to second-guess the scientific judgments made by individual scientists or by Japan, but rather to examine whether Japan, in light of JARPA II's stated research objectives, has demonstrated a reasonable basis for annual sample sizes pertaining to particular research items, leading to the overall sample size of 850 (plus or minus 10 per cent) for minke whales.

186. In the JARPA II Research Plan, individual sample size calculations are presented with respect to each of the items referred to in the above illustration: age at sexual maturity, apparent pregnancy rate, blubber thickness, pathological monitoring (i.e., monitoring of contaminant levels), mixing patterns between different stocks, and "DNA mark-recapture", which Japan describes as a method for researching population trends.

187. The Court notes at the outset that the JARPA II Research Plan states that for all parameters, "a sample size needed to detect changes in a six-year period . . . has been adopted as the pertinent criterion". The JARPA II Research Plan does not explain the reason for this threshold decision, but Japan offered some explanations during these proceedings, which are discussed below (see paragraph 192).

188. The evidence shows that the JARPA II Research Plan lacks transparency in the reasons for selecting particular sample sizes for individual research items. This is a matter on which the experts called by the two Parties agreed, as described above (see paragraphs 158–159).

With the exception of one variable (discussed in the next paragraph), the JARPA II Research Plan provides very limited information regarding the selection of a particular value for a given variable. For example, in the Court's view, there is no consistent effort to explain why, for the various research items relating to the monitoring of biological parameters, JARPA II is designed to detect one particular rate or degree of change over another that would result in a lower sample size. These shortcomings of the JARPA II Research Plan have particular prominence in light of the fact that the particular choices of rate and degree of change consistently lead to a sample size of approximately 850 minke whales per year.

189. An exception to this pattern is arguably the discussion of the sample size applicable to the study of the age at sexual maturity of minke whales, as to which the JARPA II Research Plan furnishes some details about the factors that Japan considered in selecting the particular rate of change to detect. For this research item, the Research Plan also offers an indication of the relationship between the data sought and the first two JARPA II research objectives. The Court finds no comparable reasoning given as to the five other research items that were expressly used to set the overall sample size of 850 whales (i.e., those research items set forth in Figure 5-4 from Japan's Counter-Memorial above). This highlights the absence of evidence, at least in the JARPA II Research Plan, that could support a finding that the sample size for the lethal take of minke whales, a key component of the design of JARPA II, is reasonable in relation to achieving the programme's objectives.

190. The Court also recalls that one of the experts called by Australia, Mr. Mangel, asserted that nearly the same level of accuracy that JARPA II seeks could be obtained with a smaller lethal take of minke whales and further posited that a smaller take and higher margin of error might be acceptable, depending on the hypothesis under study. Japan did not refute this expert opinion.

191. The Court turns next to the evidence regarding Japan's decision to use a six-year period to calculate the sample sizes for research items corresponding to minke whales, rather than a 12-year period as was used for fin and humpback whales. That decision has a considerable effect on sample size because the shorter time-period generally requires a higher figure, as the JARPA II Research Plan demonstrates (see paragraph 165 above).

192. Japan, in discussing one research item (age at sexual maturity) in the Counter-Memorial, attributes the use of a six-year period to the need to obtain at least three data points from each JARPA II research area (since whales are taken from each area in alternating seasons), because it would be "highly uncertain" to detect a trend on the basis of only two data points. Japan also refers to the desirability of detecting change "as promptly as possible". In the oral proceedings, Japan offered two different rationales for the six-year period. After initially suggesting that the six-year period was intended to coincide with JARPA II's six-year review by the Scientific Committee, Japan withdrew that explanation and asserted that the six-year period for minke whales was chosen because it "coincides with the review period for the RMP". This corresponds to the explanation given by the expert called by Japan, Mr. Walløe, in his oral testimony, although Mr. Walløe also described the use of a six-year period to calculate sample sizes as "arbitrary".

193. In light of the evidence, the Court has no basis to conclude that a six-year research period for minke whales is not reasonable in relation to achieving the programme's objectives. However, the Court finds it problematic that, first, the JARPA II Research Plan does not explain the reason for choosing a six-year period for one of the whale species (minke whales) and, secondly, Japan did not offer a consistent explanation during these proceedings for the decision to use that research period to calculate the minke whale sample size.

194. Moreover, Japan does not address how disparate research time frames for the three whale species are compatible with JARPA II's research objectives relating to ecosystem modelling and multi-species competition. JARPA II is apparently designed so that statistically useful information regarding fin and humpback whales will only be available after 12 years of research

(and the evidence indicates that, even after 12 years, sample sizes would be insufficient to be statistically reliable based on the minimum requirements set forth in the JARPA II Research Plan). As noted above (see paragraph 181), this casts doubt on whether it will be meaningful to review the programme in respect of its two primary objectives after six years of operation, which, in turn, casts doubt on whether the minke whale target sample size is reasonable in relation to achieving the programme's objectives.

195. The Court thus identifies two overarching concerns with regard to the minke whale sample size. First, Figure 5-4 shows that the final sample size of 850 minke whales (plus or minus 10 per cent) falls within a range derived from the individual sample sizes for various research items, but there is a lack of transparency regarding the decisions made in selecting those individual sample sizes. The Court notes that a lack of transparency in the JARPA II Research Plan and in Japan's subsequent efforts to defend the JARPA II sample size do not necessarily demonstrate that the decisions made with regard to particular research items lack scientific justification. In the context of Article VIII, however, the evidence regarding the selection of a minimum sample size should allow one to understand why that sample size is reasonable in relation to achieving the programme's objectives, when compared with other possible sample sizes that would require killing far fewer whales. The absence of such evidence in connection with most of the sample size calculations described in the JARPA II Research Plan lends support to Australia's contention that a predetermined overall sample size has dictated the choice of the research period and the rate of change to be detected, rather than the other way around.

196. Secondly, as noted above (see paragraph 149), Japan justifies the increase in the minke whale sample size in JARPA II (as compared to the JARPA sample size) by reference to the research objectives relating to ecosystem research and multi-species competition. However, the evidence suggests that the programme's capacity to achieve these objectives has been compromised because of shortcomings in the programme's design with respect to fin and humpback whales. As such, it is difficult to see how these objectives can provide a reasonable basis for the target sample size for minke whales in JARPA II.

197. In addition, the Court recalls that Japan describes a number of characteristics that, in its view, distinguish commercial whaling from research whaling. Japan notes, in particular, that high-value species are taken in commercial whaling, whereas species of both high value and of less or no commercial value (such as sperm whales) may be taken in research whaling (see paragraph 89 above). The use of lethal methods in JARPA II focuses almost exclusively on minke whales. As to the value of that species, the Court takes note of an October 2012 statement by the Director-General of Japan's Fisheries Agency. Addressing the Subcommittee of the House of Representatives Committee on Audit and Oversight of Administration, he stated that minke whale meat is "prized because it is said to have a very good flavour and aroma when eaten as sashimi and the like". Referring to JARPA II, he further stated that "the scientific whaling program in the Southern Ocean was necessary to achieve a stable supply of minke whale meat". In light of these statements, the fact that nearly all lethal sampling under JARPA II concerns minke whales means that the distinction between high-value and low-value species, advanced by Japan as a basis for differentiating commercial whaling and whaling for purposes of scientific research, provides no support for the contention that JARPA II falls into the latter category.

198. Taken together, the evidence relating to the minke whale sample size, like the evidence for the fin and humpback whale sample sizes, provides scant analysis and justification for the underlying decisions that generate the overall sample size. For the Court, this raises further concerns about whether the design of JARPA II is reasonable in relation to achieving its stated objectives. These concerns must also be considered in light of the implementation of JARPA II, which the Court turns to in the next section.

(iii) Comparison of sample size to actual take

199. There is a significant gap between the JARPA II target sample sizes and the actual number of whales that have been killed in the implementation of the programme. The Parties disagree as to the reasons for this gap and the conclusions that the Court should draw from it.

200. The Court recalls that, for both fin whales and humpback whales, the target sample size is 50 whales, following a two-year feasibility study during which the target for humpback whales was zero and the target for fin whales was ten.

201. As to actual take, the evidence before the Court indicates that a total of 18 fin whales have been killed over the first seven seasons of JARPA II, including ten fin whales during the programme's first year when the feasibility of taking larger whales was under study. In subsequent years, zero to three fin whales have been taken annually. No humpback whales have been killed under JARPA II. Japan recounts that after deciding initially not to sample humpback whales during the first two years of JARPA II, it "suspended" the sampling of humpback whales as of 2007. The Court observes, however, that the permits issued for JARPA II since 2007 continue to authorize the take of humpback whales.

202. Notwithstanding the target sample size for minke whales of 850 (plus or minus 10 per cent), the actual take of minke whales under JARPA II has fluctuated from year to year. During the 2005–2006 season, Japan caught 853 minke whales, a number within the targeted range. Actual take has fallen short of the JARPA II sample size target in all subsequent years. On average, approximately 450 minke whales have been killed in each year. The evidence before the Court indicates that 170 minke whales were killed in the 2010–2011 season and that 103 minke whales were killed in the 2012–2013 season.

203. As to the reasons for the gap between target sample sizes and actual take, Japan states that it decided not to take any humpback whales in response to a request by the then-Chair of the IWC. With respect to fin whales, Japan points to sabotage activities by anti-whaling non-governmental organizations, noting in particular the Sea Shepherd Conservation Society, and to the inability of the main JARPA II research vessel, the *Nisshin Maru*, to pull on board larger whales. As to minke whales, Japan offers two reasons that actual sample sizes have been smaller than targets: a fire on board the *Nisshin Maru* in the 2006–2007 season and the aforementioned sabotage activities.

204. Japan refers in particular to incidents of sabotage during the 2008–2009 season (the ramming of vessels in February 2009 and the throwing of bottles of acid at Japanese vessels), the unauthorized boarding of the vessel *Shonan-Maru* in February 2010, which resulted in the withdrawal of that vessel from the fleet for the remainder of the 2009–2010 season for crime scene investigation, and additional harassment during the 2012–2013 season. Japan notes that the IWC has condemned such violent sabotage activities in a series of resolutions adopted by consensus.

205. Australia takes issue with Japan's account of the reasons for the gap between target sample sizes and actual take. Australia does not dispute that the decision to take no humpback whales was made in response to a request from the Chair of the IWC, but points out that this was a political decision, not a decision taken for scientific reasons. With respect to fin whales, Australia emphasizes the undisputed fact that Japan's vessels are not equipped to catch larger whales. As to minke whales, Australia points to evidence that, in its view, demonstrates that actual take is a function of the commercial market for whale meat in Japan, not the factors identified by Japan. According to Australia, Japan has adjusted the operations of JARPA II in response to lower demand for whale meat, resulting in shorter seasons and fewer whales being taken. Australia also invokes press reports of statements by Japanese officials indicating that JARPA II's research objectives do not actually require the amount of lethal sampling described in the Research Plan and can be accomplished with a smaller actual take.

206. Taking into account all the evidence, the Court considers that no single reason can explain the gap between the target sample sizes and the actual take. As to humpback whales, the gap

results from Japan's decision to accede to a request from the Chair of the IWC but without making any consequential changes to the objectives or sample sizes of JARPA II. The shortfall in fin whales can be attributed, at least in part, to Japan's selection of vessels, an aspect of the design of JARPA II criticized by the expert called by Japan (see paragraph 180 above). As to the fire on board a ship in one season, Japan did not provide information regarding the extent of the damage or the amount of time during which the vessel was compromised. The Court considers it plausible that sabotage activities could have contributed to the lower catches of minke whales in certain seasons, but it is difficult to assess the extent of such a contribution. In this regard, the Court notes that the actual take of minke whales in the 2006–2007 and 2007–2008 seasons was 505 and 551, respectively, prior to the regrettable sabotage activities that Japan has brought to the Court's attention. In this context, the Court recalls IWC Resolution 2011–2, which was adopted by consensus. That resolution notes reports of the dangerous actions by the Sea Shepherd Conservation Society and condemns "any actions that are a risk to human life and property in relation to the activities of vessels at sea".

207. The Court turns next to Australia's contention that the gap between the target sample sizes and the actual take undermines Japan's position that JARPA II is a programme for purposes of scientific research. Australia states that it welcomes the fact that the actual take under JARPA II has been smaller than the programme's target sample sizes. Australia asserts, however, that Japan has made no effort to explain how this discrepancy affects the JARPA II research objectives and has not adapted the programme to account for the smaller actual sample size. Japan also has not explained how the political decision not to take humpback whales, as well as the small number of fin whales that have been killed, can be reconciled with the emphasis of the JARPA II Research Plan on the need for the lethal sampling of those two species. Australia asks how a multi-species competition model can be constructed on the basis of data only from minke whales, if, as stated in the JARPA II Research Plan, information based on lethal sampling is required from all three species to construct such a model or to explore the "krill surplus hypothesis". Australia emphasizes that Japan has asserted that the information it needs can be obtained only by lethal take but that the actual take has been entirely different from the sample sizes on which JARPA II was premised. Citing these factors, Australia describes JARPA II's multi-species competition model goal as "illusory".

208. Japan asserts that the discrepancy between sample size and actual take, at least with regard to minke whales, likely means that "it will take several additional years of research to achieve the required sample sizes before the research objectives can be met". Along these lines, Japan states that "if we conduct the research over a longer time or are willing to accept a lower degree of accuracy then a smaller sample size will also give viable results, but it might delay the ability to detect potentially important changes in a stock's dynamics". Japan also takes the position that the under-take to date of fin and humpback whales "does not preclude existing ecosystem models . . . from being improved by use of data that JARPA II has collected in respect of these species by non-lethal means".

209. The Court observes that, despite the number of years in which the implementation of JARPA II has differed significantly from the design of the programme, Japan has not made any changes to the JARPA II objectives and target sample sizes, which are reproduced in the special permits granted annually. In the Court's view, two conclusions can be drawn from the evidence regarding the gap between the target sample sizes and actual take. First, Japan suggests that the actual take of minke whales does not compromise the programme, because smaller numbers of minke whales can nonetheless generate useful information, either because the time frame of the research can be extended or because less accurate results could be accepted. The Court recalls, however, that the minke whale sample sizes for particular research items were based on a six-year research period and on levels of accuracy that were not explained in the JARPA II Research Plan or in these proceedings. Japan's statement that the programme can achieve

scientifically useful results with a longer research period or a lower level of accuracy thus raises further doubts about whether the target sample size of 850 whales is reasonable in relation to achieving the stated objectives of JARPA II. This adds force to Australia's contention that the target sample size for minke whales was set for non-scientific reasons.

210. Secondly, despite the fact that no humpback whales and few fin whales have been caught during JARPA II, Japan's emphasis on multi-species competition and ecosystem research as the bases for the JARPA II sample sizes for all three species is unwavering. In the view of the Court, the gap between the target sample sizes for fin and humpback whales in the JARPA II Research Plan and the actual take of these two species undermines Japan's argument that the objectives relating to ecosystem research and multi-species competition justify the larger target sample size for minke whales, as compared to that in JARPA.

211. The Court also notes Japan's contention that it can rely on non-lethal methods to study humpback and fin whales to construct an ecosystem model. If this JARPA II research objective can be achieved through non-lethal methods, it suggests that there is no strict scientific necessity to use lethal methods in respect of this objective.

212. Japan's continued reliance on the first two JARPA II objectives to justify the target sample sizes, despite the discrepancy between the actual take and those targets, coupled with its statement that JARPA II can obtain meaningful scientific results based on the far more limited actual take, cast further doubt on the characterization of JARPA II as a programme for purposes of scientific research. This evidence suggests that the target sample sizes are larger than are reasonable in relation to achieving JARPA II's stated objectives. The fact that the actual take of fin and humpback whales is largely, if not entirely, a function of political and logistical considerations, further weakens the purported relationship between JARPA II's research objectives and the specific sample size targets for each species — in particular, the decision to engage in the lethal sampling of minke whales on a relatively large scale.

(c) *Additional aspects of the design and implementation of JARPA II*

213. The Court now turns to several additional aspects of JARPA II to which the Parties called attention.

(i) Open-ended time frame

214. Japan asserts that "JARPA II is a long-term research programme and has no specified termination date because its primary objective (i.e., monitoring the Antarctic ecosystem) requires a continuing programme of research". The programme is organized into six-year "research phases" and "a review will be held and revisions made to the programme if required" after each such period. The first review by the Scientific Committee is scheduled to take place in 2014 (see paragraph 119 above). According to Japan, Article VIII, paragraph 4, of the Convention contemplates such open-ended research when it states that "continuous collection and analysis of biological data . . . are indispensable to sound and constructive management of the whale fisheries".

215. Australia draws two conclusions from the absence of any specified termination date in JARPA II. First, Australia contends that this demonstrates that the design of JARPA II is geared towards the perpetuation of whaling by any means until the commercial whaling moratorium is lifted. Secondly, Australia maintains that the open-ended nature of JARPA II precludes a meaningful assessment of whether it has achieved its research objectives, distorts the process of sample size selection, and therefore renders the design of JARPA II unscientific.

216. The Court notes the open-ended time frame of JARPA II and observes that with regard to a programme for purposes of scientific research, as Annex P indicates, a "time frame with intermediary targets" would have been more appropriate.

(ii) Scientific output of JARPA II to date

217. Japan maintains that, prior to the periodic review of JARPA II, no meaningful evaluation of JARPA II's scientific output can be made. Japan does assert, however, that the Scientific

Committee has recognized the value of data derived from JARPA II, including genetic data and age data derived from lethal whaling. In addition, the expert called by Japan, Mr. Walløe, testified that in his view JARPA II has already provided valuable information relating to the RMP and the Antarctic ecosystem.

218. Australia acknowledges that JARPA II has produced some results in the form of data that has been considered by the Scientific Committee. The Parties disagree about this output, however, in the sense that Australia argues that the data obtained from lethal sampling and provided to the Scientific Committee has not proven useful or contributed "significant knowledge" relating to the conservation and management of whales.

219. The Court notes that the Research Plan uses a six-year period to obtain statistically useful information for minke whales and a 12-year period for the other two species, and that it can be expected that the main scientific output of JARPA II would follow these periods. It nevertheless observes that the first research phase of JARPA II (2005–2006 to 2010–2011) has already been completed (see paragraph 119 above), but that Japan points to only two peer-reviewed papers that have resulted from JARPA II to date. These papers do not relate to the JARPA II objectives and rely on data collected from respectively seven and two minke whales caught during the JARPA II feasibility study. While Japan also refers to three presentations made at scientific symposia and to eight papers it has submitted to the Scientific Committee, six of the latter are JARPA II cruise reports, one of the two remaining papers is an evaluation of the JARPA II feasibility study and the other relates to the programme's non-lethal photo identification of blue whales. In light of the fact that JARPA II has been going on since 2005 and has involved the killing of about 3,600 minke whales, the scientific output to date appears limited.

(iii) Co-operation with other research institutions

220. Australia points to limited co-operation between JARPA II researchers and other scientists as evidence for its contention that JARPA II is not a programme for purposes of scientific research. One of the experts called by Australia, Mr. Gales, stated that JARPA II "operates in complete isolation" from other Japanese and international research projects concerning the Antarctic ecosystem.

221. In response to a question put by a Member of the Court, Japan cited co-operation with other Japanese research institutions. The expert called by Japan, Mr. Walløe, suggested that co-operation with international research programmes "would be difficult for personal and political reasons", given that the use of lethal methods is contentious among scientists. He acknowledged that co-operation with other Japanese research institutions, such as the National Institute for Polar Research, could be improved.

222. The Court notes that the evidence invoked by Japan to demonstrate co-operation with Japanese research institutions relates to JARPA, not JARPA II. It observes that some further evidence of co-operation between JARPA II and other domestic and international research institutions could have been expected in light of the programme's focus on the Antarctic ecosystem and environmental changes in the region.

(d) *Conclusion regarding the application of Article VIII, paragraph 1, to JARPA II*

223. In light of the standard of review set forth above (see paragraph 67), and having considered the evidence with regard to the design and implementation of JARPA II and the arguments of the Parties, it is now for the Court to conclude whether the killing, taking and treating of whales under the special permits granted in connection with JARPA II is "for purposes of scientific research" under Article VIII of the Convention.

224. The Court finds that the use of lethal sampling per se is not unreasonable in relation to the research objectives of JARPA II. However, as compared to JARPA, the scale of lethal sampling in JARPA II is far more extensive with regard to Antarctic minke whales, and the programme includes the lethal sampling of two additional whale species. Japan states that this expansion is required by the new research objectives of JARPA II, in particular, the objectives relating to ecosystem research and the construction of a model of multi-species competition. In the view

of the Court, however, the target sample sizes in JARPA II are not reasonable in relation to achieving the programme's objectives.

225. First, the broad objectives of JARPA and JARPA II overlap considerably. To the extent that the objectives are different, the evidence does not reveal how those differences lead to the considerable increase in the scale of lethal sampling in the JARPA II Research Plan. Secondly, the sample sizes for fin and humpback whales are too small to provide the information that is necessary to pursue the JARPA II research objectives based on Japan's own calculations, and the programme's design appears to prevent random sampling of fin whales. Thirdly, the process used to determine the sample size for minke whales lacks transparency, as the experts called by each of the Parties agreed. In particular, the Court notes the absence of complete explanations in the JARPA II Research Plan for the underlying decisions that led to setting the sample size at 850 minke whales (plus or minus 10 per cent) each year. Fourthly, some evidence suggests that the programme could have been adjusted to achieve a far smaller sample size, and Japan does not explain why this was not done. The evidence before the Court further suggests that little attention was given to the possibility of using non-lethal research methods more extensively to achieve the JARPA II objectives and that funding considerations, rather than strictly scientific criteria, played a role in the programme's design.

226. These problems with the design of JARPA II must also be considered in light of its implementation. First, no humpback whales have been taken, and Japan cites non-scientific reasons for this. Secondly, the take of fin whales is only a small fraction of the number that the JARPA II Research Plan prescribes. Thirdly, the actual take of minke whales has also been far lower than the annual target sample size in all but one season. Despite these gaps between the Research Plan and the programme's implementation, Japan has maintained its reliance on the JARPA II research objectives — most notably, ecosystem research and the goal of constructing a model of multi-species competition — to justify both the use and extent of lethal sampling prescribed by the JARPA II Research Plan for all three species. Neither JARPA II's objectives nor its methods have been revised or adapted to take account of the actual number of whales taken. Nor has Japan explained how those research objectives remain viable given the decision to use six-year and 12-year research periods for different species, coupled with the apparent decision to abandon the lethal sampling of humpback whales entirely and to take very few fin whales. Other aspects of JARPA II also cast doubt on its characterization as a programme for purposes of scientific research, such as its open-ended time frame, its limited scientific output to date, and the absence of significant co-operation between JARPA II and other related research projects.

227. Taken as a whole, the Court considers that JARPA II involves activities that can broadly be characterized as scientific research (see paragraph 127 above), but that the evidence does not establish that the programme's design and implementation are reasonable in relation to achieving its stated objectives. The Court concludes that the special permits granted by Japan for the killing, taking and treating of whales in connection with JARPA II are not "for purposes of scientific research" pursuant to Article VIII, paragraph 1, of the Convention.

4. Conclusions regarding alleged violations of the Schedule

228. The Court turns next to the implications of the above conclusion, in light of Australia's contention that Japan has breached three provisions of the Schedule that set forth restrictions on the killing, taking and treating of whales: the obligation to respect zero catch limits for the killing for commercial purposes of whales from all stocks (para. 10 *(e)*); the factory ship moratorium (para. 10 *(d)*); and the prohibition on commercial whaling in the Southern Ocean Sanctuary (para. 7 *(b)*).

229. The Court observes that the precise formulations of the three Schedule provisions invoked by Australia (reproduced in pertinent part below, see paragraphs 231–233) differ from each other. The "factory ship moratorium" makes no explicit reference to commercial whaling, whereas the requirement to observe zero catch limits and the provision establishing the Southern Ocean

Sanctuary express their prohibitions with reference to "commercial" whaling. In the view of the Court, despite these differences in wording, the three Schedule provisions are clearly intended to cover all killing, taking and treating of whales that is neither "for purposes of scientific research" under Article VIII, paragraph 1, of the Convention, nor aboriginal subsistence whaling under paragraph 13 of the Schedule, which is not germane to this case. The reference to "commercial" whaling in paragraphs 7 *(b)* and 10 *(e)* of the Schedule can be explained by the fact that in nearly all cases this would be the most appropriate characterization of the whaling activity concerned. The language of the two provisions cannot be taken as implying that there exist categories of whaling which do not come within the provisions of either Article VIII, paragraph 1, of the Convention or paragraph 13 of the Schedule but which nevertheless fall outside the scope of the prohibitions in paragraphs 7 *(b)* and 10 *(e)* of the Schedule. Any such interpretation would leave certain undefined categories of whaling activity beyond the scope of the Convention and thus would undermine its object and purpose. It may also be observed that at no point in the present proceedings did the Parties and the intervening State suggest that such additional categories exist.

230. The Court therefore proceeds on the basis that whaling that falls outside Article VIII, paragraph 1, other than aboriginal subsistence whaling, is subject to the three Schedule provisions invoked by Australia. As this conclusion flows from the interpretation of the Convention and thus applies to any special permit granted for the killing, taking and treating of whales that is not "for purposes of scientific research" in the context of Article VIII, paragraph 1, the Court sees no reason to evaluate the evidence in support of the Parties' competing contentions about whether or not JARPA II has attributes of commercial whaling.

231. The moratorium on commercial whaling, paragraph 10 *(e)*, provides:

"Notwithstanding the other provisions of paragraph 10, catch limits for the killing for commercial purposes of whales from all stocks for the 1986 coastal and the 1985/86 pelagic seasons and thereafter shall be zero. This provision will be kept under review, based upon the best scientific advice, and by 1990 at the latest the Commission will undertake a comprehensive assessment of the effects of this decision on whale stocks and consider modification of this provision and the establishment of other catch limits."

From 2005 to the present, Japan, through the issuance of JARPA II permits, has set catch limits above zero for three species 850 for minke whales, 50 for fin whales and 50 for humpback whales. As stated above (see paragraphs 229–230), the Court considers that all whaling that does not fit within Article VIII of the Convention (other than aboriginal subsistence whaling) is subject to paragraph 10 *(e)* of the Schedule. It follows that Japan has not acted in conformity with its obligations under paragraph 10 *(e)* in each of the years in which it has granted permits for JARPA II (2005 to the present) because those permits have set catch limits higher than zero.

232. The factory ship moratorium, paragraph 10 *(d)*, provides:

> "Notwithstanding the other provisions of paragraph 10, there shall be a moratorium on the taking, killing or treating of whales, except minke whales, by factory ships or whale catchers attached to factory ships. This moratorium applies to sperm whales, killer whales and baleen whales, except minke whales."

The Convention defines a "factory ship" as a ship "in which or on which whales are treated either wholly or in part" and defines a "whale catcher" as a ship "used for the purpose of hunting, taking, towing, holding on to, or scouting for whales" (Art. II, paras. 1 and 3). The vessel *Nisshin Maru*, which has been used in JARPA II, is a factory ship, and other JARPA II vessels have served as whale catchers. As stated above (see paragraphs 229–230), the Court considers that all whaling that does not fit within Article VIII of the Convention (other than aboriginal subsistence whaling) is subject to paragraph 10 *(d)* of the Schedule. It follows that Japan has not acted in conformity with its obligations under paragraph 10 *(d)* in each of the seasons during which fin whales were taken, killed and treated in JARPA II.

233. Paragraph 7 *(b)*, which establishes the Southern Ocean Sanctuary, provides in pertinent part: "In accordance with Article V (1) *(c)* of the Convention, commercial whaling, whether by pelagic operations or from land stations, is prohibited in a region designated as the Southern Ocean Sanctuary."

As previously noted, JARPA II operates within the Southern Ocean Sanctuary (see paragraph 120). Paragraph 7 *(b)* does not apply to minke whales in relation to Japan, as a consequence of Japan's objection to the paragraph. As stated above (see paragraphs 229–230), the Court considers that all whaling that does not fit within Article VIII of the Convention (other than aboriginal subsistence whaling) is subject to paragraph 7 *(b)* of the Schedule. It follows that Japan has not acted in conformity with its obligations under paragraph 7 *(b)* in each of the seasons of JARPA II during which fin whales have been taken.

5. Alleged non-compliance by Japan with its obligations under paragraph 30 of the Schedule

234. In its final submissions, Australia asks the Court to adjudge and declare that Japan violated its obligation to comply with paragraph 30 of the Schedule, which requires Contracting Governments to make proposed permits available to the IWC Secretary before they are issued, in sufficient time to permit review and comment by the Scientific Committee. Paragraph 30 states that the proposed permits should specify: the objectives of the research, the number, sex, size and stock of the animals to be taken; opportunities for participation in the research by scientists of other nations; and the possible effect on conservation of the stock.

235. Although the alleged violation of paragraph 30 was not framed as a submission in Australia's Memorial, the Memorial addressed the issue, as did Japan's Counter-Memorial.

236. Australia raises two complaints with regard to paragraph 30 that Japan has failed to provide proposed permits for review prior to the commencement of each season of JARPA II and that the annual permits do not contain the information required by paragraph 30.

237. In response, Japan points out that, prior to the present proceedings, Australia had not complained within the Scientific Committee regarding this alleged breach of paragraph 30. Japan explained that the JARPA II Research Plan was submitted two months in advance of the IWC's June 2005 meeting, prior to the issuance of any special permits for JARPA II, and that the Scientific Committee reviewed and commented on the proposal, in keeping with the then-applicable Guidelines, reflected in Annex Y. Japan asserts that for a multi-year programme such as JARPA II, only the initial proposal is reviewed by the Scientific Committee and that "ongoing unchanged proposals that have already been reviewed" are not subject to annual review. According to Japan, this had been the practice of the Scientific Committee prior to the submission of the JARPA II Research Plan and it has been formalized by Annex P.

238. As regards the question of timing, the Court observes that Japan submitted the JARPA II Research Plan for review by the Scientific Committee in advance of granting the first permit for the programme. Subsequent permits that have been granted on the basis of that proposal must be submitted to the Commission pursuant to Article VIII, paragraph 1, of the Convention, which states that "[e]ach Contracting Government shall report at once to the Commission all such authorizations which it has granted". Australia does not contest that Japan has done so with regard to each permit that has been granted for JARPA II.

239. As regards the substantive requirements of paragraph 30, the Court finds that the JARPA II Research Plan, which constitutes the proposal for the grant of special permits, sets forth the information specified by that provision. This was also recognized by the Scientific Committee in 2005 in its review of the JARPA II Research Plan. The lack of detail in the permits themselves is consistent with the fact that the programme is a multi-year programme, as described in the JARPA II Research Plan. Japan's approach accords with the practice of the Scientific Committee.

240. The Court observes that paragraph 30 and the related Guidelines regarding the submission of proposed permits and the review by the Scientific Committee (currently, Annex P) must be

appreciated in light of the duty of co-operation with the IWC and its Scientific Committee that is incumbent upon all States parties to the Convention, which was recognized by both Parties and the intervening State. As has been discussed above (see paragraphs 199–212), the implementation of JARPA II differs in significant respects from the original design of the programme that was reflected in the JARPA II Research Plan. Under such circumstances, consideration by a State party of revising the original design of the programme for review would demonstrate co-operation by a State party with the Scientific Committee.

241. The Court notes that 63 Scientific Committee participants declined to take part in the 2005 review of the JARPA II Research Plan, citing the need for the Scientific Committee to complete its final review of JARPA before the new proposal could be assessed. Those scientists submitted a separate set of comments on the JARPA II Research Plan, which were critical of its stated objectives and methodology, but did not assert that the proposal fell short of Scientific Committee practice under paragraph 30.

242. For these reasons, the Court is persuaded that Japan has met the requirements of paragraph 30 as far as JARPA II is concerned.

* * *

243. In view of the conclusions that the Court has reached regarding the characterization of JARPA II in relation to Article VIII, as well as the implications of these conclusions for Japan's obligations under the Schedule, the Court does not need to address other arguments invoked by Australia in support of its claims.

III. REMEDIES

244. In addition to asking the Court to find that the killing, taking and treating of whales under special permits granted for JARPA II is not for purposes of scientific research within the meaning of Article VIII and that Japan thus has violated three paragraphs of the Schedule, Australia asks the Court to adjudge and declare that Japan shall:

"*(a)* refrain from authorizing or implementing any special permit whaling which is not for purposes of scientific research within the meaning of Article VIII;

(b) cease with immediate effect the implementation of JARPA II; and

(c) revoke any authorization, permit or licence that allows the implementation of JARPA II."

245. The Court observes that JARPA II is an ongoing programme. Under these circumstances, measures that go beyond declaratory relief are warranted. The Court therefore will order that Japan shall revoke any extant authorization, permit or licence to kill, take or treat whales in relation to JARPA II, and refrain from granting any further permits under Article VIII, paragraph 1, of the Convention, in pursuance of that programme.

246. The Court sees no need to order the additional remedy requested by Australia, which would require Japan to refrain from authorizing or implementing any special permit whaling which is not for purposes of scientific research within the meaning of Article VIII. That obligation already applies to all States parties. It is to be expected that Japan will take account of the reasoning and conclusions contained in this Judgment as it evaluates the possibility of granting any future permits under Article VIII, paragraph 1, of the Convention.

* * *

247. For these reasons,

THE COURT,

(1) Unanimously,

Finds that it has jurisdiction to entertain the Application filed by Australia on 31 May 2010;

(2) By twelve votes to four,

Finds that the special permits granted by Japan in connection with JARPA II do not fall within the provisions of Article VIII, paragraph 1, of the International Convention for the Regulation of Whaling;

IN FAVOUR: *President* Tomka; *Vice-President* Sepúlveda-Amor; *Judges* Keith, Skotnikov, Cançado Trindade, Greenwood, Xue, Donoghue, Gaja, Sebutinde, Bhandari; *Judge* ad hoc Charlesworth;

AGAINST: *Judges* Owada, Abraham, Bennouna, Yusuf;

(3) By twelve votes to four,

Finds that Japan, by granting special permits to kill, take and treat fin, humpback and Antarctic minke whales in pursuance of JARPA II, has not acted in conformity with its obligations under paragraph 10 *(e)* of the Schedule to the International Convention for the Regulation of Whaling;

IN FAVOUR: *President* Tomka; *Vice-President* Sepúlveda-Amor; *Judges* Keith, Skotnikov, Cançado Trindade, Greenwood, Xue, Donoghue, Gaja, Sebutinde, Bhandari; *Judge* ad hoc Charlesworth;

AGAINST: *Judges* Owada, Abraham, Bennouna, Yusuf;

(4) By twelve votes to four,

Finds that Japan has not acted in conformity with its obligations under paragraph 10 *(d)* of the Schedule to the International Convention for the Regulation of Whaling in relation to the killing, taking and treating of fin whales in pursuance of JARPA II;

IN FAVOUR: *President* Tomka; *Vice-President* Sepúlveda-Amor; *Judges* Keith, Skotnikov, Cançado Trindade, Greenwood, Xue, Donoghue, Gaja, Sebutinde, Bhandari; *Judge* ad hoc Charlesworth;

AGAINST: *Judges* Owada, Abraham, Bennouna, Yusuf;

(5) By twelve votes to four,

Finds that Japan has not acted in conformity with its obligations under paragraph 7 *(b)* of the Schedule to the International Convention for the Regulation of Whaling in relation to the killing, taking and treating of fin whales in the "Southern Ocean Sanctuary" in pursuance of JARPA II;

IN FAVOUR: *President* Tomka; *Vice-President* Sepúlveda-Amor; *Judges* Keith, Skotnikov, Cançado Trindade, Greenwood, Xue, Donoghue, Gaja, Sebutinde, Bhandari; *Judge* ad hoc Charlesworth;

AGAINST: *Judges* Owada, Abraham, Bennouna, Yusuf;

(6) By thirteen votes to three,

Finds that Japan has complied with its obligations under paragraph 30 of the Schedule to the International Convention for the Regulation of Whaling with regard to JARPA II;

IN FAVOUR: *President* Tomka; *Vice-President* Sepúlveda-Amor; *Judges* Owada, Abraham, Keith, Bennouna, Skotnikov, Cançado Trindade, Yusuf, Greenwood, Xue, Donoghue, Gaja;

AGAINST: *Judges* Sebutinde, Bhandari; *Judge* ad hoc Charlesworth;

(7) By twelve votes to four,

Decides that Japan shall revoke any extant authorization, permit or licence granted in relation to JARPA II, and refrain from granting any further permits in pursuance of that programme.

IN FAVOUR: *President* Tomka; *Vice-President* Sepúlveda-Amor; *Judges* Keith, Skotnikov, Cançado Trindade, Greenwood, Xue, Donoghue, Gaja, Sebutinde, Bhandari; *Judge* ad hoc Charlesworth;

AGAINST: *Judges* Owada, Abraham, Bennouna, Yusuf.

Done in English and in French, the English text being authoritative, at the Peace Palace, The Hague, this thirty-first day of March, two thousand and fourteen, in four copies, one of which will be placed in the archives of the Court and the others transmitted to the Government of Australia, the Government of Japan and the Government of New Zealand, respectively.

(Signed) Peter TOMKA, President.

(Signed) Philippe COUVREUR, Registrar.

Judges OWADA and ABRAHAM append dissenting opinions to the Judgment of the Court; Judge KEITH appends a declaration to the Judgment of the Court; Judge BENNOUNA appends a dissenting opinion to the Judgment of the Court; Judge CANÇADO TRINDADE appends a separate opinion to the Judgment of the Court; Judge YUSUF appends a dissenting opinion to the Judgment of the Court; Judges GREENWOOD, XUE, SEBUTINDE and BHANDARI append separate opinions to the Judgment of the Court; Judge ad hoc CHARLESWORTH appends a separate opinion to the Judgment of the Court.

(Initialled) P. T.

(Initialled) Ph. C.

B. DOMESTIC CASES

Martin John Beattie et al v United States of America (United States Court of Appeals, District of Columbia Circuit, 31 December 1984, 756 F 2d 91; 244 US App DC 70 (1984))

[Issue: whether Antarctica is a 'foreign country' within the meaning of the foreign country exception of US Federal Tort Claims Act, in a tort action alleging that US Navy air controllers in Antarctica were negligent, causing the crash of an Air New Zealand aircraft into Mount Erebus, Antarctica, on 28 November 1979.]

(Senior Circuit Judge Wilkey; Circuit Judge Wald concurring; Circuit Judge Scalia dissenting):

This case arises out of the crash of an Air New Zealand aircraft into Mount Erebus, Antarctica, on 28 November 1979. All persons on board were killed. On 12 January 1983 plaintiffs filed a complaint in the United States District Court for the District of Columbia, seeking recovery against the United States for wrongful death under the Federal Tort Claims Act (FTCA).[18] Plaintiffs' amended complaint ultimately alleged negligence of United States Navy Air Traffic Controllers at McMurdo Naval Air Station, Antarctica, as well as negligence in the selection, training, and supervision of the navy personnel at McMurdo Base by officials of the Department of Defense.

The United States filed a motion to dismiss under Rule 12(b)(1), (3), and (6), claiming that the District Court lacked subject matter jurisdiction, that plaintiffs had failed to state a cause of action upon which relief could be granted, and that venue was improper. The primary basis for the motion was the "foreign country" exception to the Federal Tort Claims Act.[19] This exception removes from the scope of the FTCA "[a]ny claim arising in a foreign country."[20]

The issue before the District Court was one of first impression: Is Antarctica, a continent which is not now subject to the sovereignty of any nation, a "foreign country" within the meaning of the FTCA? By interlocutory order on 25 June 1984 the District Court denied the government's motion to dismiss, 592 F.Supp. 780, and certified this case for consideration by this Court in conformity with 28 U.S.C. § 1292(b). The government sought permission to appeal, which we granted.

To resolve the question before us, we must deal with three broad issues. The first issue is whether the District Court has subject matter jurisdiction. This issue hinges on a determination of whether Antarctica is a foreign country within the meaning of the FTCA. The second issue is whether the venue rules of the FTCA have been satisfied. The final issue involves a determination of which forum's law to apply. Our analysis of these issues leads us to affirm the interlocutory order of the District Court.

---

[18] 28 U.S.C. §§ 1346(b), 2671 *et seq.* (1982).

[19] 28 *id.* § 2680(k) (1982).

[20] *Id.*

I. SUBJECT MATTER JURISDICTION

A. *The Exception of Section 2680(k)*

The FTCA acts as a waiver of sovereign immunity in specified types of cases. Section 2680 of the FTCA lists several exceptions to that waiver. One of those retentions of sovereign immunity is involved here: section 2680(k), which withholds FTCA jurisdiction from "[a]ny claim arising in a foreign country."[21] As previously noted, the question of whether the District Court has subject matter jurisdiction depends on whether Antarctica is a foreign country within the meaning of the FTCA.

1. The Nature of Antarctica

Antarctica can properly be characterized as something of an international anomaly. It is a large continent which has never been and is not now subject to the sovereignty of any nation. Under the Antarctica Treaty of 1959 the signatory nations agreed not to exercise sovereignty in Antarctica, although their claims to sovereignty were not extinguished.[22]

The United States currently operates four active year-round stations, several summer camps, and numerous temporary tent cities in Antarctica.[23] McMurdo Base is America's largest station, with a summer population in excess of 850 persons and a winter population of about 92. It consists of approximately 130 buildings. McMurdo Station has been assigned a zip code by the United States Postal Service.[24]

McMurdo Station has an airfield which supports frequent flights to and from New Zealand during the Antarctic summer. The airfield has two air traffic control facilities. One is Ice Tower; it is located adjacent to the runway, and has radio communication capability with incoming aircraft. The second facility is Mac Center, which has both radio capability to communicate with aircraft and radar capability to locate aircraft via radar returns.[25]

These United States activities are not set forth to demonstrate that, by virtue of extensive involvement, the United States can bring some distant land within the scope of United States sovereignty. These activities are relevant only to a fairly narrow and straightforward issue—is Antarctica a foreign country? The answer to this question is determined in part by answering the question of whether the United States treats this admittedly sovereignless land like a foreign country. The answer is that it does not.

During the pendency of the Antarctica Treaty the United States has consistently reaffirmed its position regarding Antarctica. In 1981, for example, Assistant Secretary of State James L. Malone reiterated that, while the United States does not recognize territorial sovereignty in Antarctica, it maintains its own basis to claims of sovereignty in Antarctica.[26]

[1] Based on the foregoing information, and on a common sense approach to the plain language of the statute, it would appear obvious that Antarctica is not a foreign country within any ordinary meaning of that term. That sort of "plain meaning" approach formed part of the basis of the District Court's decision. As the District Court explained:

In view of this status of Antarctica, if the words of the statute are to be the decisive guide to statutory interpretation, the government's motion must fail, for clearly the instant claim did not arise in a foreign country as that term is commonly understood. Antarctica is not a foreign country; it is not a country at all; and it is not under the domination of any other foreign nation or country. Thus, if it be deduced from the language of the law that the section 2680(k) exception applies only where the government of a foreign nation has or asserts sovereignty, the Court

[21] *Id.*

[22] The Antarctica Treaty, 12 U.S.T. 795, T.I.A.S. No. 4780, Appendix at 55–60.

[23] National Science Foundation, *Facts About the United States Antarctic Research Program* 1–3 (July 1984).

[24] *Id.* The United States Postal Service Zip Code Directory 1984. The zip code listed is 96692.

[25] National Science Foundation, *supra* note 6, at 1.

[26] *Hearings Before the Subcommittee on Arms Control, Oceans, International Operations and Environment, of the Senate Committee on Foreign Relations,* 97th Cong., 1st Sess. (1981) (testimony of Ass't Sec. of State James L. Malone).

would have to hold that with respect to Antarctica the exception does not, and the Act does, apply.[27]

2. The Legislative History

The FTCA was the product of many years of congressional drafting and redrafting. A variety of amendments were proposed to the original legislation, including several different ways to structure the foreign country exception. A look at some of the rejected language highlights the meaning which should be given to the version which was eventually passed. In 1940 language was proposed to the foreign country exception which would have delineated the geographical jurisdiction of the FTCA to approximately the area the government now contends is covered, and by a positive inclusion instead of the negative exclusion we now have. The suggested language read:

(12) This act shall be applicable only to damages or injury occurring within the geo graphical limits of the United States, Alaska, Hawaii, Puerto Rico or the Canal Zone.[28]

Obviously, this language, if it had been accepted, would have limited the geographic jurisdictional scope of the FTCA to what the government now says it is. In fact, even if such language had never been suggested in the legislative history, the government would be hard put now to explain why, if the intent was to confine the FTCA solely to the geographical United States, the statute did not use straightforward language such as, "the applicability of the FTCA is limited to United States territory," or, "limited to claims arising in this country." However, no such language was accepted, and the previous "foreign country" version was retained.[29] We find it persuasive that *Congress did not place a strict geographical limit on the scope of the FTCA, preferring simply to make an exception in the case of foreign countries.*

One instructive item of legislative history was highlighted in the only Supreme Court case to interpret this section of the FTCA, *United States v. Spelar*.[30] The Court quoted a pertinent colloquy between Assistant Attorney General Francis M. Shea, testifying to the House Committee on the Judiciary, and Congressman Robson of that Committee.

Mr. Shea: Claims arising in a foreign country have been exempted from this bill, H.R. 6463, whether or not the claimant is an alien. Since liability is to be determined by the law of the situs of the wrongful act or omission, it is wise to restrict the bill to claims arising in this country. This seems desirable because the law of the particular State is being applied. Otherwise, it will lead I think to a good deal of difficulty.

Mr. Robson: You mean by that any representative of the United States who committed a tort in England or some other country could not be reached under this?

Mr. Shea: That is right. That would have to come to the Committee on Claims in the Congress.[31]

Although Mr. Shea did testify that it would be "wise to restrict the bill to claims arising in this country," the entire basis for that statement was his premise that liability is to be determined by the law of the situs of the wrongful act or omission.[32]

[2] It should be noted that in examining legislative history, one is justified in placing greater reliance on the exact choice of words in the bill as enacted than in oral testimony to a committee hearing. Mr. Shea's words must be given their general intent, which is that liability based on the law of a foreign country was to be avoided.

---

[27] Appendix at 42 (Mem.Op. by Harold Greene, J.) (citations omitted). Reference to the legislative history and relevant case law illustrates that Congress did not intend the term "foreign country" to extend beyond its ordinary meaning.

[28] *Hearings on S. 2690 Before a Subcommittee of the Senate Committee on the Judiciary,* 76th Cong., 3d Sess. 38 (1940).

[29] *See Tort Claims Against the United States: Hearings on H.R. 7236 Before Subcommittee No. 1 of the House Judiciary Committee,* 76th Cong., 3d Sess. 3 (1940).

[30] 338 U.S. 217, 70 S.Ct. 10, 94 L.Ed. 3 (1949).

[31] *Id.* at 221, 70 S.Ct. at 12.

[32] *Id.*

Although the legislative history does not point decisively to any answer, the weight of the evidence is in favor of the concept that Congress did not intend to limit the application of the FTCA to the United States and its territories and possessions. It had the opportunity to do so and chose to retain only the "foreign country" limitation. Rather, the legislative will seems to be as the Supreme Court summarized it in *Spelar,* that "though Congress was ready to lay aside a great portion of the sovereign's ancient and unquestioned immunity from suit, it was unwilling to subject the United States to liabilities depending upon the laws of a foreign power."[33]

3. Cases Interpreting Section 2680(k)

The only Supreme Court case to interpret § 2680(k) is *United States v. Spelar.*[34] That case involved a suit for wrongful death arising out of the death of a flight engineer at a United States Air Base in Newfoundland, leased by the United States from Great Britain. The Supreme Court determined that even though the accident occurred on a United States Base, that the negligent acts complained of nevertheless arose in a foreign country. The law which would have been applied to the case was the wrongful death law of Newfoundland. The holding of *Spelar* is based on the principle that § 2680(k)'s purpose is to prevent the United States from being subject to "liabilities depending upon the laws of a foreign power,"[35] and that the mere presence of United States government activities *in a foreign country* will not convert that portion of the foreign country into something else.

Both parties in this proceeding cite a wealth of lower federal court cases relating to the issue of jurisdiction. Since the issue in this case is one of first impression, none of the cases can be said to be truly on point. However, these cases are instructive and stand for several helpful propositions.

B. ***Operative Effect Cases***

Several cases have determined that a claim arises where the act or omission complained of occurs.[36] Thus, a large body of the cases cited in the briefs illustrate that an FTCA claim may arise in the United States, because the negligent act or omission occurred here, even though the act or omission had its "operative effect," i.e., the injury occurred, in a foreign country.[37]

For example, in the case of *Sami v. United States*[38] an Afghanistani economist was arrested by German police in Germany, at the request of the United States representative for Interpol. Mr. Sami had fled to Germany with his children as a result of a child custody dispute. He sued the United States for false arrest after the State Department told Germany that the offense was not extraditable.[39]

The District Court dismissed the case as one arising in a foreign country, because the last event necessary to liability had occurred in Germany. This Court responded that the FTCA focuses on the place where the negligent or wrongful act or omission of the government employee occurred. Since the instructions to make the arrest and most of the other operative facts in *Sami* occurred in the District of Columbia, this Court determined that § 2680(k) was not a bar, because the case actually arose in the United States.

These operative effect cases relate not so much to the definition of "foreign country," but to the meaning of "arising in." They determine that "arising in" does not necessarily refer to the situs of the injury, but to the situs of the negligence. The operative effect cases support subject matter jurisdiction over a portion of the plaintiffs' claims in this case, those which have been

[33] *Id.*

[34] 338 U.S. 217, 70 S.Ct. 10, 94 L.Ed. 3 (1949).

[35] *Id.* at 221, 70 S.Ct. at 12.

[36] *See, e.g., Sami v. United States,* 617 F.2d 755 (D.C.Cir.1979) ("[T]he FTCA, for purposes of imposing liability, focuses on the place of the government employee's act or omission.").

[37] *See, e.g., id.; Leaf v. United States,* 588 F.2d 733 (9th Cir.1978); *In re Paris Air Crash of March 3, 1974,* 399 F.Supp. 732, 737 (C.D.Cal.1975).

[38] 617 F.2d 755 (D.C.Cir.1979).

[39] *Id.* at 758.

characterized as the "headquarters claims."[40] The headquarters claims are the allegations of negligent selection, training, and supervision of the McMurdo Air Traffic Controllers by officials in Washington, D.C. Since these claims allege negligent acts or omissions by government employees which occur within the United States, and which merely had their operative effect in Antarctica, they are not claims which "arise in" a foreign country. However, the operative effect cases do not support subject matter jurisdiction over the claims of negligence by the air traffic controllers at McMurdo Base, Antarctica. These "Antarctica claims" constitute a separate ground for relief, with the negligent acts or omissions complained of occurring in Antarctica.

Thus, we accept for present purposes the validity of the headquarters claims, as we must on appeal of a Rule 12(b) motion.[41] Doing so does not eviscerate the jurisdictional bar of the foreign country exception, as the government fears. For one thing, it has always been possible to allege headquarters claims in cases involving injury in a foreign land. But unless subject matter jurisdiction can be separately established for those claims truly arising in a foreign country, the parties would be left with the headquarters claims as their entire case. Since, with the exception of international anomalies such as Antarctica, those claims would be barred by § 2680(k), it is seldom worth their while to try to make a case live or die on the basis of headquarters claims standing alone.

C. *The Foreign Country Cases*

A variety of cases have been cited which merely decide that, despite outward appearances, the situs of the acts or omissions was a foreign country. For example, torts occurring on American embassies or military bases which are located in foreign countries are barred by the foreign country exception.[42] This is also related to the idea that embassies and military bases in foreign countries often operate under agreement to apply that foreign country's laws in cases occurring there.[43]

A variety of other cases make subtle distinctions as to the level of sovereignty existing in some foreign land. For example, in *Burna v. United States*,[44] an FTCA case in post World War II Japan, the court concluded that, while the applicable treaty conferred some authority over Okinawa to the United States, Okinawa was still a foreign country within the meaning of the FTCA. This and other vestiges of sovereignty in Japan led the court to conclude that the foreign country exception applied. In *Cobb v. United States*,[45] the court's extensive analysis led it to the conclusion that Japanese tort law would be applicable. The court determined that Okinawa was in a foreign country because of the fact that the United States Military Government was not free to alter the tort law of Okinawa at will but was bound to maintain the preexisting "foreign law." As the court concluded, "[s]ince Congress was unwilling to subject the United States to liability based on that sort of law, the action was properly dismissed."[46] Since Antarctica, by agreement, is not now and never has been subject to the sovereignty of any nation, the present case does not require such an analysis.

From this wealth of cases, plaintiffs have selected one case as that "most closely analogous to the present litigation,"[47] the case of *In Re "Agent Orange" Product Liability Litigation.*[48] In *Agent Orange,* Vietnam veterans, their spouses and children brought suit under the FTCA for

[40] Brief for Appellees at 33.

[41] *Schuler v. United States,* 617 F.2d 605, 608 (D.C.Cir.1979) (quoting *Conley v. Gibson,* 355 U.S. 41, 45–46, 78 S.Ct. 99, 101–102, 2 L.Ed.2d 80 (1957)).

[42] *See, e.g., United States v. Spelar,* 338 U.S. 217, 70 S.Ct. 10, 94 L.Ed. 3 (1949); *Broadnax v. United States,* 710 F.2d 865 (D.C.Cir.1983); *Meredith v. United States,* 330 F.2d 9 (9th Cir.1964).

[43] North Atlantic Treaty Organization Status of Forces Agreement, 19 June 1951, art. VIII, 4 U.S.T. 1792, T.I.A.S. No. 2846, 199 U.N.T.S. 67.

[44] 240 F.2d 720 (4th Cir.1957).

[45] 191 F.2d 604 (9th Cir.1951).

[46] *Id.* at 611.

[47] Brief for Appellees at 13.

[48] 580 F.Supp. 1242 (E.D.N.Y.1984), *aff'd,* No. 84–381 (2d Cir. 25 Sept. 1984).

alleged injuries incurred from exposure of the servicemen to the herbicide Agent Orange while they were stationed in Vietnam. The claims brought by the servicemen were dismissed pursuant to the doctrine enunciated in *Feres v. United States*.[49] However, the independent claims of the wives and children were permitted to proceed. The government put forth several grounds for dismissal, one of which was the foreign country exception, since the alleged injuries occurred in Vietnam. In examining the foreign country exception, Judge Weinstein, "[a]t the peril of restating the obvious," stated that "the purpose of the exception, then, is to ensure that 'the United States [is not subject] to liabilities dependent upon the laws of a foreign power.'"[50] He went on to say that

[t]he purpose of the "foreign claim" exception does not apply to this litigation: not only have none of the parties contended that foreign law should be applied, but there is no theoretical justification for application of foreign law.... The jurisdiction where most of the use of herbicides took place, South Vietnam, no longer exists and Cambodia appears to be an independent state in name only now taken over by Vietnam. North Vietnam, the jurisdiction that has replaced South Vietnam and Cambodia, was at war with the United States and it was in the prosecution of the war that the exposure to Agent Orange took place.[51]

Because of the procedural posture of the case, the judge noted that "[i]t is unclear at this point if the decisions relating to that misuse took place in the United States or Vietnam.... There is no reason to attribute those mistakes to Vietnam rather than to the United States and no policy reason to apply the 'foreign claim' exception."[52]

The exact reason for the court's decision that the foreign country exception did not bar the case is not clear from the language of the opinion. The court appears to have been influenced by cases such as *Sami*,[53] an operative effect case, and yet it was also clearly influenced by the apparent lack of sovereignty in South Vietnam and Cambodia. *Agent Orange,* like the present case, involved an undetermined mix of acts or omissions, some occurring within the United States and others in a distant land, all contributing to the harm complained of. *Agent Orange* supports the proposition that § 2680(k) is not a bar to jurisdiction over cases arising at least in part outside the United States, and in areas where "there is no theoretical justification for application of foreign law."[54]

For all of the above reasons, we conclude that the District Court has jurisdiction over this case. Congress, in drafting and passing section 2680(k), only intended to exclude foreign countries from the scope of the FTCA.

D. ***Analogous Statutes and Cases***

[3] Plaintiff also lists a potpourri of cases and statutes which have decided, in other contexts, that Antarctica was not a foreign country or a foreign state. By themselves, none of these cases would be persuasive, since they all involve interpretations of other statutes with other purposes. "Foreign country" is a fluid concept and Congress is capable of defining it very differently for different reasons. In addition, waiver of sovereign immunity is not to be inferred lightly. But these cases have a cumulative effect which is persuasive. They demonstrate that across a broad scheme of regulations Congress and the courts have consistently determined that Antarctica does not satisfy any definition of "foreign country."

For example, in *Larry R. Martin v. Commissioner*[55] the Tax Court held that Antarctica was not a foreign country within the meaning of income tax regulations[56] which define "foreign country" as follows:

---

49 340 U.S. 135, 71 S.Ct. 153, 95 L.Ed. 152 (1950).
50 580 F.Supp. at 1254.
51 *Id.*
52 *Id.* at 1255.
53 *Sami v. United States,* 617 F.2d 755 (D.C.Cir.1979).
54 580 F.Supp. at 1254.
55 50 T.C. 59 (1968).
56 Treas.Reg. § 1.911.1(a)(7) (in effect at the time of the *Martin* case).

> The term "foreign country" means territory under the sovereignty of a government other than that of the United States and includes the air space over such territory. It does not include a possession or territory of the United States.

The Tariff Act of 1930,[57] the Interstate Transportation of Wagering Paraphernalia Act,[58] and the State Conducted Lotteries Act[59] each defined "foreign country" as "any empire, country, dominion, colony, or protectorate, or any subdivision or subdivisions thereof (other than the United States and its possessions)." The International Flight Information Manual, published by the Federal Aviation Administration, does not list Antarctica in its designations of "foreign countries" in international aviation.[60] As previously noted,[61] the McMurdo Station has been assigned a zip code by the United States Postal Service. United States dollars are the currency of exchange at McMurdo Base, and to obtain dollars to spend at McMurdo, New Zealanders must apply for permits to export money from New Zealand.[62]

As Judge Greene noted, "to the extent that there is any assertion of governmental authority in Antarctica, it appears to be predominantly that of the United States. The United States conducts all search and rescue operations in Antarctica and, significantly, it controls all air transportation."[63]

E. *The Analogy to Outer Space*

The legal status of Antarctica has been most frequently analogized to outer space.[64] United States spokesmen suggested the 1959 Antarctic Treaty as a possible model for an outer space treaty during initial formulation discussions in 1965 and 1966.[65] Obviously, the provisions of a treaty relating to outer space are only relevant to the present case by analogy. However, they are instructive as to the way in which the United States has acted with reference to sovereign immunity and liability for acts of its agents in a context very similar to Antarctica.

The Treaty on Principles Governing the Activities of States in the Exploration and Use of Outer Space, Including the Moon and Other Celestial Bodies[66] [the Space Treaty], was signed at Washington, London, and Moscow on 27 January 1967, and entered into force on 10 October 1967. By the terms of the treaty, the United States has agreed to be internationally liable for its space objects and retain jurisdiction over its own objects and persons.

For example, Article VII of the Space Treaty provides:

> Each State Party to the Treaty that launches or procures the launching of an object into outer space ... and each State Party from whose territory or facility an object is launched, is internationally liable for damage to another State Party to the Treaty or to its natural or judicial persons by such object....[67]

In addition, Article VIII of the Space Treaty provides:

> A State Party to the Treaty on whose registry an Object launched into outer space is carried shall retain jurisdiction over such object, and over any personnel thereof, while in outer space or on a celestial body.[68]

[57] 19 U.S.C. §§ 1336(h)(3), 1338(i) (1982).

[58] 18 *id.* § 1953(d).

[59] *Id.* § 1307(c).

[60] *See* Brief for Appellees at 24 n. 22.

[61] *Supra* p. ——.

[62] *See* Brief for Appellees at 7.

[63] Appendix at 47 (Mem.Op. by Harold Greene, J.).

[64] I.A. CSABAFI, THE CONCEPT OF STATE JURISDICTION IN INTERNATIONAL SPACE LAW 66 (1971); *see also* McDougal, Lasswell, Vlasic & Smith, *The Enjoyment and Acquisition of Resources in Outer Space,* 111 U.PA.L.REV. 521, 589 (1963); Comment, *Report of the National Citizen's Commission on Space, presented to the White House Conference on International Cooperation,* Nov. 1965, 53 AM.J.INT'L L. 121, 126–31 (1959).

[65] *See* Brief for Appellees at 29 (citing S.H. LAY & H.J. TAUBENFELD, THE LAW RELATING TO ACTIVITIES OF MAN IN SPACE 59–60 (1970)).

[66] 18 U.S.T. 2410, T.I.A.S. 6347, 61 U.N.T.S. 205 (1967).

[67] Appendix at 57.

[68] *Id.* at 57–58.

The Space Treaty is obviously not couched in terms of tort claims. However, the basic principle is that in the sovereignless reaches of outer space, each state party to the treaty will retain jurisdiction over its own objects and persons. Like the decisions under the statutes discussed in section D above, holding that Antarctica is not a "foreign country" for various purposes, the treatment of outer space is persuasive by analogy.

II. VENUE

Venue of cases under the FTCA is governed by the provisions of 28 U.S.C. § 1402, which provides that any such "civil action on a tort claim against the United States ... may be prosecuted only in the judicial district where the plaintiff resides or wherein the act or omission complained of occurred."[69] Since the plaintiffs in this case are all residents of Great Britain or New Zealand, venue must be satisfied through the place of the act or omission. This would be true even if the plaintiffs were *American citizens resident in New Zealand,* which brings into stark relief the state of utter lawlessness which would be created in Antarctica by adoption of the government theories.

Plaintiffs have posited two separate grounds for relief, which may be characterized as the headquarters claims and the Antarctica claims. The headquarters claims alleged negligence by officers of the United States, occurring in Washington, D.C., and in the Pentagon. On their face, the headquarters claims satisfy the venue requirements of section 1402(b). Of course, we must analyze these claims under the settled rule for assessing the propriety of dismissal under Rule 12(b) of the Federal Rules of Civil Procedure. Many potentially dispositive facts are intensely disputed by the parties. Because there has been neither factfinding by the district court nor very much if any discovery by the parties, we must accept as true all of the material allegations in the plaintiffs' complaint. Dismissal for failure to state a claim for relief is proper only when it "appears beyond doubt that the plaintiff can prove no set of facts in support of his claim which would entitle him to relief."[70] All factual doubts must be resolved and all inferences made in favor of the plaintiffs.[71] On that basis, it is clear that the headquarters claims satisfy the requirements of section 1402(b) by complaining of acts or omissions within the jurisdiction of the District Court for the District of Columbia.

This leaves us with the claims involving negligence in Antarctica. These claims satisfy the venue requirements under two discrete but interrelated theories.

[5] The general rule is that venue must be established as to each separate cause of action.[72] However, as one commentator has explained, the focus is on the word *separate.*[73] Professor Moore notes that, whether the case involves a federal and nonfederal claim,[74] or two federal claims,[75] *if they amount to only one cause of action* with two grounds for relief, proper venue as to one federal ground will support adjudication of both grounds. His theory is that "there is no true problem of joinder of actions unless there be two or more causes of action; that a broad concept of cause of action eliminates or lessens the problem."[76] He goes on to apply to the venue context the broad definition of cause of action from *Hurn v. Oursler.*[77] This notion of venue being required only for separate causes of action is still used,[78] even though *Hurn's* concept of cause of action has been replaced with respect to subject matter jurisdiction by the doctrine of pendent jurisdiction announced in *United Mine Workers v. Gibbs.*[79]

---

[69] 28 U.S.C. § 1402(b) (1982).

[70] *Schuler v. United States,* 617 F.2d 605, 608 (D.C.Cir.1979) (quoting *Conley v. Gibson,* 355 U.S. 41, 45–46, 78 S.Ct. 99, 101–102, 2 L.Ed.2d 80 (1957)) (emphasis added).

[71] *Shear v. National Rifle Ass'n,* 606 F.2d 1251, 1253 (D.C.Cir.1979).

[72] 15 C. WRIGHT, A. MILLER & E. COOPER, FEDERAL PRACTICE AND PROCEDURE § 3808 (1976).

[73] 1 J. MOORE, MOORE'S FEDERAL PRACTICE ¶ 0.142[3] (2d ed. 1984).

[74] *Id.* ¶ 0.140[5].

[75] *Id.*

[76] *Id.*

[77] 289 U.S. 238, 53 S.Ct. 586, 77 L.Ed. 1148 (1933).

[78] *See, e.g., LaMont v. Haig,* 590 F.2d 1124, 1135 (D.C.Cir.1978); *International Patent Dev. v. Wyomont Partners,* 489 F.Supp. 226, 230 (D.Nev.1980); *Garfinkle v. Arcata Nat'l Corp.,* 360 F.Supp. 1296, 1298 (S.D.N.Y.1973).

[79] *United Mine Workers v. Gibbs,* 383 U.S. 715, 86 S.Ct. 1130, 16 L.Ed.2d 218 (1966).

[6] Applying that principle to the present case, it is clear that this litigation can accurately be described as a single cause of action with separate grounds for relief. Plaintiffs seek damages for "an essentially single wrong,"[80] i.e., wrongful death. They allege against the same defendant two separate grounds for relief. These two grounds are identical as to parties and very similar as to the proof. There will be great commonality as to witnesses and evidence. Recognizing that there is but a single cause of action, venue under § 1402(b) is satisfied for the entire case by virtue of the headquarters claims.

In the context of subject matter jurisdiction, the concept of "cause of action" has been replaced as the touchstone for analysis by the doctrine of pendent jurisdiction. This familiar concept has also spilled over into the rules of venue. The doctrine of "pendent venue" is now well established, particularly in cases where the court has previously exercised its discretion to hear a certain claim under pendent jurisdiction. As one commentator noted, "[i]t would seem that if procedural convenience is enough to avoid the constitutional limitations on the jurisdiction of the federal court, it should suffice also to dispense with the purely statutory requirements as to venue."[81] Consequently, many pendent jurisdiction cases also apply the principles of pendent jurisdiction by analogy when one or more claims arising out of a common nucleus of operative facts do not satisfy the requirements of the applicable venue statute.[82]

This has even been carried over into cases where subject matter jurisdiction was independently satisfied on each claim, although with a more limited application.[83] This extension was foreseen by the authors of another treatise, in which they explain the rule that venue must be proper for each claim.[84] They cite a Supreme Court case involving both patent and breach of contract claims.[85] Jurisdiction was proper on all claims due to the complete diversity of the parties, but venue was only proper as to the patent claim. The other claims had to be dismissed. The authors note that the case was decided long before the concept of pendent jurisdiction was developed, and that the result should be different today.[86]

It would seem that there is no practical reason for limiting the application of pendent venue to cases where pendent jurisdiction has also been applied, and judges have recognized this by utilizing pendent venue when the case has merited it.

For example, in *Laffey v. Northwest Airlines*[87] the District Court for the District of Columbia found that it "need not decide whether [venue] is proper" for the cause of action under the Civil Rights Act of 1964[88] since venue was clearly proper under the Equal Pay Act claim.[89] The Equal Pay Act claim involved allegations that Northwest Airlines paid female in-flight cabin attendants less than male in-flight cabin attendants, and sought past-due and future wages. The Civil Rights Act claim involved allegations that Northwest discriminated in its employment practices against its female in-flight cabin attendants in that it used a discriminatory employment classification scheme and employment conditions including male priority in the "chain of

[80] *Hurn v. Oursler,* 289 U.S. at 246, 53 S.Ct. at 590.

[81] C. WRIGHT, THE LAW OF FEDERAL COURTS § 10, at 32 (4th ed. 1983).

[82] The rationale of similarity of proofs was important in the pre-*Gibbs* case of *Carolyn Chenilles, Inc. v. Ostow & Jacobs, Inc.,* 168 F.Supp. 894 (S.D.N.Y.1958). The court held that when the district court has jurisdiction over the patent infringement aspect of a case, and proofs as to both the patent infringement aspect and the unfair competition aspect would undoubtedly be substantially similar, and the needs of efficient administration dictated that, if possible, they should be tried together, the district court would retain jurisdiction over the unfair competition aspect, even if there were any doubt as to the proper venue of the unfair competition aspect.

[83] Specifically, some courts have expressed reluctance about the application of pendent venue in patent infringement cases, with the special concerns those cases entail. *See, e.g., Hoffacker v. Bike House,* 540 F.Supp. 148, 149–50 (N.D.Cal.1981); *Goggi Corp. v. Outboard Marine Corp.,* 422 F.Supp. 361, 366 (S.D.N.Y.1976).

[84] 15 C. WRIGHT, A. MILLER & E. COOPER,*supra* note 55, § 3808, at 42.

[85] *Geneva Furniture Mfg. Co. v. S. Karpen & Bros.,* 238 U.S. 254, 35 S.Ct. 788, 59 L.Ed. 1295 (1915).

[86] *See supra* note 54.

[87] 321 F.Supp. 1041 (D.D.C.1971) (denial of motion to reconsider venue).

[88] 42 U.S.C. §§ 2000e–2, 2000e–5(g) (1982).

[89] 29 *id.* § 206(d)(1).

command" and unequal treatment in regard to weight and height requirements, eyeglasses, uniform cleaning, and hotel accommodations.[90] Thus, *Laffey* can be aptly characterized as two separate causes of action arising out of a common nucleus of operative facts. This Court has subsequently cited *Laffey,* with respect to the general rule that venue must be satisfied as to each cause of action, for the notion that such a rule may be undesirable "when parties and proofs for all causes of action are identical."[91]

These same principles were applied in the case of *Zenith Radio Corp. v. Matsushita Electric Industrial Co.*[92] That case involved, among other things, allegations under the Anti-Dumping Act of 1916[93] and federal antitrust law.[94] The court addressed defendant's argument that even if venue were proper under § 12 of the Clayton Act, it was not proper for the counts arising under the Anti-Dumping Act. As the court explained:

> It would be senseless for this court to bifurcate these two exceedingly complex antitrust cases by dismissing or transferring the anti-dumping counts while retaining the antitrust counts since the facts underlying both sets of issues are essentially the same. If ever a case has cried out for the exercise of pendent venue, these two antitrust actions do. Accordingly, in the interest of judicial economy this court will retain jurisdiction over the anti-dumping counts under the doctrine of pendent venue.[95]

In the case of *Seamon v. Upham,*[96] which originally was a Voting Rights Act case charging that the Texas apportionment plan in various ways diluted minority voting strength, plaintiff sought to file a supplemental complaint, adding under Federal Rule of Civil Procedure 18(a) a claim challenging the legality and constitutionality of the Texas Governor's proclamation which set a date for a special congressional election. This supplemental complaint clearly lacked venue. The court, in its examination of the doctrine of pendent venue, noted that a court exercising its discretion in a pendent venue case "should consider the same factors that it would consider in deciding whether to exercise pendent jurisdiction.... Thus it should consider whether the claims derive from a 'common nucleus of operative fact,' ... and whether the exercise of jurisdiction furthers the goals of judicial economy, convenience, and fairness to the litigants."[97] The court also noted that

> a federal court's exercise of pendent *venue* over an additional *federal* law claim—the issue presented in the case before us—does not raise either the question of the power or the propriety of federal court actions, the questions that were implicated in *Gibbs.* Nevertheless,we assume that the "common nucleus of operative fact" test should retain some weight in our discretionary deliberations, because it, in itself, embodies factors that bear upon judicial economy, convenience, and fairness.[98]

The court went on to decline to exercise pendent venue because it determined that the supplemental complaint arose out of a completely discrete set of circumstances.[99]

---

[90] 321 F.Supp. at 1042.

[91] *LaMont v. Haig,* 590 F.2d 1124, 1135 (D.C.Cir.1978); *Relf v. Gasch,* 511 F.2d 804, 807 (D.C.Cir.1975) (citing *Laffey*).

[92] 402 F.Supp. 262 (E.D.Pa.1975) (Higginbotham, J.).

[93] 15 U.S.C. § 72 (1982).

[94] Specifically the Clayton Act, *id.* § 22.

[95] 402 F.Supp. at 328 n. 38.

[96] 563 F.Supp. 396 (E.D.Tex.1983).

[97] *Id.* at 399.

[98] *Id.* at 399 n. 3.

[99] *Id.* at 399. Many of these same considerations of judicial economy prompted this court to affirm a district court's denial of pendent venue over an FTCA claim in connection with a Privacy Act claim in the case of *Reuber v. United States,* 750 F.2d 1039 (D.C.Cir.1984). This court explained that many distinct issues of proof would be presented, and that "consideration of judicial economy must keep in mind that Reuber has identical claims to those considered here, including an FTCA action, already pending in federal district court in Maryland," at 1049, a consideration not present in this case. The court also noted that the FTCA "created a strong negative presumption against courts finding discretionary pendent venue elsewhere," *id.,* that is, in some district other than

Goggi v. Outboard Marine Corp.[100] was a case where plaintiff sought to apply the concept of pendent venue to a patent claim. The court explained that, at least with regard to the special patent venue statute,[101] this area of "pendent venue" has received limited application.[102] The court in *Goggi* distinguished those cases which did apply the concept of pendent venue by noting that "the sense of these opinions was that where there is substantial identity of issues and proof, it is most economical to try the various claims at one time."[103] Certainly the present case bears the same identity of parties and proofs found in *Laffey* and other pendent venue cases.

[7] [8] Whether to apply the principle of pendent venue in any given case is a discretionary decision, based on applicable policy considerations. Some of these considerations will be the same as those that support the exercise of pendent jurisdiction—judicial economy, convenience, avoidance of piecemeal litigation, and fairness to the litigants. Other considerations unique to the context of venue will apply.[104] For example, the purpose of venue rules is generally considered to be "primarily a matter of convenience of litigants and witnesses."[105] It is also oriented to the convenience of the court system.[106]

[9] Given that all parties to this lawsuit will be properly before the district court on the headquarters claims, it does not seem too inconvenient to include the Antarctica claims in the same lawsuit. Indeed, even if the Antactica claims were sued on alone, the District of Columbia might well be the most convenient forum, since many of the witnesses will be either here in Washington, D.C. or scattered around the globe.[107] Records relating to the accident investigation of the Air New Zealand flight are located in Washington, D.C.[108] Much of the other evidence in the case will be either in the District of Columbia or at the Pentagon.[109]

Hearing the Antarctica claims also allows the district court to act in harmony with congressional intent and a rule of construction adopted by the Supreme Court, both of which are explained in *Brunette Machine Works v. Kockum Industries*.[110] The court noted that there had been and perhaps still were occasional cases in which the federal courts have jurisdiction but there is no district in which venue is proper, but that Congress had acted to close such gaps in 1966 by amending the general venue statute. The court noted that "the development supports the view that Congress does not in general intend to create venue gaps, which take away with one hand what Congress has given by way of jurisdictional ground with the other. Thus, in construing venue statutes it is reasonable to prefer the construction that avoids having such a gap."[111] In the present case, dismissal of the Antarctica claims for lack of venue creates a gap between jurisdiction and venue and works a hardship not usually found in dismissals for lack of venue, which are often done

where plaintiffs reside or where the acts or omissions complained of occurred. In *Reuber,* plaintiff attempted to try his case in the District of Columbia, a forum where he did not reside and where the acts or omissions complained of did not occur. *Id.* at 1046. Plaintiff sought to use pendent venue completely to circumvent the FTCA's venue provisions by bringing his FTCA claims under the general value provisions applicable to the Privacy Act. In the present case, pendent venue is used to satisfy venue requirements for a portion of plaintiffs' FTCA claims, based on the satisfaction of venue requirements by the remainder of plaintiffs' claims in this FTCA case.

[100] 422 F.Supp. 361 (S.D.N.Y.1976).

[101] The patent venue statute "reflects a Congressional awareness of the technical nature of patent litigation and the particular advantage in limiting its prosecution to forums where the acts of infringement occurred and the defendant is located." *Hoffacker v. Bike House,* 540 F.Supp. 148, 149 (N.D.Cal.1981).

[102] 422 F.Supp. at 366.

[103] *Id.*

[104] *See* Comment, *Ancillary Process and Venue in the Federal Courts,* 73 HARV.L.REV. 1164 (1960).

[105] *Denver & R.G.W.R. Co. v. Brotherhood of R.R. Trainmen,* 387 U.S. 556, 560, 87 S.Ct. 1746, 1748, 18 L.Ed.2d 954 (1967).

[106] *Whittier v. Emmet,* 281 F.2d 24 (D.C.Cir.), *cert. denied,* 364 U.S. 935, 81 S.Ct. 380, 5 L.Ed.2d 367 (1961); *Jones v. United States,* 407 F.Supp. 873 (N.D.Tex.1976).

[107] Brief for Appellees at 40.

[108] *Id.*

[109] *Id.* at 40–41.

[110] 406 U.S. 706, 92 S.Ct. 1936, 32 L.Ed.2d 428 (1972).

[111] *Id.* at 710 n. 8, 92 S.Ct. at 1939 n. 8.

with an eye toward another court in which subject matter jurisdiction and venue can both be established. No one contends here that venue lies elsewhere. The government, consistent with its position that there is no law in Antarctica, maintains that venue exists—nowhere.

Whether viewed as a single cause of action with two grounds for relief (two claims), or as an appropriate case to apply the principle of "pendent venue" to the headquarters and Antarctica claims, this case satisfies the venue requirements of § 1402(b).

III. CHOICE OF LAW

Choice of law issues in FTCA actions are governed by 28 U.S.C. § 1346(b), which states that the district courts "shall have exclusive jurisdiction of civil actions on claims against the United States ... under circumstances where the United States, if a private person, would be liable to the claimant in accordance with the law of the place where the act or omission occurred."[112] This section has been construed to mean that the district court should apply as a choice of law rule the whole law of the place where the act or omission occurred.[113]

In this wrongful death case, some undetermined portion of the acts or omissions complained of occurred in the District of Columbia. Thus, at least as to the headquarters claims, and probably as to the entire case, application of D.C. law would mean that this "civil action" would be tried "in accordance with the law of the place where the act or omission occurred."

The Antarctica claims presents another novel issue. By directing application of the law of the place where the act or omission occurred, § 1346 leads the court to a place where this is no civil tort law to apply.[114] As we have seen, this is a situation *directly opposite* to the fear of becoming entangled in foreign law, which produced the "foreign country" exception. Hence, for this and other reasons, contrary to the government's assertions, we do not feel that the logical conclusion to be derived therefrom is that the entire case ought to be dismissed.[115] Rather, we feel that this represents a question not answered by the statute, and turn to those factors relevant to the choice of the applicable rule of law when there is no such statutory directive. Those factors, outlined in Restatement 2d, Conflict of Laws § 6, point to the District of Columbia as the forum whose law should be applied in this case.[116]

This is not a case such as *Sami*,[117] where a foreign state's substantive law is supplanted by the law of the forum because it conflicts with a strong public policy of the forum.[118] Rather, by traditional analysis, among the two "forums" with the greatest interest in the outcome of this litigation—Antarctica and the United States—only one has any civil law to apply. And, in fact, Antarctica has no "forum" either; fundamentally, because Antarctica is not a "country," foreign or otherwise. These considerations are similar to those which influenced the court's decision in *Agent Orange*.[119] In that case the erratic ebb and flow of sovereignty in Southeast Asia led the court to conclude that "there is no theoretical justification for application of foreign law."[120]

[11] These conclusions are buttressed by the recognized principle of international law that a nation may exercise jurisdiction over its nationals as a legitimate exercise of the nationality principle. The United States recognizes the validity of the nationality principle.[121]

[12] The United States has a strong public policy interest in the outcome of this litigation. In addition, the District Court for the District of Columbia has a strong interest in bringing to a

---

[112] 28 U.S.C. § 1346(b) (1982).

[113] *See Richards v. United States,* 369 U.S. 1, 82 S.Ct. 585, 7 L.Ed.2d 492 (1962).

[114] Brief for Appellants at 17.

[115] *Id.*

[116] *See, e.g.,* E. SCOLES & P. HAY, CONFLICT OF LAWS 551–606 (1984); RESTATEMENT (SECOND) CONFLICT OF LAWS § 6 (1971).

[117] *Sami v. United States,* 617 F.2d 755 (D.C.Cir.1979).

[118] *Id.* at 763.

[119] *In re "Agent Orange" Product Liability Litigation,* 580 F.Supp. 1242 (E.D.N.Y.1984).

[120] *Id.* at 1254.

[121] RESTATEMENT OF FOREIGN RELATIONS LAW OF THE UNITED STATES § 402 (Ten.Draft No. 2, 1981).

resolution a case which has been properly filed in that court in which it has both subject matter jurisdiction and venue. In contrast to these and other strong interests of the District of Columbia forum, there is no foreign sovereign even to assert a countervailing interest in Antarctica. The proper law to be applied to the case would be District of Columbia law.

In summary, the government argument requires us to accept an analysis of the FTCA, section 2680(k), that there are two areas of the world only—first, the United States, and second, "foreign countries." There are obviously several other areas in which people operate, e.g., outer space, the high seas, and Antarctica. While the other non-United States/non-foreign country areas may be covered by some law, we have a no-man's land of law in Antarctica, unless United States law covers the actions of United States citizens—not an unfair concept—and United States law includes the Federal Tort Claims Act.

All of this attempted limitation of coverage rests on one indefensible concept—that Antarctica is a "foreign country." Such an interpretation does violence to the plain meaning of the statute and the purpose behind the "foreign country" exception. While there are theoretical procedural obstacles, these can be logically overcome once the basic concept that United States law applies at least to the actions of United States citizens in Antarctica is accepted, and the other side of the coin is visualized, i.e., that unless this concept *is* accepted, Antarctica is an area without any law whatsoever.

The decision of the District Court is *Affirmed* and the case is *Remanded* for further proceedings consistent with this opinion.

So Ordered.

[Omitted: concurring opinion of Circuit Judge Wald and dissenting opinion of Circuit Judge Scalia.]

Antarctica Legal Status Case (German Federal Fiscal Court (BFH), Case No. VI R 185/87, 14 June 1991)[122]

[Issue: whether Antarctica is sovereign territory for taxation law purposes.]

The facts

In the year in question the plaintiff was employed as a cartographer. Between November 1984 and February 1985 he worked for his employer on a scientific expedition in the Antarctic. The purpose of the expedition was to create a geological map of a surveyed area. In his 1984 income tax declaration the plaintiff requested that, in accordance with the Foreign Activities Decree (*Auslandstätigkeitserlaß*) of 31 October 1983 (*BStBl.* I 1983, p. 470, *RIW* 1983, p. 880), his pay arising out of his employment in the Antarctic in 1984 be exempted from taxation. The defendant Tax Office declined to do so, arguing that the rules of the Foreign Activities Decree did not apply in his case. After the plaintiff had lodged an objection without success, the Regional Finance Court held that the Foreign Activities Decree was not applicable, but that the plaintiff had a claim to an abatement on grounds of fairness. The plaintiff's appeal was unsuccessful, whereas that of the Tax Office led to the dismissal of the action.

GROUNDS

Contrary to the view of the Regional Finance Court, the contested administrative decisions do not infringe Section 34c(5) of the Income Tax Law (*EStG*). Under that provision the highest tax authorities of the *Länder* may, with the approval of the Federal Finance Minister, grant an abatement, in whole or in part, of German Income Tax on foreign income … if it is expedient to do so on economic grounds or where the application of subparagraph (1) (credit for foreign tax) is particularly difficult. …

[122] (Case No. VI R 185/87), Federal Republic of Germany, Federal Fiscal Court (BFH), 14 June 1991.

I.

[The Court stated that the proceedings solely concerned the question of the requirements for the direct or analogous application of the Foreign Activities Decree, and the question of which authority had the power to refuse to apply it did not need to be decided. The Court continued:]

II.

The Tax Office and the Principal Revenue Office were justified in refusing to apply the Foreign Activities Decree in the case in point.

1. …

2. As the Finance Court correctly held, the preconditions for the application of the Foreign Activities Decree are not fulfilled in the present case.

a) The Finance Court correctly stated that such a conclusion was clear from the very wording of the Foreign Activities Decree. In Section II(1) of the Foreign Activities Decree it is stated that "the foreign activity must be pursued for a continuous period of at least 3 months in States with which no Treaty for the avoidance of double taxation exists …". However, the Antarctic is not part of the sovereign territory of any State and therefore constitutes a no-man's-land from the point of view of taxation.

b) The correctness of that conclusion is confirmed by interpretation of Section 34c(5) *EStG*, which … constitutes the statutory basis for the Foreign Activities Decree.

aa) The factual precondition … for the discretionary decision under Section 34c(5) *EStG* is the existence of "foreign income". What is to be understood as foreign income for that purpose follows from the legal definition in Section 34d *EStG*. Under Section 34d(5) *EStG*, foreign income arising out of employed activity is income from such an activity which "was pursued in a foreign State or, without being pursued in Germany, … was exploited in a foreign State …". Those preconditions are not fulfilled in the case of an employed activity in the Antarctic, which does not belong to any sovereign territory.

bb) Furthermore, the non-applicability of Section 34c(5) *EStG* in the present case of an activity in a taxation no-man's-land, is made clear by that provision's history, its sense and purpose and its place within the system linking it with the other sub-paragraphs of Section 34c *EStG*.

[The Court stated that Section 34c *EStG* aimed to avoid international double taxation and allowed for taxes comparable to German Income Tax to be set off against the latter. Section 34c(5) *EStG* was intended to be a catch-all for those cases where the primary means of avoiding double taxation (double taxation treaties, tax allowances, deduction of foreign taxes from the amount charged to tax) did not lead in a particular case to satisfactory results. The Court continued:]

Section 34c *EStG*… therefore requires (also in subparagraph (5)) that the taxpayer be in receipt of "foreign income" within the meaning of Section 34d *EStG* and that such income be subject to both foreign as well as German taxation … That requirement is not satisfied here. In this case the employed activity in a taxation no-man's-land does not give rise to "foreign income" within the meaning of Section 34d(5) *EStG*. Equally, since no foreign taxation has been levied on the income earned in the Antarctic, it is not a question of preventing or reducing the untoward effect of international double taxation in foreign trade matters.

[Report: RIW 1991, p. 966 (in German)]

Environmental Defense Fund Inc. v Massey (United States Court of Appeals, District of Colombia Circuit (Chief Judge Mikva and Judges Wald and Edwards), 29 January 1993[123]

[Issue: whether a US environmental law applied extraterritorially to US activities in Antarctica, notwithstanding that the US did not claim sovereignty over that territory]

[123] 986 F.2d 528, 36 ERC 1053, 300 U.S.App.D.C. 65, 61 USLW 2490, 23 Envtl. L. Rep. 20601.

[Chief Judge Mikva, for the Court]

The Environmental Defense Fund ("EDF") appeals the district court's order dismissing its action seeking declaratory and injunctive relief under the National Environmental Policy Act ("NEPA"). EDF alleges that the National Science Foundation ("NSF") violated NEPA by failing to prepare an environmental impact statement ("EIS") in accordance with Section 102(2)(C) before going forward with plans to incinerate food wastes in Antarctica. The district court dismissed EDF's action for lack of subject matter jurisdiction. The court explained that while Congress utilized broad language in NEPA, the statute nevertheless did not contain "a clear expression of legislative intent through a plain statement of extraterritorial statutory effect;" consequently, the court was compelled by the recent Supreme Court decision in *Equal Employment Opportunity Commission v. Arabian American Oil Co* ,—U.S.—, 111 S.Ct. 1227, 113[124] L.Ed.2d 274 (1991) ("*Aramco*") to conclude that NEPA does not apply to NSF's decision to incinerate food wastes in Antarctica. *See Environmental Defense Fund, Inc. v. Massey*, 772 F.Supp. 1296, 1297 (D.D.C.1991).

We reverse the district court's decision, and hold that the presumption against the extraterritorial application of statutes described in *Aramco* does not apply where the conduct regulated by the statute occurs primarily, if not exclusively, in the United States, and the alleged extraterritorial effect of the statute will be felt in Antarctica—a continent without a sovereign, and an area over which the United States has a great measure of legislative control. We therefore remand to the district court for a determination of whether NSF actually failed to comply with Section 102(2)(C) of NEPA, as EDF alleges in its complaint.

I

As both parties readily acknowledge, Antarctica is not only a unique continent, but somewhat of an international anomaly. Antarctica is the only continent on earth which has never been, and is not now, subject to the sovereign rule of any nation. Since entry into force of the Antarctic Treaty in 1961, the United States and 39 other nations have agreed not to assert any territorial claims to the continent or to establish rights of sovereignty there. *See* The Antarctica Treaty, 12 U.S.T. 794 (Dec. 1, 1959). Hence, Antarctica is generally considered to be a "global common" and frequently analogized to outer space. *See Beattie v. United States*, 756 F.2d 91, 99 (D.C.Cir.1984).

Under the auspices of the United States Antarctica Program, NSF operates the Mc-Murdo Station research facility in Antarctica. McMurdo Station is one of three year-round installations that the United States has established in Antarctica, and over which NSF exercises exclusive control. All of the installations serve as platforms or logistic centers for U.S. scientific research; McMurdo Station is the largest of the three, with more than 100 buildings and a summer population of approximately 1200.

Over the years, NSF has burned food wastes at McMurdo Station in an open landfill as a means of disposal. In early 1991, NSF decided to improve its environmental practices in Antarctica by halting its practice of burning food wastes in the open by October, 1991. After discovering asbestos in the landfill, however, NSF decided to cease open burning in the landfill even earlier, and to develop quickly an alternative plan for disposal of its food waste. NSF stored the waste at McMurdo Station from February, 1991 to July, 1991, but subsequently decided to resume incineration in an "interim incinerator" until a state-of-the-art incinerator could be delivered to McMurdo Station. EDF contends that the planned incineration may produce highly toxic pollutants which could be hazardous to the environment, and that NSF failed to consider fully the consequences of its decision to resume incineration as required by the decisionmaking process established by NEPA.

Section 102(2)(C) of NEPA requires "all federal agencies" to prepare an EIS in connection with any proposal for a "major action significantly affecting the quality of the human environment." 42

[124] 90 *ILR* 617.

U.S.C. § 4332(2)(C). The EIS requirement, along with the many other provisions in the statute, is designed to "promote efforts which will prevent or eliminate damage to the environment and biosphere." 42 U.S.C. § 4321. Following the passage of NEPA, NSF promulgated regulations applying the EIS requirement to its decisions regarding proposed actions in Antarctica. *See* 29 Fed.Reg. 3544, 3547 (Jan. 28, 1974) (codified at 45 C.F.R. § 640.3(e) (1977)). Since the issuance of Executive Order 12114, however, NSF has contended that proposed action affecting the environment in Antarctica is governed by the Executive Order, not NEPA. *See* Exec.Order 12114, 3 C.F.R. 356 (1980) [hereinafter cited as E.O. 12114].

Executive Order 12114 declares that federal agencies are required to prepare environmental analyses for "major Federal actions significantly affecting the environment of the global commons outside the jurisdiction of any nation (e.g., the oceans or Antarctica)." E.O. 12114 § 2–3(a). According to the Executive Order, major federal actions significantly affecting the environment of foreign countries may also require environmental analyses under certain circumstances. *Id.* Although the procedural requirements imposed by the Executive Order are analogous to those under NEPA, the Executive Order does not provide a cause of action to a plaintiff seeking agency compliance with the EIS requirement. The Executive Order explicitly states that the requirements contained therein are "solely for the purpose of establishing internal procedures for Federal agencies ... and nothing in [the Order] shall be construed to create a cause of action." E.O. 12114 § 3–1. Thus, what is at stake in this litigation is whether a federal agency may decide to take actions significantly affecting the human environment in Antarctica without complying with NEPA and without being subject to judicial review

II

A. The Presumption Against Extraterritoriality

As the district court correctly noted, the Supreme Court recently reaffirmed the general presumption against the extraterritorial application of statutes in *Equal Employment Opportunity Commission v. Arabian American Oil Co.*,—U.S.—, 111 S.Ct. 1227, 113 L.Ed.2d 274 (1991) ("*Aramco*"). Extraterritoriality is essentially, and in common sense, a jurisdictional concept concerning the authority of a nation to adjudicate the rights of particular parties and to establish the norms of conduct applicable to events or persons outside its borders. More specifically, the extraterritoriality principle provides that "[r]ules of the United States statutory law, whether prescribed by federal or state authority, apply only to conduct occurring within, or having effect within, the territory of the United States."Restatement (Second) of Foreign Relations Law of the United States § 38 (1965) [hereinafter Restatement (Second)]; Restatement (Third) of Foreign Relations Law of the United States § 403, Com. (g) (1987) [hereinafter Restatement (Third)]. As stated by the Supreme Court in *Aramco*, the primary purpose of this presumption against extraterritoriality is "to protect against the unintended clashes between our laws and those of other nations which could result in international discord." *Aramco*,—U.S. at—, 111 S.Ct. at 1230.

An early example of the application of the extraterritoriality principle is *American Banana Co. v. United States Fruit Co.*, 213 U.S. 347, 29 S.Ct. 511, 53 L.Ed. 826 (1909). In that case, the plaintiff alleged that the defendant, a U.S. corporation, had violated United States antitrust laws by inducing a foreign government to take actions within its own territory which were adverse to the plaintiff's business. The Supreme Court refused, in the absence of a clear statement of extraterritorial scope, to infer congressional intent to apply the federal statute to the conduct of a foreign government because enforcement would have interfered with the exercise of foreign sovereignty.

Similarly, in *Foley Bros. v. Filardo*, 336 U.S. 281, 282, 69 S.Ct. 575, 576, 93 L.Ed. 680 (1949), the Supreme Court declined to give extraterritorial effect to the Eight Hour Law, a labor statute applying to "[e]very contract made to which the United States ... is a party." The Court recognized that extraterritorial application of the statute would have "extend[ed] its coverage beyond places over which the United States has sovereignty or has some measure of legislative control," and therefore held that the intention "to regulate labor conditions, which are the primary concern of a foreign country, should not be attributed to Congress in the absence of a clearly expressed purpose."*Id.* at 285–286, 69 S.Ct. at 578.

Most recently, in *Aramco*, the Supreme Court held that Title VII of the 1964 Civil Rights Act does not apply extraterritorially to regulate the employment practices of United States firms that employ American citizens abroad. *Aramco*,—U.S. at—, 111 S.Ct. at 1236. In that case, the discriminatory conduct that allegedly violated Title VII occurred within the jurisdiction of another sovereign, although perpetrated by a U.S. firm. Since the petitioners were advancing a construction of Title VII that would logically result in the statute's application to foreign as well as American employers, the Court held that the presumption against extraterritoriality was necessary to avoid the inevitable clash between foreign and domestic employment laws. *Id.*—U.S. at—, 111 S.Ct. at 1234.

There are at least three general categories of cases for which the presumption against the extraterritorial application of statutes clearly does not apply. First, as made explicit in *Aramco*, the presumption will not apply where there is an "affirmative intention of the Congress clearly expressed" to extend the scope of the statute to conduct occurring within other sovereign nations. *Id.*—U.S. at—, 111 S.Ct. at 1230 (quoting *Bern v. Compania Naviera Hidalgo*, S.A., 353 U.S. 138, 147, 77 S.Ct. 699, 704, 1 L.Ed.2d 709 (1957)).[125]

Second, the presumption is generally not applied where the failure to extend the scope of the statute to a foreign setting will result in adverse effects within the United States. Two prime examples of this exception are the Sherman Anti-Trust Act, 15 U.S.C. §§ 1–7 (1976), and the Lanham Trade-Mark Act, 15 U.S.C. § 1051 et seq. (1976), which have both been applied extraterritorially where the failure to extend the statute's reach would have negative economic consequences within the United States. *See, e.g., Steele v. Bulova Watch Co.*, 344 U.S. 280, 73 S.Ct. 252, 97 L.Ed. 319 (1952)[126] (Lanham Trade-Mark Act applies extraterritorially when defendant is a United States national); *United States v. Aluminum Co. of America*, 148 F.2d 416 (2d Cir.1945) (applying U.S. antitrust laws extraterritorially); *Laker Airways Ltd. v. Sabena, Belgian World Airlines*, 731 F.2d 909, 925 (D.C.Cir.1984) ("[j]urisdiction exists under United States antitrust laws whenever conduct is intended to, and results in, substantial effects within the United States"); *see also Schoenbaum v. First-brook*, 405 F.2d 200 (2d Cir.1968) (securities[127] laws apply extraterritorially when necessary to protect American investors).

Finally, the presumption against extraterritoriality is not applicable when the conduct regulated by the government occurs within the United States. By definition, an extraterritorial application of a statute involves the regulation of conduct beyond U.S. borders. Even where the significant effects of the regulated conduct are felt outside U.S. borders, the statute itself does not present a problem of extraterritoriality, so long as the conduct which Congress seeks to regulate occurs largely within the United States. *See generally Laker Airways*, 731 F.2d at 921; Restatement (Second) § 38 (rules of U.S. statutory law apply "to conduct occurring within, or having effect within the territory of the United States"); Restatement (Second) § 17 (1965); Restatement (Third) § 492(l)(a), (b) (1987).

Despite these well-established exceptions to the presumption against extraterritoriality, the district court below bypassed the threshold question of whether the application of NEPA to agency actions in Antarctica presents an extraterritoriality problem at all. In particular, the court failed to determine whether the statute seeks to regulate conduct in the United States or in another sovereign country. It also declined to consider whether NEPA would create a potential for "clashes between our laws and those of other nations" if it was applied to the decisionmaking

[125] 24 *ILR* 167.
[126] 23 *ILR* 270.
[127] 60 *ILR* 28.

of federal agencies regarding proposed actions in Antarctica. *Aramco*,—U.S. at—, 111 S.Ct. at 1230. After a thorough review of these relevant factors, we conclude that this case does not present an issue of extraterritoriality.

B. Regulated Conduct Under NEPA

NEPA is designed to control the decision-making process of U.S. federal agencies, not the substance of agency decisions. By enacting NEPA, Congress exercised its statutory authority to determine the factors an agency must consider when exercising its discretion, and created a process whereby American officials, while acting within the United States, can reach enlightened policy decisions by taking into account environmental effects. In our view, such regulation of U.S. federal agencies and their decision-making processes is a legitimate exercise of Congress' territoriality-based jurisdiction, and does not raise extraterritoriality concerns.

Section 102(2)(C) lies at the heart of NEPA and is often considered the "action-forcing" element of the statute. *See* S.Rep. No. 91–296, 91st Cong., 1st Sess. 19 (1969); *Robertson v. Methow Valley Citizens Council*, 490 U.S. 332, 350, 109 S.Ct. 1835, 1845, 104 L.Ed.2d 351 (1989). This section requires "all agencies of the Federal Government" to prepare a detailed environmental impact statement for every "major Federal action" which has the potential to significantly affect the human environment. 42 U.S.C. § 4332(2)(C). Section 102(2)(C) binds only American officials and controls the very essence of the government function: decisionmaking. Because the decisionmaking processes of federal agencies take place almost exclusively in this country and involve the workings of the United States government, they are uniquely domestic. *See* Mary A. McDougall, *Extraterritoriality and the Endangered Species Act of 1973*, 80 Geo. L. J. 435, 445 (1991).

NEPA, unlike many environmental statutes, does not dictate agency policy or determine the fate of contemplated action. *Robertson*, 490 U.S. at 350, 109 S.Ct. at 1845; *Strycker's Bay Neighborhood Council, Inc. v. Karlen*, 444 U.S. 223, 227–228, 100 S.Ct. 497, 499–500, 62 L.Ed.2d 433 (1980) (per curiam). NEPA simply mandates a particular process that must be followed by a federal agency before taking action significantly affecting the human environment. After weighing environmental considerations, an agency decisionmaker remains free to subordinate the environmental concerns revealed in the EIS to other policy concerns. *Robertson*, 490 U.S. at 350, 109 S.Ct. at 1845. As this Court observed almost two decades ago,

> [t]he harm against which NEPA's impact statement requirement was directed was not solely or even primarily adverse consequences to the environment; such consequences may ensue despite the fullest compliance. Rather NEPA was intended to ensure that decisions about federal actions would be made only after responsible decisionmakers had fully adverted to the environmental consequences of the actions, and had decided that the public benefits flowing from the actions outweighed their environmental costs.

Jones v. District of Columbia Redevelopment Land Agency, 499 F.2d 502, 512 (D.C.Cir.1974), *cert. denied*, 432 U.S. 937 (1975).

In many respects, NEPA is most closely akin to the myriad laws directing federal decisionmakers to consider particular factors before extending aid or engaging in certain types of trade. *See* Comment, *NEPA's Role in Protecting the World Environment*, 131 U. Pa.L.Rev. 353, 371 (1982). For example, the Foreign Assistance Act of 1961 requires the Agency for International Development, before approving developmental assistance, to consider the degree to which programs integrate women into the economy, as well as the possibility of using aid to "support democratic and social political trends in recipient countries." 22 U.S.C. §§ 2151k, 2218(c) (1976). Similarly, the Nuclear Nonproliferation Act requires the Nuclear Regulatory Commission to consider a nation's willingness to cooperate with American nonproliferation objectives before approving a nuclear export license. 22 U.S.C. §§ 3201–3282 (1976); 42 U.S.C. §§ 2156, 2157 (Supp. III 1979). Just as these statutes fall short of prescribing action in foreign jurisdictions, and are instead directed at the regulation of agency decisionmaking,

NEPA also creates no substantive environmental standards and simply prescribes by statute the factors an agency must consider when exercising its discretionary authority.

Moreover, NEPA would never require enforcement in a foreign forum or involve "choice of law" dilemmas. This factor alone is powerful evidence of the statute's domestic nature, and distinguishes NEPA from Title VII as well as the Federal Tort Claims Act—two statutes that have been limited in their effect by the presumption against extraterritoriality. *See Aramco,*— U.S. at—, 111 S.Ct. at 1234 (presumption against extraterritoriality applies where Congress failed to provide for overseas enforcement and failed to address the potential conflicts of law issue); *Smith v. United States*, 932 F.2d 791, 793 (9th Cir. 1991) (an "indication that the [statute] was not intended to apply to Antarctica is the choice of law problem"), *cert, granted*—U.S.—, 112 S.Ct. 2963, 119 L.Ed.2d 585 (1992).

In sum, since NEPA is designed to regulate conduct occurring within the territory of the United States, and imposes no substantive requirements which could be interpreted to govern conduct abroad, the presumption against extraterritoriality does not apply to this case.

C. The Unique Status of Antarctica

Antarctica's unique status in the international arena further supports our conclusion that this case does not implicate the presumption against extraterritoriality. The Supreme Court explicitly stated in *Aramco* that when applying the presumption against extraterritoriality, courts should look to see if there is any indication that Congress intended to extend the statute's coverage "beyond places over which the United States has sovereignty *or some measure of legislative control.*" *Aramco,*—U.S. at—, 111 S.Ct. at 1230, (quoting *Foley Bros.*, 336 U.S. at 285, 69 S.Ct. at 577 (emphasis added)). Thus, where the U.S. has some real measure of legislative control over the region at issue, the presumption against extraterritoriality is much weaker. *See, e.g., Sierra Club v. Adams*, 578 F.2d 389 (D.C.Cir.1978) (NEPA assumed to be applicable to South American highway construction where the United States had two-thirds of the ongoing financial responsibility and control over the highway construction); *People of Enewetak v. Laird*, 353 F.Supp. 811 (D.Hawaii 1973) (concluding that NEPA applies to the United States trust territories in the Pacific). And where there is no potential for conflict "between our laws and those of other nations," the purpose behind the presumption is eviscerated, and the presumption against extraterritoriality applies with significantly less force. *Aramco,*—U.S. at—, 111 S.Ct. at 1230.

Indeed, it was the general understanding that Antarctica "is not a foreign country," but rather a continent that is most frequently analogized to outer space, that led this Court to conclude in *Beattie v. United States*, 756 F.2d 91 (D.C.Cir.1984), that the presumption against extraterritoriality should not apply to cases arising in Antarctica. *But cf. Smith v. United States*, 932 F.2d 791 (9th Cir.1991). The *Beattie* Court noted that Antarctica is not a "country" at all, as it has no sovereign, and stated that "to the extent that there is any assertion of governmental authority in Antarctica, it appears to be predominately that of the United States." *Beattie*, 756 F.2d at 99.

Even aside from this Court's holding in *Beattie*, it cannot be seriously suggested that the United States lacks some real measure of legislative control over Antarctica. The United States controls all air transportation to Antarctica and conducts all search and rescue operations there. Moreover, the United States has exclusive legislative control over McMurdo Station and the other research installations established there by the United States Antarctica Program. This legislative control, taken together with the status of Antarctica as a sovereignless continent, compels the conclusion that the presumption against extraterritoriality is particularly inappropriate under the circumstances presented in this case. As stated aptly by a State Department official in congressional testimony shortly following the enactment of NEPA,

> application of [NEPA] to actions occurring outside the jurisdiction of any State, including the United States, would not conflict with the primary purpose underlying this venerable rule of interpretation—to avoid ill-will and conflict between nations arising out of one nation's

> encroachments upon another's sovereignty. … There are at least three general areas: The high seas, outer space, and Antarctica.

See Memorandum of C. Herter, Special Assistant to the Secretary of State for Environmental Affairs, *reprinted in Administration of the National Environmental Policy Act: Hearing Before the Subcommittee on Fisheries and Wildlife Conservation of the House Committee on Merchant Marine and Fisheries*, 91st Cong., 2d Sess. 551 (1970) [hereinafter cited as State Dept. Memo].

While the State Department memo is hardly a part of appropriate legislative history, and is not entitled to any particular deference, the memo does reflect the general understanding by those intimately involved in the creation and execution of U.S. foreign policy that the global commons, including Antarctica, do not present the challenges inherent in relations between sovereign nations. Thus, in a sovereign-less region like Antarctica, where the United States has exercised a great measure of legislative control, the presumption against extraterritoriality has little relevance and a dubious basis for its application.

D. Foreign Policy Considerations

Although NSF concedes that NEPA only seeks to regulate the decisionmaking process of federal agencies, and that this case does not present a conflict between U.S. and foreign sovereign law, NSF still contends that the presumption against extraterritoriality controls this case. In particular, NSF argues that the EIS requirement will interfere with U.S. efforts to work cooperatively with other nations toward solutions to environmental problems in Antarctica. In NSF's view, joint research and cooperative environmental assessment would be "placed at risk of NEPA injunctions, making the U.S. a doubtful partner for future international cooperation in Antarctica." Appellee's Brief at 45.

NSF also argues that the Protocol on Environmental Protection to the Antarctic Treaty, which was adopted and opened for signature on October 4, 1991, would, if adopted by all the proposed signatories, conflict with the procedural requirements adopted by Congress for the decisionmaking of federal agencies under NEPA. *See* Protocol on Environmental Protection to the Antarctic Treaty, with Annexes, XI ATSCM, *reprinted in* 30 Int'l Legal Materials 1461 (1991). According to NSF, since NEPA requires the preparation of an EIS for actions with potentially "significant" impacts, while the Protocol requires an environmental analysis even for actions with "minor or transitory" impacts on the Antarctic environment, the two regulatory schemes are incompatible and will result in international discord.

We find these arguments unpersuasive. First, it should be noted that the Protocol is not in effect in any form and is years away from ratification by the United States and all 26 signatories. Second, we are unable to comprehend the difficulty presented by the two standards of review. It is clear that NSF will have to perform *fewer* studies under NEPA than under the Protocol, and where an EIS is required under NEPA, it would not strain a researcher's intellect to indicate in a single document how the environmental impact of the proposed action is more than "minor" and also more than "significant."

More importantly, we are not convinced that NSF's ability to cooperate with other nations in Antarctica in accordance with U.S. foreign policy will be hampered by NEPA injunctions. We made clear in *Natural Resources Defense Council v. Nuclear Regulatory Commission*, 647 F.2d 1345, 1366 (D.C.Cir.1981) ("*NRDC*"), that where the EIS requirement proves to be incompatible with Section 102(2)(F), federal agencies will not be subject to injunctions forcing compliance with Section 102(2)(C). Section 102(2)(F) specifically requires all federal agencies to

> recognize the worldwide and long-range character of environmental problems and, where consistent with the foreign policy of the United States, lend appropriate support to initiatives, resolutions, and programs designed to maximize international cooperation …

42 U.S.C. § 4332(F). While there was no majority opinion in *NRDC*, Judge Wilkey, writing for the Court, concluded that because U.S. foreign policy interests in the area of nuclear exportation

were unique and delicate, the EIS requirement had to give way to the explicit directive in Section 102(2)(F) requiring agencies to cooperate with other nations where consistent with U.S. foreign policy. *NRDC*, 647 F.2d at 1348. Judge Robinson, in his concurrence, echoed this theme in many respects, and noted that the EIS requirement did not actually present an issue of extraterritoriality since "the licensing procedure takes place entirely within the United States, and domestic law completely expends its force then and there." *Id.* at 1384 n. 138.

NRDC was not the first case to hold that NEPA's EIS requirement must yield where overriding policy concerns are present. In *Committee for Nuclear Responsibility v. Seaborg*, 463 F.2d 796 (D.C.Cir.1971), for example, we refused to issue an injunction under NEPA, despite the real potential for significant harm to the environment, because the government made "assertions of harm to national security and foreign policy." *Id.* at 798. In that case, conservation groups sought to enjoin an underground nuclear test on the grounds that the Atomic Energy Commission failed to comply fully with NEPA. Although there was reason to believe that the petitioners would succeed on the merits of their claim, we denied the requested injunction in light of the foreign policy concerns.

NRDC and *Seaborg* illustrate that the government may avoid the EIS requirement where U.S. foreign policy interests outweigh the benefits derived from preparing an EIS. Since NEPA imposes no substantive requirements, U.S. foreign policy interests in Antarctica will rarely be threatened, except perhaps where the time required to prepare an EIS would itself threaten international cooperation, *see Flint Ridge Development Co. v. Scenic Rivers Association*, 426 U.S. 776, 791, 96 S.Ct. 2430, 2439, 49 L.Ed.2d 205 (1976) (EIS requirement must yield where a clear conflict in statutory authority is unavoidable, including conflicts which arise out of timetables imposed by statute), or where the foreign policy interests at stake are particularly unique and delicate. *See NRDC*, 647 F.2d at 1348. Thus, contrary to NSF's assertions, where U.S. foreign policy interests outweigh the benefits of the EIS requirement, NSF's efforts to cooperate with foreign governments regarding environmental practices in Antarctica will not be frustrated by forced compliance with NEPA.

E. NEPA's Plain Language and Interpretation

NSF's final argument is that even if the presumption against extraterritoriality does not apply to this case, the plain language of Section 102(2)(C) precludes its application to NSF's decisionmaking regarding proposed agency action in Antarctica. We read the plain language differently.

Section 102(2)(C), on its face, is clearly not limited to actions of federal agencies that have significant environmental effects within U.S. borders. This Court has repeatedly taken note of the sweeping scope of NEPA and the EIS requirement. *See, e.g., Calvert Cliffs' Coord. Comm. v. United States A.E. Com'n*, 449 F.2d 1109, 1122 (D.C.Cir.1971) ("[T]he sweep of NEPA is extraordinarily broad, compelling consideration of any and all types of environmental impact of federal action."); *City of Los Angeles v. NHTSA*, 912 F.2d 478, 491 (D.C.Cir.1990) ("[NEPA] was designed explicitly to take account of impending as well as present crises in this country and *in the world as a whole*.") (emphasis added).

Far from employing limiting language, Section 2 states that NEPA is intended to "encourage productive and enjoyable harmony between *man and his environment*" as well as to "promote efforts which will prevent or eliminate damage to the environment and *biosphere*." 42 U.S.C. § 4321 (emphasis added). Clearly, Congress painted with a far greater brush than NSF is willing to apply. As stated by the *Enewetak* court, "there appears to have been a conscious effort to avoid the use of restrictive or limiting terminology." *Enewetak*, 353 F.Supp. at 816.

Section 102(2)(F) further supports the conclusion that Congress, when enacting NEPA, was concerned with worldwide as well as domestic problems facing the environment. 42 U.S.C. § 4332(2)(F) (federal agencies required to "recognize the worldwide and long-range character of environmental problems"). NSF acknowledges that Section 102(2)(F) clearly addresses international environmental problems, but argues that this section announces Congress' only requirement for agencies pursuing action in the international arena.

We find nothing in the statute which supports the construction of Section 102 urged by NSF. Apparently, NSF has chosen to ignore the clear interrelationship between the Section 102 subsections and the Section 102 mandate as a whole. Section 102 lists several requirements under NEPA for "*all Federal agencies.*" 42 U.S.C. § 4332(2). Compliance with one of the subsections can hardly be construed to relieve the agency from its duty to fulfill the obligations articulated in other subsections. For example, compliance with Section 102(2)(G), which requires agencies to make environmental information available to the states, does not excuse an agency from preparing an EIS under Section 102(2)(C).

We also note, that prior to the issuance of Executive Order 12114, the Council on Environment Quality ("CEQ") maintained that NEPA applies to the decisionmaking process of federal agencies regarding actions in Antarctica. CEQ is the agency created by Congress to oversee the implementation of NEPA, and its interpretation of that statute is generally entitled to "substantial deference." *See, e.g., Andrus v. Sierra Club*, 442 U.S. 347, 358, 99 S.Ct. 2335, 2341, 60 L.Ed.2d 943 (1979). NSF contends that CEQ changed its mind after the issuance of the Executive Order, and therefore its interpretation of NEPA is not entitled to deference. Whether or not NSF is right about CEQ's change of heart, we find CEQ's original conclusion to be not only reasonable, but fully supported by the plain language of the statute.

CONCLUSION

Applying the presumption against extraterritoriality here would result in a federal agency being allowed to undertake actions significantly affecting the human environment in Antarctica, an area over which the United States has substantial interest and authority, without ever being held accountable for its failure to comply with the decisionmaking procedures instituted by Congress—even though such accountability, if it was enforced, would result in no conflict with foreign law or threat to foreign policy. NSF has provided no support for its proposition that conduct occurring within the United States is rendered exempt from otherwise applicable statutes merely because the effects of its compliance would be felt in the global commons. We therefore reverse the district court's decision, and remand for a determination of whether the environmental analyses performed by NSF, prior to its decision to resume incineration, failed to comply with Section 102(2)(C) of NEPA.

We find it important to note, however, that we do not decide today how NEPA might apply to actions in a case involving an actual foreign sovereign or how other U.S. statutes might apply to Antarctica. We only hold that the alleged failure of NSF to comply with NEPA before resuming incineration in Antarctica does not implicate the presumption against extraterritoriality.

Reversed and remanded.

Smith v United States of America
(United States Supreme Court (Rehnquist, Chief Justice; White, Blackmun, O'Connor, Scalia, Kennedy, Souter and Thomas, Justices; Justice Stevens dissenting), 8 March 1993[128]

[Issue: whether a US tort claims law applied extraterritorially to Antarctica, as a sovereignless region without a civil tort law of its own]

This case presents the question whether the Federal Tort Claims Act (FTCA), 28 USC §§1346(b), 1402(b), 2401(b), 2671–2680 (1988 ed and Supp II), applies to tortious acts or omissions occurring in Antarctica, a sovereignless region without civil tort law of its own.[129]

[128] (91-1538), 507 U.S. 197; 113 S. Ct. 1178; 122 L. Ed. 2d 548.

[129] Without indigenous human population and containing roughly one-tenth of the world's land mass, Antarctica is best described as "an entire continent of disputed territory." F. Auburn, Antarctic Law and Politics 1 (1982). Seven nations—Argentine Australia, Chile, France, New Zealand, Norway, and the United Kingdom—presently

We hold that it does not.

Petitioner Sandra Jean Smith is the widow of John Emmett Smith and the duly appointed representative of his estate. At the time of his death, Smith worked as a carpenter at McMurdo Station on Ross Island, Antarctica, for a construction company under contract to the National Science Foundation, an agency of the United States. Smith and two companions one day took a recreational hike to Castle Rock, located several miles outside of McMurdo Station. On their return, they departed from the marked route to walk across a snow field in the direction of Scott Base, a New Zealand outpost not far from McMurdo Station.

After stopping for a snack, one of the three men took a step and suddenly dropped from sight. Smith followed, and he, too, disappeared. Both men had fallen into a crevasse. Despite search and rescue efforts, Smith died from exposure and internal injuries suffered as a result of the fall.

Petitioner filed this wrongful death action against the United States under the FTCA in the District Court for the District of Oregon, the district where she resides. Petitioner alleged that the United States was negligent in failing to provide adequate warning of the dangers posed by crevasses in areas beyond the marked paths. It is undisputed that petitioner's claim is based exclusively on acts or omissions occurring in Antarctica. Upon the motion of the United States, the District Court dismissed petitioner's complaint for lack of subject-matter jurisdiction, 702 F Supp 1480 (1989), holding that her claim was barred by 28 USC § 2680(k), the foreign-country exception. Section 2680(k) precludes the exercise of jurisdiction over "[a]ny claim arising in a foreign country."

The Court of Appeals affirmed, 953 F2d 1116 (CA9 1991). It noted that the term "foreign country" admits of multiple interpretations, and thus looked to the language and structure of the FTCA as a whole to determine whether Antarctica is a "foreign country" within the meaning of the statute. Adopting the analysis and conclusion of then-Judge Scalia, see *Beattie v United States*, 244 US App DC 70, 85–109, 756 F2d 91, 106–130 (1984) (Scalia, J., dissenting), the Court of Appeals ruled that the FTCA does not apply to claims arising in Antarctica. To hold otherwise, the Court of Appeals stated, would render two other provisions of the FTCA, 28 USC §§ 1402(b), 1346(b), nonsensical. The Court of Appeals held, in the alternative, that petitioner's suit would be barred even if Antarctica were not a "foreign country" for purposes of the FTCA. Because the FTCA was a limited relinquishment of the common-law immunity of the United States, the Court of Appeals concluded that the absence of any clear congressional intent to subject the United States to liability for claims arising in Antarctica precluded petitioner's suit. We granted certiorari to resolve a conflict between two Courts of Appeals,[130] 504 US—, 119 L Ed 2d 585, 112 S Ct 2963 (1992), and now affirm.

Petitioner argues that the scope of the foreign-country exception turns on whether the United States has recognized the legitimacy of another nation's sovereign claim over the foreign land. Otherwise, she contends, the land is not a "country" for purposes of the FTCA. Petitioner points out that the United States does not recognize the validity of other nations' claims to portions of Antarctica. She asserts, moreover, that this construction of the term "foreign country" is most consistent with the purpose underlying the foreign-country exception. According to petitioner, Congress enacted the foreign-country exception in order to insulate the United States from tort

---

assert formal claims to pie-shaped portions of the continent that total about 85 percent of its expanse. Boczek, The Soviet Union and the Antarctic Regime, 78 Am J Int'l L 834, 840 (1984); Hayton, The Antarctic Settlement of 19S9, 64 Am J Int'l L 349 (1960). The United States does not recognize other nations' claims and does not itself assert a sovereign interest in Antarctica, although it maintains a basis for such a claim. Lissitzyn, The American Position on Outer Space and Antarctica, 53 Am J Int'l L 126, 128 (1959). In any event, these sovereign claims have all been suspended by the terms of the Antarctic Treaty, concluded in 1959. Antarctic Treaty, Dec. 1, 1959 [1961] 12 UST 794, TIAS No. 4780. Article 4 of the Treaty states that no claim may be enforced, expanded, or compromised while the Treaty is in force, id., Art IV, 12 UST, at 796, thus essentially freezing nations' sovereign claims as of the date of the Treaty's execution.

[130] Compare *Beattie v United States*, 244 US App DC 70, 756 F2d 91 (1984) (holding that Antarctica is not a "foreign country" within the meaning of the FTCA).

liability imposed pursuant to foreign law. Because Antarctica has no law of its own, petitioner claims that conventional choice-of-law rules control and require the application of Oregon law, the law of her domicile. Thus, petitioner concludes, the rationale for the foreign-country exception would not be compromised by the exercise of jurisdiction here, since the United States would not be subject to liability under the law of a foreign nation.

Petitioner's argument for governmental liability here faces significant obstacles in addition to the foreign-country exception, but we turn first to the language of that proviso. It states that the FTCA's waiver of sovereign immunity does not apply to "[a]ny claim arising in a foreign country." 28 USC § 2680(k). Though the FTCA offers no definition of "country," the commonsense meaning of the term undermines petitioner's attempt to equate it with "sovereign state." The first dictionary definition of "country" is simply "[a] region or tract of land." Webster's New International Dictionary 609 (2d ed 1945). To be sure, this is not the only possible interpretation of the term, and it is therefore appropriate to examine other parts of the statute before making a final determination. But the ordinary meaning of the language itself, we think, includes Antarctica, even though it has no recognized government.

Our construction of the term "foreign country" draws support from the language of § 1346(b), "[t]he principal provision of the Federal Tort Claims Act." *Richards v United States*, 369 US 1, 6, 7 L Ed 2d 492, 82 S a 585 (1962). That section waives the sovereign immunity of the United States for certain torts committed by federal employees "under circumstances where the United States, if a private person, would be liable to the claimant *in accordance with the law of the place where the act or omission occurred.*" 28 USC § 1346(b) (emphasis added). We have construed § 1346(b) in determining what law should apply in actions brought under the FTCA. See Richards, supra. But by its terms the section is more than a choice-of-law provision: it delineates the scope of the United States' waiver of sovereign immunity. If Antarctica were not a "foreign country," and for that reason included within the FTCA's coverage, § 1346(b) would instruct courts to look to the law of a place that has no law in order to determine the liability of the United States—surely a bizarre result.[131] Of course, if it were quite clear from the balance of the statute that governmental liability was intended for torts committed in Antarctica, then the failure of § 1346(b) to specify any governing law might be treated as a statutory gap that the courts could fill by decisional law. But coupled with what seems to us the most natural interpretation of the foreign-country exception, this portion of § 1346(b) reinforces the conclusion that Antarctica is excluded from the coverage of the FTCA.

Section 1346(b) is not, however, the only FTCA provision that contradicts petitioner's interpretation of the foreign-country exception. The statute's venue provision, § 1402(b), provides that claims under the FTCA may be brought "only in the judicial district where the plaintiff resides or wherein the act or omission complained of occurred." Because no federal judicial district encompasses Antarctica, petitioner's interpretation of the FTCA would lead to yet another anomalous result: the FTCA would establish jurisdiction for all tort claims against the United States arising in Antarctica, but no venue would exist unless the claimant happened to reside in the United States.[132] As we observed in *Brunette Machine Works, Ltd. v Kockum*

[131] Nor can the law of the plaintiff's domicile, Oregon here, be substituted in FTCA actions based on torts committed in Antarctica. "Congress has expressly stated that the Government's liability is to be determined by the application of a particular law, the law of the place where the act or omission occurred ..." *Richards v United States*, 369 US 1, 9, 7L Ed 2d 492, 82 S Ct 858 (1962). Petitioner does not contend that her cause of action is based on acts or omissions occurring in Oregon.

[132] The history of the FTCA reveals that Congress declined to enact earlier versions of the statute that would have differentiated between foreign and United States residents. Those versions would have barred claims "arising in a foreign country in *behalf of an alien.*" S 2690, 76th Cong, 1st Sess, § 303(12) (1939) (emphasis added); HR 7236, 76th Cong, 1st Sess, § 303(12) (1939) (emphasis added). At the suggestion of the Attorney General, the last five words of the proposed bills were dropped. See Hearings on HR 5373 and HR 6463 before the House Committee on the Judiciary, 77th Cong, 2d Sess, 29, 35, 66 (1942). As we observed in *United States*

Industries, Inc., 406 US 706, 710, n 8, 32 L Ed 2d 428, 92 S Ct 1936 (1972), "Congress does not in general intend to create venue gaps, which take away with one hand what Congress has given by way of jurisdictional grant with the other." Thus, in construing the FTCA, it is "reasonable to prefer the construction that avoids leaving such a gap," ibid., especially when that construction comports with the usual meaning of a disputed term.

Our decisions interpreting the FTCA contain varying statements as to how it should be construed. See, e. g., *United States v Yellow Cab Co.*, 340 US 543, 547, 95 L Ed 523, 71 S Ct 399 (1951); *Dalehite v United States*, 346 US 15, 31, 97 L Ed 1427, 73 S Ct 956 (1953); *United States v Orleans*, 425 US 807, 813, 48 L Ed 2d 390, 96 S Ct 1971 (1976); *Kosak v United States*, 465 US 848, 853, n 9, 79 L Ed 2d 860, 104 S Ct 1519 (1984). See also *United States v Nordic Village, Inc.*,—US—,—, 117 L Ed 2d 181, 112 S Ct 1011 (1992). A recent statement of this sort, and the one to which we now adhere, is found in *United States v Kubrick*, 444 US 111, 117–118, 62 L Ed 2d 259, 100 S Ct 352 (1979): "We should also have in mind that the Act waives the immunity of the United States and that ... we should not take it upon ourselves to extend the waiver beyond that which Congress intended. [Citations omitted.] Neither, however, should we assume the authority to narrow the waiver that Congress intended." Reading the foreign-country exception to the FTCA to exclude torts committed in Antarctica accords with this canon of construction.

Lastly, the presumption against extraterritorial application of United States statutes requires that any lingering doubt regarding the reach of the FTCA be resolved against its encompassing torts committed in Antarctica. "It is a longstanding principle of American law 'that legislation of Congress, unless a contrary intent appears, is meant to apply only within the territorial jurisdiction of the United States.'" *EEOC v Arabian American Oil Co.*, 499 US—,—, 113 L Ed 2d 274, 111 S Ct 1227 (1991)[133] (quoting *Foley Bros., Inc. v Filardo*, 336 US 281, 285, 93 L Ed 680, 69 S Ct 575 (1949)). In applying this principle, "[w]e assume that Congress legislates against the backdrop of the presumption against extraterritoriality." Arabian American Oil Co., supra, at—, 113 L Ed 2d 274, 111 S Ct 1227; accord, e.g., *Argentine Republic v Amerada Hess Shipping Corp.*, 488 US 428, 440, 102 L Ed 2d 818, 109 S Ct 683 (1989)[134] ("When it desires to do so, Congress knows how to place the high seas within the jurisdictional reach of a statute"). The applicability of the presumption is not defeated here just because the FTCA specifically addresses the issue of extraterritorial application in the foreign-country exception. To the contrary, as we stated in *United States v Spelar*, 338 US 217, 222, 94 L Ed 3, 70 S Ct 10 (1949), "[t]hat presumption, far from being overcome here, is doubly fortified by the language of this statute and the legislative purpose underlying it." Petitioner does not assert, nor could she, that there is clear evidence of congressional intent to apply the FTCA to claims arising in Antarctica.[135]

For all of these reasons, we hold that the FTCA's waiver of sovereign immunity does not apply to tort claims arising in Antarctica. Some of these reasons are based on the language and structure of the statute itself; others are based on presumptions as to extraterritorial application of Acts of Congress and as to waivers of sovereign immunity. We think these norms of statutory

v Spelar, 338 US 217, 220, 94 L Ed 3, 70 S Ct 10 (1949), "[t]he superseded draft had made the waiver of the Government's traditional immunity turn upon the fortuitous circumstance of the injured party's citizenship." The amended version, however, "identified the coverage of the Act with the scope of United States sovereignty." Id., at 220–221, 94 L Ed 3, 70 S Ct 10. At least insofar as Antarctica is concerned, petitioner's interpretation of the FTCA would effectively resurrect the scheme rejected by Congress; it would deny relief to foreign residents in circumstances where United States residents could recover.

[133] 90 *ILR* 617.

[134] 81 *ILR* 658.

[135] Petitioner instead argues that the presumption against extraterritoriality applies only if it serves to avoid "'unintended clashes between our laws and those of other nations which could result in international discord.'" Brief for Petitioner 16 (quoting *EEOC v Arabian American Oil Co.*, 499 US—,—, 113 L Ed 2d 274, 111 S Ct 1227 (1991)). But the presumption is rooted in a number of considerations, not the least of which is the common-sense notion that Congress generally legislates with domestic concerns in mind.

construction have quite likely led us to the same conclusion that the 79th Congress would have reached had it expressly considered the question we now decide: it would not have included a desolate and extraordinarily dangerous land such as Antarctica within the scope of the FTCA. The judgment of the Court of Appeals is therefore affirmed.

SEPARATE OPINION – Justice Stevens, dissenting.

In my opinion the Court's decision to grant certiorari in this case was a wise exercise of its discretion. The question whether the United States should be held responsible for the tortious conduct of its agents in the vast "sovereignless region" of Antarctica, ante, at—, 122 L Ed 2d, at 552, is profoundly important, not only because its answer identifies the character of our concern about ordinary justice, but also because Antarctica is just one of three vast sovereignless places where the negligence of federal agents may cause death or physical injury. The negligence that is alleged in this case will surely have its parallels in outer space as our astronauts continue their explorations of ungoverned regions far beyond the jurisdictional boundaries that were familiar to the Congress that enacted the Federal Tort Claims Act (FTCA) in 1946. Moreover, our jurisprudence relating to negligence of federal agents on the sovereignless high seas points unerringly to the correct disposition of this case. Unfortunately, the Court has ignored that jurisprudence in its parsimonious construction of the FTCA's "sweeping" waiver of sovereign immunity.[136]

In theory the territorial limits on the consent to sue the United States for the torts of its agents might be defined in four ways: (1) there is no such limit; (2) territory subject to the jurisdiction of a foreign country is the only exclusion; (3) it also excludes sovereignless land areas such as Antarctica, but it includes the high seas and outer space; or (4) it has an "exclusive domestic focus" that applies "only within the territorial jurisdiction of the United States."[137] The "foreign country" exclusion in § 2680(k)[138] unquestionably eliminates the first possibility. In my opinion, the second is compelled by the text of the Act.[139] The third possibility is not expressly rejected by the Court, but the reasoning in its terse opinion seems more consistent with the Government's unambiguous adoption of the fourth, and narrowest, interpretation. I shall therefore first explain why the text of the FTCA unquestionably requires rejection of the Government's submission.

I

The FTCA includes both a broad grant of jurisdiction to the federal courts in § 1346(b)[140] and a broad waiver of sovereign immunity in § 2674.[141] Neither of these sections identifies any territorial limit on the coverage of the Act. That Congress intended and understood the broad language of those two provisions to extend beyond the territory of the United States is demonstrated by its en-

[136] "The Federal Tort Claims Act waives the Government's immunity from suit in sweeping language." *United States v Yellow Cab Co.*, 340 US 543, 547, 95 L Ed 523, 71 S Ct 399 (1951).

[137] See Brief for United States 16, 21–22.

[138] "The provisions of this chapter and section 1346(b) of this title shall not apply to—

"(k) Any claim arising in a foreign country." 28 USC § 2680(k) [28 USCS § 2680(k)].

[139] In short, I agree with most of the analysis in Judge Fletcher's dissenting opinion in this case and Judge Wilkey's opinion for the Court of Appeals for the District of Columbia Circuit in *Beattie v United States*, 244 US App DC 70, 756 F2d 91 (1984). Indeed, I am persuaded that the 79th Congress would have viewed torts committed by federal agents in "desolate and extraordinarily dangerous" lands as falling squarely within the central purpose of the FTCA. Ante, at—, 122 L Ed 2d, at 556.

[140] Title 28 USC § 1346(b) provides:

"Subject to the provisions of chapter 171 of this title, the district courts, together with the United States District Court for the District of the Canal Zone and the District Court of the Virgin Islands, shall have exclusive jurisdiction of civil actions on claims against the United States, for money damages, accruing on and after January 1, 1945, for injury or loss of property, or personal injury or death caused by the negligent or wrongful act or omission of any employee of the Government while acting within the scope of his office or employment, under circumstances where the United States, if a private person, would be liable to the claimant in accordance with the law of the place where the act or omission occurred."

[141] Title 28 USC § 2674 provides, in pertinent part:

"The United States shall be liable, respecting the provisions of this title relating to tort claims, in the same manner and to the same extent as a private individual under like circumstances, but shall not be liable for interest prior to judgment or for punitive damages."

actment of two express exceptions from that coverage that would have been unnecessary if the initial grant of jurisdiction and waiver of immunity had been as narrow as the Government contends. One of those, of course, is the "foreign country" exclusion in § 2680(k). See n 6, supra. The other is the exclusion in § 2680(d) for claims asserted under the Suits in Admiralty Act or the Public Vessels Act.[142] Without that exclusion, a party with a claim against the United States cognizable under either of those venerable statutes would have had the right to elect the pre-existing remedy or the newly enacted FTCA remedy. Quite obviously that exclusion would have been unnecessary if the FTCA waiver did not extend to the sovereignless expanses of the high seas.

Indeed, it was the enactment of the FTCA in 1946 that first subjected the United States to liability for maritime negligence claims that could not be maintained under either the Suits in Admiralty Act or the Public Vessels Act,[143] in particular, claims arising from death or injury on the high seas. As enacted in 1920, the Death on the High Seas Act (DOHSA) provided a remedy against private parties but contained no waiver of sovereign immunity.[144] That changed with the enactment of the FTCA, which waived the sovereign immunity of the United States for claims arising on the high seas under the DOHSA and the general maritime law. See, e.g., *United States v Gavagan*, 280 F2d 319, 321 (CA5 1960), cert denied, 364 US 933, 5 L Ed 2d 365, 81 S Ct 379 (1961) (holding United States liable, under the FTCA and the DOHSA, for death resulting from negligent rescue efforts on the high seas); *Blumenthal v United States*, 189 F Supp 439, 446–447 (ED Pa 1960) ("In the same manner as a private person is liable under the Death on the High Seas Act, so, too, is the Government under the Federal Tort Claims Act"), aff'd, 306 F2d 16 (CA3 1962); *Kunkel v United States*, 140 F Supp 591, 594 (SD Cal 1956) (same); *Moran v United States*, 102 F Supp 275 (D Conn 1951) (holding that the FTCA waived the sovereign immunity of the United States for claims arising from both personal injury and death on' the high seas). See also *McCormick v United States*, 680 F2d 345, 349 (CA5 1982) (citing Moran with approval); *Roberts v United States*, 498 F2d 520, 525–526 (CA9 1974) (noting that prior to 1960 amendments to Suits in Admiralty Act, FTCA waived sovereign immunity for claims under the general maritime law and the DOHSA).

In 1960, Congress amended the Suits in Admiralty Act so as to bring *all* maritime torts asserted against the United States, including those arising under the DOHSA, within the purview of the Suits in Admiralty Act and thus outside the waiver of sovereign immunity in the FTCA. See *United States v United Continental Tuna Corp.*, 425 US 164, 176, n 14, 47 L Ed 2d 653, 96 S Ct 1319 (1976). There can be no disputing the fact, however, that at the time it was enacted, the FTCA waiver extended to the sovereignless reaches of the high seas. Since the geographic scope of that waiver has never been amended, the Government's submission that it is confined to territory under the jurisdiction of the United States is simply untenable.

That the 79th Congress intended the waiver of sovereign immunity in the FTCA to extend to the high seas does not, of course, answer the question whether that waiver extends to the sovereignless region of Antarctica. It does, however, undermine one premise of the Court's analysis: that the presumption against the extraterritorial application of federal statutes supports its narrow construction of the geographic reach of the FTCA. As the Court itself acknowledges, see ante, at—, 122 L Ed 2d, at 556, that presumption operates "unless a contrary intent appears." Here, the contrary intent is unmistakable. The same Congress that enacted the "foreign country" exception to the broad waiver of sovereign immunity in § 2674, subjected the United States to claims for wrongful death and injury arising well beyond the territorial jurisdiction of the United States. The presumption against extraterritorial application of federal statutes simply has no bearing on this case.

142 Title 28 USC § 2680(d) excludes from the coverage of the FTCA "[a]ny claim for which a remedy is provided by sections 741–752, 781–790 of Title 46, relating to claims or suits in admiralty against the United States."

143 See *United States v United Continental Tuna Corp.*, 426 US 164, 172, 47 L Ed 2d 653, 96 S a 1319 (1976) ("Maritime tort claims deemed beyond the reach of both Acts could be brought only on the law side of the district courts under the Federal Tort Claims Act").

144 Pub L 69–165, 41 Stat 537, codified at, 46 USC App § 761 et seq.

II

The Government, therefore, may not prevail unless Antarctica is a "foreign country" within the meaning of the exception in subsection (k). Properly, in my view, the Court inquires as to how we are to construe this exception to the FTCA's waiver of sovereign immunity. Ante, at—, 122 L Ed 2d, at 555. Instead of answering that question, however, the Court cites a nebulous statement in *United States v Kubrick*, 444 US 111, 117–118, 62 L Ed 2d 259, 100 S Ct 352 (1979), and simply asserts that construing the foreign-country exception so as to deny recovery to this petitioner somehow accords with congressional intent. Ante, at——, 122 L Ed 2d, at 555.

I had thought that canons of statutory constructions were tools to be used to *divine* congressional intent, not empty phrases used to *ratify* whatever result is desired in a particular case. In any event, I would answer the question that the Court poses, but then ignores. And as I read our cases, the answer is clear: Exceptions to the "'sweeping'" waiver of sovereign immunity in the FTCA should be, and have been, "narrowly construed." *United States v Nordic Village, Inc.*, 503 US—, 117 L Ed 2d 181, 112 S Ct 1011 (1992) (quoting *United States v Yellow Cab Co.*, 340 US 543, 547, 95 L Ed 523, 71 S Ct 399 (1951)).[145] Accordingly, given a choice between two acceptable interpretations of the term "country"—it may designate either a sovereign nation or an expanse of land—it is our duty to adopt the former.

Even without that rule of construction, we should favor the interpretation of the term that the Court has previously endorsed. Referring specifically to the term as used in the FTCA, we stated: "We know of no more accurate phrase in common English usage than 'foreign country' to denote territory subject to the sovereignty of another nation." *United States v Spelar*, 338 US 217, 219, 94 L Ed 3, 70 S Ct 10 (1949). That interpretation is consistent with a statutory scheme that imposes tort liability on the Government "in the same manner and to the same extent as a private individual under like circumstances", see n 6, supra. As we explained in Spelar: "[T]hough Congress was ready to lay aside a great portion of the sovereign's ancient and unquestioned immunity from suit, it was unwilling to subject the United States to liabilities depending upon the laws of a foreign power." 338 US, at 221, 94 L Ed 3, 70 S Ct 10. Thus, the narrow interpretation of the term "foreign country" is precisely tailored to make the scope of the subsection (k) exception coextensive with its justification.

III

The Court seeks to buttress its interpretation of the "foreign country" exception by returning to the language of the jurisdictional grant in § 1346(b). As I have noted, federal courts have jurisdiction of civil claims against the United States "for injury or loss of property, or personal injury or death caused by the negligent or wrongful act or omission of any employee of the Government while acting within the scope of his office or employment, under circumstances where the United States, if a private person, would be liable to the claimant in accordance with the law of the place where the act or omission occurred."[146] Emphasizing the last dozen words, the Court essentially argues that Antarctica is "a place that has no law" and therefore it would

[145] See also *Block v Neal*, 460 US 289, 298, 75 L Ed 2d 67, 103 S Ct 1089 (1983) and *United States v Aetna Casualty & Surety Co.*, 338 US 366, 383, 94 L Ed 171, 70 S Ct 207, 12 ALR2d 444 (1949). As we stated in the latter:

"In argument before a number of District Courts and Courts of Appeals, the Government relied upon the doctrine that statutes waiving sovereign immunity must be strictly construed. We think that the congressional attitude in passing the Tort Claims Act is more accurately reflected by Judge Cardozo's statement …: 'The exemption of the sovereign from suit involves hardship enough where consent has been withheld. We are not to add to its rigor by refinement of construction where consent has been announced.'" Ibid. (quoting *Anderson v Hays Construction Co.*, 243 NY 140, 147, 153 NE 28, 29–30 (1926)).

[146] The Court inaccurately refers to the jurisdictional grant as the section that "waives the sovereign immunity of the United States," ante, at—, 122 L Ed 2d, at 554. It is actually § 2674 that waives immunity from liability by simply providing: "The United States shall be liable, respecting the provisions of this title relating to tort claims, in the same manner and to the same extent as a private individual under like circumstances…." The Court does not quote § 2674.

be "bizarre" to predicate federal liability on its governing law. Ante, at ——, 122 L Ed 2d, at 554.[147]

Although the words the Court has italicized indicate that Congress may not have actually thought about sovereignless regions, they surely do not support the Court's conclusion. Those words, in conjunction with § 2674, require an answer to the question whether a private defendant, in like circumstances, would be liable to the complainant. The Court fails even to ask that question, possibly because it is so obvious that petitioner could maintain a cause of action against a private party whose negligence caused her husband's death in Antarctica. It is simply wrong to suggest, as the Court does, that Antarctica is "a place that has no law," ante, at—, 122 L Ed 2d, at 554.[148]

The relevant substantive law in this case is the law of the State of Oregon, where petitioner resides. As was well settled at English common law before our Republic was founded, a nation's personal sovereignty over its own citizens may support the exercise of civil jurisdiction in transitory actions arising in places not subject to any sovereign. *Mostyn v Fabrigas*, 98 Eng Rep 1021, 1032 (KB 1774). See also *Dutton v Howell*, 1 Eng Rep 17, 21 (HL 1693). This doctrine of personal sovereignty is well recognized in our cases. As Justice Holmes explained in *American Banana Co. v United Fruit Co.*, 213 US 347, 53 L Ed 826, 29 S a 511 (1909):

> "No doubt in regions subject to no sovereign, like the high seas, or to no law that civilized countries would recognize as adequate, such [civilized nations] may treat some relations between their citizens as governed by their own law, and keep to some extent the old notion of personal sovereignty alive." Id., at 355–356, 53 L Ed 826, 29 S Ct 511.

Justice Holmes was referring to the assertion of extra-territorial jurisdiction by the United States rather than an individual State, but it is clear that the States also have ample power to exercise legislative jurisdiction over the conduct of their own citizens abroad or on the high seas. As we explained in *Skiriotes v Florida*, 313 US 69, 85 L Ed 1193, 61 S Ct 924 (1941):[149]

> "If the United States may control the conduct of its citizens upon the high seas, we see no reason why the State of Florida may not likewise govern the conduct of its citizens upon the high seas with respect to matters in which the State has a legitimate interest and where there is no conflict with acts of Congress." Id., at 77, 85 L Ed 1193, 61 S Ct 924.[150]

Surely the State of Oregon, the forum State, has a substantial interest in applying its civil tort law to a case involving the allegedly wrongful death of the spouse of one of its residents. Certainly no other State has an interest in applying its law to these facts. Moreover, application of Oregon's substantive law would in no way conflict with an Act of Congress because Congress has expressly subjected the United States to the laws of the various States for torts committed by the United States and its agents. It is thus perfectly clear that were the defendant in this case

[147] Apparently the Court is assuming that private contracts made in Antarctica are unenforceable and that there is no redress for torts committed by private parties in sovereignless regions. Fortunately our legal system is not that primitive. The statutory reference to "the law of the place where the act or omission occurred" was unquestionably intended to identify the substantive law that would apply to a comparable act or omission by a private party at that place. As long as private conduct is constrained by rules of law, and it certainly is in Antarctica, see infra, at ——, 122 L Ed 2d, at 561–562, there is a governing "law of the place" within the meaning of the FTCA.

[148] Indeed, it borders on the absurd to suggest that Antarctica is governed by nothing more than the law of the jungle. The United States exercises both criminal jurisdiction, see 18 USC § 7(7), and taxing jurisdiction, see 26 USC § 863(d)(2)(A) , over the approximately 2,500 Americans that live and work in and around Antarctica each year. See National Science Foundation, Facts About the U.S. Antarctic Program 1 (July 1990). The National Science Foundation operates three year-round stations in Antarctica, the largest of which is comprised of 85 buildings and has a harbor, landing strips on sea ice and shelf ice, and a helicopter pad. Ibid. Transportation to and from New Zealand is frequent during the summer months. Id., at 2.

[149] 10 *Ann Dig* 258.

[150] Again, as Justice Holmes explained:

> "[T]he bare fact of the parties being outside the territory [of the United States] in a place belonging to no other sovereign would not limit the authority of the State, as accepted by civilized theory. No one doubts the power of England or France to govern their own ships upon the high seas." *The Hamilton*, 207 US 398, 403, 52 L Ed 264, 28 S Ct 133 (1907).

a private party, there would be law to apply to determine that party's liability to petitioner. Given the plain language of § 2674, I see no basis for the Court's refusal to follow the statutory command and hold the United States "liable ... in the same manner and to the same extent as a private individual under like circumstances."

IV

Petitioner's action was filed "in the judicial district where the plaintiff resides", as § 1402(b) authorizes; there is, therefore, no objection to venue in this case. Because that provision would not provide a forum for a comparable action brought by a nonresident alien, the statute contains an omission that is no stranger to our law. In our opinion in *Brunette Machine Works, Ltd. v Kockum Industries, Inc.*, 406 US 706, 710, n 8, 32 L Ed 2d 428, 92 S Ct 1936 (1972), we identified examples of "cases in which the federal courts have jurisdiction but there is no district in which venue is proper" and stated that "in construing *venue statutes* it is reasonable to prefer the construction that avoids leaving such a gap." (emphasis added). Neither in that case nor in any other did we suggest that a venue gap should be avoided by adopting a narrow construction of either a jurisdictional grant or the scope of a federal cause of action. Yet that is the Court's perverse solution to the narrow venue gap in the FTCA.

Because a hypothetical handful of nonresident aliens may have no forum in which to seek relief for torts committed by federal agents in outer space or in Antarctica, the Court decides that the scope of the remedy itself should be narrowly construed. This anomalous conclusion surely derives no support whatsoever from the basic decision to include aliens as well as citizens within the protection of the statute, particularly since the overwhelming majority of aliens who may have occasion to invoke the FTCA are surely residents. As Judge Fletcher accurately observed in her dissenting opinion in the Court of Appeals:

> "Those who have no problem with venue should not be foreclosed from bringing suit simply because others cannot, particularly with respect to a statute such as the FTCA the primary purpose of which, as we have seen, was to expand the jurisdiction of the federal courts." 953 F2d 1116, 1122 (CA9 1991).

At most, the imperfections in the statute indicate that in 1946 the 79th Congress did not specifically consider the likelihood of negligence actions arising in outer space or in a sovereignless territory such as Antarctica. In view of the fact that it did authorize actions against the United States arising out of negligence on the high seas, see supra, at ——, 122 L Ed 2d, at 557–559, I am bewildered by the Court's speculation that if it had expressly considered the equally dangerous area at issue in this case, it would have distinguished between the two. Ante, at—, 122 L Ed 2d, at 556. The claim asserted in this case is entirely consistent with the central purpose of the entire Act.

Indeed, given that the choice is between imposing individual liability on federal agents for torts committed in the course of their employment, on the one hand, or holding their employer responsible, on the other hand, the amendment to the FTCA adopted by Congress in 1988 sheds more light on the issue presented in this case than the Court's unfounded speculation about congressional intent. The congressional findings explaining the decision to immunize federal employees from personal liability for negligence in the performance of their duties indicate that Congress recognizes both the practical value and the justice of a generous interpretation of the FTCA.[151] Moreover, those findings are thoroughly consistent with the interpretative approach

---

[151] In enacting the Federal Employees Liability Reform and Tort Compensation Act of 1988, the stated purpose of which was "to protect Federal employees from personal liability for common law torts committed within the scope of their employment, while providing persons injured by the common law torts of Federal employees with an appropriate remedy against the United States,"§ 2(b), 102 Stat 4564, 28 USC § 2671 note Congress made the following findings:

"(1) For more than 40 years the Federal Torts Claims Act has been the legal mechanism for compensating persons injured by negligent or wrongful acts of Federal employees committed within the scope of their employment.

"(2) The United States, through the Federal Tort Claims Act, is responsible to injured persons for the common law torts of its employees in the same manner in which the common law historically has recognized the responsibility of an employer for torts committed by its employees within the scope of their employment.

of the unusually distinguished panel of Circuit Judges who, shortly after the FTCA was passed, wrote:

"When after many years of discussion and debate Congress has at length established a general policy of governmental generosity toward tort claimants, it would seem that that policy should not be set aside or hampered by a niggardly construction based on formal rules made obsolete by the very purpose of the Act itself. Particularly should this be true as to the broad terms of coverage employed in the basic grant of liability itself." *Spelar v United States*, 171 F2d 208, 209 (CA2 1948).[152]

The wisdom that prompted the Court's grant of certiorari is not reflected in its interpretation of the 1946 Act. Rather, it reflects a vision that would exclude electronic eavesdropping from the coverage of the Fourth Amendment and satellites from the coverage of the Commerce Clause. The international community includes sovereignless places but no places where there is no rule of law. Majestic legislation like the Federal Tort Claims Act should be read with the vision of the judge, enlightened by an interest in justice, not through the opaque green eyeshade of the cloistered bookkeeper. As President Lincoln observed in his first State of the Union Message:

"It is as much the duty of Government to render prompt justice against itself, in favor of citizens, as it is to administer the same between private individuals."[153]

I respectfully dissent.

R v Pesquera Concar SA (Owners of The Antonio Lorenzo) (Falkland Islands Magistrate's Court, 8 July 1996, Senior Magistrate Jeremiah)[154]

[Issue: whether domestic fisheries law prevailed over the *Convention on Marine Living Resources*, and whether the domestic law conflicted with that Convention]

This is a judgment of the Magistrate's Court of the Falkland Islands exercising the jurisdiction conferred upon it by Section 3 of the Falkland Islands Courts (Overseas Jurisdiction) Order 1989; the matter for determination being an allegation of a criminal offence contrary to the law of South Georgia and the South Sandwich Islands. I remind myself at the outset that the substantive law to be applied is that of South Georgia and the South Sandwich Islands. Matters of evidence and procedure fall to be determined in accordance with the law of the Falkland Islands.

Pesquera Concar SA are charged that on 5 March 1996 being the owners of the fishing boat *Antonio Lorenzo* the said fishing boat was used in contravention of the prohibition imposed by Article 4(1) of the Fishing (Maritime Zone) Order 1993 ("the Order"), contrary to Section 5(3) of the Fisheries (Conservation and Management) Ordinance 1993 ("the Ordinance").

Section 5(1) of the Ordinance provides:

"(3) Because Federal employees for many years have been protected from personal common law tort liability by a broad based immunity, the Federal Tort Claims Act has served as the sole means for compensating persons injured by the tortious conduct of Federal employees.

"(4) Recent judicial decisions, and particularly the decision of the United States Supreme Court in *Westfall v Erwin*, have seriously eroded the common law tort immunity previously available to Federal employees.

"(5) This erosion of immunity of Federal employees from common law tort liability has created an immediate crisis involving the prospect of personal liability and the threat of protracted personal tort litigation for the entire Federal workforce.

"(6) The prospect of such liability will seriously undermine the morale and well being of Federal employees, impede the ability of agencies to carry out their missions, and diminish the vitality of the Federal Tort Claims Act as the proper remedy for Federal employees torts." § 2(a), 102 Stat 4563, 28 USC § 2671 note.

[152] The members of the panel were Learned Hand, Chief Judge, and Augustus N. Hand and Charles E. Clark, Circuit Judges.

[153] Cong Globe, 37th Cong, 2d Sess, App 2 (1861).

[154] Unreported judgment.

> The Commissioner may by Order provide that any area of the fishing waters lying to the north of sixty degrees south of latitude specified in the order (a "specified area") fishing is prohibited unless it is authorised by a licence granted by the Director of Fisheries or is permitted under subsection (14).

The interpretation Section (Section 2) and Section 3 show that the "fishing waters" of South Georgia and the South Sandwich Islands comprise the internal waters, the territorial sea and the Maritime Zone; the last of which is the zone of that name established by and defined in a proclamation by the Commissioner for South Georgia and the South Sandwich Islands. The relevant Proclamation is that of 7 May 1993, establishing a Maritime Zone of 200 nautical miles from the points there referred to.

The Order makes provision, in accordance with Section 5(1) of the Ordinance, for "the specified area". By virtue of Articles 3(1) and (2) of the Order, the specified area is all parts of the fishing waters lying to the north of sixty degrees South of latitude.

Neither Section 5 of the Ordinance nor the Order applies to fishing which is undertaken for the purpose(s) of genuine scientific research which has been notified in advance to the Secretariat provided for by the Convention on the Conservation of Antarctic Marine Living Resources ("the Convention"); although it is not obvious to me why the Ordinance is expressed in the singular and the Order in the plural.

Article 4(1) of the Order provides:

> Subject as expressed in Article 3(1) and to paragraph (2) of this Article, all fishing operations in the specified area are prohibited unless they are authorised by a licence granted under this Order.

Paragraph (2) refers to trans-shipment of fish authorized by a licence granted under the Fisheries (Trans-shipment and Export) Regulations 1990.

Section 5(3) of the Ordinance provides:

> Where any fishing boat is used in contravention of any prohibition imposed by an Order under this section, the master, the owner and the charterer (if any) each commit an offence under this subsection and are each liable on conviction thereof to a fine without limit.

In the version of the Ordinance available to me, the "on" is printed as "an", but I treat this as a typographical error that does not change the clear meaning of the sub-section.

The effect of all of the above is that all fishing operations in the specified area are prohibited, and constitute a criminal offence, unless they are undertaken for the purpose(s) of genuine scientific research which has been notified in advance to the Secretariat provided for by the Convention, are authorized by a licence granted under the Order or they consist of trans-shipment of fish authorized by a licence granted under the Fisheries (Trans-shipment and Export) Regulations 1990. This should be borne in mind when charging offences under the Ordinance. The charge (as the amended charge does) should follow the wording of the Ordinance. A charge that does not do so, and which is expressed simply in terms of negativing an exception to a general prohibition which is not referred to, would be defective.

I turn now to the facts. No evidence has been called. The facts upon which this judgment is based have been established by admission in the course of the proceedings.

I am satisfied so that I am sure that on 5 March 1996, the *Antonio Lorenzo*, a fishing boat then owned by the defendant Pesquera Concar SA, was used for fishing operations within the specified area. This being the case, it is for the defence to show an exception provided for in Article 4(1) of the Order or otherwise which avoids the prohibition imposed by the Order in accordance with the provisions of Section 5(1) of the Ordinance. This is the effect of Section 101 of the Magistrate's Courts Act 1980 which, in any event, simply reflects the common law rule which I would be persuaded to apply if it were necessary; see *R v. Edwards* [1974] 1 QB 27. The standard of proof is that of a balance of probabilities. I am persuaded that this is the case by the decision in *Islington London Borough v. Panico* [1973] 3 All ER 485.

The defence has not called any evidence, nor has it called upon the prosecution to make any admissions of fact. There is, therefore, no evidence, nor is it asserted, that the fishing operations in the present case were undertaken for the purposes of genuine scientific research notified in advance to the Secretariat provided for by the Convention, that they were authorized by a licence granted under the Order (the contrary has been admitted) or that the fishing operations were transshipment of fish authorized by a licence granted under the Fisheries (Trans-shipment and Export) Regulations 1990 (the admitted facts also showing that the fishing operations did not amount to a trans-shipment).

Mr Kilmartin does not rely on any defence to be found within the laws referred to. He asserts that the treaty obligations to which South Georgia and the South Sandwich Islands are subject are such as to nullify the laws which it is sought to rely upon in this case. This raises the fundamental question of whether and, if so, to what extent this Court may look any further than the laws which it is empowered to apply. The Falkland Islands Courts (Overseas Jurisdiction) Order 1989 is an Order of Her Majesty, by and with the advice of Her Privy Council, which takes effect as law. It is mandatory in its terms. By virtue of Section 6(1) (the word "shall" is used), I am required, in all matters of substantive law, to apply the law of South Georgia and the South Sandwich Islands in exercising the jurisdiction conferred upon me by Section 3. However, Mr Kilmartin suggests that I should read the law of South Georgia and the South Sandwich Islands subject to its treaty obligations, even to the extent of rendering that law (or part of it) of no effect. This begs the question of whether the law of South Georgia and the South Sandwich Islands enables me to do so.

It will surprise nobody that the law of South Georgia and the South Sandwich Islands does not have a large body of established case-law, on this or any other subject. I approach this, therefore, on the basis of general principle and persuasive authorities from other jurisdictions.

I do not intend to diminish Mr Kilmartin's eloquent and erudite arguments by paraphrasing them but, in summary, they amount to this. The United Kingdom (including on behalf of South Georgia and the South Sandwich Islands) is a Contracting Party to the Convention on the Conservation of Antarctic Marine Living Resources. The Convention covers a geographical area more extensive than that covered by the Antarctic Treaty. Article I(1) of the Convention provides:

> This Convention applies to the Antarctic marine living resources of the area south of 60° South latitude and to the Antarctic marine living resources of the area between that latitude and the Antarctic Convergence which form part of the Antarctic marine ecosystem.

It is common ground that the *Antonio Lorenzo* was conducting its fishing operations on 5 March 1996 within the Antarctic Convergence, as defined in the Convention. I have not been offered any assistance as to whether the (approximately) ten tonnes of headed and gutted fish on the vessel had once formed part of the Antarctic marine ecosystem. Mr Kilmartin argues that if I look at the provisions of the Convention, as amplified by an annexed Statement by the Chairman, I will find that the Maritime Zone has been established in breach of the treaty obligations contained within the Convention. That does not seem to me to be the case; Article IV(2) of the Convention provides:

> Nothing in this Convention and no acts or activities taking place while the present Convention is in force shall:
>
> ... (b) be interpreted as a renunciation or diminution by any Contracting Party of, or as prejudicing, any right or claim or basis of claim to exercise coastal state jurisdiction under international law within the area to which this Convention applies; ...

I would have thought it obvious that this included the right to establish a Maritime Zone in accordance with the established principles of customary international law, but Mr Kilmartin argues that it was tainted, in the present instance, by the assertion of the right to establish a Maritime Zone extending south of 60° latitude south, thus breaching Article IV(2)(d) of the Convention, which confirms that:

> ... no new claim, or enlargement of an existing claim, to territorial sovereignty in Antarctica shall be asserted while the Antarctic Treaty is in force.

I doubt that the establishment of a Maritime Zone amounts to an assertion of "territorial sovereignty" (it carries with it only a claim to exercise sovereign rights for the purpose of exploring and exploiting, conserving and managing the marine natural resources therein) and, in any event, I am unable to see how the establishment of a zone extending south of 60° latitude south can prejudice any claim to that part of the zone falling north of 60° latitude south. If a person claims a hundred acres of land he does not, by reason of claiming that hundred acres, lose the sixty acres of it that he is actually found to be entitled to. In fact, presumably to avoid any argument of this type, the Ordinance (Section 5(1)) only empowers the Commissioner to prescribe a "specified area" in any area of the fishing waters lying to the north of sixty degrees south of latitude, i.e. outside of the area covered by the Antarctic Treaty. Were it necessary, I would find that there is no conflict between the domestic provisions and the treaty obligations. It is clear from the whole scheme of the Ordinance that it was drafted so as to comply with, rather than detract from, the treaty obligations.

But interesting though all of this is, I find myself constrained by the legal principles that I must apply.

The conclusion and ratification of a treaty is an Executive act, not a legislative one. The entry into a treaty obligation by or on behalf of South Georgia and the South Sandwich Islands does not, of itself, affect the domestic or municipal law of South Georgia and the South Sandwich Islands so as to give effect, in law, to those treaty obligations. As is commonly said, treaty obligations are not self-executing. It is only if there is an ambiguity (latent or otherwise) in any law enacted to give effect to those treaty obligations that, as an aid to construction, I would be able to look at and take account of a document such as the Convention. I find no ambiguity in the wording of Article 4(1) of the Order, which reads:

> Subject as expressed in Article 3(1) and to paragraph (2) of this Article, all fishing operations in the specified area are prohibited unless they are authorised by a licence granted under this Ordinance ...

Nor do I find any ambiguity in Section 5 of the Ordinance, sub-section (3) of which provides:

> Where any fishing boat is used in contravention of any prohibition imposed by an Order under this section, the master, the owner and the charterer (if any) each commit an offence under this subsection and are each liable on conviction thereof to a fine without limit.

I am persuaded that the principles set out in the cases to which I have been referred, chiefly *Chung Chi Cheung v. The King* [1939] AC 160[155] and *R v. Home Secretary, ex parte Brind* [1991] AC 697,[156] reflect what is the law of South Georgia and the South Sandwich Islands. In fact, I am probably bound by the first of these, as it is a decision of the Judicial Committee of the Privy Council. I therefore apply the clear and unambiguous provisions already referred to and being satisfied so that I am sure of the matters previously referred to, and the defence having shown no exception, exemption, proviso, excuse or qualification which could cause me to find otherwise, I find the defendant guilty.

Attorney General of the Commonwealth of Australia, Outline of Submissions as Amicus Curiae in the case of *Humane Society International Inc v Kyodo Senpaku Kaisha Ltd* (Federal Court of Australia, 25 January 2005)

[Issue: international legal issues concerning Antarctica and their relationship to domestic laws concerning Antarctica and their enforcement]

[155] 9 *Ann Dig* 264.
[156] 85 *ILR* 29.

INTRODUCTION

1. In response to the judgment of Allsop J of 23 November 2004 [2004] FCA 1510 the Attorney-General seeks leave to appear as amicus curiae for the purpose of making the following written submissions. The Attorney-General wishes to rely on the written submissions alone and does not seek to be further heard.

ISSUES RELATING TO THE EXERCISE OF THE COURT'S DISCRETION

Principles of international law relating to jurisdiction

2. Under international law, the right of a State to exercise jurisdiction depends on there being a sufficiently close connection between the subject matter and the State to justify that State in regulating the matter. (See Jennings and Watts, Oppenheim's International Law (9th ed, 1992) ('Oppenheim'), vol 1, paragraph 136, pages 457–8). Territoriality is the primary basis for jurisdiction. There are also other bases, eg a State may exercise jurisdiction, within its own territory, over its nationals travelling or residing abroad, since they remain under its personal authority.

3. A State's jurisdiction extends for certain purposes to adjacent maritime zones, even though those zones are not part of the State's sovereign territory. The United Nations Convention on the Law of the Sea, done at Montego Bay on 10 December 1982, [1994] ATS 31 ('UNCLOS') provides for an exclusive economic zone (EEZ) extending up to 200 nautical miles from the territorial sea baselines of the coastal State (Article 57 of UNCLOS). In its EEZ, the coastal State has sovereign rights for the purpose of exploring and exploiting, conserving and managing natural resources, and with regard to other activities for the economic exploitation and exploration of the zone (Article 56 of UNCLOS). In the exercise of these rights, the coastal State may take necessary measures in the EEZ to ensure compliance with its relevant laws. Those measures include, for example, boarding, inspection, arrest and judicial proceedings (Article 73 of UNCLOS).

4. The coastal State's jurisdiction in the EEZ is, thus, not as extensive as in its territory. It has only sovereign rights for limited purposes and not full sovereignty.

5. Parts of the sea that are not included in the EEZ, territorial sea or in the internal waters of a State, or in the archipelagic waters of an archipelagic State, are the 'high seas'.

No State has territorial jurisdiction over the high seas. Under international law, every vessel sailing the high seas has the nationality of the State whose flag it flies. The vessel, and persons and things aboard the vessel, are subject to the law of the flag State, and are in general subject to its exclusive jurisdiction. (Oppenheim, paragraph 287, page 731.)

The Australian Antarctic Territory (AAT) and the adjacent waters under international law

Claims to land territory in Antarctica

6. Australia considers that it has sovereignty over the Australian Antarctic Territory. Australia and six other States[157] have territorial claims in Antarctica. None of these claims is recognised by more than a limited number of other States. Only four States formally recognise Australia's territorial claim. These States are Norway, France and New Zealand, whose claims are adjacent to Australia's, and the United Kingdom.

7. In order to form a legal framework for activities in Antarctica to proceed unencumbered by arguments over the validity of claims to territorial sovereignty, the Antarctic Treaty (Washington, 1 December 1959) [1961] ATS 12, was concluded in 1959 and entered into force in 1961.

8. Article IV of the Antarctic Treaty provides that nothing in the Treaty shall be interpreted as a renunciation of a claim, or as prejudicing the position of any Party as regards its recognition or non-recognition of any other State's claim, to territorial sovereignty in Antarctica. In addition, while the Treaty is in force, no new claim, or enlargement of an existing claim, may be asserted and no acts or activities taking place while the Treaty is in force shall constitute a basis for asserting,

[157] Argentina, Chile, France, New Zealand, Norway, and the UK.

supporting or denying a claim. Thus, the Antarctic Treaty in effect provides for a balance between potentially competing interests, by preserving the status quo as it was at the time of the Treaty's completion. Australia's claim precedes the entry into force of the Antarctic Treaty.

9. Twenty-one of the 28 Consultative Parties to the Antarctic Treaty have made no claims to Antarctic Territory to date and do not recognise the existing claims. There are currently 45 Parties (consultative and non-consultative) in total. Japan is a Consultative Party to the Antarctic Treaty. Japan does not recognise Australia's claim to the AAT.

10. As a matter of practice, issues relating to territorial sovereignty in Antarctica are avoided by each Antarctic Treaty Party regulating the activities of its own nationals in Antarctica and the conduct of its scientific expeditions.

The Antarctic seas and claims to maritime zones in Antarctica

11. Article VI of the Antarctic Treaty provides that nothing in the Treaty shall prejudice or in any way affect the rights, or the exercise of the rights, of any State under international law with regard to the high seas within the region below 60° South. Under the Antarctic Treaty no provision has been made for controlling whaling in the maritime areas below 60° South. The Convention on the Conservation of Antarctic Marine Living Resources, (Canberra, 20 May 1980) [1982] ATS 9 ('CCAMLR'), which deals with fishing activities in the area, specifically preserves the operation of the International Convention for the Regulation of Whaling, (Washington, 2 December 1946) [1948] ATS 18 ('Whaling Convention').

12. Under UNCLOS, maritime zones are attributable to any territory, including in the Antarctic. Accordingly, Australia has established maritime zones off the AAT. Australia considers that this is consistent with Article IV of the Antarctic Treaty. Other States need not recognise this action. If a State does not recognise Australia's claim to the AAT, it follows that it will not recognise the related EEZ.

13. Japan does not recognise Australia's claim to the AAT or its assertion of an adjacent EEZ. Accordingly, it considers that the waters adjacent to the AAT are part of the high seas, and that Australia therefore has no sovereign rights in relation to these waters (ie no jurisdiction over non-Australian vessels or non-Australian citizens in those waters). Rather, it considers that Japan, as the flag State, has exclusive jurisdiction over Japanese vessels, and persons and things on those vessels, while they are in the waters concerned.

14. Japan would consider any attempt to enforce Australian law against Japanese vessels and its nationals, in the waters adjacent to the AAT, to be a breach of international law on Australia's part.

15. Japan's response would reflect the fact that, in the present case, Australia would be treating as criminal conduct which the Government of Japan not only does not regard as an offence, but which it specifically authorised under Japanese law, in accordance with what Japan considers to be its rights under the Whaling Convention. (The Australian Government does not consider that, even if the authorisation is consistent with the Whaling Convention, this overrides the rights of a coastal State in its EEZ, but Japan does not recognise that Australia has those rights in the area concerned.)

16. Further, enforcement of Australian law against foreigners in Antarctic waters, based on jurisdiction deriving from Australia's territorial claim to the AAT and associated EEZ, can reasonably be expected to prompt a significant adverse reaction from other Antarctic Treaty Parties. To this point, the Australian Government has not enforced its laws in Antarctica against the nationals of other States which are Parties to the Antarctic Treaty, except when such persons have voluntarily subjected themselves to Australia law (for example, by applying for permits under the applicable Australian laws), as each Party has responsibility for the activities of its own nationals under the Antarctic Treaty.

17. Japan has indicated that enforcement of Australian law against Japanese vessels would be likely to give rise to an international disagreement with Japan. Similar disputes could also arise with other countries that do not accept Australia's claim to the AAT. To this point, Australia's

claim to the AAT, although not widely recognised, has not been the subject of a dispute in an international court or tribunal. The object of Article IV of the Antarctic Treaty was to avoid such disputes, by preserving the status quo with respect to Antarctic claims. Provoking a disagreement in this instance may undermine the status quo, which would be contrary to Australia's long term national interests.

The AAT and adjacent waters under Australian law

18. In accordance with Australia's claim under international law, as a matter of Australian law, the AAT has been accepted as a territory of the Commonwealth (section 2 of the Australian Antarctic Territory Acceptance Act 1933). Similarly, in accordance with Australia's claim under international law, waters adjacent to the AAT have been proclaimed as part of Australia's EEZ under the Seas and Submerged Lands Act 1973.

19. As a matter of Australian law, therefore, the AAT is an external territory, and the relevant waters off the AAT are part of Australia's EEZ. Accordingly, the relevant provisions of the Environment Protection and Biodiversity Conservation Act 1999 (EPBC Act) apply to foreigners and foreign vessels in the waters concerned (section 5 of the EPBC Act).

Considerations relating to the enforcement of Australian law in the waters adjacent to the AAT

20. Non-recognition of Australia's claim to the AAT and associated EEZ by other States, as a matter of international law, does not preclude the application of the EPBC Act as a matter of Australian law. However, the Commonwealth considers that it is a key consideration to be taken into account in deciding whether or not to seek to enforce that legislation in relation to persons and vessels with the nationality of the States concerned.

21. The Commonwealth Government considers that it is generally more appropriate to pursue diplomatic solutions in relation to activities by foreign vessels in the EEZ off the AAT.

22. This is consistent with international practice with respect to Antarctica. As explained above, the Antarctic Treaty has successfully operated to date on the basis that each Antarctic Treaty Party is prepared to regulate the activities of its nationals in the region subject to that Treaty.

Issues of practical enforcement: utility of injunction and/or declaration

23. For the reasons discussed above, the Commonwealth has not sought to intercept, board and arrest Japanese vessels engaged in whaling activities in the EEZ adjacent to the AAT. (Attachment A sets out an extract from the brief that is given to each Australian Antarctic Division Voyage Leader, providing instructions as to what they should do in the event of sighting Japanese whalers in the EEZ off the AAT.) This is apart from the significant practical and logistical difficulties of intercepting, and then successfully boarding, fast and well equipped vessels in the remote, vast and hostile Southern Ocean environment.

24. In any case, if it were to do so, the exercise of enforcement powers would be based on contravention of the offence provisions in the EPBC Act, and not on the existence of an injunction and/or declaration.

25. Under Australian law, failure of the respondent to comply with an injunction would constitute contempt of court. However, since the defendant is not located in Australian territory, and has no assets in Australian territory, probably it will ultimately not be possible to enforce against the defendant any orders made by the Court.

26. It could not be expected that an injunction or declaration would be given any effect under Japanese law. Generally, the courts of a country decline to give effect to the public law, as distinguished from private law, of foreign States unless otherwise required by any relevant treaty. There is no relevant treaty in this case. Although in such matters courts often base their refusal to enforce foreign public law upon considerations of public policy, in international law a basis for that widespread practice is to be found in the principle of territorial authority, from which it follows that

> states have no right to perform acts of sovereignty within the territory of other states. For a state's public law to be enforced in another state would in effect involve the performance of acts of

sovereignty in foreign states in derogation of their territorial authority. (Oppenheim, paragraph 144, page 490)

27. This is a reflection of the distinction between the jurisdiction to prescribe conduct and the jurisdiction to enforce, which depends on the presence of a person in the jurisdiction of the enforcing State.

Decision on enforcement more appropriately exercised by Commonwealth

28. The Attorney-General submits that in the light of the complex factors relating to the enforcement of Australian law against foreign nationals in relation to activities in the EEZ off the AAT, it should be left to the Commonwealth Executive to decide on the appropriate action to be taken in such cases. This is particularly so where, as in this case, the Commonwealth has deliberately not taken enforcement action in the waters concerned (eg by intercepting and boarding vessels), and where it does not appear that judicial orders would be capable of effective enforcement.

29. The Attorney-General also notes that a substantive hearing of this case, the issue of an injunction and the issue of a declaration would be expected to harm Australia's relations with Japan as well as other Antarctic Treaty Parties. Moreover, as explained above, the international disagreements and challenges that enforcement could prompt could undermine the Antarctic Treaty and, ultimately, Australia's position with respect to the AAT.

30. The Attorney-General asks the Court to take these issues into account in the exercise of its discretion.

OTHER POINTS

'Recognised foreign authority'

31. The Attorney-General does not consider that the Japanese permit for scientific whaling (JARPA) is a 'recognised foreign authority' for the purposes of subsection 7(1) of the Antarctic Treaty (Environment Protection) Act 1980 ('ATEP Act'). Accordingly, the Attorney-General does not consider that the JARPA prevents the application of sections 229, 229A, 229B, 229C, 229D and 230 of the EPBC Act. The Attorney-General considers that, as a matter of Australian law, those provisions of the EPBC Act apply.

Whaling Convention

32. The Attorney-General agrees with the conclusion of the Court that whatever the rights in public international law that Japan enjoys under Article VIII of the Whaling Convention, the content of the relevant Australian municipal law can be seen to be such as to prohibit the killing of whales for any purpose ... in the Australian Whale Sanctuary. (For the reasons already given, the Attorney-General considers that the reference in the judgment to 'Australian territory, including the Antarctic EEZ' is not accurate.)

33. Australia has consistently opposed the Japanese 'scientific' whaling program, in the International Whaling Commission established by the Whaling Convention. However, the Whaling Convention does not authorise any Party to take enforcement action against another Party for breach of the Convention. Accordingly, Australia cannot claim jurisdiction over Japanese whaling vessels on the basis of the Whaling Convention. The appropriate way to deal with activities which Australia considers to be contrary to the Whaling Convention is by diplomatic action, in particular in the International Whaling Commission.

34. Australia's jurisdiction to prohibit the killing, taking etc of whales by foreign nationals in Australia's EEZ does not depend on the activities in question being inconsistent with the Whaling Convention. Rather, it relies on Australia's rights in relation to the natural resources of the EEZ and the protection and preservation of the marine environment, as provided for by UNCLOS. These rights arise by virtue of Australia's territorial claim over the AAT which, as explained above, is not widely recognised.

Meaning of 'in the Commonwealth' in the Federal Court Rules

35. The Attorney-General agrees that the case falls within the scope of rule 1(1) of Order 8 of the Federal Court Rules.

36. However, the Attorney-General submits that the expression 'in the Commonwealth', in rules 1(a), (b), and (j) of Order 8, does not include the EEZ outside the territorial sea (12 nautical miles). Order 1 rule 4 of the Federal Court Rules provides that, in the Rules, unless the contrary intention appears, Australia or the Commonwealth means the Commonwealth of Australia and when used in a geographical sense includes external territories.

37. Paragraph 15B(1)(b) of the Acts Interpretation Act 1901 provides that, except so far as the contrary intention appears, a reference to 'Australia' or to 'the Commonwealth' shall be read as including a reference to the 'coastal sea'. The 'coastal sea' is defined in subsection 15(4) as including the territorial sea of Australia and sea landward of the territorial sea, but it does not include the EEZ outside the territorial sea.

38. The presumption created by paragraph 15B(1)(b), that a reference to 'Australia' or 'the Commonwealth' includes the territorial sea, expands, rather than restricts, the ordinary meaning of those words. That ordinary meaning does not include the EEZ. The EEZ is not part of the territory over which Australia has sovereignty as a matter of international law. Rather, Australia may exercise in the EEZ sovereign rights in relation to certain matters.

39. Where a contrary intention appears, displacing the operation of paragraph 15B(1)(b) of the Acts Interpretation Act, therefore, generally the effect will be that 'Commonwealth' or 'Australia' is to be interpreted as not including the territorial sea, not that those terms are to be interpreted as including the EEZ. Those terms would encompass the EEZ, only if it is clear from the terms, or the context, of the provision in which they appear, that they are intended to have that (unusual) meaning.

40. The Australian Antarctic Territory Acceptance Act 1933, and the Australian Antarctic Territory Act 1954, do not have the effect of extending the meaning of 'Australia' or 'the Commonwealth' to include an EEZ off the AAT. They do not refer to the EEZ; the concept of an EEZ was not recognised at the time those Acts were passed. Section 10B of the Seas and Submerged Lands Act 1973 (Cth) and the proclamation of the EEZ on 29 July 1994 also do not affect the meaning of 'Commonwealth' and 'Australia'. They establish the proclaimed area as part of Australia's EEZ, for the purposes of Australian law. Section 10A of the Seas and Submerged Lands Act provides that the rights and jurisdiction of Australia in its EEZ are vested in and exercisable by the Crown in right of the Commonwealth. However, none of these provisions declares the EEZ to be part of the Commonwealth, or part of Australia, geographically speaking.

41. Some provisions of the EPBC Act, including those relating to the Australian Whale Sanctuary, expressly apply to the EEZ. The application of the EPBC Act to certain activities in the EEZ brings those activities within the scope of rule 1(l) – 'where the proceeding concerns the construction, effect or enforcement of an Act' – since that rule is not limited geographically. However, the Attorney-General submits that the scope of application of the EPBC Act does not affect the interpretation of the expression 'in the Commonwealth' in rules 1(a), (b), and (j).

42. An interpretation of 'in the Commonwealth' as not including the EEZ is also consistent with the extent of Australia's jurisdiction as a matter of international law. Australia's sovereign rights in the EEZ are restricted to certain matters. Australia cannot, consistently with international law, apply its law on other matters to non-Australian nationals in the EEZ, except by agreement with the State of nationality. For Australian courts to exercise jurisdiction generally over actions in its EEZ, on the basis that there was jurisdiction in relation to 'anything to be done in the Commonwealth or ... the doing of any act in the Commonwealth' (rule 1(j)) by foreign nationals, would not be consistent with international law.

Date: 25 January 2005
Henry Burmester QC
Benjamin Dubé
A solicitor employed by Australian Government Solicitor
Solicitor for the Attorney-General

ATTACHMENT A

Extract from instructions to Australian Antarctic Division Voyage Leaders

6.1.1 Sightings of whaling or fishing vessels

Outlined below are the procedures to follow in the event that either whaling or fishing vessels are encountered within the Convention Area of the Commission for the Conservation of Antarctic Marine Living Resources (CCAMLR), or in the vicinity of Macquarie Island. The procedures will vary according to the type of vessel encountered and/or the area in which it is encountered (see categories and procedures outlined below). However, procedures common to all encounters which should be followed as a minimum include:

- video recording any communications with vessels encountered;
- attempts to identify the vessel – this should include asking (by radio) the vessel to provide its name, call sign, Lloyd's registration number (also called the IMO number), home port and Flag State (i.e. the country where the vessel is registered);
- confirming with the vessel its position and course (so that they are on record as knowing where they are) and asking what activities they are licensed to undertake;
- obtaining photographs and video footage (if possible) of the vessel from as many different angles as possible;
- photographing of the overall vessel, with bow, port side, starboard side and stern views and close-ups of any special features (e.g. name, identifying marks, etc), to assist in further identification of the vessel; and
- completing a Vessel Activity Report form at the time of the sighting – that provides prompts about which information is needed.

It is important to provide an accurate and detailed account of any encounters as it is possible that this information may need to be submitted as evidence in legal proceedings at a later date.

The voyage leader, as the official representative of the Australian Antarctic Division, is primarily responsible for communications with any vessels encountered.

6.1.1.1 A whaling vessel within Australia's Exclusive Economic Zone (including Australia's Exclusive Economic Zone adjacent to the Australian Antarctic Territory)

The 1946 International Convention for the Regulation of Whaling allows countries that are parties to that Convention to grant special permits to their nationals authorising the killing and taking of whales for scientific research. Scientific permits issued under the Convention can only authorise research on the high seas, i.e. in waters outside any country's Exclusive Economic Zone (EEZ).

Under the international law of the sea, all vessels are entitled to freedom of navigation through a country's EEZ. However, they are subject to that country's laws relating to the exploration, exploitation, conservation and management of the natural resources of the EEZ.

The waters comprising the Australian EEZ – including the EEZ adjacent to the Australian Antarctic Territory – have been declared the Australian Whale Sanctuary under the Environment Protection and Biodiversity Conservation Act 1999. It is an offence under that Act to kill or cause injury to a cetacean within the Australian Whale Sanctuary.

Only Japan has issued scientific permits under the above-mentioned Convention to its nationals to allow them to undertake lethal research on whales in Antarctic waters. The Japanese government's position is that these special permits allow Japanese nationals to undertake lethal research on whales throughout all Antarctic waters including in the Australian EEZ off the Australian Antarctic Territory. This is because Japan does not recognise Australia's territorial claim over the Australian Antarctic Territory and to the EEZ adjacent to it.

The voyage leader should advise any vessels involved in whaling activities within Australia's EEZ that they are whaling within the Australian Whale Sanctuary and in contravention of Australian legislation. They should then be advised that their details have been passed on to the Australian authorities and be asked to leave Australian waters.

Japanese whaling vessels encountered in Australia's EEZ adjacent to the Australian Antarctic Territory are likely to claim that they are whaling on the high seas in accordance with international law (see above paragraphs) and that Australian laws cannot apply to them. As such, they may refuse to leave. If this occurs, no further enforcement action should be taken.

Sightings of whaling vessels in Australia's EEZ should be advised in the first instance via telephone to Tom Kaveney of the Approvals and Wildlife Division on 0409 127 808.2 Following this, the Vessel Activity Report form should be emailed to vessel.sightings@aad.gov.au so that other appropriate action can be taken promptly through the Australian Antarctic Division's headquarters in Kingston.

2 The Approvals and Wildlife Division of the Australian Government Department of the Environment and Heritage is responsible for whales and whaling issues occurring in Australia's EEZ.

Humane Society International Inc v Kyodo Senpaku Kaisha Ltd [2005] FCA 664 (Federal Court of Australia, Justice Allsop, 27 May 2005)

[Issue: relevance of the executive government's views on international law matters concerning Antarctica, in the exercise of a judicial discretion to serve originating process on a foreign company in respect of alleged violations of Australian environmental laws in the Antarctic area]

THE COURT ORDERS THAT:

1. To the extent necessary Parts 2.2, 3.2 and 3.3 of the *Evidence Act 1995* (Cth) not apply to the submissions filed on behalf of the Attorney-General as *amicus curiae* to prove the facts referred to therein as to the state of non-recognition of Australia's Antarctic Territory and Antarctic EEZ and the conduct of the Australian Executive in dealing with conduct of parties within the Antarctic EEZ and said submissions be marked exhibit 1.

2. The application for leave to serve the originating process on the respondent in Japan be dismissed.

Note: Settlement and entry of orders is dealt with in Order 36 of the Federal Court Rules.

REASONS FOR JUDGMENT

1. I refer to my reasons dated 23 November 2004 ([2004] FCA 1510). I will not repeat matters (including definitions) there set out. These reasons should be read in conjunction with those reasons. Since November, I have received submissions made on behalf of the Attorney-General of the Commonwealth as amicus curiae. The applicant has responded to those submissions with written submissions of its own.

2. The submissions of the Attorney-General raised a number of issues with which it is necessary to deal, these being:

(a) the nature of Australia's sovereignty over the Australian Antarctic EEZ and the grounds available under the relevant provisions of Order 8 Rule 1 of the Federal Court Rules, including the meaning of the phrase "in the Commonwealth" therein;
(b) the nature of Australia's claims to the Australian Antarctic Territory and the adjacent EEZ and the lack of international recognition of those claims;
(c) the likely consequences of any attempted curial enforcement of the EPBC Act upon Australia's international relations with Japan and other countries;
(d) the Commonwealth Government's views as to the appropriate means of dealing with activities in the Antarctic EEZ, such as those apparently conducted by the respondent, which may be seen to be in contravention of the EPBC Act; and
(e) the futility of any order permitting service in Japan.

3. The submissions of the applicant dealt with these matters as well as the two matters in respect of which I sought further assistance in my reasons of November:

(a) whether the permits issued by Japan to the respondent, apparently under Article VIII of the Whaling Convention, cannot also be seen to be permits under Article 3 rules 1 and 2 of Annex II to the Madrid Protocol; and

(b) the form of the pleading and whether it was pregnant with the proposition that the activities of the respondent exceeded what was allowed for by the relevant permit issued to it by the Government of Japan.

4. At the centre of the submissions on behalf of the Attorney-General are the international law issues attending Australia's claim to the Antarctic EEZ. There is no dispute that as a matter of Australian municipal law the Australian Antarctic Territory (that is Australian Antarctica "proper") is an external territory of Australia and the relevant adjacent waters of the Australian Antarctic Territory are part of Australia's Antarctic EEZ. Accordingly, there is no dispute that, as a matter of Australian municipal law, the provisions of the EPBC Act apply to foreigners and foreign flagged vessels (such as the respondent and its vessels) in the waters concerned.

5. The submissions on behalf of the Attorney-General reveal that Australia's claims to sovereignty over the Australian Antarctic Territory (along with the similar territorial claims of Argentina, Chile, New Zealand, Norway and the United Kingdom to different parts of the continent) are recognised by only a small number of countries. Formal recognition of Australia's claim is limited to four countries, including some of the other claimants to Antarctic territory: Norway, New Zealand, France and the United Kingdom. Japan does not recognise Australia's claim of territorial sovereignty over the Australian Antarctic Territory.

6. The legal framework (in terms of public international law) for activities in Antarctica that has been put in place to avoid arguments over fundamental claims to territorial sovereignty is found in the *Antarctic Treaty 1959*. The *Antarctic Treaty*, to which there are 28 Consultative Parties (both Australia and Japan being parties), provides (in Article IV) for the preservation of the positions of Parties in relation to their claims, or their opposition to claims of others, of territorial sovereignty.

7. Article VI of the *Antarctic Treaty* provides:

The provisions of the present Treaty shall apply to the area south of 60° South Latitude, including all ice shelves, but nothing in the present Treaty shall prejudice or in any way affect the rights, or the exercise of the rights, of any State under international law with regard to the high seas within that area.

8. The Australian domestic legislation concerning the Antarctic EEZ must (subject to any contrary intention in the domestic statute) be read conformably with the international convention providing the foundation for the legislation: *El Greco (Australia) Pty Ltd v Mediterranean Shipping Co SA* (2004) 209 ALR 448; [2004] 2 Lloyd's Rep 537 at [142] and the cases there referred to. The extension of territorial claims for control or some form of sovereignty to adjacent maritime waters is now regulated under international law in the *United Nations Conventions on the Law of the Sea*, done at Montego Bay on 10 December 1982 ("UNCLOS"). UNCLOS provides for the notion of EEZs up to 200 nautical miles beyond baselines of the coastal States from which the breadth of territorial seas are measured: see Article 57 of UNCLOS. Article 55 of UNCLOS recognises the fact that the claims for sovereignty in an EEZ are to be seen as balanced against the rights of other States and are to be found within the compromises embodied within the terms of UNCLOS. Article 55 reads:

Specific legal regime of the exclusive economic zone.

The exclusive economic zone is an area beyond and adjacent to the territorial sea, subject to the specific legal regime established in this Part, under which the rights and jurisdiction of the coastal State and the rights and freedoms of other States are governed by the relevant provisions of this Convention.

9. I referred in my earlier reasons to Article 65 of UNCLOS (see [54]). The balance between coastal States and other States can be seen in the terms of Articles 56 and 58 of UNCLOS which are in the following terms:

Article 56
Rights, jurisdiction and duties of the coastal State in the exclusive economic zone
1. In the exclusive economic zone, the coastal State has:

(a) sovereign rights for the purpose of exploring and exploiting, conserving and managing the natural resources, whether living or non-living, of the waters superjacent to the sea-bed and of the sea-bed and its subsoil, and with regard to other activities for the economic exploitation and exploration of the zone, such as the production of energy from the water, currents and winds;

(b) jurisdiction as provided for in the relevant provisions of this Convention with regard to:

(i) the establishment and use of artificial islands, installations and structures;

(ii) marine scientific research;

(iii) the protection and preservation of the marine environment;

(c) other rights and duties provided for in this Convention.

2. In exercising its rights and performing its duties under this Convention in the exclusive economic zone, the coastal State shall have due regard to the rights and duties of other States and shall act in a manner compatible with the provisions of this Convention.

3. The rights set out in this article with respect to the sea-bed and subsoil shall be exercised in accordance with Part VI.

...

Article 58
Rights and duties of other States in the exclusive economic zone
1. In the exclusive economic zone, all States, whether coastal or land-locked, enjoy, subject to the relevant provisions of this Convention, the freedoms referred to in article 87 of navigation and overflight and of the laying of submarine cables and pipelines, and other internationally lawful uses of the seas related to these freedoms, such as those associated with the operation of ships, aircraft and submarine cables and pipelines, and compatible with the other provisions of this Convention.

2. Articles 88 to 115 and other pertinent rules of international law apply to the exclusive economic zone in so far as they are not incompatible with this Part.

3. In exercising their rights and performing their duties under this Convention in the exclusive economic zone, States shall have due regard to the rights and duties of the coastal State and shall comply with the laws and regulations adopted by the coastal State in accordance with the provisions of this Convention and other rules of international law in so far as they are not incompatible with this Part.

10. Article 87 referred to in Article 58 paragraph 1 is the fundamental right of the freedom of the high seas. Article 89 provides that no State may validly purport to subject any part of the high seas to its sovereignty.

11. For a discussion of the nature of the limitations on the notion of sovereignty as used in Article 56 and in respect of the EEZ, see Koh "The Exclusive Economic Zone" 30 *Malaya Law Review* 1, reproduced in Caminos (Ed), *The Law of the Sea* (Ashgate 2001) p 155.

12. Thus, as it was submitted on behalf of the Attorney-General, the claim of Australia to the Antarctic EEZ is not one of sovereignty in the full sense over the waters adjacent to the Antarctic Territory (except for the territorial sea), but of claims (reflected in domestic legislation) to exercise the rights of exploitation, conservation, management and control, and enforcement thereof, given to coastal States by UNCLOS. (As to enforcement, see Article 73 of UNCLOS.) The recognition of the limitations (short of full claims to sovereignty) of Australia's claims to the Antarctic EEZ becomes important in assessing whether for the purposes of Order 8 Rules 1(a), (b) and (j) the acts of the respondent and the contraventions of the EPBC Act took place "in the Commonwealth". I will return to this issue. For the moment, it only needs to be recognised that Japan, by its non-recognition of the claim by Australia to sovereignty over the Antarctic Territory, does not recognise Australia's claims to the Antarctic EEZ and thus to Australia's

claim to entitlement, in international law, to pass domestic legislation such as the EPBC Act. As far as Japan is concerned, the Australian Antarctic EEZ is the high seas which is not subject to any legitimate control by Australia under UNCLOS and domestic legislation provided for thereby (such as the EPBC Act).

13. A recognition of the above has influenced the views, and affected the conduct, of the Australian Executive Government in the following manner described in the submissions on behalf of the Attorney-General. First, the Government considers that the Government of Japan would regard any attempt by Australia to enforce Australian law against Japanese vessels and its nationals in the Antarctic EEZ to be a breach of international law on Australia's part and would give rise to an international disagreement with Japan. Secondly, enforcement of Australian domestic law against foreigners in the Antarctic EEZ, based as it is on Australia's claim to territorial sovereignty to the relevant part of Antarctica, can be "reasonably expected to prompt a significant adverse reaction from other Antarctic Treaty Parties". Thirdly, up to this point, the Australian Government has not enforced the laws of the Commonwealth in Antarctica against nationals of other States which are Parties to the Antarctic Treaty, except where there has been submission to Australian law, for example by applying for permits under applicable Australian law.

14. The submissions on behalf of the Attorney-General also stated that Australia's claim to the Antarctic Territory, though not widely recognised, has not yet been disputed in an international court or tribunal (the avoidance of such disputes having been one aim of Article IV of the *Antarctic Treaty*). It was also stated that an assertion of jurisdiction by an Australian court over claims concerning rights and obligations found in the EPBC Act, in the view of the Government, would or may provoke an international disagreement with Japan, undermine the status quo attending the *Antarctic Treaty*, and "be contrary to Australia's long term national interests."

15. For the above reasons, it appears that the Commonwealth has not sought to intercept, board or arrest Japanese vessels engaged in whaling activities adjacent to the Antarctic Territory and in the Antarctic EEZ.

16. It was submitted by the Attorney-General that, whilst the EPBC Act applied as a matter of domestic legislation, the Executive Government of the Commonwealth considers what it sees (for the above reasons) as the more appropriate pursuit of diplomatic solutions in relation to activities (at least of this kind) by foreign vessels in the Antarctic EEZ to be a key consideration to be taken into account in the question of leave in these proceedings.

17. Two matters are important to note in respect of the above. First, (as could not be the case) the submissions put on behalf of (and so by) the Attorney-General did not purport to direct this Court in any way in the exercise of the judicial power of the Commonwealth arising under Chapter III of the Constitution in the Court's role as the third, and independent, arm of government (using that last word in the wider sense than it has been hitherto used in these reasons as referring to the Executive Government provided for under Chapter II of the Constitution). Secondly, the matters to which I have referred were put in submissions filed pursuant to the invitation which I gave in November 2004. No affidavit was filed seeking to prove the views of the Government, the approach and conduct of the Executive and the Government's concerns as to the effects on Australia's long term national interests and relations with other nation States, including Japan. No certificate was given by or on behalf of the Commonwealth with respect to a matter of foreign affairs.

18. The applicant submitted that because of the absence of an affidavit or a certificate, I could have no regard to these submissions. Judicial notice cannot be taken of these matters, it was submitted.

19. I reject that submission. The submissions of the Attorney-General stated the views and concerns of the Executive Government. These are matters that are, at least in the context in which they arise here, non-justiciable. At least in the framework in which the issues arise here, it is not for this Court to decide as a fact whether or not Japan will view a step taken by Australia

as a breach of international law, or whether or not Australia's long term national interests are best served by one course or another, or whether or not the use of the EPBC Act will endanger the diplomatic balance underlying the *Antarctic Treaty* or Australia's claims to sovereignty in Antarctica. These are questions, at least in the context in which they present themselves here as relevant considerations to be weighed in the exercise of a judicial discretion under Order 8, outside the purview of the Court: *Re Ditfort; Ex parte Deputy Commissioner of Taxation* (1988) 19 FCR 47, 367–73. On any view as to how one analyses the jurisprudential basis of non-justiciability (see *Re Ditfort* and Lindell "Judicial Review of International Affairs" in Opeskin and Rothwell (Eds) *International Law and Australian Federalism* pp 160–209) assessment of the conduct of foreign affairs (including the formation of relevant views about such matters and Australia's interests in such matters) will generally be outside the judicial function. I say "generally" because of the type of qualification adverted to by Brennan J in *Baker v Carr* 369 US 186, 211 (1962) and because of the need, always, to understand the operation of Chapter III of the Constitution and the context of the arising of the issue in question in the manner discussed by Gummow J in *Re Ditfort*.

20. The Chapter III context here is the decision whether or not to grant leave to serve process outside the jurisdiction. It is relevant to the exercise of the judicial power of the Commonwealth in that respect to understand the views of the Executive Government in weighing the possible consequences thereof. A consideration of those views does not involve a judicial enquiry as to the wisdom or correctness of those views. This is so because of the character of the subject matter of those views – international and foreign relations insofar as they may affect Australia and her interests. See generally: *Minister for Arts, Heritage and Environment v Peko Wallsend Ltd* (1987) 15 FCR 274, 278–79 (per Bowen CJ), 281 (per Sheppard J), 307, 308 (per Wilcox J); *Buttes Gas and Oil v Hammer (No 3)* [1982] AC 888, 937–38; *Gerhardy v Brown* (1985) 57 ALR 472, 523–24; *Petrotimor v Commonwealth* (2003) 126 FCR 354, 361 et seq. See also, in somewhat different contexts, *R v Bow Street Magistrates; Ex parte Pinochet (No 1)* [2000] 1 AC 61; *Kuwait Airways Corporation v Iraqi Airways Co (No 6)* [2002] 2 AC 883; *R v DPP; Ex parte Kebilene* [2000] 2 AC 326, 381; and *Secretary of State v Rehman* [2003] 1 AC 153.

21. To the extent that the submissions set out the understandings, views and concerns of the Executive Government of the Commonwealth of Australia, the submissions are adequate to inform me of those things. There was no suggestion that the submissions did not come with the authority of the Attorney-General and the Executive Government. They were signed by counsel, including Mr Burmester QC, on behalf of the Attorney-General, and filed by the Australian Government Solicitor. The submissions were a way of informing the Court of matters, which, on their face, were matters for the Executive Government, and not matters for investigation by the Court: *In re Westinghouse Uranium Contract* [1978] AC 547, 650–51; *Shaw Saville Albion Co Ltd v The Commonwealth* (1940) 66 CLR 344, 364; and *Attorney-General (UK) v Heinemann Publishers Australia Pty Ltd* (1988) 165 CLR 30, 51.

22. Apart from views of the Executive Government, the submissions covered factual issues – such as the state of non-recognition of Australia's claims. They also dealt with the procedures that have been followed in the control of the Antarctic EEZ. None of these matters were the subject of factual dispute. Section 190(3) of the *Evidence Act 1995* (Cth) permits me to make an order that Parts 2.2, 3.2 and 3.3 of the Evidence Act not apply to the submissions as evidence of their contents and so to have recourse to the submissions on these factual matters. The submissions will be marked on the file exhibit 1. Though I have not heard the applicant on this course under the *Evidence Act*, it is ultimately unnecessary to do so because my view as to the exercise of discretion would be the same even if I did not take into account these factual issues. The submissions are without more an adequate and proper vehicle for disclosing to the Court the views and concerns of the Executive Government, without the need for the use of s 190(3) of the *Evidence Act*.

23. There is no fundamental constitutional issue here of any fact in question being a relevant and disputed constitutional fact: *Attorney General (Commonwealth) v Tse Chu-Fai* (1998) 193 CLR 128, 149. Nor is there any question of abrogation, or usurpation, of the judicial power or function.

24. The views of the Executive Government are relevant. The views concern subject matters which are within the province of the democratically elected Government of this country. The views of the Government may not be shared by the applicant. Nevertheless, they are about considerations that are peculiarly within the field of the Executive Government, as involving political judgments (using that phrase in the broad sense) and lacking legal criteria permitting judicial assessment.

25. Those views have been laid before me. I propose to take them into account.

26. In taking them into account, I recognise that Parliament has spoken in the EPBC Act and provided an entity such as the applicant with standing to bring these proceedings. If the respondent were present in Australia the EPBC Act would plainly apply to it and no issue would arise as to jurisdiction. But it is not present. Leave, involving the exercise of a discretion, is required to permit service in a foreign country.

27. Very relevant to the exercise of that discretion are the kinds of consideration dealt with by the Attorney-General's submissions. I can conclude that Japan will view service or any attempt at service in Japan of process of this Court seeking orders under the EPBC Act as the attempted enforcement of rights that it does not recognise and as an interference with rights, under international law, of its nationals to ply the high seas and conduct themselves conformably with Japan's rights under international law, in particular by acting conformably with the Whaling Convention. I can conclude that the Australian Government has the view that the attempt to enforce the EPBC Act may upset the diplomatic status quo under the *Antarctic Treaty* and be contrary to Australia's long term national interests, including its interests connected with its claim to territorial sovereignty to the Antarctic. I can also conclude that Japan would take the view that an attempt to invoke the exercise of federal jurisdiction under the EPBC Act was itself contrary to international law and that the claim by this Court to the exercise of jurisdiction was based on an impermissible claim by Australia under international law to the Antarctic Territory. Of course, that would be no answer in this Court if the respondent were present within Australia when served or if there were to be voluntary submission by the respondent to the jurisdiction of the Court.

28. Any difficulties raised by the above would be compounded by the difficulty, if not impossibility, of enforcement of any court order. Enforcement (if the opportunity for such arose) may then place the Executive Government (as the branch of government which may assist in giving effect to and enforcing, in an administrative way, the orders of the Court by assisting in bringing people to court or levying execution on property) in the position of assisting the enforcement of an order of this Court (whether in contempt proceedings or otherwise) contrary to its view that such a course was in the best interests of this country by reference to considerations that are non-justiciable.

29. The nature of the underlying issues also illuminates the international political framework and content of the dispute. It does not involve private rights of property or liberty. It involves the protection of whales (which, subject to UNCLOS, are owned by no one) from interference and killing. To express the matter thus is not intended, in the slightest, to diminish either the statutory right sought to be enforced or the views of those who guide the applicant. The whales being killed by the respondent are seen by some as not merely a natural resource that is important to conserve, but as living creatures of intelligence and of great importance not only for the animal world, but for humankind and that to slaughter them in the manner that has occurred is deeply wrong. These views are not shared by all. It may be assumed that they are shared by many Australians. It may be assumed that they are not shared by many in Japan, and in Norway and in other places. They are views which, at an international level, are mediated through the Whaling

Commission and its procedures, by reference to the Whaling Convention and the views of nation States. They are views which contain a number of normative and judgmental premisses, the nature and content of which do not arise in any simple application of domestic law, but which do, or may, arise in a wider international context.

30. Weighed against this is the standing of the applicant and the material disclosing a clear prima facie case of contravention of Australian municipal law.

31. The issue for me is not only whether there appears to be a contravention of the EPBC Act, but also whether I should exercise a discretion to permit service of proceedings under the EPBC Act which seek a declaration and an injunction under domestic legislation dealing with these issues of international political controversy of the above character with the possible consequences referred to above and which are otherwise dealt with under international law and procedures.

32. The taking into account of the matters to which I have referred is central to the proper exercise of the discretion concerning leave to serve process claiming such orders against a Japanese company in Japan, in circumstances where Japan will view (what is in any event often called the "exhorbitant" jurisdiction) the assumption of jurisdiction as baseless by international law.

33. It was accepted in submissions that a legitimate consideration to take into account in the exercise of the discretion was the lack of means of making any injunction effectual. See *Marshall v Marshall* (1888) 38 Ch D 330; *Kinahan v Kinahan* (1890) 45 Ch D 78, 84; and cf *Watson v Daily Record* [1907] 1 KB 853; and also *ACCC v Chen* (2003) 132 FCR 309 at [45] and *ACCC v Kaye* [2004] FCA 1363 at [199]–[202]. Relevant to such a consideration here are the facts that there is no apparent reason for any of the ships of the respondent (apart from requiring refuge) to call into Australian ports and that there is no place of business of the respondent in Australia. Also, as the issue is one for public law, it cannot be expected that Japanese courts would give effect to an injunction.

34. The making of a declaration alone (a course suggested by the applicant) might be seen as tantamount to an empty assertion of domestic law (by the Court), devoid of utility beyond use (by others) as a political statement.

35. Futility will be compounded by placing the Court at the centre of an international dispute (indeed helping to promote such a dispute) between Australia and a friendly foreign power which course or eventuality the Australian Government believes not to be in Australia's long term national interests.

36. In my view, in all the circumstances, I should not exercise a discretion to place the Court in such a position.

37. For these reasons, I do not propose to grant leave to serve originating process in Japan.

38. This course may perhaps be seen as having echoes of the monist (as opposed to dualist) theory of the relationship between municipal and international law (cf Brownlie *Principles of Public International Law* (6th edn) ch 2) or of a notion of *forum non conveniens* leading to the preference of international dispute resolution mechanisms over domestic mechanisms. Neither is a correct explanation for my reasons for refusing to exercise the discretion as asked. The case is an unusual one, in which futility is deeply intertwined with powerful non-justiciable considerations, tending to make it inappropriate to exercise the discretion.

39. Nothing that I have said would necessarily determine the question of the grant of leave if there were revealed material upon which I could conclude that the grant of leave was likely to bring the respondent to the Court in circumstances tending to show that any orders made would be able to be enforced and thereby be effectual to enforce the EPBC Act.

40. This leaves a number of matters to comment upon. I sought further submissions upon whether the permit issued by the Japanese Government to the respondent was a permit under Article 3 of Annex II to the Madrid Protocol as well as being a permit issued under Article VIII of the Whaling Convention. The applicant has put on material which would indicate that Japan does not treat the permit as one issued under Article 3 of Annex II to the Madrid Protocol. Also,

the Attorney-General conceded that the permit for scientific whaling issued to the respondent by the Government of Japan, was not a recognised foreign authority for the purpose of s 7(1) of the *AT(EP)* Act. This concession, together with the submissions of the applicant, permit me to conclude that the relevant permit is not under the Article 3 of Annex II of the Madrid Protocol for the purposes of this application. However, one could see an argument being put forward, at a level of disputed application, to the effect that the permit was both a permit under Article VIII of the Whaling Convention and Article 3 of Annex II to the Madrid Protocol.

41. I indicated in my reasons in November 2004 that I needed to be persuaded why the statement of claim should not be amended to exercise the words "purported to be done" in paragraph 7 of the Statement of Claim. The submissions of the applicant in effect concede that the statement of claim should be amended in this respect, if leave were to be given. If I had been of the view that leave should be given, I would have required that amendment. There is no evidence that the respondent has engaged in conduct outside the terms of its permit. Also, for the reasons I gave in November 2004, it seems to me that that consideration is irrelevant.

42. It is unnecessary to decide whether the Antarctic EEZ is, or can be seen as, "in the Commonwealth" for the purposes of three of the four bases sought to be raised under Order 8 rule 1. It is sufficient for me to say that the submissions of the Attorney-General appear to have great force and my conclusion to the contrary in my November reasons was made, as I expressly said, subject to hearing from the Attorney-General. If I had otherwise been minded to grant leave any view that the Antarctic EEZ was not "in the Commonwealth" would not have prevented leave being granted because of the availability of Order 8 rule 1(l).

43. For the above reasons, the application for leave to serve the originating process in Japan should be dismissed.

...

Humane Society International Inc v Kyodo Senpaku Kaisha Ltd [2006] FCAFC 116 (Federal Court of Australia (Full Court), 14 July 2006)

[Issue: whether the primary judge erred in refusing leave to serve originating process on a foreign company abroad even where the claim was contrary to Australia's foreign relations]

THE COURT ORDERS THAT:

1. The appeal be allowed.
2. The order dismissing the application for leave to serve the originating process in Japan be set aside and in lieu thereof it be ordered that the appellant have leave to serve the originating application herein together with a copy of the amended statement of claim on Kyodo Senpaku Kaisha Ltd at 4–5 Toyomi-cho Chuo-ku, Tokyo, Japan.

Note: Settlement and entry of orders is dealt with in Order 36 of the Federal Court Rules.

REASONS FOR JUDGMENT

BLACK CJ AND FINKELSTEIN J

Introduction

1. The Commonwealth claims sovereignty over the Australian Antarctic Territory, but the claim is formally recognised by only four States, each of which also has a claim over part of the Antarctic. Australia's claim is not recognised by other States, including Japan.

2. The issue before the Court has come about in the following way. The appellant is a public interest organisation with one of its objects as the protection and conservation of the environment. It has commenced this action against the respondent, a Japanese company, alleging that its fleet of whalers has been unlawfully (that is, in breach of a law of the Commonwealth) killing, injuring, taking and dealing with Antarctic minke whales in that part of the Australian Whale Sanctuary that is adjacent to the Australian Antarctic Territory. The appellant seeks a declaration

to that effect and an injunction to restrain future contraventions. It applied to the Court for leave to serve outside the jurisdiction.

3. The Federal Court can only exercise *in personam* jurisdiction over the Japanese company if the appellant is given leave under O 8 r 2 of the Federal Court Rules to serve the application on the respondent in Japan. In the *ex parte* application for leave before the primary judge the appellant satisfied each of the required conditions for obtaining leave namely: (1) the Federal Court had subject-matter jurisdiction over the dispute; (2) the dispute fell within one of the classes of claims specified in O 8 r 1; and (3) the appellant had a prima facie case for the relief it seeks. At that point, leave to serve should have been given in the absence of some countervailing consideration: *Agar v Hyde* (2000) 201 CLR 552 at 575. The judge refused to grant leave for two reasons: see *Humane Society International Inc v Kyodo Senpaku Kaisha Ltd* [2005] FCA 664. Each of the reasons was put forward by counsel for the Attorney-General for the Commonwealth, following an invitation from the judge that he would be assisted by submissions from the Executive since, in his Honour's view, the matter was of importance to Australia's foreign relations: see *Humane Society International Inc v Kyodo Senpaku Kaisha Ltd* [2004] FCA 1510.

4. Two factors were decisive for the judge. First, that prosecution of the action 'may upset the diplomatic status quo under the *Antarctic Treaty* and be contrary to Australia's long term national interests, including its interests connected with its claim to territorial sovereignty to the Antarctic'. Second, that the action was futile because of 'the difficulty, if not impossibility, of enforcement of any court order': [2005] FCA 664 at [27] and [28]. The judge also said that: 'Futility will be compounded by placing the Court at the centre of an international dispute (indeed helping to promote such a dispute) between Australia and a friendly foreign power which course or eventuality the Australian Government believes not to be in Australia's long term national interests': at [35].

5. The appellant has appealed the order refusing leave. It says that the judge's discretion miscarried. We are persuaded that the appellant is correct and would reverse the judge's order for the reasons that now follow.

THE ENVIRONMENT PROTECTION AND BIODIVERSITY CONSERVATION ACT

6. The reasons must begin with an examination of the relevant legislation. The *Environment Protection and Biodiversity Conservation Act 1999* (Cth) ('the EPBC Act') was enacted by the Parliament principally to provide for the protection of the environment, to promote ecologically sustainable development, to promote the conservation of biodiversity, to promote a cooperative approach to the protection and management of the environment, and to recognise the role of indigenous people in the conservation and ecologically sustainable use of Australia's biodiversity: s 3. To achieve its object of protecting the environment and promoting the conservation of Australian biodiversity, the EPBC Act established the Australian Whale Sanctuary ('the Sanctuary'): s 225. The Sanctuary comprises an area that includes the waters of the exclusive economic zone: s 225(2)(a). Relevantly, that area encompasses the waters within 200 nautical miles seaward of the baseline of the Australian Antarctic Territory. This is the area in which the respondent's allegedly illegal activities are said to have been taking place. To the extent that the EPBC Act has effect in relation to the outer limits of the exclusive economic zone it applies in relation to '(a) all persons (including persons who are not Australian citizens); (b) all aircraft (including aircraft that are not Australian aircraft); and (c) all vessels (including vessels that are not Australian vessels)': s 5(4).

7. The Parliament may be taken to know about the remoteness and general conditions pertaining to the Sanctuary which its legislation has established. It may also be taken to have appreciated that the circumstances under which its laws may be enforced in relation to the Sanctuary are quite exceptional. It nevertheless made no provision for the exclusion of the general enforcement provisions of the EPBC Act to matters occurring within the Sanctuary, even where those matters relate to conduct by foreign persons aboard foreign vessels.

8. The EPBC Act creates offences for acts done within the Sanctuary. The offences include the reckless killing or injuring of a cetacean (the Order Cetacea includes whales) (s 229), a strict liability offence of killing or injuring a cetacean (s 229A), intentionally taking, trading, keeping, moving or interfering with a cetacean (s 229B), a strict liability offence of taking, trading, keeping, moving or interfering with a cetacean (s 229C), treating an illegally killed or taken cetacean (s 229D) and possession of cetaceans killed or taken in contravention of the Act (s 230). Each offence other than the strict liability offences is punishable on conviction by imprisonment of not more than two years or by a fine not exceeding 1,000 penalty units, or both. A strict liability offence is punishable on conviction by fine not exceeding 500 penalty units. The *Crimes Act 1914* (Cth) presently provides that one penalty unit is equal to $110: s 4AA(1). Section 231(a) provides that the provisions in the EPBC Act creating the offences relating to cetaceans will not apply if a permit has been granted by the responsible Minister under s 238 authorising the holder of the permit to take an action without breaching those provisions.

9. A prosecution for an offence against the EPBC Act must be instituted by the Commonwealth Director of Public Prosecutions. It can only be instituted against a person amenable to the jurisdiction of the relevant Australian criminal court. The decision to prosecute is made by the Director, independently of the views of the Executive. If a person has engaged or proposes to engage in conduct that would be an offence under the EPBC Act, s 475 provides that the responsible Minister, 'an interested person' (other than an unincorporated organisation) or a person acting on behalf of an unincorporated organisation that is 'an interested person' may apply to the Federal Court for an injunction restraining the person from engaging in that conduct. In the case of an organisation, 'interested person' is defined in s 475(7). It is not necessary to repeat the definition save to note that the appellant falls within it. The Minister's decision to bring or not to bring a *civil* proceeding for an injunction may be informed by policy considerations. So might a decision by an interested person to bring proceedings.

Reasons for decision

10. We take it to be settled law that provided the jurisdiction of the Federal Court is engaged by an action in respect of subject-matter with which the Court can deal, and the action is instituted by an applicant who has standing, and the action is not oppressive, vexatious or otherwise an abuse of process and, finally, the Court can assume jurisdiction over the defendant (by service or submission), the Court cannot refuse to adjudicate the dispute. The reason is explained by Brennan J in *Oceanic Sun Line Special Shipping Company Inc v Fay* (1988) 165 CLR 197 at 239:

> *'Generally speaking, it is of the nature of a legal right that the person in whom it is vested is entitled to invoke the State's power to enforce it. For that purpose the courts are at the service of litigants, and the rule of law rests on the courts' duty to exercise their jurisdiction when litigants invoke it'.*

It follows that, in our opinion, the judge was in error in refusing leave even if the pursuit of the claim was contrary to Australia's foreign relations.

11. In our view, it would in any event be both curious and anomalous if matters that could not be raised in answer to the appellant's claim by a defendant served within the jurisdiction could nevertheless be taken into account when deciding whether to allow service out of the jurisdiction.

12. We are also persuaded that the primary judge was in error in attaching weight to what we would characterise as a political consideration. It may be accepted that whilst legal disputes may occur in a political context, the exclusively political dimension of the dispute is non-justiciable. It is appropriately non-justiciable because the court lacks competence to resolve disputes and issues of an exclusively political type, the resolution of which will involve the application of non-judicial norms: compare *Japan Whaling Association v American Cetacean Society* (1986) 478 US 221 at 230.

13. Even if, in special circumstances, there is occasion for political considerations to be taken into account in deciding whether an action should be permitted to go forward, there is no room, in our view, for those considerations where, as here, the Parliament has provided that the action is justiciable in an Australian court: *R v Bow Street Metropolitan Stipendiary Magistrate; Ex parte Pinochet Ugarte* [2000] 1 AC 61 at 107.

14. On the question of futility, that is the lack of means of making an injunction effective, we also disagree with the approach of the primary judge in several respects. First, while it may be accepted that an injunction is by its nature a discretionary remedy which may be refused if it cannot be enforced, the question whether an injunction should be granted is to be dealt with either in an application (if there be one) to set aside service (*Agar v Hyde* at 574–575) or, more appropriately, when the application itself is heard and not when the court is deciding whether there should be leave to serve out of the jurisdiction (see, by analogy, *Helicopter Utilities Pty Ltd v Australian National Airlines Commission* (1963) 80 WN NSW 48 at 51).

15. Second, it seems to us that the judge in effect imposed upon the appellant the obligation of showing that an injunction would be a useful remedy. In fact the reverse is true. It is the defendant who has the onus of showing that it has no assets within the jurisdiction which could be sequestrated in punishment for contempt: *Hospital for Sick Children (Board of Governors) v Walt Disney Productions Inc* [1968] Ch 52 at 71.

16. Third, we consider that when asked to grant an injunction, the court should not necessarily contemplate that it would be disobeyed: *In re Liddell's Settlement Trusts* [1936] Ch 365 at 373–374; *Castanho v Brown & Root (UK) Ltd* [1981] AC 557 at 574; *Republic of Haiti v Duvalier* [1990] 1 QB 202 at 216; *South Bucks District Council v Porter* [2003] 2 AC 558 at 580. There are many cases where parties out of the jurisdiction have been subjected to an injunction regarding their conduct abroad. The cases to which we have referred show that if a person is properly served in accordance with the court's exorbitant jurisdiction, that person (so far as the jurisdiction of the court is concerned) is in the same position as a person who is within its territorial jurisdiction. Nevertheless, in an appropriate case the judge may refuse to grant an injunction because the defendant is outside the jurisdiction and is likely to ignore the order. It will all depend upon the circumstances and, at the present stage of these proceedings, they are not yet known.

17. The traditional view of the international community that non-monetary orders made by a foreign court should not be enforced locally is itself under review. The issue is to be considered by the Supreme Court of Canada before which judgment is presently reserved in the appeal from *Pro Swing Inc v Elta Golf Inc* (2004) 71 OR (3d) 566.

18. There is another way of considering the question of futility. The injunctive relief that the appellant seeks is relief by way of statutory injunction under s 475 of the EPBC Act. That section authorises the grant of what has been called a public interest injunction: see *ICI Australia Operations Pty Ltd v TPC* (1992) 38 FCR 248 at 256. Section 475 and the related provisions in Div 14 of Pt 17 of the EPBC Act have their counterpart in s 80 of the *Trade Practices Act 1974* (Cth) ('the TP Act') upon which they appear to have been largely modelled.

19. Parliament has determined that it is in the public interest that the enforcement provisions of the EPBC Act should be unusually comprehensive in scope. Section 475 of the EPBC Act and its related provisions form part of a much larger enforcement scheme contained in the 21 divisions of Pt 17. The provisions include the conferral of powers of seizure and forfeiture, powers to board and detain vessels and authority to continue a pursuit on the high seas.

20. It is an important and distinctive feature of Div 14 of Pt 17 of the EPBC Act that, like s 80(4) of the TP Act, the Federal Court is expressly empowered to grant an injunction restraining a person from engaging in conduct whether or not it appears to the Court that the person intends to engage again in conduct of that kind and, even, whether or not there is a significant risk of injury or damage to the environment if the person engages or continues to engage in conduct of that kind: see s 479(1)(a) and (c).

21. The public interest character of the injunction that may be granted under s 475 of the EPBC Act is also emphasised by other elements in Div 14 of Pt 17. Thus, as we have noted, standing is conferred upon 'an interested person' to apply to the Court for an injunction. Likewise, the traditional requirement that an applicant for an interim injunction give an undertaking as to damages as a condition of the grant is negated. Indeed, s 478 provides, expressly, that the Federal Court is *not* to require such an undertaking. These modifications to the traditional requirements for the grant of injunctions have the evident object of assisting in the enforcement, in the public interest, of the EPBC Act. This does not of course mean that the traditional requirements are irrelevant: see *ICI Australia Operations Pty Ltd v TPC* at 256–257.

22. Although 'deterrence' is more commonly used in the vocabulary of the law than 'education', the two ideas are closely connected and must surely overlap in areas where a statute aims to regulate conduct. Thus, there being a 'matter' (see [28] below), the grant of a statutory public interest injunction to mark the disapproval of the Court of conduct which the Parliament has proscribed, or to discourage others from acting in a similar way, can be seen as also having an educative element. For that reason alone the grant of such an injunction may be seen, here, as potentially advancing the regulatory objects of the EPBC Act. Indeed, some of those objects are expressed directly in the language of 'promotion', including the object provided for by s 3(1)(c), namely to promote the conservation of biodiversity, which is an object that the legislation links to the establishment of an Australian Whale Sanctuary 'to ensure the conservation of whales and other cetaceans': s 3(2)(e)(ii).

23. Consistently with this view it has been said in relation to s 80(4) of the TP Act that whilst the Court should not grant an injunction unless it is likely to serve some purpose, it may be that in a particular case an injunction will be of benefit to the public by marking out the Court's view of the seriousness of a respondent's conduct: see *Hughes v Western Australian Cricket Association (Inc) & Ors* (1986) ATPR 40-748 at 48,135 and *Trade Practices Commission v Mobil Oil Australia Ltd* (1984) 4 FCR 296 at 300.

24. Similarly, it has been said, again in the context of s 80 of the TP Act, that the purpose of an appropriately drafted injunction may be merely to reinforce to the marketplace that the restrained behaviour is unacceptable: *ACCC v 4WD Systems Pty Ltd* (2003) 200 ALR 491 at [217]. That is to say, a public interest injunction may have a purpose that is entirely educative. In *ACCC v 4WD Systems*, the enjoined behaviour had ceased and there was little likelihood of repetition and yet it was considered appropriate to grant an injunction.

25. More generally, we agree with the view expressed by Sackville J in *ACCC v Chen* (2003) 132 FCR 309 that the fact that an injunction granted under s 80 of the TP Act may prove difficult or even impossible to enforce is not necessarily a bar to the grant of relief, although it is a material consideration to be weighed against other circumstances relevant to the exercise of the Court's discretion: see at [45], citing I C F Spry, *The Principles of Equitable Remedies* (6th ed, 2001) at 42.

26. Accordingly, and certainly at the stage of leave to serve out of the jurisdiction, there are added reasons why the Court, at least in a case such as this, should not refuse leave on the ground of futility. To the contrary, it might well be open to the Court, in the proper exercise of its discretion at the trial, to grant the relief sought by way of statutory public interest injunction even though there might be no prospect of the conduct being repeated by the respondent or even because there is no prospect of the injunction being enforced.

27. The same considerations may operate, perhaps more strongly, in relation to the declaratory relief that is also sought by the appellant.

28. Finally, even if there is a problem with the enforcement of an injunction (if any be granted) that does not lead to the conclusion that there is no justiciable controversy or 'matter' before the court. It is of course true that a 'matter' includes both a controversy about a right, duty or liability and the existence of a remedy to enforce that right, duty or liability. If there were no remedy the controversy would not be capable of being quelled by the court. But the requirement

that there must be an available remedy is to say nothing about the effectiveness of that remedy in a particular case.

29. For these reasons we would allow the appeal and set aside the order dismissing the application for leave to serve the originating process in Japan. In lieu thereof we would grant the appellant leave to serve the originating application together with a copy of the amended statement of claim on the respondent at its address at 4–5 Toyomi-cho Chuo-ku, Tokyo, Japan. It has not been suggested that notice of the proceeding should be served in place of the originating process.

...

REASONS FOR JUDGMENT

MOORE J

30. I have had the benefit of reading the reasons of Black CJ and Finkelstein J in a draft form. It is unnecessary to repeat much of the background. The power the primary judge was being asked to exercise is conferred by O 8 r 2 of the Federal Court Rules which provides:

(2) The Court may, by order, give leave to serve originating process outside the Commonwealth in accordance with Division 2 or 3 of this Order or, subject to sub rule (2B) on such terms and conditions as it considers appropriate, if the Court is satisfied that:

(a) the Court has jurisdiction in the proceedings; and

(b) rule 1 applies to the proceeding; and

(c) the parties seeking leave has a prima face the case for the relief sought by the party in the proceeding.

On one view of the rule, particularly having regard to its structure and the subject matter it addresses, the Court would be obliged to grant leave if the preconditions in paragraphs (a), (b) and (c) are satisfied. On that view of the rule, and notwithstanding the use of the word 'may', the discretion would be a limited one of the type considered in *Commissioner of State Revenue v Royal Insurance Australia Limited* (1993) 182 CLR 51. However, it appears the matter proceeded before the primary judge on the basis that his Honour had a residual discretion to decide whether to grant leave notwithstanding the satisfaction of the preconditions. In addition, there are many authorities which say there is, or assume the existence of, a residual discretion: see *Bray v F Hoffman-La Roche Ltd and Others* (2003) 130 FCR 317 at 356; *Best (Australia) Ltd v Aquagas Marketing Pty Ltd* (1988) 83 ALR 217 at 222; *Cell Tech Communications Pty Ltd v Nokia Mobile Phones (UK) Ltd and Others* (1995) 58 FCR 365 at 371; *Century Insurance Ltd (In provisional liquidation) and Ors v New Zealand Guardian Trust Ltd and Ors* (1996) (unreported, Fed C of A, Lee J, No. WAG 81 of 1995, 16 May 1996); *Southern Cross Airlines Holdings Ltd v Arthur Anderson & Co (A firm) and Ors* (unreported, Fed C of A, Cooper J, QG 170 of 1996, 27 March 1998; *Bell Group Ltd (in liq) and Others v Westpac Banking Corporation and Others* (1996) 20 ACSR 760; *TPC v The Gillette Company and Others (No 2)* (1993) 45 FCR 366; *Quinlan v Safe International Försäkrings AB* [2005] FCA 1362 at [26]–[27]; *Equiticorp Industries Group Ltd v Hawkins* [1991] 3 NZLR 700; *Hartwell Trent (Australia) Pty Ltd v Tefal Societe Anonyme* [1968] VR 3 and *Kuwait Asia Bank EC v National Mutual Life Nominees Ltd* [1991] 1 AC 187 at 212.

31. In my opinion, the existence of a recognised residual discretion to grant leave to serve outside the jurisdiction tells against the proposition that if an applicant has standing, seeks to prosecute an action which is not oppressive, vexatious or otherwise an abuse of process, and the Court can assume jurisdiction (by service or submission), then the Court is obliged to adjudicate the dispute and a judge must grant leave to serve outside the jurisdiction. I will return to this question later.

32. It is convenient, at this point, to consider the way in which the primary judge exercised the discretion when refusing leave to serve outside the jurisdiction. On 27 May 2005, his Honour dismissed the application for leave to serve the originating process on the respondent in Japan:

Humane Society International Inc v Kyodo Senpaku Kaisha Ltd [2005] FCA 664. His Honour's decision was based upon discretionary considerations advanced on behalf of the Attorney-General for the Commonwealth appearing as *amicus curiae*. These considerations can be divided into two categories. The first relates to the international political context of the dispute, and the possible adverse ramifications that permitting service in Japan may have on Australia's relations with Japan as well as on other signatories to the Antarctic Treaty.

33. As to Australia's relations with Japan, his Honour's focus was Japan's likely response to any attempt at service, which might have the effect of developing into an international disagreement with Australia. His Honour accepted that Japan would view service as the attempt to enforce rights which it did not recognise, and in addition, would view it as an illegitimate interference with its own rights, under international law, in relation to area it regards as the high seas.

34. His Honour also appeared to accept the argument advanced by the Attorney General that service could be 'reasonably expected to prompt a significant adverse reaction from other Antarctic Treaty Parties' (besides Japan, which is also a party to the Treaty). This view appeared to be based on the notion that enforcing domestic legislation of one of the parties to the Antarctic Treaty would undermine the diplomatic status quo of that Treaty, which, in addition, was contrary to Australia's long term national interests and might endanger Australia's claims to sovereignty in Antarctica.

35. The primary judge also appeared to be influenced by the view that the issues disputed in the proceedings would better be dealt with by diplomatic solutions or other means which did not have the effect of placing a domestic court 'at the centre of an international dispute': at [29], [31] and [34].

36. The second type of discretionary consideration relied upon by the primary judge was more orthodox and related to the many difficulties said to attend the enforcement of any order. Service was unlikely to be effectual in bringing the respondent to Court, and similarly, the ultimate orders sought were unlikely to be effective in enforcing the *Environment Protection and Biodiversity Conservation Act 1999* (Cth) ('the EPBC Act').

37. In addition, there was a further consideration apparently relied on by his Honour which drew these two strands together. His Honour had regard to the position in which the Executive Government would necessarily be placed in terms of having to assist in the enforcement of any Court orders, in a situation where that Government viewed the orders as contrary to national interests on the basis of (non-justiciable) matters uniquely within the domain of the Executive Government.

38. I agree with Black CJ and Finkelstein J, for the reasons their Honours have given at [11] and [12], that the primary judge erred in the exercise of his discretion by taking into account the first category of considerations. The political repercussions of service of the process and, additionally, potentially the litigation of this application in an Australian court, are irrelevant in deciding whether to grant leave. To allow such considerations to influence the resolution of the application for leave denies this Court its proper role in our system of government. Courts must be prepared to hear and determine matters whatever their political sensitivity either domestically or internationally. To approach the matter otherwise, is to compromise the role of the courts as the forum in which rights can be vindicated whatever the subject-matter of the proceedings.

39. In taking those considerations into account, the primary judge erred in a way that authorises appellate intervention: see *House v King* (1936) 55 CLR 499 at 505, having allowed 'extraneous or irrelevant matters to guide or affect him'. This leads to a consideration of how the discretion should be exercised. I referred earlier (at [30]) to *Kuwait Asia Bank EC v National Mutual Life Nominees Ltd*. That was a judgment of the Privy Council concerning an unsuccessful application by a foreign company to set aside process invoking the jurisdiction of the New Zealand High Court. The procedural rules of that Court enabled service of proceedings outside the jurisdiction without the leave of the Court, on the basis that the rules made provision for the

person served to make an application that the proceedings be dismissed because the Court had no jurisdiction to hear and determine them. The Privy Council concluded that, in addition to the express power to dismiss conferred by the rules, the Court retained a discretionary power to set aside the service on the same principles that governed the grant of leave to serve originating process extra-territorially in relation to a rule such as O 8 r 2 of the Federal Court Rules. The then equivalent rule of the English Supreme Court Rules, O 11, was, in relevant respects, in substantially the same terms as O 8 r 2 of the rules of this Court.

40. In the course of discussing the way the discretion under O 11 should be exercised, their Lordships said at 212:

'The English R.S.C., Ord. 11, which has served as the model in most Commonwealth countries for service of process out of the jurisdiction, does not spell out the entirety of the court's discretion to refuse leave, even where the case falls within rule 1, but that the discretion exists is not in doubt: see Johnson v. Taylor Brothers & Co. Ltd *[1920] A.C. 144, 153,* per *Lord Birkenhead L.C. and Viscount Haldane, and Lord Dunedin who said, at p. 154:*

"I think it is legitimate to begin by considering the genesis of the rule. I understand that jurisdiction according to English law is based on the act of personal service and that if this is effected the English law does not feel bound by the Roman maxim 'Actor sequitur forum rei'. It is far otherwise in other systems where service is in no sense a foundation of jurisdiction, but merely a sine qua non before effective action is allowed. Now service being the foundation of jurisdiction, it follows that that service naturally and normally would be service within the jurisdiction. But there is an exception to this normal rule, and that is service out of the jurisdiction. This however is not allowed as a right but is granted in the discretion of the judge as a privilege, and the rule in question here prescribes the limits within which that discretion should be exercised."

For further statements of principle one may refer to The Brabo, Vitkovice Horni v. Korner, Siskina (Owners of cargo lately laden on board) v. Distos Compania Naviera SA *[1979] A.C. 210,* The Hagen *[1908] P 189 and* The Spiliada *[1987] A.C. 460 and, for a recent example, see* Kloeckner & Co AG v. Gatoil Overseas Inc *[1990] 1 Lloyd's Rep. 177.'*

41. It has been said by the High Court that a court should not grant leave to serve outside the jurisdiction unless '[the court] is positively persuaded that it should do so': *Voth v Manildra Flour Mills Pty Ltd* (1990) 171 CLR 538 at 565. That statement appears to continue to identify the applicable principle in relation to provisions requiring a court's leave to serve an originating process outside the jurisdiction on the *ex parte* application of a plaintiff or applicant. Differently cast provisions concerning the exercise of a court's exorbitant jurisdiction may require another approach: see *Agar v Hyde* (2000) 201 CLR 552 particularly at [51], where it is said that a plaintiff has a prima facie right to obtain leave to proceed once service outside the jurisdiction has been effected and no unconditional appearance has been filed by the defendant. In earlier times it has been said that the discretionary power to exercise jurisdiction against a foreigner by service outside the jurisdiction should be 'exercised with caution and with a bias against invading the sovereignty of a foreign State' (per Lord Simonds in *Vitkovice Horni A Hunti Tezirstvo v Korner* [1951] AC 869 at 877).

42. In an era of international commerce and global human engagement, it may not be necessary for courts to be overly cautious about exercising jurisdiction in relation to foreigners. Nonetheless there remains, on the authorities, a need for courts to approach with some circumspection the grant of leave to serve outside the jurisdiction: see, for example, the observations of Nicholson J in *Quinlan v Safe International Försäkrings AB* at [27].

43. But for one consideration, I would grant leave. The applicant has demonstrated that it has an arguable case involving, from one perspective, issues of significance and public importance. The factor which results in me not being positively satisfied that leave should be granted is the almost certain futility of the litigation the applicant wishes to pursue. There are some older

authorities to the effect that leave should not be granted if the relief sought is injunctive relief and there is no method for making the injunction effectual: see *Marshall v Marshall* (1888) 38 Ch D 330 and *Kinahan v Kinahan* (1890) 45 Ch D 78. This is qualified by the principle that leave might be given if there was a reasonable ground for believing that the injunction will be efficacious at some time in the future: see *Tozier v Hawkins* (1885) 15 QBD 650 and *Re Burland's Trade Mark* (1889) 41 Ch D 157.

44. More recent Australian authority would support that approach. The jurisdiction of courts created under Chapter III of the Australian Constitution is centrally concerned with the determination of 'matters'. It has been said that a legally enforceable remedy is as essential to the existence of a 'matter' as the right, duty or liability which gives rise to the remedy: see *Abebe v Commonwealth* (1999) 197 CLR 510 at [31] (per Gleeson CJ and McHugh J) and *Truth About Motorways Pty Ltd v Macquarie Infrastructure Investment Management Ltd* (2000) 200 CLR 591, especially Gaudron J at [49]. More generally, this Court has been enjoined not to embark upon the determination of hypothetical questions which can include the making of a declaration in default of a defence: see *Bass v Permanent Trustee Co Ltd* (1999) 198 CLR 334 especially at [47].

45. In the present matter, the relief sought is a declaration that the conduct of the respondent contravenes the EPBC Act and an injunction restraining the respondent from engaging in the contravening conduct. It is almost certain that the respondent will not submit to the jurisdiction of an Australian court having regard to the broad political context in which it engages in whaling and, in particular, having regard to the fact that it is doing so seemingly lawfully under Japanese law with the authority of the Japanese Government. On the evidence as it presently stands, the respondent has only the most tenuous connection with Australia, involving periodically entering remote Australian waters in the Antarctic to undertake the activities the subject of the relief sought by the appellant. Those circumstances are quite unusual if not unique. It is also almost certain that any proceedings in this Court will proceed *ex parte*. While the applicant may ultimately obtain relief of the type sought (though plainly discretionary considerations may militate against the grant of such relief), it is not apparent to me that it will be effective relief. That is because it is highly probable the orders will never be served or otherwise rendered efficacious. Senior counsel for the appellant accepted that any judgment could not be registered and enforced in Japan. In the unlikely event that this Court made an order under O 8 r 3 facilitating service in Japan of any order of this Court (whether by way of declaration or injunction), it would almost certainly be ignored.

46. Indeed, the position of the appellant appeared to involve an acceptance that no enforceable injunction will be granted but that, at least in part, any declaration would operate to influence the Japanese Government, which is not a party to the proceedings. In the applicant's written submissions in reply, it repeated and elaborated on a submission earlier made:

> *'...... the fact that an order is likely to prove difficult or even impossible to enforce is not necessarily a bar to the grant of relief, although it is a material consideration to be weighed against other circumstances relevant to the exercise of the Court's discretion to grant relief. The declaration sought in these proceedings does not rely upon enforcement in any foreign jurisdiction. It will remove any doubt for the respondent that it breaches Australian law by whaling within the Australian Wildlife Sanctuary. It should also not lightly be assumed that the Government of Japan will ignore the declaration by granting further permits to the respondent in such a manner as to allow contravention of Australian domestic laws. Consequently, the relief sought cannot be said to be ineffective or futile and this is not a basis for refusing to grant leave to serve the proceedings.'*

47. It is not legitimate, in my opinion, for a court to sanction the commencement of proceedings by granting leave to serve outside the jurisdiction if a purpose of the application, if not the dominant purpose, is to pressure a person or body which is not a party to the proceedings. In any event,

the making of a declaration without service of the order would not bind the respondent to any determination made by this Court of its obligations and liabilities under Australian law. It may be accepted that in litigation not intended to enforce private rights but which has a public dimension (such as enforcing a norm of conduct established by statute for the protection of the public interest), an unduly narrow view has not been adopted about the circumstances in which a bare declaration might be made: for example, *Truth About Motorways Pty Ltd v Macquarie Infrastructure Investment Management Ltd.* However, such cases have, as far as I am aware, involved litigation between parties within the jurisdiction of the Australian court seized of the matter.

48. While I do not suggest that this Court is not seized of a 'matter' (though it is a question which has not been agitated to this point in the proceedings), authorities such as those referred to at [44] above give content to the judicial power of the Commonwealth having regard to questions of public policy. Courts exist in our system of government to adjudicate real disputes and exert 'actual power', an expression used by members of the High Court in *Laurie v Carroll* (1958) 98 CLR 310. In my opinion, similar considerations can inform the exercise of a discretion to grant leave to serve outside the jurisdiction. Leave should not be given in circumstances where the proceedings only involve the adjudication of a legal controversy in form but not in substance. As I have already said, any remedy that might be granted will be incapable of enforcement. That feature of these proceedings denies them substance. I would refuse leave to serve the application on the respondent.

49. It might be thought that leave should be given on the footing that the respondent could move the court to set aside the service. But what in fact would almost certainly happen if leave to serve was granted is that the respondent would ignore any process and would not engage with this Court in exercise of its jurisdiction. It would do this for the reasons given at [45] above.

50. As I would refuse leave to serve the application, the appropriate order is that the appeal be dismissed. No question of costs arises.

...

Humane Society International Inc v Kyodo Senpaku Kaisha Ltd [2008] FCA 3 (Federal Court of Australia (Justice Allsop), 15 January 2008)

[Issue: whether the respondent company violated domestic environmental laws prohibiting the killing of whales in the Australian Whale Sanctuary]

1. THE COURT DECLARES that the respondent has killed, injured, taken and interfered with Antarctic minke whales (*Balaenoptera bonaerensis*) and fin whales (*Balaenoptera physalus*) and injured, taken and interfered with humpback whales (*Megaptera novaeangliae*) in the Australian Whale Sanctuary in contravention of sections 229, 229A, 229B and 229C of the *Environment Protection and Biodiversity Conservation Act 1999* (Cth), (the "Act"), and has treated and possessed such whales killed or taken in the Australian Whale Sanctuary in contravention of sections 229D and 230 of the Act, without permission or authorisation under sections 231, 232 or 238 of the Act.

2. THE COURT ORDERS that the respondent be restrained from killing, injuring, taking or interfering with any Antarctic minke whale (*Balaenoptera bonaerensis*), fin whale (*Balaenoptera physalus*) or humpback whale (*Megaptera novaeangliae*) in the Australian Whale Sanctuary, or treating or possessing any such whale killed or taken in the Australian Whale Sanctuary, unless permitted or authorised under sections 231, 232 or 238 of the *Environment Protection and Biodiversity Conservation Act 1999* (Cth).

Note: Settlement and entry of orders is dealt with in Order 36 of the Federal Court Rules.

REASONS FOR JUDGMENT

Background

1. These reasons should be read against the background of the earlier judgments on service: *Humane Society International Inc v Kyodo Senpaku Kaisha Ltd* (2004) 212 ALR 551, *Humane Society International Inc v Kyodo Senpaku Kaisha Ltd* [2005] FCA 664 (the two judgments containing my original reasons for refusing leave to serve outside Australia), *Humane Society International Inc v Kyodo Senpaku Kaisha Ltd* (2006) 154 FCR 425 (the Full Court judgment), and *Humane Society International Inc v Kyodo Senpaku Kaisha Ltd* [2007] FCA 124 (my reasons on substituted service). I do not propose to repeat matters there discussed. Phrases and terms used in these reasons (if otherwise undefined or unexplained) are to be understood by reference to those earlier reasons.

2. This is an application under section 475 of the *Environment Protection and Biodiversity Conservation Act 1999* (Cth) (the "EPBC Act") for injunctive relief and accompanying declarations in relation to whaling activities undertaken by the respondent in the Australian Whale Sanctuary, in contravention of ss 229-230 of the EPBC Act. References to section numbers are to provisions of the EPBC Act unless otherwise stated.

3. The respondent is a company incorporated in Japan, which the evidence reveals is the owner of a number of ships from which it has engaged, and is likely in the future to engage, in the killing of various species of whales in the Australian Whale Sanctuary. The respondent has engaged in such activity pursuant to the Japanese Whaling Research Program under Special Permit in the Antarctic (JARPA), issued under Article VIII of the *International Convention for the Regulation of Whaling* (opened for signature 2 December 1946) 1948 ATS 18 (entered into force 10 November 1948) (the "Whaling Convention") and monitored by the International Whaling Commission ("IWC"). From 2005, a second, more extensive, whaling programme has been undertaken by the respondent under a special permit, known as JARPA II.

4. The applicant is a public interest organisation incorporated in New South Wales, whose stated objectives include promotion of the "enhancement and conservation of all wild plants and animals". The applicant qualifies as an "interested person" pursuant to s 475(7) of the EPBC Act, and is therefore entitled to bring an action claiming the relief sought: see *Humane Society International Inc v Kyodo Senpaku Kaisha Ltd* (2004) 212 ALR 551 at [15].

The EPBC Act

5. The EPBC Act was enacted by the Commonwealth Parliament in 1999. The objects stated in s 3 of the EPBC Act include, amongst other things, the protection of the environment, particularly for matters of national environmental significance, conservation of biodiversity and heritage and promotion of ecologically sustainable development.

6. The EPBC Act is drafted in wide terms. It applies throughout Australia, including its external territories (s 5(1)), and to adjacent waters claimed as Australia's Exclusive Economic Zone. It applies to all persons and all vessels within territorial Australia and the exclusive economic zone, including persons who are not Australian citizens and vessels that are not registered Australian vessels: s 5(4).

7. One of the stated means by which the Parliament has expressed its intention to achieve the objects of the Act is by the establishment of the Australian Whale Sanctuary "to ensure the conservation of whales and other cetaceans": s 3(2)(e)(ii). The Australian Whale Sanctuary is established by s 225 of the EPBC Act, which is in the following terms:

(1) The Australian Whale Sanctuary is established in order to give formal recognition of the high level of protection and management afforded to cetaceans in Commonwealth marine areas and prescribed waters.

(2) The Australian Whale Sanctuary comprises:

(a) any waters of the sea inside the seaward boundary of the exclusive economic zone, except:

(i) waters, rights in respect of which have been vested in a State by section 4 of the Coastal Waters (State Title) Act 1980 or in the Northern Territory by section 4 of the Coastal Waters (Northern Territory Title) Act 1980; and

(ii) waters within the limits of a State or the Northern Territory; and

(b) any waters over the continental shelf, except:

(i) waters, rights in respect of which have been vested in a State by section 4 of the Coastal Waters (State Title) Act 1980 or in the Northern Territory by section 4 of the Coastal Waters (Northern Territory Title) Act 1980; and

(ii) waters within the limits of a State or the Northern Territory; and

(iii) waters covered by paragraph (a); and

(c) so much of the coastal waters of a State or the Northern Territory as are prescribed waters.

8. Sections 229 to 230 make it an offence to kill, injure, intentionally take or otherwise deal with a cetacean in the Australian Whale Sanctuary. The relevant provisions are as follows: ...

[text of provisions omitted]

9. A "cetacean" is defined in schedule 1 to the Act as "a member of the sub-order Mysticeti or Odontoceti of the Order Cetacea". Relevantly, Antarctic minke whales, fin whales and humpback whales are cetaceans as defined by the EPBC Act.

10. The Commonwealth Director of Prosecutions is responsible for prosecuting any offences under the EPBC Act, a decision which is made independently of the Executive Government. To date, the DPP has not sought to prosecute the respondent or others for undertaking the activity complained of by the applicant. In the absence of, or in addition to, criminal prosecution, section 475 of the Act gives the Minister, or an "interested person", standing to seek in a civil action an injunction to restrain conduct that would amount to an offence. This is what has been sought in this case. The section plainly gives *locus standi* to the applicant to seek the orders in this proceeding, without seeking the fiat of the Attorney-General and without any attendant complexities that might otherwise arise in the civil enforcement or prevention of conduct that is provided for by the criminal law (here by the same Commonwealth statute).

UNCLOS

11. Territorial claims for some form of sovereignty over waters adjacent to a state are regulated in international law by the *United Nations Convention on the Law of the Sea* done at Montego Bay, 10 December 1982 ("UNCLOS"). Article 57 of UNCLOS defines the exclusive economic zone of a coastal state as not exceeding 200 nautical miles from the baseline from which the territorial sea is measured.

12. Australia's claimed exclusive economic zone extends to the waters adjacent to the baseline of Australia's external territories, including, importantly for this matter, the Australian Antarctic Territory. By virtue of the statutory definition in s 225 of the EPBC Act, the waters within 200 nautical miles from the Australian Antarctic Territory land mass are within the Australian Whale Sanctuary.

13. Australia's claim to sovereignty over the Australian Antarctic Territory is recognised only by four nations (New Zealand, France, Norway and the United Kingdom), themselves with asserted (and otherwise disputed) claims over various parts of the Antarctic land mass. Japan rejects Australia's purported exercise of jurisdiction over waters that are considered by Japan to be the high seas. This is not a ground for invalidity of the EPBC Act: the sovereign claim by Australia to the Australian Antarctic Territory is not a matter capable of being questioned in this Court in this proceeding: cf *Mabo v Queensland (No 2)* (1992) 175 CLR 1. These matters of sovereignty and international recognition (and lack of extensiveness thereof) can be taken to have been before, and well recognised by, Parliament when it enacted the EPBC Act.

14. A claim to an exclusive economic zone does not amount to sovereignty for all purposes. See *Humane Society International Inc v Kyodo Senpaku Kaisha Ltd* [2005] FCA 664 at [11] –

[13] for a discussion of the rights flowing from a claim to the exclusive economic zone.

History of the litigation

15. The applicant commenced proceedings in this Court on 19 October 2004. On the same day, the applicant also filed a notice of motion, together with supporting affidavits, seeking leave to serve the respondent out of the jurisdiction in Japan, in accordance with Order 8 rule 2 of the Federal Court Rules. On 23 November 2004, I ordered the applicant to serve copies of documents in the proceeding on the Attorney-General for the Commonwealth, on the basis that it was appropriate that he be informed of the nature of the matter.

16. In due course, the Attorney-General filed submissions as *amicus curiae*. The substance of those submissions was that the subject matter of the proceedings was a matter best dealt with by the Executive Government, and it was not appropriate for the Court to exercise its discretion to grant relief, either to serve the respondent out of the jurisdiction, or final relief of the nature of the declarations and injunctions sought. After considering submissions both from the Attorney-General and the applicant, I gave judgment on 27 May 2005, dismissing the motion: see *Humane Society International Inc v Kyodo Senpaku Kaisha Ltd* [2005] FCA 664. I do not propose to set out my reasons enunciated therein; it is sufficient to say that, in light of the international position, including the view of Japan that the assertion of jurisdiction in this matter would be a breach of international law, including, but not limited to, the Whaling Convention, of the place of an international body, the IWC, to deal with the issue of the killing of whales for scientific or other purposes, of the expression of the Executive Government of its (non-justiciable) view of Australia's long-term national interest, of the placing of the Court at the centre of an international dispute (indeed, helping to promote such a dispute) between Australia and a friendly foreign power, and of the likelihood that any attempt to enforce an injunction against the respondent would be futile (a matter that was never seriously contested by the applicant on the application for leave to serve out of Australia), I was not persuaded that the Court's exercise of discretion to grant leave to serve the respondent outside the jurisdiction was appropriate.

17. On that day, senior counsel for the applicant made an application for leave to appeal under the Federal Court Rules, as he was entitled to do. I granted that leave.

18. The applicant was successful on appeal to the Full Court: see *Humane Society International Inc v Kyodo Senpaku Kaisha Ltd* (2006) 154 FCR 425. The Full Court unanimously held that the considerations to which I referred (which were broadly characterised by the Full Court as "political") should not affect the exercise of judicial discretion where, as here, the action is otherwise justiciable. The joint judgment of Black CJ and Finkelstein J at [12] and [13] (with which propositions Moore J concurred at [38]) stated:

> *...It may be accepted that whilst legal disputes may occur in a political context, the exclusively political dimension of the dispute is non-justiciable. It is appropriately non-justiciable because the Court lacks competence to resolve disputes and issues of an exclusively political type, the resolution of which will involve the application of non-judicial norms: compare* Japan Whaling Association v American Cetacean Society *(1986) 487 US 221 at 230.*
>
> *Even if, in special circumstances, there is occasion for political considerations to be taken into account in deciding whether an action should be permitted to go forward, there is no room, in our view, for those considerations where, as here, the Parliament has provided that the action is justiciable in an Australian court:* R v Bow Street Metropolitan Stipendiary Magistrate; Ex parte Pinochet Ugarte *[2000] 1 AC 61 at 107.*

19. Further, the majority of the Full Court (Black CJ and Finkelstein J, *contra* Moore J) stated that considerations of futility of enforcement of any final relief were premature when determining whether or not to exercise discretion to allow service out of the jurisdiction. The majority said the following at [14] – [16]:

> *On the question of futility, that is the lack of means of making an injunction effective, we also disagree with the approach of the primary judge in several respects. First, while it may be*

*accepted that an injunction is by its nature a discretionary remedy which may be refused if it cannot be enforced, the question whether an injunction should be granted is to be dealt with either in an application (if there be one) to set aside service (*Agar v Hyde *at 574–575) or, more appropriately, when the application itself is heard and not when the court is deciding whether there should be leave to serve out of the jurisdiction (see, by analogy,* Helicopter Utilities Pty Ltd v Australian National Airlines Commission *(1963) 80 WN NSW 48 at 51).*

Second, it seems to us that the judge in effect imposed upon the appellant the obligation of showing that an injunction would be a useful remedy. In fact the reverse is true. It is the defendant who has the onus of showing that it has no assets within the jurisdiction which could be sequestrated in punishment for contempt: Hospital for Sick Children (Board of Governors) v Walt Disney Productions Inc *[1968] Ch 52 at 71.*

Third, we consider that when asked to grant an injunction, the court should not necessarily contemplate that it would be disobeyed: In re Liddell's Settlement Trusts [1936] Ch 365 at 373–374; Castanho v Brown & Root (UK) Ltd *[1981] AC 557 at 574;* Republic of Haiti v Duvalier *[1990] 1 QB 202 at 216*; South Bucks District Council v Porter *[2003] 2 AC 558 at 580. There are many cases where parties out of the jurisdiction have been subjected to an injunction regarding their conduct abroad. The cases to which we have referred show that if a person is properly served in accordance with the court's exorbitant jurisdiction, that person (so far as the jurisdiction of the court is concerned) is in the same position as a person who is within its territorial jurisdiction. Nevertheless, in an appropriate case the judge may refuse to grant an injunction because the defendant is outside the jurisdiction and is likely to ignore the order. It will all depend upon the circumstances and, at the present stage of these proceedings, they are not yet known.*

Service and non-appearance of the respondent

20. Following the Full Court judgment, the applicant attempted, unsuccessfully, to serve the respondent in Japan via diplomatic channels. The Japanese Ministry of Foreign Affairs, in a note verbale dated 26 October 2006, refused to allow the documents to be accepted for service on the grounds that "this issue relates to waters and a matter over which Japan does not recognise Australia's jurisdiction". The applicant then filed a notice of motion on 31 January 2007, seeking substituted service upon the respondent in accordance with Order 7 rule 9 of the Federal Court Rules.

21. On 2 February 2007, I made the following orders for service upon the respondent:

1. The applicant be permitted to serve the originating process on the respondent in Japan by:

(a) Serving the following documents on or before 1 April 2007:

- *(i) Copies in English of the amended application and the amended statement of claim;*
- *(ii) Copies in Japanese of the amended application and the amended statement of claim; and*
- *(iii) A copy of this order in English and Japanese.*

(b) Serving the documents referred to in 1(a) on the respondent by:

- *(i) Sending by registered post addressed to the managing director of the respondent at the following address, being the respondent's registered place of business: 4–5 Toyomi-cho, Chuo-ku, Tokyo, Japan; and*
- *(ii) Serving the said documents at the respondent's registered place of business: 4–5 Toyomi-cho, Chuo-ku, Tokyo, Japan.*

22. The applicant relied on an affidavit of Emily Lucienne Besser, a solicitor of the firm representing the applicant, affirmed 6 August 2007, in relation to service upon the respondent by registered post. Ms Besser deposed that on 27 February 2007, copies of the relevant documents were sent to the respondent by registered post in accordance with order (1)(b)(i) of the orders of 2 February 2007. Exhibit ELB-2 to that affidavit is the registered post receipt, identifying the respondent's address. Exhibit ELB-3 is a copy of the envelope sent to the respondent, which

was returned on 12 March 2007. The envelope was unopened and was marked with Japanese characters, the translation of which reads "refuse to receive".

23. The applicant also relied upon an affidavit of Diana Beaton, affirmed 31 August 2007. Ms Beaton is an administrative assistant at the firm representing the applicant. Ms Beaton deposed that on 27 July 2007, she sent by registered post a further copy of the relevant documents to the respondent's registered address in Tokyo. That package was also returned, unopened, marked "RETOUR/REFUSE".

24. In relation to the personal service upon the respondent at its offices in Tokyo, the applicant read the affidavit of Mikio Hisamatsu, affirmed 24 March 2007. Mr Hisamatsu, a lawyer, attended the respondent's office in Tokyo on 21 February 2007. Mr Hisamatsu attended upon the respondent's General Affairs Department, and handed the package of service documents to a woman there, identifying the package as legal documents to be served upon the company. Mr Hisamatsu deposed that the woman took the envelope, but indicated that she was not authorised to accept service. Mr Hisamatsu was then confronted by a man who identified himself as the "sub-department leader" of the respondent. That person was holding the package, but also stated he would not accept service. Mr Hisamatsu then deposed that the sub-department leader returned with an apparently more senior person, who again refused to accept service on the grounds that "you have not identified yourself, this envelope is not sealed and there is no name on it". The senior person attempted to return the package to Mr Hisamatsu. However, Mr Hisamatsu refused to accept it and left the building, leaving the package with the employees of the respondent.

25. Based on the above, I am satisfied that the applicant has served the relevant documents on the respondent in accordance with the orders of 2 February 2007 and that the respondent was aware of the proceeding against it in this Court.

26. After reserving judgment on this matter, I directed the applicant to write to the Attorney-General for the Commonwealth to ascertain whether he remained of the same view as expressed in his submissions relating to leave to serve out of the jurisdiction. In a letter dated 12 October 2007, the Attorney-General's advisors expressed the opinion that the service by the applicant was defective and that "Japan would view neither the proceedings nor any judgment arising from them as legitimate". However, in circumstances such as these, where the Full Court of this Court has ordered that the respondent be served out of the jurisdiction, and where the Japanese Government has declined to assist in that service (as outlined above), I am of the opinion that the orders of 2 February 2007 are in accordance with the Rules. In so saying, I refer to my reasons given for granting substituted service (given on 16 February 2007): see *Humane Society International Inc v Kyodo Senpaku Kaisha Ltd* [2007] FCA 124.

27. Following substituted service, the matter was called on for hearing on 18 September 2007. The respondent did not file a notice of appearance prior to that time and did not appear on the morning of the hearing. The respondent was called outside the Court, but failed to appear. The matter then proceeded without the respondent being present. The applicant did not seek orders on a default basis, but proceeded to prove the matters required to establish the claim.

Pleadings

28. The applicant originally sought leave to serve upon the respondent a pleading to the effect that the whaling conducted pursuant to the Japanese Whaling Research Program under Special Permit in the Antarctic (JARPA) by the respondent was not scientific whaling. Leave was not given to serve a pleading containing that allegation, as the allegation was not particularised. There was no appeal from that part of the original decision to refuse leave to serve out of Australia. In the circumstances, this proceeding has been conducted on the premise that JARPA (and later JARPA II) are not challenged as lawful permits under the Whaling Convention and thus it was not asserted that the impugned activity of the respondent was and is not scientific research.

29. The amended statement of claim asserts the following:

- That the respondent has intentionally engaged in a series of activities that have resulted in Antarctic minke whales and fin whales being killed, taken and interfered with, and humpback whales being taken and interfered with, within the Australian Whale Sanctuary, and subsequently intentionally treated and possessed in contravention of ss 229, 229A, 229B, 229C, 229D and 230 of the EPBC Act;
- That the conduct was done in accordance with the Japanese Whaling Research Program under Special Permit in the Antarctic (JARPA) issued by the government of Japan under Article VIII of the Whaling Convention;
- That JARPA is not a recognised foreign authority for the purposes of subsection 7(1) of the *Antarctic Treaty (Environment Protection) Act 1980* (Cth);
- That the respondent is not permitted or authorised to kill, take, interfere with, treat or possess whales in accordance with ss 231, 232 or 238 of the EPBC Act;
- That, unless restrained, the respondent will in the future intentionally kill, take and interfere with within the Australian Whale Sanctuary, and subsequently intentionally treat and possess Antarctic minke whales, fin whales and humpback whales in contravention of the EPBC Act.

The hearing

30. The evidence reveals that the whaling activity in the waters off Antarctica was undertaken by a fleet of five vessels: the MV *Kyoshin Maru No 2*, a sighting and survey vessel that steamed ahead of the fleet to locate whale pods; the MV *Yushin Maru*, the MV *Kyo Maru No 1* and the MV *Toshi Maru No 25*, being sampling or "catcher" vessels used for hunting and killing whales; and the MV *Nisshin Maru,* being the base ship where the slaughtered whales were processed and research carried out. The MV *Toshi Maru No* 25 was retired prior to the 2002/2003 season and was replaced with the MV *Yushin Maru No 2*. The MV *Kaikoh Maru*, a second sighting and survey vessel, also participated in the 2005/2006 and 2006/2007 whaling seasons.

31. The evidence of the registration of each of the vessels *Kyoshin Maru No 2, Yushin Maru, Yushin Maru No 2, Kyo Maru No 1, Kaikoh Maru, Toshi Maru No 25* and *Nisshin Maru* discloses that the respondent is the owner of the vessels. That is sufficient *prima facie* evidence of ownership: *Tisand Pty Ltd v The Owners of the Ship MV Cape Moreton (Ex Freya)* (2005) 143 FCR 43 at 85 [171]. There was no suggestion in the evidence that the registration was, or was likely to be, in any way inaccurate. Although the respondent's purposes, as stated in its company registration certificate, include "conducting shipping and lease of vessels", there is no evidence to suggest that that the vessels were either demise or time chartered when they were engaged in the whaling activity.

32. Under JARPA, the whaling activity was conducted in two groups of areas, alternating on a biennial basis. In the 2001/2002 and 2003/2004 seasons, whaling was conducted south of latitude 60° S to the ice edge of the Antarctic land mass between longitude 35° E and longitude 130° E (referred to as Area IV and Area IIIE). In the 2000/2001, 2002/2003 and 2004/2005 seasons, whaling was conducted south of latitude 60° S to the ice edge of the Antarctic land mass between longitude 130° E and longitude 145° W (referred to as Area V and Area VIW). After the introduction of JARPA II, the internal boundaries were shifted such that in the 2005/2006 season, whaling occurred between 35° E and 175° E and in 2006/2007, between 175° E and 145° W.

33. The applicant relied upon reports submitted by the respondent to the IWC pursuant to JARPA (and from the 2005/2006 season onwards, JARPA II) to establish the respondent's whaling activity in the Antarctic. The reports identify that whale pods were located and pursued by the sighting and survey vessels in a manner that falls within the statutory definition of "interfering" with a cetacean within the scope of 229B(1) and (4).

34. The numbers of whales killed in the waters off Antarctica each season, as outlined by the reports, are as follows:

Whaling season	Number of Antarctic minke whales killed under JARPA and JARPA II	Number of fin whales killed under JARPA and JARPA II
2000/2001	440	0
2001/2002	440	0
2002/2003	440	0
2003/2004	440	0
2004/2005	440	0
2005/2006	853	10
2006/2007	505	3
Total	3,558	13

35. The reports indicate that no humpback whales were killed under the JARPA II regime during the "feasibility study" period, which comprised the 2005/2006 and 2006/2007 seasons. However, the 2006/2007 report stated that the "full-scale JARPA II will start from the 2007/08 season", during which time the respondent expected to take 50 humpback whales, 50 fin whales and 850 Antarctic minke whales each season. I therefore conclude that it is likely that the respondent will kill humpback whales in future seasons.

36. The 2005/2006 and 2006/2007 reports stated that "biopsy samples" were taken from humpback whales, as well as other whale species, by use of a compound crossbow. I am satisfied that this non-lethal method of sampling amounted to injuring, interfering with and treating a cetacean within the definition of the EPBC Act.

37. The applicant tendered photographs annexed to an affidavit of Kieran Paul Mulvaney, a Greenpeace whaling protester, which identify that after slaughter, the whales were taken aboard the MV *Nisshin Maru* and dissected. This is consistent with the respondent's cruise reports and is on its face a breach of s 230 of the EPBC Act.

38. The cruise reports filed with the IWC acknowledge the assistance of employees of the respondent in the preparation of the report. It is reasonably open to infer (and I do) that the authors of the report include employees of the company, and that the representations made in the reports go to a matter within the scope of the employees' employment and authority: the *Evidence Act 1995* (Cth), ss 87 and 88.

39. The area in which the fleet conducted its whaling activities extends beyond the boundaries of the Australian Whale Sanctuary. Nevertheless, by overlaying a map of the Australian Whale Sanctuary over the maps in the cruise reports identifying the locations at which whales were taken, I conclude that a significant number of the whales were taken inside the Australian Whale Sanctuary.

40. The Australian Government has not issued a permit under s 238 of the EPBC Act authorising these acts. On the basis of the above, the applicant has established on the balance of probabilities that the fleet has engaged in conduct that contravenes ss 229, 229A, 229B, 229C, 229D and 230 of the EPBC Act, and intends to continue doing so in the future under the JARPA II regime.

41. Attribution of acts of individuals to a body corporate for the purposes of the EPBC Act is prescribed by s 498B(1), which is in the following terms:

Any conduct engaged in on behalf of a body corporate:

(a) by a director, employee or agent of the body corporate within the scope of his or her actual or apparent authority; or

(b) by any other person at the direction or with the consent or agreement (whether express or implied) of a director, employee or agent of the body corporate, where the giving of the direction, consent or agreement is within the scope of the actual or apparent authority of the director, employee or agent;

is to be taken, for the purposes of this Act, to have been engaged in also by the body corporate unless the body corporate establishes that the body corporate took reasonable precautions and exercised due diligence to avoid the conduct.

42. The respondent is the entity authorised by the Japanese Government to conduct the whaling. No direct evidence has been adduced to establish that the crews of the vessel were employees of the respondent. I infer, however, that the crews of the various vessels in the fleet were acting in accordance with the respondent's authority, under JARPA and JARPA II.

43. Based on the facts outlined above, I am satisfied that the respondent is responsible for the actions of the whaling fleet for the purposes of the EPBC Act.

44. For the reasons already given in earlier reasons, I am satisfied that the EPBC Act applies to the Australian Whale Sanctuary and that there is no recognised foreign authority for the purposes of s 7(1) of the *Antarctic Treaty (Environment Protection) Act 1980* (Cth). In reaching this latter conclusion, I have acted on the submissions and material put on by the applicant and the concession of the Attorney-General, both referred to at [40] of my reasons published on 27 May 2005 ([2005] FCA 664). Thus, I am satisfied that the respondent has contravened the EPBC Act, as alleged.

Discretion

45. The Full Court made its views clear (unanimously) as to the taking into account of what Black CJ and Finkelstein J called in their reasons "political" questions, at the point of leave to serve out of the jurisdiction. Once leave has been granted, and the matter is before the Court to be resolved in the exercise of federal jurisdiction, it follows *a fortiori* from the Full Court's views as to the irrelevance of those matters at the point of decision whether to grant leave to serve process outside Australia that they are irrelevant at the point of final relief. Though it does not matter for the resolution of this proceeding, it may well be that the breadth or range of discretionary matters is wider at the point of deciding upon leave to serve out of Australia than at the point of decision about final relief. In any event, in accordance with the reasons of the Full Court, I can give no weight or relevance to the considerations that, when combined with futility, influenced my earlier decision. I therefore turn to futility, as a separate issue.

46. The respondent has, on the evidence, no presence or assets within the jurisdiction. Unless the respondent's vessels enter Australia, thus exposing themselves to possible arrest or seizure, the applicant acknowledges that there is no practical mechanism by which orders of this Court can be enforced (supplementary submissions, paragraph 36).

47. In addition to paragraphs [14] – [16] of the majority judgment of the Full Court of this Court on appeal (excerpted above), Black CJ and Finkelstein J said the following on futility at [18] – [20]:

There is another way of considering the question of futility. The injunctive relief that the appellant seeks is relief by way of statutory injunction under s 475 of the EPBC Act. That section authorises the grant of what has been called a public interest injunction: see ICI Australia Operations Pty Ltd v TPC *(1992) 38 FCR 248 at 256. Section 475 and the related provisions in Div 14 of Pt 17 of the EPBC Act have their counterpart in s 80 of the* Trade Practices Act 1974 *(Cth) ('the TP Act') upon which they appear to have been largely modelled. Parliament has determined that it is in the public interest that the enforcement provisions of the EPBC Act should be unusually comprehensive in scope. Section 475 of the EPBC Act and its related provisions form part of a much larger enforcement scheme contained in the 21 divisions of Pt 17. The provisions include the conferral of powers of seizure and forfeiture, powers to board and detain vessels and authority to continue a pursuit on the high seas.*

It is an important and distinctive feature of Div 14 of Pt 17 of the EPBC Act that, like s 80(4) of the TP Act, the Federal Court is expressly empowered to grant an injunction restraining a person from engaging in conduct whether or not it appears to the Court that the person intends to engage again in conduct of that kind and, even, whether or not there is a significant risk of injury or damage to the environment if the person engages or continues to engage in conduct of that kind: see s 479(1)(a) and (c).

Further, at [21], the majority said:

Although 'deterrence' is more commonly used in the vocabulary of the law than 'education', the two ideas are closely connected and must surely overlap in areas where a statute aims to regulate conduct. Thus, there being a 'matter' (see [28] below), the grant of a statutory public interest injunction to mark the disapproval of the Court of conduct which the Parliament has proscribed, or to discourage others from acting in a similar way, can be seen as also having an educative element. For that reason alone the grant of such an injunction may be seen, here, as potentially advancing the regulatory objects of the EPBC Act. Indeed, some of those objects are expressed directly in the language of 'promotion', including the object provided for by s 3(1)(c), namely to promote the conservation of biodiversity, which is an object that the legislation links to the establishment of an Australian Whale Sanctuary 'to ensure the conservation of whales and other cetaceans': s 3(2)(e)(ii).

48. The majority compared the terms of section 475 of the EPBC Act with similar provisions in s 80 of the *Trade Practices Act* (at [23] – [25]).

49. Moore J did not agree with the majority on the question of futility of enforcement. His Honour was of the opinion that both long-standing common law authorities and recent High Court dicta support the proposition that relief should not be granted unless it would be effectual (or unless it there are reasonable grounds to believe an injunction will be effacious in the future). In support of this proposition, Moore J cited the following authorities:

Abebe v Commonwealth (1999) 197 CLR 510 at [31] per Gleeson CJ and McHugh J:

The term "matter" has meaning only in the context of a legal proceeding, as the passages from South Australia v Victoria, Re Judiciary and Navigation Acts, Stack v Coast Securities (No 9) Pty Ltd and Attorney-General (NSW) v Commonwealth Savings Bank *demonstrate. A "matter" cannot exist in the abstract. If there is no legal remedy for a "wrong", there can be no "matter". A legally enforceable remedy is as essential to the existence of a "matter" as the right, duty or liability which gives rise to the remedy. Without the right to bring a curial proceeding, there can be no "matter". If a person breaches a legal duty which is unenforceable in a court of justice, there can be no "matter". Such duties are not unknown to the law. For example, in* Australian Broadcasting Corp v Redmore Pty Ltd, *this court had to consider the effect on a contract of a statutory provision which prohibited the making of the contract without the approval of a minister. The prohibition arose in a context where s 8(1) of the relevant Act imposed a duty on the board of the appellant to ensure that it did not contravene any provision of the Act but s 8(3) provided that "[n]othing in this section shall be taken to impose on the Board a duty that is enforceable by proceedings in a court". Although the point did not arise for decision, it is plain that breach of the prohibition was incapable of giving rise to a "matter".*

(footnotes omitted)

Truth About Motorways v Macquarie Infrastructure Investment Management Ltd (2000) 200 CLR 591 at [49] per Gaudron J:

Absent the availability of relief related to the wrong which the plaintiff alleges, no immediate right, duty or liability is established by the court's determination. Similarly, if there is no available remedy, there is no administration of the relevant law. Thus, as Gleeson CJ and McHugh J pointed out in Abebe v Commonwealth, *"[i]f there is no legal remedy for a 'wrong', there can be no 'matter'".*

Bass v Permanent Trustee (1999) 198 CLR 334 at [47]:

Because the object of the judicial process is the final determination of the rights of the parties to an action, courts have traditionally refused to provide answers to hypothetical questions or to give advisory opinions. The jurisdiction with respect to declaratory relief has developed with an awareness of that traditional attitude. In Re F (Mental Patient: Sterilisation*), Lord Goff of Chieveley said that:*

a declaration will not be granted where the question under consideration is not a real question, nor where the person seeking the declaration has no real interest in it, nor where the declaration is sought without proper argument, for example, in default of defence or on admissions or by consent.

By "not a real question", his Lordship was identifying what he called the "hypothetical or academic". The jurisdiction includes the power to declare that conduct which has not yet taken place will not be in breach of a contract or a law and such a declaration will not be hypothetical in the relevant sense. Barwick CJ pointed this out in Commonwealth v Sterling Nicholas Duty Free Pty Ltd. *However, that is not the present case.*

(footnotes omitted)

50. The applicant submitted that a broad range of remedies are appropriate in attempting to enforce an order for contempt. In this regard, the applicant cited the case of *Simonton v Australian Prudential Regulation Authority* (2006) 152 FCR 129, in particular [70] – [74].

51. The question of futility can, however, also be seen from a perspective of disobedience. To do so requires the setting to one side of the refusal by Japan to recognise Australia's claim to Antarctica. It is not for this Court to question Australia's claim or Parliament's mandate in the EPBC Act, which is based on Australia's claim. Thus, this perspective can be seen to be relevant for this Court to take into account (even if from another perspective, for instance that of Japan, the perspective is flawed). So viewed, it (futility arising from disobedience and an inability to bring about obedience) may bring to mind what was said by Hardie, Hutley and Bowen JJA in *Vincent v Peacock* [1973] 1 NSWLR 466 at 468:

In our opinion, it is not a ground for refusing an injunction that it would not have a practical effect, where its failure to have a practical effect is because the defendant disobeys it.

52. Further, one cannot ignore the public interest nature of the claim and the complete recognition by the Parliament of that type of claim and of the lack of wide international recognition of Australia's claim to the relevant part of Antarctica: see the majority of the Full Court reasons at 154 FCR 425 and [21] – [24]; and see also *Citron v Zündel (No 4)* (2002) 41 CHRR D/274 at [298] – [301].

53. In the light of the reasons of the majority of the Full Court, I cannot conclude that the practical difficulty (if not impossibility) of enforcement is a reason to withhold relief.

54. On the material placed before the Court, I am satisfied that the respondent has contravened ss 229, 229A, 229B, 229C, 229D and 230 of the EPBC Act in relation to Antarctic minke whales and fin whales by killing, injuring, taking and interfering with them and the treating and possessing of them and by injuring, interfering with and treating and possessing humpback whales and that, unless restrained, it will continue to kill, injure, take and interfere with them, and treat and possess them.

55. In all the circumstances, the orders of the Court will be:

1. The Court declares that the respondent has killed, injured, taken and interfered with Antarctic minke whales (*Balaenoptera bonaerensis*) and fin whales (*Balaenoptera physalus*) and injured, taken and interfered with humpback whales (*Megaptera novaeangliae*) in the Australian Whale Sanctuary in contravention of sections 229, 229A, 229B and 229C of the *Environment Protection and Biodiversity Conservation Act 1999* (Cth), (the "Act"), and has treated and possessed such whales killed or taken in the Australian Whale Sanctuary in contravention of sections 229D and 230 of the Act, without permission or authorisation under sections 231, 232 or 238 of the Act.
2. The Court orders that the respondent be restrained from killing, injuring, taking or interfering with any Antarctic minke whale (*Balaenoptera bonaerensis*), fin whale (*Balaenoptera physalus*) or humpback whale (*Megaptera novaeangliae*) in the Australian

Whale Sanctuary, or treating or possessing any such whale killed or taken in the Australian Whale Sanctuary, unless permitted or authorised under sections 231, 232 or 238 of the *Environment Protection and Biodiversity Conservation Act 1999* (Cth).

56. Neither the application nor the amended application contained a request for an order for costs. I thus make no such order.

…

PART 11
NATIONAL SUBMISSIONS TO THE COMMISSION ON THE LIMITS OF THE CONTINENTAL SHELF (CLSC) CONCERNING ANTARCTIC TERRITORIAL CLAIMS[1]

AUSTRALIA

Continental Shelf Submission of Australia: Executive Summary (15 November 2004), p. 11

...

2. Australian Antarctic Territory

The Australian Antarctic Territory comprises the part of the Antarctic continent and off-lying islands lying between 45° E and 136° E, and between 142° E and 160° E. The continental margin in this region, which formed during the break-up of Antarctica, Greater India and Australia in the Cretaceous, is the submerged prolongation of the landmass of the Australian Antarctic Territory.

The outer limit of Australia's extended continental shelf in the region of the Australian Antarctic Territory encloses an area of up to 686,821 km^2 beyond 200 M from the territorial sea baseline. The outer limit of the extended continental shelf is defined by 157 fixed points, of which:

- 60 are defined by the sediment thickness formula (article 76, paragraph 4(a)(i));
- 69 are defined by arcs 60 M from the foot of the continental slope (article 76, paragraph 4(a)(ii));
- 19 are defined by the constraint line 350 M from the territorial sea baseline (article 76, paragraph 5); and
- 9 are points where the outer limit of the extended continental shelf joins to the line 200 M from Australia's territorial sea baseline (article 76, paragraph 1).

Each successive pair of points is connected by a straight line not exceeding 60 M in length.

The list of points delineating the outer limit of Australia's extended continental shelf in the region of the Australian Antarctic Territory is given in Annexes 1 and 2.

The following provisions of article 76, as well as paragraphs 4(b) and 7, are invoked to support the submission for the outer limit of the extended continental shelf in the region:

–subparagraph 4(a)(i) and (ii),

–paragraph 5.

This region is affected by outstanding delimitations with France and Norway of the overlap between the area of continental shelf of Australia, the subject of this part of the submission, and any such area appurtenant to France or Norway that may be included in a French or Norwegian submission to the Commission. France and Norway have both indicated to Australia that they have no objection to such areas being included in this part of Australia's submission, without prejudice to the eventual delimitations between Australia and each of the two States.

Attachment: Note from the Permanent Mission of Australia to the Secretary-General of the United Nations accompanying the lodgement of Australia's submission (Note No. 89/2004)

The Permanent Mission of Australia to the United Nations presents its compliments to the Secretary-General of the United Nations and has the honour to refer to the Submission

[1] [Note: Figures have been omitted from this Part].

to the Commission on the Limits of the Continental Shelf on the Outer Limits of Australia's Continental Shelf Extending Beyond 200 Nautical Miles from the Territorial Sea Baseline (the Submission) lodged pursuant to article 76, paragraph 8, of the United Nations Convention on the Law of the Sea (UNCLOS) under cover of Note No 88/2004 of the same date as this Note.

Australia recalls the principles and objectives shared by the Antarctic Treaty and UNCLOS, and the importance of the Antarctic system and UNCLOS working in harmony and thereby ensuring the continuing peaceful cooperation, security and stability in the Antarctic area.

Australia notes also the relevant provisions of UNCLOS, including its article 77, which provides *inter alia* that the rights of the coastal State over the continental shelf do not depend on any express proclamation, and recalls the decisions of Meetings of the States Parties to UNCLOS and the rules of the Commission on the Limits of the Continental Shelf (the Commission).

Australia has regard to the circumstances of the area south of 60 degrees South latitude and the special legal and political status of Antarctica under the provisions of the Antarctic Treaty, including its article IV, and notes that appurtenant to Antarctica there exist areas of continental shelf the extent of which has yet to be defined. It is open to the States concerned to submit information to the Commission which would not be examined by it for the time being, or to make a partial submission not including such areas of continental shelf, for which a submission may be made later, notwithstanding the provisions regarding the ten-year period established by article 4 of Annex II to UNCLOS and the subsequent decision on its application taken by the Eleventh Meeting of States Parties to UNCLOS.

Consistent with the first option, Australia requests the Commission in accordance with its rules not to take any action for the time being with regard to the information in this Submission that relates to continental shelf appurtenant to Antarctica.

The Permanent Mission of Australia to the United Nations requests that this Note be placed on the website of the Division for Ocean Affairs and the Law of the Sea along with the remainder of the executive summary of the Submission in fulfilment of the requirements of the Commission's Rules of Procedure.

The Permanent Mission of Australia to the United Nations avails itself of this opportunity to renew to the Secretary-General of the United Nations the assurances of its highest consideration.

Note verbale from the USA on the Australian Submission (3 December 2004) (POL 10-04)

The Deputy Representative of the United States of America to the United Nations presents her compliments to the Secretary-General of the United Nations and refers to the recent Australian submission to the Commission on the Limits of the Continental Shelf (the Commission). The United States recalls the principles and objectives shared by the Antarctic Treaty and the United Nations Convention on the Law of the Sea (the Convention), and the importance of the Antarctic system and the Convention working in harmony and thereby ensuring the continuing peaceful cooperation, security and stability in the Antarctic area. The United States wishes to inform you that, recalling Article IV of the Antarctic Treaty, the United States does not recognize any State's claim to territory in Antarctica and consequently does not recognize any State's rights over the seabed and subsoil of the submarine areas beyond and adjacent to the continent of Antarctica. The United States acknowledges with appreciation Australia's request to the Commission that it not take any action on that portion of its submission relating to areas of the seabed and subsoil adjacent to Antarctica. The United States requests that this note be posted on the United Nations Division for Ocean Affairs and the Law of the Sea web site and made available to the Commission.

The Deputy Representative of the United States of America to the United Nations avails herself of this opportunity to renew to the Secretary-General the assurances of her highest consideration.

Note verbale from Russia on the Australian Submission (9 December 2004) (No. 739/N) (translated from Russian)

The Permanent Mission of the Russian Federation to the United Nations presents its compliments to the Secretary-General of the United Nations and has the honour to inform him that the Russian Federation, with reference to the submission of Australia to the Commission on the Limits of the Continental Shelf (notification No. CLCS.03.2004.LOS of 15 November 2004), wishes to convey the following information.

Based on the provisions of article 4 of the Antarctic Treaty of 1959, the Russian Federation does not recognize any claims in relation to territories located in the area covered by the Treaty, nor does it regard the assertion of such claims by any State as establishing rights with respect to the seabed (continental shelf) and its mineral resources in areas appurtenant to Antarctica.

In this connection, the Russian Federation takes note of and supports the request by Australia that the Commission should not take any action with regard to the part of its submission that relates to the seabed (continental shelf) appurtenant to Antarctica in the area covered by the Antarctic Treaty of 1959.

The Russian Federation requests that this note should be posted on the web site of the Division for Ocean Affairs and the Law of the Sea of the Secretariat of the United Nations and brought to the attention of the Commission on the Limits of the Continental Shelf.

The Permanent Mission of the Russian Federation to the United Nations takes this opportunity to convey to the Secretary-General of the United Nations the renewed assurances of its highest consideration.

Note verbale from The Netherlands on the Australian Submission (31 March 2005) (No. NYV/2005/690)

The Permanent Mission of the Netherlands to the United Nations presents its compliments to the United Nations Division for Ocean Affairs and the Law of the Sea, Office of Legal Affairs, and has the honor to refer to the Submission to the Commission on the Limits of the Continental Shelf on the Outer Limits of Australia's Continental Shelf Extending Beyond 200 Nautical Miles from the Territorial Sea Baseline and the accompanying note of the Permanent Mission of Australia to the Secretary-General of the United Nations, dated 15 November 2004.

Taking note that the submission of Australia includes information relating to continental shelf adjacent to Antarctica, the Netherlands wishes to reiterate its long-standing position that the Netherlands does not recognize any claim to territories in Antarctica and does not recognize that a claim to territorial sovereignty in Antarctica is capable of creating any sort of rights over continental shelf adjacent to Antarctica. It is well-established that the principle of sovereign rights over continental shelf adjacent to the coast, for the purposes of exploring and exploiting the natural resources of the shelf, derives from sovereignty of the coastal State over adjacent land territory. Accordingly, the Netherlands does not consider that the continental shelf adjacent to Antarctica is subject to the sovereign rights of any State.

The Netherlands notes that there is an unresolved land dispute in relation to Australia's claim to territory in Antarctica. It understands the reference to Article IV of the 1959 Antarctic Treaty in Australia's note to be information to the Commission on the Limits of the Continental Shelf of said dispute in accordance with paragraph 2 of Annex I of the Rules of Procedure of the Commission on the Limits of the Continental Shelf. Therefore, the Netherlands requests the Commission to act pursuant to paragraph 5(a) of Annex I of the Rules of Procedure of the

Commission on the Limits of the Continental Shelf insofar the submission of Australia includes information relating to continental shelf adjacent to Antarctica. In this respect, the Netherlands acknowledges with appreciation Australia's request to the Commission on the Limits of the Continental Shelf that it not take any action on that portion of its submission relating to continental shelf adjacent to Antarctica.

The Netherlands requests that this *note verbale* be circulated to the members of the Commission on the Limits of the Continental Shelf and Member States of the United Nations, and be posted on the web site of the United Nations Division for Ocean Affairs and the Law of the Sea.

The Permanent Mission of the Netherlands to the United Nations avails itself of this opportunity to renew to the Division for Ocean Affairs and the Law of the Sea the assurances of its highest considerations.

Note verbale from India on the Australian Submission (5 July 2005) (NY/PM/443/1/98)

The Permanent Mission of India to the United Nations presents its compliments to the Secretary-General of the United Nations and with reference to the circular note CLCS.03.2004. LOS (Continental Shelf Notification) of 15 November 2004 concerning the Australian submission to the Commission on the limits of Continental Shelf ("the Commission"), has the honour to express the position of the Government of India with regard to the submission made by the Government Australia relating to the seabed and subsoil of the submarine areas adjacent to the continent of Antarctica.

India recalls the principles and objectives shared by the Antarctic Treaty and the United Nations Convention on the Law of the Sea (the Convention), and confirms the importance of harmony between the Antarctic Treaty and the Convention and of the continuing cooperation, security and stability in the Antarctic area.

India, while referring to Article IV of the Antarctic Treaty, wishes to inform that it does not recognise any state's right or claims to territorial sovereignty in the Antarctic area, and consequently does not recognise any state's right over or claims to the water, seabed and subsoil of the submarine areas adjacent to the continent of Antarctica.

Acknowledging with appreciation Australia's request to the Commission for not taking any action on the portion of its submission relating to areas of the seabed and subsoil adjacent to Antarctica, India requests the Commission not to take any action accordingly.

India requests that this *note verbale* be made available to the Member States and the Commission.

The Permanent Mission of India to the United Nations avails of this opportunity to renew to the Secretary-General of the United Nations the assurances of its highest consideration.

NEW ZEALAND

Continental Shelf Submission of New Zealand: Note Accompanying Lodgement of Submission (19 April 2006) (NZ-CLCS-TPN-02)

The New Zealand Permanent Mission to the United Nations presents its compliments to the Secretary-General of the United Nations and has the honour to refer to the submission of the Government of New Zealand to the Commission on the Limits of the Continental Shelf pursuant to article 76, paragraph 8, of the United Nations Convention on the Law of the Sea 1982 (UNCLOS), presented under cover of Note No. NZ-CLCS-TPN-01 of the same date as this Note.

New Zealand recalls the principles and objectives shared by the Antarctic Treaty and UNCLOS, and the importance of the Antarctic system and UNCLOS working in harmony and thereby ensuring the continuing peaceful cooperation, security and stability in the Antarctic area.

New Zealand notes also the relevant provisions of UNCLOS, including its article 77, which provides *inter alia* that the rights of the coastal State over the continental shelf do not depend on any express proclamation, and recalls the decisions of Meetings of the States Parties to UNCLOS and the rules of the Commission on the Limits of the Continental Shelf (the Commission).

New Zealand has regard to the circumstances of the area south of 60 degrees South latitude and the special legal and political status of Antarctica under the provisions of the Antarctic Treaty, including its article IV, and notes that appurtenant to Antarctica there exist areas of continental shelf the extent of which has yet to be defined. It is open to the States concerned to submit information to the Commission which would not be examined by it for the time being, or to make a partial submission not including such areas of continental shelf, for which a submission may be made later, notwithstanding the provisions regarding the ten-year period established by article 4 of Annex II to UNCLOS and the subsequent decision on its application taken by the Eleventh Meeting of States Parties to UNCLOS.

New Zealand makes a partial submission, in accordance with the Commission's rules, not including areas of continental shelf appurtenant to Antarctica, for which a submission may be made later, notwithstanding the provisions regarding the ten-year period established by article 4 of Annex II to UNCLOS and the subsequent decision on its application taken by the Eleventh Meeting of States Parties to UNCLOS.

The Permanent Mission requests that this Note be placed on the website of the Division for Ocean Affairs and the Law of the Sea together with the remainder of the executive summary of the Submission in fulfilment of the requirements of the Commission's Rules of Procedure.

The New Zealand Permanent Mission to the United Nations takes this opportunity to renew to the Secretary-General of the United Nations the assurances of its highest consideration.

Note verbale from Japan on the New Zealand Submission (28 June 2006) (SC/06/459)

The Permanent Mission of Japan to the United Nations presents its compliments to the Secretariat of the United Nations and, with reference to the circular CLCS.05.2006.LOS (Continental Shelf Notification) dated 21 April 2006, concerning the receipt of the submission made by New Zealand to the Commission on the Limits of the Continental Shelf (hereinafter referred to as "the Commission"), has the honour to express the position of the Government of Japan with regard to the submission made by New Zealand, and requests that this note verbale be circulated to the members of the Commission and Member States of the United Nations, posted on the Web site of the Division for Ocean Affairs and the Law of the Sea (DOALOS) of the Secretariat of the United Nations, and made available to the Member States and the Commission.

Japan confirms the importance of keeping harmony between the Antarctic Treaty and the United Nations Convention of the Law of the Sea and thereby ensuring the continuing peaceful cooperation, security and stability in the Antarctic area.

Recalling Article IV of the Antarctic Treaty, Japan does not recognize any State's right of or claim to territorial sovereignty in the Antarctic, and consequently does not recognize any State's rights over or claims to the water, seabed and subsoil of the submarine areas adjacent to the continent of Antarctica.

From this standpoint, Japan stresses that the balance of rights and obligations in the Antarctic Treaty should not be affected in any way by the intention to submit to the Commission information on the outer limits of the continental shelf adjacent to the continent of Antarctica expressed by New Zealand.

The Permanent Mission of Japan to the United Nations avails itself of this opportunity to renew to the Secretariat of the United Nations the assurances of its highest consideration.

Note verbale from The Netherlands on the New Zealand Submission (19 December 2006) (DJZ-IR 178/2006)

The Permanent Mission of the Kingdom of the Netherlands to the United Nations presents its compliments to the United Nations Secretary-General and has the honor to refer to Note No. NZ-CLCS-TPN-02, dated 19 April 2006, relating to the Submission of the Government of New Zealand to the Commission on the Limits of the Continental Shelf pursuant to article 76, paragraph 8, of the United Nations Convention on the Law of the Sea 1982 (UNCLOS), presented under cover of Note No. NZ-CLCS-TPN-0l of the same date.

In Note No. NZ-CLCS-TPN-02, New Zealand states that "New Zealand makes a partial submission, in accordance with the Commission's rules, not including areas of continental shelf appurtenant to Antarctica, for which a submission may be made later, notwithstanding the provisions regarding the ten-year period established by article 4 of Annex II to UNCLOS and the subsequent decision on its application taken by the Eleventh Meeting of State Parties to UNCLOS".

Taking note that New Zealand makes a claim to territory in Antarctica and that this claim appears to be referred to in Note No. NZ-CLCS-TPN-02, the Netherlands wishes to reiterate its long-standing position that the Netherlands does not recognize any claim to territories in Antarctica and consequently does not recognize that a claim to territorial sovereignty in Antarctica is capable of creating any sort of rights over continental shelf adjacent to Antarctica. It is well-established that the principle of sovereign rights over continental shelf adjacent to the coast, for the purposes of exploring and exploiting the natural resources of the shelf, derives from sovereignty of the coastal State over adjacent land territory. Accordingly, the Netherlands does not consider that the continental shelf adjacent to Antarctica is subject to the sovereign rights of any State.

The Netherlands acknowledges with appreciation that New Zealand has made a partial submission that does not include areas of continental shelf appurtenant to Antarctica. However, the Netherlands stresses that the balance of rights and obligations in the Antarctic Treaty should not be affected in any way by the intention to submit to the Commission information on the outer limits of the continental shelf adjacent to the continent of Antarctica expressed by New Zealand.

The Netherlands confirms the importance of keeping harmony between the Antarctic Treaty and the United Nations Conventions on the Law of the Sea and thereby ensuring the continuing peaceful cooperation, security and stability in the Antarctic area.

The Netherlands requests that this *note verbale* be circulated to the members of the Commission on the Limits of the Continental Shelf and Member States of the United Nations, and be posted on the web site of the United Nations Division for Ocean Affairs and the Law of the Sea.

The Permanent Mission of the Kingdom of the Netherlands to the United Nations avails itself of this opportunity to renew to the United Nations Secretary-General the assurances of its highest considerations.

The Hague, 19 December 2006

UNITED KINGDOM

Continental Shelf Submission of the United Kingdom of Great Britain and Northern Island: Note accompanying Lodgement of Submission (9 May 2008) (No. 168/08)

The Permanent Mission of the United Kingdom of Great Britain and Northern Ireland to the United Nations presents its compliments to the Secretary-General of the United Nations, and, in accordance with Article 76(8) of the United Nations Convention on the Law of the Sea ("UNCLOS"), has the honour to transmit herewith the submission of the United Kingdom to the Commission on the Limits of the Continental Shelf ("the Commission") relating to the continental shelf of Ascension Island.

The United Kingdom will be preparing a number of other partial submissions to the Commission, which it will make prior to the deadline of May 2009.

However, as regards Antarctica, the United Kingdom recalls the principles and objectives shared by the Antarctic Treaty and UNCLOS, and the importance of the Antarctic system and UNCLOS working in harmony and thereby ensuring the continuing peaceful cooperation, security and stability in the Antarctic area.

The United Kingdom notes also the relevant provisions of UNCLOS, including its Article 77, which provides *inter alia* that the rights of the coastal State over the continental shelf do not depend on any express proclamation, and recalls the decisions of Meetings of the States Parties to UNCLOS and the rules of the Commission.

The United Kingdom has regard to the circumstances of the area south of 60 degrees South latitude and the special legal and political status of Antarctica under the provisions of the Antarctic Treaty, including its article IV, and notes that appurtenant to Antarctica there exist areas of continental shelf the extent of which has yet to be defined. It is open to the States concerned to submit information to the Commission which would not be examined by it for the time being, or to make a partial submission not including such areas of continental shelf, for which a submission may be made later, notwithstanding the provisions regarding the ten-year period established by article 4 of Annex II to UNCLOS and the subsequent decision on its application taken by the Eleventh Meeting of States Parties to UNCLOS.

Accordingly, in its partial submissions, made in accordance with the Commission's rules, the United Kingdom will not include areas of continental shelf appurtenant to Antarctica, for which a submission may be made later, notwithstanding the provisions regarding the ten-year period established by article 4 of Annex II to UNCLOS and the subsequent decision on its application taken by the Eleventh Meeting of States Parties to UNCLOS.

The Permanent Mission of the United Kingdom requests that this note be placed on the website of the Division for Ocean Affairs and Law of the Sea, together with the Executive Summary of the submission relating to Ascension Island, in fulfilment of the requirements of the Commission's Rules of Procedure.

The Permanent Mission of the United Kingdom to the United Nations takes this opportunity to renew to the Secretary-General of the United Nations the assurances of its highest consideration.

United Kingdom Mission to the United Nations

9 May 2008

Note verbale from The Netherlands on the UK Submission (28 August 2009) (No. NYV/2009/2184)

The Permanent Mission of the Kingdom of the Netherlands to the United Nations presents its compliments to the United Nations Secretary-General and has the honour to refer to its *note verbale* of 23 January 2007 (DJZ-IR 178/2006).

The Netherlands wishes to inform the United Nations that the views expressed in the *note verbale* of 23 January 2007 (DJZ-IR 178/2006) equally apply to the submissions of other States, which have been made or may be made, who reserve their right to make a submission relating to areas of continental shelf appurtenant to Antarctica, such as in Note No. 168/08 of the United Kingdom Mission to the United Nations New York, dated 9 May 2008, and Note HR/cl No. 69 of the Permanent Mission of France to the United Nations, dated 5 February 2009.

The Netherlands requests that this *note verbale* be posted on the web site of the United Nations Division for Ocean Affairs and the Law of the Sea.

The Permanent Mission of the Kingdom of the Netherlands to the United Nations avails itself of this opportunity to renew to the United Nations Secretary-General the assurances of its highest considerations.

Note verbale from Japan on the UK Submission (19 November 2009) (SC/09/391)

The Permanent Mission of Japan to the United Nations presents its compliments to the Secretary-General of the United Nations and, with reference to the circulars CLCS.11.2008. LOS (Continental Shelf Notification) dated 12 May 2008 and CLCS.17.2009.LOS dated 17 February 2009, concerning the receipt of the submissions made by the United Kingdom of Great Britain and Northern Ireland and the French Republic respectively, to the Commission on the Limits of the Continental Shelf (hereinafter referred to as "the Commission"), has the honour to express the position of the Government of Japan with regard to those submissions, and requests that this note verbale be circulated to the members of the Commission and Member States of the United Nations, and be posted on the web site of the Division for Ocean Affairs and the Law of the Sea (DOALOS) of the Secretariat of the United Nations.

Japan confirms the importance of keeping harmony between the Antarctic Treaty and the United Nations Convention on the Law of the Sea and thereby ensuring the continuing peaceful cooperation, security and stability in the Antarctic area.

Recalling Article IV of the Antarctic Treaty, Japan does not recognize any State's right of or claims to territorial sovereignty in Antarctica, and consequently does not recognize any State's right over or claims to the seabed and subsoil of the submarine areas adjacent to the continent of Antarctica.

From this standpoint, Japan stresses that the balance of rights and obligations in the Antarctic Treaty should not be affected in any way by the intentions to submit to the Commission information on the limits of the continental shelf adjacent to the continent of Antarctica expressed by the United Kingdom of Great Britain and Northern Ireland and the French Republic.

The Permanent Mission of Japan to the United Nations avails itself of this opportunity to renew to the Secretary-General of the United Nations the assurances of its highest consideration.

19 November 2009

FRANCE

Continental Shelf Submission of France: Note Accompanying Lodgement of Submission (5 February 2009) (HR/cl No. 69)

The Permanent Mission of France to the United Nations presents its compliments to the Secretary-General of the United Nations and has the honour to transmit to him, in accordance with article 76, paragraph 8, of the United Nations Convention on the Law of the Sea, the present partial submission relating to the continental shelf of the Kerguelen Islands and of the French overseas departments of the Antilles (Martinique and Guadeloupe).

On this occasion, France recalls the principles and objectives shared by the Antarctic Treaty and the United Nations Convention on the Law of the Sea, as well as the importance of ensuring that the Antarctic system and the Convention work in harmony, thus ensuring the continuity of peaceful cooperation, security and stability in the Antarctic region.

France also notes the relevant articles of the Convention – including article 77 thereof, which states, inter alia, that the rights of the coastal State over the continental shelf do not depend on any express proclamation – and recalls the decisions taken at the meeting of States parties to the Convention and the rules of the Commission.

Taking due account of the characteristics of the area located south of 60 degrees latitude south and of the particular legal and political status of Antarctica accorded by the provisions of the Antarctic Treaty, including article IV thereof, France notes that there are some areas adjoining Antarctica for which the limits of the continental shelf have yet to be established. Concerned States have the option either to provide the Commission with information on these areas, which the Commission would not consider as yet; or to make a partial submission which does not include these areas of the continental shelf and for which a submission might later be made, notwithstanding the provisions of Annex II, article 4, of the Convention concerning the 10-year period and the decisions regarding its application that were taken at the Eleventh Meeting of States parties thereto.

Therefore, in accordance with the Commission's regulations, France hereby makes a partial submission which does not include the areas of the continental shelf that adjoin Antarctica and for which a submission may later be made, notwithstanding the provisions of Annex II, article 4, of the Convention concerning the 10-year period and the decisions regarding its application that were taken at the Eleventh meeting of States parties thereto.

The Permanent Mission hereby requests that this note should be posted on the website of the Division for Ocean Affairs and the Law of the Sea, next to the section where the executive summary of the submission is posted in accordance with the rules of procedure of the Commission.

The Permanent Mission of France takes this opportunity to convey to the Commission on the Limits of the Continental Shelf the renewed assurances of its highest consideration.

Note verbale from The Netherlands on the French Submission (28 August 2009) (No. NYV/2009/2184)

The Permanent Mission of the Kingdom of the Netherlands to the United Nations presents its compliments to the United Nations Secretary-General and has the honour to refer to its *note verbale* of 23 January 2007 (DJZ-IR 178/2006).

The Netherlands wishes to inform the United Nations that the views expressed in the *note verbale* of 23 January 2007 (DJZ-178/2006) equally apply to the submissions of other States, which have been made or may be made, who reserve their right to make a submission relating to areas of continental shelf appurtenant to Antarctica, such as in Note No. 168/08 of the United Kingdom Mission to the United Nations New York, dated 9 May 2008, and Note HR/cl No. 69 of the Permanent Mission of France to the United Nations, dated 5 February 2009.

The Netherlands requests that this *note verbale* be posted on the web site of the United Nations Division for Ocean Affairs and the Law of the Sea.

The Permanent Mission of the Kingdom of the Netherlands to the United Nations avails itself of this opportunity to renew to the United Nations Secretary-General the assurances of its highest considerations.

Note verbale from Japan on the French Submission (19 November 2009) (SC/09/391)

The Permanent Mission of Japan to the United Nations presents its compliments to the Secretary-General of the United Nations and, with reference to the circulars CLCS.11.2008. LOS (Continental Shelf Notification) dated 12 May 2008 and CLCS.17.2009.LOS dated 17 February 2009, concerning the receipt of the submissions made by the United Kingdom of Great Britain and Northern Ireland and the French Republic respectively, to the Commission on the Limits of the Continental Shelf (hereinafter referred to as "the Commission"), has the honour to express the position of the Government of Japan with regard to those submissions, and requests that this note verbale be circulated to the members of the Commission and Member States of the United Nations,. and be posted on the web site of the Division for Ocean Affairs and the Law of the Sea (DOALOS) of the Secretariat of the United Nations.

Japan confirms the importance of keeping harmony between the Antarctic Treaty and the United Nations Convention on the Law of the Sea and thereby ensuring the continuing peaceful cooperation, security and stability in the Antarctic area.

Recalling Article IV of the Antarctic Treaty, Japan does not recognize any State's right of or claims to territorial sovereignty in Antarctica, and consequently does not recognize any State's right over or claims to the seabed and subsoil of the submarine areas adjacent to the continent of Antarctica.

From this standpoint, Japan stresses that the balance of rights and obligations in the Antarctic Treaty should not be affected in any way by the intentions to submit to the Commission information on the limits of the continental shelf adjacent to the continent of Antarctica expressed by the United Kingdom of Great Britain and Northern Ireland and the French Republic.

The Permanent Mission of Japan to the United Nations avails itself of this opportunity to renew to the Secretary-General of the United Nations the assurances of its highest consideration.

19 November 2009

ARGENTINA

Continental Shelf Submission of Argentina: Executive Summary (21 April 2009) (pp. 11–15)

d) Argentine Antarctic Sector

South of the Scotia Sea, Argentina selected both formulae. Argentina selected 8 FOS points in this area of its continental margin. From FOS-50, located on the ARG-300 line in the central sector of the Scotia Sea, to the north of the Islas Orcadas del Sur up to FOS-57, on the ARG-355 line in the Weddell Sea, to the south of the abovementioned islands. From the FOS points thus selected, Argentina generated the 60 M arcs and the corresponding envelope. The 1 per cent formula on a total of 5 fixed points was also used.

In the region of the Weddell Sea, Argentina selected a total of 12 FOS points: FOS-68 to FOS-79. From these selected FOS, Argentina determined the points with the 1 per cent sediment thickness.

Figure 6 shows a map with the fixed points of the outer limit of the Argentine continental shelf along this section. Coordinates are included in Table I.

2. Applications of constraints

In order to define the *constraint line*, Argentina applied both constraints in accordance with paragraph 5 of Art. 76, which states:

"The fixed points comprising the line of the outer limits of the continental shelf on the seabed, drawn in accordance with paragraph 4 (a)(i) and (ii), either shall not exceed 350 nautical miles from the baselines from which the breadth of the territorial sea is measured or shall not exceed 100 nautical miles from the 2,500 metre isobath, which is a line connecting the depth of 2,500 metres."

The 350 M arcs were generated from the points of the baseline selected.

Argentina identified three areas of its continental margin where the application of the 100 M constraint beyond the 2,500 m isobath is more favorable than the 350 M constraint.

In each of these areas, the 2,500 m isobath was drawn as detailed in the Main Body, which includes the description of the equipment used, the data processing, the methods and algorithms used as well as the delineation of the 2,500 m isobath, thus providing the best accuracy as this isobath constitutes the basis to draw the 100 M distance.

In order to draw the 100 M distance, Argentina selected the generating points, from which both the arcs and the envelope were generated, on the 2,500 m isobath.

3. Description of the fixed points of the outer limit of the argentine continental shelf

Argentina has used the denomination **"RA"** for the fixed points of the outer limit of its continental shelf.

The description of the fixed points of the outer limit of the Argentine continental shelf starts with the first of these, located in the northernmost area of the Argentine volcanic passive continental margin, and continues, southwards, following the numbers allocated, until it reaches the last fixed point located on the eastern limit of the Argentine Antarctic Sector, south of 70°S latitude.

The first fixed point of the outer limit of the Argentine continental shelf is RA-01, as determined by applying the 1 per cent formula, and is located close to the boundary – not yet demarcated – between Argentina's continental shelf and that of Uruguay as per the "Treaty of the Río de la Plata and its maritime front" signed by both countries on November 19, 1973.

It is followed by a group of 7 (seven) fixed points that comply with the 1 per cent formula up to RA-08 (included). Points from RA-09 to RA-179 are part of the 350 M constraint line.

From **RA-180** to **RA-481**, the outer limit fixed points become part of the 2,500 m isobath + 100 M constraint line.

From **RA-482** to **RA-740**, all fixed points are part again of the 350 M constraint line. Then, the outer limit moves to **RA-741** as determined by the 1 per cent formula.

Fixed point **RA-742** is the first one located in the sheared continental margin region, established by applying the distance formula (FOS+60 M). The same holds true for the following fixed points, up to fixed point **RA-1012.**

From fixed point **RA-1013** to **RA-1142**, these are outer limit fixed points determined by the 2,500 m isobath + 100 M constraint line.

From fixed point **RA-1143** to **RA-1312**, these are outer limit fixed points which are part of the 350 M constraint line.

From **RA-1313** to **RA-1841**, these are outer limit fixed points determined by application of the distance formula (FOS+60 M).

From fixed point **RA-1842** to **RA-2069** the outer limit fixed points are part of the 350 M constraint line.

From this last point, the following outer limit fixed points are located in the Georgias Basin area, up to fixed point **RA-2542.**

From fixed point **RA-2070** to **RA-2541** are fixed points of the outer limit established by application of the distance formula (FOS + 60 M).

Fixed point **RA-2542** is located on the 200 M line, generated from a point on the baseline located on Isla San Pedro of the Islas Georgias del Sur. It is on the straight line starting from the previous fixed point, **RA-2541**, and ending on the 60 M arc generated from FOS-40, thus fulfilling the condition that distance between fixed points should not exceed 60 M.

Proceeding southwards, in the area of the combined continental margin – North Scotia Ridge, the easternmost fixed point is **RA-2543**, generated by the intersection of the 60 M arc drawn from FOS-41 to the 200 M line.

From fixed point **RA-2544** westwards to **RA-2828**, a number of fixed points have been determined by application of the distance formula (FOS+60 M).

From fixed point **RA-2829** to **RA-2976**, the outer limit fixed points are part of the 350 M constraint line.

From fixed point **RA-2977** to **RA-3456**, the outer limit fixed points are determined by the application of the distance formula (FOS+60 M).

Fixed point **RA-3457** is the intersection of point of the 60 M arc generated from FOS-48 and the 200 M line drawn from the baseline point located in Isla de los Estados.

To the west of that fixed point, the 60 M arc drawn from FOS-49 generates fixed point **RA-3458** as the intersection with the 200 M line drawn from the baseline point located in Isla de los Estados.

From fixed point **RA-3459** up to **RA-3839**, the outer limit fixed points are determined by the application of the distance formula (FOS+60 M). From this last fixed point up to **RA-3840** all the points are located on the meridian 67° 16.0' West longitude, which in this sector constitutes the boundary between the respective sovereignties over the sea, seabed and subsoil of the Argentine Republic and the Republic of Chile according to the Peace and Friendship Treaty signed by the two countries on November 29, 1984.

The following fixed points on the outer limit of the Argentine continental shelf belong to the Argentine Antarctic Sector.

The first of these fixed points is **RA-3841**, located on the 200 M line drawn from a point on the baseline of the Islas Orcadas del Sur intersecting the 60 M arc drawn from FOS-50. The fixed points **RA 3842** to **RA 4134** are thus determined by the distance formula (FOS + 60 M). The last fixed point belonging to this arc is **RA-4135** resulting from the intersection with the 200 M line corresponding to points of the baseline of Cormorán and Negra.

The 60 M arc delineated from FOS-55 generates fixed points that go beyond the 200 M drawn from points of the baseline of Islas Sandwich del Sur and Georgias del Sur. Therefore, the resulting fixed points are **RA-4137** to **RA-4224** which are part of the 350 M constraint arc drawn from the points on the baseline of Islas Orcadas del Sur. **RA-4136** and **RA-4225** are to fixed points deriving from the intersection of that arc with the 200 M lines of isles Sandwich del Sur and Georgias del Sur.

The 350 M constraint line drawn from the points of the baseline of the Islas Orcadas del Sur determines the outer limit in the area of the corresponding arc from **RA-4226** to **RA-4398.**

The first fixed point, **RA-4226**, corresponds to the intersection of the 350 M constraint and the 200 M line drawn from the points of the baseline of Islas Sandwich de Sur.

RA-4399 to **RA-4721** are points determined by applying the 60 M formula from FOS-58 to 63, located in the feature referred to as Jane arc.

Fixed point **RA-4721** connects with **RA-4722**. The first one has been determined by the 1 per cent formula, same as the following ones up to **RA-4727**.

The following fixed point is **RA-4728**. It belongs to the 350 M constraint, up to **RA-5513.**

From there on, as well as from **RA-5514** to **RA-5668**, the outer limit line is the 2,500 m+100 M restriction.

From fixed point **RA-5669** to **RA-6237** the outer limit fixed points are part of the 350 M constraint line.

The following fixed points of the outer limit from **RA-6238** to **RA-6239** were established by the application of the 1 per cent formula.

From fixed point **RA-6240** to **RA-6328**, these outer limit fixed points are part of the 350 M constraint line.

Fixed points from **RA-6329** to **RA-6332** were determined by the 1 per cent formula. This last one finally connects, through the shortest line, to **RA-6333** located on the 25° W meridian, which is the eastern boundary of the Argentine Antarctic Sector. As the distance between this last point and **RA-6336** – generated by the intersection of the 200 M line and the eastern boundary mentioned above – exceeds 60 M, Argentina has included both fixed points **RA-6334** and **RA-6335**, in accordance with the provisions in paragraph 7 of Art. 76.

Note verbale from the UK on the Argentine Submission (6 August 2009) (No. 84/09)

The Permanent Mission of the United Kingdom of Great Britain and Northern Ireland presents its compliments to the Secretary-General of the United Nations, and with reference to his communication of 1 May 2009, CLCS.25.2009.LOS (Continental Shelf Notification), regarding receipt of the submission made by the Argentine Republic to the Commission on the Limits of the Continental Shelf, and to the contents of this submission, has the honour to convey the following:

The Falkland Islands and South Georgia and the South Sandwich Islands

The United Kingdom has no doubt about its sovereignty over the Falkland Islands, and over South Georgia and the South Sandwich Islands and the surrounding maritime areas.

The principle of self-determination, enshrined in the UN Charter, underlies the United Kingdom's position on the sovereignty of the Falkland Islands. There can be no negotiations on the sovereignty of the Falkland Islands unless and until such time as the Falkland Islanders so wish. The Islanders regularly make it clear that they have no wish either to lose British sovereignty or to become independent.

The United Kingdom would like to point out that it exercises control over the continental shelf up to 200 nautical miles from the coast of each of these Overseas Territories, in accordance with the United Kingdom's Declaration on Maritime Jurisdiction around the Falkland Islands of 29 October 1986, and its Proclamation of Maritime Zone around South Georgia and the South Sandwich Islands of 1993. The United Kingdom therefore *rejects* those parts of Argentina's submission which claim rights to the seabed and subsoil of the submarine areas appurtenant to the Falkland Islands, South Georgia and the South Sandwich Islands, *and requests that the Commission does not examine those parts of the Argentine submission – i.e. any fixed points greater than RA-481, except between fixed points RA-3458 and RA-3840,*

Antarctica

The United Kingdom recalls the principles and objectives shared by the Antarctic Treaty and UNCLOS, and the importance of the Antarctic system and UNCLOS working in harmony and thereby ensuring the continuing peaceful cooperation, security and stability in the Antarctic area.

Recalling Article IV of the Antarctic Treaty, the United Kingdom does not recognise Argentina's claim to territory in Antarctica and consequently does not recognise that Argentina has any rights over the seabed and subsoil of the submarine areas appurtenant to Antarctica (as defined in the Antarctic Treaty, 1959).

The United Kingdom noted in its Note 168/08 of 9 May 2008 that, as regards Antarctica, it was open to the States concerned to submit information pertaining to Antarctica to the

Commission, which would not be examined by it for the time being, or to make a partial submission not including such areas of continental shelf, for which a submission may be made later, notwithstanding the provisions regarding the ten-year period established by article 4 of Annex II to UNCLOS and the subsequent decision on its application taken by the Eleventh Meeting of States Parties to UNCLOS. The United Kingdom took the latter course.

Taking account of the paragraphs above, and consistent with the approach taken by the United Kingdom and other Parties to the Antarctic Treaty, the United Kingdom expects that the Commission will not, for the time being, take any action on that portion of the Argentine submission relating to areas of the seabed and subsoil appurtenant to Antarctica, i.e. all fixed points greater than RA-3840.

The United Kingdom has no objection to the examination by the Commission of the remainder of the Argentine submission, i.e. up to, and including, fixed point RA-481 and between fixed points RA-3458 and RA-3840.

The Government of the United Kingdom requests that this Note be circulated to the Members of the Commission on the Limits of the Continental Shelf, States Parties to the United Nations Convention on the Law of the Sea, and other Member States of the United Nations, and also requests that the Note be posted on the website of the Division for Ocean Affairs and the Law of the Sea of the Office of Legal Affairs of the United Nations.

The Permanent Mission of the United Kingdom of Great Britain and Northern Ireland avails itself of this opportunity to renew to the Secretary-General of the United Nations the assurances of its highest consideration.

United Kingdom Mission to the United Nations

Note verbale from the USA on the Argentine Submission (19 August 2009)

The Permanent Mission of the United States of America to the United Nations presents its compliments to the Secretariat of the United Nations (Office of Legal Affairs) and refers to the recent submission by Argentina to the Commission on the Limits of the Continental Shelf (the Commission). The United States recalls the principles and objectives shared by the Antarctic Treaty and the United Nations Convention on the Law of the Sea (the Convention), and the importance of the Antarctic system and the Convention working in harmony and thereby ensuring the continuing peaceful cooperation, security and stability in the Antarctic area. The United States wishes to inform the Secretariat that, recalling Article IV of the Antarctic Treaty, the United States does not recognize any State's claim to territory in Antarctica and consequently does not recognize any State's rights over the seabed and subsoil of the submarine areas beyond and adjacent to the continent of Antarctica. The United States understands that the Commission will not take any action on that portion of Argentina's submission relating to areas of the seabed and subsoil adjacent to Antarctica. The United States requests that this note be posted on the United Nations Division for Ocean Affairs and the Law of the Sea web site and be made available to the Commission.

The Permanent Mission of the United States of America to the United Nations takes this opportunity to renew to the United Nations the assurances of its highest consideration.

Note verbale from Russia on the Argentine Submission (24 August 2009) (No. 2282/N) (translated from Russian)

The Permanent Mission of the Russian Federation to the United Nations presents its compliments to the Secretary-General of the United Nations and, with reference to the submission made by the Republic of Argentina to the Commission on the Limits of the Continental Shelf (notification CLCS.25.2009.LOS of 1 May 2009), has the honour to inform him of the following.

The Russian Federation, as a State party to the United Nations Convention on the Law of the Sea of 1982 and a Contracting Party to the Antarctic Treaty of 1959, has an interest in ensuring that all parties comply fully, unconditionally and responsibly with these important international treaties and adhere to their fundamental goals and principles.

In accordance with article IV of the 1959 Antarctic Treaty, the Russian Federation does not recognize any rights or claims in relation to territories located in the area covered by the Treaty, and considers that the assertion of such claims by any State does not establish rights over the seabed (continental shelf) and subsoil of the areas adjacent to the continent of Antarctica.

In that connection, the Russian Federation expects that the Commission on the Limits of the Continental Shelf will not take any action with respect to the section of the above-mentioned submission by the Republic of Argentina that pertains to the seabed (continental shelf) and subsoil of the areas adjacent to the continent of Antarctica.

The Permanent Mission of the Russian Federation to the United Nations takes this opportunity to convey to the Secretary-General of the United Nations the renewed assurances of its highest consideration.

Note verbale from India on the Argentine Submission (31 August 2009) (No. NY/PM/443/1/2009)

The Permanent Mission of India to the United Nations presents its compliments to the Secretary General of the United Nations and with reference to the submission of the Argentine Republic to the Commission on the Limits of the Continental Shelf on April 21 2009, has the honor to express the following:

India recalls the principles and objectives shared by the Antarctic Treaty and the United Nations Convention on the Law of the Sea, 1982 (Convention) and the importance of harmony between the Antarctic Treaty and the Convention and of the continuing cooperation, security and stability in the Antarctic area.

In accordance with Article IV of the Antarctic Treaty, India does not recognize any State's right or claim to territorial sovereignty in the Antarctic area and consequently over the seabed and subsoil of the submarine areas adjacent to the continent of Antarctica.

Accordingly India expects that the Commission will not take any action on the part of Argentine submission relating to areas of the seabed and subsoil appurtenant to Antarctica.

India requests that this note may be circulated to the Member States and to the Commission.

The Permanent Mission of India to the United Nations avails of this opportunity to renew to the Secretary General of the United Nations the assurances of its highest consideration.

Note verbale from The Netherlands on the Argentine Submission (30 September 2009) (No. NYV/2009/2459)

The Permanent Mission of the Kingdom of the Netherlands to the United Nations presents its compliments to the Secretary-General of the United Nations and has the honor to refer to the Argentine Submission to the Commission on the Limits of the Continental Shelf on the Outer Limit of the Continental Shelf and the accompanying note of the Permanent Mission of the Argentine Republic to the United Nations to the Secretary-General of the United Nations, dated 21 April 2009 (N.U. 139/2009/600).

Taking note that the submission of Argentina includes information relating to continental shelf adjacent to Antarctica, the Kingdom of the Netherlands wishes to reiterate its long-standing position that the Kingdom of the Netherlands does not recognize any claim to territories in Antarctica and does not recognize that a claim to territorial sovereignty in Antarctica is capable of creating any sort of rights over continental shelf adjacent to Antarctica. It is well-established that the principle of sovereign rights over continental shelf adjacent to the coast, for the purposes of exploring and exploiting the natural resources of the shelf, derives from sovereignty of the coastal State over adjacent land territory. Accordingly, the Kingdom of the Netherlands does not consider that the continental shelf adjacent to Antarctica is subject to the sovereign rights of any State.

The Kingdom of the Netherlands notes that there is an unresolved land dispute in relation to Argentina's claim to territory in Antarctica. It understands the reference to Article IV of the 1959 Antarctic Treaty in Argentina's note to be information to the Commission on the Limits of the Continental Shelf of said dispute in accordance with paragraph 2 of Annex I of the Rules of Procedure of the Commission on the Limits of the Continental Shelf. Therefore, the Kingdom of the Netherlands requests the Commission to act pursuant to paragraph 5(a) of Annex I of the Rules of Procedure of the Commission on the Limits of the Continental Shelf insofar the submission of Argentina includes information relating to continental shelf adjacent to Antarctica.

The Kingdom of the Netherlands requests that this *note verbale* be circulated to the members of the Commission on the Limits of the Continental Shelf and be posted on the web site of the United Nations Division for Ocean Affairs and the Law of the Sea.

The Permanent Mission of the Kingdom of the Netherlands to the United Nations avails itself of this opportunity to renew to the Secretary-General of the United Nations the assurances of its highest considerations.

Note verbale from Japan on the Argentine Submission (19 November 2009) (SC/09/390)

The Permanent Mission of Japan to the United Nations presents its compliments to the Secretary-General of the United Nations and, with reference to the circular CLCS.25.2009.LOS (Continental Shelf Notification) dated 1 May 2009, concerning the receipt of the submission made by the Argentine Republic to the Commission on the Limits of the Continental Shelf (hereinafter referred to as "the Commission"), has the honour to express the position of the Government of Japan with regard to the submission made by the Argentine Republic and requests that this note verbale be circulated to the members of the Commission and Member States of the United Nations, and be posted on the web site of the Division for Ocean Affairs and the Law of the Sea (DOALOS) of the Secretariat of the United Nations.

Japan confirms the importance of keeping harmony between the Antarctic Treaty and the United Nations Convention on the Law of the Sea and thereby ensuring the continuing peaceful cooperation, security and stability in the Antarctic area.

Recalling Article IV of the Antarctic Treaty, Japan does not recognize any State's right of or claims to territorial sovereignty in Antarctica, and consequently does not recognize any State's right over or claims to the seabed and subsoil of the submarine areas adjacent to the continent of Antarctica.

From this standpoint, Japan stresses that the balance of rights and obligations in the Antarctic Treaty should not be affected in any way in handling the information on the limits of the continental shelf, submitted by the Argentine Republic to the Commission.

Japan understands that the Commission will not take any action on the portion of Argentina's submission relating to the seabed and subsoil of the submarine areas adjacent to the continent of Antarctica.

The Permanent Mission of Japan to the United Nations avails itself of this opportunity to renew to the Secretary-General of the United Nations the assurances of its highest consideration.

Note verbale from Argentina: Response to the UK (8 August 2012)

The Argentine Republic rejects in its entirety the content of the aforementioned note verbale from the United Kingdom of Great Britain and Northern Ireland.

At the same time, the Argentine Republic reiterates the content of its note of 20 August 2009, in which it objected to the British submission to the Commission concerning the Malvinas Islands, South Georgia Islands and South Sandwich Islands, and recalls that those archipelagos and the surrounding maritime areas are an integral part of the national territory of the Argentine Republic and that, being illegally occupied by the United Kingdom, they are the subject of a sovereignty dispute between the two countries, which has been repeatedly recognized in declarations by the United Nations and other international forums and organizations.

The Argentine Republic reaffirms its rights to sovereignty over the Malvinas Islands, South Georgia Islands and South Sandwich Islands and the surrounding maritime areas and over the Argentine Antarctic Sector. Furthermore, it rejects all claims of sovereignty by the United Kingdom of Great Britain and Northern Ireland over Antarctic Territory.

The Argentine Republic requests that this note be circulated among the States members of the Commission on the Limits of the Continental Shelf, the States parties to the United Nations Convention on the Law of the Sea and the other States Members of the United Nations. It further requests that this note be posted on the website of the Division for Ocean Affairs and the Law of the Sea of the Office of Legal Affairs of the United Nations.

Accept, Sir, the assurances of my highest consideration.

Note verbale from the UK: Response to Argentina (23 August 2012) (No. 273/12)

The Permanent Mission of the United Kingdom of Great Britain and Northern Ireland presents its compliments to the Secretary-General of the United Nations, and has the honour to refer to the note of 8 August 2012 from the Permanent Mission of the Republic of Argentina to the United Nations (336/2012).

The United Kingdom reaffirms the views conveyed in its Note of 6 August 2009 (84/09), a copy of which is attached for ease of reference. The United Kingdom has no doubt about its sovereignty over the Falkland Islands and over South Georgia and the South Sandwich Islands and their respective surrounding maritime areas. Nor, recalling Article IV of the Antarctic Treaty, does the United Kingdom recognise Argentina's claim to territory in Antarctica and consequently does not recognise that Argentina has any rights over the seabed and subsoil of the submarine areas appurtenant to Antarctica (as defined in the Antarctic Treaty, 1959).

Consequently, the United Kingdom expects that the Commission on the Limits of the Continental Shelf will not consider those parts of Argentina's submission that relate to areas appurtenant to the Falkland Islands, South Georgia and South Sandwich Islands (as detailed in its note of 6 August 2009), or which relate to areas appurtenant to Antarctica.

The Government of United Kingdom requests that this Note be circulated to the Members of the Commission on the Limits of the Continental Shelf, States Parties to the United Nations Convention on the Law of the Sea, and other Members States of the United Nations, and also requests that the Note be posted on the website of the Division for Ocean Affairs and the Law of the Sea of the Office of Legal Affairs of the United Nations.

The Permanent Mission of the United Kingdom of Great Britain and Northern Ireland avails itself of this opportunity to renew to the Secretary-General of the United Nations the assurances of its highest consideration.

NORWAY

Continental Shelf Submission of Norway: Executive Summary (4 May 2009), pp. 6–15

1. Introduction

Norway signed the United Nations Convention on the Law of the Sea (hereinafter the Convention) on the day it was opened for signature and ratified it on 24 June 1996. It entered into force for Norway on 24 July 1996.

Norway transmitted on 27 November 2006 a submission to the Commission on the Limits of the Continental Shelf in respect of areas in the Arctic Ocean, the Barents Sea and the Norwegian Sea, in accordance with Article 76 (8) of the United Nations Convention on the Law of the Sea (the Convention). It was stated that the submission only dealt with the outer limits of the continental shelf in these three areas and that a further submission might be made in respect of other areas.

The present submission fulfils the obligation Norway has under article 76 and article 4 of Annex II of the Convention to submit information on the outer limits of its continental shelf beyond 200 nautical miles from the baselines from which the breadth of the territorial sea is measured, in respect of Bouvetøya in the South Atlantic Ocean and Dronning Maud Land in the Southern Ocean.

Bouvetøya is located in the middle of the southern part of the South Atlantic Ocean. The island, at approximately 54° South Latitude, and the appurtenant maritime areas are situated beyond the area south of 60° South Latitude constituting the Antarctic Treaty area. The maritime areas appurtenant to Bouvetøya include continental shelf beyond 200 nautical miles as specified in this submission.

The maritime areas appurtenant to Dronning Maud Land are characterized by an extended continental margin. These are, however, covered by the provisions of the Antarctic Treaty of 1 December 1959. Norway therefore requests the Commission, in accordance with its rules, not to take any action for the time being with regard to the information in this submission that relates to the continental shelf appurtenant to Dronning Maud Land. Reference is made, in this regard, to section 3 below. Norway recalls the unique and comprehensive Antarctic cooperation and the need to ensure the continuing peaceful cooperation and harmony in the Antarctic area. Norway remains fully committed to its obligations and the cooperation under the Antarctic Treaty System. While fulfilling the requirements of the Convention, the documentation acquired by Norway is also believed to contribute to increased scientific knowledge of the Antarctic marine areas concerned.

The preparation of the present submission began after Norway's ratification of the Convention in 1996. Acquisition of seismic and bathymetric data, as well as processing, analysis and interpretation of data have continued until this year. The preparation has been carried out by the Norwegian Petroleum Directorate, an independent agency under the Royal Ministry of Petroleum and Energy. The Directorate is Norway's expert body for offshore geology and geophysics. Various other agencies and institutions, including in particular the Norwegian Mapping Authority, the Norwegian Polar Institute, The Norwegian Institute of Marine Research and the University of Bergen, have also made scientific or other contributions to the submission. The preparation of the submission has been undertaken under the direction of the Royal Ministry of Foreign Affairs.

2. Maritime areas, maps and coordinates

The data and information contained in this submission concern the outer limits of the continental shelf where those limits extend beyond 200 nautical miles from the baselines in two separate areas, in the South Atlantic Ocean adjacent to Bouvetøya and in the Southern Ocean adjacent to Dronning Maud Land.

Six maps are included in this executive summary. One gives an outline of the continental shelves beyond 200 nautical miles (Fig. 1). Three-dimensional overview maps show the continental margins and other characteristic morphological elements in the maritime areas concerned (Figs. 2, 3 and 4). The outer limit of the continental shelf off Bouvetøya in the South Atlantic Ocean is indicated in Fig. 6. The information pertaining to the continental shelf off Dronning Maud Land is shown in Fig. 7.

Appendix 1 provides a list of the coordinates of the fixed points on the outer limit of the continental shelf beyond 200 nautical miles off Bouvetøya, the distance between adjacent points and the provision of article 76 on which each point is based. Appendix 2 contains the corresponding information pertaining to Dronning Maud Land.

3. Particular circumstances concerning Dronning Maud Land

Norway recalls the principles and objectives shared by the Antarctic Treaty and the United Nations Convention of the Law of the Sea, and the importance of the Antarctic system and the Convention working in harmony and thereby ensuring the continuing peaceful cooperation, security and stability in the Antarctic area.

Norway notes also the relevant provisions of the Convention, including its article 77, which provides inter alia that the rights of the coastal State over the continental shelf do not depend on any express proclamation, and recalls the decisions of Meetings of the States Parties to the Convention and the rules of the Commission on the limits of the Continental Shelf (the Commission).

Norway has regard to the circumstances of the area south of 60 degrees South Latitude and the special legal and political status of Antarctica under the provisions of the Antarctic Treaty, including its article IV, and notes that appurtenant to Antarctica there exist areas of continental shelf the extent of which has yet to be defined. It is open to the States concerned to submit information to the Commission which would not be examined by it for the time being, or to make a partial submission not including such areas of continental shelf, for which a submission may be made later, notwithstanding the provisions regarding the ten-year period established by article 4 of Annex II to the Convention and the subsequent decision on its application taken by the Eleventh Meeting of States Parties to the Convention.

Consistent with the first option, Norway requests the Commission in accordance with its rules not to take any action for the time being with regard to the information in this submission that relates to continental shelf appurtenant to Antarctica.

4. Commission members who provided advice during the preparation of the submission

Norway was assisted in the preparation of the submission by Mr. Harald Brekke, member of the Commission (1997-present). No advice was provided by any other member of the Commission.

5. Provisions of article 76 invoked in support of the submission

Norway invokes the provisions of paragraphs 1, 3, 4, 5 and 6 of article 76 in support of the establishment of the outer limits of the continental shelf beyond 200 nautical miles, as specified. Both the "Hedberg" and "Gardiner" formulae lines have been used in this submission. The outer limits of the continental shelf have been delineated by fixed points connected by straight lines not exceeding 60 nautical miles as provided in article 76, paragraph 7.

6. General description of the continental margin off *Bouvetøya*

Bouvetøya is situated approximately 280 km east of the Bouvet Triple Junction where the South American, the African and the Antarctic lithospheric plates meet. The plate boundaries are constituted by three separate spreading ridge systems, the Mid-Atlantic Ridge, the South American-Antarctic Ridge, and the Southwest Indian Ridge. This explains a complicated tectono-magmatic geometry in the triple junction area.

Bouvetøya is itself located on the Antarctic lithospheric plate on the westernmost part of the Southwest Indian Ridge. With a 780 metres peak (Olavtoppen), the landmass of the island is part of a wide, submerged pedestal formed by magmatic rocks. These are associated with the hotspot mantle plume that underlies the complex Bouvet Triple Junction. By seafloor mapping, it can be demonstrated that this submerged landmass of the island includes the Shaka Ridge, along the Shaka Fracture Zone in the east (Fig. 3).

7. General description of the continental margin off Dronning Maud Land

The Antarctic continent is surrounded by the Southern Ocean. By definition (IHOS-23, 4th edition) the latter is part of the world ocean between Antarctica and 60° South Latitude. The parts of the Southern Ocean adjacent to Dronning Maud Land include, from west to east, the Weddell Sea, the Lazarev Sea, the Riiser-Larsen Sea and the Cosmonaut Sea (Figs. 1 and 4).

The continental margin of Antarctica was formed by the rifting and splitting of the Gondwana Super-Continent during the period from Triassic to Late Cretaceous. The part of the continental margin appurtenant to Dronning Maud Land was formed during Jurassic times by the rifting and separation processes between Antarctica and Africa. This rifting and breakup of the continent produced prominent ridges and elevations that are integral parts of this continental margin. These are the Maud Rise, the Astrid Ridge, the Gunnerus Ridge and Kainan Maru Seamount (Figs. 1 and 4).

The Maud Rise is an equidimensional plateau in the Lazarev Sea. The plateau is located at about 2000 – 4000 m depth rising from the general depth of 5000 m of the adjacent abyssal plain. On the landward side, the Maud Rise is connected to the rest of the continental margin by a wide saddle area generally at a depth of 4000 m.

The Astrid Ridge is a complicated seafloor high at about 1500 – 4000 m depth east of the Maud Rise. It is situated at the junction between the Antarctic Continent and a prominent fracture zone system to the north-east. The western flank of the Astrid Ridge forms part of the Maud Rise saddle area.

The Gunnerus Ridge trends northwards at less than 1500 m general depth. This feature separates the Riiser-Larsen Sea from the Cosmonaut Sea. The northern end of the Gunnerus Ridge amalgamates with the Kainan Maru Seamount. Together they form a seafloor high complex.

8. Maritime delimitations

The maritime areas off Bouvetøya are not affected by any outstanding delimitations with other States.

The maritime areas off Dronning Maud Land are affected by outstanding delimitations with Australia and the United Kingdom of Great Britain and Northern Ireland of the overlap between the area of the continental shelf of Norway, the subject of this submission, and the area appurtenant to Australia that was included in the Australian submission to the Commission on 15 November 2004 as well as any such area appurtenant to the United Kingdom of Great Britain and Northern Ireland that may be included in any submission to the Commission by the latter State. Australia and the United Kingdom of Great Britain and Northern Ireland have both indicated to Norway that they have no objection to such areas being included in the present submission, without prejudice to the eventual delimitations between Norway and each of the two States.

9.2 Dronning Maud Land

The outer limits of the continental shelf beyond 200 nautical miles adjacent to Dronning Maud Land are based on the foot of the slope established along the flanks of the major submarine promontories of the Maud Rise, the Astrid Ridge and the Gunnerus Ridge-Kainan Maru Seamount seafloor high complex.

The 200 nautical miles line and the 350 nautical miles constraint line are based on relevant basepoints along the coastline of Dronning Maud Land.

The outer limits of the continental shelf beyond 200 nautical miles in this area are defined by 936 fixed points established in accordance with article 76 of the Convention. These are as follows:

- 12 points defined by the sediment thickness formula contained in article 76, paragraph 4(a)(i);
- 364 points defined by arcs 60 nautical miles from the foot of the continental slope in accordance with article 76, paragraph 4(a)(ii);
- 278 points defined by arcs at 100 nautical miles from the 2500 m isobaths in accordance with the constraint criteria provided for in article 76, paragraphs 5 and 6;
- 281 points defined by arcs at 350 nautical miles from the relevant basepoints along the coastline of Dronning Maud Land in accordance with the constraint criteria provided for in article 76, paragraphs 5 and 6;
- 1 point at the intersection of the outer edge of the continental margin and 200 nautical miles limit line of Dronning Maud Land.

The 936 fixed points are connected by straight lines not exceeding 60 nautical miles in length as provided in article 76, paragraph 7. Fig. 7 shows the fixed points and connecting lines. A colour code indicates the article 76 criterion used to establish them (see also Appendix 2).

Norway, Note Accompanying Lodgement of Submission (4 May 2009)

The Permanent Mission of Norway to the United Nations presents its compliments to the Secretary-General of the United Nations and referring to the article 76 of the United Nations Convention on the Law of the Sea and article 4 of its Annex II, has the honour to submit to the Commission on the Limits of the Continental Shelf information on the limits of the continental shelf beyond 200 nautical miles from the baselines from which the breadth of the territorial sea is measured in respect of Bouvetøya and Dronning Maud Land.

The enclosures include particulars of such limits along with supporting scientific and technical data, as defined in a separate list of material provided.

Norway respectfully requests the Commission on the Limits of the Continental Shelf to consider the information submitted in respect of Bouvetøya.

As regards the information submitted in respect of Dronning Maud Land, Norway would like to state the following:

Norway recalls the principles and objectives shared by the Antarctic Treaty and the United Nations Convention on the Law of the Sea (hereinafter the Convention) and the importance of the Antarctic system and the Convention working in harmony and thereby ensuring the continuing peaceful cooperation, security and stability in the Antarctic area.

Norway notes also the relevant provisions of the Convention, including its article 77, which provides inter alia that the rights of the coastal State over the continental shelf do not depend on any express proclamation, and recalls the decisions of Meetings of the States Parties to the Convention and the rules of the Commission on the Limits of the Continental Shelf (hereinafter the Commission).

Norway has regard to the circumstances of the area south of 60 degrees South Latitude and the special legal and political status of Antarctica under the provisions of the Antarctic Treaty, including its article IV, and notes that appurtenant to Antarctica there exist areas of continental shelf the extent of which has yet to be defined. It is open to the States concerned to submit information to the Commission which would not be examined by it for the time being, or to make a partial submission not including such areas of continental shelf, for which a submission may be made later, notwithstanding the provisions regarding the ten-year period established by article 4 of Annex II to the Convention and the subsequent decision on its application taken by the Eleventh Meeting of States Parties to the Convention.

Consistent with the first option, Norway requests the Commission in accordance with its rules not to take any action for the time being with regard to the information in this submission that relates to continental shelf appurtenant to Antarctica, including Dronning Maud Land.

The Permanent Mission of Norway to the United Nations avails itself of this opportunity to renew to the Secretary-General of the United Nations the assurances of its highest consideration.

New York, 4 May 2009

Note verbale from the USA on the Norwegian submission (4 June 2009)

The Permanent Mission of the United States of America to the United Nations presents its compliments to the Secretariat of the United Nations (Office of Legal Affairs) and refers to the recent Norwegian submission to the Commission on the Limits of the Continental Shelf (the Commission). The United States recalls the principles and objectives shared by the Antarctic Treaty and the United Nations Convention on the Law of the Sea (the Convention), and the importance of the Antarctic system and the Convention working in harmony and thereby ensuring the continuing peaceful cooperation, security and stability in the Antarctic area. The United States wishes to inform the Secretariat that, recalling Article IV of the Antarctic Treaty, the United States does not recognize any State's claim to territory in Antarctica and consequently does not recognize any State's rights over the seabed and subsoil of the submarine areas beyond and adjacent to the continent of Antarctica. The United States acknowledges with appreciation Norway's request to the Commission that it not take any action on that portion of its submission relating to areas of the seabed and subsoil adjacent to Antarctica. The United States requests that this note be posted on the United Nations Division for Ocean Affairs and the Law of the Sea web site and be made available to the Commission.

The Permanent Mission of the United States of America to the United Nations takes this opportunity to renew to the United Nations the assurances of its highest consideration.

Note verbale from Russia on the Norwegian submission (15 June 2009) (No. 1682)

The Permanent Mission of the Russian Federation to the United Nations presents its compliments to the Secretary-General of the United Nations and, with reference to the submission made by the Kingdom of Norway to the Commission on the Limits of the Continental Shelf (see notification CLCS.30.2009.LOS dated 5 May 2009) and also to the note No. 82 dated 21 February 2007 from the Permanent Mission of the Russian Federation to the United Nations, has the honour to state the following.

On the basis of the provisions of Article IV of the Antarctic Treaty of 1959, the Russian Federation does not recognize any claims concerning areas falling within the scope of that treaty, and also considers that the making of such claims by any Government shall not create rights regarding the seabed (continental shelf) and subsoil thereof in areas adjoining the continent of Antarctica.

In that connection, the Russian Federation notes and supports the request by the Kingdom of Norway that the Commission should take no actions regarding the part of the submission by the Kingdom of Norway that relates to the seabed (continental shelf) adjoining Antarctica in the area falling within the scope of the 1959 Antarctic Treaty.

The Russian Federation also requests that this notification be placed on the website of the Division for Ocean Affairs and the Law of the Sea of the United Nations Secretariat and brought to the attention of the Commission on the Limits of the Continental Shelf

The Permanent Mission of the Russian Federation to the United Nations takes this opportunity to convey to the Secretary-General of the United Nations the renewed assurances of its highest consideration.

Note verbale from India on the Norwegian submission (31 August 2009) (No. NY/PPM/443/1/2009)

The Permanent Mission of India to the United Nations presents its compliments to the Secretary General of the United Nations and with reference to the submission of the Norway to the Commission on the Limits of the Continental Shelf on May 4, 2009 has the honor to express the following:

India recalls the principles and objectives shared by the Antarctic Treaty and the United Nations Convention on the Law of the Sea, 1982 (Convention) and the importance of harmony between the Antarctic Treaty and the Convention and of the continuing cooperation, security and stability in the Antarctic area.

In accordance with Article IV of the Antarctic Treaty, India does not recognize any State's right or claim to territorial sovereignty in the Antarctic area and consequently over the seabed and subsoil of the submarine areas adjacent to the continent of Antarctica.

India acknowledges and supports Norway's request that the Commission not take any action on the part of Norwegian submission relating to areas of the seabed and subsoil appurtenant to Antarctica.

India requests that this note may be circulated to the Member States and to the Commission.

The Permanent Mission of India to the United Nations avails of this opportunity to renew to the Secretary General of the United Nations the assurances of its highest consideration.

Note verbale from The Netherlands on the Norwegian submission (30 September 2009) (No. NYV/2009/2458)

The Permanent Mission of the Kingdom of the Netherlands to the United Nations presents its compliments to the Secretary-General of the United Nations and has the honor to refer to the Continental Shelf Submission of Norway to the Commission on the Limits of the Continental Shelf in respect of Bouvetøya and Dronning Maud Land, and the accompanying note of the Permanent Mission of Norway to the United Nations to the Secretary-General of the United Nations, dated 4 May 2009.

Taking note that the submission of Norway includes information relating to continental shelf adjacent to Antarctica, the Kingdom of the Netherlands wishes to reiterate its long-standing position that the Kingdom of the Netherlands does not recognize any claim to territories in Antarctica and does not recognize that a claim to territorial sovereignty in Antarctica is capable of creating any sort of rights over continental shelf adjacent to Antarctica. It is well-established that the principle of sovereign rights over continental shelf adjacent to the coast, for the purposes of exploring and exploiting the natural resources of the shelf, derives from sovereignty of the coastal State over adjacent land territory. Accordingly, the Kingdom of the Netherlands does not consider that the continental shelf adjacent to Antarctica is subject to the sovereign rights of any State.

The Kingdom of the Netherlands notes that there is an unresolved land dispute in relation to Norway's claim to territory in Antarctica. It understands the reference to Article IV of the 1959 Antarctic Treaty in Norway's note to be information to the Commission on the Limits of the Continental Shelf of said dispute in accordance with paragraph 2 of Annex I of the Rules of Procedure of the Commission on the Limits of the Continental Shelf. Therefore, the Kingdom of the Netherlands requests the Commission to act pursuant to paragraph 5(a) of Annex I of the Rules of Procedure of the Commission on the Limits of the Continental Shelf insofar the submission of Norway includes information relating to continental shelf adjacent to Antarctica. In this respect, the Kingdom of the Netherlands acknowledges with appreciation Norway's request to the Commission on the Limits of the Continental Shelf that it not take any action on the portion of its submission relating to continental shelf adjacent to Antarctica.

The Kingdom of the Netherlands requests that this *note verbale* be circulated to the members of the Commission on the Limits of the Continental Shelf and be posted on the web site of the United Nations Division for Ocean Affairs and the Law of the Sea.

The Permanent Mission of the Kingdom of the Netherlands to the United Nations avails itself of this opportunity to renew to the Secretary-General of the United Nations the assurances of its highest considerations.

Note verbale from Japan on the Norwegian submission (19 November 2009) (SC/09/389)

The Permanent Mission of Japan to the United Nations presents its compliments to the Secretary-General of the United Nations and, with reference to the circular CLCS.30.2009.LOS (Continental Shelf Notification) dated 5 May 2009, concerning the receipt of the submission made by the Kingdom of Norway to the Commission on the Limits of the Continental Shelf (hereinafter referred to as "the Commission"), has the honour to express the position of the Government of Japan with regard to the submission made by the Kingdom of Norway, and requests that this note verbale be circulated to the members of the Commission and Member States of the United Nations, and be posted on the web site of the Division for Ocean Affairs and the Law of the Sea (DOALOS) of the Secretariat of the United Nations.

Japan confirms the importance of keeping harmony between the Antarctic Treaty and the United Nations Convention on the Law of the Sea and thereby ensuring the continuing peaceful cooperation, security and stability in the Antarctic area.

Recalling Article IV of the Antarctic Treaty, Japan does not recognize any State's right of or claims to territorial sovereignty in Antarctica, and consequently does not recognize any State's right over or claims to the seabed and subsoil of the submarine areas adjacent to the continent of Antarctica.

From this standpoint, Japan stresses that the balance of rights and obligations in the Antarctic Treaty should not be affected in any way in handling the information on the limits of the continental shelf, submitted by the Kingdom of Norway to the Commission.

Japan understands that the Commission will not take any action on the portion of Norway's submission relating to the seabed and subsoil of the submarine areas adjacent to the continent of Antarctica.

The Permanent Mission of Japan to the United Nations avails itself of this opportunity to renew to the Secretary-General of the United Nations the assurances of its highest consideration.

PART 12: BILATERAL TREATIES

Exchange of Notes constituting an Agreement between the Governments of Australia, New Zealand and the United Kingdom of Great Britain and Northern Ireland, and the Government of the French Republic, regarding Aerial Navigation in the Antarctic (1938)[1]

Note from the British Ambassador, Paris, to the French Minister for Foreign Affairs

I

British Embassy, Paris

25 October 1938

His Excellency Monsieur Georges Bonnet

Minister for Foreign Affairs

Monsieur le Ministre

In their memorandum (*Direction politique*) of 5 March last, the Ministry of Foreign Affairs were so good as to inform His Majesty's Embassy that the Government of the Republic were prepared to recognise the free right of passage of British Commonwealth aircraft over Adélie Land on the understanding that reciprocal rights would be accorded to French aircraft over British Commonwealth territories in the Antarctic.

2. I have the honour to state that His Majesty's Governments in the United Kingdom, the Commonwealth of Australia, and New Zealand accept an arrangement on the abovementioned basis.

3. I have the honour to suggest that the present note and Your Excellency's acknowledgement thereof shall be regarded as placing the understanding on record.

I have the honour to be, with the highest consideration Monsieur le Ministre, Your Excellency's most obedient, humble servant.

[Signed]

Eric Phipps

Note on behalf of the French Minister for Foreign Affairs to the British Ambassador, Paris

II

[Translation]

French Republic

Ministry of Foreign Affairs

Direction Politique

Paris

25 October 1938

His Excellency Sir Eric Phipps

British Ambassador

Paris

Monsieur l'Ambassadeur

I have the honour to acknowledge receipt of you letter of today's date in the following terms:

[See note I.]

I hasten to inform Your Excellency of my agreement with the contents of the above letter.

I have the honour to be, etc.

For the Minister for Foreign Affairs:

[Signed]

Alexis Léger

[1] Adopted 25 October 1938, entered into force 25 October 1938.

Exchange of Notes (with Memorandum of Understandings) constituting an Agreement regarding the Provision of Facilities in New Zealand for United States Antarctic Expeditions (1958)[2]

The Right Honourable Walter Nash, Minister of External Affairs of New Zealand, to His Excellency Mr. Francis H. Russell, Ambassador of the United States of America in New Zealand

Ministry of External Affairs
Wellington
24 December 1958

Excellency,

I have the honour to refer to discussions which have taken place between the New Zealand and the United States authorities regarding the future provision of facilities in New Zealand for United States personnel, ships and aircraft engaged in operations in Antarctica. As you know, the New Zealand Government wishes to provide whatever assistance it can to the United States Government in connection with such operations, and a number of understandings regarding the provision of appropriate facilities in New Zealand have been reached during the discussions.

These understandings, which include a statement of the assistance which the United States Government has offered in respect of New Zealand operations in Antarctica, are set out in the attached memorandum.[3]

It is suggested that these arrangements should enure for the full period during which United States personnel, ships and aircraft may be in New Zealand in connection with United States operations in Antarctica during the present International Geophysical Year and for the period ending on 31 December 1959, and that the provision of any necessary facilities which may thereafter be required in New Zealand be discussed in correspondence between us at the appropriate time.

If the proposals contained in the present note, and the understandings set out in the attached memorandum are acceptable to the Government of the United States of America, I have the honour to suggest that this note and your reply thereto, should constitute an agreement between our Governments, the agreement to enter into force on the date of your note in reply.

Accept, Excellency, the renewed assurances of my highest consideration.

W. Nash

Memorandum of Understandings

1.

(a) The New Zealand Government will provide as far as possible facilities in New Zealand requested by the United States authorities in connection with United States operations in Antarctica. It agrees to the establishment of operational headquarters in New Zealand and to the transit of United States personnel, ships and aircraft through New Zealand. United States personnel may be accommodated in New Zealand and United States aircraft may be based at agreed airports within New Zealand.

(b) The New Zealand Government agrees to the establishment and operation of a military and affiliate radio station in New Zealand by the United States authorities, under arrangements to be made with the Royal New Zealand Air Force.

(c) In each case where facilities are provided by the New Zealand Government, the financial basis on which they are made available, and the conditions on which they shall be returned, will be decided by agreement between the New Zealand and the United States authorities.

2. As appropriate, the normal requirements in connection with the arrival and departure of ships and aircraft in New Zealand, as well as passport, visa and other immigration laws and

[2] Adopted 24 December 1958, entered into force 24 December 1958, 324 UNTS 111.

[3] See p. 114 of this volume.

regulations will be waived in respect of United States personnel, and ships and aircraft of the United States Navy and Air Force engaged upon operations in Antarctica.

3.

(a) Subject to such procedures as may be arranged, the Government of New Zealand will exempt from payment of taxes and customs duties, goods imported into or exported out of New Zealand by the United States authorities or United States personnel in connection with United States operations in Antarctica.

(b) The presence of United States personnel in New Zealand solely in connection with United States operations in Antarctica shall not subject them to taxation on their salary and emoluments received from the United States Government or on any tangible movable property the presence of which in New Zealand is due solely to their temporary presence there, nor constitute residence nor domicile for New Zealand tax purposes.

4.

(a) If United States personnel are alleged to have committed acts which are offences against New Zealand law, the following provisions shall apply:

   i. The New Zealand authorities, recognising the problems arising from the concurrent jurisdiction in criminal matters over such personnel in New Zealand territory, will consider alleged offences affecting only United States personnel or property, or committed in the performance of official duty, as a matter for the United States authorities.

   ii. Moreover, the New Zealand authorities will not ordinarily be concerned to institute proceedings in the New Zealand courts in respect of alleged minor offences which do not fall within the categories referred to in (i) above.

(b) For their part, the United States authorities will take measures to ensure respect for the laws of New Zealand by United States personnel and will take whatever steps are necessary to punish personnel who have committed acts which are offences against those laws.

(c) United States personnel who have been arrested or apprehended, whether by the New Zealand authorities or by the United States authorities, will be retained in custody by the United States authorities, who shall produce the personnel concerned, upon request by the New Zealand authorities, for investigation, identification or trial.

(d) It is understood that the principle of not trying an accused twice for the same offence will be followed, except that the United States authorities shall remain free to punish for violation of rules of military discipline.

5.

(a) It is the understanding of the New Zealand Government that United States law makes provision for the settlement of meritorious claims for loss or damage caused by the acts or omissions (whether committed on or off duty) of United States personnel, and acts or omissions arising out of the performance of official duty by employees of the United States forces who are nationals of or ordinarily resident in New Zealand. In this connection, it is understood that the United States compensation authorities will pay, in accordance with and to the fullest extent possible under United States claims rules and procedures, just and reasonable compensation, when accepted by claimants in full satisfaction and in final settlement, for meritorious claims for injury or death or damage to property arising out of such acts or omissions. It is understood that United States claims legislation requires that such claims be presented to United States authorities within one year after the occurrence of the accident or incident out of which the claim arises.

(b) It is further understood by the two Governments that the satisfactory procedures which have been arranged with the Office of the Solicitor-General of New Zealand for the settlement of such claims will be maintained, and accordingly that the United States compensation authorities will, in determining liability and compensation, continue to give due regard to the Solicitor-General's assessment and to the amount which he may recommend for settlement in particular cases.

6. The Government of the United States of America for its part will provide as far as possible logistic support requested by the New Zealand authorities in connection with New Zealand operations in Antarctica.

7. The Governments of New Zealand and the United States of America will cooperate in making appropriate administrative arrangements to give effect to the understandings set out in this memorandum and to resolve any other practical issues which may from time to time arise from the presence in New Zealand of personnel, ships an aircraft of United States Antarctic expeditions.

8. The term "United States personnel" includes uniformed members of the United States forces and civilian employees of the forces except those employees who are nationals of, or ordinarily resident in, New Zealand.

II

His Excellency Mr. Francis H. Russell, Ambassador of the United States of America in New Zealand, to The Right Honourable Walter Nash, Minister of External Affairs of New Zealand

American Embassy
Wellington
24 December 1958

Excellency,

I have the honour to acknowledge the receipt of your note of today's date, together with the memorandum of understandings attached thereto, the texts of which read as follows:

[See note 1]

I have the honour to inform you that the Government of the United States of America accepts the proposals contained in your note, together with the understandings set out in the memorandum attached thereto, and regards your note and my present reply as constituting an agreement between our two Governments, the agreement to enter into force on this day.

Accept, Excellency, the renewed assurances of my highest consideration.

Francis H. Russell

Exchange of Notes constituting an Agreement Extending the Operation of the Agreement between the Government of New Zealand and the Government of the United States of America regarding the Provision of Facilities in New Zealand for United States Antarctic Expeditions (1960)[4]

The Right Honourable Walter Nash, Minister of External Affairs of New Zealand, to His Excellency Mr. Francis H. Russell, Ambassador of the United States of America in New Zealand

Office of the Minister of External Affairs
Wellington
18 October 1960

Excellency,

I have the honour to refer to the Exchange of Notes constituting an Agreement between the Government of New Zealand and the Government of the United States of America regarding the Provision of Facilities in New Zealand for United States Antarctic Expeditions, which was concluded at Wellington on 24 December 1958.[5] As you know, the Agreement constituted by this

[4] Adopted and entered into force 18 October 1960, with retroactive effect from 1 January 1960, 447 UNTS 356.

[5] United Nations, *Treaty Series*, vol. 324, p. 111.

Exchange terminated, in accordance with its terms, on 31 December 1959, but discussions have been held between the United States and New Zealand authorities regarding its prolongation.

Cooperation between the Governments of New Zealand and the United States of America during and since the International Geophysical Year period made possible the fulfilment of wide programmes of scientific exploration in the Antarctic. The recently concluded Antarctic Treaty provides scope for the extension of this relationship. Accordingly the New Zealand Government wishes to provide whatever assistance it can in connection with the continuing United States operations in Antarctica. I therefore have the honour to propose an agreement between our two Governments in the following terms:

1. The Agreement constituted by the Exchange of Notes of 24 December 1958 shall, subject to the provisions of the present agreement, be regarded as remaining in force for the full period during which United States personnel, ships and aircraft continue in future to be based in New Zealand in connection with United States operations in Antarctica.

2. Each Government will arrange for the earliest possible notification to be given to the other Government, prior to the beginning of each Antarctic season, of the nature and scope of the operations which it is planning for that season.

3. The two Governments agree to consult together at any time, at the request of either, regarding the operation, application or amendment of the present agreement.

4. Either Government may at any time give to the other Government notice of intention to terminate the present agreement. In such case the present agreement shall terminate after the expiration of ninety days from the date on which the notice is received.

If the proposals contained in this note are acceptable to the Government of the United States of America, I have the honour to suggest that this note and your reply thereto, should constitute an agreement between our two Governments, with effect from 1 January 1960.

Accept, Excellency, the renewed assurances of my highest consideration.

W. NASH

II

His Excellency Mr. Francis H. Russell, Ambassador of the United States of America in New Zealand, to The Right Honourable Walter Nash, Minister of External Affairs of New Zealand

Embassy of the United States of America
Wellington
18 October 1960

Excellency,

I have the honor to acknowledge the receipt of your note of today's date, the text of which reads as follows:

[See note I]

I have the honor to inform you that the Government of the United States of America accepts the proposals contained in your note, and regards your note and my present reply as constituting an agreement between our two Governments.

Accept, Excellency, the renewed assurances of my highest consideration.

Francis H. RUSSELL

New Zealand and Federal Republic of Germany: Exchange of Letters Constituting an Agreement Concerning Antarctic Co-Operation (1981)[6]

I

Minister of Foreign Affairs
Parliament House, Wellington, New Zealand
26 June 1981
Excellency,

I have the honour to refer to discussions which have taken place between the authorities of New Zealand and the Federal Republic of Germany regarding scientific cooperation in Antarctica and the provision of access to facilities in New Zealand for personnel, ships and aircraft of the Federal Republic of Germany engaged in expeditions in Antarctica. As you know, New Zealand, by virtue of its geographical proximity to Antarctica, is well placed to provide assistance to Antarctic scientific research programmes.

For its part, New Zealand welcomes the recent admission of the Federal Republic of Germany to Consultative Party status under the Antarctic Treaty and the setting up by your Government of the Alfred Wegener Institute for Polar Research. We consider that the results of the discussions which have been held between our respective authorities will strengthen further the valuable cooperation which already exists between New Zealand and the Federal Republic of Germany in the scientific field.

Accordingly, 1 have the honour to propose that the results of those discussions will be recorded as an Agreement between our two Governments in the following terms:

1.

(a) The two Governments agree to cooperate in Antarctic scientific research for peaceful purposes and their mutual benefit and to strengthen further the valuable cooperation in the scientific field which already exists between New Zealand and the Federal Republic of Germany under the Agreement on Scientific and Technological Cooperation and the Antarctic Treaty.

(b) Each Government shall designate an agent or agency to be responsible for the coordination and facilitation of cooperative activities under this Agreement. These agents or agencies shall consult with a view to developing such cooperative activities.

(c) Cooperative activities shall be the subject of such specific arrangements as may be deemed appropriate.

(d) The two Governments agree to consult together at any time, at the request of either, regarding the implementation of this Agreement.

2. Subject to agreement on the level of such operations in any year, the Government of New Zealand undertakes to permit:

(a) The transit through and temporary accommodation in New Zealand of personnel engaged in the German Antarctic research programme, en route to and from Antarctica;

(b) Access to and usage of agreed ports, airports and other necessary services in New Zealand by ships and aircraft engaged in the German Antarctic research programme, in accordance with New Zealand law and subject to payment of the normal dues and fees.

3. The Government of New Zealand shall, consistent with its laws and regulations, facilitate as far as possible the entry into, exit from and stay in New Zealand of personnel engaged in the German Antarctic research programme, other than persons who are nationals of or ordinarily resident in New Zealand. Provided such personnel meet normal temporary entry requirements the Government of New Zealand agrees to issue to them entry permits allowing employment, valid for the period of their assignment up to a maximum of twelve months.

[6] Adopted and entered into force 26 June 1981, 1324 UNTS 299.

4. The Government of New Zealand shall facilitate, consistent with its laws and regulations including those relating to agricultural health inspection, the entry into and exit from New Zealand of ships, aircraft, equipment and materials to be used in the German Antarctic research programme, as well as the personal effects of personnel engaged in the programme. The Government of New Zealand shall exempt equipment and materials imported or exported for such purpose from payment of taxes and customs duties.

5. The Government of the Federal Republic of Germany shall, in so far as the logistic capabilities of the current German Antarctic research programme will at the time allow, provide, under modalities to be agreed upon in each case, logistic support requested in good time by the Government of New Zealand for the implementation of the New Zealand Antarctic research programme.

6. The Government of the Federal Republic of Germany shall inform the Government of New Zealand on a timely basis each year through the diplomatic channel of:

(a) The expected size of the German Antarctic research programme for the forthcoming Antarctic season in so far as the use of facilities in New Zealand may be involved;

(b) The ports, airports and other necessary services requested for use by the personnel, ships and aircraft of the German Antarctic research programme during the forthcoming Antarctic season.

7. This Agreement shall not apply to the Cook Islands, Niue or Tokelau.

8. This Agreement shall apply also to Land Berlin, provided that the Government of the Federal Republic of Germany does not make a contrary declaration to the Government of New Zealand within three months of the date of entry into force of this Agreement.

9. Either Government may at any time give to the other Government notice of intention to terminate this Agreement. In such cases the Agreement shall terminate after the expiration of one year from the date on which the notice is received.

If the proposals contained in this Note are acceptable to the Government of the Federal Republic of Germany, I have the honour to suggest that this Note and your reply thereto should constitute an Agreement between our two Governments, the Agreement to enter into force on the date of your Note in reply.

Please accept, Excellency, the renewed assurances of my highest consideration.

[Signed]

The Right Honourable

B.E. Talboys

Minister of Foreign Affairs of New Zealand, Wellington

II

[Translation]

The Ambassador of the Federal Republic of Germany

Wellington, 26 June 1981

Excellency,

I have the honour to thank you for your letter of 26 June 1981 which refers to discussions held between the authorities of New Zealand and the Federal Republic of Germany regarding scientific cooperation in Antarctica and the provision of access to facilities in New Zealand for personnel, ships and aircraft of the Federal Republic of Germany engaged in expeditions in Antarctica.

I share your view that the results of the discussions which have been held between our authorities will further strengthen the valuable cooperation which already exists between New Zealand and the Federal Republic in the scientific field.

I have the honour to accept your proposal that the results of those discussions be recorded as an Agreement between our two Governments in the following terms:

[See letter I]

I have the honour to communicate to you my Government's agreement that your Note and this reply shall constitute an Agreement between our two Governments, to enter into force on the date of my Note in reply, and take this opportunity to renew to you the assurances of my highest consideration.

[Signed] Dr. H. A. Steger
His Excellency Dr. Hans Alfred Steger
Ambassador Extraordinary and Plenipotentiary
Embassy of the Federal Republic of Germany
Wellington

Exchange of Letters Constituting Agreement between New Zealand and Sweden concerning Antarctic Cooperation (1986)[7]

I

Prime Minister of New Zealand to the Prime Minister of Sweden
Stockholm, 3 June 1986
Your Excellency,

I have the honour to refer to discussions which have taken place between the authorities of New Zealand and Sweden regarding scientific cooperation in Antarctica. In the course of those discussions it was noted that Sweden, aiming at increasing its comparative Arctic and Antarctic research, would welcome New Zealand scientists taking part in Swedish polar research programmes. It was also noted that New Zealand by virtue of its geographical proximity to Antarctica, is well placed to provide assistance to Antarctic scientific research programmes.

For its part, New Zealand welcomes the recent accession by Sweden to the Antarctic Treaty.[8] Both parties consider that the results of the discussions which have been held between our respective authorities will strengthen further the valuable cooperation which already exists between New Zealand and Sweden in the scientific field.

I have the honour to propose that the results of those discussions will be recorded as an Agreement between our two Governments in the following terms:

1.

(a) The two Governments agree to cooperate in Antarctic scientific research for peaceful purpose and for their mutual benefit.

(b) Each Government shall designate an agent or agency to be responsible for the coordination and facilitation of cooperative activities under this Agreement. These agents or agencies shall consult with a view to developing such cooperative activities.

(c) Cooperative activities shall be the subject of such specific arrangements as may be deemed appropriate.

(d) The two Governments agree to consult together at any time, at the request of either, regarding the implementation of this Agreement.

2. Subject to agreement on the level of such operations in any year, the Government of New Zealand undertakes to permit the transit through and temporary accommodation in New Zealand of personnel engaged in the Swedish research programme, en route to and from Antarctica.

3. The Government of New Zealand will, consistent with its laws and regulations, facilitate as far as possible the entry into, exit from and stay in New Zealand of personnel engaged in the Swedish Antarctic research programme, other than persons who are nationals of or ordinarily resident in New Zealand. Provided such personnel meet normal temporary entry requirements the Government of New Zealand agrees to issue them entry permits allowing employment, valid for the period of their assignment up to a maximum of twelve months.

[7] Adopted and entered into force 3 June 1986, 1563 UNTS 357.
[8] United Nations, *Treaty Series,* vol. 402, p. 71.

4. The Government of Sweden will provide, as far as possible, under modalities to be agreed upon in each case, appropriate logistical support, including scientific equipment, to the cooperative activities in Antarctica.

5. The Government of Sweden shall inform the Government of New Zealand on a timely basis each year through the diplomatic channel of the number of personnel and other facilities which they wish to include in cooperative activities in Antarctica.

6. This Agreement shall not apply to the Cook Islands, Niue or Tokelau. In conclusion, the Government of New Zealand welcomes and encourages the development of a greater Swedish participation in Antarctic Cooperation and in view of the extensive facilities which the City of Christchurch offers to Antarctic operations stands ready to extend this Agreement should the Government of Sweden so desire to facilitate access to Antarctica through Christchurch by Swedish ships or aircraft.

If the proposals contained herein are acceptable to the Government of Sweden, I have the honour to suggest that this Letter and your reply thereto, should constitute an Agreement between our two Governments, the Agreement to enter into force on the date of your Letter in reply.

I avail myself of this opportunity to express to Your Excellency the assurances of my highest consideration.

D. R. Lange

II

The Prime Minister of Sweden to the Prime Minister of New Zealand

Stockholm June 3, 1986

Your Excellency,

I have the honour to acknowledge receipt of your letter of 3 June 1986 regarding scientific cooperation in Antarctica, reading as follows:

[See letter I]

I have the honour to confirm that the Government of Sweden considers that Your Excellency's letter and this reply constitute an agreement between our two governments.

I avail myself of this opportunity to express to Your Excellency the assurances of my highest consideration.

I. Carlsson

Prime Minister of Sweden

Exchange of letters Constituting an Agreement between New Zealand and Italy on Antarctic Cooperation (1987)[9]

8 April 1987

Excellency,

I have the honour to refer to discussions which have taken place between the authorities of New Zealand and the Republic of Italy regarding scientific cooperation in Antarctica and the provision of access to facilities in New Zealand for personnel, ships and aircraft of the Republic of Italy engaged in expeditions in Antarctica.

As you know, New Zealand, by virtue of its geographical proximity to Antarctica, is well placed to provide assistance to Antarctic scientific research programmes.

For its part, New Zealand welcomes the accession by Italy to the Antarctic Treaty.[10] We consider that the results of the discussions which have been held between our respective authorities will strengthen further the valuable cooperation which already exists between New Zealand and Italy in the scientific field.

[9] Adopted 8 April 1987, entered into force 8 April 1987, 1675 UNTS 419.

[10] United Nations, *Treaty Series*, vol. 402, p. 71.

Accordingly, I have the honour to propose that the results of those discussions will be recorded as an Agreement between our two Governments in the following terms:

1.

(a) The two Governments agree to cooperate in Antarctic scientific research for peaceful purposes and their mutual benefit and to strengthen further the valuable cooperation in the scientific field which already exists between New Zealand and Italy.

(b) Each Government shall designate an agent or agency to be responsible for the coordination and facilitation of cooperative activities under this Agreement. These agents or agencies shall consult with a view to developing such cooperative activities.

(c) Cooperative activities shall be the subject of such specific arrangements as may be deemed appropriate.

(d) The two Governments agree to consult together at any time, at the request of either, regarding the implementation of this Agreement.

2. Subject to agreement between such agents or agencies on the level of such operations in any year, the Government of New Zealand undertakes to permit the transit through and temporary accommodation in New Zealand of personnel engaged in the Italian Antarctic Research Programme, en route to and from Antarctica.

3. The Government of New Zealand shall, consistent with its laws and regulations, facilitate as far as

possible the entry into, exit from and stay in New Zealand of personnel engaged in the Italian Antarctic Research Programme, other than persons who are nationals of or ordinarily resident in New Zealand. Provided such personnel meet normal temporary entry requirements the Government of New Zealand agrees to issue to them entry permits allowing employment, valid for the period of their assignment up to a maximum of twelve months.

4. The Government of New Zealand shall facilitate, consistent with its laws and regulations including those relating to agricultural health inspection, the entry into and exit from New Zealand of ships, aircraft, equipment and materials to be used in the Italian Antarctic Research Programme, as well as the personal effects of personnel engaged in the programme. The Government of New Zealand shall exempt equipment and materials imported or exported for such purpose from payment of taxes and customs duties.

5. The Government of the Republic of Italy shall provide, as far as possible, under modalities to be agreed upon in each case, appropriate logistic support for the implementation of the New Zealand Antarctic Research Programme.

6. The Government of the Republic of Italy shall inform the Government of New Zealand on a timely basis each year through the diplomatic channel of:

(a) the expected size of the Italian Antarctic Research Programme for the forthcoming Antarctic season in so far as the use of facilities in New Zealand may be involved;

(b) the ports, airports and other necessary services requested for use by the personnel, ships and aircraft of the Italian Antarctic Research Programme during the forthcoming Antarctic season.

7. This Agreement shall not apply to the Cook Islands, Niue or Tokelau.

8. Either Government may at any time give to the other Government notice of intention to terminate this Agreement. In such cases the Agreement shall terminate after the expiration of one year from the date on which the notice is received.

In conclusion, the Government of New Zealand welcomes and encourages the development of a greater Italian participation in Antarctic cooperation and in view of the extensive facilities which the City of Christchurch offers to Antarctic operations stands ready to extend this Agreement, should the Government of the Republic of Italy so desire, to facilitate access to Antarctica through Christchurch by Italian ships or aircraft.

If the proposals contained in this letter are acceptable to the Government of Italy, I have the honour to suggest that this letter and your reply thereto, should constitute an Agreement between our two Governments, the Agreement to enter into force on the date of your letter in reply.

Please accept, Excellency, the renewed assurances of my highest consideration.

David Lange
Minister of Foreign Affairs
New Zealand

Wellington, 8 April 1987

Excellency,

I have the honour to refer to your letter dated 8 April 1987 by which you propose that the results of the discussions which have taken place between the authorities of New Zealand and the Republic of Italy regarding scientific co-operation in Antarctica and the provision of access to facilities in New Zealand for personnel, ships and aircraft of the Republic of Italy engaged in expeditions in Antarctica be recorded as an Agreement between our two Governments in the following terms:

[See letter I]

You also suggest that, if the proposals contained in the above-mentioned letter are acceptable to the Government of Italy, your letter and my reply thereto should constitute an Agreement between our two Governments and that the Agreement should enter into force on the date of my letter in reply.

Accordingly I have the honour to inform you that I have been instructed by my Government and received full powers thereto to assure you that the afore-mentioned proposals are acceptable to the Government of Italy and that your letter and this reply shall constitute an Agreement between our two Governments which will enter into force on this date.

Please accept, Excellency, the renewed assurances of my highest consideration.

[Signed]
Giorgio De Andreis
Ambassador of Italy to New Zealand

Agreement Concerning Antarctic Cooperation between the Kingdom of Spain and the Argentine Republic (1991)[11]

The Kingdom of Spain and the Argentine Republic, reaffirming their desire to strengthen their bilateral ties and to promote the full implementation of the Antarctic Treaty of 1 December 1959[12] and its System,

Have agreed as follows:

Article I

1. The two Governments shall consult each other through their Ministries of Foreign Affairs on political, legal, scientific or other matters of common interest that may arise in the context of the Antarctic Treaty System.

2. Consequently, they shall endeavour to coordinate their positions in the various international forums where issues relating to Antarctica are dealt with, and, subject to the Antarctic Treaty, they shall respect each other's legitimate interests in Antarctica.

Article II

The two Governments agree to work together to make full use of the opportunities for international cooperation provided for in the Antarctic Treaty, especially to science and

[11] Adopted 21 June 1991, entered into force 13 July 1992, 1686 UNTS 275.

[12] United Nations, *Treaty Series,* vol. 402, p. 71.

technology, in order to improve their knowledge of the Antarctic Continent and its adjacent areas.

Article III

1. The two Governments express their interest in combining their efforts in Antarctica through the implementation of joint and cooperative projects in science and technology under the aegis of the National Antarctic Programme of Spain and the National Antarctic Office (Argentine Antarctic Institute), which shall act as executing agencies and as intermediaries in securing the required cooperation in the field of Antarctic science from other institutions and organizations in their respective countries.

2. In order to increase cooperation between the National Antarctic Office (Argentine Antarctic Institute) and the National Antarctic Programme, the two bodies shall exchange information about their programmes in the Antarctic region in a timely manner and shall intensify the exchange of bibliographical information.

Article IV

Joint projects for scientific and technical cooperation and logistics, and the modes of operation for their implementation as enumerated in articles V and VI, shall be the subject of specific agreements to be concluded later between the bodies responsible for their implementation.

Article V

1. The National Antarctic Office (Argentine Antarctic Institute) and the National Antarctic Programme agree to develop joint and cooperative programmes in all fields relating to the substance of this Agreement, especially oceanography, marine chemistry, physics of the upper atmosphere, geology, geophysics, geochemistry, biology, glaciology and meteorology.

2. The modes of operation for this cooperation shall in particular be the following:

(a) The participation of Argentine scientists and technicians in Antarctic expeditions carried out on board vessels utilized by the National Antarctic Programme and by Spanish scientists and technicians on board vessels utilized by the National Antarctic Office (Argentine Antarctic Institute).

(b) The exchange of scientists and technicians, and of fellowships, courses and technology and, in particular, of scientists and technicians of the two nationalities between the Argentine scientific stations and the Spanish station.

(c) The exchange of information on scientific programmes in progress.

(d) The joint use of scientific research facilities and laboratories in Antarctica to develop programmes in the disciplines mentioned.

Article VI

1. Subject to the availability of space, the National Antarctic Office and the National Antarctic Programme shall be responsible for the transport of personnel and freight to Antarctica on a reciprocal basis.

2. The National Antarctic Office shall take the necessary steps to facilitate the stay in Argentine ports of the vessels that the National Antarctic Programme uses to conduct its Antarctic activities and shall provide logistical support for the transport of Spanish personnel and equipment within the territory of the Argentine Republic.

3. The National Antarctic Office shall endeavour to ensure that fuel is supplied to Spanish vessels in Argentine ports.

4. Spanish researchers and/or technicians performing either advisory or scientific and technical cooperation duties at Argentine scientific stations may utilize free of charge the Argentine transport facilities routinely serving those areas. Their stay at the stations or encampments where they carry out their assignment shall also be free of charge.

5. In order to facilitate the exchange of technical information on logistics and the installation of stations and equipment, it is agreed that an Argentine logistics expert shall travel to Spain and a Spanish expert to the Argentine Republic.

Article VII

Any dispute arising with regard to the interpretation or application of this Agreement which cannot be settled by the executing agencies referred to in article III shall be submitted to the respective Ministries of Foreign Affairs, which shall hold direct negotiations in order to arrive at a settlement.

Article VIII

This Agreement shall be applied provisionally from the date of its signature and shall enter into force on the date on which the Parties shall have informed each other, through the diplomatic channel, of the fulfilment of their respective domestic requirements. It shall remain in force for five years and shall be renewed automatically for one-year periods unless either of the Parties indicates at least three months before the expiry date the intention to terminate it.

DONE at Madrid on 21 June 1991 in duplicate.

[Signatories omitted].

Treaty between the Argentine Republic and the Republic of Chile on the Environment (1991)[13]

Article II Scope of the Agreement

...

10. Antarctic Environment:

The Parties, in accordance with the Joint Declaration on the Antarctic, of 29 August 1990, shall strengthen their bilateral cooperation within the Antarctic Treaty System, in order to reinforce the mechanisms and measures for protection of the Antarctic environment and its dependent and associated ecosystems.

...

Specific Additional Protocol on the Protection of the Antarctic Environment between the Argentine Republic and the Republic of Chile (1991)[14]

The Government of the Argentine Republic and the Government of the Republic of Chile, hereinafter referred to as "the Parties";

Mindful of the importance of the Antarctic regions on which their land masses are projected; the influence of Antarctic weather phenomena, Antarctic marine currents and the Antarctic ecosystems with which their living resources are associated when they do not share their existence between one or other habitat; and the need to protect and preserve the Antarctic for future generations;

Evoking the Joint Declarations on the Antarctic and, in particular, the Presidential Declaration of 29 August 1990, bearing in mind the provisions contained in the Protocol to the Antarctic Treaty on the Protection of the Environment negotiated at the 11th Special Consultative Meeting on the Antarctic Treaty;

Considering the provisions of the Treaty on the Environment signed by the two Governments on 2 August 1991, especially its stipulations in Articles II and III which contain a mandate to coordinate actions in specific areas by adopting additional protocols;

Have agreed as follows:

Article I. Protection of Antarctic assets

The Parties shall promote the conservation of Antarctic natural and cultural assets, through appropriate actions to protect designated areas, the conservation and restoration of historical

[13] Adopted 2 August 1991, entered into force 17 November 1992, 1733 UNTS 201.

[14] Adopted 2 August 1991, entered into force 17 November 1992.

sites and monuments, the observance of the standards of conduct adopted for this purpose in the framework of the Antarctic Treaty, and the dissemination of intrinsic values of the Antarctic.

Article II. Exchange of information

The Parties shall exchange information on the planning and undertaking of activities in the Antarctic, with the aim of avoiding potential adverse impacts on the Antarctic environment and its dependent and associated ecosystems.

To that end, they will cooperate in preparing technical or other guidelines that serve to facilitate environmentally harmonious planning of their activities in the Antarctic.

Article III. Environmental vigilance

In their national Antarctic programs, The Parties shall prioritize the vigilance of global environmental changes that could have effects on the ozone layer over the Antarctic, on the Antarctic land, marine and atmospheric environment, and of its dependent and associated ecosystems.

The Parties undertake to set up environmental vigilance programs to verify the foreseen effects and detect possible unforeseen effects on the environment and on Antarctic living resources caused by activities undertaken in the Antarctic Treaty area, including:

(a) The disposal of wastes;
(b) Pollution from hydrocarbons or other hazardous and toxic substances;
(c) The construction and operation of stations, refuges, camps, ships, aircraft, and other forms of logistic support;
(d) Scientific programmes;
(e) Leisure activities;
(f) Activities that could affect the objectives of the zones designated as protected areas.

The Parties may establish joint or complementary vigilance programmes that will help to detect, quantify and determine the likely causes of changes observed in the quality of the air, and snow, and water, and the other essential characteristics of the environment of Antarctic biodiversity.

Article IV. Cooperation

The Parties shall promote programmes of scientific, technical and educational cooperation for the protection and preservation of the Antarctic environment and its dependent and associated ecosystems including the following aspects, among others:

(a) The training of scientific and technical personnel;
(b) Antarctic environmental management;
(c) The preparation of environmental impact assessments;
(d) The exchange of infonnation on polar technologies;
(e) Research into all types of pollutants found in the Antarctic Treaty area;
(f) Facilities for the use of installations and laboratories by researchers from both countries.

Article V. Consultations

The Parties shall consult each other on selection of sites for potential stations and other facilities to avoid undesirable effects on scientific research or cumulative impacts on the environment arising from excessive concentration in a given area.

When they deem appropriate, the Parties may consider undertaking joint expeditions, logistical operations, exchange of personnel, and any other form of coordination or joint action that could help avoid interference with existing scientific programmes or adverse impacts on the environment and damage to other established uses.

Article VI. Coordination

By common agreement, the Parties shall establish ways of preparing, disseminating and applying the environmental impact procedures that are applicable to any activities they have planned jointly in the Antarctic Treaty area, and for which prior notification is required pursuant to Article VII of the Antarctic Treaty.

The Parties shall also coordinate in adopting standard inspection procedures and for the exchange of information on inspections aimed at protecting the Antarctic environment and its dependent and associated ecosystems, and may agree to undertake joint inspections when they deem appropriate.

Article VII. Prevention and security

The Parties shall coordinate for the study, planning, application and execution of procedures applicable to natural disasters and accidents that require rapid and effective response. For that purpose they will:

(a) Constantly review the effectiveness of measures aimed at preventing or reducing environmental pollution;

(b) Cooperate in the formulation and implementation of contingency plans, as well as emergency interventions in response to environmental hazards and accidents, including joint activities as necessary;

(c) Exchange information on air and maritime safety measures, including buoy marking, cartography, meteorological information and information on marine ice, pursuant to the standards and procedures specified in the Antarctic Treaty consultative meetings.

Article VIII. Wastes and discharges

The Parties shall coordinate their action for the control of movements of radioactive, toxic and hazardous wastes originating outside the Antarctic Treaty area, to ensure that no waste materials are introduced, or discharges made in that area.

The Parties shall foster the application of new and better waste disposal methods in the Antarctic, along with waste management practices with little environmental impact, including those that allow for the conservation of energy and water.

Article IX. Legislative harmonization

The Parties shall promote the exchange of background information and experiences with a view to promoting the harmonization of their domestic legislation on issues relating to compliance, emergency response, accountability, dispute settlement, and other measures aimed at ensuring full application of the agreements on the protection of the Antarctic environment and its dependent and associated ecosystems.

Article X. Annual meetings

The Parties shall hold annual meetings for analysis, coordination and planning, to review:

(a) The degree of compliance with this protocol;

(b) The advisability of setting up additional programmes;

(c) The amendment or expansion of existing agreements; and

(d) Any other additional measure that could be considered beneficial for the protection of the Antarctic environment and its dependent and associated ecosystems.

Article XI. Obligation of the Parties

The provisions of this Protocol shall not affect more stringent obligations that may have been assumed by the Parties under the provisions of the Antarctic Treaty, its complementary instruments, or the recommendations adopted by the consultative meetings of that Treaty.

Article XII. Entry into force

This Protocol shall enter into force when the Parties notify each other, through the diplomatic channel, that their respective constitutional requirements for its approval have been completed. It shall remain valid indefinitely, and may be denounced by either of the Parties through notification through the diplomatic channel giving six months' notice. Denunciation of the Agreement shall not affect the continuation and completion of actions initiated while it was in force.

DONE at Buenos Aires on 2 August 1991 in duplicate, both copies being equally authentic.

[Signatories omitted].

Antarctic Cooperation Agreement between the Kingdom of Spain and the Republic of Chile (1993)[15]

The Kingdom of Spain and the Republic of Chile, hereinafter referred to as "the Parties",

Reaffirming their determination to strengthen their bilateral ties of friendship and cooperation, within the framework of the General Treaty of cooperation and friendship and the Economic Agreement annexed to that Treaty, signed with the Kingdom of Spain at Santiago on 19 October 1990,[16]

Taking into account the Antarctic Treaty,[17] particularly its articles II and III, and the Protocol on Environmental Protection to the Antarctic Treaty,

Bearing in mind the recommendations produced within the Antarctic Treaty system concerning the facilities to be provided in the context of international scientific cooperation,

Recalling the decision of the Parties to the Antarctic Treaty to designate the period from 1991 to 2000 as the Antarctic Decade of International Scientific Cooperation,

Further recognizing the exceptional value of the Antarctic for scientific observation and for the investigation of processes of global and regional importance,

Agree as follows:

Article I

The Parties undertake to establish through the Ministries of Foreign Affairs of Chile and Spain a mechanism for permanent consultation regarding matters of mutual interest in the political, legal and scientific areas, and any other area, in the context of the Antarctic Treaty system.

To that end, they shall endeavour to coordinate their respective positions in the various international forums having competence in this field, respecting each other's interests and acting in accordance with the spirit of the Antarctic Treaty.

Article II

The Parties shall endeavour to act jointly in order to make full use of the opportunities for cooperation provided for in the Antarctic Treaty and to optimize human and material resources, in response to the need to promote the planning of scientific work and interdisciplinary studies between their respective scientific communities.

Article III

The Parties shall cooperate in the planning and implementation of activities in the Antarctic Treaty area, by means of:

(a) Joint scientific, technical and educational research projects, mainly concerning improved knowledge and protection of the Antarctic environment and of its dependent and associated ecosystems;
(b) Cooperation in the preparation and presentation of assessments of the environmental impact of such projects;
(c) A mechanism for consultation and for exchange of information in order to avoid the cumulative impact of activities and their excessive concentration in particular areas;
(d) Joint expeditions and shared utilization of means of transport, logistics, and other facilities, as detailed in the Annex to this Agreement;
(e) Research into and protection of the historical heritage of the Antarctic.

Article IV

For these purposes, the Parties designate the Chilean Antarctic Institute and the Spanish National Antarctic Programme, respectively, as implementing agencies in these areas and as intermediaries for the management, with regard to other competent institutions and agencies in their respective countries, of appropriate collaboration for the implementation of the cooperative projects and activities which are under consideration.

[15] Adopted 22 December 1993, entered into force 18 May 1994, 1820 UNTS 281.
[16] United Nations, *Treaty Series*, vol. 1653, No. I-28441.
[17] *Ibid*, vol. 402, p. 71.

Article V

The Parties agree that the Chilean Antarctic Institute and the Spanish National Antarctic Programme shall also endeavour:

(a) To include within the framework of this Agreement the scientific collaborative activities currently existing between researchers from Chile and Spain, and the joint and coordinated implementation of scientific research projects and technological development;

(b) To establish an information exchange system for programmes in the areas of science, technological information, and logistic support;

(c) To share information which may be useful for the planning and implementation of their activities in the Antarctic Treaty area, to protect, principally, the Antarctic environment and its dependent and associated ecosystems;

(d) To exchange scientific data from joint projects for the joint compilation of results in accordance with the principles previously established under each research project;

(e) To participate, through joint scientific projects, in each other's Antarctic expeditions on board the means of transport used on each occasion, making use of the Antarctic infrastructures of both parties on that continent; and

(f) To train professionals and specialists in matters concerning the Antarctic, and to promote the exchange of such persons and give each other access to scientific installations and equipment.

Article VI

In the spirit of the Antarctic Decade of International Scientific Cooperation, and taking into account the Antarctic cooperation programmes of Chile and Spain with other countries, particularly in Latin America and Europe, the Chilean Antarctic Institute and the Spanish National Antarctic Programme shall study the feasibility of extending their bilateral cooperation to multilateral projects, and insofar as their budgetary resource permit, shall include financing and any travel by their research staff which may be necessary for the fulfilment of the aforesaid objectives.

Article VII

The Chilean Antarctic Institute and the Spanish National Antarctic Programme shall elaborate, at least one year ahead, the Joint Action Programme incorporating the objectives stated in articles III and V of this Agreement.

Within the framework of that Programme, the implementation arrangements laid down in the Annex to this Agreement shall be reviewed annually.

Article VIII

Any dispute which may arise concerning the interpretation or implementation of this Antarctic Cooperation Agreement, and which cannot be settled by the implementing agencies designated by the Parties, shall be submitted by them to their respective Ministries of Foreign Affairs, through which the necessary talks for its settlement shall take place.

Article IX

This Agreement shall enter into force on the date of the last notification by which the Parties inform each other through the diplomatic channel of the completion of the formalities required by their internal legal systems.

Article X

This Agreement shall remain in force indefinitely. It may be denounced by either of the Parties by means of notification through the diplomatic channel with six months' notice. The denunciation shall not affect the completion of activities initiated during its period of validity.

DONE at Santiago, Chile, on 22 December 1993.

[Signatories omitted].

Agreement on Antarctic Cooperation between the Government of New Zealand and the Government of the French Republic (1994)[18]

The Government of New Zealand and the Government of the French Republic,

Recalling the Joint Statement on Antarctic Cooperation issued in Christchurch on 23 December 1992, and their desire to conclude a bilateral Agreement;

Noting that New Zealand and France have a commitment to the comprehensive protection of the Antarctic environment;

Recognising that the signature of the Protocol on Environmental Protection to the Antarctic Treaty[19] ("the Protocol") by all Consultative Parties represent an historic step;

Recalling the environmental principles of the Protocol which require, inter alia, that activities in the Antarctic Treaty Area be planned and conducted so as to limit adverse impacts on the Antarctic environment and dependent and associated ecosystems;

Recalling that New Zealand is one of the most important gateways to Antarctica and that New Zealand, by virtue of its geographical proximity to Antarctica, and its territorial sovereignty over the Ross Dependency, is well placed to provide assistance to Antarctic scientific research programmes;

Recognising France's wish to develop an air support capability for its Antarctic Research Programme and that transiting New Zealand territory (including the Ross Dependency) will facilitate the operation of an air support link;

Noting that in view of the extensive facilities which the City of Christchurch offers to Antarctic operations, in particular the International Antarctic Centre at Christchurch International Airport, and those available at the International Centre for Antarctic Information and Research (ICAIR), the Government of New Zealand welcomes the use of facilities by the French Antarctic Research Programme;

Further noting that France shall be circulating a final Comprehensive Environmental Evaluation in respect of the establishment of the "Concordia" scientific station at Dome C taking full account of the observations and recommendations of the Antarctic Treaty Parties and Non-Governmental Organisations made in accordance with the Protocol;

Recalling the Agreement between New Zealand and Italy on Cooperation in Antarctic Research done at Wellington on 8 March 1987.[20]

Have agreed as follows:

1.

(a) The two Governments shall develop further their bilateral Antarctic cooperation. In particular, they will consult and cooperate about issues relating to the protection of the Antarctic environment arising from:
- Their national Antarctic Research Programmes, or
- From the consideration at an Antarctic Treaty Consultative Meeting, or by certain Consultative Parties of issues or measures relating to the protection of the Antarctic environment.

They will also consult and cooperate on any issues concerning the implementation of the Antarctic Treaty, the Protocol or other elements of the Antarctic Treaty System.

(b) The two Governments shall cooperate in Antarctic scientific research for peaceful purposes and their mutual benefit and shall develop this cooperation, particularly in light of the establishment of the "Concordia" scientific station at Dome C by France and Italy.

(c) Each Government shall designate an agent or agency to be responsible for the coordination and facilitation of cooperative activities under this Agreement. These agents or agencies shall consult with a view to developing such cooperative activities.

[18] Adopted and entered into force 16 September 1994, 1866 UNTS 345.
[19] For the Antarctic Treaty, see United Nations, *Treaty Series*, vol. 402, p. 71.
[20] Should read 8 April 1987. *See* United Nations, *Treaty Series*, vol. 1675, No. I-28952.

(d) Cooperative activities shall be the subject of such specific arrangements as may be deemed appropriate.

(e) The two Governments shall take early and frequent opportunities to consult together, and at any time at the request of either, regarding the implementation of this Agreement.

2. Subject to prior agreement between the agents or agencies referred to in Article 1 *c* on the level of such operations in any year, the Government of New Zealand undertakes to permit the transit through and temporary accommodation in New Zealand of French personnel engaged in the French Antarctic Research Programme, en route to and from Antarctica. The Government of New Zealand shall, consistent with its laws and regulations, facilitate as far as possible the transit through and temporary accommodation in New Zealand of other personnel who may be subject to separate arrangements, either already existing or to be concluded, between the Government of New Zealand and the State of nationality of the other personnel.

3. The Government of New Zealand shall, consistent with its laws and regulations, facilitate as far as possible the entry into, exit from and stay in New Zealand of French personnel engaged in the French Antarctic Research Programme, and of other personnel who may be subject to separate arrangements, either already existing, or to be concluded, between the Government of New Zealand and the State of nationality of the other personnel. Provided such personnel meet normal temporary entry requirements the Government of New Zealand agrees to issue to them an entry permit allowing employment, valid for the period of their assignment up to a maximum of twelve months, or in respect of the period the personnel are present on New Zealand territory, including the Ross Dependency.

4. The Government of New Zealand shall facilitate, consistent with its laws and regulations including those relating to agricultural health inspection, the entry into and exit from New Zealand of ships, aircraft, equipment and materials to be used in the French Antarctic Research Programme as well as the personal effects of personnel engaged in the programme. The Government of New Zealand shall exempt equipment and materials imported or exported for such purpose from payment of taxes and customs duties.

5. The Government of New Zealand shall, consistent with its laws and regulations, and with reciprocal measures taken by the Government of the French Republic vis-à-vis New Zealand in situations of a similar nature, facilitate the protection and security of personnel engaged in, and aircraft, equipment and materials to be used in, the French Antarctic Research Programme.

6. The Government of the French Republic shall inform the Government of New Zealand on a timely basis each year through the diplomatic channel of:

(a) The expected size of the French Antarctic Research Programme for the forthcoming Antarctic season in so far as the use of facilities in New Zealand may be involved;

(b) The ports, airports and other services requested for use by the personnel, ships and aircraft of the French Antarctic Research Programme during the forthcoming Antarctic season;

(c) The expected impact, if any, on the Antarctic environment arising directly, or indirectly, from logistic or other activities involving the proposed use of New Zealand ports, airports and other services requested for use by the French Antarctic Research Programme during the forthcoming season.

7. Any requests by the Government of the French Republic for the use of ports, airports and other services for use by the French Antarctic Research Programme shall relate to activities in respect of which appropriate measures have beforehand been taken, consistent with the Protocol, satisfactorily to limit adverse impacts on the Antarctic environment and dependent and associated ecosystems.

8. The Government of the French Republic shall provide, as far as possible, under modalities to be agreed upon in each case, appropriate logistic support for the implementation of the New Zealand Antarctic Programme. It shall give consideration, as appropriate, to the joint benefits which may result from France, in consultation and cooperation with other countries, basing a

Twin Otter or other aircraft at McMurdo for Dome C and Dumont d'Urville support and for its use, as appropriate, by the New Zealand Antarctic Programme.

9. This Agreement shall not apply to the Cook Islands, Niue or Tokelau.

10. Either Government may, at any time, give to the other Government notice in writing of intention to terminate this Agreement. Such notice shall take effect one year after its receipt.

11. This Agreement shall enter into force on signature.

DONE in duplicate at Wellington, on 16th September 1994, in the English and French languages, each version being equally authentic.

[Signatories omitted].

Convenio de Cooperacion Antarctica entre los Goviernos de la Republica de Chile y de la Federacion de Rusia (1995)[21]

Los Gobiernos de la República de Chile y de la Federación de Rusia, denominados de ahora en adelante como las Partes.

Considerando que los artículos II y III del Tratado Antártico, el Protocolo sobre Protección del Medio Ambiente del Tratado Antártico y las recomendaciones atribuyen una alta prioridad a la cooperación internacional en el campo de las actividades científicas.

Reconociendo el papel creciente de la Antártica en lo que respecta a investigaciones científicas destinadas a preservar el medio ambiente del planeta, y conscientes de la necesidad de elevar al máximo los beneficios de las investigaciones científicas con fines de minimizar efectos negativos sobre el medio ambiente.

Tomando en consideración la decisión de los estados miembros del Tratado Antártico de declarar el período 1991–2000 como "Decenio de Cooperación Científica Internacional en la Antártica".

Acuerdan lo siguiente:

Artículo I

Las Partes establecerán, a través de sus Ministerios de Relaciones Exteriores, un mecanismo permanente de consultas sobre cuestiones de mutuo interés en las esferas política, jurídica y científica, así como en otros campos en el marco del Tratado Antártico.

Artículo II

Las Partes cooperarán con el fin de alcanzar el mejor aprovechamiento de las posibilidades de colaboración estipuladas en el Tratado Antártico para optimizar los recursos materiales y humanos disponibles, coadyuvando a la mejor planificación y al perfeccionamiento de las investigaciones interdisciplinarias efectuadas por sus respectivas entidades científicas.

Artículo III

Las Partes cooperarán en el desarrollo de actividades encaminadas al logro de los siguientes objetivos:

a) elaborar investigaciones técnico-científicas y proyectos conjuntos con miras al enriquecimiento de conocimientos, principalmente en todo lo relativo a la protección del medio ambiente de la Antártica y de los ecosistemas dependientes y vinculados a dicho continente;
b) formar grupos mixtos de expertos para evaluar el posible impacto que pudieran tener las actividades de las Partes sobre el medio ambiente de la Antártica;
c) capacitar recursos humanos a través de la aplicación de conocimientos técnico-científicos avanzados con el fin de crear un equipo competente de investigadores, administradores y técnicos especializados en cuestiones del medio ambiente de la Antártica;
d) asimismo, y con idéntico propósito, promover el intercambio de expertos, personal técnico y científico especializado para participar en programas de capacitación que se lleven a

[21] Adopted 14 February 1995.

cabo en las instalaciones de cada una de las Partes. La formación del personal deberá ajustarse a Programas académicos y actividades conducentes a la obtención de títulos de post-grado en materias científicas (Magister en Ciencias y Doctor en Ciencias);

e) conceder mutuamente los servicios vinculados al transporte y ubicación del personal así como de los cargamentos a bordo de sus propios navíos, aviones y estaciones, como también el arriendo de los mismos durante la época de las expediciones antárticas, de acuerdo al artículo V del presente Convenio;
f) intercambiar experiencias sobre el desarrollo tecnológico de los asentamientos humanos y las actividades turísticas en las regiones polares;
g) intercambiar experiencias y organizar investigaciones médicas conjuntas sobre el comportamiento humano en las regiones polares, especialmente bajo condiciones extremas.

Artículo IV

Para alcanzar los objetivos anteriormente mencionados las Partes designan, al Instituto Antártico Chileno (INACH) del Ministerio de Relaciones Exteriores de Chile y al Instituto de Investigaciones Científicas sobre el Artico y la Antártica (IICAA) del Servicio Federal Ruso de Hidrometeorología y Monitoreo del Medio Ambiente (SFRHMMA) respectivamente, como organismos responsables de la coordinación de actividades relativas al cumplimiento del presente Convenio.

Artículo V

El Instituto Antártico Chileno y el Instituto de Investigaciones Científicas sobre el Artico y la Antártica del SFRHMMA encaminarán sus esfuerzos hacia las siguientes actividades:

a) elaborar y coordinar conjuntamente los proyectos científico-técnicos de investigación en el marco del presente Convenio;
b) crear un sistema de intercambio de información concerniente a los problemas relacionados con el apoyo científico, médico, tecnológico y logístico a las actividades de las Partes en la Antártica;
c) intercambiar información que pueda ser útil para la planificación y preparación de actividades en el marco del Tratado Antártico con el fin de proteger, inter alia, el medio ambiente antártico así como los ecosistemas vinculados a este último;
d) intercambiar información obtenida de proyectos similares para preparación de investigaciones conjuntas conforme a principios establecidos con anterioridad para cada proyecto de investigación;
e) participar, a través de proyectos científicos conjuntos, en las expediciones antárticas que lleven a cabo las Partes;
f) capacitar profesionalmente a expertos para trabajar en la Antártica, promoviendo el intercambio de estos expertos con el fin de utilizar más eficazmente las instalaciones y equipos científicos de cada una de las Partes.

Artículo VI

El Instituto Antártico Chileno y el Instituto de Investigaciones Científicas sobre el Artico y la Antártica del SFRHMMA, en el espíritu del "Decenio de Cooperación Científica Internacional en la Antártica" y tomando en consideración los programas de cooperación en la Antártica que la República de Chile y la Federación de Rusia llevan a cabo con otros países, especialmente en América Latina y Europa, examinarán las posibilidades de extender su cooperación bilateral a la ejecución de proyectos multilaterales y, dentro de sus posibilidades financieras, buscarán medios de financiamiento y formas de traslado de sus respectivos científicos, elemento esencial para el logro de estos objetivos.

Artículo VII

El Instituto Antártico Chileno y el Instituto de Investigaciones Científicas sobre el Artico y la Antártica del SFRHMMA elaborarán, por lo menos un año antes del inicio de su puesta en marcha, un programa de actividades conjuntas que incluirá los objetivos mencionados en los artículos III y V del presente Convenio.

Artículo VIII

Cualesquiera divergencias que puedan surgir respecto de la interpretación y aplicación del presente Convenio se resolverán por vía de negociaciones entre las Partes.

Artículo IX

El presente Convenio entrará en vigor al intercambiarse las notificaciones que confirmen el cumplimiento por ambas Partes de los requerimientos estatales internos necesarios para que el presente Convenio entre en vigor.

Artículo X

En el caso de que una de las Partes decida denunciar el presente Convenio, deberá notificar en forma escrita a la otra de tal decisión. El Convenio cesará en su vigencia seis meses después de hecha la referida notificación.

La denuncia del presente Convenio no impedirá el cumplimiento de compromisos previamente acordados pero no concluidos a la fecha en que el Convenio cese en su vigencia.

Hecho en la ciudad de Moscú el 14 de febrero de 1995 en dos ejemplares en los idiomas español y ruso, respectivamente, teniendo ambos textos el mismo valor.

[Signatories omitted].

Acuerdo con el Reino Unido de Gran Bretaña e Irlanda del Norte Relativo al Traspaso al Gobierno de Chile del Refugio "View Point Hut", Situado en la Antartica, Bahia Duse, Peninsula Trinidad (1996)[22]

N° SAP/002/7/96

El Ministerio de Relaciones Exteriores y de la Comunidad Británica de Naciones saluda atentamente a la Embajada de Chile y, con referencia al entendimiento en cuanto a que el Gobierno de Chile desea hacerse cargo de "View Point Hut", refugio situado en la Antártica, en Bahía Duse, Península Trinidad, señala lo siguiente:

Actualmente, el mencionado refugio es propiedad del Consejo de Investigación del Medio Ambiente Natural (NERC), organismo del cual depende el "Centro de Estudio Antártico Británico" (British Antartic Survey). Luego de consultar a ambos organismos, el Ministerio de Relaciones Exteriores y de la Comunidad Británica de Naciones tiene el agrado de informar a la Embajada de Chile que han confirmado que ya no necesitarán dicho refugio, y que el NERC está dispuesto a no hacer valer ningún derecho o título sobre el mismo y a renunciar a toda responsabilidad ulterior respecto a la estructura.

En estas circunstancias, el Ministerio de Relaciones Exteriores y de la Comunidad Británica de Naciones tiene el agrado de informar a la Embajada que si el Gobierno de Chile, actuando en el marco del Tratado Antártico y teniendo especialmente presente sus artículos II y IV, desea hacerse cargo de dicho refugio y asumir la responsabilidad de su funcionamiento y mantenimiento futuros, ni el NERC ni el Gobierno de Su Majestad tendrán objeción alguna.

Si el Gobierno de Chile desea proceder sobre esta base, el Ministerio de Relaciones Exteriores y de la Comunidad Británica de Naciones tiene el honor de proponer que la presente Nota y la respuesta afirmativa de la Embajada sean consideradas como una constancia del entendimiento de nuestros dos gobiernos en esta materia y que la adquisición de "View Point Hut" por parte del Gobierno de Chile se haga efectiva en la fecha de respuesta de la Embajada.

El Ministerio de Relaciones Exteriores y de la Comunidad Británica de Naciones, Departamento Sudatlántico y Antártico, aprovecha esta ocasión para reiterar a la Embajada de Chile las seguridades de su más alta consideración.

[22] Adopted 29 July 1996.

Firma ilegible
Timbre: Ministerio de Relaciones Exteriores y de la Comunidad Británica de Naciones-Londres.
Ministerio de Relaciones Exteriores y de la Comunidad Británica de Naciones
London SW1A 2AH
17 de Julio de 1996
Timbre: SAP 272/015/96
Santiago de Chile, a 16 de agosto de 1996.– La traductora oficial
EMBAJADA DE CHILE
12 Devonshire Street
London W1N 2DS
Teléfono: 0171 580 6392/7
Fax: 0171 4365204
Télex: 25970 PMRACHIL
FO/046/96

La Embajada de Chile saluda atentamente al Ministerio de Relaciones Exteriores y de la Comunidad Británica de Naciones, Departamento Sudatlántico y Antártico, y tiene el honor de referirse a su nota N° SAP/002/7/96 de fecha 17 de julio de 1996, por la cual el Gobierno de Su Majestad Británica comunicó su consentimiento al traspaso por parte del Consejo de Investigación del Medio Ambiente Natural (NERC) y el "Centro de Estudio Antártico Británico" (British Antartic Survey) al Gobierno de la República de Chile, de "View Point Hut", refugio situado en Bahía Duse, en el lado occidental de la Península Antártica, que el NERC ya no necesita.

Con respecto a esta materia, la Embajada de Chile tiene el honor de informar al Ministerio de Relaciones Exteriores y de la Comunidad Británica de Naciones, Departamento Sudatlántico y Antártico, que el Gobierno de Chile desea asumir la responsabilidad del refugio y de su funcionamiento y mantenimiento futuros.

En consecuencia, y de acuerdo con lo expuesto en la Nota SAP/002/7/96 del Ministerio de Relaciones Exteriores y de la Comunidad Británica de Naciones, Departamento Sudatlántico y Antártico, la Embajada de Chile tiene el honor de confirmar que la Nota antes mencionada constituiría un entendimiento de nuestros dos Gobiernos en esta materia y que la adquisición de "View Point Hut" se hará efectiva a contar de la fecha de hoy.

La Embajada de Chile aprovecha esta ocasión para reiterar al Ministerio de Relaciones Exteriores y de la Comunidad Británica de Naciones, Departamento Sudatlántico y Antártico las seguridades de su más alta consideración.

Firma ilegible
Timbre: Embajada de Chile en Gran Bretaña
Londres, 29 de Julio de 1996.
Santiago de Chile, a 16 de agosto de 1996.– La traductora oficial.

Agreement on Scientific, Technologic and Logistic Cooperation in Antarctica between the Government of the Republic of Korea and the Government of the Republic of Peru (1996)[23]

The Government of the Republic of Korea and the Government of the Republic of Peru (hereinafter referred to as "the Contracting Parties");

Conscious of the importance of the scientific research in Antarctica, and within the spirit of the Antarctic Treaty for promoting and assuring cooperation in this field;

Desiring to strengthen their bilateral links and to organize the exchange of experiences between the Contracting Parties concerning Antarctica;

[23] Adopted 13 September 1996, entered into force 11 November 1996, 2113 UNTS 355.

Have agreed as follows:

Article I

The executive committees of this Agreement shall be the Korea Ocean Research Development Institute (hereinafter referred to as "KORDI") for the Republic of Korea and the National Commission of Antarctic Affairs (hereinafter referred to as "CONAAN") for the Republic of Peru.

Article II

The Contracting Parties shall promote cooperation and scientific, technologic and logistic exchanges through the following terms:

1. exchange of scientists, technicians, and support staff;
2. implementation of joint scientific research and technologic development projects;
3. organization of and participation in scientific and technologic conferences, seminars and meetings;
4. exchange of scientific, technologic and logistic information; and
5. any other terms which provide reciprocal consultation and exchanges of experiences and which have been mutually agreed upon by the Contracting Parties in accordance with their respective countries' laws and regulations.

Article III

1. Joint research projects approved by the Contracting Parties shall last for a period of one year, and may be renewed upon agreement between KORDI and CONAAN.
2. Scientific conferences, seminars and meetings shall not exceed two weeks. In the specific case of programmed logistic courses, the Sending Party shall determine their duration.

Article IV

KORDI and CONAAN shall coordinate the actions necessary to ensure the success of each project, in collaboration with the relevant institutions in their respective countries.

Article V

The specific areas of interest where KORDI and CONAAN shall initially develop joint programs and projects are the following:

1. sciences of the sea: marine biology, physical oceanography, chemical oceanography, acoustics, and marine pollution;
2. sciences of the earth: geology;
3. sciences of the atmosphere and space: meteorology (climatology and synoptic meteorology) and astrophysics;
4. sciences of life: human biology, and
5. other areas as agreed by the Contracting Parties.

Article VI

1. For performing the terms of the scientific, technologic and logistic cooperation and the exchanges provided for by Article II, the Sending Party shall inform the Receiving Party, at least three (3) months prior to the beginning of a proposed activity, of the necessary information about the personnel and their work programs as well as the beginning and ending dates of the activity.
2. The Receiving Party shall respond to the proposal within forty-five (45) days from the date of the receipt of the proposal, indicating its consent to the program and/or suggesting modifications.

Article VII

The financing agreed upon between the Contracting Parties shall be governed by the following terms:

1. The Sending Party shall pay for the international round-trip tickets for its personnel, and the Receiving Party shall be responsible for the cost of local travel and accommodation required for the performances of the missions by the personnel from the Sending Party;

2. The Receiving Party shall grant proper medical care in case of emergencies;

3. Each Contracting Party shall be in charge of the expenses of their own personnel which result from accident, death or disability for life during the activities agreed upon by both Parties; and

4. Other terms may be included by mutual agreement of the Contracting Parties.

Article VIII

The personnel sent by the Contracting Parties pursuant to this Agreement shall be subject to the administrative rules of the Receiving Party's institutions to which they are assigned.

Article IX

KORDI and CONAAN shall agree on an annual plan of action. For that purpose, a meeting between the Contracting Parties shall be held annually on a date mutually agreed upon. The chair for this meeting shall be held in turn by the Contracting Parties, with the chair being responsible for transmitting appropriate communications concerning the meeting.

Article X

1. This Agreement shall become effective on the date when the Contracting Parties have notified each other that all legal requirements for its entry into force have been fulfilled. It shall remain effective for a period of five (5) years and shall be automatically renewed for the same period, unless one of the Contracting Parties notifies the other Party in writing not later than six (6) months before the expiration date of intention to terminate the Agreement.

2. The terms in paragraph 1 shall not alter already implemented programs and projects, which shall continue until their expiry.

Done in duplicate at Lima this 13th day of September 1996, in the Korean, Spanish and English languages, all three texts being equally authentic. In case of any divergence of interpretation, the English text shall prevail.

[Signatories omitted].

Memorandum of Understanding between the Government of the Republic of South Africa and the Government of the United Kingdom of Great Britain and Northern Ireland concerning the Convention on the Conservation of Antarctic Marine Living Resources (1997)[24]

Preamble

The Government of the Republic of South Africa and the Government of the United Kingdom of Great Britain and Northern Ireland (hereinafter referred to as the "Receiving Member" and the "Designating Member" respectively), being signatories to the Convention on the Conservation of Antarctic Marine Living Resources (hereinafter referred to as the "CCAMLR"); and

In order to promote the objectives and ensure observance of the provisions of the CCAMLR;

Have reached the following understanding:

Article I

The Receiving Member will take appropriate measures within its competence to ensure that a Scientific Observer, designated by the Designating Member, will be taken on board of a vessel, to be agreed before the beginning of each fishing season by the Receiving and Designating Member, to observe and report on the activities of said vessel as contemplated in Article XXIV. (2) of the CCAMLR and subject to any CCAMLR Conservation Measure in force for a targeted species.

Article II

(1) This programme will operate subject to the terms and conditions established by the Scheme of International Scientific Observation adopted by the CCAMLR Commission (hereinafter

[24] Adopted and entered into force 27 October 1997, 2568 UNTS 17.

referred to as "the Commission") at its XIth meeting in 1992, pursuant to Article XXIV of CCAMLR, which will include the following provisions:

(2) The Scientific Observer will be accommodated aboard the vessel specified under Article I and in accordance with the following arrangements:

(a) The Scientific Observer will be accorded the status of a ship's officer. Accommodations and meals for the Scientific Observer on board will be of a standard commensurate with this status.

(b) The Receiving Member will ensure that the vessel operator co-operates fully with the Scientific Observer to enable the Scientific Observer to carry out the tasks assigned by the Commission. This will include access to data and to those operations of the vessel necessary to fulfil the duties of a Scientific Observer as required by the Commission.

(c) The Receiving Member will take appropriate action on board the vessel to ensure the security and welfare of the Scientific Observer in the performance of his/her duties, to provide him/her with medical care and to safeguard his/her freedom and dignity.

(d) Arrangements will be made by the Receiving Member for messages to be sent and received on behalf of the Scientific Observer through the vessel's communications system. Reasonable costs of such communications will be borne by the Designating Member.

(e) Arrangements involving the transportation and boarding of the Scientific Observer will be organized so as to minimize interference with harvesting and research operations.

(f) The Scientific Observer will provide to the master of the vessel copies of such records, prepared by the Scientific Observer, as the master may request.

(g) The Designating Member will ensure that the Scientific Observer carries insurance adequate to cover accidents and/or illness while the Scientific Observer is aboard the vessel. Such insurance will be to the satisfaction of both the Receiving and Designating Member.

(h) Transportation costs of the Scientific Observer to and from the boarding points will be borne by the Receiving Member.

(i) Unless otherwise agreed, the equipment, protective clothing, salary and any related allowances of the Scientific Observer will be borne by the Receiving Member. The vessel operator of the Receiving Member will bear the costs of the accommodation and meals of the scientific observer whilst he/she is on board the vessel.

(3) A copy of this Memorandum of Understanding will be forwarded to the Commission by the Designating Member.

(4) The primary mission of the Scientific Observer will be to collect information in accordance with the instruction of the Commission's Scientific Committee, Conservation Measures adopted by the Commission and such information as may be requested by the Secretariat of the Commission during the fishing season. The instructions of the Commission's Scientific Committee will constitute the schedule of activities which is hereby agreed to. The Scientific Observer will undertake the following tasks, using the observation formats approved by the Commission's Scientific Committee:

(a) Record details of the vessel's operation (e.g. partition of time between searching, fishing transit etc., and details of hauls, which should include basic data on the method, timing and duration ["soak time"] of setting and hauling lines [including number and type of hooks, their spacing, type of bait etc.]);

(b) Take samples of catches to determine biological characteristics including a statistically adequate sample of otoliths and scales from the targeted species of subsequent analysis;

(c) Record biological data by species caught, including length frequency and weight;

(d) Record all by-catches, their quantity and other biological data, including invertebrate (e.g. crab) species;

(e) Record the interaction and incidental mortality of seabirds and mammals during as many sets and hauls of the lines as possible (preferably a minimum of 20 sets and hauls), specifically recording –
   i. the number of species of seabirds at risk from long lining operations and seabirds in close proximity to the line;
   ii. the number of baits removed, or attempt to be removed by seabirds, and
   iii. the number of seabirds taken on board, definitely hooked, probably hooked, possibly hooked and not hooked, and
   iv. the species, sex, and age of seabirds taken on board, plus ring number if applicable.

(f) Record the procedure by which declared catch weight is measured and collect data relating to the conversion factors between green weight and final product in the event that catch is recorded on the basis of weight or processed product;

(g) Submit copies of reports to the master of the vessel;

(h) Assist, if requested, the master of the vessel in the catch recording and reporting procedures, and

(i) Validate scientific information essential for the assessment of the status of populations of Antarctic marine living resources, and for the assessment of the impact of fishing on those populations.

(5) All requests to the Scientific Observer for information, data and/or specimens, other than that set out in subarticle (3) above, made by either of the parties will receive a lesser priority in the scientific observer's schedule and will be confirmed by both the Designating and Receiving Members.

(6) The Scientific Observer will be a national of the Designating Member and will conduct himself/herself in accordance with the customs and orders existing aboard the vessel of assignment.

(7) The Scientific Observer will be familiar with the activities to be observed and the provisions of CCAMLR and the Conservation Measures adopted under it. The Scientific Observer will be adequately trained to competently carry out the duties of scientific observation. The scientific observer will be able to communicate in the language of the Receiving Member. For the purpose of this Memorandum, the official language of the Receiving Member will be deemed to be English.

(8) The Scientific Observer will carry a document issued by the Designating Member which identifies the individual as a scientific observer in accordance with Article XXIV of the CCAMLR. The Scientific Observer will, on boarding the vessel, hand the master of the vessel a copy of an agreed schedule of activities (as specified in subarticle (3) above) and hand the master a copy of this Memorandum of Understanding, and

(9) Within one month of the Observer's return to the United Kingdom, the Scientific Observer will submit to the CCAMLR Secretariat, through the respective authorities, a report on his/her observations, information gathered, data and scientific specimens acquired on the cruise using the formats required by the Scientific Committee. The Designating Member will submit the report to the next annual meeting of the Scientific Committee and Commission as an information paper.

Article III

The Designating Member and the Receiving Member have entered into this memorandum of understanding in the spirit of scientific co-operation under the CCAMLR Scheme of International Scientific Observation in order to gather and present scientific information essential for the assessment of the status of populations and ecosystems in CCAMLR waters.

Article IV

The costs and travel itinerary of the Scientific Observer, and such other details, will be determined by consultation between the Receiving and Designating Member.

Article V Settlement of Disputes

Any disputes between the Members arising out of the interpretation or implementation of this Memorandum of Understanding will be settled amicably through consultation or negotiation between them.

Article VI Entry into Effect, Duration and Termination

(1) This Memorandum of Understanding will enter into effect upon signature. The date of entry into effect will be the date of signature.

(2) This Memorandum of Understanding may be amended at any time by mutual consent of the Members through an exchange of notes between the Members. Such an amendment will come into effect on the date of the last of the two Notes.

(3) This Memorandum of Understanding will remain in effect until it is terminated upon six months written notice of termination by a Member to the other Member.

Signed in duplicate copies in the English language, both being duly authentic.

[Signatories omitted].

Convenio sobre Cooperacion Antartica Entre los Gobiernos de la Republica de Chile y la Republica de Italia (1997)[25]

La República de Chile y la República de Italia, en adelante denominadas "las Partes",

Teniendo en cuenta el Convenio Básico de Cooperación Económica, Industrial, Científico-Tecnológica, Técnica y Cultural, suscrito entre ambos países el 8 de noviembre de 1990 en Santiago de Chile, y el Acuerdo de Cooperación Científica y Tecnológica, suscrito el 18 de abril de 1991.

Considerando que los Artículos II y III del Tratado Antártico, el Protocolo sobre Protección del Medio Ambiente del Tratado Antártico y las Recomendaciones, otorgan gran prioridad a la cooperación internacional en la realización de las actividades científicas.

Reconociendo la creciente importancia de la Antártica para la investigación científica, especialmente para el medio ambiente global y conscientes de la necesidad de maximizar la producción científica para que el impacto sea mínimo.

Tomando en cuenta la decisión de las Partes del Tratado Antártico de designar el período 1991–2000 como la "Década de la Cooperación Científica Internacional Antártica".

Convienen lo siguiente:

Articulo I

Las Partes convienen en establecer a través de sus respectivos Ministerios de Relaciones Exteriores, un mecanismo de consulta permanente, relativo a materias de interés común en las áreas política, jurídica, científica, medioambiental y otras, en el marco del Sistema del Tratado Antártico.

Con este objeto, las Partes se esforzarán por coordinar sus respectivas posiciones en diferentes foros internacionales con competencia en esas materias, respetando sus intereses mutuos y llevando a la práctica la letra y el espíritu del Tratado Antártico.

Articulo II

Las Partes harán todo cuanto esté a su alcance para operar conjuntamente, con el objeto de utilizar mejor las posibilidades de cooperación previstas en el Tratado Antártico y de optimizar los recursos humanos y materiales correspondientes, respondiendo a la necesidad de plantear una mejor planificación para perfeccionar los estudios interdisciplinarios entre sus respectivas comunidades científicas.

Articulo III

Las Partes cooperarán con actividades orientadas a los siguientes objetivos:

[25] Adopted 31 October 1997.

a) Desarrollar la investigación científica y tecnológica en proyectos conjuntos a objeto de obtener un conocimiento más amplio, principalmente con respecto a la protección del medio ambiente antártico y sus ecosistemas dependientes y asociados.
Del mismo modo, establecer equipos conjuntos de expertos para evaluar el posible impacto sobre el medio ambiente antártico de sus respectivas actividades en el área y, además, promover el intercambio de personal científico y logístico para colaborar en proyectos de común interés en los respectivos entes antárticos.
b) Intercambiar información y desarrollar proyectos y experiencias comunes en las respectivas estaciones de cada país, con el fin de proporcionar apoyo logístico moderno y eficiente a las actividades científicas, teniendo en cuenta el medio ambiente antártico y el impacto que produce la presencia humana en la Antártica.
c) La capacitación de recursos humanos mediante la aplicación de conocimientos científicos y tecnológicos modernos a fin de contar con un grupo de investigadores, administradores y técnicos especializados principalmente en el medio ambiente antártico.
Igualmente, en el mismo espíritu, habrá intercambio de expertos, personal científico, logístico y tecnológico para participar en programas de capacitación realizados en las instalaciones físicas de cualquiera de las Partes Contratantes. La capacitación de recursos humanos deberá considerar programas y actividades académicas conducentes a la obtención de títulos de postgrado (tales como Master en Ciencias, Doctor en Ciencias o equivalentes).
d) Las Partes podrán conforme a sus capacidades proporcionarse mutuamente transporte y alojamiento para el personal y carga a bordo de sus propios barcos, aviones y estaciones o refugios durante las campañas antárticas, de acuerdo con el Artículo V del presente Convenio.
e) El intercambio de experiencias relacionadas con el desarrollo tecnológico de asentamientos humanos y con actividades turísticas en áreas polares.

Articulo IV

Para los fines señalados precedentemente, las Partes designan respectivamente, al Instituto Antártico Chileno, organismo técnico del Ministerio de Relaciones Exteriores, en adelante "INACH", y al Ente Para las Nuevas Tecnologías, la Energía y el Medio Ambiente, organismo coordinador del Programa Antártico Italiano en adelante "ENEA-Proyecto Antártico", como las instituciones dedicadas a llevar a cabo dichos fines y que disponen de órganos intermediarios para coordinar las actividades científicas y logísticas con los organismos nacionales.

Articulo V

1. – Las Partes convienen que el INACH y el ENEA-Proyecto Antártico, harán cuanto estará a su alcance para obtener lo siguiente:

a) Desarrollar y coordinar conjuntamente proyectos de investigación científica, médica y tecnológica en virtud de este Convenio.
b) Establecer un sistema de intercambio de información en materias de orden científico, tecnológico y apoyo logístico.
c) Compartir información que pueda ser de utilidad en la planificación y desarrollo de actividades en el área del Tratado Antártico, con el objeto de proteger el medio ambiente antártico y sus ecosistemas dependientes y asociados, entre otros.
d) Intercambiar datos científicos obtenidos en proyectos similares, para la elaboración de investigación conjunta, en conformidad con los principios previamente establecidos en cada proyecto de investigación.
e) Participar a través de proyectos científicos conjuntos en sus respectivas expediciones antárticas.
f) Capacitar a profesionales y técnicos en materias antárticas, intercambiando a estas

personas con el objeto de maximizar la utilización de instalaciones y equipos científicos en cualquiera de los dos países.

g) Enfatizar y promover aspectos científicos relativos a la ciencia antártica que son de gran interés para ambos países, especialmente en áreas como: Física Atmosférica y Meteorológica, Radiación Cósmica, Cosmología, Oceanografía, Ciencias de la Tierra, Ciencias del Mar, Biología, Medicina, Ecología, estudios Medio Ambientales e investigaciones tecnológicas.

h) Intercambiar profesionales del área logística para que conozcan la aplicación y desarrollo de esta técnica de apoyo en la Antártica.

2. – Los gastos de traslados ocasionados para el cumplimiento de las actividades señaladas anteriormente, serán asumidos por el país que envía al personal científico, técnico y logístico, y los gastos de estadía serán de cargo del país receptor.

Articulo VI

En el espíritu de la Década de la Cooperación Científica Internacional en la Antártica y considerando los programas de cooperación antártica que tienen Chile e Italia con otros países, el INACH y el ENEA-Proyecto Antártico, estudiarán la posibilidad de ampliar su cooperación bilateral a nuevos proyectos multilaterales para lo cual, contando con la aprobación de los Jefes de Proyectos que se encuentran actualmente en desarrollo y, en la medida de sus posibilidades financieras, incluirán aquellos aspectos de financiamiento y transporte para sus científicos y personal logístico que sean necesarios, a fin de cumplir con estos objetivos.

Articulo VII

El INACH y el ENEA-Proyecto Antártico elaborarán con al menos un año de anticipación, el programa de acción conjunta que incluya los objetivos señalados en los Artículos III y V del presente Convenio.

Articulo VIII

Cualquiera controversia que pudiere surgir en relación con la interpretación o aplicación del presente Convenio de Cooperación Antártica, que no pueda ser resuelta por los organismos designados por las Partes en el Artículo IV, deberá ser notificada a los respectivos Ministerios de Relaciones Exteriores a través de los cuales se llevarán a cabo las negociaciones necesarias para lograr una solución.

Articulo IX

El presente Convenio entrará en vigor en la fecha de la última notificación, en que las Partes se comuniquen recíprocamente, por los canales diplomáticos, el cumplimiento de las formalidades requeridas por sus ordenamientos jurídicos internos.

Articulo X

Este Convenio permanecerá en vigencia indefinidamente. Sin embargo, podrá ser denunciado por cualquiera de las Partes. La denuncia producirá sus efectos seis meses después de su notificación a la otra Parte. La denuncia no afectará a los plazos de las acciones iniciadas durante su vigencia.

Articulo Transitorio

Las Partes continuarán con el desarrollo e implementación de los siguientes proyectos, actualmente en vigencia:

1) Radiación Cósmica o Monitoreo de Neutrones;
2) Geodinámica y Evolución de los Procesos Volcánicos en los Rifs de Bransfield y Príncipe Gustavo, y su Relación con la Región Austral;
3) Telemedicina en la Antártica.

En fe de lo cual, los representantes suscritos, debidamente autorizados por sus Gobiernos respectivos, firman el presente Acuerdo.

Hecho en la ciudad de Roma, a los 31 días del mes de octubre de 1997, en dos originales, cada uno en idioma español y en italiano, siendo todos textos igualmente auténticos.

[Signatories omitted].

Agreement concerning Antarctic Cooperation between the Government of the Argentine Republic and the Government of the Republic of Peru (2001)[26]

The Government of the Argentine Republic and the Government of the Republic of Peru,

Reaffirming their desire to strengthen their proverbial bilateral ties and to promote the full implementation of the Antarctic Treaty,

Hereby agree as follows:

Article I

The two Governments shall consult each other through their Ministries of Foreign Affairs on political, legal, scientific or other matters of common interest that may arise in the context of the Antarctic Treaty System.

Consequently, they shall endeavour to coordinate their positions in the various international forums where issues relating to Antarctica are dealt with, respecting each other's legitimate interests in Antarctica in accordance with the Antarctic Treaty.

Article II

The two Governments hereby agree to work together to make use of the opportunities for international cooperation provided for in the Antarctic Treaty System, particularly with regard to science, technology, logistics and the environment, in order to improve their knowledge of the Antarctic continent and its adjacent maritime and atmospheric areas to the south of 60 degrees south latitude.

Article III

The two Governments hereby express their interest in coordinating their efforts in Antarctica through the implementation of joint and cooperative projects in science, technology, logistics and the environment.

Article IV

The two competent national technical bodies for activities in Antarctica – the National Antarctic Office of the Argentine Republic and the National Commission for Antarctic Affairs of the Republic of Peru – shall endeavour to promote joint and cooperative programmes in those areas where it is feasible, on the basis of the national regulations in force; in particular, scientific and technological cooperation may be carried out through:

- The participation of scientists and technicians from one country in Antarctic expeditions carried out using logistical resources from the national programme of the other country;
- The exchange of scientific and technical personnel between the two countries' institutions, chiefly between the scientific bases in Antarctica and between other national institutions;
- Scientific meetings and joint research on previously agreed topics and projects;
- Share use of scientific research facilities and laboratories in Antarctica and in other places for the development of programmes relating to disciplines relevant to Antarctica;
- Training and development for scientific and support personnel;
- Increased bibliographic exchange and publication of joint scientific publications;
- Shared use of logistical resources with a view to rationalizing costs and minimizing the impact on the Antarctic environment and its associated ecosystems;
- Promotion of technology exchange with respect to logistics and basic facilities and equipment;
- Transport of Peruvian personnel and freight to Antarctica, on board an ice-breaker or other appropriate Argentine-flagged vessels assigned to the Argentine Antarctic Programme, and at the request of the National Commission for Antarctic Affairs, subject to the availability of space and the established compensation of costs

[26] Adopted 1 March 2001, entered into force 16 December 2002, 2636 UNTS 279.

- Air transport of passengers and freight on aircraft of the Argentine Air Force and the Peruvian Air Force, which operate flights to Antarctica at the request of the National Commission for Antarctic Affairs and the National Antarctic Office respectively, subject to the availability of space and the established compensation of costs;
- Taking of the necessary steps to facilitate the stay in Argentine ports of vessels used by the National Commission for Antarctic Affairs in its Antarctic activities, and also logistical support and the transport of Peruvian personnel and equipment within Argentine territory;
- Resupply of fuel and provisions for Peruvian vessels in Argentine ports.

Any cost occasioned by assistance from one Party to the other Party shall be borne by the Party that uses the services in question, in an amount that shall be determined by mutual agreement.

Article V

The National Antarctic Office and the National Commission for Antarctic Affairs, in consultation with the respective Ministries of Foreign Affairs, shall, in the second quarter of each year, agree on a plan of action to be followed and also on joint projects for scientific, technological, logistical and environmental cooperation, and shall determine arrangements and activities for the following year.

Article VI

The present Agreement shall enter into force on the date on which the respective instruments of ratification are exchanged. It shall remain in force for three (3) years and shall be renewed automatically for periods of equal duration, unless one of the Parties notifies the other, through the diplomatic channel, of its intention to terminate it, at least three (3) months before the end of each period.

The termination of the present Agreement shall not affect activities planned or under way pursuant to the Agreement, unless otherwise agreed.

DONE at Lima on 1 March 2001, in two original copies in Spanish, both being equally authentic.

[Signatories omitted].

Memorandum of Understanding between the Government of the Federative Republic of Brazil and the Government of the United Kingdom of Great Britain and Northern Ireland concerning the Scheme of International Scientific Observation of the Convention for the Conservation of Antarctic Living Marine Resources (2001)[27]

The Government of the Federative Republic of Brazil and The Government of the United Kingdom of Great Britain and Northern Ireland (hereinafter referred to as "the Members"), Being Parties to the Convention on the Conservation of Antarctic Marine Living Resources, done at Canberra on 20 May 1990 (hereinafter referred to as "CCAMLR"), In order to promote the objectives and ensure observance of the provisions of CCAMLR; Have reached the following understanding concerning their respective responsibilities in relation to taking designated Scientific Observers on board their vessels engaged in scientific research into or the harvesting of marine living resources.

Paragraph I

The Member wishing to receive a Scientific Observer (hereinafter referred to as the "Receiving Member") under the provisions of this Memorandum will take appropriate measures within its competence to ensure that a Scientific Observer, designated by the Member providing the Scientific Observer under this Memorandum (hereinafter referred to the "Designating Member"), will be taken on board a vessel, licensed by the Receiving Member to fish in the CCAMLR

[27] Adopted and entered into force 29 May 2001, 2154 UNTS 157.

Area, to observe and report on the activities of the vessel in accordance with the CCAMLR Scheme of International Scientific Observation (hereinafter referred to as "the Scheme"). In each case the vessel will be agreed by the Members.

This Memorandum will be the subject, where required, of implementing provisions in the form of exchanges of Notes between the Members.

Paragraph II

1. This Memorandum will operate in accordance with the Scheme or as otherwise provided in the specific terms of this Memorandum and the implementing provisions.

2. The Scientific Observer will be accommodated aboard the vessel agreed under Paragraph I and in accordance with the following provisions:

a) the Scientific Observer will be given the status of a ship's officer. Accommodation and the meals for the Scientific Observer on board will be of a standard commensurate with this status;
b) the Receiving Member will ensure that its vessel operators co-operate fully with the Scientific Observer to enable him/her to carry out the tasks assigned to him/her by the Commission. This will include access to data and to those operations of the vessel necessary to fulfil the duties of Scientific Observer as required by the Commission;
c) the Receiving Member will take appropriate action on board its vessel to ensure the security and welfare of the Scientific Observer in the performance of their duties, provide him/her with medical care and safeguard his/her freedom and dignity;
d) arrangements will be made by the Receiving Member for messages to be sent and received on behalf of the Scientific Observer using the vessel's communications equipment and operators. Reasonable costs of such communications will be borne by the Designating Member, unless otherwise agreed by the Members;
e) arrangements for the transportation and boarding of the Scientific Observer will be organised so as to minimise interference with harvesting and research operations;
f) the Scientific Observer will provide to the master of the vessel copies of such records prepared by the Scientific Observer as the Captain may request;
g) the Designating Member will provide to the Receiving Member, through the pertinent authority, within one month of the Scientific Observer's return to his/her home territory, a copy of the records and final reports provided by the Scientific Observer;
h) the Designating Member will ensure that the Scientific Observer is covered by satisfactory insurance;
i) the Designating Member will bear the Scientific Observer's transportation and accommodation costs before embarkation and after disembarkation. The vessel owners will be responsible for the Scientific Observer's onboard accommodation and meals.

3. The primary function of the Scientific Observer is to collect information in accordance with the instructions of the Scientific Committee of CCAMLR (hereinafter referred to as "the Scientific Committee"). In fulfilling this function, Scientific Observers will undertake the following tasks using observation formats approved by the Scientific Committee, with reference to the list of current research priorities identified by the Scientific Committee for conducting scientific observations on commercial fishing vessels:

a) record details of the vessel's operation (e.g. partition of time between searching, fishing, transit etc), and details of hauls, which should include basic data on the method, timing and duration of shooting and hauling nets;
b) take samples of catches to determine biological characteristics including a statistically adequate sample of otoliths and scales of the targeted species for subsequent analysis;
c) record biological data by species caught, including length/frequency and weight;
d) record all by-catches, their quantity and other biological data, including invertebrate (e.g. crab) species;

e) record the interactions and incidental mortality of seabirds and mammals during as many trawls as possible, specifically recording:
   - number and species of seabirds at risk from the trawling operations and seabirds in close proximity to the net;
   - number of seabirds definitely/probably/possibly not caught in the net, the number of seabirds taken on board, the species/sex/age of seabirds, plus ring number if applicable;

f) record the procedure by which declared catch weight is measured and collect data relating to the conversion factor between green weight and final product in the event that catch is recorded on the basis of weight of processed product;
g) submit copies of reports to the master of the vessel;
h) assist, if requested, the master of the vessel in the catch recording and reporting procedures;
i) validate scientific information essential for the assessment of the status of populations of Antarctic marine living resources and for the assessment of the impact of fishing on those populations;
j) prepare reports on the observations using the specified observation formats (approved by the Scientific Committee) and submit them to CCAMLR through the respective authorities not later than one month after the return of the Scientific Observer to his/her home territory.
k) as part of item (c), and in the format of item (j) collect and submit to the Commission data on the length composition of the catch (B2 data), so that the Receiving Member need not additionally submit B2 forms to the Commission.

4. All requests to the Scientific Observer for information, data and/or specimens, other than those set out in paragraph 3 above, made by either of the Members will receive a lesser priority in the Scientific Observer's schedule and will be agreed by both Members.

5. The Scientific Observer will be a national of the Designating Member and will conduct himself/herself in accordance with customs and orders existing aboard the vessel.

6. The Scientific Observer will be familiar with the activities to be observed and the provisions of CCAMLR and Conservation Measures adopted under it. The Scientific Observer will be adequately trained to carry out competently the duties of scientific observation. The Scientific Observer will be able to communicate in the language of the Receiving Member.

7. The Scientific Observer will carry a document issued by the Designating Member which identifies the individual as a Scientific Observer in accordance with Article XXIV of CCAMLR. The Scientific Observer will, on boarding the vessel, hand the master of the vessel a copy of this Memorandum, of any bilateral implementing provisions and a copy of Annex I of the Scheme.

8. Within one month of the Scientific Observer's return to his/her home territory, the Scientific Observer will submit to the Commission, through the Designating Member, a report on his/her observations, information gathered, data and scientific specimens acquired on the cruise using the formats required by the Scientific Committee.

Paragraph III

Other detailed costs, and travel itinerary of the Scientific Observer, and any other matters, will be determined through consultations between the Members.

Paragraph IV

Any dispute between the Members concerning the interpretation or implementation of this Memorandum will be settled through consultations between the Members.

Paragraph V

1. This Memorandum will come into effect upon signature.

2. This Memorandum may be amended at any time by mutual decision recorded in an exchange of notes between the Members.

3. This Memorandum will remain in effect until it is terminated by three months written notice given by either Member to the other.

4. A copy of this Memorandum will be forwarded to the CCAMLR Commission by the Designating Member.

Signed at Brasilia, on May 29, 2001 in Portuguese and English, both texts being equally authentic.

[Signatories omitted].

Memorandum of Understanding between the Government of the Republic of Korea and the Government of the United Kingdom of Great Britain and Northern Ireland concerning the Scheme of International Scientific Observation of the Commission for the Conservation of Antarctic Marine Living Resources (2001)[28]

The Government of the Republic of Korea and the Government of the United Kingdom of Great Britain and Northern Ireland (hereinafter referred to as the "Members"), being parties to the Convention on the Conservation of Antarctic Marine Living Resources ("CCAMLR");

In order to promote the objectives, and ensure observance of the provisions, of CCAMLR; and

In particular scientific co-operation under the CCAMLR Scheme of International Scientific Observation;

Have reached the following understandings:

Section 1

The Member wishing to receive a Scientific Observer ("Receiving Member") will take appropriate measures within its competence to ensure that a Scientific Observer designated by the other Member ("Designating Member"), will be taken on board such fishing vessels as may be agreed before the commencement of fishing, to observe and report on the activities of the said vessel as envisaged by Article XXIV(2) of CCAMLR. The vessel will be conducting fishing for Champsocephalus gunnari in Statistical Subarea 48.3, and will be subject to Conservation Measure 219/XX, and any other Conservation Measures in force for the targeted species.

Section 2

1. This Memorandum will operate in accordance with the terms of the Scheme of International Scientific Observation adopted by the CCAMLR Commission (the "Commission") at its XIth meeting in 1992.

2. The Scientific Observer will be accommodated aboard the vessel agreed under Section 1, and in accordance with the following arrangements:

(a) The Scientific Observer will be accorded the status of a ship's officer. Accommodation and meals for the Scientific Observer on board will be of a standard commensurate with this status.

(b) The Receiving Member will ensure that the vessel operator co-operates fully with the Scientific Observer to enable the Scientific Observer to carry out the tasks assigned by the Commission. This will include access to data and to those operations of the vessel necessary to fulfil the duties of a Scientific Observer as required by the System of Observation.

(c) The Receiving Member will take appropriate action to ensure the security and welfare of the Scientific Observer on board the vessel, to provide him/her with medical care and to safeguard his/her freedom and dignity.

(d) Arrangements will be made by the Receiving Member for messages to be sent and received on behalf of the Scientific Observer through the vessel's communications system. Unless otherwise agreed, reasonable costs of such communications will be borne by the Designating Member.

(e) Arrangements involving the transportation and boarding of the Scientific Observer will be organised so as to minimise interference with harvesting and research operations.

[28] Adopted and entered into force 20 December 2001, 2395 UNTS 271.

(f) The Scientific Observer will provide to the master of the vessel copies of such records prepared by the Scientific Observer, as the master may request.

(g) The Designating Member will ensure that the Scientific Observer carries insurance adequate to cover accidents and/or illness while the Scientific Observer is aboard the vessel. Such insurance will be to the satisfaction of both the Members.

(h) Unless otherwise agreed, the transportation costs of the Scientific Observer to and from the boarding points will be the responsibility of the Designating Member.

(i) Unless otherwise agreed, the equipment, protective clothing, salary and any related allowances of the Scientific Observer will be borne by the Designating Member. The vessel operator of the Receiving Member will bear the costs of the accommodation and meals of the Scientific Observer whilst he/she is on board the vessel.

3. A copy of this Memorandum will be forwarded to the Commission by the Designating Member.

4. The function of the Scientific Observer on board vessels engaged in scientific research or harvesting of marine living resources will be to observe and report on the operation of fishing activities in the Convention Area with the objectives and the principles of CCAMLR in mind. In fulfilling this function, scientific observers will undertake the following tasks using observation formats approved by the Scientific Committee, with reference to the list of current research priorities identified by the Scientific Committee for conducting scientific observations on commercial fishing vessels:

(a) Record details of the vessel's operation (e.g. partition of time between searching, fishing, transit etc.), and details of hauls, which should include basic data on the method, timing and duration of setting and hauling lines, trawls or other fishing gear;

(b) take samples of catches to determine biological characteristics including a statistically adequate sample of otoliths and scales of the targeted species for subsequent analysis;

(c) record biological data by species caught, including length frequency and weight;

(d) record all by-catches, their quantity and other biological data, including invertebrate (e.g. crab) species;

(e) record the interaction and incidental mortality of seabirds and mammals during as [many] trawls as possible, specifically recording:

 (i) the number of species of seabirds at risk from trawling operations and seabirds in close proximity to the net;

 (ii) the number of seabirds definitely/probably/possibly not caught in the net, the number of seabirds taken on board, the species/sex/age of seabirds, plus ring number if applicable.

(f) record the procedure by which declared catch weight is measured and collect data relating to the conversion factors between green weight and final product in the event that catch is recorded on the basis of weight or processed product;

(g) submit copies of reports to the master of the vessel;

(h) assist, if requested, the master of the vessel in the catch recording and reporting procedures;

(i) validate scientific information essential for the assessment of the status of populations of Antarctic marine living resources, and for the assessment of the impact of fishing on those populations;

(j) prepare reports on the observations using the specified observation formats (approved by the Scientific Committee) and submit them to CCAMLR through the respective authorities not later than one month after the return of the Scientific Observer to his/her home territory; and

(k) as part of item (c), and in the format of item (j) collect and submit to the Commission data on the length composition of the catch (B2 data), so that the Receiving Member need not additionally submit B2 forms to the Commission.

5. All requests to the Scientific Observer for information, data and/or specimens, other than those set out in paragraph 4 above, made by either of the Members will receive a lesser priority in the Scientific Observer's schedule and will be agreed by both Members.

6. The Scientific Observer will be a national of the Designating Member and will conduct himself/herself in accordance with the customs and orders existing on board the vessel.

7. The Scientific Observer will be familiar with the activities to be observed and the provisions of CCAMLR and Conservation Measures adopted under it. The Scientific Observer will be adequately trained to carry out competently the duties of scientific observation. The Scientific Observer will be able to communicate in the language of the Receiving Member. For the purpose of this Memorandum, the official language of the Receiving Member will be as agreed between the Members.

8. The Scientific Observer will carry a document issued by the Designating Member which identifies the individual as a Scientific Observer in accordance with Article XXIV of CCAMLR. The Scientific Observer will, on boarding the vessel, hand the master of the vessel a copy of an agreed schedule of activities (as specified in paragraph 4 above) and a copy of this Memorandum.

9. Within one month of the Scientific Observer's return to his/her home territory, the Scientific Observer will submit to the Commission, through the Designating Member, a report on his/her observations, information gathered, data and scientific specimens acquired on the cruise using the formats required by the Scientific Committee.

Section 3

Other detailed costs, and travel itinerary of the Scientific Observer, and any other matters, will be determined through consultations between the Members.

Section 4. Settlement of Disputes

Any disputes arising out of interpretation or implementation of this Memorandum will be settled through consultations between the Members.

Section 5. Entry into Effect, Duration and Termination

(1) This Memorandum will enter into effect upon signature.

(2) This Memorandum may be amended at any time by mutual decision recorded in an exchange of notes between the Members.

(3) This Memorandum will remain in effect until it is terminated by six months written notice by one Member to the other.

Signed at London on this 20th day of December 2001, in duplicate in the English Language, both versions being equally valid.

[Signatories omitted].

Memorandum of Understanding between the Government of the Republic of Korea and the Government of the United Kingdom of Great Britain and Northern Ireland concerning the Scheme of International Scientific Observation of the Commission for the Conservation of Antarctic Marine Living Resources (2002)[29]

The Government of the Republic of Korea and the Government of the United Kingdom of Great Britain and Northern Ireland (hereinafter referred to as the "Members"), being Parties to the Convention on the Conservation of Antarctic Marine Living Resources ("CCAMLR");

In order to promote the objectives, and ensure observance of the provisions, of CCAMLR: and in particular scientific co-operation under the CCAMLR Scheme of International Scientific Observation:

[29] Adopted and entered into force 5 December 2002 (No UNTS Volume number has yet been determined for this record).

Have reached the following understandings:

Section 1

The Member wishing to receive one or more Scientific Observers ("Receiving Member") will take appropriate measures within its competence to ensure that any Scientific Observer designated by the other Member ("Designating Member"), will be taken on board such fishing vessels as may be agreed before the commencement of fishing, to observe and report on the activities of the said vessel as envisaged by Article XXIV (2) of CCAMLR and subject to any CCAMLR Conservation Measures in force for the targeted species.

Section 2

1. This Memorandum will operate in accordance with the terms of the Scheme of International Scientific Observation adopted by the CCAMLR Commission ("the Commission") at its XIth meeting in 1992.

2. The Scientific Observer(s) (hereinafter referred to as "the Scientific Observer") will be accommodated aboard the vessel agreed under Section 1, and in accordance with the following arrangements:

(a) The Scientific Observer will be accorded the status of a ship's officer while on board. Accommodation and meals for the Scientific Observer on board will be of a standard commensurate with this status.

(b) The Receiving Member will ensure that the vessel operator co-operates fully with the Scientific Observer to enable the Scientific Observer to carry out the tasks assigned by the Commission. This will include access to data and to those operations of the vessel necessary to fulfil the duties of a Scientific Observer as required by the System of Observation.

(c) The Receiving Member will take appropriate action to ensure the security and welfare of the Scientific Observer in the performance of his/her duties on board the vessel, to provide him/her with medical care and to safeguard his/her freedom and dignity.

(d) Arrangements will be made by the Receiving Member for messages to be sent, and received on behalf of the Scientific Observer through the vessel's communications system. Reasonable costs of such communications will normally be borne by the Designating Member.

(e) Arrangements involving the transportation and boarding of the Scientific Observer will be organised so as to minimise interference with harvesting and research operations.

(f) The Scientific Observer will provide to the master of the vessel copies of records he/she has prepared.

(g) The Designating Member will ensure that the Scientific Observer carries insurance adequate to cover accidents and/or illness while aboard the vessel. Such insurance will be to the satisfaction of both the Members.

(h) The transportation costs of the Scientific Observer to and from the boarding points will be borne by the Designating Member.

(i) Unless otherwise agreed, the equipment, protective clothing, salary and any related allowances of the Scientific Observer will be borne by the Designating Member. The vessel operator of the Receiving Member will bear the costs of the accommodation and meals of the Scientific Observer whilst he/she is on board the vessel.

3. A copy of this Memorandum will be forwarded to the Commission by the United Kingdom. The Designating Member will inform the Commission of each deployment of International Scientific Observers.

4. The function of the Scientific Observer on board vessels engaged in scientific research or harvesting of marine living resources will be to observe and report on the operation of fishing activities in the CCAMLR Area with the objectives and the principles of CCAMLR in mind. In fulfilling this function, Scientific Observers will undertake the following tasks using observation formats approved by the Scientific Committee, with reference to the list of current

research priorities identified by the Scientific Committee for conducting scientific observations on commercial fishing vessels:

(a) Record details of the vessel's operation (e.g. partition of time between searching, fishing, transit etc. and details of hauls, which should include basic data on the method, timing and duration of setting and hauling lines, trawls or other fishing gear);

(b) take samples of all species caught (including fish, krill, crabs and other invertebrates) to determine biological characteristics including where appropriate a statistically adequate sample of otoliths, statoliths or scales of the targeted species for subsequent analysis;

(c) record biological data by species caught, including length frequency and weight, and retain biological samples as necessary;

(d) record all by-catches of all species, their quantity and biological and length frequency data, including invertebrate (e.g. crab) species, and retain biological samples as necessary;

(e) record details of the gear used and the procedure by which declared catch weight is measured and collect data relating to the conversion factors between green weight and final product in the event that catch is recorded on the basis of weight or processed product;

(f) submit copies of reports to the master of the vessel;

(g) assist, if requested, the master of the vessel in the catch recording and reporting procedures:

(h) validate scientific information essential for the assessment of the status of populations of Antarctic marine living resources, and for the assessment of the impact of fishing on those populations;

(i) prepare reports on the observations using the specified observation formats (approved by the Scientific Committee) and submit them to the Commission through the respective authorities not later than one month after the return of the Scientific Observer to his/her home territory; and

(j) as part of item (c), and in the format of item (i) collect and submit to the Commission data required by relevant Conservation Measures, so that the Receiving Member need not additionally submit such data to the Commission;

(k) record entanglement and incidental mortality of birds and mammals;

(l) collect and report factual data on sightings of fishing vessels in the CCAMLR Area, including vessel type identification, position and activity; and

(m) collect information on fishing gear loss and garbage disposal by fishing vessels at sea.

5. All requests to the Scientific Observer for information, data and/or specimens, other than those set out in paragraph 4 above, made by either of the Members will receive a lesser priority in the Scientific Observer's schedule and will be agreed by both Members.

6. The Scientific Observer will be a national of the Designating Member and will conduct himself/herself in accordance with the customs and orders existing on board the vessel.

7. The Scientific Observer will be familiar with the activities to be observed and the provisions of CCAMLR and Conservation Measures adopted under it. The Scientific Observer will be adequately trained to carry out competently the duties of scientific observation. The Scientific Observer will be able to communicate in the language of the Receiving Member. For the purpose of this Memorandum, the official language of the Receiving Member will be as agreed between the Members.

8. The Scientific Observer will carry a document issued by the Designating Member which identifies the individual as a Scientific Observer in accordance with Article XXIV of CCAMLR. The ScientificObserver will, on boarding the vessel, hand the master of the vessel a copy of an agreed schedule of activities (as specified in paragraph 4. above) and a copy of this Memorandum.

9. Within one month of the Scientific Observer's return to his/her home territory, the Scientific Observer will submit to the Commission, through the Designating Member, a report on his/her observations, information gathered, data and scientific specimens acquired on the cruise using the formats required by the Scientific Committee.

Section 3

Other detailed costs, and travel itinerary of the Scientific Observer, and any other matters, will be determined through consultations between the Members.

Section 4 Settlement of Disputes

Any disputes arising out of interpretation or implementation of this Memorandum will be settled through consultations between the Members.

Section 5 Entry into Effect, Duration and Termination

1. This Memorandum will enter into effect upon signature.

2. This Memorandum may be amended at any time by mutual decision recorded in an exchange of notes between the Members.

3. This Memorandum will remain in effect until it is terminated by six months' written notice by one Member to the other.

Signed at London on this 5th day of December 2002.

[Signatories omitted].

Treaty between the Government of Australia and the Government of the French Republic on Cooperation in the Maritime Areas Adjacent to the French Southern and Antarctic Territories (TAAF), Heard Island and the McDonald Islands (2003)[30]

THE GOVERNMENT OF AUSTRALIA AND THE GOVERNMENT OF THE FRENCH REPUBLIC, hereinafter referred to as "the Parties",

Recalling their rights and responsibilities as coastal States under the United Nations Convention on the Law of the Sea of 10 December 1982 (hereinafter referred to as "the Convention"), and as Parties to the Convention on the Conservation of Antarctic Living Marine Resources of 20 May 1980 (hereinafter referred to as "the CAMLR Convention"),

Recognising that the Parties exercise jurisdiction, in accordance with international law, for the purpose of exploring, exploiting, conserving and managing the living resources within the maritime areas adjacent to the Australian territory of Heard Island and the McDonald Islands and the French Southern and Antarctic Territories (TAAF),

Recalling the principles of the Code of Conduct for Responsible Fishing of 31 October 1995,

Noting the Parties' concerns at the continued problem of illegal fishing, within the maritime areas adjacent to these maritime areas, in continued breach of the laws and regulations of the Parties,

Mindful that cooperation between the Parties is essential to the protection of their national interests in these maritime areas,

Determined to enhance their ability to take cooperative action to preserve and protect fisheries,

Conscious that the cooperative action between the Parties should encompass cooperative surveillance and law enforcement operations, including through developing further agreements or arrangements,

Recognising the need to promote the progressive development of international law in order to further their joint objectives;

Desiring to ensure the implementation of the Agreement of 15 July 1985 between the Government of Australia and the Government of the Republic of France relating to the Exchange and Communication of Classified Information,

Conscious of the important role that the Agreement of 4 January 1982 on Maritime Delimitation between the Government of Australia and the Government of the French Republic (hereinafter referred to as "the Maritime Delimitation Agreement") will play in this Treaty,

---

[30] Adopted 24 November 2003, entered into force 1 February 2005, 2438 UNTS 253.

Desiring to also promote scientific research in those maritime areas, and to further develop friendly relations between the Parties,

As a First Step, Have Agreed as Follows:

Article 1

1. This Treaty applies to activities conducted in relation to:

(a) the territorial seas and exclusive economic zone of the Australian territory of Heard Island and the McDonald Islands as defined respectively in the Seas and Submerged Lands Act 1973, proclamations pursuant thereto; and

(b) the territorial seas and exclusive economic zone of the French territories of Kerguelen Islands, Crozet Islands, Saint-Paul Island and Amsterdam Island as defined respectively in Law No. 71-1060 of 24 December 1971 and Law No. 76-655 of l6 July 1976; Decree No. 78-112 of 11 January 1978, and Decree No. 78-144 of 3 February 1978.

2. "Area of Cooperation" means the area of application of this Treaty as defined in paragraph (1) above. The boundary between the Australian maritime areas of Heard Island and McDonald Islands and the French maritime area of Kerguelen Islands is the same as that defined in paragraph 1 (points S1 to S7) of Article 2 of the Maritime Delimitation Agreement.

3. "Fishing" includes:

(a) locating, catching, taking or harvesting fish;

(b) attempting to locate, catch, take or harvest fish;

(c) engaging in any other activity which may result in the locating, catching, taking or harvesting of fish;

(d) placing, searching for or recovering fish aggregation devices or associated electronic equipment such as radio beacons;

(e) any operations at sea directly in support of, or in preparation for, any activity described in sub-paragraphs (a) to (d) above;

(f) use of any vehicle, air or sea borne, for any activity described in sub-paragraphs (a) to (e) above except for emergencies involving the health or safety of the crew or the safety of an air or sea borne vehicle; and

(g) the processing, carrying or transshipping of fish.

4. "Fishing vessel" means any boat, ship or other craft which is used for, or equipped to be used for fishing, including mother ships and any other vessels directly engaged in, or supporting such fishing operations.

5. "Cooperative surveillance" means fisheries surveillance activities, identification and recognition of vessels, in particular vessels that appear to be in breach of national or international fisheries law. These activities shall take the form of missions carried out:

(a) within the area defined in paragraph l(a) above – by French surveillance vessels and/or aircraft and/or any other means;

(b) within the area defined in paragraph l(b) above – by Australian surveillance vessels and/or aircraft and/or any other means; or

(c) within the Area of Cooperation, by the personnel authorised by the competent authorities of one of the Parties aboard surveillance vessels and/or aircraft of the other Party pursuant to a cooperative surveillance agreement or arrangement made under Annex III.

Article 2

The object of this Treaty is to enhance:

(a) cooperative surveillance;

(b) cooperative scientific research on marine living resources.

Article 3

1. The Parties may agree by common consent on procedures and forms of assistance, to facilitate the realisation of the aims of this Treaty.

2. Cooperative surveillance missions may be undertaken, with the consent of the competent authorities of each of the Parties, in conformity with the law applicable in the Area of Cooperation and with the common procedures established under this Treaty, and in particular under Annex I thereof. The competent authorities may attach conditions to their consent.

3. Each Party may request the assistance of the other Party when engaged in a hot pursuit, within the meaning of Article III of the Convention. Without prejudice to the agreements that may be reached pursuant to Article 2 of Annex III of this Treaty, such assistance shall include logistical support required to carry out the pursuit properly, including but not limited to the provision of food supplies, fuel and means of transport.

4. The Parties shall agree on a system for the surveillance of fishing in the Area of Cooperation. This may include:

(a) a vessel monitoring system;

(b) the adoption of agreed minimum standards for the vessel marking of fishing vessels licensed to fish in the Area of Cooperation.

5. Cooperative scientific research on marine living resources may be undertaken throughout the Area of Cooperation, in conformity with the law applicable in this area and with the modalities, if any, established in accordance with Annex II of this Treaty.

Article 4

In cases of hot pursuit commenced in accordance with Article III of the Convention, in relation to the Area of Cooperation, including hot pursuit commenced during activities pursuant to Article 1(5) and Annex III, such hot pursuit by a vessel or other craft authorised by one of the Parties may continue through the territorial sea of the other Party, provided that the other Party is informed, and without taking physical law enforcement or other coercive action against the vessel pursued during this phase of the hot pursuit.

Article 5

1. The competent authorities of the Parties shall, to the extent permitted by their national law and policies, exchange, inter alia, information about:

(a) the location, movements and other details of fishing vessels within the Area of Cooperation, including those suspected of fishing illegally;

(b) licensing of fishing vessels to conduct fishing within the waters mentioned in Article 1 paragraph 1 (a) and (b) above, belonging to the Area of Cooperation;

(c) cooperative surveillance activities;

(d) prosecutions instituted by each Party relating to illegal fishing in its territorial waters or exclusive economic zone included within the Area of Cooperation; and

(e) scientific research on marine living resources relating to the Area of Cooperation.

2. The competent authorities of the Parties shall develop standard forms and procedures for regular reporting and communication of the information provided under this Article. The information referred to in paragraph 1 (d) above shall be exchanged among the competent judicial, prosecutory or investigatory authorities of the two Parties.

3. The competent authorities of the Parties shall establish a shared vessel register of fishing vessels licensed to fish in their respective waters belonging to the Area of Cooperation.

4. To the extent that information passing between the Parties in accordance with this Treaty is information to which the Parties are privy, such information shall not be provided to third Parties by the Party that received the information without the written consent of the provider. Nothing in this clause shall prevent a Party from meeting its reporting obligations under the Convention or the CAMLR Convention.

5. Each Party shall provide written notice to the other Party identifying its competent authorities and contact details for those authorities. The first notice shall be provided within one month of the commencement of the Treaty. If at any time a Party's competent authorities change, that Party shall give notice in writing of the change within one month after the change has commenced.

Article 6

The competent authorities of the Parties shall hold consultations every two years to examine the implementation and effect of this Treaty.

Article 7

Nothing in this Treaty shall be deemed to derogate from the Parties' rights and obligations arising out of other international agreements to which either of them is a party, at the time of entry into force of this Treaty.

Article 8

The Annexes to this Treaty form an integral part of it and a reference to this Treaty includes a reference to the Annexes.

Article 9

This Treaty shall enter into force on the date on which the Parties have notified each other in writing, through diplomatic channels, that their internal procedures necessary for its entry into force have been met.

Article 10

This Treaty may be terminated by formal notification by one Party, by a note verbale, to the other Party. Termination shall take effect 12 months after the note verbale is received by the other Party. This Treaty may be amended at any time by common consent of the Parties. Any amendment shall take effect conditional upon completion of the procedures laid down in Article 9 of this Treaty.

IN WITNESS WHEREOF the undersigned, being duly authorised by their respective Governments,

have signed this Treaty.

DONE in duplicate at Canberra this 24th of November 2003 in the English and French languages,

both being equally authentic.

[Signatories omitted].

Annex I Approved Procedure for Cooperative Surveillance

Article 1

The competent authorities of each of the Parties shall communicate information concerning the timetable and duration of planned cooperative surveillance missions to the other Party, so as to permit effective surveillance of the Area of Cooperation.

Article 2

The competent authorities of the Party conducting a cooperative surveillance mission shall provide a report on this mission to the other Party as soon as practicable. Each Party shall notify the Secretariat of the Commission for the Conservation of Antarctic Marine Living Resources (CCAMLR) of any information resulting from any mission which took place in its territorial waters or in its exclusive economic zone mentioned in Articles 1(1) and 1(2) of this Treaty and which must be transmitted to CCAMLR on the basis of the CAMLR Convention.

Annex II Cooperative Scientific Research

Article 1

1. The national bodies principally responsible for research on marine living resources in the Area of Cooperation will promote and coordinate the conduct of research aimed at achieving the object of the Treaty.

2. The Parties shall notify each other of the national body or bodies that are principally responsible for research on marine living resources in the Area of Cooperation.

Article 2

To facilitate the development and effective operation of research programs, scientists of each Party shall meet on dates fixed as mutually convenient. The Parties shall facilitate, as far as possible, direct scientist-to-scientist communication.

Article 3

Cooperative research activities may take any of the following forms:

(a) exchanges of scientific and other personnel;
(b) joint research projects;
(c) exchanges of information and research data;
(d) logistic and technical cooperation; or
(e) other forms of cooperation as may be mutually decided by the Parties.

Article 4

The modalities under which cooperative research projects take place shall be mutually decided as appropriate from time to time and shall address the following elements:

(a) the title, description and objectives of the planned project;
(b) a national contact point for the project;
(c) a project leader for each Party;
(d) the division of activities between the Parties;
(e) the financial responsibilities of the Parties;
(t) the logistical responsibilities of the Parties;
(g) without prejudice to the implementation of the Agreement of 15 July 1985 between the Government of Australia and the Government of the French Republic relating to the Exchange and Communication of Classified Information, the arrangements for sharing and reporting of data, including any restrictions arising from the confidentiality of data and publication of results from the project; and
(h) the duration of the planned project.

Annex III Cooperative Surveillance Actions that may be the Subject of Further Agreements

Article 1

Any agreement or arrangement on cooperative surveillance should include in particular:

(a) the modalities of the missions mentioned in Article 3 of the Treaty;
(b) the alternative means by which communication of the results of surveillance missions should take place;
(c) questions relating to the reports which the Party conducting the cooperative surveillance shall communicate to the other Party;
(d) whether the patrols can contain officials of both Parties and, if so, under what conditions;
(e) additional powers, if any, to be granted to the Party conducting cooperative surveillance missions.

Article 2

The Parties may conclude agreements or arrangements that may also provide for law enforcement operations possibly accompanied by forcible measures.

Convenio de Cooperacion Cientifica en Materias Antarcticas entre la Republica de Chile y la Republica del Ecuador (2004)[31]

El Gobierno de la República de Chile y el Gobierno de la República del Ecuador, en adelante denominados "Las Partes",

Teniendo presente la prioridad que en los respectivos países se asigna al impulso de la presencia en el territorio antártico dentro de los propósitos de fomento de la paz, cooperación y conservación ambiental de este continente.

Considerando que los artículos II y III del Tratado Antártico y del Protocolo al Tratado Antártico sobre Protección del Medio Ambiente y sus Anexos, dan prioridad a la cooperación internacional en la ejecución de actividades científicas.

[31] Adopted 20 April 2004.

Reconociendo la creciente importancia de la Antártica para la investigación científica, especialmente para la comprensión del medio ambiente global y conscientes de la necesidad de optimizar la producción científica, velar por la protección ambiental y cooperar en la planificación de las actividades y procurar que el impacto en el medio ambiente antártico y en los ecosistemas dependientes y asociados sea el mínimo.

Conscientes de la conveniencia de complementar los recursos humanos, técnicos, científicos y materiales de sus países y aunar esfuerzos e iniciativas de investigación en el ámbito del Tratado Antártico.

Tomando en especial consideración la decisión de las Partes del Tratado Antártico de declarar el período 2007–2008 como el Año Polar Internacional,

Acuerdan lo siguiente:

Artículo I

Las Partes declaran su interés en colaborar para el desarrollo de programas, proyectos y actividades conjuntas de investigación científica y tecnológica en el continente Antártico, crear mecanismos para el intercambio de información y capacitación de personal científico y técnico, así como optimizar la utilización de sus recursos materiales, instalaciones y equipos existentes.

La cooperación a que se refiere el párrafo anterior propenderá a la realización de los objetivos y principios del Protocolo al Tratado Antártico sobre Protección del Medio Ambiente y sus Anexos (Protocolo de Madrid).

Artículo II

La cooperación establecida en el presente convenio se ejecutará a través de las siguientes modalidades:

1) Realización de programas de cooperación de valor científico, técnico y educativo relativos a la protección del medio ambiente antártico y sus ecosistemas dependientes y asociados y el establecimiento de equipos conjuntos para el estudio regional y global del estado del medio ambiente antártico.
2) Establecimiento de un sistema de intercambio de información sobre asuntos científicos, tecnológicos y de apoyo logístico, así como en la planificación y desarrollo de actividades en el área del Tratado Antártico.
3) Participación a través de proyectos científicos conjuntos en las respectivas expediciones antárticas.
4) Entrega de apoyo mutuo logístico que incluya transporte y, cuando procediere, el uso compartido de estaciones y demás instalaciones.

Artículo III

Las Partes otorgan especial interés a la capacitación e intercambio de expertos, personal científico, logístico y tecnológico para participar en programas de capacitación realizados en las instalaciones y sedes de las Partes. La capacitación de recursos humanos comprenderá, asimismo, programas y actividades académicas conducentes a la obtención de títulos de post-grado en las universidades e institutos de educación superior locales.

Artículo IV

La cooperación en el ámbito del medio ambiente antártico se orientará principalmente a la:

1) Creación de un Comité Bilateral de Conservación, con adecuada representación de las disciplinas relevantes.
2) Intercambio de información relativa a cualquier riesgo potencial al medio ambiente que pueda originarse por personal de las bases, científicos y visitantes en la Antártica y asistencia para minimizar sus efectos en caso de accidentes.
3) Intercambio de información y experiencias, así como apoyo mutuo en la presentación de evaluaciones del impacto ambiental y en el debido cumplimiento de las Medidas, Decisiones y Resoluciones adoptadas por las Reuniones Consultivas del Tratado Antártico y demás componentes del Sistema Antártico.

Artículo V

Las Partes designan como instancias de programación, seguimiento y evaluación de las actividades de cooperación científica previstas en el presente convenio, al Instituto Antártico Chileno (INACH), por parte de la República de Chile y al Instituto Antártico Ecuatoriano, por parte de la República del Ecuador.

Artículo VI

Ambas partes convienen en que las instancias nacionales de seguimiento y evaluación establecidas en el artículo anterior, establecerán un sistema de consultas periódicas con reuniones alternativas en Chile y Ecuador con el propósito de:

1) Programar, hacer el seguimiento y evaluar el avance de la cooperación establecida mediante el presente instrumento;
2) Intercambiar experiencias y coordinar posiciones comunes principalmente orientadas a las Reuniones Consultivas u otras de carácter internacional tales como la Reunión de Administradores de Programas Antárticos Latinoamericanos (RAPAL) y del Consejo de Administradores de Programas Nacionales Antárticos (COMNAP) que tengan lugar en el marco del Sistema Antártico.

Artículo VII

Los programas, proyectos y actividades previstos en el presente instrumento, serán cubiertos por las Partes bajo la modalidad de costos compartidos. En el caso de envío de personal científico, especialistas y demás personal técnico, los gastos de traslado serán asumidos por el país que envía al personal científico, técnico y logístico, en tanto, que los gastos de estadía serán de cargo del país receptor.

Para la ejecución de los programas, proyectos y actividades previstos en el presente convenio, las Partes celebrarán los acuerdos complementarios correspondientes.

Artículo VIII

El presente convenio entrará en vigor en la fecha de la última notificación por la cual una de las Partes notifique a la otra, a través de la vía diplomática, el cumplimiento de los procedimientos internos necesarios para tales efectos.

El presente convenio tendrá una duración indefinida. Sin embargo, cualquiera de las Partes podrá notificar a la otra su deseo de darlo por terminado, a través de la vía diplomática, con una anticipación de por lo menos ciento ochenta días.

La denuncia del presente convenio no afectará el cumplimiento de los proyectos y actividades en ejecución acordados durante su vigencia, los que se llevarán a cabo hasta su término, salvo acuerdo en contrario de las Partes.

Hecho en la ciudad de Santiago, Chile, a los veintidós días del mes de abril del año dos mil cuatro, en dos ejemplares originales, en idioma español, siendo ambos igualmente auténticos.

[Signatories omitted].

Convenio sobre Cooperacion Antartica Entre el Gobierno de la Republica de Chile y el Gobierno de la Republica de Bulgaria (2005)[32]

El Gobierno de la República de Chile y el Gobierno de la República de Bulgaria, en adelante denominadas "las Partes".

Reafirmando su voluntad de fortalecer sus vínculos bilaterales de cooperación y amistad entre ambas Partes.

Considerando que los Artículos II y III del Tratado Antártico y el Artículo VI del Protocolo al Tratado Antártico sobre Protección del Medio Ambiente y las Recomendaciones (Medidas, Decisiones y Resoluciones) de las Reuniones Consultivas del Tratado Antártico, otorgan gran prioridad a la cooperación internacional en la realización de las actividades científicas antárticas.

[32] Adopted 3 January 2005.

Reconociendo la creciente importancia de la Antártica para la investigación científica, especialmente para el medio ambiente global y conscientes de la necesidad de que las actividades científicas tengan un impacto mínimo sobre el medio ambiente antártico y sus ecosistemas dependientes y asociados.

Convienen lo siguiente:

Artículo I

Las Partes convienen en establecer a través de sus respectivos Ministerios de Relaciones Exteriores, un mecanismo de consulta permanente, relativo a materias de interés común en las áreas políticas, jurídicas, científicas, medioambientales y otras, en el marco del Sistema del Tratado Antártico.

Con este objeto, las Partes se esforzarán por intercambiar información sobre sus respectivas posiciones en diferentes foros internacionales con competencia en esas materias, respetando sus intereses individuales y llevando a la práctica la letra y el espíritu del Tratado Antártico.

Artículo II

Las Partes realizarán los máximos esfuerzos para emprender operaciones conjuntas, con el objeto de utilizar las posibilidades de cooperación previstas en el Tratado Antártico y en su Protocolo, de optimizar los recursos humanos y materiales correspondientes, y responder a la necesidad de evitar la duplicación de esfuerzos, tendientes a perfeccionar los estudios interdisciplinarios que pudieren desarrollarse entre sus respectivas comunidades científicas antárticas.

Las Partes revisarán periódicamente la aplicación del presente Convenio, considerando sus avances y posibilidades de perfeccionamiento.

Artículo III

Las Partes cooperarán específicamente, en el área del Tratado Antártico, en las siguientes actividades:

a) Desarrollar proyectos conjuntos de investigación científica y tecnológica concordantes con los objetivos de sus respectivos programas nacionales antárticos.
b) Intercambiar información de interés mutuo sobre el posible impacto en el medio ambiente antártico y en los ecosistemas dependientes y asociados de sus respectivas actividades en sus estaciones y refugios antárticos o en otros proyectos en el área del Tratado.
c) Propender a la formación y capacitación de recursos humanos, mediante el intercambio de expertos, personal científico, logístico y técnico, cursos de adiestramiento y actividades académicas en las instituciones relevantes de cada una de las Partes.
d) Cooperar en forma acorde con sus capacidades en la mutua facilitación de medios de transporte, alojamiento, carga y otras actividades de logística asociada a sus respectivos programas nacionales antárticos.

Artículo IV

Para los fines señalados precedentemente, las Partes designan, respectivamente, al Instituto Antártico Chileno, en adelante "INACH", y al Instituto Antártico Búlgaro, en adelante "IAB", como las instituciones dedicadas a llevar a cabo dichos fines y para coordinar las actividades científicas y logísticas con las entidades mencionadas.

Artículo V

1. Las Partes convienen en que el INACH y el IAB harán los máximos esfuerzos para:

a) Desarrollar y coordinar conjuntamente proyectos de investigación científica, médica y tecnológica en virtud de este Convenio.
b) Establecer un sistema de intercambio de información en materias de orden científico tecnológico y de apoyo logístico.
c) Compartir información que pueda ser de utilidad en la planificación y desarrollo de actividades en el área del Tratado Antártico, con el objeto, entre otros, de proteger el medio ambiente antártico y sus ecosistemas dependientes y asociados.

d) Participar en las respectivas expediciones, proyectos y programas de capacitación antártica, de acuerdo a las modalidades que se convengan para tales fines.
e) Promover investigaciones de interés para las Partes en disciplinas tales como la Física Atmosférica, Radiación Cósmica, Meteorología, Ciencias de la Tierra, Ecología, Glaciología y Geofísica, Ciencias, Paleontología, Biología y Ciencias Médicas, Ecología Marina y Terrestre con énfasis en la detección de cambios de importancia mundial observados en la Antártica, así como en su observación y vigilancia.
f) Intercambiar conocimientos y experiencias en desarrollos tecnológicos de asentamientos humanos y del impacto ambiental de actividades humanas, incluyendo los efectos del turismo antártico.

2. Salvo que se estipule otra modalidad, los gastos de traslado generados por el cumplimiento de las actividades señaladas anteriormente, serán asumidos por la Parte que envía al personal científico, técnico y logístico, y los gastos de estadía serán de cargo del país receptor, en ambos casos, los gastos estarán sujetos a las disponibilidades de los presupuestos de las instituciones nacionales correspondientes.

Artículo VI

En el espíritu del Año Polar Internacional (2007–2008) y considerando los programas de cooperación antártica que mantienen la República de Chile y la República de Bulgaria con otros países, el INACH y el IAB estudiarán la posibilidad de ampliar su cooperación a nuevos proyectos multilaterales, para lo cual buscarán acceder a otras fuentes de financiamiento internacional y procurarán efectuar los aportes de recursos humanos y de orden logístico necesarios, para el cumplimiento de este objetivo.

Artículo VII

El INACH y el IAB elaborarán, con al menos un año de anticipación, el programa de acción conjunta que incluya los objetivos señalados en los Artículos III y V del presente Convenio.

Sin perjuicio de lo anterior, se examinarán por los Institutos mencionados en el Artículo IV, al inicio de cada temporada antártica, las condiciones y oportunidades existentes para facilitar y optimizar el cumplimiento de dichos objetivos.

Artículo VIII

Cualquier diferencia que pudiere surgir en relación con la interpretación o aplicación del presente Convenio de Cooperación Antártica, que no pueda ser resuelta por las entidades designadas por las Partes en el Artículo IV, deberá ser notificada a los respectivos Ministerios de Relaciones Exteriores a través de los cuales se llevarán a cabo las consultas necesarias para lograr una solución.

Artículo IX

El presente Convenio entrará en vigor treinta días después de la fecha de la última notificación, en que las Partes se comuniquen recíprocamente por los canales diplomáticos, el cumplimiento de las formalidades requeridas por sus respectivos ordenamientos jurídicos internos.

Artículo X

Este Convenio permanecerá en vigor en forma indefinida. Sin embargo, podrá ser denunciado por cualquiera de las Partes mediante notificación por la vía diplomática enviada con seis meses de anticipación. La denuncia no afectará a las acciones iniciadas durante su vigencia.

En fe de lo cual, los suscritos representantes, debidamente autorizados por sus respectivos Gobiernos, firman el presente Convenio.

Suscrito en Santiago, Chile, a los tres días del mes de enero del año dos mil cinco, en tres ejemplares originales en los idiomas español, búlgaro e inglés, siendo todos los textos igualmente auténticos y prevaleciendo este último en caso de divergencia interpretativa.

[Signatories omitted].

Agreement on Scientific Cooperation in the Antarctic between the Government of the French Republic and the Government of the Italian Republic (2005)[33]

Translation:

The Government of the French Republic and the Government of the Italian Republic, hereinafter called the Parties,

Considering the importance of the scientific cooperation between the two countries developed in the framework of the Cultural Agreement between France and Italy, signed on 4 November 1949, and the Agreement on Scientific and Technological Cooperation between the Government of the French Republic and the Government of the Italian Republic, signed at Turin on 29 January 2001;

Considering the priority attached to international scientific cooperation by the Antarctic Treaty, signed on 1 December 1959 and the Protocol on Environmental Protection to the Antarctic Treaty, signed at Madrid on 4 October 1991;

Considering the remarkable results obtained in the Antarctic in the different fields of scientific research thanks to international cooperation, including the establishment of the Franco-Italian Concordia Station, located at Dome C;

Considering the Joint Declaration by the Ministry of Education, Universities and Research of the Italian Republic and the Ministry for Research of the French Republic, signed at Rome on 9 May 2005;

Have agreed as follows:

Article 1

The Parties undertake to continue their scientific cooperation in the framework of the Antarctic Treaty system in order to take advantage of the opportunities afforded by the Concordia Station in the field of scientific and technological research.

Article II

The Parties shall instruct their respective Antarctic operators, namely, on the Italian side, the "Commissione Scientifica Nazionale per l'Antartide", hereinafter referred to as CSNA, acting through the "Consorzio per l'attuazione del Programma Nazionale di Ricerche in Antartide", hereinafter referred to as Consorzio PNRA, and, on the French side, "l'Institut Polaire Français-Paul Emile Victor", hereinafter referred to as IPEV, to implement the objectives referred to in Article I above.

To that end, the operators shall direct their attention and efforts to the following activities in particular:

- Joint and reciprocal performance of logistical operations, using existing national equipment and scientific and technical installations;
- The development of joint scientific and technological research programmes in sectors of interest to both Parties, especially in the physical, biological, and geo sciences and polar technology;
- The exchange of information;
- The provision of scientific and technical personnel.

Article III

In order to implement the cooperation referred to in Article I above, the Parties shall ask Consorzio PNRA, with the consent of the CSNA, and IPEV to sign an agreement establishing the arrangements and mechanisms for using the Concordia Station to implement scientific and technological programmes.

Article IV

The Parties shall also call upon CSNA and IPEV to:

[33] Adopted 4 October 2005, entered into force 9 January 2007, 2515 UNTS 243.

- Develop other projects of mutual interest that could lead to new cooperation agreements within the limits of their budgets;
- Elicit new ties of cooperation with scientific agencies in third countries with a view to facilitating the development of international research projects.

Article V

This Agreement shall enter into force on the date of reception of the last of the notifications in which the Contracting Parties communicate to each other that their respective internal legal procedures required for its entry into force have been fulfilled.

Article VI

In the event of a disagreement between the Parties regarding the interpretation or application of this Agreement, the Parties shall consult with one another with a view to reaching a friendly settlement.

Article VII

This Agreement shall be concluded for a period of ten years and shall be tacitly renewed thereafter for periods of one year. Each Party may denounce this Agreement by means of a note verbale, addressed to the other Party, six months prior to the date on which the Agreement expires.

IN WITNESS WHEREOF, the undersigned, being duly authorized thereto, have signed this Agreement.

DONE at Paris, on 4 October 2005, in duplicate, in the French and Italian languages, both texts being equally authentic.

[Signatories omitted].

Memorandum of Understanding on Antarctic Co-operation between the Government of the Argentine Republic and the Government of the Republic of India (2006)[34]

The Government of the Argentine Republic and the Government of the Republic of India, hereinafter, "the Parties",

Recalling that the Parties are both signatories to the Antarctic Treaty and to the Protocol to the Antarctic Treaty on Environmental Protection;

Reaffirming the commitment to jointly contributing to the development, strengthening and promotion of the Antarctic Treaty System;

Considering that the Antarctic Treaty System accords high priority to international scientific co-operation;

Expressing their interest in broadening Antarctic co-operation between the Parties;

Affirming the commitment to promoting co-operative programmes of science, technology and educational value, concerning the protection of the Antarctic environment and dependent and associated ecosystems;

Taking into account that the "International Polar Year 2007–2008" will be an excellent opportunity to develop undertakings on scientific research;

Have Agreed as Follows:

1. The Parties shall promote Antarctic co-operation through their respective official scientific organisations, the "Dirección Nacional del Antartico" of the Argentine Republic and the Ministry of Ocean Development of the Republic of India, by means of:

- the exchange of scientific and bibliographical information related to the study of Antarctica and the surrounding seas;
- opportunities for exchanges of scientists;

[34] Adopted and entered into force 5 July 2006, 2661 UNTS 97.

- the participation of scientists and technical experts involved in the national Antarctic programme of one country in the national Antarctic programme of the other;
- joint scientific conferences and workshops;
- joint scientific publications;
- training of scientific personnel:
- scientific co-operation projects involving the protection of the natural environment of Antarctica and the Southern Seas

2. Each Party shall bear the costs originated by their respective activities. In the case that joint activities implying different contributions on account of each Party are undertaken, the Parties shall agree on the respective financing in each particular case.

3. The "Dirección Nacional del Antartico" and the Ministry of Ocean Development shall be the authorities responsible for the programmes on Antarctic co-operation which may be agreed upon within the framework of this Memorandum of Understanding.

4. This Memorandum of Understanding shall enter into force on the date of its signature and shall remain in force for a period of three years, which shall be automatically extended for another period of three years. After the initial three-year period, either Party may terminate this Memorandum of Understanding by giving a six months' written notice in advance to the other Party.

Done in New Delhi on the 5th day of July, 2006, in two originals in Spanish, Hindi and English languages, being both equally authentic.

[Signatories omitted].

Agreement on Cooperative Enforcement of Fisheries Laws between the Government of Australia and the Government of the French Republic in the Maritime Areas Adjacent to the French Southern and Antarctic Territories, Heard Island and the McDonald Islands (2007)[35]

THE GOVERNMENT OF AUSTRALIA AND THE GOVERNMENT OF THE FRENCH REPUBLIC, hereinafter referred to as "the Parties",

Recalling their rights and responsibilities as coastal States under the United Nations Convention on the Law of the Sea of 10 December 1982, and as Parties to the Convention on the Conservation of Antarctic Living Marine Resources of 20 May 1980,

Recognising the strong foundation of cooperation established in the field of fisheries surveillance between the Parties by the Treaty between the Government of Australia and the Government of the French Republic on Cooperation in the Maritime Areas Adjacent to the French Southern and Antarctic Territories, Heard Island and the McDonald Islands (hereinafter referred to as "the Treaty"),

Recalling Article 2 of Annex III to the Treaty with respect to concluding agreements that provide for law enforcement operations accompanied by forcible measures,

Desiring to promote cooperative enforcement of the laws of the Parties in their respective maritime areas,

Concerned about the continued problem of illegal, unreported and unregulated fishing within and adjacent to the Parties' maritime areas,

Recognising the practical difficulties faced by the Parties of enforcing their laws in respect of illegal, unreported and unregulated fishing within their respective maritime areas in the Southern Oceans,

Determined therefore to enhance their ability to enforce effectively their fisheries laws and deter breaches of such laws,

---

[35] Adopted 8 January 2007, entered into force 7 January 2011, (No UNTS Volume number has yet been determined for this record).

HAVE AGREED AS FOLLOWS:

Article 1 – Interpretation and Application

1. This Agreement shall be interpreted consistently with the Treaty. Terms defined in the Treaty have the same meaning in this Agreement.

2. This Agreement shall have the same area of application as the Treaty.

3. "Controller" means an officer from one Party who is authorised by its respective Party to exercise cooperative enforcement activities on board an authorised vessel of the other Party.

4. "Cooperative enforcement" means fisheries enforcement activities such as the boarding, inspection, hot pursuit, apprehension, seizure and investigation of fishing vessels that are believed to have violated applicable fisheries laws, undertaken by one Party in cooperation with the other Party.

5. "Authorised vessel" means:

a. for Australia, any Australian Defence Force vessel or aircraft, or any other vessel or aircraft owned, chartered or otherwise under the control of the Australian Government and being used for the purpose of law enforcement or surveillance and which is clearly marked and identified as being on government service; and

b. for the Republic of France, any French Defence Force vessel or aircraft, or any other vessel or aircraft owned, chartered or otherwise under the control of the French Government and being used for the purpose of law enforcement or surveillance and which is clearly marked and identified as being on government service.

Article 2 – Objective

The object of this Agreement is to enhance cooperative enforcement of fisheries laws in the Area of Cooperation.

Article 3 – Cooperative Enforcement

1. Controllers shall exercise cooperative enforcement activities aboard an authorised vessel of the other Party, with the consent of the other Party. Controllers shall not be required by the other Party to conduct activities contrary to the law of the Controller's Party.

2. Cooperative enforcement activities shall only be undertaken when there is a Controller on board an authorised vessel.

3. Paragraphs 1 and 2 of this Article apply in:

a. the Area of Cooperation;

b. outside the Area of Cooperation in situations of hot pursuit pursuant to Article 4; and

c. outside the Area of Cooperation where a vessel is acting as a mother ship and one of its boats or other craft, working as a team, is within the Area of Cooperation.

4. Cooperative enforcement activities undertaken pursuant to this Agreement shall be conducted in conformity with the law applicable in the maritime zone in which the activities are undertaken or, in the case of hot pursuit, the maritime zone from which a hot pursuit is commenced.

5. Each Party shall ensure that its Controllers, when conducting cooperative enforcement activities pursuant to this Agreement, act in accordance with its applicable national laws and policies and with international law and accepted international practices.

6. To facilitate implementation of this Agreement, each Party shall ensure that the other Party is informed of applicable laws and policies.

7. Authorised vessels of each Party may engage in the use of disruptive measures, to the extent permitted by their national law and policies, and consistent with international law, as a means of hindering the activities of fishing vessels believed to be fishing illegally in the Area of Cooperation.

8. Any cooperative enforcement activity involving the use of force against a fishing vessel shall require the joint authorisation of both Parties.

9. The Parties shall, as soon as possible, enter into arrangements regarding cooperative enforcement, including:

a. operating procedures;
b. the identification of authorised vessels; and
c. the identification of officers, such as a requirement to be uniformed and to carry and display an authorized card; and
d. flags and pennants displayed by authorised vessels.

Article 4 – Hot Pursuit

1. Hot pursuit of a fishing vessel believed to be fishing illegally may be commenced by an authorised vessel of either Party pursuant to this Agreement.

2. Hot pursuit may be commenced upon fulfilling the following conditions:

a. the authorities of the relevant Party have good reason to believe that the fishing vessel or one of its boats has violated the laws of the Party within whose maritime zone the vessel is detected. The basis for such belief may include:
   i. direct visual contact with the fishing vessel or one of its boats by the authorised vessel; or
   ii. evidence obtained by or on behalf of the authorised vessel by technical means; and
b. a clear signal to stop has been given to the fishing vessel by or on behalf of the authorised vessel which enables it to be seen or heard by the fishing vessel.

3. Hot pursuit is deemed to have continued without interruption from the commencement of the hot pursuit to interception as long as the relevant authorised vessel or vessels:

a. maintain continual positive identification and tracking of the fishing vessel by, inter alia, the means described in paragraphs 2(a)(i) and (ii) of this Article; and
b. from time to time continue to signal the fishing vessel to stop.

4. An authorised vessel of one Party may take over the hot pursuit commenced by an authorised vessel of the other Party.

5. For the avoidance of doubt, the hot pursuit of a fishing vessel by a Party's authorised vessel from that Party's maritime zone is not subject to this Agreement even where an officer of the other Party is aboard the authorised vessel or the hot pursuit occurs through the maritime zone of the other Party.

Article 5 – Jurisdiction

1. The Party whose authorised vessel, and its crew, is undertaking cooperative and enforcement activities in accordance with this Agreement, shall take all appropriate measures to ensure that the laws of the other Party are observed and respected.

2. Officers of one Party shall enjoy immunity from the criminal, civil and administrative jurisdiction of the other Party for acts performed in the course of carrying out cooperative enforcement activities pursuant to and consistent with this Agreement.

3. A Party shall, where one of its officers has allegedly breached the laws of the other Party, ensure appropriate action, consistent with its laws and regulations, is taken against its officers.

Article 6 – Post-Apprehension Cooperation

1. Vessels seized by a Party pursuant to Article 3 in the maritime zone of the other Party, or following a hot pursuit undertaken on behalf of the other Party pursuant to Article 4, shall, together with the persons, equipment and any documents and catch on board, be handed over as soon as possible to the authorities of the other Party.

Article 7 – Report of Cooperative Enforcement Activities

1. The competent authorities of the Party conducting cooperative enforcement activities in the maritime zone of the other Party pursuant to this Agreement shall provide a report on those activities to the other Party as soon as practicable.

2. The report shall include:

a. The details of any enforcement activities undertaken pursuant to Article 3, including the time and position the activities were undertaken;
b. The details of any hot pursuit undertaken pursuant to Article 4;

c. The details of any vessel that enforcement activities were undertaken against, including any information held concerning the crew members or owners of the vessel;
d. Any information that could reasonably assist the prosecution of the crews, charterers, owners or beneficial owners of a relevant vessel, or beneficiaries of any illegal fishing activity, for breaches of the applicable law in the Area of Cooperation; and
e. Any other information agreed to by the Parties.

3. The Parties may agree in writing at any time, to vary the required information for inclusion in a report under this Article.

Article 8 – Financing of Cooperative Enforcement Activities

1. The costs incurred during cooperative enforcement activities shall be borne by the Party undertaking them.

2. The proceeds from any sale of vessels, fishing equipment, fuel and lubricant, or catch which has been forfeited following cooperative enforcement activities shall belong to the Party whose laws are believed to have been violated.

3. Where the costs undertaken by one Party far exceed the costs undertaken by the other Party, the Parties may agree to recover those additional costs during consultations referred to in Article 11.

Article 9 – International Cooperation

Each Party shall use its best efforts to ensure that fishing vessels considered to be fishing illegally are apprehended and that illegal catches are seized or denied transhipment in their respective ports or the ports of other States.

Article 10 – Exchange of Information

1. Additionally to Article 5 of the Treaty, the competent authorities of the Parties shall, to the extent permitted by their national law and policies, exchange information about cooperative enforcement activities.

2. Information provided by a Party pursuant to this Agreement shall not be disclosed to third Parties by the Party that received the information without the written consent of the Party providing the information. Nothing in this paragraph shall prevent a Party from meeting its reporting obligations under the Convention or the CCAMLR Convention.

Article 11 – Review

The competent authorities of the Parties shall hold consultations at least every two years to examine the implementation and effect of this Agreement, including financial arrangements.

Article 12 – Dispute Settlement

If any dispute arises between the Parties concerning the interpretation or application of this Agreement, the Parties shall consult between themselves with a view to having the dispute resolved by negotiation or other agreed peaceful means.

Article 13 – Entry into Force and Amendment

1. This Agreement shall enter into force on the date on which the Parties have notified each other in writing, through diplomatic channels, that their internal procedures necessary for its entry into force have been met.

2. This Agreement may be amended at any time by common consent of the Parties. Any amendment shall enter into force conditional upon completion of the procedures laid down in paragraph 1 of this Article.

Article 14 – Termination

1. This Agreement terminates if the Treaty is terminated.

2. This Agreement may be separately terminated by formal notification by one Party in writing, through diplomatic channels, to the other Party. This Agreement shall terminate six months after the notification is received by the other Party, except that the obligations under paragraph 2 Article 10 subsisting at the time of termination shall continue indefinitely until performance of them by one Party is waived in writing by the other Party.

IN WITNESS WHEREOF the undersigned, being duly authorised by their respective Governments, have signed this Treaty.

DONE in duplicate at Paris this Eighth day of January 2007, in the English and French languages, both being equally authentic.

[Signatories omitted].

Memorando de Entendimiento Sobre Cooperación Antártica entre el Gobierno de la República de Chile y el Gobierno de la República de la India (2008)[36]

El Gobierno de la República de Chile y el Gobierno de la República de la India, de aquí en adelante "las Partes",

Recordando que ambas Partes son signatarias del Tratado Antártico y del Protocolo del Tratado Antártico sobre Protección Ambiental;

Reafirmando el compromiso de contribuir en forma conjunta al desarrollo, fortalecimiento y promoción del Sistema del Tratado Antártico;

Expresando su interés en ampliar los programas de cooperación antártica en temas como la ciencia, la tecnología, los valores culturales y educativos, y el apoyo logístico entre las Partes;

Afirmando el compromiso de promover la investigación sobre la protección del medio ambiente antártico y sus ecosistemas dependientes y asociados;

Considerando que el "Año Polar Internacional 2007–2008" es una excelente oportunidad para desarrollar investigaciones científicas conjuntas cubriendo una amplia gama de temas científicos de interés global,

Han concordado como sigue:

1. Las Partes promoverán la cooperación antártica a través de sus respectivas organizaciones científicas oficiales, el Instituto Antártico Chileno (INACH) de la República de Chile y el Ministerio de Ciencias Terrestres de la República de la India, por medio de:
   - proyectos de cooperación científica en la Antártica y el Océano Austral;
   - participación de científicos y técnicos especializados del Programa Nacional Antártico de un país en el Programa Nacional Antártico del otro;
   - oportunidades para intercambiar científicos;
   - capacitación de personal científico y técnico;
   - intercambio de información científica y bibliográfica antártica y subantártica y aguas circumpolares antárticas;
   - publicaciones científicas conjuntas;
   - conferencias y talleres científicos conjuntos;
   - apoyo logístico y técnico en investigación antártica.
2. Cada Parte financiará los costos originados por sus respectivas actividades. En el caso que se emprendan actividades conjuntas que impliquen aportes diferentes de cada Parte, éstas acordarán el financiamiento respectivo para cada caso en particular.
3. El Instituto Antártico Chileno y el Centro Nacional para la Antártica y de Investigación Oceánica del Ministerio de Ciencias Terrestres serán las autoridades responsables de los programas de cooperación antártica que se convengan dentro del marco del Memorando de Entendimiento.
4. Este Memorando de Entendimiento comenzará a regir en la fecha de su firma y se mantendrá vigente por un período de 3 años, los que podrán extenderse automáticamente por otro período de 3 años. Una vez concluido el período inicial de 3 años, cualquiera de las Partes podrá terminar este Memorando de Entendimiento con la entrega del aviso correspondiente y con 6 meses de anticipación.

[36] Adopted 21 April 2008.

Firmado en Santiago en el día 21 del mes de abril de 2008, en hindi, español e inglés, en versiones igualmente auténticas. En caso de cualquier diferencia de interpretación el texto en inglés prevalecerá.

[Signatories omitted].

Acuerdo en Materia de Cooperación Antártica Entre el Gobierno de la República de Chile y el Gobierno de la República Checa (2009)[37]

El Gobierno de la República de Chile y el Gobierno de la República Checa (en adelante, las Partes),

- Reiterando su deseo de fortalecer la cooperación bilateral y los lazos de amistad entre ambos países;
- Teniendo presente los Artículos II y III del Tratado Antártico y el Artículo VI del Protocolo al Tratado Antártico sobre Protección del Medio Ambiente, así como las recomendaciones (medidas, decisiones y resoluciones) de las Reuniones Consultivas del Tratado Antártico que hacen hincapié en la suma importancia de la cooperación internacional en las actividades científicas que se realizan en el área de la Antártica;
- Conscientes de la creciente importancia de la Antártica para la investigación científica, particularmente en el ámbito del medio ambiente global, como asimismo de la necesidad de reducir al mínimo los efectos de las actividades científicas en el medio ambiente antártico y los ecosistemas dependientes y asociados;
- Prestando debida consideración al Acuerdo entre el Gobierno de la República de Chile y el Gobierno de la República Checa sobre Cooperación en el Ámbito de la Cultura, Educación y Ciencia y otras Disciplinas, suscrito en Santiago, Chile, el 22 de abril de 1994,

Han acordado lo siguiente:

Artículo I

1. Las Partes harán cuanto esté a su alcance por efectuar actividades conjuntas con miras a aprovechar las oportunidades de cooperación que brinda el Tratado Antártico y el Protocolo sobre Protección del Medio Ambiente Antártico a objeto de optimizar los recursos humanos y materiales, y, asimismo, por evitar duplicidades en materias destinadas a perfeccionar la labor de investigación interdisciplinaria que desarrollan las diversas comunidades científicas antárticas.
2. Las Partes revisarán en forma regular la ejecución del presente Acuerdo en lo que respecta a sus beneficios y posibilidades de perfeccionamiento.

Artículo II

Las Partes deberán, en el marco del Tratado Antártico, cooperar específicamente en los siguientes ámbitos:

a) Preparación de proyectos científicos y técnicos conjuntos acordes con los objetivos de las actividades antárticas nacionales pertinentes;

b) Intercambio de información en campos de interés común, en especial sobre las posibles repercusiones de las actividades realizadas por ellos en las estaciones antárticas o los efectos de otros proyectos realizados en el marco del Tratado Antártico sobre el medio ambiente antártico y sus ecosistemas dependientes y asociados;

c) Promoción de la educación y formación profesional de recursos humanos mediante el intercambio de expertos, personal científico, logístico y técnico, cursos de capacitación y actividades académicas en las instituciones competentes de ambas Partes Contratantes;

d) Facilitación, dentro de sus capacidades, del transporte, alojamiento, expedición y otras actividades logísticas relacionadas con las actividades nacionales en la Antártica.

[37] Adopted 29 May 2009.

Artículo III

Los órganos designados para coordinar las actividades de cooperación conforme al presente Acuerdo son:

- El Ministerio de Educación, Juventud y Deportes de la República Checa, por parte de la República Checa; y
- El Ministerio de Relaciones Exteriores, a través del Instituto Antártico Chileno (INACH), por parte de la República de Chile.

Artículo IV

Los órganos designados harán cuanto esté a su alcance por:

a) Desarrollar y coordinar proyectos conjuntos en el ámbito de las ciencias, la medicina y la investigación tecnológica en virtud de este Acuerdo;

b) Crear un sistema de intercambio de información científica y técnica y soporte logístico;

c) Compartir la información necesaria para planificar y llevar a cabo actividades incluidas en el ámbito de aplicación del Tratado Antártico con miras, inter alia, a proteger el medio ambiente antártico y sus ecosistemas dependientes y asociados – incluido el intercambio de información en foros internacionales – respetando los intereses individuales de sus respectivos Estados;

d) Participar en expediciones, proyectos y programas de capacitación en materias antárticas, siguiendo los procedimientos acordados con este fin;

e) Cooperar en las actividades de investigación en ámbitos de interés común de las Partes, en áreas tales como física atmosférica, radiación cósmica, meteorología, geología, geofísica, paleontología, ecología marina y terrestre, glaciología, biología y ciencias médicas, con énfasis en la detección de cambios de importancia global observados en la Antártica y su monitoreo;

f) Intercambiar hallazgos y experiencias en el ámbito del desarrollo de asentamientos humanos y los efectos de las actividades humanas en el medio ambiente, incluidos los efectos del turismo antártico.

Artículo V

Salvo que se acuerde algo distinto, cada Parte sufragará los gastos en que hubiere incurrido al llevar a cabo las actividades antes señaladas. Los gastos en que incurrieren las instituciones que participarán en actividades derivadas de la cooperación en el marco del presente Acuerdo serán sufragados de conformidad con las normativas legales de los respectivos Estados.

Artículo VI

En el espíritu del Año Polar Internacional (2007–2008) y considerando los programas de cooperación antártica, respaldados por la República de Chile y la República Checa junto a otros países, los órganos designados investigarán las posibilidades de ampliar la cooperación bilateral en nuevos programas multilaterales. Con dicho fin, buscarán más fuentes internacionales de financiamiento con el objeto de garantizar los recursos humanos y logísticos que se requieran.

Artículo VII

Al inicio de cada temporada antártica, los órganos designados examinarán las condiciones imperantes de modo de facilitar y optimizar las actividades destinadas a cumplir las metas que se especifican en los Artículos II y IV del presente Acuerdo.

Artículo VIII

Toda diferencia que pueda surgir en la interpretación y ejecución del presente Acuerdo y que no pueda ser resuelta por los órganos designados será resuelta mediante negociación entre las Partes.

Artículo IX

El presente Acuerdo está supeditado a la aprobación conforme a la normativa legal interna vigente en cada uno de los Estados. Las Partes se transmitirán la información respectiva mediante Notas a través de la vía diplomática. El Acuerdo entrará en vigor el día en que se entregue la última Nota a la otra Parte.

Artículo X

El presente Acuerdo permanecerá en vigor por tiempo indefinido. Sin embargo, cualquiera de las Partes podrá denunciarlo mediante aviso por escrito dado con seis (6) meses de anticipación por la vía diplomática. La terminación del presente Acuerdo no afectará las actividades iniciadas durante su período de vigencia, salvo que las Partes acuerden una manera diferente.

Hecho en Praga, a los 14 días del mes de mayo de dos mil nueve en dos originales en idiomas español, checo e inglés, siendo todos los textos igualmente auténticos. En caso de divergencia de interpretación, prevalecerá el texto en idioma inglés.

[Signatories omitted].

N° 106829/2009-MPO

El Ministerio de Relaciones Exteriores de la República Checa saluda muy atentamente a la Honorable Embajada de la República de Chile en Praga y tiene el honor de transmitir la información que el Acuerdo en Materia de Cooperación Antártica ente el Gobierno de la República Checa y el Gobierno de la República de Chile (en adelante "Acuerdo"), suscrito en Praga, el 14 de mayo de 2009, fue aprobado conforme a la normativa legal interna de la parte checa en sentido del Artículo IX. Según esta disposición, el Acuerdo entrará en vigor el día en que la República Checa estará entregada una Nota análoga de la República de Chile.

El Ministerio de Relaciones Exteriores de la República Checa aprovecha la oportunidad para renovar a la Honorable Embajada de la República de Chile en Praga los testimonios de su más alta y distinguida consideración.

Praga, 20 de mayo de 2009.

A la Honorable Embajada
de la República de Chile
Praga

República de Chile
Ministerio de Relaciones Exteriores

N° 007166

El Ministerio de Relaciones Exteriores – Dirección de Asuntos Jurídicos – saluda atentamente a la Embajada de la República Checa y tiene el honor de comunicarle que el Acuerdo en Materia de Cooperación Antártica entre los Gobiernos de la República de Chile y de la República Checa, suscrito en Praga, el 14 de mayo de 2009, ha cumplido en Chile los procedimientos internos para su entrada en vigor internacional.

Al mismo tiempo, este Ministerio se permite solicitar a esa Embajada que se sirva remitir a esta Secretaría de Estado la Nota en que su Gobierno comunique, igualmente, que se han cumplido los procedimientos internos en la República Checa, para el mismo efecto, de conformidad a lo previsto en el Artículo IX del aludido Acuerdo.

El Ministerio de Relaciones Exteriores – Dirección de Asuntos Jurídicos – se vale de esta oportunidad para reiterar a la Embajada de la República Checa las seguridades de su más alta y distinguida consideración.

Santiago, 29 de mayo de 2009.

A la
Embajada de la República Checa
en Chile
Presente.

Agreement concerning Antarctic Cooperation between the Government of the Argentine Republic and the Government of the Czech Republic (2010)[38]

[Translation]

The Government of the Argentine Republic and the Government of the Czech Republic (hereinafter referred to as "the Parties");

Confirming their intention to strengthen the ties of mutual cooperation and friendship that exist between them;

Considering articles II and III of the Antarctic Treaty and Article VI of the Protocol on Environmental Protection, and the recommendations (measures, decisions, and resolutions) of the consultative assemblies on the Antarctic Treaty;

Stressing the great importance of international cooperation when undertaking scientific activities in the region of Antarctica;

Recognizing the growing importance of the Antarctic for scientific research, particularly in the global environment field; and

Mindful of the need to maximize the effect of such scientific activities on the Antarctic environment and its dependent and associated ecosystems;

Have agreed as follows:

Article I

The Parties shall do their utmost to implement joint activities aimed at exploiting the cooperation possibilities envisaged the Antarctic Treaty and in the Protocol on Environmental Protection, particularly in the scientific, technological, logistic and environmental fields, in order to improve their knowledge of the Antarctic continent and the area below latitude 60° south.

Article II

1. In the framework of the Antarctic Treaty, the Parties shall cooperate in the following ways particularly:

(a) Participation by scientists and technicians from one country in Antarctic expeditions carried out using logistical resources from the national programme of the other country;

(b) Exchange of scientific and technical personnel, and scholarships, courses and technology and, in particular, scientists and technicians from each country, between Argentine and Czech scientific stations.

(c) Scientific meetings and joint research on previously agreed-upon topics and projects;

(d) Joint use of scientific research facilities and laboratories in Antarctica and elsewhere for the development of programmes relating to disciplines relevant to Antarctica;

(e) Exchange of information on scientific research projects and bibliography, and the production of joint publications;

(f) Joint use of logistical resources with a view to rationalizing costs and minimizing the impact on the Antarctic environment and its dependent and associated ecosystems.

2. Unless agreed otherwise for a specific case, the cost incurred in implementing the aforementioned activities will be borne by the Party causing it. The cost incurred by the respective institutions involved in the activities arising from cooperation under this Agreement will be paid in accordance with the legal provisions of the Parties.

Article III

The institutions responsible for coordinating cooperation under this Agreement are: For the Argentine Party, the National Antarctic Office of the Ministry of Foreign Relations, International Trade and Worship; For the Czech Party, the Ministry of Education, Youth, and Physical Culture.

[38] Adopted 2 March 2010, entered into force 8 April 2010.

Article IV

Any differences arising in relation to the interpretation or application of this Agreement, which cannot be resolved by the institutions mentioned in the foregoing Article, shall be resolved through negotiations between the Parties.

Article V

This Agreement shall enter into force on the date of the last of the notes whereby the Parties notify each other, through the diplomatic channel, that their respective national requirements for this purpose have been fulfilled.

Article VI

This Agreement shall remain in force indefinitely. Nonetheless, either of the Parties may denounce it by giving a minimum of six months' written notice to the other, through the diplomatic channel, of its intention to do so. The termination of this Agreement shall not affect currently executing activities that began during its lifetime.

Done in Buenos Aires, on 2 March 2010, in two original copies in the Spanish and Czech languages, each text being equally authentic.

[Signatories omitted].

Memorándum de Entendimiento para la Cooperación en Asuntos Antárticos entre el Gobierno de la República de Chile y el Gobierno de la República de Colombia (2011)[39]

El Gobierno de la República de Chile y el Gobierno de la República de Colombia (en adelante, "las Partes"),

Reiterando su deseo de fortalecer la cooperación bilateral y los lazos de amistad entre ambos países;

Teniendo presente los Artículos II y III del Tratado Antártico, así como las Recomendaciones, Medidas, Decisiones y Resoluciones de las Reuniones Consultivas del Tratado Antártico que hacen hincapié en la importancia de la cooperación internacional en las actividades científicas que se realizan en la Antártica;

Considerando la Declaración Conjunta de los Presidentes de la República de Chile y de la República de Colombia, suscrita en Santiago el 11 de octubre de 2000, en la cual ratifican el pleno respeto a los principios y normas del Tratado Antártico, asimismo, el interés de Colombia de adelantar los trámites para la ratificación del Protocolo al Tratado Antártico sobre Protección del Medio Ambiente y de Chile de cooperar en el desarrollo de las actividades científicas colombianas;

Considerando el Convenio Básico de Cooperación Técnica Científica entre la República de Chile y la República de Colombia, suscrito el 16 de julio de 1991;

Conscientes de la creciente importancia de la Antártica para la investigación científica, particularmente en el ámbito del medio ambiente global, asimismo, la necesidad de reducir los efectos del impacto ambiental de las actividades científicas a través del trabajo conjunto,

Las Partes acuerdan lo siguiente:

Artículo I

El Ministerio de Relaciones Exteriores de Chile y el Ministerio de Relaciones Exteriores de Colombia mantendrán un activo intercambio de información sobre los Programas Nacionales Antárticos de ambos países, en particular sobre la concursabilidad de proyectos científicos en diferentes ámbitos de interés, programas de estudios, cursos, seminarios, talleres y el manejo de la actividad logística en la Antártica.

[39] Adopted 16 August 2011.

Artículo II

Las Partes promoverán la cooperación antártica a través de sus respectivas organizaciones científicas oficiales, el Instituto Antártico Chileno (INACH) y la Comisión Nacional para Asuntos Antárticos de Colombia.

Artículo III

El Instituto Antártico Chileno (INACH) y la Comisión Nacional para Asuntos Antárticos de Colombia crearán una Mesa de Trabajo para suscribir un acuerdo bilateral en actividades y áreas de interés común, aprovechando la experiencia antártica de Chile para el desarrollo de la ciencia y la tecnología siendo éste, uno de los ejes estratégicos en el Plan de Desarrollo "Prosperidad para Todos" del Gobierno de Colombia.

Artículo IV

Simultáneamente se estrecharán los vínculos de cooperación científica, académica y tecnológica en asuntos antárticos en relación con la conservación y protección de la biodiversidad en la Antártica, especialmente en los siguientes ámbitos:

a) Desarrollar proyectos conjuntos de investigación científica y desarrollo tecnológico e innovación concordantes con los objetivos de sus respectivos programas nacionales antárticos,
b) Propender a la formación y capacitación de recursos humanos, mediante el intercambio de expertos, personal científico, logístico y técnico, cursos de postgrado y actividades académicas en las instituciones relevantes de cada una de las Partes.
c) Cooperar en forma acorde con sus capacidades en la mutua facilitación de medios de transporte, alojamiento, carga y otras actividades de logística asociada a sus respectivos programas nacionales antárticos.
d) Cooperar en la publicación de artículos científicos.

Artículo V

Cada Parte será responsable de los gastos en el desarrollo de todas las actividades de cooperación llevadas a cabo en el marco de este Memorándum de Entendimiento, salvo que éstas convengan por escrito de un modo diferente.

La participación en las actividades de cooperación estará sujeta a la disponibilidad de fondos, recursos y personal y se efectuará de acuerdo a las leyes y reglamentaciones vigentes en las respectivas Partes.

En el caso que se emprendan actividades conjuntas que impliquen aportes diferentes de cada Parte, éstas acordarán el financiamiento respectivo para cada caso en particular.

Artículo VI

Este Memorándum de Entendimiento entrará en vigor en la fecha de su firma y tendrá una duración de tres (3) años. Podrá ser prorrogado por períodos adicionales, por acuerdo mutuo de las Partes lo que deberá constar por escrito.

Este Memorándum de Entendimiento podrá ser modificado por acuerdo mutuo de las Partes, lo que deberá constar por escrito, señalando, asimismo, la fecha de su entrada en vigor.

Las Partes podrán poner término a este Memorándum de Entendimiento en cualquier momento. La Parte que desee poner término anticipado a este Memorándum deberá comunicarlo por escrito a la otra, al menos con noventa (90) días de antelación. Sin perjuicio de lo anterior, las Partes prevén continuar trabajando en conjunto para concluir los proyectos de cooperación específicos en marcha, salvo que las Partes acuerden un modo diferente.

Hecho en Santiago, Chile, a los dieciséis días del mes de agosto de dos mil once, en dos originales, igualmente auténticos.

[Signatories omitted].

Memorandum of Understanding between the Government of the Russian Federation and the Government of the United States of America on Cooperation in Antarctica (2012)[40]

The Government of the Russian Federation and the Government of the United States of America (hereinafter "the Parties"),

Being original parties to and architects of the Antarctic Treaty of December 1, 1959 (hereinafter "the Treaty"),

Noting the leading role of the Russian Federation and the United States of America in developing and strengthening the Antarctic Treaty system,

Highlighting the substantial contribution of the explorers and scientists of the two countries to the discovery, research and exploration of Antarctica and the importance of these achievements,

Bearing in mind that the Russian Federation and the United States of America conduct some of the most extensive and diverse activities in the Treaty area,

Taking into account the experience of their long-term and multi-dimensional bilateral cooperation in the sphere of scientific exploration in Antarctica,

Being guided by the provisions of the Treaty,

Noting the importance of bilateral collaboration with respect to protection of the Antarctic marine and terrestrial environments,

Endeavoring to enhance their bilateral relations in cooperation in Antarctica as part of their collaboration globally,

Have reached the following understandings:

1. The Parties intend to consult regularly through their respective Foreign Ministries on issues of common interest concerning implementation of the Treaty and other elements of the Antarctic Treaty system, including in preparation for Antarctic Treaty Consultative Meetings and Meetings of the Commission for the Conservation of Antarctic Marine Living Resources, and, where possible, coordinate their positions on these issues.

2. The Parties intend to cooperate in the organization and conduct of joint inspections in the Treaty area under Article VII of the Treaty and Article 14 of the Protocol on Environmental Protection to the Antarctic Treaty.

3. The Parties intend to encourage organization and implementation of joint projects and programs for research and exploration of Antarctica, participation of scientists and technical experts involved in the national Antarctic program of one state in the national Antarctic program of the other, as well as exchange of scientific and technical personnel.

4.

(a) The Parties intend to promote collaboration in scientific research and logistical and support activities between their respective national Antarctic program managers, specifically the Arctic and Antarctic Research Institute of the Russian Federal Service for Hydrometeorology and Environmental Monitoring and the Office of Polar Programs of the National Science Foundation of the United States ("Managers").

(b) To coordinate cooperation in scientific research and logistical and support activities as set forth in this Memorandum and to develop associated implementation plans, the Parties intend to establish a Working Group, which will include representatives from all interested governmental agencies and governmental institutions. Cooperation regarding logistical and support activities may be implemented through additional arrangements, as appropriate.

5. The Parties intend to facilitate scientific cooperation in the Treaty area and the exchange of associated data in important areas of scientific research, including but not limited to the following:

– climate change in Antarctica and its role in understanding global processes;

[40] Adopted 8 September 2012.

- processes leading to changes in the mass of the Antarctic ice sheet;
- monitoring the Antarctic environment, including exchange of associated data acquired by Russian and U.S. Antarctic programs and environmental monitoring satellites;
- space weather, including the impact of solar wind on the processes in the Antarctic atmosphere, and related space science research;
- modeling of the interactions among components of Antarctic physical and biological systems;
- seismological investigations of the sub-glacial lithosphere and upper mantle;
- research on the impact of human presence and changing environments on microorganisms in Antarctica;
- research on microorganisms in the Antarctic permafrost;
- oceanography of maritime areas contiguous to the Antarctic continent; and
- comprehensive research of sub-glacial environments, aquatic and sedimentary, of Antarctica as unique isolated ecosystems.

6. The Parties, through the Managers, intend to enhance collaboration in the field of national expedition logistic support in the Treaty area, in particular by providing ship and aviation support in delivering their personnel and cargo to different areas of Antarctica and exchanging best practices in this field.

7. The Parties intend to enhance collaboration in organizing, coordinating and conducting search and rescue operations in the Treaty area.

8. The Parties, through the Managers, intend to enhance collaboration in the field of training of scientific and technical personnel for participation in expedition and exploration activities in Antarctica.

9. The Parties intend to encourage the exchange of experience in developing educational and cultural projects and programs that inform the public of the results of Antarctic research.

10. Unless otherwise mutually decided, each Party intends to bear the costs of its participation in the activities conducted under this Memorandum. Cooperative activities are to be conducted in accordance with the applicable laws and regulations of each country and subject to the availability of funds.

11. This non-binding Memorandum does not constitute an international agreement or give rise to any rights and obligations for the Parties under international law.

12. Cooperation under this Memorandum commences upon signature by the Parties. Cooperation under this Memorandum may be discontinued at any time by either Party, though a Party should endeavor to provide 12 months notice if possible.

Agreement between the Government of New Zealand and the Government of the Republic of Korea on Antarctic Cooperation (2012)[41]

The Government of New Zealand and the Government of the Republic of Korea (hereinafter referred to as "the Parties"):

Conscious of the long-standing, close and wide-ranging relationship between the two countries;

Considering that the two countries are both Consultative Parties to the Antarctic Treaty, done at Washington on 1 December 1959;

Underlining the special importance that the Parties attach to the protection of the Antarctic and its dependent and associated ecosystems;

Recalling the principles of cooperation included in the Antarctic Treaty and the Environmental Protocol to the Antarctic Treaty, the latter done at Madrid on 4 October 1991;

[41] Adopted 17 August 2012, entered into force 25 October 2012 (No UNTS Volume number has yet been determined for this record).

Further recalling the objective of the Convention on the Conservation of Antarctic Marine Living Resources, done at Canberra on 20 May 1980;

Bearing in mind that New Zealand is one of the most important gateways to Antarctica and is well placed to provide assistance to Antarctic scientific research programmes;

Noting the Republic of Korea's plan to establish a new scientific research base in Terra Nova Say and that transiting through New Zealand will facilitate the operation of logistical support for the Republic of Korea's Antarctic Research Programme; and

Taking account of their mutual desire to further enhance their engagement and dialogue with each other on Antarctic matters;

Have agreed as follows:

Article 1 Cooperation and Consultation

1. The Parties agree to cooperate in Antarctic scientific research for peaceful purposes and for their mutual benefit and to further strengthen the extensive bilateral cooperation in the scientific field between the Republic of Korea and New Zealand.

2. The Parties shall, through their respective Foreign Ministries:

(a) consult regularly on Antarctic subjects of common interest, including the conservation of Antarctic marine living resources and political, scientific and environmental issues within the context of the Antarctic Treaty System; and

(b) explore possibilities for coordinating their policies in international fora that deal with Antarctic matters.

Article 2 Logistical and Scientific Cooperative Activities

1. Each Party shall designate an agency to be responsible for the coordination and facilitation of logistical and scientific cooperative activities under this Agreement, and notify the details of such agency to the other Party. The Parties shall notify each other promptly of any amendments to the details of their designated agency.

2. The designated agencies of the Parties shall consult with a view to developing logistical and scientific cooperative activities, including the provision of logistical support for each other's Antarctic programmes where possible. Logistical and scientific cooperative activities shall be the subject of specific subsidiary arrangements as may be deemed appropriate by the designated agencies of the Parties.

Article 3 Provision of Information by the Republic of Korea

The designated agencies of the Parties shall consult on a timely basis each year on:

(a) the expected size of the Korean Antarctic Research Programme for the forthcoming Antarctic summer season, including personnel, ships and aircraft, in so far as the use of facilities in New Zealand may be involved; and

(b) the ports, airports and any other necessary services requested for use in New Zealand by the Korean Antarctic Research Programme for their personnel, ships and aircraft transiting through New Zealand en route to and from Antarctica during the forthcoming Antarctic summer season.

Article 4 Facilitation by New Zealand

Subject to agreement between the Parties on the size of the Republic of Korea's Antarctic operations for which the use of facilities in New Zealand may be involved in each Antarctic summer season, New Zealand shall:

(a) consistent with its laws and regulations, facilitate as far as possible entry into, exit from and stay in New Zealand of personnel engaged in the Korean Antarctic Research Programme, other than persons who are nationals of or ordinarily resident in New Zealand.

Provided such personnel meet New Zealand's standard temporary entry requirements, New Zealand agrees to issue them visas on arrival, valid for the period of their assignment with the Korean Antarctic Research Programme, up to a maximum of 12 months; and

(b) consistent with its laws and regulations including those relating to agricultural health inspection, facilitate as far as possible the entry into and exit from New Zealand of ships, aircraft, equipment and materials to be used in the Korean Antarctic Research Programme, as well as the personal effects of personnel engaged in the Korean Antarctic Research Programme. New Zealand shall exempt equipment and materials imparted into and then exported out of New Zealand by, and for use in, the Korean Antarctic Research Programme from taxes and customs duties.

Article 5 Costs

Each Party shall meet the costs of its participation in any activities envisaged or undertaken under this Agreement.

Article 6 Consultations

The Parties agree to consult together at any time, at the request of either Party, regarding the interpretation or implementation of this Agreement.

Article 7 Application to Tokelau

This Agreement shall not apply to Tokelau.

Article 8 Entry into Force, Amendment and Termination

1. This Agreement shall enter into force 30 days after the date on which the Parties have notified each other in writing that they have completed their necessary domestic procedures for the entry into force of this Agreement.

2. This Agreement may be amended at any time with the written consent of both Parties through the exchange of diplomatic notes. Any such amendment shall enter into force in accordance with the procedures stipulated in paragraph 1 of this Article.

3. Either Party may at any time give to the other Party written notice of its intention to terminate this Agreement. In such case this Agreement shall terminate after the expiration of one year from the date on which the notice is received.

In witness whereof, the undersigned, being duly authorised by their respective Governments. have signed this Agreement.

Done in duplicate at Auckland on 17 August 2012, in the English and Korean languages, both versions being equally authentic.

[Signatories omitted].

INDEX

J

K

S

Y

Z

www.ingramcontent.com/pod-product-compliance
Lightning Source LLC
LaVergne TN
LVHW080523210926
848481LV00022B/2749
9781849467315